Bloomsbury Keys
Key Dictionary

BLOOMSBURY

All rights reserved: no part of this publication may be
reproduced, stored in a retrieval system, or transmitted in any
form or by any means, electronic, mechanical, photocopying or
otherwise, without the prior written permission of the
publisher.

First published in 1983 as the Little Macquarie Dictionary
by The Macquarie Library Pty Ltd.

This edition published 1995 by
Bloomsbury Publishing Plc,
2 Soho Square, London, W1V 6HB

Copyright © Macquarie University NSW, 1983, 1995
Copyright © additional material
Bloomsbury Publishing Plc 1995

A copy of the CIP entry for this book is available from the
British Library

ISBN 0 7475 2235 9

10 9 8 7 6 5 4 3 2 1

Typeset by Hewer Text Composition Services, Edinburgh
Printed in Britain by HarperCollins Manufacturing, Glasgow

Contents

Explanatory Notes	vii
Abbreviations and Symbols used in the Dictionary	x
Pronunciation Guide	xii
Key Dictionary	1

Appendices

Countries of the World	611
Metric Conversion	618
Common Prefixes	620
Common Suffixes	623

Key to Structure of Entries

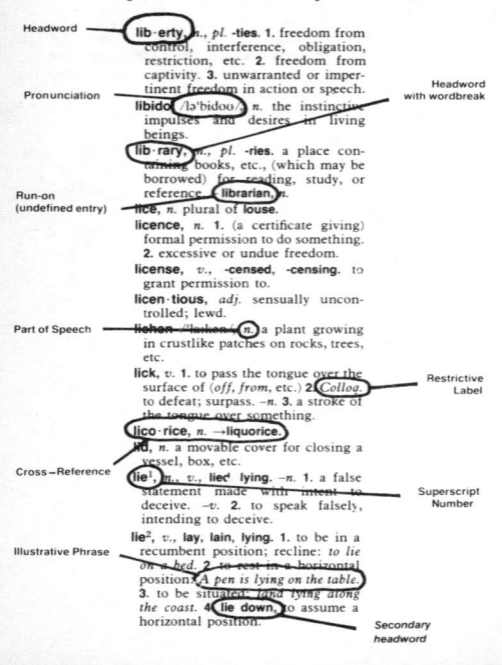

lib·erty, *n., pl.* **-ties. 1.** freedom from control, interference, obligation, restriction, etc. **2.** freedom from captivity. **3.** unwarranted or impertinent freedom in action or speech.

libido /lə'bidoʊ/, *n.* the instinctive impulses and desires in living beings.

li·brary, *n., pl.* **-ries.** a place containing books, etc., (which may be borrowed) for reading, study, or reference. **librarian,** *n.*

lice, *n.* plural of **louse.**

licence, *n.* **1.** (a certificate giving) formal permission to do something. **2.** excessive or undue freedom.

license, *v.,* **-censed, -censing.** to grant permission to.

licen·tious, *adj.* sensually uncontrolled; lewd.

lichen /'laɪkən/ *n.* a plant growing in crustlike patches on rocks, trees, etc.

lick, *v.* **1.** to pass the tongue over the surface of (*off, from*, etc.) **2.** *Colloq.* to defeat; surpass. –*n.* **3.** a stroke of the tongue over something.

lico·rice, *n.* →**liquorice.**

lid, *n.* a movable cover for closing a vessel, box, etc.

lie¹, *n., v.,* **lied, lying.** –*n.* **1.** a false statement made with intent to deceive. –*v.* **2.** to speak falsely, intending to deceive.

lie², *v.,* **lay, lain, lying. 1.** to be in a recumbent position; recline: *to lie on a bed.* **2.** to rest in a horizontal position: *A pen is lying on the table.* **3.** to be situated: *pond lying along the coast.* **4. lie down,** to assume a horizontal position.

Explanatory Notes

HEADWORD

The headword is the word or words which are being defined in a particular entry; it appears in large bold-face type at the left, slightly farther into the left margin than the usual line of text.

Words which, though spelt identically, are of quite distinct derivation, are given separate entries; in such cases, each headword is followed by a small superscript number. (Example: **gum**[1] and **gum**[2].) Entries are arranged under headwords in strict alphabetical order. A particular headword can be located by taking each successive letter of the headword in alphabetical order, ignoring hyphens, apostrophes, word spaces and wordbreak markers.

PRONUNCIATION

The pronunciation, where given, follows the headword within slant brackets. It is given in the International Phonetic Alphabet, for which keys may be found on pages xii and xiii.

For some headwords more than one pronunciation is given, the first of these being the one more widely used.

INFLECTED FORMS

If a headword has irregularly inflected forms, the summary of these forms is given immediately after the headword (or pronunciation). Regularly inflected forms, not generally shown, include:

- Nouns forming a plural merely by the addition of *-s* or *-es*, such as *dog* (*dogs*) or *class* (*classes*);
- Verbs forming the past tense by adding *-ed*, such as *halt* (*halted*);
- Verbs forming the present tense by adding *-s* or *-es*, such as *talk* (*talks*) or *smash* (*smashes*);
- Verbs forming the present participle by adding *-ing*, such as *walk* (*walking*);
- Adjectives forming the comparative and superlative by adding *-er*, *-est*, such as *black* (*blacker*, *blackest*).

PARTS OF SPEECH

The definitions are preceded by a label indicating their grammatical form, e.g. *n., adj.*, etc.

If the headword is used in more than one form, the part-of-speech label precedes each set of definitions to which it applies.

RESTRICTIVE LABELS

Entries that are limited in usage as to the level, region, time, or subject are marked with such labels as *Colloq., U.S., Obs., Music.*, etc.

If the restrictive label applies to the entire entry, it appears before the definition(s). If, however, the restrictive label applies to only one grammatical form, it appears after that part-of-speech label but before the definition numbers to which it applies. If the restrictive label applies to only one definition, it appears before that definition, after the definition number.

DEFINITIONS

Definitions are individually numbered; numbers appear in a single sequence which does not begin afresh with each grammatical form.

Where a definition contains a preposition in brackets and italic type, it is indicative that the headword is often used with that preposition, for example: **marvel** . . . –*v.* **2.** to wonder (*at*). This verb can be used with *at* following, as in *I marvelled at her courage*.

Some definitions provide an example of usage. The example sentence or phrase, preceded by a colon, is shown in italic type at the end of the definition.

Where two parts of speech with different meanings are given for the same words, brackets are used to present the separate definitions in a minimum of space. The part of speech which refers to the main definition is given first. The main definition is to be read by including the bracketed word or words. The definition for the second part of speech is read by discarding the bracketed section, for example:
invertebrate, *n., adj., Zool.* (an animal) without a backbone.
is read –
invertebrate *noun* an animal without a backbone.
invertebrate *adjective* without a backbone.

VARIANT SPELLINGS AND TERMS

Definitions appear under the most common spelling or term for a given meaning. In many cases, less common variants are given cross-references to the main headword. For example, the word **cab** appears as a headword followed by → **taxi**, indicating that the reader should seek information at that headword.

Regularly formed variants are usually not given. These include:
- the *-ize* variant of verbs ending in *-ise*, such as *realise/realize*.
- the *-or* variant of words ending in *-our*, such as *honour/honor*.

WORDBREAKS

These rules and guidelines can be used to explain the wordbreaks suggested in the *Key*.

The primary consideration in deciding where to break a word has been its sound, the secondary one its structure.

There are three rules:
1. Never break words of one syllable (e.g. *strength*).
2. Never break words with six letters, or fewer (e.g. *sorbet*).
3. Never break a word which is already hyphenated (e.g. *ill-gotten*).

The rules are supplemented by some general guidelines:
- The part of the word following the break should, where possible, begin with a consonant (e.g. *insu-late*).
- Where possible, meaningful prefixes, suffixes, and compound word parts should be left intact (e.g. *ultra-sound*; *hard-ship*; *hand-book*).
- In general, words should not be broken in such a way as to leave fewer than three letters on a line.

These guidelines should not be enforced if to do so would be to mislead the reader. The part of the word before the division should, if possible, suggest the whole word. For example, *limerick* should be broken *limer-ick*, not *lime-rick*, to avoid confusion with the word *lime*.

Abbreviations and Symbols used in the Dictionary

· indicates wordbreak

A'asian	Australasian	**def.**	definite
abbrev.	abbreviation	**derog.**	derogatory
adj.	adjective		
adv.	adverb	**eastn**	eastern
Aeron.	Aeronautics	**Eccles.**	Ecclesiastical
Agric.	Agriculture	**Econ.**	Economics
Alg.	Algebra	**e.g.**	for example
Anat.	Anatomy	**Elect.**	Electrical
Archaeol.	Archaeology	**Engin.**	Engineering
Archit.	Architecture	**esp.**	especially
art.	article	**etc.**	et cetera
Astrol.	Astrology	**euph.**	euphemistic
Astron.	Astronomy		
Aus./Aust.	Australia(n)	**fem.**	feminine
aux.	auxiliary	**fig.**	figurative
		fol.	followed
Biol.	Biology		
Bot.	Botany	**Geog.**	Geography
Bldg Trades	Building Trades	**Geol.**	Geology
Brit.	British	**Geom.**	Geometry
		Govt	Government
Cf.	compare	**Gram.**	Grammar
Chem.	Chemistry		
Colloq.	Colloquial	**Hist.**	History
Comm.	Commerce		
compar.	comparative	**i.e.**	that is

indef.	indefinite	**prec.**	preceded
indic.	indicative	**prep.**	preposition
interj.	interjection	**pres. part.**	present participle
		pron.	pronoun
joc.	jocular	**Psych.**	Psychiatry
			Psychology
Lit.	Literature	**p.t.**	past tense
masc.	masculine	**rel.**	relative
Mech.	Mechanics		
Med.	Medicine	**Scot.**	Scottish
Mil.	Military	**sing.**	singular
Myth.	Mythology	**sth(n)**	south(ern)
		superl.	superlative
n.	noun	**subj.**	subjunctive
Naut.	Nautical		
nth(n)	north(ern)	**Tech.**	Technical
N.Z.	New Zealand	**Theat.**	Theatre
obs.	obsolete	**U.S.**	United States of America
oft.	often		
orig.	originally	**usu.**	usually
Parl.	Parliament		
Photog.	Photography	**v.**	verb
pl.	plural		
p.p.	past participle	**westn.**	western

International Phonetic Alphabet

(a) Vowels		
	i as in "peat"	/pit/
	ɪ as in "pit"	/pɪt/
	ɛ as in "pet"	/pɛt/
	æ as in "pat"	/pæt/
	a as in "part"	/pat/
	ɒ as in "pot"	/pɒt/
	ʌ as in "but"	/bʌt/

(b) Diphthongs		
	aɪ as in "buy"	/baɪ/
	eɪ as in "bay"	/beɪ/
	ɔɪ as in "boy"	/bɔɪ/
	aʊ as in "how"	/haʊ/

(c) Consonants			
	(i) Plosives		
		p as in "pet"	/pɛt/
		b as in "bet"	/bɛt/
		t as in "tale"	/teɪl/
		d as in "dale"	/deɪl/
		k as in "came"	/keɪm/
		g as in "game"	/geɪm/
	(ii) Fricatives		
		f as in "fine"	/faɪn/
		v as in "vine"	/vaɪn/
		θ as in "thin"	/θɪn/
		ð as in "then"	/ðɛn/
		s as in "seal"	/sil/
		z as in "zeal"	/zil/
		ʃ as in "show"	/ʃoʊ/
		ʒ as in "measure"	/ˈmɛʒə/
		h as in "heat"	/hit/
		r as in "rain"	/reɪn/

(d) Stress	
	ˈ as in "clatter"
	ˌ as in "multimillionaire"

Symbols used in the Dictionary

ɔ as in "port"	/pɔt/
ʊ as in "put"	/pʊt/
u as in "pool"	/pul/
ɜ as in "pert"	/pɜt/
ə as in "apart"	/ə'pat/
ō as in "bon voyage"	/bō vwa'ʒaʒ/

oʊ as in "hoe"	/hoʊ/
ɪə as in "here"	/hɪə/
ɛə as in "hair"	/hɛə/
ʊə as in "tour"	/tʊə/

(iii) *Affricatives*
tʃ as in "choke"	/tʃoʊk/
dʒ as in "joke"	/dʒoʊk/

(iv) *Nasals*
m as in "mile"	/maɪl/
n as in "neat"	/nit/
ŋ as in "sing"	/siŋ/

(v) *Semi-vowels*
j as in "you"	/ju/
w as in "woo"	/wu/

(vi) *Laterals*
l as in "last"	/last/

/'klætə/
/ˌmʌltimɪljə'neə/

Aa

A, a, *n., pl.* **A's a's** or **As. 1.** the first letter of the English alphabet. **2.** the first in any series.

a[1], *adj. or indef. article.* a word used esp. before nouns beginning with a consonant to mean: **1.** some (indefinite singular referring to one individual of a class). **2.** (used before proper nouns) another: *He is quite a Romeo.* **3.** one. **4.** any (a single). **5.** indefinite plural: *a few.* Also, *before a vowel,* **an.**

a[2], *adj. or indef. article.* each; every: *twice a day.*

A, 1. argon. **2.** ampere.

aback, *adv. in the phrase* **taken aback,** suddenly disconcerted.

abacus, *n., pl.* **-ci** /-si/. a contrivance for calculating, consisting of beads strung on wires set in a frame.

abalone /æbəˈlouni/, *n.* a type of univalve, marine mollusc.

aban·don[1], *v.* **1.** to leave completely and finally; desert. **2.** to give up (something begun) without finishing.

aban·don[2], *n.* freedom from constraint or conventionality: *to dance with abandon.*

abase, *v.,* **abased, abasing.** to reduce or lower, as in rank, office, estimation; humble; degrade.

abash, *v.* to destroy the self-possession of; make ashamed or embarrassed.

abate, *v.,* **abated, abating.** to reduce or become less in amount, intensity, etc.; lessen.

abat·toirs /ˈæbətwaz, -tɔːz/, *n. pl.* a place where animals are slaughtered for food. Also, **abattoir.**

abbess, *n.* the female superior of a convent.

abbey, *n., pl.* **-beys.** a monastery or convent.

abbot, *n.* the male superior of a monastery.

abbrevi·ate, *v.,* **-ated, -ating.** to make shorter by contraction or omission. – **abbreviation**, *n.*

abdi·cate, *v.,* **-cated, -cating.** to renounce a throne, claim, right, power, or trust.

abdo·men /ˈæbdəmən, əbˈdoumən/, *n.* that part of the body of a mammal between the thorax and the pelvis; the belly. – **abdominal,** *adj.*

abduct, *v.* to carry off by force; kidnap. – **abduction,** *n.*

aber·rant, *adj.* deviating from the right or usual course or the normal type.

aber·ration, *n.* **1.** the act of wandering from the normal course. **2.** deviation from truth. **3.** lapse from a sound mental state.

abet, *v.,* **abetted, abetting.** to encourage or allow (usu. something wrong) by aid or approval.

abey·ance, *n.* temporary inactivity or suspension.

abhor, *v.,* **-horred, -horring.** to regard with repugnance; loathe.

abhor·rent, *adj.* **1.** exciting horror; detestable. **2.** utterly opposed (*to*).

abide, *v.,* **abode** or **abided, abiding. 1.** to remain; continue; stay. **2.** *Colloq.* to put up with; tolerate.

1

ability

abil·ity, n., pl. **-ties.** power or capacity to do or act.

abject, adj. **1.** utterly humiliating or disheartening. **2.** humble; servile.

abjure, v., **-jured, -juring. 1.** to renounce; retract, esp. with solemnity. **2.** to forswear.

abla·tion, n. Med. removal of organs, growths, etc. **2.** the melting or wearing away of a solid body.

ablaze, adj. **1.** (gleaming as if) on fire. **2.** excited.

able, adj., **abler, ablest. 1.** having sufficient power, strength, or qualifications. **2.** showing talent or knowledge. – **ably,** adv.

ablu·tion, n. **1.** ceremonial purification with water or other liquid. **2.** (pl.) the act of washing oneself.

abne·gate, v., **-gated, -gating.** to refuse or deny to oneself; renounce.

ab·normal, adj. deviating from the usual type.

aboard, adv., prep. on board; on or in a ship, train, etc.

abode, n. **1.** a dwelling place. **2.** continuance in a place; sojourn. –v. **3.** past tense and past participle of **abide**.

abol·ish, v. to put an end to; annul. – **abolition,** n.

abomi·nable, adj. detestable; loathsome.

abomi·nation, n. **1.** an object greatly disliked. **2.** intense aversion; detestation. **3.** a detestable action.

abor·igi·nal /æbəˈrɪdʒənəl/, adj. **1.** of or pertaining to an aborigine (def. 2). **2.** (usu. cap.) of or pertaining to the Aust. Aborigines. –n. **3.** (usu. cap.) an aborigine (def. 1).

abor·igine /æbəˈrɪdʒəni/, n. **1.** (usu. cap.) one of a race of tribal peoples,

abridge

the earliest inhabitants of Aust. **2.** (pl.) (generally) the people living in a country at the earliest period.

abort, v. **1.** to (cause to) miscarry before the foetus is capable of living. **2.** to (cause to) come to nothing; fail. – **abortive,** adj.

abor·tion, n. **1.** the expulsion or removal of a human foetus before it is capable of living. **2.** anything which fails before it is matured. – **abortionist,** n.

abound, v. **1.** to be in great plenty. **2.** to be rich (in). **3.** to be filled; teem (with). – **abounding,** adj.

about, prep. **1.** of; concerning; in regard to. **2.** near; close to. **3.** on every side of. **4.** on the point of (fol. by an infinitive). **5.** concerned with; engaged in doing. –adv. **6.** near in time, number, degree, etc.; approximately. **7.** on every side. **8.** half round; in the reverse direction. **9.** to and fro; here and there. **10.** in rotation or succession. –adj. **11. up and about,** astir; active (after sleep).

above, adv. **1.** in or to a higher place. **2.** higher in rank or power. **3.** before in order, esp. in a book or writing. –prep. **4.** in or to a higher place than. **5.** more in quantity or number than. **6.** superior to, in rank or authority. **7.** not capable of (an undesirable thought, action, etc.). –adj. **8.** said, mentioned, or written above.

abrade, v., **abraded, abrading.** to scrape off, wear down, or injure by rubbing. – **abrasive,** adj., n.

abra·sion, n. the act, process, or result of rubbing or abrading.

abreast, adv. **1.** side by side. **2.** alongside, in progress or attainment (of or with).

abridge, v., **abridged, abridging.** to

abridge

shorten by condensation or omission; rewrite on a smaller scale.

abroad, *adv.* 1. in or to a foreign country or countries. 2. at large; in circulation.

abro·gate, *v.,* **-gated, -gating.** to abolish by an authoritative act; repeal.

abrupt, *adj.* 1. ending or changing suddenly. 2. sudden or rude.

ab·scess, *n. Med.* a localised collection of pus in a cavity. **– abscessed,** *adj.*

ab·scind, *v.* to cut off; sever. **– abscission,** *n.*

ab·scond, *v.* to depart in a sudden and secret manner, esp. to avoid facing legal action.

absent /'æbsənt/, *adj.*; /əb'sent/, *v.* **-adj.** 1. not in a certain place at a given time. 2. lacking. 3. forgetful. **-v.** 4. to take or keep (oneself) away. **– absence,** *n.*

absen·tee, *n.* one who is absent.

absen·tee·ism, *n.* the practice of (irresponsibly) absenting oneself from duties, etc.

abso·lute, *adj.* 1. complete; perfect. 2. free from restriction or limitation. 3. arbitrary or despotic. 4. not comparative or relative. 5. positive. 6. *Physics.* as nearly independent as possible of arbitrary standards or of properties of special substances or systems.

ab·solve, *v.,* **-solved, -solving.** 1. to free (from) the consequences of actions. 2. to set free, as (from) some duty, obligation, or responsibility. **– absolution,** *n.*

absorb, *v.* 1. to swallow up the identity or individuality of. 2. to engross wholly. 3. to suck up or drink in (liquids). 4. to assimilate

abysmal

(ideas, knowledge, etc.). **– absorption,** *n.* **– absorbent,** *n.*

ab·stain, *v.* to refrain voluntarily, esp. (from) doing or enjoying something. **– abstention,** *n.* **– abstinence,** *n.*

abstemi·ous, *adj.* moderate in the use of food and drink.

ab·stract, *adj.* 1. thought of separately from matter, practice and particular examples. 2. theoretical; not applied. 3. difficult to understand. **-n.** 4. a summary of a statement, document, etc. 5. an idea or term considered apart from some material basis or object. **-v.** 6. to draw or take away; remove. 7. to consider as a general object apart from special circumstances.

abstrac·tion, *n.* 1. an abstract or general idea or term. 2. the act of taking away or separating; withdrawal. 3. absent-mindedness; reverie.

ab·struse, *adj.* difficult to understand; esoteric.

absurd, *adj.* contrary to reason or common sense; ridiculous. **– absurdity,** *n.*

abun·dant, *adj.* 1. present in great or sufficient quantity. 2. possessing in great quantity; abounding (in). **– abundance,** *n.*

abuse /ə'bjuːz/, *v.,* **abused, abusing;** /ə'bjuːs/, *n.* **-v.** 1. to use wrongly or improperly. 2. to revile; malign. **-n.** 3. wrong or improper use. 4. insulting language. **– abusive,** *adj.*

abut, *v.,* **abutted, abutting.** to be adjacent to (on, upon, or against). **– abuttal,** *n.*

abys·mal, *adj.* 1. immeasurable. 2. immeasurably bad.

3

abyss

abyss, *n.* any deep, immeasurable space. – **abyssal,** *adj.*

acacia, *n.* a tree or shrub native in warm regions; usu. known as wattle in Aust.

aca·de·mic, *adj.* 1. pertaining to an advanced institution of learning; relating to higher education and the subjects studied. 2. theoretical; not practical. –*n.* 3. a member of a college or university.

aca·de·my, *n., pl.* **-mies.** 1. an association or institution for the promotion of literature, science, or art. 2. a school for instruction in a particular art or science.

accede, *v.,* **-ceded, -ceding.** 1. to give consent; yield. 2. to come, as (*to*) a high office: *to accede to the throne.*

accel·er·ate, *v.,* **-rated, -rating.** 1. to (cause to) move or advance faster. 2. *Physics.* to change the magnitude and/or direction of the velocity of (a body). – **acceleration,** *n.* – **accelerator,** *n.*

accent, *n.* 1. the distinctive character of a vowel or syllable determined by its degree or pattern of stress or musical tone. 2. a mark indicating stress, musical tone, or vowel quality. 3. characteristic style of pronunciation as of a dialect. 4. *Music.* stress or emphasis given to certain notes. –*v.* 5. to pronounce or mark (a vowel, syllable, etc.) with an accent.

accen·tu·ate, *v.,* **-ated, -ating.** to emphasise.

accept, *v.* 1. to take or receive (something offered). 2. to admit and agree to. 3. to accommodate oneself to. 4. to understand. – **acceptable,** *adj.* – **acceptance,** *n.*

accommodation

accepted, *adj.* customary; established; approved.

access, *n.* 1. the act or privilege of coming (*to*). 2. way, means, or opportunity of approach. 3. a parent's right to see a child. – **accessible,** *adj.*

acces·sion, *n.* 1. the act of coming into the possession of a right, office, etc. 2. an increase by something added. 3. consent.

acces·sory, *n., pl.* **-ries.** 1. something added or attached for convenience, attractiveness, etc. 2. *Law.* one who is not the chief actor at a crime, nor present when it is committed, but yet is in some way involved in it.

acci·dent, *n.* 1. an undesirable or unfortunate happening; mishap. 2. anything that happens unexpectedly by chance. – **accidental,** *adj.*

ac·claim, *v.* 1. to salute with words or sounds of joy or approval; applaud. 2. to announce or proclaim by shouts or other demonstrations of welcome, etc. –*n.* 3. strong approval or applause. – **acclamation,** *n.* – **acclamatory,** *adj.*

acclima·tise, *v.,* **-tised, -tising.** to accustom or become accustomed to a new climate or environment.

accol·ade, *n.* 1. a ceremony used in conferring knighthood. 2. any award; honour.

accom·mo·date, *v.,* **-dated, -dating.** 1. to do a favour to. 2. to provide suitably. 3. to make suitable or consistent. 4. to adjust; reconcile. 5. to find or provide space for (something).

accom·mo·dation, *n.* 1. the act or result of accommodating. 2. lodging, or food and lodging.

accompaniment

accom·pani·ment, *n.* 1. something added for ornament, symmetry, etc. 2. *Music.* that part of a composition which provides the harmonic and rhythmic backing to a melody.

accom·pany, *v.,* -nied, -nying. 1. to go or be in company with. 2. *Music.* to play or sing an accompaniment to.

accom·plice, *n.* a partner in a crime or wrongdoing.

accom·plish, *v.* to carry out; finish.

accom·plished, *adj.* 1. completed. 2. skilled; expert. 3. perfected in the ways of polite society.

accom·plish·ment, *n.* 1. the act of carrying into effect; fulfilment. 2. anything accomplished; achievement. 3. (*oft. pl.*) an acquired art or grace.

accord, *v.* 1. to be in harmony; agree. 2. to grant; concede. –*n.* 3. harmony of relation. 4. consent or concurrence of opinions or wills; agreement. 5. **of one's own accord**, voluntarily. 6. **with one accord**, with spontaneous agreement.

accord·ing, *adv. in the phrase* **according to, a.** in accordance with. **b.** proportionately. **c.** on the authority of; as stated by.

accor·dion, *n.* 1. a portable wind instrument with bellows and button-like keys. –*adj.* 2. having folds like the bellows of an accordion.

accost, *v.* to approach, esp. with a greeting or remark.

ac·count, *n.* 1. a verbal or written recital of particular transactions and events; narrative. 2. a statement of pecuniary transactions. 3. *Bookkeeping.* a formal record of debits and credits. 4. **bring** or **call to**

accursed

account, demand explanation or justification of actions. 5. **on account of, a.** because of; by reason of. **b.** for the sake of. 6. **on** or **to account**, as an interim payment. –*v.* 7. to give an explanation (*for*). 8. to cause death, capture, etc. (*for*). 9. to count; consider as.

account·able, *adj.* answerable.

account·ant, *n.* a person who inspects and audits business accounts.– **accountancy**, *n.*

account·ing, *n.* the art of analysing the financial position and operating results of a business firm from a study of its sales, purchases, overheads, etc.

accout·rements /əˈkuːtrəmənts/, *n.pl.* equipment or trappings.

ac·credit, *v.* 1. to attribute: *He was accredited with the discovery. The discovery is accredited to him.* 2. to supply (a recognised agent) with credentials. 3. to certify as meeting official requirements.

ac·cre·tion, *n.* 1. an increase by natural growth. 2. an extraneous addition. 3. the growing together of separate parts into a single whole.

accrue, *v.,* -crued, -cruing. to happen or result as a natural growth; come as an addition. – **accrual**, **accruement**, *n.*

accumu·late, *v.,* -lated, -lating. 1. to heap up; gather as into a mass. 2. to grow into a heap or mass or an increasing quantity. – **accumulation**, *n.* – **accumulative**, *adj.*

accu·rate, *adj.* in exact conformity to truth, etc.; free from error or defect. – **accuracy, accurateness,** *n.* – **accurately,** *adv.*

ac·cursed /əˈkɜːsəd, əˈkɜːst/, *adj.* 1. subject to a curse. 2. detestable.

5

accusation

accu·sation, *n.* 1. a charge of wrongdoing. 2. the specific offence charged.

accuse, *v.*, **-cused, -cusing.** 1. to charge with the fault or crime (*of*). 2. to blame. – **accusatory,** *adj.*

accus·tom, *v.* to familiarise by custom or use; habituate.

ace, *n.* 1. a single spot or mark on a card or die. 2. (in tennis, badminton, etc.) a serve which the opponent fails to touch. 3. a highly skilled person. –*adj. Colloq.* 4. excellent.

acer·bity, *n., pl.* **-ties.** 1. sourness. 2. harshness or severity as of temper or expression. – **acerbic,** *adj.*

acet·ate, *n.* a salt or ester of acetic acid. – **acetated,** *adj.*

acetic /ə'siːtɪk/, *adj.* of vinegar.

acet·one, *n.* a colourless, inflammable liquid, used as a solvent and in varnishes, etc.

acety·lene, *n.* a colourless gas, used in metal welding, etc.

ache, *v.,* ached, aching. –*v.* 1. to have or be in continuous pain. –*n.* 2. pain of some duration, as opposed to sudden twinges.

achieve, *v.,* achieved, achieving. to bring to a successful end.

achieve·ment, *n.* 1. something accomplished; a great deed. 2. the act of achieving.

acid¹, *n.* 1. a substance with a sour taste. –*adj.* 2. sharp or sour. – **acidic,** *adj.* – **acidity,** *n.*

acid², *n. Colloq.* LSD.

acknowl·edge, *v.,* **-edged, -edging.** 1. to grant to be real or true; recognise the existence, etc., of. 2. to express recognition or realisation of. 3. to recognise the claims of. 4. to indicate appreciation for. 5. to certify the receipt of. – **acknowledgeable,** *adj.* – **acknowledgment,** *n.*

acme /'ækmi/, *n.* the highest point; culmination.

acne /'ækni/, *n.* an inflammatory disease of the skin, esp. of the face, characterised by eruptions (oft. pustular).

aco·lyte, *n.* an attendant; an assistant.

acorn, *n.* a nut, the fruit of the oak.

acous·tic, *adj.* 1. Also, **acoustical.** pertaining to the sense of hearing, or the science of sound. 2. *Music.* of instruments whose sound is not electronically amplified.

ac·quaint, *v.* to make more or less familiar (*with*).

acquaint·ance, *n.* 1. person(s) known to one, but not intimately. 2. the state of being acquainted; personal knowledge.

acqui·esce /ˌækwiˈɛs/, *v.,* **-esced, -escing.** to assent tacitly; agree; consent (*in*).

ac·quire, *v.,* **-quired, -quiring.** to come into possession of. – **acquisition,** *n.*

acquisi·tive, *adj.* fond of acquiring possessions.

acquit, *v.,* **quitted, -quitting.** to release or discharge (a person) from a charge of a crime, or an obligation. – **acquittal,** *n.*

acre, *n.* a unit of land measurement in the imperial system, equal to 4840 square yards. – **acreage,** *n.*

acrid, *adj.* sharp or biting to the taste.

acri·mony, *n., pl.* **-nies.** sharpness or severity of temper; bitterness of expression. – **acrimonious,** *adj.*

acrobat

acro·bat, *n.* a performer who can

acrobat

walk on a tightrope, perform on a trapeze, etc. – **acrobatic**, *adj.*

acro·nym, *n.* a word formed from the initial letters of other words, as ANZAC (from Australian and New Zealand Army Corps).

across, *prep.* 1. from side to side of. 2. on the other side of. 3. so as to meet with. –*adv.* 4. from one side to another. 5. on the other side.

acros·tic, *n.* a series of lines or verses in which the first, last, or other letters form a word or phrase, etc.

acry·lic, *adj.* of synthetic fibres or fabrics woven from such fibres.

act, *n.* 1. anything done or performed. 2. the process of doing. 3. a decree, law, statute, etc. 4. one of the main divisions of a play or opera. 5. an individual performance forming part of a variety show, etc. 6. behaviour which is contrived and artificial. –*v.* 7. to do something; exert force; be employed or operative. 8. to behave (as: *to act badly; to act the fool*). 9. to pretend. 10. to perform as an actor. 11. to substitute (*for*). 12. **act up**, *Colloq.* to misbehave.

actin·ium, *n.* a radioactive chemical element occurring in pitchblende. *Symbol:* Ac

action, *n.* 1. the process or state of being active. 2. something done; deed. 3. way of moving. 4. military or naval combat. 5. the main subject of a story, play, etc. 6. *Law.* a proceeding instituted by one party against another.

acti·vate, *v.*, -vated, -vating. 1. to make active. 2. *Physics.* to render radioactive. – **activation**, *n.*

active, *adj.* 1. in a state of action; in actual progress or motion. 2. constantly engaged in action; busy. 3. nimble. 4. capable of exerting influence. 5. *Gram.* denoting a voice of verb inflection, in which the subject performs the action expressed by the verb (opposed to *passive*). 6. (of a volcano) in eruption. 7. (of a communications satellite) able to retransmit signals.

acti·vist, *n.* a zealous worker for a cause, esp. political.

acti·vity, *n.*, *pl.* **-ties.** 1. the state of action. 2. a specific deed or sphere of action. 3. liveliness.

actor, *n.* one who plays the part of a character in a play, etc. – **actress**, *n.fem.*

actual, *adj.* 1. existing in fact; real. 2. now existing.

actu·ality, *n.*, *pl.* **-ties.** 1. reality. 2. (*pl.*) actual conditions or circumstances.

actu·ally, *adv.* as an actual or existing fact.

actu·ary, *n.*, *pl.* **-ries.** one who computes risks, rates, etc., according to probabilities shown by statistics. – **actuarial**, *adj.*

actu·ate, *v.*, -ated, -ating. to incite or to put into action.

acuity, *n.* sharpness of the senses, etc.; acuteness.

acumen /ˈækjəmən/, *n.* quickness of perception; mental acuteness.

acu·punc·ture, *n.* a Chinese medical practice, diagnostic and therapeutic, involving puncturing specific areas of skin with long sharp needles. – **acupuncturist**, *n.*

acute, *adj.* 1. sharp at the end; ending in a point (opposed to *blunt* or *obtuse*). 2. sharp in effect; intense. 3. severe. 4. brief and severe, as disease (opposed to *chronic*). 5.

7

acute

sharp or penetrating in intellect, etc. **6.** *Geom., etc.* (of an angle) less than 90°.

ad, *n. Colloq.* advertisement.

adage /'ædɪdʒ/, *n.* a proverb.

ad·a·mant /'ædəmənt/, *adj.* firm in purpose or opinion.

adapt, *v.* **1.** to make suitable to requirements. **2.** to adjust oneself. – **adaptable,** *adj.* – **adaptive,** *adj.* – **adaptation,** *n.*

add, *v.* **1.** to unite so as to increase the number, quantity, size, or importance. **2.** to total (*up*). **3.** to say or write further. **4.** to include (*in*). **5.** to perform the arithmetical operation of addition. **6.** to be or serve as an addition (*to*). **7. add up, a.** to amount (*to*). **b.** *Colloq.* to make sense, to be logically consistent.

adden·dum, *n., pl.* **-da.** a thing to be added.

adder, *n.* a small poisonous snake of Europe.

addict, *n.* **1.** one who is addicted to something. –*v.* **2.** to give (oneself) over, as (*to*) a habit or pursuit. – **addiction,** *n.* – **addictive,** *adj.*

addi·tion, *n.* **1.** the act or process of adding. **2.** the process of uniting 2 or more numbers into one sum. **3.** the result of adding; anything added. – **additional,** *adj.*

addi·tive, *n.* something added, esp. as an ingredient.

addled, *adj.* **1.** (of eggs) rotten. **2.** muddled; confused.

address, *n.* **1.** a formal speech. **2.** a direction as to name and residence inscribed on a letter, etc. **3.** a place where a person lives or may be reached. **4.** manner of speaking to persons. –*v.* **5.** to speak to a person in an official position, using his

adjourn

formal title. **6.** to direct to the ear or attention. **7.** to direct the energy or force of: *She addressed herself to her work.* – **addresser, addressor,** *n.* – **addressee,** *n.*

adduce, *v.,* **-duced, -ducing.** to bring forward in argument; cite as conclusive.

ade·noid, *n.* (*usu. pl.*) an enlarged mass of lymphoid tissue in the upper pharynx, common in children.

adept, *adj.* highly skilled; proficient.

ade·quate, *adj.* sufficient or suitable (*to* or *for*). – **adequacy,** *n.*

adhere, *v.,* **-hered, -hering. 1.** to stick fast; cling (*to*). **2.** to be attached as a follower (*to*). – **adhesion,** *n.*

adher·ent, *n.* one who follows a leader, cause, etc.; supporter (*of*). –*adj.* **2.** sticking.

adhe·sive, *adj.* **1.** sticking fast. –*n.* **2.** a substance for sticking things together.

ad hoc, *adj.* **1.** for this (special purpose); an **ad hoc committee** is one set up to deal with one subject only. **2.** impromptu; an **ad hoc decision** is one made with regard to the needs of the moment. –*adv.* **3.** with respect to this (subject or thing).

ad infinitum /ˌæd ɪnfɪˈnaɪtəm/, *adv.* to infinity; endlessly.

adja·cent, *adj.* lying near or close; adjoining.

adjec·tive, *n. Gram.* one of the major parts of speech comprising words used to modify or limit a noun. –**adjectival,** *adj.*

adjoin, *v.* **1.** to be in contact with; abut on. **2.** to lie to or be next to. – **adjoining,** *adj.*

ad·journ, *v.* **1.** to suspend the meet-

8

adjourn

ing of, as a public or private body, to another time or place. 2. to postpone or transfer proceedings. – adjournment, n.

ad·judge, v., -judged, -judging. 1. to pronounce formally. 2. to award judicially.

adjudi·cate, v., -cated, -cating. 1. to pass judgment on; to determine (an issue or dispute). 2. to sit in judgment (*upon*). – adjudication, n. – adjudicator, n.

ad·junct, n. 1. something added to another thing but not essentially a part of it. 2. a person joined to another in some duty or service.

adjure, v., -jured, -juring. 1. to bind or command, earnestly and solemnly, often under oath. 2. to entreat earnestly.

adjust, v. 1. to make conformable; adapt. 2. to put in working order; bring to a proper state. 3. to settle or bring to a state of agreement between parties. 4. *Insurance*. to fix or settle (the sum to be paid on a claim). 5. to adapt oneself. – adjustable, adj. – adjustment, n.

adju·tant /'ædʒətənt/, n. *Mil*. A staff officer who assists the commanding officer. – adjutancy, n.

ad lib, adv. 1. in an impromptu manner. –adj. 2. of an improvised performance.

admin·ister, v. 1. to manage (affairs, government, etc.). 2. to bring into use or operation. 3. to impose. 4. to perform the duties of an administrator. Also, **administrate**.

admin·is·tration, n. 1. the management or direction of any office, etc. 2. the function of exercising governmental duties. 3. any body of people with administrative powers. – administrator, n. – administrative, adj.

adore

admir·able /'ædmərəbəl/, adj. worthy of admiration. – admirably, adv.

admiral, n. a naval officer of high rank. – admiralty, n.

admire, v., -mired, -miring. to regard with wonder and approbation. – admiration, n. – admirer, n.

admis·sible, adj. 1. that may be allowed or conceded. 2. *Law*. allowable as evidence.

admis·sion, n. 1. the act of allowing to enter. 2. the price paid for entrance, as to a theatre, etc. 3. the act or condition of being accepted in a position or office. 4. a point or statement admitted.

admit, v., -mitted, -mitting. 1. to allow to enter. 2. to permit. 3. to permit to exercise a certain function or privilege. 4. to allow as valid. 5. to acknowledge; confess.

admo·nish, v. 1. to caution or advise against something. 2. to reprove for a fault, esp. mildly. 3. to incite to duty. – admonition, n.

ad nauseam /æd 'nɔziəm, -si-/, adv. to a sickening extent.

ado, n. activity; fuss.

ado·les·cence, n. the period between puberty and adult stages of development. – adolescent, adj. n.

adopt, v. 1. to choose for or take to oneself. 2. to take as one's own child, by a formal legal act. 3. to vote to accept. – adoptive, adj. – adopter, n. – adoption, n.

ador·ation, n. 1. worship. 2. devoted love.

adore, v., adored, adoring. 1. to regard with the utmost love and

9

adore

respect. 2. to honour as divine. – **adorable**, *adj.*

adorn, *v.* **1.** to make more attractive. **2.** to lend beauty to, as ornaments; decorate.

adrenalin, *n.* a whitish hormone used as a drug to speed heart action, etc. Also, **adrenaline**.

adrift, *adj.* **1.** not fastened by any kind of moorings. **2.** swayed by any chance impulse. **3.** *Colloq.* confused; wide of the mark.

adroit, *adj.* expert in the use of the hand or mind.

adulate, *v.*, **-lated**, **-lating**. to show pretended or undiscriminating devotion to. – **adulation**, *n.* – **adulater**, *n.* – **adulatory**, *adj.*

adult, *adj.* **1.** having attained full size and strength; mature. **2.** pertaining to or designed for adults. –*n.* **3.** a person who is of age. **4.** a fullgrown animal or plant.

adulterate, *v.*, **-rated**, **-rating**. to make impure by admixture. – **adulterator**, *n.* – **adulteration**, *n.* – **adulterant**, *adj.*, *n.*

adultery, *n.*, *pl.* **-teries**. voluntary sexual intercourse between a married person and another, not the lawful spouse. – **adulterous**, *adj.*

advance, *v.*, **-vanced**, **-vancing**, –*v.* **1.** to move forwards in place. **2.** to bring to view or notice. **3.** to improve; further. **4.** to raise in rate. **5.** to bring forwards in time. **6.** to supply beforehand. **7.** to supply in expectation of reimbursement. **8.** to move or go forwards. **9.** to make progress. **10.** to increase in quantity, value, etc. –*n.* **11.** a moving forwards. **12.** (*usu. pl.*) an effort to bring about acquaintance, understanding, etc. **13.** addition to price. **14.** *Comm.* **a.** a giving beforehand. **b.** a loan against securities, or in advance of payment due.

advantage, *n.*, *v.*, **-taged**, **-taging**. –*n.* **1.** any favourable state, circumstance, opportunity, or means to a desired end. **2.** benefit; gain. **3.** *Tennis*. the first point scored after deuce. **4. take advantage of**, to make use of. –*v.* **5.** to be of service to; benefit. – **advantageous**, *adj.*

advent, *n.* a coming into place, view, or being; arrival.

adventitious, *adj.* accidentally or casually acquired or added.

adventure, *n.* **1.** an undertaking (often hazardous) of uncertain outcome. **2.** an exciting experience. **3.** participation in exciting undertakings. **4.** a venture. – **adventurous**, *adj.*

adverb, *n.* a part of speech comprising words used to limit a verb, adjective, or another adverb, by expressing time, manner, place, cause, degree, etc. – **adverbial**, *adj.*

adversary /ˈædvəsri, -səri/, *n.*, *pl.* **-saries**. an opponent in a contest.

adverse /ˈædvɜs, -ˈvɜs/, *adj.* antagonistic in purpose or effect. – **adversity**, *n.*

advert /ədˈvɜt/, *v.* to make a remark (about); refer (*to*).

advertise, *v.*, **-tised**, **-tising**. **1.** to give information to the public about (something). **2.** to praise by advertisement in order to sell. **3.** to ask (*for*) by placing an advertisement in a newspaper, etc. – **advertisement**, *n.*

advice, *n.* **1.** an opinion recommended, or offered, as worthy to be followed. **2.** a communication, esp. from a distance, containing information.

advisable

advis·able, *adj.* proper to be advised or to be recommended.

advise, *v.*, **-vised, -vising. 1.** to give counsel to. **2.** to recommend as wise, prudent, etc. **3.** to give (a person, etc.) information or notice (*of*). **4.** to give advice. – **adviser**, *n.* – **advisory**, *adj.*

advo·cate, *v.*, **-cated, -cating.** *n.* **-v. 1.** to plead in favour of; urge by argument; recommend publicly. **–***n.* **2.** one who defends, vindicates, or espouses a cause by argument (*of*). – **advocacy**, *n.* – **advocator**, *n.* – **advocatory**, *adj.*

aegis /'iːdʒəs/, *n.* protection; sponsorship.

aeon /'iːən/, *n.* an indefinitely long period of time.

aerate, *v.*, **-rated, -rating.** to charge or treat with air or a gas, esp. with carbon dioxide.

aerial, *n.* **1.** that part of a radio system which radiates or receives electromagnetic waves into or from free space. *–adj.* **2.** of, in, or produced by the air. **3.** inhabiting or frequenting the air. **4.** unsubstantial. **5.** pertaining to aircraft. – **aerially**, *adv.*

aero·drome, *n.* a landing field (usu. small) for aeroplanes, esp. private aeroplanes.

aero·dynam·ics, *n.* the study of air in motion and of the action of solids moving through the air.

aero·gram, *n.* a sheet of lightweight paper which serves both as the envelope and the writing paper for an airmail letter. Also, **aerogramme**.

aero·naut·ics, *n.* the science of flight. – **aeronautic**, *adj.*

aero·plane, *n.* an aircraft, heavier than air, driven by propellers, jet propulsion, etc.

aero·sol container, *n.* a small metal container for storing under pressure, and subsequently dispensing as a spray, insecticides, waxes, lacquers, etc.

aes·thetic, *adj.* pertaining to the sense of the beautiful.

aeti·ology /iːtiˈɒlədʒi/, *n.* the study of the causes of anything, esp. diseases.

afar, *adv.* from a distance (usu. prec. by *from*).

aff·able, *adj.* easy to talk to or to approach; polite.

affair, *n.* **1.** anything done or to be done; business; concern. **2.** (*pl.*) matters of interest or concern. **3.** an event or a performance. **4.** → **liaison**.

affect[1], *v.* **1.** to act on; produce a change in. **2.** to impress; move (in feelings).

affect[2], *v.* **1.** to make a show of. **2.** to use or adopt by preference.

affec·tation, *n.* **1.** pretence. **2.** artificiality of manner or conduct.

affected[1], *adj.* **1.** acted upon; influenced. **2.** influenced injuriously; impaired. **3.** moved; touched.

affected[2], *adj.* **1.** artificial (in manner). **2.** pretending to have characteristics which are not natural.

affec·tion, *n.* a settled goodwill, love, or attachment. – **affectionate**, *adj.*

affi·davit, *n.* a written statement on oath, often used as evidence in court proceedings.

affi·li·ate, *v.*, **-ated, -ating.** *–v.* **1.** to attach as a branch or part (*with*). **2.** to bring into close connection. **3.** to associate oneself in action or in-

affiliate

11

affiliate

terest. –*n.* **4.** one who or that which is affiliated. – **affiliation**, *n.*

affin·ity, *n.*, *pl.* **-ties. 1.** a natural liking for, or attraction to, a person or thing. **2.** close resemblance. **3.** relationship by marriage.

affirm, *v.* **1.** to state or assert positively. **2.** to establish or confirm. – **affirmation**, *n.*

affir·ma·tive, *adj.* **1.** giving affirmation or assent. –*n.* **2.** an affirmative word or phrase, as *yes* or *I do*.

affix, *v.* **1.** to fix; fasten or attach (*to*). –*n.* **2.** that which is attached.

afflict, *v.* to distress greatly with mental or bodily pain. – **affliction**, *n.*

afflu·ent, *adj.* rich. – **affluence**, *n.*

afford, *v.* **1.** to be able to meet the expense of: *I can afford it.* **2.** to be able to give or spare: *I may afford you a loan of £5.* **3.** to give or confer upon.

af·front, *n.* **1.** a personally offensive act or word often intentional. –*v.* **2.** to offend by open disrespect.

afield, *adv.* **1.** abroad; away from home. **2.** far and wide.

afloat, *adj.* **1.** borne on the water. **2.** flooded.

afoot, *adj.* in progress.

afraid, *adj.* **1.** feeling fear. **2.** regretfully of the opinion (*that*).

afresh, *adv.* anew; again.

aft, *adv. Naut.* at, in, or towards the stern.

after, *prep.* **1.** behind in place or time. **2.** in pursuit of; in search of; with or in desire for. **3.** concerning: *I asked after him.* **4.** subsequent to and in consequence of. **5.** below in rank or excellence; next to. **6.** in imitation of (the style of): *poetry after Milton.* **7.** with name of. **8.** in proportion to. **9.** according to the nature of; in agreement or unison with. –*adv.* **10.** behind. –*adj.* **11.** later in time; next. **12.** *Naut.* farther aft. –*conj.* **13.** subsequent to the time that.

after·birth, *n.* the placenta, etc., expelled from the uterus after parturition.

after·math, *n.* resultant conditions, esp. of a catastrophe.

after·noon, *n.* the time from noon until evening.

after·wards, *adv.* in later or subsequent time. Also, **afterward**.

again, *adv.* **1.** once more; in addition. **2.** moreover; besides; furthermore. **3.** on the other hand. **4.** to the same place or person.

against, *prep.* **1.** in an opposite direction to, so as to meet; upon. **2.** in contact with, or pressing on. **3.** in opposition to. **4.** in resistance to or defence from. **5.** in preparation for. **6.** in contrast with; having as background. **7.** in exchange for; as a balance to. **8.** instead of, in contrast with (sometimes prec. by *as*).

agape, *adv.* **1.** in an attitude of wonder or eagerness; with the mouth wide open. –*adj.* **2.** wide open.

agate /ˈægət/, *n.* a variety of quartz showing coloured bands of other markings.

age, *n., v.,* **aged**, **ageing** or **aging**, *n.* **1.** the length of time of something's existence. **2.** the lifetime of an individual; an average lifetime. **3. of age**, having full adult rights and responsibilities. **4.** one of the periods or stages of human life. **5. old age. 6.** a particular period of history; a historical epoch. **7.** a generation. **8.** *Colloq.* a great length

age

of time. 9. *Geol.* a part of the world's history distinguished by special features. –*v.* 10. to make or become old or mature.

agency, *n.*, *pl.* **-cies.** 1. a commercial or other organisation furnishing some form of service. 2. the office of agent; the business of an agent. 3. the state of being in action or of exerting power; operation. 4. a mode of exerting power.

agenda, *n. pl.*, *sing.* **-dum.** 1. things to be done. 2. (construed as *sing.*) a list of things to be done, discussed, etc.

agent, *n.* 1. a person acting on behalf of another. 2. one who or that which acts or has the power to act. 3. a representative of a business firm, esp. a commercial traveller.

agglome·rate, *v.*, **-rated, -rating**, *adj.*, *n.* –*v.* 1. to collect into a mass. –*adj.* 2. gathered into a ball or mass. –*n.* 3. a rock formation of large angular volcanic fragments. – **agglomeration,** *n.*

aggluti·nate, *v.*, **-nated, -nating.** to unite or cause to adhere, as with glue. – **agglutination**, *n.*

aggran·dise, *v.*, **-dised, -dising.** 1. to make great or greater in power, wealth, etc. 2. to make (something) appear greater. – **aggrandisement**, *n.*

aggra·vate, *v.*, **-vated, -vating.** 1. to make worse or more severe. 2. *Colloq.* to provoke; irritate.

aggre·gate, *adj.*, *n.*, *v.*, **-gated, -gating.** –*adj.* 1. formed by the conjunction or collection of particulars into a whole mass or sum; combined. –*n.* 2. a sum, or assemblage of particulars; a total. 3. any hard material added to cement to make concrete. –*v.* 4. to collect into one sum, mass, or body. 5. to amount to (the number of).

agree

aggres·sion, *n.* 1. any offensive action; an inroad or encroachment. 2. *Psychol.* the emotional drive to attack. – **aggressive**, *adj.* – **aggressor**, *n.*

ag·grieve, *v.*, **-grieved, -grieving.** to oppress or wrong grievously (used now chiefly in the passive). – **aggrieved**, *adj.*

aghast, *adj.* struck with amazement; stupefied with fright or horror.

agile, *adj.* 1. quick and light in movement. 2. active. – **agility**, *n.*

agist, *v.* to take in and feed or pasture (livestock) for payment. – **agistment**, *n.*

agi·tate, *v.*, **-tated, -tating.** 1. to move or force into violent irregular action. 2. to disturb, or excite into tumult. 3. to arouse or attempt to arouse public feeling as on some political or social question.

agnos·tic, *n.* one who holds that God is unknown or unknowable or that human knowledge is limited to experience.

ago, *adv.* in past time.

agog, *adj.* highly excited by eagerness or curiosity.

agony, *n.*, *pl.* **-nies.** extreme, and generally prolonged, pain; intense suffering. – **agonise**, *v.*

agrar·ian, *adj.* relating to land or land tenure. 2. rural; agricultural.

agree, *v.*, **agreed, agreeing.** 1. to consent; say yes (*to*). 2. to be of one mind (*with*). 3. to come to one opinion or mind; come to an understanding (*upon*). 4. to be health-giving, or compatible (*with*): *This food does not agree with me.* 5. to concede (fol. by noun clause). 6.

agree

to determine (usu. fol. by noun clause). – **agreed**, *adj.*

agree·able, *adj.* 1. pleasing. 2. ready to agree or consent.

agree·ment, *n.* 1. (the act of coming to) a mutual arrangement. 2. the state of being in accord; conformity.

agri·cul·ture, *n.* the cultivation of land, including crop-raising, forestry, stock-raising, etc. – **agricultural**, *adj.*

ahead, *adv.* 1. in or to the front. 2. forward.

ahoy, *interj.* (a call used in hailing, esp. on ships).

aid, *v.* 1. to help. –*n.* 2. help; support.

aide-de-camp /eɪd-də-'kɒm/, *n.*, *pl.* **aides-de-camp**. a military or naval officer assisting a superior, esp. a general, governor, etc.

ail, *v.* 1. to affect with pain; trouble. 2. to feel pain; be unwell. – **ailing**, *adj.* – **ailment**, *n.*

aim, *v.* 1. to direct or point (something) at something. 2. to point (a gun); give direction to (a blow, missile, etc.). 3. to direct efforts towards an object. –*n.* 4. the act of aiming. 5. something intended or desired to be attained; purpose.

air, *n.* 1. a mixture of oxygen, nitrogen and other gases, which forms the earth's atmosphere. 2. the general character of anything. 3. (*pl.*) affected manner. 4. *Music.* a tune; a melody. 5. **off the air**, no longer being broadcast. 6. **on the air**, in the act of broadcasting. –*v.* 7. to expose to the air. 8. to expose ostentatiously; bring into public notice.

air·craft, *n.*, *pl.* **-craft**. any machine supported for flight in the air such as balloons, etc., or aeroplanes, helicopters, gliders, etc.

air force, *n.* the branch of armed forces concerned with military aircraft.

air·line, *n.* (a company that owns or operates) a system of (scheduled) air transport between specified points.

air·lock, *n.* 1. an obstruction to a flow of liquid in a pipe caused by an air bubble. 2. airtight compartment.

air·mail, *n.* the system of transmitting mail by aircraft.

air·play, *n.* the amount of time given to broadcasting a record.

air·port, *n.* a large airfield usu. equipped with a control tower, hangars, and areas for passengers and cargo in transit.

air·tight, *adj.* so tight or close as to be impermeable to air.

air·y, *adj.* **airier**, **airiest**. 1. open to a free current of air. 2. light in appearance. 3. light in manner; lively. 4. casual; flippant.

aisle /aɪl/, *n.* a passageway between seats in a church, hall, etc.

ajar, *adv.* 1. partly opened. –*adj.* 2. partly open.

akimbo, *adv.* with hand on hip and elbow bent outwards.

akin, *adj.* 1. related by blood. 2. allied by nature.

ala·bas·ter, *n.* a finely granular variety of gypsum, often white and translucent, used for ornamental objects, such as lamp bases, figurines, etc.

alac·ri·ty, *n.* 1. liveliness; briskness. 2. cheerful willingness.

alarm, *n.* 1. a sudden fear or painful suspense caused by apprehension

alarm

of danger; fright. **2.** any sound or information giving notice of approaching danger. **3.** a self-acting contrivance calling attention, rousing from sleep, warning of danger, etc. –*v.* **4.** to surprise with sudden fear.

alas, *interj.* (an exclamation expressing sorrow, grief, pity, concern, or apprehension of evil.)

alba·tross, *n.* a large seabird related to the petrels.

albeit /ɔl'biːt, æl-/, *conj.* although.

albino /æl'biːnoʊ/, *n., pl.* **-nos.** a person with a pale skin, light hair, and pink eyes, born lacking pigmentation.

album, *n.* **1.** a book consisting of blank leaves for the insertion of photographs, stamps, etc. **2.** a long-playing recording containing a collection of songs or pieces.

alchemy, *n.* medieval chemistry, esp. seeking to change metals into gold.

alco·hol, *n.* **1.** a colourless, flammable liquid, the intoxicating principle of fermented liquors. **2.** any intoxicating liquor containing this spirit.

alco·holic, *adj.* **1.** pertaining to alcohol. –*n.* **2.** one addicted to intoxicating drinks.

alco·hol·ism, *n.* a disease due to overuse of alcohol (def. 2).

alcove, *n.* a recess opening out of a room.

alder·man, *n., pl.* **-men.** an elected local government representative.

ale, *n.* beer.

alea·tory, *adj.* dependent on chance.

alert, *adj.* **1.** vigilantly attentive. –*n.* **2.** an attitude of vigilance or caution. –*v.* **3.** to prepare (troops, etc.) for action.

all

alga /'ælgə/, *n., pl.* **-gae** /-dʒiː/. any of various chlorophyll-containing plants such as seaweed, etc.

alge·bra, *n.* a branch of mathematics involving reasoning by the use of symbols. – **algebraic,** *adj.*

algo·rithm, *n.* a procedure for solving a particular mathematical problem. Also, **algorism.**

alias, *adv., n., pl.* **aliases.** –*adv.* **1.** at another time; in another place: *Simpson alias Smith.* –*n.* **2.** an assumed name; another name: *Simpson's alias is Smith.*

alibi, *n., pl.* **-bis.** *Law.* a provable claim not to have been in a place suggested, esp. by investigating police.

alien, *n.* one born in or belonging to another country and not yet granted citizenship.

alien·ate, *v.,* **-nated, -nating. 1.** to make indifferent or averse; estrange. **2.** to send or turn away.

alight[1], *adj.* (as if) on fire.

alight[2], *v.,* **alighted** or **alit, alighting. 1.** to get down from a horse or out of a vehicle.

align, *v.* **1.** to adjust to a line. **2.** to come into line; be in line.

alike, *adv.* **1.** in the same manner or form; equally. –*adj.* **2.** having resemblance or similarity.

ali·men·tary canal, *n.* the digestive passage in any animal from mouth to anus. Also, **alimentary tract.**

ali·mony, *n.* →**maintenance** (def. 2).

alive, *adj.* **1.** in existence; living. **2.** in force or operation. **3.** full of life.

alkali, *n., pl.* **-lis, -lies.** *Chem.* any of various bases which neutralise acids to form salts. – **alkaline,** *adj.* – **alkalinity,** *n.*

all, *adj.* **1.** the whole of (with refer-

all

ence to quantity, extent, duration, or degree). 2. the whole number of (with reference to individuals or particulars). –*pron*. 3. the whole quantity or amount. –*n*. 4. a whole; a totality of things or qualities. 5. one's whole interest, concern, or property. –*adv*. 6. wholly; quite. 7. only; exclusively. 8. each; apiece. 9. by so much; to that extent: *all the better to see you with*.

allay, *v*., **-layed**, **-laying**. 1. to put at rest; quiet (fear, suspicion, etc.); appease (wrath). 2. to mitigate.

allege, *v*., **-leged**, **-leging**. 1. to assert without proof. 2. to declare as if upon oath. 3. to declare with positiveness. – **allegation**, *n*.

alle·giance, *n*. 1. a citizen's duty owed to a sovereign or state. 2. faithfulness to any person or thing.

alle·gory, *n*., *pl*. **-ries**. figurative treatment of a subject presenting an abstract or spiritual meaning under concrete or material forms. – **allegorical**, *adj*.

allergy, *n*., *pl*. **-gies**. a physical hypersensitivity to certain things, as pollens, food, fruits, etc., which are harmless to others. – **allergic**, *adj*.

allevi·ate, *v*., **-ated**, **-ating**. to make more endurable; lessen.

alley, *n*., *pl*. **alleys**. a narrow back-street or lane.

alli·ance, *n*. 1. the state of being allied or connected; the resultant relationship. 2. any joining together by persons, families, states, or organisations.

alli·gator, *n*. the broad-snouted representative of the crocodile group.

allit·eration, *n*. the commencement

almanac

with the same sound of 2 or more words of a word group.

allo·cate, *v*., **-cated**, **-cating**. to set apart for a particular purpose. – **allocation**, *n*.

allot, *v*., **-lotted**, **-lotting**. to divide or distribute as by lot; apportion.

allot·ment, *n*. 1. a portion, share, or thing allotted. 2. a block of land.

allo·trope, *n*. one of 2 or more existing forms of a chemical element.

allow, *v*. 1. to grant permission to or for; permit. 2. to admit; acknowledge; concede. 3. allow for, to make concession, allowance, or provision for. – **allowance**, *n*.

alloy, *n*. a substance composed of 2 or more metals (or, sometimes, a metal and a non-metal).

allude, *v*., **-luded**, **-luding**. to refer casually or indirectly (*to*).

allure, *v*., **-lured**, **-luring**. 1. to attract by the offer of some real or apparent good. –*n*. 2. fascination; charm.

allu·sion, *n*. a passing or casual reference or mention either directly or by implication.

allu·vial, *adj*. 1. of or pertaining to alluvium. 2. of a mine, claim, diggings, etc., on alluvial soil.

allu·vium, *n*., *pl*. **-via -viums**. a deposit of sand, mud, etc., formed by flowing water.

ally, *v*., **-lied**, **lying**; *n*., *pl*. **-lies**. –*v*. 1. to unite by marriage, treaty, league, or confederacy (*to* or *with*). –*n*. 2. an allied person, nation, sovereign, etc. 3. one who helps another or cooperates with him; associate.

alma·nac /'ɔlmənæk, 'æl-/, *n*. a calendar with information regarding events, tides, etc.

al·mighty, *adj.* possessing all power.

almond, *n.* a nut grown in warm temperate regions.

almost, *adv.* very nearly.

alms /amz/, *n. sing.* or *pl.* that which is given to the poor or needy.

aloft, *adv.*, high up; in or into the air.

alone, *adj.* (used in the predicate or following the noun) **1.** apart from another or others. **2.** to the exclusion of all others or all else. –*adv.* **3.** solitarily. **4.** only; merely.

along, *prep.* **1.** by the length of; parallel to. –*adv.* **2.** in a line, or with a progressive motion. **3.** by the length. **4.** in company (*with*).

aloof, *adv.* **1.** at a distance, but within view; withdrawn. –*adj.* **2.** reserved; unsympathetic.

aloud, *adv.* **1.** with the natural tone of the voice. **2.** with a loud voice; loudly.

alp, *n.* **1.** a high mountain. **2.** (*pl.*) a high mountain system, usu. with snowy peaks. – **alpine**, *adj.*

alpha·bet, *n.* the letters of a language in their customary order. – **alphabetical**, *adj.*

al·ready, *adv.* by this (or that) time.

Alsa·tian, *n.* a large intelligent breed of dog, much used in police work.

also, *adv.* in addition; too.

altar, *n.* an elevated place or structure at which religious rites are performed.

alter, *v.* to make different in some particular; modify. – **alteration**, *n.*

alter·cation, *n.* a heated or angry dispute.

alter·nate /'ɒltəneɪt, 'ɒl-/, *v.*, -nated, -nating; /'ɒl'tənət, ɒl-/, *adj.* –*v.* **1.** to follow one another in time or place reciprocally. **2.** to perform by turns, or one after another. –*adj.* **3.** following each after the other, in succession. **4.** every other one of a series.

alter·na·tive, *n.* **1.** a possibility of one out of 2 (or, less strictly, more) things. –*adj.* **2.** affording a choice between 2 things.

al·though, *conj.* even though (practically equivalent to *though*, but often preferred to it in stating fact).

alti·meter /'æltɪmiːtə/, *n.* an instrument for measuring height.

alti·tude, *n.* **1.** the height above sea-level of any point on the earth's surface or in the atmosphere. **2.** distance upwards.

alto, *n., pl.* -**tos**. *Music.* **1.** the lowest female voice; contralto. **2.** the highest male voice.

al·together, *adv.* **1.** wholly; entirely; completely; quite. **2.** in all. **3.** on the whole.

altru·ism /'æltruɪzəm/, *n.* the seeking of the welfare of others (opposed to *egoism*). – **altruistic**, *adj.*

alu·mi·nium, *n.* a silver-white, ductile, malleable, rust-resistant, metallic element. *Symbol:* Al

always, *adv.* **1.** all the time; uninterruptedly. **2.** every time (opposed to *sometimes* or *occasionally*).

am, *v.* 1st person singular present indicative of **be**.

amal·gam, *n.* **1.** a mixture or combination. **2.** an alloy of mercury with another metal or metals.

amal·ga·mate, *v.*, -**mated**, -**mating**. to mix so as to make a combination; unite. – **amalgamation**, *n.*

amanu·en·sis /əˌmænjuˈɛnsəs/, *n., pl.* -**ses** /-siːz/. a person employed to

17

amanuensis

write or type what another dictates or has written.

amass, v. to collect into a mass or pile.

ama·teur /'æmətə, 'æmətʃə/, n. 1. one involved in a study, art or activity for personal pleasure rather than for gain. 2. an athlete who has never competed for money.

ama·tory, adj. pertaining to lovers or lovemaking.

amaze, v., **amazed**, **amazing**. to overwhelm with surprise.

amazon /'æməzən/, n. a tall, powerful, aggressive woman.

am·bas·sador, n. a diplomat of the highest rank representing his or her country in a foreign country.

amber, n. 1. a pale yellow, sometimes reddish or brownish, fossil resin of vegetable origin. –adj. 2. resembling amber.

ambi·dex·trous, adj. able to use both hands equally well. – **ambidexter**, n.

ambi·ence, n. environment; surrounding atmosphere.

ambi·ent, adj. 1. completely surrounding. 2. circulating.

ambig·uous, adj. open to various interpretations. – **ambiguity**, n.

ambit, n. 1. boundary; limits; sphere. 2. scope; extent.

ambi·tion, n. 1. an eager desire for distinction, power, etc. 2. the object desired. – **ambitious**, adj.

ambi·val·ence /æm'bɪvələns/, n. 1. the existence in one person of conflicting feelings on one subject. 2. uncertainty, esp. due to inability to make up one's mind. – **ambivalent**, adj.

amble, v., -**bled**, -**bling**, n. –v. 1. to go at an easy pace. –n. 2. an ambling gait.

ambu·lance, n. a vehicle for carrying sick or wounded persons.

ambush, n. 1. the act of attacking unexpectedly from a concealed position. –v. 2. to attack by ambush.

amelio·rate, v., -**rated**, -**rating**. to make or become better.

amen /eɪ'mɛn, ɑ–/, interj. so be it (used after a prayer, creed, or other formal statement).

amen·able /ə'mɛnəbəl, ə'miːn-/, adj. 1. disposed or ready to answer, yield, or submit. 2. legally responsible.

amend, v. 1. to alter (a motion, bill, constitution, etc.) by formal procedure. 2. to change for the better. 3. to remove or correct faults in. – **amendment**, n.

amends, n. sing. or pl. reparation for a loss, damage, etc.; recompense.

amen·ities /ə'mɛnətiz, ə'miːn-/, n.pl. 1. agreeable features, circumstances, etc. 2. public toilets.

ame·thyst, n. Mineral. a purple or violet quartz used in jewellery.

ami·able, adj. having agreeable qualities, as good temper, kindness, etc.

ami·cable, adj. characterised by or exhibiting friendliness.

amid, prep. in the midst of or surrounded by. Also, **amidst**.

amino acid /ə'minoʊ 'æsəd, ˌæmənoʊ–/, n. a protein-forming organic compound.

amiss, adv. out of the proper course or order; wrongly.

amity, n., pl. -**ties**. friendship; harmony.

am·meter, n. an instrument for

ammeter

measuring electric currents in amperes.

am·mo·nia, *n.* a colourless, pungent, suffocating gas, a compound of nitrogen and hydrogen, soluble in water.

ammu·nition, *n.* **1.** projectiles that can be discharged from firearms, etc., as bullets, etc. **2.** *Colloq.* evidence used to support an argument.

amne·sia /'æmnəzɪə/, *n.* loss of memory.

amnesty /'æmnəsti/, *n., pl.* **-ties.** a general pardon for offences against a government.

amoeba /ə'mibə/, *n., pl.* **-bae** /-bi/, **-bas.** a microscopic, one-celled animal. **– amoebic,** *adj.*

among, *prep.* **1.** in or into the midst of. **2.** included in a group of. **3.** to each of. **4.** each with the group. Also, **amongst.**

amoral, *adj.* neither moral nor immoral.

amo·rous, *adj.* **1.** disposed to love. **2.** enamoured.

amor·phous, *adj.* lacking definite form.

amor·tise /ə'mɔtaɪz, 'æmətaɪz/, *v.,* **-tised, -tising.** to liquidate (an indebtedness or charge) usu. by periodic payments to a creditor or to an account.

amount, *n.* **1.** quantity or extent. *–v.* **2.** to reach, extend, or be equal in number, quantity, effect, etc. (*to*).

ampere, *n.* the base SI unit of current. *Symbol:* A

amper·sand, *n.* the name of the character &, meaning *and.*

ampheta·mine /æm'fɛtəmin, -main/, *n.* a drug inhaled to relieve congestion, or taken internally as a stimulant.

amphib·ian, *n.* **1.** an animal that

anaesthetic

lives on land but breeds in water, as a frog, etc. **2.** a vehicle used on both land and water, as a tank.

amphib·ious, *adj.* able to move and live on land and in water.

amphi·theatre, *n.* **1.** a level area, usu. oval or circular, surrounded by rising ground. **2.** an arena. **3.** a semi-circular sloping gallery in a modern theatre.

ample, *adj.,* **-pler, -plest. 1.** in full or abundant measure. **2.** bulky in form or figure.

amplify, *v.,* **-fied, -fying. 1.** to make larger or greater. **2.** to expand in stating or describing, as by details, illustration, etc. **3.** to make louder. **– amplifier,** *n.* **– amplification,** *n.*

ampli·tude, *n.* **1.** extension in space, esp. breadth or width. **2.** large or full measure; abundance.

ampu·tate, *v.,* **-tated, -tating.** to cut off (a limb, arm, etc.) by surgery.

amuck, *adv.* in the phrase **run amuck,** to rush about wildly. Also, **amok.**

amuse, *v.,* **amused, amusing. 1.** to hold the attention of agreeably. **2.** to excite mirth in. **– amusement,** *n.*

an, *adj.* or *indefinite article.* the form of *a* before an initial vowel sound. See a¹.

anach·ron·ism /ə'nækrənɪzəm/, *n.* something out of its proper time. **– anachronistic,** *adj.*

anae·mia /ə'nimiə/, *n.* a deficiency in red blood cells. **– anaemic,** *adj.*

anaes·thesia /ænəs'θiʒə, -ziə/, *n. Med.* general or local insensibility, as to pain, etc., induced by certain drugs.

anaes·thetic, *n.* a substance such as ether, chloroform, cocaine, etc., that produces anaesthesia. **– anaesthetise,** *v.* **– anaesthetist,** *n.*

19

an·a·gram, *n.* a word or sentence formed from letters of another word or sentence, as *caned* is an anagram of *dance*.

anal /'eɪnəl/, *adj.* of, pertaining to, or near the anus.

anal·gesic /ænəl'dʒɪzɪk, -sɪk/, *n.* a remedy that relieves or removes pain.

analog, *adj. Electronics.* pertaining to the use of physical quantities (such as voltages, etc.) as analogues to the variables in a mathematical problem, as in an analog computer. Also, **analogue**.

analo·gous /ə'næləgəs, -dʒəs/, *adj.* corresponding in some particular.

ana·logue, *n.* **1.** something having analogy to something else. –*adj.* **2.** →**analog**.

anal·ogy /ə'nælədʒi/, *n., pl.* **-gies.** a partial similarity in particular circumstances on which a comparison may be based.

ana·lyse, *v.,* **-lysed, -lysing. 1.** to resolve into constituent parts; determine the essential features of. **2.** to examine critically.

anal·ysis, *n., pl.* **-ses. 1.** separation of a whole into its constituent elements. **2.** an outline or summary, as of a book. **- analyst**, *n.* **- analytic**, *adj.*

an·archy, *n.* **1.** a state of society without government or law. **2.** total disorder. **- anarchic**, *adj.* **- anarchist**, *n.*

anath·ema /ə'næθəmə/, *n., pl.* **-mas. 1.** any curse of divine punishment. **2.** a person or thing detested.

anat·omy, *n., pl.* **-mies.** (the science of) the structure of an animal or plant, or of any of its parts. **- anatomical**, *adj.*

ances·tor, *n.* one from whom a person is descended, usually distantly. **- ancestral**, *adj.*

ances·try, *n., pl.* **-tries.** ancestral descent.

anchor, *n.* **1.** a device for holding boats, floating bridges, etc., in place. **2.** a means of stability. **3.** **weigh anchor**, to take up the anchor. –*v.* **4.** to hold fast by an anchor. **5.** to affix firmly. **6.** to drop anchor. **7.** to be firmly fixed. **- anchorage**, *n.*

ancho·rite, *n.* one living in a solitary place for a life of religious seclusion; a hermit.

ancho·vy, *n., pl.* **-vies.** a small, herring-like fish.

ancient, *adj.* **1.** of or in time long past. **2.** of great age.

ancil·lary, *adj.* accessory; auxiliary.

and, *conj.* **1.** (along) with; together with; besides; also; moreover (used to connect grammatically coordinate words, phrases, or clauses). **2.** as well as. **3.** *Colloq.* to (used between verbs): *Go and see if he will help.*

anec·dote /'ænɪkdoʊt/, *n.* a short narrative of a particular incident or occurrence. **- anecdotal**, *adj.*

anem·one /ə'nɛmənɪ/, *n.* a plant with mostly red and blue flowers.

aneroid, *adj.* using no fluid.

aneu·rism /'ænjərɪzəm/, *n.* abnormal widening of the wall of a weakened blood vessel. Also, **aneurysm**.

anew, *adv.* **1.** once more. **2.** in a new form.

angel, *n.* **1.** a spiritual being, an attendant of God. **2.** a messenger, esp. of God. **3.** a person like an angel in beauty, kindliness, etc. **- angelic**, *adj.*

anger, *n.* **1.** strong displeasure

aroused by real or supposed wrongs; wrath; ire. –*v.* 2. to excite to anger.

angle[1], *n.*, **-gled**, **-gling**. –*n.* 1. *Maths.* the space within two lines or three planes diverging from a common point, or within two planes diverging from a common line. 2. a corner. 3. a point of view. 4. *Colloq.* a devious, artful scheme, etc. –*v.* 5. to move, direct, etc., at an angle or in an angular course.

angle[2], *v.*, **-gled**, **-gling**. to fish with hook and line. – **angler**, *n.*

Angora, *n.* (yarn or fabric made from) the long, silky hair of certain goats and rabbits.

angry, *adj.*, **-grier**, **-griest**. 1. feeling or showing anger or resentment. 2. inflamed, as a sore. – **angrily**, *adv.*

anguish, *n.* agonising pain of either body or mind.

angular, *adj.* 1. having an angle or angles. 2. situated at or forming an angle. 3. gaunt. – **angularity**, *n.*

animadvert, *v.* to comment critically (*on* or *upon*). – **animadversion**, *n.*

animal, *n.* 1. any living thing that is not a plant. 2. any animal other than man. 3. a brutish person. –*adj.* 4. of or derived from animals. 5. pertaining to the physical or carnal nature of man.

animate, *v.*, **-mated**, **-mating**. –*v.* 1. to give life to. 2. to make lively. 3. to move to action. 4. to cause to appear as if alive. –*adj.* 5. alive. – **animation**, *n.*

animosity, *n.*, *pl.* **-ities**. an active feeling of ill will or enmity (*between* or *towards*).

aniseed, *n.* a seed used in medicine, cookery, etc.

ankle, *n.* the joint connecting the foot with the leg.

annals, *n.pl.* history of events recorded year by year.

anneal, *v.* to heat (glass, earthenware, metals, etc.) to strengthen.

annex, *v.* 1. to attach, join, or add, esp. to something larger or more important. 2. to take possession of. – **annexation**, *n.*

annexe, *n.* a subsidiary building.

annihilate, *v.*, **-lated**, **-lating**. to reduce to nothing; destroy utterly.

anniversary, *n.*, *pl.* **-ries**. the yearly recurrence of the date of a past event.

annotate, *v.*, **-tated**, **-tating**. to remark upon in notes. – **annotator**, *n.* – **annotation**, *n.*

announce, *v.*, **-nounced**, **-nouncing**. 1. to make known publicly. 2. to state the approach or presence of. – **announcement**, *n.*

annoy, *v.* to disturb (a person) in a way that displeases or irritates. – **annoyance**, *n.* – **annoying**, *adj.*

annual, *adj.* 1. yearly. –*n.* 2. a plant living only one year or season.

annuity, *n.*, *pl.* **-ties**. a specified income payable during the recipient's life, in consideration of a premium paid. – **annuitant**, *n.*

annul, *v.*, **annulled**, **annulling**. to make void or null; abolish.

annunciate, *v.*, **-ated**, **-ating**. to announce.

anode /ˈænoʊd/, *n.* the positive pole of a battery or other source of current.

anoint, *v.* to apply an unguent or oily liquid to, esp. to consecrate.

anomaly, *n.*, *pl.* **-lies**. deviation

anomaly

from the common rule. – **anomalous**, *adj.*

anony·mous, *adj.* 1. without any name acknowledged, as that of author, contributor, etc. 2. lacking individuality. – **anonymity**, *n.*

ano·rexia /ænəˈrɛksiə/, *n.* lack of appetite.

another, *adj.* 1. a second; an additional: *Give me another one.* 2. a different; a distinct: *That is another breed of dog.* – *pron.* 3. one more: *Give me another.*

answer, *n.* 1. a reply to a question, letter, etc., or to an accusation. 2. a solution to a problem, esp. in mathematics. – *v.* 3. to reply. 4. to respond to (a stimulus, direction, command, etc.). 5. to declare oneself responsible (*for*). 6. to act or suffer in consequence of (*for*). 7. to correspond (*to*). 8. to make a defence against (a charge or argument).

answer·able, *adj.* 1. responsible (*for* a person, act, etc.). 2. liable to be asked to defend one's actions.

ant, *n.* any of certain very small, usu. wingless, insects, very widely distributed in thousands of species, and having some social organisation.

antago·nise, *v.*, **-nised**, **-nising.** to make hostile.

antago·nism, *n.* 1. active opposition. 2. an opposing force, principle, or tendency. – **antagonist**, *n.*

ant·arc·tic, *adj.* of, at, or near the South Pole.

ante, *n.* a stake of money in a card game, etc.

ant·eater, *n.* any of various mammals which eat ants.

ante·ced·ent, *adj.* 1. going or being

anticipate

before. – *n.* 2. (*pl.*) **a.** ancestry. **b.** one's past history. 3. a preceding circumstance, event, etc. 4. *Gram.* a word or phrase which is later replaced by a pronoun.

ante·date, *v.*, **-dated**, **-dating.** 1. to precede in time. 2. to affix an earlier date to (a document, etc.).

ante·lope, *n.*, *pl.* **-lopes**, (*esp. collectively*) **-lope.** a slenderly built, hollow-horned ruminant allied to cattle, etc., found chiefly in Africa and Asia.

antenna, *n.*, *pl.* **-tennae** for def. 1; **-tennas** for def. 2. 1. one of the pair of long, thin growths on the heads of insects, crustaceans, etc.; feeler. 2. a radio or television aerial.

anter·ior, *adj.* 1. situated more to the front. 2. going before in time.

anthem, *n.* a hymn, as of praise, devotion, or patriotism.

anthol·ogy, *n.*, *pl.* **-gies.** a collection of literary pieces, esp. poems, of varied authorship.

anthro·poid, *adj.* resembling man.

anthro·pology, *n.* the science that treats of the origin, development and varieties, and usu. the cultural development, of mankind. – **anthropologist**, *n.* – **anthropological**, *adj.*

anti·biotic, *n.* a chemical substance used in the treatment of bacterial infections.

anti·body, *n.*, *pl.* **-bodies.** a substance in the blood which counteracts bacterial or viral poisons in the system.

antic, *n.* (*oft. pl.*) a grotesque or ludicrous gesture or posture.

antici·pate, *v.*, **-pated**, **-pating.** 1. to expect, or realise beforehand. 2. to

anticipate

consider, do, or mention before the proper time. – **anticipation**, *n*.

anti·climax, *n*. an abrupt descent in dignity of thought or expression; disappointing conclusion.

anti·clock·wise, *adv.*, *adj.* in a direction opposite to that of the rotating hands of a clock.

anti·dote, *n*. a remedy for counteracting the effects of poison, disease, etc.

antin·omy /æn'tɪnəmi/, *n.*, *pl.* -mies. opposition between laws or principles.

anti·pathy /æn'tɪpəθi/, *n.*, *pl.* -thies. 1. a natural or settled dislike. 2. an instinctive opposition in feeling.

anti·podes /æn'tɪpədiz/, *n.pl.* 1. points diametrically opposite to each other on the earth or any globe. 2. the Antipodes, Australia. – **antipodean**, *adj.*, *n*.

anti·quary /æn'tɒkwəri/, *n.*, *pl.* -quaries. an expert on or collector of ancient things.

anti·quate, *v.*, -quated, -quating. to make out-of-date by substituting something newer and better. – **antiquated**, *adj*.

antique, *adj*. 1. belonging to former times. –*n*. 2. an object of art or a furniture piece of a former period.

anti·quity, *n.*, *pl.* -ties. 1. the quality of being ancient. 2. ancient times. 3. (*usu. pl.*) something belonging to ancient times.

anti·septic, *n*. an agent which destroys the micro-organisms that produce septic disease.

anti·social, *adj*. 1. unwilling or unable to be sociable. 2. opposing or damaging to social order.

anti·thesis /æn'tɪθəsəs/, *n.*, *pl.* -ses

anywhere

/-siz/. 1. opposition; contrast. 2. the direct opposite (*of* or *to*).

anti·toxin, *n*. a substance which counteracts a specific toxin. – **antitoxic**, *adj*.

anti·venene, *n*. an antitoxic serum which counteracts venom of snakes, etc. Also, **antivenin**.

antler, *n*. one of the solid deciduous horns, usually branched, of a deer, etc.

anto·nym, *n*. a word opposed in meaning to another.

anus, *n*. the opening at the lower end of the alimentary canal.

anvil, *n*. a heavy iron block on which hot metals are hammered into desired shapes.

anxi·ety, *n.*, *pl.* -ties. distress or uneasiness of mind caused by fear.

anx·ious, *adj*. 1. full of anxiety or solicitude. 2. earnestly desirous (fol. by infinitive of *for*).

any, *adj*. 1. one, a, an, or (with plural noun) some; whatever or whichever it may be. 2. in whatever quantity or number. 3. every. –*pron*. 4. (construed as *sing.*) any person; anybody, or (construed as *pl.*) any persons. 5. any quantity or number. –*adv*. 6. in any degree; at all.

any·body, *pron.*, *n.*, *pl.* -bodies. 1. any person. 2. a person of importance: *Anyone who is anybody will be invited.*

any·how, *adv*. 1. in any case. 2. in a careless manner.

anyone, *pron*. any person; anybody.

any·thing, *pron*. 1. any thing whatever; something. –*n*. 2. a thing of any kind.

anyway, *adv*. in any case; anyhow.

any·where, *adv*. in, at, or to any place.

aorta

aorta /eɪˈɔːtə/, n., pl. **-tas, -tae.** the main artery, conveying blood from the left ventricle of the heart to all the body except the lungs.

apart, adv. **1.** in or to pieces. **2.** separately or aside. **3.** to or at one side. **4.** individually in consideration. **5.** aside (used with a gerund or noun). –adj. **6.** separate; independent.

apart·heid /əˈpeɪtɪt/, n. (esp. in South Africa) racial segregation.

apart·ment, n. **1.** a single room in a building. **2.** a home unit.

apathy, n., pl. **-thies.** lack of emotion or excitement. – **apathetic**, adj.

ape, n., v., **aped, aping.** –n. **1.** a tailless monkey or one with a very short tail. –v. **2.** to mimic.

aper·ture, n. a hole, slit, or other opening.

apex, n., pl. **apexes, apices** /ˈeɪpəsiːz/. the tip or highest point of anything.

aphid, n. a plant-sucking insect.

aphor·ism, n. a terse saying embodying a general truth.

aphro·disiac, n. a drug or food that arouses sexual desire.

apiary, n., pl. **-ries.** a place in which bees are kept. – **apiarist**, n.

apiece, adv. for each one; each.

aplomb, n. imperturbable self-possession or poise.

apoca·lypse, n. revelation; discovery. – **apocalyptic**, adj.

apocry·phal, adj. **1.** of doubtful authorship. **2.** false. **3.** mythical.

apolo·gise, v., **-gised, -gising.** to offer excuses or regrets. – **apologetic**, adj.

apol·ogy, n., pl. **-gies. 1.** an expression of regret. **2.** a poor specimen or substitute. **3.** a formal defence.

appease

apo·plexy /ˈæpəplɛksɪ/, n. loss of bodily function due to haemorrhage in the brain. – **apoplectic**, adj.

apos·tasy, n., pl. **-sies.** rejection of one's religion, party, cause, etc.

apos·tle, n. a zealous supporter (of a principle, cause, etc.). – **apostolic**, adj.

apos·trophe /əˈpɒstrəfɪ/, n. the sign (') used to indicate: **1.** the omission of one or more letters in a word, as in *o'er* for *over.* **2.** the possessive case, as in *lion's, lions'* **3.** certain plurals, as in *many M.D.'s.* – **apostrophic**, adj.

apothe·cary /əˈpɒθɪkərɪ, -kərɪ/, n., pl. **-ries.** *Archaic.* a pharmacist.

appal, v., **-palled, -palling. 1.** to overcome with fear and horror. *Colloq.* to shock; dismay.

appa·ratus /ˌæpəˈreɪtəs, -ˈreɪtəs/, n., pl. **-tus, -tuses.** equipment etc., for a particular use.

appa·rel, n. a person's outer clothing.

appar·ent /əˈpærənt/, adj. **1.** plain or clear to the eye or mind. **2.** ostensible. **3.** open to view.

appar·ition, n. **1.** a ghost. **2.** anything that appears, esp. something remarkable.

appeal, n. **1.** a call for aid, mercy, etc. **2.** a request to some authority for confirmation, decision, etc. **3.** power to move the feelings. –v. **4.** to make an appeal (*to*). **5.** to be attractive (*to*).

appear, v. **1.** to come into sight. **2.** to seem. **3.** to be obvious. **4.** to come before the public. **5.** *Law.* to come before a court, etc. – **appearance**, n.

ap·pease, v., **-peased, -peasing. 1.** to bring to a state of peace or ease. **2.** to satisfy.

appel·lation, *n.* a name or title.

append, *v.* to add, as an accessory. – **appendage**, *n.* – **appendant**, *adj.*

appen·di·citis, *n.* inflammation of the appendix.

appen·dix, *n., pl.* **-dixes, -dices. 1.** matter which supplements the main text of a book. **2.** *Anat.* a small outgrowth at the beginning of the large intestine.

appe·tis·ing, *adj.* appealing to the appetite.

appe·tite, *n.* a desire for food or drink or any bodily wants.

applaud, *v.* **1.** to express approval by clapping hands, etc. **2.** to praise. – **applause**, *n.*

apple, *n.* an edible fruit, usu. round, crisp, and with red, yellow or green skin.

appli·ance, *n.* a device, usu. operated by electricity and designed for household use.

appli·cable /əˈplɪkəbəl, ˈæp-/, *adj.* capable of being applied; relevant.

appli·cant, *n.* one who applies.

appli·cation, *n.* **1.** the act of putting to a special use. **2.** the quality of being useable for a particular purpose. **3.** something applied. **4.** (a written) request or appeal, as for a job, loan, etc. **5.** close, persistent attention.

apply, *v.*, **-plied, -plying. 1.** to lay on; bring into contact. **2.** to put into operation, as a rule, etc. **3.** to employ. **4.** to give earnestly. **5.** to be pertinent. **6.** to make (an) application.

appoint, *v.* **1.** to assign to a position or to a function: *to appoint a secretary*. **2.** to fix; settle. **3.** to equip.

appoint·ment, *n.* **1.** the act of appointing or placing in office. **2.** an office held by a person appointed. **3.** an engagement to meet.

appor·tion, *v.* to distribute proportionally.

appo·site, *adj.* suitable; pertinent.

appo·sition, *n.* a placing together; juxtaposition.

ap·praise, *v.*, **-praised, -praising. 1.** to estimate generally, as to quality, weight, etc. **2.** to value in current money. – **appraisal**, *n.*

appre·ciable, *adj.* **1.** capable of being perceived. **2.** fairly large.

appre·ci·ate, *v.*, **-ated, -ating. 1.** to place a sufficiently high estimate on. **2.** to be aware of. **3.** to be pleased with. **4.** to increase in value. – **appreciation**, *n.* – **appreciative**, *adj.*

appre·hend, *v.* **1.** to take into custody. **2.** to grasp the meaning of. – **apprehension**, *n.*

appre·hensive, *adj.* fearful.

appren·tice, *n.* **1.** one who works for another whilst learning a trade. **2.** a learner.

apprise, *v.*, **-prised, -prising.** to inform; advise (*of*).

ap·proach, *v.* **1.** to come near or nearer (to). **2.** to make a proposal to. **–***n.* **3.** the act of drawing near. **4.** any means of access. **5.** the method used in setting about a task.

appro·bation, *n.* approval. – **approbatory**, *adj.*

appro·pri·ate, *adj., v.*, **-ated, -ating.** **–***adj.* **1.** suitable for a particular purpose, occasion, etc. **–***v.* **2.** to set apart for a specific use. **3.** to take for oneself. – **appropriation**, *n.* – **appropriateness**, *n.*

ap·proval, *n.* **1.** the act of approving. **2.** sanction. **3. on approval**, for

approval

examination, without obligation to buy.

ap·prove, *v.*, **-proved, -proving. 1.** to agree to officially. **2.** to be in favour (of).

ap·prox·i·mate, *adj., v.,* **-mated, -mating.** *–adj.* **1.** nearly exact. **2.** inaccurate; rough. *–v.* **3.** to come or make near to.

apri·cot, *n.* a downy yellow fruit resembling a small peach. **2.** a pinkish yellow.

apron, *n.* a protective garment covering the front of a worker in a kitchen, factory, etc.

apse, *n.* a vaulted recess esp. in a church.

apt, *adj.* **1.** inclined. **2.** quick to learn. **3.** suited to the purpose or occasion.

apti·tude, *n.* **1.** a tendency or inclination. **2.** readiness in learning; talent. **3.** special fitness or suitability.

aqua-lung, *n.* a diver's underwater breathing apparatus.

aqua·marine, *n., adj.* light blue-green.

aquar·i·um, *n., pl.* **aquariums, aquaria**, a pond, tank, etc., for keeping living aquatic animals or plants.

aqua·tic /ə'kwɒtɪk/, *adj.* **1.** of or pertaining to water. **2.** living or growing in water.

aque·duct, *n.* an artificial channel for conducting water.

aqui·line /'ækwəlaɪn/, *adj.* **1.** of or like the eagle. **2.** (of the nose) curved like an eagle's beak.

arable /'ærəbl/, *adj.* able to be tilled to produce crops.

arach·nid /ə'ræknɪd/, *n.* any arthropod of the class which includes the spiders, scorpions, mites, etc.

archbishop

arbi·ter /'ɑːbɪtə/, *n.* a person empowered to decide points at issue; judge.

arbi·trary, *adj.* **1.** subject to individual will or judgment. **2.** not attributable to any rule or law. **3.** unreasonable. **4.** selected at random.

arbi·trate, *v.,* **-trated, -trating. 1.** to decide as arbiter; determine. **2.** to settle by arbitration. – **arbitrator**, *n.*

arbi·tration, *n.* the hearing and resolving of disputes, esp. industrial, by an appointed 3rd party.

arbor·eal /ɑː'bɔːrɪəl/, *adj.* **1.** of or pertaining to trees. **2.** *Zool.* living in trees.

arbour, *n.* a bower formed by trees, shrubs, or vines, etc.

arc, *n.* **1.** any part of a circle or other curve. **2.** *Elect.* the luminous bridge formed by the passage of a current across a gap between 2 conductors or terminals.

arcade, *n.* a pedestrian way with shops usu. on both sides.

arcane, *adj.* mysterious; secret.

arch[1], *n.* **1.** a curved structure supported at both ends. *–v.* **2.** to span with an arch. **3.** to curve.

arch[2], *adj.* cunning; sly.

archae·ology, *n.* the study of any culture, esp. a prehistoric one, by excavation of its remains.

arch·aic, *adj.* **1.** characteristic of an earlier period. **2.** no longer used in ordinary speech or writing. – **archaism**, *n.*

arch·angel /'ɑːkeɪndʒəl/, *n.* a chief angel.

arch·bishop, *n.* a bishop of the highest rank.

archer, *n.* one who shoots with a bow and arrow. – **archery**, *n.*

arche·type /'akitaip/, *n.* the original pattern or model. – **archetypal**, *adj.*

archi·pelago /akə'pɛləgou/, *n., pl.* **-gos, -goes.** (sea with) group of many islands.

archi·tect, *n.* a professional designer of buildings.

archi·tec·ture, *n.* 1. the art or science of designing and constructing buildings. 2. the style of building.

archi·trave, *n.* a band of mouldings, etc., about a door or other opening.

arch·ives, *n. pl.* (place for keeping) historical documents or records of a family, organisation, etc.

arctic, *adj.* of, at, or near the North Pole.

ardent, *adj.* 1. glowing with feeling or zeal; passionate. 2. burning.

ardour, *n.* warmth of feeling; fervour.

ardu·ous, *adj.* laborious; difficult.

are[1] /a/, *v.* present indicative plural of be.

are[2] /ɛə/, *n.* a hundredth of a hectare.

area, *n., pl.* **areas, areae.** 1. any particular extent of surface; region. 2. extent or scope. 3. an open space. 4. *Maths.* 2 dimensional extent.

arena, *n.* 1. an enclosure for sports contests, etc. 2. a field of conflict or endeavour.

argon, *n.* a colourless, odourless, chemically inactive, gaseous element. Symbol: Ar

argot /'agou/, *n.* the jargon of any class or group.

argu·able, *adj.* 1. plausible. 2. open to argument. 3. able to be argued. – **arguably**, *adv.*

argue, *v.,* **-gued, -guing.** 1. to present reasons for or against (a thing). 2. to dispute.

argu·ment, *n.* 1. a debate. 2. a matter of contention. 3. a statement supporting a point.

argu·men·ta·tive, *adj.* given to argument.

aria /'ariə/, *n.* a melody for a single voice in an opera, oratorio, etc.

arid, *adj.* dry; parched.

arise, *v.,* **arose, arisen, arising.** 1. to come into being; originate. 2. to rise; get up from sitting, etc.

aris·toc·racy /ærə'stɒkrəsi/, *n., pl.* **-cies.** a class of hereditary nobility.

aris·to·crat /'ærəstəkræt/, *n.* 1. one belonging to a superior group or class. 2. (one of) the best of its kind. – **aristocratic**, *adj.*

arith·metic, *n.* the art of computation with figures. – **arithmetical**, *adj.*

ark, *n.* 1. a wooden chest. 2. a large, floating vessel, as Noah's Ark.

arm[1], *n.* 1. the human limb from the shoulder to the hand. 2. any arm-like part. 3. the sleeve of a garment. 4. the side part of a chair to support the arm.

arm[2], *n.* 1. (*usu. pl.*) a weapon. –*v.* 2. to equip with arms. 3. to fit (a thing) for any specific purpose.

armada /a'madə/, *n.* a fleet of warships.

arma·dillo, *n., pl.* **-los.** an armoured, burrowing mammal of Central and Sth America.

arma·ment, *n.* the weapons with which a military unit is equipped.

arma·ture, *n.* protective covering.

armchair

arm·chair, *n.* a chair with arms to support the forearms or elbows.

armi·stice, *n.* a truce.

armour, *n.* 1. defensive equipment or covering. 2. that which serves as a protection.

arm·oury, *n., pl.* **-ries.** a storage place for weapons and other war equipment.

armpit, *n.* the hollow under the arm at the shoulder.

arms, *n. pl.* weapons.

army, *n., pl.* **-mies.** a large body of men trained and armed for war.

aroma, *n.* a smell, esp. an agreeable smell; fragrance. – **aromatic**, *adj.*

arose, *v.* past tense of **arise**.

around, *adv.* 1. in a circle; on every side. 2. here and there; about. –*prep.* 3. about; on all sides. 4. *Colloq.* approximately.

arouse, *v.*, **aroused, arousing.** 1. to excite into action; call into being. 2. to wake from sleep. – **arousal**, *n.*

arrange, *v.*, **-ranged, -ranging.** 1. to place in proper order; adjust properly. 2. to come to an agreement regarding. 3. to prepare or plan. – **arrangement**, *n.*

arrant, *adj.* downright; thorough.

array, *v.* 1. to place in proper order, as troops for battle. 2. to clothe, esp. with ornamental garments. –*n.* 3. regular arrangement. 4. attire.

arrear, *n.* 1. (*usu. pl.*) that which is behind in payment. 2. **in arrear** or **in arrears,** behind in payments.

arrest, *v.* 1. to seize (a person) by legal warrant. 2. to bring to a standstill; stop. –*n.* 3. the lawful taking of a person into custody.

arrive, *v.*, **-rived, -riving.** 1. to reach

arthritis

one's destination. 2. to reach in any process (*at*). – **arrival**, *n.*

arro·gant, *adj.* pretending to superior importance or rights. – **arrogance**, *n.*

arrow, *n.* 1. a slender, long, pointed, missile shot from a bow. 2. a figure of an arrow used to indicate direction.

arrow·root, *n.* a tropical American plant whose rhizomes yield a nutritious starch.

arse, *n. Colloq.* rump; buttocks.

arsenal, *n.* a repository of arms and military stores.

arsenic, *n.* a greyish-white element having a metallic lustre, and forming poisonous compounds. *Symbol:* As

arson, *n.* the unlawful burning of any property.

art, *n.* 1. the production or expression of what is beautiful (esp. visually) or appealing. 2. (*pl.*) a branch of learning or university study. 3. skilled workmanship. 4. a skill or knack. 5. cunning.

arte·fact, *n.* any object made by man. Also, **artifact.**

arterio·sclerosis /ɑːˌtɪəriəʊskləˈrəʊsəs/, *n.* a disease causing thickening of the artery walls, with lessened blood flow.

artery, *n., pl.* **-teries.** 1. a blood vessel carrying blood from the heart to any part of the body. 2. a main channel, as in systems of communication and transport.

arte·sian bore, *n.* a bore in which the water level, under pressure, rises above ground.

arth·ritis, *n.* inflammation of a joint, as in gout or rheumatism. – **arthritic**, *adj., n.*

arthro·pod, *n.* any of the phylum of segmented invertebrates, having jointed legs, as the insects, arachnids, crustaceans, and myriapods.

arti·choke, *n.* a herbaceous, thistle-like plant with an edible flower head.

article, *n., v.,* **-cled, -cling.** –*n.* **1.** a piece of writing on a specific topic. **2.** an individual piece or thing; an item. **3.** In English, the words *a*, *an* and *the*. **4.** a clause, item or point in a contract, treaty, statute, etc. **5.** (*pl.*) a document drawn up in articles. –*v.* **6.** to bind by articles.

articu·late, *v.,* **-lated, -lating,** *adj.* –*v.* **1.** to utter clearly. **2.** to unite by a joint or joints. –*adj.* **3.** uttered clearly. **4.** capable of speech or self-expression.

arti·fice, *n.* **1.** a clever trick or stratagem. **2.** trickery.

arti·ficial, *adj.* **1.** made by human skill and labour. **2.** made in imitation of; not genuine. **3.** feigned.

artil·lery, *n.* mounted guns, movable or stationary, as distinguished from small arms.

arti·san /'atəzən/, *n.* a skilled worker, esp. in a craft.

artist, *n.* **1.** one who practises one of the fine arts, esp. a painter or a sculptor. **2.** an actor or singer, etc. – **artistic**, *adj.*

artis·try, *n., pl.* **-tries.** artistic workmanship, effect, or quality.

art union, *n.* a lottery.

as, *adv.* **1.** to such a degree or extent. **2. as well as**, as much as; just as; equally as; in addition to. **3. as well as, a.** equally; also; too. **b.** equally well; better; advisable. –*conj.* **4.** used in the correlations *as* (or *so*)...*as*, *same*...*as*, etc., denoting degree, extent, manner, etc. (*as good as gold, in the same way as before*), or in the correlations *so as*, *such as*, denoting purpose or result. **5.** in the degree, manner, etc., of or that: *Speak as he does.* **6.** though: *Bad as it is, it could be worse.* **7.** as if; as though. **8.** when or while. **9.** since; because. **10.** for instance. **11. as for, as to**, with regard or respect to. **12. as if, as though**, as it would be if. **13. as it were**, so to speak. **14. as yet, a.** up to now. **b.** for the moment. –*rel. pron.* **15.** that; who; which (esp. after *such* and *the same*). **16.** (of) which fact, contingency, etc. (referring to a statement). –*prep.* **17.** in the role, or manner of.

asbes·tos, *n.* (fireproof article made from) a fibrous mineral.

ascend, *v.* **1.** to climb upwards; rise. **2.** to climb; mount. – **ascension**, *n.*

ascen·dant, *n.* **1.** a position of controlling influence. (*adj.*) **2.** superior. – **ascendancy**, *n.*

ascent, *n.* **1.** the act of ascending; upward movement. **2.** gradient.

ascer·tain, *v.* to determine by trial, examination, or experiment.

ascetic, *n.* **1.** one who leads an abstemious life. –*adj.* **2.** austere.

ascor·bic acid /əskɔbik 'æsəd/, *n.* vitamin C, found in citrus fruits, tomatoes, etc.

ascribe, *v.,* **ascribed, ascribing.** to attribute or impute.

ash[1], *n.* (usu. *pl.*, but also used as *sing.*) the powdery residue that remains after burning.

ash[2], *n.* **1.** a tree of the Nthn Hemisphere producing hard, valuable timber. **2.** any of many Sthn Hemisphere trees with timber and foliage like that of the ash.

ashamed, *adj.* **1.** feeling shame or

ashamed

guilt. 2. unwilling through fear of shame. 3. loath to acknowledge (of).

ashore, adv. 1. to shore; on or to the land. –adj. 2. on land: *The crew is ashore.*

aside, adv. 1. on or to one side; away from some position or direction. 2. away from one's thoughts. –n. 3. words spoken so as not to be heard by everyone. 4. a remark incidental to the main subject.

asi·nine /'æsənaɪn/, adj. stupid; obstinate.

ask, v. 1. to put a question to. 2. to seek information. 3. to request. 4. to make a request (for). 5. to call for. 6. to invite.

askance, adv. with suspicion or disapproval.

askew, adv. to one side; awry.

asleep, adv. 1. in a state of sleep. –adj. 2. sleeping. 3. (of the foot, hand, leg, etc.) numb.

asp, n. any of several poisonous snakes.

aspar·a·gus, n. a plant cultivated for its edible shoots.

aspect, n. 1. appearance to the eye or mind. 2. a view or direction: *a southerly aspect.* 3. side facing a particular direction.

asper·i·ty /æs'pɛrəti, əs-/, n., pl. **-ties**. 1. sharpness of temper. 2. hardship. 3. roughness of surface.

asper·sion, n. a damaging or derogatory remark.

asphalt /'æsfɛlt, 'æsfælt/, n. any of various solid bituminous substances occurring naturally in various parts of the earth.

asphy·xia, n. the condition caused by lack of oxygen in the blood, resulting from interference with breathing. – **asphyxiant**, adj., n. – **asphyxiate**, v.

assess

aspic, n. a jellied mould of meat, fish, etc.

aspire, v., **-spired**, **-spiring**. to aim or seek ambitiously, esp. something great or lofty. – **aspiration**, n.

aspi·rin, n. (a tablet of) a white crystalline substance, used to relieve pain.

ass, n. 1. a long-eared mammal related to the horse; the donkey. 2. a fool.

assail, v. 1. to assault. 2. to set upon vigorously with arguments, abuse, etc. – **assailant**, n., adj.

assas·sin, n. one who murders from fanaticism or for a reward.

assas·si·nate, v., **-nated**, **-nating**. to kill for political or religious motives. – **assassination**, n.

assault, n. 1. an attack; onslaught. 2. *Law.* an attempt to attack another, as by threatening with a weapon. –v. 3. to make an assault upon.

assay /ə'seɪ/, v. 1. to examine by test or trial. 2. to judge the quality of.

assem·blage, n. a number of persons or things assembled.

assem·ble, v., **-bled**, **-bling**. 1. to bring or come together. 2. to put or fit (parts) together.

assem·bly, n., pl. **-blies**. 1. a company of persons gathered together. 2. the putting together of complex machinery.

assent, v. 1. to express agreement or concurrence. –n. 2. agreement, as to a proposal.

assert, v. 1. to state as true. 2. to put (oneself) forward insistently. – **assertion**, n. – **assertive**, adj.

assess, v. 1. to estimate officially the

value of. 2. to determine the amount of. – **assessor**, *n*.

asset, *n*. 1. a useful thing or quality. 2. an item of property. 3. (*pl*.) financial resources, including property.

assid·uous, *adj.* 1. constant; unremitting. 2. constant in application. – **assiduity**, *n*.

assign, *v*. 1. to give, as in distribution; allot. 2. to appoint, as to a duty: *assigned to stand guard*. 3. to ascribe; attribute. – **assigner**, *n*.

assig·nation, *n*. 1. an appointment for a meeting. 2. the act of assigning.

assign·ment, *n*. something assigned, as a particular task or duty.

assimi·late, *v*., **-lated**, **-lating**. 1. to absorb or become absorbed into the body, mind, society, etc. 2. to make or become like (*to* or *with*). – **assimilation**, *n*.

assist, *v*. 1. to give support or aid (to). 2. to be an assistant. – **assistance**, *n*.

assis·tant, *n*. 1. one who assists a superior. – *adj*. 2. helpful. 3. associated with a superior.

asso·ciate, *v*., **-ated**, **-ating**; *n*., *adj*. -*v*. 1. to connect by some relation, as in thought. 2. to join as a companion or ally. 3. to unite. 4. to enter into a union. 5. to keep company, as a friend. – *n*. 6. a partner, as in business. – *adj*. 7. having subordinate membership.

associ·ation, *n*. 1. an organisation of people with a common purpose and having a formal structure. 2. companionship. 3. connection or combination. 4. the connection of ideas in thought.

asso·nance, *n*. resemblance of sounds.

assort·ment, *n*. 1. distribution according to kind; classification. 2. a miscellaneous collection.

assuage /əˈsweɪdʒ/, *v*., **-suaged**, **-suaging**. 1. to make milder or less severe. 2. to satisfy.

assume, *v*., **-sumed**, **-suming**. 1. to suppose as a fact. 2. to undertake. 3. to pretend to have or be. 4. to appropriate. – **assumption**, *n*.

assur·ance, *n*. 1. a positive declaration. 2. pledge; guarantee. 3. full confidence or trust. 4. freedom from timidity; self-reliance. 5. insurance (now usu. restricted to life insurance).

assure, *v*., **-sured**, **-suring**. 1. to inform or tell positively. 2. to convince, as by a promise or declaration. 3. to make (a future event) sure. 4. to secure or confirm. 5. to give confidence to.

aster·isk, *n*. the figure of a star (*), used in writing and printing as a reference mark.

aster·oid, *n*. 1. a marine animal having a starlike body with radiating arms or rays, as the starfishes. 2. one of several hundred small planets with orbits mostly between those of Mars and Jupiter.

asthma /ˈæsmə/, *n*. a paroxysmal disorder of respiration with laboured breathing. – **asthmatic**, *adj*., *n*.

aston·ish, *v*. to surprise greatly; amaze.

astound, *v*. to overwhelm with amazement; astonish greatly.

astral, *adj*. pertaining to the stars.

astray, *adv*. out of the right way; straying.

astride

astride, *adv.* **1.** in the posture of straddling. *–prep.* **2.** with a leg on each side of.

astrin·gent, *adj.* **1.** (as affecting the skin) refreshing, tightening. **2.** severe, sharp. *–n.* **3.** an astringent agent (esp. cosmetic).

astrol·ogy, *n.* a study professing to interpret the supposed influence of the celestial bodies on human affairs. **– astrologer,** *n.* **– astrological,** *adj.*

astro·naut, *n.* one trained as a pilot, navigator, etc., of a spacecraft.

astron·omy, *n.* the science or study of the celestial bodies. **– astronomer,** *n.* **– astronomical,** *adj.*

astute, *adj.* of keen discernment; shrewd.

asunder, *adv.* into separate parts.

asylum, *n.* **1.** *Archaic.* an institution for the care of the insane, the blind, orphans, etc. **2.** an inviolable refuge; a sanctuary. **3.** *Internat. Law.* temporary refuge granted political offenders, esp. in a foreign legation.

at, *prep.* a particle specifying a point occupied, attained, sought, etc., and used in many phrases expressing position, degree or rate, action, manner: *at noon, at home, at length.*

ata·vism, *n.* reversion to an earlier type. **– atavistic,** *adj.*

ate, *v.* past tense of **eat.**

athe·ism, *n.* (belief of) the doctrine that there is no God. **– atheist,** *n.*

ath·lete, *n.* **1.** one trained in physical agility and strength. **2.** one trained for running, hurdling, throwing, etc. **– athletic,** *adj.*

ath·letics, *n.* (*usu.* construed as *pl.*) athletic sports, as running, rowing, boxing, etc.

attaché

atlas, *n.* a bound collection of maps.

atmos·phere, *n.* **1.** the gaseous fluid surrounding the earth; the air. **2.** pervading influence. **– atmospheric,** *adj.*

atoll, *n.* a ringlike coral island enclosing a lagoon.

atom, *n.* the smallest unitary constituent of a chemical element.

atomic, *adj.* **1.** pertaining to atoms. **2.** driven by atomic energy. **3.** using or having developed atomic weapons.

atomic bomb, *n.* a bomb whose explosion is extremely violent and attended by great heat, brilliant light and strong radiation. Also, **atom bomb, A-bomb.**

atomic energy, *n.* the energy obtained from changes within the atomic nucleus, chiefly through nuclear fission or fusion, and useful as a source of power.

atom·iser, *n.* an apparatus for reducing liquids to a fine spray.

atone, *v.,* atoned, atoning. to make amends or reparation. **– atonement,** *n.*

atro·cious, *adj.* **1.** shockingly wicked or cruel. **2.** shockingly bad or lacking in taste.

atroc·ity /'ætrəfi/, *n., pl.* **-ties.** an atrocious deed or thing.

atrophy /'ætrəfɪ/, *n., v.,* -phied, -phying. *–n.* **1.** *Pathol.* wasting away of the body or of an organ or part. **2.** degeneration. *–v.* **3.** to affect with or undergo atrophy.

attach, *v.* **1.** to fasten to; connect. **2.** to join in action or function. **3.** to associate. **4.** to attribute. **5.** to bind by ties of affection. **– attachment,** *n.*

attaché /əˈtæfeɪ/, *n.* one attached to

attaché

an official staff, esp. that of an embassy or legation.

attaché case, n. a small rectangular case with a hinged lid, for documents, etc.

attack, v. 1. to set upon with force or weapons. 2. to blame or abuse violently. 3. to set about (a task) vigorously. 4. (of disease, destructive agencies, etc.) to begin to affect. – n. 5. onslaught; assault. 6. criticism; abuse.

attain, v. 1. to reach or accomplish by continued effort. 2. to come to or arrive at. 3. **attain to**, to arrive at; succeed in reaching or obtaining.

attempt, v. 1. to make an effort at; try. 2. to attack. – n. 3. effort to accomplish something. 4. an attack.

attend, v. 1. to be present at. 2. to go with as a result. 3. to minister to. 4. to pay heed. 5. to apply oneself.

atten·dance, n. 1. the act of attending. 2. the (number of) persons present.

atten·dant, n. 1. one who attends another. 2. one employed to direct or assist people in a public place. – adj. 3. concomitant.

atten·tion, n. 1. observant care; consideration. 2. courtesy. 3. (pl.) acts of courtesy, as in courtship.

atten·tive, adj. 1. giving attention; observant. 2. assiduous in service. – **attentiveness**, n.

atten·uate, v., -ated, -ating. 1. to make thin or fine. 2. to weaken.

attest, v. 1. to certify, esp. affirm in an official capacity. 2. to give proof or evidence of. – **attestation**, n.

attic, n. that part of a building, esp. a house, directly under a roof.

attire, v., -tired, -tiring. n. – v. 1. to dress, esp. for special occasions, ceremonials, etc. – n. 2. (rich or splendid) outer clothing.

atti·tude, n. 1. manner with regard to a person or thing. 2. position of the body.

attor·ney /əˈtɜːni/, n., pl. -neys. 1. one empowered by another to transact any business for him. 2. U.S. lawyer.

attract, v. 1. to act upon by a physical force causing approach or union (opposed to repel). 2. to invite or allure; win. – **attraction**, n. – **attractive**, adj.

attri·bute /əˈtrɪbjuːt/, v., -uted, -uting. /ˈætrəbjuːt/, n. – v. 1. to consider as belonging (to). – n. 2. something attributed as belonging; a quality or property. – **attributive**, adj.

attri·tion, n. a wearing down or away.

atyp·i·cal /eɪˈtɪpɪkəl/, adj. not typical; not conforming to the type. Also, **atypic**. – **atypically**, adv.

auber·gine /ˈoʊbədʒɪn/, n. → **eggplant**.

auburn, n. a reddish-brown or golden-brown colour.

auc·tion, n. a public sale at which buyers make bids. – **auctioneer**, n.

auda·cious, adj. 1. bold or daring. 2. reckless or bold in wrongdoing. – **audacity**, n.

audi·ble, adj. able to be heard.

audi·ence, n. 1. an assembly of hearers or spectators. 2. formal interview.

audi·ology, n. the study of hearing and esp. its impairment.

audit, n. 1. an official examination and verification of financial accounts and records. – v. 2. to make audit of. – **auditor**, n.

audi·tion, n. 1. a hearing given to a

audition

audition

musician, speaker, etc., to test voice qualities, performance, etc. –v. 2. to perform or test in an audition.

audi·torium, n., pl. -toriums, -toria. 1. the space for the audience in a concert hall, etc. 2. a large building or room for meetings, assemblies, theatrical performances, etc.

audi·tory, adj. pertaining to hearing, or to the sense or organs of hearing.

auger, n. a tool for boring holes in wood.

aug·ment, v. to make larger; increase.

augur, v. to be a sign or omen (of).

august /ɔːˈgʌst/, adj. 1. inspiring reverence or admiration; majestic. 2. venerable.

aunt, n. 1. the sister of one's father or mother. 2. the wife of one's uncle.

aura, n. a distinctive air, atmosphere, character, etc.

aural, adj. of, or perceived by, the organs of hearing. – aurally, adv.

aurif·erous, adj. yielding or containing gold.

aurora /ɔːˈrɔːrə/, n. moving bands of light in the skies, visible at high latitudes.

aus·pice, n. (usu. pl.) favouring influence; patronage.

auspi·cious, adj. of good omen; favourable.

aus·tere, adj. 1. harsh in manner; stern in appearance. 2. severe in disciplining oneself. 3. severely simple. – austerity, n.

Australian Rules, n. pl. a code of football which originated in Aust. and which is most popular in the sthn and westn States. Also, Australian National Football, Aussie Rules.

aut·archy /ˈɔːtɑːki/, n., pl. -chies. 1. absolute sovereignty. 2. self-government.

authen·tic, adj. 1. entitled to acceptance or belief. 2. of genuine origin. – authenticity, n.

authen·ti·cate, v., -cated, -cating. 1. to make authoritative or valid. 2. to establish as genuine.

author, n. a person who writes a novel, poem, essay, etc.

autho·rise, v., -rised, -rising. 1. to give legal power to. 2. to formally approve. 3. to justify. – authorisation, n.

authori·tarian, adj. favouring the principle of subjection to authority.

autho·rity, n., pl. -ties. 1. the right to determine issues or disputes; the right to control or command. 2. a person or body with such rights. 3. an accepted source of information, etc. 4. a statute, court rule, or judicial decision. 5. a warrant for action. – authoritative, adj.

autism, n. Psychiatry. a syndrome of unknown cause characterised by the sufferer's inability to understand or relate to his environment. – autistic, adj.

auto·biography, n., pl. -phies. an account of a person's life written by himself.

auto·cracy, n., pl. -cies. unlimited authority over others invested in a single person; the government or power of an absolute monarch. – autocrat, n. – autocratic, adj.

auto·graph, n. 1. a person's signature. –v. 2. to write one's name on or in.

auto·mate, v., -mated, -mating. to

automate

automate

convert (machinery, procedures, etc.) to automatic operation.

auto·matic, *adj.* 1. self-moving or self-acting; mechanical. 2. done unconsciously or from force of habit. –*n.* 3. a machine which operates automatically, as a motor car with automatic gear shift. – **automatically**, *adv.*

auto·mation, *n.* 1. the use of automatic machinery in industrial processes. 2. the act of automating a mechanical process.

autom·aton /ɔːˈtomətən/, *n.*, *pl.* **-tons, -ta**. 1. a robot. 2. a person acting mechanically or repetitively.

auto·mobile, *n. Chiefly U.S.* a motor car.

auto·motive, *adj.* 1. propelled by a self-contained power plant. 2. pertaining to motor vehicles.

auton·omous /ɔːˈtɒnəməs/, *adj.* self-governing; independent. – **autonomy**, *n.*

autopsy, *n., pl.* **-sies**. medical examination of a body to determine the cause of death.

autumn, *n.* the season between summer and winter.

auxi·liary, *adj., n., pl.* **-ries**. –*adj.* 1. giving support; helping. 2. subsidiary. –*n.* 3. a person or thing that gives aid of any kind. 4. an organisation which assists a larger one.

avail, *v.* 1. to have force; be of use. 2. to be of value. 3. to advantage. 4. **avail oneself of**, to make use of. –*n.* 5. efficacy or advantage for a purpose.

avail·able, *adj.* 1. suitable or ready for use. 2. having sufficient power or efficacy. – **availability**, *n.*

ava·lanche, *n.* a large mass of snow,

avow

ice, etc., sliding suddenly down a mountain slope.

ava·rice, *n.* insatiable greed for riches. – **avaricious**, *adj.*

avenge, *v.*, **avenged, avenging**. to take vengeance.

avenue, *n.* 1. a double row of trees, often lining a road. 2. means of access.

aver, *v.*, **averred, averring**. to affirm with confidence.

aver·age, *n., adj., v.,* **-raged, -raging**. –*n.* 1. an arithmetical mean. 2. the ordinary, normal, or typical amount, quality, etc. –*adj.* 3. estimated by average; forming an average. –*v.* 4. to find an average value for.

averse, *adj.* disinclined or opposed.

aver·sion, *n.* 1. repugnance or rooted dislike (*to*). 2. an object of repugnance.

avert, *v.* 1. to turn away or aside. 2. to ward off.

aviary, *n., pl.* **-ries**. a large cage or enclosure in which birds are kept.

avi·ation, *n.* the act or science of flying by mechanical means.

avi·ator, *n.* a pilot of an aeroplane.

avid /ˈævɪd/, *adj.* keenly desirous; eager (*for*).

avo·cado /ævəˈkɑːdoʊ/, *n., pl.* **-dos**. (a tree bearing) a tropical pear-shaped fruit, green to black in colour, used often as a salad fruit. Also, **avocado pear**.

avoid, *v.* to keep away from; evade. – **avoidance**, *n.*

avoir·dupois /ˌævədəˈpwɑː/, *n.* a former system of weight, based on 16 ounces to a pound.

avow, *v.* to admit or acknowledge frankly. – **avowal**, *n.*

35

avuncular

avun·cu·lar /ə'vʌŋkjələ/, *adj.* of or like an uncle.

await, *v.* 1. to wait for. 2. to be in store for; be ready for. 3. to wait, as in expectation.

awake, *v.* **awoke** or **awaked**, **awaking**, *adj.* –*v.* 1. to rouse from sleep. 2. to stir the interest of. 3. to disturb (the memories, fears, etc.). 4. to come to realise the truth; to rouse to action, etc. –*adj.* 5. not sleeping. 6. alert.

awaken·ing, *adj.* 1. rousing. –*n.* 2. the act of awaking from sleep. 3. an arousal or revival of interest or attention.

award, *v.* 1. to adjudge to be merited; bestow. 2. to bestow by judicial decree, as in arbitration. –*n.* 3. something awarded, as a payment or medal.

aware, *adj.* conscious or having knowledge (*of*); informed. – **aware·ness**, *n.*

away, *adv.* 1. from this or that place. 2. apart; at a distance. 3. aside. 4. continuously: *The fire blazed away.* –*adj.* 5. absent. 6. distant. 7. *Colloq.* on the move.

awe, *n., v.*, **awed**, **awing**. –*n.* 1. respectful or reverential fear. –*v.* 2. to inspire with awe.

awe·some, *adj.* inspiring awe.

awful, *adj.* 1. *Colloq.* extremely bad; unpleasant. 2. *Colloq.* very; very great. 3. inspiring fear; dreadful.

awfully, *adv. Colloq.* very.

awk·ward, *adj.* 1. clumsy. 2. ungraceful. 3. ill-adapted for use or handling. 4. requiring caution. 5. difficult to handle. 6. embarrassing or trying. 7. deliberately obstructive or difficult.

azure

awl, *n.* a pointed instrument for piercing small holes in leather, wood, etc.

awning, *n.* 1. a rooflike shelter of canvas, etc., over a window, door, deck, etc. 2. a shelter.

awoke, *v.* past tense of **awake**.

awry /ə'raɪ/, *adv., adj.* 1. with a turn or twist to one side. 2. amiss; wrong.

axe, *n., pl.* **axes**, *v.*, **axed**, **axing**. –*n.* 1. an instrument with a bladed head on a handle used for hewing, cleaving, etc. 2. **the axe**, *Colloq.* a. a drastic cutting down (of expenses). b. dismissal from a job, etc. –*v.* 3. to shape or trim with an axe. 4. *Colloq.* to dismiss from a position.

axes, *n.* plural of **axis**.

axial, *adj.* 1. of, pertaining to, or forming an axis. 2. situated in an axis or on the axis. Also, **axile**.

axiom, *n.* 1. a recognised truth. 2. an established principle. – **axiomatic**, *adj.*

axis, *n., pl.* **axes**. 1. the line about which a rotating body, such as the earth, turns. 2. a fixed line of reference for plotting a curve on a graph.

axle, *n.* the pin, shaft, etc., on which or with which a wheel or pair of wheels rotate.

ay, *adv., n., pl.* **ayes**. –*adv.* 1. yes. –*n.* 2. an affirmative vote or voter. Also, **aye**.

ayatol·lah, *n.* title of an Islamic religious leader in Iran.

azalea, *n.* a shrub with handsome, variously coloured flowers.

azure, *adj.* of a sky blue colour.

Bb

B, b, *n.*, *pl.* **B's** or **Bs**, **b's** or **bs**. the 2nd letter of the English alphabet.

babble, *v.*, **-led**, **-ling**, *n*. –*v.* 1. to utter words imperfectly or indistinctly. 2. to make a continuous murmuring sound. –*n.* 3. inarticulate speech. 4. a murmuring sound.

baboon, *n.* a large, terrestrial monkey.

baby, *n.*, *pl.* **-bies**. 1. a very young child of either sex. 2. *Colloq.* an invention or creation of which one is particularly proud.

bac·carat /ˈbækərɑː/, *n.* a card game played for money.

bach /bætʃ/, *v. Colloq.* to keep house alone when not accustomed to housekeeping. Also, **batch**.

bachelor, *n.* 1. an unmarried man. 2. a person who has taken the first or lowest degree at a university.

bacil·lus /bəˈsɪləs/, *n.*, *pl.* **-cilli** /-ˈsɪliː/. any of the group of rod-shaped bacteria which produce spores in the presence of free oxygen.

back[1], *n.* 1. the hinder part of the human body, extending from the neck to the end of the spine. 2. the part of the body of animals corresponding to the human back. 3. the part opposite to or farthest from the face or front. –*v.* 4. to support, as with authority, influence, or money (*up*). 5. to (cause to) move backwards. 6. to bet in favour of. 7. lying or being behind. 8. away from the front position or rank; remote.

back[2], *adv.* 1. at, to, or towards the rear. 2. towards the past. 3. towards the original starting point, place, or condition. 4. in reply; in return.

back·bench, *n.* the non-office-holding parliamentary membership of a political party. – **backbencher**, *n.*

back·bone, *n.* 1. the spinal or vertebral column. 2. strength of character; resolution.

back·date, *v.*, **-dated**, **-dating**. to date (something) earlier; apply retrospectively.

back·fire, *v.*, **-fired**, **-firing**. 1. (of an internal-combustion engine) to have a premature explosion in the cylinder or in the admission or exhaust passages. 2. to bring results opposite to those planned.

back·gammon, *n.* a game played by 2 persons at a board with pieces moved in accordance with throws of dice.

back·ground, *n.* 1. the portions of a picture represented as in the distance. 2. the social, historical and other earlier circumstances which explain an event or condition. –*adj.* 3. of or pertaining to the background.

back·hand, *n.* a stroke, as in tennis, by a right-handed player from the left of the body (or the reverse for a left-handed player).

back·lash, *n.* any sudden, violent, or unexpected reaction.

back·log, *n.* 1. an accumulation (of business resources, stock, etc.) acting as a reserve. 2. an accumu-

37

backlog

lation (of work, correspondence, etc.) awaiting attention.

back·side, n. Colloq. the buttocks.

back·space, v., -spaced, -spacing. (in typing) to move the carriage back one space at a time.

back·stage, adv. in the wings or dressing rooms of a theatre.

back·stop, n. 1. Sport. a person, screen, or fence placed to prevent a ball going too far. 2. a person or a thing relied on for assistance when all else fails.

back·stroke, n. Swimming. a stroke in which the swimmer is on his back.

back·track, v. 1. to return over the same course or route. 2. to pursue a reverse policy.

backup, n. 1. a pent-up accumulation, esp. of a liquid. 2. a reserve supply or resource; a second means of support.

back·ward, adj. 1. Also, **backwards**. directed towards the back or past. 2. behind in time or progress. 3. reluctant; bashful.

back·wards, adv. 1. towards the back or rear. 2. with the back foremost. 3. towards the past. 4. towards a worse condition.

back·water, n. 1. a body of stagnant water connected to a river. 2. an unprogressive place or state.

back·woods, n.pl. any unfamiliar or unfrequented area.

back·yard, n. 1. an area, sometimes with gardens and lawn, at the back of a house. –adj. 2. illegal, illicit, improper or unqualified.

bacon, n. cured meat from the back and sides of the pig.

bac·te·ria /bæk'tɪərɪə/, n., pl. of **bacterium**. microscopic organisms,

bail

various species of which produce disease. – **bacterial**, adj.

bad, adj., **worse**, **worst**. 1. not good. 2. unsatisfactory; poor; inadequate. 3. regretful; sorry; upset. 4. severe. 5. rotten.

bade /bæd/, v. past tense of **bid**.

badge, n. a mark, token or device worn as a sign of allegiance, membership, authority, achievement.

badger, n. 1. a burrowing carnivorous mammal of Europe and America. –v. 2. to harass.

badi·nage /'bædənaʒ/, n. light, playful talk; banter.

bad·min·ton /'bædmɪntən/, n. a tennis-like game played with a high net and shuttlecock.

baffle, v., -fled, -fling. 1. to thwart or frustrate disconcertingly. 2. to puzzle.

bag, n., v., **bagged**, **bagging**. –n. 1. a receptacle of leather, cloth, paper, etc. 2. (pl.) Colloq. a lot; an abundance: bags of energy. 3. a sac, as in the body of an animal or insect. –v. 4. to hang loosely like an empty bag. 5. to put into a bag. 6. to kill or catch, as in hunting.

bag·gage, n. luggage.

bag·pipes, n. a musical instrument consisting of reeded pipes protruding from a windbag into which the air is blown.

bail^1, n. 1. property given as surety that a person released from legal custody will return at an appointed time. 2. the person or persons giving such surety. –v. 3. **bail up**, to delay (someone) as in conversation.

bail^2, v., →**bale**^{2}.

bail^3, n. 1. Cricket. either of the 2 small bars or sticks laid across the

bail

tops of the stumps. **2.** a framework for securing a cow's head during milking.

bail·iff /'beɪlɪff/, *n.* an officer employed to deliver court orders, collect debts, etc.

bait, *n.* **1.** food, etc., used as a lure in fishing, trapping, etc. **2.** food containing a harmful additive used to lure and kill animals considered pests. –*v.* **3.** to prepare (a hook or trap) with bait. **4.** to add substances to (food); to kill or drug animals. **5.** to goad to anger; torment (someone) for amusement.

baize, *n.* a green cloth used for tops of billiard tables, etc.

bake, *v.,* **baked, baking. 1.** to cook by dry heat in an oven, etc. **2.** to harden by heat.

baker, *n.* one who makes and sells bread, cake, etc. – **bakery,** *n.*

bala·clava /bælə'klɑːvə/, *n.* a knitted woollen hood covering the whole head except for the face.

bal·ance, *n., v.,* **-anced, -ancing.** –*n.* **1.** an instrument for weighing, typically a bar poised or swaying on a central support according to the weights borne in scales (pans) suspended at the ends. **2.** a state of equilibrium. **3.** mental steadiness or calmness. **4.** harmonious arrangement or adjustment, esp. in design. **5.** something used to produce equilibrium. **6.** the act of balancing; comparison as to weight, amount, importance, etc. **7.** the remainder. **8.** *Comm.* **a.** equality between the totals of the 2 sides of an account. **b.** the difference between the debit and credit totals of an account. **c.** amount still owing. **9.** an adjustment of accounts. –*v.* **10.** to weigh in a balance. **11.** to estimate the relative weight or importance of. **12.** to arrange or adjust the parts of symmetrically. **13.** to be equal or proportionate to. **14.** *Comm.* **a.** to add up the 2 sides of (an account) and determine the difference. **b.** to make the necessary entries in (an account) so that the sums of the 2 sides will be equal. **c.** to pay what remains due on an account.

ballad

balance sheet, *n.* a balanced statement of the financial position of a business on a specified date.

bal·cony /'bælkəni/, *n., pl.* **-nies.** a raised and railed platform projecting from an upper storey of a building.

bald /bɔːld/, *adj.* **1.** lacking hair on some part of the scalp. **2.** (of tyres) having the rubber tread worn off. **3.** bare; plain.

bale[1], *n.* a large bundle or package prepared for storage or transportation, esp. one closely compressed and secured by cords, wires, etc.

bale[2], *v.,* **baled, baling. 1.** to remove (water) esp. from a boat, as with a bucket or a can. **2. bale out,** to make a parachute-jump from a plane (esp. in emergency).

bale·ful, *adj.* full of menacing or malign influences.

ball[1], *n.* **1.** a spherical or approximately spherical body. **2.** a round or roundish body, hollow or solid, etc., as used in various games, as cricket, football, tennis, or golf. **3.** *Colloq.* a testicle. **4. on the ball,** *Colloq.* alert.

ball[2], *n.* **1.** a social gathering (usu. formal) at which people dance. **2.** *Colloq.* an enjoyable occasion.

ballad /'bæləd/, *n.* **1.** a simple nar-

39

ballad

rative poem, in short stanzas, often adapted for singing. 2. a sentimentalised pop song.

bal·last /'bæləst/, *n.* 1. any heavy material carried by a ship or boat to ensure proper stability. 2. something heavy, as bags of sand, placed in the car of a balloon for control of altitude, etc. 3. anything that gives mental, moral, or political stability.

ball-bearing, *n.* (one of the balls from) a bearing in which moving parts turn on rolling steel balls.

bal·ler·ina /bælə'riːnə/, *n., pl.* **-nas.** a female ballet-dancer.

ballet /'bæleɪ/, *n.* (performance of) theatrical style of dance using a formal technique, usu. narrative structure, and choreography.

bal·lis·tic /bə'lɪstɪk/, *adj.* relating to projectiles.

bal·loon, *n.* a usu. spherical bag filled with some gas lighter than air.

ballot /'bælət/, *n.* 1. a ticket or paper used in voting. 2. Also, **secret ballot.** the system of secret voting by means of printed or written ballots or voting machines.

ballpoint pen, *n.* a pen in which the point is a fine ball-bearing.

balm /baːm/, *n.* 1. any fragrant ointment. 2. anything which heals or soothes.

balmy, *adj.*, **balmier, balmiest.** mild and refreshing; soft; soothing.

bal·sam /'bɒlsəm, 'bɔːl-/, *n.* 1. any of various fragrant resins from certain trees. 2. a common garden plant often with red, pink or white flowers. 3. a balm.

bamboo, *n., pl.* **-boos.** 1. any of various treelike tropical and semit-

banish

ropical grasses. 2. the hollow woody stem of such a plant, used for building, furniture making, etc.

bam·boozle, *v.*, **-zled, -zling.** 1. to deceive by trickery. 2. to perplex.

ban, *v.*, **banned, banning.** *n.* -*v.* 1. to prohibit. -*n.* 2. a prohibition.

banal /bə'nal, 'beɪnəl, '/, *adj.* hackneyed; trite. - **banality**, *n.*

banana, *n.* (a tropical plant, cultivated for) a nutritious yellow fruit.

band[1], *n.* 1. a group of people or animals. 2. a company of musicians usu. playing for performance or as an accompaniment to dancing. -*v.* 3. to unite; form a group (*together*).

band[2], *n.* 1. any strip that contrasts with its surroundings in colour, texture or material. 2. *Radio.* a well-defined range of frequencies.

ban·dage, *n.* a strip of cloth used to bind up a wound, hold a dressing in place, etc.

bandi·coot, *n.* any of various small omnivorous somewhat ratlike Aust. marsupials.

bandit, *n.* 1. an armed robber. 2. an outlaw.

bandy, *v.*, **-died, -dying.** *adj.* -*v.* 1. to pass from one to another, or back and forth. -*adj.* 2. (of legs) having a bend outward.

bane, *n.* a destructive person or thing.

bang, *n.* 1. a loud, sudden explosive noise. 2. a knock; a bump. -*v.* 3. to strike or beat resoundingly. 4. to slam. 5. to knock or bump. 6. to strike violently or noisily.

bangle, *n.* a ring-shaped bracelet without a clasp.

banish, *v.* to condemn to exile; relegate to a country or place by decree.

ban·is·ter, *n.* (one of the supports of) a stair rail. Also, **bannister**.

banjo, *n., pl.* **-jos**. a musical instrument of the guitar family, having a circular body.

bank[1], *n.* **1.** a long pile or mass. **2.** a slope or acclivity. **3.** the land bordering the course of a river. **4.** lateral inclination during a curve. –*v.* **5.** to rise in or form banks, as clouds or snow. **6.** to tip or incline laterally, as of an aeroplane, a road, a cycle racing track, etc.

bank[2], *n.* **1.** an institution for receiving and lending money and transacting other financial business. **2.** any store or reserve. –*v.* **3.** to function as a bank or banker. **4.** to keep money in, or have an account with, or deposit in a bank. **5.** *Colloq.* to rely or count (*on* or *upon*). **6. bank up**, to accumulate.

bank[3], *n.* **1.** an arrangement of objects in line. **2.** a row or tier of oars.

bank·note, *n.* paper money issued by a bank.

bank·roll, *n.* **1.** a roll of money notes. –*v.* **2.** to provide funds for.

bank·rupt, *n.* **1.** *Law.* a person adjudged insolvent by a court, and whose property is administered for and divided among his creditors. **2.** any insolvent debtor; one unable to satisfy any just claims made upon him. **3.** a person completely depleted of some human quality or resource: *a moral bankrupt.* –*adj.* **4.** *Law.* subject to legal process because of insolvency. **5.** completely depleted of some human quality or resource. **6.** pertaining to bankrupts. –*v.* **7.** to make bankrupt. – **bankruptcy**, *n.*

bank·sia, *n.* any of various shrubs and trees with leathery leaves and dense cylindrical heads of flowers, sometimes called a bottlebrush.

banner, *n.* the flag of a country, army, troop, etc.

banns, *n.pl.* public announcement in church of intended marriage.

ban·quet /'bæŋkwət/, *n.* a formal and ceremonious meal, often given for a special occasion.

bantam, *n.* (*oft. cap.*) any of certain very small varieties of domestic fowl.

banter, *n.* **1.** goodhumoured teasing. –*v.* **2.** to use banter.

bap·tism, *n.* **1.** a ceremonial immersion in or sprinkling of water, as a sacrament of the Christian church. **2.** any similar ceremony or action of initiation, dedication, etc.: *a soldier's baptism of fire.* – **baptise**, *v.*

bar, *n., v.,* **barred, barring,** *prep.* –*n.* **1.** a relatively long and evenly shaped piece of some solid substance. **2.** a bank or stripe. **3.** a ridge of sand or gravel in coastal waters. **4.** anything which obstructs, hinders, or impedes. **5.** *Music.* Also, **bar-line.** the vertical line drawn across the stave to mark the metrical accent. **6.** a counter or a room where alcoholic drinks, etc., are served to customers. **7.** practising barristers collectively. **8.** any tribunal. –*v.* **9.** to fasten with a bar or bars. **10.** to block (a way, etc.) as with a barrier. **11.** to forbid; preclude. –*prep.* **12.** except; omitting; but.

barb, *n.* **1.** a pointed part projecting backwards from a main point, as of a fishhook or a fence wire. **2.** a sharp or unkind implication in a remark.

barbarian

bar·bar·ian /baˈbeəriən/, *n.* an ignorant, uncouth and cruel person. – **barbaric, barbarous,** *adj.*

bar·be·cue, *n.*, *v.* -cued, -cuing. –*n.* **1.** a metal frame for cooking meat, etc., above an open fire. **2.** a party, usu. out of doors, where barbecued food is served. –*v.* **3.** to cook on a barbecue. Also, **barbeque, bar-b-q.**

barber, *n.* one whose occupation it is to cut and style men's hair and to shave or trim beards.

bar·bi·tu·rate /baˈbɪtʃərət/, *n.* a drug used as an anaesthetic or a sedative.

bard, *n. Archaic.* a poet.

bare, *adj.* barer, barest, *v.*, bared, baring. –*adj.* **1.** without covering; naked. **2.** without the usual furnishings, contents, etc. **3.** open to view; undisguised. **4.** unadorned; bald. **5.** just sufficient. –*v.* **6.** to make bare.

barely, *adv.* only just; no more than: *She is barely 13.*

bar·gain, *n.* **1.** an agreement between parties in a transaction. **2.** an advantageous purchase. –*v.* **3.** to discuss the terms of a bargain; haggle over terms.

barge, *n.*, *v.*, barged, barging. –*n.* **1.** a large flat-bottomed vessel, used for transporting freight. –*v.* **2.** to move aggressively or with undue energy.

bari·tone, *n.* a male voice or voice part between tenor and bass.

barium /ˈbeəriəm/, *n.* a whitish, active, metallic element. *Symbol:* Ba

bark[1], *n.* **1.** the abrupt, explosive cry of a dog. –*v.* **2.** to utter such a cry or cries, as a dog. **3.** to speak or cry out sharply or gruffly.

bark[2], *n.* the external covering of the woody stems, branches, and roots of plants, as distinct from the wood itself.

barley, *n.* a cereal plant whose grain is used as food and in the making of whisky.

barn, *n.* a building for storing hay, grain, etc., and often for stabling livestock.

barnacle, *n.* any of certain crustaceans which attach themselves to marine rocks, etc.

baro·meter /bəˈrɒmətə/, *n.* **1.** an instrument for measuring atmospheric pressure, thus determining height, weather changes, etc. **2.** anything that indicates changes.

baron, *n.* **1.** a peer of the lowest titular rank. **2.** a rich and powerful man.

baro·net, *n.* a British hereditary titled man, ranking below the barons.

ba·roque /bəˈrɒk, bəˈroʊk/, *adj.* **1.** of or pertaining to the ornate style of musical or literary composition, art and architecture of the 17th and early 18th centuries. **2.** extravagantly ornamented.

bar·rack[1], *n.* (usu. pl.) a building or buildings for lodging soldiers, esp. in garrison.

bar·rack[2], *v.* to support; shout encouragement and approval (*for*).

barra·couta /bærəˈkuːtə/, *n.* an elongated, cold water, sport and food fish.

barra·cuda /bærəˈkuːdə/, *n.* **1.** an elongated, predatory, tropical and subtropical marine fish. **2.** →**barracouta.**

bar·rage, *n.* **1.** *Mil.* a barrier of artillery fire. **2.** any overwhelming quantity.

barramundi /bærəˈmʌndɪ/, n. a large, silver-grey, food fish.

barrel, n. 1. a wooden cylindrical vessel having slightly bulging sides and flat ends. 2. the tube of a gun.

barren, adj. 1. incapable of producing, or not producing, offspring. 2. unproductive.

barricade, n., v., -caded, -cading. –n. 1. a defensive barrier hastily constructed, as in a street. –v. 2. to obstruct with a barricade. 3. to shut in and defend with or as with a barricade.

barrier, n. anything that bars passage or access.

barrister, n. a lawyer allowed to plead cases in any court.

barrow, n. 1. a pushcart or horsedrawn cart used by street vendors. 2. →wheelbarrow.

barter, v. to trade by exchange of commodities instead of using money.

basalt /ˈbæsɒlt/, n. a dark, dense igneous rock.

base[1], n., v., based, basing. –n. 1. the bottom of anything, considered as its support. 2. the principal or fundamental element or ingredient of anything. 3. a fortified or protected area or place used by any of the armed services. 4. *Maths*. the number which serves as a starting point for a logarithmic or other numerical system. 5. *Chem*. any of numerous compounds which react with an acid to form a salt. –v. 6. to form a base or foundation for. 7. to establish, as a fact or conclusion (*on* or *upon*). 8. to place or establish on a base or basis.

base[2], adj., baser, basest. 1. morally low; cowardly. 2. debased or counterfeit.

baseball, n. 1. a game played with a wooden bat and a hard ball by 2 teams of 9 players. 2. the ball used in this game.

basement, n. a storey of a building partly or wholly underground.

bash, v. to strike with a crushing or smashing blow.

bashful, adj. uncomfortably shy; timid and easily embarrassed.

basic /ˈbeɪsɪk/, adj. 1. of, pertaining to, or forming a base; fundamental. –n. 2. something that is basic or essential. – **basically**, adv.

basil /ˈbæzəl/, n. a herb used in cooking.

basilica /bəˈsɪlɪkə/, n. 1. an oblong building, esp. a church with nave higher than its aisles. 2. a Roman Catholic church with special ceremonial rights.

basin /ˈbeɪsən/, n. 1. a circular container of greater width than depth, with sloping sides, used chiefly for washing. 2. a small circular container used chiefly for mixing, cooking, etc. 3. a hollow or depression in the earth's surface.

basis /ˈbeɪsɪs/, n., pl. **-ses** /-siz/. 1. a starting point or base. 2. a groundwork or fundamental principle. 3. the principal constituent.

bask, v. to lie in or be exposed to a pleasant warmth.

basket, n. a receptacle made of firm, flexible material, woven together.

basketball, n. a ball game, the object of which is to throw the ball through an elevated basket.

bass[1] /beɪs/, adj. low in pitch; of the lowest pitch or range.

bass

bass² /bæs/, *n.* a type of freshwater fish.

basset /'bæsət/, *n.* a long-bodied, short-legged dog resembling a dachshund but larger and heavier. Also, **basset hound**.

bas·si·nette, *n.* a basket in which a baby sleeps.

bassoon, *n.* a double reed woodwind instrument.

bastard /'bastəd/, *n.* **1.** an illegitimate child. **2.** *Colloq.* an unpleasant or despicable person or thing.

baste /beɪst/, *v.*, **basted, basting**. to moisten (meat, etc.) while cooking, with dripping, butter, etc.

bas·tion, *n.* **1.** a fortified place. **2.** any person or object which supports or defends.

bat¹, *n., v.,* **batted, batting**. *—n.* **1. a.** the club used in cricket, baseball, etc., to strike the ball. **b.** a racquet, esp. one used in table tennis. **2.** *Colloq.* rate of motion. *—v.* **3.** to strike or hit with or as with a bat or club.

bat², *n.* **1.** a small, nocturnal flying mammal. **2.** *Colloq.* a cranky or silly woman.

bat³, *v.,* **batted, batting**. to wink or flutter (one's eyelids).

batch, *n.* a quantity or a number taken together. **2.** The quantity of material prepared or required for, or produced by one operation.

bath /bɑθ/, *n.* **1.** a washing of the body in water or other liquid, or vapour, etc. **2.** (a vessel for containing) water or other liquid, etc., used for a bath. **3.** (*pl.*) a public swimming pool. *—v.* **4.** to put or wash in a bath.

bathe /beɪð/, *v.,* **bathed, bathing**. **1.** to immerse in water or other liquid

battle

for cleansing, refreshment, etc. **2.** to apply water or other liquid to, with a sponge, cloth, etc.

bathos /'beɪθɒs/, *n.* **1.** *Lit.* a comical drop from an elevated to a commonplace level. **2.** insincere emotion.

batik /'bætɪk, 'bætik/, *n.* (fabric with pattern made by) method of applying wax before dyeing.

batman, *n., pl.* **-men**. an army officer's servant.

baton /'bætn/, *n.* **1.** a staff or truncheon, esp. as a mark of office or authority. **2.** *Music.* the wand used by a conductor. **3.** (in relay racing) a metal or wooden tube handed on by one relay runner to the next.

bat·ta·lion /bə'tæljən/, *n. Mil.* a ground-force unit composed of 3 or more companies or similar units.

batten, *n.* **1.** a light strip of wood used to fasten main members of a structure together. *—v.* **2.** to fasten (*down*) with battens and tarpaulins.

batter¹, *v.* **1.** to beat persistently or hard. **2.** to damage by beating or hard usage.

batter², *n.* a mixture of flour, milk or water, eggs, etc., beaten together.

bat·tery, *n., pl.* **-ries**. **1.** *Elect.* chemical cells or groups of cells which produce or store electrical energy. **2.** a group of similar items or people used together: *a battery of machine guns, experts*. **3.** a large number of cages in which chickens, etc., are reared for intensive productivity. **4.** *Law.* an unlawful attack upon, or offensive touching of another.

battle, *n., v.,* **battled, battling**. *—n.* **1.** a hostile engagement between opposing forces. **2.** any extended

44

intense fight, struggle or contest. —v. 3. to fight.

bauble /'bɔbl/, n. a cheap piece of ornament; trinket.

baulk /bɔk/, v. 1. to stop, as at an obstacle. 2. *Sport*. to make an incomplete or misleading move, esp. an illegal one.

baux·ite /'bɔksaɪt/, n. a rock, the principal ore of aluminium.

bawdy, adj. rollickingly vulgar; lewd.

bawl, v. to cry loudly and vigorously.

bay[1], n. an inlet in the shore of a sea or lake.

bay[2], n. 1. a space projecting outwards from the line of a wall, as to contain a window. 2. the aisle between parallel rows of shelves as in a library.

bay[3], n. a deep, prolonged bark, as of a hound or hounds in hunting.

bay[4], n. a reddish brown colour.

bayo·net, n. a stabbing or slashing instrument of steel, made to be attached to the muzzle of a rifle.

bazaar /bə'za:/, n. a marketplace.

be, v., *pres. sing.* 1 **am**; 2 **are**; 3 **is**; *pl.* **are**; *pt.* 1 **was**; 2 **were**; 3 **was**; *pl.* **were**; *pp.* **been**; *ppr.* **being**. 1. to exist; have reality; live; take place; occur: *I think therefore I am*; *The party is next week.* 2. (a link connecting a subject with predicate or qualifying words or serving to form infinitive and participial phrases): *He is a student*; *Are you sure?*; *Try to be fair*; *the art of being agreeable.* 3. (used as an auxiliary verb with the present participle of a principal verb to form the continuous tense (*I am waiting*), or with a past participle in passive forms (*The date was fixed*; *It must be done*).

beach, n. 1. that part of the sandy shore of the sea, or of a large river or lake, washed by the tide or waves. 2. the seaside as a place of recreation. —v. 3. to run or haul up (a ship or boat) on the beach.

beacon, n. a guiding or warning signal, such as a lighthouse, fire, etc.

bead, n. 1. a small ball of glass, pearl, wood, etc., with a hole through it, for stringing and use as an ornament or in a rosary. 2. a drop of liquid.

beagle, n. a small hound with short legs and drooping ears.

beak, n. the horny bill of a bird.

beaker, n. a large drinking vessel with a wide mouth.

beam, n. 1. a thick, long piece of timber, for structural use. 2. the side of a vessel, or the direction at right angles to the keel, with reference to the wind, sea, etc. 3. the widest part. 4. the transverse bar of a balance from which the pans are suspended. 5. a ray, or bundle of parallel rays, of light or other radiation. 6. *Radio, Aeron.* a signal transmitted to guide pilots through darkness, bad weather, etc. —v. 7. to emit beams, as of light. 8. to look or smile radiantly.

bean, n. 1. the edible fruit or seed of various plants. 2. any of various other beanlike seeds, as the coffee bean.

bear[1], v., **bore**, **borne** or **born**, **bearing**. 1. to hold up. 2. to carry. 3. to give: *to bear witness.* 4. to undergo. 5. to be fit for or worthy of. 6. to give birth (to); bring forth young. 7. to produce by natural growth. 8. to be patient (*with*). 9. to press (*on*, *against*, *down*, etc.). 10. to have an

bear

effect, reference, or bearing (on). **11.** to have relevance to. **12.** to tend in course or direction. **13. bear out**, to confirm; prove right. **14. bear up**, to hold, or remain firm, as under pressure.

bear[2], *n.* a large carnivorous or omnivorous mammal, with coarse, heavy fur, short limbs, and a very short tail.

beard, *n.* the growth of hair on the face of an adult male, sometimes exclusive of the moustache.

bear·ing, *n.* **1.** the manner in which a person carries himself, including posture, gestures, etc. **2.** reference, relation, or relevance (on). **3.** *Mach.* a part in which a pivot, etc., turns or moves. **4.** (*oft. pl.*) direction or relative position.

beast, *n.* **1.** any animal except man, but esp. a large four-footed one. **2.** a coarse, filthy, or otherwise beastlike human.

beastly, *adj.*, **beastlier**, **beastliest**. **1.** of or like a beast; bestial. **2.** *Colloq.* nasty; disagreeable.

beat, *v.*, **beat**, **beaten** or **beat**, **beating**, *n.*, *adj.* –*v.* **1.** to strike repeatedly and usu. violently, esp. as a punishment; pound. **2.** to whisk. **3.** to assault; cause damage to: *They beat him up.* **4.** to flutter or flap. **5.** to sound as (on) a drum. **6.** to hammer (metal) thin; flatten (*out*). **7.** to make (a path) by repeated treading. **8.** *Music.* to mark (time) by strokes, as with the hand or a metronome. **9.** to overcome in a contest. **10.** to be superior to. **11.** to throb. **12** to radiate intense light or heat. –*n.* **13.** a stroke or blow. **14.** a throb. **15.** a beaten path or habitual round. **16.** the marking of the met-

bed

rical divisions of music. –*adj.* **17.** *Colloq.* exhausted.

be·a·ti·fic /biəˈtɪfɪk/, *adj.* **1.** bestowing blessedness. **2.** blissful.

beatify /biˈætɪfaɪ/, *v.*, **-fied**, **-fying**. **1.** to make blissfully happy. **2.** *Rom. Cath. Ch.* to declare (a deceased person) to be entitled to specific religious honour.

beaut, *Colloq.* –*adj.* **1.** fine; good. –*interj.* **2.** Also, **you beaut!** (an exclamation of approval, delight, enthusiasm, etc.)

beau·teous, *adj.* beautiful.

beau·ti·cian, *n.* a person skilled in cosmetic treatment and beauty aids.

beau·ti·ful, *adj.* **1.** having or exhibiting beauty. **2.** very pleasant.

beau·ti·fy, *v.*, **-fied**, **-fying**. to decorate or make more beautiful.

beauty, *n.*, *pl.* **beauties**. **1.** that quality which excites an admiring pleasure, or delights the eye. **2.** something or someone beautiful. **3.** a particular advantage. –*interj.* **4.** (an exclamation of approval, delight, etc.)

beaver, *n.* an amphibious rodent which dams streams with branches, mud, etc.

because, *conj.* **1.** for the reason that. –*adv.* **2.** by reason; on account (*of*).

beckon, *v.* **1.** to summon or direct by a gesture. **2.** to lure; entice.

become, *v.*, **became**, **become**, **becoming**. **1.** to come into being; grow to be (as stated). **2.** to be the fate (*of*). **3.** to befit; suit.

becom·ing, *adj.* **1.** attractive. **2.** suitable; proper.

bed, *n.* **1.** a piece of furniture upon which a person sleeps. **2.** a piece of ground (in a garden) in which plants are grown. **3.** a part forming a foundation or base.

bedlam, *n.* a scene of wild uproar and confusion.

bedrag·gled, *adj.* limp, wet and dirty.

bed·rid·den, *adj.* confined to bed.

bee, *n.* **1.** a four-winged insect which gathers pollen. **2.** a local gathering for work, contests, etc.

beech, *n.* a type of tree growing in temperate regions.

beef, *n.* **1.** the edible flesh of a bull or cow. *-v.* **2.** *Colloq.* to complain.

been, *v.* past participle of **be**.

beer, *n.* an alcoholic beverage brewed and fermented from malted barley and flavoured with hops, etc.

beet, *n.* any of various biennial plants including the red beet and the sugar beet.

beetle, *n.* any insect with forewings modified as hard, horny structures, useless in flight.

beet·root, *n.* the edible root of the red beet.

befall, *v.*, **-fell, -fallen, -falling.** to happen (to) or occur.

before, *adv.* **1.** in front; in advance. **2.** earlier or sooner. *-prep.* **3.** in front of; in advance of. **4.** previously to; earlier than. **5.** in preference to. **6.** in precedence of. **7.** in the presence or sight of. **8.** under the jurisdiction or consideration of. *-conj.* **9.** previously to the time when. **10.** rather than.

before·hand, *adv.* in anticipation; ahead of time.

be·friend, *v.* to act as a friend; aid.

be·fuddle, *v.*, **-dled, -dling. 1.** to make stupidly drunk. **2.** to confuse, as with glib argument.

beg, *v.*, **begged, begging. 1.** to ask for in charity. **2.** to ask (for, or of) with humility or earnestness, or as a favour. **3.** to ask alms or charity; live by asking alms.

beget, *v.*, **begot, begotten** or **begot, begetting.** to procreate (used chiefly of the male parent).

beggar, *n.* **1.** one who begs alms, or lives by begging. **2.** a penniless person. **3.** (in playful use) a wretch or rogue.

begin, *v.*, **began, begun, beginning. 1.** to enter upon an action; start. **2.** to come into existence; arise. **3.** to take the first step in; set about. **4.** to be the originator of. **- beginning**, *n.*

be·grudge, *v.*, **-grudged, -grudging.** to be discontented at seeing (a person) have (something).

be·guile /bə'gaɪl, bi-/, *v.*, **-guiled, -guiling. 1.** to influence by guile; mislead. **2.** to charm.

behalf, *n.* the side or interest (prec. by *on*).

behave, *v.*, **-haved, -having. 1.** to conduct oneself or itself. **2.** to act in a socially acceptable manner. **- behaviour**, *n.*

behead, *v.* to cut off the head of; execute.

behest, *n.* bidding; command.

behind, *prep.* **1.** at the back of. **2.** after. **3.** less advanced than; inferior to. **4.** on the farther side of. **5.** supporting; promoting. **6.** hidden by. *-adv.* **7.** at or towards the back. **8.** in arrears. *-n.* *Colloq.* **9.** the buttocks.

behold, *v.*, **-held, -holding.** to observe; look at.

behove, *v.*, **-hoved, -hoving.** to be

47

behove

needful or proper for (now only in impersonal use).

beige /beɪʒ/, *n., adj.* very light brown

being, *n.* 1. (conscious) existence; life. 2. substance or nature. 3. a living thing.

be·lated, *adj.* coming or being late.

belch, *v.* 1. to eject wind spasmodically and noisily from the stomach through the mouth. 2. to emit contents violently, as a gun, geyser, or volcano. 3. to eject spasmodically or violently. –*n.* 4. a belching.

belfry, *n., pl.* **-fries.** a tower for a bell, either attached to a church or other building or standing apart.

belie, *v.,* **-lied, -lying.** 1. to misrepresent. 2. to show to be false.

belief, *n.* 1. that which is believed. 2. acceptance of the truth or reality of a thing without absolute proof. 3. confidence; trust.

believe, *v.,* **-lieved, -lieving.** 1. to have confidence in; rely through faith (*on*). 2. to accept a doctrine, principle, system, etc. (*in*). 3. to have belief in. 4. to think. – **believable**, *adj.* – **believer**, *n.*

be·little, *v.,* **-tled, -tling.** to make little or less important; disparage.

bell, *n.* 1. a cup-shaped sounding instrument, usu. of metal, rung by the strokes of a clapper suspended within it. 2. any instrument emitting a ringing signal, as a doorbell. 3. **ring a bell**, *Colloq.* to remind one; jog the memory. 4. *Naut.* the half-hourly subdivisions of a watch of 4 hours.

bell·bird, *n.* a yellowish-green honeyeater with a tinkling, bell-like call.

belli·cose, *adj.* warlike; pugnacious.

bench

belli·gerent /bəˈlɪdʒərənt/, *adj.* 1. warlike; aggressive. 2. pertaining to war. –*n.* 3. a state or nation at war.

bellow, *v.* 1. to make a hollow, loud cry, as a bull or cow. 2. to roar; bawl.

bellows, *n. sing. and pl.* an instrument which is pumped to produce a strong current of air.

belly, *n., pl.,* **-ies.** the front or underpart of a vertebrate body from the chest to the thighs, containing the stomach, etc.; the abdomen.

belong, *v.* 1. to have one's rightful place; be connected with as a member, etc. (*to*). 2. to be proper or due. 3. **belong to**, to be the property of.

belong·ings /bəˈlɒŋɪŋz, bi-/, *n.pl.* possessions.

be·loved /bəˈlʌvd, -ˈlʌvd, bi-/, *adj.* 1. greatly loved. –*n.* 2. one who is greatly loved.

below, *adv.* 1. in or to a lower place. 2. at a later point on a page or in writing. 3. in a lower rank or grade. –*prep.* 4. lower down than. 5. not worthy of.

belt, *n.* 1. a band of leather, etc., worn around the waist to support clothing, for decoration, etc. 2. any encircling or transverse band or strip. 3. a flexible band connecting 2 or more wheels, etc., to transmit motion. –*v.* 4. to gird or furnish with a belt. 5. *Colloq.* to give a blow to. 6. to sing very loudly and often raucously (*out*). 7. *Colloq.* to move quickly. 8. **belt up**, *Colloq.* to be quiet.

be·mused, *adj.* 1. confused; stupefied. 2. lost in thought.

bench, *n.* 1. a long seat with or without a back for several people.

48

bench

2. a seat for members in a house of parliament. 3. the position or office of a judge. 4. the strong work-table of a carpenter or other mechanic.

bend, *v.,* **bent, bending,** *n.* –*v.* 1. to make or become curved, crooked, or bent. 2. to turn or incline in a particular direction. 3. to (force to) bow in submission or reverence. –*n.* 4. the act of bending. 5. the state of being bent. 6. a bent thing or part; curve.

be·neath, *adv.* 1. below; in a lower place, position, state, etc. –*prep.* 2. below; under. 3. unworthy of.

bene·dic·tion, *n. Eccles.* (the act of uttering) a blessing.

bene·fac·tor, *n.* 1. a kindly helper. 2. one who makes a bequest or endowment.

bene·ficial, *adj.* conferring benefit; advantageous; helpful.

bene·fit, *n., v.,* **-fited, -fiting.** –*n.* 1. an act of kindness. 2. anything that is for the good of a person or thing. 3. a payment made by an insurance company, public agency, etc. –*v.* 4. to do good to; be of service to. 5. to gain advantage; make improvement.

bene·volent /bəˈnɛvələnt/, *adj.* 1. desiring to do good for others. 2. intended for benefits rather than profit. – **benevolence,** *n.*

be·nighted, *adj.* intellectually or morally ignorant; unenlightened.

benign, *adj.* 1. of a kind disposition; kind. 2. *Pathol.* (of a tumour, etc.) not malignant.

bent, *adj.* 1. curved; crooked. 2. determined (*on*). –*n.* 3. direction taken; inclination; leaning.

be·queath, *v.* to dispose by last will

best

of (personal property, esp. money). – **bequest,** *n.*

berate, *v.,* **-rated, -rating.** to scold.

be·reave, *v.,* **-reaved** or **-reft, -reaving.** to make desolate through loss (*of*), esp. by death.

beret /ˈbɛreɪ/, *n.* a soft, round, peakless cap that fits closely.

berry, *n., pl.* **-ries.** 1. any small, (usu.) stoneless and juicy fruit, as the gooseberry, strawberry, etc. 2. a dry seed or kernel, as of wheat.

ber·serk /bəˈzɜːk/, *adj.* violently and destructively frenzied.

berth, *n.* a shelf-like space, bunk, or whole room allotted to a traveller on a vessel or a train.

beryl /ˈbɛrɪl/, *n.* a mineral group which includes the emerald.

be·seech, *v.,* **-sought** or **-seeched, -seeching.** 1. to implore urgently. 2. to beg eagerly for.

beset, *v.,* **-set, -setting.** to attack on all sides; assail; harass.

beside, *prep.* 1. by or at the side of; near. 2. compared with.

be·sides, *adv.* 1. moreover. 2. in addition. 3. otherwise; else. –*prep.* 4. over and above; in addition to. 5. other than; except.

be·siege, *v.,* **-sieged, -sieging.** 1. to lay siege to. 2. to ply, as with requests, etc.

be·sotted, *adj.* 1. foolishly in love. 2. made stupid or drunk.

be·spoke, *adj.* made to order.

best, *adj.* (*superlative of* **good**). 1. of the highest quality or standing. 2. most advantageous or suitable. 3. favourite. –*adv.* (*superlative of* **well**). 4. most excellently or suitably; with most advantage or success. 5. in or to the highest degree; most fully. –*n.* 6. the best thing,

best

state, or part. 7. best quality. –v. 8. to defeat. 9. to outdo.

bes·tial, adj. 1. of or belonging to a beast. 2. brutal; irrational.

best man, n. the chief attendant of a bridegroom.

bestow, v. to present as a gift; confer.

bet, v., bet or betted, betting, n. –v. 1. to agree to pay a forfeit to another if one's opinion is proved wrong; wager. 2. to lay a wager. 3. to make a practice of betting. –n. 4. a pledge to be forfeited in a wager.

betide, v., -tided, -tiding. Archaic. to happen; befall; come to.

betray, v. 1. to expose to an enemy by treachery. 2. to be unfaithful in keeping or upholding. 3. to disclose in violation of confidence. 4. to show: *His face betrayed his emotions.* 5. to deceive. – **betrayal**, n.

be·troth /bɪˈtroʊð, -ˈtroʊθ, bi-/, v. 1. to promise to marry. 2. to arrange for the marriage of.

better, adj. (*comparative of* **good**). 1. of superior quality. 2. of superior value, use, etc. 3. larger. (*comparative of* **well**). 4. in a more excellent way. 5. in a superior degree. 6. **better off**, in better circumstances. 7. **had better**, would be wiser, safer, etc., to. –v. 8. to make better; improve. –n. 9. that which is superior. 10. (*usu. pl.*) one's superior(s) in wisdom, wealth, etc.

between, prep. 1. in the space separating (2 or more points, objects, etc.). 2. intermediate in, time, quantity, or degree: *between 12 and 1 o'clock, between pink and red.* 3. distinguishing one thing from another. –adv. 4. in the intervening space or time; in an intermediate position or relation.

bevel, n. a sloping edge or surface.

bev·erage, n. a drink of any kind.

bevy /ˈbɛvi/, n., pl. **bevies**. a flock.

beware, v. (*now only used as imperative or infinitive*). to be wary or careful (fol. by *of* or a clause).

be·wil·der, v. to confuse or puzzle completely; perplex.

be·witch, v. to affect by witchcraft or magic.

be·yond, prep. 1. on or to the farther side of. 2. farther on than. 3. past. 4. more than; over and above. –adv. 5. farther on or away: *as far as the house and beyond.*

bi·annual, adj. occurring twice a year.

bias, n., v., biased, biasing. –n. 1. an oblique or diagonal line of direction, esp. across a woven fabric. 2. a particular tendency oft. indicating prejudice. –v. 3. to influence, usu. unfairly; prejudice.

bib, n. a protective cloth worn under the chin by a child while eating.

Bible, n. (a copy of) the sacred book of Christianity, including the Old and New Testaments. – **biblical**, adj.

bibli·ography, n., pl. **-phies**. 1. a list of literature on a particular subject. 2. a list of source materials used in the preparation of a work.

bi·cameral, adj. having 2 branches, chambers, or houses, as a legislative body.

bi·centenary, n. a 200th anniversary. – **bicentennial**, adj.

biceps /ˈbaɪsɛps, -sɛps/, n. a muscle having 2 heads of origin, esp. the muscle on the front of the upper arm.

50

bicker

bicker, *v.* to engage in petulant argument; wrangle.

bi·cycle, *n.* a vehicle with 2 wheels driven by pedals and having a saddle-like seat for the rider.

bid, *v.*, **bade** /bæd/ or **bad** /bæd/ (*for defs 1, 2*) or **bid** (*for def 3*), **bidden** or **bid, bidding,** *n.* —*v.* 1. to command; direct. 2. to offer, as a greeting of benediction. 3. to offer, as a price at an auction or to secure a contract. —*n.* 4. an offer, as at an auction. 5. an attempt to attain some goal.

biddy, *n., pl.* **-dies.** *Colloq.* an old woman.

bide, *v.*, **bided, biding.** *in the phrase* **bide one's time,** to wait for a favourable opportunity.

bidet /ˈbiːdeɪ/, *n.* a small low bath for washing the genitals.

bi·ennial /baɪˈɛnɪəl/, *adj.* happening every 2 years.

bier /bɪə/, *n.* a stand on which a corpse, or the coffin, is laid before burial.

bi·focal /baɪˈfoʊkəl/, *adj.* (of spectacle lenses) having 2 portions, one for near and the other for far vision.

big, *adj.*, **bigger, biggest.** 1. large in size, amount, etc. 2. large in compass or conception; magnanimous.

bi·gamy, *n.* the crime of marrying while one has a spouse living and not divorced. – **bigamist,** *n.* – **bigamous,** *adj.*

bight, *n.* 1. the loop or bent part of a rope. 2. a bend or curve in the shore of a sea or a river.

bigot /ˈbɪɡət/, *n.* a person intolerantly convinced of the rightness of a particular creed, etc.

bike /baɪk/, *n. Colloq.* a bicycle, tricycle, or motorcycle.

bikini /bɪˈkiːni/, *n.* a very brief, two-piece swimming costume.

bi·lateral, *adj.* pertaining to or involving 2 sides or parties.

bile, *n.* 1. a bitter yellow or greenish liquid secreted by the liver and aiding in digestion of fats. 2. ill nature; peevishness.

bilge /bɪldʒ/, *n.* 1. the lowest portion of a ship's interior. 2. foul water that collects there.

bi·lingual, *adj.* able to speak 2 languages.

bi·lious /ˈbɪlɪəs/, *adj.* 1. pertaining to bile or to an excess secretion of bile. 2. suffering from or caused by trouble with the bile or liver. 3. nauseating.

bill[1], *n.* 1. an account of money owed for goods or services. 2. a draft of a proposed statute presented to a legislature, but not yet made law. 3. a printed public notice or advertisement. 4. a bill of exchange. 5. program; entertainment. —*v.* 6. to announce by bill or public notice. 7. to schedule as part of a program. 8. to render an account of money owed.

bill[2], *n.* the horny sheath covering the jaws of a bird.

billa·bong, *n.* a waterhole, orig. part of a river, formed when the channel connecting it to the river dries up.

bill·board, *n.* →**hoarding.**

billet, *n.* 1. lodging for a soldier, esp. in private or non-military buildings. 2. private, usu. unpaid, temporary lodgings arranged for members of a group or team.

bil·liards, *n.* a game played on a

billiards

rectangular table, with balls driven by means of cues.

bil·lion, *n.* **1.** (esp. in scientific use) a million times a million, or 10^{12}. **2.** a thousand times a million, or 10^9.

billow, *n.* **1.** a great wave or surge of the sea. –*v.* **2.** to rise or roll in or like billows.

billy, *n., pl.* **billies.** a cylindrical container for liquids, usu. having a close-fitting lid.

billy·cart, *n.* a small four-wheeled cart.

billy·goat, *n.* a male goat.

bin, *n.* **1.** a box or enclosed space used for storing grain, wool, coal, refuse, etc. **2.** a winemaker's stand for storing wine in bottles.

bi·nary /'baɪnərɪ/, *adj.* **1.** consisting of, indicating, or involving 2. **2.** using, involving, or expressed in the binary number system. **3.** *Maths.* having 2 variables.

binary code, *n.* any means of representing information by a sequence of the digits 1 and 0.

bind, *v.,* **bound, binding,** *n.* –*v.* **1.** to make fast with a band or bond. **2.** to swathe or bandage (*up*). **3.** to unite by any legal or moral tie. **4.** to hold to a particular state, place, employment, etc. **5.** (*usu. passive*) to place under obligation or compulsion. **6.** to secure within a cover, as a book. **7.** to become compact or solid; cohere. **8.** to be obligatory. –*n.* **9.** something that binds, esp. a situation with few or no choices available.

bindi·eye /'bɪndɪaɪ/, *n.* **1.** any of a number of plants with small, burr-like fruits. Also, **bindii, bindy-eye, bindy.**

birthday

binge, *n. Colloq.* a spree; a period of excessive indulgence, as in eating or drinking.

bingo, *n.* →**housie-housie.**

bi·noc·ular, *adj.* **1.** involving the use of) 2 eyes. –*n.* **2.** (*pl.*) a double telescope used by both eyes at once.

bi·nomial, *n. Maths.* an expression which is a sum or difference of 2 terms, as $3x + 2y$ and $x^2 - 4x$.

bio·de·grad·able, *adj.* capable of being decomposed.

bi·og·raphy, *n., pl.* **-phies.** a written account of a person's life. – **biographer**, *n.* – **biographical**, *adj.*

bi·ol·ogy, *n.* the science of life or living matter in all its forms and phenomena. – **biologist**, *n.* – **biological**, *adj.*

biopsy, *n.* the excision and diagnostic study of a piece of tissue from a living body.

bio·rhythms, *n. pl.* the 3 supposed cycles of human energy, the physiological, emotional, and intellectual.

bi·par·tite, *adj.* being in 2 corresponding parts.

birch, *n.* a tree or shrub with a smooth bark and close-grained wood.

bird, *n.* **1.** any of the class of warm-blooded, feathered vertebrates with wings by means of which most species fly. **2.** *Colloq.* a girl; a girlfriend.

biro, *n.* a ballpoint pen.

birth, *n.* **1.** the fact of being born. **2.** the act of bearing or bringing forth. **3.** lineage; extraction. **4.** supposedly natural heritage. **5.** any coming into existence; origin.

birth·day, *n.* (the anniversary of) the

birthday

day of one's birth, or of the origin of something.

birth·mark, *n.* a congenital mark on the body.

birth·right, *n.* any right or privilege to which a person is entitled by birth.

bis·cuit, *n.* a mixture of flour, liquid, shortening, etc., baked in small pieces.

bi·sect, *v.* to cut or divide into 2 parts.

bi·sexual, *adj.* 1. of both sexes. –*n.* 2. a person sexually attracted to both sexes.

bishop, *n.* a clergyman in charge of a diocese.

bison, *n., pl.* **-son.** a large Nth American bovine ruminant.

bistro, *n.* 1. a wine bar. 2. a small unpretentious restaurant.

bit[1], *n.* 1. the metal mouthpiece of a bridle attached to the reins. 2. anything that curbs or restrains. 3. the cutting or penetrating part of various tools.

bit[2], *n.* 1. a small piece or quantity of anything. 2. share or part of a duty, task, etc.

bitch, *n.* 1. a female dog. 2. *Colloq.* a disagreeable or malicious woman. 3. *Colloq.* a complaint. – **bitchy**, *adj.*

bite, *v.*, **bit, bitten** or **bit, biting**, *n.* –*v.* 1. to cut into or wound, or cut (*off, out*, etc.) with the teeth. 2. to press the teeth (*into, on*, etc.); snap. 3. to sting, as an insect. 4. to cheat; deceive. 5. (of fish) to take the bait. 6. to accept a deceptive offer or suggestion. –*n.* 7. the act of biting. 8. a wound made by biting. 9. pungency; sharpness.

bitter, *adj.* 1. having a harsh, disagreeable taste. 2. hard to bear;

blackboard

grievous. 3. characterised by intense sorrowing.

bittersweet, *adj.* 1. both bitter and sweet to the taste. 2. both pleasant and painful.

bitu·men /'ɪtʃəmən/, *n.* 1. any of various natural substances, as asphalt, etc. 2. **the bitumen,** a tarred or sealed road.

bi·valve /'baɪvælv/, *n.* a mollusc having 2 shells hinged together.

bi·vouac /'bɪvuæk/, *n.* 1. a temporary camp made out in the open. –*v.* 2. (**-ck-**) to camp in the open.

bi·zarre /bə'zɑː/, *adj.* singular in appearance, style, or general character; odd.

blab, *v.*, **blabbed, blabbing.** to reveal indiscreetly and thoughtlessly.

black, *adj.* 1. without brightness or colour; absorbing all or nearly all the rays emitted by a light source. 2. pertaining to a race with dark skin pigmentation. 3. soiled with dirt. 4. gloomy; dismal. 5. indicating censure, disgrace, etc. 6. illicit. 7. banned by a trade union. –*n.* 8. a colour without hue, opposite to white. 9. (*sometimes cap.*) a member of a dark-skinned people. 10. **In the black,** financially secure. –*v.* 11. to make or become black. 12. (of a trade union) to declare (a factory, etc.) black. 13. **black out,** to lose consciousness.

black·ball, *v.* 1. to ostracise. 2. to vote against.

black·berry, *n., pl.* **-ries.** a black or very dark purple fruit.

black·bird, *n.* a European songbird.

black·board, *n.* a smooth dark board for writing or drawing on with chalk.

53

blackcurrant

black·currant, *n.* (a shrub bearing) a small, black edible fruit.

black eye, *n.* bruising round the eye.

black·guard 'blægad, *n.* a coarse, despicable person; a scoundrel.

black·head, *n.* a small black-tipped pimple on the face.

black·jack, *n.* 1. black flag of a pirate ship. 2. *Cards.*→pontoon².

black·leg, *n.* 1. →scab (def. 2). 2. a swindler esp. in racing or gambling.

black magic, *n.* magic used for evil purposes.

black·mail, *n.* 1. act of demanding payment usu. by threats of damaging revelations. 2. the payment itself. –*v.* 3. to demand such payment from.

black market, *n.* an illegal market violating price controls, rationing, etc.

black·out, *n.* 1. the extinguishing or covering of all visible lights in a city, etc., as a wartime protection. 2. the loss of lighting as in a power failure. 3. temporary loss of consciousness or vision.

black sheep, *n.* a person regarded as worthless despite a good background.

black·smith, *n.* an artisan who works in iron, esp. making and fitting horseshoes.

blad·der, *n.* 1. *Anat., Zool.* a membranous and muscular sac for storage and expulsion of urine. 2. the inflatable inner bag of a football, or the like.

blade, *n.* 1. the flat cutting part of sword, knife, etc. 2. a sword. 3. the leaf of a plant, esp. of a grass or cereal. 4. a thin, flat part of some-

blaspheme

thing, as of a bone, an oar, etc. 5. a dashing or rakish young fellow.

blame, *v.*, **blamed, blaming**, –*v.t.* 1. to lay the responsibility of (a fault, error, etc.) (*on*) (a person): *I blame the mistakes on him; I blame you for the delay.* 2. **to blame**, responsible for a fault or error; culpable. –*n.* 3. imputation of fault; censure. 4. responsibility for a fault, error, etc.

blanch, *v.* to make or become white; turn pale.

blancmange blə'mɒnʒ, *n.* a sweet dessert made of thickened and flavoured milk.

bland, *adj.* 1. (of a person's manner) suave; deliberately agreeable but often without real feeling. 2. soothing or balmy, as air. 3. mild, as food or medicines.

bland·ish, *v.* to treat flatteringly; coax; cajole.

blank, *adj.* 1. (of paper, etc.) free from marks, writing or printing. 2. not filled in. 3. unrelieved by ornament or opening. 4. lacking some usual or completing feature. 5. complete or utter. –*n.* 6. a void; emptiness. 7. a space left (to be filled in) in written or printed matter. 8. *Mach.* a piece of metal prepared to be stamped or cut into a finished object, such as a coin or key.

blan·ket, *n.* 1. a large piece of soft fabric, used esp. as a bed covering. 2. any heavy concealing layer or covering. –*adj.* 3. covering a group or class of things, conditions, etc.

blare, *v.*, **blared, blaring**. to emit a loud raucous sound.

blasé blɑ'zeɪ, 'blɑzeɪ, *adj.* bored by pleasures of life.

blas·pheme, *v.*, **-phemed, -pheming**.

blaspheme

1. to speak irreverently of (God or sacred things). 2. to utter impious words. - **blasphemy**, n. - **blasphemous**, adj.

blast, n. 1. a sudden gust of wind. 2. the blowing of a trumpet, whistle, etc. 3. a forcible stream of air from the mouth, from bellows, or the like. 4. explosion. 5. severe criticism. -v. 6. to blow (a trumpet, etc.). 7. to tear (rock, etc.) to pieces with an explosive. 8. to criticise (someone) abusively. -interj. 9. (an exclamation of anger or irritation).

blast furnace, n. a furnace using a forced blast to produce molten iron.

bla·tant, adj. (of actions, etc.) flagrantly obvious or undisguised.

blaze[1], n., v. blazed, blazing. -n. 1. a bright flame or fire. 2. a sudden, intense outburst, as of fire, passion, fury. -v. 3. to burn brightly.

blaze[2], n. 1. a spot or mark made on a tree as an indicator. 2. a white spot on the face of a horse, cow, etc.

blazer, n. a jacket.

bleach, v. 1. to make white or pale. -n. 2. a bleaching agent.

bleak, adj. 1. bare, desolate. 2. cold and piercing.

bleary, adj., blearier, bleariest. (of the eyes) dim and watery.

bleat, v. 1. to cry as a sheep, goat, or calf. 2. to complain.

bleed, v., bled, bleeding. 1. to lose blood. 2. to cause to lose blood, esp. surgically. 3. to exude sap, juice, etc. 4. Colloq. to extort money from.

ble·mish, v. 1. to mar the beauty or perfection of. -n. 2. a defect; a disfigurement.

blitz

blend, v., blended, blending, n. -v. 1. to mix smoothly and inseparably together. 2. to mix (various sorts or grades). -n. 3. a mixture or kind produced by blending.

bless, v., blessed or blest, blessing. 1. to consecrate by a religious rite; pronounce holy. 2. to request the bestowal of divine favour on. 3. to bestow good of any kind upon. - **blessing**, n.

blight, n. 1. any cause of destruction or frustration. -v. 2. to destroy; frustrate.

blind, adj. 1. lacking the sense of sight. 2. unwilling or unable to understand. 3. having no outlets: *a blind alley*. 4. made without knowledge in advance. -v. 5. to make blind. -n. 6. something that obstructs vision or keeps out light. 7. a shade for a window. -adv. 8. without being able to see one's way. 9. without prior consideration.

blind·fold, v. 1. to cover the eyes of. -n. 2. a cover over the eyes.

blink, v. 1. to wink, esp. rapidly and repeatedly. 2. a glance or glimpse. 3. **on the blink**, Colloq. not working properly.

blin·ker, n. either of 2 flaps on a bridle, to prevent a horse from seeing sideways.

bliss, n. 1. blitheness; gladness. 2. supreme happiness.

blis·ter, n. 1. a watery swelling on the skin as from a burn or other injury. 2. any similar swelling, as an air bubble in a casting or a paint blister. -v. 3. to rise in blisters; become blistered.

blithe, adj. joyous, merry, or gay in disposition; glad.

blitz, n. 1. war waged by surprise,

55

swiftly and violently. 2. any swift, vigorous attack.

bliz·zard, *n.* a violent windstorm with dry, driving snow and intense cold.

bloat, *v.* 1. to make or become distended, as with air, water, etc.; cause to swell. 2. to puff up.

bloc, *n.* a group of states or territories united by some common factor.

block, *n.* 1. a solid mass of wood, stone, etc. 2. a piece of wood prepared for wood engraving. 3. a letter-press printing plate. 4. **a.** a device consisting of pulleys mounted in a casing or shell, to which a hook is attached, used for transmitting power, etc. **b.** the casing holding the pulley. 5. a blocking or obstructing, or obstructed state or condition. 6. **a.** a fairly large area of land, esp. for settlement, etc. **b.** a section of land for building a house, etc. 7. a row of contiguous buildings, or one large building, divided into separate houses, shops, etc. 8. a portion of a city, etc., enclosed by (usu. 4) streets. 9. a writing or sketching pad. –*v.* 10. to fit with blocks; mount on a block. 11. to sketch or outline roughly (*out* or *in*). 12. to obstruct (a space, progress, etc.); check or hinder (a person, etc.).

block·ade, *n.* any obstruction of passage or progress.

block·age, *n.* an obstruction.

block·buster, *n. Colloq.* anything large and spectacular.

bloke, *n. Colloq.* man; fellow; guy.

blond, *adj.* 1. light-coloured. 2. (of a person) having light-coloured hair and skin. –*n.* 3. a blond person.
– **blonde,** *n.fem.*

blood /blʌd/, *n.* 1. the fluid that circulates in the arteries and veins. 2. physical and cultural extraction. 3. descent from a common ancestor. 4. **in cold blood,** calmly, coolly, and deliberately.

blood·bath, *n.* a massacre.

blood·hound, *n.* a large, powerful dog used for tracking game, human fugitives, etc.

blood·shed, *n.* destruction of life; slaughter.

blood·shot, *adj.* (of the eyes) red from dilated blood vessels.

blood·stream, *n.* the blood flowing through a circulatory system.

blood·thirsty, *adj.* eager to shed blood; murderous.

bloody, *adj.,* **bloodier, bloodiest,** *v.,* **bloodied, bloodying,** *adv.* –*adj.* 1. stained with blood. 2. attended with bloodshed. 3. *Colloq.* (an intensive as in *bloody good* or *bloody awful*). 4. *Colloq.* difficult; obstinate; cruel. –*v.* 5. to stain with blood. –*adv.* 6. *Colloq.* very; extremely.

bloom, *n.* 1. the flower of a plant. 2. a flourishing, healthy condition. 3. a whitish, powdery surface coating. –*v.* 4. to produce blossoms. 5. to flourish.

bloo·mers, *n.* loose trousers gathered at the knee, formerly much worn by women.

blos·som, *n. Bot.* 1. the flower of a plant, esp. of one producing an edible fruit. –*v.* 2. to flourish; develop (*out*).

blot, *n., v.,* **blotted, blotting.** –*n.* 1. a spot or stain, esp. of ink on paper. –*v.* 2. to spot or stain. 3. to make indistinguishable (*out*). 4. to dry with absorbent material. 5. (of ink,

blot

etc.) to spread in a stain. **6.** to become blotted or stained.

blouse /blauz/, *n. v.*, **bloused, blousing.** −*n.* **1.** a loosely fitting bodice or shirt usu. held in at the waist. −*v.* **2.** to hang loose and full.

blow[1], *n.* **1.** a sudden stroke with hand, fist, or weapon. **2.** a sudden shock, or a calamity.

blow[2], *v.*, **blew, blown, blowing. 1.** (of the wind or air) to be in motion. **2.** to emit a current of air, as with the mouth, etc. **3.** to (cause to) give out sound, as of a trumpet, whistle, etc. **4.** (of a fuse, tyre, etc.) to burn (*out*) or perish. **5.** to extinguish, as by the wind or a puff of air (*out*). **6.** to drive by means of a current of air. **7.** *Photog.* to reproduce by enlargement (*up*). **8.** waste; squander. **9. blow up, a.** to develop, esp. to a crisis. **b.** to explode. **c.** *Colloq.* to lose one's temper.

blow·fly, *n., pl.* **-flies.** a fly which deposits its eggs or larvae on carcasses or meat, etc.

blow·lamp, *n.* a small portable apparatus which gives a hot flame under pressure.

blow-out, *n.* a rupture of a motor-car tyre.

blow·torch, *n.* a portable apparatus which gives an extremely hot flame.

blow-up, *n.* **1.** an explosion. **2.** a violent outburst of temper. **3.** *Photog.* an enlargement.

blub·ber, *n.* the fat of whales and other cetaceans from which oil is made. −*v.* **2.** to weep, usu. noisily.

bludge, *v.*, **bludged, bludging.** *n.* −*v. Colloq.* **1.** to evade responsibilities. **2.** to impose on others. (*on*). **3.** to cadge. −*n.* **4.** a job which entails next to no work. − **bludger**, *n.*

blud·geon, *n.* **1.** a short, heavy club. −*v.* **2.** to strike with a bludgeon. **3.** to force (someone) into something.

blue, *n. adj.*, **bluer, bluest.** −*n.* **1.** the pure hue of clear sky. **2.** *Colloq.* a fight. −*adj.* **3.** of the colour blue. **4.** *Colloq.* depressed in spirits. **5.** *Colloq.* obscene. **6. true blue**, loyal; genuine.

blue·bell, *n.* woodland wild flower with bell-shaped blue flowers.

blueberry, *n.* small edible blackish-blue fruit.

blue·bottle, *n.* **1.** large buzzing fly. **2.** a small sea animal found in warm seas with a deep blue body from which trail stinging tentacles.

blue-collar, *adj.* pertaining to factory or production line workers, etc.

Blue Peter, *n.* **1.** blue flag with central white square hoisted before sailing. **2.** popular British children's TV show.

blue·print, *n.* a photographic print, white on a blue ground, esp. of building plans, etc.

blue-ribbon, *adj.* **1.** (of an electorate) sure to be held by a party or candidate. **2.** of or pertaining to a prize-winner.

blues, *n. pl.* **1.** despondency; melancholy. **2.** *Jazz.* a melancholy type of song, of American Negro origin, usu. in slow tempo.

bluff[1], *adj.* somewhat abrupt and unconventional in manner. −*n.* **2.** a cliff or hill with a broad, steep face.

blunt, *adj.* **1.** having a thick or dull

blunt

edge or tip; rounded. 2. abrupt in address or manner; plain-spoken.

blur, v., **blurred, blurring**, n. –v. 1. to obscure by making confused in form or outline. 2. to make or become indistinct. –n. 3. a blurred condition; indistinctness.

blurb, n. an announcement or advertisement, usu. laudatory, esp. on the jacket flap of a book or the cover of a book.

blurt, v. to utter suddenly or inadvertently (*out*).

blush, v. 1. to redden as from embarrassment, shame, or modesty. –n. 2. a rosy or pinkish tinge.

blus·ter, v. 1. to roar and be tumultuous, as wind. –n. 2. noisy, empty menaces or protests; inflated talk.

boa, n., pl. **boas**. 1. any of various non-venomous snakes which coil around and crush their prey. 2. a long, snake-shaped wrap of silk, feathers, or other material.

boar, n. an uncastrated male pig.

board, n. 1. a long, narrow, thin piece of sawn timber. 2. daily meals, esp. as provided for pay; *bed and board*. 3. an official body of persons who direct a business, etc. 4. the border or edge of anything, as in *seaboard*. 5. **on board**, on or in a ship, aeroplane, etc. –v. 6. to cover or close with boards (*up* or *in*). 7. to go on board of or enter (a ship, train, etc.). 8. to be supplied with food and lodging at a fixed price.

boast, v. 1. to speak exaggeratedly, esp. about oneself. 2. to speak with pride (*of*). 3. to be proud of the possession of.

boat, n. a vessel for transport by water.

bohemian

boater, n. a straw hat with a flat hard brim.

boatswain /ˈbousən/, n. an officer on a ship in charge of deck equipment and crew. Also, **bo's'n, bosun**.

bob, n., v., **bobbed, bobbing**. –n. 1. a short jerky motion up and down. 2. a quick curtsy. –v. to move up and down with a bouncing motion.

bobbin, n. a reel or spool upon which yarn or thread is wound.

bobby pin, n. a tightly closing metal pin for holding the hair.

bodice, n. the fitted upper part of a woman's dress.

bodkin, n. a blunt, needle-like instrument for drawing tape, cord, etc., through a loop, hem, or the like.

body, n., pl. **bodies**. 1. the physical structure of an animal. 2. a corpse; carcass. 3. the main mass of a thing. 4. a number of things or people. 5. consistency or density; substance. 6. matter or physical substance (as opposed to *spirit* or *soul*).

body·guard, n. a personal guard.

bog, n., v., **bogged, bogging**. –v. 1. wet, spongy ground, full of decayed vegetable matter. 2. *Colloq.* a lavatory or latrine. –v. 3. to sink in or as in a bog (*down*).

bogey, n. score in golf of one more than par for hole.

boggle, v., **-gled, -gling**. to take alarm; start with fright.

bogie, n. a low truck or trolley.

bogus, adj. counterfeit; spurious.

bogy, n., pl. **bogies**. 1. a hobgoblin; evil spirit. 2. anything that haunts or annoys.

bo·he·mian /bouˈhiːmiən/, n. 1. a person, usu. artistic or intellectual,

bohemian

who lives and acts unconventionally. –*adj.* 2. pertaining to bohemians.

boil[1], *v.* 1. (to cause) to change from liquid to gas with bubbles rising through, and agitating, the liquid. 2. to be agitated by angry feeling. 3. *Colloq.* to feel very hot. 4. to cook by heating.

boil[2], *n.* a suppurating, inflammatory sore forming a central core.

boil·er, *n.* 1. a closed vessel in which steam is generated for heating or for driving engines. 2. a vessel for boiling or heating.

bois·ter·ous, *adj.* rough and noisy.

bold, *adj.* 1. not hesitating in the face of danger or rebuff. 2. disrespectful or forward. 3. (of type, etc.) with heavy lines.

bol·ster, *n.* 1. a long ornamental pillow for a bed, sofa, etc. 2. a support. –*v.* 3. to support with or as with a pillow. 4. to prop, support, or uphold (something weak, unworthy, etc.) (*up*).

bolt, *n.* 1. a movable bar which fastens a door, gate, etc. 2. a strong metal pin, with a screw thread to receive a nut. 3. a woven length of cloth. 4. any sudden dash, flight, etc. –*v.* 5. to fasten with bolts. 6. to swallow (one's food) hurriedly. 7. to run away in alarm and uncontrollably. 8. **bolt upright**, stiffly upright.

bomb, *n.* 1. a hollow projectile filled with an explosive charge. 2. *Colloq.* an old car. 3. *Colloq.* a failure. –*v.* 4. to hurl bombs (at); drop bombs (upon). 5. *Colloq.* to fail; perform badly (at).

bom·bard, *v.* to assail vigorously.

bom·bar·dier /bɒmbə'dɪə/, *n. Mil.* the member of a plane crew who releases the bombs.

bom·bast /'bɒmbæst/, *n.* high-sounding and often insincere words; verbiage. – **bombastic**, *adj.*

bomb·shell, *n.* 1. a bomb. 2. a sudden or devastating action or effect. 3. a very attractive woman.

bo·na fide /ˌboʊnə 'faɪdɪ/, *adj.* Also, **bona-fide**, performed, etc., in good faith; without fraud. – **bona fides**, evidence of good faith.

bond, *n.* 1. something that binds, fastens, confines, or holds together. 2. something that unites individuals. 3. a document guaranteeing payment of a stated sum of money on or before a specified day. 4. any binding written obligation. 5. *Law.* a written acknowledgment of a debt. 6. a document certifying the amount of a loan to a government or other corporation, and usu. bearing a fixed rate of interest. 7. →**bond money**. 8. a substance that causes particles to adhere. 9. *Chem.* any linkage between atoms in a compound. 10. **in bond**, (of goods) held until customs or excise duty is paid. –*v.* 11. to put (goods, an employee, official, etc.) in or under bond. 12. to cause (bricks, etc.) to hold together firmly by laying them in some overlapping pattern.

bond·age, *n.* the state of being bound by or subjected to external control.

bond money, *n.* an initial payment made by a tenant to guarantee against damage or failure to pay rent.

bone, *n., v.,* **boned, boning.** –*n.* 1. any of the separate pieces of which the skeleton of a vertebrate is composed. 2. any substance, such as

bone

ivory, whalebone, etc. **3.** an off-white colour. –v. **4.** to take out the bones of.

bon·fire, n. a large fire in an open place, for entertainment, celebration, or as a signal.

bongo, n., pl. **-gos, -goes.** one of a pair of small drums, played by beating with the fingers.

bonnet, n. **1.** a woman's or child's closely fitting hat, usu. tied under the chin. **2.** any of various hoods, covers, or protective devices.

bonny, adj., **-ier, -iest.** radiant with health; handsome; pretty.

bonus, n. something given or paid over and above what is due.

bonzer, adj. Colloq. excellent, attractive, pleasing. Also, **bonza, boshter.**

boob, n. Colloq. **1.** a fool; a dunce. **2.** Colloq. a woman's breast.

booby prize, n. a prize given to the worst player in a game or contest.

booby trap, n. an object so placed as to fall on or trip up an unsuspecting person.

book, n. **1.** a written or printed work of some length, esp. on consecutive sheets fastened or bound together. **2.** a number of sheets of writing paper bound together and used to record commercial transactions. **3. the books,** a record of commercial transactions. **4.** a set of tickets, cheques, stamps, etc., bound together like a book. **5.** anything that serves for the recording of facts or events. –v. **6.** to enter in a book or list; record; register. **7.** to reserve or engage (a place, ticket, performer, etc.) beforehand. **8.** to record the name of, for possible prosecution for a minor offence. **9.** to register one's name (in).

book·keeping, n. the work or skill of keeping account books. – **book-keeper,** n.

book·maker, n. a professional betting person, who accepts the bets of others, as on horses in racing.

book·worm, n. a person very fond of reading or studying.

boom[1], v. **1.** to make a deep, prolonged, resonant sound. **2.** to progress or flourish vigorously, as a business, a city, etc. –n. **3.** a deep, hollow, continued sound. **4.** a rapid increase in prices, business activity, etc.

boom[2], n. a long pole or spar used to extend the foot of certain sails.

boom·erang, n. **1.** a bent or curved piece of hard wood used as a missile by Aborigines, one form of which can be thrown so as to return to the thrower. **2.** Colloq. that which is expected to be returned by a borrower. –v. **3.** to return to, or recoil upon, the originator.

boon, n. a benefit enjoyed; a thing to be thankful for.

boor /bɔ, bʊə/, n. a rude or unmannerly person.

boost, v. **1.** to lift or raise by pushing from behind or below. **2.** to increase. –n. **3.** an upward shove or push. **4.** an aid or encouragement to success. – **booster,** n.

boot, n. **1.** a heavy shoe, esp. one reaching above the ankle. **2.** place for baggage, usu. at the rear of a vehicle. **3.** a kick.

booth, n. a small compartment for a telephone, film projector, etc.

boot-leg, v., **-legged**, **legging**. to deal in (spirits or other goods) illicitly.

booty, n., pl. **-ties**. spoil taken from an enemy in war.

booze, n. Colloq. alcoholic drink.

border, n. **1.** a side, edge, or margin. **2.** the line that separates one country, state, etc. from another. –v. **3.** **border on** or **upon**, **a.** to touch or abut at the border. **b.** to approach closely in character.

border-line, adj. **1.** on or near a border or boundary. **2.** (in examinations, etc.) qualifying or failing to qualify by a narrow margin.

bore[1], v., **bored**, **boring**, n. –v. **1.** to pierce (a solid substance) or make (a round hole, etc.) with an auger, drill, etc. **2.** to force by persistent forward thrusting. –n. **3.** a deep hole through which water is obtained from beneath the ground. **4.** the inside diameter of a hollow cylindrical object or device, such as the barrel of a gun.

bore[2], v., **bored**, **boring**, n. –v. **1.** to weary by tedious repetition, dullness, unwelcome attentions etc. –n. **2.** a dull or tiresome person. – **boredom**, n.

bore[3], v. past tense of **bear**[1].

borer, n. any insect that burrows in trees, fruits, etc.

born, adj. **1.** brought forth by birth. **2.** possessing from birth the quality or character stated: *born honest; a born liar.*

borne, v. past participle of **bear**[1].

borrow, v. **1.** to take or obtain (a thing) on the promise to return it or its equivalent. **2.** to get from another or from a foreign source.

Borstal, n. Hist. a now archaic and derog. term for a residential institution for youth custody.

bosom /ˈʊzəm/, n. **1.** the breast of a human being, esp. a woman. **2.** the breast, conceived of as the seat of thought or emotion. –adj. **3.** intimate or confidential.

boss, n. Colloq. **1.** one who employs or superintends workmen. **2.** anyone who asserts mastery, esp. one who controls a political or other body. –v. **3.** to be domineering.

bosun, n. →**boatswain**.

botany, n. the science of plants and plant life. – **botanist**, n. – **botanical**.

botch, v. to spoil by poor work; bungle.

both, adj., pron. **1.** the one and the other; the 2 together. –conj., adv. **2.** alike; equally: *both men and women; I both like and respect her.*

bother, v. **1.** to give trouble to; annoy. **2.** to trouble oneself. –n. **3.** **an annoying disturbance. 4.** worried or perplexed state. – **bothersome**, adj.

bottle, n., v., **-tled**, **-tling**. –n. **1.** a portable vessel with a neck or mouth, usu. made of glass or plastic, used for holding liquids. –v. **2.** to put into or seal in a bottle; to preserve (fruit or vegetables) in bottles.

bottle bank, n. place, site, or containers, for depositing bottles, cans, etc. for recycling.

bottle green, adj. a dark shade of green.

bottle-neck, n. **1.** a place, or stage in a process, where progress is retarded. **2. a.** a narrow part of a road between 2 wide stretches. **b.** a congested junction, road, town, etc.

bottom, n. **1.** the lowest or deepest

bottom

part of anything. **2.** the underside. **3.** the ground under any body of water. **4.** the buttocks. **5.** the basic aspect. –*v.* **6.** to be based; rest. **7.** to strike against or reach the bottom or end. –*adj.* **8.** lowest.

bougain·villea /boʊɡənˈvɪliə/, *n.* a shrub or spiny climber with brightly coloured bracts.

bough /baʊ/, *n.* a large branch of a tree.

bought, *v.* past tense and past participle of buy.

boul·der, *n.* a detached and rounded rock.

boule·vard /ˈbuːləvɑːd/, *n.* **1.** a broad avenue of a city, often having trees. **2.** a street.

bounce, *v.*, **bounced**, **bouncing**, *n.* –*v.* **1.** to (cause to) move with a bound, and rebound, as a ball. **2.** *Colloq.* (of cheques) to be returned unpaid. **3.** *Colloq.* to eject or discharge summarily. –*n.* **4.** a rebound or bound. **5.** ability to bounce; resilience.

bound[1], *adj.* **1.** tied; in bonds. **2.** made fast as by a band or bond. **3.** secured within a cover, as a book. **4.** under obligation, legally or morally. **5.** destined or sure.

bound[2], *v.* **1.** to move by leaps; spring. –*n.* **2.** a leap onwards or upwards.

bound[3], *n.* **1.** (*usu.* pl.) a limiting line, or boundary. **2. out of bounds**, forbidden of access to certain persons. –*v.* **3.** to form the boundary of.

bound[4], *adj.* going or intending to go; on the way (*to*); destined (*for*).

boun·dary, *n., pl.* **-ries.** something that indicates bounds or limits.

boun·teous, *adj.* **1.** giving or dis-

bow

posed to give freely. **2.** freely bestowed; plentiful.

bounti·ful, *adj.* **1.** liberal in bestowing gifts or favours; generous. **2.** abundant; ample.

bounty, *n., pl.* **-ties. 1.** generosity in giving. **2.** a benevolent, generous gift. **3.** a reward, esp. one offered by a government.

bou·quet /ˈbuːkeɪ, boʊˈkeɪ/, *n.* **1.** a bunch of flowers. **2.** the characteristic aroma of wine, liqueurs, etc.

bour·bon /ˈbɜːbən/, *n.* a kind of whisky distilled from maize. Also, **bourbon whisky.**

bour·geois /ˈbʊəʒwɑː, ˈbuː-/, *n., pl.* **-geois**, *adj.* –*n.* **1.** a member of the middle class. **2.** a capitalist, as opposed to a member of the wage-earning class. –*adj.* **3.** of the middle class; conventional. – **bourgeoisie**, *n.*

bout, *n.* **1.** a contest, esp. a boxing or wrestling match. **2.** period; spell.

bou·tique /buːˈtiːk/, *n.* a small shop selling fashionable or luxury articles, esp. for women.

bovine, *adj.* **1.** of a genus of horned and stocky ruminants. **2.** stolid; dull.

bow[1] /baʊ/, *v.* **1.** to bend or curve downwards; stoop. **2.** to yield; submit. **3.** to bend (the body or head) in worship, salutation, respect, or submission. –*n.* **4.** a bowing movement of head or body.

bow[2] /boʊ/, *n.* **1.** a strip of flexible material bent by a string stretched between its ends, used for shooting arrows. **2.** something curved or arc-shaped. **3.** a looped knot, as of ribbon, composed of one or 2 loops and 2 ends. **4.** *Music.* an implement designed for playing a violin, etc.

bow

–*adj.* **5.** curved; bent like a bow. –*v.* **6.** to bend into the form of a bow; curve.

bow³ /baʊ/, *n.* (*sometimes pl.*) the forward part of a ship, boat, airship, etc.

bowd·ler·ise /'baʊdləraɪz/, *v.*, **-rised, -rising.** to expurgate prudishly.

bowel /'baʊəl/, *n.* **1. a.** an intestine. **b.** (*usu. pl.*) the intestines or entrails. **2.** the inward or interior parts.

bower /'baʊə/, *n.* a leafy shelter or recess; an arbour.

bower·bird, *n.* any of various birds which build bowerlike structures to attract the females.

bowl¹, *n.* **1.** a deep, round dish used to hold liquids, etc. **2.** any bowl-shaped depression.

bowl², *n.* **1.** one of the biased or weighted balls used in the games of lawn and carpet bowls. **2.** a delivery of the ball in bowling. –*v.* **3.** to play with bowls, or at bowling. **4.** to roll or trundle (a ball, hoop, etc.). **5.** to knock or strike, as by the ball in bowling (*over* or *down*). **6.** *Cricket.* to dismiss (a batsman) by delivering a ball which breaks the batsman's wicket.

bowler, *n.* a hard felt hat with a rounded crown and narrow brim.

bowling, *n.* a game in which players roll a ball in order to knock down nine or ten pins (def. 2).

bowls, *n.* a game in which players roll a weighted ball in an effort to make it stop as near as possible to a target ball.

bowser /'baʊzə/, *n.* a petrol pump.

box¹, *n.* **1.** a receptacle with a lid or removable cover. **2.** a compartment for the accommodation of a small

brace

number of people in a public place, esp. in theatres, etc. **3.** (in a court of law) a stand or pew reserved for witnesses, the accused or the jury. –*v.* **4.** to put into a box. **5.** to enclose or confine as in a box (*up* or *in*).

box², *n.* **1.** a blow with the hand or fist. –*v.* **2.** to strike with the hand or fist, esp. on the ear. **3.** to fight in a boxing match.

boxer, *n.* **1.** one who boxes. **2.** a smooth-coated dog related to the bulldog and terrier.

box office, *n.* the office in which tickets are sold at a theatre, etc.

boy, *n.* **1.** a male child. **2.** a young servant. –*interj.* **3.** (an exclamation of surprise, delight, etc.)

boy·cott, *v.* **1.** to combine in abstaining from, or preventing dealings with, as a means of intimidation or coercion. **2.** to abstain from buying or using. –*n.* **3.** the practice or an instance of boycotting.

boysen·berry /'bɔɪzənbɛri/, *n., pl.* **-ries.** blackberry-like fruit with a flavour similar to raspberries.

bra, *n.* →**brassiere**.

brace, *n., v.,* **braced, bracing.** –*n.* **1.** something that holds parts together or in place. **2.** anything that imparts rigidity or steadiness. **3.** a device for holding and turning tools for boring or drilling. **4.** a piece of timber, metal, etc., used to support a portion of a framework. **5.** (*oft. pl.*) metal wire used to straighten irregular teeth. **6.** *Med.* an appliance for supporting a weak joint or joints. **7.** (*pl.*) straps worn over the shoulders to hold up trousers. **8.** a pair. –*v.* **9.** to furnish, fasten, or strengthen with or as with a brace. **10.** to fix firmly; make steady.

63

brace·let, *n.* 1. an ornamental band or circlet for the wrist or arm. 2. *Colloq.* a handcuff.

bracken, *n.* a large, coarse fern.

bracket, *n.* 1. a triangular support for a shelf or the like. 2. one of 2 marks, ([) or ([), used in writing or printing to enclose parenthetical matter, interpolations, etc. 3. *Maths.* (*pl.*) parentheses of various forms indicating that the enclosed quantity is to be treated as a unit. 4. a small group of musical items. –*v.* 5. to furnish with or support by a bracket or brackets. 6. to associate or mention together.

brack·ish, *adj.* slightly salt; having a salty or briny flavour.

bract, *n.* a specialised leaf or leaflike part, usu. at the base of a flower.

brag, *v.*, bragged, bragging. to use boastful language. – **braggart**, *n.*

braid, *v.* to weave together strips or strands of; plait.

braille, *n.* a system of printing for the blind, in which combinations of raised points represent letters, etc.

brain, *n.* 1. (*sometimes pl.*) the nerve substance which fills the cranium of man and other vertebrates; centre of sensation, body coordination, thought, emotion, etc. 2. (*usu. pl.*) understanding; intellectual power. – **brainy**, *adj.*

brain·storm, *n.* 1. a sudden, violent mental disturbance. 2. *Colloq.* a sudden inspiration, idea, etc.

brain·washing, *n.* systematic indoctrination to change someone's convictions, esp. political.

braise, *v.*, braised, braising. to cook (meat or vegetables) slowly in very little moisture.

brake[1], *n.* 1. any mechanical device for arresting the motion of a wheel, a motor, or a vehicle, chiefly by means of friction. –*v.* 2. to use or apply a brake.

brake[2], *n.* a place overgrown with bushes, shrubs, brambles, etc.

bram·ble, *n.* 1. the common blackberry. 2. any rough prickly shrub.

bran, *n.* the ground husk of wheat or other grain.

branch, *n.* 1. a division or subdivision of the stem of a tree, shrub, or other plant (as opposed to twigs, shoots, etc.). 2. a limb, offshoot, or ramification. 3. a section or subdivision of a body or system. 4. a tributary stream. –*v.* 5. to put forth branches; spread in branches. 6. to divide into separate parts or subdivisions; diverge.

brand, *n.* 1. a trademark or trade name to identify a product. 2. a mark made by burning or otherwise, to indicate kind, grade, make, ownership, etc. 3. any mark of infamy.

brand·ish, *v.* 1. to shake or wave, as a weapon; flourish. –*n.* 2. a wave of flourish, as of a weapon.

brandy, *n., pl.* -dies. the spirit distilled from the fermented juice of grapes or, sometimes, of apples, peaches, plums, etc.

brash, *adj.* impertinent; impudent.

brass, *n.* 1. a durable, malleable, and ductile yellow alloy, consisting essentially of copper and zinc. 2. a collective term for musical instruments of the trumpet and horn families (brass instruments). 3. **top brass**. *Colloq.* high-ranking people. 4. *Colloq.* excessive assurance; impudence. 5. *Colloq.* money.

bras·siere /'bræziə, -siə/, n. a woman's undergarment which supports the breasts.

brat, n. a child (used usu. in contempt or irritation).

bra·vado /brə'vadoʊ/, n. boasting; swaggering pretence.

brave, adj., braver, bravest, n., v., braved, braving. –adj. 1. possessing or exhibiting courage or courageous endurance. –n. 2. a Nth American Indian or other native warrior. –v. 3. to meet or face courageously. 4. to defy; challenge. – bravery, n.

brawl, n. a noisy quarrel; a squabble.

brawn, n. 1. well-developed muscles. 2. meat, esp. pork, boiled, pickled, and pressed.

bray, n. a harsh, breathy cry, as of the donkey.

brazen, adj. 1. made of brass. 2. like brass. 3. shameless or impudent.

bra·zier, n. a metal receptacle for holding burning charcoal for heating a room. Also, **brasier.**

breach, n. 1. the act or result of breaking. 2. a gap made in a wall, dyke, fortification, etc. 3. an infraction or violation, as of law, trust, etc. 4. a severance of friendly relations.

bread, n. 1. a food made of flour or meal, milk or water, etc., mixed with or without yeast or the like, and baked. 2. food or sustenance. 3. *Colloq.* money; earnings.

bread·line, n. *in the phrase* **on the breadline**, living at subsistence level.

breadth, n. 1. *Maths.* the measure of the 2nd principal diameter of a surface or solid, the first being length, and the 3rd (in the case of a solid) thickness; width. 2. freedom from narrowness or restraint. 3. extent.

bread·winner, n. one who earns a livelihood for a family.

break, v., broke, broken, breaking, n. –v. 1. to divide or separate into parts, esp. violently; reduce to pieces or fragments. 2. to violate. 3. to fracture a bone of. 4. to destroy the regularity of. 5. to put an end to; overcome. 6. to exchange for a smaller amount or smaller units. 7. to make or force one's way through; penetrate. 8. to force a way (*in, through, out,* etc.). 9. to burst (*in, forth, from,* etc.). 10. to disable or destroy. 11. to ruin financially, or make bankrupt. 12. to impair or weaken in strength, spirit, force, or effect. 13. to defeat the purpose of (a strike). 14. to train to obedience; tame. 15. *Elect.* to render (a circuit) incomplete. 16. to sever relations (*up* or *with*). 17. (of a wave) to topple forward after developing a crest. 18. to free oneself or escape suddenly, as from restraint (*away*). 19. to change state or activity (*into*). 20. to dawn, as the day. 21. (of the heart) to be overwhelmed, esp. by grief. 22. (of the voice) to vary between 2 registers, esp. in emotion or during adolescence. 23. (in a race) to start before the signal. 24. **break down, a.** to take down or destroy by breaking. **b.** to overcome. **c.** to analyse. **d.** to collapse. **e.** to cease to function. 25. **break in, a.** to interrupt. **b.** to adapt to one's convenience by use. **c.** to accustom (a horse) to harness and use. **d.** to enter (a house or the like) forcibly, as a burglar. 26. **break off, a.** to end or finish. **b.** to stop or interrupt. 27. **break out, a.** to issue

break

forth; arise. **b.** (of certain diseases) to appear in eruptions. **28. break up**, **a.** to separate; disband. **b.** to put an end to. **c.** to cut up or separate into pieces. **d.** *Colloq.* to collapse with laughter. –*n.* **29.** a forcible disruption or separation of parts; a breaking. **30.** a gap. **31.** an attempt to escape. **32.** an interruption of continuity. **33.** an abrupt or marked change, as in sound or direction. **34.** *Colloq.* an opportunity; chance. **35.** a brief rest, as from work. **36.** a premature start in racing.

break·age, *n.* **1.** an act of breaking; a break. **2.** the amount or quantity of things broken.

break·away, *n.* **1.** the formation of a splinter group in a political party, etc. **2.** a panic rush of or among a mob of cattle, horses, etc.

break·fast, *n.* the first meal of the day.

break·neck, *adj.* dangerous; hazardous.

break·through, *n.* any development which removes a barrier to progress.

break·water, *n.* a structure built to break the force of waves, esp. near a harbour.

bream /brɪm/, *n.* an edible fish.

breast, *n.* **1.** the front part of the body from neck to belly; the chest. **2.** a mammary or milk gland, esp. of a woman. **3.** the bosom regarded as the seat of thoughts and feelings.

breath, *n.* **1.** the air inhaled and exhaled in respiration. **2.** ability to breathe, esp. freely. **3.** a light current of air.

breathe, *v.*, **breathed, breathing. 1.** to inhale and exhale (air, fumes, etc.). **2.** to blow lightly, as air. **3.** to live; exist. **4.** to give utterance to; whisper.

breath·taking, *adj.* causing extreme excitement.

breathy, *adj.* (of the voice) characterised by excessive emission of breath.

breech, *n.* **1.** the posterior or buttocks. **2.** the hinder or lower part of anything. **3.** the part of a gun behind the barrel.

breeches /ˈbrɪtʃəz/, *n.pl.* trousers, esp. designed for horse-riding, or those reaching just to the knee.

breed, *v.*, **bred, breeding**, *n.* –*v.* **1.** to produce (offspring). **2.** to procure by the mating of parents. **3.** to cause to reproduce by controlled pollination or fertilisation. **4.** to cause; occasion. –*n.* **5.** a genetically similar group of animals within a species, developed and maintained by man. **6.** race; strain.

breeze, *n., v.*, **breezed, breezing.** –*n.* **1.** a light or moderate wind. **2.** *Colloq.* an easy task. –*v.* **3.** *Colloq.* to move or proceed lightheartedly (*along, in*). **4. breeze through**, *Colloq.* to perform without effort.

breth·ren, *n.* **1.** *Archaic.* plural of **brother. 2.** fellow members.

brevity, *n.* shortness of time or duration; briefness.

brew, *v.* **1.** to make (beer, ale, etc.). **2.** to make (tea) (*up*). **3.** to concoct or contrive. **4.** to be in preparation; be forming or gathering (*up*). –*n.* **5.** a quantity brewed in a single process. – **brewery**, *n.*

briar, *n.* a prickly shrub or plant, esp. the sweetbriar. Also, **brier.**

bribe, *n., v.*, **bribed, bribing.** –*n.* **1.** any payment offered to influence cor-

bribe

rupt behaviour in the performance of duty. –v. 2. to influence or corrupt by a bribe. – **bribery**, n.

brick, n. 1. a baked block of clay used for building, paving, etc. 2. Colloq. a good fellow.

bride, n. a woman newly married, or about to be married. – **bridal**, adj.

bride·groom, n. a man newly married, or about to be married.

brides·maid, n. a young unmarried woman who attends the bride at a wedding.

bridge[1], n., v., **bridged, bridging**. –n. 1. a structure spanning a river, road, etc., and affording passage. 2. the ridge or upper line of the nose. –v. 3. to make a bridge over; span.

bridge[2], n. a card game for 4 players, derived from whist.

bridle, n., v., **-dled, -dling**. –n. 1. the part of the harness of a horse, etc., about the head. –v. 2. to draw up the head and draw in the chin, as in disdain or resentment (at).

brief, adj. 1. of little duration. 2. using few words. –n. 3. an outline of all the possible arguments and information on one side of a controversy. 4. instructions or notes for a particular task. –v. 5. to instruct by a brief.

brief·case, n. a flat, rectangular leather case used for carrying documents, etc. Also, **dispatch case**.

briefing, n. a short, accurate summary of a plan or operation given to a military unit, etc., before it undertakes the operation.

brig, n. a two-masted vessel with square sails.

bri·gade, n. 1. a large body of troops. 2. a group organised for a special purpose.

bri·gand, n. a bandit.

bright, adj. 1. radiating or reflecting light; luminous. 2. vivid or brilliant, as colour. 3. quick-witted or intelligent. 4. animated; lively.

bril·liant, adj. 1. shining brightly; sparkling. 2. distinguished; illustrious. 3. having or showing great intelligence. – **brilliance**, n.

brim, n., v., **brimmed, brimming**. –n. 1. the upper edge of anything hollow. 2. a projecting edge. –v. 3. to be full to the brim or overflowing.

brin·dled, adj. grey or tawny with darker streaks or spots.

brine, n. water strongly impregnated with salt. – **briny**, adj.

bring, v., **brought, bringing**. 1. to cause to come with oneself; convey. 2. to lead or induce. 3. **bring about**, a. to cause; accomplish. 4. **bring down**, a. to shoot down or cause to fall (a plane, animal, footballer, etc). b. to reduce (a price); lower in price. c. to humble or subdue. d. to introduce (proposed legislation). 5. **bring forward**, a. to produce to view. b. to move to an earlier date or hour. 6. **bring in**, a. to introduce. b. to pronounce (a verdict). 7. **bring off**, to bring to a successful conclusion. 8. **bring out**, a. to expose. b. to encourage (a shy person). c. to induce to go on strike. 9. **bring up**, a. to care for during childhood. b. to introduce for consideration. c. to vomit.

brink, n. any extreme edge; verge.

brink·man·ship, n. Colloq. the practice of courting disaster to gain one's ends.

brisk, adj. quick and active; lively.

brisket, n. (meat from) the breast of an animal.

bristle

bris·tle, n., v., **-tled**, **-tling**. –n. 1. one of the short, stiff, coarse hairs of certain animals, esp. swine, used in making brushes, etc. –v. 2. to erect the bristles, as an irritated animal. 3. to be visibly roused to anger or resistance.

brit·tle, adj. breaking readily.

broach, v. to mention or suggest for the first time.

broad, adj. 1. of great breadth. 2. of great extent. 3. widely diffused. 4. not limited or narrow; liberal. 5. main or general. 6. (of pronunciation) strongly dialectal. –n. 7. Colloq. a woman.

broad·cast, v., **-cast** or **-casted**, **-casting**, n. –v. 1. to send (messages, speeches, music, etc.) by radio. 2. to spread widely. –n. 3. that which is broadcast.

broad·sheet, n. 1. a sheet of paper, esp. of large size, printed on one side only, as for distribution or posting. 2. a newspaper printed on the standard sheet size of paper.

broad·side, n. the whole side of a ship above the waterline.

bro·cade, n. fabric woven with an elaborate, raised design from any yarn.

broc·co·li /ˈbrɒkəli, -laɪ/, n. a plant resembling the cauliflower.

bro·chure /ˈbroʊʃə, brəˈʃʊə/, n. →pamphlet.

brogue¹, n. a broad accent, esp. Irish, in the pronunciation of English.

brogue², n. a strongly made, comfortable shoe.

broil, v. to cook by direct radiant heat; grill; pan fry.

broke, v. 1. past tense of **break**. –adj. 2. Also, **flat broke**. Colloq. completely out of money.

broken, v. 1. past participle of **break**. –adj. 2. having undergone breaking. 3. uneven; (of ground) rough; (of water) with a disturbed surface; (of weather) patchy, unsettled. 4. imperfectly spoken.

bro·ker, n. 1. an agent who buys or sells for another, on commission. 2. a middleman or agent. – **brokerage**, n.

brol·ga, n. a large, silvery-grey crane.

brol·ly, n. Colloq. an umbrella.

bromide, n. Chem. a compound of bromine with one other element.

bron·chi·tis /brɒnˈkaɪtəs/, n. an inflammation of the bronchial membranes.

bronze, n. a durable brown alloy of copper and tin.

brooch /broʊtʃ/, n. an ornament with a pin made to be fastened to clothing.

brood, n. 1. a number of young produced or hatched at one time; a family of offspring. –v. 2. to meditate morbidly. 3. to incubate (eggs). – **broody**, adj.

brook¹, n. a small, natural stream of fresh water; creek.

brook², v. to bear; suffer (usu. in a negative sentence).

broom, n. a sweeping implement on a long handle.

broth, n. thin soup of concentrated meat or fish stock.

broth·el, n. a house of prostitution.

broth·er, n., pl. **brothers**, **brethren**. 1. a male child of the same parents as one's own. 2. a male child of only one of one's parents (**half-brother**). 3. a male member of the same kinship group, nationality, profes-

brother

sion, etc.; an associate; a fellow countryman, fellow man, etc. 4. a male lay member of a religious organisation which has a priesthood.

brother-in-law, n., pl. **brothers-in-law**. 1. the brother of one's spouse. 2. the husband of one's sister. 3. the husband of one's spouse's sister.

brought, v. past tense and past participle of **bring**.

brow, n. the ridge over the eye.

brow·beat, v., -beat, -beaten, -beating. to intimidate by overbearing looks or words; bully.

brown, n. 1. a dark shade with yellowish or reddish hue. –adj. 2. of the colour brown. 3. having skin of that colour. 4. sunburned or tanned. –v. 5. to make brown.

browse, v., browsed, browsing. to glance at random through a book or books.

bruise, v., bruised, bruising. n. –v. 1. to injure by striking or pressing, without breaking the skin or drawing blood. 2. to develop a discoloured spot on the skin as the result of a blow, fall, etc. –n. 3. an injury due to bruising.

brumby, n. a wild horse, esp. one descended from runaway stock.

brunch, n. a midmorning meal that serves as both breakfast and lunch.

bru·nette, adj. (of a person) having dark or brown hair, eyes, or skin.

brunt, n. the shock or force of an attack, etc.

brush¹, n. 1. an instrument consisting of bristles, hair, or the like, set in or attached to a handle. 2. an act of brushing; an application of a brush. 3. the bushy tail of an animal. 4. a slight skimming touch. 5. a brief hostile encounter; argument. –v. 6. to sweep, rub, clean, polish, etc., with a brush. 7. to touch lightly in passing. 8. to remove by brushing (aside).

brush², n. a dense growth of bushes, shrubs, etc.

brusque /brʌsk, brusk/, adj. abrupt in manner; blunt; rough.

brussels sprout, n. a plant with small, edible, cabbage-like heads or sprouts along the stalk.

brutal, adj. 1. savage; inhuman. 2. crude; coarse; harsh. – **brutality**, n.

brute, n. 1. a non-human animal; beast. 2. a brutal person.

bubble, n., v., -bled, -bling. –n. 1. a small globule of gas in a liquid or solid. –v. 2. to send up bubbles.

bubble·gum, n. a type of chewing gum which can be blown into bubbles.

bub·bler, n. a small fountain which ejects water for drinking.

buc·ca·neer, n. a pirate.

buck¹, n. the male of certain animals, as the deer, rabbit, etc.

buck², v. 1. (of a saddle or pack animal) to leap with arched back in order to dislodge rider or pack. 2. Colloq. to resist obstinately; object strongly: *to buck at improvements*. 3. Colloq. to become more cheerful, vigorous, etc. (up).

buck³, n. in the phrase **pass the buck**, Colloq. to shift the responsibility or blame to another person.

buck⁴, n. Colloq. a dollar.

bucket, n. a vessel, with a semicircular handle, for carrying water, sand, etc. **kick the bucket**, Colloq. to die.

buckle, n., v., -led, -ling. –n. 1. a clasp used for fastening together 2 loose

buckle

ends, as of a belt. 2. a bend or kink, as in metal. –v. 3. to fasten with a buckle. 4. to bend and shrivel, by applying heat or pressure; warp. 5. to bend, warp, or give way suddenly. 6. **buckle down**, to set to work with vigour.

bu·co·lic /bju'kɒlɪk/, adj. rustic; rural.

bud, n. a small protuberance on a plant, containing the first stages of a leaf, or flower or both.

buddy, n., pl. **-dies**. Colloq. comrade; mate.

budge, v. budged, budging. to (cause to) move slightly or give way (usu. with negative).

bud·ger·i·gar, n. a small yellow and green parakeet, widely domesticated and bred in many coloured varieties. Also, **budgerygah**.

budget, n. an estimate, often itemised, of expected income and expenditure, etc. – **budgetary**, adj.

buff[1], n. 1. a kind of thick leather. 2. yellowish brown; medium or light tan. 3. Colloq. the bare skin. 4. Colloq. an enthusiast; an expert (sometimes self-proclaimed). –v. 5. to polish (metal).

buf·fa·lo, n., pl. **-loes**, **-los**, (esp. collectively) **-lo**. any of several mammals of the ox kind.

buffer, n. anything serving to neutralise the shock of opposing forces.

buffet[1] /'bʌfət/, n., v., **-feted**, **-feting**. –n. 1. a blow, as with the hand. –v. 2. to strike, as with the hand.

buffet[2] /'bʌfeɪ, 'bʊfeɪ/, n. 1. a counter, bar, or the like, for lunch or refreshments. 2. a sideboard for holding china, plate, etc. –adj. 3. (of a meal) spread on tables or buffets from which the guests serve themselves.

buf·foon, n. one who amuses others by tricks, odd gestures and postures, jokes, etc.

bug, n., v., **bugged**, **bugging**. –n. 1. any insect. 2. Colloq. a malady, esp. a virus infection. 3. Colloq. an idea or belief with which one is obsessed. 4. Colloq. a microphone hidden in a room. –v. 5. Colloq. to install a bug in (a room, etc.). 6. Colloq. to cause annoyance or distress to (a person).

bug·bear, n. any source of needless fright or fear.

bug·ger, n. 1. one who practises bestiality or sodomy. 2. Colloq. a foul, contemptible person. 3. **bugger all**, Colloq. nothing. –v. 4. Colloq. to cause damage or inconvenience to (up). –interj. 5. (a strong exclamation of annoyance, disgust, etc.). – **buggery**, n.

buggy, n., pl. **-gies**. a two-wheeled horse-drawn carriage.

bugle, n. a cornet-like military wind instrument.

build, v., **built**, **building**, n. –v. 1. to construct by assembling and combining parts. 2. to establish, increase, and strengthen (up). 3. to base; form. 4. to form a plan, system of thought, etc. (on or upon). –n. 5. manner or form of construction.

building society, n. a business organisation that lends money to house buyers.

bulb, n. 1. an underground bud with a flat, disc-shaped stem from which roots grow, as in the onion, lily, etc. 2. the glass housing holding the filament of an incandescent electric lamp. – **bulbous**, adj.

bulge, *n., v.*, **bulged, bulging.** –*n.* 1. a rounded projecting or protruding part. –*v.* 2. to swell out; be protuberant.

bulk, *n.* 1. size in 3 dimensions. 2. the greater part. 3. **in bulk, a.** unpackaged. **b.** in large quantities. – **bulky**, *adj.*

bull[1], *n.* 1. the uncastrated male of a bovine animal. 2. the male of certain other animals.

bull[2], *n. Colloq.* nonsense.

bull-dog, *n.* a large-headed, short-haired, heavily built and muscular dog of comparatively small size.

bull-dozer, *n.* a powerful tractor on continuous tracks with a front vertical blade for moving earth, tree stumps, rocks, etc.

bullet, *n.* a small metal projectile fired from small arms.

bul·le·tin, *n.* 1. a brief account or statement, as of news or events. 2. a periodical publication, as of a learned society.

bull-headed, *adj.* obstinate; blunderingly stubborn; stupid.

bul·lion, *n.* gold or silver in mass, bars or ingots.

bul·lock, *n.* a castrated male bovine animal; steer.

bulls-eye, *n.* the central spot of a target.

bull·shit, *n. Colloq.* nonsense.

bull-terrier, *n.* a breed of dog produced by crossing the bulldog and the terrier.

bully, *n., pl.* **-lies,** *v.*, **-lied, -lying.** –*n.* 1. an overbearing person who brow-beats weaker people. –*v.* 2. to be loudly arrogant and overbearing.

bul·rush /'bʊlrʌʃ/, *n.* a tall, rushlike plant from which mats, chair seats, etc., are made.

bul·wark /'bʊlwək/, *n.* 1. an earthern wall used for defence. 2. anything serving as a protection. 3. (*usu.pl.*) solid part of ship's side above deck level.

bum, *n. Colloq.* 1. the rump; buttocks. 2. a shiftless or dissolute person.

bumble, *v.*, **bumbled, bumbling.** *Colloq.* to proceed clumsily or inefficiently.

bumble-bee, *n.* any of various large, hairy, social bees. Also, **humblebee.**

bump, *v.* 1. to come more or less heavily in contact with; strike; collide with. 2. *Colloq.* to increase (in extent, etc.) (*up*). 3. **a.** to come in contact with; collide (*against, into*). **b.** to meet by chance (*into*). –*n.* 4. the act of bumping; a blow. 5. a dull thud; the noise of collision. 6. a small area raised above the level of the surrounding surface.

bumper bar, *n.* a horizontal bar affixed to the front or rear of a vehicle for protection in collisions.

bump·tious, *adj.* offensively self-assertive.

bun, *n.* 1. a round-shaped bread roll, usu. sweet, and often containing dried currants, etc. 2. hair arranged at the back of the head in a bun shape.

bunch, *n.* 1. a connected group; cluster. –*v.* 2. to group together; make a bunch of.

bundle, *n., v.*, **-dled, -dling.** –*n.* 1. a group loosely held together. 2. something wrapped for carrying; package. –*v.* 3. to send away hurriedly or unceremoniously (*off, out,* etc.).

bundy, *n. Colloq.* a clock which

bundy

records on a card inserted in it, the arrival and departure times of employees.

bung, n. 1. a stopper, as for the hole of a cask. –v. Colloq. 2. to put. 3. **bung it on**, to behave temperamentally. –adj. 4. Colloq. not in good working order.

bunga·low /'bʌŋgəloʊ/, n. a house or cottage of one storey.

bungle /'bʌŋgəl/, v., **-gled, -gling**. to do clumsily and awkwardly; botch.

bunion, n. a swelling on the foot.

bunk, n. a built-in platform bed.

bunker[1], n. 1. a chest or box; a large bin or receptacle. 2. Golf. a shallow excavation, usu. at the side of a green, partly filled with sand.

bunker[2], n. a bombproof shelter, often underground.

bunkum, n. insincere talk; humbug.

bunny, n., pl. **-nies**. Colloq. 1. a rabbit. 2. one who accepts the responsibility for a situation.

bunt·ing, n. 1. a coarse open fabric used for flags, signals. 2. decorations made from bunting, paper, etc., usu. in the form of wide streamers, etc.

bunyip, n. an imaginary creature of Aboriginal legend, said to haunt rushy swamps and billabongs.

buoy /bɔɪ/, n. Naut. 1. an anchored float, sometimes carrying a light, whistle, or bell, marking a channel or obstruction. –v. 2. to support by or as by a buoy; keep afloat in a fluid. 3. to bear up or sustain: *Hope buoyed up their courage.*

buoy·ant, adj. 1. tending to float. 2. not easily depressed.

burble, v., **-bled, -bling**. to make a bubbling sound; bubble.

burden, n. 1. that which is carried.

burn

2. that which is borne with difficulty. –v. 3. to load heavily. – **burdensome**, adj.

bureau /'bjʊəroʊ, bju'roʊ/, n., pl. **-eaus, -eaux** /-oʊz/. 1. a desk or writing table with drawers. 2. a division of a government department.

bureau·cracy /bju'rɒkrəsi/, n., pl. **-cies**. 1. the body of officials administering bureaus. 2. excessive governmental red tape and routine. – **bureaucrat**, n. – **bureaucratic**, adj.

bur·geon, v. to begin to grow, as a bud; to put forth buds or shoots (*out, forth*).

burg·lary, n., pl. **-ries**. the crime of breaking into and entering a house with intent to steal, etc. – **burglar**, n.

bur·gundy /'bɜgəndi/, n., pl. **-dies**. 1. wine of many varieties, red and white, usu. still and dry. 2. dull reddish blue colour.

burial /'bɛriəl/, n. the act of burying.

burl, n. Colloq. an attempt.

bur·lesque /bɜ'lɛsk/, n. 1. comic work which vulgarises lofty material or treats ordinary material with mock dignity. 2. a theatrical entertainment featuring coarse, often vulgar comedy.

burly, adj., **-lier, -liest**. 1. great in bodily size; sturdy. 2. bluff; brusque.

burn, v., **burnt** or **burned, burning**, n. –v. 1. to be on fire. 2. to feel heat. 3. to give light. 4. to feel strong passion. 5. to become discoloured or charred through heat. 6. to consume with fire. 7. to injure, discolour, char, or treat with heat. 8. **burn off**, to clear (land) by burning the cover. –n. 9. an injury produced

burn·ish, v. to polish (a surface) by friction.

burp, n., v., Colloq. →**belch**.

burr[1], n. the rough, prickly case around the seeds of certain plants.

burr[2], n. 1. a tool or appliance for cutting or drilling. 2. to form a rough point or edge on. Also, **bur**.

burrow, n. 1. a hole in the ground made by a rabbit, fox, or similar small animal. –v. 2. to make a hole or passage (*in*, *into*, or *under* something).

bursar, n. 1. a treasurer or business officer, esp. of a college or university. 2. a student holding a bursary.

bur·sary, n., pl. **-ries**. a scholarship.

burst, v., **burst**, **bursting**. –v. 1. to fly apart or break open with sudden violence; explode. 2. to issue forth suddenly, as from confinement. 3. to give way from violent pain or emotion. 4. to be extremely full, as if ready to break open. –n. 5. the act of bursting. 6. a sudden display or manifestation: *a burst of energy or anger*.

bury /ˈbɛri/, v., **buried**, **burying**. 1. to put in the ground and cover with earth. 2. to cover in order to conceal. 3. to occupy (oneself) completely.

bus, n., pl. **buses** or **busses**. a passenger vehicle with a long body, usu. operating as part of a scheduled service.

bush, n. 1. a woody plant with many branches which usu. arise from or near the ground. 2. something resembling or suggesting this, as a thick, shaggy head of hair. 3. a stretch of land covered with bushy vegetation or trees. 4. the countryside in general. –adj. 5. uncivilised; rough; makeshift.

bushed, adj. Colloq. 1. lost. 2. exhausted. 3. confused.

bushel, n. a unit of dry measure in the imperial system equal to 36.368 72 × 10^{-3}m^3 (8 gallons).

bush·fire, n. a fire in forest or scrub country.

bush·man, n. 1. a dweller in the bush. 2. one skilled in survival in the bush.

bush·ranger, n. (formerly) a bandit who hid in the bush and robbed travellers, etc.

bush·walking, n. the sport of hiking through the bush, sometimes for long periods through virgin terrain.

bush·whacker, n. Colloq. one who lives in the bush.

busi·ness /ˈbɪznəs/, n. 1. one's occupation, profession, or trade. 2. the purchase and sale of goods in an attempt to make a profit. 3. a person, partnership, or corporation engaged in this. 4. volume of trade. 5. that with which one is principally and seriously concerned. 6. affair; matter.

busi·ness·like, adj. conforming to the methods of business or trade.

busi·ness·man, n., pl. **-men**. a man who engages in business or commerce. – **businesswoman**, n. fem.

busker, n. an entertainer who gives performances in streets, etc.

bust[1], n. 1. the head and shoulders of a person done in sculpture. 2. the chest or breast; the bosom.

bust[2], Colloq. v. 1. to burst. 2. to (cause to) go bankrupt. 3. to part finally; quarrel and part (*up*). 4. to smash (*up*). 5. to interrupt violently

bust

(a meeting, etc.) (*up*). **6.** to reduce in rank or grade. –*n.* **7.** a complete failure; bankruptcy. **8.** a police raid. –*adj.* **9.** Also, **busted.** broken; ruined. **10.** bankrupt.

bus·tard, *n.* a large, heavy bird inhabiting the plains and open scrub of Aust. Also, **plain turkey.**

bustle[1], *v.,* **-tled, -tling.** to move or act with a great show of energy (*about*).

bustle[2], *n.* (formerly) a pad worn by women on the back below the waist, to expand and support the skirt.

busy /ˈbɪzi/, *adj.,* **busier, busiest,** *v.,* **busied, busying.** –*adj.* **1.** actively and attentively engaged. **2.** full of activity. –*v.* **3.** to keep occupied; make or keep busy.

busy·body, *n., pl.* **-bodies.** a person who meddles in the affairs of others.

but, *conj.* **1.** on the contrary; yet. **2.** except, rather than, or save. **3.** except that (fol. by a clause, oft. with *that* expressed). **4.** without the circumstance that, or that not. **5.** otherwise than. **6.** that (esp. after *doubt, deny,* etc., with a negative). **7.** who or which not. –*prep.* **8.** with the exception of; except; save. –*adv.* **9.** only; just. –*n.* **10.** a restriction or objection.

butane /ˈbjuteɪn, bjuˈteɪn/, *n.* a hydrocarbon used as a fuel.

butch, *adj. Colloq.* of a man or woman, exhibiting masculine characteristics.

butcher, *n.* **1.** a retail dealer in meat. **2.** a person guilty of cruel or indiscriminate slaughter. –*v.* **3.** to murder indiscriminately or brutally. – **butchery,** *n.*

butcher bird, *n.* any of several birds

button

which impale their prey on spikes or thorns or wedge it in the forks of trees.

butler, *n.* the head male servant of a household.

butt[1], *n.* **1.** the thicker, larger, or blunt end of anything, esp. of a rifle, fishing rod, whip handle, arrow, log, etc. **2.** a hind leg of beef on the bone. **3.** an end which is not used up. **4.** buttock.

butt[2], *n.* **1.** a person or thing that is an object of ridicule, contempt, etc. **2.** the target for archery practice. –*v.* **3.** to have an end or projection (*on*); be adjacent (*to*).

butt[3], *v.* **1.** to strike with the head or horns. **2.** to project. *Colloq.* to interrupt; interfere (*in*).

butter, *n.* the yellowish, fatty solid made from churned cream. –*v.* **2.** to put butter on or in. *Colloq.* to flatter grossly (*up*).

butter·fly, *n., pl.* **-flies. 1.** an insect with large, broad wings often conspicuously coloured and marked. **2.** *Colloq.* (*pl.*) nervousness. **3.** Also, **butterfly stroke.** a swimming stroke in prone position, with both arms flung forward simultaneously.

butter·milk, *n.* the liquid remaining after the butter has been separated from milk or cream.

butter·scotch, *n.* a kind of toffee made with butter.

but·tock, *n.* either of the 2 protuberances which form the rump.

button, *n.* **1.** a disc or knob on a garment which passes through a slit or loop to serve as a fastening. **2.** anything resembling a button. **3.** a disc pressed to close an electric circuit, as in ringing a bell. –*v.* **4.** to fasten with a button or buttons.

button·hole, n. 1. the hole, slit, or loop through which a button is passed. 2. a small flower or nosegay worn on the lapel of a jacket.

but·tress, n. 1. a stabilising structure built against a wall or building. 2. any prop or support.

buxom, adj. (of a woman) full-bosomed, plump, and attractive.

buy, v., **bought**, **buying**, n. –v. 1. to acquire the possession of by payment. 2. to get rid of (a claim, opposition, etc.) by payment; bribe (*off*). 3. to secure (an owner's or partner's) share in an enterprise (*out*). 4. to buy as much as one can of (*up*). 5. *Colloq.* to accept. 6. to be or become a purchaser. **7. buy into**, to choose to become involved in. –n. 8. *Colloq.* a bargain.

buyer, n. 1. one who buys; a purchaser. 2. a purchasing agent, as for a department store.

buzz, n. 1. a low, vibrating, humming sound, as of bees. 2. *Colloq.* a telephone call. 3. *Colloq.* a feeling of exhilaration, esp. as induced by drugs. –v. 4. to make a low, vibrating, humming sound (*with*). 5. to move busily from place to place (*about*). 6. *Colloq.* to go; leave (*off* or *along*). 7. *Colloq.* to fly an aeroplane very low over.

buz·zard, n. any of various carrion-eating birds.

by, prep. 1. near to. 2. using as a route. 3. through or on as a means of conveyance. 4. not later than. 5. to the extent of. 6. through evidence or authority of. 7. in conformity with. 8. before; in the presence of. 9. through the agency or efficacy of. 10. after; in serial order. 11. combined with in multiplication or relative dimension. –adv. 12. near to something. 13. to and past a point near something. 14. aside. 15. over; past. **16. by and by**, at some time in the future; before long. **17. by and large**, in general.

bye, n. the state of having no competitor in a contest where competitors are paired, giving the right to compete in the next round. Also, **by**.

by-election, n. a parliamentary election held between general elections, to fill a vacancy. Also, **bye-election**.

bygone, adj. 1. past; out of date. –n. 2. that which is past.

by-law, n. 1. a regulation made by a local government and enforceable only within its area. 2. a subsidiary law. Also, **bye-law**.

by-line, n. a line under the heading of a newspaper or magazine article giving the writer's name.

bypass, n. 1. a road enabling motorists to avoid towns and other heavy traffic points on a main road. –v. 2. to avoid (obstructions, etc.). 3. to go over the head of (one's immediate supervisor, etc.).

by-product, n. a secondary or incidental product, as in a process of manufacture.

byre, n. a cowhouse or shed.

by·stander, n. a person present but not involved.

byway, n. 1. a secluded, or obscure road. 2. a subsidiary field of research, endeavour, etc.

byword, n. 1. the name of a quality or concept which characterises some person or group; the epitome (*of*). 2. a word or phrase used proverbially.

Cc

C, c, *n., pl.* **C's** or **Cs, c's** or **cs.** the 3rd letter of the English alphabet.

cab, *n.* **1.** →**taxi. 2.** the covered part of a truck etc., for the driver.

cab·a·ret /ˈkæbəreɪ/, *n.* musical entertainment at a restaurant, nightclub, etc.

cab·bage, *n.* a vegetable with a compact head of edible leaves.

caber, *n.* a pole thrown as a trial of strength in a Scottish game.

cabin, *n.* **1.** a small temporary house. **2.** a room in a ship, aircraft, etc.

cabi·net, *n.* **1.** (*also cap.*) the group of ministers responsible for the government of a nation. **2.** a piece of furniture with shelves, drawers, etc.

cable, *n.* **1.** a thick, strong rope. **2.** a telegram sent abroad.

cacao /kəˈkeɪoʊ, -ˈkɑːoʊ/, *n.* a small evergreen tropical American tree, from the seeds of which cocoa and chocolate are made.

cache /kæʃ/, *n.* a hiding place.

cackle, *v.,* **-led, -ling.** to utter the shrill, broken sound of a hen.

caco·phony /kəˈkɒfəni/, *n., pl.* **-nies.** (the quality of having) a harsh sound.

cactus, *n., pl.* **-ti, -tuses.** *n.* any of various fleshy-stemmed plants of the American deserts.

cad, *n.* a contemptible person.

cada·ver /kəˈdævə, -ˈdɑːvə/, *n.* a corpse.

caddie, *n. Golf.* an attendant, hired to carry the player's clubs, etc.

caddy, *n., pl.* **-ies.** a small box, tin, or chest, esp. one for holding tea.

cadence /ˈkeɪdəns/, *n.* **1.** rhythmic flow of poetry, etc. **2.** the general modulation of the voice.

cadet, *n.* a person undergoing training, esp. in the armed services.

cadge, *v.,* **cadged, cadging.** to borrow without intent to repay.

cad·mium, *n.* a white metallic element like tin in appearance. *Symbol:* Cd

cadre /ˈkɑːdə/, *n.* a personnel unit within an organisational framework.

caesa·rean section, *n.* the operation by which a baby is born by cutting through the walls of the abdomen and womb.

cae·sium /ˈsiːziəm/, *n.* a rare, extremely active, soft, metallic element. *Symbol:* Cs

cafe, *n.* a shop where coffee and light refreshments are served. Also, **café.**

cafe·teria, *n.* an inexpensive restaurant or snack-bar, usu. self-service.

caf·feine /ˈkæfiːn/, *n.* a bitter substance obtained from coffee, tea, etc.

caftan, *n.* a long, loose garment.

cage, *n., v.,* **caged, caging.** —*n.* **1.** a box-shaped receptacle or enclosure with bars or wires for confining birds or other animals. —*v.* **2.** to confine in a cage.

cagey, *adj.* **cagier, cagiest.** *Colloq.* cautious; secretive. Also **cagy.**

cajole, v., -joled, -joling. to persuade by flattery or promises. – **cajolery**, n.

cake, n. a sweet baked food in loaf or layer form.

cala·mine, n. a liquid soothing to the skin. Also, **calamine lotion**.

calam·ity, n., pl. -ties. a disaster. – **calamitous**, adj.

cal·cify, v., -fied, -fying. to become chalky or bony.

cal·cium, n. a silver-white metal. Symbol: Ca

cal·cu·late, v., -lated, -lating. to ascertain by mathematical methods. – **calculation**, n. – **calculable**, adj.

cal·cu·lating, adj. shrewd.

cal·cu·lator, n. a machine that performs mathematical operations.

cal·cu·lus /'kælkjələs/, n., pl. -luses (def. 1) -li /-laɪ/ (def. 2). 1. a method of calculation. 2. Pathol. a stone in the body.

cal·en·dar, n. a system of reckoning time, esp. with reference to the divisions of the year.

calf[1], n., pl. **calves**. the young of the cow or certain other animals.

calf[2], n., pl. **calves**. the fleshy part of the back of the human leg below the knee.

cali·brate, v., -brated, -brating. to determine, check, or rectify the graduation or accuracy of.

cali·bre, n. 1. the diameter of something circular, esp. that of the inside of the bore of a gun. 2. personal character.

calico, n., pl. -coes, -cos. a coarse, white cotton cloth.

call, v. 1. to cry out or speak in a loud voice as to attract attention (of). 2. (of a bird or other animal) to utter its characteristic cry. 3. to command or request to come. 4. to give a name to. 5. to make a short visit. 6. **call in**, a. to collect. b. to withdraw from circulation. –n. 7. a cry or shout. 8. the cry of a bird or other animal. 9. a short visit. 10. a telephone conversation. 11. a summons; invitation. 12. a demand or claim. 13. **on call**, a. Also, **at call**, payable without advance notice. b. (of doctors, etc.) available for duty at short notice. –adj. 14. repayable on demand.

call girl, n. a prostitute who makes appointments by telephone.

calli·graphy /kə'lɪgrəfi/, n. handwriting.

call·ing, n. a vocation, profession, or trade.

cal·i·per, n. 1. (usu. pl.) a tool for measuring diameters. 2. Med. a limb brace.

cal·lis·then·ics, n.pl. light gymnastic exercises.

cal·lous, adj. hardened; insensitive.

callow, adj. immature or inexperienced.

callus, n., pl. -luses. a hardened or thickened part of the skin.

calm, adj. 1. without rough motion; still. 2. free from excitement or passion. –v. 3. to make calm.

calo·rie, n. a non-SI unit, approx. equal to 4 kilojoules, used to express the heat energy value of a food.

cal·umny /'kæləmni/, n., pl. -nies. slander. – **calumniate**, v.

calve, v., calved, calving. to give birth to a calf.

calyx /'keɪlɪks, 'kæl-/, n., pl. **calyces**, **calyxes**. the outermost parts of a flower, usu. green.

77

camaraderie

cama·raderie /kæməˈrɑːdəri/, *n.* comradeship; close friendship.

came, *v.* past tense of **come**.

camel, *n.* 1. a large humped ruminant quadruped. –*adj.* 2. a light fawn colour.

cameo, *n., pl.* **-os.** an engraving in relief upon a gem, stone, etc.

camera, *n., pl.* **-eras** for def. 1, **-erae** for def. 2. 1. an apparatus for taking photographs or moving pictures. 2. a judge's private room.

cami·sole, *n.* an ornamental underbodice, worn under a thin outer bodice.

camou·flage /ˈkæməflɑːʒ, -flɑːʒ/, *n.* the means by which any object disguises itself against its background.

camp[1], *n.* 1. a group of tents, caravans, or other temporary shelters. 2. a group of people with the same ideals, doctrines, etc. –*v.* 3. to establish or pitch a camp. 4. to live temporarily in a tent (*out*).

camp[2], *adj.* homosexual.

cam·paign, *n.* any course of aggressive activities for some special purpose.

cam·phor, *n.* 1. a crystalline substance used in medicine, etc. 2. any of various similar substances, for household use as an insect deterrent.

campus, *n.* the grounds of a university or other such institute.

can[1], *v., pt.* **could.** –*aux.* 1. to know how to; be able to. 2. *Colloq.* may; have permission.

can[2], *n., v.,* **canned, canning.** –*n.* 1. a metal container usually coated with tin. 2. *Colloq.* the blame for something. –*v.* 3. to put in a container, usu. sealed for preservation.

cannon

canal, *n.* an artificial waterway.

canary, *n., pl.* **-ries.** Also, **canary bird.** a small, yellow songbird.

cancel, *v.* **-celled, -celling.** 1. to cross out by drawing a line or lines over. 2. to make void.

cancer, *n.* a malignant growth or tumour. – **cancerous**, *adj.*

candela /kænˈdiːlə, -ˈdeɪlə/, *n.* the SI base unit of luminous intensity. *Symbol:* cd

cande·labrum, *n., pl.* **-bra.** an ornamental branched candlestick.

candid, *adj.* frank; outspoken; open and sincere.

can·di·date, *n.* one who seeks an office, an honour, etc.

candle, *n.* a long, slender piece of wax, etc., with an embedded wick, burnt to give light.

can·dour, *n.* frankness; sincerity.

candy, *n., pl.* **-dies,** *v.,* **-died, -dying.** –*n.* 1. a sweet made of sugar crystallised by boiling. –*v.* 2. to cook in heavy syrup until transparent, as fruit, fruit peel, or ginger.

cane, *n.* 1. a long, hollow or pithy, jointed woody stem, as that of bamboo, rattan, sugar cane, certain palms, etc. 2. the stem of a bamboo, etc., used as a rod for punishing school children. 3. a walking stick.

canine, *adj.* pertaining to dogs.

can·is·ter, *n.* a small container for holding tea, flour, etc.

canna·bis /ˈkænəbəs/, *n.* hashish.

canni·bal, *n.* any animal that eats its own kind.

cannon, *n., pl.* **-nons,** (*esp. collectively*) **-non.** 1. a large ancient gun mounted on a carriage. 2. any strike

78

cannon / capitalise

and rebound, as a ball striking a wall and glancing off.

canny, *adj.*, **-nier, -niest**. careful; cautious; wary.

canoe, *n.* any light and narrow boat propelled by paddles.

canon[1], *n.* 1. a church rule or law. 2. the body of such laws. 3. a fundamental principle. – **canonical**, *adj.*

canon[2], *n.* one of a body of clergy attached to a cathedral.

canopy, *n., pl.* **-pies**. a covering suspended over a throne, bed, etc.

cant[1], *n.* 1. insincere statements. 2. the words, phrases, etc., peculiar to a particular class, party, profession, etc.

cant[2], *n.* 1. a slope. 2. a sudden movement that tilts or overturns a thing.

can't, *v.* contraction of *cannot*.

canta·loupe /'kæntəlup/, *n.* →**rockmelon**. Also, **cantaloup**.

can·tan·ker·ous, *adj.* ill-natured; quarrelsome.

can·teen, *n.* 1. a restaurant or cafeteria attached to a workplace. 2. a box containing a set of cutlery. 3. a small container for carrying water.

canter, *n.* 1. a horse's gait, slower than a gallop. –*v.* 2. to ride at a canter.

canton, *n.* a small district, esp. in Switzerland.

canvas, *n.* 1. a closely woven, heavy cloth used for tents, sails, etc. 2. a piece of this used for an oil painting.

can·vass, *v.* to solicit votes, subscriptions, opinions, etc., from (a district, group of people, etc.).

canyon, *n.* a deep valley with steep sides.

cap, *n., v.,* **capped, capping**. 1. a close-fitting head covering of soft material, with a peak. 2. the detachable protective top of a fountain pen, jar, etc. 3. a noise-making device for toy pistols. –*v.* 4. to provide or cover with or as with a cap. 5. to surpass.

capa·ble, *adj.* 1. having much intelligence or ability; efficient. 2. **capable of**, qualified or fitted for. – **capability**, *n.*

capa·cious, *adj.* capable of holding much.

capa·city, *n., pl.* **-ties**. 1. cubic contents; volume. 2. power or ability, to do something. 3. position; function: *in the capacity of legal adviser.*

cape[1], *n.* a sleeveless garment fastened round the neck and falling over the shoulders.

cape[2], *n.* a piece of land jutting into the sea.

caper[1], *v.* 1. to leap about in a sprightly manner. –*n.* 2. a prank.

caper[2], *n.* the pickled flower bud of a bramble-like shrub used in cooking.

capil·lary, *adj., n., pl.* **-laries**. –*adj.* 1. pertaining to or occurring in or as in a tube of fine bore. –*n.* 2. a minute blood vessel.

capi·tal, *n.* 1. the city where the government of a country, etc. sits. 2. wealth capable of producing more wealth. 3. the ownership interest in a business. –*adj.* 4. pertaining to capital. 5. principal; highly important. 6. (of letters) of the large size. 7. involving the loss of the head or life, usu. as punishment; punishable by death.

capita·lise, *v.,* **-lised, -lising**. 1. to

capitalise

write or print in capital letters, or with an initial capital. 2. to supply with capital. 3. to take advantage of; turn to one's advantage (*on*). – **capitalisation**, *n*.

cap·i·tal·ism, *n*. a system under which the means of production, etc. are mainly privately owned. – **capitalist**, *n*.

cap·i·ta·tion, *n*. 1. a numbering or assessing by the head. 2. a fee or payment of a uniform amount for each person.

ca·pit·u·late, *v*., **-lated, -lating**. to surrender unconditionally or on stipulated terms. – **capitulation**, *n*.

ca·price, *n*. a whim. – **capricious**, *adj*.

cap·si·cum /'kæpsəkəm/, *n*. the common pepper with mild to hot, pungent seeds enclosed in a bell-shaped case.

cap·size, *v*., **-sized, -sizing**. 1. to overturn. 2. to upset.

cap·sule, *n*. 1. a gelatinous case enclosing a dose of medicine. 2. the compartment of a spacecraft containing the crew and/or instruments.

cap·tain, *n*. one who is in authority over others.

cap·tion, *n*. 1. a legend for a picture or illustration. 2. *Films*. the title of a scene, the text of a speech, etc., shown on the screen.

cap·ti·vate, *v*., **-vated, -vating**. to enthral by beauty or excellence.

cap·tive, *n*. 1. a prisoner. *–adj*. 2. made or held prisoner, esp. in war. – **captivity**, *n*.

cap·tor, *n*. a person who captures.

cap·ture, *v*., **-tured, -turing**, *n*. *–v*. 1. to take prisoner; seize. *–n*. 2. the act of capturing. 3. the thing or person captured.

carcass

car, *n*. 1. a motor car. 2. a vehicle running on rails, as a tramcar, etc.

ca·rafe /kə'raf, -'ræf, 'kærəf/, *n*. a glass bottle for water, wine, etc.

car·a·mel, *n*. burnt sugar, used for colouring and flavouring food, etc.

car·at, *n*. 1. Also, **metric carat**. a unit of weight used for gem stones. 2. a measurement of the purity of gold.

car·a·van, *n*. 1. a vehicle in which people may live, designed to be drawn by a motor car. 2. a group of merchants or others travelling together, esp. over deserts, etc.

car·bide, *n*. a compound of carbon.

car·bine, *n*. (formerly) a short rifle for cavalry use.

car·bo·hy·drate, *n*. a class of organic compounds including sugars, starch, etc., which are important food for animals.

car·bon, *n*. a widely distributed element which forms organic compounds in combination with hydrogen, oxygen, etc., and which occurs in a pure state as charcoal. *Symbol*: C

carbon dioxide, *n*. a colourless, odourless, incombustible gas, CO_2, used extensively in industry.

carbon monoxide, *n*. a colourless, odourless, poisonous gas.

carbon paper, *n*. paper faced with a preparation of carbon or other material, used to make copies as one writes or types.

car·bun·cle, *n*. a painful circumscribed mass of boils.

car·bu·ret·tor, *n*. a device in an internal-combustion engine for mixing a volatile fuel with the correct proportion of air.

car·cass, *n*. the dead body of an

carcass

animal or (now only in contempt) of a human being.

car·ci·no·gen /kəˈsɪnədʒən/, n. any substance which tends to produce a cancer in a body. – **carcinogenic**, adj.

card¹, n. 1. a piece of stiff paper or thin pasteboard. 2. one of a set of small pieces of cardboard with spots or figures, used in playing various games.

card², n. an implement used in combing out fibres of wool, flax, etc., preparatory to spinning.

card·board, n. thin, stiff pasteboard.

car·di·ac, adj. pertaining to the heart.

cardi·gan, n. a knitted jacket.

car·di·nal, adj. 1. of prime importance; chief; fundamental. –n. 2. a member of the Sacred College of the Roman Catholic Church, which elects the pope.

cardinal number, n. a number used in counting or indicating how may, as *one, two, three,* etc.

care, n., v., **cared, caring**. –n. 1. worry; concern. 2. serious attention; caution. 3. protection. 4. **care of**. Also, **c/o**. at the address of. –v. 5. to be affected emotionally. 6. to be concerned or solicitous. 7. to have a fondness or affection (*for*). 8. to look after; make provision (*for*). – **careful, careless**, adj.

careen, v. to lean or sway, as a ship.

career, n. 1. general progress of a person through life. 2. an occupation, profession, etc., followed as one's lifework. –v. 3. to move at high speed.

caress, n. 1. a gesture expressing affection. –v. 2. to touch affectionately.

carousel

caret, n. a mark (‸) in written or printed matter to show where something is to be inserted.

care·taker, n. 1. a person who maintains and protects a building or group of buildings. –adj. 2. holding office temporarily until a new appointment can be made.

cargo, n., pl. **-goes**. 1. the freight of a ship. 2. load.

caribou /ˈkærəbuː/, n., pl. **-bou**. a Nth American species of reindeer.

cari·ca·ture, n. 1. a picture, description, etc., ludicrously exaggerating the peculiarities of persons or things.

caries /ˈkɛəriz/, n. decay of bone or teeth.

caril·lon /kəˈrɪljən/, n. a set of bells hung in a tower and sounded manually, or by machinery.

car·mine, n. crimson.

car·nage, n. the slaughter of a great number.

carnal, adj. 1. pertaining to the flesh or the body; sensual. 2. sexual.

car·nation, n. a garden plant with fragrant flowers of various colours.

car·ni·val, n. 1. a festive procession. 2. a fair or amusement show, esp. one erected temporarily. 3. a series of sporting events as a racing carnival, etc.

car·ni·vore, n. a flesh-eating animal or plant. – **carnivorous**, adj.

carol, n. a song, esp. of joy.

caro·tid /kəˈrɒtɪd/, n. either of the 2 great arteries, one on each side of the neck.

carouse /kəˈraʊz/, n. a noisy or drunken feast; jovial revelry.

carou·sel /kærəˈsɛl/, n. →**merry-go-round**.

81

carp

carp[1], *v.* to find fault.

carp[2], *n., pl.* **carp.** a large, coarse freshwater food fish.

car·pen·ter, *n.* a workman who erects the wooden parts of houses etc. – **carpentry**, *n.*

carpet, *n.* a heavy fabric for covering floors.

car·riage, *n.* 1. a wheeled vehicle for passengers. 2. manner of carrying the head and body.

car·rion, *n.* dead and putrefying flesh.

carrot, *n.* a reddish root vegetable.

carry, *v.,* **-ried, -rying.** 1. to cause to be moved or brought from one place to another. 2. to bear the weight, burden, etc., of. 3. to hold (the body, head, etc.) in a certain manner. 4. to secure the election of (a candidate) or the adoption of (a motion or bill). 5. to support or give validity to (a related claim, etc.). 6. *Comm.* **a.** to keep on hand or in stock. **b.** to keep on one's account books, etc. 7. to be transmitted, propelled, or sustained. 8. **carry away, a.** to influence greatly or beyond reason. 9. **carry off, a.** to face consequences boldly. 10. **carry on, a.** to manage; conduct. **b.** to behave in an excited, foolish, or improper manner; flirt. 11. **carry out,** to accomplish or complete. 12. **carry over,** to postpone; hold off until later.

cart, *n.* a heavy horse-drawn vehicle.

cartel /kɑ'tɛl/, *n.* an international syndicate formed to regulate prices, etc.

car·ti·lage, *n.* firm, elastic, flexible connective tissue; gristle.

cart·ography, *n.* the production of maps.

cashmere

carton, *n.* a cardboard box, esp. one in which food is packaged.

car·toon, *n.* 1. a sketch or drawing caricaturing some subject or person. 2. an animated cartoon.

car·tridge, *n.* 1. Also, **cartridge case.** a cylindrical case for holding the bullet or the shot, for a rifle, etc. 2. anything resembling a cartridge, as the disposable container of ink for some types of fountain pen. 3. (in a tape recorder) a plastic container enclosing recording tape.

carve, *v.,* **carved, carving.** 1. to fashion by cutting wood, etc. 2. to cut into slices or pieces, as meat.

cas·cade, *n., v.,* **-caded, -cading.** – *n.* 1. a waterfall over steep rocks. – *v.* 2. to fall in or like a cascade.

case[1], *n.* 1. an instance of something. 2. the actual state of things. 3. a statement of facts, reasons, etc.. 4. a suit or action at law. 5. *Gram.* a category in the inflection of nouns, pronouns, and adjectives, denoting the syntactic relation of these words to other words in the sentence. 6. **in case,** if.

case[2], *n., v.,* **cased, casing.** – *n.* 1. a receptacle. 2. a sheath or outer covering. – *v.* 3. to put or enclose in a case.

case·ment, *n.* a window sash opening on hinges.

cash, *n.* 1. money, esp. money on hand. – *v.* 2. to give or obtain cash for (a cheque, etc.).

cashew, *n.* a small, edible, kidney-shaped nut.

cash·ier, *n.* one who has charge of cash and who superintends monetary transactions.

cash·mere, *n.* the fine downy wool of Kashmir goats.

casino

casino, *n.*, *pl.* **-nos.** a building or large room for gambling, etc.

cask, *n.* 1. a barrel-like container for holding liquids, etc. 2. a lightweight container, with a small tap, used for holding wine for domestic use.

casket, *n.* 1. a small chest or box, as for jewels. 2. a coffin.

casse·role /'kæsəroul/, *n.* 1. a baking dish of glass, pottery, etc., usu. with a cover. 2. any food, usu. a mixture, baked in such a dish.

cas·sette, *n.* a plastic container enclosing a recording tape.

cas·sock, *n.* a long, close-fitting garment worn by ecclesiastics.

casso·wary /'kæsəwari/, *n.*, *pl.* **-ries.** a large, flightless bird of Australasian regions.

cast, *v.*, **cast, casting**, *n.* –*v.* 1. to throw; fling; hurl (*away, off, out,* etc.) 2. to direct (the eye, a glance, etc.) 3. to shed or drop (hair, fruit, etc.), esp. prematurely. 4. to deposit (a vote, lot, etc.) 5. to let go or let loose, as a vessel from a mooring (*loose, off,* etc.). 6. to throw a fishing line or the like (*out*). 7. to shape in a mould. 8. **cast off,** *a.* to discard or reject. *b. Knitting.* to make the final row of stitches. 9. **cast on,** *Knitting.* to make the initial row of stitches. –*n.* 10. the act of casting. 11. the form in which something is made or written. 12. the actors in a play. 13. something shaped in a mould while in a fluid or plastic state; a casting. 14. any impression or mould made from an object. 15. rigid surgical bandage. 16. a permanent twist or turn, esp. a squint.

casta·net, *n.* a pair or one of a pair of shells held in the palm of the hand and struck together as an accompaniment to music and dancing.

cast·away, *n.* a ship-wrecked person.

caste, *n.* 1. a social group. 2. one of the rigid, hereditary, Hindu social classes.

casti·gate, *v.*, **-gated, -gating.** to punish in order to correct.

cast iron, *n.* an alloy of iron, carbon, and other elements.

castle, *n.* a fortified residence.

castor, *n.* a small wheel on a swivel, set under a piece of furniture, etc.

castor oil, *n.* a viscid oil used as a laxative, lubricant, etc.

cas·trate, *v.*, **-trated, -trating.** to remove the testicles from.

casual, *adj.* 1. happening by chance. 2. offhand. 3. careless; negligent. 4. occasional. 5. informal. 6. employed only irregularly.

casu·alty, *n.*, *pl.* **-ties.** 1. a soldier missing, killed, wounded, or captured in action. 2. one who is injured or killed in an accident. 3. Also, **casualty ward.** the section of a hospital to which accident or emergency cases are taken.

casua·rina, *n.* an Aust. tree or shrub with jointed stems and no real leaves.

cat, *n.* any of the carnivorous feline mammals, as the domesticated cat, or the lion, tiger, etc.

cata·clysm, *n.* any violent upheaval. –**cataclysmic**, *adj.*

cate·comb /'kætəkoum, -kum/, *n.* a series of underground tunnels and caves, used for burial.

cata·logue, *n.*, **-logued, -loguing.** –*n.* 1. a list, usu. in alphabetical or thematic order, with brief notes on

catalogue

names, articles, prices, etc., listed. –v. 2. to enter in a catalogue.

cat·a·lyst, n. 1. a substance which causes or accelerates a chemical change. 2. the manipulating agent of any event.

cat·a·maran /ˈkætəməræn/, n. any craft with twin parallel hulls.

cat·a·pult, n. a Y-shaped stick with an elastic strip for propelling stones, etc.

cat·a·ract, n. 1. a large waterfall. 2. an opacity of the lens of the eye.

catarrh, n. excessive secretions from the mucous membrane, esp. of the nasal passages.

cat·as·trophe /kəˈtæstrəfi/ n. 1. a sudden and widespread disaster. 2. a disastrous conclusion. – **catastrophic**, adj.

catch, v., caught, catching, n. –v. 1. to capture, esp. after pursuit. 2. to entrap or deceive. 3. to be in time to reach (a train, boat, etc.). 4. to surprise or detect, as in some action. 5. to strike. 6. to intercept and seize (a ball, etc.). 7. to incur or contract (often used figuratively): *to catch the blame, a cold*. 8. to become fastened or entangled. 9. to take hold. 10. to become lit, take fire. –n. 11. the act of catching. 12. a device for checking motion. 13. that which is caught, as a quantity of fish. 14. anything worth getting.

catch·cry, n. a memorable expression voicing a popular sentiment.

catch·ment area, n. Also, **catchment basin**. a drainage area, esp. of a reservoir or river.

cate·chism, n. a book of questions and answers containing a summary of the principles of the Christian religion.

causality

cat·e·gory, n., pl. -ries. 1. a classificatory division in any field of knowledge. 2. any general or comprehensive division; a class. – **categorical**, adj.

cater, v. 1. to provide food and service, etc., at functions (*for*). 2. to pander or give in (*to*).

cater·pillar, n. the wormlike larva of a butterfly or moth.

cater·waul, v. to cry as cats on heat.

cathar·sis /kəˈθɑsɪs/, n. the purifying or cleansing of strong, esp. negative emotions. – **cathartic**, adj.

cathe·dral, n. the principal church of a diocese.

cath·eter /ˈkæθətə/, n. a tube employed to drain fluids from body cavities.

cath·ode, n. the negative pole of a battery (opposed to *anode*). Also, **kathode**.

cath·olic, adj. universal in extent.

cattle, n. ruminants of the bovine kind.

cat·walk, n. 1. any narrow walking space. 2. a platform on which fashion models parade clothes.

caucus, n. a meeting of the parliamentary members of a political party.

caught, v. past tense and past participle of **catch**.

caul·dron, n. a large kettle or boiler.

cauli·flower, n. a vegetable with a compact, fleshy head.

caulk /kɔk/, v. to fill or close (a seam, joint, etc.), as in a boat.

causal, adj. of, constituting, or implying a cause.

caus·ality, n., pl. -ties. 1. the relation of cause and effect. 2. causal quality.

caus·ation, *n.* **1.** the action of causing or producing. **2.** the relation of cause to effect. **3.** anything that produces an effect.

cause, *n.*, *v.*, **caused, causing.** –*n.* **1.** that which produces an effect or result; the ground of any action or result; reason; motive. **2.** that side of a question which a person or party supports; the aim, purpose, etc., of a group. –*v.* **4.** to be the cause of.

cause·way, *n.* a raised road or path.

caus·tic /'kɒstɪk/, *adj.* **1.** capable of burning, corroding, or destroying living tissue. **2.** severely critical or sarcastic.

cau·ter·ise, *v.*, **-rised, -rising.** to burn, esp. for curative purposes.

cau·tion, *n.* **1.** prudence; carefulness. **2.** a warning. –*v.* **3.** to give warning to. – **cautionary**, *adj.* – **cautious**, *adj.*

caval·cade, *n.* any procession.

cava·lier, *n.* **1.** a courtly gentleman. –*adj.* **2.** haughty, disdainful. **3.** offhand; casual.

cav·alry, *n., pl.* **-ries.** part of an army, formerly on horseback, but now equipped with armoured vehicles.

cave, *n.*, *v.*, **caved, caving.** –*n.* **1.** a hollow opening into the side of a hill, etc. –*v.* **2.** to fall or sink (*in*).

cavern, *n.* a cave, esp. a large, deep cave. – **cavernous**, *adj.*

caviar, *n.* the salted roe of sturgeon and other large fish.

cavil, *v.*, **-illed, -illing.** to raise trivial objections.

cavity, *n., pl.* **-ties.** any hollow place.

cavort, *v. Colloq.* to prance or caper about.

cease, *v.*, **ceased, ceasing. 1.** to stop. **2.** to put a stop or end to. – **ceaseless**, *adj.*

cedar, *n.* any of several coniferous trees having fine-grained wood.

cede, *v.*, **ceded, ceding.** to yield or formally surrender to another.

ceil·ing, *n.* **1.** the overhead interior lining of a room. **2.** top limit.

cele·brant, *n.* **a.** the priest who officiates at the performance of a religious rite. **b.** the person who conducts a civil marriage.

cele·brate, *v.*, **-brated, -brating. 1.** to observe (a day) or commemorate (an event) with ceremonies or festivities. **2.** to make known publicly. **3.** to sound the praises of.

cele·brated, *adj.* well-known for outstanding achievement; famous; renowned.

celeb·rity, *n., pl.* **-ties.** a famous or well-known person.

celer·ity, *n.* swiftness; speed.

celery, *n.* a plant whose leafstalks are used raw for salad, and cooked as a vegetable.

celes·tial, *adj.* **1.** pertaining to heaven; divine. **2.** pertaining to the sky.

celi·bacy, *n.* **1.** the unmarried state. **2.** (of priests, etc.) abstention by vow from marriage. **3.** abstention from sexual intercourse. – **celibate**, *n., adj.*

cell, *n.* **1.** a small room in a convent, prison, etc. **2.** a unit within a larger organisation. **3.** the structural unit of plant and animal life. **4.** a device which generates electricity. – **cellular**, *adj.*

cellar, *n.* an underground room or store.

cello /'tʃɛloʊ/, *n., pl.* **-los, -li.** a four-stringed instrument of the

85

cello

violin family. Also, 'cello, violoncello. – **cellist**, n.

cellu·lite, n. fatty deposits, resulting in a dimply appearance of the skin.

cellu·loid, n. 1. a type of plastic. 2. films; the cinema.

cellu·lose, n. the chief constituent of the cell walls of plants.

Cel·sius, adj. denoting or pertaining to a scale of temperature in which the boiling point of water is approximately 100°C.

cement, n. a substance mixed with water and sand, used in building and which hardens when dry.

cem·etery, n., pl. **-teries**. a burial ground.

ceno·taph, n. a memorial to those killed in war.

censor, n. 1. an official who examines books, plays, films, etc., to determine, and ban, what is thought objectionable on moral, political, military, or other grounds. 2. to examine and act upon as a censor does.

cen·sor·ious, adj. fault-finding.

cen·sure, n., v., **-sured**, **-suring**. –n. 1. an expression of disapproval. –v. 2. to criticise adversely.

census, n. an official enumeration of inhabitants, with details as to age, sex, pursuits, etc.

cent, n. (a coin equal to) one hundredth part of the dollar.

cen·ten·ary /senˈtinəri, -ˈten-/, adj., n., pl. **-ries**. –adj. 1. of or pertaining to a 100th anniversary. –n. 2. a 100th anniversary. 3. a period of 100 years.

cen·ten·nial, adj. marking the completion of 100 years.

centi·pede, n. small segmented

ceremony

arthropod with a pair of legs attached to each segment.

cen·tral, adj. 1. of or forming the centre. 2. in, at, or near the centre. 3. principal; chief; dominant. – **centralise**, v.

centre, n., v. **-tred**, **-tring**. –n. 1. Geom. the middle point. 2. a point, pivot, axis, etc., round which anything rotates or revolves. 3. a central place in a town, city, etc., often set aside as an area for a particular activity. –v. 4. to place in or on a centre.

centri·fugal force, n. the force exerted outwards by a body moving in a curved path.

centri·petal force, n. a force acting on a body, which is directed towards the centre of a circle or curve, which causes it to move in the circle or curve.

century, n., pl. **-ries**. 1. a period of 100 years. 2. any group or collection of 100.

cephalic, adj. of or pertaining to the head.

cer·amic, adj. pertaining to products made from clay and similar materials, such as pottery, brick, etc. – **ceramics**, n.

cereal, n. 1. a plant yielding an edible grain, as wheat, rye, oats, rice, maize, etc. 2. a breakfast food made from grain.

cere·bral, adj. 1. of or pertaining to the brain. 2. intellectual.

cere·mony, n., pl. **-monies**. 1. the formalities observed on some important public occasion. 2. a solemn rite. 3. any formal act or observance, often used of a meaningless one. – **ceremonious**, adj. – **ceremonial**, adj., n.

cerise

cerise /sə'ris, -riz/, *adj., n.* mauve-tinged cherry red.

cer·tain, *adj.* 1. having no doubt; confident. 2. sure; inevitable. 3. unquestionable. 4. definite or particular, but not named. – **certainty**, *n.*

cer·tif·i·cate, *n.* a document certifying to the truth of something or to status, qualifications, privileges, etc.

cert·i·fy, *v.*, **-fied, -fying.** 1. to guarantee as certain; give reliable information of. 2. to declare insane.

cervix, *n.*, *pl.* **cervixes, cervices.** *Anat.* 1. the neck. 2. the neck of the uterus. – **cervical**, *adj.*

cess·ation, *n.* a ceasing or stopping.

cession, *n.* the act of ceding, as by treaty.

cess·pool, *n.* a cistern or pit for retaining the sediment of a drain or for sewage. 2. any filthy receptacle or place.

cet·acean /sə'teɪʃən/, *n.* an aquatic mammal as the whale, dolphin, etc. – **cetaceous**, *adj.*

chafe, *v.*, **chafed, chafing.** 1. to warm by rubbing. 2. to wear or abrade by rubbing. 3. to irritate; annoy.

chaff¹, *n.* the husks of grains and grasses separated from the seed.

chaff², *v.* to ridicule or tease good-naturedly.

cha·grin /'ʃægrən, ʃə'grin/, *n.* a feeling of vexation and disappointment or humiliation.

chain, *n.* 1. a connected series of metal or other links. 2. something that binds or restrains. 3. any connected series: *a chain of events.* –*v.* 4. to fasten or secure with or as with a chain.

chameleon

chain-reaction, *n. Colloq.* a series of reactions provoked by one event.

chair, *n.* 1. a seat with a back usu. for one person. 2. a seat of office or authority. 3. **take the chair**, to assume the role of chairman of a meeting. –*v.* 4. to preside over.

chair·man, *n., pl.* **-men**. the presiding officer of a meeting, committee, etc. Also, **chairperson.**

chalet /'ʃæleɪ/, *n.* a kind of cottage built for alpine regions.

cha·lice, *n.* a cup for the wine of the eucharist.

chalk, *n.* 1. a soft, white, pure limestone. 2. a prepared piece of chalk or chalk-like substance for marking. –*v.* 3. to mark or write with chalk. 4. **chalk up, a.** to score. **b.** to ascribe to.

chal·lenge, *n., v.*, **-lenged, -lenging.** –*n.* 1. a call to a contest of skill, strength, etc. 2. something that makes demands upon one's abilities, etc. 3. a calling to account or into question. –*v.* 4. to summon to a contest. 5. to make stimulating demands upon. 6. to call in question.

chamber, *n.* 1. a private room, esp. a bedroom. 2. the meeting hall, esp. of a legislature. 3. (*pl.*) a place where a judge hears matters not requiring action in court. 4. (*pl.*) a suite of rooms of barristers. 5. a compartment or enclosed space.

chamber·lain /'tʃeɪmbəlɪn/, *n.* official in charge of the household of a sovereign or nobleman.

chamber-pot, *n.* a portable vessel used chiefly in bedrooms as a toilet.

cha·meleon /kə'miliən, ʃə-/, *n.* a slow-moving lizard noted for its power to change colour.

87

chamois

chamois /ˈʃæmwɑ/ *for def. 1;* /ˈʃæmi/ *for def. 2., n., pl.* **-ois. 1.** an agile goatlike antelope. **2.** Also, **chammy**, a soft, pliable leather.

chamo·mile /ˈkæməmaɪl/, *n.* a herb used medicinally. Also, **camomile**.

champ[1], *v.* to bite upon, esp. impatiently.

champ[2], *n. Colloq.* a champion.

cham·pagne, *n.* a sparkling white wine.

cham·pignon /ʃæmpɪnjɔ̃/, *n.* a very small mushroom.

cham·pion, *n.* **1.** one who has defeated all opponents. **2.** one who fights for or defends any person or cause. –*v.* **3.** to act as champion of.

chance, *v.,* **chanced, chancing,** *adj.* –*n.* **1.** the absence of any known reason why an event should turn out one way rather than another. **2.** fortune; fate; luck. **3.** a possibility or probability of anything happening. **4.** an opportunity. **5.** a risk or hazard. –*v.* **6.** to come by chance (*on* or *upon*). **7.** *Colloq.* to take the chances of; risk. –*adj.* **8.** due to chance.

chan·cellor, *n.* the honorary head of a university.

chan·delier /ʃændəˈlɪə/, *n.* a branched support for a number of lights, suspended from a ceiling.

change, *v.,* **changed, changing.** –*v.* **1.** to alter in condition, appearance, etc. **2.** to substitute another or others for; exchange. **3.** to become different; alter (*to* or *into*). **4.** to change trains, etc. **5.** to change one's clothes. –*n.* **6.** variation; alteration. **7.** a substitution. **8.** variety or novelty. **9.** the passing from one place, or phase, etc., to another. **10.** money returned when

character

the sum offered is larger than the sum due. **11.** coins of low denomination.

chan·nel, *n., v.,* **-nelled, -nelling.** –*n.* **1.** the bed of a stream or waterway. **2.** the deeper part of a waterway. **3.** a route through which anything passes. **4.** a frequency band for one-way communication (as radio, television, etc.). –*v.* **5.** to convey through a channel. **6.** to direct towards or into some particular course.

chant, *n.* **1.** a short, simple melody, esp. with multiple syllables sung to each note. –*v.* **2.** to sing to, or in the manner of, a chant.

chaos, *n.* utter confusion or disorder. – **chaotic**, *adj.*

chap[1], *v.,* **chapped, chapping. 1.** (of cold weather) to crack, roughen, and redden (the skin). **2.** to become chapped.

chap[2], *n. Colloq.* a fellow.

chapel, *n.* a separate part of a church, or a small church, devoted to special services.

chap·er·one /ˈʃæpəroʊn/, *n.* an older person who supervises young unmarried people at social functions.

chap·lain, *n.* a clergyman attached to a royal court, military unit, college, etc.

chap·ter, *n.* a main division, usu. numbered, of a book, etc.

char·ter, *n.,* **charred, charring. 1.** to burn or reduce to charcoal. **2.** to burn slightly; scorch.

charac·ter, *n.* **1.** the aggregate of qualities that distinguishes one person or thing from others. **2.** good moral constitution or reputation. **3.** a person. **4.** *Colloq.* an odd

character

or interesting person. 5. a person represented in a drama, story, etc. 6. a symbol used in a writing system.

charac·ter·ise, v., -rised, -rising. 1. to be a characteristic of. 2. to describe the characteristic or peculiar quality of.

charac·ter·istic, adj. 1. typical; distinctive. –n. 2. a distinguishing feature or quality.

cha·rade /ʃəˈrɑːd/, n. 1. a game in which a player or players mime a word or phrase which the others try to guess. 2. a pointless act.

char·coal, n. the carbon-containing material obtained by the imperfect combustion of wood etc.

charge, v., charged, charging, n. –v. 1. to put a load on or in. 2. to fill or furnish (a thing) with the appropriate quantity. 3. to supply with a quantity of electricity. 4. to lay a command or injunction upon. 5. to lay blame upon; accuse (with). 6. to hold liable for payment. 7. to postpone payment on (a service or purchase) by having it recorded on one's account. 8. to ask as a price. 9. to attack by rushing against. 10. to rush, as to an attack. –n. 11. a load or burden. 12. the quantity an apparatus can hold. 13. a quantity of electricity. 14. (anything or anybody committed to one's) care, custody or superintendence. 15. an injunction. 16. an accusation. 17. a price charged. 18. an onset or attack, as of soldiers. 19. the quantity of electrical energy in a battery, etc. 20. in charge, having supervisory powers.

chargé d'affaires /ˌʃɑːʒeɪ dæˈfɛə/, n., pl. **chargés d'affaires**. 1. a diplomat acting for an absent ambassador. 2.

chase

an envoy to a state to which a diplomat of higher grade is not sent. Also, **chargé**.

chariot, n. a two-wheeled, horse-drawn vehicle.

char·isma /kəˈrɪzmə/, n. personal qualities that give an individual influence or authority over large numbers of people. – **charismatic**, adj.

charity, n., pl. **-ties**. 1. private or public aid to needy people. 2. a charitable fund, etc. 3. benevolent feeling, esp. towards those in need. – **charitable**, adj.

char·la·tan /ˈʃɑːlətən/, n. one who pretends to more knowledge or skill than he possesses.

charm, n. 1. a power to please and attract. 2. an object, action, verse, etc. with supposed magical power. 3. a trinket worn on a chain, bracelet, etc. 4. a verse or formula. –v. 5. to attract powerfully by beauty, etc. 6. to act upon with or as with a charm.

chart, n. 1. a sheet of information in tabulated form. 2. a map, esp. a marine map. –v. 3. to make a chart of. 4. to plan.

char·ter, n. 1. a document or contract, esp. relating to land transfers. 2. an official document giving privileges, rights, the benefit of a new invention, a peerage, etc. –v. 3. to establish by charter. 4. to hire a vehicle, etc. –adj. 5. founded, granted, or protected by a charter. 6. hired for a particular purpose or journey.

chary, adj., charier, chariest. 1. careful; wary. 2. shy.

chase[1], v., chased, chasing, n. –v. 1. to pursue in order to seize, overtake, etc. 2. to follow in pursuit. –n.

chase

3. the act of chasing. 4. a flora and fauna reserve.

chase[2], *v.*, **chased, chasing.** to ornament (metal) by engraving or embossing.

chasm /'kæzəm/, *n.* a deep cleft in the earth's surface.

chas·sis /'ʃæzi/, *n., pl.* **chassis** /'ʃæziz/. the frame, wheels, etc., of a motor vehicle, on which the body is supported.

chaste, *adj.* 1. virgin; virtuous; undefiled. 2. pure in style; simple. – **chastity,** *n.*

chas·ten /'tʃeɪsən/, *v.* to chastise.

chas·tise, *v.*, **-tised, -tising.** 1. to punish, esp. by beating. 2. to scold.

chat, *v.*, **chatted, chatting.** –*v.* 1. to converse in a familiar or informal manner. –*n.* 2. informal conversation.

chat·tel, *n.* a movable article of property.

chat·ter, *v.* to talk rapidly and to little purpose.

chatter·box, *n.* a very talkative person.

chauf·feur /'ʃoʊfə, ʃoʊ'fɜ/, *n.* a man employed to drive a private motor car. – **chauffeuse,** *n. fem.*

chauvi·nism /'ʃoʊvənɪzəm/, *n.* zealous and belligerent patriotism or devotion to any cause.

cheap, *adj.* 1. of a relatively low price. 2. of poor quality.

cheat, *n.* 1. a fraud; swindle. 2. a person who cheats. –*v.* 3. to defraud; swindle. 4. to practise fraud or deception.

check, *v.* 1. to stop the motion of, forcibly. 2. to restrain. 3. to investigate or verify as to correctness. 4. to leave in temporary custody. 5. to mark in a pattern of checks or squares. 6. *Chess.* to place (an opponent's king) under direct attack. 7. to prove to be right; to correspond accurately. 8. **check in/out**, to register one's arrival/departure. 9. **check up** or **on**, to investigate for verification. –*n.* 10. a person or thing that checks or restrains. 11. a sudden arrest or stoppage. 12. control with a view to ascertaining performance or preventing error. 13. a pattern formed of squares, as on a draughtboard.

check·mate, *n. Chess.* the act of putting the opponent's king into an inextricable check.

check·up, *n.* 1. an examination to verify accuracy, make a comparison, etc. 2. a complete physical examination.

ched·dar, *n.* a smooth white or yellow cheese.

cheek, *n.* 1. either side of the face below eye level. 2. the side wall of the mouth. 3. a buttock. 4. *Colloq.* impudence or effrontery.

cheeky, *adj.*, **cheekier, cheekiest.** *Colloq.* impudent; insolent.

cheep, *v.* to chirp; peep.

cheer, *n.* 1. a shout of encouragement, approval, congratulation, etc. 2. gladness, gaiety, or animation. –*v.* 3. to salute with shouts of approval, etc. 4. to inspire with cheer (*up*). 5. to encourage (*on*).

cheese, *n.* a food separated from the curd of milk separated from the whey.

chee·tah, *n.* an animal of the cat family resembling the leopard.

chef /ʃɛf/, *n.* a cook, esp. a head cook.

chemi·cal, *adj.* 1. of or concerned

chemical

with the science of chemistry. –*n.* **2.** a substance produced by or used in a chemical process.

chem·ist, *n.* **1.** one versed in chemistry or professionally engaged in chemical investigations. **2.** a retailer of medicinal drugs and toilet preparations.

chem·is·try, *n., pl.* **-tries. 1.** the science concerned with the composition of substances, the various elementary forms of matter, and the interactions between them. **2.** chemical properties, reactions, etc.

chemo·therapy /kɛmoʊˈθɛrəpi, kim-/, *n.* treatment of disease with chemicals which have a specific toxic effect on the disease-producing micro-organism.

chenille /ʃəˈniːl/, *n.* **1.** (a fabric with a weft of) velvety yarn. **2.** cotton fabric with a pattern of lines of tufts of cotton.

cheque, *n.* a written order, usu. on a standard printed form directing a bank to pay a specified sum of money to a payee named or to the person presenting it.

chequer, *v.* to mark with (squares of) different or contrasting colours.

cher·ish, *v.* to hold or treat as dear.

che·root /ʃəˈruːt/, *n.* a cigar having open, unpointed ends.

cher·ry, *n., pl.* **-ries.** (a tree bearing) small, round, bright red stone fruit.

cher·ub, *n., pl.* **cherubim** for def. 1; **cherubs** for def. 2. **1.** a kind of celestial being. **2.** a beautiful or innocent person, esp. a child.

chess, *n.* a game of battle strategy, played by 2 persons on a chequered board.

chest, *n.* **1.** the part of the body from

child

the neck to the waist. **2.** a storage box, usu. a large, strong one.

chest·nut, *n.* **1.** (a type of tree bearing) an edible nut. –*adj.* **2.** a reddish brown.

chew, *v.* **1.** to crush or grind with the teeth; masticate. **2.** to damage by or as if by chewing (*up*). **3.** to meditate on; consider deliberately (*over*).

chic /ʃiːk/, *adj.* stylish.

chicanery /ʃəˈkeɪnəri/, *n., pl.* **-ries.** legal trickery, quibbling, or sophistry.

chick, *n.* **1.** a young chicken or other bird. **2.** *Colloq.* a young girl.

chicken, *n.* **1.** the young of the domestic fowl (or of certain other birds). **2.** *Colloq.* a coward. –*v.* *Colloq.* **3.** **chicken out**, to withdraw because of cowardice, tiredness, etc.

chicken·pox, *n.* a mild, contagious eruptive disease, usu. of children.

chide, *v.*, **chided** or **chid**; **chided, chid** or **chidden**; **chiding. 1.** to scold; find fault. **2.** to drive, impel, etc., by chiding.

chief, *n.* **1.** the head or ruler of a clan, tribe, etc. **2.** *Colloq.* boss. –*adj.* **3.** highest in rank or authority. **4.** most important.

chief·tain, *n.* a leader of a group, band, etc.

chif·fon /ʃəˈfɒn, ˈʃɪfɒn/, *n.* sheer fabric of silk, nylon, or rayon in plain weave.

chihuahua /tʃəˈwɑːwə/, *n.* very small Mexican breed of dog.

chil·blain, *n.* (*usu. pl.*) an inflammation on the hands and feet caused by exposure to cold.

child, *n., pl.* **children. 1.** a baby or infant. **2.** a boy or girl. **3.** a childish person. **4.** any descendant.

chill

chill, *n.* **1.** a moderate but penetrating coldness. **2.** a sensation of cold, usu. with shivering. **3.** a depressing influence or sensation. **4.** a coldness of manner. –*adj.* **5.** cold; tending to cause shivering. **6.** depressing or discouraging. –*v.* **7.** to make or become cold. **8.** to make cool, but not freeze. – **chilly**, *adj.*

chilli, *n., pl.* **-ies.** the small, hot, pungent fruit of some species of capsicum.

chime, *n., v.*, **chimed, chiming.** –*n.* **1.** (sound produced by striking) a set of tuned bells or tubes. –*v.* **2.** to sound harmoniously in chimes. **3.** to harmonise; agree.

chim·ney, *n., pl.* **-neys.** a structure containing a flue for the passage of the smoke, gases, etc., of a fire or furnace.

chim·pan·zee, *n.* a highly intelligent anthropoid ape, smaller than the gorilla.

chin, *n.* the lower extremity of the face, below the mouth.

china, *n.* **1.** a vitreous, translucent earthenware. originally produced in China. **2.** plates, cups, etc., collectively.

chink[1], *n.* a crack, cleft, or fissure.

chink[2], *v.* to make a short, sharp sound, as of coins striking together.

chintz, *n., pl.* **chintzes.** a printed cotton (curtain) fabric, often shiny.

chip, *n., v.*, **chipped, chipping.** –*n.* **1.** a small piece, as of wood, separated by chopping, cutting, or breaking. **2. a.** a deep-fried finger of potato. **b.** =**crisp** (def. 3). **3.** *Electronics.* a minute square of semi-conducting material, processed in various ways to have certain electrical charac-

chlorophyll

teristics. **4. chip on the shoulder,** *Colloq.* a grudge. –*v.* **5.** to hew or cut with an axe, chisel, etc. **6.** to become chipped. **7. chip in,** *Colloq.* to contribute money, help, etc.

chip·munk, *n.* any of various small striped terrestrial squirrels.

chi·rop·o·dy /kə'rɒpədi/, *n.* the treatment of minor foot ailments. – **chiropodist**, *n.*

chi·ro·prac·tic /kaɪrə'præktɪk/, *n.* a therapeutic system based upon restoring normal nerve function by adjusting the segments of the spinal column. – **chiropractor**, *n.*

chirp, *v.* to make a short, sharp sound, as small birds and certain insects.

chirpy, *adj. Colloq.* cheerful.

chir·rup, *v.*, **-ruped, -ruping.** to chirp.

chisel, *n., v.*, **-elled, -elling.** –*n.* **1.** a steel tool with a cutting edge for shaping wood, stone, etc. –*v.* **2.** to work with a chisel.

chit, *n.* a voucher.

chiv·al·ry /'ʃɪvlri/, *n.* **1.** the rules and customs of medieval knighthood. **2.** good manners. – **chivalrous**, *adj.*

chive, *n.* a small bulbous plant related to the onion.

chlor·ide /'klɔraɪd/, *n.* a compound usu. of 2 elements only, one of which is chlorine.

chlor·ine, *n.* a greenish yellow gaseous element used as a powerful bleaching agent and in industry. *Symbol:* Cl

chloro·form, *n.* a colourless volatile liquid used as an anaesthetic and solvent.

chloro·phyll, *n.* the green colouring substances of leaves and plants necessary for photosynthesis.

chock, *n.* **1.** a block or wedge of wood, etc., used to prevent movement, as of a wheel or a cask. *–adv.* **2.** as close or tight as possible: *chock full*.

choc·o·late, *n.* a preparation made from cocoa beans.

choice, *n., adj.*, **choicer, choicest**. *–n.* **1.** the act of choosing; selection. **2.** power of choosing; option. **3.** the person or thing chosen. **4.** an abundance and variety from which to choose. *–adj.* **5.** excellent; superior. **6.** carefully selected.

choir /ˈkwaɪə/, *n.* a company of singers.

choke, *v.*, **choked, choking**, *n.* *–v.* **1.** to stop the breath of, by obstructing the windpipe; strangle; suffocate. **2.** to suffer strangling or suffocation. **3.** to make or become obstructed or clogged. **4.** to be temporarily overcome, as with emotion. *–v.* **5.** the act or sound of choking. **6.** (in internal-combustion engines) the mechanism regulating the air supply to a carburettor.

choker, *n.* a close-fitting necklace, often made of velvet or stringed pearls.

chol·era, *n.* an acute, infectious disease marked by diarrhoea, vomiting, cramp, etc.

choles·terol /kəˈlɛstərɒl/, *n.* an organic compound present in the liver, the blood and brain, the yolk of eggs, etc.

choose, *v.*, **chose, chosen**. **1.** to select from a number, or in preference to another. **2.** to prefer and decide (to do something).

choosy, *adj. Colloq.* hard to please. Also, **choosey**.

chop¹, *v.*, **chopped, chopping**, *n.* *–v.* **1.** to cut with a quick, heavy blow or series of blows, using an axe, etc. **2.** to make a quick heavy stroke or a series of strokes. *–n.* **3.** the act of chopping. **4.** a cutting blow. **5.** a slice of lamb, veal, pork, etc. containing some bone.

chop², *v.*, **chopped, chopping**. to turn, shift, or change suddenly, as the wind.

chop·per, *n.* **1.** *Colloq.* a helicopter. **2.** large-bladed axe with short handle.

chop·stick, *n.* one of a pair of thin sticks used to raise food to the mouth.

chord¹, *n.* **1.** a string of a musical instrument. **2.** a feeling of emotion.

chord², *n.* a combination of 3 or more tones, usu. in harmonic relation. – **chordal**, *adj.*

chore /tʃɔː/, *n.* a small or odd job; a piece of minor domestic work.

chore·og·ra·phy /kɒrɪˈɒgrəfɪ/, *n.* the art of composing ballets, dances, etc. – **choreographer**, *n.* – **choreographic**, *adj.* – **choreograph**, *v.*

chor·tle, *v.* to chuckle with glee.

chorus, *n., pl.* **-ruses**. **1. a.** a group of persons singing together. **b.** a part of a song in which others join the principal singer(s). **c.** any recurring refrain. **2.** simultaneous utterance in singing, speaking, etc. **3.** (in musical shows) the company of dancers and singers – **choral**, *adj.*

chose, *v.* past tense of **choose**.

chow·der, *n.* a kind of soup or stew made of clams, fish, or vegetables.

christen, *v.* to give a name to at baptism.

chro·matic, *adj.* **1.** pertaining to colour or colours. **2.** *Music.* (of a scale) moving by semitones.

chrome, *n.* chromium, esp. as a source of various pigments.

chromium

chro·mium, *n.* a metallic element used in pigments for photography, etc.; also used in corrosion-resisting chromium plating. *Symbol:* Cr

chromo·some, *n.* any of several bodies in the cell nucleus which carry the genes.

chronic, *adj.* 1. always present; constant. 2. continuing a long time.

chron·icle, *n., v.,* **-cled, -cling.** –*n.* 1. a record of events in the order of time. –*v.* 2. to record as in a chronicle.

chron·ology, *n., pl.* **-gies.** a statement of the accepted order of past events. – **chronological**, *adj.*

chron·ometer, *n.* a very accurate clock.

chrysa·lis, *n., pl.* **chrysalises, chrysalids, chrysalides.** the hard-shelled pupa of a moth or butterfly.

chrys·an·themum, *n.* a garden plant with large, colourful flowers.

chubby, *adj.,* **-bier, -biest.** round and plump.

chuck, *v.* 1. to pat or tap lightly, as under the chin. 2. to throw with a quick motion, usu. a short distance.

chuckle, *v.,* **chuckled, chuckling,** *n.* –*v.* 1. to laugh in a soft, amused manner. –*n.* 2. a soft, amused laugh.

chum, *n., v.,* **chummed, chumming.** –*n.* 1. an intimate friend. –*v.* 2. **chum up with,** to become friendly with.

chump, *n. Colloq.* a blockhead or dolt. 2. the thick blunt end of anything.

chun·der, *v., Colloq.* to vomit.

chunk, *n.* a thick mass or lump of anything.

church, *n.* 1. an edifice for public

94

circle

Christian worship. 2. (*cap.*) a Christian denomination.

churl, *n.* a rude, boorish, or surly person. – **churlish**, *adj.*

churn, *n.* 1. a vessel or machine in which butter is made. –*v.* 2. to shake or agitate with violence or continued motion.

chute, *n.* a channel, trough, etc., for conveying water, grain, etc., to a lower level.

chut·ney, *n., pl.* **-neys.** a fruit or vegetable relish.

cicada, *n., pl.* **-dae, -das.** a large insect which makes a shrill sound by vibrating membranes on the underside of the abdomen.

cider, *n.* the expressed juice of apples.

cigar, *n.* a small, shaped roll of tobacco leaves prepared for smoking.

ciga·rette, *n.* finely cut tobacco rolled in paper for smoking.

cinch, *n.* 1. a strong girth for a saddle or pack. 2. *Colloq.* something certain or easy.

cinder, *n.* 1. a burnt-out piece of coal, wood, etc. 2. (*pl.*) ashes.

cinema, *n.* 1. a film theatre. 2. **the cinema**, films collectively. – **cinematic**, *adj.*

cinna·mon, *n.* a spice from the inner bark of certain trees.

cipher, *n.* 1. an arithmetical symbol (0) which denotes no quantity or magnitude. 2. any Arabic numeral. 3. something of no value or importance. 4. (the key) to a secret method of writing. Also, **cypher.**

circa /'səkə, 'sasə/, *prep., adv.* about (used esp. in approximate dates). *Abbrev.:* c., c, or ca

circle, *n., v.,* **-cled, -cling.** –*n.* 1. a

circle

closed plane curve which is at all points equidistant from it's centre. 2. any circular object or arrangement. 3. an upper section of seats in a theatre. 4. an area of activity, influence, etc. 5. a complete series forming a connected whole. 6. a number of persons bound by a common tie. –v. 7. to enclose in a circle. 8. to move in a circle or circuit (*round*).

cir·cuit, *n.* 1. the act of going or moving round. 2. any circular or roundabout journey. 3. a number of theatres, cinemas, etc., under common control. 4. the complete path of an electric current.

cir·cu·i·tous /səˈkjuətəs/, *adj.* not direct.

cir·cu·lar, *adj.* 1. having the form of a circle. –*n.* 2. a letter, notice, etc., for general circulation or within an organisation. – **circularise**, *v.*

cir·cu·late, *v.*, -lated, -lating. 1. to move in a circle or circuit. 2. *Colloq.* to move amongst the guests at a social function.

cir·cu·la·tion, *n.* 1. the act of circulating. 2. the recurrent movement of the blood throughout the body. 3. the distribution of copies of a publication among readers.

cir·cum·cise, *v.* -cised, -cising. to remove the foreskin of (males). – **circumcision**, *n.*

cir·cum·fer·ence, *n.* the outer boundary, esp. of a circular area.

cir·cum·lo·cu·tion, *n.* a roundabout way of speaking.

cir·cum·nav·i·gate, *v.*, -gated, -gating. to sail round.

cir·cum·scribe, *v.*, -scribed, -scribing. 1. to draw a line round. 2. to enclose within bounds; limit, esp. narrowly.

cir·cum·spect, *adj.* watchful on all sides; prudent.

cir·cum·stance, *n.* 1. a condition which accompanies, determines, or modifies a fact or event. 2. ceremonious accompaniment or display. – **circumstantial**, *adj.*

cir·cum·vent, *v.* to gain advantage over by artfulness or deception.

circus, *n.* a company of performers, animals, etc., esp. a travelling company.

cirrho·sis /sɪˈroʊsəs, sə-/, *n.* a disease of the liver.

cirrus /ˈsɪrəs/, *n.* a high, thin cloud.

cis·tern, *n.* a reservoir, tank, etc., for holding water.

cita·del, *n.* any strongly fortified place.

cite, *v.*, cited, citing. 1. to quote (a passage, book, author, etc.), esp. as an authority. 2. to refer to as an example. – **citation**, *n.*

citi·zen, *n.* 1. a member of a state or nation (as distinguished from *alien*). 2. an inhabitant of a city or town. – **citizenry**, *n.*

citrus, *n.* any tree or shrub of the lemon, lime, orange, grapefruit, etc., genus.

city, *n.*, *pl.* **cities**. 1. a large or important town; a town so nominated by decree. 2. the central business area of a city.

civic, *adj.* 1. of or pertaining to a city. 2. of or pertaining to citizenship.

civil, *adj.* 1. of, consisting of, or relating to citizens. 2. of the commonwealth or state. 3. polite; courteous.

civil·ian, *n.* one engaged in civil

civilian

pursuits (distinguished from a soldier, etc.)

civi·li·sation, *n.* 1. state of human society with a high level of art, science, religion, and government. 2. the type of culture, society, etc., of a specific group. 3. the act or process of civilising.

civi·lise, *v.*, **-lised**, **-lising**. to bring out of a savage state.

civi·lised, *adj.* 1. having an advanced culture, society, etc. 2. polite or refined in behaviour.

civ·il·ity, *n., pl.* **-ties**. courtesy; politeness.

civil war, *n.* a war between parties, regions, etc., within their own country.

clack, *v.* to make a quick, sharp sound by striking or cracking.

clad, *v.* a past tense and past participle of **clothe**.

claim, *v.* 1. to demand as a right. 2. to assert as a fact. –*n.* 3. a demand for something as due. 4. a just title to something. 5. that which is claimed. 6. a payment demanded in accordance with an insurance policy, etc.

claim·ant, *n.* one who makes a claim.

clair·voyant, *adj.* 1. having supernatural powers of prediction. –*n.* 2. a clairvoyant person.

clam, *n., v.*, **clammed**, **clamming**. –*n.* 1. a type of mollusc. –*v.* 2. **clam up**, *Colloq.* to be silent.

clam·ber, *v.* to climb, using both feet and hands.

clammy, *adj.*, **-mier**, **-miest**. covered with a cold, sticky moisture.

clam·our, *n.* 1. a loud outcry. 2. popular outcry. –*v.* 3. to make a clamour.

clash

clamp, *n.* 1. a device for strengthening, supporting or fastening objects together. –*v.* 2. to fasten with or fix in a clamp. 3. **clamp down**, *Colloq.* to become more strict.

clan, *n.* a group of people of common descent. – **clannish**, *adj.*

clan·des·tine, *adj.* secret; private.

clang, *v.* 1. to give out a loud, resonant, metallic sound. –*n.* 2. such a sound.

clang·our, *n.* a loud, resonant, metallic sound, as of a trumpet.

clap, *v.*, **clapped**, **clapping**. –*v.* 1. to strike with a quick, smart blow, producing an abrupt, sharp sound. 2. to strike (the hands, etc.) together resoundingly, as to express applause. 3. to make an abrupt, sharp sound, as of bodies in collision. –*n.* 4. the act or sound of clapping. 5. a resounding blow. 6. a loud and abrupt noise, as of thunder.

claret /'klærət/, *n.* a red (originally the light red or yellowish) table wine.

clar·ify, *v.*, **-fied**, **-fying**. 1. to make or become clear, pure, or intelligible. 2. to make (a liquid) clear by removing sediment. – **clarification**, *n.* – **clarifier**, *n.*

clari·net, *n.* a wind instrument in the form of a cylindrical tube with a single reed attached to its mouthpiece. Also, **clarionet**.

clar·ion, *adj.* 1. clear and shrill. 2. inspiring.

clar·ity, *n.* clearness.

clash, *v.* 1. to make a loud, harsh noise. 2. to collide, esp. noisily. 3. to conflict; disagree, as of temperaments, colours, etc. 4. to coincide

clash

unfortunately (esp. of events). –*n.* **5.** the noise of, or as of, a collision. **6.** an unfortunate coinciding, as of events.

clasp, *n.* **1.** a fastening device, usu. of metal. **2.** a grasp. –*v.* **3.** to take hold of with an enfolding grasp.

class, *n.* **1.** a number of persons, things, animals, etc., regarded as forming one group through the possession of similar qualities. **2.** any division according to rank or grade. **3. a.** a group of pupils taught together. **b.** a period during which they are taught. **4.** a social stratum sharing similar economic and cultural characteristics. **5.** *Colloq.* acceptable style in dress or manner. **6.** a grade of accommodation in railway carriages, ships, aeroplanes, etc. –*v.* **7.** to arrange, place, or rate as to class.

classic, *adj.* **1.** serving as a standard, model, or guide. **2.** of literary or historical renown. –*n.* **3.** an author or a literary work of the first rank. **4.** (*pl.*) the literature or language of ancient Greece and Rome. **5.** something considered to be a perfect example of its type. – **classical,** *adj.*

clas·sify, *v.,* **-fied, -fying. 1.** to arrange or distribute in classes. **2.** to mark and limit access to (a secret document, information, etc.). – **classification.** *n.*

clat·ter, *v.* **1.** to make a loud rattling sound. –*n.* **2.** a clattering noise.

clause, *n.* **1.** a group of words containing a subject and a predicate. **2.** part of a legal document dealing with a section of the matter concerned, as in a contract, will, etc.

claus·tro·phobia, *n.* a dread of

clearway

confined places. – **claustrophobic,** *adj.*

clavi·cle, *n.* the collarbone.

claw, *n.* **1.** a sharp, usu. curved, nail on the foot of an animal or bird. **2.** any part or thing resembling a claw. –*v.* **3.** to tear, scratch, seize, etc., with or as with claws.

clay, *n.* **1.** a natural earthy material used for making bricks, pottery, etc. **2.** earth.

clean, *adj.* **1.** free from dirt or filth; unstained. **2.** free from defect. **3.** free from disease. **4.** shapely; trim: *the clean lines of a ship.* –*adv.* **5.** in a clean manner. **6.** wholly; completely. **7. come clean,** to make a full confession. –*v.* **8.** to make clean.

clean-cut, *adj.* **1.** distinctly outlined. **2.** definite. **3.** neatly dressed; wholesome.

cleanse /klenz/, *v.,* **cleansed, cleansing.** to make clean.

clear, *adj.* **1.** free from darkness, obscurity, or cloudiness. **2.** bright. **3.** transparent. **4.** distinct to the eye, ear, or mind. **5.** free from guilt or blame. **6.** free from obstructions. **7.** unentangled or disengaged (*of*). **8.** without limitation or qualification. **9.** free from debt. **10.** without deduction. –*v.* **11.** to make or become clear. **12.** to pass over without entanglement or collision. **13.** to gain as profit. **14.** to approve or authorise, or to obtain approval or authorisation for (a thing or person). **15.** to remove trees, undergrowth, etc., from (an area of land).

clear·ance, *n.* **1.** the act of clearing. **2.** a clear space. **3.** amount of room available or required to clear an obstacle.

clear·way, *n.* a stretch of road on

clearway

which, between stated times, motorists may not stop.

cleat, *n.* a small wedge-shaped block.

cleav·age, *n.* 1. the state of being cleft or split. 2. *Colloq.* the cleft between a woman's breasts.

cleave¹, *v.*, **cleaved, cleaving.** to stick or adhere; cling or hold fast (*to*).

cleave², *v.*, **cleft** or **cleaved** or **clove, cleft** or **cleaved** or **cloven, cleaving.** to part or split, esp. along a natural line of division.

clea·ver, *n.* a heavy knife used by butchers.

clef, *n. Music.* a symbol placed upon a stave to indicate the name and pitch of the notes.

cleft¹, *n.* a space or opening made by cleavage; a split.

cleft², *adj.* cloven; split.

cle·ment, *adj.* 1. lenient; compassionate. 2. (of the weather, etc.) mild or pleasant. – **clemency**, *n.*

clench, *v.* to close (the hands, teeth, etc.) tightly.

clergy, *n., pl.* **-gies.** the body of ordained people in the Christian Church. – **clergyman**, *n.*

cleric, *n.* a member of the clergy.

cleri·cal, *adj.* 1. pertaining to a clerk or to clerks. 2. of or pertaining to the clergy.

clerk /klak/, *n.* one employed in an office, shop, etc., to keep records, etc.

clever, *adj.* 1. having quick intelligence. 2. dexterous or nimble with the hands.

cliché /ˈkliːʃeɪ/, *n., pl.* **-chés** /-eɪz/. a trite, stereotyped expression, idea, practice, etc.

click, *n.* 1. a slight, sharp sound. –*v.* 2. to make a click or clicks. 3. to fall into place or be understood.

client, *n.* 1. one who consults a professional adviser. 2. a customer.

cli·en·tele /ˌkliənˈtɛl/, *n.* the customers, clients, etc. (of a solicitor, businessman, etc.) as a whole.

cliff, *n.* the high, steep face of a rocky mass.

cli·mate, *n.* the composite weather conditions of a region.

climax, *n.* the crisis point of anything; the culmination. –*v.* 2. to reach the climax. – **climactic**, *adj.*

climb, *v.* 1. to mount or go upwards, esp. by using both hands and feet; ascend. 2. to rise slowly by continued effort. 3. to slope upward.

clinch, *v.* 1. to secure (a driven nail, etc.) by beating down the point. 2. to settle (a matter) decisively. –*n.* 3. *Boxing, etc.* the act of a contestant holding the other so as to hinder his punches. 4. *Colloq.* an embrace or passionate kiss.

cling, *v.*, **clung, clinging.** to adhere closely.

clinic, *n.* any medical centre offering a variety of services.

clini·cal, *adj.* 1. pertaining to a clinic. 2. scientific; not affected by the emotions.

clink, *v.* to make a light, sharp, ringing sound.

clip¹, *v.*, **clipped, clipping.** –*v.* 1. to cut, or cut off or out, as with shears. 2. to punch a hole in (a ticket). 3. to omit sounds of (a word) in pronouncing. 4. *Colloq.* to hit with a quick, sharp blow. 5. to move swiftly. –*n.* 6. the act of clipping. 7. anything clipped off.

clip², *n.* a device for gripping and holding tightly.

clip·per, *n.* **1.** (*oft. pl.*) a cutting tool, esp. shears. **2.** a sailing vessel built for speed.

clique, *n.* a small set or coterie, esp. one that is snobbishly exclusive.

clit·oris, *n.* the erectile organ of the vulva.

cloak, *n.* a loose outer garment.

clob·ber, *v. Colloq.* to batter severely.

clock, *n.* **1.** an instrument for measuring and indicating time. *–v.* **2.** to time or ascertain by the clock.

clock·wise, *adj., adv.* in the direction of rotation of the hands of a clock.

clock·work, *n.* **1.** the mechanism of a clock. **2. like clockwork,** with perfect regularity or precision.

clod, *n.* **1.** a lump or mass, esp. of earth or clay. **2.** a stupid person.

clod·hoppers, *n. pl.* strong, heavy shoes.

clog, *v.,* **clogged, clogging.** *–v.* **1.** to hinder or obstruct, esp. by sticky matter. *–n.* **2.** a kind of shoe with a thick sole usu. of wood.

clois·ter, *n.* **1.** a covered walk. **2.** any quiet, secluded place. *–v.* **3.** to confine in retirement.

clone, *n., v.,* **cloned, cloning.** *–v.* **1.** an asexually produced descendant, identical to the original. *–v.* **2.** to develop such descendant(s).

close /klouz/, *v.,* **closed, closing;** /klous/, *adj.,* **closer, closest;** /klouz/ for def. 17; /klous/ for def. 18; *n. –v.* **1.** to stop or obstruct (a gap, entrance, aperture, etc.). **2.** to stop or obstruct the entrances or holes in (a container, etc.). **3.** to refuse access to or passage across. **4.** to bring together the parts of. **5.** to bring or come to an end; to shut down, temporarily or permanently. **6.** to become closed. **7.** to come together; unite. *–adj.* **8.** shut tight. **9.** confined; narrow. **10.** lacking fresh air. **11.** practising secrecy. **12.** stingy. **13.** near in space, time, or relation. **14.** intimate; confidential. **15.** not deviating from a model or original. **16.** nearly even or equal. *–n.* **17.** the end or conclusion. **18.** a cul-de-sac.

closet, *n.* **1.** a small room or cabinet for clothing, food, utensils, etc. *–adj.* **2.** secret.

clo·sure, *n.* the act of closing or shutting.

clot, *n.* **1.** a semisolid mass, as of coagulated blood. **2.** *Colloq.* a stupid person.

cloth, *n., pl.* **cloths.** a fabric formed by weaving, etc., used for garments, upholstery, etc.

clothe, *v.,* **clothed** or **clad, clothing.** to dress; attire.

clothes, *n.pl.* fitted articles, usu. of cloth, worn on the body for warmth, protection, etc.; garments.

cloud, *n.* **1.** a visible collection of particles of water or ice suspended in the air. **2.** any similar mass, esp. of smoke or dust. **3.** anything that darkens, or causes gloom, etc. *–v.* **4.** to cover with, or as with, a cloud. **–** **cloudy,** *adj.*

clout, *n.* **1.** *Colloq.* a blow, esp. with the hand. **2.** effectiveness; force.

clove^1**,** *n.* the dried flower bud of a tropical tree used as a spice.

clove^2**,** *n.* one of the small bulbs forming a mother bulb, as in garlic.

clove^3**,** *n.* past tense of **cleave**^{2}.

cloven, *adj.* divided.

clover, *n.* any of various herbs with leaves with 3 lobes.

clown, *n.* 1. a jester or buffoon in a circus, etc. –*v.* 2. to act like a clown.

cloy, *v.* to weary by an excess of food, sweetness, pleasure, etc.

club, *n., v.,* **clubbed, clubbing.** –*n.* 1. a heavy stick, usu. thicker at one end used as a weapon. 2. A stick or bat used in various ball games. 3. a group of persons organised for various social purposes and regulated by rules agreed by its members. 4. the building or rooms used by such a group. 5. a black 3-leaved figure on a playing card. –*v.* 6. to beat with a club. 7. to unite; join together.

cluck, *v.* to utter the cry of a hen.

clue, *n.* a guide or aid in the solution of a problem, mystery, etc.

clump, *n.* 1. a cluster, esp. of trees, or other plants. –*v.* 2. to walk heavily and clumsily.

clumsy, *adj.,* **-sier, -siest.** lacking dexterity or skill in movement or action.

clung, *v.* past tense and past participle of **cling**.

clus·ter, *n.* a number of things of the same kind, growing or held together.

clutch[1], *v.* 1. to seize with the hands or claws. 2. to grip tightly or firmly. –*n.* 3. (*usu. pl.*) power of disposal or control. 4. a device for gripping something. 5. (esp. in a motor vehicle) the device which engages and disengages the engine from the transmission.

clutch[2], *n.* a hatch of eggs.

clut·ter, *v.* 1. to heap or strew in a disorderly manner. –*n.* 2. a disorderly heap; litter.

coach, *n.* 1. a large, enclosed, four-wheeled carriage. 2. a bus used for long distances or for sightseeing. 3. a person who trains athletes. 4. a private tutor. –*v.* 5. to act in the capacity of a coach.

coagu·late koʊˈægjəleɪt , *v.,* **-lated, -lating.** to change from a fluid into a thickened mass.

coal, *n.* a black or brown coloured compact and earthy organic rock used as a fuel.

co·alesce /koʊəˈlɛs/, *v.,* **-lesced, -lescing.** to unite so as to form one mass, community, etc.

co·alition, *n.* an alliance, esp., a temporary one between political parties, states, etc.

coarse, *adj.,* **coarser, coarsest.** 1. of inferior or faulty quality. 2. composed of relatively large particles. 3. lacking in fineness or delicacy.

coast, *n.* 1. the land next to the sea. –*v.* 2. to move along after effort has ceased. – **coastal**, *adj.*

coast·guard, *n.* a coastal police force responsible for preventing smuggling, watching for and aiding ships in distress or danger, etc.

coat, *n.* 1. an outer garment with sleeves. 2. a natural covering, as the hair of an animal, etc. 3. anything that covers or conceals. –*v.* 4. to cover with a layer or coating.

coat of arms, *n.* a heraldic design.

coax, *v.* 1. to influence by, or use gentle persuasion, etc. 2. to get by coaxing.

cob, *n.* 1. the long, woody core in which the grains of corn or maize are embedded. 2. a short-legged, thickset horse.

cobalt, *n.* a silver-white metallic element used in alloys, ceramics,

cobalt

etc., and (as an isotope) in the treatment of cancer. *Symbol:* Co

cobber, *n. Colloq.* mate; friend.

cob·bler, *n.* **1.** one who mends shoes. **2.** a clumsy workman.

cobra, *n.* any of several extremely venomous snakes able to dilate the neck to a hoodlike form.

cobweb, *n.* a web or net spun by a spider to catch its prey.

co·caine, *n.* a bitter crystalline alkaloid used as a local anaesthetic. Also, **cocain**.

coccyx /'kɒksɪks, 'kɑkɪks/, *n.* a small triangular bone forming the lower extremity of the spinal column in man.

cochi·neal, *n.* a red dye.

cock[1], *n.* **1.** the male of any bird. **2.** a device for controlling the flow of a liquid or gas. —*v.* **3.** to pull back and set the hammer of (a firearm).

cock[2], *v.* to set or turn up or to one side, often in an assertive, jaunty, or significant manner.

cocka·too, *n.* any of several crested parrots.

cock·erel, *n.* a young domestic cock.

cocker spaniel, *n.* a breed of small spaniels used in hunting or kept as pets.

cock·eyed, *adj.* having a squinting eye.

cockle, *n.* a type of mollusc.

cock·pit, *n.* **1.** (in some aeroplanes) an enclosed space containing seats for the pilot and copilot. **2.** the driver's seat in a racing car.

cock·roach, *n.* any of various insects, usu. nocturnal, and having a flattened body.

cocks·comb, *n.* the comb of a cock.

cock·sure, *adj.* overconfident.

coelenterate

cock·tail, *n.* any of various short mixed drinks.

cocky, *adj.* **cockier, cockiest.** *Colloq.* arrogantly smart; full of conceit.

cocoa, *n.* **1.** the roasted, ground seeds of the cacao. **2.** a beverage made from this.

coco·nut, *n.* the seeds of the coconut palm, large, hard-shelled, lined with a white edible meat, and containing a milky liquid.

cocoon, *n.* the silky envelope spun by the larvae of many insects to protect them in the pupal state.

cocotte, *n.* small ovenproof dish used for cooking and serving food: *oeuf en cocotte* (egg baked in a cocotte).

cod, *n.* any of a number of freshwater or marine fishes.

coda, *n.* a passage at the end of a musical composition.

coddle, *v.*, **-dled, -dling. 1.** to cook (eggs, fruit, etc.) slowly in water just below boiling point. **2.** to treat tenderly; nurse or tend indulgently.

code, *n.* **1.** any system of rules and regulations. **2.** a system of symbols for use in communication by telegraph, etc. **3.** a system of symbols, words etc., used for secrecy.

codger, *n. Colloq.* an odd or peculiar (old) person.

codicil /'kɒdɪsɪl/, *n.* a supplement to a will, containing an addition, explanation, modification, etc.

codify, *v.*, **-fied, -fying.** to reduce (laws, etc.) to a code.

co·education, *n.* joint education of both sexes in the same institution.

co·efficient, *n.* a number or quantity placed (generally) before and multiplying another quantity.

coelen·terate /sə'lɛntəreɪt, -tərət/, *n.*

coelenterate

one of the group of invertebrate animals that includes the jellyfishes, corals, polyps, etc.

coerce /kouˈɜs/, v., **-erced, -ercing.** to compel by force. – **coercion**, n. – **coercive**, adj.

coffee, n. a beverage made from the roasted and ground beans or seeds of various tropical trees and shrubs.

coffer, n. 1. a box or chest for valuables. 2. (pl.) a treasury; funds.

coffin, n. the box in which a corpse is placed for burial.

cog, n. a tooth or projection on a wheel, etc., for transmitting motion to, or receiving motion from, a corresponding part with which it engages.

cogent /ˈkoudʒənt/, adj. compelling assent or belief. – **cogency**, n.

cogitate, v., **-tated, -tating.** to think hard; ponder.

cognac /ˈkɒnjæk/, n. French brandy.

cognate, adj. related by birth or origin.

cognisance, n. knowledge; notice. – **cognisant**, adj.

cognition, n. the act or process of knowing; perception.

cohabit, v. to live together in a sexual relationship.

cohere, v., **-hered, -hering.** 1. to hold fast, as parts of the same mass. 2. to be congruous. – **coherent**, adj.

cohesion, n. the state of cohering, uniting, or sticking together. – **cohesive**, adj.

cohort, n. any group or company.

coiffure /kwaˈfjuə/, n. a style of arranging the hair.

coil, v. 1. to wind into rings one above another. –n. 2. a connected series of spirals or rings. 3. a single such ring.

coin, n. 1. a piece of metal stamped and issued officially as money. 2. such pieces collectively. –v. 3. to make; invent.

coincide, v., **-cided, -ciding.** to be or happen at the same point in space or time.

coincidence, n. 1. the condition or fact of coinciding. 2. a striking chance occurrence of 2 or more events at one time. – **coincidental**, adj.

coitus /ˈkouətəs/, n. sexual intercourse. Also, **coition** /kouˈɪʃən/.

coke, n. a solid fuel remaining after the removal of gas from coal.

cola, n. a carbonated soft drink containing an extract made from the tropical cola nut.

colander /ˈkʌləndə, ˈkɒl-/, n. a strainer used in cookery. Also, **cullender**.

cold, adj. 1. having a relatively low temperature. 2. producing or feeling a marked lack of warmth. 3. Colloq. unconscious because of a severe blow, shock, etc. 4. not affectionate or friendly. –n. 5. the relative absence of heat. 6. the sensation produced by loss of heat from the body. 7. Also, **the common cold**. an indisposition caused by a virus, characterised by catarrh, etc.

cold-blooded, adj. 1. unsympathetic; cruel. 2. designating animals, as fishes and reptiles, whose blood temperature varies according to the temperature of their environment.

cold-shoulder, v. to ignore; show indifference to.

cold sore, n. a watery eruption on

cold sore

the face often accompanying a cold (def. 7).

cole·slaw, *n.* a salad of finely sliced white cabbage, etc. Also, **slaw**.

colic, *n.* paroxysmal pain in the abdomen. – **colicky**, *adj.*

col·lab·or·ate, *v.*, **-rated, -rating. 1.** to work, one with another. **2.** to co-operate treacherously.

col·lage /kə'lɑ:ʒ/, *n.* a picture composed of various materials.

col·lapse, *v.*, **-lapsed, -lapsing**, *n.* –*v.* **1.** to fall or cave in; crumble suddenly. **2.** to break down; come to nothing. –*n.* **3.** a sudden, complete failure.

col·laps·ible, *adj.* designed to fold into a compact size.

collar, *n.* **1.** anything worn or placed round the neck. **2.** the part of a shirt, etc., round the neck. –*v.* **3.** to put a collar on. **4.** to seize by the collar or neck.

collar·bone, *n.* a slender bone connecting the breastbone with the shoulder blade, and forming the front part of the shoulder.

col·late, *v.*, **-lated, -lating.** to put together (a document) by sorting its pages into the correct order.

col·lat·eral, *adj.* **1.** situated at the side. **2.** accompanying; auxiliary.

col·league, *n.* an associate in business, etc.

col·lect, *v.* **1.** to gather together. **2.** to accumulate; make a collection of. **3.** to regain control of (one's thoughts, etc.). **4.** to call for and remove. **5.** *Colloq.* to run into or collide with. –*adj.*, *adv.* **6.** to be paid for by the receiver. – **collection**, *n.*

col·lec·tive, *adj.* **1.** forming a collection or aggregate; combined. **2.** pertaining to a group of individuals taken together. –*n.* **3.** a collective body. **4.** a communal enterprise.

collective noun, *n.* a noun that expresses a grouping of individual objects or persons, as *herd*, *jury*, and *clergy*.

col·lege, *n.* **1.** a (usu.) post-secondary, diploma-awarding, technical or professional school. **2.** an institution for special or professional instruction often part of a university. **3.** a self-governing association of scholars incorporated within a university. **4.** a large private school. **5.** an association of persons having certain powers and engaged in a particular pursuit. – **collegian**, *n.* – **collegiate**, *adj.*

col·lide, *v.*, **-lided, -liding.** to come together with force; come into violent contact. – **collision**, *n.*

collie, *n.* a dog used for tending sheep. Also, **colly**.

col·liery, *n.*, *pl.* **-ries.** a coal mine, including all buildings and equipment.

col·lo·cate, *v.*, **-cated, -cating.** to set or place together. – **collocation**, *n.*

col·lo·qui·al, *adj.* appropriate to conversational or informal speech or writing.

col·lu·sion, *n.* secret agreement for a fraudulent purpose.

co·logne /kə'loʊn/, *n.* a perfumed toilet water.

colon[1], *n.* a point of punctuation (:) marking off a main portion of a sentence.

colon[2], *n.*, *pl.* **-lons, -la.** the large intestine excluding the rectum.

colon·nade, *n.* **1.** a series of columns set at regular intervals. **2.** a long row of trees.

103

colony

col·o·ny, *n., pl.* **-nies. 1.** a group of people who settle a new land and are subject to the parent state. **2.** the country or district so settled. **3.** any people or territory separated from but subject to a ruling power. – **colonial,** *adj.* – **colonise,** *v.* – **colonist,** *n.*

col·o·phon, *n.* a publisher's distinctive emblem.

co·los·sal, *adj.* gigantic; vast.

co·los·to·my, *n.* the surgical formation of an artificial anus.

col·our, *n.* **1.** that quality of light (reflected or transmitted by a substance) which is basically determined by its spectral composition and is perceived as (a mixture of) red, blue, yellow, etc. **2.** racial complexion other than white, esp. Negro. **3.** vivid or distinctive quality, as of literary work. **4.** that which is used for colouring; pigment. **5.** (*pl.*) a flag, ensign, etc., as of a military body or ship. –*v.* **6.** to give or apply colour to; tinge. **7.** to cause to appear different from the reality. **8.** to take on or change colour. **9.** to flush.

colour-blindness, *n.* defective colour perception. – **colour-blind,** *adj.*

colt, *n.* a male horse not past its 4th birthday.

col·umn, *n.* **1.** an upright shaft usu. serving as a support; a pillar. **2.** any column-like object, mass, or formation. **3.** one of the 2 or more vertical rows of lines of type or printed matter on a page. **4.** a regular contribution to a newspaper, usu. signed, and consisting of comment, news, etc.

co·ma, *n., pl.* **-mas.** a state of prolonged unconsciousness. – **comatose,** *adj.*

comedy

comb, *n.* **1.** a toothed piece of bone, metal, etc., for arranging or holding the hair. **2.** any comblike instrument. **3.** the fleshy growth on the head of the domestic fowl. –*v.* **4.** to dress (the hair, etc.) with a comb. **5.** to search with great thoroughness.

com·bat, *v.,* **-bated, -bating.** *n.* –*v.* **1.** to fight or contend against. –*n.* **2.** a fight between two men, armies, etc.

com·bine, *v.* **1.** to bring or join into a close union or whole. **2.** a union of persons or groups for political, commercial, or other interests. – **combination,** *n.*

com·bus·tion, *n.* the process of burning. – **combustible,** *adj.*

come, *v.,* **came, come, coming. 1.** to move towards or arrive at a particular place. **2.** to extend; reach (*to*). **3.** to issue; be derived. **4.** to arrive or appear as a result. **5.** to turn out to be. **6.** *Colloq.* to have an orgasm. **7. come about,** to come to pass. **8. come across,** to meet with, esp. by chance. **9. come down with,** to contract (a disease). **10. come from, a.** to have been born in; to live in. **b.** to derive or be obtained from. **11. come in, a.** to become useful, fashionable, etc. **12. come into, a.** to get. **b.** to inherit. **13. come out, a.** to appear; be published. **b.** to be revealed. **14. come round, a.** to relent. **b.** to recover consciousness. **c.** to change (an opinion, direction, etc.). **15. come to, a.** to recover consciousness. **b.** to amount to.

co·me·dian, *n.* an actor or writer of comedy. – **comedienne,** *n. fem.*

com·e·dy, *n., pl.* **-dies. 1.** a play, film, etc., of light and humorous character. **2.** the comic element of drama, literature, or life.

comely

comely, *adj.*, -lier, -liest. pleasing in appearance.

comet, *n.* a celestial body moving about the sun in an elongated orbit.

com·fort, *v.* 1. to soothe when in grief. –*n.* 2. relief in affliction; consolation. 3. a person or thing that consoles. 4. a state of ease. – **comfortable**, *adj.*

comic, *adj.* 1. pertaining to comedy. 2. provoking laughter. –*n.* 3. *Colloq.* a comic actor. 4. a magazine containing one or more stories in comic strip form. 5. (*pl.*) *Colloq.* comic strips.

comical, *adj.* provoking laughter, or amusing.

comic strip, *n.* a series of cartoon drawings relating a comic incident, an adventure story, etc.

comma, *n.* a mark of punctuation (,) used to indicate the smallest breaks in a sentence.

com·mand, *v.* 1. to order with authority. 2. to require with authority. 3. to have authority over. –*n.* 4. the act of commanding or ordering. 5. control; disposal: *to have influential friends at one's command.*

com·man·dant, *n.* the commanding officer of a place, group, etc.

com·man·deer, *v.* to seize (private property) for military or other public use.

com·mander, *n.* one who exercises authority; a chief officer.

com·mand·ment, *n.* a command or edict.

com·man·do, *n.*, *pl.* -dos, -does. (a member of) a small specially trained fighting force.

com·mem·o·rate, *v.* -rated, -rating. 1.

commission

to serve as a memento of. 2. to honour the memory of by some act.

com·mence, *v.*, -menced, -mencing. to begin; start.

com·mend, *v.* 1. to recommend as worthy of confidence, notice, etc. 2. to entrust. – **commendation**, *n.*

com·men·su·rate, *adj.* 1. of equal extent or duration. 2. proportionate.

com·ment, *n.* a remark, observation, or criticism.

com·men·tary, *n.*, *pl.* -taries. 1. a series of comments or annotations. 2. a description of a public event broadcast or televised as it happens.

com·men·tator, *n.* a writer or broadcaster who makes critical or explanatory remarks about news, events, or describes sporting events etc.

com·merce, *n.* interchange of goods or commodities, esp. on a large scale; trade; business.

com·mer·cial, *adj.* 1. of, or of the nature of, or engaged in commerce. 2. capable of being sold in great numbers. 3. setting possible commercial return above artistic considerations. 4. *Radio, T.V.* financially dependent on advertising. –*n.* 5. *Radio, T.V.* an advertisement.

commercial traveller, *n.* a travelling agent who solicits orders for a wholesaler's goods.

com·mis·er·ate, *v.*, -rated, -rating. to sympathise (*with*).

com·mis·sar /ˈkɒmɪsɑ/, *n.* head of a government department in the Soviet Union.

com·mis·sion, *n.* 1. the act of giving in charge. 2. an authoritative order or charge. 3. an official body charged with particular functions. 4. the condition of anything in

commission

active service or use. **5.** a task or matter committed to one's charge. **6.** authority to act as agent for another. **7.** a sum or percentage allowed to an agent, salesman, etc. **8.** the position or rank of an officer in the army or navy. *v.* **9.** to give a commission to. **10.** to send on a mission.

com·mis·sion·aire, *n.* a uniformed messenger or doorkeeper at a hotel, etc.

com·mis·sion·er, *n.* **1.** a member of a commission. **2.** a government official in charge of a department.

commit, *v.*, **-mitted**, **mitting**. **1.** to give in trust or charge. **2.** to consign to custody in a gaol, mental hospital, etc. **3.** to hand over for treatment, disposal, etc. **4.** to do; perpetrate. **5.** to bind by pledge. – **commitment**, *n.*

com·mit·tee, *n.* a group of persons appointed to investigate, report, or act in special cases.

com·mode, *n.* **1.** a piece of furniture containing drawers or shelves. **2.** a stand or cupboard containing a chamber-pot or washbasin.

com·modious, *adj.* convenient and roomy; spacious.

com·mod·i·ty, *n., pl.* **-ties**. an article of trade.

com·mo·dore, *n.* the senior captain of a line of merchant vessels.

common, *adj.* **1.** belonging equally to, or shared alike by, 2 or more. **2.** of frequent occurrence; familiar; usual. **3.** of mediocre or inferior quality.

com·moner, *n.* one of the common people.

common law, *n.* **1.** the system of law based on customs and court decision distinct from statute or ecclesiastical law. **2.** the law administered through the system of writs.

communiqué

common noun, *n. Gram,* a noun applicable to any one or all the members of a class, as *man, men, city, cities,* in contrast to *Shakespeare, London.* Cf. **proper noun.**

common·place, *adj.* ordinary; without individuality.

common sense, *n.* sound, practical understanding.

common·wealth, *n.* **1.** the whole body of people of a nation. **2.** (*cap.*) a federation of states and territories with powers and responsibilities divided between a central government and a number of smaller governments.

com·motion, *n.* violent or tumultuous motion or disturbance.

com·munal /kəˈmjunəl, ˈkɒmjənəl/, *adj.* pertaining to a commune or a community.

com·mune[1] /kəˈmjun/, *v.*, **-muned**, **-muning**. to converse; interchange thoughts or feelings.

com·mune[2] /ˈkɒmjun/, *n.* any community of like-minded people choosing to live independently.

communicant, *n.* one who receives Holy Communion.

com·muni·cate, *v.*, **-cated**, **-cating**. **-v.** **1.** to give to another as a partaker; impart; transmit. **2.** to make known. **3.** to have interchange of thoughts. – **communication**, *n.* – **communicative**, *adj.* – **communicable**, *adj.*

com·munion, *n.* **1.** the act of sharing, or holding in common. **2.** interchange of thoughts or interests; intimate talk. **3.** the celebration of the Lord's Supper.

com·muniqué /kəˈmjunəkeɪ/, *n.* an

communiqué

official bulletin or communication usu. to the press or public.

com·mu·nism, *n.* a system of social organisation based on the holding of all property in common. – **communist**, *n.* – **communistic**, *adj.*

com·mu·nity, *n., pl.* **-ties.** 1. a social group living in a specific locality, and having a common culture. 2. **the community**, the public.

com·mute, *v.*, **-muted, -muting.** 1. to change (a penalty, etc.) for one less burdensome or severe. 2. to serve as a substitute. 3. to travel regularly between home and work.

com·pact¹ /'kɒm'pækt, 'kɒmpækt/, *adj.* / kɒm'pækt/, *v.*; /'kɒmpækt/, *n.* –*adj.* 1. joined or packed together; closely and firmly united. 2. arranged within a relatively small space. 3. expressed concisely. –*v.* 4. to join or pack closely together. –*n.* 5. a small case containing a mirror, face powder, etc.

com·pact² /'kɒmpækt/, *n.* an agreement between parties.

com·pan·ion, *n.* 1. one who accompanies or associates with another. 2. a handbook.

com·pan·ion·able, *adj.* fitted to be a companion; sociable.

com·pa·ny, *n.* 1. a group of people. 2. a guest or guests. 3. a number of persons united or incorporated for joint action, esp. for business. 4. *Mil.* a subdivision of a regiment or battalion.

com·par·a·tive, *adj.* 1. pertaining to comparison. 2. estimated by comparison; not positive or absolute. 3. denoting the intermediate degree of the comparison of adjectives and adverbs.

com·pare, *v.*, **-pared, -paring.** 1. to represent as similar (*to*). 2. to note the similarities and differences of (*with*). 3. to bear comparison. – **comparable**, *adj.*

com·par·i·son, *n.* 1. the state of being compared. 2. a likening; a comparative estimate or statement.

com·part·ment, *n.* 1. a space marked or partitioned off. 2. a separate room, section, etc.

com·pass, *n.* 1. an instrument for determining directions. 2. space within limits; scope. 3. (*usu. pl.*) an instrument for describing circles, measuring distances, etc. –*v.* 4. to extend or stretch around.

com·pas·sion, *n.* pity for the sufferings or misfortunes of another. – **compassionate**, *adj.*

com·pat·ible, *adj.* capable of existing together in harmony.

com·pa·triot, *n.* a fellow citizen.

com·pel, *v.*, **-pelled, -pelling.** to force, esp. to a course of action.

com·pel·ling, *adj.* (of a person, writer, actor, etc.) demanding attention, respect.

com·pen·sate, *v.*, **-sated, -sating.** 1. to offset; make up (*for*). 2. to provide or be an equivalent. 3. make amends (*for*). – **compensation**, *n.*

com·pere, *n.* one who introduces the acts in an entertainment.

com·pete, *v.*, **-peted, -peting.** to contend with another for a prize, profit, etc.

com·pe·tent, *adj.* 1. properly qualified, capable. 2. fitting or sufficient for the purpose. – **competence**, *n.*

com·pe·ti·tion, *n.* 1. a contest for some prize or advantage. 2. rivalry, esp. in business. 3. a competitor or competitors.

com·pet·i·tive, *adj.* of, pertaining to,

competitive

or decided by competition. Also, **competitory**.

com·pet·i·tor, n. one who competes; a rival.

com·pile, v., **-piled**, **-piling**. to put together (literary materials) in one book or work. – **compilation**, n.

com·pla·cent, adv. pleased, esp. with oneself or one's own merits, etc. – **complacency**, n.

com·plain, v. to express grief, pain, uneasiness, censure, resentment, etc. – **complaint**, n.

com·ple·ment, n. 1. that which completes or makes perfect. 2. full quantity or amount. –v. 3. to complete. – **complementary**, n.

com·plete, adv., v., **–pleted**, **-pleting**. adj. 1. having all its parts or elements. 2. finished. –v. 3. to make complete. – **completion**, n.

com·plex, adj. 1. composed of interconnected parts. 2. difficult to understand. –n. 3. a complex whole or system. – **complexity**, n.

com·plex·ion, n. 11. the natural colour and appearance of the skin, esp. of the face. 2. appearance; aspect.

com·pliance /kəmˈplaɪəns/, n. the act of complying; an acquiescing.

com·pli·cate, v., **-cated**, **-cating**. to make complex or involved. – **complication**, n.

com·pli·city, n., pl. **-ties**. the state of being an accomplice.

com·pli·ment, n. 1. an expression of praise or admiration. 2. a formal expression of civility or respect. –v. 3. to pay a compliment to. – **complimentary**, adj.

complimentary, adj. given free of charge.

comprehend

com·ply, v., **-plied**, **-plying**. to act in accordance with wishes, commands, requirements, etc. (*with*).

com·po·nent, adj. 1. constituent. –n. 2. a constituent part.

com·port, v. 1. to bear or conduct (oneself). 2. to agree or accord (*with*): *to comport with the facts.*

com·pose, v., **-posed**, **-posing**. 1. to make by uniting parts or elements. 2. to devise and make (a literary or musical production). 3. to bring (the body or mind) to a condition of repose, calmness, etc. – **composer**, n.

com·po·site, adj. made up of various parts or elements.

com·po·si·tion, n. 1. the act of combining parts or elements. 2. the resulting state or product. 3. a short essay.

com·pos·i·tor, n. a person who assembles the type for a printed page.

com·post /ˈkɒmpɒst/, n. a mixture of organic matter used for fertilising land.

com·po·sure, n. serene state of mind: calmness.

com·pound[1], adj. 1. composed of 2 or more parts, elements, or ingredients. –n. 2. something formed by compounding or combining parts, etc. –v. 3. to put together into a whole. 4. to pay (interest) on the accrued interest as well as the principal. 5. to make a bargain.

com·pound[2], n. an enclosure in which people live.

compound interest, n. interest paid on a debt plus its interest as it falls due.

com·pre·hend, v. 1. to understand

comprehend

the meaning or nature of. **2.** to take in; include. – **comprehension**, *n.*

com·pre·hen·sive, *adj.* inclusive; comprehending much; of large scope.

com·press, *v.* **1.** to press together; force into less space. –*n.* **2.** a soft pad held in place by a bandage, to supply pressure, moisture, cold, etc. – **compression**, *n.*

com·prise, *v.*, **-prised, -prising. 1.** to include; contain. **2.** to be composed of.

com·pro·mise /'kɒmprəmaɪz/, *n., v.*, **-mised, -mising.** –*n.* **1.** a settlement of differences by mutual concessions. **2.** something intermediate between different things. **3.** an endangering, esp. of reputation. –*v.* **4.** to settle by a compromise. **5.** to make liable to danger, suspicion, scandal, etc.

com·pul·sion, *n.* **1.** the act of compelling; constraint. **2.** a strong irrational impulse to carry out a given act. – **compulsive**, *adj.*

com·pul·so·ry, *adj.* **1.** using compulsion. **2.** compelled; obligatory.

com·punc·tion, *n.* regret for wrongdoing or causing pain.

com·pute, *v.*, **-puted, -puting. 1.** to determine by calculation. – **computation**, *n.*

com·put·er, *n.* an apparatus for performing mathematical computations electronically according to a series of stored instructions.

com·put·er·ise, *v.*, **-ised, -ising. 1.** to process or store (data) in a computer. **2.** to provide with a computer system. – **computerisation**, *n.*

com·rade, *n.* an associate in occupation or friendship.

con[1], *adv.* **1.** against a proposition, opinion, etc. –*n.* **2.** the argument, arguer, or voter against (something).

con[2], *n., v.*, **conned, conning.** –*n.* **1.** a confidence trick. –*v.* **2.** to swindle.

con·cave, *adj.* curved like the interior of a circle.

con·ceal, *v.* to hide.

con·cede, *v.*, **-ceded, -ceding. 1.** to admit as true, just, or proper. **2.** to grant as a right or privilege.

con·ceit, *n.* **1.** an exaggerated estimate of one's own ability, etc. **2.** a fanciful thought or expression, esp. far-fetched.

con·ceiv·able, *adj.* imaginable.

con·ceive, *v.*, **-ceived, -ceiving. 1.** to form (a notion, purpose, etc.). **2.** to apprehend in the mind. **3.** to become pregnant (with). **4.** to form an idea (*of*).

con·cen·trate, *v.*, **-trated, -trating**, *n.* –*v.* **1.** to converge or draw to a common centre. **2.** make more intense, stronger, or purer by removing or reducing what is inessential. **3.** to become more intense, etc. **4.** to direct one's thoughts or actions towards one subject. –*n.* **5.** a concentrated form of something. – **concentration**, *n.*

con·cen·tric, *adj.* having a common centre, as circles or spheres.

con·cept, *n.* **1.** a generalised thought, idea, or notion. **2.** an idea that includes all that is associated with a word or other symbol. – **conceptual**, *adj.*

con·cep·tion, *n.* **1.** the act of conceiving. **2.** fertilisation. **3.** that which is conceived. **4.** beginning.

con·cern, *v.* **1.** to relate to; be of interest or importance to. **2.** to in-

concern

terest or involve. 3. to disquiet. —*n.* 4. a matter that engages one's attention, interest, or care, or that affects one's welfare. 5. (active) interest in someone's welfare. 6. a commercial or manufacturing firm.

con·cert, *n.* 1. a public performance, usu. by 2 or more musicians. 2. agreement of 2 or more in a design or plan.

con·certed, *adj.* done by agreement.

con·ces·sion, *n.* 1. the act of conceding or yielding, as a right, or a point in an argument. 2. a thing or point yielded.

conch /kɒntʃ, kɒŋk/, *n., pl.* **conchs** /kɒŋks/, **conches**, /'kɒntʃəz/. the spiral shell of a gastropod.

con·cil·i·ate, *v.*, -ated, -ating. 1. to overcome the distrust or hostility of. 2. to render compatible. – **conciliation**, *n.*

con·cise, *adj.* expressing much in few words.

con·clave, *n.* any private meeting.

con·clude, *v.*, -cluded, -cluding. 1. to bring or come to an end. 2. to determine by reasoning. 3. to arrive at an opinion or judgment; come to a decision. – **conclusion**, *n.*

con·clu·sive, *adj.* serving to settle or decide a question.

con·coct, *v.* to prepare; make up. – **concoction**, *n.*

con·com·i·tant, *adj.* accompanying; concurrent.

con·cord, *n.* agreement.

con·course, *n.* 1. an assembly. 2. an open space in a public building, esp. a railway station.

con·crete, *adj., n., v.*, -creted, -creting. —*adj.* 1. constituting an actual thing. 2. representing or applied to an actual substance or thing as

condole

opposed to an abstract quality. —*n.* 3. an artificial stone-like material. —*v.* 4. to treat or lay with concrete. – **concretion**, *n.*

con·cu·bine, *n.* (among polygamous peoples) a secondary wife.

concur, *v.*, -curred, -curring. 1. to agree in opinion. 2. to cooperate; combine. 3. to coincide. – **concurrent**, *adj., n.*

con·cus·sion, *n.* 1. the act of shaking or shocking, as by a blow. 2. shock occasioned by a blow or collision.

con·demn, *v.* 1. to express strong disapproval of. 2. to pronounce to be guilty. 3. to pronounce to be unfit for use. – **condemnation**, *n.* – **condemnatory**, *adj.*

con·dense, *v.*, -densed, -densing. 1. to make more dense or compact. 2. to reduce (a gas or vapour) to a liquid or solid state. 3. to compress into fewer words. – **condensation**, *n.*

con·de·scend, *v.* 1. to stoop or deign (to do something). 2. to behave as if one is descending from a superior rank, etc.

condi·ment, *n.* a sauce or seasoning, etc., used to give a special flavour to food.

con·dition, *n.* 1. particular mode of being of a person or thing; existing state or case. 2. fit or requisite state. 3. a circumstance indispensable to some result. 4. something demanded as an essential part of an agreement. —*v.* 5. to put in fit or proper state. 6. to subject to particular conditions or circumstances.

con·ditional, *adj.* imposing or depending on a condition or conditions.

con·dole, *v.*, -doled, -doling. to

condole

express sympathy with one in affliction. – **condolence**, n.

condom, n. a contraceptive device worn over the penis.

con·do·min·i·um, n. 1. joint rule of a territory by 2 or more foreign states. 2. →**home unit**.

con·done, v., **-doned**, **-doning**. to pardon or overlook (an offence).

con·duce, v., **-duced**, **-ducing**. to lead or contribute to a result (*to*). – **conducive**, *adj*.

con·duct, n. 1. personal behaviour. 2. direction or management. –v. 3. to behave (oneself). 4. to direct in action or course; manage. 5. to lead or guide. 6. to serve as a channel or medium for (heat, electricity, sound, etc.).

con·duc·tiv·i·ty, n., pl. **-ties**. the property of conducting heat, electricity, or sound.

con·duc·tor, n. 1. one who conducts. 2. the director of an orchestra, etc. 3. the person on a public transport vehicle, who collects fares, issues tickets, etc. 4. something that readily conducts heat, electricity, sound.

con·duit /'kɒndɪt, 'kɒndʒuət/, n. a pipe for conveying water or other fluid.

cone, n. 1. a solid which tapers to a point from a circular base. 2. the multiple fruit of the pine, fir, etc. 3. anything cone-shaped.

con·fec·tion, n. a sweet (def. 7).

con·fec·tion·ery, n., pl. **-eries**. confections or sweets collectively.

con·fed·er·a·cy, n., pl. **-cies**. an alliance of persons, parties, or states.

con·fed·er·ate, *adj*. 1. united in a league or alliance. –n. 2. an accomplice. –v. 3. to unite in a league or alliance, or a conspiracy. – **confederation**, n.

con·fer, v., **-ferred**, **-ferring**. to bestow as a gift, favour, honour, etc. (*on* or *upon*).

con·fer·ence, n. a meeting for consultation or discussion.

con·fess, v. 1. to acknowledge or avow. 2. to own or agree to being responsible for. 3. to acknowledge one's belief in. – **confession**, n.

con·fes·sor, n. a priest authorised to hear confessions of sins.

con·fet·ti, n.pl., *sing*. **-fetto**. small bits of coloured paper, thrown at weddings, etc.

con·fi·dant /ˈkɒnfɪˌdænt, ˌkɒnfəˈdænt/, n. one to whom secrets are confided. – **confidante**, n. fem.

con·fide, v., **-fided**, **-fiding**. 1. to trust by imparting secrets (*in*). 2. to tell in confidence.

con·fi·dence, n. 1. full trust; belief in the reliability of a person or thing. 2. self-reliance, self-assurance. 3. a confidential communication. 4. **in confidence**, as a secret or private matter.

confidence trick, n. a swindle in which the victim's confidence is first gained.

con·fi·dent, *adj*. 1. having strong belief or full assurance. 2. sure of oneself.

con·fi·den·tial, *adj*. 1. spoken or written in confidence. 2. enjoying another's confidence.

con·fig·u·ra·tion, n. the relative disposition of the parts of a thing.

con·fine, v., **-fined**, **-fining**. –v. 1. to enclose within bounds. –n. 2. (*usu*. pl.) a boundary or bound.

con·firm, v. 1. to make certain or sure; verify. 2. to make valid by

confirm

some formal act. **3.** to strengthen (a person) in habit, resolution, etc. – **confirmation**, n.

con·fis·cate, v., **-cated, -cating. 1.** to seize as forfeited. **2.** to seize as if by authority.

con·flict, v. **1.** to clash, or be in opposition or at variance. –n. **2.** a battle or struggle, esp. prolonged.

con·form, v. to act in accord; comply with (to). – **conformist**, n. – **conformity**, n.

con·found, v. **1.** to throw into confusion. **2.** to refute in argument.

con·front, v. **1.** to meet face to face. **2.** to oppose boldly. – **confrontation**, n.

con·fuse, v., **-fused, -fusing. 1.** to combine without order or clearness. **2.** to throw into disorder. **3.** to fail to distinguish between; associate by mistake. **4.** to perplex. – **confusion**, n.

con·geal, v. to change from a fluid to a solid state.

con·gen·ial, adj. agreeing or suited in nature or character.

con·gen·i·tal, adj. existing at or from one's birth.

con·gest, v. to fill to excess. – **congestion**, n.

con·glom·er·ate, n. **1.** anything composed of various elements. **2.** a company engaged in a wide range of activities. –adj. **3.** gathered into a rounded mass. –v. **4.** to collect or cluster together.

con·grat·u·late, v., **-lated, -lating.** to express sympathetic joy to (a person), as on a happy occasion. – **congratulation**, n. – **congratulatory**, adj.

con·gre·gate, v., **-gated, -gating.** to

connection

assemble, esp. in large numbers. – **congregation**, n.

con·gress, n. a formal meeting or assembly of representatives for discussion, etc. – **congressional**, adj.

con·gru·ent, adj. agreeing; corresponding; congruous.

con·gru·ous, adj. harmonious in character. – **congruity**, n.

con·i·fer, n. any of the cone-bearing (mostly evergreen) trees and shrubs. – **coniferous**, adj.

con·jec·ture, n., v., **-tured, -turing.** –n. **1.** an opinion formed without sufficient evidence for proof. –v. **2.** to conclude or suppose from weak or unsure evidence.

con·ju·gal, adj. marital.

con·ju·gate, v., **-gated, -gating.** to inflect (a verb). – **conjugation**, n.

con·junc·tion, n. **1.** the act or result of joining together; combination. **2.** something that joins, esp. a word joining words, clauses, etc.

con·junc·ti·va, n., pl. **-vas, -vae.** the mucous membrane lining the eyelids.

conjunctivitis kəndʒʌŋktə'vaɪtɪs/, n. a painful disease of the conjunctiva.

con·jure, v., **-jured, -juring. 1.** to effect, produce, etc., by, or as by, magic. **2.** to practise sleight of hand or magic. – **conjuration**, n.

conk, v. Colloq. **1.** to hit, esp. on the head. **2.** to faint; collapse.

con·nect, v. **1.** to bind or fasten together. **2.** to establish communication between. **3.** to think of as related. **4.** to become connected; join or unite. – **connective**, adj.

con·nec·tion, n. **1.** the act of connecting. **2.** the state of being con-

connection

nected. 3. a connecting part. 4. (*usu. pl.*) influential friends, etc.

con·nive, *v.* -nived, -niving. 1. to help wrongdoing, esp. by not opposing it. 2. to cooperate secretly (*with*).

con·nois·seur /kɒnəˈsɜː/, *n.* an expert judge of one of the fine arts, or in matters of taste.

con·note, *v.*, -noted, -noting. to signify in addition to the primary meaning. – **connotation**, *n.*

con·quer, *v.* 1. to overcome by force. 2. to gain the victory over. – **conqueror**, *n.* – **conquest**, *n.*

con·science, *n.* the sense of right and wrong as regards one's actions and motives.

con·scien·tious, *adj.* controlled by or done according to conscience.

con·scious, *adj.* 1. aware of one's own existence, sensations, cognitions, etc. 2. having the mental faculties awake. – **consciousness**, *n.*

con·script, *n.* a recruit obtained by compulsory enrolment. –*v.* 1. to enrol compulsorily for service in the armed forces. – **conscription**, *n.*

con·se·crate, *v.*, -crated, -crating. to make or declare sacred. – **consecration**, *n.*

con·sec·u·tive, *adj.* following one another without interruption.

con·sen·sus, *n.* general agreement or concord.

con·sent, *v.* 1. to give assent (fol. by *to* or infinitive). –*n.* 2. assent; permission.

con·se·quence, *n.* 1. (the act or fact of following as) an effect or result. 2. importance or significance. – **consequent**, *n., adj.* – **consequential**, *adj.*

con·ser·vation, *n.* the act of con-

consistency

serving; preservation, esp. of natural resources.

con·ser·vative, *adj.* 1. disposed to preserve existing conditions, etc. 2. having the power or tendency to conserve. –*n.* 3. a person of conservative principles. – **conservatism**, *n.*

con·serva·torium, *n.* a school of music. Also, **con**, **conservatoire**.

con·serva·tory, *n., pl.* -tries. a glass-covered house or room for plants in bloom.

con·serve, *v.*, -served, -serving. *n.* –*v.* 1. to keep safe or sound. –*n.* 2. (*oft. pl.*) fruits cooked with sugar to a jamlike consistency. – **conserver**, *n.*

con·sider, *v.* 1. to contemplate mentally. 2. to regard as. 3. to make allowance for. 4. to regard with consideration or respect.

con·sider·able, *adj.* 1. worthy of consideration. 2. fairly large.

con·sider·ate, *adj.* showing regard for another's feelings, etc.

con·sider·ation, *n.* 1. the act of considering. 2. regard or account; something taken into account. 3. a recompense for service rendered, etc. 4. thoughtfulness for others. 5. estimation; esteem.

con·sign, *v.* 1. to hand over or deliver formally (*to*). 2. to transfer to another's custody. – **consignee**, *n.*

con·sign·ment, *n.* goods sent to an agent for sale, etc.

con·sist, *v.* 1. to be made up or composed (*of*). 2. to be comprised or contained (*in*).

con·sis·tency, *n., pl.* -cies. 1. agreement between the parts of a complex thing. 2. degree of density.

113

consistency

3. adherence to the same principles, course, etc. – **consistent,** *adj.*

con·sole[1] /kən'soul/, *v.*, **-soled, -soling.** to alleviate the grief or sorrow of; comfort. – **consolation,** *n.*

con·sole[2] /'kɒnsoul/, *n.* a desk on which are mounted the controls of an electrical or electronic system.

con·sol·i·date, *v.*, **-dated, -dating.** to bring together compactly in one mass or connected whole. – **consolidation,** *n.*

con·so·nant, *n.* 1. a sound made when exhaled air is partly obstructed, as the *l, s,* and *t* of *list.* –*adj.* 2. in agreement; consistent (*to* or *with*).

con·sort, *n.* 1. a spouse, esp. of a reigning monarch. 2. a ship accompanying another. –*v.* 3. to associate; keep company.

con·sor·tium, *n., pl.* **-tia.** a combination of financial institutions, capitalists, etc., formed to provide capital for a costly undertaking.

con·spic·u·ous, *adj.* 1. easy to be seen. 2. readily attracting the attention.

con·spire, *v.*, **-spired, -spiring.** to agree together, esp. secretly, to do something wrong or illegal. – **conspiracy,** *n.* – **conspirator,** *n.*

con·sta·ble, *n.* an officer of the lowest rank in a police force.

con·stant, *adj.* 1. invariable; always present. 2. continuing without intermission. 3. standing firm in mind or purpose. –*n.* 4. something constant or unchanging.

con·stel·la·tion, *n.* a group of stars to which a name has been given.

con·ster·na·tion, *n.* amazement or dismay.

construe

con·sti·pa·tion, *n.* a condition of the bowels marked by defective or difficult evacuation.

con·stit·u·en·cy, *n., pl.* **-cies.** –**electorate.**

con·stit·u·ent, *adj.* 1. serving to make up a thing. 2. having power to frame or alter a political constitution or fundamental law. –*n.* 3. a constituent element, material, etc. 4. a voter, or (loosely) a resident, in an electorate.

con·sti·tute, *v.*, **-tuted, -tuting.** 1. (of elements, etc.) to compose; form. 2. to appoint to an office or function. 3. to give legal form to (an assembly, etc.).

con·sti·tu·tion, *n.* 1. the way in which anything is constituted. 2. the physical character of the body. 3. the act of constituting; establishment. 4. any established arrangement or custom. 5. the system of fundamental principles according to which a nation, state, etc., is governed. – **constitutional,** *adj.*

con·strain, *v.* 1. to force, compel, or oblige. 2. to confine forcibly. 3. to repress or restrain. – **constraint,** *n.*

con·strict, *v.* 1. to draw together; compress. 2. to restrict. – **constriction,** *n.* – **constrictive,** *adj.*

con·struct, *v.* 1. to form by putting together parts; build. –*n.* 2. a complex image or idea.

con·struc·tion, *n.* 1. the act of constructing. 2. the way in which a thing is constructed. 3. that which is constructed. 4. explanation or interpretation.

con·struc·tive, *adj.* constructing; helpful: *constructive advice.*

con·strue, *v.*, **-strued, -struing.** 1. to

construe

show the meaning of. 2. to deduce by interpretation.

con·sul, *n.* a government agent residing in a foreign state and discharging certain administrative duties. – **consular**, *adj.* – **consulate**, *n.*

con·sult, *v.* 1. to refer to for information or advice. 2. to consider or deliberate.

con·sul·tant, *n.* one who gives professional or expert advice.

con·sul·ta·tion, *n.* 1. the act of consulting. 2. a meeting for deliberation. 3. a meeting to request professional advice.

con·sume, *v.*, **-sumed, -suming.** 1. to use up. 2. to eat or drink up. 3. to absorb.

con·sum·er, *n.* one who uses a commodity or service.

con·sum·er·ism, *n.* 1. a movement which aims at educating consumers to protect themselves from dishonest trading practices. 2. a theory that the economy of a capitalist society requires an ever increasing consumption of goods.

con·sum·mate /ˈkɒnsjuːmeɪt/, *v.*, **-mated, -mating;** /ˈkɒnsjumət, ˈkɒnsəmət/, *adj.* –*v.* 1. to bring to completion or perfection. –*adj.* 2. complete or perfect.

con·sump·tion, *n.* 1. the act of consuming. 2. the amount consumed. 3. the using up of goods and services. 4. a wasting disease, esp. tuberculosis of the lungs. – **consumptive**, *adj., n.*

con·tact, *n.* 1. the state or fact of touching. 2. immediate proximity or association. 3. a person through whom an association is established.

contemptible

–*v.* 4. to put or bring into contact. 5. to get in touch with (a person).

contact lens, *n.pl.* small lenses to aid defective vision, usu. of plastic, which cover the irises and are held in place by eye fluid.

con·ta·gious, *adj.* (of a disease) easily transmitted to another.

con·tain, *v.* 1. to have within itself; hold within fixed limits. 2. to have as contents or constituent parts. 3. to restrain.

con·tain·er, *n.* 1. anything that can contain, as a carton, tin, etc. 2. a box-shaped unit for transporting goods.

con·tam·i·nate, *v.*, **-nated, -nating.** to render impure by contact or mixture. – **contamination**, *n.*

con·tem·plate, *v.*, **-plated, -plating.** 1. to observe thoughtfully. 2. to have as a purpose. 3. to think studiously; consider deliberately. – **contemplation**, *n.*

con·tem·pla·tive /ˈkɒntəmˌpleɪtɪv, kənˈtemplətɪv/, *adj.* given to or characterised by contemplation.

con·tem·po·ra·neous, *adj.* contemporary.

con·tem·po·rary, *adj., n., pl.* **-raries.** –*adj.* 1. belonging to, existing, or occurring at the same time. 2. of the present time. –*n.* 3. one belonging to the same time or period with another or others.

con·tempt, *n.* 1. the feeling one has for anything mean, vile, or worthless. 2. the state of being despised. 3. *Law.* disobedience to, or open disrespect of, the rules or orders of a court or legislature.

con·tempt·i·ble, *adj.* deserving of or held in contempt; despicable.

115

contemptuous

con·temp·tu·ous, *adj.* manifesting or expressing contempt.

con·tend, *v.* **1.** to struggle in opposition. **2.** to assert earnestly.

con·tent[1] /'kɒntɛnt/, *n.* **1.** (*usu. pl.*) that which is contained. **2.** (*usu. pl.*) (a list) of the chapters or chief topics of a book or document. **3.** substance or purport, as of a document.

con·tent[2] /kən'tɛnt/, *adj.* **1.** being satisfied with what one has. **2.** willing or resigned.

con·ten·tion, *n.* **1.** a struggling together in opposition. **2.** strife in debate; a dispute. – **contentious**, *adj.*

con·test, *n.* struggle for victory. –*v.* **2.** to struggle or fight for. **3.** to argue against.

con·tes·tant, *n.* one who takes part in a contest or competition.

con·text, *n.* **1.** the parts of a discourse or writing which precede or follow a given passage or word. **2.** the circumstances surrounding a particular situation, event, etc. – **contextual**, *adj.*

con·tig·u·ous, *adj.* **1.** touching. **2.** in close proximity.

con·ti·nence, *n.* **1.** self-restraint, esp. in regard to sexual activity. **2.** ability to exercise control over natural functions. Also, **continency**.

con·ti·nent, *n.* **1.** one of the main land masses of the globe. –*adj.* **2.** able to exercise control over natural impulses or functions.

con·tin·gent, *adj.* **1.** dependent for existence, occurrence, character, etc., on something not yet certain (*on* or *upon*). **2.** accidental or unpredictable. –*n.* **3.** a share to be contributed or furnished. **4.** any

contract

one of the representative groups composing an assemblage. – **contingency**, *n.*

con·tin·ual, *adj.* **1.** proceeding without interruption or cessation. **2.** of regular or frequent recurrence.

con·tin·ue, *v.*, **-ued, -uing. 1.** to go forwards or onwards in any course or action. **2.** to go on after interruption. **3.** to remain in a particular state. **4.** to go on with. **5.** to extend from one point to another in space. – **continuation**, *n.*

con·ti·nu·ity, *n., pl.* **-ties.** the state or quality of being continuous.

con·tin·u·ous, *adj.* **1.** having successive parts connected. **2.** uninterrupted in time.

con·tin·u·um, *n., pl.* **-tinuums, -tinua.** a continuous extent, series, or whole.

con·tort, *v.* to twist; bend or draw out of shape. – **contortion**, *n.*

con·tour, *n.* the outline of a figure or body.

contra·band, *n.* any prohibited imports or exports.

contra·ception, *n.* the prevention of conception by deliberate measures; birth control. – **contraceptive**, *adj., n.*

con·tract, *n.* **1.** an agreement between 2 or more parties for the doing or not doing of some definite thing. **2.** an agreement enforceable by law. –*v.* **3.** to draw together or into smaller limits or area. **4.** to shorten (a word, etc.) by combining or omitting some of its elements. **5.** to acquire, as by habit or contact; incur, as a liability or obligation. **6.** to settle by agreement. – **contrac-**

contract

tion, n. – contractor, n. – contractual, adj. – contractile, adj.

contra·dict, v. to assert the contrary of. – contradiction, n. – contradictory, adj.

con·tralto, n., pl. -ti. the lowest female voice.

con·trap·tion, n. a contrivance; a device.

con·trary /ˈkɒntrəri/; for def. 3 also /kənˈtreəri/ adj., n., pl. -ries. –adj. 1. opposite in nature. 2. opposite in direction or position. 3. perverse; self-willed. –n. 4. that which is contrary or opposite. – contrariety, n. – contrariness, n.

con·trast, v. 1. to compare by observing differences. 2. to afford or form a contrast in. 3. to exhibit unlikeness on comparison. –n. 4. the state of being contrasted or unlike. 5. something strikingly unlike. 6. variation in tones and forms in a work of art, photograph, etc.

contra·vene, v., -vened, -vening. to violate or infringe. – contravention, n.

con·tri·bute, v., -uted, -uting. to give to a common stock. – contribution, n. – contributor, n. – contributory, adj.

con·tri·tion, n. sincere penitence. – contrite, adj.

con·trive, v., -trived, -triving. 1. to plan with ingenuity. 2. to bring about or effect by a device, stratagem, etc.; manage (to do something). – contrivance, n.

con·trol, v., -trolled, -trolling, n. –v. 1. to exercise restraint or direction over. –n. 2. the act or power of controlling. 3. check or restraint. 4. a standard of comparison in scien-

conversant

tific experimentation. 5. (pl.) an arrangement of devices for regulating a machine.

contro·versy /ˈkɒntrəvəsi, kənˈtrɒvəsi/, n., pl. -sies. dispute, debate, or contention. – controversial, adj.

con·tumely /ˈkɒntʃuməli, kənˈtjuməli/, n., pl. -lies. contemptuous or humiliating treatment.

con·tuse, v., -tused, -tusing. to bruise. – contusion, n. – contusive, adj.

co·nun·drum, n. a riddle.

con·va·lesce, v., -lesced, -lescing. to grow stronger after illness. – convalescence, n. – convalescent, adj., n.

con·vec·tion, n. the transference of heat by the circulation of the heated parts of a liquid or gas.

con·vene, v., -vened, -vening. to (cause to) assemble, usu. for a public purpose. – convener, n.

con·ven·ient, adj. 1. suited to the needs or purpose. 2. easily accessible. – convenience, n.

con·vent, n. 1. a community of nuns devoted to religious life. 2. a Roman Catholic or other school where children are taught by nuns.

con·ven·tion, n. 1. a meeting or assembly, esp. a formal one. 2. general agreement or consent; accepted usage, or procedure. – conventional, adj.

con·verge, v., -verged, -verging. 1. to tend to meet in a point or line. 2. to tend to a common result, conclusion, etc. – convergence, n. – convergent, adj.

con·ver·sant /kənˈvɒsənt, ˈkɒnvəsənt/, adj. familiar by use or study (with).

117

con·ver·sation, *n.* informal interchange of thoughts by spoken words.

con·verse[1] /kənˈvɜs/, *v.*, **-versed, -versing.** to talk informally with another.

con·verse[2] /ˈkɒnvɜs/, *adj.* 1. turned about. –*n.* 2. a thing which is the opposite of another.

con·vert, *v.* 1. to change into something of different form or properties. 2. to cause to adopt a different religion, party, opinion, etc. –*n.* 3. one who has been converted. – **conversion,** *n.*

con·vertible, *adj.* 1. capable of being converted. 2. (of a motor car) having a removable top.

convex, *adj.* bulging and curved.

convey, *v.* 1. to carry or transport. 2. to communicate.

con·veyance, *n.* 1. the act of conveying; transmission. 2. a means of transport, esp. a vehicle. 3. *Law.* the transfer of property from one person to another.

con·veyancing, *n.* that branch of legal practice concerned with the transfer of property.

con·veyor belt, *n.* a flexible band used to transport objects, esp. in a factory.

con·vict, *v.* 1. to prove or declare guilty of an illegal act. –*n.* 2. a person proved or declared guilty of an offence. 3. a person serving a prison sentence.

con·vic·tion, *n.* 1. the fact or state of being convicted. 2. the state of being convinced. 3. a firm belief.

con·vince, *v.*, **-vinced, -vincing.** to persuade by argument or proof.

con·viv·ial, *adj.* agreeable; sociable; merry.

con·vo·lution, *n.* a rolled up or coiled condition.

convoy, *n.* any group of vehicles travelling together.

con·vulse, *v.*, **-vulsed, -vulsing.** 1. to shake violently. 2. to cause to laugh violently. 3. to cause to suffer violent muscular spasms. – **convulsion,** *n.* – **convulsive,** *adj.*

coo, *v.* to utter the soft, murmuring sound characteristic of pigeons or doves.

cooee, *n.* a prolonged clear call, rising in pitch, used in the bush as a signal.

cook, *v.* 1. to prepare (food) by the action of heat. 2. (of food) to undergo cooking. –*n.* 3. one who cooks. – **cookery,** *n.*

cool, *adj.* 1. moderately cold. 2. not excited; deliberate; aloof. 3. deficient in ardour or enthusiasm. 4. *Colloq.* attractive; excellent. –*n.* 5. the cool part, place, time, etc. –*v.* 6. to make cool.

coola·bah, *n.* a species of eucalypt. Also, **coolibah.**

co-op, *n.* a cooperative shop, store, or society.

coop, *n.* 1. an enclosure, usu. with bars or wires, in which fowls, etc., are confined. –*v.* 2. to place in, or as in, a coop; confine narrowly (*up* or *in*).

co·operate, *v.*, **-rated, -rating.** to work or act together or jointly. – **cooperation,** *n.*

co·operative, *adj.* 1. cooperating. 2. helpful. –*n.* 3. a cooperative society or shop.

co·ordi·nate, /kouˈɔdnət, -neɪt/, *adj.; n.;* /kouˈɔdɪneɪt/, *v.*, **-nated, -nating.** –*adj.* 1. of the same order or degree. –*n.* 2. an equal in rank

coordinate

or importance. **3.** any of the magnitudes which define the position of a point, line, or the like. –*v.* **4.** to make or become coordinate. **5.** to arrange or act in harmonious combination. – **coordination**, *n.*

cop, *n., v.,* **copped, copping.** *Colloq.* –*n.* **1.** a policeman. –*v.* **2.** to accept resignedly.

cope, *v.,* **coped, coping.** to struggle or contend, esp. with a degree of success (*with*).

copi·ous, *adj.* large in quantity or number.

copper[1], *n.* **1.** a metallic element of a reddish brown colour. *Symbol:* Cu **2.** a large vessel for boiling clothes.

copper[2], *n. Colloq.* a policeman.

copper·plate, *n.* style of handwriting, formerly much used in engravings.

cop·pice, *n.* a wood or thicket, of small trees or bushes. Also, **copse.**

copra, *n.* the dried kernel or meat of the coconut.

copula, *n., pl.* **-lae. 1.** something that connects or links together. **2.** a word, as the verb *be*, which acts as a connecting link between subject and predicate.

copu·late, *v.,* **-lated, -lating.** to unite in sexual intercourse.

copy, *n., pl.* **copies,** *v.,* **copied, copying.** –*n.* **1.** a transcript, reproduction, or imitation of an original. **2.** matter intended to be reproduced in print. –*v.* **3.** to make a copy of; transcribe. **4.** to follow as a pattern or model.

copy·right, *n.* the exclusive right granted by law to control a literary, musical, dramatic, or artistic work.

coral, *n.* **1.** the chalky skeleton of

corner

any of various marine animals. **2.** such skeletons collectively, as forming reefs, islands, etc.

cord, *n.* **1.** a string or small rope. **2.** a ribbed fabric.

cordial, *adj.* **1.** hearty; warmly friendly. –*n.* **2.** a flavoured concentrated syrup to be mixed with water as a drink.

cordu·roy, *n.* a cotton pile fabric with lengthwise ridges.

core, *n., v.,* **cored, coring. 1.** the central part of a fleshy fruit, containing the seeds. **2.** the most essential part of anything. –*v.* **3.** to remove the core of (fruit).

corgi, *n.* a short-legged Welsh dog with erect ears.

cork, *n.* **1.** the outer bark of a certain type of oak tree. **2.** a piece of cork, or other material (as rubber), used as a stopper for a bottle, etc.

cork·age, *n.* a charge made by a restaurant, etc., for serving liquor brought in by the customers.

cork·screw, *n.* an instrument used to draw corks from bottles.

cor·mo·rant, *n.* any of several large voracious waterbirds with a long neck and a pouch under the beak.

corn[1], *n.* **1.** collectively, any edible grain, esp. maize in Nth America and Aust. –*v.* **2.** to lay down in brine, as meat.

corn[2], *n.* a horny callus, usu. with a central core, esp. on the toes.

cornea, *n., pl.* **-neas, -neae.** the transparent outer membrane of the eye, covering the iris and the pupil.

corner, *n.* **1.** (the space at) the meeting place of 2 converging lines or surfaces. **2.** the place where 2 streets meet. **3.** any situation from which escape is impossible.

119

corner

monopoly of the available supply of a stock or commodity. **5.** a region; quarter. **6. cut corners, a.** to take short cuts habitually. **b.** to bypass an official procedure, or the like. *–v.* **7.** to place in or drive into a corner. **8.** to form a corner in (a stock, etc.). **9.** in a motor vehicle, to turn a corner, esp. at speed. *–adj.* **10.** situated at a junction of 2 roads. **11.** made to be fitted or used in a corner.

cor·net, *n.* a wind instrument of the trumpet class.

corn·flour, *n.* a starchy flour made from maize, rice, or other grain.

cor·nice, *n.* the moulding between the walls and ceiling.

corny, *adj.*, **-nier**, **-niest**. **1.** *Colloq.* old-fashioned; lacking subtlety. **2.** *Colloq.* sentimental; mawkish.

corol·lary, *n.*, *pl.* **-ries**. a natural consequence or result.

corona, *n.*, *pl.* **-nas**, **-nae**. a circle of light seen round a luminous body. **– coronal**, *adj.*

coro·nary /'korənri/, *adj.* **1.** pertaining to the arteries which supply the heart tissues. *–n.* **2.** a heart attack.

coro·nation, *n.* the ceremony of crowning a sovereign.

coro·ner, *n.* an officer, as of a county or municipality, who investigates by inquest any death not clearly due to natural causes. **– coronial**, *adj.*

coro·net, *n.* a small or inferior crown.

cor·poral, *adj.* of the human body; physical.

cor·po·rate, *adj.* forming, or of a corporation.

cor·po·ration, *n.* an association of individuals, created by law and having powers and liabilities distinct from those of its members.

cor·po·real /kɔ'pɔriəl/, *adj.* of the nature of the physical body.

corps /'kɔ:/, *n.*, *pl.* **corps** /kɔ:z/. a group of persons associated or acting together.

corpse, *n.* a dead body, usu. of a human being.

cor·pu·lent, *adj.* stout; fat.

corpus, *n.*, *pl.* **-pora**. a large or complete collection of writings, laws, etc.

cor·puscle, *n.* one of the minute bodies which form a portion of the blood.

cor·rect, *v.* **1.** to set right; remove the errors or faults of. **2.** to mark the errors in. *–adj.* **3.** conforming to fact or truth. **4.** in accordance with an acknowledged or accepted standard. **– correction**, *n.* **– corrective**, *adj.*

cor·re·lation, *n.* mutual relation of 2 or more things, parts, etc. **– correlate**, *v.* **– correlative**, *adj.*

cor·re·spond, *v.* **1.** to be in agreement or conformity (*with* or *to*). **2.** to be similar or analogous. **3.** to communicate by letters.

cor·re·spond·ence, *n.* **1.** Also, **correspondency**. the act or fact of corresponding. **2.** letters between correspondents.

cor·re·spon·dent, *n.* **1.** one who communicates by letters. **2.** one employed to contribute news, etc., regularly from a distant place. **3.** a thing that corresponds to something else. *–adj.* **4.** corresponding.

cor·ri·dor, *n.* a passage connecting parts of a building.

cor·rob·or·ate, *v.*, **-rated** **-rating**. to

corroborate

confirm. – **corroboration**, *n.* – **corroborative**, *adj.*

cor·rode, *v.*, **-roded, -roding.** to eat away gradually as by chemical action. – **corrosion**, *n.* – **corrosive**, *n., adj.*

cor·ru·gate, *v.*, **-gated, -gating.** to draw or bend into alternate furrows and ridges. – **corrugation**, *n.*

cor·rupt, *adj.* **1.** guilty of dishonesty, esp. involving bribery. –*v.* **2.** to destroy the integrity of. **3.** to lower morally; pervert. – **corruption**, *n.*

cor·sage /kɔːˈsɑːʒ/, *n.* a small bouquet worn on the clothes.

corset, *n.* (*oft. pl.*) an undergarment worn to support the body.

cor·tege /kɔːˈteɪʒ, -ˈteɪʒ/, *n.* a train of attendants.

cortex, *n., pl.* **-tices.** the layer of grey matter around the brain. – **cortical**, *adj.*

cortisone, *n.* a synthetic hormone used to reduce swelling and treat allergies.

cor·vette, *n.* a small, lightly armed, fast ship.

cosh, *n.* any instrument, usu. flexible, used as a bludgeon.

cos·metic, *n.* **1.** a preparation for beautifying the skin, etc. –*adj.* **2.** serving to beautify.

cosmo·pol·i·tan, *adv.* **1.** belonging to all parts of the world. **2.** free from provincial or national ideas, prejudices, etc.

cosmos, *n.* the physical universe. – **cosmic**, *adj.*

cosset, *v.* to pamper.

cost, *n., v.*, **cost** or (def. 5) **costed, costing.** –*n.* **1.** the price paid for anything. **2.** outlay or expenditure of money, time, labour, trouble, etc. **3.** (*pl.*) *Law.* expenses incurred in litigation, often awarded to the successful party. –*v.* **4.** to require the expenditure of (money, time, labour, etc.). **5.** to estimate or determine the cost of.

costly, *adj.*, **-lier, -liest.** of great price or value.

cos·tume, *n.* the style of dress, esp. that of a nation or period.

cosy, *adj.*, **-sier, -siest.** snug; comfortable.

cot, *n.* a child's bed with enclosed sides.

cote·rie, *n.* a group of people, usu. friends, with a common interest.

cot·tage, *n.* a small bungalow.

cottage cheese, *n.* a kind of soft, unripened, white cheese.

cotton, *n.* **1.** the soft, white, downy fibres used in making fabrics, thread, etc. **2.** a plant yielding cotton. **3.** cloth, thread, etc., made of cotton. –*v.* **4. cotton on,** *Colloq.* to understand.

cotton-wool, *n.* raw cotton for surgical dressings, etc.

couch[1] /kaʊtʃ/, *n.* **1.** a seat for 2 to 4 people, with a back and sometimes armrests. **2.** a similar piece of upholstered furniture, without a back but with a headrest at one end. –*v.* **3.** to arrange or frame (words, a sentence, etc.); put into words.

couch[2] /kutʃ/, *n.* any of various grasses popular as lawn grass.

cougar /ˈkuːɡə/, *n.* →**puma.**

cough, *v.* **11.** to expel the air from the lungs suddenly and with a characteristic noise. –*n.* **2.** the act or sound of coughing.

could, *v.* past tense of **can**[1].

cou·lomb /ˈkuːlɒm/, *n.* the derived SI unit of electric charge. *Symbol:* C

council

coun·cil, *n.* **1.** an assembly convened for consultation, deliberation, or advice. **2.** the local administrative body of a city, municipality, or shire. – **councillor**, *n.*

coun·sel, *n., v.,* -**selled**, -**selling**. –*n.* **1.** advice. **2.** interchange of opinions as to future procedure; consultation. **3.** the barrister(s) engaged in the direction of a cause in court. **4.** to give counsel to. –*v.* – **counsellor**, *n.*

count[1], *v.* **1.** to check over one by one (the individuals of a collection) in order to ascertain their total number. **2.** to include in a reckoning. **3.** to esteem; consider. **4.** to depend or rely (*on* or *upon*). **5.** to be accounted or worth. **6.** to enter into consideration. –*n.* **7.** the act of counting. **8.** the total number. **9.** *Law.* a distinct charge or cause of action in a declaration or indictment.

count[2], *n.* (in some European countries) the equivalent of an English earl. – **countess**, *n. fem.*

coun·te·nance, *n., v.,* -**nanced**, -**nancing**. –*n.* **1.** appearance, esp. the look of the face. **2.** encouragement; moral support. –*v.* **3.** to show favour to; encourage. **4.** to tolerate.

coun·ter[1], *n.* **1.** a table or board in a shop, bank, etc., over which business is transacted. **2.** (in a cafe, restaurant or hotel) a long, narrow table, shelf, bar, etc., at which customers eat. **3.** anything used in keeping count or account.

coun·ter[2], *adv.* **1.** in the wrong way; in the reverse direction. –*adj.* **2.** opposite. –*n.* **3.** that which is opposite or contrary to something else. –*v.* **4.** to go counter to. **5.** to meet or answer (a move, blow, etc.)

courier

by another in return. **6.** to make an opposing move.

counter·act, *v.* to act in opposition to.

counter·feit, *adj.* **1.** not genuine. –*n.* **2.** an imitation designed to pass as an original.

counter·mand, *v.* to revoke (a command, order, etc.).

counter·part, *n.* **1.** a copy; duplicate. **2.** one of 2 parts which fit each other.

counter·sign, *v.* to sign (a document) in addition to another's signature, esp. in confirmation.

coun·try, *n., pl.* -**tries. 1.** a large tract of land. **2.** any considerable territory demarcated by geographical conditions or by a distinctive population. **3.** the territory of a nation. **4.** the public. **5.** rural districts.

county, *n.* an area of land delineated for local government purposes.

coup /ku/, *n., pl.* **coups** /kuz/. an unexpected and successfully executed strategem.

coup d'état /– deɪˈta/, *n.* a sudden change of government, esp. one brought about illegally or by force.

coupé /ˈkupeɪ/, *n.* an enclosed two-door motor car.

couple, *n.* **1.** a combination of 2. **2.** 2 of the same sort.

coupon, *n.* **1.** a separable part of a certificate, ticket, advertisement, etc., entitling the holder to something. **2.** a printed entry form for lotteries, newspaper competitions, etc.

cou·rage, *n.* ability to meet danger without fear. – **courageous**, *adj.*

cour·gette /kɔˈʒɛt/, *n.* →**zucchini**.

cou·rier, *n.* a messenger.

course

course, n., v., **coursed, coursing**. –n. 1. onward movement. 2. the path along which anything moves. 3. a particular manner of proceeding. 4. a systematised or prescribed series. 5. a part of a meal. 6. a circuit for racing, golf, etc. 7. **of course**, a. certainly; obviously. b. in the natural order. –v. 8. to run; move swiftly.

court, n. 1. an open space, usu. enclosed by a wall, buildings, etc. 2. an area on which to play tennis, netball, etc. 3. the residence of a sovereign or other high dignitary. 4. the body of persons forming his retinue. 5. assiduous attention directed to gain favour, affection, etc. 6. *Law*. a. a place where justice is administered. b. the judge(s) who sit in a court. –v. 7. to endeavour to win the favour of.

cour·te·ous, *adj.* having or showing good manners.

cour·te·san /'kɔːtəzæn/, n. 1. a court mistress. 2. any prostitute.

cour·tesy, n., pl. **-sies**. 1. excellence of manners or behaviour. 2. a courteous act or expression.

court martial, n., pl. **court martials, courts martial**. a court consisting of military officers which tries offenders against military law.

court·ship, n. 1. the wooing of a woman. 2. solicitation, esp. of favours.

court·yard, n. a space enclosed by walls.

cousin, n. 1. the son or daughter of an uncle or aunt. 2. a kinsman or kinswoman.

cou·tu·rier /kuːˈtjʊəriə/, n. a designer and seller of fashionable clothes for women.

coy

cove[1] /kouv/, n. a small indentation or recess in a shoreline.

cove[2], n. *Colloq.* a man.

coven, n. a gathering of witches.

cov·en·ant, n. 1. an agreement; a contract. –v. 2. to enter into a covenant.

cover, v. 1. to put something over or upon. 2. to extend over; occupy the surface of. 3. to shelter; serve as a defence to. 4. to hide from view. 5. to spread thickly the surface of. 6. to include; take in. 7. to suffice to meet (a charge, expense, etc.). 8. to act as reporter of (occurrences, performances, etc.). 9. to travel over. 10. to serve as substitute for one who is absent. –n. 11. that which covers. 12. protection; concealment.

cover note, n. a document given to provide temporary insurance protection until a policy is issued.

covert /'kʌvət, 'kouvət/, *adj.* 1. covered. 2. concealed; disguised.

covet, v. to desire (another's possessions) greedily.

cow[1], n. 1. the female of a bovine animal. 2. the female of various other large animals, as the elephant, whale, etc. 3. *Colloq.* an ugly or bad-tempered woman.

cow[2] /kau/, v. to intimidate.

coward, n. one who is basely timid. – **cowardice**, n.

cower, v. to crouch in fear or shame.

cowry, n., pl. **-ries**. a glossy, tropical shell. Also, **cowrie**.

cox·comb, n. a conceited dandy.

cox·swain /'kɒksən, -sweɪn/, n. the helmsman of a boat. Also, **cox**.

coy, *adj.* affectedly shy.

123

coyote /kɔɪˈoʊti/, *n.* a wild, wolf-like animal.

cozen /ˈkʌzən/, *v.* to cheat.

crab, *n.* a crustacean having a short, broad, more or less flattened body.

crack, *v.* 1. to make a sudden, sharp sound in, or as in, breaking. 2. to break with a sudden, sharp sound. 3. to break without complete separation of parts. 4. *Colloq.* to break into (a safe, vault, etc.). 5. to utter, as a joke. 6. **crack up**, *Colloq.* to suffer a physical, mental or moral breakdown. –*n.* 7. a sudden, sharp noise, as of something breaking. 8. a break without complete separation of parts. 9. a slight opening, as one between door and doorpost. 10. *Colloq.* a try.

cracker, *n.* 1. a thin, crisp biscuit. 2. a kind of firework which explodes with a loud report.

crackle, *v.*, **-led**, **-ling**. –*v.* 1. to (cause) to make slight, sudden, sharp noises, rapidly repeated. –*n.* 2. a crackling noise.

crack·ling, *n.* 1. slight cracking sounds rapidly repeated. 2. the crisp browned skin or rind of roast pork.

cradle, *n.*, *v.*, **-dled**, **-dling**. –*n.* 1. a cot for an infant, usu. built on rockers. 2. the place where anything is nurtured during its early existence. –*v.* 3. to place or rock in or as in a cradle.

craft, *n.* 1. skill; ingenuity. 2. cunning. 3. an art, trade, or occupation requiring special skill, esp. manual skill. 4. (construed as pl.) boats, ships, etc.

crafty, *adj.*, **-tier**, **-tiest**. skilful in underhand or evil schemes; cunning, deceitful.

crag, *n.* a steep, rugged rock.

craggy, *adj.*, **-gier**, **-giest**. rugged.

cram, *v.*, **crammed**, **cramming**. 1. to fill (something) by force. 2. to prepare for an examination by hastily learning facts.

cramp[1], *n.* a sudden, involuntary, persistent contraction of a muscle. –*v.* 2. to affect with, or as with, a cramp.

cramp[2], *n.* 1. a small metal bar with bent ends, for holding together planks, masonry, etc. –*v.* 2. to confine narrowly; hamper.

crane, *n.*, *v.*, **craned**, **craning**. –*n.* 1. any of a group of large wading birds. 2. a device with a hoisting tackle, for lifting and moving heavy weights. –*v.* 3. to stretch (the neck) as a crane does.

cra·nium, *n.*, *pl.* **-nia**. the skull of a vertebrate.

crank, *n.* 1. *Mach.* a device for communicating motion. 2. *Colloq.* an eccentric person. –*v.* 3. to cause (a shaft) to revolve by applying force to a crank.

crank·shaft, *n.* a shaft driving or driven by a crank.

cranky, *adj.*, **-kier**, **-kiest**. 1. ill-tempered. 2. eccentric.

cranny, *n.*, *pl.* **-nies**. a small, narrow opening (in a wall, rock, etc.).

crap, *n.* *Colloq.* 1. excrement. 2. nonsense; rubbish.

crash, *v.* 1. to break in pieces violently and noisily. 2. to force or drive with violence and noise. 3. to damage a car, aircraft, etc., in a collision. 4. to make a loud, clattering noise as of something dashed to pieces. 5. to collapse or fail suddenly, as a financial enterprise. 6. of an aircraft, to fall to the ground. –*n.* 7. a breaking or falling

crash

to pieces with loud noise. 8. the shock of collision and breaking. 9. a sudden collapse of a financial enterprise or the like. 10. a sudden loud noise.

crass, *adj.* gross; stupid.

crate, *n.* a box or framework, usu. of wooden slats, for packing and transporting fruit, furniture, etc.

crater, *n.* the cup-shaped cavity at the top of a volcano.

cravat /krə'væt/, *n.* a scarf worn round the neck.

crave, *v.*, **craved**, **craving**. 1. to long for or desire eagerly. 2. to need greatly. 3. to ask earnestly for (something).

craven, *adj.* cowardly.

craw, *n.* 1. the crop of a bird or insect. 2. the stomach of an animal.

crawl, *v.* 1. to move by dragging the body along the ground, as a worm, or on the hands and knees. 2. to progress slowly. 3. to behave abjectly. 4. to be, or feel as if, over-run with crawling things. –*n.* 5. a slow, crawling motion. 6. Also, **Australian crawl**. *Swimming*. a stroke in prone position characterised by alternate overarm movements and a continuous up and down kick.

cray·fish, *n.*, *pl.* **-fishes** (*esp. collectively*) **-fish**. any of various freshwater decapod crustaceans.

crayon, *n.* 1. a pencil of coloured wax, chalk, etc., used for drawing. 2. a drawing in crayons.

craze, *v.*, **crazed**, **crazing**, *n.* –*v.* 1. to make small cracks on the surface of (pottery, etc.). 2. to drive insane. –*n.* 3. a popular fashion, etc., usu. shortlived.

credit

crazy, *adj.*, **-zier**, **-ziest**. 1. demented; mad. 2. eccentric. 3. unrealistic.

creak, *v.* 1. to make a sharp, harsh, grating, or squeaking sound. 2. to move with creaking. –*n.* 3. a creaking sound.

cream, *n.* 1. the fatty part of milk, which rises to the surface. 2. any creamlike substance. 3. the best part of anything. 4. yellowish white. –*v.* 5. to work (butter and sugar, etc.) to a smooth, creamy mass.

crease, *n.*, *v.*, **creased**, **creasing**. –*n.* 1. a line or mark produced in anything by folding. –*v.* 2. to make a crease or creases in or on.

create, *v.*, **-ated**, **-ating**. 1. to bring into being. 2. to evolve from one's own thought or imagination. 3. to make by investing with new character or functions. – **creator**, *n.*

cre·ation, *n.* 1. the act of creating. 2. that which is created. 3. the world; universe. 4. an original work, esp. of the imaginative faculty.

cre·ative, *adj.* 1. having the power of creating. 2. resulting from originality of thought or expression.

crea·ture, *n.* an animate being.

creche /kreɪʃ, kreʃ/, *n.* a nursery for children of working mothers.

cre·dence, *n.* (cause for) belief or confidence.

cre·den·tial, *n.* 1. that which gives a basis for belief or confidence. 2. (*usu. pl.*) a letter, etc., confirming the bearer's right to confidence or authority.

cred·ible, *adj.* 1. capable of being believed. 2. worthy of belief or confidence.

credit, *n.* 1. influence or authority

credit

resulting from the confidence of others. **2.** trustworthiness. **3.** commendation or honour given for some action, quality, etc. **4.** (*pl.*) a list, appearing at the beginning or end of a film, which shows the names of those associated with its production. **5.** time allowed for payment for goods, etc., obtained on trust. **6.** confidence in a purchaser's ability and intention to pay. **7.** the balance in one's favour in an account. **8.** any deposit or sum against which one may draw. **9. on credit**, by deferred payment. –*v.* **10.** to believe. **11.** to give reputation or honour to. **12.** to ascribe (something) to a person, etc. **13.** to enter upon the credit side of an account.

credi·table, *adj.* bringing credit, honour, reputation, or esteem.

credit card, *n.* a card which the holder uses to charge purchases to an account. Also, **credit plate**.

credi·tor, *n.* one to whom money is owed.

credit union, *n.* a lending organisation usu. formed by workers in some industry or at some place of employment.

credu·lous, *adj.* ready to believe, esp. on weak or insufficient evidence. – **credulity**, *n.*

creed, *n.* **1.** any system of belief or opinion. **2.** any formula of religious belief.

creek, *n.* a small stream.

creep, *v.*, **crept**, **creeping**, *n.* –*v.* **1.** to move with the body close to the ground, as a reptile or an insect. **2.** to move slowly, imperceptibly, or stealthily. **3.** to have a sensation as of something creeping over the skin: *My skin crept as I watched the horror movie.* –*n.* **4.** the act of creeping. **5.** (*usu. pl.*) a frightening sensation, as of something creeping over the skin **6.** *Colloq.* an unpleasant, obnoxious, or insignificant person.

creeper, *n.* a plant which grows upon the surface of the ground, or other surface.

cre·mate, *v.*, **-mated**, **-mating**. to reduce (a corpse) to ashes by fire. – **cremation**, *n.*

crema·torium, *n.* an establishment for cremating dead bodies.

cren·el·ated, *adj.* having battlements. – **crenellation**, *n.*

creole, *n.* a language which has changed from a pidgin to a community's native language.

crepe, *n.* **1.** a thin, light fabric with a finely crinkled surface. **2.** Also, **crepe paper**. thin paper wrinkled to resemble crepe. **3.** a thin pancake.

crept, *v.* past tense and past participle of **creep**.

cre·scendo /krəˈʃɛndo/, *n.*, *pl.* **-dos**. a gradual increase in force or loudness.

cres·cent, *n.* the shape of the moon in its first or last quarter.

cress, *n.* a plant used for salad or as a garnish.

crest, *n.* **1.** a tuft or other natural growth of the top of an animal's head. **2.** anything resembling such a tuft. **3.** the head or top of anything. **4.** a figure or design used as a family emblem.

crest·fallen, *adj.* dejected; disheartened.

cretin, *n.* *Colloq.* a fool; a stupid person. – **cretinous**, *adj.*

cre·vasse, *n.* a deep cleft in the ice of a glacier.

cre·vice, *n.* a crack forming an opening.

crew[1], *n.* a group of persons engaged upon a particular work.

crew[2], *v.* past tense of **crow**[2].

crew cut, a very closely cropped haircut.

crib, *n., v.,* **cribbed, cribbing.** *–n.* 1. a child's bed. 2. *Colloq.* a translation or other aid used by students. *–v.* 3. *Colloq.* to pilfer or steal, as a passage from an author.

crib·bage, *n.* a game at cards.

crick, *n.* a sharp, painful spasm of the muscles, as of the neck or back.

cricket[1], *n.* any of the insects noted for the ability of the males to produce shrill sounds by friction of their leathery forewings.

cricket[2], *n.* 1. an outdoor game played with ball, bats, and wickets, by 2 sides of 11 players each. 2. *Colloq.* fair play.

crime, *n.* an act committed or an omission of duty, injurious to the public welfare, and punishable by law.

crimi·nal, *adj.* 1. of or pertaining to crime or its punishment. 2. of the nature of or involving crime. *–n.* 3. a person convicted of a crime.

crimi·nology, *n.* the science dealing with the causes and treatment of crimes and criminals.

crimp, *v.* to press into small regular folds.

crim·son, *adj.* deep purplish red.

cringe, *v.,* **cringed, cringing.** to shrink, bend, or crouch, esp. from fear or servility.

crinkle, *v.,* **-kled, -kling.** to wrinkle.

crino·line, *n.* a hoop skirt.

crip·ple, *n., v.,* **-pled, -pling.** *–n.* 1. one who is partially or wholly deprived of the use of one or more of his limbs. *–v.* 2. to disable.

crisis, *n., pl.* **-ses.** a decisive or vitally important time or occasion.

crisp, *adj.* 1. hard but easily breakable. 2. firm and fresh. *–n.* 3. a wafer of potato, fried, dried, and usu. served cold.

cri·terion, *n., pl.* **-teria, -terions.** an established rule or principle for testing anything.

critic, *n.* 1. a person skilled in judging the qualities or merits of some class of things. 2. one who censures or finds fault.

criti·cal, *adj.* 1. of or pertaining to critics or criticism. 2. pertaining to, or of the nature of, a crisis.

criti·cise, *v.,* **-cised, -cising.** 1. to make judgments as to merits and faults. 2. to find fault. – **criticism,** *n.*

cri·tique, *n.* an article or essay criticising a literary or other work.

croak, *v.* 1. to utter a low, hoarse, dismal cry, as a frog or a raven. 2. to speak with a low, hollow voice. 3. *Colloq.* to die.

cro·chet /'krouʃə, 'krouʃeɪ/, *n., v.,* **-cheted** /-ʃəd, -ʃeɪd/, **-cheting** /-ʃətɪŋ, -ʃeɪɪŋ/. *–n.* 1. a kind of needlework done with a small hook for drawing the thread or yarn into intertwined loops. *–v.* 2. to form by crochet.

crock, *n.* an earthen pot, jar, etc.

crock·ery, *n.* china in general, esp. as for domestic use.

croco·dile, *n.* a large, thick-skinned, lizard-like reptile.

crois·sant /'krwɑsɒ̃/, *n.* a crescent-shaped roll of bread or puff pastry.

crone, *n.* an old woman.

crony

crony, *n., pl.* **-nies.** an intimate friend or companion.

crook¹, *n.* **1.** a bent or curved implement, piece, appendage, etc. **2.** any bend, turn, or curve. **3.** *Colloq.* a dishonest person, esp. a swindler, or thief.

crook², *adj. Colloq.* **1.** sick. **2.** bad; inferior.

crooked /'krʊkəd/, *adj.* bent; not straight.

croon, *v.* to sing softly, esp. with exaggerated feeling.

crop, *v.,* **cropped, cropping.** –*n.* **1.** the cultivated produce of the ground, as grain or fruit, etc. **2.** the handle of a whip. **3.** a style of wearing the hair cut short. **4.** a special pouchlike enlargement of the gullet of many birds. –*v.* **5.** to cut off the ends or a part of. **6.** to cut short. **7.** to bear or yield a crop or crops. **8.** to appear unexpectedly (*up* or *out*).

crop·per, *n.* **1.** a fall. **2. come a cropper,** *Colloq.* to fall heavily.

cro·quet /'kroʊkeɪ -kɪ/, *n.* an outdoor game played by knocking wooden balls through a series of iron arches.

cross, *n.* **1.** a structure consisting essentially of an upright and a transverse piece, upon which persons were formerly put to death. **2.** the cross as the symbol of Christianity. **3.** any burden, etc., that one has to bear. **4.** any object, figure, or mark resembling a cross, as 2 intersecting lines. **5.** a mixing of breeds. **6.** something intermediate in character between 2 things. –*v.* **7.** to make the sign of the cross upon or over. **8.** to mark with a cross. **9.** to put or draw (a line, etc.) across. **10.** to lie, pass or be across. **11.** to move, pass, or extend from one side to the other side of (a street, river, etc.). **12.** to meet and pass. **13.** to oppose; thwart. **14.** to interbreed. **15. cross the floor,** *Parl.* to vote with an opposing party. –*adj.* **16.** lying or passing crosswise or across each other. **17.** involving interchange. **18.** contrary. **19.** adverse. **20.** ill-humoured.

cross-examine, *v.,* **-ined, -ining.** to examine by questions intended to check a previous examination.

cross-eye, *n.* a disorder in which both eyes turn towards the nose. – **cross-eyed,** *adj.*

cros·sing, *n.* **1.** the act of one who or that which crosses. **2.** a place where lines, tracks, etc., cross each other. **3.** a place at which a road, river, etc., may be crossed.

cross-reference, *n.* a reference from one part of a book, etc., to a word, item, etc., in another part.

cross-section, *n.* **1.** a section made by cutting anything transversely, esp. at right angles. **2.** a typical selection.

cross·word puzzle, *n.* a puzzle in which the answers to various clues must be fitted into a grid-like figure.

crotch, *n.* **1.** a forked piece, part, support, etc. **2.** a place of forking, as of the human body between the legs.

crot·chet, *n. Music.* a note having half the value of a minim.

crot·chety, *adj. Colloq.* irritable, difficult, or cross.

crouch, *v.* **1.** (of people) to lower the body with one or both knees bent, and incline the trunk forward. **2.** (of animals) to lie close to or on the

crouch

ground with legs bent ready to spring.

crou·pier, *n.* an attendant who collects and pays the money at a gaming table.

crow[1], *n.* 1. large, lustrous black bird with a harsh call. 2. **as the crow flies**, in a straight line.

crow[2], *v.,* **crowed** *or* **crew** *for def. 1*), **crowed, crowing.** 1. to utter the characteristic cry of a cock. 2. to utter an inarticulate cry of pleasure, as an infant does. 3. to exult loudly.

crow·bar, *n.* a bar of iron, for use as a lever, etc.

crowd, *n.* 1. a large number of persons gathered closely together. 2. a large number of things gathered or considered together. –*v.* 3. to gather in large numbers. 4. to press forward. 5. to press closely together; force into a confined space. 6. to fill to excess.

crown, *n.* 1. a decorative covering for the head, worn as a symbol of sovereignty. 2. the power of a sovereign. 3. the highest part of anything. –*v.* 4. to invest with a regal crown. 5. to honour as with a crown. 6. to surmount as with a crown.

cru·cial, *adj.* involving a final and supreme decision.

cru·ci·ble, *n.* a vessel for heating substances to high temperatures.

cru·ci·fix, *n.* a cross, esp. one with the figure of Jesus crucified upon it.

cruciform, *adj.* cross-shaped.

cru·ci·fy, *v.,* **-fied, -fying.** to put to death by nailing or binding the body to a cross. – **crucifixion**, *n.*

crude, *adj.,* **cruder, crudest.** 1. in a raw or unprepared state. 2. lacking

crush

culture, refinement, tact, etc. – **crudity,** *n.*

cruel, *adj.* 1. disposed to inflict suffering. 2. causing great pain or distress. – **cruelty,** *n.*

cruet, *n.* a set, on a stand, of containers for salt, pepper, etc.

cruise, *v.,* **cruised, cruising**, *n.* –*v.* 1. to sail to and fro, or from place to place. 2. (of a car, aeroplane, etc.) to move along at a moderate speed. 3. **to cruise over.** –*n.* 4. a voyage made by cruising.

crumb, *n.* 1. a small particle of bread, cake, etc. 2. a small particle or portion of anything. 3. to dress or prepare with breadcrumbs. 4. to break into crumbs.

crum·ble, *v.,* **-bled, -bling.** to break into small fragments or crumbs.

crummy, *adj.,* **-mier, -miest.** *Colloq.* very inferior, mean, or shabby.

crum·pet, *n.* a kind of light, soft bread served toasted and buttered.

crum·ple, *v.,* **-pled, -pling.** 1. to draw or press into irregular folds. 2. to collapse.

crunch, *v.* 1. to crush with the teeth; chew with a crushing noise. –*n.* 2. *Colloq.* a moment of crisis.

cru·sade, *n.* any vigorous, aggressive movement for the defence or advancement of an idea, cause, etc.

crush, *v.* 1. to press and bruise between 2 hard bodies. 2. to break into small fragments or particles. 3. to force out by pressing or squeezing. 4. to put down, overpower, or subdue completely. 5. to oppress harshly. 6. to become crushed. 7. to press or crowd forcibly. –*n.* 8. the act of crushing. 9. the state of

129

crush   **cuff**

being crushed. **10.** *Colloq.* a great crowd. **11.** *Colloq.* an infatuation.

crust, *n.* **1.** the hard outer part of a loaf of bread, a pie, etc. **2.** any hard coating or outer part.

crus·ta·cean, *n.* any of a class of (chiefly marine) animals with a hard shell, as the lobsters, crabs, barnacles, etc.

crusty, *adj.,* **crustier, crustiest. 1.** of the nature of or resembling a crust; having a crust. **2.** harsh; surly.

crutch, *n.* **1.** a support to assist a lame or infirm person in walking. **2.** the crotch of the human body. **3.** *Colloq.* anything relied on or trusted.

crux, *v.,* *pl.* **cruxes, cruces.** a vital, basic, or decisive point.

cry, *v.,* **cried, crying,** *n.,* *pl.* **cries.** –*v.* **1.** to utter inarticulate sounds, esp. of grief or suffering, usu. with tears. **2.** to shed tears. **3.** to call loudly. **4.** to utter or pronounce loudly. **5.** to disparage (*down*). **6. cry off,** to break (an appointment, etc.). –*n.* **7.** the act or sound of crying. **8.** the call of an animal.

cryo·gen·ics, *n.* that branch of physics concerned with the properties of materials at very low temperatures.

crypt, *n.* an underground vault used as a burial place, etc.

cryp·tic, *adj.* hidden; secret.

crys·tal, *n.* **1.** a clear, transparent mineral or glass resembling ice. **2.** *Chem., Mineral.* a solid body having a characteristic internal structure.

crys·tal·lise, *v.,* **-lised, -lising. 1.** to form into crystals. **2.** to (cause to) assume definite form: *A plan crystallised in his mind.*

cu., *abbrev.* cubic.

cub, *n.* **1.** the young of certain animals, as the fox, bear, etc. **2.** a novice or apprentice, esp. a reporter.

cubby-hole, *n.* a cupboard for storage.

cube, *n., v.,* **cubed, cubing.** –*n.* **1.** a solid bounded by 6 equal squares. **2.** the 3rd power of a quantity. –*v.* **3.** to make into a cube or cubes. **4.** to raise to the 3rd power; find the cube of. – **cubic,** *adj.*

cu·bi·cle, *n.* any small space or compartment partitioned off.

cuck·old, *n.* the husband of an unfaithful wife.

cuckoo, *n.* **1.** any of a number of Aust. or European birds noted for their habit of laying eggs in the nests of other birds. **2.** *Colloq.* a fool.

cu·cum·ber, *n.* a long fleshy fruit used in salads or for pickling.

cud, *n.* food which a ruminating animal returns from the first stomach to the mouth to chew a 2nd time.

cud·dle, *v.,* **-dled, -dling.** –*v.* **1.** to hold close in an affectionate manner. –*n.* **2.** the act of cuddling; a hug.

cudg·el, *n.* a short, thick stick used as a weapon.

cue[1]**,** *n.* anything said or done on or behind the stage that is followed by a specific line or action. **2.** a hint; a guiding suggestion.

cue[2]**,** *n.* a long tapering rod used in billiards, etc.

cuff[1]**,** *n.* **1.** a fold or band serving as a trimming for the bottom of a

cuff

sleeve or trouser leg. **2. off the cuff**, impromptu.

cuff², v. to strike with the open hand.

cuff·link, n. a link which fastens a shirt cuff.

cul-de-sac, n. a street, lane, etc., closed at one end.

culi·nary, adj. pertaining to the kitchen or to cookery.

cull, v. to choose: *to cull the best cattle from the herd*.

cul·mi·nate, v., -nated, -nating. to reach the highest point.

culp·able, adj. deserving blame or censure.

cul·prit, n. one guilty of a specified offence or fault.

cult, n. 1. a particular system of religious worship, esp. with reference to its rites and ceremonies. 2. an almost religious veneration for a person or thing.

culti·vate, v., -vated, -vating. 1. to work (land) in raising crops. 2. to develop or improve by education or training. 3. to seek the acquaintance or friendship of (a person).

cul·tural, adj. of or pertaining to culture or cultivation.

cul·ture, n. 1. the action or practice of cultivating the soil. 2. development or improvement by education or training. 3. skills, arts, customs, etc., of a people passed from generation to generation.

cum·ber·some, adj. 1. burdensome. 2. clumsy.

cumu·lative, adj. increasing or growing by successive additions.

cumu·lus /ˈkjumjələs/, n., pl. **-li** /-li/. a cloud made up of rounded heaps, and with a flat base.

cuneiform /ˈkjunəfɔm/, adj. 1. wedge-shaped. 2. pertaining to the writing of ancient Persia, etc.

cunni·lingus, n. oral stimulation of the female genitals.

cun·ning, n. 1. skill employed in a crafty manner. —adj. 2. exhibiting or done with ingenuity or craftiness.

cup, n., v., **cupped**, **cupping**. —n. 1. a small, open container used mainly to drink from. 2. *(oft. cap.)* an ornamental cup or other article, esp. of precious metal, offered as a prize for a contest: *Melbourne Cup, Davis Cup*. 3. any cuplike utensil, organ, part, cavity, etc. —v. 4. to take or place in or as in a cup.

cup·board, n. a place or article of furniture used for storage.

cur, n. 1. a snarling, worthless dog. 2. a despicable person.

curate, n. a clergyman employed as assistant or deputy of a rector or vicar.

cura·tor, n. the person in charge of a museum, art collection, etc.

curb, n. 1. anything that restrains or controls. —v. 2. to control as with a curb.

curd, n. *(oft. pl.)* a substance obtained from milk by coagulation, used for making into cheese or eaten as food.

curdle, v., -dled, -dling. to change into curd.

cure, n., v., **cured**, **curing**. —n. 1. a method or course of remedial medical treatment. 2. restoration to health. —v. 3. to relieve or rid of something troublesome or detrimental, as an illness, a bad habit, etc. 4. to prepare (meat, fish, etc.) for preservation, by salting, drying,

cure

etc. – **curable**, *adj.* – **curative**, *n.*, *adj.*

curfew, *n.* a regulation which establishes strict controls on movement after nightfall.

curie, *n.* a unit of radioactivity.

curio, *n., pl.* **-s.** a rare or unusual object, sometimes antique.

cur·i·ous, *adj.* 1. desirous of learning or knowing. 2. exciting attention or interest because of strangeness or novelty. 3. odd. – **curiosity**, *n.*

curl, *v.* 1. to form into ringlets, as the hair. 2. to form into a spiral or curved shape. —*n.* 3. a ringlet of hair. 4. anything of a spiral or curved shape.

cur·rant, *n.* a small seedless raisin.

cur·ren·cy, *n., pl.* **-cies.** 1. the money in actual, current use in a country. 2. the fact or quality of being passed on, as from person to person. 3. general acceptance.

cur·rent, *adj.* 1. belonging to the time actually passing. 2. circulating as coin. 3. prevalent. —*n.* 4. a flowing; flow, as of a river.

cur·ric·u·lum, *n., pl.* **-lums, -la.** the aggregate of courses of study given in a school, etc. – **curricular**, *adj.*

curry[1], *n.* any of several hot sauces or dishes originating in India.

curry[2], *v.*, **-ried, -rying.** to rub and clean (a horse, etc.) with a comb.

curse, *n., v.*, **cursed** or **curst, cursing.** —*n.* 1. the expression of a wish that evil, etc., befall another. 2. a profane oath. —*v.* 3. to wish or invoke evil, calamity, etc. 4. to utter curses.

cur·sive, *adj.* (of writing or printing type) in flowing strokes, with the letters joined together.

cursor, *n.* 1. the sliding part of a measuring tool. 2. a moving dot, as on a computer screen.

custom

cur·so·ry, *adj.* going rapidly over something without noticing details.

curt, *adj.* rudely brief in speech, manner, etc.

cur·tail, *v.* to cut short.

cur·tain, *n.* 1. a piece of fabric hung at a window to shut out light. 2. anything that shuts off, covers, or conceals.

curtsy, *n., pl.* **-sies**, *v.*, **-sied, -sying.** —*n.* 1. a bow by women in recognition or respect. —*v.* 2. to make a curtsy.

curva·ture, *n.* curved condition, often abnormal.

curve, *n., v.*, **curved, curving.** —*n.* 1. a continuously bending line without angles. 2. a line on a graph, diagram, etc. —*v.* 3. to bend in a curve.

cush·ion, *n.* 1. a soft bag filled with feathers, air, etc., used to sit, kneel, or lie on. 2. anything similar in appearance or use. 3. something to absorb a shock or jar, as a body of air or steam. —*v.* 4. to lessen the effects of.

cusp, *n.* 1. a point; pointed end. 2. *Astrol.* the period of change from one sign to the next.

cus·tard, *n.* a sauce made from milk, eggs and sugar.

custard-apple, *n.* a tropical fruit with a soft pulp.

cus·to·dy, *n., pl.* **-dies.** 1. keeping; guardianship. 2. arrest or imprisonment by officers of the law. – **custodian**, *n.* – **custodial**, *adj.*

custom, *n.* 1. a habitual practice; the usual way of acting in given circumstances. 2. habits or usages

custom

collectively. 3. (*pl.*) customs duties. 4. business patronage.

cus·tom·ary, *adj.* according to or depending on custom.

cus·tom·er, *n.* one who purchases goods from another; a patron.

custom-made, *adj.* made to individual order.

cut, *v.*, **cut, cutting**, *n.* –*v.* 1. to penetrate (something) with, or as with, a sharp-edged instrument. 2. to divide with or as with, a sharp-edged instrument. 3. to reap; mow. 4. to halt the running of: *He cut the engine.* 5. to reduce. 6. to make or fashion by cutting. 7. *Colloq.* to absent oneself from. 8. to make an incision. 9. to allow incision or severing: *The metal will not cut easily.* 10. to pass, go, or come, esp. in the most direct way. 11. to stop filming or recording. 12. **cut one's losses,** to abandon a project so as not to incur more losses. –*n.* 13. the act or result of cutting. 14. *Colloq.* share. 15. manner or fashion in which anything is cut: *the cut of his clothes.* 16. a passage or course straight across: *a short cut.* 17. a reduction in price, salary, etc.

cute, *adj.*, **cuter, cutest.** *Colloq.* pleasingly pretty or dainty.

cu·ti·cle, *n.* the skin around the edges of the fingernail or toenail.

cut·lass, *n.* a short, heavy, slightly curved sword.

cut·lery, *n.* instruments for dinner-table use.

cut·let, *n.* a cut of meat, usu. lamb or veal.

cut·tle·fish, *n.*, *pl.* **-fishes,** (*esp. collectively*) **-fish.** any of various marine animals which eject a black, inklike fluid.

cya·nide, *n.* a highly poisonous chemical.

cyber·netics, *n.* the scientific study of methods of control and communication common to animals and machines, esp. computers.

cycla·mate, *n.* artificial sweetener.

cycla·men, *n.* any of various plants with white, purple, pink or red flowers whose petals fold backwards.

cycle, *n.*, *v.*, **-cled, -cling.** –*n.* 1. a recurring period of time, esp. one in which certain events or phenomena are repeated in the same order and at the same intervals. 2. any round of operations or events. 3. a bicycle, tricycle, etc. –*v.* 4. to ride or travel by a bicycle, etc. 5. to move or revolve in cycles. – **cyclic**, *adj.*

cyclone, *n.* a tropical hurricane.

cygnet, *n.* a young swan.

cylin·der, *n. Geom.* a tube-like figure. – **cylindrical**, *adj.*

cymbal, *n.* one of a pair of brass or bronze plates struck together to produce a sharp ringing sound.

cynic, *n.* one who doubts or denies the goodness of human motives. – **cynical**, *adj.*

cypher, *n.*, *v.* →**cipher.**

cypress, *n.* any of several coniferous evergreen trees.

cyst, *n.* a closed bladder-like sac formed in animal tissues, containing fluid or semifluid morbid matter.

cys·titis, *n.* inflammation of the urinary bladder.

czar /za/, *n.* →**tsar.** – **czardom**, *n.*

133

Dd

D, d, *n., pl.* **D's** or **Ds, d's** or **ds.** the 4th letter of the English alphabet.

'd, contraction of: **1.** had. **2.** would.

dab, *v.,* **dabbed, dabbing.** to tap lightly, as with the hand.

dabble, *v.,* **-bled, -bling. 1.** to play in water, as with the hands or feet. **2.** to do anything in a slight or superficial manner.

dachs·hund /ˈdæksənd, ˈdæʃhənd/, *n.* one of a German breed of small dogs with a long body and very short legs.

dad, *n.* father.

daddy, *n., pl.* **-dies.** (in children's speech) dad; father.

daddy-long-legs, *n. sing.* and *pl.* a small web-spinning spider with long, thin legs, frequently found indoors.

daf·fo·dil, *n.* a plant with single or double yellow nodding flowers.

daft, *adj.* simple or foolish.

dag[1], *n.* wool on a sheep's rear quarters, often dirty with mud and excreta.

dag[2], *n. Colloq.* an untidy, slovenly person.

dagger, *n.* a short-edged and pointed weapon, like a small sword, used for thrusting and stabbing.

dago, *n., pl.* **-gos, -goes.** (*oft. offensive*) a person of Latin race.

dahlia /ˈdeɪljə/, *n.* a plant widely cultivated for its showy, variously coloured flowers.

daily, *adj.* **1.** of, done, occurring, or issued each day or each weekday. –*adv.* **2.** every day.

dainty, *adj.,* **-tier, -tiest.** of delicate beauty or charm; exquisite.

dairy, *n., pl.* **dairies.** a place where milk and cream are kept and made into butter and cheese.

dais /ˈdeɪəs/, *n.* a raised platform, as at the end of a room, for a throne, a lecturer's desk, etc.

daisy, *n., pl.* **-sies.** a plant whose flower heads have a yellow disc and white rays.

dale, *n.* a vale; valley.

dally, *v.,* **-lied, -lying.** to waste time; loiter; delay.

Dal·matian, *n.* one of a breed of dogs of a white colour profusely marked with small black or liver-coloured spots.

dam[1], *n., v.,* **dammed, damming.** –*n.* **1.** a barrier to obstruct the flow of water, esp. one of earth, masonry, etc., built across a stream. **2.** a body of water confined by such a barrier. –*v.* **3.** to stop up; block up.

dam[2], *n.* a female parent (used esp. of quadrupeds).

damage, *n., v.,* **-aged, -aging.** –*n.* **1.** injury or harm that impairs value or usefulness. **2.** (*pl.*) *Law.* the estimated money equivalent for detriment or injury sustained. –*v.* **3.** to cause damage to; injure or harm.

damask, *n.* a reversible fabric of linen, silk, cotton, or wool, woven with patterns.

dame, *n.* **1.** (*cap.*) a form of address to any woman of rank or authority. **2.** *Colloq.* a woman.

damn

damn, *v.* **1.** to declare (something) to be bad, unfit, invalid or illegal. **2.** to bring condemnation upon. *–n.* **3.** a negligible amount. *–interj.* **4.** (an expression of anger, annoyance, or emphasis.) **– damnation,** *n.* **– damnable,** *adj.*

damp, *adj.* **1.** moderately wet; moist. *–v.* Also, **dampen. 2.** to make moist. **3.** to stifle or suffocate; extinguish.

damper, *n.* a simple flour and water dough with or without a raising agent, cooked in the coals or in a camp oven.

dance, *v.,* **danced, dancing.** *n.–v.* **1.** to move with the feet or body rhythmically, esp. to music. **2.** to bob up and down. *–n.* **3.** a successive group of rhythmical steps, generally performed to music. **4.** an act or round of dancing. **5.** a social gathering for dancing; ball.

dande·lion, *n.* a common weed, with golden yellow flowers.

dand·ruff, *n.* a scurf which forms on the scalp and comes off in small scales.

dandy, *n., pl.* **-dies. 1.** a man who is excessively concerned about clothes and appearance. **2.** *Colloq.* something very fine or first rate.

danger, *n.* liability or exposure to harm or injury. **– dangerous,** *adj.*

dangle, *v.,* **-gled, -gling.** to hang loosely with a swaying motion.

dank, *adj.* unpleasantly moist or humid.

dapper, *adj.* neat; trim; smart.

dapple, *n.* mottled marking, as of an animal's skin or coat.

Darby and Joan, *n.* **1.** devoted couple. **2.** club for elderly people.

dare, *v.,* **dared** or **durst, dared, daring. 1.** to have the necessary courage or boldness for something. **2.** to meet defiantly. **3.** to challenge or provoke to action, esp. by doubting one's courage; defy. **4. dare say,** to assume as probable; have no doubt.

dare-devil, *n.* **1.** a recklessly daring person. *–adj.* **2.** recklessly daring.

dark, *adj.* **1.** without light; with very little light. **2.** not pale or fair. **3.** gloomy. **4.** evil; wicked. *–n.* **5.** absence of light. **6.** ignorance.

dar·ling, *n.* a person very dear to another; person dearly loved.

darn[1], *v.* to mend (clothes, etc., or a tear or hole) with rows of stitches, sometimes crossing and interwoven.

darn[2], *v. Colloq.* to damn; curse.

dart, *n.* **1.** a long, slender, pointed, missile weapon propelled by the hand or otherwise. *–v.* **2.** to move swiftly.

dash[1], *v.* **1.** to strike violently, esp. so as to break to pieces. **2.** to throw or thrust violently or suddenly. **3.** to ruin or frustrate (hopes, plans, etc.). **4.** to write, make, sketch, etc., hastily (*off* or *down*). **5.** to move with violence; rush. *–n.* **6.** a violent and rapid blow or stroke. **7.** a small quantity of anything thrown into or mixed with something else. **8.** a hasty stroke, esp. of a pen. **9.** a horizontal line (–) used in writing and printing as a mark of punctuation to indicate an abrupt break or pause in a sentence, etc. **10.** an impetuous movement; a rush. **11.** *Athletics.* a short race or sprint.

dash[2], *v.* **1.** to confound. *–interj.* **2.** (a mild expletive).

dash·board, *n.* the instrument board of a motor car or an aeroplane.

135

dashing

dash·ing, *adj.* **1.** spirited; lively. **2.** brilliant; stylish.

das·tardly /'dæstədli/, *adj.* cowardly; meanly base; sneaking.

data /'deɪtə, 'datə/, *n.* **1.** plural of *datum.* **2.** (*construed as sing. or pl.*) figures, etc., known or available; information.

data·base, *n.* any large collection of information, esp. computerised. Also, **databank.**

date[1], *n.*, **dated, dating.** –*n.* **1.** a particular point or period of time when something happens or happened. **2.** *Colloq.* an appointment made for a particular time. **3.** *Colloq.* a person, usu. of the opposite sex, with whom one has a social appointment. **4. to date,** to the present time. –*v.* **5.** to belong to a particular period. **6.** to ascertain or fix the date or time of. **7.** to have a romantic relationship or date(s) with: *She dated him for a few months; He is dating her tonight.* **8.** to show to be of a certain age, or old-fashioned.

date[2], *n.* the oblong, fleshy fruit of the date palm.

datum /'deɪtəm, 'datəm/, *n., pl.* **-ta** /-tə/. **1.** any proposition assumed or given, from which conclusions may be drawn. **2.** (*oft. pl.*) any fact assumed to be a matter of direct observation.

daub, *v.* to cover or coat with soft, adhesive matter, such as plaster, mud, etc.

daugh·ter, *n.* **1.** a female child or person in relation to her parents. **2.** any female descendant. **3.** one re-lated as if by the ties binding daughter to parent. – **daughterly,** *adj.*

deacon

daughter-in-law, *n., pl.* **daughters-in-law.** the wife of one's son.

daunt, *v.* **1.** to overcome with fear. **2.** to lessen the courage of.

daunt·less, *adj.* not to be daunted; fearless; intrepid; bold.

dawdle, *v.,* **-dled, -dling. 1.** to waste time. **2.** to walk slowly or lag behind others.

dawn, *n.* **1.** the first appearance of daylight in the morning. **2.** the beginning or rise of anything. –*v.* **3.** to begin to open or develop. **4.** to begin to be perceived: *The truth dawned on him.*

day, *n.* **1.** the interval of light between 2 successive nights; the time between sunrise and sunset. **2.** a period of 24 hours, esp. from midnight to succeeding midnight. **3.** the light of day; daylight. **4.** a day as a point or unit of time, or on which something occurs. **5.** a day of contest, or the contest itself: *He won the day.* **6.** (*oft. pl.*) a particular time or period. **7.** period of power or influence.

day·dream, *n.* **1.** a visionary fancy indulged in while awake; reverie. –*v.* **2.** to indulge in daydreams.

daylight-saving, *n.* a system of reckoning time as being one or more hours later than the standard time, usu. used during summer months to give more hours of daylight after the working day.

daze, *v.* **dazed, dazing. 1.** to stun or stupefy with a blow, a shock, etc. **2.** to confuse; bewilder; dazzle.

dazzle, *v.,* **-zled, -zling. 1.** to overpower or dim (the vision) by intense light. **2.** to bewilder by brilliance or display of any kind.

deacon, *n.* **1.** a low-ranking clergy-

deacon

man. 2. a church official with variously defined duties. – **deaconess**, n. fem.

dead, adj. 1. no longer living. 2. not endowed with life; inanimate. 3. a. without sensation; insensible; numb. b. asleep. 4. no longer in existence or use. 5. Colloq. very tired; exhausted. 6. a. without resonance. b. without resilience or bounce. 7. not glossy, bright, or brilliant. 8. complete; absolute. –adv. 1. absolutely; completely. 10. with abrupt and complete stoppage of motion, etc.

deaden, v. 1. to make less sensitive, active, energetic, or forcible. 2. to make impervious to sound.

dead·line, n. the latest time for finishing something.

dead·lock[1], n. a state of affairs in which progress is impossible.

dead·lock[2], n. a type of lock which can only be opened from inside and outside with a key.

deadly, adj., -lier, -liest. causing or tending to cause death.

dead·pan, adj. Colloq. (of a person or his face) completely lacking expression or reaction.

deaf, adj. unable to hear. – **deafen**, v. – **deafness**, n.

deal, v., dealt, dealing, n. –v. 1. to occupy oneself or itself (with or in). 2. to take action with respect to a thing or person (with). 3. to trade or do business. 4. to distribute, esp. the cards required in a game. 5. to give to one as his share; apportion (out). 6. to deliver (blows, etc.). –n. 7. Colloq. a business transaction. 8. an indefinite but large amount or extent. 9. Cards. a. the distribution to the players of the cards in a game. b. the turn of a player to

debauch

deal. 10. any undertaking, organisation, etc.; affair. – **dealer**, n.

dealt /dɛlt/, v. past tense and past participle of **deal**.

dean, n. 1. Educ. the head of a medical school, university faculty, or the like. 2. any of various ecclesiastical dignitaries, as the head of a division of a diocese.

dear, adj. 1. beloved or loved. 2. (in the salutation of a letter) highly esteemed. 3. precious in one's regard. 4. high-priced; expensive.

dearth /dɜθ/, n. scarcity or scanty supply; lack.

death, n. 1. the act of dying; the end of life; the total and permanent cessation of the vital functions of an animal or plant. 2. the state of being dead. 3. extinction; destruction.

death adder, n. poisonous snake of Aust. and New Guinea with thick body and broad head.

de·bacle /deɪˈbɑkəl, də-/, n. a general break-up or rout; sudden overthrow or collapse; overwhelming disaster.

debar, v. to exclude or prohibit.

debase, v., -based, -basing. 1. to reduce in quality or value. 2. to lower in rank or dignity.

debate, n., v., -bated, -bating. –n. 1. a discussion, esp. of a public question in an assembly. 2. deliberation; consideration. 3. a systematic contest of speakers in which 2 opposing points of view of a proposition are advanced. –v. 4. to engage in discussion, esp. in a legislative or public assembly. 5. to dispute about. – **debater**, n. – **debatable**, adj.

de·bauch /dəˈbɔtʃ/, v. to corrupt by

debauch

sensuality, intemperance, etc.; seduce. – **debauchery**, n.

deben·ture, n. a note or certificate acknowledging a debt, as given by an incorporated company; a bond or one of a series of bonds.

de·bil·i·tate, v., -tated, -tating. to make weak or feeble. – **debility**, n.

debit, n. 1. the recording of an entry of debt in an account. 2. the balance shown to be owing in an account. –v. 3. to charge with a debt. 4. to enter upon the debit side of an account.

debo·nair, adj. of pleasant manners; courteous.

debris /'dɛbri, 'deɪbriː, də'briː/, n. the remains of anything broken down or destroyed; ruins; fragments; rubbish.

debt, n. 1. that which is owed. 2. the condition of being under such an obligation. 3. **bad debt**, a debt of which there is no prospect of payment. – **debtor**, n.

debunk, v. Colloq. to strip of false sentiment, etc.; to make fun of.

debut /'deɪbjuː, -bu, də'bu/, n. a first public appearance.

debu·tante /'dɛbjətɒnt/, n. a girl making a debut, esp. into society.

decade /'dɛkeɪd/, n. 1. a period of 10 years. 2. a group, set, or series of 10.

deca·dence, n. the act or process of falling into an inferior condition or state, esp. moral; decay. – **decadent**, adj.

decant, v. 1. to pour off gently, as liquor, without disturbing the sediment. 2. to pour from one container into another.

decanter, n. a vessel from which wine, water, etc., are served.

decibel

de·capi·tate, v., -tated, -tating. to cut off the head of; behead.

decath·lon, n. an athletic contest comprising 10 different events, and won by the contestant having the highest total score.

decay, v. 1. to fall away from a state of excellence, prosperity, health, etc.; deteriorate. 2. to become decomposed; rot. –n. 3. a gradual falling into an inferior condition. 4. decomposition; rotting.

decease, n. departure from life; death.

deceased, adj. dead.

de·ceive, v., -ceived, -ceiving. 1. to mislead by a false appearance or statement. 2. to be unfaithful to; commit adultery against. – **deceit**, n. – **deceitful**, adj.

decel·erate, v. to decrease in velocity.

decent, adj. 1. conforming to recognised standards of propriety, good taste, modesty, etc. 2. Colloq. kind; obliging. – **decency**, n.

de·centra·lise, v., -lised, -lising. 1. to disperse (industry, population, etc.), esp. from large cities to relatively undeveloped rural areas. 2. to undo the centralisation of administrative powers (of an organisation, government, etc.). – **decentralisation**, n.

decep·tion, n. 1. the act or result of deceiving. 2. something that deceives or is intended to deceive. – **deceptive**, adj.

deci·bel, n. a unit expressing difference in power, usu. between electric or acoustic signals, or between one particular signal and a reference level understood. Symbol: dB

decide

decide, *v.*, **-cided, -ciding. 1.** to bring (a person) to a decision. **2.** to settle (something in dispute or doubt). **3.** to pronounce a judgment; come to a conclusion.

decided, *adj.* resolute; determined.

de·cid·u·ous, *adj.* **1.** shedding the leaves annually, as trees, shrubs, etc. **2.** falling off at a particular season, stage of growth, etc., as leaves, teeth, horns, etc.

deci·mal, *adj.* **1.** pertaining to 10ths, or to the number 10. **2.** proceeding by tens. –*n.* **3.** a decimal fraction. **4.** a decimal number.

decimal fraction, *n.* a fraction whose denominator is some power of 10, usu. indicated by the decimal point written before the numerator, as $0.4 = \frac{4}{10}$.

decimal number, *n. Maths.* any finite or infinite string of digits containing a decimal point. 1.0, 5.23, 3.14159 ... are decimal numbers.

decimal point, *n.* (in the decimal system) a dot preceding the fractional part of a number.

deci·mate, *v.*, **-mated, -mating.** to destroy a great number or proportion of.

de·ci·pher, *v.* **1.** to make out or discover the meaning of. **2.** to interpret by the use of a key, as something written in cipher.

de·ci·sion, *n.* **1.** the act of deciding; determination (of a question or doubt). **2.** a judgment, as one formally pronounced by a court.

deci·sive /dəˈsaɪsɪv/, *adj.* **1.** having the power or quality of determining; putting an end to controversy. **2.** decided; determined.

deck, *n.* **1.** a horizontal platform extending from side to side of a

decompression

ship or of part of a ship, forming a covering for the space below and itself serving as a floor. **2.** a floor, platform or tier. **3.** a pack of playing cards. –*v.* **4.** to clothe in something ornamental.

de·claim, *v.* **1.** to speak aloud rhetorically; make a formal speech. **2.** to inveigh (*against*). – **declamatory**, *adj.*

de·clare, *v.*, **-clared, -claring. 1.** to make known, esp. in explicit or formal terms. **2.** to speak emphatically. **3.** to state emphatically. **4.** to make due statement of (dutiable goods, etc.). – **declaration**, *n.* – **declaratory**, *adj.*

de·clen·sion, *n.* **1.** *Gram.* the inflection of nouns, etc., for categories such as case and number. **2.** a bending, sloping, or moving downward.

de·cline, *v.*, **-clined, -clining.** –*v.* **1.** to withhold consent to do, enter upon, or accept. **2.** to cause to slope or incline downward. **3.** *Gram.* to inflect (a noun, pronoun, or adjective). **4.** to express courteous refusal. **5.** to bend or slant down; slope or trend downward. **6.** to fail in strength, vigour, character, value, etc. –*n.* **7.** a downward incline or slope. **8.** a failing or gradual loss, as in strength, character, value, etc.

decode, *v.*, **-coded, -coding.** to translate from code into the original language or form.

de·com·pose, *v.*, **-posed, -posing. 1.** to separate or resolve into constituent parts or elements. **2.** to rot; putrefy. – **decomposition**, *n.*

de·com·pression, *n.* **1.** the act or process of relieving pressure. **2.** the gradual return of persons, as divers or construction workers, to normal atmospheric pressure.

decongestant

de·con·gest·ant, *n.* a substance used to relieve congestion esp. in the upper respiratory tract.

decor /ˈdeɪkɔ, ˈdɛkɔ/, *n.* 1. decoration in general. 2. a style of decoration.

dec·or·ate, *v.*, -rated, -rating. 1. to furnish or deck with something becoming or ornamental. 2. to confer distinction upon by a badge, a medal of honour, etc. – **decoration**, *n.* – **decorator**, *n.* – **decorative**, *adj.*

decorum, *n.* propriety of behaviour, speech, dress, etc. – **decorous**, *adj.*

decoy, *n.* one who entices or allures, as into a trap, danger, etc.

de·crease, *v.*, -creased, -creasing. –*v.* 1. to diminish gradually in extent, quantity, strength, power, etc. –*n.* 2. a process of growing less, or the resulting condition. 3. the amount by which a thing is lessened.

decree, *n.*, *v.*, -creed, -creeing. –*n.* 1. a decision or edict promulgated by civil or other authority. –*v.* 2. to ordain or decide by decree.

dec·rep·it, *adj.* broken down or weakened by old age; feeble; infirm. – **decrepitude**, *n.*

decry, *v.* to speak badly of.

ded·i·cate, *v.*, -cated, -cating. 1. to set apart and consecrate to a deity or to a sacred purpose. 2. to give up wholly or earnestly, as to some person or end; set apart. – **dedication**, *n.* – **dedicatory**, *adj.*

deduce, *v.*, -duced, -ducing. to derive as a conclusion from something known or assumed; infer.

deduct, *v.* to take away, as from a sum or amount.

deed, *n.* that which is done, performed, or accomplished; an act.

defect

deem, *v.* to form or have an opinion; judge; think.

deep, *adj.* 1. extending far downwards, inwards, or backwards. 2. having a specified dimension downwards, inwards, or backwards. 3. situated far or a certain distance down, in, or back. 4. difficult to penetrate or understand. 5. not superficial; profound. 6. intense: *deep sleep.* 7. dark and vivid: *deep red.* 8. low in pitch, as sound. 9. absorbed. –*n.* 10. the deep part of the sea, etc. –*adv.* 11. to or at a considerable or specified depth.

deer, *n.*, *pl.* **deer.** a type of ruminant with solid antlers (usu. the male only).

deface, *v.*, -faced, -facing. 1. to mar the face or appearance of. 2. to blot out; obliterate.

de facto /diˈfæktoʊ, də, deɪ/, *adj.* 1. in fact; in reality. 2. actually existing, whether with or without right. 3. living with, but not married to, one's partner.

defame, *v.*, -famed, -faming. to attack the good name or reputation of, as by uttering or publishing maliciously anything injurious; slander; libel. – **defamation**, *n.* – **defamatory**, *adj.*

de·fault, *n.* 1. failure to act, perform or participate. –*v.* 2. to fail to perform or pay.

defeat, *v.* 1. to overcome in a contest, battle, etc.; vanquish. 2. to frustrate; thwart. –*n.* 3. the act or result of defeating.

defe·cate /ˈdɛfəkeɪt/, *v.*, -cated, -cating. to void excrement. – **defecation**, *n.*

defect, *n.* 1. a falling short; a fault or imperfection. –*v.* 2. to desert a

defect

country, cause, etc. – **defection**, n. – **defector**, n. – **defective**, adj.

de·fence, n. 1. resistance against attack; protection. 2. the defending of a cause or the like by speech, argument, etc. 3. Law. the denial or pleading of the defendant in answer to the claim or charge against him.

defend, v. 1. to ward off attack; guard against assault or injury (*from* or *against*). 2. to maintain by argument, evidence, etc. 3. to contest (a legal charge, claim, etc.). 4. to act as counsel for (an accused man).

defen·dant, n. Law. the party against whom a claim or charge is brought in a proceeding.

defen·sive, adj. 1. serving to defend; protective. 2. made or carried on for the purpose of resisting attack.

defer[1], v., -ferred, -ferring. to put off (action, etc.) to a future time. – **deferment, deferral**, n.

defer[2], v. -ferred, -ferring. to yield in judgment or opinion (*to*). – **deference**, n.

defi·ance, n. 1. a daring or bold resistance to authority or to any opposing force. 2. open disregard. – **defiant**, adj.

defi·cient, adj. lacking some element or characteristic; inadequate. – **deficiency**, n.

defi·cit /ˈdɛfəsɪt/, n. the amount by which a sum of money falls short of the required amount.

defile, v., -filed, -filing. 1. to make foul, dirty, or unclean. 2. to violate the chastity of.

define, v., -fined, -fining. 1. to explain the nature or essential qualities of;

defy

describe. 2. to fix or lay down definitely. – **definition**, n.

defi·nite, adj. 1. clearly defined or determined; not vague or general. 2. *Colloq.* certain; sure.

defini·tive /dəˈfɪnɪtɪv/, adj. 1. having the function of deciding or settling; determining; conclusive; final. 2. having its fixed and final form.

de·flate, v., -flated, -flating. 1. to release the air or gas from (something inflated, as a tyre). 2. to reduce (currency, prices, etc.) from an inflated condition. 3. to reduce in esteem, esp. self-esteem (a person or a person's ego). – **deflation**, n.

de·flect, v. 1. to bend or turn aside. 2. to cause to turn from a true course or right line. – **deflection**, n.

de·foli·ate, v., -ated, -ating. to strip or deprive (a tree, etc.) of leaves. – **defoliant**, n.

deform, v. to mar the natural form, shape, or beauty of; disfigure; spoil. – **deformity**, n. – **deformed**, adj.

de·fraud, v. to deprive of a right or property by fraud; cheat.

defray, v. to bear or pay (the costs, expenses, etc.).

defrost, v. remove ice from; cause (food, ice, etc.) to thaw.

deft, adj. dexterous; nimble; skilful; clever.

de·funct, adj. 1. deceased; dead; extinct. 2. no longer operative; not in use.

defuse, v., -fused, -fusing. 1. to remove the fuse from (a bomb). 2. to calm (a situation or action).

defy, v., -fied, -fying. 1. to challenge the power of; resist boldly or

141

defy

openly. 2. to challenge (one) to do something deemed impossible.

de·gene·rate, v., -rated, -rating, adj., n. –v. 1. to decline in physical, mental, or moral qualities or powers. –adj. 2. having declined in physical or moral qualities; degraded. –n. 3. one who has retrogressed from a normal type or standard, as in morals, or character. – degenerative, adj. – degeneracy, n. – degeneration, n.

de·grade, v., -graded, -grading. 1. to reduce from a higher to a lower rank, degree, etc., esp. as punishment. 2. to lower in character or quality. 3. to lower in dignity or estimation. – degradation, n.

degree, n. 1. a step or stage in an ascending or descending scale, or in a course or process. 2. the angle between two radii of a circle which cut off on the circumference an arc equal to $\frac{1}{360}$ of that circumference (often indicated by the sign °). 3. a unit in the measurement of temperature. 4. Geog. the unit of measurement of latitude or longitude. 5. a qualification conferred by a university, etc., for successful work.

de·hydrate /'dihaɪdreɪt/, v., -drated, -drating. 1. to deprive of water. 2. to free (vegetables, etc.) of moisture, for preservation. 3. to lose water or moisture. – dehydration, n.

deify /'diːəfaɪ, 'deɪ-/, v. to make fit or in -fied, -fying. 1. to make a god of; exalt to the rank of a deity. 2. to adore or regard as a deity.

deign /deɪn/, v. to think fit or in accordance with one's dignity; condescend.

deity /'diːəti, 'deɪ-/, n., pl. -ties. 1. a

delicatessen

god or goddess. 2. divine character or nature.

dejected, adj. depressed in spirits; disheartened.

delay, v. 1. to put off to a later time; defer. 2. to impede the progress of. –n. 3. the act of delaying; procrastination. 4. an instance of being delayed.

delec·table, adj. delightful; highly pleasing.

dele·gate, n., v., -gated, -gating. –n. 1. one delegated to act for or represent another or others, esp. at a conference, or the like. –v. 2. to send or appoint (a person) as deputy or representative. 3. to commit (powers, functions, etc.) to another as agent or deputy.

dele·gation, n. a group of delegates.

delete, v., -leted, -leting. to strike out or take out (anything written or printed). – deletion, n.

dele·teri·ous /dɛləˈtɪərɪəs/, adj. 1. injurious to health. 2. hurtful; injurious.

delib·erate, adj., v., -rated, -rating. –adj. 1. carefully weighed or considered; intentional. 2. careful or slow in deciding. –v. 3. to think carefully or attentively; reflect. – deliberation, n.

deli·cacy, n., pl. -cies. 1. quality of being delicate. 2. something delightful or pleasing, esp. to the palate.

deli·cate, adj. 1. fine in texture, quality, construction, etc. 2. so fine or slight as to be scarcely perceptible. 3. easily damaged; fragile. 4. requiring great care, caution, or tact. 5. distinguishing subtle differences. 6. fastidious.

deli·ca·tessen, n. a shop selling

delicatessen

(usu. continental or exotic) small-goods, cheeses, and other cooked or tinned foods.

deli·cious, *adj.* highly pleasing to the senses, esp. to taste or smell.

de·light, *n.* a high degree of pleasure or enjoyment; joy. – **delightful,** *adj.*

delin·eate, *v.,* **-ated, -ating.** to trace the outline of; represent pictorially.

delin·quent, *adj.* **1.** guilty of a misdeed or offence. –*n.* **2.** one who is delinquent, esp. a young person. – **delinquency,** *n.*

delir·ium, *n.,* *pl.* **-liriums, -liria.** a temporary mental disorder marked by excitement, hallucinations, etc. – **delirious,** *adj.*

deliver, *v.* **1.** to give up or surrender; give into another's possession or keeping. **2.** to strike (a blow). **3.** to assist (a female) in giving birth. **4.** to set free. – **delivery,** *n.,* for defs 1-3. – **deliverance,** *n.,* for def 4.

delta, *n.* a nearly flat plain of alluvial deposit between diverging branches of the mouth of a river.

delude, *v.* **-luded, -luding.** to mislead the mind or judgment of. – **delusion,** *n.*

deluge /ˈdɛljudʒ/, *n.* a flood.

deluxe /dəˈlʌks/, *adj.* of special elegance, sumptuousness, or fineness. Also, **de luxe.**

delve, *v.,* **delved, delving.** to carry on intensive research for information, etc.

dema·gogue, *n.* an unprincipled popular orator or agitator.

demand, *v.* **1.** to ask for with authority; claim as a right. –*n.* **2.** the act of demanding. **3.** an urgent or pressing requirement. **4.** the state of being in request for purchase or use. **5. on demand,** subject to payment upon presentation and demand.

demar·cation, *n.* **1.** the marking off of the boundaries of something. **2.** a division between things, esp. the division between types of work carried out by members of different trade unions.

demean, *v.* to lower in dignity or standing; debase.

demea·nour, *n.* conduct; behaviour; bearing.

demented, *adj.* out of one's mind; insane.

de·merit, *n.* **1.** censurable or punishable quality; fault. **2.** a mark against a person for misconduct or deficiency.

demili·tarise, *v.* to withdraw military forces from (a zone, area, etc.).

demise, *n.* death or decease.

demist, *v.* to direct air, usu. heated, onto car windscreen, to clear it of mist. – **demister,** *n.*

democ·racy, *n.,* *pl.* **-cies.** a form of government in which the supreme power is vested in the people and exercised by them under a free electoral system. – **democrat,** *n.* – **democratic,** *adj.*

de·molish, *v.* to throw or pull down (a building, etc.); reduce to ruins. – **demolition,** *n.*

demon, *n.* an evil spirit; a devil. – **demonic, demoniac,** *adj.*

demon·strate, *v.,* **-strated, -strating. 1.** to make evident by arguments or reasoning; prove. **2.** to describe and explain with the help of specimens or by experiment. **3.** to manifest or exhibit. – **demonstration,** *n.*

demon·stra·tive dəˈmɒnstrətɪv, *adj.* **1.** characterised by showing

demonstrative

demonstrative

feelings openly. **2.** serving to demonstrate.

de·mora·lise /dɪˈmɒrəlaɪz/, *v.*, **-lised, -lising.** to deprive of spirit, courage, etc.

demote, *v.*, **-moted, -moting.** to reduce to a lower grade or class (opposed to *promote*). – **demotion**, *n.*

demur, *v.*, **-murred, -murring.** –*v.* **1.** to make objection; take exception. –*n.* **2.** an objection raised. – **demurral**, *n.*

demure, *adj.*, **-murer, -murest.** affectedly or unnaturally modest, decorous, or prim.

den, *n.* **1.** a cave, etc., serving as the habitation of a wild beast. **2.** a cosy or secluded room for personal use.

denial, *n.* **1.** a contradiction of a statement, etc. **2.** refusal.

deni·grate, *v.*, **-grated, -grating. 1.** to sully; defame. **2.** to blacken.

denim, *n.* a heavy twilled cotton for overalls, trousers, etc.

deni·zen /ˈdɛnəzən/, *n.* an inhabitant.

denomi·nation, *n.* **1.** a class or kind of persons or things distinguished by a specific name. **2.** a religious group.

denomi·nator, *n. Maths.* that term of a fraction (usu. under the line) which shows the number of equal parts into which the unit is divided.

denote, *v.*, **-noted, -noting.** to be a mark or sign of; indicate. – **denotation**, *n.*

de·nounce, *v.*, **-nounced, -nouncing.** to condemn openly; assail with censure.

dense, *adj.*, **denser, densest. 1.** having the component parts closely compacted together; compact. **2.** obtuse; stupid. – **density**, *n.*

deplete

dent, *n.* a hollow or depression in a surface, as from a blow.

dental, *adj.* **1.** of or pertaining to the teeth. **2.** of or pertaining to dentistry.

den·tis·try, *n.* the science or art dealing with the prevention and treatment of oral disease. – **dentist**, *n.*

den·tition, *n.* the arrangement of teeth.

den·ture, *n.* an artificial restoration of teeth.

denude, *v.*, **-nuded, -nuding.** to make naked or bare; strip.

denun·ci·ation, *n.* a denouncing.

deny, *v.*, **-nied, -nying. 1.** to assert the negative of; declare not to be true. **2.** to refuse to grant (a claim, request, etc.). **3.** to refuse to recognise or acknowledge; repudiate.

de·odor·ant, *n.* an agent for destroying odours.

depart, *v.* **1.** to go away. **2.** to turn aside (*from*). – **departure**, *n.*

depart·ment, *n.* a distinct part or division of a complex whole or organised system.

depend, *v.* **1.** to rely; trust. **2.** to be conditioned or contingent. – **dependable**, *adj.*

depen·dant, *n.* one who depends on or looks to another for support, favour, etc.

depen·dent, *adj.* depending on something else. – **dependence**, *n.*

depict, *v.* to represent by or as by painting; portray; delineate.

depila·tory /dəˈpɪlətri/, *adj.*, *n.*, *pl.* **-ries.** –*adj.* **1.** capable of removing hair. –*n.* **2.** a depilatory agent.

de·plete, *v.*, **-pleted, -pleting.** to dep-

deplete

rive of that which fills; reduce the stock or amount of.

de·plor·able, *adj.* 1. causing grief; lamentable. 2. causing censure; bad; wretched. – **deplore**, *v.*

deploy, *v.* to spread out or place efficiently.

deport, *v.* to expel (an undesirable alien) from a country.

deport·ment, *n.* manner of bearing; carriage.

depose, *v.*, -posed, -posing. 1. to remove from office or position. 2. to declare or testify. – **deposition**, *n.*

deposit, *v.* 1. to put or lay down. 2. to place for safekeeping or in trust. –*n.* 3. anything laid or thrown down, as matter precipitated from a fluid; sediment. 4. an accumulation. 5. money placed in a bank. 6. anything given as security or in part payment.

depot /'depoʊ/, *n.* a storehouse.

de·prave, *v.*, -praved, -praving. to make bad or worse; vitiate; corrupt. – **depravity**, *n.*

depre·cate, *v.*, -cated, -cating. to express earnest disapproval of. – **deprecatory**, *adj.*

de·preci·ation, *n.* 1. a decrease in value due to wear and tear, decay, decline in price, etc. 2. a decrease in the purchasing or exchange value of money. – **depreciate**, *v.*

depre·dation, *n.* 1. robbery. 2. destruction.

de·press, *v.* 1. to lower in spirits. 2. to press down. – **depression**, *n.*

de·prive, *v.*, -prived, -priving. to divest of something; dispossess. – **deprivation**, *n.*

depth, *n.* 1. measure or distance downwards, inwards, or backwards. 2. intensity, as of silence, colour,

descendant

etc. 3. lowness of pitch. 4. extent of intellectual penetration or sagacity.

depu·tation, *n.* 1. appointment to represent or act for another or others. 2. the person(s) so appointed.

deputy, *n.*, *pl.* -ties. 1. a person appointed or authorised to act for another or others. 2. a person appointed or elected as assistant to a public official.

de·ranged, *adj.* insane.

dere·lict, *adj.* 1. left or abandoned, as by the owner or guardian. –*n.* 2. a person forsaken or abandoned, esp. by society.

dere·lic·tion, *n.* culpable neglect, as of duty; delinquency; fault.

deride, *v.*, -rided, -riding. to laugh at in contempt. – **derision**, *n.* – **derisive**, *adj.*

derive, *v.*, -rived, -riving. 1. to receive or obtain (*from*) a source or origin. 2. to trace, as from a source or origin. 3. to obtain by reasoning. 4. to come from a source; originate. – **derivation**, *n.* – **derivative**, *n.*, *adj.*

derma·titis, *n.* inflammation of the skin.

derogatory /də'rɒgətri, -ətəri/, *adj.* disparaging.

der·rick, *n.* a tower-like structure, esp. for lifting weights, etc.

descant /'deskænt/, *n. Music.* an additional, usu. higher melody accompanying a simple theme.

de·scend, *v.* 1. to move or pass from a higher to a lower place; fall; sink. 2. to be derived by birth or extraction. 3. to come down in a hostile manner, as an army. – **descendent**, *adj.*

de·scen·dant, *n.* one descended from an ancestor.

descent

descent, *n.* 1. the act of descending. 2. a downward slope. 3. derivation from an ancestor.

de·scribe, *v.*, **-scribed, -scribing.** 1. to set forth in written or spoken words; give an account of. 2. *Geom.* to draw or trace, as an arc. – **description**, *n.* – **descriptive**, *adj.*

dese·crate /'dɛsəkreɪt/, *v.*, **-crated, -crating.** to divest of sacred or hallowed character.

de·sert[1] /'dɛzət/, *n.* an area so deficient in moisture as to support little or no vegetation.

de·sert[2] /dəˈzɜt/, *v.* 1. to abandon. 2. (esp. of a soldier or sailor) to forsake one's duty, etc. – **desertion**, *n.*

de·sert[3] /dəˈzɜt/, *n.* that which is deserved; a due reward or punishment.

de·serve, *v.*, **-served, -serving.** to merit (reward, punishment, esteem, etc.) in return for actions, qualities, etc.

desic·cate, *v.*, **-cated, -cating.** to dry thoroughly; dry up.

design, *v.* 1. to plan or fashion artistically or skilfully, usu. in working detail. 2. to intend for a definite purpose. 3. to form or conceive in the mind. –*n.* 4. an outline, sketch, or plan. 5. the combination of details or features of a picture, building, etc. 6. the end in view; intention.

desig·nate, *v.*, **-nated, -nating,** *adj.* –*v.* 1. to nominate or select for a duty, office, purpose, etc.; appoint. –*adj.* 2. appointed to an office but not yet in possession of it.

desire /dəˈzaɪə/, *v.*, **-sired, -siring,** *n.* –*v.* 1. to wish or long for; crave. –*n.* 2. a longing or craving. 3. an expressed wish. – **desirable**, *adj.*

detach

desir·ous /dəˈzaɪrəs/, *adj.* having or characterised by desire; desiring.

desist /dəˈzɪst/, *v.* to cease, as from some action or proceeding.

desk /dɛsk/, *n.* a table specially adapted for convenience in writing or reading.

deso·late, *adj., v.*, **-lated, -lating.** –*adj.* 1. devastated. 2. deserted. 3. left alone; lonely. –*v.* 4. to devastate. 5. to depopulate. – **desolation**, *n.*

des·pair, *n.* total loss of hope.

des·per·ate, *adj.* 1. reckless from despair. 2. very serious or dangerous. – **desperation**, *n.*

des·pise, *v.*, **-spised, -spising.** to look down upon as, in contempt. – **despicable**, *adj.*

des·pite, *prep.* in spite of.

des·pond·ent, *adj.* depressed or dejected. – **despondency**, *n.*

despot /'dɛspɒt/, *n.* a ruler who has unlimited powers. – **despotic**, *adj.*

des·sert /dəˈzɜt/, *n.* the final, sweet course of a meal.

des·ti·nation, *n.* the predetermined end of a journey or voyage.

des·tined, *adj.* 1. bound for a certain destination. 2. predetermined.

des·tiny, *n., pl.* **-nies.** 1. a predetermined course of events. 2. the power or agency which determines the course of events.

des·ti·tute, *adj.* bereft of means or resources.

des·troy, *v.* 1. to ruin; spoil; demolish. 2. to put an end to. – **destruction**, *n.* – **destructive**, *adj.*

desul·tory /'dɛsəltri, -tɔri, 'dɛz-/, *adj.* disconnected, unmethodical, or fitful.

detach, *v.* to unfasten and separate.

detail

detail, *n.* 1. an individual or minute part; an item or particular. 2. fine, intricate decoration.

detain, *v.* 1. to keep from proceeding; keep waiting. 2. to keep under restraint or in custody. – **detention,** *n.*

detect, *v.* to discover or notice a fact, process, or action. – **detection,** *n.*

detec·tive, *n.* a person, usu. a member of the police force, who investigates crimes.

détente /deɪˈtɒnt/, *n.* a relaxing of international tension.

deter, *v.,* -**terred,** -**terring.** to discourage or restrain (one) from acting or proceeding. – **deterrent,** *adj., n.*

deter·gent, *n.* any cleaning agent, including soap.

deterio·rate, *v.,* -**rated,** -**rating.** to become worse.

deter·mi·nation, *n.* 1. the act or result of determining. 2. the quality of being determined or resolute.

deter·mine, *v.,* -**mined,** -**mining.** 1. to settle or decide (a dispute, question, etc.) by an authoritative decision. 2. to conclude or ascertain, as after reasoning, observation, etc. 3. to fix or condition (an outcome).

deter·mined, *adj.* resolute; firm.

detest, *v.* to feel abhorrence of; hate. – **detestable,** *adj.*

deto·nate, *v.,* -**nated,** -**nating.** to cause to explode. – **detonator,** *n.*

detour /ˈdituə, -tuə, -ˌtʊə/, *n.* a roundabout or circuitous way or course, esp. one used temporarily instead of the main route.

de·tract, *v.* to take away a part, as from quality, value, or reputation.

detri·ment, *n.* loss, damage, or injury. – **detrimental,** *adj.*

devise

detri·tus /dəˈtraɪtəs/, *n.* any disintegrated material; debris.

deuce, *n.* 1. a card, or the side of a dice, having 2 pips. 2. *Tennis, etc.* a juncture in a game at which the scores are level at 40 all.

de·value, *v.,* -**valued,** -**valuing.** 1. to lower the legal value of (a currency). 2. to diminish the worth or value of. – **devaluation,** *n.*

devas·tate, *v.,* -**stated,** -**stating.** to lay waste; ravage; render desolate.

de·velop, *v.* 1. to bring out the capabilities or possibilities of. 2. to (cause to) grow into a more mature or advanced state. 3. to bring or come gradually into being or activity; evolve. 4. to build on (land). 5. to treat (a photographic plate, etc.) with chemical agents so as to bring out the latent image. – **development,** *n.*

devi·ant, *adj.* 1. deviating from an accepted norm, esp. in politics or sex. – *n.* 2. one who or that which is deviant.

devi·ate, *v.,* -**ated,** -**ating.** 1. to turn aside (from a way or course). 2. to depart or swerve, as from a procedure, course of action, or acceptable standard. – **deviation,** *n.*

device, *n.* 1. an invention or contrivance. 2. a plan or scheme for effecting a purpose. 3. a design used as an emblem, badge, etc.

devil, *n.* 1. *Theol.* (*sometimes cap.*) the supreme spirit of evil. 2. an atrociously wicked, cruel, or ill-tempered person.

devi·ous, *adj.* 1. departing from the accepted way; roundabout. 2. not straightforward; deceptive.

devise, *v.,* -**vised,** -**vising.** to order or

devise

arrange the plan of; contrive; invent.

de·void, *adj.* empty, not possessing, or destitute (*of*).

de·volve, *v.*, **-volved**, **-volving**. **1.** to transfer or delegate (a duty, responsibility, etc.) to or upon another. **2.** to fall as a duty or responsibility on a person.

de·vote, *v.*, **-voted**, **-voting**. to give up to or concentrate on a particular pursuit, occupation, purpose, cause, person, etc.. – **devotion**, *n.* – **devotee**, *n.*

de·vour, *v.* to swallow or eat up voraciously or ravenously.

de·vout, *adj.* devoted to divine worship or service; pious.

dew, *n.* moisture condensed from the atmosphere, esp. at night, and deposited in the form of small drops upon any cool surface.

dex·terity, *n.* adroitness or skill in using the hands or the mind. – **dexterous**, *adj.*

dia·betes /daɪəˈbiːtɪz/, *n.* a disease in which the ability of the body to use sugar is impaired. – **diabetic**, *n.*, *adj.*

dia·bolic, *adj.* having the qualities of a devil; fiendish. Also, **diabolical**.

diag·nosis, *n.*, *pl.* **-ses**. *Med.* the process of determining by examination the nature and circumstances of a diseased condition. – **diagnose**, *v.* – **diagnostic**, *adj.*

diag·onal, *adj. Maths.* connecting, as a straight line, 2 non-adjacent angles, as between opposite corners of a square.

dia·gram, *n.* a drawing or plan that outlines and explains, the parts, operation, etc., of something.

dial, *n.* **1.** a face upon which time is indicated by hands, pointers, or

diatribe

shadows. **2.** a plate or disc with graduations or figures, as for measuring, or on a telephone, etc.

dia·lect, *n.* the language of a particular district or class.

dia·logue, *n.* **1.** conversation between 2 or more persons. **2.** an exchange of ideas or opinions on a particular issue.

dialy·sis /daɪˈæləsɪs/, *n.* (in cases of defective kidney function) the artificial removal of waste products from the blood.

dia·meter, *n. Geom.* a straight line passing through the centre of a circle or sphere and terminated at each end by the circumference or surface.

dia·metri·cal, *adj.* **1.** pertaining to or along a diameter. **2.** absolute; complete: *diametrical opposites.* Also, **diametric**.

dia·mond, *n.* **1.** an extremely hard, pure or nearly pure form of carbon, which, when used as a precious stone, has great brilliance. **2.** an equilateral quadrilateral, esp. as placed with its diagonals vertical and horizontal.

diapha·nous /daɪˈæfənəs/, *adj.* transparent; translucent.

dia·phragm, *n.* **1.** *Anat.* the partition separating the thoracic cavity from the abdominal cavity in mammals. **2.** a contraceptive membrane covering the cervix.

diar·rhoea, *n.* an intestinal disorder characterised by morbid frequency and fluidity of faecal evacuations.

diary, *n.*, *pl.* **-ries**. a daily record, esp. of the writer's own experiences or observations. – **diarist**, *n.*

dia·tribe, *n.* a bitter and violent denunciation, attack, or criticism.

dice

dice, *n. pl., sing.* **die**, *v.*, **diced**, **dicing**. –*n.* **1.** small cubes marked on each side with a different number of spots (1 to 6), or with symbols, usu. used in pairs in games of chance or in gambling. –*v.* **2.** to cut into small cubes.

dichot·omy /daɪˈkɒtəmi/, *n., pl.* **-mies**. division into 2 parts or into twos.

dick, *n. Colloq.* the penis.

dic·tate, *v.*, **-tated**, **-tating**. **1.** to say or read aloud (something) to be taken down in writing or recorded mechanically. **2.** to prescribe positively; command with authority. – **dictation**, *n.*

dic·tator, *n.* a person exercising absolute power. – **dictatorial**, *adj.*

dic·tion, *n.* style of speaking or writing as dependent upon choice of words.

dic·tion·ary, *n., pl.* **-aries**. a book containing a selection of the words of a language, usu. arranged alphabetically, with explanations of their meanings, pronunciations, and other information concerning them.

did, *v.* past tense of **do**.

di·dac·tic, *adj.* **1.** intended for instruction. **2.** inclined to teach or lecture others too much.

diddle, *v.*, **-dled**, **-dling**. *Colloq.* to cheat; swindle. – **diddler**, *n.*

didgeri·doo, *n.* an Aboriginal wind instrument. Also, **didjeridu**.

die[1], *v.*, **died**, **dying**. **1.** to cease to live; undergo the complete and permanent cessation of all vital functions. **2.** to pass gradually; fade or subside gradually (*away, out,* or *down*).

die[2], *n., pl.* **dies** for def. 1, **dice** for

difficult

def. 2. **1.** any of various devices for cutting or forming material in a press or a stamping or forging machine. **2.** singular of **dice**.

diesel engine, *n.* a type of internal-combustion engine in which an oil is used as fuel.

diet, *n., v.*, **-eted**, **-eting**. –*n.* **1.** a particular selection of food, esp. as prescribed to improve health or regulate weight. **2.** the usual or regular food(s) a person eats most frequently. –*v.* **3.** to follow a diet (def. 1). – **dietitian**, *n.* – **dietary**, *adj.*

differ, *v.* **1.** to be unlike, dissimilar, or distinct in nature or qualities (*from*). **2.** to disagree in opinion, belief, etc. (*with* or *from*).

dif·fer·ence, *n.* **1.** the state or relation of being different; dissimilarity. **2.** a significant change in or effect upon a situation. **3.** a disagreement in opinion; dispute; quarrel. **4.** *Maths.* the amount by which one quantity is greater or less than another.

dif·fer·ent, *adj.* **1.** differing in character; having unlike qualities. **2.** various; several. **3.** unusual; not ordinary.

dif·feren·tial, *adj.* **1.** constituting a difference; distinctive. –*n.* **2.** *Mach.* a set of gears in a motor car which permit the driving wheels to revolve at different speeds while the car is turning.

dif·feren·tiate, *v.*, **-ated**, **-ating**. **1.** to mark off by differences; distinguish; alter; change. **2.** to make a distinction; discriminate.

dif·fi·cult, *adj.* **1.** hard to do, perform, or accomplish; requiring much effort. **2.** hard to deal with or get on with. – **difficulty**, *n.*

149

diffident

dif·fi·dent, *adj.* lacking confidence; timid. – **diffidence**, *n.*

dif·frac·tion, *n.* the breaking up of light. – **diffract**, *v.*

dif·fuse /dəˈfjuz/, *v.*, **-fused, -fusing**; /dəˈfjus/, *adj.* –*v.* 1. to spread or scatter widely or thinly. –*adj.* 2. widely spread or scattered. – **diffusion**, *n.*

dig, *v.*, **dug, digging**, *n.* –*v.* 1. to break up and turn over, or penetrate and loosen (the ground). 2. to make (a hole, tunnel, etc.) by removing material. 3. to obtain or remove by digging (*up* or *out*). –*n.* 4. thrust; poke. 5. a cutting, sarcastic remark. 6. an archaeological site undergoing excavation. 7. (*pl.*) lodgings.

digest, *v.* 1. to prepare (food) in the alimentary canal for assimilation into the system. 2. to assimilate mentally. –*n.* 3. a collection or summary, esp. of literary, historical, legal, or scientific matter. – **digestion**, *n.*

digger, *n.* 1. a miner, esp. a gold-miner.

dig·gings, *n. pl.* a mining operation or locality.

digit, *n.* 1. a finger or toe. 2. any of the figures 0, 1, . . . 9.

dig·it·al, *adj.* 1. of or pertaining to a digit. 2. *Electronics.* of or pertaining to information represented by patterns made up from qualities existing in 2 states only, on and off, as pulses (opposed to *analog*).

digitalis, *n.* a heart-stimulating drug made from the foxglove flower.

dig·ni·tary, *n. pl.* **-taries**. one who holds a high rank or office, esp. in the church.

dig·nity, *n., pl.* **-ties**. 1. nobility of

dine

manner or style; stateliness; gravity. 2. nobleness or elevation of mind; worthiness. – **dignify**, *v.*

di·gress /daɪˈgrɛs/, *v.* to deviate or wander away from the main purpose. – **digression**, *n.*

dilapi·dated, *adj.* reduced to, or fallen into, ruin or decay.

dilate, *v.*, **-lated, -lating**. 1. to make wider or larger. 2. to speak at length. – **dilation**, *n.*

dila·tory /ˈdɪlətri, -təri/, *adj.* inclined to delay or procrastinate; slow.

dilemma, *n.* a situation requiring a choice between equally undesirable alternatives.

dili·gent /ˈdɪlədʒənt/, *adj.* constant and persistent in an effort to accomplish something. – **diligence**, *n.*

dill, *n.* a plant bearing a seedlike fruit used in medicine and for flavouring pickles, etc.

dilly-dally, *v.* to dawdle or loiter.

dilute, *v.*, **-luted, -luting**, *adj.* –*v.* 1. to make thinner or weaker by the addition of water or the like. –*adj.* 2. reduced in strength. – **dilution**, *n.*

dim, *adj.*, **dimmer, dimmest**, *v.*, **dimmed, dimming**. –*adj.* 1. not bright or strong. –*v.* 2. to make or become dim.

dimension, *n.* 1. magnitude measured in a particular direction. 2. an aspect; appearance.

diminish, *v.* to make, or cause to seem, smaller; lessen; reduce. – **diminution**, *n.*

diminu·tive, *adj.* small; little; tiny.

dimple, *n.* a small natural hollow, esp. in the cheek.

din, *n.* a loud, confused noise.

dine, *v.*, **dined, dining**. to eat the

dine

principal meal of the day; have dinner.

ding, *v.* 1. to sound, as a bell; ring, esp. with wearisome continuance. –*n.* 2. a blow or stroke. 3. the sound of a bell or the like. 4. *Colloq.* a minor accident involving a car, etc.

dinghy /'dɪŋi/, *n., pl.* **-ghies.** a small rowing or sailing boat.

dingo, *n., pl.* **-goes, gos.** the Aust. wild dog, often tawny-yellow in colour, with erect ears, a bushy tail, and with a call resembling a howl or yelp rather than a bark.

dingy /'dɪndʒi/, *adj.,* **-gier, -giest.** of a dark, dull, or dirty colour or aspect.

dinkum, *Colloq. adj.* 1. Also, **dinkydi.** true; honest; genuine. –*adv.* 2. truly.

dinner, *n.* the main meal, taken either about noon or in the evening.

dino·saur, *n.* an extinct reptile of gigantic size.

dint, *n.* force; power: *by dint of argument*.

dio·cese /'daɪəsəs/, *n., pl.* **dioceses** /'daɪəsəsəz, 'daɪəsiz/. the district, with its population, falling under the care of a bishop.

dip, *v.,* **dipped, dipping.** –*v.* 1. to plunge temporarily or quickly into a liquid. 2. to lower and raise. 3. to sink or drop down, as if plunging into water. 4. to incline or slope downwards. –*n.* 5. the act of dipping; a plunge into water, etc. 6. a liquid into which something is dipped. 7. a lowering momentarily; a sinking down. 8. downward extension, inclination, or slope. 9. a hollow or depression in the land. 10. a soft savoury mixture into

directly

which biscuits, etc., are dipped before being eaten.

diph·theria /dɪf'θɪəriə/, *n.* an infectious disease marked by the growth of a false membrane in the air passages.

diph·thong, *n.* a combination of 2 vowel sounds with only one syllabic peak, as *ei* in *vein*.

dip·loma, *n., pl.* **-mas.** a document stating one's success in an examination, etc.

dip·lo·macy, *n., pl.* **-cies.** 1. the conduct by government officials of negotiations and other relations between states. 2. skill in managing any negotiations. – **diplomat,** *n.* – **diplomatic,** *adj.*

dipso·maniac, *n.* one who suffers from an irresistible craving for intoxicants.

dire, *adj.,* **direr, direst.** causing or attended with great fear or suffering; dreadful; awful.

direct, *v.* 1. to guide. 2. to give authoritative instructions to; command. 3. to organise and supervise the artistic production of a play or film. –*adj.* 4. proceeding in a straight line or by the shortest course. 5. without intervening agency; personal. 6. going straight to the point; straightforward. –*adv.* 7. in a direct manner; straight. – **director,** *n.*

direc·tion, *n.* 1. the act of directing, pointing, aiming, etc. 2. the line along which anything lies, faces, moves, etc., with reference to the point or region towards which it is directed. 3. management.

direc·tive, *n.* an authoritative instruction or direction.

directly, *adv.* 1. in a direct line, way,

151

directly

or manner; straight. **2.** without delay; immediately. **3.** presently.

direc·tory, *n.*, *pl.* **-ries.** a book or the like containing names, addresses, telephone numbers, etc.

dirge, *n.* a funeral song or tune.

dirk, *n.* short dagger.

dirt, *n.* **1.** earth or soil, esp. when loose. **2.** any foul or filthy substance, as excrement, mud, etc. **3.** unsavoury or malicious gossip.

dirty, *adj.*, **dirtier, dirtiest**, *v.* **dirtied, dirtying.** –*adj.* **1.** soiled with dirt; foul. **2.** morally unclean; indecent. **3.** stormy or squally, as the weather. –*v.* **4.** to make or become dirty.

dis·abil·ity, *n.*, *pl.* **-ties,** lack of competent power, strength, or physical or mental ability.

dis·able, *v.* **-bled, -bling. 1.** to weaken or destroy the capability of; incapacitate. **2.** to make legally incapable; disqualify.

dis·ad·van·tage, *n.*, *v.* **-taged, -taging.** –*n.* **1.** an unfavourable circumstance or condition. –*v.* **2.** to subject to disadvantage.

dis·a·gree, *v.*, **-greed, -greeing. 1.** to fail to agree; differ (*with*). **2.** to differ in opinion; dissent. – **disagreement,** *n.*

dis·a·gree·able, *adj.* unpleasant.

dis·al·low, *v.* to refuse to admit the truth or validity of.

dis·ap·pear, *v.* **1.** to cease to appear or be seen; vanish from sight. **2.** to cease to exist or be known; end gradually. – **disappearance,** *n.*

dis·ap·point, *v.* **1.** to fail to fulfil the expectations or wishes of (a person). **2.** to defeat the fulfilment of (hopes, plans, etc.); thwart. – **disappointment,** *n.*

dis·ap·prove, *v.*, **-proved, proving.** to

discipline

have an unfavourable opinion (*of*). – **disapproval,** *n.*

dis·arm, *v.* **1.** to deprive of means of attack or defence. **2.** to divest of hostility, suspicion, etc.; make friendly. – **disarmament,** *n.*

dis·ar·ray, *n.* disorder; confusion.

dis·as·ter, *n.* any unfortunate event, esp. a sudden or great misfortune. – **disastrous,** *adj.*

dis·a·vow, *v.* to disclaim knowledge of connection with, or responsibility for; disown.

dis·band, *v.* to break up or disorganise (a band or company).

dis·burse, *v.*, **-bursed, -bursing.** to pay out (money); expend.

disc, *n.* **1.** any thin, flat, circular plate or object. **2.** a round, flat area.

dis·card, *v.* **1.** to cast aside; reject; dismiss, esp. from use. **2.** *Cards.* to throw out (a card or cards) from one's hand. –*n.* **3.** one who or that which is cast out or rejected.

dis·cern, *v.* to perceive by the sight or some other sense or by the intellect. – **discernment,** *n.*

dis·charge, *v.*, **-charged, -charging.** *n.* –*v.* **1.** to relieve of a charge or load. **2.** to fulfil or perform. **3.** to dismiss from service. **4.** to give out (liquid, etc.); emit. –*n.* **5.** the act of discharging a ship, load, etc. **6.** a sending or coming forth; ejection; emission. **7.** a relieving or a getting rid of something of the nature of a charge.

dis·ci·ple, *n.* an adherent of the doctrines of another.

dis·ci·pline, *n.*, *v.*, **-plined, -plining.** –*n.* **1.** training to act in accordance with rules. **2.** punishment inflicted by way of correction and training. **3.** the training effect of experience,

152

adversity, etc. **4.** a branch of instruction or learning. –*v.* **5.** to bring to a state of order and obedience by training and control.

disc jockey, *n.* one who comperes radio programs of gramophone records.

dis·claim, *v.* to repudiate or deny interest in or connection with; disavow.

dis·close, *v.*, **-closed, -closing. 1.** to cause to appear; allow to be seen; make known; reveal. **2.** to uncover.

dis·colour, *v.* to change or spoil the colour of.

dis·com·fi·ture, *n.* **1.** frustration of hopes or plans. **2.** confusion.

dis·com·fort, *n.* absence of comfort or pleasure; uneasiness; pain.

dis·con·cert /dɪskənˈsɜːt/, *v.* to disturb the self-possession of.

dis·con·so·late, *adj.* without consolation or solace; unhappy.

dis·cord, *n.* lack of harmony. – **discordant**, *adj.*

dis·co·theque /ˈdɪskətɛk/, *n.* a place of public entertainment or a club in which patrons may dance, esp. to recorded music. Also, **discothèque, disco.**

dis·count, *v.* **1.** to deduct. **2.** to leave out of account; disregard. –*n.* **3.** the act of discounting. **4.** amount deducted. **5. at a discount,** below usual retail price. –*adj.* **6.** (of stores) selling goods at a lower price than most competitors.

dis·cour·age, *v.*, **-raged, -raging. 1.** to deprive of courage; dishearten. **2.** to dissuade (*from*).

dis·course, *n.* communication of thought by words; conversation.

dis·cov·er, *v.* to learn of, or find out; gain sight or knowledge of (something previously unseen or unknown). – **discovery**, *n.*

dis·cred·it, *v.* to injure the credit or reputation of.

dis·creet, *adj.* **1.** wise or judicious in avoiding mistakes or faults. **2.** not given to careless talk.

dis·crep·an·cy, *n., pl.* **-cies.** an instance of difference or inconsistency.

dis·crete, *adj.* detached from others; separate; distinct.

dis·cre·tion, *n.* **1.** freedom of judgment or choice. **2.** the quality of being discreet. – **discretionary**, *adj.*

dis·crim·i·nate, *v.*, **-nated, -nating. 1.** to make a distinction, as in favour of or against a person or thing. **2.** to note or observe a difference; distinguish accurately. – **discrimination**, *n.*

dis·cur·sive, *adj.* rambling.

dis·cus, *n., pl.* **discuses, disci** /ˈdɪsaɪ/. a disc, usu. made of wood rimmed with metal, thrown by athletes.

dis·cuss, *v.* to examine by argument; sift the considerations for and against. – **discussion**, *n.*

dis·dain, *n.* a feeling of contempt for anything regarded as unworthy; haughty contempt.

disease, *n.* a morbid condition of the body, or of some organ or part; illness.

dis·embark, *v.* to go on shore; land.

dis·embowel, *v.*, **-elled, -elling.** to remove the bowels or entrails from.

dis·figure, *v.*, **-ured, -uring.** to mar the figure, appearance, or beauty of.

dis·gorge, *v.* to throw up (as) from the throat; vomit.

dis·grace, *n., v.*, **-graced, -gracing.** –*n.* **1.** the state of being in dishonour. **2.** the state of being out of

disgrace

favour. –v. 3. to bring or reflect shame or reproach upon. – **disgraceful**, adj.

dis·gruntled, adj. mildly upset; discontented.

dis·guise, v., -guised, -guising, n. –v. 1. to conceal the identity of –n. 2. that which disguises.

dis·gust, v. 1. to cause nausea or loathing in. –n. 2. strong distaste; loathing.

dish, n. 1. an open, more or less shallow container of pottery, glass, metal, wood, etc., used for various purposes, esp. for holding or serving food. 2. a particular article or preparation of food.

dishev·elled /dɪˈʃɛvəld/, adj. untidy.

dis·honest, adj. not honest; disposed to lie, cheat, or steal. – **dishonesty**, n.

dis·honour, n. 1. lack of honour; dishonourable character or conduct. 2. disgrace; ignominy. –v. 3. to bring reproach or shame on. 4. to refuse or fail to pay (a cheque, etc.). – **dishonourable**, adj.

dis·illu·sion, v. to free from illusion; disenchant.

dis·infec·tant, n. any chemical agent that destroys bacteria. – **disinfect**, v.

dis·in·herit, v. to deprive of the right to inherit. – **disinheritance**, n.

dis·inte·grate, v., -grated, -grating. to fall apart; break up. – **disintegration**, n.

dis·inter·ested, adj. unbiased by personal involvement or advantage.

dis·jointed, adj. disconnected; incoherent.

dis·like, v., -liked, -liking. to regard with displeasure or aversion.

disparate

dis·locate, v., -cated, -cating. 1. to displace. 2. to put out of joint.

dis·lodge, v., -lodged, -lodging. to remove or drive from a place of rest or lodgment.

dis·loyal, adj. not loyal.

dismal, adj. 1. gloomy; dreary. 2. terrible; dreadful.

dis·mantle, v., -tled, -tling. to pull down; take apart; take to pieces.

dismay, v. 1. to dishearten utterly; daunt. –n. 2. consternation.

dis·member, v. 1. to deprive of limbs; divide limb from limb. 2. to separate into parts.

dis·miss, v. 1. to bid or allow (a person) to go; give permission to depart. 2. to discharge or remove, as from office or service. 3. to put off or away; to put aside from consideration. 4. Law. to put out of court, as a complaint or appeal. – **dismissal**, n.

dis·obey, v. to neglect or refuse to obey (an order, person, etc.). – **disobedient**, adj.

dis·order, n. 1. lack of order or regular arrangement; confusion. 2. a derangement of physical or mental health or functions. – **disorderly**, adj.

dis·orga·nise, v., -nised, -nising. to destroy the organisation of.

dis·orien·tate, v., -tated, -tating. 1. to confuse as to direction. 2. to perplex; to confuse. Also, **disorient**.

dis·own, v. to deny the ownership of or responsibility for; renounce.

dis·par·age, v., -raged, -raging. to speak of or treat slightingly; belittle.

dis·parate /ˈdɪspərət/, adj. essentially different; dissimilar. – **disparity**, n.

dispassionate — dissident

dis·pas·sion·ate, *adj.* free from or unaffected by passion; devoid of personal feeling or bias.

dis·patch, *v.* **1.** to send off; put under way. —*n.* **2.** the sending off of a messenger, letter, etc., to a destination. **3.** prompt or speedy transaction, as of business. **4.** a written message sent in haste.

dispel /dɪsˈpɛl/, *v.*, **-pelled, -pelling.** to drive off in various directions; scatter.

dis·pen·sa·ble, *adj.* that may be dispensed with or done without.

dis·pen·sary, *n., pl.* **-saries.** a place where something is dispensed, esp. medicines.

dis·pen·sa·tion, *n.* **1.** the act of dispensing. **2.** *Rom. Cath. Ch.* the relaxation of a law in a specific case.

dis·pense, *v.*, **-pensed, -pensing. 1.** to deal out; distribute. **2.** to administer (laws, etc.). **3. dispense with**, **a.** to do without; forgo. **b.** to grant exemption from (a law, promise, etc.).

dis·perse, *v.*, **-persed, -persing.** to scatter.

dis·place, *v.*, **-placed, -placing.** to put out of the usual or proper place.

dis·play, *v.* **1.** to show; exhibit. **2.** to reveal; betray. **3.** to show ostentatiously. —*n.* **4.** the act of displaying; exhibition; show. **5.** the thing(s) displayed.

dis·please, *v.*, **-pleased, -pleasing.** to annoy.

dis·pose, *v.*, **-posed, -posing. 1.** to put in a particular or the proper order or arrangement. **2.** to incline. **3. dispose of,** to deal with definitely; get rid of. — **disposal**, *n.*

dis·po·si·tion, *n.* **1.** mental or moral constitution; character. **2.** arrangement.

dis·pos·sess, *v.* to put (a person) out of possession, esp. of real property; oust.

dis·pute, *v.*, **-puted, -puting,** *n.* —*v.* **1.** to engage in argument or discussion. **2.** to argue or debate about. —*n.* **3.** argumentation; strong difference of opinion or desires; a quarrel.

dis·qual·i·fy, *v.*, **-fied, -fying.** to render unfit or ineligible.

dis·qui·et, *v.* **1.** to disturb; make uneasy. —*n.* **2.** unrest; uneasiness.

dis·re·gard, *v.* **1.** to pay no attention to; leave out of consideration. —*n.* **2.** lack of regard or attention.

dis·re·pair, *n.* the state of being out of repair; impaired condition.

dis·re·pute, *n.* ill repute; loss of good reputation. — **disreputable**, *adj.*

dis·re·spect, *n.* lack of respect.

dis·rupt, *v.* to break or rend asunder. — **disruption**, *n.* — **disruptive**, *adj.*

dis·sect, *v.* **1.** to cut apart (an animal body, plant, etc.) to examine it. **2.** to examine minutely part by part.

dis·sem·ble, *v.*, **-bled, -bling. 1.** to conceal the real nature of. **2.** to speak or act hypocritically.

dis·sem·i·nate, *v.*, **-nated, -nating.** to scatter, or spread.

dis·sent, *v.* **1.** to disagree. —*n.* **2.** difference in sentiment or opinion. — **dissension**, *n.*

dis·ser·ta·tion, *n.* a written essay, treatise, or thesis.

dis·serv·ice, *n.* harm; injury; an ill turn.

dis·si·dent, *n.* one who differs; a dissenter, esp. against a particular political system.

dis·sim·u·la·tion, *n.* a false appearance; the disguising of one's real feelings or motives.

dis·si·pate, *v.*, **-pated**, **-pating**. 1. to scatter in various directions; disperse. 2. to scatter wastefully; squander.

dis·so·ci·ate, *v.*, **-ated**, **-ating**. to sever the association of; separate. – **dissociation**, *n.*

dis·so·lute, *adj.* given to immoral behaviour.

dis·solve, *v.*, **-solved**, **-solving**. 1. to make a solution of in a solvent. 2. to break up (an assembly or organisation); dismiss. 3. to bring to an end; destroy; dispel. 4. *Law.* to deprive of force; annul. 5. to become dissolved, as in a solvent. 6. to disappear gradually.

dis·so·nance, *n.* 1. discord, harsh sound. 2. disagreement.

dis·suade, *v.*, **-suaded**, **-suading**. to persuade not to do something.

dis·tance, *n.* 1. the extent of space intervening between things or points. 2. remoteness. 3. reserve or aloofness.

dis·tant, *adj.* 1. far off or apart in space; not near; remote (*from*). 2. far apart in any respect. 3. reserved; not familiar or cordial.

dis·taste, *n.* dislike; disinclination.

dis·tem·per[1], *n.* an infectious disease of young dogs.

dis·tem·per[2], *n.* a water paint used for the decoration of interior walls and ceilings.

dis·tend, *v.* to swell.

dis·til, *v.*, **-tilled**, **-tilling**. 1. to subject to a process of vaporisation and subsequent condensation, as for purification or concentration. 2. to fall in drops; trickle; exude. – **distillery**, *n.* – **distillation**, *n.*

dis·tinct, *adj.* 1. distinguished as not being the same; separate (fol. by *from* or used absolutely). 2. clear to the senses or intellect; definite.

dis·tinc·tion, *n.* 1. a marking off or distinguishing as different. 2. a discrimination made between things as different. 3. a distinguishing characteristic. 4. a mark of special favour. 5. marked superiority; eminence. – **distinctive**, *adj.*

dis·tin·guish, *v.* 1. to mark off as different (*from*). 2. to recognise as distinct or different; discriminate. 3. to perceive clearly by sight or other sense; discern. 4. to be a distinctive characteristic of; characterise. 5. to make prominent, conspicuous, or eminent. 6. to indicate or show a difference (*between*). 7. to recognise or note differences.

dis·tort, *v.* 1. to twist awry or out of shape; make crooked or deformed. 2. to pervert; misrepresent. – **distortion**, *n.*

dis·tract, *v.* 1. to draw away or divert as, the mind or attention. 2. to entertain; amuse; divert. – **distraction**, *n.*

dis·traught, *adj.* 1. distracted; deeply agitated. 2. crazed.

dis·tress, *v.*, *n.* (to cause) great pain, anxiety, or sorrow.

dis·trib·ute, *v.*, **-uted**, **-uting**. to divide and bestow in shares; deal out. – **distribution**, *n.* – **distributor**, *n.*

dis·trict, *n.* a region or locality.

dis·turb, *v.* 1. to interfere with; interrupt. 2. to throw into commo-

disturb

tion or disorder; agitate. 3. to perplex; trouble. – **disturbance**, n.

disuse, n. discontinuance of use.

ditch, n. 1. a long, narrow hollow in the earth, esp. made by digging, for draining or irrigating land. –v. 2. Colloq. to get rid of; get away from.

dither, v. to be vacillating or uncertain.

ditto, n., pl. **-tos**. the aforesaid; the same (used in accounts, lists, etc., to avoid repetition). Symbol: " ; abbrev.: do.

ditty, n., pl. **-ties**. a simple song.

diur·nal, adj. 1. daily. 2. of or belonging to the daytime.

divan /dəˈvæn/, n. a low bed.

dive, v., **dived**, **diving**, n. –v. 1. to plunge, esp. head first, as into water. 2. to dart. –n. 3. the act of diving. 4. Colloq. a disreputable place, as for gambling, etc.

di·verge, v., **-verged**, **-verging**. to move or lie in different directions from a common point; branch off. – **divergence**, n. – **divergent**, adj.

di·verse, adj. different; varied. – **diversity**, n.

divert, v. 1. to turn aside or from a path or course. 2. to draw off to a different object, purpose, etc. 3. to distract from serious occupation; entertain or amuse. – **diversion**, n.

divest, v. 1. to strip of clothing etc. 2. to strip or deprive of anything; dispossess.

divide, v., **-vided**, **-viding**. 1. to separate. 2. to deal out in parts; apportion; share. 3. Maths. to separate into equal parts by the process of division. 4. to become divided or separated. 5. to share something with others. – **divisible**, adj.

divi·dend, n. 1. Maths. a number to be divided by another number (the divisor). 2. Finance. **a.** a sum of money paid to shareholders of a company or trading concern out of earnings. **b.** interest payable on public funds. 3. a payment to creditors and shareholders in a liquidated company. 4. a share of anything divided.

divine, adj., v., **-vined**, **-vining**. –adj. 1. of or pertaining to a god. –v. 2. to discover (water, metal, etc.,) by magical means. 3. to prophesy; know the future.

divin·ity, n., pl. **-ties**. 1. the quality of being divine; divine nature. 2. the science of divine things; theology.

di·vision, n. 1. the act of dividing; partition. 2. the state of being divided. 3. Maths. the operation inverse to multiplication; the finding of a quantity (the quotient) which, when multiplied by a given quantity (the divisor), gives another given quantity (the dividend). Symbol: ÷. 4. one of the parts into which a thing is divided.

di·visive, adj. creating division or discord.

di·visor, n. Maths. a number by which another number (the dividend) is divided.

di·vorce, n. the dissolution of the marriage contract.

di·vulge, v., **-vulged**, **-vulging**. to disclose or reveal.

dizzy, adj., **-zier**, **-ziest**. 1. affected with a sensation of whirling, with tendency to fall; giddy. 2. Colloq. foolish or stupid. – **dizziness**, n.

do, v., pres. sing. 1 do, 2 do, 3 does; pl. do; pt. did; pp. done; ppr. doing; n. –v. 1. to perform (acts, duty, penance, a part, etc.). 2. to be the

do

cause of (good, harm, credit, etc.); bring about. **3.** to render (homage, justice, etc.) **4.** to serve (a period of time) in a prison. **5.** to make. **6.** to study. **7.** to get along or fare (*well* or *ill*); manage (*with, without*, etc.). **8.** to serve or be satisfactory, as for the purpose; suffice; be enough. **9.** to deal (*by*): *He did well by me—gave me a fair price.* –*aux. v.* **10.** (used without special meaning in interrogative, negative, and inverted constructions): *Do you swim every day?* **11.** (used to lend emphasis to a principal verb): *I do mean what I say.* –*n.* **12.** *Colloq.* a festivity or treat. **13.** (*pl.*) rules; customs, etc.

dob, *v.*, **dobbed, dobbing.** *Colloq.* to betray, report (someone), as for a misdemeanour (*in*).

docile, *adj.* easily managed or handled; tractable.

dock[1], *n.* **1.** a wharf. **2.** the space or waterway between 2 piers or wharves, as for receiving a ship while in port. **3.** a semi-enclosed structure which a plane, truck, etc., can enter for loading, repair, etc.

dock[2], *n.* **1.** the solid or fleshy part of an animal's tail. **2.** the part of a tail left after cutting or clipping. –*v.* **3.** to cut off the end of (a tail, etc.). **4.** to deduct a part from (wages, etc.).

dock[3], *n.* an enclosed place in a courtroom where the accused is placed during trial.

docket, *n.* a receipt.

doctor, *n.* **1.** a person licensed to practise medicine. **2.** a person who has received the highest degree conferred by a faculty of a university. – **doctoral**, *adj.* – **doctorate**, *n.*

doc‧trine, *n.* a body or system of teachings relating to a particular subject.

docu‧ment, *n.* **1.** a written or printed paper furnishing information or evidence; a legal or official paper. –*v.* **2.** to furnish with documents, evidence, or the like. – **documentation**, *n.*

docu‧men‧tary, *adj., n., pl.* **-ries.** –*adj.* **1.** pertaining to, consisting of, or derived from documents. –*n.* **2.** a factual television or radio program, film, etc.

dodge, *v.*, **dodged, dodging. 1.** to move aside or change position suddenly, as to avoid a blow or to get behind something. **2.** to use evasive methods. **3.** to elude by a sudden shift of position or by strategy.

doe, *n.* the female of the deer, antelope, and certain other animals.

does, *v.* 3rd person singular present indicative of **do.**

doff, *v.* **1.** to remove (the hat) in salutation.

dog, *n., v.*, **dogged, dogging.** –*n.* **1.** a domesticated carnivore, bred in a great many varieties. **2.** any animal belonging to the same family, including the wolves, jackals, foxes, etc. –*v.* **3.** to follow or track like a dog, esp. with hostile intent; hound.

dog‧gerel, *n.* comic verse, usu. poor in quality.

dogma, *n., pl.* **-mas, -mata. 1.** a system of principles or tenets, as of a church. **2.** prescribed doctrine.

dog‧matic, *adj.* **1.** of, pertaining to, or of the nature of a dogma or dogmas. **2.** asserting opinions in an

dogmatic

authoritative, positive, or arrogant manner.

dolly, *n., pl.* **-lies.** a small ornamental mat, as of embroidery or lace.

dol·drums, *n.pl.* **1.** the region of relatively calm winds near the equator. **2. the doldrums,** a period of dullness, depression, etc.

dole, *n., v.,* doled, doling. *–n.* **1.** a payment by a government to an unemployed person. *–v.* **2.** to give (*out*) sparingly or in small quantities.

dole·ful, *adj.* full of grief; sorrowful; gloomy.

doll, *n.* **1.** a toy representing a child or other human being. *–v.* **2.** to dress (*up*) rather too smartly or too much.

dollar, *n.* the monetary unit of the USA, Australia and various other countries. *Symbol:* $.

dollop, *n.* lump of food, etc.

dolly, *n., pl.* **dollies 1.** a child's name for a doll. **2.** a low truck or platform with small wheels for moving loads.

dol·phin, *n.* any of the various cetaceans, some of which are commonly called porpoises.

domain, *n.* **1.** an estate; any land held in possession. **2.** a field of action, thought, etc. **3.** a region with specific characteristics, types of growth, animal life, etc.

dome, *n. Archit.* a large, hemispherical roof.

dom·estic, *adj.* **1.** of or pertaining to the home, the household, or household affairs. **2.** living with man; tame. **3.** belonging, produced, or existing within a country; not foreign. **– domesticate,** *v.* **– domesticity,** *n.*

domi·cile, *n.* a place of residence; a house or home.

dope

domi·nate, *v.,* **-nated, nating. 1.** to rule (over); govern, control. **2.** to tower above; overshadow. **– dominant,** *adj.* **– domination,** *n.*

domi·neer, *v.* to govern arbitrarily; tyrannise.

do·minion, *n.* **1.** the power or right of governing and controlling. **2.** a territory, usu. of considerable size, in which a single rulership holds sway.

domino, *n., pl.* **-noes. 1.** (*pl.* construed as sing.) any of various games played with flat, oblong pieces, the face of which is divided into 2 parts, each left blank or marked with pips, usu. from 1 to 6. **2.** one of these pieces.

don, *v.* donned, donning. to put on (clothing, etc.).

donate, *v.,* **-nated, -nating.** to present as a gift, esp. to a fund or cause. **– donation,** *n.* **– donor,** *n.*

done, *v.* past participle of **do.**

donkey, *n., pl.* **-keys.** *n.* a domesticated ass used as a beast of burden.

doodle, *v.,* **-dled, -dling.** to scribble idly.

doom, *n.* **1.** fate or destiny, esp. adverse fate. *–v.* **2.** to destine, esp. to an adverse fate. **3.** to pronounce judgment against.

door, *n.* a movable barrier of wood, etc., commonly turning on hinges or sliding in a groove, for closing and opening a passage or opening, etc.

dope, *n., v.,* doped, doping. *–n.* **1.** *Colloq.* any drug, esp. a narcotic. **2.** *Colloq.* information or data. **3.** *Colloq.* a stupid person. *–v.* **4.** *Colloq.* to affect with dope or drugs.

dormant

dor·mant, *adj.* lying asleep; inactive as in sleep.

dormi·tory, *n., pl.* **-tories.** a (large) room for sleeping, for the inmates of a school or other institution.

dorsal, *adj. Zool.* of, pertaining to, or situated on the back.

dosage, *n.* 1. the administration of medicine in doses. 2. the amount of a medicine to be given.

dose, *n.* a quantity of medicine prescribed to be taken at one time.

doss, *v. Colloq.* to make a temporary sleeping place for oneself (*down*).

dos·sier, *n.* a bundle of documents on the same subject, esp. information about a particular person.

dot, *n., v.,* **dotted, dotting.** –*n.* 1. a small spot on a surface. 2. a small, roundish mark made with or as with a pen. 3. anything relatively small or specklike. 4. a full stop; a decimal point. –*v.* 5. to mark with or as with a dot or dots.

dote, *v.,* **doted, doting.** 1. to bestow excessive love or fondness (*on* or *upon*). 2. to be weak-minded, esp. from old age. – **dotage,** *n.*

dotty, *adj.,* **-tier, -tiest.** *Colloq.* crazy; eccentric.

double, *adj., n., v.,* **-led, -ling,** *adv.* –*adj.* 1. twice as great, heavy, strong, etc. 2. twofold in form, size, amount, extent, etc. 3. composed of 2 like parts or members; paired. –*n.* 4. a twofold size or amount. 5. a duplicate; a counterpart. 6. *Films, etc.* a substitute actor who takes another's place, as in dangerous scenes. 7. (*pl.*) a game in which there are 2 players on each side. –*v.* 8. to make or become double or twice as great. 9. to bend or fold with one part upon another (*over,* *up, back,* etc.) 10. to convey a second person on a horse, bicycle or motorcycle. 11. to turn (*back*) on a course. 12. to share quarters, etc. (*up*). 13. to serve in 2 capacities.

double bass, *n.* the largest instrument of the violin family.

double-cross, *v. Colloq.* to prove treacherous to; betray.

doubt, *v.* 1. to be uncertain in opinion about. 2. to distrust. 3. to feel uncertainty as to something. –*n.* 4. undecidedness of opinion or belief; a feeling of uncertainty. 5. distrust; suspicion.

doubt·ful, *adj.* 1. admitting of or causing doubt; uncertain. 2. undecided in opinion or belief; hesitating.

douche /duʃ/, *n.* a jet or current of water applied to a body part, organ, or cavity for medicinal, hygienic, or contraceptive purposes.

dough, *n.* 1. flour or meal combined with water, milk, etc., in a mass for baking into bread, cake, etc. 2. *Colloq.* money.

dough·nut, *n.* a small ring-shaped cake.

dour /'daʊə, dʊə/, *adj.* hard; severe; stern.

douse, *v.,* **doused, dousing.** 1. to plunge into water or the like; drench. 2. *Colloq.* to put out or extinguish (a light).

dove, *n.* a bird of the pigeon family.

dowa·ger, *n.* a woman who holds some title or property from her deceased husband, esp. the widow of a king, duke, or the like.

dowdy, *adj.,* **-dier, -diest.** ill-dressed; not smart, or stylish.

dowel, *n.* a wooden pin, usu. round,

dowel

fitting into corresponding holes in 2 adjacent pieces.

down[1], *adv.* **1.** into or in a lower position or condition: *to jump down.* **2.** on or to the ground. **3.** to a point of submission, inactivity, etc. **4.** to or in a position spoken of as lower, as the south, etc. **5.** from a greater to less bulk, strength, etc. **6.** in due position or state. **7.** on paper or in a book: *Take this letter down.* **8.** in cash; at once. **9. down to earth**, practical; realistic. –*prep.* **10.** to, towards, or at a lower place or on or in: *We climbed down the mountain.* **11.** to, towards, near, or at a lower station, condition, or rank in. –*adj.* **12.** downwards; going or directed downwards. **13.** *Games.* losing or behind an opponent by a specified number of points, holes, etc. **14.** depressed; unhappy. –*n.* **15.** a downward movement; descent. **16.** *Colloq.* a grudge. –*v.* **17.** to put or throw down; subdue. **18.** to drink down.

down[2], *n.* **1.** the first feathering of young birds. **2.** a soft hairy growth.

down[3], *n.* (*usu. pl.*) open, rolling, upland country with fairly smooth slopes.

down·fall, *n.* **1.** descent to a lower position or standing; overthrow; ruin. **2.** a fall, as of rain or snow.

down·pour, *n.* a heavy, continuous fall of water, rain, etc.

dow·ry, *n., pl.* **-ries.** the money, goods, or estate which a woman in some cultures brings to her husband at marriage.

doy·en, *n.* the senior member of a body, class, profession, etc.

doze, *v.*, **dozed, dozing.** to sleep lightly or fitfully.

drain

doz·en, *n., pl.* **dozen, dozens.** a group of 12 units or things.

drab, *adj.*, **drabber, drabbest. 1.** having a dull grey colour. **2.** dull.

draft, *n.* **1.** a drawing, sketch, or design. **2.** a first or preliminary form of any writing. **3.** conscription. **4.** a written order for payment of money. **5.** an animal or animals selected and separated from the herd or flock. –*v.* **6.** to draw the outlines or plan of, or sketch. **7.** to draw up in written form, as a first draft.

drag, *v.*, **dragged, dragging.** –*v.* **1.** to draw with force, effort, or difficulty; pull heavily or slowly along. **2.** to introduce, as an irrelevant matter (*in*). **3.** to protract or pass tediously (*out* or *on*). **4.** to be drawn or hauled along. **5.** to trail on the ground. **6.** to proceed or pass with tedious slowness. –*n.* **7.** something used by or for dragging. **8.** the force due to the relative airflow exerted on an aeroplane or other body tending to reduce its forward motion. **9.** *Colloq.* somebody or something that is extremely boring. **10.** *Colloq.* women's clothes, when worn by men.

drag·net, *n.* a net to be drawn along the bottom of a river, pond, etc., or along the ground, to catch something.

drag·on, *n.* **1.** a mythical monster, usu. a huge winged reptile and often spouting fire. **2.** a fierce, violent person. **3.** any of various lizards, as the frill-necked lizard of Aust.

drag·on·fly, *n., pl.* **-flies.** a large, harmless insect which feeds on mosquitoes and other insects.

drain, *v.* **1.** to draw off gradually, as

161

drain

a liquid. **2.** to draw off or take away completely. –*n.* **3.** that by which anything is drained, as a pipe or conduit. **4.** gradual or continuous outflow, withdrawal, or expenditure.

drain·age, *n.* **1.** the act or process of draining. **2.** a system of drains, artificial or natural.

drake, *n.* a male duck.

dram, *n.* **1.** a unit of measurement in the imperial system. **2.** a small quantity of anything.

drama, *n.* **1.** a composition in prose or verse presenting in dialogue a story involving conflict, esp. one intended to be acted; a play. **2.** any series of events having dramatic interest or results.

dra·matic, *adj.* **1.** of or pertaining to the drama. **2.** characteristic of or appropriate to the drama; involving conflict or contrast.

drank, *v.* past tense and former past participle of **drink**.

drape, *v.*, **draped, draping.** to cover or hang with cloth or some fabric.

draper, *n.* a dealer in textiles and cloth goods, etc. – **drapery**, *n.*

drastic, *adj.* acting with force or violence; violent.

draught, *n.* **1.** a current of air, esp. in a room, chimney, stove, or any enclosed space. **2.** an act of drawing or pulling, or that which is drawn. **3.** the drawing of a liquid from its receptacle, as of ale from a cask. **4.** an amount drunk as a continuous act. **5.** (*pl.* construed *as sing.*) a game played by 2 people each with 12 pieces on a chequered board. –*adj.* **6.** being on draught; drawn as required. **7.** used or suited for drawing loads.

dray

draughts·man, *n.*, *pl.* -**men.** one who draws sketches, plans, or designs.

draw, *v.*, **drew, drawn, drawing**, *n.* –*v.* **1.** to cause to come in a particular direction as by a pulling force; pull; drag; lead (*along, away, in, out, off,* etc.). **2.** to bring towards oneself or itself, as by inherent force or influence; attract. **3.** to pick or choose at random. **4.** to sketch in lines or words. **5.** to frame or formulate, as a distinction. **6.** to pull out to full or greater length; stretch. **7.** to write or sign a draft, cheque, etc. **8.** to use or practise the art of tracing figures; practise drawing. **9.** *Games.* to leave a contest undecided. –*n.* **10.** the act of drawing. **11.** that which is drawn, as a lot. **12.** *Sport.* a drawn or undecided contest.

draw·back, *n.* a hindrance or disadvantage.

draw·bridge, *n.* a bridge of which the whole or a part may be drawn up or aside to prevent access or to leave a passage open for boats, etc.

drawer, *n.* **1.** a sliding compartment, as in a piece of furniture, that may be drawn out. **2.** (*pl.*) pants (def. 2). **3.** *Finance.* one who draws an order, draft, etc.

drawing-pin, *n.* a short broad-headed tack designed to be pushed in by the thumb. Also, **thumbtack**.

drawing room, *n.* a room for the reception and entertainment of visitors.

drawl, *v.* **1.** to say or speak with slow, lingering utterance. –*n.* **2.** the act or utterance of one who drawls.

drawn, *v.* **1.** past participle of **draw**. –*adj.* **2.** haggard; tired; tense.

dray, *n.* a low, strong cart.

dread, v. 1. to fear greatly. –n. 2. terror or apprehension. 3. deep awe. –adj. 4. greatly feared.

dread·ful, adj. 1. causing great dread, fear, or terror. 2. *Colloq.* extremely bad, unpleasant, ugly, etc.

dream, n., v., **dreamed** or **dreamt, dreaming.** –n. 1. a succession of images or ideas present in the mind during sleep. 2. a vision voluntarily indulged in while awake; daydream. 3. something or somebody of an unreal beauty or charm. 4. a hope; an inspiration; an aim. –v. 5. to have a dream or dreams (of).

dreary, adj., **drearier, dreariest.** 1. causing sadness or gloom. 2. dull.

dredge, n., v., **dredged, dredging.** –n. 1. a contrivance for gathering material or objects from the bed of a river, etc. –v. 2. to clear out with a dredge. 3. to find, usu. with some difficulty (*up*).

dreg, n. 1. (*usu. pl.*) the sediment of wine or other drink. 2. (*usu. pl.*) any waste or worthless residue.

drench, v. 1. to wet thoroughly; steep; soak. 2. *Vet. Sci.* to administer medicine to (an animal), esp. by force.

dress, n., adj., v., **dressed** or **drest, dressing.** –n. 1. the chief outer garment worn by women, consisting of a skirt and a bodice. 2. clothing; apparel; garb. –adj. 3. of or for a dress or dresses. 4. of or for a formal occasion. –v. 5. to equip with clothing, ornaments, etc.; attire. 6. to arrange a display in; ornament or adorn. 7. to prepare (fowl, skins, timber, stone, ore, etc.) by special processes. 8. to treat (wounds or sores). 9. to clothe oneself, esp. in formal or evening clothes. 10. **dress down**, to scold severely.

dress·age /'drɛsaʒ/, n. the art of training a horse in deportment, etc.

dress circle, n. the first gallery above the floor in a theatre, etc.

dresser, n. a kitchen sideboard.

dressing-gown, n. a loose gown or robe generally worn over night attire.

dressing-table, n. a table or stand, usu. surmounted by a mirror.

drew, v. past tense of **draw**.

drib·ble, v., **-bled, -bling.** 1. to (let) fall or flow in drops or small quantities. 2. to drivel; slaver. 3. *Soccer, Hockey, etc.* to advance (a ball) by a series of short kicks or pushes.

dried, v. past tense and past participle of **dry**.

drift, n. 1. a driving movement or force; impulse; impetus. 2. *Navig.* movement or course under the impulse of water currents, wind, etc. 3. the course of anything; tendency; aim. 4. something driven, or formed by driving. –v. 5. to be carried along by currents of water or air, or by the force of circumstances. 6. to wander aimlessly.

drill[1], n. 1. a tool or machine for drilling or boring holes. 2. *Mil.* training in formal marching or other precise military or naval movements. 3. any strict, methodical training or exercise. –v. 4. to pierce or bore a hole in (anything). 5. to impart (knowledge) by strict training or discipline.

drill[2], n. strong twilled cotton.

drink, v., **drank, drunk, drinking**, n. –v. 1. to swallow water or other liquid. 2. to take in alcoholic bev-

drink

erages, esp. habitually or to excess. 3. to take in (a liquid) in any manner; absorb. 4. to take in through the senses, esp. with eagerness and pleasure. —n. 5. any liquid which is swallowed to quench thirst, for nourishment, etc.

drip, v., dripped or dript, dripping, n. —v. 1. to fall in drops, as a liquid. —n. 2. the liquid that drips. 3. *Med.* the continuous slow infusion of fluid containing nutrients or drugs to a patient. 4. *Colloq.* an insipid or colourless person; a fool.

drip·ping, n. fat exuded from meat in cooking.

drive, v., drove, driven, driving. —v. 1. to send along, away, off, in, out, back, etc., by compulsion; force along. 2. to overwork. 3. to cause and guide the movement of (an animal, vehicle, etc.). 4. to convey or travel in a vehicle. 5. to go along before an impelling force; be impelled. 6. to rush or dash violently. 7. to make an effort to reach or obtain; aim (at). —n. 8. the act of driving. 9. *Psychol.* a source of motivation. 10. a vigorous onset or onward course. 11. a united effort to accomplish some purpose, esp. to raise money. 12. energy and initiative. 13. a trip in a driven vehicle.

drive-in, n. 1. a cinema so designed that patrons park in front of an outdoor screen and view the film while seated in their cars. —*adj.* 2. (of any shop, etc.) catering for customers in cars.

drivel, v., -elled, -elling. —v. 1. to let saliva flow from the mouth or mucus from the nose. —n. 2. childish, idiotic, or silly talk.

driz·zle, v., -zled, -zling. —v. 1. to

dross

rain gently and steadily in fine drops. —n. 2. a very light rain; mist.

droll, *adj.* amusingly odd.

drone[1], n. the male of the honey bee and other bees, stingless and making no honey.

drone[2], v., droned, droning. 1. to make a dull, continued, monotonous sound; hum; buzz. 2. to speak in a monotonous tone.

drool, v. *Colloq.* →drivel (def. 1).

droop, v. to sink, bend, or hang down, as from weakness or exhaustion.

drop, n., v., dropped or dropt, dropping. —n. 1. a small quantity of liquid which falls in a more or less spherical mass. 2. a minute quantity of anything. 3. something like or likened to a drip. 4. the distance or depth to which anything drips or falls. 5. a steep slope. 6. a fall in degree, amount, value, etc. —v. 7. to (let) fall in globules or small portions, as water or other liquid. 8. to (let) fall vertically like a drop. 9. to withdraw; disappear (out). 10. to fall lower in condition, degree, etc.; sink. 11. to fall or move (back, behind, to the rear, etc.). 12. to make a visit, come or go casually or unexpectedly (in, by, across, etc.). 13. to utter or express casually or incidentally, as a hint. 14. to send or post (a note, etc.). 15. to set down, as from a ship, car, etc. 16. to omit (a letter or syllable) in pronunciation or writing. 17. to cease to keep up or have to do with.

drop-out, n. one who decides to opt out of conventional society, or an educational institution.

drop·pings, n. *pl.* animal dung.

dross, n. waste matter, esp. that

dross

drought, n. 1. dry weather; lack of rain. 2. scarcity.

drove[1], v. past tense of **drive**.

drove[2], n., v., **droved, droving**. –n. 1. a number of oxen, sheep, or swine driven in a group; herd; flock. 2. a large crowd of human beings, esp. in motion. –v. 3. to drive (herds of cattle or flocks of sheep) usu. over long distances to market. – **drover**, n.

drown, v. 1. to suffocate by immersion in water or other liquid. 2. to make inaudible; muffle; obscure.

drowse, v., **drowsed, drowsing**. to be sleepy; be half asleep. – **drowsy**, adj.

drudge, n. one who labours at servile or uninteresting tasks; a hard toiler. – **drudgery**, n.

drug, n., v., **drugged, drugging**. –n. 1. a chemical substance given to prevent or treat disease. 2. a habit-forming medicinal substance; a narcotic. –v. 3. to stupefy or poison with a drug.

drum, n., v., **drummed, drumming**. –n. 1. a musical instrument consisting of a hollow body covered at one or both ends with a tightly stretched membrane, which is struck with the hand, or stick(s). 2. something resembling a drum in shape or structure, or in the noise it produces. –v. 3. to beat or play a drum. 4. to beat rhythmically; perform (a tune) by drumming. 5. to drive or force by persistent repetition. 6. to seek or obtain (trade, customers, etc.) (up).

drunk, adj. 1. intoxicated or affected with, or as with, strong drink. –n. Colloq. 2. a drunken person. –v. 3.

duck

past participle and former past tense of **drink**. – **drunkard**, n.

dry, adj., **drier, driest**, v., **dried, drying**, n., pl. **dries**. –adj. 1. free from moisture; not moist; not wet. 2. having little or no rain. 3. not under, in, or on water. 4. not yielding water or other liquid. 5. desiring drink; thirsty. 6. dull; uninteresting 7. humorous or sarcastic in an unemotional or impersonal way. 8. (of wines) not sweet. –v. 9. to make or become dry; to free from or lose moisture. –n. 10. a dry state, condition, or place. 11. Colloq. **dry ginger ale**: brandy and dry. – **dryly, drily**, adv.

dry-clean, v. to clean (garments, etc.) with chemical solvents, etc., rather than water.

dual /ˈdjuəl/, adj. 1. of or pertaining to 2. 2. composed of consisting of 2 parts; twofold.

dub[1], v., **dubbed, dubbing**. to strike lightly with a sword in the ceremony of conferring knighthood; make, or designate as, a knight.

dub[2], v., **dubbed, dubbing**. to change the soundtrack (of a film or videotape), as in substituting a dialogue in another language.

dubi·ous, adj. 1. doubtful; marked by or occasioning doubt. 2. wavering or hesitating in opinion; inclined to doubt.

duch·ess, n. the wife or widow of a duke.

duck[1], n. any of numerous wild or domesticated web-footed swimming birds.

duck[2], v. 1. to plunge the whole body or the head momentarily under water. 2. to avoid a blow, unpleasant task, etc.

duck

duck³, *n. Cricket.* a batsman's score of nought.

duck·ling, *n.* a young duck.

duct, *n.* any tube, canal, or conduit by which fluid or other substances are conducted or conveyed.

duc·tile, *adj.* 1. capable of being hammered out thin, as certain metals; malleable. 2. capable of being moulded or shaped; plastic.

dud, *Colloq. n.* 1. any thing or person that proves a failure; useless; defective. –*adj.* 2. useless; defective.

dud·geon, *n.* a feeling of offence or resentment; anger.

due, *adj.* 1. immediately payable. 2. owing, irrespective of whether the time of payment has arrived. 3. rightful; proper; fitting. 4. attributable, as to a cause. 5. expected to be ready, be present, or arrive. –*n.* 6. (*usu. pl.*) a payment due, as a charge, a fee, a membership subscription, etc.

duel, *n.* a prearranged combat between 2 persons, fought with deadly weapons according to an accepted code of procedure.

duet, *n.* a musical composition for 2 voices or performers.

duffer, *n.* a plodding, stupid, or incompetent person.

dug, *v.* past tense and past participle of **dig**.

dugong /'dugɒn/, *n.* a tropical plant-eating water mammal with flipper-like forelimbs.

duke, *n.* 1. a sovereign prince, the ruler of a small state. 2. (in Britain) a nobleman of the highest rank after that of a prince. – **ducal**, *adj.*

dulcet, *adj.* agreeable to the feelings, the eye, or, esp., the ear; soothing.

dull, *adj.* 1. slow of understanding;

dun

obtuse; stupid. 2. not intense or acute. 3. listless; spiritless. 4. tedious; uninteresting. 5. not bright, intense, or clear. –*v.* 6. to make or become dull.

duly, *adv.* 1. in a due manner; properly. 2. in due season; punctually. 3. adequately.

dumb, *adj.* 1. without the power of speech. 2. made, done, etc., without speech. 3. stupid; dull.

dumb·found, *v.* to strike dumb with amazement.

dummy, *n., pl.* -mies; *adj.* –*n.* 1. an imitation or copy of something, as for display, to indicate appearance, exhibit clothing, etc. 2. *Colloq.* a stupid person. 3. (esp. in buying land) one put forward to act for others while ostensibly acting for himself. 4. *Cards.* a. (in bridge) the dealer's partner whose hand is exposed and played by the dealer. b. the cards so exposed. 5. a rubber teat, etc., given to a baby to suck. –*adj.* 6. counterfeit; sham; imitation.

dump, *v.* 1. to throw down in a mass; fling down or drop heavily. 2. to get rid of; hand over to somebody else. –*n.* 3. a place where rubbish is deposited. 4. *Mil.* a collection of ammunition, stores, etc., to be distributed for use. 5. *Colloq.* a place, house, or town that is poorly kept up, and generally of wretched appearance.

dump·ling, *n.* a rounded mass of steamed dough.

dumps, *n.pl. Colloq.* in the phrase **the dumps**, a dull, gloomy state of mind.

dumpy, *adj.*, dumpier, dumpiest. short and stout; squat.

dun¹, *v.*, dunned, dunning. to make

dun

repeated and insistent demands upon, esp. for the payment of a debt.

dun², *adj.* dull or greyish brown.

dunce, *n.* a dull-witted or stupid person.

dune, *n.* a sand hill or sand ridge formed by the wind, usu. in desert regions or near lakes and oceans.

dung, *n.* manure; excrement, esp. of animals.

dun·geon, *n.* any strong, close cell, esp. underground.

dunk, *v.* 1. to immerse in water. 2. to dip (biscuits, etc.) into coffee, milk, etc.

duo, *n.*, *pl.* **duos**, **dui**. a pair of singers, entertainers, etc.

duo·denum, *n.* the first portion of the small intestine. – **duodenal**, *adj.*

dupe, *n.* a person who is imposed upon or deceived.

duple, *adj.* double; twofold.

duplex, *adj.* 1. twofold; double. –*n.* 2. a two-storey block of flats or home units, one flat occupying each floor.

dup·li·cate, *adj.*, *n.*, *v.*, -**cated**, -**cating**. –*adj.* 1. exactly like or corresponding to something else. 2. double; consisting of or existing in 2 corresponding parts. –*n.* 3. a copy exactly like an original. –*v.* 4. to make an exact copy of; repeat; – **duplication**, *n.*

duplicator, *n.* machine for producing copies of text or pictures, now largely replaced by the *photocopier*.

dup·li·ci·ty, *n.*, *pl.* -**ties**. 1. the quality or state of being double. 2. deceitfulness in speech or conduct.

dur·able, *adj.* having the quality of lasting or enduring. – **durability**, *n.*

dur·ation, *n.* 1. continuance in time.

dye

2. the length of time anything continues.

duress /djuˈrɛs/, *n.* 1. constraint; compulsion. 2. forcible restraint of liberty; imprisonment.

Durex, *n.* condom, proprietary name often used generically.

during, *prep.* 1. throughout the continuance of. 2. in the course of.

dusk, *n.* a state between light and darkness; twilight.

dusky, *adj.*, **duskier**, **duskiest**. somewhat dark; dark-coloured.

dust, *n.* 1. earth or other matter in fine, dry particles. 2. any finely powdered substance, as sawdust. –*v.* 3. to free from dust; wipe the dust from. 4. to sprinkle with dust or powder. – **dusty**, *adj.*

duty, *n.*, *pl.* -**ies**. 1. that which one is bound to do by moral or legal obligation. 2. action required by one's position or occupation. 3. a levy imposed by law on the import, export, sale, or manufacture of goods, the legal recognition of deeds and documents, etc. – **dutiful**, *adj.* **dutiable**, *adj.*

dwarf, *n.* 1. an unusually small person or thing. –*adj.* 2. of unusually small stature or size. –*v.* 3. to cause to appear or seem small in size, extent, character, etc.

dwell, *v.*, **dwelt** or **dwelled**, **dwelling**. 1. to abide as a permanent resident. 2. to continue for a time. 3. to linger over in thought, speech, or writing; to emphasise (*on* or *upon*).

dwelling, *n.* a place to live; home.

dwin·dle, *v.*, -**died**, -**dling**. to become smaller and smaller.

dye, *n.*, *v.*, **dyed**, **dyeing**. –*n.* 1. a colouring material or matter. –*v.* 2. to colour or stain.

dying, *adj.* 1. ceasing to live; approaching death. 2. given, uttered, or manifested just before death. 3. drawing to a close.

dyke, *n.* an embankment for restraining the waters of the sea or a river.

dy·nam·ic, *adj.* 1. of or pertaining to force not in equilibrium (opposed to *static*) or to force in any state. 2. pertaining to or characterised by energy or effective action.

dy·nam·ics, *n.* the science or principles of forces acting in any field.

dy·na·mite, *n.* 1. a high explosive. 2. *Colloq.* anything or anyone potentially dangerous and liable to cause trouble. 3. *Colloq.* anything or anyone exceptional.

dy·na·mo, *n., pl.* **-mos.** 1. any rotating machine in which mechanical energy is converted into electrical energy. 2. *Colloq.* a forceful, energetic person.

dyn·as·ty /'dɪnəsti/, *n., pl.* **-ties.** a sequence of rulers from the same family or stock. – **dynastic**, *adj.*

dyne, *n.* the unit of force in the centimetre-gram-second system, equal to 10×10^{-6} newtons. *Symbol:* dyn

dys·en·tery, *n.* an infectious disease marked by inflammation and ulceration of the lower part of the bowels, with diarrhoea and bleeding.

dys·lex·ia, *n.* impairment in reading ability, often associated with other disorders esp. in writing and co-ordination. – **dyslectic**, *n., adj.*

dys·pep·sia, *n.* upset digestion; indigestion.

Ee

E, e, *n., pl.* **E's** or **Es, e's** or **es.** the 5th letter of the English alphabet.

each, *adj.* **1.** every, of 2 or more considered individually. –*pron.* **2.** each one. –*adv.* **3.** apiece.

eager, *adj.* keen or ardent in desire or feeling.

eagle, *n.* a large bird of prey.

ear[1], *n.* **1.** the organ of hearing. **2.** attention, esp. favourable.

ear[2], *n.* that part of a cereal plant which contains the grains or kernels.

earl, *n.* a British nobleman.

early, *adv.,* **-lier, -liest,** *adj.* –*adv.* **1.** in or during the first part of some division of time, or of some course or series. **2.** before the usual or appointed time. –*adj.* **3.** occurring in the first part of some division of time, or of some course or series. **4.** occurring before the usual or appointed time. **5.** belonging to a period far back in time.

earn, *v.* **1.** to gain by labour or service. **2.** to gain (interest or profit). **3.** to merit or deserve. – **earnings,** *n.pl.*

earn·est, *adj.* serious in intention, or effort.

ear·phone, *n.* a small device for converting electric signals from soundwaves, fitted into the ear or held close to it.

ear·shot, *n.* range of hearing.

earth, *n.* **1.** (*oft. cap.*) the planet which we inhabit. **2.** the softer part of the land, as distinguished from rock; soil. **3.** *Elect.* a conducting connection between an electric circuit or equipment and the ground. – **earthen,** *adj.*

earth·quake, *n.* tremors or earth movements in the earth's crust.

earthy, *adj.,* **earthier, earthiest. 1.** of the nature of soil. **2.** coarse or unrefined. **3.** direct; unaffected.

ease, *n., v.,* **eased, easing.** –*n.* **1.** freedom from pain or annoyance of any kind. **2.** freedom from stiffness or constraint. –*v.* **3.** to give rest or relief to. **4.** to make or become less in severity, pressure, etc. **5.** to facilitate. **6.** to move slowly and with great care.

easel, *n.* a frame for supporting an artist's canvas, etc.

ease·ment, *n. Law.* a right held by one person to make use of the land of another.

east, *n.* **1.** a cardinal point of the compass corresponding to the point where the sun is seen to rise. –*adj.* **2.** directed or proceeding towards the east. **3.** (of wind) coming from the east. –*adv.* **4.** in the direction of the sunrise; towards or in the east. – **eastern,** *adj.* – **easterly,** *adj., n.*

easy, *adj.,* **easier, easiest. 1.** not difficult; requiring no great effort. **2.** free from pain, worry, or care. **3.** *Colloq.* having no firm preferences in a particular matter. **4.** free from constraint or embarrassment.

easy·going, *adj.* taking matters in an easy way.

eat, *v.,* **ate, eaten, eating. 1.** to take (food) into the mouth and swallow for nourishment. 2. to consume by or as by devouring. 3. to make a way as by gnawing or corrosion.

eaves, *n.pl.* the overhanging lower edge of a roof.

eaves·drop, *v.*, **-dropped, -dropping.** to listen secretly.

ebb, *n.* 1. the falling of the tide. –*v.* 2. to flow back or away. 3. to decline or decay.

ebony, *n.* a hard, durable wood, usu. black.

ebul·lient /əˈbʊljənt, əˈbʌl-, əˈbjul-/, *adj.* bubbling like a boiling liquid.

eccen·tric, *adj.* 1. not conventional; odd. 2. not concentric, as 2 circles or spheres. –*n.* 3. an eccentric person. – **eccentricity**, *n.*

ecclesi·as·tical /əklɪziˈæstəkəl/, *adj.* of or pertaining to the church or the clergy.

eche·lon /ˈɛʃəlɒn/, *n.* a level of command.

echidna, *n., pl.* **-nas, -nae.** a spine-covered insectivorous monotreme; spiny anteater.

echo, *n., pl.* **echoes**, *v.*, **echoed, echoing.** 1. a repetition of sound, produced by the reflection of soundwaves from an obstructing surface. –*v.* 2. to emit an echo; resound with an echo. 3. to repeat by or as by an echo.

eclec·tic, *adj.* selecting; choosing from various sources.

ec·lipse, *n., v.*, **eclipsed, eclipsing.** –*n.* 1. *Astron.* the obscuring of the light of a satellite by the intervention of its primary planet between it and the sun. –*v.* 2. to make dim by comparison.

ecol·ogy, *n.* the branch of biology which treats of the relations between organisms and their environment.

eco·nomi·cal, *adj.* avoiding waste or extravagance; thrifty.

eco·nomics, *n.* the science treating of the production, distribution, and consumption of goods and services. – **economist**, *n.* – **economic**, *adj.*

econo·mise, *v.*, **-mised, -mising.** to be thrifty; avoid waste.

economy, *n., pl.* **-mies.** 1. thrifty management; frugality. 2. the management of the resources of a community.

ecstasy, *n., pl.* **-sies.** overpowering emotion, esp. delight. – **ecstatic**, *adj.*

ecu·meni·cal, *adj.* tending to work towards unity among all Christian Churches.

eczema, *n.* an inflammatory disease of the skin.

eddy, *n., pl.* **eddies.** a current at variance with the main current in a stream of liquid or gas.

edge, *n., v.*, **edged, edging.** –*n.* 1. a brim or margin. 2. a brink or verge. 3. one of the narrow surfaces of a thin, flat object. 4. the line in which 2 surfaces of a solid object meet. 5. sharpness or keenness. –*v.* 6. to put an edge on. 7. to move, advance or force gradually.

edible, *adj.* fit to be eaten.

edict /ˈidɪkt/, *n.* an authoritative proclamation or command.

edi·fice, *n.* a building, esp. large.

edify, *v.*, **-fied, -fying.** to instruct or benefit, esp. morally. – **edification**, *n.*

edit, *v.* 1. to direct the preparation of (a newspaper, magazine, etc.). 2. to make (a film, sound recording, etc.)

edit

by cutting and arranging, etc. **3.** to revise and correct. – **editor**, n.

edi·tion, n. one of a number of printings of the same book, newspaper, etc.

edit·orial, n. **1.** an article, in a newspaper or the like, presenting the opinion or comment of an editor. –adj. **2.** of or pertaining to an editor.

edu·cate, v., **-cated, -cating.** to develop the faculties and powers of by teaching. – **education**, n.

eel, n. a snakelike fish.

eerie, adj., **eerier, eeriest.** weird or uncanny.

efface, v., **effaced, effacing.** to wipe out; destroy.

effect, n. **1.** a result; consequence. **2.** power to produce results. **3.** the state of being operative. **4.** a mental impression produced, as by a painting, speech, etc. **5.** (of stage properties) a sight, sound, etc., giving a particular impression. **6.** (pl.) personal property. –v. **7.** to produce as an effect. – **effective**, adj.

effec·tual, adj. producing, or capable of producing, an intended effect.

effemi·nate, adj. (of a man) soft or delicate to an unmanly degree.

effer·vesce, v., **-vesced, -vescing.** to give off bubbles of gas, as fermenting liquors. – **effervescence**, n.

effete /ə'fiːt/, adj. that has lost its vigour or energy.

effi·cacy, n. capacity to produce effects. – **efficacious**, adj.

effi·cient, adj. **1.** competent; capable. **2.** avoiding waste. – **efficiency**, n.

either

effigy, n., pl. **-gies.** a representation or image, as of a person.

efflu·ent /'efluənt/, adj. **1.** flowing out. –n. **2.** that which flows out. – **effluence**, n.

effort, n. exertion of power, physical or mental.

effron·tery, n. shameless or impudent boldness.

effu·sive, adj. unduly demonstrative.

egali·tarian, adj. asserting the equality of all people.

egg[1], n. **1.** the female reproductive cell. **2.** this cell with a hard shell, produced by birds, esp. the domestic hen.

egg[2], v. to incite or urge; encourage.

egg·plant, n. a plant with purple egg-shaped fruit; aubergine.

ego, n. the 'I' or self of any person.

ego·tism /'egətɪzəm, 'igə-/, n. **1.** self-conceit. **2.** selfishness.

egress, n. a means or place of going out.

egret, n. any of various herons.

eider·down, n. (a quilt filled with) down or soft feathers, esp. from a type of duck.

eight, n. a cardinal number, 7 plus 1. – **eighth**, adj., n.

eigh·teen, n. a cardinal number, 10 plus 8. – **eighteenth**, adj., n.

eighty, n., pl. **eighties.** a cardinal number, 10 times 8. – **eightieth**, adj., n.

eisted·dfod /ə'stedfəd/, n. a competitive music festival.

either, adj. **1.** one or the other of 2: *Sit at either end of the table.* **2.** each of the 2; the one and the other: *trees on either side of the river.* –pron. **3.** one or the other but not

either

both: *Take either.* –*conj.* 4. (used as one of 2 coordinate alternatives): *Either phone or write by Tuesday.* –*adv.* 5. (used after negative sentences coordinated by *and*, *or*, *nor*).

ejac·u·late, *v.*, **-lated**, **-lating**. 1. to utter suddenly and briefly. 2. to discharge seminal fluid. – **ejaculation**, *n.*

eject, *v.* 1. to drive or force out. 2. to propel oneself out of an aeroplane, etc., by means of a mechanical device. – **ejection**, *n.*

eke, *v.*, **eked**, **eking**. 1. to use (resources) frugally (*out*). 2. to contrive to make (a living).

elabo·rate, *adj.*, *v.*, **-rated**, **-rating**. –*adj.* 1. worked out with great care and nicety of detail. –*v.* 2. to give additional or fuller treatment (*on* or *upon*). – **elaboration**, *n.*

elapse, *v.*, **elapsed**, **elapsing**. (of time) to slip by or pass away.

elas·tic, *adj.* 1. rebounding or returning to the original shape. –*n.* 2. elastic material.

elate, *v.*, **elated**, **elating**. to put in high spirits. – **elation**, *n.*

elbow, *n.* 1. the bend or joint of the arm between upper arm and forearm. –*v.* 2. to push with or as with the elbow; jostle.

elder[1], *adj.* 1. older; senior. –*n.* 2. a person who is older than oneself. 3. one of the older and more influential men of a tribe or community.

elder[2], *n.* a type of flowering shrub or tree of the Nthn Hemisphere.

elder·ly, *adj.* approaching old age.

eldest, *adj.* oldest.

elect, *v.* 1. to select by vote, as for an office. 2. to determine in favour of (a course of action, etc.). –*adj.* 3. selected for an office, but not yet

electron

inducted: *the Chairman elect.* – **elector**, *n.*

elec·tion, *n.* the selection by vote of a person or persons for office.

elec·tive, *adj.* 1. (of an office) filled by election. –*n.* 2. an option.

elec·tor·al, *adj.* pertaining to electors or election.

elec·tor·ate, *n.* the body of voters and geographical subdivision represented by an elected member; constituency.

elec·tric, *adj.* pertaining to, derived from, produced by, or involving electricity. Also, **electrical**.

elec·tri·cian, *n.* one who installs, operates, maintains, or repairs electrical devices.

elec·tri·city, *n.* an agency producing various physical phenomena, due to the presence and movements of electrons, protons, and other electrically charged particles.

elec·tri·fy, *v.*, **-fied**, **-fying**. 1. to charge with or subject to electricity. 2. to excite.

elec·tro·cute, *v.*, **-cuted**, **-cuting**. to kill by electricity. – **electrocution**, *n.*

elec·trode, *n.* a conductor of electricity through which a current enters or leaves an electrolytic cell, etc.

elec·trol·ysis /əlɛkˈtrɒləsəs, i-, ˌɛlakˈtrɒləsəs/, *n.* 1. the decomposition of a chemical compound by an electric current. 2. *Surg.* the destruction of tumours, hair roots, etc., by an electric current. – **electrolytic**, *adj.*

electro·magnetic, *adj.* relating to the interaction of electricity and magnetism.

elec·tron, *n.* an elementary particle which is a constituent of all atoms.

electronics

elec·tronics, *n.* the investigation and application of phenomena involving the movement of electrons in valves, transistors, etc. – **electronic**, *adj.*

ele·gant, *adj.* tastefully fine or luxurious in dress, manner, etc. – **elegance**, *n.*

elegy, *n., pl.* **-gies.** a mournful or plaintive poem, esp. a lament for the dead. – **elegiac**, *adj.*

ele·ment, *n.* **1.** a component or constituent part of a whole. **2.** (*pl.*) the rudimentary principles of an art, science, etc. **3.** (*pl.*) atmospheric agencies or forces. **4.** *Chem.* one of a class of substances which consist entirely of atoms having the same number of protons in the nucleus. **5.** *Elect.* the heating unit of an electric domestic appliance. – **elemental**, *adj.*

elemen·tary, *adj.* pertaining to or dealing with elements, rudiments, or first principles.

ele·phant, *n.* a very large, herbivorous mammal, having a long, prehensile trunk and curved tusks. – **elephantine**, *adj.*

ele·vate, *v.,* **-vated, -vating.** to move or raise to a higher place or position; lift up.

ele·vation, *n.* **1.** height above sea or ground level. **2.** the act of elevating. **3.** the state of being elevated. **4.** *Archit.* a drawing or design of a face of a building.

ele·vator, *n.* →**lift** (def. 6).

eleven, *n.* a cardinal number, 10 plus 1. – **eleventh**, *adj., n.*

elf, *n., pl.* **elves.** one of a class of imaginary beings, usu. a diminutive human. – **elfish, elvish**, *adj.*

emaciated

elfin, *adj.* small and sprightly or delicate.

elicit /ə'lɪsət/, *v.* to draw or bring out or forth; evoke.

elig·ible /'elədʒəbəl/, *adj.* fit or proper to be chosen.

elimi·nate, *v.,* **-nated, -nating.** to get rid of; expel; remove. – **elimination**, *n.*

elite, *n.* (construed as *pl.*) persons of the highest (esp. social) class.

elixir, *n.* **1.** a medicine. **2.** a preparation formerly believed to prolong life.

elk, *n., pl.* **elks** or **elk.** the largest existing European and Asiatic deer.

ellipse, *n.* a plane figure, oval in shape or outline. – **elliptical**, *adj.*

ellip·sis, *n., pl.* **-ses.** *Gram.* the omission from a sentence of something which would complete or clarify the construction. – **elliptical**, *adj.*

elm, *n.* a large, deciduous tree.

elo·cution, *n.* manner of speaking or reading in public.

elon·gate, *v.,* **-gated, -gating.** to draw out to greater length. – **elongation**, *n.*

elope, *v.,* **eloped, eloping.** to run away with a lover, usu. in order to marry without parental consent.

elo·quent, *adj.* characterised by fluent, persuasive expression.

else, *adv.* other than the person or the thing mentioned.

else·where, *adv.* somewhere else.

elu·ci·date, *v.,* **-dated, -dating.** to make lucid or clear; explain.

elude, *v.,* **eluded, eluding.** to avoid or escape by dexterity or artifice.

emaci·ated, *adj.* lean; wasted, as by disease.

173

emanate

ema·nate, *v.*, -nated, -nating. to flow out, issue, or proceed as from a source or origin. – **emanation**, *n.*

eman·ci·pate, *v.*, -pated, -pating. to free from restraint.

emas·cu·late, *v.*, -lated, -lating. 1. to castrate. 2. to deprive of strength or vigour.

embalm, *v.* to treat (a dead body) in order to preserve from decay.

em·bank·ment, *n.* a bank, mound, dyke, or the like, raised to hold back water, carry a road, etc.

em·bargo, *n.*, *pl.* -goes. 1. an order of a government prohibiting the movement of merchant vessels from or into its ports. 2. any restriction imposed upon commerce by law.

embark, *v.* to board a ship, plane, etc., as for a voyage.

em·bar·rass, *v.* to disconcert; make uncomfortable, self-conscious, etc.

em·bassy, *n.*, *pl.* -sies. the official headquarters of an ambassador.

em·bel·lish, *v.* to beautify by or as by ornamentation; enhance.

ember, *n.* a small coal, still glowing.

em·bezzle, *v.*, -zled, -zling. to appropriate (money, etc.) fraudulently to one's own use.

emblem, *n.* an object or representation which identifies persons, things, qualities, etc.; symbol.

embody, *v.* to give bodily or concrete form to. – **embodiment**, *n.*

embol·ism, *n.* a blockage in the blood.

emboss, *v.* to raise designs on the surface of (leather, etc.).

em·brace, *v.*, -braced, -bracing, *n.* – *v.* 1. to hug. 2. to accept (an idea, etc.) willingly. 3. to include or contain. – *n.* 4. a hug.

emotion

em·broi·der, *v.* 1. to decorate with ornamental needlework. 2. to adorn or embellish rhetorically, esp. with fictitious additions. – **embroidery**, *n.*

em·broil, *v.* 1. to involve in contention or strife. 2. to throw into confusion; complicate.

embryo /ˈɛmbriəʊ/, *n.*, *pl.* -os. an organism in the earlier stages of its development, as a mammal still in its mother's body.

emend, *v.* to free from faults or errors; correct. – **emendation**, *n.*

emer·ald, *n.* a green gemstone.

emerge, *v.*, emerged, emerging. to rise or come forth, as from concealment or obscurity.

emer·gency, *n.*, *pl.* -cies. a sudden and urgent occasion for action.

emer·gent, *adj.* (of a nation) recently independent or newly formed as a political entity. – **emergence**, *n.*

emery, *n.* a granular mineral substance used for grinding and polishing.

emetic, *adj.* inducing vomiting, as a medicinal substance.

emi·grate, *v.*, -grated, -grating. to leave one country or region to settle in another. – **emigration**, *n.* – **emigrant**, *n.*

emi·nent, *adj.* 1. high-ranking; distinguished. 2. conspicuous. – **eminence**, *n.*

emis·sary /ˈɛmɪsəri, -əsri/, *n.*, *pl.* -saries. an agent sent on a mission.

emit, *v.*, emitted, emitting. to give out or forth; discharge. – **emission**, *n.*

emol·lient, *adj.* soothing.

emo·tion, *n.* 1. any of the feelings of

joy, sorrow, fear, hate, love, etc. 2. a state of agitation of the feelings.

emo·tional, *adj.* 1. easily affected by emotion. 2. appealing to the emotions.

emo·tive, *adj.* exciting emotion.

em·pathy, *n.* an entering into the feeling or spirit of another; understanding. – **empathetic**, *adj.* – **empathise**, *v.*

em·peror, *n.* the sovereign or supreme ruler of an empire. – **empress**, *n.fem.*

em·phasis, *n.*, *pl.* -ses. 1. stress laid upon, or importance or significance attached to anything. 2. intensity or force of expression, action, etc. – **emphasise**, *v.* – **emphatic**, *adj.*

empire, *n.* an aggregate of nations or peoples ruled over by an emperor or other powerful sovereign or government.

empiri·cal, *adj.* derived from or guided by experience or experiment.

employ, *v.* 1. to use the services of (a person). 2. to make use of (an instrument, means, etc.). 3. to occupy or devote (time, energies, etc.). –*n.* 4. service: *He is in my employ.* – **employment**, *n.* – **employer**, *n.* – **employee**, *n.*

empty, *adj.*, -tier, -tiest, *v.*, -tied, -tying. –*adj.* 1. containing nothing. 2. vacant; unoccupied. –*v.* 3. to make empty.

emu, *n.* a large, flightless, Aust. bird.

emu·late, *v.*, -lated, -lating. to imitate with intent to equal or excel.

emul·sion, *n.* a suspension of a liquid in another liquid.

enable, *v.*, -bled, -bling. to make able; give power, means, or ability to.

enact, *v.* 1. to make into an act or statute. 2. to act the part of.

enamel, *n.* 1. a glassy substance, usu. opaque, applied by fusion to the surface of metal, pottery, etc. 2. a paint, varnish, etc. 3. *Anat., Zool.* the hard outer structure of the crowns of the teeth.

en·cap·su·late, *v.*, -lated, -lating. to enclose in or as in a capsule. – **encapsulation**, *n.*

en·chant, *v.* 1. to cast a spell over; bewitch. 2. to delight; charm.

en·clave /ˈɛnkleɪv/, *n.* a portion of a country surrounded by the territory of another country.

en·close, *v.*, -closed, -closing. 1. to shut in; close in on all sides. 2. to insert in the same envelope, etc., with the main letter, etc. – **enclosure**, *n.*

en·compass, *v.* 1. to encircle; surround. 2. to enclose; contain.

en·counter, *v.* 1. to come upon; meet with, esp. unexpectedly. 2. to meet (a person, military force, etc.) in conflict. –*n.* 3. a meeting with a person or thing, esp. casually or unexpectedly. 4. a meeting in conflict or opposition; battle; combat.

en·courage, *v.*, -raged, -raging. 1. to inspire with courage, spirit, or confidence. 2. to stimulate by assistance, approval, etc. – **encouragement**, *n.*

en·croach, *v.* to trespass (*on* or *upon*) the property or rights of another.

en·cumber, *v.* to impede or hamper. – **encumbrance**, *n.*

ency·clo·paedia, *n.* a work treating separately various topics from all branches of knowledge, usu. in alphabetical arrangement.

end

end, *n.* **1.** an extreme or farthermost part of anything extended in space. **2.** anything that bounds an object at one of its extremities. **3.** the act of coming to an end; termination. **4.** a purpose or aim. **5.** a remnant or fragment. –*v.* **6.** to bring to an end or natural conclusion. **7.** to form the end of. **8.** to come to an end; terminate; cease. **9.** to issue or result.

endear, *v.* to make dear, esteemed, or beloved.

en·deavour, *v.* **1.** to make an effort; try; strive. –*n.* **2.** an attempt.

en·demic, *adj.* peculiar to a particular people or locality, as a disease.

endive, *n.* a herb, used in salads and as a cooked vegetable.

endo·crine gland, *n.* a gland (as the thyroid gland) which secretes hormones directly to the blood or lymph.

en·dorse, *v.*, **-dorsed, -dorsing. 1.** to write (something) on the back of a document, etc. **2.** to sign one's name on (a commercial document or other instrument), esp. to acknowledge payment. **3.** (of a branch of a political party) to select as a candidate for an election. Also, **indorse**. – **endorsement**, *n.*

endow, *v.* **1.** to provide with a permanent fund or source of income. **2.** to furnish as with some gift, faculty, or quality; equip. – **endowment**, *n.*

endue, *v.*, **-dued, -duing.** to invest or endow with some gift, quality, or faculty.

endure, *v.*, **-dured, -during. 1.** to sustain without impairment or yielding; undergo. **2.** to bear without

engrave

resistance or with patience; tolerate. – **endurance**, *n.*

enema, *n.*, *pl.* **enemas, enemata.** a fluid injected into the rectum, as to evacuate the bowels.

enemy, *n.*, *pl.* **-mies. 1.** one who cherishes hatred or harmful designs against another; an adversary or opponent. **2.** a (subject of a) hostile nation or state. **3.** something harmful or prejudicial.

energy, *n.*, *pl.* **-gies. 1.** (the capacity or habit of) vigorous activity. **2.** ability to produce action or effect. – **energetic**, *adj.*

ener·vate, *v.*, **-vated, -vating.** to deprive of nerve, force, or strength; weaken.

en·force, *v.*, **-forced, -forcing. 1.** to put or keep in force; compel obedience to. **2.** to obtain (payment, obedience, etc.) by force or compulsion.

engage, *v.*, **-gaged, -gaging. 1.** to occupy the attention or efforts of (a person, etc.). **2.** to secure for aid, employment, use, etc.; hire. **3.** to reserve or secure. **4.** to attract or please. **5.** to betroth (usu. used in the passive). **6.** to bring (troops) into conflict. **7.** *Mech.* to cause to become interlocked; interlock with.

en·gen·der, *v.* to produce, cause, or give rise to.

engine, *n.* any mechanism or machine designed to convert energy into mechanical work.

engi·neer, *n.* **1.** one versed in the design, construction, and use of engines or machines. –*v.* **2.** to plan, construct, or manage as an engineer. **3.** to arrange, manage or carry through by skilful or artful contrivance.

en·grave, *v.*, **-graved, -graving.** to cut

176

engrave

(letters, designs, etc.) on a hard surface.

en·gross, *v.* to occupy wholly, as the mind or attention.

engulf, *v.* to swallow up in or as in a chasm.

en·hance, *v.*, **-hanced**, **-hancing**. to raise to a higher degree.

enigma /əˈnɪgmə/, *n.* somebody or something puzzling or inexplicable. – **enigmatic**, *adj.*

enjoy, *v.* 1. to experience with joy; take pleasure in. 2. to have the benefit of. 3. to find or experience pleasure for (oneself). – **enjoyment**, *n.*

en·large, *v.*, **-larged**, **-larging**. 1. to make larger. 2. to speak or write at length. – **enlargement**, *n.*

en·lighten, *v.* to give knowledge; instruct.

enlist, *v.* to (secure someone to) enter into some cause or activity.

enmity, *n.*, *pl.* **-ties**. a feeling or condition of hostility.

enor·mous, *adj.* 1. greatly exceeding the common size, extent, etc.; huge; immense. 2. outrageous or atrocious. – **enormity**, *n.*

enough, *adj.* 1. adequate for the want or need; sufficient. –*n.* 2. an adequate quantity or number. –*adv.* 3. sufficiently.

en·quire, *v.*, **-quired**, **-quiring**. to seek information by questioning; ask. Also, **inquire**. – **enquiry**, *n.*

enrage, *v.*, **-raged**, **-raging**. to put into a rage; infuriate.

enrich, *v.* 1. to supply with riches. 2. to enhance; make finer.

enrol, *v.*, **-rolled**, **-rolling**. to insert the name of (a person) in a roll or register. – **enrolment**, *n.*

enthusiasm

en·sconce, *v.*, **-sconced**, **-sconcing**. to settle securely or snugly.

ensem·ble /ɒnˈsɒmbəl/, *n.* 1. all the parts of a thing taken together. 2. a harmonious set of clothes and accessories.

ensign /ˈɛnsaɪn/, *n.* 1. a flag or banner, as of a nation. 2. any sign, token, or emblem.

en·slave, *v.*, **-slaved**, **-slaving**. to make a slave of.

en·snare, *v.*, **-snared**, **-snaring**. to trap.

ensue, *v.*, **-sued**, **-suing**. to follow, esp. in immediate succession.

ensure, *v.*, **-sured**, **-suring**. to make sure or certain to come, occur, etc.

entail, *v.* 1. to bring on or involve by necessity or consequences. 2. to cause (anything) to be inherited by a fixed series of possessors.

en·tangle, *v.*, **-gled**, **-gling**. to involve in difficulties, etc.

entente /ɒnˈtɒnt/, *n.* an understanding or agreement between parties.

enter, *v.* 1. to come or go in. 2. to make a beginning (*on* or *upon*). 3. to become a member of, or join. 4. to make a record of, as in a register.

enter·prise, *n.* 1. a project, esp. one that requires boldness or energy. 2. boldness or readiness in undertaking. 3. a company organised for commercial purposes.

enter·tain, *v.* 1. to hold the attention of agreeably; divert; amuse. 2. to receive as a guest. 3. to admit into the mind; consider. – **entertainment**, *n.*

en·thral /ɛnˈθrɒl, ən-/, *v.*, **-thralled**, **-thralling**. to captivate; charm.

en·thu·siasm, *n.* absorbing or controlling possession of the mind by any interest or pursuit; lively in-

177

enthusiasm

terest. – **enthusiast**, *n.* – **enthusiastic**, *adj.* – **enthuse**, *v.*

entice, *v.*, **-ticed**, **-ticing**. to draw on by exciting hope or desire.

entire, *adj.* 1. whole; complete. 2. full or thorough. – **entirety**, *n.*

en·title, *v.*, **-tled**, **-tling**. to give (a person or thing) a title, right, or claim to something.

entity, *n., pl.* **-ties**. something that has a real existence; thing.

entomology, *n.* the branch of zoology that treats of insects.

entour·age /ɒntʊˈrɑːʒ, -rɑʒ-/, *n.* any group of people accompanying or assisting someone.

en·trails /ˈɛntreɪlz/, *n.pl.* the inner organs of the body, esp. the intestines.

en·trance[1] /ˈɛntrəns/, *n.* 1. the act of entering. 2. a point or place of entering.

en·trance[2] /ɛnˈtrɑːns, -ˈtræns, ən-/, *v.*, **-tranced**, **-trancing**. to fill with delight.

entrant, *n.* a competitor in a contest.

en·treat, *v.* to make supplication to (a person); beseech; implore. – **entreaty**, *n.*

entrée /ˈɒntreɪ/, *n.* a dish served before the main course.

en·trench, *v.* 1. to dig trenches for defensive purposes around (oneself, a military position, etc.). 2. to establish very strongly.

entre·preneur /ɒntrəprəˈnɜː/, *n.* one who organises and manages any enterprise.

en·trust, *v.* 1. to invest with a trust or responsibility. 2. to give (something) in trust (*to*).

entry, *n., pl.* **-tries**. 1. an act of entering. 2. a place of entrance.

epicure

en·twine, *v.*, **-twined**, **-twining**. to twine with, about, or around.

enumer·ate, *v.*, **-rated**, **-rating**. to name one by one.

enun·ci·ate, *v.*, **-ated**, **-ating**. to utter or pronounce (words, etc.), esp. in a particular manner.

envelop, *v.* to wrap up in or as in a covering.

enve·lope, *n.* a cover for a letter, etc., usu. sealable.

envi·able /ˈɛnviəbəl/, *adj.* that is to be envied; highly desirable.

envi·ous, *adj.* full of envy.

environ·ment, *n.* the aggregate of surrounding things, conditions, or influences. – **environmental**, *adj.*

en·virons /ɛnˈvaɪrənz, ən-/, *n.pl.* surrounding parts or districts.

en·visage /ɛnˈvɪzɪdʒ, -zɪdʒ, ən-/, *v.*, **-aged**, **-aging**. to form a mental image of.

envoy, *n.* a diplomatic agent.

envy, *n., pl.* **-vies**, *v.*, **-vied**, **-vying**. –*n.* 1. a feeling of discontent at another's good fortune, etc. 2. desire for some advantage possessed by another. –*v.* 3. to regard with envy.

enzyme, *n.* any protein capable of catalysing a chemical reaction necessary to the cell.

eon, *n.* →**aeon**.

epaulet, *n.* an ornamental shoulder piece worn on uniforms.

ephem·eral, *adj.* short-lived; transitory.

epic, *adj.* 1. of or pertaining to poetry dealing with a series of heroic achievements or events, in a long narrative with elevated style. –*n.* 2. an epic poem. 3. any novel or film depicting great events.

epi·cure, *n.* one who cultivates a

epicure

refined taste, esp. in food. – **epicurean**, adj., n.

epi·demic, adj. 1. affecting at the same time a large number of people in a locality. –n. 2. a temporary prevalence of a disease.

epi·dermis, n. Anat. the outer layer of the skin. – **epidermal**, adj.

epi·dural /ɛpi'djurəl/, adj. situated on or over the membrane forming the outermost covering of the brain and spinal cord: *an epidural anaesthetic*.

epi·gram, n. any witty or pointed saying tersely expressed.

epi·lepsy, n. a nervous disease usu. characterised by convulsions. – **epileptic**, adj., n.

epi·logue, n. 1. a speech by one of the actors after the conclusion of the action of a play. 2. a concluding part added to a literary work.

epis·co·pal, adj. pertaining to a bishop.

epi·sode, n. 1. an incident in the course of a series of events. 2. (in radio, television, etc.) any of the separate programs constituting a serial. – **episodic**, adj.

epis·tle, n. a letter, esp. one of formal or didactic character.

epi·taph, n. a commemorative inscription on a tomb, etc.

epi·thet, n. a term applied to a person or thing to express an attribute.

epi·tome /əˈpɪtəmi/, n. something typically representing or characteristic of something else. – **epitomise**, v.

epoch, n. a period of time of distinct character.

equable, adj. 1. uniform, as motion or temperature. 2. tranquil, as the mind.

equity

equal, adj., n., v., **equalled, equalling.** adj. 1. like or alike in quantity, degree, value, etc. 2. evenly proportioned or balanced. 3. having adequate powers, ability, or means. –n. 4. one who or that which is equal. –v. 5. to make, be, or become equal to. – **equalise**, v. – **equality**, n.

equa·nimity, n. calmness of mind or temper; composure.

equate, v., **equated, equating.** 1. to state the equality of or between. 2. to regard, treat, or represent as equivalent.

equa·tion, n. Maths. an expression of, or a proposition asserting, the equality of 2 quantities, employing the sign = between them.

equa·tor, n. the great circle of the earth, midway between the Nth and Sth Poles. – **equatorial**, adj.

eques·trian, adj. of or pertaining to horsemen or horsemanship.

equi·lateral, adj. having all the sides equal.

equi·librium, n. a state of rest due to the action of forces that counteract each other.

equine, adj. of or resembling a horse.

equi·nox, n. the time when the sun crosses the plane of the earth's equator, making night and day all over the earth of equal length. – **equinoctial**, adj.

equip, v., **equipped, equipping.** to furnish or provide with whatever is needed for any task or services.

equip·ment, n. tools, machines, resources, etc., needed for a job.

equity, n., pl. **-ties.** 1. fairness; impartiality. 2. the interest of a shareholder of common stock in a company. 3. the value of an owner's

equity

share (in an asset subject to a mortgage). – **equitable**, *adj.*

equi·va·lent, *adj.* 1. equal in value, measure, force, effect, significance, etc. 2. corresponding in position, function, etc. –*n.* 3. that which is equivalent.

equi·vocal /ə'kwɪvəkəl, i-/, *adj.* questionable; dubious; suspicious.

equivo·cate /ə'kwɪvəkeɪt, i-/, *v.*, **-cated, -cating.** to use equivocal or ambiguous expressions, esp. in order to mislead.

era, *n.* 1. an epoch. 2. a system of chronological notation reckoned from a given date.

eradi·cate, *v.*, **-cated, -cating.** to remove or destroy utterly.

erase, *v.*, **erased, erasing.** to rub or scrape out, as written letters, etc.

erect, *adj.* 1. upright in position or posture. –*v.* 2. to build; construct; raise. 3. to raise and set in an upright or perpendicular position. – **erection**, *n.*

ermine /'ɜmən/, *n.*, *pl.* **-mines** (*esp. collectively*) **-mine.** a weasel of nthn regions, which turns white in winter. See **stoat**.

erode, *v.*, **eroded, eroding.** to wear away, esp. by action of wind and water. – **erosion**, *n.* – **erosive**, *adj.*

erogen·ous /ə'rɒdʒənəs, ɛ-, i-/, *adj.* arousing or tending to arouse sexual desire. – **erogeneity**, *n.*

erotic, *adj.* 1. of or pertaining to sexual love. 2. arousing or satisfying sexual desire.

err, *v.* to be mistaken or incorrect.

errand, *n.* a short journey for a specific purpose.

errant, *adj.* wandering or travelling. – **errantry**, *n.*

erratic, *adj.* 1. irregular in conduct

esquire

or opinion. 2. having no certain course; wandering.

erro·neous, *adj.* containing error; mistaken; incorrect.

error, *n.* 1. deviation from accuracy or correctness. 2. a mistake.

eru·dition, *n.* learning; scholarship. – **erudite**, *adj.*

erupt, *v.* 1. (of a volcano, geyser, etc.) to eject matter. 2. to break out suddenly or violently, as if from restraint. – **eruption**, *n.*

esca·late, *v.*, **-lated, -lating.** to intensify. – **escalation**, *n.*

esca·lator, *n.* a continuously moving staircase.

esca·pade, *n.* a reckless proceeding; a wild prank.

escape, *v.*, **-caped, -caping,** *n.* –*v.* 1. to slip or get away, as from confinement or restraint. 2. to slip away from or elude (pursuers, captors, etc.). 3. to fail to be noticed or recollected by (a person). –*n.* 4. an act or instance of escaping.

escarp·ment, *n.* a long, cliff-like ridge of rock, or the like.

eschew /əs'tʃu, ɛs-/, *v.* to abstain from; avoid.

escort, *n.* 1. one or more people or things accompanying another or others for protection, guidance, or courtesy. –*v.* 2. to attend or accompany as an escort.

eso·teric /ɛsə'tɛrɪk, ɛsoʊ-/, *adj.* understood by or meant for a select few; profound; recondite.

espi·onage, *n.* the practice of spying on others.

espla·nade, *n.* any open level space serving for public walks, etc.

esquire, *n.* a polite title (usu. abbreviated to *Esq.*) after a man's family name.

essay

essay, *n.* 1. a short literary composition on a particular subject. 2. an attempt. –*v.* 3. to try; attempt. 4. to put to the test; make trial of.

essence, *n.* 1. intrinsic nature; important elements or features of a thing. 2. a concentrated extract. – **essential**, *adj.*

establish, *v.* 1. to set up on a firm or permanent basis; institute; found. 2. to settle or install in a position, business, etc.. 3. to show to be valid or well grounded; prove.

establishment, *n.* 1. a place of business or residence. 2. an institution. 3. the act of establishing.

estate, *n.* 1. a piece of landed property, esp. a large one. 2. *Law*. a. property or possessions. b. the property of a deceased person, a bankrupt, etc., viewed as an aggregate. 3. a housing development. 4. social status or rank.

esteem, *v.* 1. to regard highly or favourably. 2. to set a value on; value. –*n.* 3. favourable opinion or judgment; respect or regard.

ester, *n.* a compound formed by the reaction between an organic acid and an alcohol.

estimable, *adj.* 1. worthy of esteem. 2. capable of being estimated.

estimate, *v.*, -mated, -mating, *n.* –*v.* 1. to form an approximate judgment or opinion regarding the value, amount, size, weight, etc., of; calculate approximately. –*n.* 2. an approximate judgment or calculation. – **estimation**, *n.*

estrange, *v.*, estranged, estranging. to alienate the affections of.

estuary, *n., pl.* -aries. 1. that part of the mouth of a river in which its current meets the sea's tides. 2. an arm or inlet of the sea.

et cetera, and others; and so forth; and so on. *Abbrev.*: etc.

etch, *v.* 1. to engrave (metals, etc.) with an acid or the like. 2. to fix in the memory.

eternity, *n., pl.* -ties. infinite time; duration without beginning or end. – **eternal**, *adj.*

ether, *n.* 1. *Chem.* a volatile, inflammable, colourless liquid used as an anaesthetic. 2. the upper regions of space; the heavens.

ethereal, *adj.* 1. light, airy or tenuous. 2. heavenly or celestial.

ethical, *adj.* pertaining to or dealing with moral principles.

ethics, *n.pl.* a system of moral principles, by which human actions and proposals may be judged good or bad or right or wrong.

ethnic, *adj.* 1. pertaining to or peculiar to a population, esp. to a language group, loosely also to a race. 2. of or pertaining to members of the community whose native language is not English.

ethos /ˈiːθɒs/, *n. Sociol.* the fundamental spiritual characteristics of a culture.

etiquette, *n.* conventional requirements as to social behaviour.

etymology, *n., pl.* -gies. 1. the study of historical linguistic change, esp. as applied to individual words. 2. the derivation of a word.

eucalyptus, *n., pl.* -tuses, -ti. any of a large genus of tall trees native to Aust. used for timber and oil; gum tree. Also, **eucalypt**.

eucharist, *n.* the celebration of the Lord's Supper.

eucharist

181

eulogy

eulogy, *n., pl.* **-gies.** a speech or writing in praise of a person or thing. – **eulogise,** *v.* – **eulogistic,** *adj.*

eunuch, *n.* a castrated man.

euphe·mism, *n.* 1. the substitution of a mild, indirect, or vague expression for a harsh or blunt one. 2. the expression so substituted. – **euphemistic,** *adj.*

eupho·ria, *n.* a feeling or state of well-being or elation. – **euphoric,** *adj.*

eutha·nasia, *n.* 1. painless death. 2. the putting to death of a person suffering from an incurable and painful disease.

eva·cu·ate, *v.,* **-ated, -ating.** 1. to leave empty; vacate. 2. to move (persons or things) from a threatened place, disaster area, etc.

evade, *v.,* **evaded, evading.** 1. to escape from by trickery or cleverness. 2. to avoid answering directly.

eval·uate, *v.,* **-ated, -ating.** to ascertain the value of.

evan·gelist, *n.* one who spreads the gospel. – **evangelical,** *adj.*

evapo·rate, *v.,* **-rated, -rating.** to turn to vapour; pass off in vapour. – **evaporation,** *n.*

evasion, *n.* the act or an instance of evading. – **evasive,** *adj.*

eve, *n.* the evening, or often the day, before a particular date or event.

even, *adj.* 1. level; flat; without irregularities; smooth. 2. on the same level; parallel. 3. uniform in action, character, or quality. 4. equal in measure or quantity. 5. divisible by 2 (opposed to *odd*). 6. leaving no balance of debt on either side. 7. equitable, impartial, or fair. –*adv.* 8. evenly. 9. still; yet

evoke

(used to emphasise a comparative). 10. indeed (used for stressing identity or truth of something). –*v.* 11. to make even; level; smooth.

evening, *n.* the latter part of the day and the early part of the night.

event, *n.* anything that happens; an occurrence, esp. one of some importance. – **eventful,** *adj.*

event·ual, *adj.* consequent; ultimate.

even·tu·ality, *n., pl.* **-ties.** a possible occurrence or circumstance.

ever, *adv.* 1. at all times. 2. continuously. 3. at any time.

every, *adj.* 1. each (referring one by one) to all the members of an aggregate). 2. all possible.

every·body, *pron.* every person.

every·day, *adj.* 1. daily. 2. ordinary; commonplace.

every·one, *pron.* every person.

every·thing, *pron.* every thing or particular of an aggregate or total; all.

every·where, *adv.* in every place.

evict, *v.* to expel (a person, esp. a tenant) from land, a building, etc., by legal process. – **eviction,** *n.*

evi·dence, *n.* 1. that which tends to prove or disprove something. 2. something that makes evident; an indication or sign.

evi·dent, *adj.* plain or clear to the sight or understanding.

evil, *adj.* 1. violating or inconsistent with the moral law; wicked. 2. harmful; injurious. 3. characterised by anger, irascibility, etc. –*n.* 4. that which is evil.

evince, *v.,* **evinced, evincing.** to show clearly; make evident.

evoke, *v.,* **evoked, evoking.** to call up

evoke

or forth, or produce (memories, feelings, etc.). **– evocation**, *n.* **– evocative**, *adj.*

evol·ution, *n.* **1.** any process of formation or growth; development. **2.** *Biol.* the continuous genetic adaptation of organisms or species to the environment.

evolve, *v.*, **evolved, evolving**. to develop gradually.

ewe, *n.* a female sheep.

ewer, *n.* a pitcher with a wide spout.

exacer·bate /ɛkˈsæsəbeɪt/, *v.*, **-bated, -bating**. to increase the bitterness or violence of (disease, ill feeling, etc.).

exact, *adj.* **1.** strictly accurate or correct. **2.** strict or rigorous. *–v.* **3.** to call for, demand, or require. **4.** to force or compel the payment, yielding, or performance of. **– exactitude, exactness**, *n.*

exagger·ate, *v.*, **-rated, -rating**. to magnify beyond the limits of truth. **– exaggeration**, *n.*

exalt, *v.* **1.** to elevate in rank, honour, power, character, quality, etc. **2.** to praise; extol. **– exaltation**, *n.*

exam, *n.* an examination (see **examine**, def. 2).

examine, *v.*, **-ined, -ining**. **1.** to inspect or scrutinise carefully; inquire into or investigate. **2.** to test the knowledge of, as by questions. **3.** to interrogate. **– examination**, *n.*

exam·ple, *n.* **1.** one of a number of things, or a part of something, taken to show the character of the whole. **2.** something to be imitated; a pattern or model. **3.** an instance serving for illustration; specimen.

exas·per·ate, *v.*, **-rated, -rating**. to

excise

irritate to a high degree. **– exasperation**, *n.*

exca·vate, *v.*, **-vated, -vating**. to make a hole or cavity in, as by digging. **– excavation**, *n.*

exceed, *v.* to go beyond in quantity, degree, rate, etc.

excel, *v.*, **-celled, -celling**. to surpass others.

excel·lence, *n.* the fact or state of excelling; superiority; eminence. **– excellent**, *adj.*

except, *prep.* **1.** with the exclusion of; excluding. *–conj.* **2.** with the exception (that).

excep·tion, *n.* **1.** something excepted; an instance or case not conforming to the general rule. **2.** opposition of opinion; objection; demurral.

excep·tion·al, *adj.* unusual; extraordinary.

excerpt, *n.* a passage taken out of a book or the like.

excess, *n.* **1.** the amount or degree by which one thing exceeds another. **2.** an extreme amount or degree. **3.** immoderate indulgence. **– excessive**, *adj.*

ex·change, *v.*, **-changed, -changing**, *n.* *–v.* **1.** to replace by something else; change for another. *–n.* **2.** the act or process of exchanging. **3.** a place for buying and selling commodities, securities, etc.: *the stock exchange.* **4.** a central office or station: *a telephone exchange.* **5.** the reciprocal transference of equivalent sums of money, as in the currencies of 2 different countries.

ex·chequer, *n.* a treasury, as of a state or nation.

excise[1] /ɛkˈsaɪz, ˈɛksaɪz/, *n.* **1.** an inland tax or duty on certain com-

183

excise

modities, as spirits, tobacco, etc. 2. a tax levied for a licence to carry on certain employments, pursue certain sports, etc. – **excisable**, *adj.*

excise[2] /'ɛksaɪz/, *v.*, **-cised, -cising.** to cut out or off. – **excision**, *n.*

ex·cite, *v.*, **-cited, -citing.** 1. to arouse or stir up the feelings of 2. to stir to action; stir up. 3. *Physiol.* to stimulate. – **excitement**, *n.* – **excitation**, *n.*

ex·claim, *v.* to cry out or speak suddenly and vehemently. – **exclamation**, *n.*

ex·clude, *v.*, **-cluded, -cluding.** to shut out or keep out; prevent the entrance of. – **exclusion**, *n.*

ex·clu·sive, *adj.* 1. excluding from consideration or account. 2. shutting out all other activities, means, etc. 3. single or sole. 4. disposed to shut out outsiders from association, intimacy, etc. 5. *Colloq.* fashionable.

ex·com·mu·ni·cate, *v.*, **-cated, -cating.** to cut off from communion or membership, esp. from the church.

ex·cre·ment /'ɛkskrəmənt/, *n.* waste matter discharged from the body, esp. the faeces.

ex·cres·cence /ɛks'krɛsəns/, *n.* abnormal growth or increase.

ex·crete, *v.*, **-creted, -creting.** to separate and eliminate from the blood or tissues, as waste matter. – **excreta**, *n.pl.* – **excretion**, *n.* – **excretory**, *adj.*

ex·cru·ci·at·ing, *adj.* very painful.

ex·cul·pate /'ɛkskʌlpeɪt, ɛks'kʌlpeɪt/, *v.*, **-pated, -pating.** to free from blame.

ex·cur·sion, *n.* 1. a short journey or trip for a special purpose. 2. deviation or digression.

exercise

excuse, *v.*, **-scused, -scusing**, *n.* – *v.* 1. to pardon or forgive. 2. to apologise for. 3. to justify. 4. to release from an obligation or duty. – *n.* 5. that which is offered as a reason for being excused. 6. an inferior or inadequate example of something specified.

exe·crable /'ɛksəkrəbəl/, *adj.* abominable.

exe·cute, *v.*, **-cuted, -cuting.** 1. to carry out; accomplish. 2. to put to death according to law. – **execution**, *n.*

execu·tive, *adj.* 1. of the kind requisite for practical performance or direction. 2. charged with or pertaining to execution of laws, or administration of affairs. – *n.* 3. a person or body having administrative authority.

execu·tor, *n. Law.* a person named by a testator in his will to carry out the provisions of his will. – **executrix**, *n.fem.*

exem·plary, *adj.* 1. worthy of imitation; commendable. 2. serving as a model, pattern or example.

ex·em·pli·fy, *v.*, **-fied, -fying.** 1. to show or illustrate by example. 2. to furnish, or serve as, an example of.

exempt, *v.* to free from an obligation or liability to which others are subject; release. – **exemptible**, *adj.* – **exemption**, *n.*

exer·cise, *n.*, *v.*, **-cised, -cising.** – *n.* 1. bodily or mental exertion. 2. something done or performed as a means of practice or training. 3. a putting into action, use, operation, or effect. – *v.* 4. to put through forms of practice or exertion, designed to train, develop, etc. 5. to put (faculties, rights, etc.) into action, practice, or use. 6. to discharge (a function); perform.

exert, v. to put forth, as power, ability or influence. – **exertion,** n.

exhale, v., **-haled, -haling.** to breathe out.

ex·haust, v. 1. to empty by drawing out the contents. 2. to use up or consume completely. 3. to drain of strength or energy. –n. 4. Mach. the escape of gases from the cylinder of an engine. – **exhaustion,** n. – **exhaustive,** adj.

ex·hi·bit, v. 1. to present for inspection. 2. to manifest or display. 3. to place on show. –n. 4. that which is exhibited. – **exhibition,** n.

exhila·rate, v., **-rated, -rating.** to enliven; stimulate; invigorate.

ex·hort, v. to urge, advise, or caution earnestly; admonish urgently. – **exhortation,** n.

ex·hume, v., **-humed, -huming.** to dig (something buried, esp. a dead body) out of the earth; disinter.

exigent /ˈɛksədʒənt/, adj. requiring immediate action or aid; urgent; pressing. – **exigency, exigence,** n.

exile, n., v., **-iled, -iling.** –n. 1. prolonged forced separation from one's country or home. –v. 2. to separate from country, home, etc.

exist, v. 1. to have actual being; be. 2. to have life or animation; live.

exit, n. 1. a way or passage out. 2. a going out or away; departure. –v. 3. to depart; go away.

exodus, n. a departure or emigration, usu. of a large number of people.

exon·erate, v., **-rated, -rating.** to clear, as of a charge; free from blame; exculpate.

exor·bi·tant, adj. exceeding the bounds of custom, propriety, or reason, esp. in amount or extent.

exor·cise, v., **-cised, -cising.** to seek to expel (an evil spirit) by religious or solemn ceremonies. – **exorcism,** n.

exotic, adj. 1. of foreign origin or character. 2. strikingly unusual or colourful in appearance or effect. – **exotically,** adv.

expand, v. 1. to increase in extent, size, volume, scope, etc. 2. to express in fuller form or greater detail; develop. – **expansion,** n.

ex·panse, n. an uninterrupted space or area; a wide extent of anything.

ex·pati·ate /əksˈpeɪʃieɪt, ɛk-/, v., **-ated, -ating.** to enlarge in discourse or writing.

ex·patri·ate, v., **-ated, -ating,** adj., n. –v. 1. to banish (a person) from his native country. 2. to withdraw (oneself) from residence in and/or allegiance to one's native country. –adj. 3. expatriated; exiled. –n. 4. an expatriated person.

expect, v. 1. to regard as likely to happen. 2. to look for with reason or justification. – **expectation,** n. – **expectancy,** n. – **expectant,** adj.

expec·torate, v., **-rated, -rating.** to eject or expel (phlegm, etc.) from the mouth; spit. – **expectorant,** n.

ex·pedi·ent, adj. 1. tending to promote some proposed or desired object. 2. conducive to advantage or interest, as opposed to right. –n. 3. a means to an end. – **expediency,** n.

ex·pe·dite /ˈɛkspədaɪt/, v., **-dited, -diting.** to speed up the progress of; hasten. – **expeditious,** adj.

ex·pe·dition, n. 1. an excursion, journey, or voyage made for some

expedition

specific purpose. 2. promptness or speed in accomplishing something.

expel, v., -pelled, -pelling. 1. to drive or force out or away. 2. to cut off from membership or relations.

expend, v. to use up. – expendable, adj.

expen·di·ture, n. 1. the act of expending. 2. that which is expended; expense.

expense, n. 1. cost or charge. 2. a cause or occasion of spending.

expen·sive, adj. costly.

ex·peri·ence, n., v., -enced, -encing. –n. 1. a particular instance of personally encountering or undergoing something. 2. the process or fact of personally observing, encountering, or undergoing something. 3. knowledge or practical wisdom gained from what one has observed, encountered, or undergone. –v. 1. to have experience of; meet with; undergo; feel. – experienced, adj., experiential, adj.

ex·peri·ment, n. 1. an act or operation for the purpose of discovering something unknown or testing a principle, supposition, etc. –v. 2. to try or test in order to find something out. – experimental, adj. – experimentation, n.

expert, n., adj. (a person) having special skill or knowledge in some particular field.

exper·tise /ɛkspɜ'tiːz/, n. expert skill or knowledge.

ex·pi·ate, v., -ated, -ating. to make amends or reparation for.

expire, v., -pired, -piring. 1. to come to an end; terminate. 2. to die. – expiration, expiry, n.

ex·plain, v. 1. to make plain or clear; render intelligible. 2. to make known in detail. 3. to give a meaning to; interpret. – explanation, n. – explanatory, adj.

ex·ple·tive /ək'spliːtɪv, ɛk-/, n. an exclamatory oath.

ex·pli·cate, v., -cated, -cating. to make plain or clear; explain; interpret. – explication, n.

ex·pli·cit, adj. leaving nothing merely implied; clearly expressed; unequivocal.

ex·plode, v., -ploded, -ploding. to expand with force and noise because of rapid chemical change or decomposition, as gunpowder, nitroglycerine, etc. – explosion, n. – explosive, adj, n.

ex·ploit[1] /'ɛksplɔɪt/, n. a striking or notable deed.

ex·ploit[2] /ək'splɔɪt, ɛk-/, v. 1. to turn to practical account; use for profit. 2. to use selfishly for one's own ends. – exploitation, n.

ex·plore, v., -plored, -ploring. 1. to traverse or range over (a region, etc.) for the purpose of discovery. 2. to look into closely; scrutinise; examine. – exploration, n. – exploratory, adj.

ex·ponent, n. 1. one who or that which expounds, explains, or interprets. 2. Maths. A symbol placed above and at the right of another symbol (the base), to denote to what power the latter is to be raised, as in x^3. – exponential, adj.

export, v. 1. to send (commodities) to other countries or places for sale, exchange, etc. –n. 2. the act of exporting; exportation. 3. an article exported. – exportation, n.

expose, v., -posed, -posing. 1. to lay

expose

open. 2. to uncover. 3. to display. 4. to hold up to public censure or ridicule. 5. *Photog.* to subject (a plate, film or paper) to the action of light. – **exposure**, *n.*

exposé, *n.* 1. a formal explanation. 2. public exposure of something discreditable.

ex·po·si·tion, *n.* 1. an exhibition or show. 2. an act of expounding, setting forth, or explaining.

ex·pos·tu·late, *v.*, -lated, -lating. to reason earnestly.

ex·pound, *v.* 1. to set forth or state in detail. 2. to explain; interpret.

ex·press, *v.* 1. to put (thought) into words. 2. to show, manifest, or reveal. 3. to press or squeeze out. –*adj.* 4. clearly indicated; distinctly stated. 5. special; particular; definite. 6. specially direct or fast, as a train, etc. –*n.* 7. an express train or bus. – **expressive**, *adj.*

ex·pres·sion, *n.* 1. the act of expressing or setting forth in words. 2. a particular word, phrase, or form of words. 3. indication of feeling, spirit, character, etc.

ex·pro·pri·ate, *v.*, -ated, -ating. to take, esp. for public use.

ex·pul·sion, *n.* the act of driving out or expelling.

ex·punge, *v.*, -punged, -punging. to erase; obliterate. – **expunction**, *n.*

ex·pur·gate /'ɛkspɜgeɪt, -pəgeɪt/, *v.*, -gated, -gating. to amend by removing offensive or objectionable matter.

ex·qui·site /'ɛkskwəzət, ək'skwɪzət, ɛk-/, *adj.* 1. of peculiar beauty or charm, or rare and appealing excellence. 2. intense or keen, as pleasure, pain, etc.

extra

extant /ɛk'stænt, 'ɛkstənt/, *adj.* in existence; still existing.

ex·tem·pore /ək'stɛmpəri, ɛk-/, *adv.* without premeditation or preparation.

extend, *v.* 1. to stretch out. 2. to increase the length or duration of. 3. to stretch out in various or all directions; expand. 4. to hold forth as an offer or grant. – **extension**, *n.*

ex·ten·sive, *adj.* of great extent.

extent, *n.* the space or degree to which something extends; length, area or volume.

ex·ten·u·ate, *v.*, -ated, -ating. to represent (a fault, offence, etc.) as less serious.

ex·te·ri·or, *adj.* 1. outer; being on the outer side. –*n.* 2. the outer surface or part; the outside; outward form or appearance.

ex·ter·mi·nate, *v.*, -nated, -nating. to get rid of by destroying; extirpate.

ex·ter·nal, *adj.* 1. of or pertaining to the outside or outer part; outer. 2. pertaining to the outward or visible appearance or show.

ex·tinct, *adj.* 1. extinguished, as a volcano. 2. having come to an end; without a living representative, as a species. – **extinction**, *n.*

ex·tin·guish, *v.* 1. to put out (a fire, light, etc.). 2. to put an end to or bring to an end.

ex·tir·pate /'ɛkstɜpeɪt, -stə-/, *v.*, -pated, -pating. to remove utterly; destroy totally.

extol, *v.*, -tolled, -tolling. to praise highly.

extort, *v.* to obtain (money, information, etc.) by force, torture, threat, or the like. – **extortion**, *n.* – **extortionate**, *adj.*

extra, *adj.* 1. beyond or more than

extra

what is usual, expected, or necessary; additional. –*n.* **2.** something extra or additional. –*adv.* **3.** over the usual or specified amount.

ex·tract, *v.* **1.** to draw forth or get out by force, as a tooth. **2.** to derive or obtain from a particular source. **3.** to take or copy out (matter from a book, etc.). **4.** to separate or obtain (a juice, ingredient, etc.) from a mixture. –*n.* **5.** something extracted. – **extraction**, *n.*

extra·dite, *v.*, **-dited, -diting.** to give up (a fugitive or prisoner) to another nation, state, or authority. – **extradition**, *n.*

ex·tra·neous, *adj.* not belonging or proper to a thing; foreign; not essential.

extra·ordinary, *adj.* **1.** beyond what is ordinary. **2.** exceptional; unusual; remarkable.

ex·trap·o·late /ek'stræpəleɪt/, *v.*, **-lated, -lating.** to infer (what is not known) from that which is known; conjecture.

extra·sensory, *adj.* outside the normal sense perception.

ex·trav·a·gant, *adj.* **1.** wasteful. **2.** exceeding the bounds of reason. – **extravagance**, *n.*

ex·trav·a·ganza, *n.* a lavish, elaborate opera or other entertainment.

ex·treme, *adj.*, **-tremer, -tremist.** –*adj.* **1.** of a character or kind farthest removed from the ordinary or average. **2.** utmost or exceedingly great in degree. **3.** last or final. –*n.* **4.** the utmost or highest degree, or a very high degree. **5.** one of 2 things as remote or different from each other as possible. – **extremity**, *n.*

ex·tri·cate, *v.*, **-cated, -cating.** to disentangle; disengage; free.

eyrie

ex·trin·sic, *adj.* extraneous.

extro·vert, *n. Psychol.* a person concerned chiefly with things outside his own self and thoughts.

ex·trude, *v.*, **-truded, -truding.** to force or press out.

exu·ber·ant /əg'zjubərənt, eg-/, *adj.* **1.** lavish; effusive. **2.** full of vigour; abounding in high spirits.

exude, *v.*, **-uded, -uding.** to come out gradually in drops like sweat through pores. – **exudation**, *n.*

exult, *v.* to show or feel a lively or triumphant joy.

eye, *n.*, *pl.* **eyes;** *v.*, **eyed, eyeing** or **eying.** –*n.* **1.** the organ of sight. **2.** the region surrounding the eye: *a black eye.* **3.** sight; vision. **4.** appreciative or discriminating visual perception: *an eye for colour.* **5.** (*oft. pl.*) look, glance, or gaze. **6.** (*oft. pl.*) estimation, or opinion. **7.** something resembling or suggesting the eye. **8.** *Meteorol.* the central region of low pressure in a tropical hurricane, where calm conditions prevail. –*v.* **9.** to fix the eyes upon; view. **10.** to observe or watch narrowly.

eye·ball, *n.* the ball or globe of the eye.

eye·brow, *n.* **1.** the arch or ridge above the eye. **2.** the fringe of hair growing upon it.

eye·lash, *n.* one of the short, thick, curved hairs growing as a fringe on the edge of an eyelid.

eyelid, *n.* the movable lid of skin which serves to cover and uncover the eyeball.

eye·sore, *n.* something unpleasant to look at.

eyrie, *n.* **1.** the nest of a bird of prey. **2.** an elevated habitation.

Ff

F, f, *n., pl.* **F's** or **Fs, f's** or **fs.** the 6th letter of the English alphabet.

fable, *n.* a short tale to teach a moral.

fabric, *n.* **1.** cloth, esp. woven. **2.** framework.

fab·ri·cate, *v.,* **-cated, -cating. 1.** to construct. **2.** to assemble. **3.** to invent (a legend, lie, etc.). – **fabrication,** *n.*

fabu·lous, *adj.* **1.** *Colloq.* wonderful. **2.** told about in fables; not true or real.

facade /fəˈsad, fæ-/, *n.* **1.** *Archit.* a face or front of a building. **2.** an appearance, esp. a misleading one.

face, *n., v.,* **faced, facing.** –*n.* **1.** the front part of the head. **2.** a look or expression on the face, e.g. showing ridicule, disgust, etc. **3.** *Colloq.* impudence. **4.** a surface. **5.** any one of the surfaces of a solid figure. **6.** *Print.* the style or appearance of type; typeface. –*v.* **7.** to have the front towards. **8.** to confront. **9.** to be turned (*to, towards*).

facet, *n.* **1.** one of the polished surfaces of a cut gem. **2.** aspect.

fac·etious /fəˈsiʃəs/, *adj.* intended or trying to be amusing.

facial, *adj.* **1.** of the face. –*n.* **2.** *Colloq.* a massage or treatment for the face.

facile /ˈfæsaɪl/, *adj.* **1.** proceeding, etc., with ease. **2.** glib.

facili·tate, *v.,* **-tated, -tating.** to make easier.

facil·ity, *n., pl.* **-ties. 1.** freedom from difficulty. **2.** building(s) designed for a specific purpose.

fac·simile /fækˈsɪməli/, *n.* an exact copy.

fact, *n.* **1.** truth; reality. **2.** something known to have happened. – **factual,** *adj.*

fac·tion, *n.* a smaller group of people within a larger group.

factor, *n.* **1.** one of the elements that contribute to bringing about any given result. **2.** *Maths.* one of 2 or more numbers, algebraic expressions, or the like, which when multiplied together produce a given product.

fac·torial, *n., Maths.* the product of an integer multiplied by all the lower integers.

fac·tory, *n., pl.* **-ries.** building(s), usu. with equipment, where goods are manufactured.

facul·ty, *n., pl.* **-ties. 1.** one of the powers of the mind, as memory, reason, speech, etc. **2.** *Educ.* one of the branches of learning in a university.

fad, *n.* a temporary, usu. irrational, pursuit, fashion, etc.

fade, *v.,* **faded, fading. 1.** to lose freshness or strength. **2.** to disappear or die gradually (*away, out*).

faeces /ˈfisiz/, *n.pl.* waste matter from the intestines; excrement.

fag, *v.,* **tagged, fagging.** –*v.* **1.** to tire (*out*). –*n.* **2.** *Colloq.* a cigarette.

faggot, *n.* a bundle of sticks.

Fahren·heit /ˈfærənhaɪt/, *adj.* of or pertaining to a scale of temperature in which the boiling point of water is 212°F.

fail

fail, *v.* **1.** to be unsuccessful. **2.** to become smaller or less. **3.** to neglect to perform or observe. **4.** to take (an examination, etc.) without passing. **5.** to declare (a person) unsuccessful in a test, course of study, etc. – *failure, n.*

faint, *adj.* **1.** lacking brightness, loudness, strength, etc. **2.** feeling weak. –*v.* **3.** to lose consciousness temporarily.

fair[1], *adj.* **1.** free from bias, dishonesty, or injustice. **2.** proper according to the rules. **3.** moderately good, large, or satisfactory. **4.** (of the weather) fine. **5.** of a light hue. **6.** beautiful. –*adv.* **7.** in a fair manner.

fair[2], *n.* **1.** an amusement show. **2.** an exhibition or display, esp. industrial.

fair·way, *n.* **1.** an unobstructed passage or way. **2.** *Golf.* that part of the course between tees and greens where the grass is kept short.

fairy, *n., pl.* **-ries.** a small magical being.

faith, *n.* **1.** confidence or trust in a person or thing. **2.** belief which is not based on proof. **3.** belief in the teachings of religion. **4.** a system of religious belief.

faith·ful, *adj.* **1.** strict or thorough in the performance of duty. **2.** that may be relied upon, or believed. **3.** true to fact or an original.

fake, *v.,* faked, faking, *n., adj. Colloq.* –*v.* **1.** to pretend. –*n.* **2.** something faked. **3.** one who fakes. –*adj.* **4.** designed to deceive or cheat.

falcon /ˈfælkən, ˈfɔlkən, ˈfɔːkən/, *n.* any of various birds of prey.

fall, *v.,* fell, fallen, falling, *n.* –*v.* **1.** to drop or come down suddenly. **2.** to become less or lower. **3.** to extend downwards. **4.** to succumb to temptation. **5.** to succumb to attack. **6.** to happen. **7.** to be naturally divisible (*into*). **8.** to lose animation, as the face. **9.** to slope, as land. **10. fall away, a.** to withdraw support. **b.** to decline; decay; perish. **11. fall in with,** to meet; retreat. **12. fall back on, a.** *Mil.* to retreat to. **b.** to have recourse to. **13. fall down,** *Colloq.* to fail. **14. fall flat,** to fail to have a desired effect. **15. fall for,** *Colloq.* to be deceived by. **b.** to fall in love with. **16. fall foul, a.** to come into collision, as ships. **b.** to come into conflict. **17. fall in, a.** to sink inwards. **b.** to take one's proper place in line, as a soldier. **c.** to agree. **18. fall in with, a.** to meet and become acquainted with. **b.** to agree. **19. fall off, a.** to drop off. **b.** to separate or withdraw. **c.** to decrease in number, amount, intensity, etc. **20. fall on** or **upon, a.** to assault; attack. **b.** to chance upon. **21. fall short, a.** to fail to reach a particular amount, degree, standard, etc. **b.** to prove insufficient. **22. fall through,** to come to naught; miscarry. **23. fall to, a.** to apply oneself; begin: *to fall to work, argument, etc.* **b.** to begin to eat. **24. fall under,** to be classed as; be included in. –*n.* **25.** the act of falling. **26.** (*usu. pl.*) a waterfall. **27.** *Chiefly U.S.* autumn.

fal·la·cy, *n., pl.* **-cies,** a misleading, or false notion, belief, etc. – *fallacious, adj.*

fal·li·ble, *adj.* liable to be deceived or mistaken; liable to err.

fallow, *adj.* ploughed and left unseeded for a season or more; uncultivated.

false — **fart**

false, *adj.*, **falser, falsest. 1.** not true or correct. **2.** used to deceive. **3.** not genuine. – **falsify**, *v.*

false·hood, *n.* a lie.

fal·setto, *n., pl.* **-tos.** an unnaturally or artificially high-pitched voice, esp. in a man.

falter, *v.* to hesitate or waver.

fame, *n.* widespread reputation. – **famed**, *adj.*

fami·liar, *adj.* **1.** commonly or generally known or seen. **2.** well-acquainted. **3.** easy; informal. – **familiarity**, *n.* – **familiarise**, *v.*

family, *n., pl.* **-lies. 1.** parents and their children, whether dwelling together or not. **2.** all those persons descended from a common ancestor. **3.** any group of related things. – **familial**, *adj.*

famine, *n.* extreme and general scarcity of food.

fam·ished, *adj. Colloq.* very hungry.

famous, *adj.* celebrated in fame; well known.

fan[1], *n., v.,* **fanned, fanning.** –*n.* **1.** any device for causing a current of air. –*v.* **2.** to move or agitate (the air) with, or as with, a fan. **3.** to spread (something) (*out*) like a fan.

fan[2], *n. Colloq.* an enthusiastic devotee or follower.

fan·atic, *n.* a person with an extreme and unreasoning enthusiasm or zeal, esp. in religious matters. – **fanatical**, *adj.* – **fanaticism**, *n.*

fancy, *n., pl.* **-cies,** *adj.,* **-cier, -ciest,** *v.,* **-cied, -cying.** –*n.* **1.** imagination. **2.** a mental image. whim; vagary. –*adj.* **3.** adapted to please the taste or fancy; of delicate or refined quality. –*v.* **5.** to picture to oneself. **6.** to take a liking to.

fan·fare, *n.* a flourish or short air played on trumpets or the like.

fang, *n.* **1.** one of the teeth of a snake, by which venom is injected. **2.** a canine tooth.

fan·light, *n.* a fan-shaped or other window above a door.

fan·tas·tic, *adj.* **1.** odd or grotesque. **2.** extravagantly fanciful. **3.** *Colloq.* very good. Also, **fantastical**.

fan·tasy, *n., pl.* **-sies.** imagination, esp. when unrestrained. – **fantasise**, *v.*

far, *adv., adj.,* **further** *or* **farther, furthest** *or* **farthest.** –*adv.* **1.** at or to a great distance; a long way off; to a remote point. **2.** to or at a remote time, etc. **3.** to a great degree; very much: *I far prefer the blue hat.* –*adj.* **4.** distant. **5.** more distant of the 2.

farad, *n.* the derived SI unit of electric capacitance. *Symbol:* F

far·away, *adj.* **1.** distant; remote. **2.** abstracted or dreamy, as a look.

farce, *n.* **1.** a light, humorous play. **2.** a ridiculous thing. – **farcical**, *adj.*

fare, *n., v.,* **fared, faring.** –*n.* **1.** the price of travelling on a bus, train, plane, etc. **2.** the person or persons who pay to be conveyed in a vehicle. **3.** food. –*v.* **4.** to experience good or bad fortune, treatment, etc.; get on. **5.** to happen (used impersonally).

fare·well, *interj.* goodbye.

farm, *n.* **1.** a tract of land devoted to agriculture or some other industry. –*v.* **2.** to cultivate (land). **3.** to raise (livestock, fish, etc.) on a farm. **4.** to distribute (responsibilities, duties, etc.) (*out*).

fart, *Colloq. n.* **1.** an emission of wind from the anus, esp. an audible

191

fart

one. –*v.* 2. to emit wind from the anus.

far·ther, *adj., adv.* comparative of far. – **farthest**, *adj., adv.*

far·thing, *n.* a former British coin.

fas·ci·nate, *v.,* -nated, -nating. to attract and hold irresistibly the attention of. – **fascination**, *n.*

fas·cism /ˈfæʃɪzəm/, *n.* (*oft. cap.*) a governmental system with strong centralised power, permitting no opposition or cricitism, emphasising an aggressive nationalism, and (often) anticommunist.

fash·ion, *n.* 1. a prevailing custom or style of dress or behaviour. 2. manner; way; mode. 3. the make or form of anything. –*v.* 4. to give a particular shape or form to; make. – **fashionable**, *adj.*

fast[1], *adj.* 1. moving or able to move quickly. 2. done in comparatively little time. 3. indicating a time in advance of the correct time, as a clock. 4. securely attached. 5. deep or sound, as sleep. 6. deceptive or unreliable. –*adv.* 7. tightly. 8. soundly. 9. rapidly. – **fasten**, *v.*

fast[2], *v.* 1. to abstain from all food. 2. to eat sparingly or of certain kinds of food, esp. as a religious observance. –*n.* 3. a fasting.

fas·tid·i·ous, *adj.* hard to please; excessively critical.

fat, *adj.,* fatter, fattest, *n.* –*adj.* 1. having much flesh other than muscle; stout; obese. –*n.* 2. the yellowish, greasy substance forming the storage material of animals, also found in plants. 3. the richest or best part of anything. – **fatty**, *adj.*

fa·tal, *adj.* 1. causing death. 2. causing destruction or ruin.

fa·tal·ism, *n.* the doctrine that all events are influenced by fate. 2. the acceptance of all things and events as inevitable. – **fatalist**, *n.* – **fatalistic**, *adj.*

fa·tal·i·ty, *n., pl.* -ties. 1. a disaster, often one resulting in death. 2. one who is killed in an accident or disaster.

fate, *n., v.,* fated, fating. –*n.* 1. fortune; destiny. –*v.* 2. to predetermine (usu. in passive).

fate·ful, *adj.* decisively important.

fa·ther, *n.* 1. a male parent. 2. any male ancestor. 3. (*oft. cap.*) a title of reverence. –*v.* 4. to beget. – **fatherly**, *adj.*

father-in-law, *n., pl.* fathers-in-law. the father of one's spouse.

fath·om, *n., pl.* fathoms, (*esp. collectively*) fathom, *v.* –*n.* 1. a unit of depth in the imperial system. Symbol: fm –*v.* 2. to penetrate to or find the bottom or extent of.

fa·tigue, *n., v.,* -tigued, -tiguing. –*n.* 1. weariness from bodily or mental exertion. 2. a weakening as of metal subjected to stress. –*v.* 3. to weary with bodily or mental exertion.

fat·u·ous, *adj.* foolish, esp. in an unconscious, complacent manner.

fault, *n.* 1. a defect or failing. 2. an error. 3. culpability. 4. a break in the continuity of a body of rock. 5. **to a fault**, excessively. –*v.* 6. to find fault with.

fau·na, *n., pl.* -nas, -nae. the animals of a given region or period.

fa·vour, *n.* 1. a kind act; something done or granted out of goodwill. 2. a state of being approved. 3. **in favour of**, **a.** in support of. **b.** to the advantage of. **c.** (of a cheque, etc.)

favour

favour payable to. –*v.* 4. to regard with favour. 5. to have a preference for.

fa·vour·a·ble, *adj.* promising well; helpful.

fa·vour·ite, *n.* 1. a person or thing regarded with special favour or preference. 2. *Sport.* a competitor considered likely to win. *–adj.* 3. regarded with particular favour or preference.

fa·vour·it·ism, *n.* the favouring of one person or group over others having equal claims.

fawn^1, *n.* 1. a young deer. *–adj.* 2. light yellowish brown.

fawn^2, *v.* to seek notice or favour by servile demeanour.

fear, *n.* 1. a painful feeling of impending danger, trouble, etc. 2. reverential awe, esp. towards God. *–v.* 3. to regard with fear; be afraid of.

fear·some, *adj.* causing fear.

feas·ible, *adj.* 1. capable of being done. 2. likely; probable. **– feasibility, feasibleness**, *n.* **– feasibly**, *adv.*

feast, *n.* 1. a commemorative celebration of religious or other character. 2. a sumptuous entertainment or meal, esp. one for many guests. *–v.* 3. to have, or partake of, a feast; eat sumptuously.

feat, *n.* a noteworthy act or achievement.

feath·er, *n.* 1. one of the quills which constitute the plumage of birds. 2. something like a feather. *–v.* 3. to provide with feathers, as an arrow. 4. **to feather one's nest**, to provide for oneself.

fea·ture, *n.*, *v.*, **-tured, -turing.** *–n.* 1. any part of the face, as the nose, chin, etc. 2. a prominent or conspicuous part or characteristic. 3. a special article, column, cartoon, etc., in a newspaper or magazine. *–v.* 4. to make or be a feature of.

feck·less, *adj.* 1. ineffective; feeble. 2. worthless.

fed, *v.* past tense and past participle of **feed**.

fed·er·a·cy, *n.* →**confederacy**.

fed·er·al, *adj.* of or pertaining to a league, esp. a league between nations or states.

fed·er·ate, *v.* **-rated, -rating.** to unite in a federation.

fee, *n.* a payment for services.

fee·ble, *adj.*, **-bler, -blest.** 1. physically weak, as from age, sickness, etc. 2. weak intellectually or morally.

feed, *v.*, **fed, feeding,** *n.* *–v.* 1. to give food to; supply with nourishment. 2. to satisfy. 3. to eat. *–n.* 4. food, esp. for cattle, etc.

feed·back, *n.* 1. an indication of reaction, as of an audience. 2. the input of a signal into a microphone from the output of the same system, usu. causing a high-pitched screech.

feel, *v.*, **felt, feeling,** *n.* *–v.* 1. to perceive or examine by touch. 2. to perceive by intuition, emotion, etc. 3. to be emotionally affected by. 4. to experience the effects of. 5. to have sympathy or compassion (*with* or *for*). 6. **feel like**, to have a desire for. *–n.* 7. a quality of an object that is perceived by feeling or touching.

feel·er, *n. Zool.* an organ of touch, as an antenna or a tentacle.

feel·ing, *n.* 1. the function or the power of perceiving by touch. 2. a consciousness or impression. 3. an intuition or premonition. 4. capacity for emotion; pity. 5. (*pl.*) sensibilities.

feet

feet, *n.* plural of **foot**.

feign, *v.* **1.** to invent (an excuse, etc.). **2.** to pretend. **3.** to imitate deceptively.

feint, *n.* a movement made with the object of deceiving an adversary.

felic·i·tate, *v.*, **-tated, -tating.** to compliment upon a happy event; congratulate. – **felicitation**, *n.*

felic·i·ty, *n., pl.* **-ties. 1.** the state of being happy. **2.** excellence, as of expression or taste. – **felicitous**, *adj.*

feline, *adj.* belonging or pertaining to the cat family.

fell[1], *v.* past tense of **fall**.

fell[2], *v.* to cause to fall; cut down.

fellow, *n.* **1.** *Colloq.* a man; boy. **2.** one of a pair; a mate or match. **3.** (*usu. cap.*) a member of any of certain learned or professional societies. –*adj.* **4.** belonging to the same class or group. – **fellowship**, *n.*

felony, *n., pl.* **-nies.** *Law.* any of various indictable offences, as murder, burglary, etc., of graver character than those called misdemeanours. – **felon**, *n.* – **felonious**, *adj.*

felt[1], *v.* past tense and past participle of **feel**.

felt[2], *n.* a non-woven fabric.

female, *n.* **1.** a human being of the sex which conceives and brings forth young; a woman or girl. **2.** any animal of corresponding sex. –*adj.* **3.** pertaining to or characteristic of this sex.

femi·nine, *adj.* pertaining to a woman. – **femininity**, *n.*

femi·nism, *n.* advocacy of equal rights and opportunities for women. – **feminist**, *n.*

femur /ˈfiːmə/, *n., pl.* **femurs, femora** /ˈfemərə/. *Anat.* the thighbone.

fertilise

fence, *n., v.*, **fenced, fencing.** –*n.* **1.** an enclosure or barrier. **2.** *Colloq.* a person who receives and disposes of stolen goods. –*v.* **3.** to enclose by some barrier.

fen·cing, *n.* the art of using a sword, foil, etc., for defence and attack.

fend, *v.* **1.** to ward (*off*). **2.** *Colloq.* to provide (*for*).

fender, *n.* a metal guard as before an open fire.

fennel, *n.* a plant bearing aromatic fruits used in cookery and medicine.

feral, *adj.* wild, or existing in a state of nature.

fer·ment, *n.* **1.** any of various agents or substances which cause fermentation. –*v.* **2.** to act upon as a ferment. **3.** to seethe with agitation or excitement.

fer·men·tation, *n. Biochem.* a change brought about by a ferment, such as yeast enzymes which convert grape sugar into alcohol, etc. – **fermentative**, *adj.*

fern, *n.* a leafy plant bearing spores.

fero·cious, *adj.* savagely fierce or cruel. – **ferocity**, *n.*

ferret, *n.* a small animal used for hunting rabbits and rats in their burrows.

fer·rous, *adj.* of or containing iron.

ferry, *n., pl.* **-ries,** *v.*, **-ried, -rying.** –*n.* **1.** (a vessel used in) a service for transport across a body of water. –*v.* **2.** to carry or convey over water in a boat or plane.

fer·tile, *adj.* **1.** (capable of) bearing abundantly, as land or soil. **2.** abundantly productive or inventive. **3.** able to produce offspring.

fer·ti·lise, *v.*, **-lised, -lising. 1.** *Biol.* to render (an egg, ovum, or female

fertilise

cell) capable of development by union with the male cell or sperm. 2. to enrich (soil, etc.) for crops, etc. – **fertility**, *n.* – **fertilisation**, *n.*

fervour, *n.* great warmth and earnestness of feeling. – **fervid**, *adj.*

fester, *v.* 1. to generate pus; suppurate. 2. to rankle, as a feeling of resentment.

fes·ti·val, *n.* a public festivity, with performances of music, processions, exhibitions, etc.

fes·tive, *adj.* joyful; merry.

fes·ti·vi·ty, *n., pl.* **-ties.** a festive celebration or occasion.

fes·toon, *v., n.* (to decorate with) a string or chain of flowers, foliage, ribbon, etc.

fetch, *v.* 1. to go and return with, or bring to or from a particular place. 2. to bring in (a price, etc.).

fetch·ing, *adj.* charming; captivating.

fete, *n., v.*, **feted, feting.** –*n.* 1. a function to raise money for charity, church, school, etc. –*v.* 2. to give a hospitable public reception to.

fetid /ˈfetəd, ˈfiːtəd/, *adj.* having a strong, offensive smell. Also, **foetid**.

fetish /ˈfetɪʃ/, *n.* an obsession or fixation.

fet·lock, *n.* lower part of a horse's leg.

fetter, *n.* (*usu. pl.*) anything that confines or restrains.

fettle, *n.* state; condition.

feud, *n.* 1. a bitter, continuous hostility, esp. between 2 families, clans, etc. –*v.* 2. to conduct a feud.

feudal, *adj.* of or pertaining to a medieval system of holding land in return for service.

fidelity

fever, *n.*, a morbid condition of the body, characterised by undue rise of temperature.

feverfew, *n.* plant formerly used to treat fever, now migraines.

few, *adj.* 1. not many; a small number (of). –*n.* 2. **a few**, a small number.

fey, *adj.* 1. as if enchanted. 2. slightly crazy.

fiancée /fiˈɑːnseɪ/, *n.* a woman engaged to be married. – **fiancé**, *n. masc.*

fiasco, *n. pl.* **-cos.** a complete and usu. ignominious failure.

fib, *n. v.*, **fibbed, fibbing.** –*n.* 1. a trivial falsehood. –*v.* 2. to tell a fib.

fibre, *n.* a fine threadlike piece, as of cotton, jute, or asbestos. – **fibrous**, *adj.*

fibre·glass, *n.* a material consisting of extremely fine filaments of glass.

fibro, *n.* compressed asbestos and cement used for building materials.

fibula /ˈfɪbjulə, jələ/, *n., pl.* **-lae / -las.** *Anat.* one of the 2 bones of the lower leg. – **fibular**, *adj.*

fickle, *adj.* likely to change.

fic·tion, *n.* the branch of literature comprising (prose) works of imaginative narration.

fiddle, *n., v.*, **-dled, -dling.** –*n.* 1. a violin. 2. *Colloq.* an illegal or underhand transaction. –*v.* 3. *Colloq.* to play on the fiddle. 4. to make aimless movements, as with the hands.

fiddly, *adj. Colloq.* difficult or exacting, as something small done with the hands.

fidel·ity, *n., pl.* **-ties.** 1. loyalty; faithfulness. 2. quality of sound reproduction.

195

fidget, *v.* to move about restlessly or impatiently.

field, *n.* 1. a piece of open or cleared ground. 2. a piece of ground devoted to sports or contests. 3. a sphere, or range of activity. –*v.* 4. *Cricket, etc.* to stop, or catch, and throw (the ball).

fiend, *n.* 1. any evil spirit. 2. a diabolically cruel or wicked person.

fierce, *adj.*, **fiercer, fiercest.** 1. wild or vehement in temper, appearance, or action. 2. violent in force, intensity, *etc.*.

fiery /'faɪəri/, *adj.*, **fierier, fieriest.** 1. characterised by or containing fire. 2. flashing or glowing, as the eye. 3. easily angered.

fiesta /fi'ɛstə/, *n.* a festival.

fife, *n.* a high-pitched flute.

fifteen, *n.* a cardinal number, 10 plus 5. – **fifteenth**, *n., adj.*

fifty, *n., pl.* **-ties.** a cardinal number, 10 times 5. – **fiftieth**, *adj., n.*

fig, *n.* (a tree bearing) a small, pear-shaped fruit.

fight, *n., v.*, **fought, fighting.** –*n.* 1. a battle or combat. 2. any quarrel, contest, or struggle. 3. ability or inclination to fight. –*v.* 4. to engage in battle or in single combat. 5. to contend (with) in any manner.

fig·ment, *n.* a mere product of the imagination.

fig·ur·a·tive, *adj.* metaphorical; not literal.

figure, *n., v.*, **-ured, -uring.** –*n.* 1. a written symbol other than a letter. 2. an amount or value expressed in numbers. 3. shape or appearance. 4. *Geom.* a particular form or shape, as triangle, curve, cube, *etc.* 5. a representation, esp. of the human form. 6. a series of movements in skating. –*v.* 7. to conclude, judge, or reason. 8. to solve; understand (*out*). 9. to compute or work with numerical figures. 10. to be conspicuous.

figure·head, *n.* a person who is nominally the head of a society, community, *etc.*, but has no real authority or responsibility.

fig·u·rine /'fɪgjurin/, *n.* a small ornamental figure of pottery, metalwork, *etc.*

fila·ment, *n.* a very fine thread or threadlike structure.

filch, *v.* to steal (esp. something of small value).

file[1], *n., v.*, **filed, filing.** –*n.* 1. any device, as a cabinet, in which papers, *etc.*, are arranged or classified for convenient reference. 2. a line of persons or things arranged one behind another. –*v.* 3. to place in a file. 4. *Law.* to bring (a suit) before a court of law.

file[2], *n., v.*, **filed, filing.** –*n.* 1. a tool for smoothing or cutting. –*v.* 2. to reduce, or smooth, as with a file.

filial, *adj.* pertaining to or befitting a son or daughter.

fili·buster /'fɪləbʌstə/, *n.* the use of obstructive tactics, esp. long speeches to delay legislative action.

fili·gree, *n.* ornamental work of fine wires.

fill, *v.* 1. to make or become full. 2. to supply to fullness or plentifully. 3. to extend throughout. 4. to occupy and perform the duties of (a position, post, *etc.*). 5. to execute (a business order). 6. **fill in, a.** to complete (a document, design, *etc.*) by filling blank spaces. **b.** to act as a substitute; replace. 7. **fill out,** to complete the details of (a plan,

fill

form, etc.). –n. 8. a full supply; enough to satisfy want or desire: *He has eaten his fill.*

fillet, *n. Cookery.* 1. a boneless piece of fish. 2. a cut of beef or pork.

filly, *n., pl.* **-lies.** a young mare.

film, *n.* 1. a thin layer or coating. 2. a strip or roll of cellulose used in photography. 3. **a.** a series of pictures or photographs on a strip of film. **b.** such a film strip representing an event, story, etc. –v. 4. to reproduce in the form of a film or films.

filter, *n.* 1. any device through which liquid is passed to remove suspended impurities or recover solids. –v. 2. to remove by the action of a filter.

filth, *n.* 1. offensive or disgusting dirt or condition. 2. moral impurity. – **filthy**, *adj.*

fin, *n.* 1. an organ of fishes used for propulsion, steering, or balancing. 2. anything resembling a fin.

final, *adj.* 1. coming at the end; last in place, order, or time. 2. conclusive or decisive. –n. 3. that which is last, esp. of a series. – **finalise**, *v.* – **finality**, *n.*

finance, *n., v.,* **-nanced, -nancing.** –n. 1. the conduct or transaction of money matters. 2. (*pl.*) pecuniary resources. –v. 3. to supply with means of payment. – **financial**, *adj.* – **financier**, *n.*

finch, *n.* a small bird common in Aust. and elsewhere.

find, *v.,* **found, finding.** –v. 1. to come upon by chance; meet. 2. to discover. 3. to recover (something lost). 4. *Law.* to pronounce (a verdict or judgment). –n. 5. a discovery.

fire

fine[1], *adj.,* **finer, finest.** 1. of very high grade or quality. 2. consisting of minute particles. 3. very thin or slender.

fine[2], *n., v.,* **fined, fining.** –n. 1. a sum of money exacted as a penalty for an offence. –v. 2. to punish by a fine.

finery, *n., pl.* **-ries.** fine or showy dress, ornaments, etc.

fin·esse, *n.* delicacy of execution.

finger, *n.* 1. any of the terminal members of the hand, esp. one other than the thumb. 2. something like a finger. –v. 3. to handle; toy or meddle with.

finger·print, *n.* an impression of the markings of the end of the thumb or a finger.

fin·icky, *adj.* fussy about details.

finish, *v.* 1. to bring or come to an end or to completion. 2. to use completely (*up* or *off*). 3. to put the final touches on. –n. 4. the end or last stage. 5. the quality of being completed with smoothness, elegance, etc. 6. the surface coating or texture of wood, metal, etc.

finite, *adj.* having bounds or limits.

fink, *n.* a contemptible or undesirable person.

fiord /'fiəd/, *n.* a long, relatively narrow arm of the sea, bordered by steep cliffs. Also, **fjord.**

fir, *n.* a pyramidal coniferous tree.

fire, *n., v.,* **fired, firing.** –n. 1. the active principle of burning as seen in the production of light and heat. 2. a burning mass of material, as on a hearth or in a furnace. 3. the destructive burning of a building, town, forest, etc. 4. burning passion; enthusiasm. 5. the discharge of firearms. –v. 6. to (be) set on fire.

197

fire

7. to apply heat to in a kiln. 8. to discharge (a gun). 9. to dismiss from a job. 10. (of an internal-combustion engine) to cause the air-fuel mixture in the cylinders to burn.

fire·arm, *n.* a gun that fires bullets.

fire·break, *n.* a strip of ploughed or cleared land made to check the spread of fire.

fire·fly, *n., pl.* **-flies.** a beetle with abdominal light-producing organs.

fire·fighter, *n.* a person employed to extinguish or prevent fires.

fire·place, *n.* that part of a chimney which opens into a room and in which fuel is burnt.

fire·works, *n.pl.* combustible or explosive devices for producing a striking display of light, etc.

firing squad, *n.* a small military force assigned to execute a condemned person by shooting.

firm[1], *adj.* 1. fairly solid or stiff. 2. securely fixed in place. 3. steady; not shaking or trembling.

firm[2], *n.* 1. a business organisation or partnership. 2. the name or title under which associated parties transact business.

fir·ma·ment, *n.* the vault of heaven; the sky.

first, *adj.* 1. being before all others: *the first person to arrive.* –*adv.* 2. before all others: *she arrived first.* 3. before doing anything else: *first, eat your dinner.* 4. for the first time: *when I first saw you.* –*n.* 5. that which is first in time, order, rank, etc.: *the first to arrive.*

first aid, *n.* emergency aid or treatment given to persons suffering from an accident, etc.

first-class, *adj.* 1. of the highest or best class or quality. –*adv.* 2. by first-class conveyance: *to travel first-class.*

first-hand,, *adj.* direct from the original source: *a first-hand account of events.*

first person, *n.* the class of a pronoun or verb in which the speaker is the subject. See **person**.

fis·cal, *adj.* 1. of or pertaining to the public treasury or revenues. 2. pertaining to financial matters in general.

fish, *n., pl.* **fishes**, (*esp. collectively*) **fish**, *v.* –*n.* 1. any of various cold-blooded, completely aquatic vertebrates, having gills, commonly fins, and typically an elongated body usu. covered with scales. –*v.* 2. to draw as by fishing (*up, out,* etc.). 3. to catch or attempt to catch fish. 4. to seek to obtain something indirectly (*for*).

fish·er·man, *n., pl.* **-men.** one engaged in fishing.

fish·y, *adj.*, **fishier, fishiest.** 1. fish-like. 2. *Colloq.* of questionable character.

fis·sion, *n.,* the act of cleaving or splitting into parts.

fis·sure, *n.* a narrow opening produced by cleavage or separation of parts; a cleft.

fist, *n.* the hand closed tightly, with the fingers doubled into the palm.

fisti·cuffs, *n.pl.* combat with the fists.

fit[1], *adj.*, **fitter, fittest,** *v.,* **fitted, fitting,** *n.* –*adj.* 1. well adapted or suited. 2. proper or becoming. 3. in good health. –*v.* 4. to be suitable (for a purpose, etc.). 5. to conform or adjust to something. 6. to furnish;

fit

equip. 7. to be of the right size or shape. —*n.* 8. the manner in which a thing fits: *The shirt is a good fit.*

fit², *n.* 1. a sudden, acute attack, as of a disease. 2. a burst or period of emotion, activity, etc. 3. a convulsion.

fit·ful, *adj.* happening irregularly.

fit·ting, *adj.* appropriate; proper.

five, *n.* a cardinal number, 4 plus one. — **fifth**, *n., adj.*

fix, *v.*, **fixed, fixing**. —*v.* 1. to make fast, firm, or stable. 2. to settle definitely; determine. 3. to direct (the eyes, the attention, etc.) steadily. 4. to put or place (responsibility, blame, etc.) on a person. 5. to repair. —*n.* 6. *Colloq.* a predicament. 7. *Colloq.* a hit (def. 7).

fix·ation, *n. Psychol.* the state of being fixed in one idea, stage of development, etc.; an obsession.

fix·ed·ly, *adv.* intently.

fix·ture, *n.* 1. something or someone securely fixed in position. 2. a sporting event.

fizz, *v.* 1. to make a hissing or sputtering sound. —*n.* 2. a hissing sound; effervescence.

fiz·zle, *v.*, **-zled, -zling**. 1. to make a hissing or sputtering sound, esp. one that dies out weakly. 2. *Colloq.* to fail ignominiously after a good start (*out*).

flab, *n. Colloq.* bodily fat.

flab·ber·gast, *v.*, to overcome with surprise and bewilderment; astound.

flac·cid /'flæsəd/, *adj.* soft and drooping.

flag¹, *n., v.*, **flagged, flagging**. —*n.* 1. a piece of cloth, bearing a design, used as a symbol, signal, decoration, etc., esp. one used as the emblem of a country. —*v.* 2. to signal or warn as with a flag.

flannel

flag², *v.*, **flagged, flagging**. to fall off in vigour, interest, etc.

fla·gel·late /'flædʒəleɪt/, *v.*, **-lated, -lating**. to whip oneself or another.

flag·on, *n.* a large bottle.

fla·grant /'fleɪgrənt/, *adj.* blatant; scandalous.

flag·ship, *n.* a ship which carries the admiral of a fleet, etc.

flail, *v.* to strike out wildly (at).

flair, *n.* talent, aptitude.

flak, *n.* anti-aircraft fire.

flake, *n., v.*, **flaked, flaking**. —*n.* 1. a small, flat, thin piece of anything. —*v.* 2. to peel off or separate in flakes. 3. Also, **flake out**. *Colloq.* to collapse, faint, or fall asleep.

flam·boy·ant, *adj.* flaming; gorgeous. 2. florid, ornate.

flame, *n., v.*, **flamed, flaming**. —*n.* 1. burning gas or vapour, as from wood, etc., undergoing combustion. 2. heat or ardour. 3. *Colloq.* a sweetheart. —*v.* 4. to burn with a flame; blaze.

fla·min·go, *n., pl.* **-gos, -goes**. an aquatic bird with very long neck and legs and pinkish plumage.

flam·mable, *adj.* easily set on fire. — **flammability**, *n.*

flan, *n.* an open tart.

flange, *n.* a projecting rim.

flank, *n.* 1. the side of an animal or a human being between the ribs and hip. 2. the side of anything, as of a building. —*v.* 3. to stand or be placed or posted at the flank or side of.

flan·nel, *n.* 1. a warm, soft fabric. 2. small cloth for washing.

199

flannelette

flannel·ette, *n.* a cotton fabric made to imitate flannel.

flap, *v.*, **flapped, flapping**, *n.* –*v.* 1. to swing or sway about loosely, esp. with noise. 2. to move (wings) up and down. –*n.* 3. a flapping motion. 4. something that hangs loosely, attached at one side only. 5. *Colloq.* a state of panic or nervous excitement.

flare, *v.*, **flared, flaring.** *n.* 1. to burn with an unsteady flame. 2. to blaze (*up*) with a sudden burst of flame. 3. to burst out in sudden fierce activity. 4. to spread outwards as the end of a trumpet. –*n.* 5. a sudden blaze of fire or light used as a signal, etc. 6. a sudden burst, as of zeal or of temper.

flash, *n.* 1. a sudden burst of flame or light. 2. a sudden, brief outburst or display of joy, wit, etc. 3. an instant. 4. ostentatious display. –*v.* 5. to gleam. 6. to move like a flash. 7. to emit or send forth (fire or light) in sudden flashes. –*adj.* 8. showy or ostentatious.

flash·back, *n.* a representation, during the course of a novel, film, etc., of some event or scene which occurred at a previous time.

flashing, *n.* strip to stop water penetration at joints (on roof, etc.).

flask, *n.* a bottle-shaped container.

flat[1], *adj.*, **flatter, flattest**, *adv.*, *n.* –*adj.* 1. level, even, as of land, etc. 2. lying at full length, as a person. 3. (of feet) having little or no arch. 4. spread out. 5. collapsed; deflated. 6. unqualified; downright, or positive: *a flat refusal.* 7. uninteresting, dull, or tedious. 8. (of beer, etc.) having lost its effervescence. –*adv.* 9. in a flat position; horizontally;

fleece

levelly. 10. *Music.* below the true pitch. 11. **flat out**, *Colloq.* **a.** as fast as possible. **b.** very busy. –*n.* 12. *Music.* (the sign ♭), indicating) a note lowered one semitone below another.

flat[2], *n.*, *v.*, **flatted, flatting.** –*n.* 1. a suite of rooms, usu. rented. –*v.* 2. to live in a flat.

flat·ter, *v.* 1. to compliment or praise, esp. insincerely. 2. to show to advantage. –**flattery**, *n.*

flatu·lent, *adj.* 1. generating gas in the alimentary canal. 2. pretentious; empty. –**flatulence**, *n.*

flaunt, *v.* to parade or display oneself conspicuously or boldly.

flaut·ist, *n.* a flute player.

fla·vour, *n.* 1. (a noticeable element in) the taste of a thing. 2. the characteristic quality of a thing.

flaw, *n.* a defect.

flax, *n.* 1. a plant cultivated for its fibre and seeds. 2. the fibre of this plant, manufactured into linen yarn.

flaxen, *adj.* 1. made of flax. 2. of a pale yellowish colour.

flay, *v.* 1. to strip off the skin or outer covering of. 2. to criticise severely.

flea, *n.* any of numerous small, wingless, blood-sucking insects.

fleck, *n.* 1. a spot or mark; speck. –*v.* 2. to mark with flecks.

fled, *v.* past tense and past participle of **flee**.

fledg·ling, *n.* 1. a young bird. 2. an inexperienced person. Also, **fledge·ling.**

flee, *v.*, **fled, fleeing.** to run away (from).

fleece, *n.*, *v.*, **fleeced, fleecing.** –*n.* 1. the coat of wool that covers a sheep

fleece

or some similar animal. –v. 2. to plunder; swindle.

fleet[1], n. 1. the largest organised unit of naval ships. 2. the vessels, aeroplanes or vehicles collectively of a single transport company or undertaking.

fleet[2], adj. swift; rapid.

fleet·ing, adj. passing swiftly; transient.

flesh, n. 1. the soft substance of an animal body, consisting of muscle and fat. 2. the soft pulpy portion of a fruit, vegetable, etc.

flew, v. past tense of fly[1].

flex, v. 1. to bend (something pliant or jointed). –n. 2. an insulated electric cable or wire.

flex·ible, adj. 1. easily bent. 2. adaptable. – flexibility, n.

flexi·time, n. the arrangement of working hours, meal-breaks, etc., to suit the employee. Also, **gliding time**.

flick, n. 1. a sudden light blow or stroke, as with a whip or the finger. 2. (usu. pl.) Colloq. a cinema film. –v. 3. to remove with a flick.

flicker, v. 1. to burn or shine unsteadily. –n. 2. an unsteady flame or light. 3. a brief spark.

flight[1], n. 1. the act, manner, or power of flying. 2. the distance covered or the course pursued by a flying object. 3. a journey by air, esp. by aeroplane. 4. Archit. the series of steps or stairs between 2 adjacent landings.

flight[2], n. the act of fleeing.

flighty, adj., -tier, -tiest. given to flights of fancy, caprice, etc.

flimsy, adj., -sier, -siest. without material strength or solidity.

flinch, v. to draw back from what is dangerous, painful, etc.

fling, v., flung, flinging, n. –v. 1. to throw, esp. with violence. 2. to put suddenly or violently. –n. 3. a spell of unrestrained indulgence of one's impulses.

flint, n. a hard kind of stone.

flip, v., flipped, flipping, n. –v. 1. to toss with a snap of a finger and thumb; flick. –n. 2. a smart tap or strike. 3. a somersault.

flip·pant, adj. 1. clever or pert in speech. 2. characterised by a shallow or disrespectful levity.

flip·per, n. 1. a broad, flat limb, as of a seal, whale, etc. 2. a swimming aid resembling in form an animal's flipper.

flirt, v. 1. to trifle in love. –n. 2. a person given to flirting.

flit, v., flitted, flitting. to move lightly and swiftly.

float, v. 1. to rest on the surface of a liquid; be buoyant. 2. to move or drift about free from attachment. 3. to launch (a company, scheme, etc.). 4. (of currency) to allow the rate of exchange of a currency to find its own level in a foreign exchange market. –n. 5. something that floats, as a raft, a life jacket, etc. 6. a decorated platform on wheels drawn in a procession.

flock[1], n. 1. a number of animals or of birds of one kind. –v. 2. to gather or go in a flock.

flock[2], n. a lock or tuft of wool, hair, etc.

floe, n. a field of floating ice formed on the surface of the sea, etc.

flog, v., flogged, flogging. 1. to beat hard with a whip. 2. Colloq. to sell

flog

or attempt to sell. **3.** *Colloq.* to steal.

flood, *n.* **1.** an overflowing of water, esp. over land not usu. submerged. **2.** any great outpouring or stream. –*v.* **3.** to flow or pour in or as in a flood. **4.** to overwhelm with an abundance of something.

floor, *n.* **1.** that part of a room or the like upon which one walks. **2.** a storey of a building. **3.** any more or less flat extent or surface. **4.** the part of a legislative chamber, etc., where the members sit. –*v.* **5.** to cover or furnish with a floor. **6.** *Colloq.* to confound or puzzle completely: *She floored me with her ideas.*

flop, *v.,* **flopped, flopping,** *n. Colloq.* –*v.* **1.** to drop or turn with a sudden bump or thud. **2.** to yield or break down suddenly; fail. –*n.* **3.** a failure.

flora, *n., pl.* **floras, florae.** the plants of a particular region.

floral, *adj.* pertaining to or consisting of flowers.

florid, *adj.* highly coloured or ruddy, as complexion, cheeks, etc.

florin, *n.* a former silver coin worth 2 shillings.

flor·ist, *n.* a retailer of flowers.

floss, *n.* **1.** silky thread-like matter. **2.** Also, **dental floss.** soft, waxed thread used for cleaning between the teeth.

flo·ta·tion, *n.* **1.** the act or state of floating. **2.** the launching of a commercial venture, a loan, etc.

flo·til·la, *n.* a number of small naval vessels.

flotsam and jetsam, *n.* the wreckage of a ship and its cargo found either floating upon the sea or washed ashore.

flounce[1], *v.,* **flounced, flouncing.** to go with an impatient or angry fling of the body.

flounce[2], *n.* a gathered strip of material on a skirt, etc.

floun·der[1], *v.* to struggle with stumbling or plunging movements.

floun·der[2], *n., pl.* **-der.** any of numerous species of flatfishes.

flour, *n.* the finely ground meal of wheat or other grain.

flou·rish, *v.* **1.** to be in a vigorous state; be successful. **2.** to brandish or wave (a sword, etc.) about in the air. –*n.* **3.** a parade or ostentatious display. **4.** *Music.* a trumpet call or fanfare.

flout, *v.* to mock; scoff at.

flow, *v.* **1.** to move along smoothly and continuously as in a stream. –*n.* **2.** the act of flowing. **3.** any continuous movement, as of thought, speech, trade, etc.

flower, *n.* **1.** the blossom of a plant. **2.** the best or finest member or part of a number, body, or whole. –*v.* **3.** to blossom, as a plant. **4.** to reach the stage of full development.

flowery, *adj.,* **-rier, -riest. 1.** abounding in or covered with flowers. **2.** containing highly ornate language.

flown, *v.* past participle of **fly**[1].

flu, *n. Colloq.* →**influenza.**

fluc·tu·ate, *v.,* **-ated, -ating. 1.** to change continually, as from one course to another. **2.** to move in waves or like waves.

flue, *n.* any duct or passage for air, gases, or the like.

fluent, *adj.* **1.** flowing smoothly and easily. **2.** able to speak or write readily.

fluff

fluff, *n.* **1.** light, downy particles, as of cotton. **2.** *Colloq.* a blunder or error.

fluid, *n.* a substance which is capable of flowing; a liquid or a gas.

fluke[1], *n.* any accidental advantage; a lucky chance.

fluke[2], *n.* a type of flounder.

flum·mox, *v. Colloq.* to bewilder; confuse.

flung, *v.* past tense and past participle of **fling**.

flunk, *v. Colloq.* to fail, as a student in an examination.

flun·key, *n., pl.* **-keys. 1.** a male servant in uniform; a lackey. **2.** a servile follower; a toady.

flu·or·es·cence, *n.* a light emitted by certain substances. — **fluorescent,** *adj.*

fluo·ride, an organic compound used to prevent tooth decay.

fluo·rine, *n.* a pale yellow corrosive gas. *Symbol:* F

flurry, *n.* **1.** a sudden gust of wind. **2.** commotion.

flush[1], *n.* a blush; a rosy glow. *v.* **2.** a rushing or overspreading flow, as of water. **3.** waves of heat, as during fever, menopause, etc.

flush[2], *adj.* **1.** even or level, as with a surface; in one plane. **2.** well-supplied, as with money.

flush[3], *v.* to cause (others) to reveal themselves (*out*).

flush[4], *n.* a hand of cards all of one suit.

flus·ter, *v.* to confuse; make nervous.

flute, *n.* **1.** a musical wind instrument consisting of a tube with a series of fingerholes or keys. **2.** a channel or furrow.

focus

flut·ter, *v.* **1.** to flap or wave lightly in air, as a flag. **2.** to beat fast and irregularly, as the heart. — *n.* **3.** a fluttering movement. **4.** *Colloq.* a small wager or bet.

flux, *n.* a flowing or flow.

fly[1], *v.,* **flew, flown, flying,** *n., pl.* **flies.** — *v.* **1.** to move through the air on wings, as a bird. **2.** to (cause to) be carried through the air. **3.** to move or pass swiftly. **4.** to flee. — *n.* **5.** a strip sewn along one edge of a garment, to aid in concealing the buttons or other fasteners. **6.** (*pl.*) *Theat.* the space and apparatus above the stage.

fly[2], *n., pl.* **flies. 1.** any of various two-winged insects, esp. the common housefly. **2.** *Angling.* a fishhook dressed with silk, tinsel, etc., to resemble an insect.

flying saucer, *n.* any of various disc-shaped objects allegedly seen flying at high speeds and altitudes.

fly·leaf, *n., pl.* **-leaves.** a blank leaf in the front or at the back of a book.

foal, *n.* **1.** the young of a horse. — *v.* **2.** to bring forth a foal.

foam, *n.* **1.** minute bubbles formed on the surface of a liquid. **2.** the froth of perspiration or saliva.

fob[1], *n.* Also, **fob pocket.** a small pocket just below the waistline in trousers. **2.** a short chain for a watch.

fob[2], *v.,* **fobbed, fobbing. 1.** to palm off: *to fob off a watch.* **2.** to put off: *to fob someone off with promises.*

focus, *n., pl.* **-ci** /-sai, -kai/, **-cuses,** *v.,* **-cused, -cusing,** or **-cussed, -cussing.** — *n.* **1.** clear and sharply defined condition of an image. **2.** a central point, as of attention. — *v.* **3.**

203

focus

to bring to a focus or into focus. 4. to concentrate. – **focal**, adj.

fodder, n. food for livestock.

foe, n. an enemy or opponent.

foe·tus /'fitəs/, n. the young of an animal in the womb or in the egg. – **foetal**, adj.

fog, n. 1. a thick mist. 2. a state of mental confusion or obscurity.

fogy, n., pl. **-gies**. an old-fashioned or excessively conservative person. Also, **fogey**.

foible, n. a weakness or failing of character.

foil[1], v. to frustrate (a person, an attempt, a purpose).

foil[2], n. 1. a metallic substance formed into very thin sheets. 2. anything that serves to set off another thing by contrast.

foil[3], n. a flexible, light sword for use in fencing.

foist, v. to palm off or impose fraudulently or unwarrantably (*on* or *upon*).

fold[1], v. 1. to bend (cloth, paper, etc.) over upon itself. 2. to shut by bending and laying parts together (*up*). 3. *Cookery.* to mix (*in*) gently. 4. to be closed or brought to an end, usu. with financial loss. –n. 5. a part that is folded; pleat; layer. 6. a hollow place in undulating ground.

fold[2], n. 1. an enclosure for domestic animals, esp. sheep. 2. a church or congregation.

folder, n. an outer cover, usu. a folded sheet of light cardboard, for papers.

foli·age, n. the leaves of a plant, collectively.

folio, n. 1. a sheet of paper folded once to make 2 leaves (4 pages) of

204

food

a book. 2. a paper size. 3. *Print.* the page number of a book.

folk, n., pl. **folk**, **folks**. people in general, esp. the common people.

folk-lore, n. the traditional beliefs, legends, customs, etc., of a people.

fol·li·cle, n. 1. *Bot.* a seed vessel. 2. *Anat.* a small cavity, sac, or gland.

follow, v. 1. to come after in natural sequence, order of time, etc. 2. to move behind in the same direction. 3. to accept as a guide or leader. 4. to move forward along (a path, etc.). 5. to watch the movements, progress, or course of. 6. to occur as a consequence: *It follows that you are penalised for the error.* 7. **follow suit**, to follow the example of another. 8. **follow through**, to carry out completely. 9. **follow up**, a. to pursue closely, or to a conclusion. b. to take further action.

folly, n., pl. **-lies**. 1. the state or quality of being foolish. 2. a foolish action, practice, idea, etc.

foment, v. 1. to foster (discord, rebellion, etc.). 2. to apply (cloths dipped in) warm water or medicated liquid to (the surface of the body).

fond, adj. 1. liking (*of*). 2. loving. 3. foolishly tender; doting.

fondle, v., **-dled**, **-dling**. to show fondness, as by manner, words, or caresses.

fondue, n. a dish of melted cheese or other sauce into which pieces of bread, meat, etc., are dipped.

font[1], n. a receptacle for the water used in baptism.

font[2], n. a complete assortment of printing type of one style and size. Also, **fount**.

food, n. 1. what is eaten, or taken

food

into the body, for nourishment. 2. more or less solid nourishment (as opposed to *drink*).

fool, *n*. 1. a silly or stupid person. 2. a professional jester. –*v.* 3. to make a fool of. 4. to act like a fool. – **foolish**, *adj.*

fool·hardy, *adj.*, **-dier, -diest**. bold without judgment.

fools·cap, *n.* a printing paper size, usu. 337 × 206 mm.

foot, *n.*, *pl.* **feet**, *v.* –*n.* 1. the part of the leg below the ankle joint on which the body stands and moves. 2. a unit of length in the imperial system, equal to 0.3048 m. 3. any thing or part resembling a foot, as in function. 4. the part of a stocking, etc., covering the foot. 5. the part of anything opposite the top or head. –*v.* 6. *Colloq.* to pay or settle (a bill).

foot·age, *n.* 1. length or extent in feet. 2. a length of film.

foot·ball, *n.* 1. any game in which the kicking of a ball has a large part. 2. the ball used in such a game.

foot·ing, *n.* 1. a secure position; foothold. 2. the basis on which anything is established. 3. position or status assigned to a person: *on an equal footing with colleagues*.

foot·lights, *n.pl. Theat.* a row of lights at the front of the stage.

foot·loose, *adj.* free to go or travel about.

foot·man, *n.*, *pl.* **-men**. a male servant in livery.

foot·note, *n.* a note or comment at the foot of a page.

foot·step, *n.* a step or tread of the foot, or the sound produced by it.

fop, *n.* a man who is excessively

forceps

concerned about his manners and appearance.

for, *prep.* 1. with the object or purpose of: *The meat was bought for dinner*. 2. intended to belong to or be used in connection with: *Those shoes are for dancing*. 3. in order to obtain: *He sang for his supper*. 4. in consideration of, or in return for: *You can have it for nothing*. 5. during the continuance of: *for the rest of the performance*. 6. in favour of, or on the side of: *to stand for open government*. 7. in place of, or instead of: *to act for the governor*. 8. by reason of, or because of: *famed for its beauty*.

for·age /'forɪdʒ/, *n.*, *v.*, **-raged, -raging**. –*n.* 1. food for horses and cattle. –*v.* 2. to hunt or search about.

for·ay, *n.* a raid for the purpose of taking plunder.

for·bear, *v.*, **-bore, -borne, -bearing**. to refrain from; cease.

for·bear·ance, *n.* patience.

for·bid, *v.*, **-bade** or **-bad, -bidden** or **-bid, -bidding**. 1. to command (a person, etc.) not to do, have, use, etc., something. 2. to prohibit (something).

force, *n.*, *v.*, **forced, forcing**. –*n.* 1. strength; power. 2. *Law*. violence offered to persons or things. 3. (*oft. pl.*) a large body of armed men; an army. 4. any body of persons combined for joint action. 5. *Physics*. an influence which tends to produce motion. 6. value; meaning. –*v.* 7. to compel or move (someone) to do something. 8. to break open (a door, lock, etc.).

for·ceps, *n.*, *pl.* **-ceps, -cipes** /-səpiz/. an instrument, as pincers or tongs, for seizing and holding objects.

205

forcible

forc·ible, *adj.* 1. effected by force. 2. having force; effective.

ford, *n.* 1. a place where a river or other body of water may be crossed by wading. –*v.* 2. to cross (a river, etc.) by a ford.

fore, *adj.* situated at or towards the front, as compared with something else.

fore·arm, *n.* the part of the arm between the elbow and the wrist.

fore·bear, *n.* (*usu. pl.*) an ancestor. Also, **forbear**.

fore·bode, *v.*, **-boded, -boding.** to foretell or predict (esp. something bad); portend. – **foreboding**, *n.*

fore·cast, *v.*, **-cast** or **-casted, -casting.** –*v.* 1. to predict. –*n.* 2. a prediction, esp. as to the weather.

fore·close, *v.*, **-closed, -closing.** *Law.* to deprive (a mortgagor or pledgor) of the right to redeem his property.

fore·finger, *n.* the first or index finger next to the thumb.

forego, *v.*, **-went, -gone, -going.** to go before.

fore·ground, *n.* the area represented as situated in the front.

fore·hand, *Sport. adj.* (of a stroke, etc.) made to the right side of the body (when the player is right-handed).

fore·head /ˈfɒrɪd/, *n.* the part of the face above the eyes; the brow.

for·eign, *adj.* 1. pertaining to another country or nation. 2. not related to the thing under consideration. – **foreigner**, *n.*

fore·lock, *n.* the lock of hair that grows from the front part of the head.

fore·man, *n.*, *pl.* **-men.** 1. a man in charge of a group of workers. 2. the spokesman of a jury.

forgo

fore·most, *adj.*, *adv.* first in place, order, rank, etc.

foren·sic /fəˈrɛnsɪk, -zɪk/, *adj.* 1. pertaining to courts of law or public discussion and debate. 2. adapted or suited to argumentation.

fore·see, *v.*, **-saw, -seen, -seeing.** to know beforehand.

fore·shore, *n.* the part of the shore between the ordinary high-water mark and low-water mark.

fore·sight, *n.* care or provision for the future.

fore·skin, *n.* →**prepuce**.

forest, *n.* a large tract of land covered with trees. – **forestry**, *n.*

fore·stall, *v.* to take measures to prevent or thwart (a thing) in advance.

for·ever, *adv.* 1. without ever ending. 2. continually.

fore·word, *n.* a preface or introductory statement in a book, etc.

for·feit /ˈfɔːfɪt/, *n.* 1. a fine; a penalty. –*v.* 2. to lose, or become liable to lose, in consequence of fault, broken agreement, etc.

forge[1], *n.*, *v.*, **forged, forging.** –*n.* 1. the special furnace in which metal is heated before shaping. –*v.* 2. to form by heating and hammering. 3. to imitate (a signature, etc.) fraudulently. – **forgery**, *n.*

forge[2], *v.*, **forged, forging.** to move ahead slowly.

forget, *v.*, **-got; -gotten** or **-got; -getting.** 1. to cease or fail to remember. 2. to overlook.

for·give, *v.*, **-gave, -given, -giving.** 1. to cease to feel resentment against. 2. to pardon (an offence or an offender).

forgo, *v.*, **-went, -gone, -going.** to do without.

fork, *n.* 1. (anything resembling) an instrument having 2 or more prongs for holding, lifting, etc. 2. a branch of a river, road, etc. –*v.* 3. to lift, dig, etc., with a fork. 4. to divide into 2 branches.

for·lorn, *adj.* 1. unhappy or miserable, as in appearance. 2. desperate or hopeless, as in outlook.

form, *n.* 1. external shape or appearance considered apart from colour or material. 2. a document with blank spaces to be filled in. 3. procedure or conduct, as judged by social standards. 4. condition, esp. good condition, with reference to fitness. 5. a single division of a school containing pupils of about the same age or of the same level of scholastic progress. 6. a bench or long seat. 7. to construct or frame. 8. to make or produce; serve to make up, or constitute. 9. to develop (habits, friendships, etc.). 10. to give shape to; fashion. 11. to take or assume form.

formal, *adj.* 1. marked by form or ceremony. 2. made or done in accordance with forms. – **formalise**, *v.* – **formality**, *n.*

for·malde·hyde /ˈfɔːmældəhaɪd/, *n.* a disinfectant and preservative gas.

format, *n.* 1. the general physical appearance of a book, newspaper, or magazine, etc. 2. the plan or style of something.

for·ma·tion, *n.* 1. the manner in which a thing is formed. 2. a group of things arranged according to a fixed plan.

for·ma·tive, *adj.* giving form or shape.

former, *adj.* 1. preceding in time. 2. being the first of 2.

for·mid·able /ˈfɔːmədəbəl, fɔːˈmɪdəbəl/, *adj.* that is to be feared or dreaded.

for·mu·la, *n., pl.* **-las, -lae** /-liː/. 1. a set form of words. 2. *Maths.* a rule or principle, frequently expressed in algebraic symbols. 3. a recipe or prescription.

for·mu·late, *v.*, **-lated, -lating.** to state precisely, definitely or systematically.

for·ni·cation, *n.* voluntary sexual intercourse between unmarried persons. – **fornicate**, *v.*

for·sake, *v.*, **-sook, -saken, -saking.** 1. to desert or abandon. 2. to give up or renounce (a habit, way of life, etc.).

fort, *n.* a strong or fortified place.

forth, *adv.* 1. forwards; onwards or outwards: *to go forth into the world.* 2. out into view or consideration: *He brought forth new ideas.*

forth·coming, *adj.* 1. about to appear. 2. ready or available when required.

forth·right, *adj.* going straight to the point.

forth·with, *adv.* without delay.

for·tify, *v.*, **-fied, -fying.** 1. to strengthen against attack. 2. to increase the strength of, as by adding alcohol, vitamins, etc. – **fortification**, *n.*

forti·tude, *n.* moral strength or endurance.

fort·night, *n.* 2 weeks.

for·tress, *n.* a large fortified place.

for·tui·tous /fɔːˈtjuːətəs/, *adj.* happening or produced by chance.

for·tu·nate, *adj.* 1. having good fortune. 2. bringing or presaging good fortune.

fortune

for·tune, *n.* **1.** position in life as determined by wealth. **2.** great wealth. **3.** chance; luck.

forty, *n., pl.* **-ties**, *adj.* a cardinal number, 10 times 4. – **fortieth**, *adj., n.*

forum, *n., pl.* **forums, fora.** an assembly for the discussion of questions of public interest.

for·ward, *adj.* **1.** moving ahead; onward. **2.** well-advanced. **3.** presumptuous, pert, or bold. **4.** situated in the front. –*n.* **5.** *Aust. Rules, etc.* a player placed in front of the rest of the team. –*adv.* **6.** Also, **forwards**, towards a place or time in advance; ahead. –*v.* **7.** to send forward, esp. to a new address. **8.** to advance or help onwards.

fos·sick, *v.* to search systematically or in a small way, esp. for gold.

fossil, *n.* any remains or trace of an animal or plant of a former geological age.

foster, *v.* **1.** to encourage. **2.** to bring up or rear, as a foster-child.

foster-child, *n., pl.* **-children.** a child brought up by someone not its own mother or father.

fought, *v.* past tense and past participle of **fight**.

foul, *adj.* **1.** grossly offensive to the senses. **2.** filthy or dirty. **3.** unfavourable or stormy, as weather. **4.** wicked or vile. **5.** contrary to the rules. –*adv.* **6.** in a foul manner. –*n.* **7.** a violation of the rules of a sport or game. –*v.* **8.** to make foul. **9.** to defile; disgrace.

found[1], *v.* past tense and past participle of **find**.

found[2], *v.* **1.** to set up or establish. **2.** to lay the lowest part of (a structure) on a firm base. **3.** to base or ground (*on* or *upon*).

foun·dation, *n.* **1.** that on which something is founded. **2.** the lowest division of a building, wall, or the like, usu. below the surface of the ground. **3.** the act of establishing, etc. **4.** an endowed institution.

foun·der, *v.* **1.** to fill with water and sink, as a ship. **2.** to go lame, as a horse.

found·ling, *n.* an infant found abandoned.

foundry, *n.* a factory for producing metal casts.

fount, *n.* **1.** a spring of water; fountain. **2.** a source or origin.

foun·tain, *n.* **1.** a spring, source or mechanical jet of water. **2.** the source or origin of anything.

fountain pen, *n.* a pen holding ink which is supplied to the point of the nib.

four, *n.* a cardinal number, 3 plus one. – **fourth**, *n., adj.*

four·teen, *n.* a cardinal number, 10 plus 4. – **fourteenth**, *n., adj.*

fowl, *n., pl.* **fowls**, (*esp. collectively*) **fowl. 1.** the domestic or barnyard hen or cock, or similar bird. **2.** any bird (now chiefly in combination).

fox, *n.* **1.** any of certain carnivores of the dog family. **2.** a cunning or crafty person. –*v.* **3.** *Colloq.* to deceive or trick.

foy·er, *n.* **1.** (in theatres and cinemas) the area between the outer lobby and the auditorium. **2.** a hall or entrance, esp. in a hotel.

fracas /ˈfrækɑ, -kəs/, *n.* an uproar.

frac·tion, *n.* **1.** *Maths.* one or more parts of a unit or whole number. **2.** a part as distinct from the combination of anything. – **fractional**, *adj.*

fraction

208

fractious

frac·tious, *adj.* 1. peevish. 2. unmanageable or stubborn.

frac·ture, *n., v.,* -tured, -turing. –*n.* 1. a break or split. –*v.* 2. to break or crack, as a bone, etc.

fra·gile, *adj.* easily broken or damaged. – **fragility**, *n.*

frag·ment, *n.* 1. a part broken off or detached. 2. an odd piece, bit, or scrap. – **fragmentary**, *adj.*

fra·grant, *adj.* having a pleasant odour. – **fragrance**, *n.*

frail, *adj.* 1. having delicate health. 2. easily broken; weak. – **frailty**, *n.*

frame, *n., v.,* framed, framing. –*n.* 1. an enclosing border as for a picture. 2. a structure. 3. the body with reference to its build. 4. a particular state, as of the mind. 5. one of the successive small pictures on a strip of film. –*v.* 6. to construct as by fitting and uniting parts. 7. *Colloq.* to incriminate unjustly by a plot.

frame·work, *n.* 1. a structure composed of parts fitted together. 2. a structure designed to support or enclose something.

fran·chise, *n.* 1. the rights of a citizen, esp. the right to vote. 2. permission granted by a manufacturer to a distributor or retailer to sell his products.

frangi·panni, *n., pl.* -nies. a shrub or tree with yellow and white, occasionally pink, flowers.

frank, *adj.* 1. open or unreserved in speech. 2. undisguised. –*v.* 3. to mark (a letter, parcel, etc.) for transmission free of the usual charge.

frank·furt, *n.* a reddish variety of sausage. Also, **frankfurter, frank**.

fran·tic, *adj.* wild with excitement, pain, etc.

freehand

fra·ter·nal frəˈtɜːnəl, *adj.* brotherly.

fra·ter·nise ˈfrætənaɪz, *v.,* -nised, -nising. to associate in a fraternal or friendly way.

fra·ter·nity, *n., pl.* -ties. a body of persons associated as by ties of brotherhood.

freud, *n.* 1. deceit by which it is sought to gain some unfair or dishonest advantage. 2. one who makes deceitful pretences. – **fraudulent**, *adj.*

fraught, *adj.* involving; attended: *fraught with danger*.

fray[1], *n.* a fight, skirmish, or battle.

fray[2], *v.* 1. to exasperate; upset. 2. to be worn to threads, as cloth, etc.

fraz·zled, *adj.* weary; tired out.

freak, *n.* 1. a sudden and apparently causeless turn of events. 2. any curiously unusual object. –*adj.* 3. unusual; odd.

freckle, *n.* a small brownish spot in the skin.

free, *adj.,* freer, freest, *v.,* freed, freeing. –*adj.* 1. enjoying personal rights or liberty. 2. not literal, as a translation. 3. clear of obstructions. 4. available; unoccupied. 5. exempt or released from something specified: *free from obligations*. 6. that may be used by or open to all. 7. easy, firm, or swift in movement. 8. not held fast or attached. 9. ready in giving. 10. provided without charge. –*v.* 11. to set at liberty. 12. to disengage (*from* or *of*).

free·dom, *n.* 1. exemption from external control. 2. absence of obligations, etc. 3. ease of movement or action.

free·hand, *adj.* done by the hand without aids.

209

free·hold, *n.* unconditional ownership of property for unlimited time.

free lance, *n.* a journalist, commercial artist, editor, etc., who does not work on a regular salaried basis for any one employer.

freesia 'friːzə, *n.* a fragrant flowering plant.

free·style, *n.* →crawl (def. 6).

free·way, *n.* a road designed for high speed traffic. Also, **expressway.**

freeze, *v.,* **froze, frozen, freezing,** *n.* —*v.* **1.** to (cause something to) change from the liquid to the solid state by loss of heat. **2.** to be extremely cold. **3.** to (cause something to) suffer the effects of intense cold. **4.** to stop suddenly, as through fear, shock, etc. **5.** to exclude from society, business, etc., as by chilling behaviour, severe competition, etc. (*out*). **6.** to fix (wages, prices, etc.) at a specific level. —*n.* **7.** the act of freezing. **8.** legislative action by a government to fix wages, prices, etc., at a specific level.

freight, *n.* **1.** cargo carried for pay. **2.** the charge made for transporting goods. —*v.* **3.** to transport as freight; send by freight.

French horn, *n.* a mellow-toned brass wind instrument.

fren·etic, *adj.* frantic.

fren·zy, *n., pl.* **-zies. 1.** wild excitement or enthusiasm. **2.** mental derangement. – **frenzied,** *adj.*

fre·quen·cy, *n., pl.* **-cies. 1.** frequent occurrence. **2.** rate of recurrence. **3.** *Physics.* the number of cycles or vibrations of a wave motion in unit time.

fre·quent, *adj.* **1.** occurring at short intervals. **2.** constant; regular. —*v.* **3.** to visit often.

fres·co, *n., pl.* **-coes, -cos.** the art of painting on fresh lime plaster.

fresh, *adj.* **1.** newly made or obtained, etc. **2.** newly arrived. **3.** not previously known. **4.** (of water) not salt. **5.** not deteriorated. **6.** pure, cool, or refreshing, as air. **7.** cheeky.

fret[1]**,** *v.,* **fretted, fretting. 1.** to give oneself up to feelings of resentful discontent. **2.** to torment or vex. – **fretful,** *adj.*

fret[2]**,** *n.* an interlaced, angular design; fretwork.

fret·work, *n.* ornamental work consisting of interlacing parts.

fri·a·ble, *adj.* easily crumbled.

friar, *n.* a brother or member of one of certain Christian religious orders.

fric·tion, *n.* **1.** clashing or conflict, as of opinions, etc. **2.** *Mech., Physics.* the resistance to the relative motion (sliding or rolling) of surfaces of bodies in contact. **3.** the rubbing of the surface of one body against that of another.

fridge, *n. Colloq.* →refrigerator.

fried, *v.* past tense and past participle of fry[1].

friend, *n.* someone with whom one is on good terms and likes well. – **friendly,** *adj.* – **friendship,** *n.*

frieze, *n.* any decorative band or feature, as on a wall.

frig·ate /'frɪgət/, *n.* a general-purpose warship.

fright, *n.* **1.** sudden and extreme fear. **2.** a person or thing of shocking or ridiculous appearance. – **frighten,** *v.*

fright·ful, *adj.* terrible or alarming.

frigid, *adj.* **1.** very cold in temperature. **2.** without warmth of feeling.

frill, *n.* a strip of material or lace gathered at one edge; a ruffle.

fringe, *n., adj. –n.* **1.** an ornamental bordering of lengths of thread, cord, etc. **2.** hair falling over the brow. **3.** a border or extremity. *–adj.* **4.** accessory; supplementary: *fringe benefits.* **5.** of persons living on the outskirts of social acceptability.

frisk, *v.* **1.** to dance or gambol, as in frolic. **2.** *Colloq.* to search (a person) for concealed weapons, etc. – **frisky,** *adj.*

frit·ter[1], *v.* to waste (money, etc.) little by little (*away*).

frit·ter[2], *n.* a small cake of batter fried.

fri·vo·lous, *adj.* **1.** not worthy of serious notice. **2.** not serious, as persons.

frizz, *v.,* **frizzed, frizzing,** *n., pl.* **frizzes.** *–v.* **1.** to make into small, crisp curls. *–n.* **2.** something frizzed, as hair. Also, **friz.** – **frizzy,** *adj.*

friz·zle, *v.,* **-zled, -zling.** to make a sizzling or sputtering noise in frying or the like.

fro, *adv.* in the phrase **to and fro,** back and forth.

frock, *n.* a dress, esp. for a small girl.

frog, *n.* **1.** a tailless amphibian. **2.** a slight hoarseness of voice.

frog·man, *n., pl.* **-men.** a swimmer specially equipped for swimming underwater.

frolic, *n., v.,* **-icked, -icking.** *–v.* **1.** merry play; fun. *–v.* **2.** to play merrily; have fun.

from, *prep.* a particle specifying a starting point, and hence used to express removal or separation in space, time, order, etc., distinction, source and cause.

frond, *n.* a finely divided leaf, often large.

front, *n.* **1.** the foremost part or surface of anything. **2.** someone or something which serves as a cover for another activity, esp. an illegal or disreputable one. **3.** *Meteorol.* a surface separating 2 dissimilar air-masses. *–adj.* **4.** of or pertaining to the front. *–v.* **5.** to have or turn the front towards; face. **6.** Also, **front up.** *Colloq.* to arrive; turn up. – **frontal,** *adj.*

fron·tier, *n.* that part of a country which borders another country.

frontis·piece, *n.* an illustrated leaf preceding the titlepage of a book.

frost, *n.* **1.** a covering of minute ice needles, formed from the atmosphere at night on cold surfaces. *–v.* **2.** to cover with frost. **3.** to give a frostlike surface to (glass, etc.).

frost·bite, *n.* an inflammation on a part of the body due to excessive exposure to extreme cold.

frost·ing, *n.* a kind of cake icing.

froth, *n.* a mass of bubbles; foam.

frown, *v.* to contract the brow as in displeasure.

frozen, *v.* past participle of **freeze.**

frugal, *adj.* economical in use or expenditure. – **frugality,** *n.*

fruit, *n.* **1.** any product of vegetable growth useful to men or animals. **2.** *Bot.* the developed ovary of a seed plant, with its contents and related parts. **3.** anything produced; effect; profit.

fru·i·tion /fruˈɪʃən/, *n.* attainment of maturity; realisation of results.

fruity, *adj.,* **-tier, -tiest. 1.** having the taste or flavour of fruit. **2.** (of wine)

fruity

having body and fullness of flavour.

frump, *n.* a dowdy, drably dressed woman.

frus·trate, *v.,* **-trated, -trating. 1.** to make (plans, efforts, etc.) ineffective. **2.** to disappoint or thwart (a person). – **frustration,** *n.*

fry[1], *v.,* **fried, frying.** to cook in fat, oil, etc., usu. over direct heat.

fry[2], *n., pl.* **fry. 1.** the young of fishes. **2. small fry,** unimportant or insignificant people; young children.

fuchsia /ˈfjuʃə/, *n.* any of several plants with handsome drooping flowers.

fuck, *Colloq.* –*v.* **1.** to have sexual intercourse with. –*n.* **2.** the act of sexual intercourse.

fuddy-duddy, *n.* a fussy, stuffy, or old-fashioned person.

fudge[1], *n.* a soft sweet made of sugar, butter, etc.

fudge[2], *v.,* **fudged, fudging. 1.** to put together in a makeshift, clumsy, or dishonest way; fake. **2.** (in games and contests) to cheat.

fuel, *n.* a combustible matter used to maintain fire, as coal, wood, oil, etc.

fugi·tive /ˈfjudʒətɪv, ɪv/, *n.* a runaway.

fugue /fjug/, *n. Music.* a composition based upon one, 2, or even more interwoven themes.

ful·crum /ˈfʊlkrəm/, *n., pl.* **-crums, -cra** /-krə/. the support on which a lever turns in moving a body.

ful·fil, *v.,* **-filled, -filling. 1.** to carry out, as a prophecy, promise, etc. **2.** to satisfy (requirements, etc.).

full, *adj.* **1.** containing all that can be held. **2.** complete; entire; maxi-

funicular railway

mum. **3.** (of garments, etc.) wide, ample.

full stop, *n.* the point or character (.) used to mark the end of a sentence, indicate an abbreviation, etc.; a period. Also, **full point.**

ful·mi·nate, *v.,* **-nated, -nating.** to issue denunciations or the like (*against*).

ful·some, *adj.* immoderate, esp. in flattery.

fumble, *v.,* **-bled, -bling.** to feel or grope about clumsily.

fume, *n., v.,* **fumed, fuming.** –*n.* **1.** (*oft. pl.*) any smokelike or vaporous exhalation. –*v.* **2.** to show irritation or anger.

fumi·gate, *v.,* **-gated, -gating.** to expose to smoke or fumes, as in disinfecting.

fun, *n.* merry amusement; joking; playfulness.

func·tion, *n.* **1.** an activity proper to a person, thing, or institution. **2.** any ceremonious public or social gathering or occasion. –*v.* **3.** to act; serve; operate; carry out normal work or processes. – **functional,** *adj.*

fund, *n.* **1.** a stock of money. **2.** a store or stock of something: *She is a fund of knowledge.* –*v.* **3.** to provide funds for.

funda·mental, *adj.* serving as a foundation; underlying.

funeral, *n.* the ceremonies connected with the disposal of the body of a dead person. – **funereal,** *adj.*

fungus /ˈfʌŋɡəs/, *n., pl.* **fungi, funguses. 1.** a plant without chlorophyll, as mushrooms, moulds, or mildews. **2.** *Pathol.* a spongy morbid growth.

funi·cular railway, *n.* a railway

funicular railway

system of cable-linked cars operating up steep gradients.

funk, *n. Colloq.* a state of abject terror.

funnel, *n.* 1. a cone-shaped utensil for pouring liquid, etc., through a small opening. 2. a metal chimney, esp. of a ship or a steam-engine.

funnel-web, *n.* either of 2 species of large, aggressive, venomous, eastn Aust. spiders.

funny, *adj.*, **-nier**, **-niest**. 1. amusing; comical. 2. strange; queer; odd.

fur, *n.* 1. the skin of certain animals, covered with a thick, hairy coating. 2. the cured and treated skin of animals used in garments, etc.

fur·bish, *v.* to restore to freshness of appearance or condition (*up*).

furi·ous, *adj.* 1. full of rage. 2. intensely violent, as wind, storms, etc.

furl, *v.* to draw into a compact roll, as a sail, etc.

fur·long, *n.* a unit of distance in the imperial system, equal to 201.168 m. *Symbol:* fur

fur·lough, *n.* leave of absence from official duty, usu. for a longish period.

fur·nace, *n.* a structure or apparatus in which to generate heat.

fur·nish, *v.* 1. to provide or supply. 2. to fit up (a house, room, etc.) with necessary appliances, esp. furniture.

fur·ni·ture, *n.* the movable articles required for use or ornament in a house, office, or the like.

furore /'fjuro/, *n.* a general outburst of enthusiasm or excited disorder.

furphy, *n.*, *pl.* **-phies.** a rumour; a false story.

furrow, *n.* a narrow trench or groove.

fuzz

fur·ther, *compar. adv. and adj.*, *superl.* **furthest**, *v.* –*adv.* 1. at or to a greater distance; farther. 2. at or to a more advanced point; to a greater extent; farther. 3. in addition; moreover. –*adj.* 4. more distant or remote; farther: *the further horizon.* 5. additional; more: *further assistance.* –*v.* 6. to help forward (a cause, etc.).

fur·tive, *adj.* 1. taken, done, used, etc., by stealth. 2. sly; shifty.

fury, *n.*, *pl.* **-ries.** unrestrained violent passion, esp. anger.

fuse[1], *n.* 1. *Elect.* a device for preventing an excessive current from passing through a circuit. 2. a tube, ribbon, or the like, filled or saturated with combustible matter, for igniting an explosive.

fuse[2], *v.*, **fused**, **fusing.** to combine or blend by melting together.

fuse·lage /'fjuzəlaʒ, -lɪdʒ/, *n.* the body of an aircraft.

fusion, *n.* 1. the act or process of fusing. 2. that which is fused.

fuss, *n.* 1. an excessive display of useless activity. 2. a commotion or dispute. –*v.* 3. to make a fuss; move fussily about. – **fussy**, *adj.*

futile, *adj.* incapable of producing any result; ineffective. – **futility**, *n.*

future, *n.* 1. the time that is to be or come. 2. what will exist or happen in future time. –*adj.* 3. pertaining to or connected with time to come.

futur·is·tic, *adj.* (of design) anticipating the age of space travel and living; ultra-modern.

fuzz, *n.* 1. loose, light, fibrous, or fluffy matter. 2. *Colloq.* a blur. 3. *Colloq.* the police force. – **fuzzy**, *adj.*

Gg

G, g, *n., pl.* **G's** or **Gs, g's** or **gs.** the 7th letter of the English alphabet.

gaber·dine, *n.* a closely woven twill fabric of cotton or spun rayon.

gable, *n.* the triangular wall formed by the 2 slopes of a roof.

gadget, *n.* a mechanical contrivance or device.

gaffe, *n.* a social blunder.

gaffer, *n.* old man, boss, foreman, chief electrician in film unit.

gag¹, *v.,* **gagged, gagging,** *n.* —*v.* **1.** to stop up the mouth so as to prevent speech. **2.** to restrain by force or authority from freedom of speech or expression. **3.** to heave with nausea. —*n.* **4.** something thrust into or bound around the mouth to prevent speech.

gag², *v.,* **gagged, gagging,** *n.* —*v.* **1.** to make jokes. —*n.* **2.** a joke.

gage, *n.* a pledge or pawn.

gaggle, *n.* a flock of geese.

gaiety, *n., pl.* **-ties.** the state of being gay or cheerful.

gain, *v.* **1.** to obtain (something desired). **2.** to acquire as an increase or addition. **3.** to reach by effort; arrive at. **4.** to improve; make progress. **5.** profit; advantage. **6.** an increase or advance.

gain·say, *v.,* **-said, -saying.** **1.** to deny. **2.** to speak or act against.

gait, *n.* **1.** a particular manner of walking. **2.** the pace of a horse.

gaiter, *n.* a covering for the ankle and instep.

gala, *n.* a festive occasion.

galaxy, *n., pl.* **-axies.** a large system of stars. — **galactic**, *adj.*

gale, *n.* a strong wind.

gall¹, *n.* **1.** bile. **2.** something very bitter or severe. **3.** bitterness of spirit. **4.** impudence; effrontery.

gall², *n.* **1.** a sore on the skin, esp. of a horse. —*v.* **2.** to irritate.

gall³, *n.* an abnormal growth on a plant.

gal·lant, /ˈgælənt, gəˈlɒnt/, *adj.* **1.** brave and dashing. **2.** polite and attentive to women. **3.** generous or sporting.

gall bladder, *n.* a small sac attached to the liver containing bile.

gal·leon, /ˈgælɪən, ˈgæljən/, *n.* a kind of large sailing vessel.

gal·lery, *n., pl.* **-leries.** **1.** a covered walk. **2.** a platform in a church, theatre, etc., to provide extra seats. **3.** any audience. **4.** a place for exhibiting works of art.

galley, *n., pl.* **-leys.** **1.** an early ship propelled by oars. **2.** the kitchen of a ship or airliner.

galli·vant, *v.* to go from place to place in a light-hearted manner.

gallon, *n.* a unit of capacity in the imperial system.

gallop, *v.* **1.** to ride a horse at full speed. **2.** to race or hurry. —*n.* **3.** fastest gait of a horse.

gal·lows, *n., pl.* **-lows, -lowses.** a wooden frame used for the hanging of criminals.

gall·stone, *n.* a stone formed in the bile ducts or gall bladder.

gallup poll, *n.* the questioning of a

gallup poll   **garland**

cross-section of the population in order to assess voting intentions.

galore, *adv. (used only after nouns)* in abundance.

ga·loshes, *n.pl.* a pair of rubber shoes worn over shoes in wet weather.

galva·nise, *v.*, **-nised**, **-nising**. 1. to startle into sudden activity. 2. to coat (iron or steel) with zinc.

gambit, *n.* an opening move in chess, in which the player sacrifices a pawn so as to obtain some advantage.

gamble, *v.*, **-bled**, **-bling**, *n.* –*v.* 1. to play at any game of chance for stakes. 2. to act on favourable hopes or assessment. –*n.* 3. anything risky or uncertain.

gambol, *v.*, **-bolled**, **-bolling**. to frolic and run or skip about.

game, *n., adj.*, **gamer**, **gamest**. –*n.* 1. an amusement or pastime. 2. a contest; match. 3. sport of any kind; joke. 4. wild animals hunted for sport, food, or profit. –*adj.* 5. pertaining to animals hunted as game. 6. with fighting spirit; plucky.

gamete /'gæmiːt, gə'miːt/, *n.* either of the 2 germ cells which unite to form a new organism.

gamin, *adj.* (of a person's appearance, or hairstyle) elfin.

gammon, *n.* a smoked or cured ham.

gamut, *n.* the whole scale or range.

gander, *n.* 1. a male goose. 2. *Colloq.* a look at something.

gang, *n.* a band or group, esp. of persons associated for some disreputable purpose. – **gangster**, *n.*

gan·gling /'gæŋglɪŋ/, *adj.* awkwardly tall and spindly.

gang·plank, *n.* a plank used as a bridge into a ship, etc.

gan·grene, *n.* the dying of tissue, as from interruption of circulation. – **gangrenous**, *adj.*

gang·way, *n.* a passageway.

gannet, *n.* a large seabird.

gantry, *n., pl.* **-tries**. a spanning framework.

gaol /dʒeɪl/, *n.* a prison. Also, **jail**.

gap, *n.* 1. a break or opening. 2. a vacant space or interval.

gape, *v.*, **gaped**, **gaping**. 1. to stare with open mouth, as in wonder. 2. to split or become wide open.

garage, *n.* 1. a building for housing cars, etc. 2. a place where cars, etc., are repaired and petrol is sold.

garb, *n.* fashion or mode of dress.

gar·bage, *n.* rubbish.

garble, *v.*, **-bled**, **-bling**. to distort, corrupt or confuse (statements, etc.).

garden, *n.* 1. a plot of ground for the cultivation of plants. –*v.* 2. to lay out or cultivate a garden. – **gardener**, *n.*

gar·denia, *n.* a plant cultivated for its fragrant, waxlike, white flowers.

gar·fish, *n., pl.* **-fishes**, *(esp. collectively)* **-fish**. a fish having a slender body and a needle-like lower jaw.

gar·gan·tuan /ɡɑːˈɡæntʃuən/, *adj.* gigantic; prodigious.

gargle, *v.*, **-gled**, **-gling**. to wash or rinse (the throat or mouth) with a liquid held in the throat.

gar·goyle, *n.* a spout, often terminating in a grotesque head.

garish /'ɡɛərɪʃ, ɡɑr-/, *adj.* glaring, or excessively bright.

gar·land, *n.* a wreath or string of flowers, etc.

215

garlic

garlic, *n.* a hardy plant, with a strong-scented bulb used in cookery and medicine.

gar·ment, *n.* any article of clothing.

garnet, *n.* a deep red gemstone.

gar·nish, *v.* 1. to fit out with something that adorns or decorates. –*n.* 2. something that decorates, esp. food.

garret, *n.* → attic.

garri·son, *n.* a body of troops stationed in a fortified place.

gar·rotte, *n.* a Spanish mode of capital punishment, originally by strangulation.

garru·lous, *adj.* given to much talking, esp. about trifles.

garter, *n.* a fastening to keep up stockings or long socks.

gas[1], *n.*, *pl.* **gases**, *v.*, **gassed**, **gassing**. –*n.* 1. *Physics.* a substance whose molecules are sufficiently mobile for it to occupy the whole of the space in which it is contained. –*v.* 2. to overcome with gas or fumes. – **gaseous**, *adj.*

gas[2], *n. Chiefly U.S. Colloq.* 1. petrol. 2. **step on the gas**, to hurry.

gash, *n.* a long, deep wound or cut.

gasket, *n.* anything used as a packing or jointing material for making joints fluid-tight.

gasp, *n.* 1. a sudden, short breath. 2. a short, convulsive utterance. –*v.* 3. to catch the breath or struggle for breath with open mouth.

gas·tric, *adj.* pertaining to the stomach.

gastro·nome, *n.* a gourmet.

gastro·nomic, *adj.* pertaining to the art or science of good eating.

gastro·pod, *n.* a mollusc of the snail class.

gaze

gate, *n.* 1. a movable barrier in a fence or wall, or across a passageway. 2. a device for regulating the passage of water, etc., as in a dam, pipe, etc.; valve.

gate·crash, *v.* to attend (a party) uninvited.

gather, *v.* 1. to bring or come together into one company or aggregate. 2. to learn or infer from observation. 3. to draw (someone or something) close. 4. to draw up (cloth) on a thread in fine folds. 5. to increase (speed, etc.).

gauche /gouʃ/, *adj.* awkward; clumsy. – **gaucheness**, **gaucherie**, *n.*

gaudy, *adj.*, **-dier**, **-diest**. brilliant; excessively showy.

gauge, *v.*, **gauged**, **gauging**, *n.* –*v.* 1. to appraise, estimate, or judge. 2. to determine the dimensions, capacity, quantity, or force of. –*n.* 3. a standard of measure. 4. a means of estimating or judging; criterion; test. 5. any instrument for measuring pressure, volume, or dimensions.

gaunt, *adj.* abnormally thin; emaciated; haggard.

gaunt·let, *n.* 1. a medieval glove. 2. **throw down the gauntlet**, to extend a challenge, originally to a duel.

gauze, *n.* any thin transparent fabric.

gave, *v.* past tense of **give**.

gavel, *n.* a small mallet used by a presiding officer to signal for attention or order.

gawk, *v. Colloq.* to stare stupidly.

gay, *adj.*, **gayer**, **gayest**, *n.* 1. having or showing a joyous mood. 2. bright or showy. 3. *Colloq.* camp; homosexual. –*n.* 4. *Colloq.* a homosexual.

gaze, *v.*, **gazed**, **gazing**, *n.* –*v.* 1. to

gaze

look steadily or intently. –*n.* **2.** a steady or intent look.

gazebo, *n.*, *pl.* **-bos**, **-boes**. a structure, esp. in garden, etc., commanding an extensive view.

gazelle, *n.* a small antelope.

gazette, *n.*, *v.*, **-zetted**, **-zetting**. –*n.* **1.** a newspaper. **2.** an official government journal, containing lists of government appointments, etc. –*v.* **3.** to publish, announce, or list in a gazette.

gear, *n.* **1.** *Mach.* **a.** a mechanism for transmitting or changing motion, as by toothed wheels. **b.** a toothed wheel which engages with another wheel or part. **2.** tools or apparatus; harness; tackle.

gecko, *n.* a small nocturnal lizard.

geese, *n.* plural of **goose**.

Geiger counter /'gaɪgə/, *n.* an instrument for detecting radioactivity.

gel, *n.* a jellylike substance.

gelatine, *n.* an organic substance, obtained by boiling in water the ligaments, bones, skin, etc., of animals, and forming the basis of jellies, glues, and the like. – **gelatinous**, *adj.*

geld, *v.*, **gelded** or **gelt**, **gelding**. to castrate (esp. animals).

gelding, *n.* a castrated animal, esp. a horse.

gelignite, *n.* an explosive.

gem, *n.* **1.** a stone used in jewellery. **2.** something likened to, or prized as, a gem, esp. something small.

gender, *n.* *Gram.* (in many languages) a set of classes, such as masculine, feminine and neuter, which together include all nouns.

gene, *n.* the unit of inheritance, situated on the chromosome, which passes on hereditary character.

genealogy, *n.*, *pl.* **-gies**. an account of the descent of a person or family through an ancestral line.

genera, *n.* plural of **genus**.

general, *adj.* **1.** pertaining to the whole, or to all members of a class or group; not partial or particular. **2.** not specific or special.

generalise, *v.*, **-lised**, **-lising**. **1.** to give a general (rather than specific or special) character to. **2.** to infer (a general principle, etc.) from facts, etc. **3.** to form general notions.

generality, *n.*, *pl.* **-ties**. **1.** a general or vague statement. **2.** general principle; general rule or law.

general practitioner, *n.* a non-specialist doctor. *Abbrev.:* G.P.

generate, *v.*, **-rated**, **-rating**. to bring into existence; give rise to; produce.

generation, *n.* **1.** the whole body of individuals born about the same time. **2.** production by natural or artificial processes; evolution, as of heat or sound.

generator, *n.* a machine which converts mechanical energy into electrical energy.

generic, *adj.* **1.** pertaining to a genus. **2.** referring to all the members of a genus or class.

generous, *adj.* **1.** bountiful; unselfish. **2.** free from meanness or smallness of mind or character. – **generosity**, *n.*

genesis, *n.*, *pl.* **-ses** /-siz/. origin; production; creation.

genetics, *n.* the science of heredity, dealing with resemblances and

genetics

differences of related organisms. – **geneticist**, *n.* – **genetic**, *adj.*

genial, *adj.* sympathetically cheerful.

genie, *n.* a spirit of Arabian mythology.

geni·tals, *n.pl.* the reproductive organs, esp. the external organs. Also, **genitalia**.

genius, *n.* **1.** the highest natural capacity for creative and original ideas. **2.** a person having such capacity.

geno·cide, *n.* planned extermination of a national or racial group. – **genocidal**, *adj.*

genre /'ʒɒnrə/, *n.* genus; kind; sort; style.

gen·teel, *adj.* belonging or suited to polite society. – **gentility**, *n.*

gen·tile, *adj.* of or pertaining to any people not Jewish.

gentle, *adj.*, **-tler**, **-tlest**. **1.** mild, kindly, or amiable. **2.** not severe, rough, or violent. **3.** moderate; gradual. **4.** of good birth or family.

gentle·man, *n., pl.* **-men**. **1.** a man of good breeding, education, and manners. **2.** (as a polite form of speech) any man.

gentry, *n.* the class below the nobility.

genu·flect, *v.* to bend the knee in reverence.

genu·ine, *adj.* **1.** being truly such; real; authentic. **2.** free from pretence or affectation.

genus, *n., pl.* **genera**. **1.** a kind; sort; class. **2.** *Biol.* the usual major subdivision of a family or subfamily.

geog·raphy, *n., pl.* **-phies**. the study of the earth's surface, climate, vegetation, population, etc. – **geographer**, *n.* – **geographical**, *adj.*

geol·ogy, *n., pl.* **-gies**. the science

gerund

which treats of the composition and changes in structure of the earth. – **geological**, *adj.* – **geologist**, *n.*

geom·etry, *n.* that branch of mathematics which deduces the properties of figures (def. 4). – **geometric**, *adj.*

geo·phys·ics, *n.* the physics of the earth, dealing esp. with the study of inaccessible portions of the earth.

gera·nium, *n.* a plant cultivated for its showy flowers.

geri·atric, *n.* an aged person, esp. an incapacitated one.

germ, *n.* **1.** a micro-organism, esp. when disease-producing. **2.** that from which anything springs as if from a seed.

german, *adj.* **1.** sprung from the same father and mother (always placed after the noun). **2.** sprung from the brother or sister of one's father or mother, or from brothers or sisters.

ger·mane, *adj.* closely related; pertinent.

German measles, *n.* a contagious disease accompanied by fever and a rash and which may cause serious defects in the unborn child of a pregnant woman.

German shepherd dog, *n.* →**Alsatian**.

ger·mi·nate, *v.,* **-nated**, **-nating**. to begin to grow or develop.

gerry·mander, *n. Politics.* an arbitrary arrangement of electoral boundaries made so as to give one party an unfair advantage in elections.

gerund, *n. Gram.* a noun formed

from a verb, as *skiing* in *Skiing is fun*.

ges·tate /ˈdʒɛsteɪt/, *v.*, -tated, -tating. to carry in the womb from conception to delivery. – **gestation**, *n.*

ges·tic·u·late /-/, *v.*, -lated, -lating. to make or use gestures, esp. in an animated or excited manner, with or instead of speech.

ges·ture /ˈdʒɛstʃə/, *n., v.,* -tured, -turing. –*n.* 1. movement of the body that expresses an idea or an emotion. 2. any action or proceeding intended for effect or as a formality; demonstration. –*v.* 3. to make or use gestures.

get, *v.*, got; getting. 1. to obtain, gain, or acquire by any means. 2. to fetch or bring. 3. to hear or understand. 4. to be afflicted with (an illness, etc.). 5. *Colloq.* to hit. 6. to come to or arrive. 7. to become; grow. 8. to succeed in coming or going (*away, in, into, out, over, through,* etc.). 9. **get across**, to make understood. 10. **get at, a.** to reach; make contact with. **b.** *Colloq.* to hint at or imply. **c.** *Colloq.* to influence, as by bribery. 11. **get away with,** to avoid punishment or blame for. 12. **get by,** to manage in spite of difficulties. 13. **get even with,** to square accounts with; be revenged against. 14. **get his, hers,** etc. To get a just reward. 15. **get on, a.** to age. **b.** to make progress; proceed; advance. **c.** to agree or be friendly (*with*). 16. **get one's own back,** to be revenged. 17. **get round, a.** to outwit. **b.** to cajole or ingratiate oneself with (someone). **c.** to overcome (difficulties, etc.). 18. **get (someone) down,** to depress, discourage (someone). 19. **get (stuck) into,** *Colloq.* **a.** to attack (a person), physically or verbally. **b.** to set about a task vigorously. 20. **get to (someone). a.** to arouse deep feeling in (someone). **b.** to annoy or irritate (someone). 21. **get up, a.** to arise. **b.** to dress elaborately. **c.** to prepare, arrange, or organise. 22. **get up to,** to be involved in (mischief, etc.).

geyser /ˈgiːzə, ˈgaɪzə/, *n.* a hot spring which intermittently sends up jets of water and steam into the air.

ghastly, *adj.*, -lier, -liest. frightful; dreadful; horrible.

gher·kin /ˈgɜːkən/, *n.* a small immature cucumber used in pickling.

ghetto, *n., pl.* **ghettos, ghettoes.** an area in a city in which any minority group lives.

ghost, *n.* 1. the disembodied spirit of a dead person imagined as haunting living persons. –*v.* 2. to write for someone else who is publicly known as the author.

ghoul, *n.* 1. an evil demon. 2. a grave robber. 3. one who revels in what is revolting. – **ghoulish**, *adj.*

giant /ˈdʒaɪənt/, *n.* 1. a huge imaginary human being. 2. a person or thing of unusually great size, endowments, importance, etc. –*adj.* 3. gigantic; huge.

gibber¹ /ˈdʒɪbə/, *v.* to speak inarticulately; chatter. – **gibberish**, *n.*

gibber² /ˈgɪbə/, *n.* a stone; boulder.

gibbon, *n.* a kind of small ape.

gibe, *v.*, gibed, gibing. –*v.* 1. to utter mocking words; scoff; jeer. –*n.* 2. a taunting or sarcastic remark. Also, **jibe.**

giblet /ˈdʒɪblət/, *n.* (*usu. pl.*) the heart, liver, or gizzard from a fowl.

giddy, *adj.*, -dier, -diest. 1. frivolously light; flighty. 2. affected with vertigo; dizzy.

gift

gift /gɪft/, *n.* **1.** something given; a present. **2.** a special ability; natural endowment; talent.

gig[1], *n.* a light horse carriage.

gig[2], *n. Colloq.* (a booking for a band, etc., to perform at) a jazz or pop concert.

gi·gan·tic, *adj.* **1.** of, like, or for a giant. **2.** huge.

gig·gle, *v.,* -**gled,** -**gling.** *n.* -*v.* **1.** to laugh in a silly, undignified way; titter. -*n.* **2.** a silly laugh. **3.** *Colloq.* an amusing occasion.

gig·o·lo /ˈʒɪgəloʊ/, *n., pl.* -**los.** a young man supported by an older woman in return for companionship.

gild, *v.,* **gilded** or **gilt, gilding.** to coat with gold, gold leaf, etc.

gill /gɪl/, *n.* an aquatic respiratory organ.

gim·let /ˈgɪmlət/, *n.* a small tool for boring holes.

gim·mick, *n. Colloq.* a pronounced eccentricity, esp. one exploited to gain publicity.

gin[1], *n.* an alcoholic beverage obtained by redistilling spirits with juniper berries, orange peel, angelica root, etc.

gin[2], *n.* **1.** a machine for separating cotton from its seeds. **2.** a trap or snare for game, etc.

gin[3], *n.* a card game similar to rummy. Also, **gin rummy.**

gin·ger /ˈdʒɪndʒə/, *n.* **1.** a pungent, spicy rhizome used in cookery and medicine. **2.** (of hair) red. -*v.* **3.** *Colloq.* to impart spiciness or piquancy to; make lively.

gin·ger·ly, *adv.* with extreme care or caution; warily. — **gingerliness,** *n.*

ging·ham, *n.* yarn-dyed, plain-weave cotton fabric.

give

gip·sy, *n., pl.* -**sies. 1.** (*oft. cap.*) one of a nomadic Caucasian minority race of Hindu origin. **2.** a person who resembles or lives like a gipsy. Also, **gypsy.**

gi·raffe, *n.* a tall, long-necked, spotted ruminant of Africa.

gird, *v.,* **girt** or **girded, girding. 1.** to encircle with a belt or girdle. **2.** to prepare (oneself) mentally for action (*up*).

gird·er, *n.* a main horizontal supporting beam.

gir·dle, *n., v.,* -**dled, dling.** -*n.* **1.** a belt, etc., worn about the waist. **2.** a lightweight undergarment which supports the abdominal region of the body. -*v.* **3.** to encompass; enclose.

girl, *n.* a female child or young person.

girth, *n.* **1.** the measure around anything; circumference. **2.** a band passed under the belly of a horse, etc., to secure a saddle.

gist /dʒɪst/, *n.* the substance or pith of a matter; essential part.

give, *v.,* **gave, given, giving.** *n.* -*v.* **1.** to deliver freely; hand over: *to give a present.* **2.** to deliver to another in exchange for something; pay: *She gave £5 for it.* **3.** to grant permission or opportunity to. **4.** to present (as to an audience): *I give you the Mayor.* **5.** to suppose; assume: *given these facts.* **6.** to assign to someone as his right, lot, etc.: *to give him the benefit of the doubt.* **7.** *Orig. U.S. Colloq.* tell; offer as explanation: *Don't give me that.* **8.** to furnish or provide. **9.** to produce; present: *to give a play.* **10.** to yield under pressure or strain. **11. give in, a.** to yield; acknowledge defeat. **b.** to hand in. **12. give up, a.** to lose all

give

hope. **b.** to abandon as hopeless. **c.** to desist from; forsake: *give up a task.* **d.** to surrender. **e.** to devote entirely. **f.** to inform against. Also, **give away.** –*n.* **13.** the act or fact of yielding to pressure; elasticity.

giz·zard, *n.* the grinding or muscular stomach of birds.

gla·cier /'gleisiə, 'glæsiə/, *n.* an extended mass of ice formed from falling snow and moving very slowly. – **glacial**, *adj*

glad, *adj.* delighted or pleased.

glade, *n.* an open space in a forest.

gladi·a·tor, *n. Rom. Hist.* a person, often a slave or captive, who fought in public to entertain the people.

gladi·o·lus, *n., pl.* **-lus, -li** /ˈlaɪ/, **-luses.** a plant with spikes of variously coloured flowers.

glam·our, *n.* alluring and often illusory charm; fascination. – **glamorous**, *adj.*

glance, *v.,* **glanced, glancing,** *n.* –*v.* **1.** to look quickly or briefly. **2.** to gleam or flash. **3.** to go off in an oblique direction from an object struck. –*n.* **4.** a quick or brief look.

gland, *n. Anat.* an organ or tissue which secretes a substance which is used elsewhere in the body or is eliminated. – **glandular**, *adj.*

glare, *n., v.,* **glared, glaring.** –*n.* **1.** a strong, dazzling light. –*v.* **2.** to shine with a strong, dazzling light. **3.** to be conspicuous. **4.** to stare fiercely.

glass, *n.* **1.** a hard, brittle, usu. transparent substance produced from silica. **2.** (*pl.*) glass lenses set in a frame worn to help defective eyesight; spectacles. **3.** a glass container for drinking water, beer, etc.

glisten

glaze, *v.,* **glazed, glazing,** *n.* –*v.* **1.** to furnish, fit or cover with glass. **2.** to produce a vitreous or glossy surface on (pottery, pastry, etc.). –*n.* **3.** a smooth, glossy surface or coating.

gleam, *n.* **1.** a flash or beam of light. **2.** dim or subdued light. –*v.* **3.** to send forth a gleam or gleams. **4.** to appear suddenly and clearly.

glean, *v.* **1.** to gather slowly and laboriously in bits. **2.** to gather (grain, etc.) after the reapers. **3.** to discover or find out.

glee, *n.* demonstrative joy.

glen, *n.* a small, narrow, secluded valley.

glib, *adj.,* **glibber, glibbest.** spoken or speaking fluently, often thoughtlessly or insincerely so.

glide, *v.,* **glided, gliding.** **1.** to move smoothly and effortlessly along. **2.** *Aeron.* to move in the air, esp. gradually downwards, by gravity or momentum already acquired. –*n.* **3.** a gliding movement, as in dancing.

glider, *n. Aeron.* a motorless aeroplane for gliding from a higher to a lower level by gravity, or from a lower to a higher level by air currents.

glim·mer, *n.* a faint or unsteady light; gleam.

glimpse, *n., v.,* **glimpsed, glimpsing.** –*n.* **1.** a momentary sight or view. –*v.* **2.** to catch a glimpse of.

glint, *n.* **1.** a gleam or glimmer; flash. **2.** glinting brightness; lustre. –*v.* **3.** to gleam or flash.

glis·ten /'glɪsən/, *v.* **1.** to shine with a sparkling light. –*n.* **2.** a glistening; sparkle.

221

glitch

glitch, *n. Colloq.* a hitch; snag; malfunction.

glit·ter, *v.* to shine with a brilliant, sparkling light.

gloat, *v.* to smile smugly or scornfully.

globe, *n.* 1. the earth. 2. a sphere with a map of the earth. 3. anything spherical. – **globular**, *adj.*

glob·ule, *n.* a small spherical body.

glock·en·spiel /ˈglɒkənspil, -kənˌʃpil/, *n.* a set of steel bars mounted in a frame and struck with hammers.

gloom, *n.* 1. a state of melancholy or depression. 2. darkness. – **gloomy**, *adj.*

glo·ri·ous, *adj.* 1. full of glory. 2. brilliantly beautiful.

glory, *n., pl.* **glories**, *v.*, **gloried**, **glorying**. –*n.* 1. exalted praise, honour, or distinction, accorded by common consent. 2. resplendent beauty or magnificence. 3. the splendour and bliss of heaven; heaven. –*v.* 4. to be boastful; exult arrogantly (*in*).

gloss[1] /glɒs/, *n.* a superficial lustre. – **glossy**, *adj.*

gloss[2] /glɒs/, *n.* 1. an explanation by means of a note in a manuscript text. –*v.* 2. to give a specious interpretation of; explain away (*over*).

glos·sary, *n., pl.* **-ries**. a list of basic technical, and difficult terms in a subject or field, with definitions.

glove, *n.* a covering for the hand.

glow, *n.* 1. light emitted by a substance heated to luminosity; incandescence. 2. warmth of emotion or passion; ardour. –*v.* 3. to emit bright light and heat without flame. 4. to be animated with emotion.

gnomic

glower /ˈglouə, ˈglauə/, *v.* to stare with sullen dislike or discontent.

glu·cose, *n. Chem.* a sugar occurring in many fruits, animal tissues and fluids, etc.

glue, *n., v.*, **glued**, **gluing**. –*n.* 1. any adhesive substance made from any natural or synthetic resin, etc. –*v.* 2. to join or fasten with glue.

glum, *adj.*, **glummer**, **glummest**. gloomily sullen or silent; dejected.

glut /glʌt/, *v.*, **glutted**, **glutting**, *n.* 1. to feed or fill to satiety; sate. 2. to overstock. –*n.* 3. a full supply. 4. a surfeit.

gluten, *n.* the tough, viscid nitrogenous substance remaining when the flour of wheat or other grain is washed to remove the starch.

glu·ti·nous, *adj.* gluey; viscid; sticky.

glut·ton, *n.* 1. one who eats to excess. 2. one who accepts an inordinate amount of unpleasantness, etc.: *a glutton for punishment*. – **gluttonous**, *adj.* – **gluttony**, *n.*

glyc·erol, *n.* a colourless, odourless, liquid alcohol, of syrupy consistency and sweet taste, used as a solvent, plasticiser, or sweetener. Also, **glycerine**.

gnarled, *adj.* 1. (of trees) knotty. 2. (of persons) having a rugged, weatherbeaten appearance.

gnash, *v.* to grind (the teeth).

gnat, *n.* a small winged insect.

gnaw, *v.*, **gnawed** or **gnawn**, **gnawing**. 1. to bite persistently. 2. to consume with passion; torment. – **gnawer**, *n.*

gnome /noum/, *n.* (in fairy stories) a shrivelled little old man.

gnomic /ˈnoumɪk, ˈnɒm-/, *adj.* like or containing aphorisms.

gnu /nu/, *n., pl.* **gnus**, (*esp. collectively*) **gnu**. a large African antelope with an oxlike head.

go, *v.,* **went**, **gone**, **going**, *n., pl.* **goes**. –*v.* 1. to move or pass (along); proceed. 2. to move away or out; depart (opposed to *come* or *arrive*). 3. to keep or be in motion; act, work, or run. 4. to become: *to go mad*. 5. to reach or extend: *This road goes to the city*. 6. to belong; have a place: *That book goes on the top shelf*. 7. (of colours, etc.) to harmonise; be compatible. 8. to develop, esp. with reference to success, or failure: *How did the exam go?* 9. to fail; give way. 10. to carry final authority: *What I say goes*. 11. to be contained (into): *4 goes into 12*. 12. to be about, intending, or destined (used in the pres. part. fol. by an infinitive): *I am going to drive to town*. 13. **go at**, a. to undertake with vigour. b. to attack. 14. **go down**, a. to descend; slope down. b. to be defeated. c. to be remembered for posterity. 15. **go into**, to investigate thoroughly. 16. **go off**, a. to discharge; explode. b. (of food, etc.) to deteriorate. c. to take place (in a specified manner): *The party went off well*. d. *Colloq.* to come to dislike. 17. **go over**, a. to read or reread. b. to repeat. c. to examine. d. to have an effect (as specified): *Our suggestion went over badly*. –*n.* 18. the act of going. 19. *Colloq.* energy, spirit, or animation. 20. one's turn to play or to make an attempt at something. 21. *Colloq.* a success: *to make a go of something*. 22. **fair go**, *Colloq.* adequate opportunity. 23. **have (give) it a go**, *Colloq.* to make an attempt; try. 24. **on the go**, *Colloq.* very active.

goad, *n.* 1. a stick with a pointed end, for driving cattle, etc. –*v.* 2. to prick or drive with or as with a goad; incite.

goal, *n.* 1. that towards which effort is directed; aim or end. 2. an area, basket or structure into which players in a game try to send the ball.

goanna, *n.* a large Aust. monitor lizard.

goat, *n.* 1. an agile hollow-horned ruminant closely related to the sheep. 2. *Colloq.* a fool.

goatee, *n.* a man's beard trimmed to a tuft or a point on the chin.

gob, *n.* a mass or lump.

gobble[1], *v.,* **-bled, -bling**. to swallow hastily in large pieces; gulp.

gobble[2], *v.,* **-bled, -bling**. to make the characteristic throaty cry of a turkey cock.

gobble·de·gook, *n. Colloq.* language characterised by circumlocution and jargon.

goblet, *n.* a drinking glass with a foot and stem.

goblin, *n.* a grotesque mischievous sprite or elf.

God, *n.* 1. the one Supreme Being considered by many as the creator and ruler of the universe. 2. (*l.c.*) a deity, esp. male, presiding over some portion of worldly affairs.

god·child, *n., pl.* **-children**. one for whom a person (godparent) stands sponsor at baptism.

god·dess, *n.* a female god or deity.

god·ly, *adj.,* **-lier, -liest**. pious.

goggle, *n., v.,* **-gled, -gling**. –*n.* 1. (*pl.*) special spectacles designed to protect the eyes from wind, dust, water, or glare. –*v.* 2. to stare with bulging eyes. 3. to roll the eyes.

goitre, *n.* an enlargement of the

goitre

thyroid gland, on the front and sides of the neck.

gold, *n.* 1. a precious yellow metal, highly malleable and ductile, and free from liability to rust. *Symbol.*: Au 2. something like gold in brightness, preciousness, etc. 3. bright yellow-brown. – **golden**, *adj.*

gold·fish, *n., pl.* **-fishes**, (*esp. collectively*) **-fish**. a small fish of the carp family.

golf, *n.* an outdoor game, in which a small ball is driven with special clubs into a series of holes. – **golfer**, *n.*

gonad, *n.* the sex gland, male or female, in which gametes develop and appropriate sex hormones are produced.

gon·dola /'gɒndələ/, *n.* a long, narrow boat used on the Venetian canals. – **gondolier**, *n.*

gone, *adj.* departed; left.

gong, *n. Music.* an oriental bronze disc to be struck with a soft-headed stick.

gonor·rhoea, *n.* a contagious disease causing purulent inflammation mainly of the urethra and cervix.

good, *adj.*, **better**, **best**, *n.*, *interj.* –*adj.* 1. morally excellent; righteous; pious. 2. satisfactory in quality, quantity, or degree; excellent. 3. right; proper. 4. fresh and palatable. 5. reliable; safe. 6. pleasant. 7. (of clothes) best or newest. 8. competent or skilful; clever. 9. **a.** valid (*for*). **b.** giving rights or entitlement (*for*: *This coupon is good for 2 free tickets.* **c.** (of a person) willing to provide (*for*: *He is good for a loan.* 10. **good luck**, *Colloq.* (an expression wishing a person well). –*n.* 11. profit;

gorgeous

worth; advantage; benefit. 12. excellence or merit; righteousness; kindness; virtue. 13. (*pl.*) possessions. 14. (*pl.*) articles of trade; wares; merchandise. 15. **be up to no good**, *Colloq.* to do wrong; behave in a suspicious manner. 16. **for good** or **for good and all**, finally and permanently; for ever. 17. **make good**, **a.** to make recompense for; pay for. **b.** to keep to an agreement. **c.** to be successful. **d.** to prove the truth of; substantiate. –*interj.* 18. (an expression of approval or satisfaction). 19. **good on** or **for you**, *Colloq.* (an expression of approval, encouragement, or satisfaction).

good·bye, *interj.* farewell (a conventional expression used at parting).

good·will, *n.* friendly disposition; benevolence; favour.

goose, *n., pl.* **geese.** 1. a web-footed bird, larger and with a longer neck than a duck. 2. the female of this bird, as distinguished from the male (or gander). 3. a foolish person; simpleton.

goose·berry /'gʊzbəri, -bri/, *n., pl.* **-ries.** the small fruit or berry of certain prickly shrubs.

gore¹, *n.* blood that is shed, esp. when clotted. – **gory**, *adj.*

gore², *v.*, **gored**, **goring.** (of an animal) to pierce with the horns or tusks.

gorge, *n., v.*, **gorged**, **gorging.** –*n.* 1. a narrow cleft with steep, rocky walls, esp. one through which a stream runs. 2. the throat; gullet. –*v.* 3. to stuff (oneself, etc.) with food.

gor·geous, *adj.* sumptuous; magnificent in appearance or colouring.

gorilla

go·ril·la, *n.* the largest of the anthropoid apes.

gorm·less, *adj. Colloq.* (of a person) dull; stupid.

gos·ling, *n.* a young goose.

gos·pel, *n.* 1. (*oft. cap.*) (the writings containing) the body of doctrine taught by Christ and the apostles. 2. something regarded as true and implicitly believed.

gos·sa·mer, *n.* a fine filmy cobweb.

gos·sip, *n., v.,* **-siped** or **-sipped, -siping** or **-sipping.** —*n.* 1. idle talk, esp. about the affairs of others. 2. a person, esp. a woman, given to tattling or idle talk. —*v.* 3. to talk idly, esp. about the affairs of others; go about tattling.

got, *v.* past tense and past participle of **get**.

gouache, *n.* opaque water-colour paint.

gouge, *n., v.,* **gouged, gouging.** —*n.* 1. a chisel whose blade is curved. —*v.* 2. to dig or force out with or as with a gouge.

gourd, *n.* the fruit of various melon or pumpkin plants, whose dried shell is used for bottles, bowls, etc.

gour·met /'guəmeɪ, 'gɔ-/, *n.* a connoisseur in the delicacies of the table; an epicure.

gout, *n.* a constitutional disease characterised by painful inflammation of the joints.

gov·ern, *v.* 1. to rule by right of authority. 2. to exercise a directing or restraining influence over; guide.

gov·er·ness, *n.* a woman who directs the education of children, generally in their own homes.

gov·ern·ment, *n.* 1. the authoritative direction and restraint exercised over societies and states. 2. (*sometimes construed as pl.*) the governing body of persons in a state.

gov·er·nor, *n.* one charged with the direction or control of an institution, society, etc.

governor-general, *n., pl.* **governor-generals, governors-general**. the principal representative of the sovereign in certain independent Commonwealth countries.

gown, *n.* 1. a woman's dress. 2. a loose, flowing outer garment.

grab, *v.,* **grabbed, grabbing.** 1. to seize suddenly and eagerly; snatch. 2. *Colloq.* to affect; impress: *The film did not grab me.*

grace, *n., v.,* **graced, gracing.** —*n.* 1. elegance or beauty of form, motion, etc. 2. mercy; clemency; pardon. 3. (*pl.*) affected manner. 4. a short prayer before or after a meal. —*v.* 5. to lend or add grace to; adorn. – **graceful**, *adj.*

grace·less, *adj.* lacking charm, elegance and grace.

gra·cious, *adj.* kind; benevolent; courteous.

gra·da·tion, *n.* any process or change taking place through a series of stages, by degrees, or gradually.

grade, *n., v.,* **graded, grading.** —*n.* 1. a degree in a scale, as of rank, advancement, quality, value, intensity, etc. 2. a step or stage in a course or process. 3. →**gradient** (def. 2). —*v.* 4. to arrange in a series of grades; class; sort. 5. to determine the grade of.

gra·di·ent, *n.* 1. the degree of inclination, or the rate of ascent or descent, in a railway, etc. 2. an inclined surface; grade; ramp.

gradual

grad·u·al, *adj.* **1.** taking place, changing, moving, etc., by degrees or little by little. **2.** rising or descending at an even, moderate inclination.

grad·u·ate, *n., v.* -ated, -ating. –*n.* **1.** one who has received a degree from a university or college. –*v.* **2.** to receive a degree or diploma on completing a course of study. **3.** to divide into or mark with degrees or other divisions, as the scale of a thermometer. – **graduation**, *n.*

graf·fi·ti, *n.pl., sing.* **graffito** /grəˈfitoʊ/. drawings or words, sometimes obscene, sometimes political, etc., written on public walls.

graft[1], *n.* **1.** *Hort.* part of a plant inserted in a groove in another plant so as to become united with it. **2.** a portion of living tissue surgically transplanted. –*v.* **3.** to cause (a plant) to reproduce through grafting. **4.** to transplant (a portion of living tissue) as a graft.

graft[2], *n.* **1.** work, esp. hard work. **2.** gain or advantage achieved by dishonest or unfair means.

grail, *n.* a cup or chalice which according to medieval legend was used by Jesus at the Last Supper.

grain, *n.* **1.** a small hard seed. **2.** any small, hard particle, as of sand, gold, pepper, gunpowder, etc. **3.** the arrangement or direction of fibres in wood. **4.** temper or natural character.

gram, *n.* a metric unit of mass, $\frac{1}{1000}$ of a kilogram. *Symbol:* g

gram·mar, *n.* the features of a language (sounds, words, formation and arrangement of words, etc.) considered systematically as a whole, esp. with reference to their mutual contrasts and relations. – **grammarian**, *n.* **grammatical**, *adj.*

gramo·phone, *n.* →record-player.

gram·pus, *n.* **1.** a marine mammal of the dolphin family. **2.** the killer whale.

gran·ary, *n., pl.* -ries. a storehouse or repository for grain. –*adj.* **2.** a type of brown bread, with a nutty flavour.

grand, *adj.* **1.** imposing in size or appearance or general effect. **2.** magnificent or splendid. **3.** of great importance, distinction, or pretension. – **grandeur**, *n.*

grand·child, *n., pl.,* -children. a child of one's son or daughter.

gran·dil·o·quent, *adj.* speaking or expressed in a lofty or pompous style; bombastic.

grandi·ose, *adj.* grand in an imposing or pompous way.

grand·parent, *n.* a parent of a parent.

grand·stand, *n.* **1.** the principal stand for spectators at a racecourse, athletic field, etc. –*v.* **2.** to behave ostentatiously in order to impress or win approval.

gran·ite, *n.* a granular igneous rock.

grant, *v.* **1.** to bestow or confer, esp. by a formal act. **2.** to give or accord. **3.** to admit or concede; accept for the sake of argument. **4. take for granted**, to accept without appreciation. –*n.* **5.** something given, as a privilege or right, a sum of money, or a tract of land.

granu·lar, *adj.* **1.** of the nature of granules. **2.** composed of or bearing granules.

granu·late, *v.* -lated, -lating. to form into granules or grains. – **granulator**, *n.* – **granulation**, *n.*

granule

gran·ule, *n.* a little grain, pellet, or particle.

grape, *n.* the edible, pulpy, smooth-skinned fruit which grows in clusters on certain vines.

grape·fruit, *n.* a large roundish, yellow-skinned citrus fruit.

graph, *n.* 1. a diagram representing a system of connections or inter-relations among 2 or more things by a number of distinctive dots, lines, bars, etc. –*v.* 2. to draw a graph of.

graphic, *adj.* 1. life-like; vivid. 2. pertaining to the use of diagrams, graphs, etc. 3. pertaining to writing.

graph·ite, *n.* a very common mineral, soft native carbon.

grap·nel, *n.* a device consisting of one or more hooks or clamps, for grasping or holding something.

grap·ple, *n., v.,* -**pled,** -**pling.** –*n.* 1. →grapnel. –*v.* 2. to make or keep fast to something. 3. to seize another, or each other, in a firm grip, as in wrestling. 4. to try to overcome or deal (*with*).

grasp, *v.* 1. to seize and hold; grip. 2. understand; comprehend. –*n.* 3. a grasping or gripping. 4. hold, possession, or mastery. 5. broad or thorough comprehension.

grass, *n.* 1. a plant with jointed stems, sheathing leaves, flower spikelets, and fruit consisting of a seed-like grain. 2. *Colloq.* →marijuana.

grass·hopper, *n.* a terrestrial, herbivorous insect with long hind legs for leaping.

grate[1], *n.* a frame of metal bars for holding burning fuel in a fireplace or furnace.

grate[2], *v.,* **grated, grating.** 1. to have an irritating or unpleasant effect on the feelings. 2. to make a sound as of rough scraping. 3. to rub together with a harsh, jarring sound. 4. to reduce to small particles by rubbing against a rough surface.

grate·ful, *adj.* warmly or deeply appreciative of kindness or benefits received; thankful. – **gratitude**, *n.*

grat·ify, *v.,* -**fied,** -**fying.** to give pleasure to (persons) by satisfying desires or humouring inclinations or feelings. – **gratification**, *n.*

gra·tu·itous /grə'tjuətəs/, *adj.* 1. freely bestowed or obtained; free. 2. being without reason, cause, or justification.

gra·tuity /grə'tjuəti/, *n., pl.* -**ties.** a gift, usu. of money, over and above payment due for service; tip.

grave[1], *n.* an excavation made in the earth to receive a dead body in burial.

grave[2], *adj.* 1. dignified; sedate; serious; earnest; solemn. 2. important or critical; involving serious issues.

gravel, *n.* small stones and pebbles, or a mixture of these with sand.

gravi·tate, *v.,* -**tated,** -**tating.** 1. to move or tend to move under the influence of gravitational force. 2. to have a natural tendency to be strongly attracted (*to* or *towards*).

gravi·ta·tion /grævə'teɪʃən/, *n. Physics.* that force of attraction between all particles or bodies, or that acceleration of one towards another, of which the fall of bodies to the earth is an instance. – **gravitational**, *adj.* – **gravitationally**, *adv.*

grav·ity, *n., pl.* -**ties.** 1. the force of attraction by which terrestrial

gravity

bodies tend to fall towards the centre of the earth. 2. seriousness; dignity; solemnity. 3. serious or critical character.

gravy, n., pl. -vies. a sauce made with meat drippings as its basic ingredient.

graze[1], v., **grazed, grazing**. to feed on growing herbage, as cattle, sheep etc.

graze[2], v., **grazed, grazing**, n. –v. 1. to touch or rub lightly in passing. 2. to scrape the skin from (the leg, arm, etc.); abrade. –n. 3. a slight scratch in passing; abrasion.

gra·zier, n. a farmer, usu. a substantial landowner.

grease /gris/, n.; /griz, gris/, v. **greased, greasing**. –n.1. soft melted or rendered fat of animals. 2. fatty or oily matter in general; lubricant. –v. 3. to smear with grease.

great, adj. 1. large. 2. notable or remarkable. 3. important. 4. being such in an extreme degree. 5. *Colloq.* first-rate; very good; fine.

greed, n. inordinate or rapacious desire, esp. for food or wealth. – **greedy**, adj.

green, adj. 1. of the colour of growing foliage, between yellow and blue in the spectrum. 2. covered with herbage or foliage; verdant. 3. not fully developed; unripe. 4. immature; inexperienced. 5. uncooked; raw. –n. 6. green colour. 7. a playing area for golf or bowls.

green·grocer, n. a retailer of fresh vegetables and fruit.

green·house, n. a building, chiefly of glass, for the cultivation or protection of plants.

grievous

greet, v. to address with some form of salutation; welcome.

greet·ing, n. 1. the act or words of one who greets; salutation. 2. (*usu. pl.*) a friendly message.

gregar·i·ous, adj. 1. living or growing in groups or clusters. 2. fond of company; sociable.

gre·nade, n. a small explosive shell thrown by hand or fired from a rifle.

gre·villea, n. one of a large genus of mainly Aust. flowering shrubs and trees.

grew, v. past tense of **grow**.

grey, adj. 1. of a colour between white and black, having no definite hue; ash-coloured. 2. dark, overcast, dismal, gloomy. 3. grey-haired. –n. 4. grey colour. 5. a grey horse.

grey·hound, n. one of a breed of tall, slender dogs, notable for keen sight and for fleetness.

grid, n. 1. a grating of crossed bars. 2. a network of cables, pipes, etc., for the distribution and supply of electricity, gas, water, etc. 3. a network of horizontal and vertical reference lines on a map.

grid·dle, n. a flat, heated surface on top of a stove.

grief, n. 1. keen mental suffering or distress over affliction or loss. 2. **come to grief**, to come to a bad end; turn out badly.

grie·vance, n. a wrong, real or fancied, considered as grounds for complaint.

grieve, v., **grieved, grieving**. to (cause to) feel grief or sorrow.

grie·vous /'grivəs/, adj. 1. causing grief or sorrow. 2. flagrant; atrocious.

grill

grill, *n.* 1. →**griller.** 2. a meal of grilled meat. –*v.* 3. to cook by means of a griller. 4. *Colloq.* to subject to severe questioning.

grille, *n.* a metal openwork screen forming a window or gate or used on the front of a motor car. – **grilled,** *adj.*

griller, *n.* a cooking device, or that part of a stove, in which meat, etc., is cooked by exposure to direct radiant heat.

grim, *adj.,* **grimmer, grimmest.** 1. stern; unrelenting; uncompromising. 2. of a fierce or forbidding aspect.

gri·mace /ˈgrɪməs, grəˈmeɪs/, *n., v.,* **-maced, -macing.** –*n.* 1. a wry face; facial contortion; ugly facial expression. –*v.* 2. to make grimaces.

grime, *n.* dirt or foul matter, esp. on or ingrained in a surface.

grin, *v.,* **grinned, grinning,** –*v.* 1. to smile broadly. –*n.* 2. a broad smile.

grind, *v.,* **ground, grinding.** –*v.* 1. to wear, smooth, or sharpen by friction; whet. 2. to reduce to fine particles, as by pounding or crushing. –*n.* 3. *Colloq.* laborious or monotonous work or study.

grip, *n., v.,* **gripped** or **gript, gripping.** –*n.* 1. the act of grasping; a seizing and holding fast; firm grasp. 2. mental or intellectual hold; competence. 3. a special mode of clasping hands. –*v.* 4. to grasp or seize firmly; hold fast. 5. to take hold on; hold the interest of.

gripe, *v.,* **griped, griping.** –*v.* 1. *Colloq.* to complain constantly; grumble. –*n.* 2. an objection; complaint.

grisly, *adj.,* **-lier, -liest.** such as to

grope

cause a shuddering horror; gruesome.

grist, *n.* corn to be ground.

gristle, *n.* →**cartilage.**

grit, *n., v.,* **gritted, gritting.** –*n.* 1. fine, stony, or hard particles such as are deposited like dust from the air or occur as impurities in food, etc. 2. firmness of character; indomitable spirit; pluck. –*v.* 3. to grate or grind.

griz·zle, *v.,* **-zled, -zling.** to whimper; whine; complain fretfully.

griz·zled, *adj.* greyhaired with age.

groan, *n.* 1. a low, inarticulate sound uttered in pain or grief. 2. a deep murmur uttered in derision, disapproval, etc. –*v.* 3. to utter a groan.

grocer, *n.* a dealer in general food supplies, soaps, etc. – **grocery,** *n.*

grog, *n. Colloq.* alcohol.

groggy, *adj.,* **-gier, -giest.** *Colloq.* 1. staggering, as from exhaustion or blows. 2. drunk.

groin, *n.* the fold or hollow on either side of the body where the thigh joins the abdomen.

groom, *n.* 1. a man or boy in charge of horses or the stable. 2. a man newly married, or about to be married; bridegroom. –*v.* 3. to tend carefully as to person and dress; make neat or tidy. 4. to prepare for a position, election, etc.

grooms·man, *n., pl.* **-men.** a man who attends the bridegroom at a wedding.

groove, *n.* 1. a furrow or channel cut by a tool. 2. a fixed routine.

groovy, *adj. Colloq.* 1. exciting, satisfying, or pleasurable. 2. appreciative.

grope, *v.,* **groped, groping.** 1. to feel about with the hands; feel one's

grope

way. **2.** to search blindly or uncertainly.

groper, *n., pl.* **-pers,** *(esp. collectively)* **-per.** a large Aust. or N.Z. marine fish.

gross, *adj.* **1.** whole, entire, or total, esp. without having had deductions made. **2.** glaring or flagrant. **3.** morally coarse; indelicate or indecent. **4.** large, big, or bulky. —*n.* **5.** a unit consisting of 12 dozen, or 144. —*v.* **6.** to total a total of.

gro·tesque, *adj.* odd or unnatural; fantastically ugly or absurd; bizarre.

grotto, *n., pl.* **-toes. -tos.** a cave or cavern.

grotty, *adj. Colloq.* **1.** dirty; filthy. **2.** useless; rubbishy.

grouch, *Colloq. v.* **1.** to be sulky or morose; show discontent; complain. —*n.* **2.** a sulky or morose person.

ground[1], *n.* **1.** the earth's solid surface; firm or dry land. **2.** earth or soil. **3.** *(oft. pl.)* a tract of land given over to a special use. **4.** *(oft. pl.)* a motive; reason. **5.** the underlying or main surface or background, in painting, etc. **6. common ground,** matters on which agreement exists. **7. gain ground,** to advance; make progress. **8. hold** or **stand one's ground,** to maintain one's position. **9. lose ground,** to lose what one has gained; retreat; give way. **10. run to ground,** to hunt down; track down. —*adj.* **11.** situated on or at, or adjacent to, the surface of the earth. —*v.* **12.** to lay or set on the ground. **13.** to place on a foundation; found; fix firmly; settle or establish. **14.** to prevent (an aircraft or a pilot) from flying. **15.** to restrict, or withdraw privileges from.

grudge

ground[2], *v.* past tense and past participle of **grind.**

group, *n.* **1.** an assemblage; cluster; aggregation. **2.** a number of persons or things ranged or considered together as being related in some way. —*v.* **3.** to place in a group, as with others.

grouse[1], *n., pl.* **grouse.** an important game bird of the Nthn Hemisphere.

grouse[2], *v.*, **groused, grousing.** *Colloq.* to grumble; complain.

grouse[3], *adj. Colloq.* **1.** very good. **2. extra grouse,** excellent.

grout, *n.* a mortar poured into the joints of masonry, brickwork and tilework.

grove, *n.* a small wood or plantation of trees.

grovel, *v.*, **-elled, -elling.** to humble oneself or act in an abject manner, as in fear or in mean servility.

grow, *v.*, **grew, grown, growing. 1.** (to cause) to increase by natural development. **2.** to increase gradually; become greater. **3.** to become by degrees. **4. grow up,** to attain maturity.

growl, *v.* **1.** to utter a deep guttural sound of anger or hostility. —*n.* **2.** the act or sound of growling.

growth, *n.* **1.** the act, process, or manner of growing; development; gradual increase. **2.** *Pathol.* a morbid mass of tissue, as a tumour.

grub, *n.* **1.** the bulky larva of certain insects. **2.** *Colloq.* food or victuals.

grubby, *adj.*, **-bier, -biest.** dirty; slovenly.

grudge, *n.* a feeling of ill will or resentment excited by some special cause, as a personal injury or insult, etc.

gruel, *n.* a light, thin porridge.

gruel·ling, *adj.* exhausting; very tiring; severe.

grue·some, *adj.* inspiring horror.

gruff, *adj.* 1. low and harsh; hoarse. 2. rough; surly.

grum·ble, *v.*, -bled, -bling, *n.* -*v.* 1. to complain ill-humouredly; murmur. -*n.* 2. an ill-humoured complaining; murmur.

grumpy, *adj.*, -pier, -piest. surly; ill-tempered. – **grump**, *n.*

grunt, *v.* to utter the deep guttural sound characteristic of a pig.

guaran·tee, *n.*, *v.*, -teed, -teeing. -*n.* 1. a promise or assurance, usu. written, as to the quality of goods, with an undertaking to make good any defects under certain conditions. 2. →**guaranty** (def. 1 or 2). 3. to secure, as by giving or taking security. 4. to make oneself answerable for on behalf of one primarily responsible. 5. to undertake to secure to another, as rights or possessions. 6. to serve as a warrant or guarantee for. 7. to engage to protect or indemnify (*from*, *against*, or *in*). 8. to promise.

guarantor, *n.* one who makes or gives a guarantee or guaranty.

guaranty, *n.*, *pl.* -ties, *v.*, -tied, -tying. -*n.* Also, **guarantee.** 1. a warrant, pledge, or promise accepting responsibility for the discharging of another's liabilities, as the payment of a debt. 2. that which is taken or presented as security. -*v.* 3. to guarantee.

guard, *v.* 1. to keep safe from harm; protect; watch over. 2. to keep under close watch in order to prevent escape, outbreaks, etc. 3. to take precautions (*against*). -*n.* 4. one who guards, protects, or restrains. 5. something intended or serving to guard or protect; a safeguard. 6. an official in general charge of a railway train.

guar·dian, *n.* 1. one who guards, protects, or preserves. 2. one who is entrusted by law with the care of the person or property, or both, of another. -*adj.* 3. guarding; protecting.

guava, *n.* a tropical tree or shrub with a fruit used for jelly, etc.

guer·rilla, *n.* a member of a small, independent band of soldiers which harasses the enemy by surprise raids, attacks on communication and supply lines, etc.

guess, *v.* to form an opinion of at random or from evidence admittedly uncertain.

guest, *n.* a person entertained at the house or table of another.

guffaw, *n.* 1. a loud, coarse burst of laughter. -*v.* 2. to laugh loudly.

guide, *v.*, **guided**, **guiding**, *n.* -*v.* 1. to show the way to. 2. to direct the movement or course of. -*n.* 3. one who guides. – **guidance**, *n.*

guild, *n.* an organisation of persons with common professional or cultural interests formed for mutual aid and protection.

guile, *n.* insidious cunning.

guillo·tine, *n.* 1. a machine for beheading persons by means of a heavy blade falling in 2 grooved posts. 2. a device with a long blade for trimming paper. 3. a time restriction imposed by resolution on a parliamentary debate.

guilt, *n.* 1. the fact or state of having committed an offence or crime. 2. a feeling of responsibility or

231

guilt

remorse for some crime, wrong, etc. – **guilty**, *adj.*

guinea·pig, *n.* a short-eared, short-tailed rodent much used in scientific experiments.

guise, *n.* 1. external appearance in general; aspect. 2. assumed appearance or mere semblance.

guitar, *n.* a musical stringed instrument with a long fretted neck and a flat body.

gulf, *n.* 1. a portion of an ocean or sea partly enclosed by land. 2. a deep hollow; chasm; abyss.

gull, *n.* a web-footed, aquatic bird.

gullet, *n.* the oesophagus, or tube by which food and drink pass to the stomach.

gul·li·ble, *adj.* easily deceived or cheated. – **gullibility**, *n.*

gully, *n.* a small valley cut by running water.

gulp, *v.* 1. to gasp or choke, as when taking large draughts of liquids. 2. to eat (food) hastily or greedily. –*n.* 3. the act of gulping.

gum[1], *n., v.,* **gummed, gumming.** –*n.* 1. any of various viscid, amorphous exudations from plants. 2. a preparation of such a substance. 3. a eucalypt. –*v.* 4. to smear, stiffen, or stick together with gum. 5. to clog with or as with some gummy substance (*up*).

gum[2], *n.* (*oft. pl.*) the firm, fleshy tissue enveloping the bases of the teeth.

gum·boot, *n.* a rubber boot reaching to the knee or thigh.

gump·tion, *n. Colloq.* 1. initiative or courage; resourcefulness. 2. shrewd, practical common sense.

gum tree, *n.* 1. →**eucalyptus**. 2. **up a gum tree,** *Colloq.* **a.** in difficulties; in a predicament. **b.** completely baffled. Also, **gumtree.**

gun, *n., v.,* **gunned, gunning.** *adj.* –*n.* 1. a weapon consisting of a metallic tube from which missiles, ammunition, etc., are thrown by the force of an explosive. 2. any similar device for projecting something. 3. *Colloq.* a champion, esp. in shearing. –*v.* 4. to shoot with a gun (*down*). –*adj.* 5. *Colloq.* of or pertaining to one who is expert, esp. in shearing.

gun·nery, *n.* 1. the art and science of constructing and managing guns, esp. large guns. 2. the firing of guns. 3. guns collectively.

gun·powder, *n.* an explosive mixture of saltpetre (potassium nitrate), sulphur, and charcoal, used esp. in gunnery.

gun·wale /'gʌnəl/, *n.* the upper edge of a ship's or boat's side.

gunyah, *n.* an Aborigine's hut made of boughs and bark; humpy.

gurgle, *v.,* **-gled, -gling.** 1. to flow in a broken, irregular, noisy current. 2. to make a sound as of water doing this.

guru, *n.* (in Hinduism) a spiritual guide.

gush, *v.* 1. to flow suddenly and copiously. 2. *Colloq.* to express oneself extravagantly or emotionally.

gusset, *n.* an angular piece of material inserted in a garment.

gust, *n.* a sudden, strong blast, as of wind. – **gusty**, *adj.*

gusto, *n.* keen relish or hearty enjoyment.

gut, *n., v.,* **gutted, gutting.** *adj.* –*n.* 1. →**intestine**. 2. (*pl.*) the bowels or entrails. 3. (*pl.*) *Colloq.* courage;

gut

stamina; endurance. 4. (*pl.*) *Colloq.* essential information. –*v.* 5. to take out the guts or entrails of; disembowel. 6. to destroy the interior of. –*adj.* 7. of or pertaining to feelings, emotion, intuition. – **gutsy**, *adj.*

gutter, *n.* 1. a channel at the side of a road for leading off surface water. 2. Also, **guttering**. a channel at the eaves or on the roof of a building, for carrying off rainwater.

gut·tural, *adj.* 1. pertaining to the throat. 2. harsh; throaty.

guy[1], *n. Colloq.* a fellow or man.

guy[2], *n.* a rope or appliance used to guide and steady a thing being hoisted or lowered.

guzzle, *v.*, -zled, -zling. to eat or drink frequently and greedily.

gym, *n.* 1. →**gymnasium**. 2. gymnastic exercises.

gym·khana, *n.* a horseriding event featuring games and novelty contests.

gym·na·sium, *n.*, *pl.*, -siums, -sia. a building or room equipped with facilities for gymnastics and sport.

gym·nas·tic, *adj.* pertaining to exercises which develop flexibility, strength, and agility. – **gymnast**, *n.* – **gymnastics**, *n.*

gynae·col·o·gy, *n.* that department of medical science which deals with the functions and diseases peculiar to women. – **gynaecologist**, *n.*

gyp, *v.*, gypped, gypping, *n. Colloq.* –*v.* 1. to swindle; cheat; defraud or rob by some sharp practice. –*n.* 2. a swindle.

gypsum, *n.* a very common mineral, used to make plaster of Paris, as an ornamental material, as a fertiliser, etc.

gypsy, *n.*, *pl.* -sies, *adj.* →**gipsy**.

gyrate, *v.*, -rated, -rating. to move in a circle or spiral, or round a fixed point; whirl. – **gyration**, *n.* – **gyratory**, *adj.*

gyre, *n.* a ring or circle.

gyro·scope, *n.* an apparatus consisting of a rotating wheel so mounted that its axis can turn freely in certain or all directions, and capable of maintaining the same absolute direction in space in spite of movements of the mountings and surroundings parts. – **gyroscopic**, *adj.*

Hh

H, h, *n.*, *pl.* **H's** or **Hs**, **h's** or **hs**. a consonant, the 8th letter of the English alphabet.

haber·dashery, *n.*, *pl.* **-ries.** (a shop selling) goods such as buttons, needles, etc. – **haberdasher,** *n.*

habit, *n.* **1.** a tendency, constantly shown, to act in a certain way. **2.** garb of a particular religious order, etc. – **habitual,** *adj.*

habi·table, *adj.* capable of being inhabited.

habi·tat, *n.* the native environment of an animal or plant.

habi·tation, *n.* a place of abode; dwelling.

habit·uate, *v.* to make used (*to*); accustom.

hack[1], *v.* **1.** to cut irregularly, as with heavy blows. **2.** to damage by cutting harshly. –*n.* **3.** a short, broken cough.

hack[2], *n.* **1.** a horse kept for general work, esp. ordinary riding. **2.** a person who for a living undertakes literary or other work of little or no originality. –*v.* **3.** *Colloq.* to put up with; endure.

hackle, *n.* a neck feather of certain birds, as the domestic cock. **2.** (*pl.*) the hair on a dog's neck.

hack·neyed, *adj.* overused and trite.

hack·work, *n.* the routine aspects of creative or artistic work, considered as of an inferior quality.

had, *v.* past tense and past participle of **have.**

haemo·globin, *n.* a protein responsible for the red colour of blood.

haemo·philia, *n.* a hereditary disease in which blood fails to coagulate. – **haemophiliac,** *n.*

haemor·rhage, *n.* a discharge of blood, as from a ruptured blood vessel.

haemor·rhoid, *n.* a swelling of a vein of the anus; pile.

haft, *n.* a handle, as of a knife.

hag, *n.* a repulsive old woman.

hag·gard, *adj.* thin and wild-looking, as from prolonged suffering, anxiety, etc.

haggis, *n.* a dish made of the heart, liver, etc., of a sheep, etc.

haggle, *v.*, **-gled, -gling.** to bargain in a petty and tedious manner.

hail[1], *v.* **1.** to salute or greet; welcome. **2.** to acclaim. **3.** to call out to, in order to attract attention. – **hail from,** to belong to as the place of residence, etc.

hail[2], *n.* **1.** pellets of ice falling from the clouds in a shower. –*v.* **2.** to pour down hail.

hair, *n.* **1.** the natural covering of the human head. **2.** (one of) the mass of the numerous fine, usu. cylindrical filaments growing from the skin and forming the coat of most mammals.

hairdo, *n.*, *pl.* **-dos.** the style in which a person's hair is arranged.

hair·dresser, *n.* one who arranges or cuts hair, esp. women's hair.

hal·cyon, *adj.* **1.** calm, tranquil, or peaceful. **2.** carefree; joyous.

hale, *adj.*, **haler, halest.** free from

hale

disease or infirmity; robust; vigorous.

half, n., pl. **halves**, adj., adv. —n. 1. one of the 2 equal parts into which anything may be divided. 2. Sport. either of the 2 periods of a game. 3. one of a pair. —adj. 4. being one of the 2 equal parts into which anything may be divided. 5. being equal to only about half of the full measure. —adv. 6. to the extent or measure of half. 7. to some extent.

half-back, n. Sport. a player positioned between the centre line and the back line, or next behind the forward line.

half-caste, n. a person of mixed race.

half-life, n. the time required for one half of a sample of unstable material to undergo chemical change, as the disintegration of radioactive material, etc.

half-way, adv. 1. to or at half the distance. —adj. 2. midway, as between 2 places or points.

hali·tosis, n. bad breath.

hall, n. 1. the entrance room of a building. 2. a corridor or passageway in a building. 3. a large building or room for public meetings, etc.

halle·lujah, interj. Praise ye the Lord!

hall·mark, n. 1. an official mark or stamp indicating a standard of purity, used in marking gold and silver articles. 2. any outstanding feature.

hallow, v. to make holy.

hal·luci·nation, n. subjective perceptions for which there is no appropriate external source, as 'hearing voices'. – **hallucinate**, v.

halo, n., pl. **-loes**, **-los**. 1. a radiance

hamper

surrounding the head in the representation of a sacred personage. 2. a circle of light, appearing round the sun or moon.

halt[1], v. 1. to make a temporary stop, as in marching, etc. —n. 2. a temporary stop.

halt[2], v. to falter as in speech, reasoning, etc.

halter, n. a rope or strap with a noose or harness for leading or fastening horses or cattle.

halve, v., **halved**, **halving**. 1. to divide in halves; share equally. 2. to reduce to half.

halves, n. plural of **half**.

hal·yard, n. a rope or tackle used to hoist or lower a sail, yard, flag, etc. Also, **halliard**.

ham, n. 1. (the meat from) the rear quarters of a pig. 2. Colloq. an actor who overacts. 3. Colloq. an amateur.

ham·burger, n. (a bread roll containing) a cooked cake of minced beef.

hamlet, n. a small village.

hammer, n. 1. a tool with a solid metal head set crosswise on a handle, used for beating metals, driving in nails, etc. 2. any tool or device resembling a hammer. —v. 3. to beat or drive with or as with a hammer. 4. to hit with some force; pound.

hammer·head, n. a shark with a head resembling a double-headed hammer.

ham·mock, n. a kind of hanging bed made of canvas, etc.

hamper[1], v. to impede; hinder.

hamper[2], n. 1. a large basket. 2. a package of foods.

hamster

ham·ster, *n.* a short-tailed, burrowing rodent.

ham·string, *n., v.,* **-strung**, **-stringing**. —*n.* 1. one of the tendons at the back of the knee. —*v.* 2. to cripple; thwart.

hand, *n.* 1. the terminal, prehensile part of the arm, consisting of the palm and 5 digits. 2. something resembling a hand. 3. a manual labourer. 4. (*oft. pl.*) power, control or custody: *to have someone's fate in your hands*. 5. a side of a subject, question, etc.: *on the other hand*. 6. style of handwriting. 7. a person, with reference to action or ability. 8. a pledge of marriage. 9. a unit used in measuring the height of horses, etc., equal to approx. 10 cm. 10. *Cards*. the cards dealt to or held by each player at one time. 11. a bunch of fruit, leaves, etc. 12. a round of applause. 13. **at hand**, **a.** within reach. **b.** near in time. **c.** ready for use. 14. **free hand**, freedom to act as desired. 15. **give a hand**, to help. 16. **in hand**, **a.** under control. **b.** in immediate possession. **c.** in process: *keep to the matter in hand*. 17. **on hand**, **a.** in immediate possession. **b.** before one for attention. **c.** present. —*v.* 18. to pass with the hand. 19. to pass on: *to hand on an infection*. 20. **hand it to**, to give due credit to.

hand·book, *n.* a small book serving as a guide to study, etc.

hand·cuff, *n.* one of a pair of ring-shaped shackles for the wrist.

handi·cap, *n., v.,* **-capped**, **-capping**. —*n.* 1. (a contest involving) disadvantages or advantages of weight, distance, etc., placed upon competitors to equalise their chances of winning. 2. any encumbrance or

hang

disadvantage. 3. a physical disability. —*v.* 4. to serve as a handicap or disadvantage to.

handi·craft, *n.* 1. manual skill. 2. a manual art or occupation.

handi·work, *n.* work done or a thing or things made by the hands.

hand·ker·chief /ˈhæŋkətʃif/, *n.* a small, usu. square piece of fabric for wiping the nose, etc. Also, *Colloq.* **hankie**, **hanky**.

han·dle, *n., v.,* **-dled**, **-dling**. —*n.* 1. a part of a thing which is intended to be grasped by the hand in using or moving it. —*v.* 2. to touch or feel with the hand. 3. to manage, direct, or control. 4. to deal with or treat in a particular way. 5. to deal or trade in (goods, etc.). 6. to respond to handling.

hand·some, *adj.,* **-somer**, **-somest**. 1. of fine or admirable appearance; comely. 2. ample, or liberal in amount.

hand·writ·ing, *n.* (a kind or style of) writing done with the hand.

hand·y, *adj.,* **-dier**, **-diest**. 1. conveniently accessible. 2. ready for use. 3. skilful with the hands; deft; dexterous. 3. convenient or useful.

hang, *v.,* **hung** or (*esp. for capital punishment and suicide*) **hanged**, **hanging**. —*v.* 1. to fasten something so that it is supported only from above. 2. to be suspended; dangle. 3. to hang (someone) by the neck until dead. 4. to (let) droop or bend downwards. 5. to fasten into position: *to hang a painting*. 6. to attach (paper, etc.) to walls. 7. to cling, or adhere; rest for support (*on* or *upon*). 8. to be dependent: *His fate hangs on the jury's decision*. 9. to be doubtful; remain unfinished. 10. **hang about** or **around**, to

hang

loiter. **11. hang on, a.** to persevere. **b.** to linger. **c.** to wait. **12. hang out,** *Colloq.* to live at or frequent a particular place. **13. hang up, a.** to suspend on a hook, etc. **b.** to break off a telephone conversation by putting down the receiver. *–n.* **14.** the way in which a thing hangs.

hangar, *n.* a shed or shelter, usu. for an aircraft.

hang-glider, *n.* a simple kite-like glider with a framework from which a person hangs.

hangover, *n. Colloq.* the after-effects of drinking too much alcohol.

hang-up, *n. Colloq.* something which causes unease, inhibition, or conflict in an individual.

hank, *n.* a skein.

hanker, *v.* to have a restless or incessant longing (fol. by *after*, *for*, or an infinitive).

hanky-panky, *n. Colloq.* **1.** trickery; subterfuge. **2.** sexual play.

haphazard, *adj.* dependent on mere chance.

hapless, *adj.* unlucky.

happen, *v.* **1.** to take place, or occur. **2.** to befall, as to a person or thing. **3.** to come by chance (*on* or *upon*).

happy, *adj.*, **-pier, -piest. 1.** feeling or expressing pleasure, contentment, or gladness. **2.** delighted, as over a particular thing. **3.** fortunate or lucky.

harangue, *n.*, **-rangued, -ranguing.** *–n.* **1.** a passionate, vehement speech. *–v.* **2.** to address in a harangue.

harass /ˈhærəs, həˈræs/, *v.* to disturb persistently.

harbinger /ˈhabɪŋə, -bɪndʒə/, *n.* **1.** one who goes before and makes known the approach of another. **2.** an omen.

harbour, *n.* **1.** a body of water along the shore deep enough for ships. **2.** any place of shelter or refuge. *–v.* **3.** to conceal or shelter. **4.** to entertain in the mind: *to harbour ill will*.

hard, *adj.* **1.** solid and firm to the touch; not soft. **2.** tightly formed. **3.** difficult to do or accomplish; troublesome. **4.** involving or with great exertion or persistence. **5.** violent; harsh. **6.** callous. **7.** unpleasant to the eye, ear, etc. **8.** severe in terms: *a hard bargain*. **9.** alcoholic or addictive: *hard drink or drugs*. **10.** (of water) containing mineral salts which interfere with the action of soap. *–adv.* **11.** with great exertion; with vigour or violence. **12.** harshly or severely; badly. **13.** intently: *to look hard at something*. **–harden,** *v.*

hard-line, *adj.* not deviating from a set doctrine, policy, etc.

hardly, *adv.* **1.** barely; almost not at all. **2.** not quite.

hardship, *n.* something hard to bear, as severe toil, oppression, need, etc.

hardware, *n.* **1.** building materials, tools, etc. **2.** the physical components of a computer system, as the circuitry, magnetic tape units, etc. (opposed to *software*).

hardy, *adj.*, **-dier, -diest.** capable of enduring fatigue, hardship, exposure, etc.

hare, *n.*, *pl.* **hares,** (*esp.* collectively) **hare.** a rabbit-like mammal.

harelip, *n.* a congenitally deformed lip.

harem /ˈhɛərəm, haˈrim/, *n.* the wives

harem

and concubines in an oriental household.

hark, v. 1. (*chiefly imperative*) to listen. 2. **hark back**, to return to a previous point.

harlot, n. a promiscuous woman; prostitute.

harm, n. 1. injury; damage; hurt. –v. 2. to injure; damage; hurt.

har·mon·i·ca, n. a musical instrument played by the breath; mouth organ.

har·mo·ny, n., pl. **-nies**. 1. agreement; accord. 2. a consistent, orderly, or pleasing arrangement of parts. 3. *Music.* **a.** part(s) supporting the melody. **b.** chordal structure. – **harmonise**, v. – **harmonic**, adj. – **harmonious**, adj.

har·ness, n. 1. the combination of straps, etc., forming the working gear of a horse, etc. 2. a similar combination worn by persons for protection, restraint, etc. –v. 3. to put harness on (a horse, etc.). 4. to bring under conditions for working.

harp, n. 1. a triangular stringed instrument, played with the hands. –v. 2. to dwell (*on, upon*) persistently or tediously in speaking or writing.

har·poon, n. a spear attached to a rope.

harp·si·chord, n. a keyboard instrument, with strings being plucked (rather than struck as in a piano).

har·ri·dan, n. a disreputable violent woman.

har·row, n. 1. an implement for levelling soil, etc. –v. 2. to disturb keenly or painfully.

har·ry, v., **-ried, -rying**. 1. to torment; worry. 2. to ravage, as in war.

haul

harsh, adj. 1. ungentle and unpleasant in action or effect. 2. rough to the touch, etc.

hart, n., pl. **harts**, (*esp. collectively*) **hart**. a male deer.

har·vest, n. 1. (the gathering of) a crop, as of grain. 2. the product of any process. –v. 3. to gather, as a crop.

has, v. 3rd person singular present indicative of **have**.

hash, n. 1. a dish of reheated food. 2. a mess, jumble, or muddle.

hash·ish /ˈhæʃiʃ, ˈhæʃiʃ/, n. the resin from Indian hemp, smoked, chewed, etc., as a narcotic.

hasp, n. a clasp for a door, lid, etc.

has·sle, n., v., **-led, -ling**. –n. 1. a quarrel. 2. a struggle; period of unease. –v. 3. to worry; harass.

has·sock, n. a thick, firm cushion used for kneeling.

haste, n. 1. speed in motion or action. 2. thoughtless or rash speed. – **hasty**, adj.

has·ten, v. to proceed with haste.

hat, n. a shaped covering for the head, usu. worn outdoors.

hatch[1], v. 1. to bring forth (young) from the egg. 2. to contrive; devise.

hatch[2], n. a cover for an opening in a ship's deck, etc.

hatch[3], v. to mark with (usu. parallel) lines, as for shading in drawing.

hat·chet, n. a small, short-handled axe.

hate, v., **hated, hating**. to regard with a strong dislike; detest. – **hateful**, adj. – **hatred**, n.

haugh·ty, adj., **-tier, -tiest**. disdainfully proud; arrogant.

haul, v. 1. to pull or draw with force.

haul

2. (of the wind) to change direction (round or to). –n. 3. a strong pull or tug. 4. the distance over which anything is hauled.

haunch, n. the hip.

haunt, v. 1. to visit habitually as a ghost. 2. to worry or disturb. 3. to visit frequently. –n. 4. (oft. pl.) a place visited frequently.

have, v., pres. 1 **have**, 2 **have**, 3 **has**, pl. **have**; pt. and past part. **had**, pres. part. **having**. –v. 1. to hold or possess. 2. to get, receive, or take. 3. to be required (to). 4. to experience: *to have fun*. 5. to require or cause: *Have it finished by tomorrow*. 6. to engage in. 7. to permit or allow. 8. to give birth to. 9. *Colloq*. to outwit, or deceive. –aux. v. 10. (used with the past participle of a verb to form a compound or perfect tense).

haven, n. 1. a harbour or port. 2. any place of shelter and safety.

haver·sack, n. a bag carried on the back.

havoc, n. ruinous damage; devastation.

hawk[1], n. a bird of prey.

hawk[2], v. to clear the throat noisily.

hawker, n. one who travels from place to place selling goods.

haw·thorn, n. a thorny shrub.

hay, n. dried grass used as fodder.

hay fever, n. inflammation of the eyes, nose and throat, caused by pollen.

hay·wire, adj. 1. in disorder. 2. out of control; crazy.

haz·ard, n. 1. a risk; exposure to danger. –v. 2. to venture ∷o offer (a guess, etc.). 3. to take a risk; expose to risk. – **hazardous**, adj.

headmaster

haze, n. a thin mist, caused by dust, heat, etc. – **hazy**, adj.

hazel, n. 1. a small tree which bears edible nuts. 2. light reddish brown.

he, pron., poss. **his**, obj. **him**, pl. **they**. 1. the male being in question. 2. anyone; that person.

head, n. 1. the upper part of the body, joined to the trunk by the neck. 2. the head as the seat of thought, memory, etc. 3. the position of leadership. 4. the top, summit, or upper end of anything. 5. the foremost part; a projecting part. 6. a person or animal considered merely as one of a number (with pl. **head**). 7. culmination or crisis; conclusion. 8. something resembling a head. 9. a projecting point of a coast. 10. the side of a coin, bearing a head (opposed to *tail*). 11. the source of a river. 12. froth, as that formed on beer when poured. 13. a section of a discourse; topic. –adj. 14. situated at the top or front. 15. being in the position of leadership or superiority. –v. 16. to go in front of; lead. 17. to be the head or chief of. 18. **head for**, to move towards a certain point. 19. **head off**, to intercept (something) and force (it) to change course.

head·ache, n. 1. a pain in the head. 2. *Colloq*. a worrying problem.

head·ing, n. a title or caption of a page, chapter, etc.

head·land, n. a promontory extending into the sea, etc.

head·light, n. a light on the front of any vehicle.

head·line, n. a display line over an article, etc., as in a newspaper.

head·mas·ter, n. the male principal of a school.

239

headmistress

head·mistress, *n.* the female principal of a school.

head·quarters, *n.pl. or sing.* any centre of operations.

head start, *n.* an initial advantage in a race, competition, etc.

head·stone, *n.* a stone set at the head of a grave.

head·strong, *adj.* bent on having one's own way; wilful.

head·way, *n.* progress.

head·wind, *n.* a wind that blows directly against the course of a ship.

heady, *adj.*, **-ier**, **-iest**. 1. rashly impetuous. 2. intoxicating.

heal, *v.* to restore to health.

health, *n.* 1. freedom from disease or ailment. 2. the general condition of the body or mind. – **healthy**, *adj.*

heap, *n.* 1. an assemblage of things, lying one on another; pile. 2. *Colloq.* a great quantity or number. –*v.* 3. to gather in a heap; pile (*up*, *on*, *together*, etc.).

hear, *v.*, **heard, hearing. 1.** to perceive (something) by the ear. 2. to listen (to). 3. to give a formal hearing to, as a judge does.

hearing, *n.* 1. the sense by which sound is perceived. 2. *Law.* the trial of an action. 3. earshot.

hear·say, *n.* gossip; rumour.

hearse, *n.* a funeral vehicle.

heart, *n.* 1. a hollow muscular organ which pumps blood throughout the body. 2. this organ considered as the seat of life, thought, or emotion. 3. the seat of emotions (often in contrast to the *head* as the seat of the intellect). 4. spirit, courage, or enthusiasm. 5. the innermost part of anything. 6. a figure with rounded sides meeting in a point at the bottom and curving inwards to a cusp at the top.

heavy

heart attack, *n.* sudden heart failure.

heart·burn, *n.* a burning sensation above the abdomen.

hearten, *v.* to give courage to; cheer.

hearth, *n.* 1. that part of the floor on which the fire is made. 2. the fireside; home.

hearty, *adj.*, **-tier, -tiest. 1.** warm-hearted; affectionate; cordial; friendly. 2. enthusiastic; vigorous. 3. substantial or satisfying.

heat, *n.* 1. the quality, condition or sensation of hotness. 2. hot weather. 3. warmth or intensity of feeling. 4. a single division of a race. 5. *Zool.* sexual excitement in animals, esp. females. –*v.* 6. to make or become hot or warm.

heath, *n.* 1. a tract of open, uncultivated land, esp. in European countries. 2. a low, evergreen shrub.

heathen, *n.*, *pl.* **-thens, -then.** an irreligious person.

heather, *n.* a heath plant.

heave, *v.*, **heaved** or (*Chiefly Naut.*) **hove, heaving. 1.** to lift with effort; hoist. 2. to rise and fall with a swelling motion. 3. to vomit; retch.

heaven, *n.* 1. the abode of God, the angels, and the spirits of the righteous after death. 2. (*chiefly pl.*) the sky. 3. a place or state of supreme bliss. – **heavenly**, *adj.*

heavy, *adj.*, **-ier, -iest,** *n.*, *pl.* **-ies.** –*adj.* 1. of great weight; hard to lift or carry. 2. burdensome. 3. concerned with the manufacture of heavy goods. 4. serious; grave. 5. exceptionally dense. 6. (of music, literature, etc.) intellectual or deep. –*n.* 7. *Colloq.* an influential person.

heckle, v., -led, -ling. to harass, esp. a public speaker, with questions and gibes.

hec·tare, n. a surface measure. the common unit of land measure in the metric system, equal to 10 000 square metres (approx. 2.47 acres). *Symbol:* ha

hectic, adj. characterised by great excitement, activity, confusion, haste.

hedge, n., v., hedged, hedging. –n. 1. a row of closely planted bushes as forming a fence or boundary. –v. 2. to close (*off, in,* etc.) by a hedge. 3. to protect (a bet, etc.) by taking some offsetting risk. 4. to avoid taking an open or decisive course.

hedge·hog, n. a small spiny mammal.

hedon·ism, n. the doctrine that pleasure or happiness is the highest good. – **hedonist**, n.

heed, v. to give attention to; notice.

heel[1], n. 1. the back part of the foot. below and behind the ankle. 2. the part of a stocking, etc., covering the heel. 3. *Colloq.* a despicable person; cad. –v. 4. to furnish with heels, as shoes.

heel[2], v. (of a ship, etc.) to lean.

heeler, n. a cattle or sheep dog which rounds up stock by following at their heels.

hefty, adj., -tier, -tiest. *Colloq.* 1. heavy. 2. big and strong; powerful.

hege·mony /'hɛgəmənɪ, 'hɛdʒ-, həˈgɛmənɪ/, n., pl. -nies. leadership; predominance.

heifer /'hɛfə/, n. a cow that has not produced a calf and is under 3 years of age.

height, n. 1. the state of being high. 2. extent upwards; altitude; stature. 3. a high place as a hill, etc. 4. the highest point; utmost degree.

heinous /'heɪnəs, 'hi-/, adj. hateful.

heir /ɛə/, n. 1. *Law.* one who inherits the property and liabilities of a deceased person. 2. one to whom something falls or is due. – **heiress**, *n. fem.*

heir·loom, n. any family possession transmitted from generation to generation.

held, v. past tense and past participle of **hold**.

heli·copter, n. an aircraft which is lifted and sustained in the air by horizontal rotating blades.

helium, n. an inert gaseous element present in the sun's atmosphere. *Symbol:* He

helix, n., pl. **helices, helixes.** a spiral. – **helical**, adj.

hell, n. 1. the abode of evil and spirits of the wicked condemned to punishment after death. 2. any place or state of torment or misery. 3. the powers of evil. – **hellish**, adj.

hello, interj. (an exclamation to attract attention, express greeting, etc.)

helm, n. 1. the wheel which controls the rudder of a vessel. 2. the place or post of control.

helmet, n. a protective covering for the head.

help, v. 1. to cooperate effectively with a person; aid; assist. 2. to rescue. 3. to relieve (someone) in distress. 4. to refrain from; avoid: *He cannot help it.* 5. to remedy, or prevent: *Nothing will help now.* 6. **help oneself (to)**, to take or appropriate at will. –n. 7. (a person or thing that gives) aid, assistance or relief. – **helpful**, adj.

helpless

help·less, *adj.* unable to help oneself; weak or dependent.

helter-skelter, *adv.* in disorderly haste.

hem, *v.*, **hemmed, hemming**, *n.* –*v.* 1. to enclose or confine (*in*, *round*, or *about*). 2. to fold back and sew down the edge of (cloth, etc.). –*n.* 3. the folded and sewn border of a garment.

hemi·sphere, *n.* 1. half of the terrestrial globe or celestial sphere. 2. the half of a sphere. – **hemispherical**, *adj.*

hem·lock, *n.* a poisonous herb.

hemp, *n.* 1. a tall, Asian herb yielding hashish, etc. 2. the tough fibre of this plant used for making coarse fabrics, ropes, etc.

hen, *n.* a female bird, esp. of the domestic fowl.

hence, *adv.* as an inference from this fact; therefore.

hence·forth, *adv.* from now on. Also, **henceforwards**.

hench·man, *n., pl.* **-men**. a trusted attendant or follower.

hen·na, *n.* (the reddish-orange dye from) a small Asian tree.

hepa·titis, *n.* a serious viral disease of the liver causing jaundice.

her, *pron.* 1. the objective case of *she*. –*adj.* 2. the possessive form of *she*, used before a noun (cf. **hers**): *That is her book.*

her·ald, *n.* 1. a messenger; harbinger. 2. one who announces. –*v.* 3. to give tidings of; proclaim. 4. to usher in.

heral·dic, *adj.* pertaining to heralds or heraldry.

heral·dry, *n., pl.* **-dries**. (the science of) the use of emblems and design on shields, armour, etc.

heroin

herb, *n.* 1. a flowering plant whose stem is not woody and persistent. 2. such a plant as used for its medicinal properties, flavour, etc. – **herbal**, *adj.* – **herbaceous**, *adj.*

herbi·vorous, *adj.* feeding on plants. – **herbivore**, *n.*

herd, *n.* a number of animals, esp. cattle, kept, feeding, or travelling together.

here, *adv.* 1. in this place (opposed to *there*). 2. to or towards this place; hither. 3. at this point.

heredi·tary, *adj.* 1. passing naturally from parents to offspring. 2. *Law.* descending by inheritance.

hered·ity, *n., pl.* **-ties**. the transmission of genetic characteristics from parents to progeny.

heresy, *n., pl.* **-sies**. (the holding of) a doctrine contrary to the orthodox doctrine of a church or religious system. – **heretic**, *n.* – **heretical**, *adj.*

heri·tage, *n.* that which belongs to one by reason of birth; an inheritance.

hermaph·ro·dite, *n.* a person or animal with male and female sexual organs and characteristics.

hermit, *n.* one who has retired to a solitary place, esp. for religious seclusion. – **hermitage**, *n.*

hernia, *n., pl.* **-nias**. the protrusion of an organ through an opening in its surrounding tissues, esp. in the abdomen.

hero, *n., pl.* **-roes**. 1. a man distinguished by his great courage and noble qualities. 2. the principal male character in a story, etc. – **heroic**, *adj.* – **heroine**, *n.fem.*

heroin, *n.* an addictive drug derived from morphine.

heron

heron, *n.* a wading bird with a long neck, bill, and legs.

herpes /'hɜpiz/, *n.* blistering of the skin or mucous membranes caused by a viral infection.

herring, *n., pl.* **-rings**, (*esp. collectively*) **-ring**. a food fish.

herring·bone, *n.* a pattern of parallel lines arranged in the form of a V.

hers, *pron.* 1. form of the possessive *her: That book is hers.* 2. the person(s) or thing(s) belonging to her.

her·self, *pron.* 1. a reflexive form of *her: She could have hugged herself for joy.* 2. an emphatic form of *her* or *she: She said it for herself; She herself did it.* 3. her normal state of mind: *She felt quite herself again.*

hesi·tate, *v.*, **-tated**, **-tating**. 1. to hold back in doubt or indecision. 2. to pause. – **hesitation**, *n.* – **hesitant**, *adj.*

hessian /'hɛʃən/, *n.* a strong fabric made from jute, used for sacks, etc.

hetero·dox, *adj.* not in accordance with established doctrines, esp. in theology; unorthodox.

hetero·geneous, *adj.* composed of (parts) of different kinds.

hetero·sexuality, *n.* sexual feeling for persons of the opposite sex. – **heterosexual**, *n., adj.*

heu·ristic, *adj.* 1. furthering investigation. 2. (of a teaching method) encouraging the student to discover for himself.

hew, *v.*, **hewed**, **hewed** or **hewn**, **hewing**. to strike forcibly with an axe, etc.; chop.

hex, *n.* an evil spell or charm.

hexa·gon, *n.* a polygon with 6 sides.

hey, *interj.* (an exclamation used to call attention, etc.)

high

heyday, *n.* the period of greatest vigour or strength.

hiatus, *n., pl.* **-tuses**, **-tus**. a break, with a part missing; an interruption.

hiber·nate, *v.*, **-nated**, **-nating**. to spend the winter in a dormant condition, as certain animals.

hibis·cus, *n.* a tree or bush with showy flowers.

hiccup, *n.* an involuntary respiratory spasm producing a characteristic sound. Also, **hiccough**.

hick·ory, *n., pl.* **-ries**. a Nth American nut-bearing tree.

hide^1, *v.*, **hid**, **hidden** or **hid**, **hiding**. 1. to prevent (oneself) from being seen or discovered. 2. to keep secret.

hide^2, *n.* 1. the skin of an animal. 2. *Colloq.* impudence.

hid·eous, *adj.* very ugly.

hiding, *n.* 1. a beating. 2. a defeat.

hier·archy, *n., pl.* **-chies**. any graded order of persons or things.

hiero·glyphic, *n.* 1. (*usu. pl.*) writing (esp. of Ancient Egypt) using pictures or symbols to represent words or sounds. – *adj.* 2. written in hieroglyphics.

high, *adj.* 1. having a great extent upwards; lofty; tall. 2. having a specified extent upwards. 3. elevated. 4. of more than average height or depth. 5. intensified; strong; energetic. 6. shrill. 7. of great amount, force, etc. 8. chief; principal. 9. (of a period of time) at its fullest point of development: *the High Renaissance.* 10. *Colloq.* intoxicated with alcohol or drugs. 11. smelly; bad. – *adv.* 12. at or to a high point, place, level, rank, amount, price, degree. – *n.* 13. that

243

high

which is high; a high level. **14.** *Meteorol.* a pressure system with high pressure at its centre.

high-handed, *adj.* overbearing; arbitrary.

high·land, *n.* an elevated region; plateau.

high·light, *v.*, **-lighted, -lighting**, *n.* –*v.* **1.** to emphasise or make prominent. –*n.* **2.** a conspicuous part. **3.** (*pl.*) gleaming flecks of colour.

high·ness, *n.* **1.** the state of being high; dignity. **2.** (*cap.*) a title of honour given to royalty (prec. by *His, Your*, etc.).

high·way, *n.* a main road.

high·way·man, *n., pl.* **-men.** a robber on the highway, esp. one on horseback.

hijack, *v.* **1.** to steal (something) in transit, as a lorry and its goods. **2.** to seize by threat of force (a vehicle, esp. an aircraft).

hike, *v.*, **hiked, hiking**, *n.* –*v.* **1.** to walk a long distance for pleasure. –*n.* **2.** a long walk, esp. in the country. **3.** an increase in wages, prices, etc.

hilari·ous, *adj.* **1.** boisterously gay. **2.** funny. – **hilarity**, *n.*

hill, *n.* a conspicuous natural elevation of the earth's surface, smaller than a mountain.

hill·billy, *n., pl.* **-lies.** *Orig. U.S.* a person living in the backwoods or mountains; yokel.

hilt, *n.* the handle of a sword or dagger.

him, *pron.* objective case of *he*.

him·self, *pron.* **1.** a reflexive form of *him*: *He works himself too hard.* **2.** an emphatic form of *him* or *he*: *He used it for himself; He himself did it.* **3.** his normal state of mind: *He is now himself after his fit.*

his

hind[1], *adj.*, **hinder, hindmost** or **hindermost**, situated at the back; posterior.

hind[2], *n.* a female deer.

hinder, *v.* **1.** to interrupt; retard. **2.** to prevent from taking place; stop. – **hindrance**, *n.*

hind·sight, *n.* perception of what should have been done after the event.

hinge, *n., v.*, **hinged, hinging.** –*n.* **1.** the joint on which a door, gate, etc., turns or moves. –*v.* **2.** to depend or turn on, or as if on, a hinge.

hint, *n.* **1.** an indirect or covert suggestion or implication; an intimation. **2.** a barely perceptible amount. –*v.* **3.** to make indirect suggestion or allusion.

hinter·land, *n.* the land lying behind a coastal district.

hip[1], *n.* the projection of the side of the pelvis and the upper part of the femur.

hip[2], *n.* the ripe fruit of a rose.

hippo·potamus, *n., pl.* **-muses, -mi.** a large, hairless, herbivorous, African mammal.

hire, *v.*, **hired, hiring**, *n.* –*v.* **1.** to engage or grant the temporary use of, or the services of, for a payment. –*n.* **2.** (payment received for) the act of hiring.

hire-purchase, *n.* a purchasing system whereby a person has full use of a commodity being paid for by instalments.

hir·sute, *adj.* hairy.

his, *pron.* **1.** the possessive form of *he*. **2.** the person(s) or thing(s) belonging to him. –*adj.* **3.** pertaining to, or owned by him; made, experienced, etc., by him.

hiss, *v.* 1. to make a sharp sound like that of the letter *s* prolonged, esp. in disapproval or contempt. —*n.* 2. a hissing sound.

hista·mine, *n.* a substance released by the tissues in allergic reactions.

his·tory, *n., pl.* **-ries**. 1. the branch of knowledge dealing with past events. 2. a written record of past events as relating to a particular people, period, etc. — **historian**, *n.* — **historic, historical**, *adj.*

histri·onics, *n.pl.* melodramatic behaviour, speech, etc., for effect. — **histrionic**, *adj.*

hit, *v.*, **hit, hitting**, *n., adj.* —*v.* 1. to come against with an impact or collision. 2. to strike with a missile, weapon, blow, etc. 3. to affect severely. 4. to reach (a particular level). —*n.* 5. an impact or collision, as of one thing against another. 6. a successful stroke, performance, etc. 7. *Colloq.* a shot of heroin or any drug; fix. —*adj.* 8. successful; achieving popularity.

hitch, *v.* 1. to fasten, esp. temporarily, by a hook, rope, etc.; tether. 2. to raise (*up*) with jerks. 3. *Colloq.* to (seek to) obtain (a ride) from a passing vehicle. —*n.* 4. a halt; obstruction.

hitch·hike, *v.*, **-hiked, -hiking**. *Colloq.* to travel by obtaining rides in passing vehicles.

hither, *adv.* to or towards this place; here.

hither·to, *adv.* until now.

hive, *n.* 1. an artificial shelter for honeybees. 2. a place swarming with busy occupants.

hives, *n.* a skin rash.

hoard, *n.* 1. something accumulated for preservation or future use. —*v.* 2. to accumulate for preservation or future use, esp. secretly.

hoard·ing, *n.* 1. a temporary fence enclosing a building site. 2. a large billboard for displaying advertisements or notices.

hoarse, *adj.*, **hoarser, hoarsest**. 1. having a raucous voice. 2. husky.

hoary, *adj.*, **hoarier, hoariest**. grey or white with age.

hoax, *n.* 1. a humorous deception. 2. a deception, esp. of the public, and usu. for gain.

hobble, *v.*, **-bled, -bling**. 1. to walk lamely; limp. 2. to fasten together the legs of (a horse, etc.) so as to prevent free motion.

hobby, *n., pl.* **-bies**. a spare-time activity or pastime, etc.

hob·goblin, *n.* anything causing superstitious fear.

hobnob, *v.*, **-nobbed, -nobbing**. to associate (*with*) on very friendly terms.

hobo, *n., pl.* **-bos, -boes**. a tramp or vagrant.

hock[1], *n.* the joint in the hind leg of the horse, etc., corresponding to the ankle in man.

hock[2], *n.* a dry white wine.

hock[3], *v. Colloq.* →**pawn**[1].

hockey, *n.* a team game in which curved sticks are used to drive the ball.

hod, *n.* a trough for carrying mortar, bricks, etc.

hoe, *n., v.*, **hoed, hoeing**. —*n.* 1. a long-handled implement with a thin, flat blade used to break up the soil. —*v.* 2. to dig, etc., with a hoe.

hog, *n., v.*, **hogged, hogging**. —*n.* 1. a

hog domesticated pig, esp. a castrated boar. **2.** *Colloq.* a selfish, gluttonous, or filthy person. *–v.* **3.** *Colloq.* to take more than one's share of.

hogget, *n.* (the meat of) a young sheep before the cutting of its first 2 adult teeth.

hoist, *v.* **1.** to raise or lift, esp. mechanically. *–n.* **2.** an apparatus for hoisting, as a lift.

hold[1], *v.*, **held, holding**, *n.* *–v.* **1.** to have or keep in the hand; grasp. **2.** to retain; set aside. **3.** to support with the hand, arms, etc. **4.** to (cause to) remain in a specified state, relation, etc. **5.** to (be able to) contain. **6.** to regard or consider. **7.** to remain valid; be in force. **8. hold back, a.** to restrain. **b.** to withhold. **9. hold out, a.** to offer or present. **b.** to continue to exist; last. **10. hold to,** to abide by. **11. hold up, a.** to display. **b.** to delay. **c.** to stop in order to rob. *–n.* **12.** the act of holding fast by the hand, etc.; grasp; grip. **13.** a controlling force, or dominating influence. **– holder**, *n.*

hold[2], *n.* *Naut.* The space inside a ship for storing cargo.

hold·ing, *n.* (*oft. pl.*) property owned, esp. stocks and shares, and land.

hold-up, *n.* *Colloq.* **1.** a forcible stopping and robbing of a person, bank, etc. **2.** a delay; stoppage.

hole, *n.* **1.** an opening through anything; an aperture. **2.** a hollow place in a solid body; cavity. **3.** a small, shabby dwelling or town.

hol·i·day, *n.* **1.** a day on which ordinary business is suspended in commemoration of some event, person, etc. **2.** (*oft. pl.*) a break from work, for recreation; vacation. *–v.* **3.** to take a holiday.

homoeopathy

hollow, *adj.* **1.** having a hole or cavity within; not solid; empty. **2.** sunken, as the cheeks or eyes. *–v.* **3.** to make hollow.

holly, *n., pl.* **-lies.** a plant with glossy, spiny-edged leaves and red berries.

holo·caust /ˈhɒləkɒst, -kɔst/, *n.* great or wholesale destruction of life, esp. by fire.

hol·ster, *n.* a leather case for a pistol, attached to a belt.

holy, *adj.*, **-lier, -liest. 1.** declared sacred by religious use or authority; consecrated. **2.** dedicated or devoted to the service of God, the Church, or religion. **– holiness**, *n.*

homage, *n.* respect or reverence given.

home, *n.* **1.** a house, or other shelter that is the fixed residence of a person, etc. **2.** (*oft. cap.*) an institution for the homeless, sick, etc. **3.** the region where something is native or most common. **4.** one's native place or own country. *–adv.* **5.** to, towards, or at home.

homely, *adj.*, **-lier, -liest. 1.** plain and unpretentious. **2.** not good-looking.

home·sick, *adj.* longing for home.

home·stead, *n.* the main residence on a large farm, etc.

home unit, *n.* one of a number of dwelling apartments in the same building, each owned under separate title (def. 5).

homi·cide, *n.* the killing of one human being by another. **2.** a murderer. **– homicidal**, *adj.*

homily, *n., pl.* **-lies.** a religious address to a congregation; sermon.

homoeo·pathy /ˌhoʊmiˈɒpəθi/, *n.* a method of treating disease by minute doses of drugs, which produce in a healthy person symptoms

homoeopathy

similar to those of the disease. – **homoeopathic**, *adj.* – **homoeopath**, *n.*

homo·geneous /houməˈdʒiniəs, homə-/, *adj.* (composed of parts) of the same kind; not heterogeneous. – **homogeneity**, *n.*

homog·enise /həˈmɒdʒənaɪz/, *v.*, **-nised, -nising** to make homogeneous.

homog·enous /həˈmɒdʒənəs/, *adj.* 1. corresponding in structure because of a common origin. 2. →**homogeneous**.

homolo·gous /həˈmɒləgəs/, *adj.* corresponding in relative position, structure, etc., but not necessarily in use.

homonym, *n.* a word like another in sound and perhaps in spelling, but different in meaning, as *meat* and *meet*.

homo·sexuality, *n.* sexual feeling for a person of the same sex. – **homosexual**, *n., adj.*

hone, *n., v.*, **honed, honing.** –*n.* 1. a stone of fine texture, as for sharpening razors. –*v.* 2. to sharpen (as) on a hone.

honest, *adj.* 1. honourable in principles, intentions, and actions; upright. 2. open; sincere 3. genuine or unadulterated. – **honesty**, *n.*

honey, *n.* a sweet, viscid fluid produced by bees from the nectar collected from flowers.

honey·comb, *n.* 1. a wax structure of hexagonal cells, formed by bees for keeping honey, pollen and eggs. –*v.* 2. to pierce with many holes or cavities.

honey·eater, *n.* a bird which feeds on the nectar from flowers.

honey·moon, *n.* a holiday spent by a newly married couple after the wedding.

honey·suckle, *n.* a fragrant, climbing plant.

honk, *n.* 1. the cry of the wild goose. 2. any similar sound, as a motor-car horn. –*v.* 3. to emit a honk.

honky-tonk, *n.* ragtime piano music.

hono·rarium, *n., pl.* **-rariums, raria**. a fee for professional services.

hono·rary, *adj.* 1. (holding a position) given for honour only, without the usual duties, etc. 2. (of a position, job, etc.) unpaid. 3. (of an obligation) depending on one's honour for fulfilment.

hono·rific, *n., adj.* (a title) conferring honour.

honour, *n.* 1. high public esteem; fame; glory. 2. reputation for worthy behaviour. 3. a source of credit: *to be an honour to one's family*. 4. a special privilege: *May I have the honour of your company?* 5. high principles; fine sense of one's obligations. 6. (*pl.*) (in universities) academic achievement in a degree examination higher than that required for a pass degree. –*v.* 7. to hold in honour or high respect; revere. 8. to confer honour upon. 9. to accept and pay (a cheque, etc.) when due. 10. to accept the validity of (a document, etc.) – **honourable**, *adj.*

hood, *n.* 1. a soft covering for the head and neck, sometimes attached to a cloak, etc. 2. something resembling this. 3. a motor-car bonnet. 4. *Colloq.* a hoodlum.

hood·lum, *n.* 1. a petty gangster. 2. a young person given to street fighting, vandalism, etc.

hood·wink, v. to deceive.

hoof, n., pl. **hoofs**, **hooves**. the horny covering protecting the foot in certain mammals, as the ox, horse, etc.

hook, n. 1. a curved or angular piece of metal, etc., for catching or supporting something. 2. that which catches; a trap. 3. something resembling a hook. 4. *Boxing*. a curving blow made with the arm bent. –v. 5. to seize, or fasten with a hook. 6. to become attached by a hook; join on.

hookah, n. a pipe filled with water for cooling the smoke of tobacco, marijuana, etc.

hooked, adj. 1. bent like a hook. 2. *Colloq.* addicted; obsessed (*on*).

hooli·gan, n. *Colloq.* a hoodlum (def. 2).

hoop, n. a circular band of wood, metal, etc., or something resembling it.

hooray, interj. (an exclamation of joy, applause, etc.)

hoot, v. 1. to cry out or shout, esp. in disapproval. 2. (of an owl) to utter its cry. 3. to blow a horn; honk. –n. 4. the cry of an owl. 5. any similar sound.

hooves, n. a plural of **hoof**.

hop¹, v., **hopped**, **hopping**. –v. 1. to jump on one foot. 2. *Colloq.* to get (*in*, *on* or *off*) a car, train, etc. 3. *Colloq.* to jump (*off*) something elevated, or (*over*) a fence, ditch, etc. –n. 4. a leap on one foot. 5. *Colloq.* a dance, or dancing party.

hop², n. a plant used in brewing.

hope, n., v., **hoped**, **hoping**. –n. 1. expectation of something desired. 2. confidence in a future event. –v. 3. to look forward (*to*) with desire and confidence. 4. to trust in the truth of a matter (fol. by a clause). – **hopeless**, adj.

hope·ful, adj. 1. full of hope. 2. promising advantage or success. –n. 3. a promising young person.

horde, n. (*oft. derog.*) a multitude.

hori·zon, n. the line forming the apparent boundary between earth and sky.

hori·zontal, adj. 1. at right-angles to the vertical. 2. near, on, or parallel to the horizon.

hor·mone, n. 1. a substance, secreted into the body fluids by an endocrine gland, which activates specific nerve cells. 2. a synthetic substance having the same effect.

horn, n. 1. a hard, often curved, outgrowth (usu. one of a pair) on the head of certain mammals. 2. any hornlike projection. 3. *Music*. a wind instrument of the brass family. 4. an instrument for sounding a warning signal.

hornet, n. a large wasp.

horo·scope, n. 1. the art or practice of foretelling future events by observation of the stars and planets. 2. the diagram of the heavens used for this purpose.

horren·dous, adj. dreadful; horrible.

hor·rible, adj. 1. causing horror; dreadful. 2. extremely unpleasant; deplorable.

horrid, adj. 1. horrible; abominable. 2. *Colloq.* extremely unpleasant or disagreeable.

hor·rific, adj. causing horror.

hor·rify, v., **-fied**, **-fying**. to shock or strike with horror.

horror, n. 1. great fear or abhorrence. 2. *Colloq.* something considered

horror

atrocious or bad. 3. intense aversion or repugnance.

horse, n., pl. **horses**, (esp. collectively) **horse**. 1. a large, solid-hoofed four-legged animal often used for riding. 2. a vaulting block, used for gymnastics.

horse·play, n. rough or boisterous play.

horse·power, n. a unit of measurement of power in the imperial system, defined as 550 pounds-force per second (approx. 745 watts).

horse·radish, n. a plant with a pungent root used as a flavouring.

horse·shoe, n. 1. a U-shaped iron plate nailed to a horse's hoof to protect it. 2. a symbol of good luck.

horta·tory, adj. encouraging; exhorting.

horti·culture, n. the science or art of growing plants.

hose, n., pl. **hose**, v., **hosed, hosing**. -n. 1. a stocking. 2. a flexible tube for conveying water, etc. -v. 3. to apply water, etc., to by means of a hose.

hosiery, n. stockings of any kind.

hos·pice, n. 1. a refuge for pilgrims, etc., esp. one kept by a religious order. 2. a hospital for dying patients.

hospi·tal, n. an institution for the treatment of sick or injured persons.

hospi·tality, n., pl. **-ties**. the kind and generous treatment of guests or strangers. – **hospitable**, adj.

host[1], n. 1. one who entertains guests. 2. the landlord of an inn. 3. an animal or plant from which a parasite obtains nutrition.

host[2], n. a multitude.

house

hos·tage /'hɒstɪdʒ/, n. a person held as a security for the performance of certain actions as the payment of ransom, etc.

hostel, n. a supervised place of low cost accommodation, as for students, nurses, etc.

host·ess, n. a woman who entertains guests.

hos·tile, adj. unfriendly; antagonistic. – **hostility**, n.

hot, adj., **hotter, hottest**. 1. having or communicating heat; having a high temperature. 2. having or producing a sensation of great bodily heat. 3. new; fresh: *hot off the press*. 4. close: *hot on one's heels*. 5. (of motor cars) modified for high speeds. 6. *Colloq*. recently stolen.

hotch·potch, n. a heterogeneous mixture; jumble.

hot dog, n. a hot frankfurter or sausage, esp. as served in a bread roll.

hotel, n. a building providing accommodation, food, and (alcoholic) drinks.

hot plate, n. a heated metal plate upon which food may be cooked.

hound, n. 1. a (hunting) dog. -v. 2. to hunt with hounds; pursue. 3. to harass unceasingly.

hound's-tooth, n. a pattern of contrasting jagged checks.

hour, n. 1. a space of time equal to one 24th part of a mean solar day; 60 minutes. 2. a particular time. 3. distance normally covered in an hour's travelling.

house, n., pl. **houses**, v., **housed, housing**. -n. 1. a building for human habitation. 2. a household. 3. the audience of a theatre, etc. 4. (the meeting place of) a legislative

249

house

body. 5. a commercial establishment. 6. a subdivision of a school, comprising children of all ages and classes. −v. 7. to provide with a house. 8. to put in a safe place.

house·hold, n. 1. all the people of a house; a family, including servants, etc. −adj. 2. pertaining to a household; domestic. 3. ordinary or common.

house·keep·er, n. an employee hired to run a house.

house·wife, n.; pl. -wives. a married woman in charge of a household.

house·work, n. the work of cleaning, cooking, etc.

housie-housie, n. a gambling game in which players put markers on numbered squares on a card according to the numbers drawn and announced by a caller.

housing, n. 1. (something serving as) a shelter, etc. 2. the providing of houses for the community. 3. *Mach.* a frame, plate, etc., that supports a part of a machine, etc.

hovel, n. a small, shabby dwelling.

hover, v. 1. to hang suspended in the air. 2. to wait near at hand.

hover·craft, n. a vehicle able to travel above the ground or water, on a cushion of air.

how, adv. 1. in what way; by what means: *How did you do it?* 2. to what extent, etc.: *How much is it?* 3. in what condition: *How are you?* −conj. 4. concerning the way in which: *I wonder how you managed it.* 5. concerning the extent to which: *I wonder how far you can go.* 6. concerning the condition in which: *I wonder how you are.*

how·ev·er, conj. 1. nevertheless; yet. −adv. 2. to whatever extent; no

hum

matter how (far, much, etc.). 3. in whatever condition, state, or manner. 4. Also, **how ever**. (interrogatively) how in any circumstances.

howl, v. 1. to utter a loud, prolonged, mournful cry, as that of a dog or wolf. −n. 2. the cry of a dog, wolf, etc. 3. a cry or wail, as of pain or rage.

hub, n. 1. the central part of a wheel supporting the spokes. 2. the central part around which all else revolves.

huddle, v., -dled, -dling, n. −v. 1. to gather or crowd together confusedly. −n. 2. a confused heap, mass, or crowd; jumble.

hue[1], n. 1. colour: *all hues of the rainbow*. 2. variety of a colour; tint.

hue[2], n. outcry.

huff, n. 1. a sudden fit of anger. −v. 2. to puff or blow.

hug, v., hugged, hugging, n. −v. 1. to clasp tightly in the arms, esp. with affection; embrace. −n. 2. a tight clasp with the arms; a warm embrace.

huge, adj., huger, hugest. extraordinarily large.

hulk, n. 1. the body of an old or dismantled ship. 2. a bulky or unwieldy person or mass of anything.

hull[1], n. 1. the outer covering of a seed or fruit, or the calyx of a strawberry, etc. −v. 2. to remove the hull of.

hull[2], n. the frame or body of a ship.

hul·la·baloo, n. a clamorous noise; uproar.

hum, v., hummed, humming. 1. to make a low, continuous, droning sound. 2. *Colloq.* to be busy and active.

human

human, *adj.* **1.** of, pertaining to, or characteristic of man. **2.** a human being.

humane, *adj.* characterised by compassion for the suffering.

humani·tarian, *adj.* **1.** having regard to the interests of all mankind. –*n.* **2.** a philanthropist.

human·ity, *n., pl.* **-ties. 1.** the human race; mankind. **2.** the quality of being humane.

humanly, *adv.* within the capabilities of a human; in a human way.

humble, *adj.*, **-bler**, **-blest**, *v.* **-bled**, **-bling.** –*adj.* **1.** low in rank, importance, etc.; lowly. **2.** modest; meek. –*v.* **3.** to lower in dignity; abase.

humbug, *n. Colloq.* (someone who practises) falseness or deception.

hum·drum, *adj.* lacking variety; dull.

humerus, *n., pl.* **-meri.** (in man) the long bone in the arm, from the shoulder to the elbow.

humid, *adj.* moist or damp. – **humid·ity**, *n.*

humili·ate, *v.*, **-ated**, **-ating.** to lower the pride or self-respect of; mortify.

humil·ity, *n.* the quality of being humble; modesty.

humming·bird, *n.* a small bird whose narrow wings vibrate very rapidly, producing a humming sound.

hum·mock, *n.* a small hill.

humor·ous, *adj.* **1.** amusing; funny. **2.** droll; facetious.

humour, *n.* **1.** the quality of being funny. **2.** (speech, writing, etc., showing) the ability to perceive what is amusing. **3.** frame of mind. **4.** *Obs.* one of the 4 supposed chief bodily fluids, blood, yellow bile, phlegm, and melancholy or black bile. –*v.* **5.** indulge: *to humour a child.*

hump, *n.* **1.** a rounded protuberance, esp. on the back. **2.** a low, rounded rise of ground; hummock.

humus, *n.* the dark organic material in soils, produced by the decomposition of vegetable or animal matter.

hunch, *v.* **1.** to (be) thrust out or up in a hump. –*n.* **2.** a hump. **3.** *Colloq.* a premonition or suspicion.

hun·dred, *n., adj.* **-dreds** (*as after a numeral*), **-dred.** a cardinal number, 10 times 10.

hung, *v.* past tense and past participle of **hang**.

hunger, *n.* **1.** the painful sensation caused by need of food. **2.** strong desire. – **hungry**, *adj.*

hunk, *n.* a large piece or lump; chunk.

hunt, *v.* **1.** to (engage in the) chase for the purpose of catching or killing (game, etc.). **2.** to search or seek (*for, after*). –*n.* **3.** the act of hunting game, etc.; the chase. **4.** pursuit; search.

hurdle, *n., v.*, **-dled**, **-dling.** –*n.* **1.** a barrier in a racetrack, to be leapt by the contestants. **2.** a difficult problem to be overcome; obstacle. –*v.* **3.** to leap over (a hurdle, etc.) as in a race. **4.** to master (a difficulty, problem, etc.).

hurl, *v.* to throw with great force.

hurri·cane, *n.* a violent tropical cyclonic storm.

hurry, *v.*, **-ried**, **-rying**, *n.* –*v.* **1.** to move (someone or something) with (often undue) haste. –*n.* **2.** need or desire for haste.

hurry, *v.*, **hurt**, **hurting**, *n.* –*v.* **1.** to cause injury or pain (to). **2.** to

hurt

harm. −n. 3. (a blow that inflicts) injury.

hurtle, v., -tled, -tling. to rush violently and noisily.

hus·band, n. the man of a married pair (correlative of *wife*).

hus·bandry, n. agriculture; farming.

hush, v. 1. to make silent. 2. to suppress mention of; keep concealed.

husk, n. the dry external covering of certain fruits or seeds.

husky[1], adj., -kier, -kiest. 1. *Colloq.* big and strong; burly. 2. spoken in a half-whisper.

husky[2], n., pl. -kies. an Eskimo dog used in a team to pull sledges over snow.

hussy /'hʌsi, 'hʌzi/, n., pl. -sies. 1. an ill-behaved girl. 2. a lewd woman.

hus·tings, n.pl. (a platform for) election proceedings.

hustle, v., -tled, -tling. −v. 1. to proceed energetically. 2. to force roughly or hurriedly. −n. 3. energetic activity.

hut, n. a simple, small house.

hutch, n. a coop for confining small animals.

hya·cinth, n. a bulbous plant with spikes of fragrant, bell-shaped flowers.

hybrid, n. 1. the offspring of 2 animals or plants of different breeds. 2. anything composed of different or incongruous elements.

hydran·gea, n. a shrub with large showy flower clusters.

hydrant, n. an outlet from a water main.

hyd·raulic, adj. operated by or employing liquid, esp. water.

hyperbolic

hydro·carbon, n. a compound containing only hydrogen and carbon.

hydro·foil, n. a boat fitted with skis which, at speed, lifts above the surface of the water.

hydro·gen, n. a colourless, odourless, inflammable gas, which combines chemically with oxygen to form water. Symbol: H

hydro·plane, n. an aeroplane provided with floats for landing on water.

hydro·ponics, n. the cultivation of plants by placing the roots in nutrient solutions rather than in soil.

hyena, n. a doglike nocturnal carnivore feeding chiefly on carrion.

hygiene, n. (the science which deals with) the preservation of health.

hygienic, adj. 1. sanitary; clean. 2. pertaining to hygiene.

hygro·meter, n. an instrument for determining the humidity of the atmosphere.

hymen, n. a membrane partially closing the external orifice of the vagina.

hymn, n. a song in praise of God, a nation, etc.

hymnal, n. Also, **hymnbook**. a book of hymns for use in divine worship.

hype, n. manufactured excitement.

hyper·bola /haɪ'pɜbələ/, n., pl. -las. a curve formed by the intersection of a plane with a cone when the plane makes an angle to the base greater than that of the side of the cone to the base.

hyper·bole /haɪ'pɜbəli/, n. obvious exaggeration, for serious or comic effect.

hyper·bolic /haɪpə'bɒlɪk/, adj. 1. exaggerated. 2. of or pertaining to the hyperbola.

hyphen

hyphen, *n.* a short stroke (-) used to connect the parts of a compound or divided word. – **hyphenate**, *v.*

hypno·sis, *n., pl.* **-ses.** *Psychol.* a trance-like mental state induced in a cooperative subject by suggestion. – **hypnotise**, *v.* – **hypnotism**, *n.*

hyp·notic, *adj.* **1.** pertaining to hypnosis or hypnotism. –*n.* **2.** a drug that produces sleep; sedative.

hypo·chondria, *n. Psychol.* a condition characterised by depressed spirits and fancies of ill health. – **hypochondriac**, *n., adj.*

hypoc·risy, *n., pl.* **-sies. 1.** the act of pretending to have a character, beliefs, etc., that one does not possess. **2.** pretence of virtue or piety.

hysteria

hypo·crite, *n.* one given to hypocrisy. – **hypocritical**, *adj.*

hypo·dermic, *n.* a needle used to introduce liquid medicine, etc., under the skin.

hypot·enuse, *n.* the side of a right-angled triangle opposite the right angle.

hypo·thesis, *n., pl.* **-ses. 1.** a proposed explanation for the occurrence of some specified group of phenomena. **2.** a proposition assumed as a premise in an argument. – **hypothetical**, *adj.*

hyster·ectomy, *n., pl.* **-mies.** the excision of the uterus.

hys·teria, *n.* emotional frenzy. – **hysterical**, *adj.*

Ii

I, i, *n., pl.* **I's** or **Is** or **i's** or **is.** 1. the 9th letter of the English alphabet. 2. the Roman numeral for one. See **Roman numerals.**

iamb /'aɪæmb, 'aɪəm/, *n.* a metrical foot of 2 syllables, a short followed by a long. – **iambic,** *adj.*

ibidem, *adv.* in the same book, chapter, page, etc.

ibis, *n.* a wading bird with a long, down-curved bill.

ice, *n., v.,* **iced, icing.** –*n.* 1. frozen water. –*v.* 2. to cover (cakes, etc.) with icing. – **icy,** *adj.*

ice·berg, *n.* a large mass of ice floating in the sea.

ice-cream, *n.* a frozen food made of cream, or milk, sweetened and flavoured.

ichthy·ology, *n.* the branch of zoology that treats of fishes.

icicle, *n.* a hanging mass of ice formed by the freezing of dripping water.

icing, *n.* a preparation of sugar for covering cakes, etc.

icon, *n.* a representation in painting, enamel, etc., of Christ or a saint, itself venerated as sacred.

icono·clast /aɪ'kɒnəklæst/, *n.* 1. a destroyer of images, esp. those set up for religious veneration. 2. one who attacks cherished beliefs as based on error or superstition.

idiosyncrasy

id, *n.* the part of the psyche which is the source of instinctive energy.

idea, *n.* any conception or new thought resulting from mental understanding or activity.

ideal, *n.* 1. a conception of something in its highest perfection. 2. that which exists only in idea. –*adj.* 3. conceived as a standard of perfection or excellence. 4. not real or practical.

ideal·ise, *v.,* **-lised, -lising.** to regard or represent as ideal.

ideal·ism, *n.* the cherishing or pursuit of ideals. – **idealist,** *n.* – **idealistic,** *adj.*

idem, *pron., adj.* the same as previously mentioned.

identi·cal, *adj.* 1. agreeing exactly. 2. same, or being the same one.

iden·tify, *v.,* **-fied, -fying.** 1. to recognise or establish as being a particular person or thing. 2. to associate in feeling, interest, action, etc. (*with*). – **identification,** *n.*

iden·tity, *n., pl.* **-ties.** 1. the state or fact of being the same. 2. the condition of being oneself or itself, and not another.

ideol·ogy /aɪdɪ'ɒlədʒi/, *n., pl.* **-gies.** the body of doctrine of a social movement, institution, class, etc. – **ideological,** *adj.* – **ideologist,** *n.*

id est, that is.

idiom, *n.* 1. a form of expression peculiar to a language, esp. one having a significance other than its literal one. 2. distinct style or character, as in music, art, etc. – **idiomatic,** *adj.*

idio·syn·crasy, *n., pl.* **-sies.** any behaviour, mode of expression, or the like, peculiar to an individual.

idiosyncrasy

– **idiosyncratic**, *adj.* – **idiosyncratically**, *adv.*

idiot, *n.* an utterly foolish person. – **idiotic**, *adj.* – **idiotically**, *adv.* – **idiocy**, *n.*

idle, *adj.*, **idler**, **idlest**, *v.*, **idled**, **idling**. –*adj.* 1. unemployed, or doing nothing. 2. habitually doing nothing or avoiding work; lazy. –*v.* 3. to pass time in idleness.

idol, *n.* 1. an image or object representing a deity, to which religious worship is addressed. 2. any person or thing blindly adored or revered. – **idolatry**, *n.* – **idolise**, *v.*

idyll, *n.* 1. a poem or prose composition describing pastoral scenes or events. 2. an episode or scene of simple or poetic charm. – **idyllic**, *adj.*

if, *conj.* 1. in case that; granting that; on condition that. 2. whether.

igloo, *n.*, *pl.* **-loos**. a dome-shaped Eskimo hut, built of blocks of hard snow.

igneous rock, *n.* rock formed from magma.

ignite, *v.*, **-nited**, **-niting**. 1. to set on fire; kindle. 2. to begin to burn.

ig·nition, *n.* 1. the act of igniting. 2. the state of being ignited. 3. (in an internal-combustion engine) the process which ignites the fuel in the cylinder.

ig·noble, *adj.* of low character, aims, etc.; mean; base.

igno·miny /'ɪgnəmɪni/, *n.*, *pl.* **-minies**. disgrace; dishonour. – **ignominious**, *adj.*

igno·ramus, *n.*, *pl.* **-muses**. an ignorant person.

igno·rant, *adj.* destitute of knowledge. – **ignorance**, *n.*

image

ignore, *v.*, **-nored**, **-noring**. to refrain from noticing or recognising.

iguana, *n.* a large tropical American lizard.

ilk, *n.* family, class, or kind.

ill, *adj.*, **worse**, **worst**, *n.*, *adv.* –*adj.* 1. unwell or sick. 2. evil, wicked, or bad. –*n.* 3. evil. 4. harm or injury. 5. a disease or ailment. –*adv.* 6. unsatisfactorily or poorly. 7. with displeasure or offence. 8. faultily or improperly. – **illness**, *n.*

il·legal, *adj.* not legal. – **illegality**, *n.*

il·legible, *adj.* impossible or hard to read or decipher.

il·legit·i·mate, *adj.* 1. not legitimate. 2. born out of wedlock.

ill-gotten, *adj.* acquired by dishonest means.

illicit, *adj.* not permitted or authorised; unlawful.

il·liter·ate, *adj.* 1. unable to read and write. –*n.* 2. an illiterate person.

il·lumi·nate, *v.*, **-nated**, **-nating**. 1. to supply with light; light up. 2. to enlighten, as with knowledge. 3. to decorate (a manuscript, etc.) with colour, gold, or the like.

illu·sion, *n.* something that deceives by producing a false impression. – **illusory**, *adj.*

illus·trate, *v.*, **-strated**, **-strating**. 1. to make clear or intelligible, as by examples. 2. to furnish (a book, etc.) with drawings or pictorial representations. – **illustration**, *n.*

illus·trious, *adj.* 1. highly distinguished; famous. 2. glorious, as deeds, etc.

image, *n.* 1. a likeness or representation of a person, animal, or thing. 2. an optical counterpart or appearance of an object. 3. an idea or conception. 4. the public

image

impression made by a politician, etc. 5. a counterpart or copy. 6. a figure of speech, esp. a metaphor or simile. – **imagery**, n.

imagi·nary, adj. existing only in the imagination.

imagi·nation, n. the action of forming mental images or concepts of what is not actually present to the senses. – **imaginative**, adj.

imagine, v., -ined, -ining. 1. to form a mental image of (something not actually present to the senses). 2. to think, believe, or suppose.

imbecile, n. 1. a mentally defective person. 2. Colloq. a silly person.

imbibe, v., -bibed, -bibing. to drink in, or drink (liquid).

imbro·glio /im'brouliou/, n., pl. -os. a complicated or confused situation, esp. involving disagreement.

imbue, v., -bued, -buing. to impregnate or inspire, as with feelings, opinions, etc.

imi·tate, v., -tated, -tating. 1. to follow in action or manner. 2. to mimic or counterfeit. 3. to make a copy of. – **imitation**, n.

immacu·late, adj. spotlessly clean.

imma·nent, adj. remaining within; indwelling; inherent.

im·material, adj. 1. unimportant. 2. not material; spiritual.

immedi·ate, adj. 1. occurring without delay; instant. 2. nearest or next. – **immediacy**, n.

im·memorial, adj. extending back beyond memory or record.

immense, adj. vast; huge; immeasurable.

immerse, v., -mersed, -mersing. to plunge into or place under a liquid. – **immersion**, n.

immi·grate, v., -grated, -grating. to

impassive

come to live in a country of which one is not a native. – **immigration**, n. – **immigrant**, n., adj.

immi·nent, adj. likely to occur at any moment.

immo·late, v., -lated, -lating. to sacrifice.

immoral, adj. not conforming to the moral law or accepted patterns of conduct. – **immorality**, n.

immortal, adj. 1. not liable to subject to death; undying. 2. remembered or celebrated through all time. – **immortality**, n. – **immortalise**, v.

immune, adj. 1. protected from a disease or the like, as by inoculation. 2. exempt. – **immunise**, v. – **immunisation**, n. – **immunity**, n.

immu·nology, n. that branch of medical science which deals with immunity from disease.

immure, v., -mured, -muring. 1. to enclose within walls. 2. to imprison.

immut·able, adj. unchangeable.

imp, n. 1. a little devil or demon. 2. a mischievous child.

impact, n. 1. the striking of one body against another. 2. the effect exerted by a new idea, etc. –v. 3. to drive firmly into something; pack in.

impair, v. to diminish in value, excellence, etc.

impala, n. an African antelope.

impale, v., -paled, -paling. to fix upon a sharpened stake or the like.

impart, v., to give or bestow.

im·partial, adj. unbiased.

impasse /'impas/, n. a position from which there is no escape.

im·passive, adj. without emotion; apathetic.

impatient

im·pa·tient, *adj.* not bearing pain, opposition, etc., with composure. – **impatience**, *n.*

impeach, *v.* 1. to challenge the credibility of. 2. to accuse of a grave criminal offence.

impec·cable, *adj.* faultless or irreproachable.

im·pecu·nious, *adj.* poor; penniless.

impede, *v.*, **-peded**, **-peding**. to obstruct; hinder.

impedi·ment, *n.* 1. some physical defect, esp. a speech disorder. 2. obstruction or hindrance.

impel, *v.*, **-pelled**, **-pelling**. to drive or urge forward.

impend, *v.* to be imminent.

im·pera·tive, *adj.* 1. not to be avoided or evaded. 2. of the nature of or expressing a command.

im·perfect, *adj.* 1. having defects. 2. *Gram.* designating a tense which denotes incomplete past action.

im·perial, *adj.* 1. of or pertaining to an empire. 2. of a commanding quality, manner, or aspect. 3. (of weights and measures) conforming to the former official British standards.

im·peri·ous, *adj.* domineering; dictatorial.

im·personal, *adj.* without personal reference or connection. 2. *Gram.* (of a verb) having only 3rd person singular forms.

im·person·ate, *v.*, **-nated**, **-nating**. to mimic or pretend to be.

im·perti·nent, *adj.* rude or presumptuous.

im·per·vious, *adj.* not penetrable.

impetigo, *n.* a contagious skin disease.

imposing

im·petu·ous, *adj.* characterised by a sudden or rash energy.

impetus, *n.*, **-tuses**. moving force; impulse; stimulus.

impinge, *v.*, **-pinged**, **-pinging**. 1. to collide. 2. to encroach (*on* or *upon*).

im·plac·able, *adj.* not to be appeased or pacified.

implant, *v.* to instil or inculcate.

imple·ment, *n.* 1. an instrument, tool, or utensil. –*v.* 2. to put (a plan, etc.) into effect.

impli·cate, *v.*, **-cated**, **-cating**. 1. to involve in a matter, affair, etc. 2. to imply. – **implication**, *n.*

implicit, *adj.* 1. (of belief, etc.) unquestioning, unreserved, or absolute. 2. implied, rather than expressly stated.

implore, *v.*, **-plored**, **-ploring**. to urgently or piteously beseech.

imply, *v.*, **-plied**, **-plying**. 1. to involve as a necessary circumstance. 2. to indicate or suggest.

import, *v.* 1. to bring in from another country, as merchandise or commodities. 2. to convey as a meaning. –*n.* 3. that which is imported from abroad. 4. meaning. 5. consequence or importance.

im·por·tant, *adj.* 1. of much significance or consequence. 2. mattering much (*to*). 3. of considerable influence or authority. – **importance**, *n.*

impor·tune /ɪmˈpɔːtʃʊn, ɪmpəˈtjuːn/, *v.*, **-tuned**, **-tuning**. to beg urgently or persistently. – **importunate**, *adj.*

impose, *v.*, **-posed**, **-posing**. 1. to lay (a burden, charge, penalty, etc.) on. 2. to obtrude oneself or one's requirements. – **imposition**, *n.*

im·posing, *adj.* making an impres-

imposing

sion as by great size, stately appearance, etc.

im·pos·si·ble, *adj.* 1. that cannot be, exist, or happen. 2. that cannot be done. – **impossibility**, *n.*

im·pos·tor, *n.* one who practises deception under an assumed character or name. – **imposture**, *n.*

im·po·tent, *adj.* 1. lacking power or ability. 2. (of a male) wholly lacking in sexual power. – **impotence**, *n.*

im·pound, *v.* 1. to shut up in a pound, as a stray animal. 2. to seize, take, or appropriate summarily.

im·pov·er·ish, *v.* to reduce to poverty.

im·preg·na·ble, *adj.* strong enough to resist attack.

im·preg·nate, *v.*, **-nated, -nating.** 1. to make pregnant. 2. to saturate.

impress, *v.*, **-pressed** or (*Archaic*) **-prest, -pressing.** 1. to cause a strong response or influence, esp. a favourable one, in the mind. 2. to urge, as something to be remembered or done. 3. to stamp or imprint (a mark, figure, etc.). – **impressive**, *adj.*

im·pres·sion, *n.* 1. a strong effect produced on the mind, etc. 2. a notion. 3. a mark, indentation, etc., produced by pressure. 4. an imitation of the idiosyncrasies of some well-known person or type. – **impressionable**, *adj.*

imprint, *n.* 1. a mark, etc., impressed or printed on something. –*v.* 2. to impress (a quality, character, or distinguishing mark). 3. to fix firmly on the mind, memory, etc.

im·prison, *v.* to confine in a prison.

im·promp·tu, *adj.* made or done without previous preparation.

improve, *v.*, **-proved, -proving.** to

incalculable

(cause to) increase in value, excellence, etc.; make or become better. – **improvement**, *n.*

im·pro·vise, *v.*, **-vised, -vising.** to provide or perform without previous preparation. – **improvisation**, *n.*

im·pu·dent, *adj.* shamelessly bold. – **impudence**, *n.*

impugn /ɪmˈpjuːn/, *v.* to challenge as false.

impulse, *n.* 1. sudden, involuntary inclination to act. 2. an impelling action or force. – **impulsive**, *adj.*

im·pu·ni·ty, *n.* exemption from punishment or ill consequences.

impute, *v.*, **-puted, -puting.** to attribute or ascribe. – **imputation**, *n.*

in, *prep.* 1. a particle expressing inclusion within space, limits, a whole, material or immaterial surroundings, etc.: *in a box; in the country; in politics.* –*adv.* 2. in or into some place, position, state, relation, etc.: *to push a button in.* –*adj.* 3. internal; inward; incoming.

in·ad·ver·tent /ˌɪnədˈvɜːtnt/, *adj.* 1. not attentive. 2. unintentional.

inane, *adj.* lacking sense or ideas; silly. – **inanity**, *n.*

in·an·i·mate, *adj.* 1. lifeless. 2. spiritless; dull.

in·au·gu·rate, *v.*, **-rated, -rating.** 1. to make a formal beginning of. 2. to install in office with formal ceremonies. – **inaugural**, *adj.* – **inauguration**, *n.*

in·born, *adj.* implanted by nature; innate.

in·breed, *v.*, **-bred, -breeding.** to breed (animals) repeatedly within the same strain. – **inbred**, *adj.*

in·cal·cu·la·ble, *adj.* that cannot be calculated.

in camera, *adj.* (of a case) heard by a judge in his private room.

in·can·des·cence, *n.* the state of a body caused by approximately white heat, when it may be used as a source of artificial light. – **incandesce**, *v.* – **incandescent**, *adj.*

in·can·ta·tion, *n.* a magic spell; charm.

in·ca·pac·i·tate, *v.*, -tated, -tating. to make incapable or unfit.

in·car·cer·ate, *v.*, -rated, -rating. to imprison; confine.

in·car·nate, *adj.*, *v.*, -nated, -nating. –*adj.* 1. invested with a bodily, esp. a human, form. 2. to be the embodiment or type of. – **incarnation**, *n.*

in·cen·di·ar·y, *adj.* used or adapted for setting property on fire.

incense[1] /ˈɪnsɛns/, *n.* an aromatic gum producing a sweet smell when burnt.

incense[2] /ɪnˈsɛns/, *v.*, -censed, -censing. to make angry; enrage.

in·cen·tive, *n.* that which encourages action, greater effort, etc.

incep·tion, *n.* beginning; start.

in·ces·sant, *adj.* continuing without interruption.

incest, *n.* sexual intercourse between persons closely related by blood. – **incestuous**, *adj.*

inch, *n.* 1. a unit of length in the imperial system, $\frac{1}{12}$ foot or 25.4×10^{-3} m (25.4 mm). –*v.* 2. to move by small degrees.

in·cho·ate /ˈɪnkoʊeɪt/, *adj.* just begun.

inci·dence, *n.* the range of occurrence or influence of a thing.

inci·dent, *n.* an occurrence or event.

inci·dental, *adj.* 1. happening in fortuitous or subordinate conjunction with something else. 2. incurred casually and in addition to the regular or main amount.

incin·erate, *v.*, -rated, -rating. to reduce to ashes. – **incinerator**, *n.*

in·cip·i·ent, *adj.* in an initial stage.

incise, *v.*, -cised, -cising. to cut into. – **incision**, *n.*

in·ci·sive, *adj.* penetrating, trenchant, or biting.

in·ci·sor, *n.* a tooth in the front part of the jaw.

incite, *v.*, -cited, -citing. to urge on; stimulate or prompt to action.

incle·ment /ɪnˈklɛmənt/, *adj.* (of weather) wet or harsh.

incline, *v.*, -clined, -clining, *n.* –*v.* 1. to (cause to) be influenced or disposed in mind, habit, etc. (to). 2. to bow (the head, etc.). 3. to (cause to) lean or bend in a particular direction. –*n.* 4. an inclined surface; a slope. – **inclination**, *n.*

include, *v.*, -cluded, -cluding. 1. to contain, embrace, or comprise, as a whole does parts or any part or element. 2. to place in an aggregate, class, category, or the like. – **inclusive**, *adj.*

in·cog·nito, *adv.* with the real identity concealed.

income, *n.* the returns that come in from one's work, property, business, etc.; revenue.

in·com·mu·ni·cado, *adj.* deprived of communication with others.

in·con·gru·ous, *adj.* 1. out of keeping or place; inappropriate. 2. lacking harmony of parts, etc. – **incongruity**, *n.*

in·con·sequen·tial, *adj.* 1. of no consequence; trivial. 2. illogical.

in·con·veni·ent, *adj.* arranged or

259

inconvenient

happening in such a way as to be awkward, troublesome, etc. – **inconvenience**, n.

in·con·vert·i·ble, adj. 1. (of paper money) not capable of being converted into coins. 2. not interchangeable.

in·cor·po·rate, v., -rated, -rating. 1. to form into a society or corporation. 2. to put into a whole as an integral part or parts.

in·cor·ri·gi·ble, adj. bad beyond correction or reform.

in·crease, v., -creased, -creasing. n. –v. 1. to (cause to) become greater or more numerous. –n. 2. growth or augmentation. 3. that by which something is increased.

in·cred·i·ble, adj. 1. seeming too extraordinary to be possible. 2. that cannot be believed.

in·cred·u·lous, adj. 1. indisposed to believe; sceptical. 2. indicating unbelief.

in·cre·ment, n. an addition or increase, esp. in salary.

in·crim·i·nate, v., -nated, -nating. 1. to charge with a crime or fault. 2. to involve in a crime or fault.

in·cu·bate, v., -bated, -bating. 1. to sit upon (eggs) for the purpose of hatching. 2. to keep at even temperature, as prematurely born infants. – **incubator**, n.

in·cul·cate, v., -cated, -cating. to teach persistently and earnestly; instil (*upon* or *in*).

in·cum·bent, adj. obligatory.

incur, v., -curred, -curring. to run or fall into (some consequence, usu. undesirable or injurious).

in·cur·sion, n. an invasion.

in·debted, adj. 1. owing money. 2.

index

being under an obligation for assistance, etc., received.

in·de·cent, adj. offending against recognised standards of propriety or good taste.

indeed, adv. in fact; truly.

in·de·fat·i·ga·ble, adj. incapable of being tired out.

in·de·fen·si·ble, adj. that cannot be justified; inexcusable.

in·del·i·ble, adj. incapable of being deleted or obliterated.

in·del·i·cate, adj. offensive to a sense of propriety, or modesty.

in·dem·ni·ty, n., pl. -ties. 1. protection or security against damage or loss. 2. compensation for damage or loss sustained. 3. legal insurance against penalties incurred by one's actions.

indent, v. 1. to form deep recesses in. 2. to set in or back from the margin, as the first line of a paragraph. 3. to order, as commodities. –n. 4. a toothlike notch or deep recess. 5. an order for goods.

in·den·ta·tion, n. 1. a cut, notch, or deep recess. 2. a series of incisions or notches.

in·den·ture, n. a contract by which a person, as an apprentice, is bound to service.

in·de·pen·dent, adj. 1. not subject to another's authority or influence; autonomous. 2. not depending on something or someone else for existence, operation, etc. 3. (of a school) non-government. –n. 4. a politician who is not formally affiliated with a political party. – **independence**, n.

inde·ter·mi·nate, adj. not fixed in extent; indefinite.

index, n., pl. -dexes, -dices, v. –n. 1.

index

a detailed alphabetical key to names, places, and topics in a book with reference to their page number, etc. 2. a sign, token, or indication. –v. 3. to provide with an index, as a book.

in·dex·ation, n. the adjustment of one variable in the light of changes in another variable, esp. the adjustment of wages to compensate for rises in the cost of living.

index finger, n. →forefinger.

in·di·cate, v., -cated, -cating. 1. to be a sign of; imply. 2. to point out; direct attention to. – **indication**, n.

in·dica·tive, adj. 1. that indicates; suggestive (of). –n. 2. Gram. the mood used in ordinary statements, questions, etc.

in·di·ca·tor, n. a pointing or directing instrument, as a flashing light on a car.

indices, n. plural of **index**.

indict, v. to charge with an offence or crime. – **indictment**, n.

in·differ·ent, adj. 1. without interest or concern; apathetic. 2. neither good nor bad. 3. not very good. 4. immaterial or unimportant.

in·dig·e·nous /ɪnˈdɪdʒənəs/, adj. originating in and characterising a particular region or country; native (to).

in·di·gent /ˈɪndədʒənt/, adj. poor.

in·di·gestion, n. difficulty in digesting food; dyspepsia. – **indigestive**, adj.

in·dig·na·tion, n. strong displeasure at something deemed unworthy, unjust, or base. – **indignant**, adj.

in·dig·ni·ty, n., pl. -ties. injury to dignity.

indigo, n., pl. -gos. 1. a blue dye. 2. a deep violet blue.

industrial

in·dis·crim·i·nate, adj. not discriminating; making no distinction.

in·dis·pen·sable, adj. absolutely necessary.

in·dis·posed, adj. 1. sick, esp. slightly. 2. disinclined or unwilling. – **indisposition**, n.

indi·vidual, adj. 1. single; particular; separate. 2. pertaining or peculiar to a single person or thing. 3. distinguished by unique characteristics. –n. 4. a single human being or thing. – **individuality**, n. – **individualise**, v. – **individualist**, n.

in·doc·tri·nate, v., -nated, -nating. to teach or inculcate.

indo·lent, adj. avoiding exertion; lazy. – **indolence**, n.

in·domi·table, adj. that cannot be subdued or overcome.

indoor, adj. occurring, used, etc., in a house or building. – **indoors**, adv.

in·du·bi·table, adj. that cannot be doubted; unquestionable. – **indubitably**, adv.

induce, v., -duced, -ducing. 1. to lead or move by persuasion, as to some action, state of mind, etc. 2. to bring about, produce, or cause. 3. to initiate (labour) artificially in pregnancy.

induct, v. to introduce, esp. formally, as into a place, office, etc.

in·duc·tion, n. 1. a bringing forward, as of facts, evidence, etc. 2. the act of inducing. 3. the act of inducting.

indulge, v., -dulged, -dulging. 1. to yield to one's own inclinations (in). 2. to yield to (desires, feelings, etc.). 3. to yield to the wishes or whims of. – **indulgence**, n. – **indulgent**, adj.

in·dus·tri·al, adj. 1. of or pertaining

261

industrial

to, or resulting from industry or productive labour. 2. having highly developed industries. 3. pertaining to the workers in industries.

in·dus·trious, *adj.* hard-working; diligent.

in·dus·try, *n., pl.* -tries. 1. a particular branch of trade or manufacture. 2. manufacture or trade as a whole. 3. assiduous activity at any work or task.

in·ebri·ated /ɪˈniːbrieɪtɪd/, *adj.* drunk; intoxicated.

in·ef·fable, *adj.* that cannot be uttered or expressed.

inept, *adj.* 1. not apt, fitted, or suitable. 2. absurd or foolish. 3. clumsy; incompetent.

inert, *adj.* 1. having no inherent power of action or motion. 2. *Chem.* non-reactive under normal conditions.

in·er·tia, *n.* 1. inert condition; inactivity; sluggishness. 2. *Physics.* that tendency of matter to retain its state of rest or of uniform motion in a straight line.

in·esti·mable, *adj.* too great to be estimated. – **inestimably**, *adv.*

in·evi·table, *adj.* that cannot be avoided; certain or necessary.

in·exo·rable /ɪnˈɛksərəbəl, ɪnˈɛgz-/, *adj.* unyielding or unalterable.

in·fal·lible, *adj.* exempt from liability to error or failure.

in·fam·ous /ˈɪnfəməs/, *adj.* having or causing an extremely bad reputation. – **infamy**, *n.*

infant, *n.* 1. a young child or a baby. –*adj.* 2. of or relating to infants. 3. of anything in its initial or developing stages: *an infant industry*. – **infancy**, *n.*

infinitive

in·fan·tile, *adj.* of or befitting an infant; babyish; childish.

infan·try, *n.* soldiers who fight on foot.

in·fatu·ated, *adj.* blindly in love (*with*). – **infatuation**, *n.*

infect, *v.* 1. to impregnate with disease-producing germs. 2. to affect morally or so as to influence feelings or actions. – **infection**, *n.*

in·fec·tious, *adj.* tending to spread from one to another.

infer, *v.*, -ferred, -ferring. 1. to conclude or judge by reasoning. 2. *Colloq.* to indicate or suggest. – **inference**, *n.*

in·ferior, *adj.* 1. lower in station, rank, or degree (*to*). 2. poor in quality. 3. lower in place or position. –*n.* 4. one inferior to another or others, as in rank. – **inferiority**, *n.*

in·ferno, *n., pl.* -nos. hell. – **infernal**, *adj.*

infest, *v.* to be numerous in, as anything troublesome. – **infestation**, *n.*

in·fidel, *n.* an unbeliever.

in·fidel·ity, *n., pl.* -ties. 1. unfaithfulness. 2. a breach of trust.

in·fil·trate, *v.*, -trated, -trating. 1. to (cause to) pass in by, or as by, filtering. 2. to join (an organisation) for the unstated purpose of influencing it.

in·fin·ite, *adj.* 1. immeasurably great. 2. unbounded or unlimited; endless. – **infinity**, *n.*

in·fini·tesi·mal /ˌɪnfɪnɪˈtɛzməl, -ˈtsɛməl/, *adj.* indefinitely or exceedingly small.

in·fini·tive, *n. Gram.* the simple form of the verb (as *come, take, eat*) used after certain other verbs (I

infinitive

didn't *eat*), or preceded by *to* (I wanted *to come*).

in·firm, *adj.* **1.** feeble in body or health. **2.** not steadfast, as persons, the mind, etc. – **infirmity**, *n.*

in·fir·mary, *n., pl.* **-ries.** a hospital.

in·flame, *v.*, **-flamed, -flaming. 1.** to set aflame or afire. **2.** to kindle or excite (passions, anger, etc.). – **inflammatory**, *adj.*

in·flam·ma·ble, *adj.* capable of being set on fire.

in·flam·ma·tion, *n. Pathol.* a reaction of the body to injurious agents, commonly characterised by heat, redness, swelling, pain, etc.

inflate, *v.*, **-flated, -flating. 1.** to (cause to) swell or puff out, esp. with gas. **2.** to (cause to) puff up with pride, satisfaction, etc. **3.** to expand (currency, prices, etc.) unduly.

in·fla·tion, *n.* **1.** undue expansion of the currency of a country, esp. by the issuing of paper money not redeemable in coin. **2.** a substantial rise of prices caused by this. **3.** the act of inflating. **4.** the state of being inflated. – **inflationary**, *adj.*

in·flec·tion, *n.* **1.** change in pitch or tone of voice. **2.** a grammatical change in the form of a word. **3.** a bend or angle. Also, **inflexion**. – **inflect**, *v.*

inflict, *v.* to impose (anything unwelcome). – **infliction**, *n.*

in·flu·ence, *n., v.*, **-enced, -encing.** –*n.* **1.** power of producing effects by invisible means on another person or thing. **2.** these effects. **3.** a thing or person that affects by invisible or insensible means. –*v.* **4.** to exercise influence on. – **influential**, *adj.*

ingest

in·flu·en·za, *n. Pathol.* an acute, contagious, viral disease.

influx, *n.* the act of flowing in.

inform, *v.* **1.** to impart knowledge of a fact or circumstance (to). **2.** to animate or inspire. – **informant**, *n.*

in·for·mal, *adj.* **1.** not according to prescribed or customary forms; irregular. **2.** without formality; unceremonious. –*adv.* **3. vote informal,** to mark a ballot-paper incorrectly thereby invalidating one's vote. – **informality**, *n.*

in·for·ma·tion, *n.* knowledge communicated concerning some fact or circumstance; news. – **informative**, *adj.*

infra-red, *n.* the part of the invisible spectrum contiguous to the red end of the visible spectrum.

infra-structure, *n.* **1.** the basic framework (as of an organisation or a system). **2.** the buildings or permanent installations associated with an organisation, operation, etc.

in·fringe, *v.*, **-fringed, -fringing. 1.** to violate or transgress (a law, etc.). **2.** to encroach or trespass (*on* or *upon*). – **infringement**, *n.*

in·fu·ri·ate, *v.*, **-ated, -ating.** to make furious; enrage.

infuse, *v.*, **-fused, -fusing. 1.** to cause to penetrate; instil (*into*). **2.** to steep in a liquid to extract soluble properties or ingredients. – **infusion**, *n.*

in·gen·ious, *adj.* having or showing cleverness in invention or construction. – **ingenuity**, *n.*

in·gen·u·ous, *adj.* artless; innocent.

ingest, *v. Physiol.* to put or take (food, etc.) into the body. – **ingestion**, *n.* – **ingestive**, *adj.*

ingot

in·got, *n.* an (oblong) cast of metal.

in·grain, *v.* to fix deeply and firmly, as in the mind.

in·grate, *n.* an ungrateful person.

in·gra·ti·ate, *v.,* **-ated, -ating.** to establish (oneself) in the favour of others.

in·grati·tude, *n.* the state of being ungrateful.

in·gredi·ent, *n.* an element in a mixture.

in·habit, *v.* to live in (a place). – **inhabitant,** *n.*

in·hale, *v.,* **-haled, -haling.** to breathe in. – **inhalation,** *n.*

in·her·ent, *adj.* existing in something as a natural and permanent quality or attribute. – **inhere,** *v.*

in·herit, *v.* **1.** to take or receive (property, a right, a title, etc.) as an heir. **2.** to possess as a hereditary characteristic. – **inheritance,** *n.* – **inheritor,** *n.*

in·hibit, *v.* to restrain or check (an action, impulse, etc.). – **inhibition,** *n.*

in·imi·cal, *adj.* **1.** adverse in tendency or effect. **2.** unfriendly or hostile. – **inimicality,** *n.*

in·imi·table, *adj.* incapable of being imitated.

in·iquity, *n., pl.* **-ties.** gross injustice; wickedness. – **iniquitous,** *adj.*

initial, *adj., n., v.,* **-ialled, -ialling.** – *adj.* **1.** of or pertaining to the beginning. – *n.* **2.** the first letter of a word. – *v.* **3.** to mark or sign with initials, esp. as an indication of responsibility for or approval of the contents.

in·iti·ate, *v.,* **-ated, -ating.** **1.** to begin, set going, or originate. **2.** to introduce into the knowledge of some art or subject. **3.** to admit with

innate

formal rites into secret knowledge, a society, etc. – **initiation,** *n.*

in·itia·tive, *n.* **1.** an introductory act or step. **2.** readiness and ability in setting action going; enterprise.

inject, *v.* **1.** to force (a fluid) into (a part of the body, etc.). **2.** to introduce (something new or different) into (a thing). – **injection,** *n.*

in·junc·tion, *n. Law.* a judicial order requiring a person or persons to do or (more commonly) not to do a particular thing.

injure, *v.,* **-jured, -juring.** **1.** to do or cause harm to; damage. **2.** to do wrong or injustice to. – **injurious,** *adj.* – **injury,** *n.*

in·jus·tice, *n.* **1.** the quality or fact of being unjust. **2.** unjust action or treatment.

ink, *n.* a fluid used for writing or printing.

ink·ling, *n.* a hint, intimation, or slight suggestion.

inland, *adj., n.* **1.** (pertaining to or situated in) the interior part of a country or region. – *adv.* **2.** in or towards the interior of a country.

in-law, *n.* a relative by marriage.

inlay, *v.,* **-laid, -laying.** to decorate (an object) with veneers of fine materials set in its surface.

inlet, *n.* a narrow stretch of water reaching into a shore line or between islands.

inmate, *n.* one of those confined in a hospital, prison, etc.

inn, *n.* a small hotel that provides lodging, food, etc., for travellers.

innards, *n.pl.* the inward parts of the body; entrails.

innate, *adj.* **1.** inborn; existing in one from birth. **2.** inherent.

in·ner, *adj.* 1. interior. 2. mental or spiritual.

in·nings, *n.pl.* (*construed as sing.*) 1. *Cricket.* the turn of any one member of the batting team, or of the whole team, to bat. 2. any opportunity for some activity; turn.

in·no·cent, *adj.* 1. free from any moral wrong; pure. 2. free from legal or specific wrong; guiltless. 3. harmless. —*n.* 4. an innocent person. — **innocence**, *n.*

in·noc·u·ous, *adj.* causing no harm.

in·no·vate, *v.*, **-vated, -vating**. to bring in (something new). — **innovative**, *adj.* — **innovation**, *n.* — **innovator**, *n.*

in·nu·en·do, *n., pl.* **-dos, -does**. an indirect hint about a person or thing, esp. of a derogatory nature.

in·nu·mer·a·ble, *adj.* 1. very numerous. 2. incapable of being definitely counted.

in·oc·u·late, *v.*, **-lated, -lating**. to inject (a person or animal) with a serum, or vaccine in order to secure immunity from a disease. — **inoculation**, *n.*

in·op·por·tune, *adj.* inappropriate; untimely.

in·or·di·nate, *adj.* excessive.

in-patient, *n.* a patient who is staying in a hospital.

input, *n.* that which is put in.

in·quest, *n.* a legal or judicial inquiry.

inquire, *v.*, **-quired, -quiring**. to make investigation (*into*). — **inquiry**, *n.*

in·qui·si·tion, *n.* an investigation, or process of inquiry. — **inquisitor**, *n.* — **inquisitorial**, *adj.*

in·quis·i·tive, *adj.* 1. unduly curious; prying. 2. inquiring; eager for knowledge.

in·road, *n.* forcible or serious encroachment.

in·sane, *adj.* 1. mentally deranged. 2. set apart for mentally deranged persons. 3. utterly senseless. — **insanity**, *n.*

in·sa·tia·ble, *adj.* incapable of being satisfied.

in·scribe, *v.*, **-scribed, -scribing**. 1. to write or engrave (words, characters, etc.). 2. to mark (a surface) with words, characters, etc. 3. to address or dedicate (a book, photograph, etc.) with writing. 4. to enrol, as on an official list. — **inscription**, *n.*

in·scru·ta·ble, *adj.* not easily understood; mysterious.

insect, *n. Zool.* a small, air-breathing arthropod with a body clearly divided into 3 parts, and with 3 pairs of legs, and usu. 2 pairs of wings.

in·sec·ti·cide, *n.* a substance used for killing insects.

in·sec·tiv·o·rous, *adj.* adapted to feeding on insects.

in·se·cure, *adj.* 1. exposed to danger. 2. not firm or safe. 3. not free from fear, doubt, etc. — **insecurity**, *n.*

in·sem·i·nate, *v.*, **-nated, -nating**. to introduce semen into (a female) to cause fertilisation. — **insemination**, *n.*

in·sen·si·ble, *adj.* incapable of feeling or perceiving; unconscious.

insert, *v.* 1. to put or set in. —*n.* 2. something inserted, or to be inserted. — **insertion**, *n.*

inset, *n., v.* **-set, -setting**. —*n.* 1. something inserted. —*v.* 2. to set in; insert.

inside, *prep.* 1. on the inner side of; within. 2. before the elapse of: *inside an hour.* —*adv.* 3. in or into the inner part. 4. indoors. 5. by nature; fundamentally: *She's very kind inside.* interior. –adj. 7. situated or being on or in the inside; interior.

in·sid·i·ous, adj. stealthily deceitful.

in·sight, n. 1. an understanding gained: *an insight into country life.* 2. faculty of seeing into inner character or underlying truth.

in·sig·ni·a /in'signiə/, n.pl., sing. insigne /-ni/. badges or distinguishing marks of office or honour.

in·sin·u·ate, v., -ated, -ating. 1. to suggest or hint slyly. 2. to bring or introduce into a position by indirect or artful methods. – insinuation, n.

in·sip·id, adj. without distinctive, interesting, or attractive qualities.

insist, v. 1. to be firm, or persistent about some desire, demand, intention, etc. 2. to assert or maintain positively. – insistent, adj.

in·so·lent, adj. boldly rude or disrespectful. – insolence, n.

in·som·ni·a, n. inability to sleep, esp. when chronic. – insomniac, n.

in·spect, v. 1. to look carefully at or over. 2. to examine officially. – inspection, n. – inspector, n.

in·spire, v., -spired, -spiring. 1. to infuse an animating or exalting influence into. 2. to produce or arouse (a feeling, thought, etc.). 3. to give rise to, or cause. 4. to inhale. – inspiration, n.

in·stall, v. 1. to place in position for service or use. 2. to establish in any office, position, or place. – installation, n.

in·stal·ment, n. 1. any of several parts into which a debt is divided for payment. 2. a single portion of something issued by parts at successive times.

in·stance, n., v., -stanced, -stancing. –n. 1. a case or example of anything. –v. 2. to cite as an example.

in·stant, n. 1. a moment. 2. a particular moment. –adj. 3. immediate. 4. (of a foodstuff) processed for immediate and simple preparation.

in·stan·ta·neous, adj. occurring, done, or completed in an instant.

in·stead, adv. 1. in the place (of): *I want a new book instead of this.* 2. in one's (its, their, etc.) stead: *She was sick, so her husband came instead.*

instep, n. the arched upper surface of the human foot between the toes and the ankle.

in·sti·gate, v., -gated, -gating. to incite to some action or course. – instigation, n.

instil, v., -stilled, -stilling. to infuse slowly or by degrees into the mind or feelings.

in·stinct, n. 1. innate impulse or natural inclination. 2. a natural aptitude for something. 3. natural intuitive power. – instinctive, adj.

in·sti·tute, v., -tuted, -tuting, n. –v. 1. to set up or establish. 2. to set in operation. 3. to establish in an office or position. –n. 4. a society or organisation esp. of a literary, scientific, or educational character.

in·sti·tu·tion, n. 1. an organisation or establishment, usu. one for some public, educational, charitable, or similar purpose. 2. any established law, custom, etc. 3. the act of instituting or setting up.

in·sti·tu·tion·al, adj. 1. of, pertaining to, or established by institution. 2.

institutional

characterised by uniformity and dullness. – **institutionalise**, v.

in·struct, v. 1. to direct or command. 2. to teach; train; educate. 3. to inform or apprise. – **instructive**, adj. – **instructor**, n.

in·struc·tion, n. 1. the act or practice of instructing or teaching; education. 2. (usu. pl.) an order or direction.

in·stru·ment, n. 1. a tool or implement. 2. a contrivance for producing musical sounds. 3. a thing with or by which something is effected; a means. 4. a legal document. – **instrumental**, adj.

in·sub·or·di·nate, adj. disobedient; rebellious. – **insubordination**, n.

in·suf·fer·able, adj. not to be endured; unbearable.

in·su·lar, adj. 1. of or pertaining to an island or islands. 2. narrow or illiberal. – **insularity**, n.

in·su·late, v., -lated, -lating. 1. to cover or surround (an electric wire, etc.) with non-conducting material. 2. to place in an isolated situation. 3. to install a material in the roof of (a house), to retain warmth in winter and keep out heat in summer. – **insulation**, n. – **insulator**, n.

in·su·lin, n. a hormone produced in the pancreas, a deficiency of which produces diabetes.

insult, v. 1. to treat with contemptuous rudeness; affront. –n. 2. a contemptuously rude action or speech.

in·su·per·able, adj. incapable of being passed over, overcome, or surmounted.

in·sur·ance, n. the act, system, or business of insuring property, life, the person, etc., against specified

intelligence

loss or harm in consideration of a payment proportionate to the risk involved.

insure, v., -sured, -suring. 1. to guarantee against risk of loss or harm. 2. to secure indemnity to or on, in case of loss, damage, or death. 3. to issue or procure an insurance policy on.

in·sur·gent, n., adj. (one) rising in forcible opposition to established authority.

in·sur·rec·tion, n. the act of rising in arms or open resistance against established authority.

intact, adj. remaining uninjured or whole; unimpaired.

intake, n. 1. the act of taking in. 2. that which is taken in.

in·te·ger /'ɪntədʒə/, n. 1. Also, **positive integer**. a whole number. 2. a complete entity.

in·te·gral, adj. belonging as a part of the whole.

in·te·grate, v., -grated, -grating. 1. to bring together (parts) into a whole. 2. to amalgamate (a racial or religious minority group) with the rest of the community. – **integration**, n.

integrated circuit, n. an assembly of miniature electronic components simultaneously produced in batch processing. Also, **IC**

in·teg·ri·ty, n. 1. uprightness; honesty. 2. unimpaired condition.

in·tel·lect, n. the power or faculty of the mind by which one knows, understands, or reasons.

in·tel·lec·tu·al, adj. 1. of, appealing to or engaging the intellect. 2. possessing mental capacity, esp. to a high degree. –n. 3. an intellectual person.

in·tel·li·gence, n. 1. aptitude in

intelligence

grasping truths, facts, meaning, etc. **2.** news; information. **3.** (the gathering or distribution of) secret information which might prove detrimental to an enemy. – **intelligent,** *adj.*

in·tel·li·gent·sia, *n.pl.* the intellectuals of a society.

in·tel·li·gible, *adj.* capable of being understood.

in·tem·per·ate, *adj.* **1.** indulging excessively in intoxicating drink. **2.** unrestrained or unbridled. – **intemperance,** *n.*

in·tend, *v.* to have in mind as something to be done or brought about.

in·tense, *adj.* **1.** of an extreme kind. **2.** having or showing great strength or vehemence of feeling. – **intensify,** *v.*

in·ten·sity, *n., pl.* -**ties. 1.** the quality or condition of being intense. **2.** the degree or extent to which something is intense.

in·ten·sive, *adj.* **1.** of, pertaining to, or characterised by intensity. **2.** *Econ.* of or denoting methods designed to increase effectiveness, as, in agriculture.

intent[1], *n.* that which is intended; purpose; aim.

intent[2], *adj.* firmly or steadfastly fixed or directed (upon something).

in·ten·tion, *n.* the act of determining mentally upon some action or result; a purpose or design. – **intentional,** *adj.*

inter /ɪn'tɜː/, *v.,* -**terred,** -**terring.** to bury (a dead body), esp. with ceremonies.

inter·act, *v.* to act on each other. – **interaction,** *n.* – **interactive,** *adj.*

inter·cede, *v.,* -**ceded,** -**ceding.** to act or speak on behalf of one in difficulty or trouble, as by pleading or petition. – **intercession,** *n.*

interfere

inter·cept, *v.* **1.** to take or seize on the way from one place to another. **2.** to stop or check (passage, etc.).

inter·change, *v.,* -**changed,** -**changing,** *v.* **1.** to (cause to) change places, as 2 persons or things. –*n.* **2.** the act of interchanging; reciprocal exchange.

inter·com, *n. Colloq.* an electronic system for sending spoken messages within an office complex, school, etc.

inter·course, *n.* **1.** dealings or communication between individuals. **2.** →**sexual intercourse.**

inter·dict /'ɪntədɪkt, -daɪt/, *n.* **1.** *Civil Law.* an official prohibitory act or decree. –*v.* **2.** to forbid; prohibit. – **interdictory,** *adj.* – **interdiction,** *n.*

inter·est, *n.* **1.** the feeling of one whose attention or curiosity is particularly engaged by something. **2.** the power of exciting such feeling. **3.** a share in the ownership of property, in a commercial or financial undertaking, or the like. **4.** something in which one has an interest, as of ownership, advantage, attention, etc. **5.** benefit or advantage. **6.** *Comm.* **a.** a sum paid for the use of money borrowed. **b.** the rate per cent per unit of time represented by such payments. –*v.* **7.** to engage or excite the attention or curiosity of.

inter·face, *n.* **1.** a surface regarded as the common boundary to 2 bodies or spaces. **2.** the point or area at which any 2 systems interact.

inter·fere, *v.,* -**fered,** -**fering.** **1.** to clash; be in opposition. **2.** to come between people or things for a

268

interfere

particular purpose. 3. to take a part in the affairs of others; meddle.

inter·fer·ence, *n.* 1. the act or fact of interfering. 2. *Radio.* the jumbling of radio signals by receiving signals other than the desired ones.

in·ter·im, *adj., n.* (belonging to or connected with) an intervening period of time.

in·te·ri·or, *adj.* 1. being within; internal. 2. pertaining to the inland. 3. inner, private, or secret. —*n.* 4. the internal part; the inside. 5. the inland parts of a region, country, etc.

inter·ject, *v.* to throw (a remark) abruptly into a speech or conversation.

inter·jec·tion, *n.* 1. (the utterance of) an ejaculation or exclamation. 2. something, as a remark, interjected. 3. *Gram.* (in many languages) a form class, or 'part of speech', comprising words which constitute utterances or clauses in themselves, without grammatical connection.

inter·lace, *v.*, **-laced, -lacing.** 1. to cross (threads, etc.) so that they pass alternately over and under. 2. to mingle; blend.

inter·lock, *v.* 1. to (cause to) fit into each other, as parts of machinery, so that all action is simultaneous. 2. to (cause to) lock one with another. — **interlocker**, *n.*

inter·loc·u·tor /ɪntəˈlɒkjətə/, *n.* one who takes part in a conversation. — **interlocutory**, *adj.* — **interlocution**, *n.*

inter·lope, *v.*, **-loped, -loping.** to intrude into the affairs of others.

inter·lude, *n.* 1. an intervening episode, period, space, etc. 2. a period of inactivity; lull.

inter·me·di·ate¹ /ɪntəˈmiːdiət, -dʒət/, *adj.* being, situated, or acting between 2 points, stages, things, persons, etc. — **intermediacy**, *n.*

inter·me·di·ate² /ɪntəˈmiːdieɪt/, *v.* **-ated, -ating.** to act as an intermediary; mediate. — **intermediation**, *n.* — **intermediator**, *n.*

in·ter·mi·na·ble, *adj.* unending.

inter·mis·sion, *n.* a break between items in an entertainment, esp. in the cinema; interval.

inter·mit·tent, *adj.* alternately ceasing and beginning again.

intern¹ /ɪnˈtɜːn/, *v.* to oblige to reside within prescribed limits.

intern² /ˈɪntɜːn/, *n.* a resident doctor at a hospital, usu. a recent graduate still in partial training.

inter·nal, *adj.* 1. in, or pertaining to, the interior of something. 2. existing or occurring within a country; domestic.

inter·na·tion·al, *adj.* 1. between or among nations. 2. of or pertaining to different nations or their citizens.

inter·ne·cine /ɪntəˈniːsaɪn/, *adj.* mutually destructive.

inter·play, *n.* reciprocal play, action, or influence.

inter·po·late, *v.*, **-lated, -lating.** 1. to alter (a text, etc.) by the insertion of new matter. 2. to introduce (something additional or extraneous) between other things or parts. — **interpolation**, *n.*

inter·pose, *v.*, **-posed, -posing.** 1. to (cause to) come between other things. 2. to put in (a remark) by way of interruption.

in·ter·pret, *v.* 1. to explain or elu-

interpret

cidate. 2. to explain, construe, or understand in a particular way. 3. to translate. – **interpretation**, n. – **interpreter**, n.

inter·reg·num, n., pl. -nums, -na. 1. an interval of time between the reigns of 2 successive sovereigns. 2. any interruption in continuity.

inter·ro·gate, v., -gated, -gating. to question (a person), esp. closely or formally. – **interrogation**, n.

inter·rog·a·tive, adj. 1. pertaining to or conveying a question. 2. Gram. an interrogative word, element, or construction, as 'who?' and 'what?' – **interrogative**, adv.

inter·rupt, v. 1. to make a break in (something otherwise continuous). 2. to stop (a person) in the midst of doing or saying something, esp. as by an interjected remark. – **interruption**, n. – **interruptive**, adj.

inter·sect, v. to cut or divide by passing through or lying across.

inter·sec·tion, n. 1. the act of intersecting. 2. a place where 2 or more roads meet.

inter·sperse, v., -spersed, -spersing. 1. to scatter among other things. 2. to diversify with something scattered. – **interspersion**, n.

inter·state, adj. 1. between or jointly involving states. –adv. 2. to, from or in another state. Cf. **intrastate**.

inter·stice /ɪnˈtɜstɪs/, n. a small or narrow opening between things or parts.

inter·val, n. 1. an intervening period of time; pause. 2. a space intervening between things, points, limits, qualities, etc. 3. Music. the difference in pitch between 2 notes.

inter·vene, v., -vened, -vening. 1. to come between in action; intercede.

intoxicate

2. to fall or happen between other events or periods. – **intervention**, n.

inter·view, n. 1. a meeting of persons face to face, in which one asks questions of the other. –v. 2. to have an interview with. – **interviewer**, n.

intes·tate, adj. (of a person) dying without having made a will. – **intestacy**, n.

intes·tine, n. (oft. pl.) the lower part of the alimentary canal. – **intestinal**, adj.

inti·mate[1] /ˈɪntəmət/, adj. 1. associated in close or friendly personal relations. 2. private; closely personal. 3. maintaining sexual relations. 4. arising from close personal connection or familiar experience. 5. detailed; deep. –n. 6. an intimate friend or associate. – **intimacy**, n.

inti·mate[2] /ˈɪntəmeɪt/, v., -mated, -mating. to make known indirectly; hint. – **intimation**, n.

in·tim·i·date, v., -dated, -dating. 1. to inspire with fear; overawe. 2. to force into or deter by inducing fear. – **intimidation**, n.

into, prep. 1. in and to (expressing motion or direction towards the inner part of a place or thing). 2. Maths. being the divisor of.

in·to·na·tion, n. the pattern or melody of pitch changes revealed in connected speech.

intone, v., -toned, -toning. to speak or recite in a singing voice, esp. in monotone.

intox·i·cate, v. -cated, -cating. 1. to make drunk. 2. to excite mentally beyond self-control or reason. – **intoxication**, n. – **intoxicant**, n.

intractable

in·trac·ta·ble, *adj.* not docile; stubborn.

in·tran·si·gent, *adj.* uncompromising.

in·tran·si·tive verb, *n.* a verb that is not accompanied by a direct object, as *come, sit, lie*, etc.

intra·state, *adj.* within a state.

intra·venous, *adj.* within a vein or the veins.

in·trepid, *adj.* fearless.

intri·cate, *adj.* perplexingly entangled or involved. – **intricacy**, *n.*

in·trigue, *v.* -trigued, -triguing, *n.* – *v.* 1. to excite the curiosity or interest of by puzzling qualities. 2. to plot craftily. – *n.* 3. the use of underhand plots to accomplish designs. 4. a clandestine or illicit love affair.

in·trin·sic, *adj.* belonging to a thing by its very nature.

intro·duce, *v.* -duced, -ducing. 1. to bring into notice, knowledge, use, vogue, etc. 2. to bring forward with preliminary matter. 3. to bring (a person) (*to*) the knowledge or experience of something. 4. to bring (a person) into the acquaintance of another. – **introductory**, *adj.*

intro·duc·tion, *n.* 1. the act of introducing. 2. something introduced. 3. a preliminary part, as of a book.

intro·spec·tion, *n.* examination of one's own mental states. – **introspective**, *adj.*

intro·vert, *n.* 1. *Psychol.* a person concerned chiefly with his own self and thoughts. – *v.* 2. to turn inwards. – **introversion**, *n.*

intrude, *v.*, -truded, -truding. 1. to thrust or bring in without reason, permission, or welcome. 2. to

inverse

thrust oneself in; come uninvited. – **intrusion**, *n.* – **intrusive**, *adj.*

in·tui·tion, *n.* direct perception (of truth, facts, etc.) independent of any reasoning process. – **intuitive**, *adj.*

in·un·date, *v.*, -dated, -dating. to overspread with or as with a flood. – **inundation**, *n.*

inure, *v.*, inured, inuring. to accustom; habituate (*to*).

invade, *v.*, -vaded, -vading. 1. to enter as an enemy. 2. to intrude upon.

in·valid[1] /ˈɪnvəlɪd, -lɪd/, *n.* 1. a chronically ill person. – *adj.* 2. deficient in health; sick. 3. of or for invalids. – *v.* 4. to make or become an invalid.

in·valid[2] /ɪnˈvælɪd/, *adj.* not valid. – **invalidity**, *n.* – **invalidate**, *v.*

in·valu·able, *adj.* of inestimable value.

invari·able, *adj.* unchangeable.

in·va·sion, *n.* 1. the act of invading or entering as an enemy. 2. infringement by intrusion.

in·vec·tive, *n.* an utterance of violent censure or reproach.

in·veigh, *v.* to attack vehemently in words; rail (*against*).

inveigle, *v.*, -gled, -gling. to draw by beguiling inducements (*into, from, away*, etc.).

invent, *v.* to originate by one's own contrivance; think up. – **inventive**, *adj.* – **inventor**, *n.*

in·ven·tion, *n.* 1. the act of inventing. 2. anything invented or devised. 3. imagination. 4. falsehood; a lie.

in·ven·tory /ˈɪnvəntri, ɪnˈvɛntəri/, *n.* a detailed descriptive list of articles.

in·verse, *adj.* 1. reversed in position,

271

inverse direction, or tendency. –n. 2. an inverted state or condition. 3. that which is inverse; the direct opposite.

invert, v. 1. to turn upside down, inside out, or inwards. 2. to reverse in position, direction, order, or tendency. – **inversion**, n.

in·ver·te·brate, n., adj. Zool. (an animal) without a backbone.

invest, v. 1. to put (money) in something offering profitable returns, esp. interest or income. 2. to endow. 3. to install in an office or position. – **investor**, n.

in·ves·ti·gate, v., -gated, -gating. to search or inquire into the particulars of. – **investigation**, n. – **investigative**, adj.

in·ves·ti·ture, n. (a ceremony involving) the formal bestowal or presentation of certain rights or powers.

in·vest·ment, n. the investing of money or capital in order to secure profitable returns. 2. a thing invested in. 3. that which is invested.

in·vet·er·ate, adj. 1. confirmed in a habit, practice, etc. 2. firmly established by long continuance.

in·vid·i·ous, adj. such as to bring hatred or envy.

in·vig·or·ate, v., -rated, -rating. to give vigour to.

in·vin·ci·ble, adj. that cannot be conquered.

in·vi·o·lable, adj. that must not be violated, as something sacred.

in·vi·o·late, adj. free from injury, desecration, or outrage.

in·vis·i·ble, adj. not visible.

invite, v., -vited, -viting. 1. to ask courteously to come or go somewhere or to do something. 2. to act so as to bring on or render probable. – **invitation**, n.

in vitro, adv., adj. in an artificial environment, as a test tube.

in·voice, n., v., -voiced, -voicing. –n. 1. a written list of merchandise, with prices, or an itemised bill, delivered or sent to a buyer. –v. 2. to present an invoice to (a customer)

invoke, v., -voked, -voking. 1. to call for with earnest desire. 2. to call on (a divine being, etc.), as in prayer. 3. to put (a law, etc.) into use. – **invocation**, n.

in·volve, v., -volved, -volving. 1. to include as a necessary circumstance, condition, or consequence. 2. to include. 3. to bring into an intricate or complicated form or condition. 4. to implicate, as in guilt or crime. 5. to be highly or excessively interested in.

inward, adj. 1. proceeding or directed towards the inside or interior. 2. situated within; interior, internal. –adv. 3. inwards.

in·wards, adv. towards the inside or interior.

iodine /'aɪədiːn, 'aɪədaɪn/, n. a nonmetallic element, used in medicine as an antiseptic. *Symbol:* I

ion, n. an electrically charged atom, radical, or molecule, formed by the loss or gain of one or more electrons.

iota, n. a very small quantity.

IOU, n. a written acknowledgment of a debt (I owe you).

iras·ci·ble, adj. easily provoked to anger.

irate, adj. angry; enraged.

ire, n. anger; wrath.

iri·des·cent, *adj.* displaying colours like those of the rainbow.

iris, *n.*, *pl.* **irises, irides.** 1. *Anat.* the contractile circular membrane forming the coloured portion of the eye around the pupil. 2. a plant with handsome flowers and sword-shaped leaves.

irk, *v.* to weary, annoy, or trouble.

iron, *n.* 1. *Chem.* a ductile, malleable, silver-white metallic element, commonly used for making tools, implements, machinery, etc. *Symbol:* Fe 2. an iron or steel implement used heated for smoothing or pressing cloth, etc. 3. an iron-headed golf club. 4. (*pl.*) an iron shackle or fetter. *adv.* 5. made of iron. 6. resembling iron in colour, firmness, etc. –*v.* 7. to smooth or press with a heated iron, as clothes, etc.

iron lung, *n.* a chamber in which alternate pulsations of high and low pressure can be used to force normal lung movements.

irony, *n.*, *pl.* **-nies.** 1. a figure of speech or literary device in which the literal meaning is the opposite of that intended. 2. an outcome of events contrary to what was, or might have been, expected. – **ironic, ironical,** *adj.*

ir·ra·di·ate, *v.*, **-ated, -ating.** 1. to shed rays of light or shine (upon). 2. to illumine intellectually or spiritually. 3. to radiate (light, heat, etc.). 4. to expose to radiation. – **irradiation,** *n.* – **irradiant,** *adj.*

ir·ra·tion·al, *adj.* 1. without the faculty of reason. 2. without, or deprived of, sound judgment.

irresistible, *adj.* too strong, charming, attractive, etc. to be resisted.

ir·re·spec·tive, *adj.* without regard to something else; independent (*of*).

ir·rev·o·ca·ble /ɪˈrevəkəbəl/, *adj.* not to be revoked, recalled or undone.

ir·ri·gate, *v.*, **-gated, -gating.** 1. to supply (land) with water by means of canals passing through it. 2. *Med.* to supply (a wound, etc.) with a constant flow of some liquid. – **irrigation,** *n.*

ir·ri·ta·ble, *adj.* easily irritated.

ir·ri·tate, *v.*, **-tated, -tating.** 1. to excite to impatience or anger. 2. *Physiol., Biol.* to excite (a living system) to some characteristic action or function. 3. *Pathol.* to bring (a bodily part, etc.) to a sensitive condition. – **irritating,** *adj.* – **irritation,** *n.* – **irritant,** *n., adj.*

is, *v.* 3rd person singular present indicative of **be.**

island, *n.* 1. a tract of land completely surrounded by water, and not large enough to be called a continent. 2. something resembling an island. – **islander,** *n.*

isle, *n.* a small island.

isobar, *n. Meteorol., etc.* a line drawn on a weather map, etc., connecting all points having the same barometric pressure. – **isobaric,** *adj.*

iso·late, *v.*, **-lated, -lating.** to detach or separate so as to be alone. – **isolation,** *n.*

iso·metric, *adj.* Also, **isometrical.** 1. pertaining to or having equality of measure. –*n.* 2. (*pl.*) a system of physical exercises in which muscles are pitted against each other or against a fixed object.

isos·ce·les, *adj.* (of a triangle) having 2 sides equal.

iso·tope, *n.* any of 2 or more forms

isotope

of a chemical element, having the same number of protons but different numbers of neutrons in the nucleus. – **isotopic**, *adj*.

is·thmus, *n.*, *pl.* **-muses**. a narrow strip of land, bordered on both sides by water, connecting 2 larger bodies of land.

issue, *n.*, *v.*, **issued**, **issuing**. –*n.* 1. the act of sending, giving out, or promulgation. 2. that which is issued. 3. a point in question or dispute. 4. a point or matter of special or public importance. 5. offspring or progeny. –*v.* 6. to put out; deliver for use, sale, etc.; put into circulation. 7. to send out; discharge; emit. 8. to go, pass, or flow out; come forth; emerge. 9. to arise as a result or consequence.

it, *pron.*, *poss.* **its**, *obj.* **it**, *pl.* **they**. a personal pronoun of the 3rd person and neuter gender, which corresponds to *he* and *she*, and which is used: 1. as a substitute for a neuter noun or a noun representing something possessing sex when sex is not particularised or considered: *The baby lost its rattle.* 2. to refer to some matter expressed or understood, or some thing or notion not definitely conceived: *Did you like it in Melbourne?* 3. as the grammatical subject of a clause of which the logical subject is a phrase or clause, generally following, regarded as in apposition to it: *It was agreed that she would go.* 4. in impersonal constructions: *It is raining.* 5. without definite force after an intransitive verb: *They decided to walk it.*

italic, *adj.* 1. designating or pertaining to a style of printing types in which the letters usu. slope to the right (thus, *italic*), used for emphasis, etc. –*n.* 2. (*oft. pl.*) italic type. – **italicise**, *v.*

itch, *v.* 1. to have or feel a peculiar irritation of the skin which causes a desire to scratch. 2. to have a restless desire to do or get something. –*n.* 3. the sensation of itching. – **itchy**, *adj*.

item, *n.* 1. a separate article or particular. 2. a separate piece of information or news.

item·ise, *v.*, **-mised**, **-mising**. to state by items.

itin·er·ant, *adj*. travelling from place to place, or on a circuit, as a preacher, etc.

itin·er·ary, *n.*, *pl.* **-ries**. 1. an account of a journey. 2. a plan of travel.

its, *adj.*, *pron.* possessive form of *it*.

it's, contraction of *it is*.

it·self, *pron.* 1. the reflexive form of *it*: *The sleeve caught itself.* 2. an emphatic form of *it*: *The play itself was not worth watching; It exists only for itself.* 3. in its normal state: *The house is itself again.*

ivory, *n.*, *pl.* **-ries**. the hard white substance composing teeth or tusks.

ivy, *n.* an evergreen climbing plant.

Jj

J, j, *n., pl.* **J's** or **Js, j's** or **js.** the 10th letter of the English alphabet.

jab, *v.,* **jabbed, jabbing,** *n.* –*v.* **1.** to thrust or poke (something) smartly or sharply. –*n.* **2.** a poke with the end or point of something.

jabber, *v.* to utter rapidly, indistinctly, or nonsensically.

jaca·randa, *n.* a tall tropical tree with lavender-blue flowers.

jack, *n.* **1.** a man or fellow. **2.** a contrivance for raising heavy weights short distances. **3.** any of the 4 knaves in playing cards. **4.** a knucklebone or plastic imitation used in a children's game. –*v.* **5.** to lift or raise with or as with a jack. **6. jack up,** *Colloq.* to refuse; be obstinate; resist.

jackal, *n.* any of several types of wild dog.

jackass, *n.* **1.** a male donkey. **2.** a very stupid or foolish person.

jackboot, *n.* a large boot reaching above the knee, often used for riding.

jackdaw, *n.* a small bird of the crow family.

jacket, *n.* **1.** a short coat. **2.** Also, **dust jacket.** a detachable paper cover for protecting the binding of a book.

jack·hammer, *n.* a hand-held drill operated by compressed air, used for drilling rocks.

jack-in-the-box, *n.* a toy consisting of a figure, enclosed in a box, which springs out when the lid is unfastened.

jack·knife, *n., pl.* **-knives,** *v.,* **-knifed, -knifing.** –*n.* **1.** a large knife with a blade that folds into the handle. –*v.* **2.** to bend or fold up, like a jackknife.

jack·pot, *n.* the chief prize to be won in a lottery, a game or contest.

Jacobite, *n.* a supporter of James II or of the Stuarts.

Jacuzzi, *n.* a large bath or tub with swirling underwater jets.

jade, *n.* a mineral, sometimes green, highly esteemed as an ornamental stone.

jaded, *adj.* **1.** worn out. **2.** sated.

jagged, *adv.* having notches, teeth, or ragged edges.

jaguar, *n.* a large, ferocious, spotted feline.

jail, *n.* →**gaol.**

jalopy, *n., pl.* **-lopies.** *Colloq.* an old, decrepit, or unpretentious motor car.

jam[1], *v.,* **jammed, jamming.** –*v.* **1.** to press or squeeze tightly between bodies or surfaces. **2.** to fill or block up by crowding. **3.** to (cause to) become wedged, caught, or displaced, so that it cannot work. **4.** *Radio.* to interfere with (signals, etc.) by sending out others of approximately the same frequency. **5.** to apply (brakes) forcibly (*on*). –*n.* **6.** the act of jamming. **7.** the state of being jammed. **8.** a mass of vehicles, people, or objects jammed together. **9.** Also, **jam session.** *Music.* a meeting for improvisation, esp. of jazz. **10.** *Colloq.* a difficult or awkward situation; a fix.

275

jam

jam², *n.* a preserve of boiled and crushed fruit.

jamb, *n.* a vertical piece forming the side of a doorway or window.

jam·bo·ree, *n.* a large gathering or rally.

jangle, *v.,* **-gled, -gling,** *n.* (to produce) a harsh or discordant sound.

jan·i·tor, *n.* a doorkeeper or porter.

japon·ica, *n.* a garden shrub with white, pink or red flowers.

jar¹, *n.* a broad-mouthed earthen or glass vessel.

jar², *v.,* **jarred, jarring. 1.** to produce a harsh, grating sound. **2.** to have a harshly unpleasant effect upon the nerves, feelings, etc. **3.** to be at variance; conflict.

jargon, *n.* the language peculiar to a trade, profession, or other group.

jas·mine, *n.* a climbing plant with fragrant flowers.

jasper, *n.* a coloured variety of quartz.

jaun·dice, *n., v.,* **-diced, -dicing.** —*n.* **1.** *Pathol.* a disease characterised by yellowness of the skin, etc. —*v.* **2.** to distort or prejudice, as with pessimism, jealousy, resentment, etc.

jaunt, *v., n.* (to make) a short journey, esp. for pleasure.

jaunty, *adj.,* **-tier, -tiest.** easy and sprightly in manner or bearing.

javelin, *n.* a spear to be thrown by hand.

jaw, *n.* one of the 2 bones or structures (upper and lower) which form the framework of the mouth.

jay-walk, *v. Colloq.* to cross a street ignoring the road rules.

jazz, *n.* **1.** a type of popular music marked by frequent improvisation and unusually accented rhythms. —*v.* **2.** *Colloq.* to put vigour or liveliness into.

jea·lous, *adj.* **1.** inclined to or troubled by suspicions or fears of rivalry. **2.** solicitous or vigilant in maintaining or guarding something. — **jealousy,** *n.*

jeans, *n.pl.* trousers made of denim or other sturdy fabric.

jeep, *n.* a small military motor vehicle.

jeer, *v.* to speak or shout derisively.

Jehovah, *n.* name of God in the Old Testament.

jell, *v.* set as a jelly; to take definite shape or form.

jelly, *n., pl.* **-lies.** a food preparation of a soft, elastic consistency.

jelly-fish, *n., pl.* **-fishes.** (*esp.* collectively) **-fish.** any of various marine invertebrates of a soft, jelly-like structure.

jemmy, *n.* a short crowbar.

jeop·ardy, *n.* hazard or risk of loss or harm. — **jeopardise,** *v.*

jerk, *n.* **1.** a quick, sharp thrust, pull, throw, or the like. **2.** *Colloq.* a stupid or naive person. —*v.* **3.** to move or throw with a quick, suddenly arrested motion.

jersey, *n.* **1.** a close-fitting, usu. woollen, outer garment; jumper. **2.** a machine-knitted fabric.

jest, *n.* **1.** a witticism, joke, or pleasantry. **2.** sport or fun. —*v.* **3.** to speak in a playful or humorous way.

jet¹, *n., v.,* **jetted, jetting.** —*n.* **1.** a stream of fluid from a nozzle, orifice, etc. **2.** a jet plane. —*v.* **3.** to spout.

jet², *n.* a hard black coal, used when polished for making beads, jewellery, buttons, etc.

jet plane, *n.* an aeroplane operated

jet plane

by jet propulsion, where a high-velocity jet of gas is discharged towards the rear.

jetsam, *n*. goods thrown overboard to lighten a vessel in distress. See **flotsam**.

jetti·son, *v*. to throw (cargo, etc.) overboard, esp. to lighten a vessel or aircraft in distress.

jetty, *n., pl.* **-ties**. a landing pier.

jewel, *n*. a cut and polished precious or semiprecious stone. – **jeweller**, *n*.

jewel·lery, *n*. jewels for personal adornment.

jew·fish, *n., pl.* **-fishes**, (*esp. collectively*) **-fish**. any of several species of large food fishes.

jib[1], *n*. a triangular sail.

jib[2], *n., v.,* **jibbed, jibbing**. to hold back or baulk at doing something.

jiffy, *n., pl.* **-fies**. *Colloq*. a very short time. Also, **jiff**.

jig[1], *n*. a device for holding the work in a machine tool.

jig[2], *n., v.,* **jigged, jigging**. – *n*. 1. a rapid, lively dance. – *v*. 2. to move with a jerky or bobbing motion.

jigger, *n*. a measure for alcohol used in cocktails.

jiggery-pokery, *n., Colloq*. dishonest dealings, trickery, swindling.

jiggle, *v.,* **-gled, -gling**. to move up and down or to and fro with short, quick jerks.

jigsaw puzzle, *n*. small, irregularly shaped pieces of cardboard, which, when correctly fitted together, form a picture.

jihad, *n*. holy war waged on behalf of Islam against unbelievers.

jilt, *v*. to cast off (a lover or sweetheart) after encouragement or engagement.

jingle, *v.,* **-gled, -gling**, *n*. – *v*. 1. to make clinking or tinkling sounds. – *n*. 2. a clinking or tinkling sound. 3. a simple, repetitious, catchy rhyme set to music.

jingo·ism, *n*. fervent and excessive patriotism.

jinx, *Colloq. n*. 1. a person, thing, or influence supposed to bring bad luck. – *v*. 2. to bring bad luck to someone.

jit·ters, *n. pl. Colloq*. nervousness; nerves (usu. prec. by *the*).

jive, *n*. a dance performed to beat music.

job, *n., v.,* **jobbed, jobbing**. – *n*. 1. an individual piece of work done in the routine of one's occupation or trade. 2. a post of employment. – *v*. 3. to work at jobs, or odd pieces of work.

jobless, *adj*. unemployed.

jockey, *n*. one who professionally rides horses in races.

jock·strap, *n. Colloq*. a support for the genitals worn by male athletes, dancers, etc.

jocose /dʒəˈkoʊs/, *adj*. characterised by joking; humorous. – **jocosity**, *n*.

jocu·lar, *adj*. given to, characterised by, intended for, or suited to joking or jesting.

jocund /ˈdʒɒkənd/, *adj*. cheerful; merry.

jodh·purs, *n.pl*. riding breeches reaching to the ankle, and fitting closely from the knee down.

jog, *v*. **jogged, jogging**. 1. to move or shake with a push or jerk. 2. to stir up by hint or reminder. 3. to run at a slow, regular pace.

joggle, *v.,* **-gled, -gling**. to shake slightly; move to and fro as by repeated jerks.

john

john, *n. Colloq.* a toilet.

John Dory, *n.* a thin, deep-bodied food fish.

join, *v.* **1.** to come, be, or put together, in contact or connection. **2.** to become a member of. **3.** to come into the company of. **4.** to take part with others (*in*). –*n.* **5.** a place or line of joining; a seam.

joiner, *n.* a worker in wood who constructs the fittings of a house, furniture, etc. – **joinery,** *n.*

joint, *n.* **1.** the place or part in which 2 things, or parts of one thing, are joined. **2.** one of the portions into which a carcass is divided by a butcher, esp. one ready for cooking. **3.** *Colloq.* one's house, unit, office, etc. **4.** *Colloq.* a marijuana cigarette. –*adj.* **5.** shared by or common to 2 or more. **6.** sharing or acting in common. –*v.* **7.** to unite by a joint or joints. **8.** to divide at a joint, or separate into pieces.

joist, *n.* any of the parallel lengths of timber, steel, etc., used for supporting floors, ceilings, etc.

joke, *n., v.,* **joked, joking.** –*n.* **1.** something said or done to excite laughter or amusement. **2.** an amusing or ridiculous circumstance. –*v.* **3.** to speak or act in a playful or merry way. **4.** to say something in mere sport, rather than in earnest.

joker, *n.* **1.** one who jokes. **2.** an extra playing card in a pack, used in some games.

jolly, *adj.,* **-lier, -liest,** *adv.* –*adj.* **1.** in good spirits. –*adv.* **2.** *Colloq.* extremely; very.

jolt, *v.* **1.** to jar or shake as by a sudden rough thrust. –*n.* **2.** a jolting shock or movement.

judge

jon·quil, *n.* a species of narcissus.

jostle, *v.,* **-tled, -tling. 1.** to strike or push roughly or rudely against. **2.** to collide (*with*) or strike or push (*against*) as in passing or in a crowd.

jot, *n., v.,* **jotted, jotting.** –*n.* **1.** the least part of something; a little bit. –*v.* **2.** to write or mark briefly (*down*).

joule, *n.* the derived SI unit of work or energy. *Symbol:* J

jour·nal, *n.* **1.** a daily record; diary. **2.** a newspaper, esp. a daily one. **3.** any periodical or magazine, esp. one published by an academic or other society.

jour·nal·ism, *n.* the occupation of writing for, editing, and conducting newspapers and other periodicals. – **journalist,** *n.*

jour·ney, *n., pl.* **-neys,** *v.,* **-neyed, -neying.** –*n.* **1.** a course of travel. –*v.* **2.** to make a journey; travel.

joust, *n.* a combat in which 2 armoured knights on horseback opposed each other with lances.

jovial, *adj.* having or showing a hearty, joyous humour.

jowl, *n.* **1.** a jaw, esp. the underjaw. **2.** the cheek. **3.** a fold of flesh hanging from the jaw.

joy, *n.* an emotion of keen or lively pleasure; great gladness.

JP, *abbrev.* Justice of the Peace.

Jr., *abbrev.* Junior.

jubi·lant, *adj.* expressing or exciting joy.

jubi·lation, *n.* the act of rejoicing.

jubi·lee, *n.* the celebration of any of certain anniversaries, esp. the 25th, 50th, etc.

judge, *n., v.,* **judged, judging.** –*n.* **1.** a public officer authorised to bear

278

judge

and determine causes in a court of law. 2. a person appointed to decide in any competition or contest. –v. 3. to try (a person or a case) as a judge does; pass sentence (on or in). 4. to form a judgment or opinion (of or upon).

judg·ment, n. 1. the act of judging. 2. *Law.* the judicial decision of a case in court. 3. ability to judge justly or wisely. 4. the forming of an opinion, estimate, notion, or conclusion. Also, **judgement**.

judi·cial, adj. 1. pertaining to legal justice. 2. pertaining to courts of law or to judges. 3. proper to the character of a judge; judgelike.

judi·ciary, n., pl. **-aries**. the system of courts of justice in a country.

judi·cious, adj. having, exercising, or showing good judgment; wise.

judo, n. a style of self-defence derived from Japanese wrestling.

jug, n. a vessel for holding liquids, commonly having a handle.

jugger·naut, n. any large, relentless, destructive force.

juggle, v., **-gled, -gling**. 1. to keep (several objects) in continuous motion in the air by tossing and catching. 2. to manipulate or alter by artifice or trickery.

jug·ular, adj. 1. *Anat.* of or pertaining to the throat or neck. –n. 2. one of the large veins in the neck.

juice, n. the liquid part of plant or animal substance. – **juicy**, adj.

ju-jitsu, n. Japanese system of unarmed combat.

juke-box, n. a coin-operated record-player permitting selection of the record to be played.

jumble, v., **-bled, -bling**, n. –v. 1. to put or throw together without order. –n. 2. a confused mixture.

jumbo, n., pl. **-bos**, adj. *Colloq.* –n. 1. an elephant. –adj. 2. very large.

jump, v. 1. to spring clear of the ground or over an obstacle, etc., by a sudden muscular effort; leap. 2. to move suddenly or abruptly, as from surprise or shock; start. 3. to pass abruptly, ignoring intervening stages. –n. 4. the act of jumping; a leap. 5. a space or obstacle or apparatus cleared in a leap. 6. a sudden rise in amount, price, etc. 7. an abrupt transition from one point or thing to another.

jumper, n. an outer garment for the upper part of the body.

jumpy, adj., **jumpier, jumpiest**. showing nervousness, fear, excitement, etc.

junc·tion, n. 1. the act of joining; combination. 2. a place of joining or meeting.

junc·ture, n. 1. a point of time, esp. a critical or important one. 2. the line or point at which 2 bodies are joined.

jungle, n. a thick tropical rainforest.

junior, adj. 1. younger. 2. of lower rank or standing. –n. 3. a person who is younger than another. 4. any minor or child, esp. a male. 5. one employed as the subordinate of another.

juni·per, n. any of several coniferous evergreen shrubs or trees.

junk[1], n. 1. any old or discarded material. 2. *Colloq.* anything regarded as worthless.

junk[2], n. a kind of seagoing ship used in Chinese and other waters.

junket, n. 1. a sweet custard-like

junket

food. 2. a feast or merrymaking; a picnic.

junkie, n. Colloq. a drug addict.

junta, n. a small ruling group in a country, esp. one which has come to power after a revolution.

juris·dic·tion, n. 1. the right, power, or authority to administer justice by hearing and determining controversies. 2. power; authority; control.

juris·pru·dence, n. 1. the science or philosophy of law. 2. a body or system of laws. – jurisprudent, n., adj. – jurisprudential, adj.

jurist, n. one versed in the law.

juror, n. a member of any jury.

jury, n., pl. -ries. 1. a body of people selected and sworn to inquire into a court case and to render a verdict. 2. a body of persons chosen to judge prizes, etc., as in a competition.

just, adj. 1. actuated by truth, justice, and lack of bias. 2. based on right; lawful. 3. true; correct. 4. deserved, as a sentence, punishment, reward, etc. –adv. 5. within a brief preced-

juxtapose

ing time, or but a moment before. 6. exactly; or precisely. 7. by a narrow margin; barely. 8. only or merely. 9. Colloq. actually; truly; positively.

jus·tice, n. 1. the quality of being just. 2. that which is just. 3. the maintenance or administration of law, as by judicial or other proceedings. 4. a judicial officer; a judge or magistrate.

jus·tify, v., -fied, -fying. 1. to show (an act, claim, etc.) to be just, right, or warranted. 2. Print. to adjust exactly; make (lines) of the proper length by spacing. – justification, n.

jut, v., jutted, jutting. to extend (out) beyond the main body or line.

jute, n. a strong fibre used for making fabrics, rope, etc.

juve·nile, adj. 1. pertaining to or intended for young persons. 2. inappropriately suggestive of the behaviour or sentiments of a young person. –n. 3. a young person; a youth.

jux·ta·pose, v., -posed, -posing. to place in close proximity or side by side. – juxtaposition, n.

280

Kk

K, k, *n., pl.* **K's** or **Ks**, **k's** or **ks**. the 11th letter of the English alphabet.

kaftan, *n.* →caftan.

kaleido·scope, *n.* an optical instrument in which pieces of coloured glass, etc., in a rotating tube are shown by reflection in continually changing symmetrical forms. – **kaleidoscopic,** *adj.*

kamikaze, *n.* volunteer pilot of explosive-laden Japanese aircraft deliberately crashed on target.

kanga·roo, *n.* any of several herbivorous marsupials of the Aust. region, with powerful hind legs developed for leaping.

kaput, *adj. Colloq.* 1. smashed; ruined. 2. broken; not working.

karaoke, *n.* entertainment in clubs, bars, etc. with customers singing to recorded music.

karma, *n.* Buddhist and Hindu belief that a person's actions in life decide their fate in next.

kayak, *n.* an Eskimo hunting canoe.

kebab, *n.* →shish kebab.

keel, *n.* 1. a long piece of timber, iron plates, or the like supporting the whole frame of a ship. –*v.* 2. **keel over,** *Colloq.* to collapse suddenly.

keen[1], *adj.* 1. sharp. 2. strong and clear, as hearing, eyesight, etc. 3. having or showing great mental penetration or acumen. 4. intense, as feeling, desire, etc. 5. having a fondness or devotion: *keen on rock music*.

keen[2], *v.* to wail in lamentation for the dead.

keep, *v.,* **kept, keeping,** *n.* –*v.* 1. to (cause to) continue in some place, state, or course specified. 2. to have habitually in stock or for sale. 3. to withhold from use; reserve. 4. to maintain or carry on, as an establishment, business, etc.; manage. 5. to maintain or support (a person, etc.). 6. to save, or retain in possession. 7. to continue unimpaired or without spoiling. 8. to stay (*away, back, off, out,* etc.). –*n.* 9. subsistence; board and lodging. 10. the central tower of a medieval castle. 11. **for keeps,** *Colloq.* permanently.

keep·ing, *n.* proper conformity in things or elements associated together.

keepsake, *n.* anything kept as a token of remembrance, friendship, etc.

keg, *n.* a barrel, esp. of beer.

kelp, *n.* any of the large brown seaweeds.

kelpie, *n.* one of a breed of sheepdogs.

kelvin, *n.* the base SI unit of thermodynamic temperature. One Kelvin is equivalent to one degree Celsius.

ken, *n.* 1. range of vision. 2. knowledge; mental perception.

kennel, *n.* 1. a dog house. 2. (*usu. pl.*) an establishment where dogs are bred or boarded.

kept, v. past tense and past participle of **keep**.

kerb, n. a line of joined stones, concrete, or the like at the edge of a street, wall, etc.

kernel, n. 1. the softer, usu. edible, part contained in the shell of a nut or the stone of a fruit. 2. the central part of anything; the core.

kero·sene, n. a mixture of liquid hydrocarbons used for lamps, engines, heaters. Also, **kerosine**.

kestrel, n. small falcon.

ket·chup, n. any of several sauces for meat, fish, etc. Also, **catsup**, **catch-up**.

kettle, n. a portable container in which to boil water.

kettle·drum, n. a tunable drum with a half-spherical base.

key, n., pl. **keys**, adj., v., **keyed**, **keying**. —n. 1. an instrument for fastening or opening a lock by moving its bolt. 2. a means of attaining, understanding, solving, etc. 3. a systematic explanation of abbreviations, symbols, etc. 4. one of a set of levers or parts pressed in operating a telegraph, typewriter, musical instrument, etc. 5. *Music.* the keynote or tonic of a scale. —adj. 6. chief; indispensable. 7. identifying. —v. 8. to bring (*up*) to a particular degree of intensity of feeling. 9. to adjust (one's speech, actions, etc.) to external factors, as the level of understanding of one's hearers.

key·board, n. the row or set of keys on a piano, typewriter, etc.

key·note, n. 1. *Music.* the note on which a system of notes is founded; tonic. 2. the main interest or determining principle of a speech, campaign, etc.

khaki, n., pl. **-kis**. 1. dull yellowish brown. 2. stout cloth of this colour, worn esp. by soldiers.

kibble, v., **-bled**, **-bling**. to grind into small particles.

kib·butz, n., pl. **kibbutzim**. (in Israel) a communal agricultural settlement.

kick, v. 1. to strike (*out*) with the foot. 2. to drive, force, make, etc., by or as by kicks. 3. *Football.* to score (a goal) by a kick. 4. *Colloq.* to resist, object, or complain. 5. to recoil, as a firearm when fired. 6. **kick out**, *Colloq.* to dismiss; get rid of. —n. 7. the act of kicking; a blow or thrust with the foot. 8. a recoil, as of a gun. 9. *Colloq.* any thrill or excitement that gives pleasure. 10. *Colloq.* vigour or energy.

kick·back, n. *Colloq.* 1. a response, usu. vigorous. 2. any sum paid for favours received or hoped for.

kid[1], n. 1. (leather made from the skin of) a young goat. 2. *Colloq.* a child or young person.

kid[2], v., **kidded**, **kidding**. *Colloq.* to tease; banter; jest with.

kidnap, v., **-napped**, **-napping**. to carry off (a person) by unlawful force or by fraud, often with a demand for ransom. – **kidnapper**, n.

kidney, n., pl. **-neys**. either of a pair of bean-shaped glandular organs which excrete urine.

kidney bean, n. the dried, somewhat kidney-shaped seed of the French bean.

kikuyu, n. a lawn grass.

kill, v. 1. to deprive of life. 2. to destroy. 3. to defeat or veto (a legislative bill, etc.). —n. 4. the act

kill

of killing (game, etc.). 5. an animal or animals killed.

kil·ling, *n. Colloq.* a stroke of extraordinary success.

kiln, *n.* a furnace or oven, esp. one for baking bricks.

kilo, *n. Colloq.* a kilogram.

kilo·gram, *n.* a unit of mass equal to 1000 grams. *Symbol:* kg

kilo·joule, *n.* one thousand joules. *Symbol:* kJ

kilo·metre /ˈkɪləmitə/; *deprecated* /kəˈlɒmətə/, *n.* a unit of length, the common measure of distances equal to 1000 metres. *Symbol:* km

kilt, *n.* any short, pleated skirt, esp. one worn by men in the Scottish Highlands.

kilter, *n.* good condition; order.

kimono /kɪˈmoʊnoʊ, kəˈmoʊnoʊ/, *pl.* **-nos**. a wide-sleeved robe characteristic of Japanese costume.

kin, *n.* relatives collectively.

kind[1], *adj.* of a good or benevolent nature or disposition. – **kindness**, **kindliness**, *n.* – **kindly**, *adj., adv.*

kind[2], *n.* 1. a class or group of individuals of the same nature or character. 2. nature or character as determining likeness or difference between things. 3. **in kind**, in something of the same kind in the same way. 4. **of kind** (used adverbially), *Colloq.* after a fashion; to some extent.

kinder·garten, *n.* a school or class for young children, usu. under the age of 5 or 6.

kindle, *v.*, **-dled, -dling.** 1. to set (a fire, flame, etc.) burning or blazing. 2. to excite (feelings, etc.).

kin·dred, *n.* 1. a body of persons related to one another. –*adj.* 2.

kitsch

associated by origin, nature, qualities, etc.

kin·etic, *adj.* 1. pertaining to motion. 2. caused by motion.

king, *n.* a male sovereign.

king·dom, *n.* 1. a state having a king or queen as its head. 2. a realm or province of nature.

king·fisher, *n.* any of numerous fish- or insect-eating birds.

king·pin, *n. Colloq.* the principal person or element in a company or system, etc.

kink, *n.* 1. a twist or curl. 2. a deviation, esp. sexual. – **kinky**, *adj.*

kin·ship, *n.* 1. the state or fact of being of kin. 2. relationship by nature, qualities, etc.; affinity.

kiosk, *n.* a small, light structure for the sale of newspapers, cigarettes, etc.

kip, *n. Colloq.* a sleep.

kipper, *n.* a smoked fish, esp. a herring.

kirk, *n. Scot.* a church.

kismet, *n.* fate; destiny.

kiss, *v.* 1. to touch or press (someone or something) with the lips in token of greeting, affection, etc. –*n.* 2. the act of kissing.

kit, *n.* 1. a set or collection of tools, supplies, etc., for a specific purpose. 2. a set or collection of parts to be assembled.

kit·chen, *n.* a room or place for cooking.

kite, *n.* 1. a light frame covered with some thin material, to be flown in the wind at the end of a long string. 2. any of various medium-sized hawks.

kitsch, *n.* pretentious or worthless art, literature, etc.

283

kitten

kitten, *n.* a young cat.

kitty, *n., pl.* **-ties.** a jointly held fund or collection.

kiwi, *n.* any of several flightless birds of N.Z.

Kiwi fruit, *n.* a small, green, hairy fruit; Chinese gooseberry.

klaxon, *n.* a type of warning hooter, originally used in motor vehicles.

klep·to·mania, *n.* an irresistible desire to steal, without regard to personal needs. – **kleptomaniac,** *n.*

knack, *n.* a faculty or power of doing something with ease; aptitude.

knacker, *n.* one who buys old or useless horses for slaughter. – **knackery,** *n.*

knap·sack, *n.* a leather or canvas case for clothes and the like, carried on the back.

knave, *n.* 1. an unprincipled or dishonest fellow. 2. *Cards.* a playing card bearing the formalised picture of a prince; jack. – **knavery,** *n.* – **knavish,** *adj.*

knead, *v.* to work (dough, etc.) into a uniform mixture by pressing, folding and stretching.

knee, *n., v.,* **kneed, kneeing.** –*n.* 1. the joint between the thigh and the lower part of the leg. –*v.* 2. to strike or touch with the knee.

knee·cap, *n.* the flat, movable bone at the front of the knee.

kneel, *v.,* **knelt** or **kneeled, kneeling.** to fall or rest on the knees or a knee.

knell, *n.* the sound made by a bell rung slowly for a death or a funeral.

knew, *v.* past tense of **know.**

knicker·bockers, *n.pl.* loosely fitting breeches gathered in at the knee.

knockout

knick·ers, *n. pl.* 1. →**pants** (def. 2). 2. →**knickerbockers.**

knick-knack, *n.* a pleasing trifle; a trinket.

knife, *n., pl.* **knives,** *v.,* **knifed, knifing.** –*n.* 1. a cutting instrument consisting of a thin blade attached to a handle. –*v.* 2. to cut, stab, etc., with a knife.

knight, *n. Hist.* 1. a man, usu. of noble birth, bound to chivalrous conduct. 2. a man upon whom the honorific *Sir* is conferred because of personal merit or for services rendered to the country. –*v.* 3. to dub or create (a man) a knight.

knit, *v.,* **knitted** or **knit, knitting,** *n.* –*v.* 1. to make (a garment, fabric, etc.) by interlacing loops of yarn either with knitting needles or by machine. 2. to join or become joined closely and firmly together, as members or parts. 3. to contract, as the brow does in a frown. –*n.* 4. fabric produced by interlooping of a yarn or yarns.

knob, *n.* 1. a projecting part forming the handle of a door or the like. 2. a rounded lump or protuberance.

knock, *v.* 1. to strike a sounding blow with the fist or anything hard, esp. on a door, as in seeking admittance, etc. 2. (of an internal-combustion engine) to make a metallic noise as a result of faulty combustion. 3. to collide (*against* or *into*). 4. to drive, force, or render by a blow or blows. 5. *Colloq.* to criticise; find fault with. 6. **knock off,** *Colloq.* to stop an activity, esp. work. 7. **knock out,** to render senseless. –*n.* 8. the act or sound of knocking.

knock·out, *n.* 1. the act of knocking out. 2. *Colloq.* a person or thing of

284

knockout overwhelming success or attractiveness.

knoll, *n.* a small, rounded hill.

knot, *n., v.,* **knotted, knotting.** –*n.* 1. an interlacement of a cord, rope, or the like, drawn tight, as for fastening 2 cords. 2. the hard mass of wood where a branch joins the trunk of a tree. 3. a unit of speed, used in marine and aerial navigation, and in meteorology. –*v.* 4. to tie or become tied in a knot or knots.

know, *v.,* **knew, known, knowing.** 1. to perceive or understand as fact or truth. 2. to have fixed in the mind or memory. 3. to be acquainted with (a thing, person etc.), as by experience or report. 4. to understand from experience or attainment: *to know how to swim.* – **knowledge**, *n.*

knuckle, *n., v.,* **-led, -ling.** –*n.* 1. a joint of a finger. –*v.* 2. to apply oneself vigorously or earnestly, as (*down*) to a task. 3. to yield or submit (*down* or *under*).

knurl, *n.* 1. a small ridge or the like, esp. one of a series. –*v.* 2. to make knurls or ridges on.

koala, *n.* a sluggish, tailless, grey, furry, small Aust. marsupial, which eats the leaves of certain eucalypts. Also, **koala bear.**

kook, *n. Colloq.* a strange or eccentric person. – **kooky**, *adj.*

kooka·burra, *n.* either of 2 Aust. kingfishers renowned for their call resembling human laughter.

kosher /ˈkɒʃə, ˈkoʊʃə/, *adj.* fit, lawful, or ritually permitted, according to the Jewish law.

kowtow /kaʊˈtaʊ/, *v.* to act in an obsequious manner.

kryp·ton, *n.* an inert gaseous element. *Symbol:* Kr

kudos /ˈkjuːdɒs/, *n.* glory; renown.

kum·quat /ˈkʌmkwɒt/, *n.* a small, round, citrus fruit.

kung-fu, *n.* karate in the form developed in China.

kurra·jong, *n.* a tree valued as fodder.

L l

L, l, *n., pl.* **L's** or **Ls, l's** or **ls.** the 12th letter of the English alphabet.
label, *n., v.,* **-belled, -belling.** —*n.* 1. a slip of paper, etc., for affixing to something to indicate its nature, ownership, etc. 2. *Colloq.* the trade name, esp. of a record or clothing company. —*v.* 3. to affix a label to.
labora·tory, *n., pl.* **-ries.** (a part of) a building fitted with apparatus for conducting scientific investigations or for manufacturing chemicals, medicines, etc.
labor·ious, *adj.* requiring much labour, exertion, or perseverance.
labour, *n.* 1. physical work done for money. 2. hard or fatiguing work. 3. the time during which the pangs and efforts of childbirth take place. —*v.* 4. to perform labour; work; toil.
labra·dor, *n.* one of a breed of dogs with black or golden coats.
laby·rinth, *n.* a complicated arrangement of passages in which it is difficult to find one's way or to reach the exit.
lace, *n., v.,* **laced, lacing.** —*n.* 1. a netlike ornamental fabric. 2. a cord for holding or drawing together: *shoe laces.* —*v.* 3. to fasten or draw together by a lace: *to lace shoes.* 4. to intermix, as coffee with spirits.
lacer·ate, *v.,* **-rated, -rating.** 1. to tear roughly; mangle. 2. to hurt.
lack, *n.* the absence of something required, desirable, etc. —*v.* 2. to be deficient in, or without.
laco·nic /ləˈkɒnɪk/, *adj.* using few words.
lac·quer, *n.* a resinous varnish.
lac·tate, *v.* **-tated, -tating.** to produce milk.
lad, *n.* a boy or youth.
lad·der, *n.* 1. a structure of wood, etc., with 2 sidepieces joined by a series of spaced bars, forming a means of ascent or descent. 2. a line in a stocking, etc., where a series of stitches have come undone. —*v.* 3. to cause a ladder in (a stocking, etc.).
laden, *adj.* 1. loaded; burdened. 2. filled: *a tree laden with fruit.*
ladle, *n., v.,* **-dled, -dling.** —*n.* 1. a long-handled utensil with a cup-shaped bowl for holding liquids. —*v.* 2. to convey with a ladle.
lady, *n., pl.* **-dies.** 1. a woman of good breeding, refinement, etc. 2. (*cap.*) a prefix to a title of honour or respect. 3. a woman.
lady·bird, *n.* a small beetle with usu. orange back spotted with black.
lady-in-waiting, *n., pl.* **ladies-in-waiting,** a lady in attendance upon a queen or princess.
lag, *v.,* **lagged, lagging.** to move slowly; fall behind.
lager, *n.* a German type of beer.
lagoon, *n.* any small, pondlike body of water.
laid, *v.* past tense and past participle of **lay¹**.
lain, *v.* past participle of **lie²**.
lair¹, *n.* the den of a wild beast.
lair², *n. Colloq.* a brash, flashily dressed young man.
laissez faire /ˌleɪseɪ ˈfɛə/, *n.* the

laissez faire

doctrine of non-interference, esp. in the conduct of others. Also, **laisser faire.**

lai·ty, *n.* laymen, as distinguished from clergymen. – **laic**, *adj.*

lake, *n.* a large body of water surrounded by land.

lama, *n.* a Buddhist priest of Tibet, Mongolia, etc.

lamb, *n.* a young sheep.

lame, *adj.*, **lamer**, **lamest**. physically disabled esp. in the foot or leg.

lamé /ˈlæmeɪ/, *n.* an ornamental fabric in which metallic threads are woven with silk, etc.

lament, *v.* 1. to feel or express sorrow or regret (for). –*n.* 2. an expression of grief or sorrow. – **lamentable**, *adj.*

lami·nate, *v.*, **-nated, -nating. 1.** to separate into thin layers. **2.** to construct by placing layer upon layer.

laming·ton, *n.* a cube of sponge cake covered in chocolate icing and shredded coconut.

lamp, *n.* a device using gas or electricity, etc., to generate heat or light.

lam·poon, *n.* a satire upon a person, government, etc., in either prose or verse.

lam·prey, *n., pl.* **-preys.** an eel-like fish.

lance, *n., v.*, **lanced, lancing.** –*n.* **1.** a long, spearlike weapon with a metal head. –*v.* **2.** to pierce (as) with a lance.

land, *n.* the solid substance of the earth's surface. **2.** agricultural areas as opposed to urban. –*v.* **3.** to bring to or put on land or shore. **4.** to alight upon the ground as from an aeroplane, or after a jump. **5.** land

lantana

with, to give (someone) a task which they may be unwilling to perform.

land·ing, *n.* the floor at the head or foot of a flight of stairs.

land·lord, *n.* **1.** one who owns and leases land, buildings, etc., to another. **2.** the master of a hotel, boarding house, etc. – **landlady,** *n.*

land·lubber, *n. Naut.* one who lives on land.

land·mark, *n.* **1.** a conspicuous object on land that serves as a guide, esp. to vessels at sea. **2.** a prominent feature, event, etc.

land·scape, *n.* an expanse of rural scenery visible from a single point.

land·slide, *n.* **1.** the sliding down of a mass of soil, etc., on a steep slope. **2.** an overwhelming electoral victory.

lane, *n.* a narrow passage, track, etc., as between fences, houses, etc.

lan·guage, *n.* **1.** communication by voice using sound symbols in conventional ways with conventional meanings. **2.** any system of such symbols used in such a way as to enable people to communicate intelligibly with one another.

lan·guid, *adj.* **1.** lacking in spirit; indifferent. **2.** lacking in vigour; slack; dull. – **languor**, *n.*

lan·guish, *v.* **1.** to be or become weak or feeble. **2.** to lose activity and vigour. **3.** to pine with longing for.

lank, *adj.* **1.** lean; gaunt. **2.** (of hair) straight and limp. – **lanky**, *adj.*

lano·lin, *n.* a fatty substance, extracted from wool, used in ointments. Also, **lanoline**.

lan·tana, *n.* a tropical plant, now a troublesome weed in some areas.

lantern

lan·tern, *n.* a transparent, protective case for enclosing a portable light.

lap¹, *n.* the front portion of the body from the waist to the knees when one sits.

lap², *v.,* **lapped, lapping.** *-v.* **1.** to fold or wrap over or about something. **2.** to get a lap or more ahead of (a competitor) in racing. *-n.* **3.** a single circuit of the course in racing.

lap³, *v.,* **lapped, lapping. 1.** to lick (*up*) (liquid). **2. lap up,** to receive avidly.

lapel, *n.* that part of a coat collar folded back on the breast.

lapi·dary, *n., pl.* **-ries.** a person who cuts, polishes, etc., precious or semiprecious stones.

lapse, *n., v.,* **lapsed, lapsing.** *-n.* **1.** a slip or slight error. **2.** a passing away, as of time. **3.** a sinking to a lower condition. *-v.* **4.** to pass slowly, silently, or by degrees. **5.** to cease to be in force or use.

lar·ceny, *n., pl.* **-nies.** *Law.* the theft of the personal goods of another.

lard, *n.* melted pig fat used in cooking.

larder, *n.* a place where food is kept; a pantry.

large, *adj.,* **larger, largest.** being of more than common size, amount, or number.

largely, *adv.* to a great extent.

lar·gess, *n.* generosity, esp. with money. Also, **largesse.**

lark¹, *n.* a small singing bird.

lark², *n. Colloq.* a merry adventure; prank.

larva, *n., pl.* **-vae.** *Entomol.* the young of any insect which undergoes metamorphosis. – **larval,** *adj.*

late

laryngitis /lærən'dʒaɪtəs/, *n.* inflammation of the larynx.

larynx, *n., pl.* **larynges, larynxes.** the upper part of the throat containing the vocal cords.

las·civious, *adj.* inclined to lust; lewd.

laser, *n.* a device for producing a strong, sharply defined, single-colour beam of radiation with waves in phase.

lash, *n.* **1.** the flexible, cord-like part of a whip. **2.** a swift stroke with a whip, etc., as a punishment. **3.** an eyelash. *-v.* **4.** to strike (*out*) vigorously (at) as with a weapon, whip, etc. **5.** to fasten with a rope, cord, etc.

lass, *n.* a girl or young woman.

lassi·tude, *n.* weariness.

lasso /læ'su/, *n., pl.* **-sos, -soes.** a long rope with a running noose at one end, used for catching horses, etc.

last¹, *adj.* **1.** coming after all others, as in time, order, or place. **2.** latest; most recent. **3.** being the only remaining. **4.** conclusive: *the last word in an argument.* *-adv.* **5.** after all others. **6.** most recently. *-n.* **7.** that which is last.

last², *v.* to continue in progress or existence; endure.

last³, *n.* a model of the human foot.

latch, *n.* a device for holding a door, etc., closed.

late, *adj.,* **later** or **latter, latest** or **last,** *adv.,* **later, latest.** *-adj.* **1.** coming after the usual or proper time. **2.** far advanced in time: *a late hour.* **3.** having died recently. *-adv.* **4.** after the usual or proper time, or after delay. **5.** until after the usual time; until late at night.

lately, *adv.* recently.

latent, *adj.* hidden; present, but not apparent. – **latency**, *n.*

lat·eral, *adj.* relating to the side: *a lateral view*.

latex, *n., pl.* **latices**, **latexes**. *Bot.* a milky liquid in certain plants, as rubber trees.

lath, *n., pl.* **laths**. a thin, narrow strip of wood.

lathe, *n.* a machine for use in working metal, wood, etc.

lather, *n.* foam made from soap moistened with water.

lati·tude, *n.* 1. *Geog.* the angular distance nth or sth from the equator of a point on the earth's surface, measured on the meridian of the point. 2. freedom of action, attitude, etc., from narrow restrictions.

lat·rine, *n.* a toilet, esp. in a camp, etc.

latter, *adj.* 1. being the 2nd mentioned of 2 (opposed to *former*). 2. later in time. 3. nearer to the end or close.

lat·tice, *n.* a structure of crossed wooden, etc., strips with open spaces between, used as a screen, etc.

laud /lɔːd/, *v.* to praise.

laugh, *v.* 1. to express mirth, joy, contempt, etc., by an explosive, inarticulate sound of the voice, facial expressions, etc. –*n.* 2. the act or sound of laughing. 3. (*oft. ironic*) a cause for laughter: *That's a laugh*. – **laughter**, *n.*

launch[1], *n.* a heavy, open or half-covered boat.

launch[2], *v.* 1. to set (a boat) afloat. 2. to set going.

laun·der, *v.* 1. to wash and iron (clothes, etc.). 2. to make (money from illegal sources) appear legal.

laun·dry, *n., pl.* **-dries**. 1. articles of clothing, etc., to be washed. 2. (a room in a house, etc., used for) the washing of clothes.

laurel, *n.* 1. a small evergreen tree. 2. (*usu. pl.*) honour won, as by achievement.

lava, *n.* the molten rock which issues from a volcano.

lava·tory, *n., pl.* **-ries**. (a room with) a toilet.

lav·en·der, *n.* a plant with fragrant, pale purple flowers.

lavish, *adj.* 1. using or giving generously (*of*): *lavish of praise*. –*v.* 2. to use or give generously.

law, *n.* 1. the principles and regulations made by government. 2. the profession which deals with law and legal procedure. 3. (in philosophical and scientific use) a statement of a relation between events which is consistent under the same conditions. – **lawful**, *adj.*

lawn[1], *n.* a stretch of grass-covered land, esp. one closely mowed.

lawn[2], *n.* a light linen or cotton fabric.

lawyer, *n.* one whose profession it is to give legal advice and represent people in court.

lax, *adj.* 1. not strict; careless or negligent. 2. loose or slack.

laxa·tive, *n., adj. Med.* (a substance) mildly stimulating to the bowels.

lay[1], *v.*, **laid**, **laying**. –*v.* 1. to place in a position of rest. 2. to bring forth and deposit (eggs). 3. to set (a table). 4. to present as a claim, charge, etc. 5. to place on or over a surface, as paint, coverings, etc. 6. **lay about** or **into**, to attack with

lay

blows. **7. lay by,** to put away for future use. **8. lay off, a.** to dismiss, esp. temporarily, as a workman. **b.** *Colloq.* to desist. **9. lay on,** to provide or supply. –*n.* **10.** the position in which a thing is laid.

lay², *v.* past tense of **lie²**.

lay³, *adj.* relating to the people or laity, as distinguished from the clergy.

lay-by, *n.* the reserving of an article by payment of a cash deposit.

layer, *n.* a thickness of some material laid on a surface.

layman, *n., pl.* **-men.** one not a clergyman or not a member of a profession.

laze, *v.,* **lazed, lazing.** to be lazy.

lazy, *adj.,* **-zier, -ziest.** disinclined to exertion or work; idle.

leach, *v.* to cause (water, etc.) to percolate through something.

lead¹ /liːd/, *v.,* **led, leading,** *n., adj.* –*v.* **1.** to go before or with (someone) to show the way. **2.** to go first. **3.** to guide in direction, opinion, etc.; to influence: *to lead astray.* **4.** to bring (water, wire, etc.) in a particular course. **5.** to command, or direct (an army, organisation, etc.). **6.** to go through or pass (life, etc.): *to lead a life of crime.* **7.** to afford passage (*to*) a place, etc.: *The road leads to the town.* –*n.* **8.** the first or foremost position. **9.** the extent of advance. **10.** a strap for holding a dog or other animal in check. **11.** a clue. **12.** *Elect.* an insulated wire used to connect pieces of electrical apparatus. –*adj.* **13.** solo or dominating: *a lead guitar.*

lead² /lɛd/, *n.* *Chem.* a heavy, comparatively soft, malleable bluish-grey metal. *Symbol:* Pb **2.** a

leap year

plumbline for measuring the depth of water.

leaden, *adj.* **1.** made of lead. **2.** inertly heavy, and hard to move.

leader, *n.* **1.** one who or that which leads. **2.** the main editorial article, as in a newspaper.

leaf, *n., pl.* **leaves.** *v.* –*n.* **1.** one of the flat, usu. green, organs on the stem of a plant. **2.** both sides of a page of a book, considered as a unit. **3.** a thin sheet of metal, etc. **4.** a detachable flat part, as of a tabletop, etc. –*v.* **5. leaf through,** to turn the pages of quickly.

leaf·let, *n.* a small sheet of printed matter, as for distribution.

league¹, *n.* (a group of people, nations, etc., making) an agreement for mutual benefit and promotion of common interests.

league², *n.* a former unit of distance.

leak, *n.* **1.** an unintended hole, etc., allowing fluid, gas, etc., to enter or escape. **2.** an (apparently) accidental disclosure of information. –*v.* **3.** to (let water, etc.) pass in or out through a hole, etc. **4.** to give out (confidential information), esp. to the media. **5. leak out,** to become known, not by design. – **leakage,** *n.*

lean¹, *v.,* **leant** or **leaned, leaning. 1.** to bend in a particular direction. **2.** to rest against something for support. **3.** to depend or rely.

lean², *adj.* **1.** (of persons or animals) thin; not plump. **2.** (of meat) containing little fat.

leap, *v.,* **leapt** or **leaped, leaping.** –*v.* **1.** to spring or jump (over). **2.** to pass, come, rise, etc., as if with a bound: *to leap to a conclusion.* –*n.* **3.** a spring, jump, or bound.

leap year, *n.* a year containing 366

leap year

days, or one day (29 February) more than the ordinary year.

learn, *v.*, **learnt** or **learned**, **learning**. to acquire knowledge of, or skill in, by study, instruction, or experience.

learned /'lɜnəd/, *adj.* having much knowledge gained by study; scholarly.

lease, *n.*, *v.*, **leased**, **leasing**. –*n.* 1. a contract conveying property to another for a definite period in return for regular rent payments. –*v.* 2. to grant the temporary possession or use of (lands, etc.) to another for rent; let. 3. to hold by a lease, as a flat, house, etc.

leash, *n.* a strong lead for a dog.

least, *adj.* 1. smallest; slightest. –*n.* 2. the least amount, quantity, degree, etc.

leather, *n.* the skin of animals prepared for use by tanning.

leave[1], *v.*, **left**, **leaving**. 1. to go away depart (from). 2. to let stay or be as specified. 3. to omit or exclude (out). 4. to give for use after one's death or departure. 5. to have as a remainder after subtraction: *2 from 4 leaves 2*.

leave[2], *n.* 1. permission to do something. 2. permission to be absent, or the period of absence, as from duty. 3. a farewell.

leaven /'lɛvən/, *n.* a mass of fermenting dough reserved for producing fermentation in a new batch of dough.

lecher, *n.* a man constantly seeking sexual indulgence. – **lechery**, *n.* – **lecherous**, *adj.*

lectern, *n.* a reading desk, esp. in a church.

lecture, *n.*, *v.*, **-tured**, **-turing**. –*n.* 1.

legation

a speech delivered before an audience, esp. for instruction. –*v.* 2. to give a lecture (to).

led, *v.* past tense and past participle of **lead**[1].

ledge, *n.* any relatively narrow, horizontal projecting part.

ledger, *n. Bookkeeping.* an account book of final entry, containing all the accounts.

lee, *n.* the side sheltered from the wind.

leech, *n.* a bloodsucking worm.

leek, *n.* an onion-like plant.

leer, *n.* a sideways glance, esp. a sly or insulting one.

lee·way, *n. Colloq.* extra space, time, money, etc.

left[1], *adj.* 1. relating to the side which is turned towards the west when a person or thing is facing north (opposed to *right*). 2. holding socialist or reformist political ideas.

left[2], *v.* past tense and past participle of **leave**[1].

left·over, *n.* something remaining.

leg, *n.* 1. one of the limbs which support and move the body. 2. something resembling a leg in use, position, or appearance. 3. a portion of a race, journey, etc.

legacy, *n., pl.* **-cies.** 1. *Law.* a gift of property, esp. money, by will; a bequest. 2. a consequence.

legal, *adj.* 1. appointed, established, or authorised by law. 2. of or pertaining to law.

legate, *n.* an official representative of the pope.

lega·tee, *n.* one who receives a legacy.

lega·tion, *n.* a diplomatic minister

legation

(not of ambassadorial rank) and his staff.

legend, *n*. 1. a story handed down by tradition and popularly accepted as based on historical fact. 2. an inscription. – **legendary**, *adj*.

leg·ging, *n*. (*usu. pl*.) a covering for the leg.

legible, *adj*. able to be read (easily). – **legibility**, *n*.

legion, *n*. 1. an infantry brigade in the army of ancient Rome. 2. a type of modern military body, as the Foreign Legion. 3. a multitude of persons or things.

legis·lation, *n*. (the act of making) a law or a body of laws. – **legislate**, *v*. – **legislative**, *adj*.

legis·lature, *n*. the legislative body of a country or state.

legi·ti·mate, *adj*. 1. according to law; lawful. 2. born in wedlock. 3. genuine; not spurious. – **legitimacy**, *n*.

legume, *n*. (the edible pod of) a pod-bearing plant.

leisure, *n*. time free from the demands of working; ease.

leisure·ly, *adj*. unhurried.

lem·ming, *n*. a small rodent noted for its mass migrations in periods of population increase.

lemon, *n*. 1. a yellowish acid fruit. 2. a clear, light yellow colour. 3. *Colloq*. something disappointing or unpleasant.

lemon·ade, *n*. a (carbonated) soft drink made of lemons, sugar, etc.

lend, *v*., **lent**, **lending**. 1. to give the temporary use of (money, etc.) for a fee. 2. to grant the use of (something) with the understanding that it shall be returned. 3. to impart: *Moonlight lends charm to the view*. 4. to adapt (oneself or itself) to something: *The room lends itself to study*.

lessen

length, *n*. 1. the measure of anything from end to end. 2. extent from beginning to end of a series, book, etc. 3. a piece of known length: *a length of fabric*.

leni·ent, *adj*. gentle or merciful, as in treatment, spirit, etc.

lens, *n*., *pl*. **lenses**. a piece of transparent substance, usu. glass, with one or both surfaces curved, used for converging or dispersing light rays, as in magnifying, or in correcting defective eyesight.

Lent, *n*. the season of fasting and penitence, of 40 days, in preparation for Easter.

lentil, *n*. an annual plant with flattened, edible seeds.

leo·nine, *adj*. lionlike.

leopard, *n*. a large, ferocious, spotted carnivore of the cat family.

leo·tard /ˈlɪətɑːd/, *n*. a close-fitting garment worn by acrobats, dancers, etc.

leper, *n*. a person affected with leprosy.

lepre·chaun /ˈlɛprəkɔːn/, *n*. in Irish folklore, a little sprite, or goblin.

lep·rosy, *n*. a mildly infectious disease marked by sores, loss of fingers and toes etc.

les·bian, *n*. a female homosexual.

lesion, *n*. an injury; wound.

less, *adv*. 1. to a smaller amount or degree. –*adj*. 2. smaller. –*prep*. 3. minus; without.

lessee, *n*. one to whom a lease is granted.

lessen, *v*. to become less.

lesser, *adj.* being smaller or less important, etc., (than another).

lesson, *n.* 1. something to be learned. 2. a length of time during which a pupil or class studies one subject.

lessor, *n.* one who grants a lease.

lest, *conj.* 1. for fear that. 2. (after words expressing fear, danger, etc.) that.

let[1], *v.*, **let**, **letting**. 1. to allow or permit. 2. to grant the use of (property) for rent. 3. to be rented or leased. 4. to cause or make: *to let one know*. 5. (as an auxiliary used to propose or order): *Let me see*.

let[2], *n.* in Tennis, etc. an interference with the course of the ball on account of which the stroke must be replayed.

lethal, *adj.* deadly.

leth·argy, *n.*, *pl.* **-gies.** a state of drowsy dullness; apathy; inactivity. – **lethargic**, *adj.*

letter, *n.* 1. a written communication. 2. one of the signs used in writing and printing to represent speech sounds; an alphabetic character.

let·tuce, *n.* a leafy plant, much used in salads.

leu·kae·mia /lukimiə/, *n.* a disease, often fatal, characterised by excessive production of white blood cells.

levee /'lɛvi/, *n.* a raised riverside.

level, *adj.*, *v.*, **-elled**, **-elling**. –*adj.* 1. having no part higher than another. 2. horizontal. 3. even or uniform. –*n.* 4. a device used for testing whether something is horizontal. 5. a horizontal position with respect to height: *The water level is falling*. –*v.* 6. to make level. 7. to bring (something) to the level of the ground. 8. to make (2 or more things) equal in status, condition, etc. 9. to aim at a mark, as a weapon, criticism, etc. **10. level out**, to arrive at a stable level: *Food prices levelled out last year*.

lever, *n.* a rigid bar rotating about a fixed point (fulcrum) which lifts a weight at one end when a force is applied to the other.

lever·age, *n.* 1. the action of a lever. 2. power of action; influence.

levi·tate, *v.*, **-tated**, **-tating**. to rise or float in the air, esp. through some allegedly supernatural power. – **lexical**, *adj.*

levity, *n.*, *pl.* **-ties.** lack of proper seriousness or earnestness.

levy /'lɛvi/, *n.*, *pl.* **-ies**, *v.*, **-ied**, **-ying**. –*n.* 1. the collecting of money or troops, etc., by authority or force. –*v.* 2. to impose (a tax).

lewd, *adj.* characterised by lust or lechery.

lexi·con, *n.* 1. a dictionary, esp. of Greek, Latin, or Hebrew. 2. the total stock of words in a given language. – **lexical**, *adj.*

lia·bility, *n.*, *pl.* **-ties.** 1. an obligation, esp. for payment (opposed to *asset*). 2. something disadvantageous.

liable, *adj.* 1. subject to something possible or likely, esp. something undesirable. 2. legally responsible.

liai·son, *n.* 1. a connection or communication. 2. a sexual relationship outside marriage.

liar, *n.* one who tells lies.

libel, *n. Law.* defamation by written or printed words, pictures, etc., as distinct from spoken words.

liberal, *adj.* 1. favourable to progress or reform, as in religious or political affairs. 2. favourable to the

liberal

policy of freedom of self-expression for the individual. **3.** generous. **4.** not strict or rigorous. –*n.* **5.** a person of liberal principles, esp. in religion or politics.

liber·ate, *v.*, **-rated, -rating.** to set free. – **liberation**, *n.* – **liberator**, *n.*

libertine, *n.* one free from restraint or control, esp. in moral or sexual matters.

lib·erty, *n., pl.* **-ties. 1.** freedom from control, interference, obligation, restriction, etc. **2.** freedom from captivity. **3.** unwarranted or impertinent freedom in action or speech.

libido /ləˈbidoʊ/, *n.* the instinctive impulses and desires in living beings.

lib·rary, *n., pl.* **-ries.** a place containing books, etc., (which may be borrowed) for reading, study, or reference. – **librarian**, *n.*

lice, *n.* plural of **louse**.

licence, *n.* **1.** (a certificate giving) formal permission to do something. **2.** excessive or undue freedom.

license, *v.*, **-censed, -censing.** to grant permission to.

licen·tious, *adj.* sensually uncontrolled; lewd.

lichen /ˈlaɪkən/, *n.* a plant growing in crustlike patches on rocks, trees, etc.

lick, *v.* **1.** to pass the tongue over the surface of (*off, from,* etc.) **2.** *Colloq.* to defeat; surpass. –*n.* **3.** a stroke of the tongue over something.

lico·rice, *n.* →**liquorice**.

lid, *n.* a movable cover for closing a vessel, box, etc.

lie[1], *n., v.*, **lied, lying.** –*n.* **1.** a false statement made with intent to deceive. –*v.* **2.** to speak falsely, intending to deceive.

ligament

lie[2], *v.*, **lay, lain, lying. 1.** to be in a recumbent position; recline: *to lie on a bed.* **2.** to rest in a horizontal position: *A pen is lying on the table.* **3.** to be situated: *land lying along the coast.* **4.** *lie down,* to assume a horizontal position.

lieu /lu, lju/, *n. in the phrase* **in lieu of,** instead of.

lieu·tenant, *n.* a deputy or subordinate officer acting for a superior.

life, *n., pl.* **lives. 1.** the condition which distinguishes animals and plants from inorganic objects and dead organisms. **2.** (the term of) animate existence of an individual. **3.** the term of effectiveness of something inanimate, as a machine, lease, etc. **4.** a living being. **5.** manner of existence: *married life.* **6.** liveliness. **7.** a prison sentence covering the rest of the convicted person's natural life.

life·line, *n.* **1.** a line or rope for saving life, as one attached to a lifeboat. **2.** any vital line of communication.

life-saver, *n.* one of a group of volunteers who patrol surfing beaches, etc., ensuring the safety of swimmers.

lift, *v.* **1.** to move (something) upwards, as from the ground etc., to some higher position. **2.** to raise in rank, condition, estimation, etc. **3.** to rise and disperse, as clouds, fog, etc. **4.** *Colloq.* to steal or plagiarise. –*n.* **5.** the act of lifting, raising, or rising. **6.** a moving platform or cage for conveying goods, people, etc., from one level to another, as in a building. **7.** a ride in a vehicle, free of charge. **8.** exaltation or uplift, in feeling.

liga·ment, *n., pl.* **ligaments,**

ligament

lig·a·men·ta. *Anat.* a band of fibrous tissue, serving to connect bones, hold organs in place, etc.

lig·a·ture, *n.* a tie or bond.

light[1], *n., adj., v.,* lit or lighted, lighting. —*n.* 1. that which makes things visible, or gives illumination. 2. an illuminating source, as the sun, a lamp, etc. 3. the illumination from the sun, or daylight. 4. the aspect in which a thing appears or is regarded. 5. a traffic light. —*adj.* 6. illuminated; not dark. —*v.* 7. to (cause) take fire or burn, as a match, candle, etc. 8. to brighten (*up*) with animation or joy, as the face, eyes, etc.

light[2], *adj.* 1. of little weight; not heavy. 2. gentle; delicate. 3. easy to endure or perform. 4. free from care: *a light heart.* 5. frivolous: *light conduct.*

light[3], *v.,* lighted or lit, lighting. 1. to descend, as from a horse or a vehicle. 2. to come by chance, happen, or hit (*on* or *upon*).

light·house, *n.* a tower displaying a light for the guidance of mariners.

light·ning, *n.* a sudden flash of light in the sky, caused by the discharge of atmospheric electricity.

light-year, *n.* the distance traversed by light in one year (9.460 55 × 10[15] metres), used as a unit in measuring stellar distances. *Symbol:* l.y.

lig·ne·ous /'lɪgnɪəs/, *adj.* resembling wood.

like[1], *prep.* 1. similarly to: *to live like a king.* 2. bearing resemblance to. 3. for example; as; such as: *the basic needs, like food and shelter.* 4. indicating a probability of: *It looks like rain.* 5. desirous of: *to feel like a drink.* —*adj.* 6. of the same or similar kind, amount, etc. —*n.* 7. something of a similar nature (prec. by *the*): *oranges, lemons and the like.*

like[2], *v.,* -liked, liking. 1. to find agreeable.

like·ly, *adj.,* -lier, -liest. 1. probably or apparently going (to do, be, etc.). 2. seeming like truth, fact, or certainty, or reasonably to be believed or expected; probable. — **likelihood,** *n.*

lik·en, *v.* to compare.

like·wise, *adv.* in like manner.

li·lac, *n.* a shrub with large clusters of fragrant purple or white flowers.

lilt, *n.* rhythmic cadence.

lil·y, *n., pl.* -ies. a bulbous plant with showy, bell-shaped flowers.

li·ma bean, a bean with a broad, flat, edible seed.

limb, *n.* 1. a part of an animal body distinct from the head and trunk, as a leg, arm, or wing. 2. a main branch of a tree.

lim·ber, *adj.* 1. bending readily; flexible; supple. —*v.* 2. limber up, to make oneself limber.

lim·bo, *n.* (*oft. cap.*) a supposed region on the border of hell or heaven.

lime[1], *n.* the oxide of calcium, used in making mortar and cement.

lime[2], *n.* a small, greenish yellow, acid fruit allied to the lemon.

lime·light, *n.* 1. (formerly) a strong light, made by heating a cylinder of lime. 2. the glare of public interest or notoriety.

lim·er·ick, *n.* a type of humorous verse of 5 lines.

lime·stone, *n.* a rock consisting of calcium carbonate.

limestone

295

limit, *n.* 1. the furthest point or boundary. –*v.* 2. to restrict by fixing limits (*to*): *to limit phone calls to 3 minutes.* – **limitation**.

limou·sine, *n.* any large, luxurious car.

limp[1], *v.* 1. to walk with difficulty, as when lame. –*n.* 2. a lame gait.

limp[2], *adj.* lacking stiffness or firmness.

limpet, *n. Zool.* a marine mollusc found adhering to rocks.

limpid, *adj.* clear.

line[1], *n., v.,* **lined, lining.** –*n.* 1. a long, very narrow mark or stroke made with a pen, etc., on a surface. 2. something like a line, as a band of colour, a seam, etc. 3. a row of written or printed letters, words, etc. 4. a verse of poetry. 5. a course of action, thought, etc.: *to agree with the party line.* 6. a chronological succession of persons or animals, esp. in family descent. 7. a kind of occupation or business: *What line are you in?* 8. any transport company or system. 9. a railway track or system. 10. *Maths.* a continuous extent of length, straight or curved, without thickness; the trace of a moving point. 11. a supply of commercial goods of the same general class. 12. the line of arrangement of an army, etc., as drawn up ready for battle. 13. a thread, string, etc. 14. a telephonic channel: *The line is busy.* –*v.* 15. to take a position in a line; queue (*up*). 16. to bring (*up*) into line with others. 17. to mark with a line.

line[2], *v.,* **lined, lining.** to apply a layer of material to the inner side of.

lin·eage, *n.* lineal descent from an ancestor.

lineal, *adj.* being in the direct line, as a descendant, ancestor, etc.

linear, *adj.* 1. extended in a line. 2. relating to a line or length.

linen, *n.* (tablecloths, etc.) made (of) fabric woven from flax.

liner, *n.* one of a commercial line of steamships or aeroplanes.

lines·man, *n., pl.* **-men.** *Sport.* an official on the sidelines who assists the referee or umpire in determining whether the ball is still in play. Also, **lineman.**

linger, *v.* 1. to remain in a place longer than is usual or expected. 2. to take more time than usual, esp. out of enjoyment: *I lingered over my cup of tea.*

lin·gerie /ˈlɒnʒəreɪ/, *n.* women's underwear.

lingo, *n., pl.* **-goes.** *Colloq.* 1. language. 2. jargon.

lin·guist, *n.* 1. a person who is skilled in foreign languages. 2. a person who specialises in linguistics.

lin·guistics, *n.* the science of language. – **linguistic**, *adj.*

lini·ment, *n.* an oily liquid for rubbing on to the skin, as for sprains, bruises, etc.

link, *n.* 1. one of the separate pieces making up a chain. 2. anything connecting one thing with another; a bond or tie. –*v.* 3. to join (as) by a link.

links, *n.pl.* a golf course.

lino·leum, *n.* a type of smooth, hard floor covering. Also, **lino.**

lin·seed, *n.* the seed of flax.

lint, *n.* a soft material for dressing wounds, etc.

lintel, *n.* a horizontal supporting

lintel

member above a window or a door. Also, **lintol**.

lion, n. a large member of the cat family, the male of which usu. has a mane. – **lioness**, n. fem.

lip, n. 1. either of the 2 fleshy parts or folds forming the margins of the mouth and performing an important function in speech. 2. a liplike part or structure. 3. any edge or rim.

lip-service, n. insincere profession of devotion or goodwill.

lip·stick, n. a cosmetic preparation for colouring the lips. Also, **lippie**.

liquefy, v., -fied, -fying. to make or become liquid.

liqueur /ləˈkjuə, ləˈkɜː/, n. a strong, sweet, and highly flavoured alcoholic liquor.

liquid, adj. 1. such as to flow like water; fluid. 2. in cash: *liquid assets*. –n. 3. a liquid substance. – **liquidity**, n.

liqui·date, v., -dated, -dating. 1. to settle or pay (a debt, etc.). 2. (of a company) to pay off debts and wind up business. 3. to convert into cash. 4. to get rid of, esp. by killing or other violent means.

liqui·dator, n. a person appointed to conclude the affairs of a company because of bankruptcy, etc.

liquor, n. spirits (as brandy or whisky) as distinguished from fermented beverages (as wine or beer).

liquo·rice, n. (an extract from) the sweet-tasting dried root of a certain plant, used in medicine, confectionery, etc.

lisp, n. 1. a speech defect consisting in pronouncing *s* and *z* like the *th* sounds of *thin* and *this*, respectively. –v. 2. to speak with a lisp.

litigant

lissom, adj. lithe; limber.

list[1], n. 1. a record consisting of a series of names, words, etc. –v. 2. to set down together in a list.

list[2], v. (of a ship) to incline to one side.

listen, v. to give attention with the ear.

list·less, adj. feeling no interest in anything.

lit, v. past tense and past participle of **light**[1] and **light**[3].

litany, n., pl. -nies. a form of prayer consisting of a series of invocations with responses from a congregation.

lit·eral, adj. 1. following the exact words, of the original, as a translation. 2. being the natural or strict meaning of the word; not figurative or metaphorical.

liter·ary, adj. relating to books and writings, esp. those classed as literature.

liter·ate, adj. 1. able to read and write. 2. educated. – **literacy**, n.

lit·era·ture, n. 1. writings in which expression and form, together with ideas of universal interest, are characteristic features, as poetry, biography, essays, etc. 2. *Colloq.* printed matter of any kind, as advertising circulars, etc.

lithe, adj. pliant; supple.

lith·ium, n. a soft silver-white metallic element, the lightest of all metals. *Symbol*: Li

lith·ography, n. the process of printing a picture, etc., from a flat surface of aluminium, zinc or stone. – **lithograph**, n.

liti·gant /ˈlɪtɪɡənt/, n. 1. one engaged in a lawsuit. –adj. 2. engaged in a lawsuit.

litigate

liti·gate, *v.*, **-gated, -gating. 1.** to contest at law. **2.** to dispute (a point, etc.). – **litigable**, *adj.* – **litigator**, *n.* – **litigation**, *n.*

litmus, *n.* a blue colouring matter which is turned red by acid solutions and blue by alkaline solutions.

litre, *n.* a unit of capacity in the metric system equal to 10^{-3} m^3 volume of water. Symbol: L

litter, *n.* **1.** scattered rubbish. **2.** a condition of disorder or untidiness. **3.** a number of young animals brought forth at one birth. **4.** a couch, often covered and curtained, carried between shafts by men or animals. –*v.* **5.** to strew (a place) with scattered objects.

litter·bug, *n.* one who drops rubbish, esp. in public places.

little, *adj.*, **less** or **lesser, least**; or **littler, littlest**; *adv.*, **less, least**; *n.* –*adj.* **1.** small in size, number or amount. **2.** short; brief. –*adv.* **3.** not at all (before a verb). **4.** rarely; infrequently. –*n.* **5.** a small amount, quantity, or degree.

lit·urgy, *n., pl.* **-gies.** a form of public worship; a ritual. – **liturgical**, *adj.*

live^1 /lɪv/, *v.*, **lived, living. 1.** to be alive, as an animal or plant. **2.** to last: *to live in one's memory.* **3.** to subsist (on or upon): *to live on potatoes.* **4.** to dwell or reside. **5.** to pass (life): *to live a happy life.*

live^2 /laɪv/, *adj.* **1.** living, or alive. **2.** characterised by the presence of living creatures. **3.** burning or glowing, as a coal. **4.** unexploded, as a cartridge or shell. **5.** *Elect.* electrically charged. **6.** (of a radio program, etc.) broadcast at the moment it is being presented at the studio.

loading

liveli·hood, *n.* means of maintaining life.

lively, *adj.*, **-lier, -liest. 1.** active, vigorous, or brisk. **2.** vivacious or spirited. **3.** eventful or exciting.

liven, *v.* to put life into; cheer (*up*).

liver, *n.* an organ secreting bile and performing various metabolic functions.

livery, *n., pl.* **-ries. 1.** a kind of uniform worn by servants. **2.** a distinctive dress worn by an official, a member of a company or guild, etc.

live·stock, *n.* the horses, cattle, sheep, etc., kept or bred on a farm.

livid, *adj.* **1.** discoloured due to bruising. **2.** enraged.

living, *adj.* **1.** alive, or not dead. –*n.* **2.** the act or condition of someone or something which lives. **3.** livelihood.

lizard, *n.* a reptile with a long body and tail and usu. short legs, as geckos, monitors, etc.

'll, a contraction of *will* or *shall*.

llama, *n.* a woolly-haired Sth American ruminant, related to the camel.

lo, *interj.* look! see! behold!

load, *n.* **1.** that which is carried on a cart, etc. **2.** anything borne or sustained: *a load of fruit on a tree.* **3.** something that weighs down: *a load on one's mind.* **4.** the amount of work required of a person, machine, etc. **5.** the weight supported by a structure or part. –*v.* **6.** to put a load on or in. **7.** to supply abundantly with something. **8.** to give emotional or other bias to: *to load a question; to load dice.* **9.** to charge (a firearm, camera, etc.)

load·ing, *n.* **1.** an extra rate paid to

loading

employees in recognition of a particular aspect of their employment, as shift work. 2. *Insurance.* an addition to the normal premium for something seen as a risk by the insurance company.

loaf[1], *n., pl.* **loaves.** 1. a portion of bread, etc., baked in a particular form. 2. a shaped mass of food, as of sugar, chopped meat, etc.

loaf[2], *v.* to lounge or saunter lazily and idly.

loaf·ers, *n.pl.* casual shoes.

loam, *n.* a loose soil composed of clay and sand.

loan, *n.* 1. something lent on condition of being returned, as money lent at interest. –*v. Colloq.* 2. to lend; make a loan of.

loath, *adj.* reluctant, or unwilling.

loathe, *v.*, **loathed, loathing.** to feel disgust, or intense hatred for. – **loathing**, *n.* – **loathsome**, *adj.*

lob, *v.*, **lobbed, lobbing.** 1. *Tennis.* to strike (a ball) high into the air. 2. to fling in a careless fashion.

lobby, *n., pl.* **-bies,** *v.*, **-bied, -bying.** –*n.* 1. a corridor, or entrance hall. 2. a group of persons who attempt to enlist popular and political support for some particular cause. –*v.* 3. to frequent the lobby of a legislative chamber to influence the members.

lobe, *n.* a roundish projection.

lo·bot·omy, *n.* the cutting into or across a lobe of the brain.

lob·ster, *n.* a large, edible, marine crustacean.

local, *adj.* 1. pertaining to or characterised by place, or position in space. 2. relating to a particular place or part.

locust

lo·cal·ity, *n., pl.* **-ties.** a place, spot, or district.

locate, *v.*, **-cated, -cating.** to discover the place or location of.

lo·ca·tion, *n.* 1. a place of business or residence. 2. *Films.* a place, outside the studio, with a suitable environment for filming plays, incidents, etc., hence, **on location**.

loch, *n. Scot.* a lake.

lock[1], *n.* 1. a device for securing a door, lid, etc., in position when closed. 2. an enclosed portion of a canal, river, etc., with gates at each end, for raising or lowering vessels from one level to another. 3. the radius of turning in the steering mechanism of a vehicle. –*v.* 4. to secure (a door, building, etc.) by the operation of a lock (*up*). 5. to restrain by shutting (*up*) in a place fastened by a lock. 6. to exclude (as) by a lock (*out*). 7. to join by interlinking or intertwining. 8. to become locked.

lock[2], *n.* a tress or portion of hair.

locker, *n.* a chest, drawer, etc., that may be locked.

locket, *n.* a small case for a miniature portrait, a lock of hair, etc., usu. worn on a chain hung round the neck.

lock·jaw, *n.* →**tetanus**.

lo·co·motion, *n.* the act of moving from place to place.

lo·co·motive, *n.* a self-propelled vehicle which pulls railway carriages, etc., along a railway track.

locum, *n.* a temporary substitute for a doctor, lawyer, etc. Also, **locum tenens**.

locus /'loʊkəs, 'loʊkəs/, *n., pl.* **loci** /'loʊki, 'loʊki/. a place; a locality.

locust, *n.* 1. a type of grasshopper

299

locust

which swarms in immense numbers and strips plants. 2. *Colloq.* →cicada.

lode, *n.* a veinlike deposit, usu. metal bearing.

lodge, *n., v.,* **lodged, lodging.** –*n.* 1. a cabin or hut. 2. a cottage, as on an estate, occupied by a caretaker, etc. 3. the meeting place of a branch of a secret society. –*v.* 4. to have or provide with living quarters, esp. temporarily. 5. to be fixed or implanted. 6. to lay (information, a complaint, etc.) before a court, etc.

loft, *n.* the space between the ceiling and the roof.

lofty, *adj.,* **-tier, -tiest.** 1. extending high in the air. 2. elevated in style or sentiment, as writings, etc. 3. haughty; proud.

log, *n., v.,* **logged, logging.** –*n.* 1. an uncut portion of the trunk or a large branch of a felled tree. 2. the official record of significant data concerning a ship's journey, a machine's operation, etc. –*v.* 3. to cut (trees) into logs. 4. to cut down trees or timber on (land). 5. to record in a log.

logan·berry, *n., pl.* **-ries.** a large, dark red, acid berry.

loga·rithm, *n.* the exponent of that power to which a fixed number (called the *base*) must be raised in order to produce a given number (called the *antilogarithm*). – **logarithmic,** *adj.*

logic, *n.* 1. the principles of reasoning applicable to any branch of knowledge or study. 2. reasons or sound sense, as in utterances or actions. – **logical,** *adj.*

logis·tics, *n.* the branch of military science concerned with the transportation, housing and supply of bodies of troops.

longitude

logo·type, *n.* a trademark or symbol designed to identify a company, organisation, etc. Also, **logo**.

loin, *n.* (*usu. pl.*) the part of the body of man or of a quadruped animal on either side of the spine, between the ribs and hipbone.

loiter, *v.* to linger idly or aimlessly in or about a place.

loll, *v.* to recline in a relaxed or lazy manner; lounge.

lolli·pop, *n.* a kind of boiled sweet, often on the end of a stick.

lollop, *v.* to move with bounding, ungainly leaps.

lolly, *n.* any sweet, esp. a boiled one.

lone, *adj.* solitary.

lonely, *adj.,* **-lier, -liest.** 1. lone; solitary. 2. without sympathetic or friendly companionship.

lone·some, *adj.* depressed by a sense of being alone.

long¹, *adj.,* **longer, longest,** *adv.* –*adj.* 1. having considerable or great extent from end to end; not short. 2. lasting a considerable or great time. 3. having a specified length in space, duration, etc.: *30 minutes long.* 4. tall. –*adv.* 5. for or through a great extent of space or, esp., time. **6. so long,** *Colloq.* goodbye.

long², *v.* to have a very strong or unceasing desire, for something not immediately (if ever) attainable.

lon·gevity /lɒn'dʒɛvəti/, *n.* long life.

long·hand, *n.* writing of the ordinary kind, in which the words are written out in full (distinguished from *shorthand*).

longi·tude, *n. Geog.* angular distance east or west on the earth's

longitude

surface, measured along the equator. – **longitudinal**, *adj.*

long·winded, *adj.* tediously wordy in speech or writing.

look, *v.* 1. to fix the eyes upon something or in some direction in order to see. 2. to glance or gaze, in a manner specified: *to look disapprovingly at someone.* 3. to use the sight in searching, examining, etc. 4. to tend, as in bearing or significance: *Conditions look towards war.* 5. to appear or seem. 6. to direct the mind or attention. 7. to afford a view: *The house looks onto the park.* 8. to face or front: *The garden looks north.* 9. **look after**, to take care of. 10. **look forward to**, to anticipate with pleasure. 11. **look in**, **a**. to take a look into a place. **b**. to come in for a brief visit. 12. **look into**, to investigate. 13. **look like**, to seem likely to. 14. **look lively** or **sharp**, to make haste; be alert. 15. **look on**, to be a mere spectator. 16. **look on the bright (the worst) side**, to consider something with optimism (with pessimism). 17. **look out**, **a**. to look forth, as from a window, etc. **b**. to be on guard. **c**. to take watchful care (*for*). 18. **look over**, to inspect or examine. 19. **look to**, **a**. to direct the glance or gaze to. 20. **look up**, to try to find; seek. –*n.* 21. the act of looking. 22. a visual search or examination. 23. way of appearing to the eye or mind: *the look of a scoundrel.* 24. (*pl.*) general appearance.

look·out, *n.* 1. (a person or group stationed to keep) watch, as for something that may happen. 2. a high place, esp. a mountain, from which one can admire the view.

loom[1], *n.* a machine for weaving yarn into a fabric.

loom[2], *v.* to come into view in indistinct and enlarged form.

loop, *n.* 1. a folding of a cord, etc., upon itself, so as to leave an opening between the parts. 2. anything shaped like a loop. –*v.* 3. to form into a loop or loops.

loop·hole, *n.* an outlet, or means of escape or evasion.

loose, *adj.*, **looser**, **loosest**, *v.*, **loosed**, **loosing**. –*adj.* 1. not bound or fettered. 2. not attached or fastened. 3. not bound together: *loose papers.* 4. not put in a package or other container. 5. lax, as the bowels. 6. not fitting closely, as garments. 7. not compact in structure or arrangement: *cloth of a loose weave.* 8. not exact, or precise: *loose thinking.* –*v.* 9. to free from bonds or restraint. 10. to unfasten. 11. to make less tight; slacken or relax. 12. to render less firmly fixed, or loosen. – **loosen**, *v.*

loot, *n.* 1. spoils or plunder. 2. *Colloq.* money. –*v.* 3. to plunder or pillage (a city, house, etc.), as in war.

lop, *v.*, **lopped**, **lopping**. to cut off (protruding parts) of a tree, etc.

lope, *v.*, **loped**, **loping**. to move or run with a long, easy stride.

lop·sided, *adj.* heavier, larger, or more developed on one side than on the other; asymmetrical.

loqua·cious, *adj.* talkative. – **loquacity**, *n.*

loquat /ˈloʊkwɒt, -kwæt/, *n.* (a small, evergreen tree bearing) a yellow plumlike fruit.

lord, *n.* 1. one who has power over others; a master, chief, or ruler. 2.

lord

a titled nobleman. –v. 3. to behave in a lordly manner; domineer: *to lord it over someone.*

Lord's Supper, n. (the sacrament of) the last meal taken by Christ with his disciples.

lore, n. the body of knowledge, esp. of a traditional, or popular nature, on a particular subject.

lori·keet, n. a small, brightly-coloured parrot.

lorry, n. →**truck**¹ (def. 1).

lose, v., lost, losing. 1. to come to be without, by some chance, and not know the whereabouts of. 2. to suffer loss (of). 3. to become separated from and ignorant of (the way, etc.). 4. to leave far behind in a chase, race, etc. 5. to fail to win (a prize, etc.). 6. to engross (oneself) in something.

loss, n. 1. disadvantage from failure to keep, have, or get: *to bear the loss of a robbery.* 2. that which is lost. 3. amount or number lost. 4. a being deprived of something that one has had. 5. a failure to win.

lot, n. 1. one of a set of objects drawn from a receptacle, etc., to decide a question by chance. 2. The decision or choice so made. 3. one's destiny. 4. a distinct portion of anything: *Our land is lot no. 49.* 5. *Colloq.* a great many or a great deal. 6. **the lot**, the entire amount or quantity.

lotion, n. a liquid medicine, etc., for applying to the skin.

lot·tery, n., pl. -teries. any scheme for the distribution of prizes by chance.

lotus, n. 1. the fruit of a plant which, according to Greek legend, induced a state of contented forgetfulness

lovebird

in those who ate it. 2. any of various water-lilies.

loud, adj. 1. striking strongly upon the organs of hearing, as sound, noise, the voice, etc. 2. showy, as colours, dress, etc.; garish.

loud·speaker, n. any of various devices by which speech, music, etc., can be made audible throughout a room, etc.

lounge, v., lounged, lounging, n. –v. 1. to pass time idly. 2. to lie back lazily; loll. –n. 3. a living room. 4. a large room in a hotel, etc., used by guests for relaxation purposes.

lour, v. 1. to be dark and threatening, as the sky or the weather. 2. to frown, scowl, or look sullen.

louse, n., pl. lice or (def. 2) louses; v., loused, lousing. –n. 1. a small, wingless, blood-sucking insect. 2. *Colloq.* a despicable person. –v. 3. **louse up**, *Colloq.* to spoil.

lousy, adj., lousier, lousiest. 1. infested with lice. 2. *Colloq.* mean, contemptible or unpleasant. 3. *Colloq.* inferior, no good.

lout, n. *Colloq.* a rough, uncouth and sometimes violent young man.

louvre, n. an arrangement of slats covering a window or other opening.

lov·able, adj. of such a nature as to attract love. Also, **loveable**.

love, n., v., loved, loving. –n. 1. a passionate affection for another person. 2. a feeling of warm personal attachment. 3. strong liking for anything. 4. *Tennis, etc.* nothing; no score. –v. 5. to have love or affection for.

love·bird, n. a small parrot; budgerigar.

lovelorn

love·lorn, *adj.* forlorn or pining from love.

lovely, *adj.*, **-lier, -liest.** charmingly or exquisitely beautiful.

lover, *n.* 1. someone who loves another, esp. a man in love with a woman. 2. a sexual partner.

lovey-dovey, *adj.* loving.

low[1], *adj.* 1. situated not far above the ground floor, or base. 2. below the general level: *low ground.* 3. relating to regions near the sea or sea-level as opposed to highland or inland regions. 4. rising only slightly from a surface. 5. feeble; weak. 6. small in amount, degree, force, etc.: *a low number.* 7. attributing no great value, or excellence: *a low opinion.* 8. depressed or dejected. 9. far down in the scale of rank or estimation; humble. 10. lacking in dignity or elevation, as of thought or expression. 11. *Biol.* having a relatively simple structure. 12. produced by relatively low vibrations, as sounds. 13. not loud. *–adv.* 14. in or to a low position, point, degree, etc. *–n.* 15. that which is low. 16. *Meteorol.* a pressure system characterised by relatively low pressure at the centre. 17. a point of least value, amount, etc.

low[2], *v.* to utter the sound characteristic of cattle.

lowboy, *n.* a piece of furniture, not as tall as a wardrobe, for holding clothes.

low·down, *n. Colloq.* the unadorned facts on some subject.

lower, *adj.* 1. comparative of **low**[1]. *v.* 2. to reduce in amount, price, degree, force, etc. 3. to cause to descend, or let down.

lull

lower case, *n.* the small letters of the alphabet. *Abbrev.*: l.c.

low-key, *adj.* underplayed; restrained.

lowly, *adj.*, **-lier, -liest.** humble.

low profile, *n.* a low-keyed, uncommitted policy or reticent style of behaviour.

loyal, *adj.* 1. faithful to the duty owed to one's king, country, etc. 2. faithful to one's obligations.

loz·enge, *n.* a small flavoured sweet, often medicated.

lubri·cate, *v.*, **-cated, cating.** to apply some grease in order to diminish friction. – **lubricant**, *n.* – **lubrication**, *n.*

lu·cerne /ˈlusən/, *n.* a plant used as feed for animals.

lucid, *adj.* 1. shining or bright. 2. clear.

luck, *n.* 1. that which happens to a person, either good or bad, as if by chance. 2. good fortune. – **lucky**, *adj.*

lucra·tive, *adj.* profitable; remunerative.

lucre, *n.* money as the object of sordid desire.

ludi·crous, *adj.* causing laughter or scorn; ridiculous.

lug, *v.* **lugged, lugging.** to pull along or carry with effort.

lug·gage, *n.* suitcases, etc., used in travelling; baggage.

lugu·bri·ous, *adj.* mournful; doleful; dismal.

luke·warm, *adj.* 1. moderately warm; tepid. 2. not enthusiastic; indifferent.

lull, *v.* 1. to soothe or quiet, as into sleep. *–n.* 2. a temporary quiet or stillness.

lullaby

lul·la·by, *n.* a song intended to put a baby to sleep.

lumbar, *adj.* of or pertaining to the loin(s).

lumber[1], *n.* **1.** timber split into planks, boards, etc. –*v.* **2.** to cut timber and prepare it for market. **3.** to fill with various useless articles. **4.** *Colloq.* to leave (somebody) with (something or someone unpleasant).

lumber[2], *v.* to move clumsily or heavily.

lumber·jack, *Chiefly U.S. and Canada. n.* one who cuts and prepares timber.

lumi·nary, *n., pl.* **-naries. 1.** a celestial body, as the sun or moon. **2.** a person whose knowledge, etc., enlightens mankind.

lumi·nescence, *n.* an emission of light without the production of heat (opp. to *incandescence*). – **luminescent**, *adj.*

lumi·nous, *adj.* **1.** radiating or reflecting light; shining. **2.** well lighted. **3.** clear; readily intelligible. – **luminosity**, *n.*

lump[1], *n.* **1.** a mass of solid matter without regular shape. –*v.* **2.** to unite into one collection, or mass.

lump[2], *v. Colloq.* to put up with (a disagreeable necessity).

lunacy, *n., pl.* **-cies.** insanity. – **lunatic**, *n., adj.*

lunar, *adj.* relating to the moon.

lunch, *n.* **1.** a meal taken at around midday. –*v.* **2.** to eat lunch.

lunch·eon, *n.* (a formal) lunch.

lung, *n.* either of the 2 saclike respiratory organs in the chest of man and the higher vertebrates.

lunge[1], *n., v.,* lunged, lunging. –*n.* **1.** a thrust, as in fencing. –*v.* **2.** to make a lunge.

lunge[2], *n.* a long rope used to guide a horse during training or exercise.

lupine, *adj.* relating to or resembling the wolf.

lurch[1], *v.* **1.** a sudden leaning to one side, as of a ship or a staggering person. –*v.* **2.** to make a lurch; stagger.

lurch[2], *n.* the position of one in a helpless plight.

lure, *n., v.,* lured, luring. –*n.* **1.** anything that attracts or entices. –*v.* **2.** to decoy; entice; allure.

lurid, *adj.* **1.** glaringly vivid or sensational. **2.** unnatural or ghastly in hue.

lurk, *v.* **1.** to remain in a place secretly. –*n. Colloq.* **2.** a convenient, often unethical, method of performing a task, earning a living, etc.

lus·cious, *adj.* **1.** highly pleasing to the taste or smell. **2.** very luxurious; extremely attractive.

lush[1], *adj.* **1.** succulent or luxuriant, as plants. **2.** *Colloq.* characterised by luxury and comfort.

lush[2], *n.* one who drinks too much alcohol.

lust, *n.* **1.** passionate or overmastering desire, esp. sexual. –*v.* **2.** to have strong or inordinate desire, esp. sexual (*for* or *after*).

lustre, *n.* glitter, or gloss. – **lustrous**, *adj.*

lusty, *adj.,* **-tier, -tiest.** full of healthy vigour.

lute, *n.* a stringed musical instrument. – **lutenist**, *n.*

lux·uri·ant, *adj.* abundant in growth, as vegetation.

lux·uri·ate, *v.,* **-ated, -ating. 1.** to

luxuriate

indulge in luxury; revel. 2. to take great delight.

luxury, *n.* anything conducive to sumptuous, elegant living, which is not a necessity. – **luxurious**, *adj.*

lymph, *n.* a clear, yellowish fluid derived from the tissues of the body and conveyed via the lymph glands to the bloodstream. – **lymphatic**, *adj.*

lymph gland, *n.* a glandlike body, e.g. the tonsils, where antibodies and white blood cells are produced.

lynch, *v.* to put (a person) to death without authority or process of law. – **lynching**, *n.*

lyricist

lynx, *n.*, *pl.* **lynxes**, (*esp. collectively*) **lynx**. any of various wildcats having long limbs and short tail.

lyre, *n.* a stringed musical instrument of ancient Greece.

lyre·bird, *n.* either of 2 ground-dwelling birds of sth-east Aust., the males of which have long tails, spread in mating displays.

lyric, *adj.* Also, **lyrical**. 1. (of poetry) having the form and musical quality of a song. 2. relating to or using singing. –*n.* 3. a lyric poem. 4. (*oft. pl.*) the words of a song.

lyri·cist, *n.* one who writes the words for songs.

Mm

M, m, *n., pl.* **M's** or **Ms, m's** or **ms.** the 13th letter of the English alphabet.
mac·abre /məˈkabə, -brə/, *adj.* gruesome; horrible; grim; ghastly.
maca·damia nut, *n.* a small tree which bears edible hard-shelled nuts.
mac·a·roni, *n.* a kind of pasta.
mac·a·roon, *n.* a sweet cake or biscuit, usu. with coconut.
macaw, *n.* a large, brightly-coloured parrot with a harsh voice.
mace, *n.* 1. *Hist.* a clublike weapon. 2. a staff borne as a symbol of office.
macer·ate, *v.,* -rated, -rating. 1. to soften by steeping in a liquid. 2. to cause to grow thin.
machete /məˈʃeti/, *n.* a large, heavy knife.
machi·nate, *v.,* -nated, -nating. to contrive or devise, esp. artfully or with evil purpose.
mach·ine, *n., v.,* -chined, -chining. –*n.* 1. an apparatus consisting of interrelated parts with separate functions, which is used in the performance of some kind of work. 2. a device which transmits and modifies force or motion. –*v.* 3. to make, prepare, or finish with a machine.
machine-gun, *n.* a gun able to fire rapidly and continuously.
machin·ery, *n., pl.* -ries. 1. machines or mechanical apparatus. 2. the parts of a machine, collectively.
mach·ismo /məˈtʃizmoʊ, məˈkɪzmoʊ/, *n.* masculine display emphasising strength.
macho /ˈmætʃoʊ, ˈmækoʊ/, *n.* 1. a man who displays machismo. –*adj.* 2. showily virile.
mack·erel, *n.* a common food fish.
mack·in·tosh, *n.* a raincoat.
macramé, *n.* ornamental ware made by knotting thread or cord in patterns.
mad, *adj.,* madder, maddest. disordered in intellect; insane.
madam, *n., pl.* madams, mesdames. 1. a polite term of address to a woman. 2. the woman in charge of a brothel.
made, *v.* 1. past tense and past participle of **make.** –*adj.* 2. assured of success or fortune.
madeira, *n.* a rich, strong, white wine.
madri·gal, *n.* an unaccompanied part-song.
mael·strom, *n.* a restless confusion of affairs, influence, etc.
maes·tro, *n., pl.* -tri. an eminent musical composer, teacher, or conductor.
maga·zine, *n.* 1. a periodical publication. 2. a place for keeping gunpowder, etc. 3. a metal receptacle for a number of cartridges. 4. a light-proof enclosure containing film.
magenta, *n., adj.* reddish purple.
maggot, *n.* the legless larva of a fly.
magic, *n.* 1. the producing of effects claimed to be beyond the natural. 2. any extraordinary or irresistible influence. 3. a conjuring. –*adj.* 4. of, pertaining to, or due to magic.

magisterial

magis·terial, *adj.* 1. of or befitting a magistrate or his office. 2. authoritative.

mag·is·trate, *n.* a justice of the peace who officiates in a magistrate's court.

magma, *n.* molten rock under the earth's crust.

mag·nanimous, *adj.* generous in forgiving. **– magnanimity,** *n.*

mag·nate, *n.* a person of eminence or distinction in any field.

mag·nesium, *n.* a light, ductile, silver-white metallic element used in lightweight alloys. *Symbol:* Mg

magnet, *n.* 1. a body (as a piece of iron or steel) which possesses the property of attracting certain substances. 2. a thing or person that attracts. **– magnetic,** *adj.*

magnetic north, *n.* the direction in which the needle of a compass points, differing in most places from true north.

magnetic tape, *n.* a plastic tape used to record sound, video signals, digital information, etc.

magne·tism, *n.* 1. (the science of) phenomena associated with magnetic fields. 2. charm or power of attraction.

mag·neto /mæg'ni:tou/, *n., pl.* **-tos.** a small electric generator, the poles of which are permanent magnets.

magnifi·cation, *n.* 1. a magnified copy or reproduction. 2. (of an optical instrument) the ratio of the linear dimensions of the final image to that of the object.

mag·nifi·cent, *adj.* extraordinarily fine.

mag·nify, *v.,* **-fied, -fying.** 1. to increase the apparent size of, as a lens does. 2. to make greater in size; enlarge.

mag·ni·tude, *n.* 1. size; extent. 2. great amount, importance, etc..

mag·no·lia, *n.* a shrub or tree with large fragrant flowers.

magnum, *n., pl.* **-nums.** a bottle for wine or spirits, holding about 2.25 litres.

magpie, *n.* a common black and white bird.

mah-jong, *n.* a game of Chinese origin, with 136 domino-like pieces or tiles. Also, **mah-jongg.**

mahog·any, *n., pl.* **-nies.** 1. any of certain tropical American trees yielding a hard, reddish brown wood. 2. a reddish brown colour.

maid, *n.* 1. a girl; unmarried woman. 2. a female servant.

maiden, *n.* 1. a girl; young unmarried woman; virgin. **–***adj.* 2. made, tried, appearing, etc., for the first time.

maiden name, *n.* a woman's surname before marriage.

maiden over, *n.* (in cricket) an over in which no runs are made.

mail¹, *n.* 1. letters, packages, etc., carried by post. 2. the system of sending letters, etc., by post. **–***adj.* 3. of or pertaining to mail. **–***v.* 4. to send by mail; place in a post office or postbox for sending.

mail², *n.* flexible armour of interlinked rings.

maim, *v.* 1. to mutilate; cripple. 2. to impair; make defective.

main, *adj.* 1. chief; principal; leading. **–***n.* 2. a principal water or gas pipe. 3. strength; force; violent effort. 4. the chief or principal part or point.

main·land, *n.* the principal land

mainland

mass as distinguished from nearby islands and peninsulas.

main·stream, *n.* the dominant trend; chief tendency.

main·tain, *v.* 1. to keep in existence; preserve. 2. to affirm; assert.

main·te·nance, *n.* 1. the act of maintaining. 2. *Law.* the money paid for the support of the other spouse or infant children, usu. after divorce.

maize, *n.* a cereal plant bearing grain in large ears.

ma·jes·tic, *adj.* inspiring awe or reverence.

maj·es·ty, *n., pl.* **-ties.** 1. supreme greatness or authority; sovereignty. 2. (*usu. cap.*) a title used when speaking of or to a sovereign (prec. by *his, her, your,* etc.).

ma·jor, *adj.* 1. greater, as in size, amount, extent, importance, rank, etc. 2. of full legal age. –*n.* 3. a principal field of study chosen by a student.

ma·jor·i·ty, *n., pl.* **-ties.** 1. the greater part or number. 2. the state or time of being of full legal age.

make, *v.,* made, making, *n.* –*v.* 1. to produce by any action or causative agency. 2. to cause to be or become; render. 3. to put into proper condition for use. 4. to cause, induce, or compel (to do something). 5. to do; effect. 6. to become by development; prove to be. 7. to estimate; reckon. 8. to arrive at or reach. 9. to arrive in time for. 10. to pursue the course: *to make for home.* 11. **make a face**, to grimace. 12. **make believe**, to pretend. 13. **make do**, to operate or carry on using minimal or improvised resources. 14. **make love**, *Colloq.* to have sexual intercourse. 15. **make out**, **a.** to discern;

malice

decipher. **b.** to present as; impute to be. 16. **make up**, **a.** to put together; construct; compile. **b.** to compensate for. **c.** to bring to a definite conclusion, as one's mind. **d.** to apply cosmetics to, as the face. **e.** Also, **make it up**. to become reconciled after a quarrel. –*n.* 17. style or manner of being made; form; build.

make·shift, *adj., n.* (being) a temporary expedient; substitute

make-up, *n.* 1. cosmetics. 2. the manner of being made up or put together; composition. 3. physical or mental constitution.

makings, *n.pl.* material of which something may be made.

mal·a·dy, *n., pl.* **-dies.** a bodily disorder or disease.

mal·a·prop·ism, *n.* a word ridiculously misused.

ma·lar·ia, *n.* a disease characterised by attacks of chills, fever, and sweating.

mal·con·tent, *adj.* 1. dissatisfied, esp. with the existing administration; inclined to rebellion. –*n.* 2. a malcontent person.

male, *adj.* 1. belonging to the sex which begets young. 2. pertaining to or characteristic of this sex; masculine. –*n.* 3. a male person or animal.

mal·e·vo·lent /məˈlɛvələnt/, *adj.* wishing evil to another or others; showing ill will.

mal·for·ma·tion, *n.* faulty or anomalous formation or structure, esp. in a living body. – **malformed**, *adj.*

mal·ice, *n.* 1. desire to inflict injury or suffering on another. 2. *Law.* evil intent on the part of one who

308

malice

commits a wrongful act injurious to others.

ma·lign, v. 1. to speak ill of; slander. 2. to speak contemptuously to. –adj. 3. malevolent.

ma·lig·nant, adj. very dangerous; harmful in influence or effect.

mal·in·ger, v. to feign sickness or injury, esp. in order to avoid work, etc.

mall /mɔl, mæl/, n. 1. a shaded walk, usu. public. 2. a shopping complex.

mallard, n. a kind of large wild duck.

mal·le·a·ble, adj. 1. capable of being extended or shaped by hammering or by pressure with rollers. 2. adaptable or tractable.

mallet, n. a hammer-like tool.

mal·nu·tri·tion, n. unhealthy condition resulting from lack of nourishing food.

mal·prac·tice, n. improper professional action.

malt, n. germinated grain (usu. barley), used in brewing and distilling.

mal·treat, v. to handle roughly or cruelly; abuse.

mamba, n. venomous African snake.

mambo, n. dance of Haitian origin resembling the rumba and cha-cha.

mammal, n. a member of the class of vertebrates whose young feed upon milk from the mother's breast. – **mammalian**, adj.

mam·mary, adj. of or pertaining to the breast.

mam·moth, n. 1. a large, extinct elephant. –adj. 2. huge; gigantic.

man, n., pl. **men**, v., **manned**, **manning**. –n. 1. the human race; mankind. 2. a human being; a person. 3. the adult male human being. 4. a male servant; a valet. 5. one of the pieces used in playing certain games, as chess or draughts. –v. 6. to furnish with men, as for service or defence. 7. to take one's place for service, as at a gun, post, etc.

manganese

man·a·cle, n., v., -cled, -cling. –n. (usu. pl.) 1. a shackle for the hand; handcuff. 2. a restraint. –v. 3. to handcuff.

manage, v., -aged, -aging. 1. to bring about; succeed in accomplishing. 2. to take charge or care of. 3. to contrive to get along. 4. to direct or control affairs.

man·age·ment, n. 1. the act or manner of managing. 2. the person or persons managing an institution, business, etc.

man·ager, n. one charged with the management or direction of an institution, business, or entertainer. – **managerial**, adj.

man·da·rin, n. a small, flattish citrus fruit.

man·date, n. 1. a commission given to a nation by a group such as the League of Nations, to administer a backward territory. 2. *Politics*. the instruction as to policy given or supposed to be given by electors to a legislative body.

man·da·tory, adj. obligatory.

man·dible, n. the bone of the lower jaw.

man·do·lin, n. a musical instrument with a pear-shaped wooden body and metal strings.

mane, n. the long hair growing on the back of or about the neck of some animals.

man·ga·nese, n. a hard, brittle, greyish white metallic element used in alloys. *Symbol*: Mn

309

mange

mange, *n.* a skin disease characterised by loss of hair and scabby eruptions. – **mangy**, *adj.*

manger, *n.* a box or trough from which horses or cattle eat.

mangle[1], *v.*, **-gled**, **-gling**. to cut, slash, or crush so as to disfigure.

mangle[2], *n.* a machine for pressing water out of cloth by means of rollers.

mango, *n., pl.* **-goes**, **-gos**. the oval yellow fruit of a tropical tree.

man·grove, *n.* a tree found in subtropical and tropical countries on salt or brackish mud-flats.

man·handle, *v.*, **-dled**, **-dling**. to handle roughly.

man·hole, *n.* a hole, usu. with a cover, through which a man may enter a sewer, drain, etc.

mania, *n.* **1.** great excitement or enthusiasm; craze. **2.** a form of insanity. – **manic**, *adj.*

maniac, *n.* a lunatic or madman.

mani·cure, *n.* (professional) care of the hands and fingernails.

mani·fest, *adj.* **1.** readily perceived by the eye or the understanding. –*v.* **2.** to make manifest. –*n.* **3.** a list of goods or cargo carried by a ship, truck, etc. – **manifestation**, *n.*

mani·festo, *n., pl.* **-tos** or **-toes**. a public declaration making known intentions, objects, motives, etc.

mani·fold, *adj.* **1.** of many kinds, numerous and varied. **2.** having many different parts, elements, features, forms, etc. **3.** a pipe or chamber with a number of inlets or outlets. –*v.* **4.** to make copies of, as with carbon paper.

manip·ulate, *v.*, **-lated**, **-lating**. **1.** to handle or use. **2.** to adapt or change (accounts, figures, etc.) to suit one's purpose or advantage.

man·kind, *n.* the human race.

manly, *adj.* displaying so-called masculine virtues.

man·ne·quin, *n.* **1.** a model of the human figure for displaying or fitting clothes. **2.** →**model** (def. 4).

manner, *n.* **1.** way of doing, being done, or happening. **2.** (*pl.*) ways of behaving. **3.** kind; sort.

manner·ism, *n.* a habitual peculiarity of manner.

man·oeuvre, *n., v.*, **-vred**, **-vring**. –*n.* **1.** a planned and regulated movement of troops, war vessels, etc. –*v.* **2.** to manipulate with skill or adroitness. **3.** to perform a manoeuvre. **4.** to scheme; intrigue.

manor, *n. Brit.* (the main house on) a country estate.

manse, *n.* the house and land occupied by a minister or parson.

man·sion, *n.* an imposing house.

man·slaughter, *n. Law.* the killing of a human being unlawfully but without malice (def. 1).

mantel·piece, *n.* the structure around a fireplace.

mantel·shelf, *n.* the projecting part of a mantelpiece.

mantis, *n., pl.* **-tises**, **-tes**. an insect which holds the forelegs doubled up as if in prayer. Also, **praying mantis**.

mantle, *n.* **1.** Also, **mantua**. a loose, sleeveless cloak. **2.** something that covers, envelops, or conceals. **3.** the middle layer of the earth.

manual, *adj.* **1.** of or pertaining to the hand or hands. **2.** using or involving human energy, power, etc. –*n.* **3.** a book, giving information or instructions.

manufacture

manu·fac·ture, *n.*, *v.*, **-tured, -turing.** *–n.* 1. the making of goods or wares by manufacturing. *–v.* 2. to make or produce by hand or machinery, esp. on a large scale. 3. to invent fictitiously; concoct.

manure, *n.* excrement, esp. of animals, used as fertiliser.

manu·script, *n.* 1. a book, document, letter, musical score, etc., written by hand. 2. an author's copy of his work, used as the basis for typesetting. 3. writing, as distinguished from print.

many, *adj.*, **more, most.** 1. constituting or forming a large number. 2. relatively numerous (prec. by *as, so, too,* or *how*): *How many books are there?* 3. each of a large number (*a* or *an*): *Many a man has failed.* *–n.* 4. a great number. 5. (as a collective plural) many persons or things.

map, *n.* a representation of the earth's surface, the heavens, etc.

maple, *n.* a Nthn Hemisphere tree from which maple syrup is made.

mar, *v.*, **marred, marring.** to damage; impair; spoil.

mara·thon, *n.* a long-distance race.

maraud, *v.* to rove in quest of plunder.

marble, *n.* 1. a crystalline limestone much used in sculpture and architecture. 2. something hard, cold or smooth. 3. *Games.* **a.** a little ball of glass, etc., used in a children's game. **b.** (pl. construed as sing.) the game itself. *–adj.* 4. consisting of marble. 5. like marble, as being hard, cold, unfeeling, etc. 6. of variegated or mottled colour. *–v.* 7. to colour or stain like a variegated marble.

march, *v.* 1. to (cause to) walk with regular tread, as soldiers. 2. to proceed; advance. *–n.* 3. the act or course of marching. 4. a piece of music with a marching rhythm.

mare, *n.* a female horse.

marga·rine, *n.* a butter-like product made from refined vegetable or animal oils.

margin, *n.* 1. a border or edge. 2. *Comm.* the difference between the cost and the selling price. – **marginal**, *adj.*

mari·gold, *n.* a golden-flowered plant.

mari·juana /mærə'wanə/, *n.* the dried leaves and flowers of Indian hemp, used in cigarettes as a narcotic and intoxicant. Also, **marihuana**.

mari·nade, *n.* a liquid, esp. wine or vinegar with oil and seasonings, in which meat, fish, vegetables, etc., may be steeped before cooking.

mari·nate, *v.*, **-nated, -nating.** to let stand in a liquid before cooking or serving in order to impart flavour.

marine, *adj.* 1. of or pertaining to the sea. 2. pertaining to navigation or shipping.

mari·ner /'mærənə/, *n.* a sailor; seaman.

mari·tal, *adj.* of or pertaining to marriage.

mari·time, *adj.* of or pertaining to the sea.

mark, *n.* 1. a visible trace or impression upon anything. 2. a sign, token, or indication. 3. a symbol used in rating conduct, proficiency, attainment, etc., as of pupils in a school. 4. something aimed at, as a target. *–v.* 5. to be a distinguishing feature of. 6. to put a mark or marks on. 7. to indicate

mark

or designate by or as by marks. 8. to notice, observe, or consider. 9. **mark down/up**, to reduce/increase the price of.

market, n. 1. a (place for a) meeting of people for selling and buying, esp. of food. 2. a body of persons dealing in a specified commodity. 3. demand for a commodity. -v. 4. to buy or sell in a market.

market·able, adj. readily saleable.

market research, n. the gathering of information by a firm about the preferences, purchasing powers, etc., of consumers.

marlin, n. a large, powerful gamefish.

mar·ma·lade, n. a jelly-like citrus preserve.

marmot, n. a bushy-tailed, thickset rodent.

maroon¹ /məˈroon, məˈrun/, n. 1. dark brownish red. -adj. 2. of a dark brownish red colour.

maroon² məˈrun/, v. to put ashore and leave on a desolate island or coast.

mar·quee, n. a large tent or tentlike shelter, sometimes with open sides.

mar·riage, n. 1. the legal union of a man with a woman for life. 2. any close union.

married, adj. united in marriage; wedded.

marrow, n. 1. a soft, fatty, vascular tissue inside bones. 2. an elongated fruit used as a cooked vegetable.

marry, v., -ried, -rying. 1. to take in marriage. 2. to unite in marriage.

mar·sala, n. a sweet, dark, fortified wine.

marsh, n. a tract of low, wet land.

mar·shal, n., v., -shalled, -shalling. -n. 1. the title of various officials

masochism

having certain police duties. -v. 2. to arrange in an orderly manner.

marsh·mallow, n. a confection with an elastic, spongy texture.

mar·su·pial, n. any member of the order which includes all non-placental mammals such as kangaroos, wombats, possums, etc.

mart, n. market.

mar·tial, adj. pertaining to or appropriate for war.

mar·ti·net /matəˈnɛt/, n. a rigid disciplinarian, esp. a military one.

mar·ti·ni, n. a type of cocktail.

martyr, n. one who is put to death or endures great suffering for any belief, principle, or cause.

marvel, n., v., -velled, -velling. -n. 1. something that arouses wonder or admiration. -v. 2. to wonder (at).

mar·vel·lous, adj. 1. wonderful; surprising; extraordinary. 2. excellent; superb. 3. improbable or incredible.

mar·zi·pan, n. a confection made of almond paste.

mas·cara, n. a substance used as a cosmetic to colour the eyelashes.

mascot, n. a person, animal, or thing supposed to bring good luck.

mas·cu·line, adj. pertaining to or characteristic of a man.

mash, n. 1. a soft, pulpy mass. 2. mashed potatoes. -v. 3. to reduce to a soft, pulpy mass.

mask, n. 1. a disguise or protection for the face. 2. a disguise; pretence. -v. 3. to disguise or conceal.

maso·chism, n. a condition in which one compulsively seeks, and sometimes derives pleasure from, suffering.

mason, *n.* one who builds or works with stone. – **masonry**, *n.*

maso·nite, *n.* a kind of wood-fibre material, pressed in sheets and used for partitions, insulation, etc.

mas·que·rade, *n., v.,* **-raded, -rading.** –*n.* **1.** a party at which everyone wears a mask. **2.** disguise, or false outward show. –*v.* **3.** to disguise oneself.

mass[1], *n.* **1.** a body of coherent matter, usu. large and of indefinite shape. **2.** an aggregation of particles, parts, or objects regarded as forming one body. **3. the masses,** the common people. –*v.* **4.** to come or gather together; assemble.

mass[2], *n. Rom. Cath. Ch., etc.* the celebration of the Eucharist.

mass·acre, *n., v.,* **-cred, -cring.** –*n.* **1.** the unnecessary, indiscriminate slaughter of human beings. –*v.* **2.** to kill indiscriminately or in large numbers.

mas·sage, *n., v.,* **-saged, -saging.** –*n.* **1.** the act or art of treating the body by rubbing, kneading, etc. –*v.* **2.** to treat by massage.

mas·seur, *n.* a man who practises massage. – **masseuse**, *n. fem.*

mas·sive, *adj.* consisting of or forming a large mass; bulky and heavy.

mass media, *n.* the means of communication, as radio, television, newspapers, magazines, etc., that reach large numbers of people. Also, **the media.**

mass-produce, *v.,* **-duced, -ducing.** to manufacture in large quantities by standardised mechanical processes.

mast, *n.* a tall spar which supports the yards, sails, etc., of a ship.

mas·tec·tomy, *n., pl.* **-mies.** the operation of removing a breast.

master, *n.* **1.** one who has the power of controlling, using, or disposing of something. **2.** the male head of a household. **3.** a workman qualified to teach apprentices and to carry on his trade independently. **4.** the head teacher in a particular subject department in a secondary school. –*adj.* **5.** being master. **6.** chief or principal. –*v.* **7.** to conquer or subdue. **8.** to rule or direct as master. **9.** to make oneself master of. – **mastery**, *n.*

master·piece, *n.* a consummate example of skill or excellence of any kind.

master·stroke, *n.* a masterly action or achievement.

mas·ti·cate, *v.* **-cated, -cating.** to chew.

mas·tur·bation, *n.* the stimulation by friction of the genitals, resulting in orgasm. – **masturbate**, *v.*

mat, *n., v.,* **matted, matting.** –*n.* **1.** a piece of fabric made of plaited or woven fibre, used to cover a floor, to wipe the shoes on, etc. **2.** a small piece of material, often ornamental, set under a dish of food, a lamp, vase, etc. **3.** a tangled mass. –*v.* **4.** to form into a mat, as by interweaving. **5.** to form tangled masses.

mata·dor, *n.* the bullfighter who kills the bull in a bullfight.

match[1], *n.* a short, slender piece of wood or other material tipped with a chemical substance which produces fire when rubbed on a rough surface.

match[2], *n.* **1.** an equal or likeness. **2.** a contest or game. **3.** a matrimonial compact or alliance. –v. 4. to equal, or be equal (to). 5. to (make to) correspond; adapt. 6. to fit together, as 2 things.

mate, n., v., **mated, mating.** –n. 1. one of a pair, esp. of mated animals. 2. **a.** a friend. **b.** (a form of address amongst men). 3. an assistant to a tradesman. –v. 4. to join as a mate or as mates. 5. (of animals) to copulate.

ma·ter·ial, n. 1. the substance of which a thing is made or composed. 2. information, ideas, or the like on which a report, thesis, etc., is based. 3. a textile fabric. –adj. 4. formed or consisting of matter; physical; corporeal. 5. pertaining to the physical rather than the spiritual or intellectual aspect of things. 6. pertinent or essential (to).

materi·al·ise, v., **-lised, -lising.** 1. to assume material or bodily form. 2. to come into perceptible existence; appear.

materi·al·ist, n. one absorbed in material interests. – **materialistic,** adj.

mat·er·nal, adj. 1. of or pertaining to a mother. 2. related through a mother.

mat·er·nity, n. motherhood.

math·emat·ics, n. the science that treats of the measurement, properties, and relations of quantities, including arithmetic, geometry, algebra, etc. – **mathematician,** n. – **mathematical,** adj.

maths, n. →**mathematics.**

mati·nee, n. an entertainment held in the daytime.

matri·arch, n. a woman holding a position of leadership in a family or tribe.

mat·rices, n. a plural form of **matrix.**

matri·cu·late, v., **-lated, -lating.** to pass matriculation.

matri·cu·la·tion, n. a secondary-school examination that qualifies for admission to a tertiary education institution.

matri·mony, n., pl. **-nies.** the rite, ceremony, or sacrament of marriage. – **matrimonial,** adj.

matrix, n., pl. **matrices, matrixes.** 1. that which gives origin or form to a thing, or which serves to enclose it. 2. Maths, Computers. a rectangular array of numbers.

matron, n. 1. a married woman. 2. a woman in charge of the domestic arrangements in a school, prison, etc. 3. a woman in charge of nursing, etc. in a hospital.

matt, adj. lustreless and dull in surface.

matter, n. 1. the substance of which physical objects consist or are composed. 2. importance or significance. 3. a topic, subject, or item. 4. **the matter,** the trouble or difficulty. –v. 5. to be of importance; signify.

matter-of-fact, adj. adhering to actual facts; not imaginative; commonplace.

mat·tock, n. an instrument for loosening soil.

mat·tress, n. a case filled with soft material, often reinforced with springs, used as or on a bed.

mature, adj., v., **-tured, -turing.** –adj. 1. complete in natural growth or development. –v. 2. to make or become mature; ripen. – **maturity,** n.

maud·lin, adj. tearfully or weakly emotional or sentimental.

maul

maul, *v.* to handle roughly; to injure by rough treatment.

mauso·le·um, *n., pl.* **-leums, -lea.** 1. a stately and magnificent tomb. 2. *Colloq.* a large, old, gloomy building.

mauve /mouv/, *n.* 1. pale bluish purple. –*adj.* 2. of the colour of mauve.

maw, *n.* 1. the mouth, throat, or gullet of an animal. 2. the stomach.

mawk·ish, *adj.* sickly or slightly nauseating: *mawkish sentimentality.*

maxim, *n.* an expression, esp. an aphoristic or sententious one, of a general truth, esp. as to conduct.

maxi·mise, *v.,* **-mised, -mising.** to increase to the greatest possible amount or degree.

maxi·mum, *n., pl.* **-ma, -mums.** *adj., n.* (being) the greatest quantity or amount possible, assignable, allowable, etc.

may, *v., p.t.* **might.** used as an auxiliary to express: **a.** possibility, opportunity, or permission. **b.** wish or prayer. **c.** contingency, esp. in clauses expressing condition, concession, purpose, result, etc.

maybe, *adv.* perhaps.

mayhem, *n.* 1. *Law.* the crime of violently inflicting a bodily injury. 2. any tumult, fracas, or fight.

may·on·naise, *n.* a thick dressing used for salads or vegetables.

mayor, *n.* the principal officer of a municipality; the chief magistrate of a city or borough. –**mayoress** *fem.*

maze, *n.* a confusing network of intercommunicating paths or passages; labyrinth.

means test

me, *pers. pron.* objective case of the pronoun *I*.

mead, *n.* an alcoholic liquor made by fermenting honey and water.

meadow, *n. Chiefly Brit.* a piece of grassland.

meagre, *adj.* deficient in quantity or quality.

meal[1], *n.* food eaten at regular times of the day.

meal[2], *n.* the edible part of a grain ground to a (coarse) powder.

mealy-mouthed, *adj.* avoiding the use of plain language, as from timidity, excessive delicacy, or hypocrisy.

mean[1], *v.,* **meant, meaning.** 1. to have in the mind as in intention or purpose. 2. to intend for a particular purpose, destination, etc. 3. (of words, things, etc.) to signify. 4. to be minded or disposed; have intentions. –**meaning,***n.*

mean[2], *adj.* 1. inferior in grade, quality or character. 2. penurious, stingy, or miserly. 3. *Colloq.* powerful, effective.

mean[3], *n.* 1. (usu. pl. but oft. construed as sing.) an agency, instrumentality, method, etc., used to attain an end. 2. (*pl.*) disposable (money) resources. 3. *Maths.* a quantity having a value intermediate between the values of other quantities; an average. –*adj.* 4. occupying a middle position.

meander /mi'ændə/, *v.* to proceed by a winding course.

mean·ing, *n.* something which is intended to be, or is, said or shown; significance; import.

means test, *n.* an evaluation of the income and resources of a person,

means test

in order to determine eligibility for a pension, grant, allowance, etc.

mean·time, *n.* **1.** the intervening time. *–adv.* **2.** meanwhile.

mean·while, *adv.* in the intervening time; at the same time.

meas·les, *n.* an acute infectious disease occurring mostly in children.

meas·ly, *adj.*, **-lier, -liest.** *Colloq.* wretchedly poor or unsatisfactory; very small.

measure, *n., v.*, **-ured, -uring.** *–n.* **1.** size, dimensions, quantity, etc. **2.** a unit or standard of measurement. **3.** a system of measurement. **4.** any standard of comparison, estimation, or judgment. **5.** an action intended as a means to an end. *–v.* **6.** to ascertain the extent, capacity, etc., of, esp by comparison with a standard. **7.** to mark (*off*) or deal (*out*) in a certain quantity. **8.** to take measurements. **9.** to be of a specified size, quantity, etc.

meat, *n.* **1.** the flesh of animals as used for food. **2.** the edible part of a fruit, nut, etc. **3.** the main substance of something, as an argument.

me·chan·ic, *n.* a skilled worker with tools or machines.

me·chan·i·cal, *adj.* **1.** having to do with machinery. **2.** pertaining to, or controlled or effected by, physical forces.

me·chan·ics, *n.* **1.** the branch of knowledge concerned with machinery. **2.** the science dealing with the action of forces on bodies and with motion.

mech·a·nise, *v.*, **-nised, -nising.** to introduce machinery into (an industry, etc.).

meditate

mech·a·nism, *n.* **1.** the machinery, or the agencies or means, by which a particular effect is produced or a purpose is accomplished. **2.** the way in which a thing works or operates.

medal, *n.* a flat piece of inscribed metal, given as a reward for bravery, merit, etc. – **medallist**, *n.*

me·dal·lion, *n.* a large medal.

meddle, *v.*, **-dled, -dling.** to concern oneself with or in something without warrant or necessity; interfere.

media, *n.* **1.** a plural of **medium**. **2.** →**mass media**.

me·dial, *adj.* situated in or pertaining to the middle.

me·dian, *adj.* **1.** situated in or pertaining to the middle. *–n.* **2.** the middle number in a given sequence of numbers.

median strip, a dividing area, often raised or landscaped between opposing traffic lanes on a highway.

me·di·ate, *v.*, **-ated, -ating.** to act between parties to effect an agreement, compromise, or reconciliation. – **mediator**, *n.*

med·i·cal, *adj.* **1.** of or pertaining to the science or practice of medicine. *–n.* **2.** a medical examination.

med·i·cate, *v.*, **-cated, -cating.** to treat with medicine. – **medication**, *n.*

med·i·cine, *n.* **1.** any substance or substances used in treating disease. **2.** the art or science of restoring or preserving health. **3.** the medical profession.

me·di·eval, *adj.* of or pertaining to the Middle Ages. Also, **mediaeval**.

me·di·ocre, *adj.* of middling quality; ordinary.

med·i·tate, *v.*, **-tated, -tating.** to

316

meditate

engage in thought or contemplation; reflect.

medium, n., pl. **-dia**, **-diums**. adj. –n. 1. a middle state or condition. 2. an intervening substance, as air, etc., through which a force acts or an effect is produced. 3. the element in which an organism has its natural habitat. 4. an agency, means, or instrument. –adj. 5. intermediate in degree, quality, etc..

medley, n. a mixture.

meek, adj. humbly patient or submissive.

meet, v., met, meeting. –v. 1. to come into contact, junction, or connection with. 2. to go to the place of arrival of, as to welcome. 3. to come into personal acquaintance with. 4. to cope or deal effectively with. 5. to come together in opposition or conflict. –n. 6. a meeting, as of huntsmen for a hunt, or cyclists for a ride, etc.

meet·ing, n. an assembly or gathering.

megalo·mania, n. a form of mental alienation marked by delusions of greatness, wealth, etc.

mega·phone, n. a funnel-shaped device for increasing the volume of a speaker's voice.

megaton, n. 10^6 tons. 2. an explosive force equal to that of 10^6 tons of TNT.

melan·choly, n., pl. **-cholies**, adj. –n. 1. a gloomy state of mind, esp. when habitual or prolonged; depression. –adj. 2. affected with melancholy.

mela·nin, n. the dark pigment in the body of man and certain animals.

melee me'lei, -'li/, n. 1. a confused general hand-to-hand fight. 2. any noisy or confused situation.

mel·lif·luous, adj. sweetly or smoothly flowing.

mellow, adj. 1. soft and full-flavoured from ripeness, as fruit. 2. soft and rich, as sound, colour, etc. 3. genial; jovial. –v. 4. to make or become mellow.

mel·odic, adj. 1. melodious. 2. pertaining to melody as distinguished from harmony and rhythm.

melo·drama, n. a play in which the drama is exaggerated.

melody, n., pl. **-dies**. musical sounds in agreeable succession or arrangement. – **melodious**, adj.

melon, n. a type of large, juicy fruit.

melt, v., melted, melted or molten, melting. 1. to liquefy by heat. 2. to pass, change, or blend gradually (into). 3. to soften in feeling, as a person, the heart, etc.

member, n. a constituent part of any structural or composite whole.

mem·brane, n. any thin connecting layer.

mem·ento, n., pl. **-tos**, **-toes**. something that serves as a reminder of what is past or gone.

memo, n., pl. **memos**. →memorandum.

mem·oirs /'memwaz/, n.pl. records of one's own life and experiences.

memo·ra·ble, adj. worthy of being remembered.

memo·ran·dum, n., pl. **-dums**, **-da**. a note made of something to be remembered.

memor·ial, n. something designed to preserve the memory of a person, event, etc.

memo·rise, v., -rised, -rising. to

memorise

commit to memory, or learn by heart.

memory, *n., pl.* **-ries. 1.** the mental capacity or faculty of retaining and reviving impressions, or of recalling or recognising previous experiences. **2.** a mental impression retained; a recollection. **3.** the state or fact of being remembered. **4.** *Computers.* the part of a digital computer in which data and instructions are held until they are required.

men, *n.* plural of **man**.

menace, *n., v.,* **-aced, -acing.** –*n.* **1.** a threat. **2.** *Colloq.* a nuisance. –*v.* **3.** to threaten.

men·agerie, *n.* a collection of wild or strange animals, esp. for exhibition.

mend, *v.* **1.** to make whole or sound by repairing. **2.** to set right; make better.

menial, *adj.* **1.** pertaining or proper to domestic servants. **2.** servile.

menin·gitis /mɛnɪnˈdʒaɪtɔs/, *n.* inflammation of the 3 membranes covering the brain and spinal cord.

meno·pause, *n.* the period of the cessation of menstruation.

menses, *n.pl.* the monthly discharge of blood and mucous membrane tissue from the uterus.

men·struate, *v.,* **-ated, -ating.** to discharge the menses. – **menstruation**, *n.* – **menstrual**, *adj.*

men·suration, *n.* the act, art, or process of measuring.

mental, *adj.* **1.** of or pertaining to the mind. **2.** for or pertaining to those with disordered minds. **3.** *Colloq.* foolish or mad.

men·tality, *n., pl.* **-ties.** mental capacity or endowment.

meringue

men·tion, *v.* **1.** to refer to briefly or incidentally. –*n.* **2.** a referring or reference.

mentor, *n.* a wise and trusted counsellor.

menu, *n.* a list of the dishes served at a meal.

mer·cantile, *adj.* of or pertaining to merchants or to trade; commercial.

mer·cenary, *adj., n., pl.* **-naries.** –*adj.* **1.** working or acting merely for gain. –*n.* **2.** a professional soldier serving in a foreign army.

mer·chandise, *n., v.,* **-dised, -dising.** –*n.* **1.** the stock of a store. –*v.* **2.** to trade (in).

mer·chant, *n.* **1.** one who buys and sells commodities for profit; a wholesaler. –*adj.* **2.** pertaining to trade or commerce.

merchant navy, *n.* the vessels of a nation engaged in commerce.

mer·cury, *n.* *Chem.* a heavy, silver-white metallic element, remarkable for its fluidity at ordinary temperatures; quicksilver. *Symbol:* Hg

mercy, *n., pl.* **-cies. 1.** compassionate or kindly forbearance. **2. at the mercy of**, defenceless or unprotected against. – **merciful**, *adj.*

mere, *adj., superl.* **merest.** being nothing more nor better than that stated. – **merely**, *adv.*

merge, *v.,* **merged, merging. 1.** to unite or combine. **2.** to become swallowed up or absorbed (**in** or **into**).

merger, *n.* a statutory combination of 2 or more companies.

meridian, *n.* *Geog.* a line of longitude.

meringue /məˈræŋ/, *n.* a mixture of sugar and beaten eggwhites, baked.

merino

merino, *n.*, *pl.* **-nos**. one of a variety of sheep valued for its fine wool.

merit, *n.* 1. excellence; worth 2. (*pl.*) the essential right and wrong of a matter. –*v.* 3. to be worthy of; deserve.

meritorious, *adj.* deserving of reward or commendation.

mermaid, *n.* an imaginary creature with the torso of a woman and the tail of a fish.

merry, *adj.*, **-rier**, **-riest**. full of cheer or gaiety.

merry-go-round, *n.* a machine on which children ride for amusement.

mesh, *n.* 1. a network or net. 2. light woven or welded interlocking links or wires. –*v.* 3. to entangle or become entangled. 4. *Mach.* to engage, as gear teeth.

mesmerise, *v.*, **-rised**, **-rising**. to hypnotise.

mess, *n.* 1. a dirty or untidy condition. 2. a place used by service personnel, etc., for eating, recreation, etc. 3. excrement, esp. of an animal. –*v.* 4. to make dirty or untidy (*up*). 5. to eat in company, esp. as a member of a mess. 6. **mess around/about**, to waste time.

message, *n.* information, etc. transmitted through a messenger or other agency.

messenger, *n.* one who bears a message or goes on an errand.

Messrs, *pl.* of Mr.

met, *v.* past tense and present participle of **meet**.

metabolism, *n.* the sum of the processes in an organism by which food is built up into living protoplasm and protoplasm is broken down into simpler compounds, with the exchange of energy.

methane

metal /ˈmetl/, *n.* 1. an opaque, ductile, conductive, elementary substance, as silver, copper, etc. 2. an alloy or mixture of these. – **metallic**, *adj.*

metallurgy /ˈmeəlɒdʒi, məˈtælədʒi/, *n.* the art or science of separating metals from their ores, of compounding alloys or working metals.

metamorphosis /metəˈmɔfəsəs, *n.*, *pl.* **-ses** -siz/. 1. any complete change in appearance, character, circumstances, etc. 2. a form resulting from this. – **metamorphic**, *adj.* – **metamorphose**, *v.*

metaphor, *n.* a figure of speech applying a term to something quite different in reality, in order to suggest a likeness. – **metaphorical**, *adj.*

metaphysical, *adj.* concerned with abstract thought or subjects.

metaphysics, *n.* philosophy, esp. in its more abstruse branches.

mete, *v.*, **meted**, **meting**. to distribute or measure; allot (*out*).

meteor, *n.* a transient fiery streak in the sky produced by a comet, etc., passing through the earth's atmosphere. – **meteoric**, *adj.*

meteorite, *n.* a mass of stone or metal that has reached the earth from outer space.

meteorology, *n.* the science of weather.

meter, *n.* an instrument that measures.

methadone, *n.* a powerful analgesic drug used for the treatment of drug withdrawal symptoms.

methane /ˈmiθein/, *n.* a colourless, odourless, inflammable gas.

method

method, *n.* a way of doing something, esp. in accordance with a definite plan.

meth·od·i·cal, *adj.* systematic.

methylated spirits, *n.* an alcohol, made unfit for drinking by adding a poisonous substance, used for burning, cleaning, etc.

metic·ulous, *adj.* minutely careful.

metre[1], *n.* the base SI unit of measurement of length equal to approx. 39.4 inches. *Symbol:* m

metre[2], *n.* arrangement of words in rhythmic lines or verses.

metric /'metrk/, *adj.* pertaining to the metre or to the system of measures and weights originally based upon it.

metro·nome, *n.* a mechanical contrivance for marking time in music.

metro·polis, *n., pl.* **-lises** /-lsiz/. the chief city (not necessarily the capital) of a country, state, or region. – **metropolitan,** *adj.*

mettle, *n.* **1.** characteristic disposition or temper. **2.** spirit; courage.

mew, *n.* **1.** the sound a cat makes. –*v.* **2.** to make this sound.

mews, *n.pl. usu. construed as sing.* a set of stables or garages.

mezza·nine, *n.* a low storey between 2 other storeys.

mica, *n.* any member of a group of minerals that separate readily (by cleavage) into thin, tough, often transparent laminae.

mice, *n.* plural of **mouse**.

mic·robe, *n.* a microscopic organism; germ.

micro·computer, *n.* a small computer which has its central processor functions contained on a single printed circuit board.

micro·copy, *n., pl.* **-ies.** a greatly

middle-aged

reduced photographic copy of a book, page, etc.

micro·cosm, *n.* anything regarded as a world in miniature (opposed to *macrocosm*).

micro·fiche, *n.* a transparency in microfilm about the size and shape of a filing card which may have on it many pages of print.

micro·film, *n.* a very small photograph, inspected by optical enlargement.

micro·light, *n.* a small motorised hang-glider.

micro·phone, *n.* an instrument which is capable of transforming the air-pressure waves of sound into changes in electric currents or voltages.

micro·processor, *n.* a small computer, often dedicated to specific functions.

micro·scope, *n.* an optical instrument for inspecting objects too small to be seen clearly by the naked eye.

micro·scopic, *adj.* **1.** so small as to be invisible or indistinct without the use of the microscope. **2.** of or pertaining to the microscope or its use.

mid, *adj.* central; at or near the middle point.

midair, *n.* any elevated position above the ground.

midday, *n.* the middle of the day; noon.

middle, *adj.* **1.** equally distant from extremes or limits. **2.** medium. –*n.* **3.** the point, part, etc., equidistant from extremes or limits.

middle-aged, *adj.* intermediate in age between youth and old age.

middle class

middle class, *n.* a social class comprising esp. business and professional people and public servants of middle income.

middle·man, *n., pl.* **-men. 1.** a trader who makes a profit by buying from producers and selling to retailers or consumers. **2.** one who acts as an intermediary between others.

mid·dling, *adj.* medium in size, quality, grade, rank, etc.

middy, *n., pl.* **-dies.** a medium-size beer glass.

midge, *n.* a small flying insect.

midget, *n.* something very small of its kind.

mid·night, *n.* **1.** 12 o'clock at night. **2.** dark, like midnight. **3. burn the midnight oil,** to study or work far into the night.

mid·riff, *n.* **1.** the middle part of the body, between the chest and the waist. *–adj.* **2.** of a dress, blouse etc., which exposes this part.

mid·ship·man, *n., pl.* **-men.** a probationary rank held by naval cadets before qualifying as officers.

midst, *n.* the middle point, part, or stage.

mid·stream, *n.* **1.** the middle of the stream. **2. in midstream,** *Colloq.* in the middle; at a critical point.

midway, *adv.* **1.** halfway. *–adj.* **2.** in the middle.

mid·wifery /ˈmɪdwɪfəri/, *n.* the art or practice of assisting women in childbirth. **- midwife,** *n.*

mien /miːn/, *n.* air, bearing, or aspect, as showing character, feeling, etc.

miffed, *adj. Colloq.* annoyed; displeased.

might[1], *v.* past tense of **may**.

militate

might[2], *n.* power or force, esp. military, political, etc. **- mighty,** *adj.*

mi·graine /ˈmaɪgreɪn, ˈmiːgreɪn/, *n.* a severe headache, usu. associated with nausea.

migrant, *n.* **1.** one who migrates. **2.** an immigrant. *–adj.* **3.** of or pertaining to migration or migrants.

migrate, *v.,* **-grated, -grating. 1.** to pass periodically from one region to another, as certain birds, fishes, and animals. **2.** *Colloq.* to immigrate or emigrate. **- migration,** *n.* **- migratory,** *adj.*

mike, *n. Colloq.* →**microphone.**

mild, *adj.* **1.** amiably gentle or temperate in feeling or behaviour towards others. **2.** gentle or moderate in force, effect or intensity.

mildew, *n.* a plant disease usu. characterised by a whitish coating.

mile, *n.* **1.** a unit of measurement of length in the imperial system, equal to 5280 feet (1609.34 m). **2.** (*oft. pl.*) a large distance or quantity.

mile·age, *n.* **1.** the total length or distance expressed in miles. **2.** the number of miles travelled by a motor vehicle on a specified quantity of fuel.

mile·stone, *n.* **1.** a stone set up to mark the distance to or from a town, as along a highway. **2.** a significant point in one's life or career.

milieu, *n.* medium or environment.

mili·tant, *adj.* engaged in warfare; warring.

mili·tary, *adj.* **1.** of or pertaining to the army or war. *–n.* **2.** the armed forces.

mili·tate, *v.,* **-tated, -tating.** to operate

militate (*against* or *in favour of*); have effect or influence.

mili·tia, *n.* a body of citizen soldiers as distinguished from professional soldiers.

milk, *n.* 1. an opaque white liquid food secreted by the mammary glands of female mammals. –*v.* 2. to press or draw milk by hand or machine from (a cow, etc.). 3. to extract (something) as if by milking.

milk bar, *n.* a shop where milk drinks, ice-cream, sandwiches, etc., are sold.

milk·shake, *n.* a frothy drink made of milk, flavouring, and sometimes ice-cream, shaken together.

milk tooth, *n.* a temporary tooth eventually replaced by a permanent tooth. Also, **baby tooth**.

mill, *n.* 1. a building fitted with machinery, in which some mechanical operation or form of manufacture is carried on. 2. a machine which does its work by rotary motion. 3. **run of the mill**, conventional; commonplace. –*v.* 4. to grind, work, treat, or shape in or with a mill. 5. to move confusedly in a circle (*about*).

mil·len·nium, *n., pl.* **-niums, -nia.** a period of 1000 years.

millet, *n.* a cereal grass.

milli·bar, *n.* a unit of atmospheric pressure.

mil·li·ner, *n.* one who makes or sells hats for women. – **millinery,** *n.*

mil·lion, *n.* 1. a cardinal number, 1000 times 1000, or 10^6. 2. a very great number. –*adj.* 3. amounting to 10^6 in numbers. – **millionth,** *adj., n.*

million·aire, *n.* a person worth a million or millions, as of pounds, dollars, or francs.

milli·pede, *n.* an insect with a segmented body and many legs.

mill·stone, *n.* 1. either of a pair of circular stones used for grinding. 2. a heavy burden.

mime, *n., v.,* **mimed, miming.** –*n.* 1. the art of expressing emotion, character, action, etc., by gestures and movements alone. 2. a performance or performer in mime. –*v.* 3. to make such gestures.

mimeo·graph, *n.* 1. a stencil device for duplicating letters, drawings, etc. –*v.* 2. to make copies of, using a mimeograph.

mimic, *v.,* **-icked, -icking.** –*v.* 1. to imitate or copy. –*n.* 2. one apt at imitating the characteristic voice or gesture of others. – **mimicry,** *n.*

min·aret, *n.* a tall, thin tower attached to a mosque.

mince, *v.,* **minced, mincing.** –*v.* 1. to cut or chop into very small pieces. 2. to act or utter with affected elegance. –*n.* 3. minced meat.

mince·meat, *n.* 1. a mixture composed of minced apples, suet, candied peel, etc., with raisins, currants, etc., for filling a pie (**mince pie**). 2. meat chopped fine. 3. anything cut up very small.

mind, *n.* 1. that part of a person which thinks, feels, and wills, exercises perception, judgment, reflection, etc. 2. intellectual power or ability. 3. purpose, intention, or will. 4. **make up one's mind**, to come to a decision. 5. **out of one's mind**, demented; delirious. 6. **to one's mind**, in one's opinion or judgment. –*v.* 7. to apply oneself or attend to. 8. to be careful, cautious,

mind

or wary concerning. **9.** to perceive or notice. **10.** to object to.

minded, *adj.* inclined or disposed.

mind·ful, *adj.* attentive; careful (*of*).

mine[1], *pron.* possessive form of *I*, used without a noun following.

mine[2], *n., v.,* **mined, mining.** –*n.* **1.** an excavation made in the earth to get out ores, coal, etc. **2.** an abounding source or store of anything. **3.** an explosive device. –*v.* **4.** to dig (a mine). **5.** to extract (ores, coal, etc.) from a mine. **6.** to dig or lay an explosive device under.

miner, *n.* one who works in a mine, esp. a coalmine.

min·eral, *n.* **1.** a substance obtained by mining; ore. **2.** any of a class of inorganic substances occurring in nature, having a definite chemical composition and crystal structure.

mineral water, *n.* **1.** water containing dissolved mineral salts or gases. **2.** carbonated water.

mingle, *v.,* **-gled, -gling. 1.** to become mixed, blended, or united. **2.** to mix, blend or combine. **3.** to associate or mix in company.

mini, *n. Colloq.* something small of its kind, as a skirt or motor vehicle.

mini·ature, *n.* **1.** a representation or image of anything on a very small scale. –*adj.* **2.** on a very small scale; reduced.

mini·mise, *v.,* **-mised, -mising.** to reduce to the smallest possible amount or degree.

mini·mum, *n., pl.* **-mums, -ma,** *adj.* –*n.* **1.** the least quantity or amount possible, assignable, allowable, etc. **2.** the lowest amount, value, or degree attained or recorded (opposed to *maximum*). –*adj.* **3.**

minute

pertaining to a minimum. – **mini·mal,** *adj.*

minion, *n.* a servile or base favourite, esp. of a prince or patron.

minis·ter, *n.* **1.** one authorised to conduct religious worship; clergyman; pastor. **2.** one appointed to manage some important area of government. –*v.* **3.** to give service, care, or aid. – **ministerial,** *adj.* – **ministry,** *n.*

mink, *n., pl.* **minks.** (*esp. collectively*) **mink. 1.** a semi-aquatic weasel-like animal. **2.** its valuable fur.

minor, *adj.* **1.** lesser, as in size, extent, or importance, or being the lesser of 2. **2.** under legal age. –*n.* **3.** a person under legal age.

min·or·i·ty, *n., pl.* **-ties,** *adj.* –*n.* **1.** the smaller part or number. **2.** the state or period of being a minor. –*adj.* **3.** of or pertaining to a minority.

min·strel, *n.* a medieval musician who sang or recited to the accompaniment of instruments.

mint[1], *n.* **1.** an aromatic herb. **2.** a mint-flavoured sweet.

mint[2], *n.* **1.** a place where money is coined by public authority. –*v.* **2.** to coin (money).

minuet, *n.* a slow stately dance of French origin.

minus, *prep.* **1.** less by the subtraction of; decreased by. –*adj.* **2.** algebraically negative. –*n.* **3.** a deficiency or loss.

minu·scule /'mɪnəskjul/, *adj.* very small; tiny.

minute[1] /'mɪnət/, *n.* **1.** the 60th part of an hour; 60 seconds. **2.** a point of time; an instant or moment. **3.** (*pl.*) the official record of the proceedings at a meeting.

minute[2] /maɪ'njut/, *adj.,* **-nuter,**

minute
-nutest. 1. extremely small. 2. attentive to or concerned with even very small details or particulars.

min·u·tia /maɪˈnjuːʃə, -tɪə-/, n., pl. **-tiae** /-ʃiː, -tiː/. (usu. pl.) a small or trivial detail.

minx, n. a pert, impudent, or flirtatious girl.

miracle, n. a wonderful thing; a marvel. – **miraculous**, adj.

mirage, n. an optical illusion by which reflected images of distant objects are seen, often inverted.

mire, n., v., **mired**, **miring**. –n. 1. a piece of wet, swampy ground. –v. 2. to cause to stick fast in mire.

mirror, n. 1. a reflecting surface, usu. glass with a metallic backing; a looking glass. –v. 2. to reflect in or as in a mirror, or as a mirror does.

mirth, n. rejoicing; joyous gaiety.

mis·adventure, n. an accident.

mis·an·thropy, n. hatred, dislike, or distrust of mankind.

mis·appro·priate, v., **-ated**, **-ating**. to apply wrongfully or dishonestly to one's own use. – **misappropriation**, n.

mis·carriage, n. 1. failure to attain the right or desired result. 2. premature expulsion of a foetus from the uterus, esp. before it is viable. – **miscarry**, v.

mis·cel·laneous, adj. consisting of members or elements of different kinds.

mis·cel·lany /məˈsɛlənɪ/, n., pl. **-nies**. a miscellaneous collection.

mis·chief, n. 1. teasing or playfully annoying conduct. 2. an injury due to some cause. – **mischievous**, adj.

mis·creant, n. 1. base; villainous. –n. 2. a criminally evil person.

mis·demean·our, n. Law. a criminal offence.

miser, n. a niggardly, avaricious person.

mis·erable, adj. 1. wretchedly unhappy. 2. attended with or causing misery.

misery, n., pl. **-ries**. 1. great distress of mind. 2. wretchedness of condition or circumstances.

mis·fire, v., **-fired**, **-firing**. 1. to fail to fire or explode. 2. to be unsuccessful.

misfit, n. one who feels ill at ease or out of place in a given environment.

mis·giving, n. a feeling of doubt, distrust, or apprehension.

mishap /ˈmɪshæp/, n. an unfortunate accident.

mish·mash, n. a hotchpotch; jumble.

mislay, v., **-laid**, **-laying**. to put in a place afterwards forgotten.

mis·lead, v., **-led**, **-leading**. to lead or guide wrongly; lead astray.

mis·nomer, n. a misapplied name or designation.

mis·ogyny, n. hatred of women.

mis·print, n. a mistake in printing.

miss^1, v. 1. to fail to hit, light upon, meet, catch, receive, obtain, attain, accomplish, see, hear, (something). 2. to perceive the absence or loss of, often with regret. 3. to be unsuccessful. 4. **miss out**, to fail to receive, esp. something desired. 5. a failure to hit, meet, obtain, or accomplish something.

miss^2, n., pl. **misses**. (usu. cap.) the conventional title of respect for an unmarried woman.

misshapen

mis·shap·en, *adj.* badly shaped; deformed.

mis·sile, *n.* an object or weapon that can be thrown, hurled, or shot.

miss·ing, *adj.* lacking; absent; not found.

mis·sion, *n.* **1.** a body of persons sent to a foreign country to conduct negotiations, establish relations, or the like. **2.** the business with which an agent, envoy, etc., is charged. **3.** an establishment for propagating religion.

mis·sion·ary /'mɪʃənri/, *n.* a person sent to work for the propagation of his religion in another land.

mis·sive, *n.* a written message; a letter.

mist, *n.* a cloudlike aggregation of minute globules of water in the air.

mis·take, *n., v.,* **-took, -taken, -taking.** *–n.* **1.** an error in action, opinion or judgment. *–v.* **2.** to conceive of or understand wrongly.

mis·ter, *n.* (*cap.*) the conventional title of respect for a man, prefixed to the name (usu. written *Mr*).

mis·tle·toe, *n.* a parasitic plant, traditionally used in Christmas decorations.

mis·tress, *n.* **1.** a woman who has authority or control. **2.** a female head teacher in a particular subject department in a secondary school. **3.** a woman who has a continuing sexual relationship with one man outside marriage.

mis·trust, *n.* **1.** lack of trust or confidence. *–v.* **2.** to regard with mistrust; distrust.

mis·un·der·stand·ing, *n.* **1.** disagreement or dissension. **2.** failure to understand.

misuse, *n., v.,* **-used, -using.** *–n.* **1.** wrong or improper use. *–v.* **2.** to ill-use; maltreat.

mobile

mite, *n.* any of various small arachnids, many being parasitic on plants and animals.

mit·i·gate, *v.,* **-gated, -gating. 1.** to moderate the severity of (anything distressing). **2.** to become milder. – **mitigation,** *n.*

mitre, *n.* **1.** the ceremonial headdress of a bishop. **2.** a right-angled joint, as of a picture frame.

mitten, *n.* a kind of hand-covering enclosing the 4 fingers together and the thumb separately.

mix, *v.,* **mixed, mixing,** *n. –v.* **1.** to put (elements) together, evenly spread, in one mass or assemblage. **2.** to become mixed. **3.** to associate, as in company. *–n.* **4.** a mixture.

mixed, *adj.* composed of different constituents or elements.

mix·ture, *n.* any combination of differing elements.

mix-up, *n.* a confused state of things; muddle; tangle.

mnem·on·ic, *adj.* **1.** assisting, or intended to assist, the memory. *–n.* **2.** a verse or the like intended to assist the memory.

moan, *n.* **1.** a prolonged, low, inarticulate sound uttered in suffering. *–v.* **2.** to utter moans.

moat, *n.* a large water-filled trench surrounding a castle, etc.

mob, *n., v.,* **mobbed, mobbing.** *–n.* **1.** a large number, esp. of people, sheep or cattle. **2.** a disorderly, riotous or destructive group of people. *–v.* **3.** to surround and attack with riotous violence.

mobile, *adj.* **1.** movable; moving readily. *–n.* **2.** a construction or

325

mobile

sculpture of delicately balanced movable parts. – **mobility**, *n*.

mobil·ise, *v*., **-lised**, **-lising**. to put (armed forces) into readiness for active service.

mocca·sin /ˈmɒkəsən/, *n*. a shoe made entirely of soft leather.

mocha /ˈmɒkə/, *n*. 1. a choice variety of coffee. 2. a coffee or coffee and chocolate flavouring.

mock, *v*. 1. to attack with ridicule. 2. to scoff; jeer. 3. to mimic, imitate, or counterfeit. –*adj*. 4. being an imitation; pretended.

mock·ery, *n*., *pl*. **-ries**. 1. ridicule or derision. 2. a mere travesty, or mocking pretence.

mocking·bird, *n*. any of various scrub birds noted for their ability as mimics.

mock-up, *n*. a model, built to scale, of a machine, apparatus, or weapon, used in testing, teaching, etc.

mod cons, *n.pl*. *Colloq*. modern conveniences.

mode[1], *n*. 1. manner of acting or doing; method; way. 2. the natural disposition or the manner of existence or action of anything; form.

mode[2], *n*. a prevailing style or fashion.

model, *n*., *adj*., *v*., **-elled**, **-elling**. –*n*. 1. a standard or example for imitation or comparison. 2. a representation in miniature to show the construction of something. 3. a person who poses for a painter, etc. 4. one employed to wear clothes to display them to customers; mannequin. 5. a typical or specific form or style. –*adj*. 6. worthy to serve as a model; exemplary. –*v*. 7. to form or plan according to a model. 8. to

moisture

display, esp. by wearing. 9. to serve or be employed as a model.

mod·er·ate, *adj*., *n*., *v*., **-rated**, **-rating**. –*adj*. 1. not extreme, excessive, or intense. –*n*. 2. one who is moderate in opinion or action, esp. in politics or religion. –*v*. 3. to make or become less violent, severe, intense, or rigorous.

modern, *adj*. 1. of or pertaining to present and recent time; not ancient or remote. 2. one whose views and tastes are modern.

modest, *adj*. 1. moderate or humble about one's merits, importance, etc. 2. moderate. 3. decent in behaviour, speech, dress, etc. – **modesty**, *n*.

modi·cum, *n*. a moderate or small quantity.

modify, *v*., **-fied**, **-fying**. 1. to change somewhat the form or qualities of; alter somewhat. 2. to become changed. 3. to reduce in degree. – **modification**, *n*.

modu·late, *v*., **-lated**, **-lating**. to regulate by or adjust to a certain measure; soften; tone down. – **modulation**, *n*.

module, *n*. 1. a selected unit of measure used as a basis for planning and standardisation of building materials. 2. a structural component. 3. *Astronautics*. a detachable section of a space vehicle. – **modular**, *adj*.

mogul, *n*. an important person.

mohair, *n*. (a fabric made from) the yarn from the hair of the Angora goat.

moiety, *n*., *pl*. **-ties**. a half.

moist, *adj*. moderately or slightly wet; damp.

mois·ture, *n*. water or other liquid rendering anything moist.

molar, *n.* a tooth adapted for grinding.

molas·ses, *n.* the syrup drained from raw sugar.

mole[1], *n.* a small congenital spot or blemish on the human skin.

mole[2], *n.* a small insectivorous mammal living chiefly underground.

mole[3], *n.* the SI base unit of measurement of amount of substance. Symbol: mol

mol·ecule, *n. Chem., Physics.* the smallest physical unit of an element or compound. – **molecular**, *adj.*

molest, *v.* to interfere with so as to annoy or hurt.

mol·lify, *v.*, **-fied, -fying.** to soften in feeling or temper.

mol·lusc /'mɒləsk/, *n.* any of a phylum of invertebrates including the snails, bivalves, squids, octopuses, etc.

molly·coddle, *v.*, **-dled, -dling.** to coddle; pamper.

molten, *adj.* liquefied by heat.

moment, *n.* **1.** an indefinitely short space of time; instant. **2.** importance or consequence.

momen·tary, *adj.* lasting but a moment; very brief.

momen·tous, *adj.* of great importance or consequence.

momen·tum, *n.*, *pl.* **-ta. 1.** the quantity of motion of a moving body, equal to the product of its mass and velocity. **2.** impetus, as of a moving body.

mon·arch, *n.* a hereditary ruler.

mon·ar·chy, *n.*, *pl.* **-chies.** a government or state in which the supreme power is actually or nominally lodged in a monarch.

mon·as·tery, *n.*, *pl.* **-teries.** a place occupied by a community of monks living in seclusion from the world under religious vows. – **monastic**, *adj.*

mon·et·ary, *adj.* of or pertaining to money.

money, *n.*, *pl.* **-eys, -ies.** coin or notes generally accepted as payment of goods and debts.

money order, *n.* an order for the payment of money, as one issued by one post office and payable at another.

mon·grel, *n.* **1.** any animal or plant resulting from the crossing of different breeds or varieties. –*adj.* **2.** inferior.

mon·itor, *n.* **1.** a device used to check, observe, or record the operation of a machine or system. **2.** a large lizard. –*v.* **3.** to check, observe, or record, the operation of (a machine, etc.).

monk, *n.* a man living in seclusion under religious vows.

monkey, *n.*, *pl.* **-keys**, *v.*, **-keyed, -keying.** –*n.* **1.** a long-tailed member of the mammalian order Primates. **2.** any of various mechanical devices. –*v.* **3.** *Colloq.* to play or trifle idly.

monkey-wrench, *n.* a spanner or wrench with an adjustable jaw.

mono·chro·matic, *adj.* of, producing, or pertaining to one colour or one wavelength.

mon·ocle, *n.* an eyeglass for one eye.

mon·ogamy, *n.* marriage of one woman with one man.

monogram

mono·gram, *n.* a design made up of initial letters.

mono·graph, *n.* a treatise on a particular subject.

mono·lith, *n.* 1. a single huge block of stone. 2. something having a massive, uniform, or unyielding quality or character. — **monolithic,** *adj.*

mono·logue, *n.* a prolonged talk by a single speaker.

mono·plane, *n.* an aeroplane with only one pair of wings.

mono·po·lise, *v.,* **-lised, -lising. 1.** to exercise a monopoly of (a market, commodity, etc.). 2. to retain entirely for oneself.

mon·opoly, *n., pl.* **-lies.** exclusive control of a commodity or service.

mono·rail, *n.* a railway with coaches running on a single rail.

mono sodium glutamate, *n.* a sodium salt used in cooking to enhance the natural flavour of a dish.

mono·syl·labic, *adj.* 1. having only one syllable, as a word. 2. having a vocabulary composed exclusively of monosyllables.

mono·theism, *n.* the belief that there is only one God.

mono·tone, *n.* a tone without harmony or variation in pitch.

mon·ot·ony, *n.* 1. lack of variety, or wearisome uniformity, as in occupation, scenery, etc. 2. sameness of tone or pitch, as in utterance. — **monotonous,** *adj.*

mono·treme, *n.* a mammal which both lays eggs and suckles its young, as the platypus and echidna.

mon·soon, *n.* seasonal wind, often with rain, in tropical and Indian ocean areas.

moonshine

mon·ster, *n.* 1. a legendary animal compounded of brute and human shape. —*adj.* huge; enormous; monstrous.

mons·trous, *adj.* 1. huge; extremely great. 2. revolting; outrageous; shocking. 3. distorted from the natural form. — **monstrosity,** *n.*

mon·tage, *n.* the combination in one picture, etc., of composition elements from several sources.

month, *n.* 1. a period of 4 weeks or of 30 days. 2. the period (**lunar month**) of a complete revolution of the moon. – **monthly,** *adj., n.*

monu·ment, *n.* something erected in memory of a person, event, etc.

monu·men·tal, *adj.* 1. massive or imposing. 2. of lasting significance.

mooch, *v. Colloq.* to hang or loiter about.

mood¹, *n.* frame of mind, or state of feeling.

mood², *n. Gram.* a set of verb forms which show the speaker's attitude towards the action expressed by the verb.

moody, *adj.,* **-dier, -diest. 1.** given to gloomy or sullen moods; ill-humoured. 2. exhibiting sharply varied moods; temperamental.

moon, *n.* 1. the body which revolves around the earth monthly. 2. a month. 3. any planetary satellite. –*v.* 4. *Colloq.* to wander about or gaze idly, dreamily, or listlessly.

moon·light, *n.* 1. the light of the moon. —*adj.* 2. pertaining to or lit by moonlight. –*v.* 3. to work at an extra job.

moon·shine, *n.* 1. the light of the moon. 2. empty or foolish talk, ideas, etc.; nonsense. 3. *Colloq.*

moonshine

smuggled or illicitly distilled liquor.

moon·stone, *n.* a white translucent variety of felspar with a bluish pearly lustre, used as a gem.

moor[1], *n.* a tract of open waste land; heath.

moor[2], *v.* to secure (a ship, etc.) in a particular place. – **moorage**, *n.*

moor·ings, *n.pl.* the place where a ship is moored.

moose, *n., pl.* **moose**. a large animal of the deer family.

moot, *adj.* subject to argument or discussion; debatable; doubtful.

mop, *n., v.*, **mopped, mopping**. –*n.* **1.** a bundle of coarse yarn, etc., fastened at the end of a stick or handle, used for washing floors, dishes, etc. **2.** a thick mass, as of hair. –*v.* **3.** to rub, wipe, clean, or remove with a mop.

mope, *v.*, **moped, moping**. to be sunk in listless apathy or dull dejection.

mopoke, *n.* an Aust. and N.Z. owl.

moral, *adj.* **1.** pertaining to or concerned with right conduct or the distinction between right and wrong. **2.** conforming to the rules of right conduct (opposed to *immoral*). –*n.* **3.** the moral teaching or practical lesson contained in a fable, tale, experience, etc. **4.** (*pl.*) principles or habits with respect to right or wrong conduct; ethics.

morale, *n.* mental condition with respect to cheerfulness, confidence, zeal, etc.

moral·ise, *v.*, **-lised, -lising**. to make moral reflections.

mora·lity, *n., pl.* **-ties**. conformity to the rules of right conduct.

morass, *n.* a tract of low, soft, wet ground.

morse code

mora·torium, *n., pl.* **-toria, -toriums**. a legal authorisation to delay payment of money due.

morbid, *adj.* affected by, proceeding from, or characteristic of, disease.

mor·dant, *adj.* caustic or sarcastic.

mor·dent, *n.* a musical ornament.

more, *adj., superl.* **most**, *n., adv.* –*adj.* **1.** in greater quantity, amount, measure, degree, or number (as the comparative of *much* and *many*). **2.** additional or further. –*n.* **3.** an additional quantity, amount, or number. **4.** a greater quantity, amount, or degree. –*adv.* **5.** in or to a greater extent or degree. **6. more or less**, to a certain extent; approximately.

more·over, *adv.* beyond what has been said; further; besides.

mores, *n.pl.* accepted moral customs or conventions.

morgue, *n.* a place in which the bodies of persons found dead are exposed for identification.

mori·bund, *adj.* dying.

mornay, *adj.* covered with a thick white cheese sauce.

mor·ning, *n.* the first part of the day.

morocco, *n.* a fine leather made from goatskins.

moron, *n.* a person of arrested intelligence.

morose, *adj.* gloomily or sullenly ill-humoured.

mor·phine, *n.* a drug used to dull pain, induce sleep, etc. Also, **morphia**.

mor·phol·ogy, *n.* the study of form, structure, and the like.

morrow, *n.* the day after.

morse code, *n.* a system of dots, dashes, and spaces used to represent the letters of the alphabet, numerals, etc.

morsel, *n.* a small piece or amount of anything; scrap; bit.

mortal, *adj.* 1. liable or subject to death. 2. of or pertaining to man as subject to death; human. 3. causing death. –*n.* 4. a human.

mortality, *n., pl.* **-ties.** 1. the condition of being mortal. 2. relative frequency of death in a district or community.

mortar[1], *n.* 1. a bowl in which drugs, etc., are reduced to powder with a pestle. 2. a type of cannon.

mortar[2], *n.* a cement which binds bricks together.

mortar·board, *n.* a kind of cap with a stiff, square top, worn by university graduates, etc.

mort·gage /'mɔgɪdʒ/, *n., v.,* **-gaged, -gaging.** *Law.* –*n.* 1. a security by way of conveyance or assignment of property securing the payment of a debt. –*v.* 2. to put (property, esp. houses or land) under a mortgage.

mor·tice, *n.* a rectangular cavity in a piece of wood, etc., for receiving a corresponding projection (tenon) on another piece, so as to form a joint.

mor·tify, *v.,* **-fied, -fying.** to humiliate. – **mortification**, *n.*

mor·tu·ary, *n., pl.* **-ries.** a place where dead bodies are temporarily kept.

mosaic, *n.* a picture or decoration made of small pieces of stone, glass, etc.

moselle, *n.* a light white wine.

mosque, *n.* a Muslim temple.

mos·quito, *n., pl.* **-toes, -tos.** a bloodsucking insect.

moss, *n.* a small leafy-stemmed plant growing in tufts in moist places.

most, *adj., superl.* of **more**, *n., adv.* –*adj.* 1. in the greatest quantity, amount, measure, degree, or number. –*n.* 2. the greatest quantity, amount, or degree. 3. the majority of persons (construed as *pl.*). –*adv.* 4. in or to the greatest extent or degree.

mostly, *adv.* for the most part; in the main.

mote, *n.* a particle or speck, esp. of dust.

motel, *n.* a roadside hotel with self-contained units.

moth, *n.* an insect similar to the butterfly.

moth·ball, *n.* a small ball of a moth-repellent substance stored with clothes, etc.

mother, *n.* 1. a female parent. 2. the head or superior of a female religious community. –*adj.* 3. pertaining to or characteristic of a mother. –*v.* 4. to give origin or rise to. 5. to care for or protect. – **motherly**, *adj.*

mother-in-law, *n., pl.* **mothers-in-law.** the mother of one's spouse.

mother-of-pearl, *n.* a hard, iridescent substance which forms the inner layer of certain shells, as that of the pearl oyster.

motif /mou'tif, 'moutəf/, *n.* a recurring subject or theme as in art, literature, or music.

motion, *n.* 1. the process of moving, or changing place or position. 2. a bodily movement or gesture. 3. a proposal formally made to a deliberative assembly. 4. →**faeces**. –*v.* 5. to direct by a significant motion or gesture, as with the hand.

moti·vate, v. -vated, -vating. to provide with a motive. – **motivation**, n.

moti·vated, adj. ambitious; determined; energetic.

motive, n. 1. something that prompts a person to act in a certain way. –adj. 2. causing, or tending to cause, motion.

motley, adj. diverse; various.

motor, n. 1. a comparatively small and powerful engine. 2. any self-powered vehicle. –adj. 3. causing or imparting motion.

motor·cade, n. a procession or parade of motor cars.

motor car, n. a motor-driven vehicle, esp. for passengers, for travel on roads.

motor·cycle, n. a motor vehicle resembling a bicycle.

motor·ist, n. one who drives a motor car.

motor vehicle, n. a road vehicle driven by a motor.

mot·tled, adj. spotted or blotched in colouring.

motto, n., pl. -toes, -tos. a maxim adopted as expressing one's guiding principle.

mould[1], n. 1. a hollow form used to shape something in a molten or plastic state. 2. something formed in or on a mould. –v. 3. to work into a required shape or form; shape.

mould[2], n. a growth of minute fungi forming on vegetable or animal matter.

moul·der, v. to turn to dust by natural decay.

moult, v. to cast or shed old feathers or skin.

mound, n. 1. a hillock or knoll. 2. a heap or raised mass.

mount[1], v. 1. to go up or ascend. 2. to get up on (a platform, horse, etc.). 3. to go or put on (guard). 4. to fix on or in a support, backing, setting, etc. –n. 5. a horse, bicycle, etc., used for riding. 6. a support, backing or setting.

mount[2], n. a mountain or hill.

moun·tain, n. a high natural elevation of the earth's surface.

moun·tain·eer, n. 1. a climber of mountains. –v. 2. to climb mountains. – **mountaineering**, n.

moun·tain·ous, adj. 1. abounding in mountains. 2. like a mountain.

mounte·bank, n. a charlatan or quack.

mourn, v. to feel or express sorrow or grief, esp. for (the dead).

mourn·ful, adj. 1. full of or showing sorrow or grief. 2. gloomy, sombre or dreary.

mourn·ing, n. the conventional manifestation of sorrow for a person's death, esp. by the wearing of black, the hanging of flags at half-mast, etc.

mouse, n., pl. mice, v., moused, mousing. –n. 1. a small rodent. 2. Colloq. a quiet, shy person. –v. 3. to hunt for or catch mice.

mousse /mus/, n. any of various preparations of whipped cream, beaten eggs, gelatine, etc., flavoured and usu. chilled.

mous·tache, n. the hair growing on the upper lip.

mouth, n. 1. the opening through which an animal takes in food. 2. utterance or expression. –v. 3. to utter with unnecessarily noticeable use of the mouth or lips.

mouth·ful, *n.*, *pl.* **-fuls**. as much as a mouth can hold.

mouth organ, *n.* →harmonica.

mouth·piece, *n.* **1.** the part of a musical instrument held in or at the mouth. **2.** a person, a newspaper, etc., that voices the opinions, decisions, etc., of another; spokesperson.

move, *v.*, **moved**, **moving**, *n.* –*v.* **1.** to change (the) place or position (of). **2.** (of the bowels) to operate. **3.** to make a formal request, application, or proposal. **4.** to prompt or impel to some action. **5.** to affect with emotion; touch. –*n.* **6.** the act of moving; a movement. **7.** a change of abode or residence. – **movable**, **moveable**, *adj.*, *n.*

move·ment, *n.* **1.** the act or process or result of moving. **2.** (*Chiefly pl.*) a series of actions of a person. **3.** the works of a mechanism, as a watch. **4.** *Music.* a principal division or section of a sonata, symphony, etc.

movie, *n.* →film (def. 3b).

mow, *v.*, **mowed**, **mown** or **mowed**, **mowing**. **1.** to cut down (grass, grain, etc.). **2. mow down**, to destroy or kill indiscriminately.

much, *adj.*, **more**, **most**, *n.*, *adv.* –*adj.* **1.** in great quantity, amount, measure, or degree. –*n.* **2.** a great quantity or amount. **3. make much of**, to treat (a person) with great, flattering, or fond consideration. –*adv.* **4.** to a great extent or degree; greatly; far.

muck, *n.* **1.** farmyard dung, decaying vegetable matter, etc.; manure. **2.** filth; dirt. –*v.* **3.** to remove muck from (*out*). **4.** *Colloq.* to spoil; make a mess of. **5. muck about**, or **around**, *Colloq.* to idle; potter; fool about. **6. muck up**, *Colloq.* to misbehave.

muck-up, *n.* *Colloq.* fiasco; muddle.

mucous, *adj.* **1.** pertaining to, consisting of, or resembling mucus. **2.** containing or secreting mucus.

mucus, *n.* a viscid secretion of the mucous membranes.

mud, *n.* **1.** wet, soft earth or earthy matter. **2. one's name is mud**, *Colloq.* one is in disgrace. **3. throw (sling) mud at**, *Colloq.* speak ill of; abuse. – **muddy**, *adj.*

muddle, *v.*, **-dled**, **-dling**, *n.* –*v.* **1.** to mix up or jumble together in a confused or bungling way. **2.** to make mentally confused. –*n.* **3.** a muddled condition. **4.** a confused mental state.

mud·guard, *n.* a guard or shield shaped to fit over the wheels of a vehicle to prevent splashing of water, mud etc.

muesli, *n.* a breakfast cereal of oats, wheatgerm, chopped fruit and nuts, etc.

muff, *n.* **1.** a wrap for the hands. **2.** *Colloq.* a failure. –*v.* **3.** to bungle (something).

muffin, *n.* a thick, flat yeast cake, grilled and served with butter.

muffle, *v.*, **-fled**, **-fling**. **1.** to wrap or envelop in a cloak, scarf, etc. **2.** to wrap with something to deaden or prevent sound. **3.** to deaden (sound).

muf·fler, *n.* **1.** a heavy neck scarf used for warmth. **2.** any device that reduces noise, esp. on an engine.

mug, *n.*, *v.*, **mugged**, **mugging**. –*n.* **1.** a drinking cup. **2.** *Colloq.* the face. **3.** *Colloq.* a fool; one who is easily duped. –*v.* **4.** *Colloq.* to assault and rob.

muggy

muggy, *adj.*, **-gier**, **-giest**. humid and oppressive.

mulberry, *n.*, *pl.* **-ries**. 1. a type of berry. 2. a dull, dark, reddish purple colour.

mulch, *n.* straw, leaves, loose earth, etc., spread on the ground.

mule, *n.* 1. the offspring of a male donkey and a mare, used *esp* as a beast of burden. 2. *Colloq.* a stupid or stubborn person.

mull[1], *v.* to study or ruminate (*over*).

mull[2], *v.* to heat, sweeten and spice (wine, etc.) for drinking.

mullet, *n.*, *pl.* **-lets**, (*esp.* collectively) **-let**. a type of freshwater or marine fish.

mulligatawny, *n.* highly-seasoned soup of Indian origin, with a curried flavour.

multi-coloured, *adj.* of many colours.

multi-cultural, *adj.* of or pertaining to a society which embraces a number of minority cultures.

multifarious, *adj.* of or having many different parts, elements, forms, etc.

multilateral, *adj.* 1. many-sided. 2. *Govt.* denoting an agreement, etc., in which 3 or more nations participate; multipartite.

multilingual, *adj.* able to speak 3 or more languages.

multinational, *adj.* 1. of, pertaining to, or spreading across many nations. –*n.* 2. a large, usu. powerful, company with branches, offices or subsidiaries in several nations.

multipartite, *adj.* 1. divided into many parts; having many divisions. 2. *Govt.* →**multilateral** (def. 2).

multiple, *adj.* 1. consisting of, having, or involving many individuals,

municipal

parts, elements, relations, etc.; manifold. –*n.* 2. *Maths.* a number which contains another number some number of times without a remainder.

multiple sclerosis, *n.* a disease of the nervous system caused by loss of part of the sheath around certain nerve fibres. *Abbrev.:* M.S.

multiplicity, *n.*, *pl.* **-ties**. a multitude or great number.

multiply, *v.*, **-plied**, **-plying**. 1. to make or become many; increase (in) the number, quantity, etc., of. 2. *Maths.* to take by addition a given number of times. 3. to produce (animals or plants) by propagation. – **multiplication**, *n.*

multitude, *n.* 1. a great number; host. 2. a crowd or throng. **multitudinous**, *adj.*

mum[1], *adj.* silent; not saying a word.

mum[2], *n. Colloq.* mother.

mumble, *v.*, **-bled**, **-bling**, *n.* –*v.* 1. to speak or utter indistinctly or unintelligibly. –*n.* 2. a low, indistinct utterance or sound.

mumbo-jumbo, *n.* 1. meaningless ritual. 2. confusing or complicated language which renders meaning unintelligible. 3. nonsense.

mummy[1], *n.*, *pl.* **-mies**. the dead body of a human being or animal preserved by embalming.

mummy[2], *n. Colloq.* mother.

mumps, *n.pl.*, construed as *sing.* an infectious, viral disease causing swelling of the salivary glands.

munch, *v.* to chew steadily or vigorously, and often audibly.

mundane, *adj.* ordinary; boring.

mung bean, *n.* a bushy annual herb, a chief source of beansprouts.

municipal /mjuˈnɪsɪpəl/

municipal

mjunə'sipəl/, adj. of or pertaining to a municipality, its government, facilities, etc.

mu·ni·ci·pal·i·ty, n., pl. -ties. 1. an area of land delineated for the purposes of local government; borough. 2. the governing body of such an area.

mu·ni·fi·cent, adj. extremely generous in giving or bestowing.

mu·ni·tions, n.pl. materials used in war, esp. weapons and ammunition.

mural, adj. 1. of or pertaining to a wall. –n. 2. a painting on a wall.

murder, n. 1. Law. the unlawful killing of another human being with malice aforethought. 2. Colloq. an uncommonly laborious or difficult task. –v. 3. Law. to kill by an act constituting murder. – **murderous**, adj.

murky, adj., -kier, -kiest. cloudy and dirty, as water.

murmur, n. 1. any low, continuous sound. 2. a mumbled or private expression of discontent. –v. 3. to make a low or indistinct continuous sound. 4. to speak in a low tone or indistinctly. 5. to complain quietly, or in private.

muscat, n. a type of sweet wine. Also, **muscatel**.

muscle, n., v., -cled, -cling. –n. 1. a bundle of contractile fibres that produce bodily movement. 2. muscular strength. 3. ruthless political or financial strength. –v. 4. **muscle in (on)**, to force one's way in(to). – **muscular**, adj.

muscular dystrophy, n. a disease causing muscular deterioration and wastage.

muse¹, v., mused, musing. to reflect or meditate in silence.

must

muse², n. 1. one of 9 Greek goddesses of literature, the arts and science. 2. the inspiration of poets.

museum, n. a building or place for the keeping, exhibition, and study of objects of scientific, artistic, and historical interest.

mush, n. 1. any thick, soft mass. 2. Colloq. weak or maudlin sentiment or sentimental language.

mushroom, n. 1. any of various fleshy edible fungi. 2. anything of similar shape or of correspondingly rapid growth. –adj. 3. of or made of mushrooms. 4. resembling a mushroom in shape. –v. 5. to spread or grow quickly.

music, n. 1. an art of organising sound in significant forms to express ideas and emotions through the elements of rhythm, melody, harmony, and colour. 2. musical work or compositions. 3. the score of a musical composition. 4. **face the music**, to face the consequences, usu. unpleasant, cf one's actions.

mu·si·cal, adj. 1. of, pertaining to, or producing music. 2. fond of or skilled in music.

mu·si·cian, n. one skilled in playing a musical instrument.

musk, n. 1. a substance secreted by certain animals, having a strong smell, and used in perfumery. 2. a synthetic imitation of this substance.

musket, n. the predecessor of the modern rifle. – **musketeer**, n.

muslin, n. a fine cotton fabric.

mussel, n. an edible bivalve mollusc.

must, aux. v. 1. to be obliged or compelled to. 2. may reasonably be

334

must

supposed to. —*n. Colloq.* **3.** anything necessary or vital.

mus·tard, *n.* **1.** a pungent food condiment. —*adj.* **2.** brownish-yellow in colour.

mustard gas, *n.* a colourless oily liquid whose vapour is a powerful irritant inducing blisters. Used as a poison gas in warfare.

muster, *v.* **1.** to gather, summon, or round up. **2.** to come together, collect, or gather. —*n.* **3.** the act of mustering. **4. pass muster**, to measure up to specified standards.

musty, *adj.*, **-tier**, **-tiest**. having a smell or flavour suggestive of mould.

mutant, *n.* a new type of organism produced as the result of mutation.

mutate, *v.*, **-tated**, **-tating**. to change; undergo mutation.

muta·tion, *n.* **1.** the act or process of changing. **2.** a change or alteration, as in form, qualities, or nature.

mute, *adj.*, *n.*, *v.*, **muted**, **muting**. —*adj.* **1.** silent; refraining from speech. **2.** incapable of speech; dumb. —*n.* **3.** one unable to speak. **4.** a mechanical device for muffling the tone of a musical instrument. —*v.* **5.** to deaden or muffle the sound of (a musical instrument, etc.).

muti·late, *v.*, **-lated**, **-lating**. to remove parts of a body so as to disable or disfigure it. — **mutilation**, *n.*

mutineer, *n.* one who mutinies.

mutiny, *n.*, *pl.* **-nies**, *v.*, **-nied**, **-nying**. —*n.* **1.** a revolt or rebellion against authority, esp. by soldiers or seamen. —*v.* **2.** to commit mutiny. — **mutinous**, *adj.*

mutt, *n. Colloq.* **1.** a dog, esp. a mongrel. **2.** a simpleton; a stupid person.

mutter, *v.* **1.** to utter (words) indistinctly or in a low tone; murmur; grumble. **2.** to make a low, rumbling sound.

mutton, *n.* the flesh of sheep, used as food.

mutton-chops, *n.pl.* large side-whiskers.

mutual, *adj.* possessed, experienced, performed, etc., by each of 2 or more with respect to the other; reciprocal.

muzzle, *n.*, *v.*, **-zled**, **-zling**. —*n.* **1.** the mouth of a gun barrel. **2.** the jaws, mouth, and nose of an animal. **3.** a harness or cage on an animal's jaw. —*v.* **4.** to put a muzzle on. **5.** to restrain (by physical, legal, or procedural means) from speech or the expression of opinion; gag.

muzzy, *adj.*, **-ier**, **-iest**. blurred, fuzzy, indistinct, dazed.

my, *pron.* **1.** the possessive form of the pronouns *I* and *me.* —*interj.* **2.** *Colloq.* (an exclamation of surprise).

myna, *n.* **1.** a noisy scavenging bird with yellow legs and beak. **2.** any of various Asian birds known for their ability to talk. Also, **mina, mynah.**

myopia, *n.* near-sightedness. — **myopic**, *adj.*

myriad, *n.* **1.** an indefinitely great number. —*adj.* **2.** innumerable.

myrrh, *n.* an aromatic resinous exudation from certain plants used for incense, perfume, etc.

myrtle, *n.* a type of shrub with fragrant white flowers.

myself, *pron.* a reflexive form of *me.* **2.** an emphatic form of *me* or *I*, used: **a.** as object. **b.** in apposition to a subject or object. —*n.* **3.**

myself

one's proper or normal self: *I feel myself again today.*

mystery, *n., pl.* **-ries. 1.** anything that is kept secret or remains unexplained or unknown. **2.** obscure or puzzling qualtiy. **3.** any truth unknowable except by divine revelation. – **mysterious**, *adj.*

mystic, *adj.* **1.** spiritually significant or symbolic. **2.** of occult character, power, or significance. **3.** of or pertaining to mystics or mysticism. –*n.* **4.** one who claims extraordinary spiritual insight or who lives in religious contemplation.

mysti·cism, *n.* **1.** the beliefs, ideas, or mode of thought of mystics. **2.** obscure thought or speculation.

mys·tify, *v.*, **-fied, -fying. 1.** to involve (a subject, etc.) in mystery or obscurity. **2.** to confuse (someone). – **mystification**, *n.*

mys·tique, *n.* an air of mystery or mystical power surrounding something.

myth, *n.* **1.** a traditional story which attempts to explain natural phenomena. **2.** any invented story. – **mythical**, *adj.*

myth·ology, *n., pl.* **-gies.** myths collectively.

myxo·mato·sis /mɪksəmə'tousəs/, *n.* a highly infectious viral disease of rabbits.

myxomatosis

Nn

N, n, *n., pl.* **N's** or **Ns, n's** or **ns.** the 14th letter of the English alphabet.

nab, *v.,* **nabbed, nabbing.** *Colloq.* to catch or seize, esp. suddenly.

nadir, *n.* the lowest point.

nag[1], *v.,* **nagged, nagging. 1.** to torment by persistent fault-finding, etc. **2.** to keep up an irritating complaining or the like (*at*). **3.** to cause continual pain, discomfort, or depression.

nag[2], *n. Colloq.* a horse.

nail, *n.* **1.** a slender pointed piece of metal for driving into or through wood, etc. **2.** a thin, horny plate growing on the upper side of the end of a finger or toe. −*v.* **3.** to fasten with a nail or nails.

naive /naːˈiːv, naː-/, *adj.* unsophisticated; ingenuous. Also, **naïf, naïve.** − **naivety,** *n.*

naked, *adj.* without clothing or covering; nude.

name, *n., v.,* **named, naming.** −*n.* **1.** a word or a combination of words by which a person, place, object, etc., is known or described. **2.** a reputation of a particular kind given by common report. −*v.* **3.** to give a name to. **4.** to specify or mention by name.

namely, *adv.* that is to say.

name·sake, *n.* **1.** one having the same name as another. **2.** one named after another.

nanny, *n., pl.* **-ies. 1.** a nurse for children. **2.** a grandmother.

nanny-goat, *n.* a female goat.

nap[1], *v.,* **napped, napping.** −*v.* **1.** to have a short sleep; doze. −*n.* **2.** a short sleep; doze.

nap[2], *n.* the short fuzzy ends of fibres on the surface of cloth.

napalm /ˈneɪpɑːm, ˈnæpɑːm/, *n.* a sticky aluminium gel used in flame throwers and fire bombs.

nape, *n.* the back (of the neck).

napery, *n.* table linen.

naph·tha·lene, *n.* a white crystalline hydrocarbon used in dyes and as a moth-repellent, etc.

napkin, *n.* **1.** →**serviette. 2.** a piece of linen, cotton cloth or paper used as a towel or as a baby's nappy.

nappy, *n., pl.* **-pies.** a piece of cloth, etc., fastened round a baby to absorb and contain its excrement.

nar·cis·sism, *n.* an excessive self-love. − **narcissist,** *n.* − **narcissistic,** *adj.*

nar·co·sis, *n.* a state of sleep or drowsiness.

nar·cotic, *n.* any of a class of substances that blunt the senses and induce sleep.

nark, *n. Colloq.* **1.** an informer. **2.** a scolding, complaining person.

nar·rate, *v.,* **-rated, -rating.** to tell the story of (events, experiences, etc.). − **narrator,** *n.* − **narration,** *n.*

narra·tive, *n.* a story, whether true or fictitious.

narrow, *adj.* **1.** not broad or wide. **2.** limited in extent or space. **3.** lacking breadth of view or sympathy. −*v.* **4.** to make or become narrower. −*n.* **5.** a narrow part, place or thing.

nasal

nasal, *adj.* of or pertaining to the nose.

nas·cent, *adj.* beginning to exist or develop.

nas·tur·tium, *n.* a garden plant with showy flowers.

nasty, *adj.*, **-tier**, **-tiest**. vicious, spiteful, or ugly.

natal, *adj.* of or pertaining to birth.

nation, *n.* a body of people associated with a particular territory who possess or seek a government peculiarly their own. – **national**, *adj.*

nation·al·ise, *v.*, **-lised**, **-lising**. to bring under the control or ownership of a government.

nation·al·ism, *n.* devotion to the interests of one's own nation. – **nationalistic**, *adj.*

nation·al·ity, *n.*, *pl.* **-ties**. the quality of membership in a particular nation.

native, *adj.* 1. belonging to a person, place or thing by birth or nature (*to*). 2. born or originating in a particular place or country. –*n.* 3. one of the original inhabitants of a place or country. 4. one born in a particular place or country. 5. an animal or plant indigenous to a particular region.

nati·vity, *n.*, *pl.* **-ties**. birth.

natu·ral, *adj.* 1. existing in or formed by nature; not artificial. 2. free from affectation or constraint. 3. in accordance with the nature of things. 4. being such by nature; born such. 5. *Music.* without sharps or flats. –*n.* 6. *Colloq.* a thing or a person that is by nature satisfactory or successful. 7. *Music.* the sign ♮, placed before a note cancelling the effect of a previous sharp or flat.

natu·ral·ise, *v.*, **-lised**, **-lising**. to

338

near

confer the rights and privileges of citizenship upon.

natu·ral·ist, *n.* a zoologist or botanist.

nature, *n.* 1. the qualities belonging to a person or thing by birth or constitution. 2. character, kind, or sort. 3. the material world or its forces. 4. reality, as distinguished from any effect of art. 5. an uncultivated state.

naught, *n.* negation or complete failure.

naughty, *adj.*, **-tier**, **-tiest**. 1. disobedient; mischievous (esp. in speaking to or about children). 2. improper; obscene.

nausea, *n.* sickness at the stomach; a sensation of impending sickness. – **nauseous**, *adj.* – **nauseate**, *v.*

nauti·cal, *adj.* of or pertaining to seamen, ships, or navigation.

nave, *n.* the main body, lengthwise, of a church.

navel, *n.* a pit or depression in the surface of the belly.

navi·gate, *v.*, **-gated**, **-gating**. 1. to traverse (the sea, a river, etc.) in a vessel, or (the air) in an aircraft. 2. to direct the course of travel, as by map-reading. – **navigator**, *n.* – **navigable**, *adj.*

navy, *n.*, *pl.* **-vies**. 1. the whole body of warships and auxiliaries belonging to a country or ruler. 2. Also, **navy blue**. a dark blue, as of a naval uniform. – **naval**, *adj.*

nay, *adv.* no (used in dissent, denial, or refusal).

neap, *adj.* designating the lowest tides, those midway between spring tides.

near, *adv.* 1. close: *Do you live near?* 2. at, within, or to a short distance;

near

nigh. **3.** close at hand in time. –*adj.* **4.** being close by; not distant: *a house in the near distance.* **5.** closely related or connected: *a near relation.* –*prep.* **6.** at, within, or to a short distance, or no great distance, from: *We live near the town.* **7.** close to (doing something). –*v.* **8.** to approach.

nearby, *adj., adv.* close at hand.

nearly, *adv.* **1.** all but; almost: *nearly there.* **2.** with close approximation: *nearly identical.*

neat, *adj.* **1.** orderly in appearance, condition, etc. **2.** clever, dexterous, or apt. **3.** unadulterated or undiluted, as liquors.

nebula, *n., pl.* **-lae, -las.** *Astron.* a diffuse, cloudlike patch of gases, particles, etc.

nebulous, *adj.* hazy, or confused.

necessary, *adj.* **1.** that cannot be dispensed with. **2.** happening or existing by necessity.

necessitate, *v.*, **-tated, -tating.** to make necessary.

necessity, *n., pl.* **-ties. 1.** something necessary or indispensable. **2.** an imperative requirement or need for something. **3.** a state of being in difficulty or need; poverty.

neck, *n.* **1.** the part of the animal body that connects the head to the trunk. **2.** any narrow, connecting, or projecting part, as of a bottle. –*v.* **3.** *Colloq.* to play amorously.

neckerchief, *n.* a cloth worn round the neck.

necklace, *n.* an ornament worn esp. by women round the neck.

necromancy, *n.* magic; sorcery.

nectar, *n.* **1.** *Bot.* the sweet secretion of a plant. **2.** any delicious drink.

nectarine, *n.* a form of the common peach, having a completely smooth skin.

nee /neɪ/, *adj.* born (placed after the name of a married woman to introduce her maiden name.)

need, *n.* **1.** a case or instance in which some necessity or want exists; a requirement. **2.** (a condition marked by) urgent want, as extreme poverty. –*v.* **3.** to lack or require. **4.** to be necessary. **5.** to be under a necessity or be obliged (to): *He need only come tomorrow.*

needle, *n., v.,* **-dled, -dling.** –*n.* **1.** a small, slender, pointed instrument with a hole for thread, used in sewing. **2.** a slender, rodlike implement for use in knitting, etc. **3.** *Bot.* a needle-shaped leaf, as of a conifer. –*v.* **4.** to tease or heckle.

needlework, *n.* the process or the product of working with a needle.

needy, *adj.* **-dier, -diest.** very poor.

nefarious, *adj.* wicked.

negate, *v.,* **-gated, -gating.** to deny; nullify.

negative, *adj.* **1.** expressing refusal or denial. **2.** lacking positive attributes; undistinguished. **3.** not positive. **4.** *Maths.* denoting a quantity less than zero. **5.** *Elect.* pertaining to the kind of electricity present at the pole from which electrons leave an electric generator or battery, having an excess of electrons. –*n.* **6.** something negative. **7.** *Photog.* an image in which the gradations of light and shade are represented in reverse.

neglect, *v.* **1.** to pay no attention to. **2.** to be careless about, or not to care for. –*n.* **3.** the act or fact of neglecting. **4.** the fact or state of being neglected.

339

neg·li·gee /'nɛgləʒeɪ/, *n.* a woman's dressing-gown, esp. a very flimsy one.

neg·li·gent, *adj.* guilty of or characterised by neglect. – **negligence**, *n.*

neg·lig·ible, *adj.* able to be neglected or disregarded.

nego·tiate, *v.*, **-ated, -ating. 1.** to bring about by discussion and settlement of terms. **2.** to clear or pass (an obstacle, etc.). **3.** to dispose of by sale or transfer. – **negotiation**, *n.* – **negotiable**, *adj.*

neigh, *n.* the sound a horse makes; whinny.

neigh·bour, *n.* one who lives near another.

neigh·bour·hood, *n.* the region near or about some place or thing, often with reference to its character or inhabitants.

neither, *adj., pron., conj.* not either.

nemesis, *n., pl.* **-ses.** an agent of retribution or punishment.

neolo·gism /nɪ'ɒlədʒɪzəm/, *n.* a new word or phrase.

neon, *n.* a chemically inert gaseous element chiefly used in lamps. *Symbol:* Ne

neo·nate, *n.* a newborn child.

neo·phyte, *n.* **1.** a converted heathen, heretic, etc. **2.** a beginner.

nephew, *n.* **1.** a son of one's brother or sister. **2.** a son of one's spouse's brother or sister.

neph·ritis, *n.* inflammation of the kidneys.

nepo·tism, *n.* patronage bestowed because of family relationship and not of merit.

nerve, *n.* **1.** one or more bundles of fibres, forming part of a system which conveys impulses of sensation, motion, etc., between the brain or spinal cord and other parts of the body. **2.** firmness or courage in trying circumstances. **3.** (*pl.*) nervousness. **4.** *Colloq.* impertinent assurance.

nerv·ous, *adj.* **1.** of or pertaining to the nerves. **2.** characterised by uneasiness or apprehension.

nervy, *adj.*, **-vier, -viest. 1.** nervous. **2.** excitable; irritable.

nest, *n.* **1.** a structure used by a bird for incubation and the rearing of its young. **2.** an assemblage of things that fit within each other. –*v.* **3.** to build or have a nest.

nest egg, *n.* money saved as the basis of a fund or for emergencies.

nestle, *v.*, **-tled, -tling.** to lie close and snug.

net[1], *n.* **1.** a mesh of cotton, silk, etc. **2.** a piece or bag of net for catching fish, butterflies, etc.

net[2], *adj., n., v.*, **netted, netting.** –*adj.* **1.** remaining after deductions, as tax, have been made. **2.** final; conclusive. –*n.* **3.** net income, profits, or the like. –*v.* **4.** to gain or produce as clear profit. Also, **nett.**

net·ball, *n.* a game similar to basketball.

nether, *adj.* lower or under.

nettle, *n.* a plant with stinging hairs.

net·work, *n.* a system of interconnected people, companies, television stations, etc.

neural, *adj.* of or pertaining to a nerve or the nervous system.

neuro·sis, *n., pl.* **-ses.** an emotional disorder in which feelings of anxiety, obsessional thoughts, etc., dominate the personality. – **neurotic**, *adj., n.*

neuter, *adj.* **1.** *Gram.* of a gender which is neither masculine or feminine. **2.** sexless, or of indeterminate sex.

neutral, *adj.* **1.** (of a person or state) refraining from taking part in a controversy or war between others. **2.** *Chem.* indefinite. **3.** *Chem.* neither acid nor alkaline. **4.** *Elect.* neither positive nor negative. *-n.* **5.** a person or a state that remains neutral, as in a war. **6.** *Mach.* the position or state of disengaged gears, etc. – **neutralise**, *v.* – **neutrality**, *n.*

neutron, *n.* an elementary particle which is a constituent of all atomic nuclei except normal hydrogen.

neutron bomb, *n.* a nuclear weapon which kills people but causes relatively little damage to property. Also, **clean bomb**.

never, *adv.* at no time.

nevertheless, *adv.* notwithstanding; however.

new, *adj.* **1.** of recent origin or production. **2.** of a kind appearing for the first time. **3.** unfamiliar or strange (*to*). **4.** further; additional. **5.** fresh or unused. *-adv.* **6.** recently or lately. **7.** freshly; anew or afresh.

news, *n.pl.* (*construed as sing.*) **1.** the report of events as published in a newspaper, journal, radio, television, etc. **2.** information not previously known.

newspaper, *n.* a printed publication issued at regular intervals, containing news, comment, features, and advertisements.

newsprint, *n.* paper to print newspapers on.

newsreel, *n.* a short film presenting current news events.

newt, *n.* any of various small, semi-aquatic salamanders.

newton, *n.* the derived SI unit of force. *Symbol:* N

next, *adj.* (*superl. of* **nigh**), *adv. –adj.* **1.** immediately following. **2.** nearest. *–adv.* **3.** in the nearest place, time, importance, etc. **4.** on the first subsequent occasion.

nexus, *n., pl.* **nexus**. a tie or link.

nib, *n.* the point of a pen, esp. with a split tip for drawing up ink and for writing.

nibble, *v.*, **-bled**, **-bling**, *n. –v.* **1.** to bite off small bits of (a thing). *–n.* **2.** a small morsel or bit.

nice, *adj.*, **nicer**, **nicest**. **1.** agreeable; delightful. **2.** requiring great accuracy or delicacy. **3.** minute, fine, or subtle, as a distinction. – **nicety**, *n.*

niche, *n.* **1.** an ornamental recess in a wall, etc. **2.** a place suitable or appropriate for a person or thing.

nick, *n.* **1.** a notch, groove, or the like, cut into something. *–v.* **2.** to notch. **3.** *Colloq.* to steal.

nickel, *n.* *Chem.* a hard, silvery white, ductile and malleable metallic element. *Symbol:* Ni

nickname, *n.* a name substituted for the proper name of a person, place, etc.

nicotine, *n.* a poisonous alkaloid, the active principle of tobacco.

niece, *n.* **1.** a daughter of one's brother or sister. **2.** a daughter of one's spouse's brother or sister.

nifty, *adj.*, **-tier**, **-tiest**. *Colloq.* smart; stylish; fine.

niggard, *n.* a stingy person. – **niggardly**, *adj.*

nigger, *n.* (*derog.*) a person with a dark skin.

niggle

niggle, *v.,* **-gled, -gling. 1.** to make constant petty criticisms. **2.** to irritate; annoy.

nigh, *adv., adj.* **nigher, highest** or **next.** –*adv.* **1.** near in space, time, or relation. –*adj.* **2.** being near; not distant; near in relationship. **3.** short or direct.

night, *n.* the interval of darkness between sunset and sunrise.

night·cap, *n. Colloq.* an alcoholic or other drink taken before going to bed.

night·ingale, *n.* a small migratory bird of the thrush family, noted for the melodious song of the male.

nightly, *adj.* **1.** coming, occurring, etc., at night. **2.** coming or occurring each night. –*adv.* **3.** at or by night. **4.** on every night.

night·mare, *n.* a condition during sleep, or a dream, marked by painful emotion.

nihil·ism /'naɪəlɪzəm, 'nɪ-/, *n.* total disbelief in religion or moral principles or in established laws and institutions.

nil, *n.* nothing.

nimble, *adj.,* **-bler, -blest.** quick and light in movement.

nimbus, *n., pl.* **-bi, -buses.** a radiance about the head of a divine or sacred personage.

nin·com·poop, *n.* a fool.

nine, *n.* a cardinal number, 8 plus 1. – **ninth,** *adj., n.*

nine·teen, *n.* a cardinal number, 10 plus 9. – **nineteenth,** *adj., n.*

ninety, *n.* a cardinal number, 10 times 9. – **ninetieth** *adj., n.*

ninny, *n., pl.* **-nies.** a fool.

nip[1]**,** *v.,* **nipped, nipping. 1.** to pinch or bite. **2.** to check in growth or development. **3.** to affect painfully or injuriously, as cold does. **4.** *Colloq.* to move or go suddenly or quickly, or slip (*away, off, up,* etc.).

nip[2]**,** *n.* **1.** a sip. **2.** a small measure of spirits.

nipple, *n.* a protuberance of the breast where, in the female, the milk ducts discharge; teat.

nippy, *adj.,* **-pier, -piest.** biting, as the cold.

nit, *n.* the egg of a louse.

nitro·gen, *n.* a colourless, odourless, gaseous element which forms about $\frac{4}{5}$ of the volume of the atmosphere. *Symbol:* N – **nitrogenous,** *adj.*

nitro·glycerine, *n.* a colourless, highly explosive oil.

nitty-gritty, *n. Colloq.* the hard core of a matter.

nitwit, *n.* a slow-witted or foolish person.

nix, *n. Colloq.* nothing.

no[1]**,** *adv., n., pl.* **noes.** –*adv.* **1.** a word used: to express dissent, denial, or refusal, as in response (opposed to *yes*). **2.** not in any degree; not at all (used with a comparative): *no better weapon.* –*n.* **3.** a denial or refusal.

no[2]**,** *adj.* **1.** not any: *No gold was found.* **2.** not at all: *He's no genius.*

nobble, *v.,* **-bled, -bling.** *Colloq.* to disable (a horse) by drugging it.

noble, *adj.,* **nobler, noblest,** *n.* –*adj.* **1.** distinguished by birth, rank, or title. **2.** of an exalted moral character or excellence. –*n.* **3.** a person of noble birth or name. – **nobility,** *n.*

nobody, *pron., n., pl.* **-bodies.** –*pron.* **1.** no person. –*n.* **2.** a person of no importance; person esp. socially.

noc·turnal, *adj.* **1.** of or pertaining to the night. **2.** active by night.

nod, v., nodded, nodding, n. –v. 1. to make a slight, quick inclination of (the head). 2. **nod off**, Colloq. to go to sleep. –n. 3. a short, quick inclination of the head, as in assent, greeting, command, or drowsiness.

node, n. 1. a knot, protuberance, or knob. 2. a centring point of component parts. – **nodal**, adj.

no-fault, adj. of or pertaining to legislation, insurance, etc., which does not depend on the assignation of guilt or blame to any of the parties involved.

noggin, n. 1. a small measure of spirits. 2. Colloq. the head.

Noh, n. Japanese drama.

noise, n. sound, esp. of a loud, harsh, or confused kind. – **noisy**, adj.

noisome, adj. offensive.

nomad, n. one of a race or tribe without fixed abode. – **nomadic**, adj.

nomenclature /nə'mɛnklətʃə, 'noumənkleɪtʃə/, n. a set or system of names or terms.

nominal, adj. 1. being such in name only. 2. (of a price, consideration, etc.) trifling in comparison with the actual value. 3. Gram. used as or like a noun.

nominate, v., -nated, -nating. to propose as a proper person for appointment or election to an office. – **nomination**, n.

nominee, n. one nominated as to fill an office or stand for election.

nonagenarian, adj. between 90 and 100 years old.

nonagon, n. a polygon having 9 angles and 9 sides.

nonchalant /'nɒnʃələnt/, adj. coolly unconcerned; casual. – **nonchalance**, n.

non-committal, adj. not committing oneself to a particular view, course, or the like.

non-conformity, n. 1. lack of conformity or agreement. 2. failure or refusal to conform. – **nonconformist**, n., adj.

nondescript, adj. of no particular type or kind.

none, pron. 1. no one; not one: *There is none left*. 2. not any, as of something indicated: *I want none of that cake*. 3. no part; nothing. 4. (construed as pl.) no, or not any, persons or things: *None turned up*. –adv. 5. to no extent: *It's none too soon*.

nonentity, n., pl. -ties. a person or thing of no importance.

nonetheless, adv. however.

nonplussed, adj. confused; perplexed.

nonsense, n. that which makes no sense or is lacking in sense. – **nonsensical**, adj.

non sequitur /nɒn 'sɛkwɪtə/, n. an inference or a conclusion which does not follow from the premises.

noodle, n. a type of pasta cut into long, narrow, flat strips.

nook, n. any secluded or obscure corner.

noon, n. midday; 12 o'clock.

no-one, pron. nobody.

noose, n. a loop with a running knot which tightens as the rope is pulled.

nor, conj. a negative conjunction used: **a.** as the correlative to a preceding *neither*: *He could neither read nor write*. **b.** to continue the force of a negative, such as *not*, *no*, *never*, etc., occurring in a preceding clause. **c.** in the sense of *and-*

343

nor ...*not: They are happy; nor need we mourn.*

norm, *n.* 1. a standard, model, or pattern. 2. a mean or average.

normal, *adj.* 1. conforming to the standard or the common type; regular, usual. –*n.* 2. the standard or type. 3. the average or mean. – **normality,** *n.*

north, *n.* 1. a cardinal point of the compass lying to the right of a person facing the setting sun or west. –*adj.* 2. directed or proceeding towards the north. 3. coming from the north, as a wind. –*adv.* 4. towards or in the north. Also, *esp. Naut.,* **nor'**. – **northerly,** *adj., adv.* – **northern,** *adj.*

nose, *n., v.,* **nosed, nosing.** –*n.* 1. the part of the face or head which contains the nostrils. 2. this part as the organ of smell. –*v.* 3. to perceive as by the nose. 4. to touch or rub with the nose. 5. to smell or sniff. 6. to seek as if by smelling or scent (*after, for,* etc.); pry (*about, into,* etc.).

nose-dive, *n.* a plunge of an aeroplane with the fore part vertically downwards.

nose-gay, *n.* a bunch of flowers or herbs.

nosh, *v., n. Colloq.* (to have) a snack or a meal.

nos-talgia, *n.* a longing for home, family and friends, or the past. – **nostalgic,** *adj.*

nos-tril, *n.* one of the external openings of the nose.

nos-trum, *n.* 1. a patent medicine. 2. a quack medicine.

nosy, *adj.,* **-sier, -siest.** *Colloq.* prying; inquisitive. Also, **nosey.**

not, *adv.* (a word expressing nega-

not negotiable

tion, denial, refusal, or prohibition).

not·able, *adj.* 1. noteworthy. 2. prominent or distinguished, as persons.

nota·tion, *n.* a system of graphic symbols for a specialised use, other than ordinary writing.

notch, *n.* 1. a more or less angular cut in a narrow surface or an edge. –*v.* 2. to cut or make a notch or notches in. 3. to score, as in a game (*up*).

note, *n., v.,* **noted, noting.** –*n.* 1. a brief record of something set down, as to assist the memory. 2. a short informal letter. 3. a banknote 4. importance or consequence. 5. notice or heed. 6. *Music.* a sign or character used to represent a sound. 7. a quality or character. –*v.* 8. to mark down, as in writing. 9. to observe carefully; give heed to.

note·worthy, *adj.* worthy of notice.

nothing, *n.* 1. not anything; naught. 2. a cipher or nought. –*adv.* 3. in no respect or degree: *We had nothing like the numbers.*

notice, *n., v.,* **-ticed, -ticing.** –*n.* 1. information. 2. a warning. 3. a note, placard, or the like. 4. a notification of the termination of an agreement. 5. observation or heed. –*v.* 6. to pay attention to. 7. to perceive.

notify, *v.,* **-fied, -fying.** to inform of something. – **notification,** *n.*

notion, *n.* a more or less general idea of something.

not negotiable, *adj.* (of a cheque which is crossed) indicating that the person to whom it is given has no better title to it than the person had from whom he received it.

notorious

noto·ri·ous, *adj.* widely but unfavourably known. – **notoriety**, *n.*

not·with·stand·ing, *prep.* 1. in spite of. –*adv.* 2. nevertheless. –*conj.* 3. although.

nougat /'nuga/, *n.* a hard, pastelike sweet.

nought, *n.* a cipher (0); zero.

noun, *n.* the part of speech comprising words denoting person, places, things.

nour·ish, *v.* 1. to sustain with food. 2. to foster or promote. – **nourishment**, *n.*

nous /naʊs/, *n. Colloq.* common sense.

novel[1], *n.* a fictitious prose narrative of considerable length. – **novelist**, *n.*

novel[2], *adj.* different from anything seen or known before.

novelty, *n., pl.* **-ties.** 1. newness, or strangeness. 2. a novel thing, experience, or proceeding.

novice, *n.* one who is new to the circumstances, work, etc., in which he is placed.

novi·tiate, *n.* the state or period of being a novice of a religious order or congregation.

now, *adv.* 1. at the present time or moment. 2. (more emphatically) immediately or at once. 3. at the time or moment only just past. 4. nowadays. –*conj.* 5. since, or seeing that.

nowa·days, *adv.* at the present day; in these times.

no·where, *adv.* not anywhere.

nox·ious, *adj.* 1. harmful to health. 2. (of an animal, insect, plant, etc.) declared harmful by statute.

null

nozzle, *n.* a projecting spout or the like, as of a hose or rocket.

nuance, *n.* a shade of meaning, feeling, etc.

nub, *n.* 1. a knob or protuberance. 2. *Colloq.* the point or gist of anything.

nubile, *adj.* (of a girl or young woman) marriageable, esp. as to age or physical development.

nuclear, *adj.* 1. of or forming a nucleus. 2. pertaining to or powered by atomic energy.

nucleus, *n., pl.* **-clei, -cleuses.** 1. a central part or thing about which other parts or things are grouped. 2. *Biol.* a differentiated mass of protoplasm in the cell, forming an essential element in its growth metabolism and reproduction. 3. *Physics.* the central core of an atom, composed of protons and neutrons.

nude, *adj.* 1. naked or unclothed. 2. without the usual coverings, furnishings, etc. – **nudity**, *n.*

nudge, *v.,* nudged, nudging, *n.* –*v.* 1. to push slightly or jog, esp. with the elbow. –*n.* 2. a slight push or jog.

nudism, *n.* the practice of going nude as a means of healthful living. – **nudist**, *n.*

nuga·tory, *adj.* worthless.

nugget, *n.* a lump of something, esp. gold.

nug·getty, *adj. Colloq.* short and heavily built.

nui·sance, *n.* 1. a highly annoying thing or person. 2. something offensive or annoying to individuals or to the community.

null, *adj.* 1. of no effect or significance. 2. non-existent. – **nullify**, *v.*

345

nulla-nulla *n.* an Aboriginal club or heavy weapon. Also, **nulla**.

numb, *adj.* deprived of the power of sensation and movement.

numbat, *n.* a small, slender reddish-brown, insectivorous Aust. marsupial.

number, *n.* 1. the sum of a collection of units or any generalisation of this concept. 2. the particular numeral assigned to anything in order to fix its place in a series. 3. a word or symbol used in counting or to denote a total. 4. a quantity (large or small) of individuals. 5. (*pl.*) numerical strength or superiority, as in a political party, organisation, etc. –*v.* 6. to number or be numbered. 7. to mark with or distinguish by a number or numbers. 8. to amount to in number.

numeral, *n.* 1. a word or words expressing a number. 2. a letter or figure denoting a number.

numer·ate, *v.*, **-rated, -rating.** to number; count.

numer·ator, *n. Maths.* that term (usu. written above the line) of a fraction which shows how many parts of a unit are taken.

numeri·cal, *adj.* pertaining to or denoting number.

numer·ous, *adj.* very many.

numis·matics, *n.* the science of coins and medals.

nun, *n.* a woman devoted to a religious life under vows.

nun·nery, *n., pl.* **-neries.** a religious house for nuns; convent.

nup·tial, *adj.* of or pertaining to marriage.

nurse, *n., v.,* **nursed, nursing.** –*n.* 1. a woman or man who has the care of the sick or infirm. –*v.* 2. to (act as) nurse. 3. to seek to cure (a cold, etc.) by taking care of oneself. 4. to look after carefully so as to promote growth, etc. 5. to hold in the arms; embrace. 6. to suckle (an infant).

nurs·ery, *n., pl.* **-eries.** 1. a room or place set apart for young children. 2. a place where young trees or other plants are raised for transplanting or for sale.

nur·ture, *v.,* **-tured, -turing.** to feed, nourish, or support during the stages of growth.

nut, *n.* 1. a dry fruit consisting of an edible kernel enclosed in a woody shell. 2. *Colloq.* an enthusiast. 3. *Colloq.* an eccentric or insane person. 4. a perforated block with an internal thread used to screw on the end of a bolt, etc.

nutmeg, *n.* an aromatic spice.

nutri·ent /'njutrint/, *adj.* 1. nourishing. –*n.* 2. a substance that nourishes.

nutri·ment, *n.* that which nourishes.

nutri·tion, *n.* the act or process of nourishing or of being nourished.

nutri·tious, *adj.* nourishing, esp. in a high degree.

nutri·tive, *adj.* serving to nourish.

nuzzle, *v.,* **-zled, -zling.** 1. to burrow or root with the nose, as an animal does. 2. to snuggle or cuddle up with someone or something.

nylon, *n.* a synthetic material used for yarn, bristles, etc.

nymph, *n.* 1. a mythological divinity supposed to inhabit nature as a beautiful maiden. 2. a beautiful or graceful young woman.

nympho·mania, *n.* uncontrollable sexual desire in women.
– **nymphomaniac**, *adj., n.*

Oo

O, o, *n., pl.* **O's** or **Os; o's, os,** or **oes.** 1. the 15th letter of the English alphabet. 2. the Arabic cipher; zero; nought (o).

o', *prep.* an abbreviated form of *of*.

oaf, *n.* a stupid or loutish person.

oak, *n.* a large deciduous tree.

oar, *n.* a long shaft of wood with a blade at one end, used for propelling a boat.

oasis, *n., pl.* **oases.** a fertile place in a desert region.

oat, *n.* 1. (*usu. pl.*) a cereal grass cultivated for its edible seed. 2. **sow (one's) wild oats,** to indulge in the excesses or follies of youth.

oath, *n., pl.* **oaths.** 1. a solemn appeal to God, or to some revered person or thing, in attestation of the truth of a statement, etc. 2. a curse.

obdurate, *adj.* hardened against persuasions or tender feelings.

obedient, *adj.* obeying, or willing to obey. – **obedience,** *n.*

obeisance, *n.* deference or homage.

obelisk, *n.* a tapering, four-sided shaft of stone.

obese, *adj.* excessively fat. – **obesity,** *n.*

obey, *v.* 1. to fulfil the commands or instructions of. 2. (of things) to act in conformity with. 3. to be obedient.

obituary, *n.* a notice of the death of a person, often with a brief biographical sketch.

object, *n* 1. a visible or tangible thing. 2. the end towards which effort is directed. 3. *Gram.* the noun or its substitute which represents the goal or end of an action. –*v.* 4. to express or feel disapproval.

objection, *n.* something adduced or said in disagreement or disapproval.

objectionable, *adj.* unpleasant; offensive.

objective, *n.* 1. an end towards which efforts are directed. –*adj.* 2. *Gram.* denoting the object of transitive verbs. 3. unbiased. 4. of or pertaining to objects. – **objectivity,** *n.*

obligation, *n.* 1. a binding requirement as to action; duty. 2. a benefit for which gratitude is due. – **obligate,** *v.*

obligatory /ɒˈblɪɡətəri, -trɪ/, *adj.* required as a matter of obligation.

oblige, *v.,* **obliged, obliging.** 1. to require or constrain, as by law or necessity. 2. to place under a debt of gratitude for some benefit. 3. to favour or accommodate (*with*). 4. to do something as a favour.

obliging, *adj.* disposed to do favours or services.

oblique, *adj.* 1. neither perpendicular nor parallel to a given line or surface. 2. not straight or direct.

obliterate, *v.,* **-rated, -rating.** to remove all traces of.

oblivion, *n.* the state of being forgotten.

oblivious, *adj.* forgetful; unmindful; unconscious (*of* or *to*).

oblong, *adj.* in the form of a rect-

347

oblong

angle of greater length than breadth.

obnox·ious, *adj.* offensive; odious.

oboe, *n.* a woodwind instrument.

obscene, *adj.* offensive to modesty or decency. – **obscenity**, *n.*

obscure, *adj.*, **-scurer**, **-scurest**, **-scured**, **-scuring**. –*adj.* 1. (of meaning) not clear or plain. 2. inconspicuous or indistinct. –*v.* 3. to make obscure, indistinct, etc. – **obscurity**, *n.* – **obscuration**, *n.*

obsequi·ous, *adj.* weakly compliant or deferential.

obser·vant, *adj.* quick to notice or perceive.

obser·va·tory, *n., pl.* **-tories**. a place in or from which observations, esp. astronomical or meteorological, are made.

observe, *v.*, **-served**, **-serving**. 1. to see or notice. 2. to regard with attention. 3. to comment. 4. to show regard for by some appropriate procedure, ceremonies, etc. – **observation**, *n.*

obses·sion, *n.* a persistent feeling, idea, or the like, which a person cannot escape. – **obsess**, *v.*

obsoles·cent, *adj.* becoming obsolete.

obso·lete, *adj.* fallen into disuse, or no longer in use.

obsta·cle, *n.* something that stands in the way of progress.

obstet·rics, *n.* the branch of medicine dealing with childbirth. – **obstetrician**, *n.* – **obstetric**, *adj.*

obsti·nate, *adj.* firmly and often perversely adhering to one's purpose, opinion, etc. – **obstinacy**, *n.*

obstrep·erous, *adj.* resisting control in a noisy manner; unruly.

obs·truct, *v.* 1. to block or close up.

occur

2. to interrupt, make difficult, or oppose the passage, progress, course, etc., of. – **obstruction**, *n.*

obtain, *v.* 1. to get or acquire. 2. to be prevalent or in vogue.

obtru·sive, *adj.* undesirably obvious.

obtuse, *adj.* 1. blunt in form. 2. not sensitive or observant.

obvi·ate, *v.*, **-ated**, **-ating**. to meet and dispose of or prevent (difficulties, etc.).

obvi·ous, *adj.* clearly perceptible or evident.

occa·sion, *n.* 1. a particular time. 2. the immediate or incidental cause of some action or result. –*v.* 3. to bring about. 4. **on occasion**, now and then.

occa·sion·al, *adj.* 1. occurring now and then. 2. intended for use whenever needed.

occlude, *v.*, **-cluded**, **-cluding**. to stop up (a passage, etc.). – **occlusion**, *n.*

occult, *adj.* 1. beyond the bounds of ordinary knowledge. –*n.* 2. the supernatural.

occu·pant, *n.* a tenant of a house, estate, office, etc. – **occupancy**, *n.*

occu·pation, *n.* 1. one's habitual employment or calling. 2. the period during which a country is under the control of foreign military forces.

occupational therapy, *n.* a method of therapy consisting of light work, such as basketry, carpentry, etc.

occupy, *v.*, **-pied**, **-pying**. 1. to take up (space, time, etc.). 2. to engage (the mind, attention, etc.). 3. to take possession of (a place), as by invasion. 4. to hold (a position, office, etc.).

occur, *v.*, **-curred**, **-curring**. 1. to come

occur

to pass. **2.** to suggest itself in thought (*to*). – **occurrence**, *n*.

ocean, *n.* the vast body of salt water which covers almost ¾ of the earth's surface.

ochre, *n.* any of a class of natural earths used as pigments, ranging from pale yellow to an orange or reddish yellow.

ocker, *n. Colloq.* the archetypal uncultivated Aust. working man.

o'clock, *adv.* of or by the clock: *It's 2 o'clock.*

octa·gon, *n.* a polygon having 8 angles and 8 sides.

octave, *n.* a series or group of 8.

octet, *n.* any group of 8. Also, **octette**.

octo·gen·arian, *n., adj.* (someone) between 80 and 90 years of age.

octo·pus, *n., pl.* **-puses, -pi.** a sea animal with 8 arms.

ocu·list, *n.* an ophthalmologist.

OD, *n., v.,* **OD'd, OD·ing.** *Colloq.* **1.** an overdose, esp. of an injected addictive drug, as heroin. –*v.* **2.** to give oneself an overdose (*on*).

odd, *adj.* **1.** differing in character from what is ordinary or usual. **2.** (of a number) leaving a remainder of one when divided by 2 (opposed to **even**). **3.** more or less: *There were 30 odd present.* **4.** (of a pair) not matching. **5.** occasional or casual. **6.** not forming part of any particular group, set, or class: *odd man out.* – **oddity**, *n.*

odd·ball, *n. Colloq.* an eccentric.

odd·ment, *n.* a remnant, or the like.

odds, *n. pl.* **1.** the amount by which the bet of one party to a wager exceeds that of the other. **2.** balance of probability in favour of something occurring or being the case. **3. at odds**, in disagreement. **4. make no odds**, not to matter. **5. odds and ends**, remnants; fragments.

ode, *n.* a lyric poem.

odium, *n.* hatred or repulsion. – **odious**, *adj.*

odom·eter /ɒˈdɒmətə, oʊ-/, *n.* an instrument for measuring distance. Also, **hodometer**.

odour, *n.* **1.** that property of a substance which affects the sense of smell. **2.** a fragrance. **3.** a bad smell.

oeso·pha·gus /əˈsɒfəgəs/, *n., pl.* **-gi.** a tube connecting the mouth or pharynx with the stomach.

oestro·gen, *n.* any one of a group of female sex hormones.

of, *prep.* a particle indicating: **1.** distance or direction from, separation, deprivation, riddance, etc.: *within a metre of; to cure of.* **2.** derivation or source: *of good family.* **3.** occasion or reason: *to die of hunger.* **4.** material or contents: *a packet of sugar.* **5.** a relation of identity: *the city of Sydney.* **6.** reference or respect: *to talk of peace.* **7.** the attribution of a quality to: *good of you to come.*

off, *adv.* **1.** away from a position occupied, or from contact. **2.** as a deduction: *5 percent off.* **3.** distant (in future time). **4.** disconnected: *The electric current is off.* **5.** away from employment or service: *The night sister is now off.* **6.** into execution or effect: *The games didn't come off.* **7.** on one's way or journey. –*prep.* **8.** away from. **9.** from by subtraction. **10.** away or disengaged from (duty, work, etc.). **11.** *Colloq.* refraining from: *off the grog.* –*adj.* **12.** no longer in effect or operation. **13.** in bad taste. **14.** (of food)

349

tainted. **15. off and on.** Also, **on and off.** intermittently.

offal, *n.* 1. the inedible parts of a meat carcass. 2. the organs of an animal used as food.

off-beat, *adj.* unconventional.

off-chance, *n.* a remote possibility.

off-colour, *adj. Colloq.* unwell.

off-cut, *n.* that which is cut off, as from paper or meat.

offence, *n.* 1. a wrong; sin. 2. a crime which is not indictable, being punishable summarily (**summary offence**). 3. a feeling of resentful displeasure. 4. attack or assault. – **offensive**, *adj.*

offend, *v.* 1. to cause resentful displeasure in. 2. to affect (the sense, taste, etc.) disagreeably. 3. to commit a sin, crime, or fault.

offer, *v.* 1. to present for acceptance. 2. to propose or volunteer (to do something). 3. to tender or bid, as a price. 4. to occur. –*n.* 5. a bid. 6. something offered.

offer·ing, *n.* something offered.

off-hand, *adv.* 1. without previous thought or preparation. –*adj.* 2. informal or casual.

office, *n.* 1. a room or place for the transaction of business, or the like. 2. official position.

offi·cer, *n.* one who holds a position of authority.

offi·cial, *n.* 1. one who is charged with some form of official duty. *adj.* 2. of or pertaining to a position of duty, trust, or authority.

offi·cial·ese, *n.* a style of language found in official documents and characterised by pretentiousness, pedantry, obscurity, and the use of jargon.

offi·ciate, *v.*, **-ated, -ating.** to perform the duties of any office or position.

offi·cious, *adj.* pushing one's services upon others.

offing, in the phrase **in the offing**, not very distant.

off-peak, *adj.* of or pertaining to a period of time of less activity than the normal.

off-putting, *adj. Colloq.* disconcerting; discouraging.

off-season, *adj.* (of a time of year) unpopular for a specific activity.

offset, *v.*, **-set, -setting**, *n.* –*v.* 1. to balance by something else as an equivalent. –*n.* 2. a compensating equivalent.

off-shoot, *n.* a shoot from a main stem.

off·side, *adj. Sport.* in an illegal position.

off·spring, *n.* children or young of a particular parent.

oft, *adv.* often.

often, *adv.* in many cases; frequently.

ogle, *v.*, **ogled, ogling.** to eye with amorous or impertinently familiar glances.

ogre, *n.* a hideous giant.

oh, *interj.* (an expression denoting surprise, pain, etc., or for attracting attention.)

ohm, *n.* the derived SI unit of resistance. *Symbol:* Ω

oil, *n.* 1. any of a large class of insoluble viscous substances. 2. *Painting.* (a painting done in) oil colour(s). –*v.* 3. to smear or supply with oil. –*adj.* 4. concerned with the production or use of oil. 5. using oil, esp. as a fuel.

oil colour

oil colour, *n.* a colour or paint made by grinding a pigment in oil.

oil·skin, *n.* a cotton fabric made waterproof by treatment with oil.

oint·ment, *n.* medicated cream for application to the skin.

okay, *Colloq.* –*adj.* 1. all right. –*adv.* 2. well; acceptably. –*v.* 3. to endorse; approve; accept. –*n.* 4. an approval or acceptance. Also, **ok**, **OK**, **O.K.**, **o.k.**

old, *adj.*, **older**, **oldest** or **elder**, **eldest**, *n.* –*adj.* 1. far advanced in years or life. 2. having reached a specified age. 3. familiar. 4. belonging to a past time. 5. deteriorated through age or long use. –*n.* 6. (used in combination) a person or animal of a specified age or age-group: *nursery for 2 year olds.*

olden, *adj.* of old; ancient.

old-fashioned, *adj.* out of fashion.

old hat, *Colloq.* old-fashioned.

old-timer, *n.* an old man.

oli·garchy, *n.*, *pl.* **-chies**. a form of government in which the power is vested in a few.

olive, *n.* 1. (the oily fruit of) an evergreen tree. 2. a shade of green or yellowish green.

olive branch, *n.* an emblem of peace.

ombuds·man /'ɒmbʌdzmən/, *n.* an official appointed to investigate complaints by citizens against the government or its agencies.

omel·ette, *n.* a dish consisting of eggs beaten and fried.

omen, *n.* a prophetic sign.

omi·nous, *adj.* portending evil; inauspicious.

omit, *v.*, **omitted**, **omitting**. to leave out or fail to do. – **omission**, *n.*

omni·bus, *n.*, *pl.* **-buses**. 1. →**bus**. 2.

one

a volume of reprinted works by a single author or ones related in interest or nature.

omni·potent /ɒm'nɪpətənt/, *adj.* almighty; all-powerful.

omni·present, *adj.* present everywhere at the same time.

omnis·cient /ɒm'nɪsiənt, ɒm'nɪʃənt/, *adj.* knowing all things.

omni·vorous, *adj.* eating both animal and plant foods.

on, *prep.* a particle expressing: 1. position above and in contact with a supporting surface: *on the table.* 2. contact with any surface: *on the wall.* 3. support, suspension, dependence, reliance, or means of conveyance: *on foot.* 4. time or occasion: *on Monday.* 5. with reference to something else: *on the left.* 6. membership or association: *on a jury.* –*adv.* 7. on oneself or itself: *to put clothes on.* 8. fast to a thing, as for support: *to hold on.* 9. forwards, onwards or along, as in any course or process: *to go on.* 10. with continuous procedure: *to work on.* 11. into or in active operation or performance: *to turn a machine on.* 12. operating or in use. 13. taking place. 14. **be on about**, be concerned about. 15. **not on**, *Colloq.* not a possibility; not allowable.

once, *adv.* 1. (at one time) in the past. –*conj.* 2. if or whenever. –*n.* 3. **all at once**, suddenly. 4. **at once**, immediately. 5. **once and for all**, finally and decisively. 6. **once upon a time**, long ago.

once-over, *n. Colloq.* a quick or superficial examination.

on·coming, *adj.* approaching.

one, *adj.* 1. being a single unit or individual. 2. some (day, etc., in the future). 3. single through union,

351

one

agreement, or harmony. **4.** a certain: *He introduced us to one Bill Smith.* **5.** a particular (time, etc. in the past). *–n.* **6.** the first and lowest whole number. **7.** a single person or thing. **8.** one and all, everybody. *–pron.* **9.** a person or thing understood. **10.** (*in certain pronominal combinations*) a person unless definitely specified otherwise: *every one.* **11.** anyone: *as good as one would desire.* **12.** a person or thing of the kind just mentioned: *The portraits are fine ones.*

oner·ous, *adj.* burdensome or troublesome.

one·self, *pron.* **1.** a person's self (often used for emphasis or reflexively). **2.** one's proper or normal self.

onion, *n.* (a widely cultivated plant with) an edible bulb.

on·looker, *n.* a spectator.

only, *adv.* **1.** without others or anything further. **2.** as recently as: *only yesterday.* **3.** only too, very; extremely. *–adj.* **4.** being the single one or the relatively few of the kind. *–conj.* **5.** but (introducing a single restriction). **6.** except that.

ono·mato·poeia /ˌɒnəmætəˈpiːə/, *n.* a figure of speech applied to a word the sounds of which reflect its meaning, as *buzz.*

onset, *n.* **1.** an assault or attack. **2.** a beginning.

on·shore, *adj.* **1.** towards or located on the shore. *–adv.* **2.** towards the shore.

onside, *adj.* in agreement.

on·slaught, *n.* an onset, esp. a vigorous or furious one.

onto, *prep.* to a place or position on.

onus, *n.* a burden; responsibility.

opening

onward, *adj.* directed or moving forwards.

on·wards, *adv.* towards a point ahead.

onyx, *n.* a quartz which consists of straight layers of differing colour.

oodles, *n.pl. Colloq.* a large quantity.

oomph, *n. Colloq.* vitality; energy.

oops, *interj.* (an exclamation of surprise or shock)

ooze[1], *v.,* **oozed, oozing.** (of moisture, etc.) to percolate or exude, as through pores or small openings.

ooze[2], *n.* soft mud, or slime.

opal, *n.* a mineral, some varieties of which are valued as gems.

opaque, *adj.* **1.** impenetrable to light. **2.** hard to understand; obscure. – **opacity,** *n.*

open, *adj.* **1.** not shut or closed, as a door, house, box, etc. **2.** not enclosed by barriers. **3.** that may be entered, used, etc., by all. **4.** (of shops, etc.) ready to do business. **5.** undecided, as a question. **6.** liable or subject. **7.** unobstructed, as a passage, view, etc. **8.** without prohibition: *open hunting season.* **9.** exposed to general view or knowledge. **10.** expanded or spread out. **11.** generous. *–v.* **12.** to make or become open. **13.** to give or afford access to. **14.** to render accessible to knowledge, etc. **15.** to set in action. **16.** to become receptive to, as the mind. **17.** to disclose or reveal (one's feelings, etc.). **18.** to become less close together. *–n.* **19.** an open or clear space. **20.** the open air. **21.** an open competition.

open-and-shut, *adj.* easily decided.

open-ended, *adj.* without fixed limits.

open·ing, *n.* **1.** a gap, hole, or aperture. 2. the initial stage of anything. 3. a vacancy. 4. an opportunity. 5. a formal or official beginning.

opera[1], *n.* an extended dramatic musical composition.

opera[2], *n.* plural form of opus.

oper·able, *adj.* 1. that can be put into practice. 2. admitting of a surgical operation.

oper·ate, *v.*, **-rated, -rating.** 1. to (make) work or run, as a machine. 2. to act effectively. 3. *Surg.* to perform surgery on a patient. 4. to carry on transactions, esp. speculatively or on a large scale. – **operation**, *n.*

oper·ational, *adj.* ready for use; in working order.

oper·ative, *adj.* 1. exerting force or influence. 2. pertaining to work or productive activity.

oper·ator, *n.* 1. one who deals in shares, currency, etc. 2. *Colloq.* one who successfully manipulates people or situations.

oph·thal·mic, *adj.* of or pertaining to the eye.

oph·thal·mology, *n.* the science dealing with the anatomy, functions, and diseases of the eye. – **ophthalmologist**, *n.*

opiate, *n.* a medicine that contains opium and induces sleep.

opinion, *n.* a personal view, attitude, or estimation.

opin·ion·ated, *adj.* obstinate or conceited in one's opinions.

opium, *n.* a narcotic, used in medicine to induce sleep, relieve pain, etc.

oppo·nent, *n.* one who is on the opposing side.

oppor·tune, *adj.* 1. appropriate or favourable. 2. occurring at an appropriate time; timely.

oppor·tun·ism, *n.* the practice of adapting actions, etc., to expediency.

oppor·tun·ity, *n., pl.* **-ties.** an appropriate occasion.

opportunity shop, *n.* a shop run by a charity, etc., for the sale of second-hand goods. Also, **op-shop.**

oppose, *v.*, **-posed, -posing.** 1. to act or contend in opposition to. 2. to hinder. 3. to be or act in opposition (to).

oppo·site, *adj.* 1. placed over against something else or in a corresponding position. –*n.* 2. one who or that which is opposite or contrary. –*prep.* 3. in a complementary role or position. –*adv.* 4. on opposite sides.

oppo·sition, *n.* 1. the action of opposing, or combating. 2. an opposing group.

oppress, *v.* 1. to lie heavily upon, as care, sorrow, etc. 2. to burden with cruel or unjust impositions or restraints. – **oppression**, *n.* – **oppressive**, *adj.*

opprob·rium, *n.* the disgrace incurred by shameful conduct. – **opprobrious**, *adj.*

opt, *v.* 1. to make a choice. 2. opt out, to decide not to participate.

opti·cal, *adj.* 1. acting by means of sight or light, as instruments. 2. visual.

opti·cian, *n.* a maker or seller of optical glasses and instruments.

opti·mism, *n.* disposition to hope for the best. – **optimist**, *n.* – **optimistic**, *adj.*

opti·mum, *n., pl.* **-ma, -mums,** *adj.* (the) best or most favourable.

option

option, *n.* 1. power or liberty of choosing. 2. something which may be or is chosen; choice. 3. the right to buy within a certain time. – **optional,** *adj.*

optom·etry, *n.* the practice or art of testing the eyes for glasses. – **optometrist,** *n.*

opu·lent, *adj.* wealthy, as persons or places. – **opulence,** *n.*

opus /'oʊpəs/, *n., pl.* **opera.** a work or composition. *Abbrev.:* op.

or, *conj.* a particle used: 1. to connect words, phrases, or clauses representing alternatives: *to be or not to be.* 2. often in correlation: *either ... or; or ... or; whether ... or.*

oracle, *n.* any person or thing serving as an agency of divine communication.

oral, *adj.* 1. pertaining to or uttered by the mouth. 2. employing speech.

orange, *n.* 1. a common citrus fruit. 2. a reddish yellow colour.

orang-outang, *n.* a large, long-armed anthropoid ape. Also, **orang, orang-utan.**

ora·tion, *n.* a formal speech.

orator /'ɒrətə/, *n.* a public speaker, esp. one of great eloquence.

ora·tory, *n.* the art of an orator.

orb, *n.* a sphere or globe.

orbit, *n.* 1. the curved path described by a planet, satellite, etc., about a body, as the earth or sun. –*v.* 2. to travel in such a path around. – **orbital,** *adj.*

orchard, *n.* a place where fruit trees are grown.

orches·tra, *n.* a group of performers on various musical instruments.

orches·trate, *v.,* -trated, -trating. 1. to compose or arrange (music) for

354

organ

performance by an orchestra. 2. to put together cohesively. – **orchestration,** *n.*

orchid, *n.* a tropical plant noted for its beautiful flowers.

ordain, *v.* to appoint authoritatively; decree; enact. – **ordination,** *n.*

ordeal, *n.* any severe test or trial.

order, *n.* 1. an authoritative command. 2. the disposition of things following one after another. 3. a condition in which everything is in its proper place. 4. any class, kind, or sort. 5. a quantity of goods purchased. 6. a written direction to pay money or provide or deliver goods. 7. **in order that,** to the end that. 8. **in order to,** as a means to. 9. **in short order,** speedily; promptly. 10. **on order,** ordered but not yet received. –*v.* 11. to give an order to or for. 12. to regulate or manage.

order·ly, *adj., n., pl.* -lies. –*adj.* 1. arranged in order or in a tidy manner. 2. characterised by order or discipline. –*n.* 3. a person employed, as in a hospital, for general duties.

ordinal number, *n.* any of the numbers *first, 2nd, 3rd, etc.,* which indicate the order in which things occur.

ordi·nance, *n.* 1. an authoritative command. 2. a public regulation.

ordi·nary, *adj., n., pl.* -ries. –*adj.* 1. of the usual kind. 2. somewhat inferior. –*n.* 3. the ordinary condition.

ordure, *n.* filth; excrement.

ore, *n.* a metal-bearing mineral or rock.

oreg·ano, *n.* a plant of the mint family, used in cookery.

organ, *n.* 1. a keyboard instrument

organ

consisting of one or more sets of pipes sounded by means of compressed air. 2. (in an animal or a plant) a part or member, as the heart, having some specific function.

organ·die, *n., pl.* **-dies.** a fine, thin, stiff, cotton fabric.

organ·ic, *adj.* 1. pertaining to (a class of chemical compounds derived from) living organisms. 2. of or pertaining to the organs of an animal or plant. 3. characterised by the systematic arrangement of parts.

organ·ic·ally, *adv.* 1. in an organic manner. 2. *Hort.* without the use of chemical fertilisers or pesticides.

organ·isation, *n.* 1. the process of organising. 2. the manner of being organised. 3. any organised whole. 4. the administrative personnel or apparatus of a business. – **organisational**, *adj.*

organ·ise, *v.,* **-nised, -nising.** 1. to systematise. 2. to give organic structure or character to.

organ·ism, *n.* any form of animal or plant life.

orgasm, *n.* a complex series of responses of the genital organs and skin at the culmination of a sexual act.

orgy, *n., pl.* **-gies.** wild revelry.

orient, *n.* 1. the Orient, the East, comprising the countries of Asia, esp. eastn Asia. –*v.* 2. →orientate.

orien·tal, *adj.* (*sometimes cap.*) of the Orient or East.

orien·tate, *v.,* **-tated, -tating.** to adjust with relation to surroundings, etc. – **orientation**, *n.*

orien·teer·ing, *n.* a race over a course consisting of a number of checkpoints which must be located with the aid of maps, compasses, etc.

oscillate

ori·fice, *n.* a mouthlike opening or hole.

ori·gami, *n.* the art of folding paper into shapes of flowers, birds, etc.

origin, *n.* 1. that from which anything is derived. 2. derivation from a particular source. 3. birth; parentage; extraction.

origi·nal, *adj.* 1. pertaining to the origin or beginning of something. 2. fresh; novel. 3. arising from a thing itself. 4. being that from which a copy or the like is made. –*n.* 5. a primary form or type from which varieties are derived. – **originality**, *n.*

origi·nate, *v.,* **-nated, -nating.** 1. to arise; spring. 2. to initiate; invent.

orna·ment, *n.* 1. an accessory or detail used to beautify the appearance. –*v.* 2. to furnish with ornaments. – **ornamental**, *adj.* – **ornamentation**, *n.*

ornate, *adj.* elaborately adorned.

ornith·ology, *n.* the branch of zoology that deals with birds.

orphan, *n.* 1. a child bereaved of his parents. –*v.* 2. to bereave of parents or a parent.

orphan·age, *n.* an institution for orphans.

ortho·dontics, *n.* the branch of dentistry that is concerned with the straightening of irregular teeth.

ortho·dox, *adj.* (of doctrine, ideas, etc.) accepted or approved. – **orthodoxy**, *n.*

ortho·paedics, *n.* the correction or cure of deformities and diseases of the skeletal system.

oscil·late, *v.,* **-lated, -lating.** 1. to

355

oscillate

swing as a pendulum. 2. to fluctuate or vibrate. – **oscillation**, *n.*

osmium, *n.* a hard, heavy, metallic element used for electric-light filaments, etc. *Symbol:* Os

osmo·sis, *n.* the diffusion of fluids through membranes.

osten·sible, *adj.* outward; professed; pretended.

osten·tation, *n.* pretentious show. – **ostentatious**, *adj.*

osteo·arthritis, *n.* a degenerative type of chronic arthritis.

osteo·pathy /ɒstɪˈɒpəθi/, *n.* the curing of disease by manipulation of parts of the body.

ostra·cise, *v.*, **-cised, -cising.** to exclude by general consent from society, privileges, etc.

ostrich, *n.* a large flightless bird.

other, *adj.* 1. additional. 2. different in kind. 3. being the remaining one or ones. 4. **every other**, every alternate. –*pron.* 5. the other one. 6. another person or thing.

other·wise, *adv.* 1. under other circumstances. 2. differently. 3. in other respects.

otter, *n.* a furred, carnivorous, aquatic mammal with webbed feet.

otto·man, *n., pl.* **-mans.** a low cushioned seat or stool.

ouch, *interj.* (an exclamation expressing sudden pain).

ought, *aux. v.* 1. to be bound in duty or moral obligation. 2. should according to necessity, justice, etc. (fol. by infinitive).

ouija /ˈwiːdʒə, -dʒi/, *n.* a board or table covering marked with words, letters of the alphabet, etc., used during seances.

ounce, *n.* a unit of mass in the imperial system, equal to $\frac{1}{16}$ lb.

outfit

our, *pron., adj.* the possessive form corresponding to *we* and *us*, used before a noun. Cf. **ours**.

ours, *pron.* a form of *our* used without a noun following.

our·selves, *pron. pl.* 1. a reflexive form of *us*: *We hurt ourselves.* 2. an emphatic form of *us* or *we*: *We used it for ourselves; We ourselves did it.*

oust, *v.* to expel from a position occupied.

out, *adv.* 1. forth from, away from, or not in a place, position, state, etc. 2. into the open. 3. to the end: *The fire burnt itself out.* –*adj.* 4. extinguished. 5. not in vogue or fashion. 6. into or in public notice or knowledge: *The secret is out.* 7. on strike. 8. from a source, etc., (*of*). 9. having used the last (*of*). 10. incorrect or inaccurate. 11. unconscious. –*prep.* 12. forth from: *out the door.* –*n.* 13. a means of escaping. – **outer**, *adj.*

out-and-out, *adj.* thoroughgoing.

out·back, *n.* (*sometimes cap.*) remote, sparsely inhabited back country.

out·break, *n.* 1. an outburst. 2. a public disturbance.

out·building, *n.* a detached building subordinate to a main building.

out·burst, *n.* a sudden and violent outpouring.

out·cast, *n.* a person who is cast out, as from home or society.

out·come, *n.* that which results from something.

out·crop, *n.* an emerging part.

out·cry, *n., pl.* **-cries.** loud or widespread protest or indignation.

out·dated, *adj.* old-fashioned.

out·doors, *adv., n.* (in) the open air.

outfit, *n., v.*, **-fitted, -fitting.** –*n.* 1. a set

outfit

of articles, clothes, etc., for any purpose. –v. 2. to equip.

out·go·ing, adj. 1. departing. 2. interested in and responsive to others.

out·growth, n. 1. a natural development or result. 2. an offshoot.

outing, n. an excursion.

out·landish, adj. freakish.

outlaw, n. 1. a habitual criminal. –v. 2. to prohibit.

outlay, n., v., -laid, -laying. –n. 1. an amount expended. –v. 2. to expend, as money.

outlet, n. 1. a vent or exit. 2. a market for goods.

out·line, n., v., -lined, -lining. –n. 1. the line by which a figure or object is bounded. 2. a general sketch or report, indicating only the main features. –v. 3. to give or draw an outline of.

out·look, n. the view from a place.

outmoded, adj. old-fashioned; obsolete.

out·patient, n. a patient receiving treatment at a hospital but not being an inmate.

out·post, n. any remote settlement.

output, n. 1. the amount produced, as in a given time. 2. information obtained from a computer on the completion of a calculation.

out·rage, n., v., -raged, -raging. –n. 1. any gross violation of law or decency. –v. 2. to shock. –**outrageous**, adj.

out·right, adj. 1. complete or total. –adv. 2. completely; entirely.

outset, n. the beginning or start.

out·side, n. 1. the exterior. 2. the space beyond an enclosure, boundary, etc. –adj. 3. done or originating beyond an enclosure, boundary, etc. 4. external. 5. not connected with an institution, society, etc. 6. extremely unlikely: *an outside chance*. –adv., prep. 7. on or to the outside (of).

out·sider, n. one not belonging to a particular group, etc.

out·skirts, n.pl. outer parts or districts.

out·spoken, adj. unreserved in speech.

out·standing, adj. prominent; striking.

out·strip, v., -stripped, -stripping. to do better than.

out·ward, adj. 1. directed towards the outside. 2. of or pertaining to the outside. –adv. 3. outwards.

out·ward·ly, adv. as regards appearance or outward manifestation.

out·wards, adv. towards the outside; out. Also, **outward**.

outwit, v., -witted, -witting. to get the better of by superior ingenuity.

ouzo /'uzoʊ/, n. an aniseed-flavoured liqueur of Greece.

ova, n. plural of ovum.

oval, adj. 1. egg-shaped. –n. 2. any of various oval things. 3. a flat area on which sporting activities can take place.

ovary, n., pl. -ries. 1. *Anat., Zool.* the female reproductive gland. 2. *Bot.* a container for unfertilised seed. –**ovarian**, adj.

ovate, adj. egg-shaped.

ovation, n. enthusiastic applause.

oven, n. a chamber or receptacle for baking or heating.

over, prep. 1. above in place or position. 2. above and to the other side

over

of. **3.** on or upon. **4.** here and there on or in: *Debris fell over the town.* **5.** more than. **6.** in preference to. **7.** throughout the duration of: *over the long weekend.* **8.** in reference to: *to quarrel over a debt.* **9.** by the agency of: *The news came over the radio.* **10.** besides. –*adv.* **11.** over the top or upper surface, or edge of something. **12.** so as to cover the surface. **13.** through a region, area, etc. **14.** all through: *to read a letter over.* **15.** so as to bring the upper end or side down or under. **16.** in repetition: *10 times over.* **17.** **all over, a.** thoroughly; entirely. **b.** done with; finished. –*adj.* **18.** higher in authority, station, etc. **19.** serving as an outer covering. **20.** in excess or addition. **21.** at an end. –*n.* **22.** *Cricket.* the number of balls delivered between successive changes of bowlers.

over·all, *adj.* **1.** covering or including everything. –*n.* **2.** (*oft. pl.*) trousers with a bib and shoulder straps. –*adv.* **3.** covering or including everything.

over·arm, *adj.* **1.** performed with the arm being raised above the shoulder, as bowling or swimming. –*adv.* **2.** in an overarm manner.

over·awe, *v.,* -awed, -awing. to subdue by inspiring awe.

over·balance, *v.,* -anced, -ancing. to (cause to) lose balance.

over·bearing, *adj.* domineering; rudely arrogant.

over·board, *adv.* over the side of a ship or boat.

over·cast, *adj.* **1.** overspread with clouds. **2.** dark; gloomy.

over·charge, *v.,* -charged, -charging, *n.* –*v.* **1.** to charge (a person) too high a price. –*n.* **2.** a charge in excess of a just price.

overlap

over·come, *v.,* -came, -come, -coming. to conquer (someone).

over·do, *v.,* -did, -done, -doing. **1.** to carry to excess. **2.** to overcook.

over·dose, *n., v.,* -dosed, -dosing. –*n.* **1.** an excessive dose. –*v.* **2.** to take an overdose of a drug.

over·draft, *n.* a draft in excess of one's credit balance.

over·draw, *v.,* -drew, -drawn, -drawing. to draw upon (an account, allowance, etc.) in excess of the balance at one's disposal.

over·due, *adj.* past due, as a late train, or a bill not paid by the assigned date.

over·flow, *v.,* -flowed, -flown, -flowing, *n.* –*v.* **1.** to flow or run over. **2.** to be supplied in overflowing measure (*with*). –*n.* **3.** that which flows or runs over.

over·hang, *v.,* -hung, -hanging, *n.* –*v.* **1.** to hang over. **2.** to extend or jut over. –*n.* **3.** an overhanging; projection.

over·haul, *v.* **1.** to examine thoroughly. –*n.* **2.** a thorough examination.

over·head, *adv.* **1.** over one's head. –*adj.* **2.** situated above. –*n.* **3.** (*pl.*) the general cost of running a business.

over·hear, *v.,* -heard, -hearing. to hear (speech, etc.) without the speaker's intention or knowledge.

over·kill, *n.* the use of more resources or energy than is necessary to achieve one's aim.

over·lap, *v.,* -lapped, -lapping, *n.* –*v.* **1.** to cover and extend beyond (something else). **2.** to correspond partly with. **3.** to wrap over. –*n.* **4.**

overlap

the extent or amount of overlapping.

over·leaf, *adv.* on the other side of the page or sheet.

over·look, *v.* 1. to fail to notice or consider. 2. to afford a view down over. 3. to supervise.

over·night, *adv.* 1. during the night. 2. suddenly: *Everything changed overnight.* –*adj.* 3. occurring during the night. 4. staying for one night.

over·pass, *n.* a bridge over a road or railway.

over·power, *v.* to overwhelm.

over·reach, *v.* 1. to reach beyond. 2. to defeat (oneself) by overdoing matters.

over·riding, *adj.* prevailing over all other considerations.

over·rule, *v.,* -ruled, -ruling. to rule against, by higher authority.

over·run, *v.,* -ran, -run, -running. 1. to spread over rapidly and occupy. 2. to exceed. 3. to overflow.

over·seas, *adv.* 1. beyond the sea; abroad. –*n.* 2. (*construed as sing.*) countries or territories overseas.

over·see, *v.,* -saw, -seen, -seeing. to direct (work or workers).

over·shadow, *v.* to tower over.

over·shoot, *v.,* -shot, -shooting. 1. to go beyond (a point, limit, etc.). 2. to shoot too far.

over·sight, *n.* 1. failure to notice or take into account. 2. an omission or mistake.

overt, *adj.* not concealed or secret.

over·take, *v.,* -took, -taken, -taking. to pass (another vehicle).

over·throw, *v.,* -threw, -thrown, -throwing. –*v.* 1. to depose as from a position of power. 2. to overturn. –*n.* 3. the act of overthrowing.

over·time, *n.* 1. time during which one works before or after regularly scheduled working hours. 2. pay for such time.

over·tone, *n.* (*usu. pl.*) additional meaning or implication.

over·ture, *n.* 1. an introductory part. 2. an opening of negotiations, or offer.

over·turn, *v.* 1. to overthrow. 2. to turn over on its side, face, or back; capsize.

over·view, *n.* a comprehensive survey.

over·whelm, *v.* 1. to overcome completely in mind or feeling. 2. to defeat, esp. by force of numbers.

over·wrought, *adj.* worked up or excited excessively.

ovoid, *adj.* egg-shaped.

ovu·late, *v.,* -lated, -lating. to shed eggs from an ovary or ovarian follicle. – **ovulation,** *n.*

ovum, *n., pl.* **ova.** the female reproductive cell; egg.

owe, *v.,* owed, owing. 1. to be under obligation (*to*). 2. to be in debt to.

owing, *adj.* 1. owed or due. 2. **owing to, a.** because of. **b.** attributable to.

owl, *n.* a nocturnal bird of prey, with broad head and large eyes, and a distinctive cry.

own, *adj.* 1. relating to oneself or itself. 2. **get one's own back,** to have revenge. 3. **on one's own,** *Colloq.* responsible for onself; independent. –*v.* 4. to possess. 5. to admit. 6. **own up,** to confess.

ox, *n., pl.* **oxen.** a castrated bull, or any member of the bovine family.

oxide, *n.* a compound, usu. contain-

oxide

ing 2 elements only, one of which is oxygen.

oxi·dise, *v.*, **-dised**, **-dising. 1.** to combine with oxygen. **2.** to (cover with) rust.

oxygen, *n.* a colourless, odourless gaseous element, constituting about $\frac{1}{5}$ of the volume of the atmosphere. *Symbol:* O

oyster, *n.* any of various edible marine bivalve molluscs.

ozone, *n. Chem.* a form of oxygen.

Pp

P, p, *n., pl.* **P's** or **Ps, p's** or **ps.** the 16th letter of the English alphabet.

pace, *n., v.,* **paced, pacing.** –*n.* 1. rate of stepping, or of movement in general. 2. rate or style of doing anything. 3. the distance covered in a single step. 4. manner of stepping; gait. –*v.* 5. to set the pace for, as in racing. 6. to traverse with paces or steps. 7. to walk, esp. in a state of nervous excitement.

pace·maker, *n. Med.* an instrument implanted beneath the skin to control the rate of the heartbeat.

pachy·derm, *n.* a large thick-skinned animal, as the elephant, hippopotamus, and rhinoceros.

paci·fic, *adj.* 1. peaceable; not warlike. 2. peaceful; at peace.

paci·fism, *n.* opposition to war or violence of any kind. – **pacifist,** *n.*

pacify, *v.,* **-fied, -fying.** to bring into a state of peace; calm.

pack¹, *n.* 1. a quantity of anything wrapped or tied up; a parcel. 2. a load or burden for carrying. 3. a company of certain animals of the same kind. 4. a group of things, usu. abstract. 5. a complete set, as of playing cards, usu. 52 in number. –*v.* 6. to make into a pack or bundle. 7. to put (down, animals, ice, etc.) into a group or compact form. 8. to press or crowd together (within); cram. 9. to send summarily (*off, away,* etc.).

pack², *v.* to collect, arrange, or manipulate (cards, persons, facts, etc.) so as to serve one's own purposes.

pack·age, *n., v.,* **-aged, -aging.** –*n.* 1. a bundle or parcel. 2. a unit, group of parts, or the like, considered as a single entity. –*v.* 3. to put into wrappings or a container.

packet, *n.* a small pack or package.

pact, *n.* an agreement; a compact.

pad¹, *n., v.,* **padded, padding.** –*n.* 1. a cushion-like mass of some soft material, for comfort, protection, or stuffing. 2. Also, **writing pad.** a number of sheets of paper held together at the edge. 3. one of the cushion-like protuberances on the underside of the feet of dogs, foxes, etc. –*v.* 4. to furnish or stuff with a pad or padding. 5. to expand (writing or speech) with unnecessary words or matter.

pad², *v.,* **padded, padding.** –*n.* 1. a dull sound, as of footsteps on the ground. –*v.* 2. to walk softly.

paddle¹, *n., v.,* **-dled, -dling.** –*n.* 1. a short oar held in the hands (not resting in the rowlock). –*v.* 2. to propel (a canoe or the like) by using a paddle.

paddle², *v.,* **-dled, -dling.** to dabble or play in or as in shallow water.

pad·dock, *n.* an enclosed field or piece of land.

paddy, *n.* a wet, often flooded field on which rice is grown.

paddy·whack, *n. Colloq.* 1. Also, **paddy.** a rage. 2. a spanking.

pad·lock, *n.* a portable or detachable lock.

padre /'padreɪ/, *n.* a military or naval chaplain.

paedi·atrics, *n.* the study and treat-

paediatrics

ment of the diseases of children. – **paediatrician**, n.

pagan, n., adj. (a person who is) irreligious or heathenish.

page[1], n. one side of a leaf of a book, manuscript, letter, or the like.

page[2], n., v., **paged**, **paging**. –n. 1. a boy servant or attendant. –v. 2. to seek (a person) by calling out his name.

pageant, n. an elaborate public spectacle. – **pageantry**, n.

pagoda, n. (in India, Burma, China, etc.) a temple or sacred building, usu. more or less pyramidal.

paid, v. past tense and past participle of **pay**[1].

pail, n. a bucket.

pain, n. 1. bodily or mental distress. 2. (pl.) laborious or careful efforts. –v. 3. to inflict pain on.

pains·taking, adj. assiduously careful.

paint, n. 1. a substance composed of solid colouring matter mixed with a liquid and applied as a coating. –v. 2. to execute (a picture, design, etc.) in colours or pigment. 3. to coat, cover, or decorate (something) with colour or pigment. 4. to apply like paint, as a liquid medicine, etc. – **painter**, n.

painter, n. a rope for fastening a boat to a ship, stake, etc.

paint·ing, n. a picture or design executed in paints.

pair, n., pl. **pairs**, **pair**, v. –n. 1. 2 things of a kind, used or associated together. –v. 2. to arrange in pairs. 3. to join in a pair; mate.

pais·ley, n., pl. **-leys** (a soft fabric made from wool and woven with) a colourful and minutely detailed pattern.

palliate

pal, n. Colloq. a comrade; friend.

palace, n. the official residence of a sovereign, a bishop, etc.

palaeon·tology, n. the science of the forms of prehistoric life represented by fossil animals and plants.

pal·at·able, adj. agreeable to the taste.

palate, n. 1. the roof of the mouth. 2. the sense of taste. – **palatal**, adj.

pala·tial, adj. of the nature of, or befitting a palace.

pala·ver, 1. n. a conference or discussion. 2. profuse and idle talk.

pale[1], adj., **paler**, **palest**, v., **paled**, **paling**. –adj. 1. of a whitish appearance; without intensity of colour. –v. 2. to become pale.

pale[2], n. 1. a stake or picket, as of a fence. 2. a barrier.

pal·ette /ˈpælɪt/, n. a board used by painters to lay and mix colours on.

pal·in·drome, n. a word, verse, etc., reading the same backwards as forwards, as *Madam, I'm Adam*.

pali·sade, n. a fence of pales or stakes, as for enclosure or defence.

pall[1], n. 1. a cloth for spreading over a coffin, or tomb. 2. something that covers, esp. with darkness or gloom.

pall[2], v. to have a wearying effect (on or upon).

pall·bearer, n. one of those who carry or attend the coffin at a funeral.

pallet[1], n. a bed or mattress of straw.

pallet[2], n. a movable platform on which goods are placed for storage or transportation.

pal·li·ate, v., **-ated**, **-ating**. 1. to cause (an offence, etc.) to appear less

palliate

grave; excuse. 2. to mitigate or alleviate. – **palliative**, *adj.*

pallid, *adj.* pale. – **pallor**, *n.*

palm[1], *n.* 1. that part of the inner surface of the hand which extends from the wrist to the bases of the fingers. –*v.* 2. to conceal in the palm, as in cheating at cards.

palm[2], *n.* 1. a tropical, tall, unbranched tree surmounted by a crown of large fan-shaped leaves. 2. a palm leaf as an emblem of victory.

palm·istry, *n.* the art or practice of telling fortunes and predicting character by the lines of the palm of the hand. – **palmist**, *n.*

palo·mino, *n.*, *pl.* -nos. a tan or cream-coloured horse with a white mane and tail. Also, **palamino**.

pal·pable, *adj.* 1. obvious. 2. that can be touched or felt.

pal·pate, *v.*, -pated, -pating. to examine by the sense of touch.

pal·pi·tate, *v.*, -tated, -tating. to pulsate with unnatural rapidity, as the heart. – **palpitation**, *n.*

palsy, *n.* paralysis.

paltry, *adj.*, -trier, -triest. petty.

pamper, *v.* to indulge.

pam·phlet, *n.* a short publication.

pan[1], *n.*, *v.*, panned, panning. –*n.* 1. a metal dish, usu. broad and shallow. 2. a depression in the ground containing salt water, mineral salts etc. –*v.* 3. to wash (auriferous gravel, sand, etc.) in a pan, to separate the gold, etc. 4. *Colloq.* to criticise or reprimand severely.

pan[2], *v.*, panned, panning. *Films, Television, etc.* to move continuously while filming.

pana·cea, *n.* a remedy for all diseases.

pansy

panache, *n.* a grand or flamboyant manner.

pan·cake, –*n.* a thin flat cake made from batter.

pan·creas, *n.* a gland situated near the stomach. – **pancreatic**, *adj.*

panda, *n.* a mammal closely related to the bear.

pan·demic, *adj.* (of a disease) prevalent throughout an entire country or the whole world.

pan·de·mo·nium, *n.* (a place of) riotous uproar or lawless confusion.

pander, *v.* to show excessive indulgence (*to*).

pane, *n.* (one of the divisions of a window, etc., consisting of a single plate of glass.

pan·egyric /pænəˈdʒɪrɪk/, *n.* a speech or writing in praise of a person or thing.

panel, *n.*, *v.*, -elled, -elling. –*n.* 1. a distinct portion or division, as of a door, wall, etc. 2. a broad strip of material set vertically, as for ornament, in or on a woman's dress, etc. 3. a surface or section of a machine on which controls, dials, etc., are mounted. 4. the body of persons composing a jury, etc. –*v.* 5. to arrange in, or furnish with, panels.

pang, *n.* a sharp pain.

panic, *n.*, *v.*, -icked, -icking. –*n.* 1. a sudden demoralising terror. –*v.* 2. to (cause to) be stricken with panic.

pano·ply, *n.*, *pl.* -plies. a complete covering or array of something.

pano·rama, *n.* an unobstructed view or prospect over a wide area. – **panoramic**, *adj.*

pansy, *n.* 1. a plant with brightly-coloured velvety flowers. 2. *Colloq.*

pansy

a. an effeminate man. b. a male homosexual.

pant, v. 1. to breathe hard and quickly, as after exertion. —n. 2. a short, quick, laboured way of breathing; a gasp.

pan·tech·ni·con, n. a furniture van.

pan·ther, n., pl. **-thers**, (esp. collectively) **-ther**. the leopard, esp. in its black form.

panto·mime, n. a form of theatrical entertainment, esp. using stock characters, farce, music, etc.

pantry, n., pl. **-tries**. a room or cupboard in which food or silverware, dishes, etc., are kept.

pants, n.pl. 1. trousers. 2. an item of underwear.

pap, n. books, ideas, etc., lacking intellectual content.

papa, n. →father.

papacy, n., pl. **-cies**. 1. the office or authority of the pope. 2. the system of ecclesiastical government in which the pope is the supreme head.

papal, adj. of or pertaining to the pope, the papacy, or the Roman Catholic Church.

paper, n. 1. a substance made from rags, straw, wood, etc., usu. in thin sheets, for writing or printing on, wrapping things in, etc. 2. paper money. 3. (pl.) documents establishing identity, status, etc. 4. a set of questions for an examination. 5. an essay, article, etc. 6. a newspaper or journal. —v. 8. to decorate with wallpaper.

paper·back, n. a book bound in a flexible paper cover.

papier-mâché /peɪpə-ˈmæʃeɪ/, n. a substance made of pulped paper

paraffin

and glue which becomes hard and strong when dry.

pap·rika, n. the dried fruit of a cultivated form of capsicum, ground as a condiment.

papyrus /pəˈpaɪrəs/, n., pl. **-pyri** /-ˈpaɪraɪ/. 1. a tall aquatic plant of the Nile valley, Egypt, and elsewhere. 2. a material for writing on, prepared from the pith of this plant.

par, n. 1. an equality in value or standing. 2. an average or normal amount, degree, quality, condition, or the like. 3. Golf. the number of strokes per hole or course, as a target standard.

para·ble, n. a short allegorical story, designed to convey some truth or moral lesson.

para·bola, n. Geom. a plane curve formed by the intersection of a cone with a plane parallel to its side.

para·chute, n. an umbrella-shaped apparatus used in descending safely through the air, esp. from an aircraft.

parade, n., v., **-raded, -rading**. —n. 1. show, display, or ostentation. 2. the orderly assembly of troops for inspection, display, etc. 3. a public procession. —v. 4. to display ostentatiously. 5. to march or proceed with display. 6. to promenade or show oneself.

para·digm, n. a pattern or example.

para·dise, n. 1. heaven. 2. a place of extreme beauty or delight.

para·dox, n. a statement or proposition seemingly self-contradictory or absurd, and yet expressing a truth.

par·af·fin, n. 1. Chem. any hydro-

364

paraffin

carbon of the methane series. **2.** Also, **paraffin oil**, a mixture of hydrocarbons obtained from petroleum, used for lighting, etc.

para·gon, *n.* a model or pattern of excellence.

para·graph, *n.* a distinct portion of written or printed matter dealing with a particular point, and usu. beginning (commonly with indentation) on a new line.

para·keet, *n.* a small, slender parrot.

par·al·lax, *n.* the apparent displacement of an observed object due to a change or difference in position of the observer.

par·al·lel, *adj., n., v.,* **-leled, -leling** or **-lelled, -lelling.** – *adj.* **1.** corresponding; similar; analogous. **2.** *Geom.* (of straight lines) lying in the same plane but never meeting. – *n.* **3.** anything parallel in direction, course, or tendency. **4.** *Geog.* a line of latitude. – *v.* **5.** to form a parallel to.

par·al·lelo·gram, *n.* a quadrilateral the opposite sides of which are parallel.

pa·ral·y·sis, *n., pl.* **-ses** /-siz/. **1.** *Pathol.* loss of power of a voluntary muscular contraction. **2.** a more or less complete crippling, as of powers or activities. – **paralyse**, *v.* – **paralytic**, *n., adj.*

para·medical, *adj.* related to the medical profession in a supplementary capacity, as an ambulance man, etc.

param·eter, *n.* any constituent variable quality.

para·mount, *adj.* chief in importance.

para·mour, *n.* an illicit lover.

para·noia, *n.* a psychotic disorder

parent

characterised by systematised delusions. – **paranoiac**, *n., adj.*

para·pet, *n.* any protective wall on a balcony, roof, bridge, or the like.

para·pher·nalia, *n.pl.* (sometimes construed as sing.) any collection of miscellaneous articles.

para·phrase, *n., v.,* **-phrased, -phrasing.** – *n.* **1.** a restatement of the sense of a text or passage, as for clearness. – *v.* **2.** to restate in a paraphrase.

para·plegia, *n.* paralysis of both lower or upper limbs. – **paraplegic**, *adj., n.*

para·site, *n.* an animal or plant which lives on or in another organism from the body of which it obtains nutrients. – **parasitic**, *adj.*

para·sol, *n.* a woman's small or light sun umbrella.

par·boil, *v.* to boil partially, or for a short time.

parcel, *n., v.,* **-celled, -celling.** – *n.* **1.** a quantity of something wrapped or packaged together. **2.** a part or portion of anything. – *v.* **3.** to distribute in parcels or portions (*out*).

parch, *v.* to make dry or thirsty.

parch·ment, *n.* the skin of sheep, goats, etc., prepared for use as a writing material, etc.

pardon, *n.* **1.** courteous excusing of fault or seeming rudeness. **2.** *Law.* a remission of penalty. – *v.* **3.** to remit the penalty of (an offence). **4.** to release (a person) from liability for an offence. **5.** to excuse (an action or circumstance, or a person).

pare, *v.,* **pared, paring.** to cut off the outer part of.

parent, *n.* **1.** a father or a mother. **2.**

365

parent

an author or source. – **parental,** *adj.* – **parentage,** *n.*

paren·the·sis, *n., pl.* **-ses.** the upright brackets ( ) collectively, or either of them separately. – **parenthetic, parenthetical,** *adj.*

pa·ri·ah, *n.* an outcast.

pa·ri·etal, *adj. Anat.* referring to the side of the skull, or to any wall or wall-like structure.

parish, *n.* an ecclesiastical district having its own church and clergyman. – **parishioner,** *n.*

parity, *n.* **1.** equality, as in amount, status, or character. **2.** quivalence; similarity or analogy. **3.** *Finance.* equivalence in value in the currency of another country.

park, *n.* **1.** an area of land within a town set aside for public recreational use. –*v.* **2.** to put or leave (a car, etc.) for a time in a particular place.

parka, *n.* a strong waterproof jacket with a hood.

par·lance, *n.* way of speaking or language; idiom.

parley, *n.* a discussion.

par·lia·ment, *n.* **1.** (*usu. cap.*) the assembly of elected representatives, often comprising an upper and lower house, which forms the legislature of a nation or state within a nation. **2.** any one of similar legislative bodies in other countries. – **parliamentary,** *adj.* – **parliamentarian,** *n.*

par·lour, *n.* a room for the entertainment of visitors.

pa·ro·chial, *adj.* **1.** of or pertaining to a parish or parishes. **2.** narrow in range or interest.

parody, *n., pl.* **-dies,** *v.,* **-died, -dying.** –*n.* **1.** a humorous or satirical imitation of a serious piece of literature or writing. **2.** a poor imitation; a travesty. –*v.* **3.** to imitate in such a way as to ridicule.

parole, *n.* the liberation of a person from prison, conditional upon good behaviour, prior to the end of sentence.

par·oxysm, *n.* a fit of violent action or emotion.

par·quetry, *n.* mosaic work of wood used for floors, wainscoting, etc.

parrot, *n.* a hook-billed, gaily coloured bird.

parry, *v.,* **-ried, -rying.** to ward off (a thrust, stroke, weapon, etc.).

parse, *v.,* **parsed, parsing.** to describe (a word or series of words) grammatically.

parsi·mony /ˈpɑsəmɒni/ *n.* extreme or excessive economy or frugality. – **parsimonious,** *adj.*

pars·ley, *n.* a garden herb used to garnish or season food.

pars·nip, *n.* (a plant with) a large, whitish, edible root.

parson, *n.* a clergyman.

part, *n.* **1.** a portion or division of a whole. **2.** (*usu. pl.*) a region, quarter, or district. **3.** one of the sides to a contest, question, agreement, etc. **4.** a character sustained in a play or in real life; a role. **5.** a parting in the hair. –*v.* **6.** to divide (a thing) into parts; divide. **7.** to comb (the hair) away from a dividing line. **8.** to put or keep asunder; separate. **9.** to go apart from each other, as persons. –*adj.* **10.** in part; partial.

par·take, *v.,* **-took, -taken, -taking.** to take or have a part or share (*in*).

par·tial, *adj.* **1.** being such in part only; incomplete. **2.** biased or pre-

partial

judiced in favour of a person, group, side, etc. – **partiality**, n.

par·ti·ci·pate, v., **-pated**, **-pating**. to take or have a part or share (in). – **participant**, n., adj. – **participation**, n.

par·ti·ci·ple, n. an adjective form derived from verbs. – **participial**, adj.

par·ti·cle, n. 1. a minute portion, piece, or amount. 2. a small word of functional or relational use, such as an article, preposition, or conjunction.

par·tic·u·lar, adj. 1. pertaining to some one person, thing, group, class, occasion, etc.; special, not general. 2. attentive to or exacting about details or small points.

par·ti·san, n. an adherent or supporter of a person, party, or cause.

par·ti·tion, n. 1. division into or distribution in portions of shares. 2. something that separates. –v. 3. to divide into parts or portions.

part·ner, n. 1. a sharer or partaker; an associate. 2. *Comm.* one associated with another or others in a business or a joint venture. 3. either member of an established couple. –v. 4. to be, or act as, the partner of. – **partnership**, n.

par·tridge, n., pl. **-tridges**, (*esp. collectively*) **-tridge**. a game bird.

par·tu·ri·tion, n. the act of bringing forth young; childbirth.

par·ty, n., pl. **-ties**. 1. a group gathered together for some purpose, as for amusement or entertainment. 2. (*oft. cap.*) a number or body of persons united in purpose or opinion, in opposition to others, as in politics, etc. 3. one who participates in some action or affair. 4. a person in general.

passion

paschal, adj. of Passover, of Easter.

pass, v., **passed** or (*Rare*) **past**, **passed** or **past**, **passing**. –v. 1. to go by something, or move onwards. 2. to go by without acting upon or noticing; leave unmentioned. 3. to go or get through. 4. to undergo successfully (an examination, etc.). 5. to exist through; spend. 6. to convey, transfer, or transmit. 7. to discharge or void, as excrement. 8. to sanction or approve. 9. to express or pronounce, as an opinion or judgement. 10. to elapse, as time. 11. to die (*on* or *away*). 12. to happen; occur. 13. to be interchanged, as between 2 persons. 14. to go unheeded, uncensured, or unchallenged. –n. 15. a narrow route across a depression in a mountain barrier. 16. a permission or licence to pass, go, come, or enter. 17. the passing of an examination, etc. 18. the transference of a ball, etc., from one player to another, as in football.

pas·sage, n. 1. an indefinite portion of a writing, speech, or the like. 2. the act of passing. 3. liberty, leave, or right to pass. 4. a means of passing; a way, route, avenue, channel, etc. 5. a voyage across the sea from one port to another.

passageway, n. narrow alley or corridor.

passé, adj. outmoded.

pas·senger, n. one who travels by some form of conveyance.

passion, n. 1. any kind of feeling or emotion, esp. when of compelling force. 2. a strong enthusiasm, or desire for anything. 3. the object of this. – **passionate**, adj.

passionfruit

pas·sion·fruit, *n.* (the edible fruit of) a type of climbing vine.

pas·sive, *adj.* 1. not acting. 2. suffering action, acted upon (opposed to *active*). 3. submitting without resistance. 4. *Gram.* denoting a verb form or voice, in which the subject is represented as being acted on. For example, in the sentence *He was hit, was hit* is in the passive voice.

pass·port, *n.* an official document authenticating the identity and citizenship of a person visiting foreign countries.

pass·word, *n.* a secret word, made known only to authorised persons for their use in passing through a line of guards.

past, *v. Rare.* 1. past participle and occasional past tense of **pass**. –*adj.* 2. gone by in time. 3. belonging to, or having existed or having occurred in a previous time. –*n.* 4. (the events of) the time gone by. –*adv.* 5. so as to pass by or beyond. –*prep.* 6. beyond in time, position or amount.

pasta, *n.* a preparation made from a dough, such as spaghetti, macaroni, etc.

paste, *n., v.,* **pasted, pasting**. –*n.* 1. a mixture of flour and water, used for causing paper, etc., to adhere. 2. any material or preparation in a soft or plastic mass. 3. a brilliant, heavy glass, used for making artificial gems. –*v.* 4. to fasten or stick with paste or the like.

pastel, *n.* 1. a soft, subdued shade. 2. a crayon. 3. a drawing done with crayons.

pas·teur·ise, *v.,* **-rised, -rising.** to expose (milk, etc.) to a high tem-

pate

perature in order to destroy certain micro-organisms.

pas·tille, *n.* a lozenge.

pas·time, *n.* that which serves to make time pass agreeably.

pastor, *n.* a minister or clergyman with reference to his congregation.

pas·to·ral, *adj.* 1. used for pasture, as land. 2. pertaining to the country or life in the country. 3. pertaining to a minister or clergyman, or to his duties, etc. –*n.* 4. a poem, play, or the like, dealing with the life of shepherds, or with simple rural life generally.

pastry, *n., pl.* **-tries.** food made of a biscuit-like dough.

pas·ture, *n.* ground used or suitable for the grazing of cattle, etc.; grassland.

pasty /'pæsti, 'pasti/, *n., pl.* **pasties.** a circular piece of pastry folded around a filling of vegetables, meat, etc., and baked. Also, **Cornish pasty**.

pat[1], *v.,* **patted, patting,** *n.* –*v.* 1. to strike lightly with something flat. –*n.* 2. a light stroke or blow with something flat. 3. a small mass of something, as butter.

pat[2], *adj.* 1. exactly to the point or purpose. 2. apt; opportune. –*adv.* 3. exactly or perfectly.

patch, *n.* 1. a piece of material used to mend a hole or break. 2. a small piece or scrap of anything. –*v.* 3. to mend as with a patch or patches. 4. to repair or restore, esp. in a hasty or makeshift way (*up*).

patch·work, *n.* work made of pieces of cloth or leather of various colours or shapes sewn together.

pate, *n.* the head.

pâté

pâ·té, *n.* a paste or spread made of finely minced liver, meat, fish, etc.

pa·tel·la, *n., pl.* **-tellae** /-'tcli/. *Anat.* the kneecap.

pa·tent, *n.* 1. a government grant for a stated period of time, conferring the exclusive right to make, use, and vend an invention or discovery. –*adj.* 2. of a kind specially protected by a patent. 3. open to view or knowledge; evident. –*v.* 4. to take out a patent on (an invention).

patent leather, *n.* leather lacquered to produce a hard, glossy, smooth finish.

pa·ter·nal, *adj.* 1. fatherly. 2. related on the father's side.

path, *n.* 1. a way beaten or trodden by the feet of men or beasts. 2. a course of action, conduct, or procedure.

path·et·ic, *adj.* exciting pity or sympathetic sadness.

pa·thol·o·gy, *n., pl.* **-gies.** the science of the origin, nature, and course of diseases. – **pathologist,** *n.* – **pathological,** *adj.*

pa·thos, *n.* the quality or power, as in speech, music, etc., of evoking a feeling of pity or sympathetic sadness.

pa·tient, *n.* 1. one who is under medical or surgical treatment. –*adj.* 2. quietly persevering or diligent. 3. quietly enduring strain, annoyance, etc. – **patience,** *n.*

pat·i·na, *n.* 1. an attractive film of green on old bronze. 2. the shiny quality of well polished old timber.

pa·ti·o, *n., pl.* **-tios.** an area adjoining a house, used for outdoor living.

pa·tri·arch, *n.* 1. the male head of a family or tribal line. 2. a high-ranking bishop in some Eastern Christian churches.

pauper

pa·tri·arch·y, *n., pl.* **-archies.** a form of social organisation in which the father is head of the family, and in which descent is reckoned in the male line.

pa·tri·cian, *n.* 1. a member of the aristocracy in ancient Rome. 2. any noble or aristocrat.

pa·tri·cide, *n.* 1. one who kills his father. 2. the act of killing one's father. – **patricidal,** *adj.*

pa·tri·ot, *n.* a person who loves and defends his country zealously. – **patriotic,** *adj.* – **patriotism,** *n.*

pa·trol, *v.,* **-trolled, -trolling.** *n.* –*v.* 1. to walk or march round as a guard. –*n.* 2. a person or a body of persons charged with patrolling. 3. the act of patrolling. – **patronage,** *n.*

pa·tron, *n.* 1. one who spends money at a shop, hotel, or the like. 2. a protector or supporter, as of a person, cause, institution, art, or enterprise. – **patronage,** *n.*

pat·ro·nise, *v.,* **-nised, -nising.** 1. to be a customer of (a shop, restaurant, etc.). 2. to treat in a condescending way.

pat·ter¹, *v.* 1. to strike or move with a succession of slight tapping sounds. –*n.* 2. the act of pattering.

pat·ter², *n.* the glib and rapid speech used by a salesman, etc.

pat·tern, *n.* 1. a decorative design. 2. style or type in general. 3. anything serving as a model or guide for something to be made. –*v.* 4. to make after a pattern.

pat·ty, *n., pl.* **-ies.** a little pie.

pau·ci·ty, *n.* smallness of quantity.

paunch, *n.* the belly, esp. if large.

pau·per, *n.* a very poor person.

369

pause

pause, *n.*, *v.*, **paused, pausing.** –*n.* 1. a temporary stop or rest. –*v.* 2. to make a pause; stop; hesitate.

pave, *v.*, **paved, paving.** 1. to cover or lay (a road, walk, etc.) with stones, concrete, etc. 2. to prepare (the way) (*for*).

pave·ment, *n.* a paved footway at the side of a street or road.

pavil·ion, *n.* a light structure for purposes of shelter, pleasure, etc., as in a park.

pav·lova, *n.* a dessert made of a large soft-centred meringue.

paw, *n.* 1. the foot of an animal with nails or claws. 2. to touch with, or as if with, the paws.

pawl, *n.* a pivoted bar adapted to engage with the teeth of a ratchet or the like.

pawn[1], *v.* to deposit as security, as for money borrowed. – **pawnbroking**, *n.*

pawn[2], *n. Chess.* one of the 16 pieces of lowest value.

pawn·broker, *n.* one who lends money at interest on pledged personal property. – **pawnbroking**, *n.*

pawpaw, *n.* a large yellow melon-like fruit. Also, **papaw, papaya.**

pay, *v.*, **paid, paying.** –*v.* 1. to discharge (a debt, obligation, etc.), as by giving or doing something. 2. to give compensation for. 3. to yield a return profit to. 4. to give or render (attention, regard, court, compliments, etc.) 5. to make (a call, visit, etc.). 6. to suffer, or be punished, as for something. –*n.* 7. payment, as of wages, salary, or stipend. 8. paid employ. – **payment**, *n.*

pay·master, *n.* an officer or an official responsible for the payment of wages or salaries.

peasant

pay·roll, *n.* 1. a roll or list of persons to be paid, with the amounts due. 2. the aggregate of these amounts.

pea, *n.* a small, round, green vegetable.

peace, *n.* 1. freedom from war, hostilities, strife or dissension. 2. a state of being tranquil or serene. – **peaceful**, *adj.*

peace·able, *adj.* 1. disposed to peace. 2. peaceful.

peach, *n.* a juicy, yellow-orange, stone fruit.

pea·cock, *n.*, *pl.* **-cocks**, (*esp. collectively*) **cock.** the male of the peafowl distinguished for its long, colourful, erectile tail.

pea·fowl, *n.* a kind of pheasant.

peahen, *n.* the female peafowl.

peak, *n.* 1. the pointed top of a mountain. 2. the highest point or degree of anything. 3. a projecting front piece, or visor, of a cap.

peal, *n.* a loud, prolonged sound of bells, thunder, laughter, etc. –*v.* 2. to sound forth in a peal; resound.

peanut, *n.* the fruit (pod) or the edible seed of a leguminous plant native to Brazil. Also, **groundnut**.

peanut butter, *n.* Also, **peanut paste, peanut spread.** a paste or spread made from ground peanuts.

pear, *n.* an edible fruit, typically rounded but growing smaller towards the stem.

pearl, *n.* 1. a hard, smooth concretion, white or variously coloured, secreted within the shell of various molluscs, and often valuable as a gem. 2. something precious or choice.

peasant, *n.* a person living in the country and engaged usu. in agricultural labour. – **peasantry**, *n.*

peat, n. a highly organic soil of partially decomposed vegetable matter, in marshy or damp regions, used as fuel.

pebble, n. a small, rounded stone.

pecan /'pɪkæn, pɪ'kæn/, n. (the oval, smooth-skinned nut of) a type of hickory tree.

pecca·dillo, n., pl. **-loes**, **-los**. a petty sin or offence.

peck[1], n. a dry measure in the imperial system, equal to 8 quarts or $9.092\ 18 \times 10^{-3}$ m^3.

peck[2], v. 1. to strike or indent with the beak, as a bird does, or with some pointed instrument. 2. to kiss in a hasty dabbing manner. –n. 3. a pecking stroke. 4. a hasty kiss.

peck·ish, adj. Colloq. hungry.

pectin, n. a substance in ripe fruits which helps form a gel in jam-making.

pec·to·ral, adj. of or pertaining to the breast or chest.

pecu·liar, adj. 1. strange, odd, or queer. 2. belonging characteristically (to).

pecu·li·arity, n., pl. **-ties**. an odd trait or characteristic.

pecu·ni·ary, adj. consisting of or pertaining to money.

peda·gogue, n. a teacher of children.

pedal, n., v., **pedalled**, **-alling**. –n. 1. a lever worked by the foot. –v. 2. to work with the pedals, as of a bicycle, organ, etc.

pedant, n. one who makes an excessive or tedious show of learning. – **pedantic**, adj.

peddle, v., **-dled**, **-dling**. to carry about for sale.

ped·er·asty, n. homosexual relations, esp. between an adult male and a boy.

ped·es·tal, n. a supporting structure or piece; a base.

pedes·trian, n. 1. one who goes on foot. –adj. 2. prosaic; dull.

pedi·cure, n. professional care or treatment of the feet.

pedi·gree, n. an ancestral line.

pedi·ment, n. Archit. a low triangular gable.

pedlar, n. one who peddles.

peek, v. to peep; peer.

peel, v. to strip off the skin, rind, bark, etc.

peep[1], v. 1. to peer through a small aperture or from a hiding place. –n. 2. a peeping look.

peep[2], n. 1. a peeping cry or sound. –v. 2. to utter a shrill little cry; cheep. 3. to speak in a thin, weak voice.

peer[1], n. 1. one who ranks with another in respect to endowments, status, etc.; an equal. 2. a nobleman. – **peerless**, adj.

peer[2], v. to look narrowly, as in the effort to discern clearly.

peev·ish, adj. cross, querulous, or fretful.

peg, n., v., **pegged**, **pegging**. –n. 1. a pin of wood or other material used to fasten parts together, to hang things on, or to mark some point etc. –v. 2. to fasten with or as with pegs. 3. to mark with pegs.

pejo·rative, adj. deprecatory.

peli·can, n. a bird with a large fish-catching bill.

pellet, n. a small round or spherical body.

pel·lu·cid, adj. 1. allowing the pas-

pellucid

sage of light; translucent. **2.** clear in meaning.

pel·met, *n.* a drapery or board, placed across the top of a window in order to hide the curtain rail.

pelt[1], *v.* **1.** to assail with repeated blows or with missiles. **2.** (of rain) to fall very heavily. –*n.* **3.** the act of pelting. **4. full pelt**, the utmost energy or speed.

pelt[2], *n.* the skin of an animal.

pel·vis, *n., pl.* **-ves** /-viz/. the basin-like cavity in the lower part of the trunk of many vertebrates.

pen[1], *n., v.,* **penned, penning.** –*n.* **1.** an instrument for writing with ink. –*v.* **2.** to write with a pen.

pen[2], *n.* an enclosure for domestic animals.

pe·nal, *adj.* of or pertaining to punishment.

pen·al·ty, *n., pl.* **-ties. 1.** a punishment for a violation of law or rule. **2.** any disadvantageous consequence. **- penalise**, *v.*

pen·ance, *n.* punishment undergone in token of penitence for sin.

pence, *n.* a plural of **penny**.

pen·chant, *n.* a taste or liking (for something).

pen·cil, *n., v.,* **-cilled, -cilling.** *n.* **1.** a thin tube of wood, etc., with a core of graphite, chalk, the like, for drawing or writing. –*v.* **2.** to execute, draw, colour, or write with or as with a pencil.

pen·dant, *n.* a hanging ornament, as of a necklace or earring.

pen·dent, *adj.* **1.** hanging or suspended. **2.** overhanging.

pend·ing, *prep.* **1.** until: *pending a decision.* **2.** during: *All should be in attendance pending his visit.* –*adj.* **3.** remaining undecided.

pentagon

pen·du·lous, *adv.* hanging freely.

pen·du·lum, *n.* a body so suspended from a fixed point as to move to and fro.

pen·e·trate, *v.,* **-trated, -trating. 1.** to pierce into or through. **- penetrable**, *adj.* **- penetrative**, *adj.*

pen·guin, *n.* a flightless aquatic bird of the Sthn Hemisphere, with webbed feet, and wings reduced to flippers.

pen·i·cil·lin, *n.* a powerful anti-bacterial substance.

pen·in·su·la, *n.* a piece of land almost surrounded by water.

pe·nis, *n., pl.* **-nes, -nises.** the male organ of copulation and urination.

pen·i·tent, *adj.* sorry for sin or fault and disposed to atonement and amendment. **- penitence**, *n.* **- penitential**, *adj.*

pen·i·ten·tia·ry, *n., pl.* **-ries.** *U.S.* a prison.

pen·nant, *n.* **1.** Also, **pendant, pennon.** a long triangular flag. **2.** any flag serving as an emblem, as of success in an athletic contest.

pen·ni·less, *adj.* having no money.

pen·ny, *n., pl.* **pennies**, (*esp. collectively*) **pence. 1.** a former unit of currency. *abbrev.:* d. **2.** Also, **new penny.** a unit of currency, one hundredth of one pound (£) sterling. *abbrev.:* p.

pen·sion, *n.* a fixed periodical payment made in consideration of past services, injury, poverty, etc. **- pensioner**, *n.*

pen·sive, *adj.* deeply or sadly thoughtful.

pent, *adj.* shut in; confined (*up*).

pen·ta·gon, *n.* a polygon having 5 angles and 5 sides.

372

pen·tath·lon, *n.* an athletic contest consisting of 5 different exercises or events.

pent·house, *n., pl.* **-houses**. a separate flat on a roof.

pen·ul·ti·mate, *adj.* next to the last.

pe·num·bra, *n., pl.* **-brae** /-bri/, **-bras**. the partial or imperfect shadow outside the complete shadow (umbra) of an opaque body.

penury, *n.* extreme poverty. **– penurious**, *adj.*

peony, *n., pl.* **-nies**. a garden plant with large showy flowers.

people, *n., pl.* **-ple**, **-ples** for def. 1, *v.,* **-pled**, **-pling**. *–n.* 1. the whole body of persons constituting a community, tribe, race or nation. 2. the populace. *–v.* 3. to furnish with people; populate.

pep, *n. Colloq.* vigour.

pepper, *n.* 1. a pungent condiment obtained from the dried berries of certain plants. 2. any species of capsicum. *–v.* 3. to season with or as with pepper. 4. to shower with shot, etc.

pep·per·mint, *n.* 1. a herb cultivated for its aromatic pungent oil. 2. a lozenge or confection flavoured with peppermint.

peptic, *adj.* pertaining to or concerned in digestion.

per, *prep.* through; by; for each.

per·am·bu·la·tor, *n.* →pram.

per capita, *adv.* by the individual person.

per·ceive, *v.,* **-ceived**, **-ceiving**. 1. to gain knowledge of through one of the senses. 2. to apprehend with the mind; understand. **– perception**, *n.* **– perceptive**, *adj.*

per cent, *adv.* by the hundred; for or in every hundred (used in expressing proportions, rates of interest, etc.).

per·cent·age, *n.* 1. a rate or proportion per 100. 2. a proportion in general.

per·cen·tile, *n.* one of the values of a variable which divides the variable into 100 groups having equal frequencies.

per·cep·ti·ble, *adj.* capable of being perceived.

perch[1], *n.* 1. a pole or rod as a roost for birds. 2. a rod, or linear measurement in the imperial system of 5½ yards or 16½ feet, equal to 5.0292 m *– v.* to alight or rest upon, or as upon a perch.

perch[2], *n., pl.* **perches**. (*esp. collectively*) **perch**. *n.* a food and sport freshwater fish.

per·co·late, *v.,* **-lated**, **-lating**. 1. to pass through a porous substance; filter. 2. to become known gradually.

per·co·la·tor, *n.* a kind of coffeepot in which boiling water is forced up a hollow stem and filters back through ground coffee.

per·cus·sion, *n.* 1. the striking of one body against another with some violence. 2. *Music.* (collectively) the instruments in an orchestra which are played by striking.

per·di·tion, *n.* final spiritual ruin or damnation.

per·emp·tory, *adj.* 1. imperative. 2. imperious or dictatorial.

per·en·ni·al, *adj.* 1. lasting for an indefinitely long time; enduring. 2. *Bot.* having a life cycle lasting more than 2 years. *–n.* 3. a perennial plant.

per·fect, *–adj.* 1. having all essential

perfect

elements, characteristics, etc.; lacking in no respect; complete. 2. in a state of complete excellence. 3. *Gram.* designating a tense denoting an action or state brought to a close prior to some temporal point of reference. –v. 4. to bring to completion. 5. to make perfect or faultless. – perfection, n. – perfected, adj.

per·fi·dy, n., pl. **-dies**. a deliberate breach of faith or trust; treachery. – perfidious, adj.

per·fo·rate, v., -rated, rating. to make a hole or holes through. – perforation, n.

per·form, v. 1. to carry out (a command, promise, undertaking, etc.); execute. 2. to act (a play, a part, etc.), as on the stage. 3. to render (music), as by playing or singing. 4. to display anger.

per·for·mance, n. 1. a musical, dramatic or other entertainment. 2. the act of performing. 3. the way in which something fulfils the purpose for which it was intended.

per·fume, n. a substance imparting a fragrant or agreeable smell.

per·func·to·ry, adj. performed merely as an uninteresting or routine duty.

per·haps, adv. maybe; possibly.

peril, n. risk; danger. – perilous, adj.

pe·rim·e·ter, n. the outer boundary of a two-dimensional figure.

period, n. 1. an indefinite portion of time, characterised by certain features or conditions. 2. any specified division or portion of time. 3. menstruation. 4. →full stop. –adj. 5. pertaining to, denoting, characteristic of, imitating, or representing a specific period of history.

permit

peri·od·ic, adj. 1. occurring or appearing at regular intervals. 2. intermittent.

peri·odi·cal, n. a magazine, journal, etc., issued at regularly recurring intervals.

pe·riph·er·y, n., pl. -ries. the external boundary of any surface or area. – peripheral, adj.

peri·phras·tic, adj. circumlocutory; roundabout.

peri·scope, n. an optical instrument by which a view at the surface of water, etc., may be seen from below or behind. – periscopic, adj.

perish, v. 1. to die or be destroyed. 2. to decay and disappear. 3. to rot.

perish·able, adj. 1. subject to decay or destruction. –n. 2. (*usu.* pl.) a perishable thing, as food.

per·jure, v., -jured, -juring. to render (oneself) guilty of wilfully making a false statement under oath. – perjury, n.

perk, v. to regain liveliness or vigour (up).

per·ma·nent, adj. lasting or intended to last indefinitely; enduring; abiding. – permanence, n.

per·me·able, adj. capable of being permeated. – permeability, n.

per·me·ate, v., -ated, -ating. 1. to penetrate through the pores, interstices, etc., of. 2. to be diffused through; pervade.

per·mis·sion, n. formal or express allowance or consent.

per·mis·sive, adj. sexually or morally tolerant.

permit, v., -mitted, -mitting, n. –v. 1. to allow (a person, etc.) to do something. 2. to let (something) be done or occur. –n. 3. a written order

374

permit

granting leave to do something, as a licence.

per·mu·ta·tion, *n.* 1. *Maths.* **a.** the act of changing the order of elements arranged in a particular order (as, *abc* into *acb*, *bac*, etc.). **b.** any of the resulting arrangements or groups. 2. any rearrangement.

per·ni·cious, *adj.* ruinous; highly hurtful.

per·oxide, *n. Chem.* that oxide of an element or radical which contains an unusually large amount of oxygen.

perpen·dicular, *adj.* 1. vertical; upright. 2. *Geom.* meeting a given line or surface at right angles.

per·pe·trate, *v.*, -trated, -trating. to perform, execute, or commit (a crime, deception, etc.). – perpetration, *n.* – perpetrator, *n.*

per·pet·ual, *adj.* continuing or enduring for ever or indefinitely. – perpetuate, *v.* – perpetuity, *n.*

per·plex, *v.* to cause to be puzzled; bewilder; confuse mentally.

per·qui·site, *n.* an incidental benefit over and above fixed income, salary, or wages.

per se, *adv.* by or in itself; intrinsically.

per·se·cute, *v.*, -cuted, -cuting. 1. to harass persistently. 2. to oppress with injury or punishment for adherence to principles or religious faith. – persecution, *n.*

per·se·vere, *v.*, -vered, -vering. to persist in anything undertaken in spite of difficulty or obstacles. – perseverance, *n.*

per·sim·mon /ˈpəsəmən, pəˈsɪmən/, *n.* (a tree bearing) an astringent plumlike fruit.

per·sist, *v.* to continue steadily or

perspire

firmly, esp. in spite of opposition. – **persistent**, *adj.*

person, *n.* 1. a human being. 2. the living body of a human being. 3. *Gram.* (in some languages) a category of verb inflection and of pronoun classification, distinguishing between the speaker (**first person**), the one addressed (**second person**), and anyone or anything else (**third person**). 4. **in person**, in one's own bodily presence.

per·son·able, *adj.* of pleasing personality or appearance.

per·son·age, *n.* 1. a person of importance. 2. any person.

per·sonal, *adj.* 1. of, pertaining to, or directed to a particular person; individual; private. 2. done, affected, held, etc., in person. 3. pertaining to the person, body, or bodily aspect.

per·son·ality, *n., pl.* -ties. 1. distinctive or notable personal character. 2. a well-known or prominent person.

per·son·ify, *v.*, -fied, -fying. 1. to attribute human nature or character to (an inanimate object or an abstraction). 2. to be an embodiment of; typify.

per·son·nel, *n.* the body of persons employed in any work, undertaking, or service.

per·spec·tive, *n.* 1. the art of depicting on a flat surface, various objects in such a way as to express dimensions and spatial relations. 2. a mental view or prospect.

per·spex, *n.* a plastic substitute for glass.

per·spi·cacious, *adj.* having keen mental perception; discerning.

per·spire, *v.*, -spired, -spiring.

375

perspire excrete watery fluid through the pores; sweat. – **perspiration**, *n.*

per·suade, *v.*, **-suaded**, **-suading**. to prevail on (a person, etc.), by reasons, inducements, etc., to do or believe something. – **persuasion**, *n.* – **persuasive**, *adj.*

pert, *adj.* bold; cheeky; saucy.

pertain, *v.* to have reference or relation; relate.

perti·nacious, *adj.* extremely persistent.

per·ti·nent, *adj.* pertaining or relating to the matter in hand; relevant.

per·turb, *v.* to disturb or disquiet greatly in mind; agitate.

peruse, *v.*, **-rused**, **-rusing**. to read through, as with thoroughness or care. – **perusal**, *n.*

per·vade, *v.*, **-vaded**, **-vading**. to go, pass, or spread throughout. – **pervasive**, *adj.*

per·verse, *adj.* disposed to go counter to what is expected or desired; contrary.

per·ver·sion, *n.* 1. the act of perverting. 2. a perverted form of something. 3. *Psychol.* unnatural or abnormal condition of the sexual instincts.

per·vert, *v.* 1. to turn away what is considered right. 2. to distort. 3. *Pathol.* to change to what is unnatural or abnormal. –*n.* 4. *Psychol., Pathol.* one affected with perversion.

pes·sary, *n., pl.* **-ries**. *Med.* 1. an instrument worn in the vagina to remedy uterine displacement. 2. a vaginal suppository.

pes·si·mism, *n.* disposition to take the gloomiest possible view. – **pessimist**, *n.* – **pessimistic**, *adj.*

pest, *n.* a noxious, destructive, or troublesome thing or person; nuisance.

pester, *v.* to harass with petty annoyances; torment.

pes·ti·cide, *n.* a chemical substance for destroying insect pests.

pes·ti·lence, *n.* a deadly epidemic disease. – **pestilential**, *adj.*

pes·ti·lent, *adj.* destructive to life; deadly.

pestle, *n.* an instrument for grinding substances in a mortar.

pet, *n., adj., v.*, **petted**, **petting**. –*n.* 1. any domesticated or tamed animal that is cared for affectionately. –*adj.* 2. treated as a pet, as an animal. 3. favourite. –*v.* 4. to treat as a pet; fondle; indulge.

petal, *n.* one of the members of a corolla.

peter, *v.* to diminish gradually and then disappear or cease (*out*).

petite, *adj.* (of women) small.

pe·ti·tion, *n.* 1. a formally drawn-up request addressed to a person or a body of persons in authority or power. –*v.* 2. to address a formal petition to.

petrel, *n.* a sea-bird.

pet·ri·fy, *v.*, **-fied**, **-fying**. 1. to convert into stone or a stony substance. 2. to stupefy or paralyse with fear, or other strong emotion.

petrol, *n.* a mixture of volatile liquid hydrocarbons used as a solvent and extensively as a fuel in internal-combustion engines.

pe·tro·leum, *n.* Also, **rock-oil**. an oily, usu. dark-coloured liquid (a form of bitumen or mixture of various hydrocarbons).

petti·coat, *n.* an underskirt, worn by women and girls; a slip.

petty, *adj.*, **-tier**, **-tiest**. 1. of small

petty

importance; trifling. 2. having or showing narrow ideas, interests, etc.

petty cash, n. a small cash fund set aside to meet incidental expenses.

petu·lant, adj. showing sudden, impatient irritation, esp. over some trifling annoyance.

petu·nia, n. a plant with funnel-shaped flowers of various colours.

pew, n. (in a church) a fixed bench-like seat with a back.

pewter, n. any of various alloys in which tin is the chief constituent.

phal·lus, n., pl. **phalluses, phalli** /ˈfælaɪ/. an image of the erect male reproductive organ. – **phallic**, adj.

phan·tom, n. 1. an image appearing in a dream or formed in the mind. 2. an apparition or spectre.

pharma·ceuti·cal, adj. pertaining to pharmacy. Also, **pharmaceutic**.

pharma·cology, n. the science of drugs, their preparation, uses, and effects.

phar·macy, n., pl. **-cies**. 1. the art or practice of preparing and dispensing drugs and medicines. 2. a dispensary; chemist's shop. – **pharmacist**, n.

pharyn·gitis, n. inflammation of the mucous membrane of the pharynx.

pharynx /ˈfærɪŋks/, n., pl. **pharynges, pharynxes**. the tube or cavity which connects the mouth and nasal passages with the oesophagus.

phase, n., v., **phased, phasing**. –n. 1. a stage of change or development. –v. 2. **phase in**, to introduce gradually into a system, or the like. **phase out**, to withdraw gradually from a system.

phea·sant, n. a large, long-tailed, edible fowl.

phoenix

phen·om·enon, n., pl. **-na**. 1. a fact, occurrence, or circumstance observed or observable. 2. a remarkable thing or person. – **phenomenal**, adj.

phial, n. a small vessel, usu. of glass, for liquids.

phi·lan·der, v. (of a man) to make love, esp. without serious intentions.

phil·an·thropy, n., pl. **-pies**. love of mankind, esp. as manifested in deeds of practical beneficence. – **philanthropist**, n. – **philanthropic**, adj.

phil·ately, n. the collecting and study of postage stamps. – **philatelic**, adj. – **philatelist**, n.

philis·tine, n. one lacking in and indifferent to culture, aesthetic refinement, etc.

phil·ology, n. the study of written records, their authenticity, etc.

philo·sophi·cal, adj. 1. of or pertaining to philosophy. 2. sensibly calm in trying circumstances.

phi·losophy, n., pl. **-phies**. 1. the study or science of the truths or principles underlying all knowledge and being (or reality). 2. a system of principles for guidance in practical affairs. 3. wise composure throughout the vicissitudes of life. – **philosopher**, n.

phlegm /flɛm/, n. Physiol. the thick mucus secreted in the respiratory passages and discharged by coughing, etc.

phleg·matic /flɛgˈmætɪk/, adj. not easily excited to action or feeling.

phobia, n. any obsessing or morbid fear or dread.

phoenix, n. a mythical bird.

phone, n., v., phoned, phoning. *Colloq.* →telephone.

phon·etics, n. the science of speech sounds and their production. – **phonetician**, n. – **phonetic**, adj.

phoney, adj., -nier, -niest. *Colloq.* not genuine; counterfeit; fraudulent.

phospho·res·cence, n. the property of being luminous at temperatures below incandescence. – **phosphorescent**, adj.

phos·phorus, n. pl. -ri. *Chem.* a solid non-metallic element used in matches and fertilisers. Symbol: P – **phosphoric**, adj.

photo, n., pl. -tos. →photograph.

photo·copy, n., pl. -copies; v., -copied, -copying. →photostat (defs 2 and 3).

photo·electric cell, n. a device used for the detection of light.

photo·genic, adj. (of a person) looking attractive when photographed.

photo·graph, n. 1. a picture produced by photography. –v. 2. to take a photograph of.

pho·tog·raphy, n. the process or art of producing images of objects on sensitised surfaces by the chemical action of light or of other forms of radiant energy. – **photographer**, n. – **photographic**, adj.

photo·stat, n. 1. a special camera for making facsimile copies of documents, etc., which photographs directly as a positive on sensitised paper. 2. a copy so made. –v. 3. to make a photostatic copy or copies (of).

photo·syn·thesis, n. the synthesis of complex organic materials by plants from carbon dioxide, water, and inorganic salts using sunlight as the source of energy and a catalyst such as chlorophyll.

phrase, n., v., phrased, phrasing. –n. 1. *Gram.* a sequence of two or more words acting as a unit in the sentence. 2. a characteristic, current, or proverbial expression. 3. *Music.* a group of notes making up a recognisable entity. –v. 4. to express or word in a particular way. – **phrasal**, adj.

phrase·ology, n. manner or style of verbal expression.

phre·netic, adj. frantic; frenzied.

phren·ology, n. the theory that one's mental powers are indicated by the shape of the skull.

phylum, n., pl. -la. *Biol.* a primary division of the animal or vegetable kingdom.

physi·cal, adj. 1. pertaining to the body. 2. of or pertaining to tangible or material nature. 3. of or pertaining to physics.

phys·ician, n. one legally qualified to practise medicine.

phys·ics, n. the science dealing with natural laws and processes, and the states and properties of matter and energy. – **physicist**, n.

physi·ognomy, n., pl. -mies. the face or countenance, esp. as considered as an index to the character.

physi·ology, n. the science dealing with the functioning of living organisms or their parts. – **physiologist**, n. – **physiological**, adj.

physio·therapy, n. treatment using physical remedies, such as massage, gymnastics, etc. Also, **physio**. – **physiotherapist**, n.

phys·ique, n. human bodily structure or type.

pi /paɪ/, n., pl. **pis**. *Maths.* the ratio

pi

(3.141 592) of the circumference of a circle to its diameter.

piano, *n.* a musical instrument in which hammers, operated from a keyboard, strike upon metal strings. – **pianist**, *n.*

piano accordion, *n.* an accordion having a piano-like keyboard for the right hand.

piano·forte /pɪænəʊˈfɔːteɪ, pɪənəʊ-/, *n.* →**piano**.

pia·nola, *n.* a mechanical piano operated by pedals.

pica·dor, *n.* a mounted bullfighter who pricks the bull with lances.

pic·colo, *n., pl.* **-los.** a small flute, sounding an octave higher than the ordinary flute.

pick[1], *v.* **1.** to choose or select carefully. **2.** to choose (one's way or steps), as over rough ground or through a crowd. **3.** to steal the contents of (a person's pocket, purse, etc.). **4.** to open (a lock) as for robbery. **5.** to pierce, indent, dig into, or break up (something) with a pointed instrument. **6.** to pluck or gather. **7.** *Music.* to pluck (the strings of an instrument). **8.** to eat with dainty bites. **9. pick on**, *Colloq.* **a.** to annoy; tease; criticise or blame. **b.** to choose (a person) indiscriminately, esp. for an unpleasant task. **10. pick out**, **a.** to choose. **b.** to distinguish (a thing) from surrounding or accompanying things. **c.** to make out (sense or meaning). **11. pick (someone's) brains**, to find out as much as one can, from someone else's knowledge of a subject. **12. pick to pieces**, to criticise. **13. pick up**, **a.** to take up; lift and hold. **b.** to learn without special teaching. **c.** to get casually. **d.** to take (a person or

picture

thing) into a car, ship, etc., or along with one. **e.** to have within the range of reception, observation, etc. **f.** to get faster. **g.** *Colloq.* to improve. **h.** *Colloq.* to arrest. –*n.* **14.** the choicest or most desirable part or example. **15.** →**plectrum**.

pick[2], *n.* a hand tool for loosening and breaking up soil, etc. Also, **pickaxe**.

picket, *n.* **1.** a pointed post or stake. **2.** anyone stationed by a trade union before a place of work and attempting to dissuade or prevent workers from entering the building during a strike. –*v.* **3.** to stand or march by a place of employment as a picket.

pickle, *n., v.,* **-led, -ling.** –*n.* **1.** (*oft. pl.*) vegetables preserved in vinegar, etc., and eaten as a relish. **2.** a liquid or marinade prepared with salt or vinegar for the preservation of food or for the hardening of wood, leather, etc. **3.** *Colloq.* a predicament. –*v.* **4.** to preserve or steep in pickle.

pick·pocket, *n.* one who steals from the pockets, handbags, etc., of people in public places.

picnic, *n., v.,* **-nicked, -nicking.** –*n.* **1.** an outing or excursion with a meal in the open air. **2.** *Colloq.* an enjoyable experience or time. **3.** *Colloq.* an easy undertaking. –*v.* **4.** to hold, or take part in, a picnic.

pic·torial, *adj.* pertaining to, expressed in, or of the nature of, a picture or pictures.

pic·ture, *n., v.,* **-tured, -turing.** –*n.* **1.** a representation, upon a surface, as a painting, photograph, etc. **2.** any visible image, however produced. **3.** →**film** (def. 3b). **4. the pictures**, a

379

cinema. –v. 5. to form a mental image of.

pic·tu·resque, *adj.* visually charming or quaint.

pidgin, *n.* a language used for communication between groups having different first languages, and which typically has features deriving from those languages. Also, **pigeon**.

pie, *n.* a baked dish consisting of a sweet or savoury filling in pastry.

pie·bald, *adj.* having patches of black and white or of other colours.

piece, *n., v.,* **pieced, piecing.** –*n.* 1. a limited portion or quantity, of something. 2. one of the parts into which something may be divided or broken. 3. an individual article of a set. 4. a disc, block or other small shape used in a board game. 5. a short musical composition. 6. a firearm. –*v.* 7. to mend (something broken); reassemble (*together*). 8. to fit together, as pieces or parts.

piece·meal, *adv.* piece by piece; gradually.

pier, *n.* 1. a structure built out into the water to serve as a landing place for ships. 2. one of the supports of a span of a bridge.

pierce, *v.,* **pierced, piercing.** 1. to penetrate or run into or through (something); puncture. 2. to penetrate with the eye or mind. 3. to sound sharply through (the air, stillness, etc.) as a cry.

piety, *n., pl.* **-ties.** reverence for God, or regard for religious obligations.

pig, *n.* 1. an omnivorous non-ruminant mammal; a sow, hog, or boar; swine. Cf. **hog.** 2. *Colloq.* a greedy, dirty person.

pigeon, *n.* a bird with a compact body and short legs, often bred for racing, etc.

pigeon·hole, *n., v.,* **-holed, -holing.** –*n.* 1. one of a series of small compartments in a desk, cabinet, etc. –*v.* 2. to put away for future reference. 3. to assign a definite place in some orderly system.

piggy·back, *adv.* on the back or shoulders.

pig-headed, *adj.* stupidly obstinate.

piglet, *n.* a young pig.

pig·ment, *n.* a colouring matter or substance used as paint, ink, etc.

pig·tail, *n.* a braid of hair hanging down the back of the head.

pike[1], *n., pl.* **pikes,** (*esp. collectively*) **pike.** a freshwater fish.

pike[2], *n.* a sharp point; spike.

pike·let, *n.* a small thick, sweet pancake.

piker, *n.* a coward or half-hearted person.

pil·chard, *n.* a small abundant fish.

pil·chers, *n. pl.* flannel or plastic pants worn by an infant over a nappy.

pile[1], *n., v.,* **piled, piling.** –*n.* 1. an assemblage of things lying or lying one upon another. –*v.* 2. to lay or dispose in a pile (*up* or *on*). 3. to accumulate (*up*).

pile[2], *n.* a heavy timber stake driven vertically into the ground or the bed of a river, etc., to support some structure.

pile[3], *n.* 1. hair, esp. soft, fine hair or down. 2. a raised surface on cloth.

pile[4], *n.* (*usu. pl.*) →**haemorrhoid.**

pilfer, *v.* to steal (a small amount or object). – **pilferage**, *n.*

pil·grim, *n.* one who journeys to

pilgrim

some sacred place as an act of devotion. – **pilgrimage**, n.

pill, n. a small rounded mass of medicinal substance, to be swallowed whole; tablet.

pil·lage, v., -laged, -laging. –v. 1. to strip of money or goods by open violence, as in war; plunder. –n. 2. the act of plundering.

pillar, n. a tall, relatively narrow, upright supporting part.

pil·lion, n. an extra seat behind the driver's seat on a bicycle, etc.

pil·lo·ry, n., pl. -ries, v., -ried, -rying. –n. 1. a wooden structure into which an offender is locked to be exposed to public scorn or abuse. v. 2. to expose to public scorn or abuse.

pillow, n. a bag filled with some soft material, commonly used as a support for the head during sleep.

pilot, n. 1. one who steers ships through difficult waters. 2. one who controls an aircraft. 3. a guide or leader. 4. a sample episode for a television series. –v. 5. to steer. 6. to guide or conduct.

pimp, n. one who solicits for a prostitute, or brothel; a procurer.

pimple, n. a small, usu. inflammatory swelling on the skin.

pin, n., v., pinned, pinning. –n. 1. a small, slender, sometimes tapered or pointed piece of wood, metal, etc., used to fasten, or hold things together, etc. 2. a bottle-shaped piece knocked down in bowling. –v. 3. to fasten or attach with a pin. 4. to hold (a man, etc.) fast in a spot or position.

pina·fore, n. an apron. Also, **pinny**.

pin·ball, n. game played on a sloping board, in which a ball, driven by a spring, hits pins or bumpers which electrically record the score.

pince-nez /'pæns-neɪ, 'pɪns-neɪ/, n. a pair of spectacles kept in place by a spring which pinches the nose.

pin·cers, n.pl. or sing. 1. a gripping tool consisting of two pivoted limbs forming a pair of jaws and a pair of handles. 2. Zool. a grasping organ or pair of organs resembling this.

pinch, v. 1. to compress between the finger and thumb, the jaws of an instrument, or any two opposed surfaces. 2. to cramp. 3. to stint. 4. Colloq. to steal. 5. Colloq. to arrest. 6. to cause sharp discomfort or distress. –n. 7. the act of pinching; squeeze. 8. a very small quantity of anything. 9. sharp or painful stress.

pine[1], n. an evergreen coniferous tree with long needle-shaped leaves.

pine[2], v., pined, pining. to suffer with longing, or long painfully (for).

pine·apple, n. a large juicy tropical fruit.

ping-pong, n. →**table tennis**.

pinion[1], n. Mach. a small cogwheel engaging with a larger cogwheel or with a rack.

pinion[2], n. 1. (the end joint of) a bird's wing. –v. 2. to cut off a bird's pinions or bind its wings, to prevent it flying. 3. to bind (a person's arms or hands) so as to deprive him of the use of them.

pink[1], n. 1. a light tint of crimson. 2. the highest form or degree: *in the pink of condition.* –adj. 3. of the colour pink.

pink[2], v. 1. to pierce with a rapier or the like; stab. 2. to finish (cloth) at the edge with a notched pattern.

pin·na·cle, *n.* 1. a lofty peak. 2. the highest or culminating point.

pin-up, *n. Colloq.* 1. a picture, usu. pinned to the wall, of an attractive member of the opposite sex. 2. the girl or man depicted.

pio·neer, *n.* 1. one of those who first enter or settle a region. 2. one of those who are first or earliest in any field of inquiry, enterprise, or progress. –*v.* 3. to open or prepare (a way, etc.), as a pioneer does. 4. to open a way for. 5. to be a pioneer in.

pious, *adj.* 1. fervently religious or dutiful in religious observance. 2. sanctimonious.

pip¹, *n.* 1. one of the spots on dice, playing cards, or dominoes. 2. *Mil. Colloq.* a badge of rank worn on the shoulders of certain commissioned officers.

pip², *n.* a small fruit seed.

pip³, *n.* 1. a brief high-pitched sound made by a radio receiver, echosounder, etc. 2. the signal on the screen of a radar set.

pipe, *n.* 1. a hollow cylinder for carrying water, gas, steam, etc.; tube. 2. a tube of wood, clay, etc., with a small bowl at one end, used for smoking tobacco, opium, etc. 3. a musical wind instrument. –*v.* 4. to play on a pipe. 5. to convey by means of pipes. 6. to utter in a shrill tone.

pipe dream, *n.* a futile hope, far-fetched fancy, or fantastic story.

pipe·line, *n.* 1. pipe(s) used for the transmission of petroleum, etc. 2. **in the pipeline**, on the way; in preparation.

pip·ette, *n.* a slender graduated tube for measuring and transferring liquids from one vessel to another. Also, **pipet**.

pipi, *n.* an edible, smooth-shelled, burrowing, bivalve mollusc.

piping, *n.* 1. a cordlike ornamentation made of icing, used on cakes, pastry, etc. 2. a tubular band of material, sometimes containing a cord, for trimming garments, chair covers, etc.

pip·squeak, *n. Colloq.* a small or insignificant person or thing.

piquant, *adj.* 1. agreeably pungent or sharp in taste. 2. agreeably stimulating, interesting, or attractive. – **piquancy**, *n.*

pique, *v.*, **piqued, piquing**, *n.* –*v.* 1. to affect with sharp irritation and resentment, esp. by some wound to pride. 2. to excite (interest, curiosity, etc.). –*n.* 3. ill feeling from wounded pride; offence taken.

pir·anha /pəˈranə/, *n.* a small fish noted for its voracious habits.

pirate, *n., v.*, **-rated, -rating**. –*n.* 1. one who robs or commits illegal violence at sea or on the shores of the sea. 2. any plunderer. 3. one who uses the literary or other work of another as his own. 4. Also, **pirate radio**. a radio station broadcasting on an unauthorised wavelength so as to avoid legal restrictions. –*v.* 5. to act as a pirate. – **piracy**, *n.*

pirou·ette, *n.* a whirling about on one foot or on the points of the toes, as in dancing.

pisca·torial, *adj.* of or pertaining to fishermen or fishing.

piss, *Colloq.* –*v.* 1. to urinate. 2. **piss off**, (*sometimes offensive*) to go away. –*n.* 3. urine. 4. urination.

pis·tachio /pɪsˈtɑːfioʊ/, *n., pl.* **-chios**.

pistachio

a hard-shelled nut with an edible greenish kernel.

pistil, *n. Bot.* the organ of a flower bearing the rudimentary or unfertilised seed.

pistol, *n.* a short firearm intended to be held and fired with one hand.

piston, *n.* a movable disc or cylinder fitting closely within a tube and capable of being driven alternately forwards and backwards in the tube by pressure, as in an internal-combustion engine.

pit[1], *n., v.,* **pitted, pitting.** –*n.* 1. a hole or cavity, esp. in the ground. 2. an excavation made in digging for some mineral deposit. 3. an enclosure for combats, as of dogs or cocks. 4. an area beside the motor-racing track in which competing cars undergo running repairs, are refuelled, etc., during a race. –*v.* 5. to mark with pits or depressions. 6. to set in active opposition, as one against another.

pit[2], *n.* the stone of a fruit.

pitch[1], *v.* 1. to set up or erect (a tent, camp, etc.). 2. *Music.* to set at a particular pitch (def. 8). 3. to throw, fling or toss. 4. to plunge or fall forward or headlong. 5. to plunge with alternate fall and rise of bow and stern, as a ship, aeroplane, etc. (opposed to *roll*). 6. **pitch in,** *Colloq.* to contribute or join in. –*n.* 7. relative point, position, or degree. 8. *Acoustics, Music.* the apparent predominant frequency of a sound from an acoustical source, musical instrument, etc. 9. inclination or slope. 10. **a.** *Sport.* the playing area. **b.** *Cricket.* the area between the wickets. 11. a sales talk.

pitch[2], *n.* a dark viscous substance used for covering the seams of vessels after caulking, for making pavements, etc.

pitch·blende, *n.* a mineral, the principal ore of uranium and radium.

pitch·er, *n.* a container for holding and pouring liquids.

pitch·fork, *n.* a fork for lifting and pitching hay, etc.

pit·e·ous, *adj.* such as to excite or deserve pity.

pit·fall, *n.* any trap or danger for the unwary.

pith, *n.* 1. any soft, spongy tissue or substance. 2. *Bot.* the central cylinder of soft tissue in the stems of certain plants. 3. the important or essential part; essence.

pith·y, *adj.,* **-i·er, -i·est.** full of vigour, substance, or meaning; terse.

piti·a·ble, *adj.* 1. piteous; lamentable; deplorable. 2. such as to excite a contemptuous pity; miserable; contemptible.

piti·ful, *adj.* 1. piteous. 2. contemptibly small or mean.

pit·tance, *n.* 1. a small allowance or sum for living expenses. 2. a scanty income or remuneration.

pitu·i·tary gland, *n.* a small, oval, endocrine gland attached to the base of the brain.

pity, *n., pl.* **pities,** *v.,* **pitied, pitying.** –*n.* 1. sympathetic or kindly sorrow excited by the suffering or misfortune of another. –*v.* 2. to feel pity or compassion for.

pivot, *n.* 1. a pin or short shaft on the end of which something rests and turns, or upon and about which something rotates or oscillates. 2. that on which something turns, hinges, or depends. –*v.* 3. to turn on or as on a pivot.

pixy, *n.*, *pl.* **pixies**. a fairy or sprite. Also, **pixie**.

pizza, *n.* an Italian dish made from yeast dough covered with tomato, grated cheese, anchovies, etc.

pla·card, *n.* a written or printed notice to be posted in a public place; poster.

pla·cate, *v.*, **-cated**, **-cating**. to appease; pacify. – **placatory**, *adj.*

place, *n.*, *v.*, **placed**, **placing**. –*n.* 1. a particular portion of space: *to look out over a wide place.* 2. space in general: *time and place.* 3. any part or spot: *the wrong place to look.* 4. a space or seat in a theatre, train, etc. 5. position, situation, or circumstances: *I wouldn't like to be in your place.* 6. a short street. 7. a job, post, or office. 8. stead or lieu: *to use gas in place of coal.* 9. *Arith.* the position of a figure in a series. 10. *Sport.* a position among the leading competitors. –*v.* 11. to put in a particular place; set. 12. to fix (confidence, esteem, etc.) in a person or thing. 13. to appoint (a person) to a post or office. 14. to put or set in a particular situation, or relation. 15. to identify: *His face is familiar but I can't place him.*

pla·cebo, *n.*, *pl.* **-bos**, **-boes**. *Med.* a medicine which performs no physiological function but may benefit the patient psychologically.

pla·centa, *n.*, *pl.* **-tas**, **-tae**. the organ providing for the nourishment of the foetus and the elimination of its waste products.

placid, *adj.* pleasantly calm.

plagia·rism, *n.* the appropriation or imitation of another's ideas and manner of expressing them, as in art, literature, etc., to be passed off as one's own. – **plagiarist**, *n.* – **plagiaristic**, *adj.* – **plagiarise**, *v.* .

plague, *n.*, *v.*, **plagued**, **plaguing**. –*n.* 1. an epidemic disease of high mortality; pestilence. 2. any cause of trouble or vexation. –*v.* 3. to trouble or torment in any manner.

plaid /plæd/, *n.* any fabric woven of different coloured yarns in a cross-barred pattern.

plain, *adj.* 1. clear or distinct to the eye or ear. 2. clear to the mind; evident, manifest, or obvious. 3. easily understood. 4. ordinary. 5. not beautiful; unattractive. 6. without pattern, device, or colouring. 7. flat or level. –*adv.* 8. simply; absolutely. 9. clearly or intelligibly. –*n.* 10. a large (fairly) flat area of land.

plain·tiff, *n. Law.* one who brings an action in a civil case.

plain·tive, *adj.* expressing sorrow or melancholy discontent; mournful.

plait /plæt/, *n.* 1. a woven strip, as of hair or straw. –*v.* 2. to braid (hair, etc.).

plan, *n.*, *v.*, **planned**, **planning**. –*n.* 1. a scheme of action or procedure. 2. a design or scheme of arrangement. 3. a representation, as a map or diagram. –*v.* 4. to arrange a plan or scheme for (any work, enterprise, or proceeding). 5. to form a plan, project, or purpose of.

plane¹, *n.*, *adj.*, *v.*, **planed**, **planing**. –*n.* 1. a flat or level surface. 2. *Maths.* a surface such that the straight line joining any two distinct points in it lies entirely within it. 3. an aeroplane or a hydroplane. –*adj.* 4. flat or level, as a surface. 5. *Maths.* on one plane only, not multi-dimensional: *a plane figure.*

384

plane

—v. 6. to lift partly out of water at high speed, as a racing boat.

plane², n., v., **planed, planing.** —n. 1. a tool with an adjustable blade for smoothing or finishing the surface of wood, etc. —v. 2. to smooth or dress with or as with a plane.

planet, n. a solid body revolving around a star. - **planetary**, adj.

plank, n. a long, flat piece of timber thicker than a board.

plankton, n. the small animal and plant organisms that float or drift in the water, esp. at or near the surface.

plant, n. 1. any member of the vegetable group of living organisms. 2. the equipment, including the fixtures, machinery, tools, etc., and often the buildings, necessary to carry on any industrial business. 3. Colloq. a. something or someone intended to trap, decoy, or lure, as criminals. b. a spy. —v. 4. to put or set in the ground for growth, as seeds, young trees, etc. 5. to introduce and establish (principles, doctrines, etc.) 6. to insert or set firmly in or on the ground or some other body or surface. 7. to put or place. 8. Colloq. to hide or conceal, as stolen goods. 9. to place (evidence) so that it will be discovered and incriminate an innocent person.

plantation, n. a farm or estate, esp. in a (semi)tropical country, on which cotton, tobacco, coffee, sugar, etc., is cultivated.

plaque, n. 1. a thin, flat plate or tablet of metal, porcelain, etc., intended for ornament, as on a wall, or set in a piece of furniture. 2. a film on teeth harbouring bacteria.

platform

plasma, n. the liquid part of blood or lymph, as distinguished from the corpuscles.

plas·ter, n. 1. a pasty composition, as of lime, sand, water, and often hair, used for covering walls, ceilings, etc., where it hardens in drying. 2. an adhesive covering for a wound. —v. 3. to cover (walls, etc.) with plaster. 4. to overspread with anything, esp. too thickly.

plas·tic, adj. 1. capable of being moulded or of receiving form. 2. produced by moulding. —n. 3. any of a group of synthetic or natural organic materials which may be shaped when soft and then hardened.

plas·ti·cine, n. a plastic modelling compound, in various colours.

plastic surgery, n. surgery which attempts to remodel malformed or damaged parts of the body.

plate, n., v., **plated, plating.** —n. 1. a shallow, usu. circular dish, now usu. of earthenware or porcelain, from which food is eaten. 2. a plate of sandwiches, cakes, etc., brought to a social occasion. 3. domestic dishes, utensils, etc., of gold or silver. 4. a thin, flat sheet or piece of metal or other material. 5. plated metallic ware. 6. Dentistry. a piece of metal or plastic with artificial teeth attached. —v. 7. to coat (metal) with a thin film of gold, silver, nickel, etc.

plat·eau, n., pl. **-eaus**, **-eaux.** 1. a tabular surface of high elevation, often of considerable extent. 2. any period of minimal growth or decline.

plat·form, n. 1. a raised floor or structure. 2. a plan or set of principles.

385

platinum

plat·i·num, *n. Chem.* a heavy, greyish white, highly malleable and ductile metallic element. *Symbol:* Pt

plat·i·tude, *n.* a flat, dull, or trite remark.

pla·ton·ic, *adj.* purely spiritual; free from sensual desire.

pla·toon, *n.* a group of soldiers forming a unit.

plat·ter, *n.* a large, shallow dish.

platy·pus, *n., pl.* **-puses, -pi.** an amphibious, egg-laying monotreme with webbed feet and a muzzle like the bill of a duck.

plau·dit, *n.* (*usu. pl.*) a demonstration or round of applause.

plau·si·ble, *adj.* having an appearance of truth or reason.

play, *n.* 1. a dramatic composition or piece; a drama. 2. exercise or action by way of amusement or recreation. 3. fun, jest, or trifling, as opposed to earnest. 4. action, activity, or operation. 5. freedom of movement, as within a space, as of a part of a mechanism. –*v.* 6. to act or sustain (a part) in a dramatic performance or in real life. 7. to engage in (a game, pastime, etc.). 8. to contend against in a game. 9. to perform on (a musical instrument). 10. to perform (music) on an instrument. 11. to do, perform, bring about, or execute. 12. to amuse oneself or toy; trifle (*with*). 13. to work on (the feelings, weaknesses, etc., of another) for one's own purposes (*on* or *upon*).

play·house, *n.* a theatre.

play·wright, *n.* a writer of plays.

plaza, *n.* a public square.

plea, *n.* 1. an excuse; pretext. 2. *Law.* an allegation made by, or on behalf of, a party to a legal suit, in support of his claim or defence. 3. an appeal or entreaty.

plenary

plead, *v.*, **pleaded** or **plead, pleading. 1.** to make earnest appeal or entreaty. 2. *Law.* **a.** to make any allegation or plea in an action at law. **b.** to address a court as an advocate. 3. to allege or urge in defence, justification, or excuse.

pleas·ant, *adj.* pleasing, agreeable; giving enjoyment.

pleas·ant·ry, *n., pl.* **-tries.** pleasant humour in conversation.

please, *v.*, **pleased, pleasing. 1.** to act to the pleasure or satisfaction of. 2. to be the pleasure or will of; seem good to.

pleas·ur·able, *adj.* such as to give pleasure; agreeable; pleasant.

pleas·ure, *n.* 1. the state or feeling of being pleased. 2. enjoyment or satisfaction derived from what is to one's liking; gratification; delight.

pleat, *n.* 1. a fold made by doubling cloth upon itself. –*v.* 2. to fold or arrange in pleats.

ple·bei·an /plə'biən/, *adj.* 1. belonging or pertaining to the common people. –*n.* 2. a plebeian person.

ple·bi·scite, *n.* a direct vote of electors of a state on some important question.

plec·trum, *n., pl.* **-tra, -trums.** a piece of metal, plastic, etc., for plucking the strings of a guitar, etc.

pledge, *n., v.*, **pledged, pledging.** –*n.* 1. a solemn promise. 2. anything given or regarded as a security of something. 3. a toast. –*v.* 4. to bind by or as by a pledge. 5. to promise solemnly. 6. to give or deposit as a pledge; pawn.

ple·nary, *adj.* 1. complete; entire;

plenary

absolute. 2. attended by all qualified members, as a council.

pleni·poten·tiary, n., pl. **-ries**, adj. –n. 1. a person, esp. a diplomatic agent, invested with full power or authority to transact business. –adj. 2. invested with full power or authority.

pleni·tude, n. abundance.

plenti·ful, adj. existing in great plenty; abundant. Also, **plenteous**.

plenty, n., pl. **-ties**. 1. a full or abundant supply. 2. abundance.

ple·thora /'plɛθərə/, n. overfullness.

pleu·risy, n. an inflammation of the membrane surrounding the lungs.

pli·able, adj. 1. easily bent; flexible; supple. 2. easily influenced; yielding; adaptable.

pliant, adj. pliable.

pliers, n.pl. small pincers with long jaws, for bending wire, etc.

plight, n. condition, state, or situation (usu. bad).

plinth, n. Archit. the lower square part of the base of a column.

plod, v., **plodded, plodding**. 1. to walk heavily; trudge; move laboriously. 2. to work with dull perseverance.

plonk[1], v. to place or drop heavily or suddenly (*down*).

plonk[2], n. *Colloq.* cheap wine.

plop, v., **plopped, plopping**. to make a sound like that of a flat object striking water without a splash.

plot[1], n., v., **plotted, plotting**. –n. 1. a secret plan to accomplish some purpose, esp. a hostile, unlawful, or evil purpose. 2. the plan, scheme, or main story of a play, novel, poem, or the like. –v. 3. to plan secretly (something hostile or evil). 4. to determine and mark (points), as on graph paper, by means of measurements or coordinates.

plot[2], n. a small piece or area of ground.

plough, n. 1. an agricultural implement for cutting and turning over the soil. –v. 2. to furrow, remove, etc., or make (a furrow, groove, etc.) with or as with a plough. 3. to till (the soil) with a plough. 4. to work at something persistently and laboriously (*on, through* or *ahead*).

ploy, n. a manoeuvre or stratagem.

pluck, v. 1. to pull off or out from the place of growth. 2. to pull with a jerk. 3. to sound (by the strings of a musical instrument) by plucking at them. –n. 4. the act of plucking; a pull, tug, or jerk. 5. courage or resolution in the face of difficulties. – **plucky**, adj.

plug, n., v., **plugged, plugging**. –n. 1. a piece of rubber or plastic for stopping the flow of water from a basin, etc. 2. a pronged device for establishing contact between an electrical appliance and a power supply. –v. 3. to stop or fill with or as with a plug. 4. *Colloq.* to mention (a product, etc.) favourably and, often. 5. to connect (an electrical device) with a power supply (*in*).

plum, n. 1. a purplish-coloured stone fruit. 2. a good or choice thing.

plu·mage, n. feathers collectively.

plumb, n. 1. a small mass of lead or heavy material, used for various purposes. 2. **out of plumb**, a. not perpendicular. b. not functioning properly. –adj. 3. true according to a plumbline; perpendicular. –adv. 4. in a vertical direction. 5. exactly, precisely, or directly. –v. 6. to make

plumb

vertical. 7. to sound (the ocean, etc.) with or as with a plumbline.

plumb·ing, n. the system of pipes and drains for carrying water, liquid wastes, etc., into or out of a building. – **plumber,** n.

plumb·line, n. a string to one end of which is attached a metal weight, used to determine perpendicularity, find the depth of water, etc.

plume, n., v., **plumed, pluming.** –n. 1. a feather. –v. 2. to display or feel satisfaction with or pride in (oneself); pride (oneself) complacently (on or upon).

plum·met, v. to plunge.

plump[1], adj. well filled out or rounded in form; somewhat fat.

plump[2], v. 1. to fall heavily or suddenly and directly. 2. **plump for,** to choose; vote for.

plun·der, v. to rob of goods or valuables by open force. –n. 2. the act of plundering; pillage. 3. loot.

plunge, v., **plunged, plunging,** n. 1. to cast or thrust (oneself) forcibly or suddenly into a liquid, etc. 2. to rush or dash with headlong haste. 3. to throw oneself impetuously or abruptly into some condition, situation, matter, etc. 4. to descend abruptly or precipitously, as a cliff, a road, etc. –n. 5. the act of plunging.

plural, adj. consisting of, containing, or pertaining to more than one.

plus, prep. 1. with the addition of; with. –adj. 2. involving or denoting addition. 3. positive. –n. 4. a plus quantity. 5. a surplus or gain.

plush, adj. luxurious and costly, esp. a room or furnishings.

plu·toc·ra·cy, n., pl. -**cies.** the rule or power of wealth or of the wealthy.

poem

plu·to·ni·um, n. Chem. a radioactive element. Symbol: Pu

plu·vial, adj. 1. of or pertaining to rain; rainy. 2. Geol. due to rain.

ply[1], v., **plied, plying.** 1. to use; employ busily, or work with or at. 2. to carry on, practise, or pursue. 3. to supply pressingly with. 4. to address persistently or importunately; importune. 5. to travel or run regularly over a fixed course or between certain places, as a boat.

ply[2], n., pl. **plies.** 1. a fold; a thickness. 2. a strand of yarn.

ply·wood, n. a material consisting of an odd number of thin sheets or strips of wood glued together.

pneu·matic, adj. 1. of or pertaining to air, or gases in general. 2. operated by air. 3. containing air.

pneu·monia, n. inflammation of the lungs.

poach[1], v. 1. to take game or fish illegally. 2. to encroach on another's rights.

poach[2], v. to simmer in liquid in a shallow pan.

pock, n. a pustule on the body in an eruptive disease, as smallpox.

pocket, n. 1. a small bag inserted in a garment, for carrying a purse, etc. 2. money, means, or financial resources. 3. a small isolated area. –adj. 4. small enough to go in the pocket; diminutive. –v. 5. to put into one's pocket. 6. to take possession of as one's own, often dishonestly.

pod, n. a long, hinged seed case.

poddy, n. a handfed calf.

podium, n., pl. -**dia.** a small platform for the conductor of an orchestra, a public speaker, etc.

poem, n. a composition in verse, esp.

poem

one characterised by artistic construction and imaginative or elevated thought.

poet, *n.* 1. one who composes poetry. 2. one having the gift of poetic imagination and creation, together with eloquence of expression.

poetry, *n.* the art of rhythmical composition, written or spoken, for exciting pleasure by beautiful, imaginative, or elevated thoughts. – **poetic,** *adj.*

poig·nant, *adj.* keenly affecting the feelings, esp. of sorrow. – **poignancy,** *n.*

poin·ci·ana, *n.* a tree or shrub with showy orange or scarlet flowers.

poin·set·tia, *n.* a perennial with brilliant, usu. scarlet, bracts.

point, *n.* 1. a sharp or tapering end. 2. a mark made (as) with a sharp end of something; dot. 3. something that has position but not extension, as the intersection of 2 lines. 4. any definite position, as in a scale, course, etc. 5. a degree or stage. 6. a particular instant of time. 7. the important or essential thing. 8. a particular aim, end, or purpose. 9. a single unit, as in counting, scoring a game, etc. –*v.* 10. to direct (the finger, a weapon, the attention, etc.) at, to, or upon something. 11. to direct attention to: *Point him out to me; to point out a problem.* 12. to have a tendency, as towards something. 13. to face in a particular direction, as a building.

point-blank, *adj.* 1. aimed or fired at close range; direct. 2. straightforward, plain, or explicit.

poise, *n., v.,* **poised, poising.** –*n.* 1. a state of balance or equilibrium. 2. composure; self-possession. –*v.* 3. to balance evenly; adjust, hold, or

polemic

carry in equilibrium. 4. to hold supported or raised, as in position for casting, using, etc.

poison, *n.* 1. a substance with the inherent property of being harmful to life or health. –*v.* 2. to administer poison to (a person or animal). – **poisonous,** *adj.*

poke, *v.,* **poked, poking.** –*v.* 1. to thrust against or into (something) with the finger, a stick, etc.; prod. 2. to thrust obtrusively. 3. to pry; search curiously (*about* or *around*). –*n.* 4. a thrust or push.

poker[1], *n.* a metal rod for poking or stirring a fire.

poker[2], *n.* a card game, usu. involving gambling.

poker machine, *n.* a coin-operated gambling machine.

poky, *adj.,* **-kier, -kiest.** (of a place) small and cramped.

polarise, *v.* to send in different, esp. opposite, directions.

pole[1], *n., v.,* **poled, poling.** –*n.* 1. a long, rounded, usu. slender piece of wood, metal, etc. –*v.* 2. to push, strike, propel, etc., with a pole.

pole[2], *n.* 1. each of the extremities of the axis of the earth or of any more or less spherical body. 2. *Physics.* each of the 2 regions or parts of a magnet, electric battery, etc., at which certain opposite forces are manifested or appear to be concentrated. 3. one of 2 opposites. – **polar,** *adj.*

pole·axe, *n.* an axe, usu. with a hammer opposite the cutting edge, used in felling or stunning animals.

pole·cat, *n.* a mammal of the weasel family.

pol·emic, *n.* 1. a controversial argu-

389

polemic

ment; argumentation against some opinion, doctrine, etc. –*adj.* **2.** Also, **polemical.** of or pertaining to disputation; controversial.

police, *n., v.,* **-liced, -licing.** –*n.* **1.** (the members of) an organised civil force for maintaining order, preventing and detecting crime, and enforcing the laws. –*v.* **2.** to regulate, control, or keep in order (as) by police.

policy[1], *n., pl.* **-cies. 1.** a definite course of action adopted as expedient. **2.** prudence, practical wisdom, or expediency.

policy[2], *n., pl.* **-cies.** a document embodying a contract of insurance.

polio·myelitis, *n.* an acute viral disease resulting in paralysis. Also, **polio.**

polish, *v.* **1.** to make smooth and glossy, esp. by friction. **2.** to render finished, refined or elegant. **–polish off,** *Colloq.* to finish, or dispose of quickly. –*n.* **4.** the act of polishing. **5.** (a substance used to give) smoothness or gloss. **6.** superior or elegant finish; refinement; elegance.

polite, *adj.* showing good manners towards others, as in behaviour, speech, etc.; courteous; civil.

poli·tic, *adj.* **1.** sagacious; prudent; judicious. **2.** shrewd; artful; expedient.

politi·cal, *adj.* **1.** pertaining to the science or art of politics. **2.** pertaining to a political party. **3.** pertaining to the state or its government.

poli·tics, *n.* (construed as *sing.* or *pl.*) **1.** the science or art of political government. **2.** (the practice or profession of conducting) political affairs. **3.** the interplay of relationships within an organisation. **– politician,** *n.*

polka, *n.* a lively dance.

poll, *n.* **1.** the registering of votes, as at an election. **2.** the number of votes cast. **3.** an analysis of public opinion on a subject, usu. by selective sampling. **4.** the head, esp. the part of it on which the hair grows. –*v.* **5.** to receive at the polls, as votes. **6.** to take or register the votes of, as persons. **7.** to cut off or cut short.

pollen, *n.* the fertilising cells of flowering plants.

pol·li·nate, *v.,* **-nated, -nating.** to convey pollen for fertilisation to.

pol·lute, *v.,* **-luted, -luting.** to make foul or unclean. **– pollution,** *n.* **– pollutant,** *n.*

polo, *n.* a game resembling hockey, played on horseback.

pol·ter·geist /ˈpɒltəgaɪst/, *n.* a ghost or spirit which manifests its presence by noises, knockings, etc.

poly·andry, *n.* the practice or the condition of having more than one husband at one time.

poly·ester, *n.* a synthetic polymer used in fabrics, etc.

poly·gamy, *n.* the practice of having several spouses at one time. **– polygamous,** *adj.*

poly·gon, *n.* a figure, esp. a closed plane figure, having many (more than 4) angles and sides.

poly·gyny, *n.* the practice of having more than one wife at one time.

poly·hedron, *n., pl.* **-drons, -dra.** a solid figure having many faces.

poly·mer, *n.* a compound of high molecular weight derived by the combination of many smaller molecules. **– polymerise,** *v.*

polyp

polyp, *n.* **1.** *Zool.* an animal form with a more or less fixed base and free end with mouth and tentacles. **2.** *Pathol.* a projecting growth from a mucous surface, as of the nose.

poly·styrene, *n.* a clear plastic, easily coloured and moulded, and used as an insulating material.

poly·theism, *n.* the doctrine of, or belief in, many gods.

poly·thene, *n.* a plastic used for containers, electrical insulation, packaging, etc.

poly·un·satu·rated, *adj. Chem.* **1.** of or pertaining to, a fat or oil with bonds not saturated with hydrogen. **2.** of or pertaining to foodstuffs based on polyunsaturated oils, mainly of vegetable origin.

pome·granate, *n.* a several-chambered, many-seeded fruit.

pommel, *n.* Also, **pummel**. **1.** a terminating knob. **2.** the protuberant part at the front and top of a saddle.

pommy, *n., pl.* **-mies.** *Colloq.* an Englishman.

pomp, *n.* stately or splendid display.

pompom, *n.* an ornamental tuft or ball of feathers, wool, or the like.

pom·pous, *adj.* **1.** characterised by an ostentatious parade of dignity or importance. **2.** (of language, style, etc.) ostentatiously lofty.

ponce, *v.,* **ponced, poncing.** *Colloq.* –*n.* **1.** →**pimp.** –*v.* **2.** to flounce; behave in a foolishly effeminate fashion (*about*). –**poncy**, *adj.*

poncho, *n., pl.* **-chos.** a blanket-like cloak.

pond, *n.* a body of water smaller than a lake, often man-made.

ponder, *v.* to consider deeply; weigh in the mind; meditate.

pon·der·ous, *adj.* **1.** heavy; massive.

pop

2. without graceful lightness or ease; dull.

pon·tiff, *n.* **1. a.** a bishop. **b.** the bishop of Rome (the pope). – **pontifical**, *adj.*

pon·tifi·cate, *v.* **-cated, -cating.** to speak in a pompous manner.

pon·toon[1], *n.* a boat, or some other floating structure, used as one of the supports for a temporary bridge over a river.

pon·toon[2], *n.* a card game.

pony, *n., pl.* **-nies.** a small horse.

pony·tail, *n.* a bunch of hair tied at the back of the head.

poo, *n. Colloq.* (*euph.*) →**faeces.**

poodle, *n.* one of a breed of intelligent pet dogs with thick curly hair.

poofter, *n. Colloq.* a male homosexual.

pool[1], *n.* **1.** a small body of standing water; pond. **2.** a swimming pool.

pool[2], *n.* **1.** a combination of interests, funds, etc., for common advantage, esp. in business. **2.** a facility or service that is shared by a number of people. **3.** any of various games played on a billiard table in which the object is to drive all the balls into the pockets with the cue ball. –*v.* **4.** to put (interests, money, etc.) into a pool.

poop[1], *n.* the enclosed space at the stern of a ship.

poop[2], *v. Colloq.* to tire or exhaust.

poor, *adj.* **1.** having little or nothing in the way of wealth, goods, or means of subsistence. **2.** of an inferior, inadequate, or unsatisfactory kind. **3.** humble. **4.** unfortunate.

pop[1], *v.,* **popped, popping.** –*v.* **1.** to (cause to) make a short, quick,

pop

explosive sound or report. **2.** to burst open with such a sound. **3.** to come or go quickly, suddenly or unexpectedly (*in, into, out,* etc.). –*n.* **4.** a short, quick, explosive sound.

pop², *adj. Colloq.* **1.** popular. **2.** denoting or pertaining to a type of tune or song having great but ephemeral popularity, esp. among the young. **3.** denoting or pertaining to a singer or player of such music.

pop³, *n. Colloq.* father, or grandfather.

pop·corn, *n.* any of several varieties of maize whose kernels burst open and puff when subjected to heat.

pope, *n.* (*oft. cap.*) the bishop of Rome as head of the Roman Catholic Church.

poplar, *n.* a tall, spire-shaped tree.

poplin, *n.* a strong, finely ribbed, mercerised cotton material.

poppadom, *n.* thin crisp Indian bread.

poppet, *n.* a term of endearment for a girl or child.

poppy, *n., pl.* **-pies.** a plant with showy flowers of various colours.

popu·lace, *n.* the common people of a community.

popu·lar, *adj.* **1.** regarded with general favour or approval. **2.** pertaining to the (common) people. – **popularity**, *n.*

popu·late, *v.*, **-lated**, **-lating**. **1.** to inhabit. **2.** to furnish with inhabitants, as by colonisation; people.

popu·lation, *n.* **1.** the total number of persons inhabiting a country, town, or any area. **2.** the body of inhabitants of a place.

popu·lous, *adj.* full of people or inhabitants, as a region.

portend

por·ce·lain, *n.* a vitreous, more or less translucent, ceramic material; china.

porch, *n.* an exterior appendage to a building, forming a covered approach to a doorway.

por·cine, *adj.* of or resembling pigs.

por·cu·pine, *n.* a rodent covered with stout, erectile spines or quills.

pore¹, *v.*, **pored**, **poring**. to meditate or ponder intently (*over, on,* or *upon*).

pore², *n.* a minute opening or orifice, as in the skin or a leaf, a rock, etc. **-porous**, *adj.*

pork, *n.* the flesh of pigs used as food.

porn·ography, *n.* erotic literature, art, or photography, designed to excite sexual desire. – **pornographic**, *adj.*

por·poise, *n., pl.* **-poises**, (*esp. collectively*) **-poise**. a gregarious cetacean, usu. blackish above and paler beneath and having a blunt, rounded snout.

por·ridge, *n.* an oatmeal breakfast dish.

port¹, *n.* **1.** a town or place where ships load or unload. **2.** a place along the coast where ships may take refuge from storms.

port², *n.* the left-hand side of a ship or aircraft facing forward (opposed to *starboard*).

port³, *n.* a fortified wine, usu. red.

port·able, *adj.* capable of being carried.

Portakabin, *n.* prefabricated building.

portal, *n.* a door, gate, or entrance.

Portaloo, *n.* mobile prefabricated toilet.

por·tend, *v.* to indicate beforehand, as an omen does. – **portent**, *n.*

392

porter

por·ter[1], *n.* one employed to carry luggage.

por·ter[2], *n.* one who has charge of a door or gate; janitor.

port·fo·lio, *n., pl.* **-lios. 1.** a portable case for loose papers, prints, etc. **2.** the office or post of a minister of state or member of a cabinet. **3.** an itemised list of financial assets.

port·hole, *n.* a window in the side of a ship.

por·tion, *n.* **1.** a part of any whole, whether actually separated from it or not. **2.** the part of a whole allotted to or belonging to a person; share. *–v.* **3.** to divide into or distribute in portions; parcel (*out*).

port·ly, *adj.,* **-lier, -liest.** stout.

port·man·teau, *n., pl.* **-teaus, -teaux.** a suitcase.

por·trait, *n.* a likeness of a person, esp. of the face.

por·tray, *v.* **1.** to represent by a drawing, painting, etc. **2.** to represent dramatically, as on the stage. **– portrayal**, *n.*

pose, *v.,* **posed, posing.** *–v.* **1.** to affect a particular character in order to impress others. **2.** to assume or hold a position for some artistic purpose. *–n.* **3.** posture of body. **4.** a studied attitude or mere affectation.

posh, *adj. Colloq.* elegant or luxurious.

po·si·tion, *n.* **1.** condition with reference to place; location. **2.** proper or appropriate place. **3.** a post of employment. **4.** mental attitude; way of viewing a matter; stand. **5.** condition (of affairs, etc.). *–v.* **6.** to put in a particular or appropriate position; place.

post

pos·i·tive, *adj.* **1.** explicitly laid down or expressed. **2.** admitting of no question. **3.** confident in opinion or assertion, as a person. **4.** absolute. **5.** characterised by optimism. **6.** *Elect.* having a deficiency of electrons. See **negative** (def. **5**). **7.** *Maths.* denoting a quantity greater than zero.

pos·sess, *v.* **1.** to have as property; to have belonging to one. **2.** to have as a faculty, quality, or the like. **3.** (of a spirit, esp. an evil one) to occupy and control.

pos·ses·sion, *n.* **1.** the act or fact of possessing. **2.** ownership. **3.** a thing possessed. **4.** control over oneself, one's mind, etc.

pos·ses·sive, *adj.* **1.** exerting or seeking to exert excessive influence on the affections, behaviour, etc., of others. **2.** *Gram.* showing possession.

pos·si·ble, *adj.* that may or can be, exist, happen, be done, be used, etc. **– possibility**, *n.*

pos·si·bly, *adv.* perhaps, it is possible that.

pos·sum, *n.* a herbivorous, largely arboreal, Aust. marsupial.

post[1], *n.* **1.** a strong piece of timber, metal, or the like, set upright as a support. *–v.* **2.** to affix (a notice, etc.) to a post, wall, or the like.

post[2], *n.* a position of duty, employment, or trust to which one is appointed.

post[3], *n.* **1.** a single collection or delivery of letters, packages, etc. **2.** the letters, packages, etc., themselves; mail. *–v.* **3.** to place (a letter, etc.) in a post-box, etc., for transmission. **4.** to supply with up-to-date information; inform. **– postage**, *n.*

post·code, *n.* a group of numbers or letters added as part of the address.

post·date, *v.*, **-dated**, **-dating**. 1. to date (a document, cheque, invoice, etc.) with a date later than the current date. 2. to follow in time.

poster, *n.* a large placard or bill.

pos·terior, *adj.* 1. situated behind, or hinder (opposed to *anterior*). –*n.* 2. (*sometimes pl.*) the hinder parts of the body; the buttocks.

pos·ter·ity, *n.* succeeding generations collectively.

post·graduate, *n.* one studying at a university for a higher degree.

post·haste, *adv.* with all possible speed or promptness.

post·humous /ˈpɒstfəməs/, *adj.* 1. (of books, music, medals, etc.) published or awarded after a person's death. 2. arising, existing, or continuing after one's death.

post·mark, *n.* an official mark stamped on letters or other mail, to indicate the place and date of sending.

post-mortem, *adj.* 1. after death. –*n.* 2. an examination of the body after death; autopsy.

post·pone, *v.*, **-poned**, **-poning**. to put off to a later time; defer.

post·script, *n.* a paragraph, sentence, etc., added to a letter which has already been concluded and signed by the writer. *Abbrev.:* P.S.

pos·tu·late, *v.*, **-lated**, **-lating**. 1. to ask, demand, or claim. 2. to claim or assume the existence or truth of, esp. as a basis for reasoning.

pos·ture, *n.*, *v.*, **-tured**, **-turing**. *n.* 1. the relative disposition of the various parts of anything, esp. of the body and limbs. –*v.* 2. to place in or assume a particular posture or attitude.

posy, *n.*, *pl.* **-sies**. a bouquet (def. 1).

pot, *n.*, *v.*, **potted**, **potting**. *n.* 1. a container, usu. round and deep, and usu. for domestic purposes. 2. a wickerwork vessel for trapping fish or crustaceans. 3. *Colloq.* →**marijuana**. –*v.* 4. to put into a pot. 5. to preserve or cook (food) in a pot. 6. to plant in a pot of soil. 7. *Colloq.* to capture, secure, or win.

potas·sium, *n.* a silvery white metallic element whose compounds are used as fertiliser and in special high glasses. *Symbol:* K – **potassic**, *adj.*

potato, *n.*, *pl.* **-toes**. the round and white edible tuber of a cultivated plant.

potch, *n.* an inferior opal or opal matrix.

potent, *adj.* 1. powerful; mighty. 2. having sexual power. – **potency**, *n.*

poten·tate, *n.* one who possesses great power.

poten·tial, *adj.* 1. possible as opposed to actual. 2. capable of being or becoming; latent. –*n.* 3. possibility; latent skill or capability.

pot·hole, *n.* a hole in the surface of a road.

potion, *n.* a drink or draught, esp. one of a medicinal, poisonous, or magical kind.

pot·pourri /ˈpotˈpuəri, pouˈpriː/, *n.*, *pl.* **-ris**. a mixture of dried petals, spices, etc., kept in a jar for the fragrance.

potter[1], *n.* one who makes earthen pots or other vessels. – **pottery**, *n.*

potter[2], *v.* to busy or occupy oneself in an ineffective manner.

potty, *adj. Colloq.* foolish; crazy.

pouch, *n.* 1. a small bag or sack. 2. *Zool.* a baglike or pocket-like part, as the sac beneath the bill of pelicans, or the receptacle for the young of marsupials.

pouf, *n.* a stuffed cushion of thick material forming a low seat.

poul·tice, *n.* a soft, moist mass of bread, meal, linseed, etc., applied as a medication to the body.

poul·try, *n.* domestic fowls collectively, as chickens, turkeys, etc.

pounce, *v.*, pouncing, *n.* 1. to leap or swoop down suddenly and lay hold (as a bird does of its prey). —*n.* 2. a sudden leap or swoop.

pound[1], *v.* 1. to strike (heavy blows) repeatedly and with great force. 2. to beat or throb violently, as the heart. —*n.* 3. the act of pounding.

pound[2], *n.*, *pl.* **pounds**, *(collectively)* **pound**. 1. a unit of mass, varying in different periods and different countries. 2. a British monetary unit (**pound sterling**) of the value of 100 new pence.

pound[3], *n.* 1. an enclosure maintained by public authorities for confining stray or homeless animals. 2. a place of confinement or imprisonment.

pour, *v.* 1. to send (a liquid or fluid, or anything in loose particles) flowing or falling, as from a container (or *into*, *over*, or *on* something). 2. to issue, move, or proceed in great quantity or number. 3. to rain heavily. —*n.* 4. the act or process of pouring molten metal, concrete, etc., into a mould.

pout, *v.* to thrust out the lips in displeasure or sullenness.

pov·er·ty, *n.* the condition of being poor with respect to money, goods, or means of subsistence.

poverty line, *n.* officially, the level of income below which one cannot afford to obtain the necessities of life.

powder, *n.* 1. any solid substance in the state of fine, loose particles; dust. —*v.* 2. to reduce to powder; pulverise. 3. to sprinkle or cover (as) with powder.

power, *n.* 1. ability to do or act. 2. great or marked ability to do or act; strength; might; force. 3. the possession of control or command over others; dominion; authority. 4. a state or nation having international authority or influence. 5. mechanical energy as distinguished from hand labour. 6. *Maths.* the product obtained by multiplying a quantity by itself one or more times. – **powerful**, *adj.*

pox, *n.* 1. a disease characterised by multiple skin pustules, as smallpox. 2. *Colloq.* any venereal disease.

prac·ti·ca·ble, *adj.* capable of being put into practice, done, or effected, esp. with prudence; feasible.

prac·ti·cal, *adj.* 1. pertaining or relating to practice or action. 2. pertaining to or connected with the ordinary activities, business, or work of the world. 3. adapted for actual use. 4. mindful of the results, usefulness, disadvantages, etc., of action or procedure. 5. matter-of-fact; prosaic. 6. being such in practice or effect; virtual. – **practicality**, *n.*

practical joke, *n.* a trick played upon a person, often involving physical action.

prac·tice, *n.* 1. habitual or custom-

practice

ary performance. **2.** repeated performance or systematic exercise for the purpose of acquiring skill. **3.** the action or process of performing or doing something (opposed to *theory*). **4.** the exercise of a profession or occupation, esp. law or medicine.

prac·tise, *v.*, **-tised, -tising. 1.** to carry out, perform, or do habitually or usually. **2.** to perform or do repeatedly in order to acquire skill or proficiency. **3.** to pursue (a profession).

prac·ti·tioner, *n.* one engaged in the practice of a profession or the like.

prag·matic, *adj.* concerned with practical consequences or values.

prai·rie, *n.* an extensive or slightly undulating treeless tract of land.

praise, *n., v.*, **praised, praising.** —*n.* **1.** the expression of approval or admiration. —*v.* **2.** to express approval or admiration of. — **praiseworthy**, *adj.*

pram, *n.* a small, four-wheeled vehicle used for carrying a baby.

prance, *v.*, **pranced, prancing. 1.** to spring, or move by springing, from the hind legs, as a horse. **2.** to move or go in an elated manner; swagger.

prang, *v. Colloq.* **1.** to crash (a car or the like). —*n.* **2.** a crash, esp. a minor one, in a car.

prank, *n.* a playful or malicious trick.

prate, *v.*, **prated, prating.** to talk too much; talk foolishly or pointlessly.

prat·tle, *v.*, **-tled, -tling.** to talk or chatter in a simple-minded or foolish way; babble.

prawn, *n.* a shrimplike crustacean, often used as food.

precipitate

pray, *v.* to make earnest or devout petition to (a person, God, etc.).

prayer, *n.* **1.** a devout petition to, or any form of spiritual communion with, God or an object of worship. **2.** a petition or entreaty.

praying mantis, *n.* →mantis.

preach, *v.* **1.** to proclaim or make known by sermon (the gospel, good tidings, etc.). **2.** to deliver a sermon.

pre·am·ble, *n.* an introductory statement; preface.

pre·car·i·ous, *adj.* **1.** uncertain; unstable; insecure. **2.** dangerous; perilous.

pre·cau·tion, *n.* a measure taken beforehand to ward off possible evil or secure good results.

pre·cede, *v.*, **-ceded, -ceding.** to go before.

pre·ced·ence, *n.* **1.** the act or fact of preceding. **2.** priority in order, rank, importance, etc.

prece·dent, *n.* a preceding instance or case which may serve as an example or justification in subsequent cases.

pre·cen·tor, *n.* one who leads a church choir or congregation in singing.

pre·cept, *n.* a commandment or direction given as a rule of action or conduct.

pre·cinct, *n.* a place or space of definite limits.

pre·cious, *adj.* **1.** of great price or value; valuable; costly. **2.** dear or beloved.

preci·pice, *n.* a steep cliff.

pre·cip·i·tate, *v.*, **-tated, -tating,** *adj., n.* —*v.* **1.** to hasten the occurrence of; bring about in haste or suddenly. **2.** *Chem.* to separate (a substance) in solid form from a solu-

precipitate

tion. **3.** to cast down headlong; fling or hurl down. *–adj.* **4.** proceeding rapidly or with great haste. **5.** exceedingly sudden or abrupt. *–n.* **6.** *Chem.* a substance precipitated from a solution.

pre·cip·i·ta·tion, *n.* **1.** the act of precipitating. **2.** falling products of condensation in the atmosphere, as rain, snow, hail.

pre·cip·i·tous, *adj.* **1.** extremely or impassably steep. **2.** hasty or sudden; precipitate.

precis /'preɪsiː/, *n., pl.* **-cis.** an abstract or summary.

pre·cise, *adj.* **1.** definite or exact. **2.** carefully distinct, as the voice. **3.** excessively or rigidly particular. **– precision,** *n.*

pre·clude, *v.,* **-cluded, -cluding.** to shut out or exclude.

pre·co·cious, *adj.* unusually highly developed in mind.

pre·con·ceive, *v.,* **-ceived, -ceiving.** to form an idea of in advance. **– preconception,** *n.*

pre·cur·sor, *n.* one who or that which precedes; predecessor.

preda·tory, *adj.* **1.** pertaining to plundering, pillaging, or robbery. **2.** *Zool.* habitually preying upon other animals. **– predator,** *n.*

pre·de·ces·sor, *n.* one who precedes another in an office, position, etc.

pre·des·tine, *v.,* **-tined, -tining.** to appoint or determine beforehand.

pre·dic·a·ment, *n.* an unpleasant, trying, or dangerous situation.

predi·cate, *v.,* **-cated, -cating,** *n. –v.* **1.** to proclaim; declare; affirm or assert. *–n.* **2.** *Gram.* the active verb in a sentence or clause together with all the words it governs and

prefix

those which modify it, as *is here* in *Jack is here.* **– predicative,** *adj.*

pre·dict, *v.* to foretell (the future); prophesy. **– prediction,** *n.*

pre·di·lec·tion, *n.* a predisposition of the mind in favour of something.

pre·dispose, *v.,* **-posed, -posing. 1.** to give a previous inclination or tendency to. **2.** to render subject, susceptible, or liable.

pre·domi·nate, *v.,* **-nated, -nating. 1.** to be the stronger or leading element. **2.** to have or exert controlling power (*over*). **– predominant,** *adj.*

pre-eminent, *adj.* superior to or surpassing others; distinguished beyond others.

pre-empt, *v.* to acquire or appropriate beforehand. **– pre-emptive,** *adj.*

preen, *v.* **1.** to trim or dress with the beak, as a bird does its feathers. **2.** to prepare, dress, or array (oneself) carefully.

pre·face, *n., v.,* **-aced, -acing.** *–n.* **1.** a preliminary statement by the author or editor of a book. **2.** something preliminary or introductory. *–v.* **3.** to provide with or introduce by a preface. **4.** to serve as a preface to.

pre·fect, *n.* a person appointed to any of various positions of command, authority, or superintendence. **– prefecture,** *n.*

pre·fer, *v.,* **-ferred, -ferring. 1.** to like better; choose rather. **2.** to put forward (a statement, suit, charge, etc.) for consideration or sanction. **3.** to put forward or advance, as in rank or office. **– preference,** *n.* **– preferential,** *adj.*

prefix, *n.* *Gram.* an affix which is

prefix

put before a word to add to or qualify its meaning (as *un-* in *unkind*). –*v.* **2.** to fix or put before or in front.

preg·nant, *adj.* **1.** being with child or young; having a foetus in the womb. **2.** full of meaning; highly significant. –**pregnancy**, *n.*

pre·hen·sile, *adj.* adapted for seizing, grasping, or laying hold of anything.

prej·u·dice, *n.*, *v.*, **-diced, -dicing.** –*n.* **1.** any preconceived opinion or feeling, favourable or unfavourable. **2.** disadvantage resulting from some judgment or action of another. –*v.* **3.** to affect with a prejudice, favourable or unfavourable. **4.** to affect disadvantageously. –**prejudicial**, *adj.*

pre·late /'prɛlət/, *n.* an ecclesiastic of a high order, as an archbishop, bishop, etc.

pre·lim·i·nary *n.*, *pl.* **-naries**, *adj.* **1.** (something) introductory or preparatory.

pre·lude, *n.*, *v.*, **-uded, -uding.** –*n.* **1.** a preliminary to an action, event, condition, or work of broader scope and higher importance. *Music.* **2.** a piece which precedes a more important movement. –*v.* **3.** to serve as a prelude or introduction to.

pre·mar·i·tal, *adj.* before marriage.

pre·ma·ture, *adj.* coming into existence or occurring too soon.

pre·med·i·tate, *v.*, **-tated, -tating.** to plan beforehand.

pre·mier, *n.* **1.** the leader of a State government. –*adj.* **2.** first in rank; chief; leading. **3.** earliest.

prem·i·ere, *n.* a first public performance of a play, etc.

pre·mise, *n.*, *v.*, **-ised, -ising.** –*n.* **1.**

preposterous

(*pl.*) a house or building with the grounds, etc., belonging to it. **2.** Also, **premiss.** *Logic.* a proposition (or one of several) from which a conclusion is drawn. –*v.* **3.** to set forth beforehand, as by way of introduction or explanation.

pre·mi·um, *n.* **1.** a bonus, prize, or the like. **2.** the amount paid or agreed to be paid, in one sum or periodically, for a contract of insurance. **3. at a premium**, in high esteem; in demand. –*adj.* **4.** of highest quality; best.

pre·mon·i·tion, *n.* **1.** a forewarning. **2.** →**presentiment**.

pre·oc·cu·py, *v.*, **-pied, -pying.** to absorb or engross to the exclusion of other things.

prep·a·ra·tion, *n.* **1.** a proceeding, measure, or provision by which one prepares for something. **2.** the act of preparing. **3.** something prepared, manufactured, or compounded.

pre·pare, *v.*, **-pared, -paring.** **1.** to make ready, or put in due condition, for something. **2.** to get ready for eating. **3.** to manufacture, or compose. –**preparatory**, *adj.*

pre·pon·der·ate, *v.*, **-rated, -rating.** to be superior in power, force, influence, number, amount, etc.; predominate. –**preponderance**, *n.*

prep·o·si·tion, *n.* a word placed before a noun to indicate its relation to other words or their function in the sentence. *By, to, in, from* are prepositions in English.

pre·pos·sess·ing, *adj.* impressing favourably beforehand.

pre·pos·ter·ous, *adj.* directly contrary to nature, reason, or common sense; absurd, senseless.

prepuce, *n.* the fold of skin covering the head of the penis or clitoris.

pre·rog·a·tive, *n.* an exclusive right or privilege.

pres·age, *v.*, **-saged**, **-saging**. -*n.* 1. an omen. -*v.* 2. to forecast; predict.

pre·scribe, *v.*, **-scribed**, **-scribing**. 1. to lay down as a rule or a course to be followed; appoint, ordain, or enjoin. 2. *Med.* to designate or order for use, as a remedy or treatment. - **prescriptive**, *adj.*

pre·scrip·tion, *n. Med.* a direction (usu. written) by the doctor to the pharmacist for the preparation and use of a medicine.

pres·ence, *n.* 1. the state or fact of being present, with others or in a place. 2. personal appearance or bearing, esp. of a dignified or imposing kind. 3. a divine or spiritual being.

pre·sent[1], *adj.* 1. being, existing, or occurring at this time or now. 2. being here or there, rather than elsewhere. -*n.* 3. the present time.

pre·sent[2], *v.* 1. to furnish or endow with a gift. 2. to afford or furnish (an opportunity, possibility, etc.). 3. to hand or send in, as a bill or a cheque for payment. 4. to introduce (a person) to another. 5. to show or exhibit. 6. to level or aim (a weapon, esp. a firearm). -*n.* 7. a thing presented as a gift. - **presentation**, *n.*

pre·sent·able, *adj.* fit to be seen.

pre·sen·ti·ment, *n.* a feeling or impression of something about to happen, esp. something evil; foreboding.

pres·ently, *adv.* 1. in a little while or soon. 2. at this time, currently.

pre·ser·va·tive, *n.* a chemical substance used to preserve foods, etc.

pre·serve, *v.*, **-served**, **-serving**. -*v.* 1. to keep safe from harm or injury; save. 2. to keep up; maintain. 3. to prepare (food or any perishable substance) so as to resist decomposition or fermentation. -*n.* 4. something preserved, as food. 5. something reserved exclusively for someone's use.

pre·side, *v.*, **-sided**, **-siding**. to occupy the place of authority or control.

presi·dent, *n.* 1. (*oft. cap.*) the highest official in a republic. 2. an officer appointed or elected to preside over a society, etc. - **presidency**, *n.* - **presidential**, *adj.*

press[1], *v.* 1. to act upon with weight or force. 2. to compress or squeeze, as to alter in shape or size. 3. to make flat by subjecting to weight. 4. to iron (clothes, etc.). 5. to urge (a person, etc.). 6. to compel haste. 7. to crowd or throng. -*n.* 8. printed publications collectively, esp. newspapers and periodicals. 9. a machine used for printing. 10. an establishment for printing books, etc. 11. an instrument or machine for exerting pressure. 12. a crowd or throng. 13. pressure or urgency, as of affairs or business. 14. a piece of furniture, for holding clothes, books, etc.

press[2], *v.* to force into service, esp. naval or military service.

pres·sure, *n.* 1. the exertion of force upon a body by another body in contact with it; compression. 2. harassment; oppression. 3. a constraining or compelling force or influence.

pres·sur·ise, *v.*, **-rised**, **-rising**. to

pressurise

maintain normal air pressure in an aeroplane designed to fly at high altitudes.

pres·tige, *n.* reputation or influence arising from success, achievement, rank, etc. – **prestigious**, *adj.*

pre·sume, *v.*, **-sumed, -suming. 1.** to take for granted, assume, or suppose. **2.** to act or proceed with impertinent boldness. – **presumption**, *n.*

pre·sump·tuous, *adj.* impertinently bold; forward.

pre·sup·pose, *v.* to suppose (def. 3).

pre·tence, *n.* **1.** pretending or feigning. **2.** a false show of something. **3.** an alleged or pretended reason or excuse, or a pretext. **4.** insincere or false profession.

pre·tend, *v.* **1.** to put forward a false appearance of; feign. **2.** to allege or profess, esp. insincerely or falsely. **3.** to make believe. **4.** to lay claim (to).

pre·ten·sion, *n.* the assumption of or a claim to dignity or importance. – **pretentious**, *adj.* – **pretentiousness**, *n.*

pret·er·ite, *adj. Gram.* designating a tense usu. denoting an action or state which was completed in the past.

pre·text, *n.* that which is put forward to conceal a true purpose or object; an ostensible reason.

pret·ty, *adj.*, **-tier, -tiest**, *adv.*, *v.*, **-tied, -tying.** –*adj.* **1.** pleasing; fair or attractive to the eye. –*adv.* **2.** moderately. **3.** quite; very. –*v.* **4.** to make pretty.

pre·vail, *v.* **1.** to be widespread or current; to exist everywhere or generally. **2.** to be or prove superior in strength, power, or influence. **3.**

pride

to persuade successfully (*on*, *upon*, or *with*).

prev·a·lent, *adj.* widespread.

pre·var·i·cate, *v.*, **-cated, -cating.** to act or speak evasively; equivocate; quibble.

pre·vent, *v.* to keep from doing or occurring; hinder. – **prevention**, *n.*

pre·vent·ive, *adj.* **1.** *Med.* warding off disease. **2.** serving to prevent or hinder. Also, **preventative**.

pre·view, *n.* a view in advance, as of a film.

pre·vi·ous, *adj.* coming or occurring before something else; prior.

prey, *n.* **1.** an animal hunted or seized for food. **2.** a person or thing that falls a victim to an enemy, a disease, etc. –*v.* **3.** to seek for and seize prey.

price, *n.*, *v.*, **priced, pricing.** –*n.* **1.** the amount of money for which anything is bought or sold. **2.** that which must be given, done, or undergone in order to obtain a thing. –*v.* **3.** to fix the price of.

prick, *n.* **1.** a puncture made by a needle, thorn, or the like. **2.** the act of pricking. –*v.* **3.** to pierce with a sharp point; puncture. **4.** to (cause to) stand erect or point upwards.

prick·le, *n.*, *v.*, **-led, -ling.** –*n.* **1.** a sharp point. **2.** a small, pointed process growing from the bark of a plant. –*v.* **3.** to prick. **4.** to cause a pricking sensation in.

pride, *n.*, *v.*, **prided, priding.** –*n.* **1.** high or inordinate opinion of one's own dignity, importance, merit, or superiority. **2.** self-respect. **3.** the best or most admired part of anything. **4.** a company of lions. –*v.* **5.** to indulge or plume (oneself) in a feeling of pride (*on* or *upon*).

priest, *n.* one whose office it is to perform religious rites.

prig, *n.* one who is precise to an extreme in attention to principle or duty, esp. in a self-righteous way.

prim, *adj.* **primmer, primmest**. affectedly precise or proper.

pri·ma·cy, *n., pl.* **-cies. 1.** the state of being first in order, rank, importance, etc. **2.** the office, rank, or dignity of an archbishop.

primal, *adj.* first; original; primeval.

pri·ma·ry, *adj.* **1.** first or highest in rank or importance; chief; principal. **2.** constituting or belonging to, the first stage in any process. **3.** original, not derived or subordinate; fundamental; basic. **– primarily**, *adv.*

pri·mate, *n.* **1.** *Eccles.* an archbishop. **2.** any mammal of the order that includes man, the apes, the monkeys, etc.

prime, *adj., n., v.,* **primed, priming.** *–adj.* **1.** first in importance, excellence, or value. **2.** original; fundamental. *–n.* **3.** the most flourishing stage or state. **4.** the choicest or best part of anything. *–v.* **5.** to prepare or make ready for a particular purpose or operation. **6.** to supply (a firearm) with powder for communicating fire to a charge. **7.** to supply or equip with information, words, etc., for use.

prime minister, *n.* (*oft. cap.*) the first or principal minister of certain governments; the chief of the cabinet or ministry. **– prime ministry**, *n.*

primer, *n.* **1.** an elementary book for teaching children to read. **2.** any small book of elementary principles.

pri·me·val, *adj.* of or pertaining to the first age or ages, esp. of the world. Also, **primaeval**. **– primevally**, *adv.*

prim·i·tive, *adj.* **1.** early in the history of the world or of mankind. **2.** characteristic of early ages of or of an early state of human development. **3.** unaffected or little affected by civilising influences.

prim·rose, *n.* a garden plant usu. with yellow flowers.

prince, *n.* **1.** a non-reigning male member of a royal family. **2.** a sovereign or monarch; king. **3.** the ruler of a small state.

prin·cess, *n.* **1.** a female member of a royal family. **2.** the consort of a prince.

prin·ci·pal, *adj.* **1.** first or highest in rank, importance, value, etc.; chief; foremost. *–n.* **2.** a chief or head. **3.** something of principal or chief importance. **4.** *Law.* a person authorising another (an agent) to represent him. **5.** a person primarily liable for an obligation (opposed to an *endorser*). **6.** *Comm.* a capital sum, as distinguished from interest or profit.

prin·ci·pal·i·ty, *n., pl.* **-ties.** a state ruled by a prince.

prin·ci·ple, *n.* **1.** an accepted or professed rule of action or conduct. **2.** a fundamental, primary, or general truth, on which other truths depend. **3.** guiding sense of the requirements and obligations of right conduct. **4.** a rule or law exemplified in natural phenomena, in the construction or operation of a machine, the working of a system, or the like.

print, *v.* **1.** to produce (a text, a picture, etc.) by applying inked types, plates or blocks, or the like, with

print

direct pressure to paper or other material. 2. to write in letters like those commonly used in print. 3. to produce or fix (an indentation, mark, etc.) by pressure. 4. *Photog.* to produce a positive picture from (a negative) by the transmission of light. 5. *Computers.* to produce (a result, data, etc.) in a legible form on paper (*out*). –*n.* 6. the state of being printed: *in print.* 7. printed lettering. 8. printed matter. 9. (cotton cloth with) a printed design. 10. *Photog.* a picture made from a negative.

prior[1], *adj.* 1. preceding in time, or in order; earlier or former; anterior or antecedent. –*adv.* 2. previously (*to*).

prior[2], *n.* the superior of certain monastic orders and houses.

pri·or·i·ty, *n., pl.* **-ties.** 1. the state of being earlier in time, or of preceding something else. 2. precedence in order, rank, etc.

prise, *v.,* **prised, prising.** to raise, move, or force with or as with a lever.

prism, *n.* 1. *Optics.* a transparent, usu. triangular body used for decomposing light into its spectrum or for reflecting light beams. 2. *Geom.* a solid whose bases or ends are any congruent and parallel polygons, and whose sides are parallelograms. – **prismatic**, *adj.*

prison, *n.* a public building for the confinement or safe custody of criminals and others committed by law.

pris·on·er, *n.* one who is confined in prison or kept in custody, esp. as the result of legal process.

prissy, *adj.,* **-sier, -siest.** *Colloq.* precise; prim; affectedly nice.

402

probability

pris·tine, *adj.* 1. of or pertaining to the earliest period or state; original; primitive. 2. having its original purity.

pri·vate, *adj.* 1. belonging to some particular person; being one's own. 2. confidential: *a private meeting.* 3. not holding public office or employment, as a person. 4. removed from or out of public view or knowledge; secret. 5. alone; secluded. – **privacy**, *n.*

pri·va·tion, *n.* lack of the usual comforts or necessaries of life.

privet, *n.* a hardy European shrub, heavily perfumed with white flowers, now considered a noxious plant.

privi·lege, *n., v.,* **-leged, -leging.** –*n.* 1. a right or immunity enjoyed by a person or persons beyond the common advantages of others: *parliamentary privilege.* 2. an advantage, or opportunity enjoyed by anyone in a favoured position (as distinct from a right). –*v.* 3. to grant a privilege to.

privy, *adj., n., pl.* **privies.** –*adj.* 1. participating in the knowledge of something private or secret (*to*). –*n.* 2. an outhouse serving as a toilet. – **privity**, *n.*

prize[1], *n.* 1. a reward of victory or superiority, as in a contest or competition. 2. that which is won in a lottery or the like.

prize[2], *v.,* **prized, prizing.** to value or esteem highly.

pro, *adv., n., pl.* **pros.** –*adv.* 1. in favour of a proposition, opinion, etc. (opposed to *con*). –*n.* 2. an argument, consideration, vote, etc., for something.

proba·bil·i·ty, *n., pl.* **-ties.** 1. the

probability

quality or fact of being probable. 2. a likelihood or chance of something. 3. a probable event, circumstance, etc.

prob·able, *adj.* 1. likely to occur or prove true. 2. affording ground for belief.

pro·bate, *n. Law.* the official proving of a will as authentic or valid.

pro·bation, *n.* 1. the act of testing. 2. *Law.* a method of dealing with offenders, esp. young persons guilty of minor crimes or first offences, by allowing them to go free conditionally and under supervision.

probe, *v.*, probed, probing, *n.* –*v.* 1. to search into or examine thoroughly; question closely. –*n.* 2. the act of probing. 3. a slender surgical instrument for exploring a wound, sinus, etc.

pro·bity, *n.* integrity; uprightness; honesty.

prob·lem, *n.* 1. any question or matter involving doubt, uncertainty, or difficulty. 2. a question proposed for solution or discussion. – problematic, problematical, *adj.*

pro·boscis /prəˈbɒskəs, prəˈboʊsɪs/, *n., pl.* -boscises, -boscides. 1. an elephant's trunk. 2. any long flexible snout.

pro·cedure, *n.* the act or manner of proceeding in any action or process; conduct.

pro·ceed, *v.* 1. to go on with or carry on any action or process. 2. to take legal proceedings (*against*). 3. to be carried on, as an action, process, etc. 4. to go or come forth; issue. –*n.* 5. (*usu. pl.*) the sum derived from a sale or other transaction.

prodigious

pro·ceed·ing, *n.* 1. action, course of action, or conduct. 2. (*pl.*) records of the doings of a society. 3. *Law.* a. the instituting or carrying on of an action at law. b. a legal step or measure.

pro·cess, *n.* 1. a systematic series of actions directed to some end. 2. the whole course of the proceedings in an action at law. 3. a protuberance or appendage. 4. the action of going forward or on. 5. the condition of being carried on. 6. course or lapse, as of time. –*v.* 7. to treat or prepare by some particular process, as in manufacturing.

pro·ces·sion, *n.* a line of persons, vehicles, etc., moving along in an orderly or ceremonious manner.

pro·claim, *v.* to announce or declare, publicly and officially. – proclamation, *n.*

pro·cliv·ity, *n., pl.* -ties. natural or habitual inclination or tendency.

pro·cras·ti·nate, *v.*, -nated, -nating. to defer action; delay. – procrastinator, *n.*

pro·cre·ate, *v.*, -ated, -ating. 1. to beget or generate (offspring). 2. to produce; bring into being.

pro·cure, *v.*, -cured, -curing. 1. to obtain or get by care, effort, or the use of special means. 2. to effect; cause; bring about, esp. by unscrupulous or indirect means.

prod, *v.*, prodded, prodding, *n.* –*v.* 1. to poke or jab with something pointed. –*n.* 2. a poke or jab. 3. a pointed instrument, as a goad.

prod·i·gal, *adj.* 1. wastefully or recklessly extravagant. –*n.* 2. a spendthrift.

pro·di·gious, *adj.* 1. extraordinary in

prodigious

size, amount, extent, degree, force, etc. 2. wonderful or marvellous.

prod·igy, *n., pl.* **-gies.** a person, esp. a child, endowed with extraordinary gifts or powers.

pro·duce, *v.,* **-duced, -ducing,** *n.* –*v.* 1. to bring into existence. 2. to make; create. 3. *Econ.* to create (something having an exchangeable value). 4. to yield. 5. to bring forward. 6. to bring (a play, film, etc.) before the public. –*n.* 7. that which is produced; yield; product. 8. agricultural or natural products collectively. – **production**, *n.* – **productive**, *adj.* – **productivity**, *n.*

pro·ducer, *n.* one who supervises the production of a film, play, television or radio show, etc.

pro·duct, *n.* 1. a thing produced by any action or operation, or by labour; an effect or result. 2. a thing produced by nature or by a natural process. 3. *Maths.* the result obtained by multiplying 2 or more quantities together.

pro·fane, *adj.* characterised by irreverence or contempt for God or sacred things. – **profanity**, *n.*

pro·fess, *v.* 1. to lay claim to (a feeling, etc.), often insincerely; pretend to. 2. to declare openly; announce or affirm; avow or acknowledge.

pro·fes·sion, *n.* a vocation requiring knowledge of some department of learning or science.

pro·fes·sional, *adj.* 1. following an occupation as a means of livelihood or for gain. 2. pertaining or appropriate to a profession. 3. earning a living by an occupation ordinarily engaged in as a pastime. –*n.* 4. one belonging to one of the learned or skilled professions. 5. one who earns a living by an art or sport, etc., in which amateurs engage for amusement or recreation.

pro·fes·sor, *n.* a teacher of the highest rank, usu. holding a chair in a particular branch of learning, in a university or college.

prof·fer, *v.* to put before a person for acceptance; offer.

pro·fi·cient, *adj.* well advanced or expert in any art, science, or subject; skilled. – **proficiency**, *n.*

pro·file, *n.* 1. the outline or contour of the human face, esp. as seen from the side. 2. the outline of something seen against a background. 3. a vivid and concise sketch of the biography or personality of an individual.

profit, *n.* 1. (*oft. pl.*) monetary gain resulting from any transaction. 2. *Econ.* the surplus left to the producer or employer after deducting wages, rent, cost of raw materials, etc. 3. advantage; benefit; gain. –*v.* 4. to gain advantage or benefit. 5. to make profit. – **profitable**, *adj.*

profi·teer, *n.* one who makes exorbitant profits out of public need.

prof·li·gate, *adj.* utterly and shamelessly immoral.

pro·found, *adj.* 1. penetrating or entering deeply into subjects of thought or knowledge. 2. deep. – **profundity**, *n.*

pro·fuse, *adj.* 1. extravagant. 2. abundant; in great amount. – **profusion**, *n.*

pro·geny, *n., pl.* **-nies.** offspring; issue; descendants. – **progenitor**, *n.*

prog·nosis, *n., pl.* **-noses.** a forecasting of the probable course and

prognosis

prog·no·sis termination of a disease. – **prog·nostic**, *adj.*

prog·nos·ti·cate, *v.*, -cated, -cating. to prophesy.

pro·gram, *n., v.*, -grammed, -gramming. –*n.* 1. a plan or policy to be followed. 2. a list of items in an entertainment. 3. an entertainment with reference to its items. 4. a prospectus or syllabus. 5.computer instructions. –*v.* 6. *Computers.* to organise and arrange (data, etc.) relevant to a problem so that it can be solved by a computer. 7. to plan a program. Also, **programme**. – **programmer**, *n.*

pro·gress, *n.* 1. advancement, growth or development. 2. course of action, of events, of time, etc. –*v.* 3. to advance.

pro·gres·sion, *n.* 1. forward or onward movement. 2. a passing successively from one member of a series to the next; succession; sequence.

pro·gres·sive, *adj.* 1. favouring progress or reform, esp. in political matters. 2. progressing or advancing.

pro·hibit, *v.* to forbid by authority. – **prohibition**, *n.*

pro·hibi·tive, *adj.* 1. that prohibits or forbids something. 2. serving to prevent the use, purchase, etc., of something. Also, **prohibitory**.

pro·ject, *n.* 1. a plan; scheme; undertaking. 2. to propose, contemplate, or plan. 3. to throw, cast, or impel forwards or onwards. 4. to communicate; make known (an idea, impression, etc.). –*v.* 5. to (cause to) extend or protrude.

pro·jec·tile, *n.* an object set in motion by an exterior force which then continues to move by its own inertia.

promissory note

pro·jec·tor, *n.* an apparatus for throwing an image on a screen.

pro·lapse, *n. Pathol.* a falling down of an organ or part, as the uterus, from its normal position.

pro·le·tar·iat, *n.* 1. the unpropertied class. 2. the working class, or wage-earners in general.

pro·lif·er·ate, *v.*, -rated, -rating. to grow or produce by multiplication of parts, as in budding or cell division. – **proliferation**, *n.*

pro·lif·ic, *adj.* producing offspring, fruit, work, etc., esp. abundantly; fruitful.

prolix, *adj.* tediously long.

pro·logue, *n.* an introduction or introductory speech to a discourse, play, etc.

pro·long, *v.* to make longer.

prom·en·ade, *n., v.*, -naded, -nading. –*n.* 1. a walk, esp. in a public place for pleasure or display. –*v.* 2. to take a promenade.

prom·i·nent, *adj.* 1. standing out so as to be easily seen; conspicuous. 2. important; leading; well-known. – **prominence**, *n.*

promis·cu·ous, *adj.* mingling indiscriminately, esp. in sexual intercourse with a number of partners. – **promiscuity**, *n.*

promise, *n., v.*, -ised, -ising. –*n.* 1. an express assurance on which expectation is to be based. 2. indication of future excellence or achievement. –*v.* 3. to engage or undertake by promise (with an infinitive or clause). 4. to make a promise of. 5. to afford ground for expectation (*well* or *fair*).

promis·sory note, *n.* a written pro-

405

promissory note

mise to pay a specified sum of money to a person designated.

pro·mon·to·ry, *n., pl.* **-ries.** a high point of land or rock projecting into the sea; headland.

pro·mote, *v.*, **-moted, -moting. 1.** to advance in rank, dignity, position, etc. **2.** to further the growth, development, progress, etc., of; encourage. – **promotion,** *n.*

prompt, *adj.* **1.** done at once or without delay. **2.** quick to act as occasion demands. –*v.* **3.** to move or incite to action. **4.** to assist (a person speaking) by suggesting something to be said. –*n.* **5.** something that prompts.

promul·gate, *v.*, **-gated, -gating. 1.** to make known by open declaration. **2.** to set forth or teach publicly (a creed, doctrine, etc.).

prone, *adj.* **1.** having a natural inclination or tendency to something; disposed; liable. **2.** lying face downwards. **3.** lying flat; prostrate.

prong, *n.* one of the pointed divisions or tines of a fork.

pro·noun, *n.* a word used as a substitute for a noun. – **pronominal,** *adj.*

pro·nounce, *v.*, **-nounced, -nouncing. 1.** to enunciate or articulate (words, etc.). **2.** to utter or sound in a particular manner in speaking. **3.** to declare (a person or thing) to be as specified. **4.** to utter or deliver formally or solemnly. **5.** to give an opinion or decision (*on*). – **pronunciation,** *n.*; for defs 1-2. – **pronouncement,** *n.*; for defs 3-5.

pro·nounced, *adj.* **1.** strongly marked. **2.** clearly indicated.

proof, *n.* **1.** evidence sufficient to establish a thing as true. **2.** the establishment of the truth of anything; demonstration. **3.** an arithmetical operation serving to check the correctness of a calculation. **4.** *Photog.* a trial print from a negative. **5.** *Print.* a trial impression as of composed type, taken to correct errors and make alterations. –*adj.* **6.** impenetrable, impervious, or invulnerable. **7.** of tested or proved strength or quality.

prop, *v.*, **propped, propping,** *n.* –*v.* **1.** to support or sustain (*up*). –*n.* **2.** a stick, rod, pole, beam, or other rigid support. **3.** a person or thing serving as support or stay.

propa·ganda, *n.* dissemination of ideas, information or rumour for the purpose of injuring or helping an institution, a cause or a person.

propa·gate, *v.*, **-gated, -gating. 1.** to cause (plants, animals, etc.) to multiply by natural reproduction. **2.** to transmit (traits, etc.) in reproduction, or through offspring. **3.** to spread (a report, doctrine, practice, etc.) from person to person; disseminate. **4.** to cause to extend to a greater distance, or transmit through space or a medium.

pro·pane, *n.* a gaseous hydrocarbon found in petroleum.

propel, *v.*, **-pelled, -pelling.** to drive, or cause to move, forwards.

pro·pel·lant, *n.* **1.** a propelling agent. **2.** *Aeron.* one or more substances used in rocket motors for the chemical generation of gas at the controlled rates required to provide thrust.

pro·pel·ler, *n.* a device having a revolving hub with radiating blades, for propelling a ship, aircraft, etc.

pro·pen·si·ty, *n., pl.* **-ties.** natural or habitual inclination or tendency.

proper, *adj.* 1. adapted or appropriate to the purpose or circumstances; fit; suitable. 2. conforming to established standards of behaviour; correct or decorous. 3. belonging exclusively or distinctly to a person or thing. 4. strict; accurate.

proper noun, *n.* a noun that is not usu. preceded by an article, and is the name of a single person or thing, or a unique class of persons or things. See **common noun**.

prop·er·ty, *n., pl.* **-ties.** 1. the possession or possessions of a particular owner. 2. a piece of land owned. 3. a farm, station, orchard, etc. 4. an essential or distinctive attribute or quality of a thing. 5. *Theat.* Also, **prop.** an object, item of furniture, ornament, or decoration in a stage setting.

proph·e·cy, *n., pl.* **-cies.** prediction.

proph·e·sy, *v.*, **-sied, -sying.** to foretell or predict. – **prophetic**, *adj.*

proph·et, *n.* 1. one who speaks for God or a deity, or by divine inspiration. 2. one who predicts what is to come.

pro·phy·lac·tic, *adj.* 1. defending or protecting from disease, as a drug. –*n.* 2. →**contraceptive**. – **prophylaxis**, *n.*

pro·pi·ti·ate, *v.*, **-ated, -ating.** to make favourably inclined; appease.

pro·pi·tious, *adj.* favourable.

pro·po·nent, *n.* 1. one who puts forward a proposal. 2. one who supports a cause or doctrine.

pro·por·tion, *n.* 1. comparative relation between things; ratio. 2. proper relation between things or parts. 3. (*pl.*) dimensions. 4. a portion or part, esp. in its relation to the whole. 5. symmetry; harmony; balanced relationship. – **proportional**, *adj.* – **proportionate**, *adj.*

pro·pose, *v.*, **-posed, -posing.** 1. to put forward (a matter, subject, case, etc.) for consideration, acceptance, or action. 2. to present (a person) for some position, office, membership, etc. – **proposal**, *n.* – **proposition**, *n.*

pro·pound, *v.* to put forward for consideration, acceptance, or adoption.

pro·pri·e·tar·y, *adj.* 1. belonging to a proprietor. 2. manufactured and sold only by the owner of the patent, formula, brand name, or trademark associated with the product.

pro·pri·e·tor, *n.* the owner of a business establishment, a hotel, newspaper, etc. – **proprietorship**, *n.*

pro·pri·e·ty, *n., pl.* **-ties.** 1. conformity to established standards of behaviour or manners. 2. appropriateness to the purpose or circumstances; suitability.

pro·pul·sion, *n.* the act of propelling or driving forward or onward.

pro rata, *adv.* 1. in proportion; according to a certain rate. –*adj.* 2. proportionate.

pro·rogue, *v.*, **-rogued, -roguing.** to discontinue meetings of (parliament) until the next session.

pro·sa·ic, *adj.* commonplace or dull; matter-of-fact.

pro·sce·ni·um, *n., pl.* **-nia.** (in the modern theatre) the decorative arch or opening between the stage and the auditorium.

pro·scribe, *v.*, **-scribed, -scribing.** 1. to denounce or condemn (a thing)

proscribe

as dangerous; to prohibit. **2.** to banish, exile or outlaw.

prose, *n.* the ordinary form of spoken or written language, without metrical structure (as distinguished from poetry or verse).

pros·e·cute, *v.,* -cuted, -cuting. *Law.* **1.** to institute legal proceedings against (a person, etc.). **2.** to seek to enforce or obtain by legal process. **3.** to conduct criminal proceedings in court against. – **prosecution,** *n.* – **prosecutor,** *n.*

pros·e·lyte, *n.* a convert.

pros·o·dy, *n.* the science or study of poetic metres and versification.

pros·pect, *n.* **1.** (*usu. pl.*) an apparent probability of advancement, success, profit, etc. **2.** the outlook for the future. **3.** a view or scene. –*v.* **4.** to search or explore (a region), as for gold. – **prospector,** *n.*

pros·pec·tive, *adj.* **1.** of or in the future. **2.** potential; likely; expected.

pros·pec·tus, *n.* **1.** an advertisement inviting applications from the public to subscribe for securities of a (proposed) corporation. **2.** a pamphlet issued by an institution giving details about itself.

pros·per·ous, *adj.* **1.** having or characterised by continued good fortune; flourishing; successful. **2.** well-to-do or well-off. – **prosper,** *v.* – **prosperity,** *n.*

pros·tate gland, *n.* the gland which surrounds the urethra of males at the base of the bladder.

pros·the·sis, *n., pl.* -ses. the addition of an artificial part to supply a defect of the body.

pros·ti·tute, *n.* a person, esp. a woman, who engages in sexual intercourse for money as a livelihood.

pros·trate, *v.,* -trated, -trating, *adj.* –*v.* **1.** to throw down level with the ground. –*adj.* **2.** submissive. **3.** lying flat on the ground.

pro·tag·o·nist, *n.* the leading character in a play, novel, etc.

pro·te·an, *adj.* readily assuming different forms or characters.

pro·tect, *v.* to defend or guard or shield from attack, injury or danger. – **protective,** *adj.* – **protection,** *n.*

pro·tec·to·rate, *n.* **1.** the relation of a strong state towards a weaker state or territory which it protects and partly controls. **2.** a state or territory so protected.

protégé, *n.* one who is under the protection or friendly patronage of another.

pro·tein, *n.* *Biochem.* any of the polymers formed from amino acids, which are found in all cells and which include enzymes, plasma and proteins.

pro·test, *n.* **1.** an expression or declaration of objection or disapproval. –*v.* **2.** to give formal expression to objection or disapproval; remonstrate. **3.** to declare solemnly or formally; affirm; assert. – **protestation,** *n.*

pro·to·col, *n.* the customs and regulations dealing with the etiquette of the diplomatic corps and others at a court or capital.

pro·ton, *n.* a positively-charged elementary particle present in every atomic nucleus.

pro·to·type, *n.* the original or model after which anything is formed.

pro·tract, *v.* **1.** to prolong. **2.** *Survey.,*

408

protract

etc. to plot; to draw by means of a scale and protractor.

pro·trac·tor, *n.* a flat instrument, graduated around the semicircular edge, used to measure angles.

pro·trude, *v.*, -truded, -truding. to jut out.

pro·tuber·ant, *adj.* bulging.

proud, *adj.* 1. feeling or showing pleasure or satisfaction over something conceived as highly creditable to oneself (*of*). 2. (of things) stately, majestic, or magnificent.

prove, *v.*, proved, proved or proven, proving. 1. to establish the truth or genuineness of, as by evidence or argument. 2. to put to the test; try or test. 3. to determine the characteristics of by scientific analysis.

pro·ven·ance, *n.* the place of origin, as of a work of art, etc.

pro·ven·der, *n.* dry food for livestock, as hay; fodder.

pro·verb, *n.* a short popular saying, in use for a long time, expressing some familiar truth or useful thought. – **proverbial**, *adj.*

pro·vide, *v.*, -vided, -viding. 1. to furnish or supply. 2. to supply means of support, etc. (*for*).

pro·vided, *conj.* on the condition or supposition (*that*).

provi·dence, *n.* 1. the foreseeing care and guardianship of God over His creatures. 2. provident or prudent management of resources; economy.

provi·dent, *adj.* having or showing foresight; careful in providing for the future.

pro·viding, *conj.* provided.

prov·ince, *n.* 1. an administrative division or unit of a country. 2. **the provinces**, the parts of a country

prudence

outside the capital or the largest cities. 3. the sphere or field of action of a person, etc.

pro·vincial, *adj.* 1. local. 2. countrified; rustic. 3. unsophisticated or narrow.

pro·vision, *n.* 1. a clause in a legal instrument, a law, etc., providing for a particular matter; stipulation; proviso. 2. arrangement or preparation beforehand. 3. (*pl.*) supplies of food.

pro·visional, *adj.* temporary; conditional.

pro·viso, *n., pl.* -sos, -soes. a stipulation or condition.

pro·voke, *v.*, -voked, -voking. 1. to anger, enrage, exasperate, or vex. 2. to stir up, arouse, or call forth. 3. to give rise to, induce, or bring about. – **provocation**, *n.* – **provocative**, *adj.*

pro·vost, *n.* a person appointed to superintend or preside. – **provostship**, *n.*

prow, *n.* the front part of a ship or boat above the waterline; the bow.

prow·ess, *n.* 1. valour; bravery. 2. outstanding ability.

prowl, *v.* to rove or go about stealthily in search of prey, plunder, etc.

prox·imity, *n.* nearness.

proxy, *n., pl.* proxies. the agency of a person deputed to act for another.

prude, *n.* a person who affects extreme modesty or propriety. – **prudery**, *n.*

pru·dence, *n.* 1. cautious practical wisdom; good judgment; discretion. 2. provident care in management; economy or frugality. – **prudential**, *adj.* – **prudent**, *adj.*

prune

prune[1], *n.* a purplish black dried plum.

prune[2], *v.,* pruned, pruning. to cut superfluous twigs, branches, or roots from; trim.

pruri·ent, *adj.* inclined to or characterised by lascivious thought.

pry, *v.,* pried, prying. **1.** to look closely or curiously; peer, or peep. **2.** to search or inquire curiously or inquisitively into something.

psalm, *n.* a sacred or solemn song, or hymn.

pseudo·nym, *n.* an assumed name adopted by an author to conceal his identity.

psyche, *n.* the human soul, spirit, or mind.

psyche·delic, *adj.* **1.** pertaining to a mental state of enlarged consciousness, esp. as experienced through drugs. **2.** *Colloq.* having bright colours and imaginative patterns.

psych·iatry, *n.* the practice or the science of treating mental diseases. – **psychiatric**, *adj.* – **psychiatrist**, *n.*

psychic, *adj.* Also, **psychical**. **1.** of or pertaining to the human soul or mind; mental (opposed to *physical*). **2.** *Psychol.* pertaining to super- or extra-sensory mental functioning, such as clairvoyance, telepathy. –*n.* **3.** a person specially susceptible to psychic influences.

psycho·analysis, *n.* a technical procedure for investigating unconscious mental processes, and for treating neuroses. – **psychoanalyse**, *v.*

psych·ology, *n.,* *pl.* **-gies**. **1.** the science of mind, or of mental states. **2.** the science of human and animal behaviour. – **psychologist**, *n.* – **psychological**, *adj.*

psycho·path, *n.* one affected with a mental disorder. – **psychopathic** – **psychopathy**, *n.*

psy·chosis, *n.,* *pl.* **-ses**. *Pathol.* a severe mental disorder. – **psychotic**, *adj., n.*

psycho·somatic, *adj.* denoting a physical disorder which is caused by or notably influenced by the emotional state of the patient.

pto·maine, *n.* any of a class of basic nitrogenous substances, some of them very poisonous, produced during putrefaction of animal or plant proteins.

pub, *n. Colloq.* a hotel.

puberty, *n.* sexual maturity.

pubic, *adj.* pertaining to the lower part of the abdomen.

public, *adj.* **1.** pertaining to the people as a whole or the community, state, or nation. **2.** open to all the people. **3.** pertaining to or engaged in the affairs or service of the community or nation. –*n.* **4.** the people of a community, state, or nation.

pub·li·can, *n.* the owner or manager of a hotel.

publi·cation, *n.* **1.** the publishing of a book, piece of music, etc. **2.** that which is published.

pub·licity, *n.* **1.** the measures, process, or business of securing public notice. **2.** advertisement matter intended to attract public notice. – **publicise**, *v.* – **publicist**, *n.*

pub·lish, *v.* **1.** to issue in printed copies for sale or distribution to the public. **2.** to make publicly or generally known.

puce, *n.* dark or purplish brown.

pucker, *v.* to draw or gather into wrinkles or irregular folds.

pudding, *n.* 1. a sweet or savoury dish made in many forms and of various ingredients. 2. a course in a meal following the main or meat course.

puddle, *n.* 1. a small pool of water left on a road, etc., after rain. 2. a small pool of any liquid.

pue·rile, *adj.* 1. of or pertaining to a child or boy. 2. childishly foolish, irrational, or trivial.

puff, *n.* 1. a short, quick blast, as of wind or breath. 2. a swelling; protuberance. 3. inflated or exaggerated praise. –*v.* 4. to blow with short, quick blasts, as the wind. 5. to send forth (air, vapour, etc.) in short quick blasts. 6. to inflate or distend, esp. with air.

puffin, *n.* a seabird with a brightly coloured bill.

puffy, *adj.*, **puffier**, **puffiest**. inflated or distended.

pugi·list /'pjudʒəlɪst/, *n.* a boxer.

pug·nacious, *adj.* given to fighting; quarrelsome; aggressive.

pull, *v.* 1. to draw or haul towards oneself or itself. 2. to exert a drawing, tugging, or hauling force (*at*). 3. to draw, or tear (apart, to pieces, etc.). 4. to pluck away from a place of growth, attachment, etc. 5. to cause to form: *to pull a face.* 6. to strain, as a ligament. 7. **pull out**, **a.** to leave; depart. **b.** *Colloq.* to withdraw, from an agreement or enterprise. 8. **pull through**, *Colloq.* to recover or survive. 9. **pull up**, **a.** to stop. **b.** to correct or rebuke. –*n.* 10. the act of pulling or drawing. 11. force used in pulling; pulling power. 12. *Colloq.* influence, as with persons able to grant favours.

pullet, *n.* a young hen.

pulley, *n.*, *pl.* **-leys.** a wheel with a grooved rim for carrying a line, esp. as part of a block (def. 4a).

pull·over, *n.* →**jumper**.

pul·monary, *adj.* of or pertaining to the lungs.

pulp, *n.* 1. the succulent part of a fruit. 2. any soft, moist, slightly cohering mass.

pulpit, *n.* a platform or raised structure in a church, from which the priest or minister delivers a sermon, etc.

pul·sate, *v.*, **-sated**, **-sating**. 1. to expand and contract rhythmically, as the heart; beat; throb. 2. to vibrate; quiver.

pulse, *n.*, *v.*, **pulsed**, **pulsing**. –*n.* 1. the regular throbbing of the arteries caused by the successive contractions of the heart, esp. as felt in an artery at the wrist. 2. a single stroke, vibration, or undulation. 3. a throb of life, emotion, etc. –*v.* 4. to beat or throb; pulsate.

pul·verise, *v.*, **-rised**, **-rising**. to reduce to dust or powder, as by pounding, grinding, etc.

puma, *n.* a large tawny feline.

pumice, *n.* a porous or spongy form of volcanic glass, used, esp. when powdered, as an abrasive, etc.

pummel, *v.*, **-melled**, **-melling**. to beat or thrash with rapid blows, as with the fists.

pump[1], *n.* 1. an apparatus for raising, driving, exhausting, or compressing fluids, as by means of a piston, etc. –*v.* 2. to raise or drive (water) with a pump. 3. to free from water, etc., by means of a pump. 4. to try

pump

to get information from. **5.** to operate as a pump does.

pump², *n.* a type of low light shoe.

pump·kin, *n.* a large, melon-like vegetable.

pun, *n.* a play on words.

punch¹, *n.* **1.** a thrusting blow, esp. with the fist. –*v.* **2.** to give a sharp thrust or blow to, esp. with the fist.

punch², *n.* a tool for perforating tickets, leather, etc.

punch³, *n.* a beverage consisting of wine or spirits mixed with water, fruit juice, etc.

punc·til·i·ous, *adj.* strict in the observance of forms in conduct or actions.

punc·tual, *adj.* strictly observant of an appointed or regular time; not late. – **punctuality**, *n.*

punc·tu·a·tion, *n.* (the inserting of) marks or points in writing or printing in order to make the meaning clear.

punc·ture, *n., v.,* -tured, -turing. –*n.* **1.** a perforation. –*v.* **2.** to prick, pierce or perforate.

pundit, *n.* *Colloq.* a self-appointed expert.

pun·gent, *adj.* sharply affecting the taste; biting; acrid.

punish, *v.* to subject to a penalty, or to pain, loss, confinement, death, etc., for some offence, transgression, or fault. – **punishment**, *n.* – **punitive**, *adj.*

punk, *n.* **1.** *Colloq.* something or someone worthless, degraded, or bad. –*adj.* **2.** relating to a style of dress, rock music, etc., characterised by extreme rejection of social values.

punnet, *n.* a small, shallow basket, as for strawberries.

purgatory

punt¹, *n.* **1.** a shallow, flat-bottomed, square-ended boat. **2.** a ferry for carrying vehicles across rivers, etc.

punt², *v.* to gamble; wager.

puny, *adj.,* -nier, -niest. small and weak.

pup, *n.* **1.** Also, **puppy**, a young dog. **2.** a young seal.

pupa, *n., pl.* -pae. an insect in the non-feeding, usu. immobile, transformation stage between the larva and the imago. – **pupal**, *adj.*

pupil¹, *n.* one learning from an instructor or teacher; student.

pupil², *n.* the expanding and contracting opening in the iris of the eye, through which light passes to the retina.

puppet, *n.* an artificial figure with jointed limbs, moved by wires, etc., as on a miniature stage. – **puppeteer**, *n.* – **puppetry**, *n.*

pur·chase, *v.,* -chased, -chasing, *n.* –*v.* **1.** to acquire by the payment of money or its equivalent; buy. –*n.* **2.** something which is purchased or bought.

pure, *adj.,* purer, purest. **1.** free from extraneous matter, or from mixture with anything of a different, inferior, or contaminating kind. **2.** abstract or theoretical (opposed to *applied*). **3.** absolute; utter; sheer. **4.** being that and nothing else; mere. **5.** spotless, or unsullied. **6.** untainted with evil; innocent. – **purify**, *v.* – **purity**, *n.*

puree, *n.* a cooked and sieved vegetable or fruit.

purga·tive, *adj.* purging; cleansing; specifically, causing evacuation of the bowels.

purga·tory, *n., pl.* -ries. any condi-

purgatory

tion, situation, or place of temporary suffering, expiation, or the like.

purge, v., purged, purging. –v. 1. to cleanse; rid of whatever is impure or undesirable; purify. –n. 2. the elimination, esp. by killing, of political opponents and others.

purism, n. scrupulous or excessive observance of or insistence on purity in language, style, etc. – purist, n.

puri·tan, n. one who aspires to great purity or strictness of life in moral and religious matters. – puritanical, adj.

purl, n. a stitch used in hand knitting to make a rib effect.

pur·loin, v. to steal.

purple, n. 1. any colour having components of both red and blue, esp. a dark shade of such a colour. –adj. 2. of the colour of purple.

pur·port, v. 1. to profess or claim. 2. to convey to the mind as the meaning or thing intended; express; imply. –n. 3. tenor, import, or meaning. 4. purpose or object.

pur·pose, n. 1. the object for which anything exists or is done, made, used, etc. 2. an intended or desired result; end or aim. 3. intention or determination. – purposeful, adj.

purr, v. to utter a low, continuous murmuring sound.

purse, n. 1. a small bag for carrying money on the person. 2. a sum of money offered as a prize.

purser, n. an officer, esp. on board a ship, charged with keeping accounts, etc.

pursu·ant, adv. according (to).

pursue, v., -sued, -suing. 1. to follow with the view of overtaking, capturing, killing, etc.; chase. 2. to seek to attain or accomplish. 3. to carry on (action, thoughts, etc.). 4. to continue to discuss (a subject). – pursuit, n.

purvey, v. to provide, furnish, or supply (esp. food or provisions). – purveyance, n.

pur·view, n. range of operation, activity, concern, etc.

pus, n. a yellow-white substance produced by suppuration and found in abscesses, sores, etc.

push, v. 1. to exert force upon or against (a thing) in order to move it away; shove. 2. to press or urge (a person, etc.) to some action or course. 3. to peddle (narcotics). –n. 4. the act of pushing; a shove or thrust. 5. a determined pushing forward or advance. 6. the pressure of circumstances.

push·over, n. Colloq. anything done easily.

pusil·lani·mous, adj. faint-hearted; cowardly.

pussy[1] /'pʊsi/, n., pl. pussies. a cat. Also, **puss**.

pussy[2] /'pʌsi/, adj. containing pus.

pus·tule, n. Pathol. a small elevation of the skin containing pus.

put, v., put, putting. 1. to move or place (anything) so as to get it into or out of some place or position. 2. to bring into some relation, state, etc.: *to put everything in order*. 3. to estimate: *He puts the distance at 2 metres*. 4. to express or state: *to put it in writing*. 5. to set, give, or make: *to put an end to a practice*. 6. to throw or cast, esp. with a forward motion of the hand when raised close to the shoulder: *to put the shot*. 7. **put across**, to communicate; cause to be understood. 8. **put**

put

down, a. to write down. b. to repress or suppress. c. to attribute (to). d. to pay as a lump sum. e. to destroy an animal, for reasons of disease, etc. f. to nominate. **9. put in, a.** *Naut.* to enter a port or harbour. b. to apply (for). c. to devote, as time, work, etc. **10. put off, a.** to postpone. b. to disgust or displease. **11. put on, a.** to assume: *to put on airs.* b. to dress in (clothing). c. to produce; stage. d. to cause to speak on the telephone. **12. put out, a.** to extinguish (fire, etc.). b. to confuse or embarrass. c. to disturb or interrupt. d. to irritate. **13.** *Naut.* to go out to sea. **14. put up, a.** to erect. b. to provide (money, etc.). c. to give lodging to. **15. put up to,** to persuade to do. **16. put up with,** to tolerate or endure.

puta·tive /'pjutətɪv/, *adj.* commonly regarded as such; supposed.

putrefy, *v.*, **-fied, -fying.** to become putrid; rot.

putrid, *adj.* **1.** in a state of foul decay or decomposition. **2.** disgustingly objectionable or bad.

putt, *v. Golf.* to strike (the ball) gently and carefully.

putty, *n., pl.* **-ties.** a cement, of doughlike consistency, used for securing panes of glass, stopping up holes in woodwork, etc.

puzzle, *n., v.,* **-zled, -zling.** –*n.* **1.** a toy or game that presents difficulties to be solved by ingenuity or patient effort. **2.** something puzzling; a puzzling matter or person. –*v.* **3.** to cause to be at a loss; bewilder; confuse. **4.** to come to understand by careful study or effort (out).

pygmy, *n., pl.* **-mies.** a small or dwarfish person.

pyja·mas, *n.* (*construed as pl.*) nightclothes consisting of loose trousers and jacket.

pylon, *n.* **1.** a steel tower or mast carrying high-tension, telephonic or other cables and lines. **2.** a structure at either side of a gate, bridge, or avenue, marking an entrance or approach.

pyra·mid, *n.* **1.** *Archit.* a massive stone structure with usu. square base and sloping sides meeting at an apex, such as those built by the ancient Egyptians. **2.** anything of such form. **3.** *Geom.* a solid having a triangular, square, or polygonal base, and triangular sides which meet in a point.

pyre, *n.* a pile or heap of wood or other combustible material, esp. one for burning a dead body.

pyro·mania, *n.* a mania for setting things on fire. – **pyromaniac**, *n.*

pyro·technics, *n.* **1.** the making and use of fireworks for display, military purposes, etc. **2.** a brilliant or sensational display.

python, *n.* a large non-venomous snake which kills by constriction.

Qq

Q, q, *n.*, *pl.* **Q's** or **Qs**, **q's** or **qs**. the 17th letter of the English alphabet.

quack[1], *v.* to utter the cry of a duck, or a sound resembling it.

quack[2], *n.* one who pretends to skills or qualifications which he does not possess. – **quackery**, *n.*

quad, *n. Colloq.* 1. →**quadruplet**. 2. →**quadrangle**.

quad·ran·gle, *n.* 1. a plane figure having 4 angles and 4 sides, as a square. 2. a quadrangular space or court. – **quadrangular**, *adj.*

quad·rant, *n.* the quarter of a circle; an arc of 90°.

quad·rat·ic, *adj.* 1. square. 2. *Alg.* involving the square and no higher power of the unknown quantity.

quadri·lat·er·al, *adj.* 1. having 4 sides. –*n.* 2. a plane figure having 4 sides and 4 angles.

quad·rille, *n.* a square dance for 4 couples.

quadri·ple·gia, *n.* a condition in which the arms and legs are paralysed. – **quadriplegic**, *n.*, *adj.*

quad·ruped, *adj.* 1. four-footed. –*n.* 2. an animal having 4 feet.

quad·ru·ple, *adj.*, *v.*, -**pled**, -**pling**. –*adj.* 1. consisting of 4 parts. –*v.* 2. to make or become 4 times as great.

quad·ru·plet, *n.* 1. any group or combination of 4. 2. one of 4 children born at one birth.

quaff, *v.* to drink (a beverage, etc.), copiously and heartily.

quag·mire, *n.* a piece of miry or boggy ground.

quail[1], *n.*, *pl.* **quails**, (*esp. collectively*) **quail**. a small ground-dwelling bird.

quail[2], *v.* to lose heart or courage in difficulty or danger.

quaint, *adj.* strange or odd in an interesting, pleasing, or amusing way.

quake, *v.*, **quaked**, **quaking**, *n.* –*v.* 1. to shake from cold, weakness, fear, anger, or the like. –*n.* 2. an earthquake.

qual·ify, *v.*, -**fied**, -**fying**. –*v.* 1. to invest with or possess proper or necessary skills etc.; make or become competent. 2. to attribute some quality or qualities to; characterise, call, or name. 3. to modify in some way. – **qualification**, *n.*

quali·ta·tive, *adj.* pertaining to or concerned with quality or qualities.

qual·ity, *n.*, *pl.* -**ties**. 1. a characteristic, property, or attribute. 2. high grade; superior excellence.

qualm, *n.* an uneasy feeling as to conduct.

quan·da·ry, *n.*, *pl.* -**ries**. a state of uncertainty, esp. as to what to do; dilemma.

quan·ti·fy, *v.*, -**fied**, -**fying**. to determine the quantity of; measure.

quanti·ta·tive, *adj.* of or pertaining to the measuring of quantity.

quan·ti·ty, *n.*, *pl.* -**ties**. 1. a particular, indefinite, or considerable amount of anything. 2. amount or measure.

quar·an·tine, *n.*, *v.*, -**tined**, -**tining**. –*n.* 1. a strict isolation designed to prevent the spread of disease. –*v.* 2. to put in or subject to quarantine.

quarrel

quar·rel, *n.*, *v.*, **-relled, -relling.** –*n.* **1.** an angry dispute or altercation. –*v.* **2.** to disagree angrily; squabble. – **quarrelsome**, *adj.*

quarry[1], *n.*, *pl.* **-ries**, *v.*, **-ried, -rying.** –*n.* **1.** an open excavation or pit from which building stone, slate, or the like is obtained. –*v.* **2.** to obtain (stone, etc.) from, or as from, a quarry.

quarry[2], *n.*, *pl.* **-ries.** an animal or bird hunted or pursued.

quart, *n.* a liquid measure in the imperial system, equal to 1/4 of a gallon, or 1.136 5225 litres.

quar·ter, *n.* **1.** one of the 4 equal parts into which anything is or may be divided. **2.** *Astron.* a 4th of the moon's period or monthly revolution. **3.** a region, district, or place. **4.** (*usu. pl.*) a place of stay. **5.** a part or member of a community, government, etc., which is not specified. **6.** to divide into 4 equal parts. **7.** to provide with lodgings in a particular place.

quarter·deck, *n.* the upper deck between the mainmast and the stern.

quar·terly, *adj.*, *n.*, *pl.* **-lies.** –*adj.* **1.** occurring, done, etc., at the end of every 3 months. –*n.* **2.** a periodical issued every 3 months.

quarter·master, *n. Mil.* a regimental officer in charge of quarters, rations, clothing, equipment, and transport.

quar·tet, *n.* a group of 4 singers or players.

quarto, *n.*, *pl.* **-tos.** a paper size, usu. 260 x 206 mm.

quartz, *n.* one of the commonest minerals, having many varieties which differ in colour, lustre, etc.

quench

quart·zite, *n.* a granular rock consisting essentially of quartz in interlocking grains.

quasar /ˈkweɪsɑ/, *n.* one of many very massive sources of high-energy, radio-frequency, electromagnetic radiation of unknown constitution or structure, existing outside the galaxy.

quash, *v.* **1.** to put down or suppress completely; subdue. **2.** to make void; annul, or set aside (a law, indictment, decision, etc.).

qua·ter·nary, *adj.* **1.** consisting of 4. **2.** arranged in fours.

quat·rain, *n.* a stanza or poem of 4 lines.

quaver, *v.* **1.** to quiver, or tremble (now said usu. of the voice). –*n.* **2.** a quavering or tremulous shake, esp. in the voice. **3.** *Music.* a note equal in length to half a crotchet.

quay /kiː/, *n.* an artificial landing place for vessels.

queasy, *adj.*, **-sier, -siest.** inclined to nausea.

queen, *n.* **1.** the wife or consort of a king. **2.** a female sovereign or monarch. **3.** a fertile female of ants, bees, etc. **4.** *Colloq.* a male homosexual.

queer, *adj.* **1.** strange from a conventional point of view; odd. **2.** out of the normal state of feeling physically. **3.** *Colloq.* mentally unbalanced or deranged. **4.** *Colloq.* homosexual. –*n.* **5.** *Colloq.* a male homosexual.

quell, *v.* **1.** to suppress (disorder, mutiny, etc.). **2.** to quiet or allay (feelings, etc.).

quench, *v.* **1.** to slake, as thirst; allay; satisfy. **2.** to suppress; stifle; subdue.

querulous

queru·lous, *adj.* full of complaints; complaining.

query, *n., pl.* **-ries**, *v..* **-ried, -rying.** *–n.* 1. a question; enquiry. 2. a doubt; uncertainty. *–v.* 3. to ask or enquire about. 4. to question (a statement, etc.) as doubtful or obscure. 5. to ask questions of.

quest, *n.* a search or pursuit made in order to find or obtain something.

ques·tion, *n.* 1. a sentence in an interrogative form, addressed to someone in order to elicit information. 2. a matter for investigation. 3. a matter or point of uncertainty or difficulty: *a question of etiquette*. *–v.* 4. to ask a question or questions of. 5. to make a question of; doubt. 6. to challenge; dispute. **– questionable**, *adj.*

question mark, *n.* a mark indicating a question, as (?).

ques·tion·naire /kwɛstʃənˈɛə, kɛs-/, *n.* a list of questions, usu. printed on a form, to obtain opinions on some subject.

queue, *n., v.*, **queued, queuing.** *–n.* 1. a file or line of people, vehicles, etc., waiting. *–v.* 2. to form in a line while waiting.

quib·ble, *n., v.*, **-bled, -bling.** *–n.* 1. trivial or carping criticism. *–v.* 2. to make trivial criticisms.

quiche /kiʃ/, *n.* a savoury tart with a filling of eggs, milk, etc.

quick, *adj.* 1. done or proceeding with promptness or rapidity. 2. hasty; impatient. 3. lively or keen, as feelings. 4. of ready intelligence. *–n.* 5. tender sensitive flesh, esp. that under the nails. **– quickly**, *adv.*

quick·sand, *n.* an area of soft or loose wet sand of considerable depth, dangerous to persons, animals, etc.

quick·silver, *n.* mercury.

quid, *n., pl.* **quid, quids.** *Colloq.* 1. (formerly) a pound in money. 2. (*pl.*) money, esp. a large amount.

qui·es·cent /kwiˈɛsənt/, *adj.* being at rest, inactive or motionless.

quiet, *n.* 1. freedom from disturbance or tumult. *–adj.* 2. making no disturbance or trouble. 3. free from disturbing emotions, etc. 4. refraining or free from activity. 5. motionless or moving gently. 6. making no noise or sound. 7. restrained in speech, manner, etc. *–v.* 8. to make or become quiet.

quill, *n.* 1. one of the large feathers of a bird. 2. a feather, as of a goose, formed into a pen for writing. 3. one of the hollow spines on a porcupine or hedgehog.

quilt, *n.* 1. a cover for a bed. *–v.* 2. to stitch together (2 pieces of cloth with a soft interlining).

quin, *n. Colloq.* one of 5 children born at one birth.

quince, *n.* a hard, yellowish, acid fruit.

quin·ine, *n.* a bitter colourless alkaloid, used in medicine as a stimulant and to treat malaria.

quin·tes·sence, *n.* 1. the pure and concentrated essence of a substance. 2. the most perfect embodiment of something. **– quintessential**, *adj.*

quin·tet, *n.* a set of 5 singers or players.

quin·tu·ple, *adj., v.*, **-pled, -pling.** *–adj.* 1. consisting of 5 parts. *–v.* 2. to make or become 5 times as great.

quin·tuplet, *n.* 1. any group or

quintuplet

quintuplet

combination of 5. **2.** one of 5 children born at one birth.

quip, n., v., **quipped, quipping.** –n. **1.** a clever or witty saying. –v. **2.** to utter quips.

quirk, n. **1.** a trick or peculiarity. **2.** a sudden twist, turn, or curve.

quis·ling, n. a person who betrays his own government.

quit, v., **quitted** or **quit, quitting,** adj. –v. **1.** to cease from doing (something); discontinue. **2.** to depart (from); leave. **3.** to give up (one's job or position); let go. –adj. **4.** released from obligation, penalty, etc.; free, clear, or rid (of).

quite, adv. **1.** completely, wholly. **2.** actually, really, or truly. **3.** Colloq. to a considerable extent.

quiver[1], v. to shake with a slight but rapid motion; tremble.

quiver[2], n. a case for holding arrows.

quix·otic, adj. extravagantly chivalrous or romantic.

quiz, v., **quizzed, quizzing,** n., pl. **quizzes.** –v. **1.** to question closely. **2.** to examine or test informally by questions. –n. **3.** a general knowledge test.

quiz·zi·cal, adj. odd or comical.

quoin /kɔin/, n. an external solid angle of a wall or the like.

quoit, n. **1.** Also, **deck quoit.** a flattish ring thrown in play to encircle a peg. **2.** (pl., construed as sing.) the game so played.

quorum, n. the number of members of a body required to be present to transact business legally.

quota, n. **1.** a proportional share of a fixed total quantity. **2.** the number of persons allowed to immigrate to a country, join an institution, etc.

quo·tation, n. **1.** that which is quoted, from a book, speech, etc. **2.** a price nominated for services, goods, etc.

quote, v., **quoted, quoting,** n. –v. **1.** to repeat (a passage, etc.) from a book, speech, etc. **2.** to bring forward, adduce, or cite. **3.** to state the current price of. –n. **3.** a quotation.

quo·tient, n. (in mathematics) the result of division.

Rr

R, r, *n., pl.* **R's** or **Rs, r's** or **rs.** the 18th letter of the English alphabet.

rabbi, *n., pl.* **-bis.** the spiritual leader of a Jewish community.

rabbit, *n., v.,* **-bited, -biting.** –*n.* **1.** a small, long-eared, burrowing mammal. –*v.* **2.** to hunt rabbits.

rabble, *n.* **1.** a disorderly crowd. **2.** (*derog.*) the lowest class of people (prec. by *the*).

rabid, *adj.* **1.** irrationally extreme in opinion or practice. **2.** furious or raging. **3.** affected with or pertaining to rabies; mad.

rabies, *n.* a fatal, infectious disease of the brain, transmitted by the bite of an afflicted animal, generally the dog.

rac·coon, *n.* any of several small nocturnal carnivores with a bushy ringed tail.

race[1], *n., v.,* **raced, racing.** –*n.* **1.** a contest of speed, as in running, riding, etc. **2.** (*pl.*) a series of races, esp. horseraces or greyhound races. **3.** any contest or competition. **4.** a narrow passageway. –*v.* **5.** to compete (against) in a contest of speed; run a race (with). **6.** to (cause to) run in a race or races. **7.** to engage in horseracing. **8.** to run or go swiftly.

race[2], *n. Ethnol.* a subdivision of a stock, characterised by a more or less unique combination of physical traits which are transmitted in descent.

racial, *adj.* **1.** pertaining to or characteristic of race or races. **2.** pertaining to the relations between people of different races.

racism, *n.* the belief that human races have distinctive characteristics which determine their respective cultures. – **racist,** *n., adj.*

rack[1], *n.* **1.** a framework of bars, wires, or pegs on which articles are arranged. **2.** an apparatus formerly in use for torturing persons by stretching the body. **3.** violent strain. –*v.* **4.** to strain in mental effort.

rack[2], *v. Colloq.* to leave; go (*off*).

racket[1], *n.* **1.** a loud noise. **2.** *Colloq.* an organised illegal activity.

racket[2], *n.* →**racquet.**

racon·teur, *n.* a person skilled in relating stories.

rac·quet, *n.* a light bat having a network of cord, catgut or similar, stretched in a frame, used in tennis, etc.

racy, *adj.,* **-cier, -ciest. 1.** vigorous; lively; spirited. **2.** suggestive; risqué.

radar, *n.* a device using radio waves to determine the presence and location of an object.

radial, *adj.* of, or pertaining to a radius or a ray.

radian /'reɪdɪən/, *n.* the supplementary SI unit of measurement of plane angle. Symbol: rad

radi·ant, *adj.* emitting rays of light; shining; bright.

radi·ate, *v.,* **-ated, -ating. 1.** to spread or move like rays or radii from a centre. **2.** to emit rays, as of light or heat. **3.** (of persons) to exhibit

radiate

abundantly (good humour, benevolence, etc.).

radi·ation, *n. Physics.* the emission and spreading of particles or waves such as by a radioactive substance.

radi·ator, *n.* a device which radiates heat.

radi·cal, *adj.* 1. going to the root or origin; fundamental. 2. thoroughgoing or extreme. 3. (*oft. cap.*) favouring drastic political, social or other reforms. 4. *Maths.* pertaining to or forming a root. –*n.* 5. one who holds or follows extreme principles, esp. leftist political principles. 6. *Chem.* a group of atoms which behaves as an unchangeable unit in many reactions.

radio, *n., pl.* **-dios,** *v.,* **-dioed, -dioing.** –*n.* 1. wireless telegraphy or telephony. 2. an apparatus for receiving radio broadcasts. –*v.* 3. to transmit (a message) by radio.

radio·activity, *n.* the property of spontaneous disintegration possessed by certain elements due to changes in their atomic nuclei. – **radioactive,** – *adj.*

radi·ography, *n.* the production of images by the action of X-rays on a photographic plate.

radish, *n.* the crisp, pungent, edible root of a plant.

radium, *n.* a naturally occurring radioactive metallic element. *Symbol:* Ra

radius, *n., pl.* **-dii, -diuses.** 1. a straight line extending from the centre of a circle or sphere to the circumference or surface. 2. that one of the 2 bones of the forearm which is on the thumb side.

raffia, *n.* a fibre from certain palms

raillery

used for making matting, baskets, etc.

raffle, *n., v.,* **-fled, -fling.** –*n.* 1. a lottery in which the prizes are usu. goods rather than money. –*v.* 2. to dispose of by a raffle (*off*).

raft, *n.* a floating platform assembled for the conveyance of people, goods, etc., on or over water.

rafter, *n.* one of the sloping timbers that form the framework of a roof.

rag[1], *n.* 1. a worthless piece of cloth, etc. esp. an old or worn one. 2. *Colloq.* a newspaper or magazine, esp. one considered as being of little value.

rag[2], *v.,* **ragged, ragging.** to tease; torment.

raga·muffin, *n.* a ragged child.

rage, *n., v.,* **raged, raging.** –*n.* 1. angry fury. 2. the object of widespread enthusiasm. –*v.* 3. to show or feel violent anger.

ragged, *adj.* 1. clothed in tattered garments. 2. torn or worn to rags. 3. full of rough or sharp projections; jagged.

raglan, *n.* a garment whose sleeves are cut so as to continue up to the collar.

raid, *n.* 1. a sudden attack, as upon something to be seized. –*v.* 2. to make a raid on.

rail[1], *n.* 1. a horizontal bar of wood or metal used as a barrier or support. 2. one of a pair of steel bars that provide a running surface for the wheels of vehicles. 3. the railway, as a means of transportation.

rail[2], *v.* to utter bitter complaint or vehement denunciation (*at* or *against*).

rail·lery, *n., pl.* **-ries.** good-humoured ridicule.

420

rail·way, *n.* 1. a permanent road or way, laid with rails on which trains run. 2. the company owning or operating it.

rai·ment, *n.* Archaic or Poetic. clothing; apparel; attire.

rain, *n.* 1. water in drops falling from the sky to the earth. 2. (*pl.*) the seasonal rainfalls in tropical regions. –*v.* 3. (of rain) to fall. 4. to fall like rain. 5. to offer or give abundantly. 6. **rain cats and dogs**, to rain heavily. – **rainy**, *adj.*

rain·bow, *n.* 1. a bow or arc of colours appearing in the sky opposite the sun, due to the refraction and reflection of the sun's rays in drops of rain. 2. the spectrum. –*adj.* 3. multicoloured.

rain·fall, *n.* 1. a shower of rain. 2. the amount of water falling as rain, snow, etc., within a given time and area.

rain forest, *n.* dense forest found in tropical and temperate areas.

raise, *v.*, **raised, raising**, *n.* –*v.* 1. to move to a higher position. 2. to cause to rise or stand up. 3. to build; erect. 4. to cause to be or appear. 5. to cultivate, produce, breed (crops, plants, animals, etc.). 6. to bring up; rear (children, etc.). 7. to give rise to; bring up or about. 8. to give vigour to; animate (the mind, spirits, hopes). 9. to gather together. 10. to increase in degree, intensity, pitch, or force. 11. to increase in amount, as rent, prices, wages, etc. –*n.* 12. a rise (in wages). 13. a raising, lifting, etc.

raisin, *n.* a dried grape.

rake[1], *n., v.*, **raked, raking**. –*n.* 1. a long-handled tool with teeth, used for various purposes. –*v.* 2. to gather together, draw, or remove (leaves, grass, etc.) with or as with a rake. 3. to collect, esp. with difficulty (*up*). 4. to search as with a rake. 5. to scrape or sweep (*against, over,* etc.).

rake[2], *n.* a profligate or dissolute man.

rally, *v.*, **-lied, -lying**, *n., pl.* **-lies**. –*v.* 1. to bring together in order once again. 2. to draw or call (persons) together for common action. 3. to come to the assistance of a person, party, or cause. 4. to acquire fresh strength or vigour. –*n.* 5. a recovery from dispersion or disorder, as of troops. 6. a renewal or recovery of strength, etc. 7. a drawing or coming together of persons, as for common action. 8. *Tennis, etc.* a relatively long exchange of strokes.

ram, *n., v.*, **rammed, ramming**. –*n.* 1. an uncastrated male sheep. 2. a device for battering, crushing, driving, or forcing something. –*v.* 3. to drive or force by heavy blows. 4. to push firmly.

ramble, *v.*, **-bled, -bling**, *n.* –*v.* 1. to wander about in a leisurely manner. –*n.* 2. a leisurely walk.

rami·fi·cation, *n.* 1. a division or subdivision derived from a main stem or source. 2. an implied result or complication.

ramp, *n.* 1. a sloping surface connecting 2 different levels. –*v.* 2. to act violently; rage; storm.

ram·page, *n., v.*, **-paged, -paging**. –*n.* 1. violent or furious behaviour. –*v.* 2. to rush, move, or act furiously or violently.

ram·pant, *adj.* in full sway; unchecked.

ram·rod, *n.* 1. a rod for ramming down the charge of a muzzle-loading firearm. 2. any person or

ramrod

thing considered as exemplifying or exercising stiffness.

ram·shackle, *adj.* loosely made or held together; rickety.

ran, *v.* past tense of **run**.

ranch, *n.* (U.S.) any large farm, esp. for cattle, horses, etc.

rancid, *adj.* having a rank, stale smell or taste.

ran·cour, *n.* a continuing bitter resentment or ill will. – **rancorous**, *adj.*

random, *adj.* 1. without aim, pattern or method; haphazard. –*n.* 2. **at random**, in a haphazard way.

randy, *adj.* sexually aroused.

rang, *v.* past tense of **ring**².

range, *n., v.,* **ranged, ranging.** –*n.* 1. the extent of the operation or efficacy of something. 2. an area in which shooting at targets is practised. 3. a row or line, as of persons or things. 4. the region over which something is distributed, is found, or occurs. 5. a chain of mountains. 6. a cooking stove. –*v.* 7. to set in order; arrange. 8. to make straight or level as lines of type. 9. to pass over or extend through (an area or region) in all directions, as in exploring or searching. 10. to vary within certain limits. 11. to have range of operation. 12. to extend in a certain direction.

ranger, *n.* a person employed to patrol a public reserve, wildlife park, etc.

rank¹, *n.* 1. position or standing in the social scale or in any graded body. 2. a row or series of things or persons. –*v.* 3. to assign to or take up or occupy a particular position, station, class, etc.

rank², *adj.* 1. growing with excessive

rare

luxuriance. 2. having an offensively strong smell or taste. 3. utter; unmistakable. 4. grossly coarse or indecent.

rankle, *v.,* **-kled, -kling.** to produce within the mind keen irritation or bitter resentment.

ran·sack, *v.* to search thoroughly through.

ransom, *n.* 1. the redemption of a prisoner, slave, kidnapped person, captured goods, etc., for a price. 2. the sum or price paid or demanded. –*v.* 3. to redeem from captivity, bondage, etc., by paying a price demanded.

rant, *v.* to talk in a wild or vehement way.

rap, *v.,* **rapped, rapping,** *n.* –*v.* 1. to strike, esp. with a quick, smart, or light blow. 2. to utter sharply or vigorously (*out*). 3. to knock smartly or lightly. –*n.* 4. a quick, smart, or light blow.

rapa·cious, *adj.* 1. given to plundering. 2. extraordinarily greedy.

rape, *n., v.,* **raped, raping.** –*n.* 1. the crime of having sexual intercourse with anyone against his or her will. –*v.* 2. to commit rape on.

rapid, *adj.* 1. moving or acting with great speed. –*n.* 2. (*usu. pl.*) a part of a river where the current runs very swiftly. – **rapidity**, *n.*

rapier, *n.* a slender sword used only for thrusting.

rap·port /ræ'pɔ/, *n.* relation; connection, esp. of a harmonious or sympathetic kind.

rapt, *adj.* 1. deeply engrossed or absorbed. 2. transported with emotion.

rap·ture, *n.* ecstatic joy or delight.

rare¹, *adj.,* **rarer, rarest.** 1. few in

422

rare

number. **2.** of low density or pressure. **3.** remarkable or unusual, esp. in excellence or greatness.

rare², *adj.*, **rarer, rarest**. (of meat) not thoroughly cooked; underdone.

rarefy, *v.*, **-fied, -fying**. to make or become rare, more rare, or less dense. – **rarefaction**, *n.*

rarity, *n.*, *pl.* **-ties**. something rare or uncommon.

rascal, *n.* a base, dishonest person.

rash¹, *adj.* acting too hastily or without due consideration.

rash², *n.* **1.** an eruption on the skin. **2.** a proliferation.

rasher, *n.* a thin slice of bacon.

rasp, *v.* **1.** to scrape or grate with a rough instrument. **2.** to utter with, or make, a grating sound. –*n.* **3.** a coarse form of file, having separate pointless teeth.

rasp·berry¹, *n.*, *pl.* **-ries**. a small red, black, or pale yellow berry.

rasp·berry², *n.*, *pl.* **-ries**. *n. Colloq.* a sound expressing contempt, made with the tongue and lips.

rat, *n.*, *v.*, **ratted, ratting**. –*n.* **1.** any of certain long-tailed rodents. **2.** *Colloq.* one who abandons his friends or associates, esp. in time of trouble. **smell a rat**, *Colloq.* to be suspicious. –*v.* **3.** *Colloq.* to desert one's party or associates, esp. in time of trouble. **4.** *Colloq.* to inform (on).

ratchet, *n.* a toothed bar with which a pawl engages.

rate, *n.*, *v.*, **rated, rating**. –*n.* **1.** a certain quantity or amount of one thing considered in relation to a unit of another thing and used as a standard of measure: *a rate of 5 per cent per year.* **2.** a fixed charge per unit of quantity. **3.** degree of speed, of travelling, working, etc. **4.** degree of excellence: *first-rate.* **5.** (*usu. pl.*) a tax on property, imposed by a local authority. –*v.* **6.** to estimate the value or worth of; appraise. **7.** to fix at a certain rate, as of charge or payment. **8.** to have value, standing, etc.

rather, *adv.* **1.** more so than not; to a certain extent. **2.** in preference.

ratify, *v.*, **-fied, -fying**. to confirm by expressing consent or formal sanction.

rating, *n.* **1.** classification according to grade or rank. **2.** a person's or firm's credit standing.

ratio, *n.*, *pl.* **-tios**. proportional relation; rate; quotient of 2 numbers.

ration, *n.* **1.** a fixed allowance of provisions or food. –*v.* **2.** to put on, or restrict to, rations.

rational, *adj.* **1.** agreeable to reason; sensible. **2.** endowed with the faculty of reason. **3.** proceeding or derived from reason. **4.** *Maths.* expressible as the quotient of 2 integers. – **rationality**, *n.*

rationale, *n.* a reasoned exposition of principles.

rationalise, *v.*, **-lised, -lising**. **1.** *Psychol.* to justify (behaviour) by inventing a rational, acceptable explanation. **2.** to employ reason; think in a rational manner. **3.** to reorganise and integrate (an industry).

rat-race, *n.* **1.** the fiercely competitive struggle for success, esp. in career. **2.** the frantic pace of city life.

rattan, *n.* the tough stems of certain palms, used for wickerwork, etc.

rattle, *v.*, **-tled, -tling**, *n.* –*v.* **1.** to (cause to) give out a rapid succes-

rattle

sion of short sharp sounds. 2. to utter or perform in a rapid or lively manner. 3. *Colloq.* to disconcert or confuse (a person). –n. 4. a rapid succession of short, sharp sounds. 5. an instrument contrived to make a rattling sound, as a child's toy.

rattle·snake, *n.* any of various venomous American snakes with a rattling appendage on the tail.

rau·cous, *adj.* hoarse; harsh-sounding, as a voice.

ravage, *n., v.,* -aged, -aging. –n. 1. havoc; ruinous damage. –v. 2. to damage or work havoc upon.

rave, *v.,* raved, raving. –v. 1. to talk wildly, as in delirium. –n. 2. extravagant enthusiastic praise. –adj. 3. praising with extravagant enthusiasm.

ravel, *v.,* -elled, -elling. 1. to tangle or become tangled. 2. to become separated thread by thread; fray.

raven, *n.* 1. either of 2 large, glossy black birds with loud harsh calls. –adj. 2. lustrous black.

rav·en·ous, *adj.* extremely hungry.

ravine, *n.* a long, deep, narrow valley, esp. one eroded by water.

ra·vi·oli, *n. pl.* small pieces of filled pasta.

ravish, *v.* 1. to fill with strong emotion, esp. joy. 2. to seize and carry off by force.

ravish·ing, *adj.* entrancing; enchanting.

raw, *adj.* 1. not having undergone processes of preparing, refining, or manufacture. 2. painfully open, as a sore, wound, etc. 3. *Colloq.* harsh or unfair.

ray[1], *n.* 1. a narrow beam of light. 2. *Maths.* one of a system of straight lines emanating from a point.

read

ray[2], *n.* a flat fish living on the sea bottom.

rayon, *n.* a synthetic textile.

raze, *v.,* razed, razing. to tear down, demolish.

razor, *n.* a sharp-edged instrument used esp. for shaving hair from the skin.

re /ri, reɪ/, *prep.* in the case of; with reference to: *re my memorandum*.

reach, *v.* 1. to get to, or get as far as, in moving, travelling, etc. 2. to stretch or extend so as to touch or meet. 3. to stretch in space; extend in direction, length, distance, etc. 4. to establish communication with. 5. to make a stretching movement, as with the hand or arm. –n. 6. the act of reaching. 7. the extent of reaching. 8. a continuous stretch of something, as a river.

react, *v.* 1. to act in return on an agent or influence. 2. to act in opposition, as against some force. – **reactor**, *n.* – **reactive**, *adj.*

re·action, *n.* the act or an instance of reacting.

read[1] /riːd/, *v.,* read /rɛd/, reading. –v. 1. to peruse and understand (something written, etc.). 2. to render in speech (something written, etc.) (*out, aloud*). 3. to understand (something read or observed) in a particular way: *to read a look as a sign of disapproval*. 4. to introduce (something not expressed or directly indicated) into what is read or considered. 5. to register or indicate, as a thermometer or other instrument. 6. to obtain knowledge by reading. 7. to be able to be read or interpreted (as stated). –n. 8. the act or process of reading.

read² /rēd/, *adj.* having knowledge gained by reading.

ready, *adj.*, **readier, readiest,** *v.*, **readied, readying,** *n.* –*adj.* 1. completely prepared for immediate action or use. 2. willing. 3. prompt or quick in perceiving, speaking, writing, etc. 4. present or convenient. –*v.* 5. to make ready; prepare. –*n.* 6. *Colloq.* ready money. 7. the condition or position of being ready.

re·agent, *n.* a substance which, on account of the reactions it causes, is used in chemical analysis.

real, *adj.* 1. true. 2. genuine; not counterfeit, artificial, or imitation. 3. *Law.* pertaining to immoveable property as lands and buildings (opposed to *personal*). –*adv.* 4. *Colloq.* very.

real estate, *n.* land and whatever is part of it, as minerals, buildings, etc. Also, **real property**.

real·ise, *v.*, **-lised, -lising.** 1. to understand clearly. 2. to give reality to (a hope, fear, plan, etc.). 3. to convert (property or goods) into cash or money. 4. to obtain (as a profit) by trade, labour, or investment.

realism, *n.* 1. the taking of a practical rather than a moral view in human problems, etc. 2. the tendency to view or represent things as they really are. **–realistic**, *adj.* **– realist**, *n.*

reality, *n.* 1. the state of being real. 2. a real thing or fact.

realm, *n.* the region, sphere, or domain within which anything rules or prevails.

real·tor, *n.* an estate agent who acts as an intermediary between the buyer and seller of real estate.

realty, *n.* →**real estate**.

ream, *n.* a standard quantity among paper dealers meaning 500 sheets (formerly 480 sheets).

reap, *v.* to gather or cut (a crop, harvest, etc.) with a sickle, machine etc.

rear¹, *n.* 1. the back of anything, as opposed to the front. 2. the space or position behind anything. –*adj.* 3. situated at or pertaining to the rear.

rear², *v.* 1. to care for and support up to maturity. 2. to raise to an upright position. 3. to rise on the hind legs, as a horse or other animal.

reason, *n.* 1. a cause, as for a belief, action, fact, event, etc. 2. the mental powers concerned with drawing conclusions or inferences. 3. sound judgment or good sense. –*v.* 4. to think (*out*) (a problem, etc.) logically. 5. to conclude or infer (*that*). 6. to bring, persuade, etc., by reasoning.

reason·able, *adj.* 1. endowed with reason. 2. agreeable to reason or sound judgment. 3. moderate, as in price etc.

re·assure, *v.*, **-sured, -suring.** to restore (a person, etc.) to assurance or confidence.

rebate, *n.*, *v.*, **-bated, -bating.** –*n.* 1. a return of part of an original amount paid for some service or merchandise. –*v.* 2. to allow as a discount.

rebel, *n.*, *adj.*, *v.*, **-belled, -belling.** –*n.* 1. one who resists, or rises in arms against, the established government or ruler. –*adj.* 2. of or pertaining to rebels. –*v.* 3. to rise in

rebel

arms or active resistance against one's government or ruler. – **rebellious**, *adj.*

rebel·lion, *n.* the act of rebelling.

re·bound, *v.* 1. to bound or spring back from force of impact. –*n.* 2. the act of rebounding; recoil.

rebuff, *n.* 1. a peremptory refusal of a request, offer, etc.; a snub. 2. a check to action or progress. –*v.* 3. to give a rebuff to.

rebuke, *v.*, **-buked, -buking.** –*v.* 1. to reprove or reprimand. –*n.* 2. a reproof; a reprimand.

rebut, *v.*, **-butted, -butting.** to refute by evidence or argument. – **rebuttal**, *n.*

recal·ci·trant, *adj.* 1. resisting authority or control. –*n.* 2. a recalcitrant person. – **recalcitrance, recalcitrancy**, *n.*

recall, *v.* 1. to recollect or remember. 2. to call back; summon to return. –*n.* 3. the act of recalling. 4. memory; recollection.

recant, *v.* to withdraw or disavow (a statement, etc.), esp. formally.

re·capi·tu·late, *v.*, **-lated, -lating.** to review (statements or matters) by way of an orderly summary.

recede, *v.*, **-ceded, -ceding.** 1. to go or move back, or towards a more distant point. 2. to slope backwards.

re·ceipt /rəˈsiːt/, *n.* 1. a written acknowledgment of having received money, goods, etc. 2. (*pl.*) the amount or quantity received. 3. the state of being received.

re·ceive, *v.*, **-ceived, -ceiving.** 1. to take (something) into one's possession. 2. to take into the mind. 3. to meet with; experience. 4. to greet (guests, etc.) upon arriving. 5. to accept as authoritative, valid,

reciprocate

true, or approved. 6. *Radio.* to convert incoming electromagnetic waves into the original signal.

re·ceiv·er, *n.* 1. a device or apparatus which receives electrical signals, and renders them perceptible to the senses. 2. *Comm.* one appointed to receive money due. 3. one who receives stolen goods.

recent, *adj.* lately happening, done, made, etc.

recep·tacle, *n.* that which serves to receive or hold something.

recep·tion, *n.* 1. the act of receiving. 2. a manner of being received. 3. a function where people are formally received. 4. a place, office, desk, or the like where callers are received.

recep·tion·ist, *n.* a person employed to receive and direct callers, as in an office or hotel.

recep·tive, *adj.* able or quick to receive ideas, etc.

recess, *n.* 1. a part or space that is set back or recedes. 2. withdrawal or cessation for a time from the usual occupation, work, or activity. –*v.* 3. to place or set in a recess. 4. to make a recess or recesses in. 5. to take a recess.

reces·sion, *n.* 1. a receding part of a wall, etc. 2. a period of adverse economic circumstances.

reces·sive, *adj.* tending to recede; receding.

recipe, *n.* any formula, esp. one for preparing a dish in cookery.

recip·ient, *n.* one who or that which receives something given or offered, as a favour, etc.

recip·ro·cate, *v.*, **-cated, -cating.** 1. to give, feel, etc., (something) in return. 2. to give and receive

426

reciprocally; interchange. – **reciprocity,** n. – **reciprocal,** adj.

recital, n. a musical or other entertainment given usu. by a single performer.

recite, v., **-cited, -citing.** to repeat the words of, (a poem, etc.) as from memory, esp. in a formal manner.

reck·less, adj. utterly careless of the consequences of action.

reckon, v. 1. to count, compute, or make a calculation (as to number or amount). 2. to esteem or consider (as stated). 3. *Colloq.* to think or suppose. 4. to settle accounts. 5. to count or rely (*on*), as in expectation.

re·claim, v. to bring (waste, or marshy land) into a useable condition. – **reclamation,** n.

re·cline, v., **-clined, -clining.** to (cause to) lean or lie back (on something).

re·cluse, n. a person who lives in seclusion.

recog·nise, v., **-nised, -nising.** 1. to identify from knowledge of appearance or character. 2. to perceive as existing or true. 3. to acknowledge or treat as valid. – **recognition,** n.

recoil, v. 1. to draw back, as in alarm, disgust, etc. 2. to spring or fly back, as from force of impact, as a firearm. –n. 3. the act of recoiling.

recol·lect, v. to recall to mind; remember.

recom·mend, v. to present as worthy of confidence, acceptance, use, etc. – **recommendation,** n.

recom·pense, v., **-pensed, -pensing,** n. –v. 1. to make compensation to or reward or repay (a person, etc.). –n. 2. compensation made, as for loss, injury, or wrong.

recon·cile, v., **-ciled, -ciling.** to bring into agreement; make compatible or consistent. – **reconciliation,** n.

recon·dite, adj. dealing with abstruse or profound matters.

recon·noitre, v., **-tred, -tring.** to examine (a region, etc.) for engineering, geological, or other purposes. – **reconnaissance,** n.

record, v. 1. to set down or register (something) in some permanent form. –n. 2. an account, esp. written, preserving the memory or knowledge of facts or events. 3. information or knowledge so preserved. 4. a disc for reproducing sound. 5. the highest or best recorded rate, amount, degree, etc. attained. 6. **off the record,** unofficially; without intending to be quoted. –adj. 7. making or affording a record.

recor·der, n. 1. a recording or registering apparatus or device. 2. a soft-toned flute played in vertical position.

record-player, n. a machine that reproduces sound from a record.

re·count, v. to relate or narrate.

recoup, v. 1. to obtain an equivalent for (money lost, time spent, etc.). 2. to regain or recover. 3. to reimburse or compensate. –n. 4. the act of recouping.

re·course, n. 1. application to a person or thing for help or protection. 2. *Comm.* the right to apply to a person for compensation in money.

re·cover, v. 1. to get again, or regain (something lost or taken away). 2. to make up for or make good (loss,

recover

damage, etc., to oneself). 3. to regain the strength, composure, balance, etc., of (oneself). 4. to regain a former (and better) state or condition. – recovery, n.

recre·ation, n. (an agreeable pastime, exercise etc. affording) refreshment and relaxation. – recreate, v.

re·crimi·nate, v., -nated, -nating. to accuse in return.

rec·ruit, n. 1. a newly secured member of any body or class. –v. 2. to enlist (men) for service in the armed forces.

rec·tangle, n. a parallelogram with all its angles right angles. – rectangular, adj.

rec·tify, v., -fied, -fying. to set right; remedy; correct.

rec·ti·tude, n. rightness of principle or practice.

rector, n. C. of E. a cleric who has the charge of a parish.

rectum, n., pl. -ta. the comparatively straight terminal section of the intestine, ending in the anus.

re·cumbent, adj. lying down; reclining; leaning.

re·cuper·ate, v., -rated, -rating. to recover from sickness, exhaustion, loss, etc.

recur, v., -curred, -curring. to occur again, as an event, experience, etc. – recurrent, n.

re·cycle, v., -cycled, -cycling. to treat (waste materials) so that new products can be manufactured from them.

red, adj., redder, reddest, n. –adj. 1. of a hue beyond orange in the spectrum. 2. (oft. cap.) politically extreme, esp. communist. –n. 3. any of the hues adjacent to orange in the spectrum, such as scarlet, vermilion, cherry. 4. red wine. 5. **the red**, loss or deficit, as recorded in red ink in accounting practice.

red-back spider, n. a small, venomous, Aust. spider.

red-blooded, adj. vigorous; virile.

redeem, v. 1. to buy or pay off. 2. to recover (something pledged or mortgaged) by payment etc. 3. to make amends for. 4. to obtain the release or restoration of, as from captivity, by paying a ransom. – redemption, n.

red-handed, adj., adv. in the very act of a crime or other deed.

red herring, n. something to divert attention; a false clue.

redo·lent, adj. 1. having a pleasant smell; fragrant. 2. odorous or smelling (of). 3. suggestive; reminiscent (of).

redoubt·able, adj. that is to be feared; formidable.

re·dound, v. to come back or recoil, as upon a person.

re·dress, n. 1. the setting right of what is wrong. 2. compensation for wrong or injury. –v. 3. to set right; remedy (wrongs, injuries, etc.).

reduce, v., -duced, -ducing. 1. to bring down to a smaller extent, size, amount, etc. 2. to lower in degree, intensity, etc. 3. to lower in price. 4. to bring to a certain state, condition, etc. 5. to bring under control or authority; subdue. 6. to thin (paints, etc.) with oil or turpentine. 7. to become reduced. – reduction, n.

redun·dant, adj. 1. being in excess. 2. pertaining to an employee who is no longer needed by his employer.

reed, *n.* 1. the straight stalk of any of various tall grasses. 2. a small piece of reed, fitted into the mouthpiece of some instruments, as clarinets, etc.

reef, *n.* a narrow ridge of rocks, sand, coral, etc., at or near the surface of water.

reefer, *n. Colloq.* a marijuana cigarette.

reef knot, *n.* a kind of flat knot.

reek, *n.* 1. a strong, unpleasant smell. –*v.* 2. to smell strongly and unpleasantly.

reel¹, *n.* 1. a cylinder, frame, etc., turning on an axis, on which to wind something. –*v.* 2. to draw with a reel, or by winding. 3. to say, write, or produce in an easy, continuous way (*off*).

reel², *v.* to sway or rock from dizziness, intoxication, or under a blow, shock, etc.; stagger.

reel³, *n.* a lively dance popular in Scotland.

refectory, *n., pl.* **-ries.** a dining hall in an institution.

refer, *v.,* **-ferred, -ferring.** 1. to direct for information or requirements. 2. to hand over or submit for information, consideration, decision, etc. 3. to have relation; relate; apply. 4. to direct a remark or mention. – **referral**, *n.*

referee, *n.,* **-reed, -reeing.** –*n.* 1. one to whom something is referred, esp. for decision or settlement; arbitrator; umpire. –*v.* 2. to preside over as referee; act as referee in.

reference, *n.* 1. the act or fact of referring. 2. a mention; allusion. 3. a direction, as to some source of information. 4. use or recourse for purposes of information. 5. (a person to whom one refers for) testimony as to one's character, abilities, etc. 6. relation, regard, or respect.

referendum, *n., pl.* **-da, -dums.** the procedure of referring measures proposed or passed by a legislative body to the vote of the electorate for approval or rejection.

refine, *v.,* **-fined, -fining.** 1. to free or become free from impurities. 2. to make or become more elegant or cultured. – **refinery**, *n.*

reflect, *v.* 1. to cast back (light, heat, sound, etc.). 2. to give back or show: *The results reflect her hard work.* 3. to be turned, reflected, or cast back. 4. to serve or tend to bring reproach or discredit. 5. to think, ponder, or meditate.

reflex, *adj.* 1. occurring in reaction; responsive. 2. bent or turned back. –*n.* 3. *Physiol.* a reflex action or movement.

reflexive, *adj. Gram.* 1. (of a verb) having identical subject and object, as *shave* in *He shaved himself.* 2. (of a pronoun) indicating identity of object with subject, as *himself* in the example above.

reform, *n.* 1. the improvement or amendment of what is wrong, corrupt, etc. –*v.* 2. to improve by alteration, substitution, abolition, etc. 3. (to cause a person to) abandon wrong or evil ways.

reformatory, *n., pl.* **-ries.** Also, **reform school.** a penal institution for the reformation of young offenders.

refraction, *n. Physics.* the change of direction of a ray of light, heat, or the like, in passing obliquely from one medium into another.

refractory

refrac·tory, *adj.* stubborn; unmanageable.

re·frain[1], *v.* to keep oneself back (*from*).

re·frain[2], *n.* a phrase or verse recurring at intervals in a song or poem; chorus.

re·fresh, *v.* 1. to reinvigorate or be revived by rest, food, etc. 2. to stimulate (the memory).

refresh·ment, *n.* that which refreshes, esp. food or drink.

refrig·er·ate, *v.*, -rated, -rating. to make or keep cold or cool.

refrig·er·ator, *n.* a room, or cabinet in which food, drink, etc., are kept cool.

refuge, *n.* shelter or protection from danger, trouble, etc.

refu·gee, *n.* one who flees for refuge or safety, esp. to a foreign country.

refund, *v.* 1. to give back or restore (esp. money); repay. 2. to make repayment to; reimburse. –*n.* 3. a repayment.

re·fur·bish, *v.* to renovate.

refu·sal, *n.* 1. the act of refusing. 2. priority in refusing or taking something; option.

refuse[1] /rəˈfjuːz/, *v.*, -fused, -fusing. 1. to decline to accept (something offered). 2. to deny (a request, demand, etc.). 3. to express a determination not (to do something).

refuse[2] /ˈrɛfjuːs/, *n.* something discarded as worthless; rubbish.

refute, *v.*, -futed, -futing. to prove to be false.

regal, *adj.* 1. of or pertaining to a king; royal. 2. (of a woman) tall, dignified, and elegant.

register

regale, *v.*, -galed, -galing. to entertain agreeably; delight.

regard, *v.* 1. to look upon or think of with a particular feeling. 2. to have or show respect or concern for. 3. to take into account; consider. 4. to look at; pay attention (to). 5. to relate to; concern. –*n.* 6. reference; relation. 7. a point or particular: *satisfactory in this regard.* 8. thought; attention; concern. 9. look; gaze. 10. respect; deference. 11. kindly feeling; liking. 12. (*pl.*) sentiments of esteem or affection.

regatta, *n.* a boat race.

re·gener·ate, *v.*, -rated, -rating. *adj.* –*v.* 1. to re-create or make over or reform esp. in a better form or condition. 2. to come into existence or be formed again. –*adj.* 3. reconstituted in a better form. 4. reformed.

regent, *n.* one who exercises the ruling power in a kingdom during the minority, absence, or disability of the sovereign. – **regency**, *n.*

regime /reɪˈʒiːm/, *n.* a mode or system of rule or government.

regi·men, *n.* any prevailing system, as a regulated course of diet, exercise, etc.

regi·ment, *n.* 1. *Mil.* a unit of ground forces. –*v.* 2. to form into an organised body or group. – **regimentation**, *n.* – **regimental**, *adj.*

region, *n.* 1. any more or less extensive, continuous part of a surface or space. 2. a district without respect to boundaries or extent.

regis·ter, *n.* 1. a record of acts, occurrences, attendances, etc. 2. a mechanical device by which certain data are automatically recorded, as

430

a cash register. –v. 3. to enter or have entered formally in a register. 4. to indicate or show, as on a scale. 5. to show (surprise, joy, anger, etc.) 6. to enter one's name in an electoral or other register; enrol. 7. *Colloq.* to make an impression. – **registration**, *n.*

regis·trar, *n.* one who keeps official records.

regis·try, *n., pl.* **-tries.** a place where a register is kept.

re·gress, *v.* to move backwards, esp. to an earlier (undesirable) state. – **regression**, *n.*

regret, *v.*, **-gretted, -gretting,** *n.* – 1. to feel sorry about (anything disappointing, unpleasant, etc.). 2. to think of with a sense of loss. –*n.* 3. a sense of loss, disappointment, etc. 4. the feeling of being sorry for some fault, act, omission, etc., of one's own.

regu·lar, *adj.* 1. usual; normal; customary. 2. conforming in form or arrangement; symmetrical. 3. adhering to rule or procedure. 4. orderly. 5. *Colloq.* complete; thorough. –*n.* 6. *Colloq.* a regular customer.

regu·late, *v.*, **-lated, -lating.** 1. to control or direct by rule, principle, method, etc. 2. to adjust to some standard or requirement. – **regulation**, *n.*

regur·gi·tate, *v.*, **-tated, -tating.** to cause to surge or rush back; vomit.

re·habil·i·tate, *v.*, **-tated, -tating.** to restore to a good condition.

re·hearse, *v.*, **-hearsed, -hearsing.** to perform in private by way of practice (a play, part, etc.). – **rehearsal**, *n.*

reign /reɪn/, *n.* 1. the period or term of ruling, as of a sovereign. –*v.* 2. to possess or exercise sovereign power or authority.

re·imburse, *v.*, **-bursed, -bursing.** to make repayment to for expense or loss incurred.

rein /reɪn/, *n.* 1. a long, narrow strap for guiding a horse. 2. any means of curbing, controlling, or directing; a check; restraint. –*v.* 3. to curb; restrain; control.

re·incar·nation, *n.* rebirth of the soul in a new body after death.

rein·deer, *n., pl.* **-deer,** (*occasionally*) **-deers.** any of various species of large deer.

re·inforce, *v.*, **-forced, -forcing.** 1. to strengthen; make more forcible or effective. 2. to augment; increase.

re·instate, *v.*, **-stated, -stating.** to put back or establish again, as in a former position or state.

re·iter·ate, *v.*, **-rated, -rating.** to repeat; say or do again.

reject, *v.* 1. to refuse to have, take, recognise, etc. 2. to cast out or off. –*n.* 3. something rejected, as an imperfect article.

re·joice, *v.*, **-joiced, -joicing.** to be glad; take delight (*in*).

re·joinder, *n.* an answer to a reply; response.

re·juven·ate, *v.*, **-nated, -nating.** to make young again.

re·lapse, *v.*, **-lapsed, -lapsing,** *n.* –*v.* 1. to fall or slip back into a former state, practice, etc. –*n.* 2. the act of relapsing.

re·late, *v.*, **-lated, -lating.** 1. to tell. 2. to bring into association, connection, or have some relation (*to*). 3. to have reference (*to*).

rel·ation, *n.* 1. an existing connection; a particular way of being re-

431

relation

lated. 2. connection between persons by blood or marriage. 3. a relative. 4. reference; regard; respect.

rela·tive, *n.* 1. one who is connected with another or others by blood or marriage. 2. something having, or standing in, some relation to something else, as opposed to *absolute.* –*adj.* 3. considered in relation to something else. 4. having relation or connection. 5. correspondent; proportionate. – **relativity,** *n.*

relax, *v.* 1. to make or become lax, or less tense, rigid, or firm. 2. to diminish the force of. 3. to become less strict or severe. 4. to slacken in effort, application, etc.

relay, *n.* 1. a set of persons relieving others or taking turns; a shift. 2. an electrical device for operating the controls of a larger piece of equipment. –*v.* 3. to carry forward by or as by relays: *to relay a message.*

re·lease, *v.,* -leased, -leasing, *n.* –*v.* 1. to free from restraint as confinement, bondage, obligation, pain, etc. 2. to allow to become known, be issued or exhibited. –*n.* 3. (a device for effecting) liberation from anything that restrains or fastens. 4. the releasing of something for public exhibition or sale. 5. the article so released.

rele·gate, *v.,* -gated, -gating. to send or consign to some obscure position, place, or condition.

relent, *v.* to soften in feeling, temper, or determination.

rele·vant, *adj.* bearing upon the matter in hand; to the purpose; pertinent.

remain

reli·able, *adj.* that may be relied on; trustworthy.

reli·ant, *adj.* dependent.

relic, *n.* 1. a surviving memorial of something of historical interest. 2. a surviving trace of something.

relief, *n.* 1. (something affording) deliverance or ease through the removal of pain, distress, oppression, monotony, etc. 2. the person or persons relieving another or others. 3. prominence, distinctness, or vividness due to contrast. 4. projection of a figure from its background.

re·lieve, *v.,* -lieved, -lieving. 1. to ease or free from (pain, distress, anxiety, need, etc.). 2. to make less tedious, unpleasant, or monotonous. 3. to bring into relief or prominence. 4. to release (one on duty) by providing a substitute. 5. to take the place of (an absent worker). 6. **relieve oneself,** to empty the bowels or bladder.

reli·gion, *n.* belief in a controlling superhuman power entitled to obedience, reverence, and worship.

reli·gious, *adj.* 1. pertaining to religion. 2. scrupulously faithful; conscientious.

relin·quish, *v.* to renounce or surrender (a possession, right, etc.).

relish, *n.* 1. pleasurable appreciation or enjoyment. 2. something appetising or savoury added to a meal, as chutney. 3. a taste or flavour. –*v.* 4. to take pleasure in; like; enjoy.

reluc·tant, *adj.* unwilling; disinclined.

rely, *v.,* -lied, -lying. to put trust in; depend confidently (*on* or *upon*).

remain, *v.* 1. to continue in the same state or place; continue to be (as

remain

specified). **2.** to be left after the removal, departure, loss, etc., of another or others. –*n.* **3.** that which remains or is left; a remnant.

remain·der, *n.* **1.** that which remains or is left. –*v.* **2.** to dispose of or sell at reduced price, as unsold copies of a book.

remand, *v.* **1.** to send back, remit, or consign again. –*n.* **2.** the state of being remanded.

remark, *v.* **1.** to say (something) casually, as in making a comment (*on* or *upon*). **2.** to note; perceive. –*n.* **3.** a casual or brief expression of thought or opinion.

remark·able, *adj.* worthy of notice; unusual; outstanding.

remedy, *n.*, *pl.* **-dies**, *v.*, **-died**, **-dying**. –*n.* **1.** something that corrects or removes an evil or illness of any kind. –*v.* **2.** to cure or heal. **3.** to put right, or restore to the natural or proper condition. – **remedial**, *adj.*

remem·ber, *v.* **1.** to recall to the mind by an act or effort of memory. **2.** to retain in the memory; bear in mind. **3.** to mention to another as sending kindly greetings. **4.** to possess or exercise the faculty of memory. – **remembrance**, *n.*

remind, *v.* to cause to remember.

remi·ni·scence, *n.* the act or process of remembering one's past. – **reminiscent**, *adj.* – **reminisce**, *v.*

remiss, *adj.* characterised by negligence or carelessness.

remit, *v.*, **-mitted**, **-mitting**. **1.** to send (money, etc.) to a person or place. **2.** to refrain from exacting, as a payment or service. **3.** to slacken; abate. **4.** to put back into a previous position or condition. – **remission**, *n.*

remit·tance, *n.* **1.** the remitting of money, etc., to a recipient at a distance. **2.** money etc., so sent.

rem·nant, *n.* a part, quantity, or number (usu. small) remaining.

remon·strance, *n.* a protest. – **remonstrate**, *v.*

re·morse, *n.* deep and painful regret for wrong-doing; compunction.

remote, *adj.*, **-moter**, **-motest**. **1.** distant in time or space. **2.** out-of-the-way; secluded. **3.** slight or faint. **4.** abstracted; cold and aloof.

re·moval, *n.* **1.** the act of removing. **2.** a change of residence, position, etc. **3.** dismissal, as from an office.

remove, *v.*, **-moved**, **-moving**. –*v.* **1.** to move from a place or position; take away; take off. **2.** to take, withdraw, or separate (*from*). **3.** to move from one place to another, esp. to another locality or residence. –*n.* **4.** the act of removing. **5.** a step or degree, as in a graded scale.

re·moved, *adj.* remote; separate; distinct from.

remu·nerate, *v.*, **-rated**, **-rating**. to pay, recompense, or reward for work, trouble, etc. – **remuneration**, *n.* – **remunerative**, *adj.*

renal, *adj.* of or pertaining to the kidneys.

rend, *v.*, **rent**, **rending**. to tear apart, split, or divide.

render, *v.* **1.** to make, or cause, to be or become. **2.** to do; perform. **3.** to present for consideration, approval, payment, action, etc., as an account. **4.** to give in return, as reward or retaliation. **5.** to cover

render

433

render

(brickwork, stone etc.) with plaster. – **rendition**, n.

rendez·vous /'rɒndeɪvu, rɒndeɪ'vu/, n. an appointment to meet at a fixed place and time.

renegade, n. one who deserts a party or cause for another.

renege /rəˈneɡ, -ˈnɪɡ/, v., **-neged**, **-neging**. Colloq. to go back on one's word.

renew, v. 1. to begin or take up again (an acquaintance, conversation etc.) 2. to make effective for an additional period, as a lease etc. 3. to restore or replenish. – **renewal**, n.

re·nounce, v., **-nounced**, **-nouncing**. 1. to give up voluntarily. 2. to repudiate; disown.

reno·vate, v., **-vated**, **-vating**. to make new or as if new again.

renown, n. widespread and high repute; fame.

re·nowned, adj. celebrated; famous.

rent[1], n. 1. a payment made periodically by a tenant to an owner or landlord for the use of land or building. –v. 2. to grant the possession and use of (property) in return for regular payments. 3. to take and hold (property) in return for regular payments.

rent[2], n. 1. an opening made by rending or tearing; slit. –v. 2. past tense and past participle of **rend**.

rental, n. 1. an amount received or paid as rent. –adj. 2. available for rent.

renun·ci·ation, n. the formal abandoning of a right, title, etc.

rep, n. Colloq. 1. a travelling salesman. 2. a union representative.

repair[1], v. 1. to restore to a good or sound condition; mend. –n. 2. the act, process, or work of repairing.

repetition

3. the good condition resulting from repairing. – **reparable**, adj.

repair[2], v. to take oneself off or go, as to a place.

reparation, n. the making of amends for wrong or injury done.

repartee, n. skill in making witty replies.

repast, n. a meal.

re·patriate, v., **-ated**, **-ating**. to bring or send back (a person) to his own country.

repay, v., **-paid**, **-paying**. 1. to pay back or refund (money, etc.). 2. to make return for.

repeal, v. 1. to revoke or withdraw formally or officially. –n. 2. the act of repealing; revocation; abrogation.

repeat, v. 1. to do, make or say again (something already done, made or said by oneself or another). –n. 2. something repeated. 3. a duplicate or reproduction of something.

repel, v., **-pelled**, **-pelling**. 1. to drive or force back (an assailant, invader, etc.). 2. to keep off or out; fail to mix with. 3. to excite feelings of distaste or aversion in. – **repellent**, adj., n.

repent, v. 1. to feel self-reproach, compunction, or contrition for past conduct. 2. to feel sorry for; regret. – **repentance**, n.

reper·cussion, n. an after-effect, often an indirect result, of some event or action.

repertoire /'rɛpətwɑ/, n. the list of dramas, operas, parts, pieces, etc., which a company, actor, singer etc., is prepared to perform.

reper·tory, n., pl. **-ries**. a theatrical company.

repe·tition, 1. n. the act of repeating.

434

2. a repeated action, performance, etc. – **repetitive**, adj.

re·place, v., **-placed**, **-placing**. 1. to take the place of or provide a substitute for (a person or thing). 2. to restore to a former or the proper place. – **replacement**, n.

re·plen·ish, v. to bring back to a state of fullness or completeness.

re·plete, adj. gorged with food and drink.

rep·li·ca, n. an exact copy or reproduction.

re·ply, v., **-plied**, **-plying**, n., pl. **-plies**. –v. 1. to make answer in words or writing. 2. to respond by some action, performance, etc. 3. to return as an answer: *He replied that he would come today.* –n. 4. an answer or response.

report, n. 1. an account brought back or presented. 2. a statement generally circulated; rumour. 3. repute; reputation. 4. a loud noise, as from an explosion. –v. 5. to relate or tell (what has been learned by observation or investigation). 6. to give or render a formal account or statement (of). 7. to lay a charge against (a person), as to a superior. 8. to present oneself duly, as at a place.

repor·ter, n. 1. one employed to gather and report news. 2. one who prepares official reports, as of legal or legislative proceedings.

repose, n., v., **-posed**, **-posing**. –n. 1. the state of resting; sleep. 2. dignified calmness, as of manner or demeanour. –v. 3. to lie at rest; take rest. 4. to lay to rest; rest; refresh (oneself) by rest.

re·pos·i·tory, n., pl. **-tories**. a place where things are deposited, stored, or offered for sale.

re·pos·sess, v. 1. to possess again; regain possession of. 2. to put again in possession of something: *They repossessed him of his property.*

repre·hen·sible, adj. deserving to be censured or reproved.

repre·sent, v. 1. to serve to express, designate, stand for, or denote, as a word or symbol. 2. to speak and act for by delegated authority. 3. to present in words; set forth; describe. 4. to serve as an example or specimen of; exemplify. 5. to be the equivalent of.

repre·sen·tative, adj. 1. serving to represent; typical. 2. representing a constituency or community or the people generally in legislation or government. 3. characterised by, founded on, or pertaining to representation of the people in government. –n. 4. one who represents another or others; an agent or deputy. 5. a commercial traveller; a travelling salesman.

re·press, v. to keep under control or suppress.

re·prieve, v., **-prieved**, **-prieving**, n. –v. 1. to relieve temporarily from any punishment or evil. –n. 2. respite from impending punishment, esp. from execution of a sentence of death.

repri·mand, n. 1. a severe reproof, esp. a formal one by a person in authority. –v. 2. to reprove severely, esp. in a formal way.

repri·sal, n. (an act of) retaliation.

re·proach, v. 1. to find fault with (a person, etc.); censure. 2. to reprove severely (*with*). –n. 3. an expression of censure or reproof.

repro·bate /'reprəbeɪt/, n. 1. an unprincipled, or reprehensible per-

reprobate

son. –*adj.* 2. morally depraved; unprincipled; bad.

re·pro·duce, *v.*, **-duced, -ducing. 1.** to make a copy, representation, or close imitation of. **2.** to produce (its kind), as an animal or plant; propagate. **3.** to produce, form, make, again or anew in any manner. **4.** to turn out (well, etc.) when copied. – **reproducible**, *adj.* – **reproduction**, *n.*

re·proof, *n.* an expression of censure or rebuke.

re·prove, *v.*, **-proved, -proving.** to address words of disapproval to (a person, etc.). – **reproval**, *n.*

rep·tile, *n.* any of various cold-blooded creeping or crawling animals, as lizards, snakes, etc.

re·pub·lic, *n.* a state, especially a democratic state, in which the head of the government is an elected or nominated president, not a hereditary monarch.

re·pub·li·can, *adj.* **1.** of, pertaining to, or of the nature of a republic. **2.** favouring a republic. –*n.* **3.** one who favours a republican form of government. – **republicanism**, *n.*

re·pu·di·ate, *v.*, **-ated, -ating. 1.** to reject as having no authority or binding force. **2.** to disown or cast off. **3.** to refuse to acknowledge and pay, as a debt.

re·pug·nant, *adj.* distasteful or objectionable. – **repugnance**, *n.*

re·pulse, *v.*, **-pulsed, -pulsing.** to drive back, or repel, as an assailant, etc.

re·pul·sive, *adj.* causing strong dislike. – **repulsion**, *n.*

re·pu·ta·ble, *adj.* held in good repute; honourable.

reservation

re·pu·ta·tion, *n.* the estimation in which a person or thing is held.

re·pute, *n.* estimation in the view of others; reputation.

re·quest, *n.* **1.** the act of asking for something. –*v.* **2.** to ask for, esp. politely or formally. **3.** to make request to, (a person, etc.) to do something.

re·qui·em, *n.* any musical service, or funeral hymn, for the repose of the dead.

re·quire, *v.*, **-quired, -quiring. 1.** to have need of; need. **2.** to ask for authoritatively or imperatively; demand. **3.** to place under an obligation or necessity.

req·ui·si·tion, *n.* **1.** an authoritative or official demand. **2.** the state of being required for use or called into service. –*v.* **3.** to require or take for use; press into service.

re·scind, *v.* to invalidate or repeal (an act, measure, etc.) by a later action or a higher authority. – **recission**, *n.*

res·cue, *v.*, **-cued, -cuing,** *n.* –*v.* **1.** to free or deliver from confinement, violence, danger, or evil. –*n.* **2.** the act of rescuing.

re·search, *n.* **1.** diligent and systematic enquiry or investigation into a subject. –*v.* **2.** to make researches; investigate carefully. –*adj.* **3.** of or pertaining to research.

re·sem·ble, *v.*, **-bled, -bling.** to be like or similar to. – **resemblance**, *n.*

re·sent, *v.* to feel or show a sense of injury or insult.

res·er·va·tion, *n.* **1.** the making of some exception or qualification. **2.** →**reserve** (def.5). **3.** the allotting or the securing of accommodation at a hotel, on a train or boat, etc.

436

reserve

re·serve, *v.,* **-served, -serving,** *n., adj.* –*v.* **1.** to keep back or save for future use, disposal, etc. **2.** to secure or book in advance, as accommodation, theatre seats, etc. **3.** *Law.* to delay handing down (a judgment or decision). –*n.* **4.** something reserved, as for some purpose or contingency. **5.** a tract of public land set apart for a special purpose, as a nature reserve. –*adj.* kept in reserve; forming a reserve.

re·served, *adj.* **1.** kept in reserve. **2.** reticent or silent in disposition, manner, etc.

reserve price, *n.* the lowest price at which a person is willing that his property shall be sold at auction. Also, **reserve.**

res·er·voir, *n.* a natural or artificial place where water is collected and stored.

re·shuffle, *v.,* **-fled, -fling.** to make a new allocation of jobs, esp. within a government or cabinet.

reside, *v.,* **-sided, -siding. 1.** to dwell (*in*) for a considerable time. **2.** to rest or be vested, as powers, rights, etc. – **resident,** *adj., n.*

resi·dence, *n.* **1.** the place, esp. the house, in which one resides. **2.** a large house. **3.** the time during which one resides in a place. – **residential,** *adj.*

resi·due, *n.* that which remains after a part is removed; remainder. – **residual,** *adj.*

resign, *v.* **1.** to give up formally (an office, position, etc.). **2.** to submit (oneself, one's mind, etc.); yield. – **resignation,** *n.*

resil·ient, *adj.* **1.** returning to the original form after being bent, compressed, or stretched. **2.** readily recovering, as from sickness, reverses, etc. – **resilience,** *n.*

resin, *n.* any of a class of organic substances used esp. in the making of varnishes and plastics.

resist, *v.* **1.** to act in opposition; oppose; withstand.

resis·tance, *n.* **1.** the opposition offered by one thing, force, etc., to another. **2.** *Elect.* the property of a device which opposes the flow of an electric current.

reso·lute, *adj.* firmly resolved or determined.

reso·lution, *n.* **1.** a resolve or determination. **2.** the mental state or quality of being resolute. **3.** the act or process of resolving or separating into constituent parts.

re·solve, *v.,* **-solved, -solving,** *n.* –*v.* **1.** to fix or settle on by deliberate choice and will; determine (to do something). **2.** to separate into constituent or elementary parts. **3.** to deal with (a question, etc.) conclusively. **4.** to clear away (doubts, etc.), as by explanation. **5.** to come to a determination; make up one's mind (*on* or *upon*). **6.** to break up or disintegrate. –*n.* **7.** a resolution or determination made. **8.** determination; firmness of purpose.

reso·nance, *n.* the state or quality of resounding or re-echoing; reverberation. – **resonate,** *v.* – **resonant,** *adj.*

resort, *v.* **1.** to have recourse for use, service, or help. –*n.* **2.** a place frequented by the public. **3.** a resorting to some person or thing for aid, service, etc. **4.** a person or thing resorted to for aid, service, etc.

re·sound, *v.* **1.** to re-echo (a sound) or ring with sound. **2.** to be echoed, or ring, as sounds. 3. to proclaim loudly (praises, etc.).

re·source, n. 1. a source of supply, support, or aid. 2. (pl.) monetary or other wealth, esp. of a country.

re·source·ful, adj. skilful in dealing with situations, meeting difficulties, etc.

res·pect, n. 1. a particular, detail, or point (in phrases prec. by in): *to be defective in some respect.* 2. relation or reference (prec. by in or with). 3. esteem or deferential regard felt or shown. 4. (pl.) deferential or friendly compliments. –v. 5. to hold in esteem or honour. 6. to treat with consideration; refrain from interfering with.

res·pec·table, adj. 1. worthy of respect or esteem. 2. having socially accepted standards of moral behaviour. 3. of presentable appearance.

res·pec·tive, adj. pertaining individually or severally to each of a number of persons, things, etc. – respectively, adv.

res·pi·ration, n. the inhalation and exhalation of air; breathing.

res·pite /'rɛspaɪt, 'rɛspaɪt/, n., v., -pited, -piting. –n. 1. a cessation for a time, esp. of anything distressing. –v. 2. to relieve temporarily.

re·splen·dent, adj. shining brilliantly; splendid.

re·spond, v. to answer; give a reply.

re·spon·dent, n. Law. a defendant, esp. in divorce cases.

re·sponse, n. an answer or reply in words, action, etc.

re·spon·si·ble, adj. 1. answerable or accountable (to or for), as for something within one's power. 2. able to discharge obligations or pay debts. 3. reliable in business or other dealings. – responsibility, n.

re·spon·sive, adj. responding readily to influences, appeals, etc.

rest[1], n. 1. refreshing ease or inactivity after exertion or labour. 2. relief or freedom, esp. from anything that wearies or disturbs. 3. cessation or absence of motion. 4. a pause or interval. 5. a support, or supporting device. –v. 6. to refresh oneself, as by sleeping or relaxing. 7. to be quiet or still. 8. to bring or come to rest, or stop. 9. to remain without further action or notice. 10. to lie, sit or lean (in, on, against etc.). 11. to base or be based or founded (on or upon). 12. to be a responsibility, as something to be done (in or with).

rest[2], n. that which is left or remains.

res·taur·ant, n. an establishment where meals are served to customers.

res·ti·tu·tion, n. the restoration of property or rights previously surrendered or removed.

res·tive, adj. impatient of control, restraint, or delay.

re·store, v., -stored, -storing. 1. to bring back to a former, original, or normal condition. 2. to put back to a former place, position, rank, etc. 3. to give back. – restoration, n.

re·strain, v. to hold back from action; keep in check.

re·straint, n. 1. a means of restraining. 2. the state or fact of being restrained.

re·strict, v. to confine or keep within limits, as of space, action, choice, quantity, etc. – restriction, n. – restrictive, adj.

**result, ** n. 1. that which results; the outcome. –v. 2. to arise, or proceed as a consequence. 3. to end in a specified manner or thing.

**resume, ** v., -sumed, -suming. to take up or go on with (something) again after interruption.

**résumé, ** n. a summary.

**resurgent, ** adj. rising again. – **resurgence, ** n.

**resurrect, ** v. 1. to raise from the dead; bring to life again.

**re·sus·ci·tate, ** v. -tated, -tating. to revive, esp. from apparent death or from unconsciousness.

**retail, ** n. 1. the sale of (small quantities of) goods directly to the consumers (opposed to *wholesale*). –adj. 2. pertaining to or engaged in sale at retail. –adv. 3. at a retail price or quantity. –v. 4. to sell directly to the consumer. 5. to be sold at retail.

**retain, ** v. 1. to continue to use, practise, etc. 2. to continue to hold or have. 3. to keep in mind; remember. – **retention, ** n.

**re·tainer, ** n. 1. a fee paid to secure services, as of a barrister. 2. a reduced rent paid during absence as an indication of future requirement.

**retaliate, ** v., -ated, -ating. to return like for like, esp. evil for evil.

**retard, ** v. 1. to delay or hinder the progress of. 2. to delay or limit (a person's intellectual or emotional development).

**retch, ** v. 1. to make efforts to vomit. –n. 2. the act or an instance of retching.

**retentive, ** adj. 1. tending or serving to retain something. 2. having power or capacity to retain.

**reticent, ** adj. inclined to be silent. – **reticence, ** n.

**retina, ** n., pl. -nas, -nae. the innermost coat of the back part of the eyeball, serving to receive the image.

**reti·nue, ** n. a body of people in attendance upon an important personage.

**retire, ** v., -tired, -tiring. 1. to withdraw, or go away to a place of abode, shelter, or seclusion. 2. to go to bed. 3. to withdraw from office, business, or active life.

**retirement, ** n. the state of being retired.

**retort, ** v. 1. to reply in retaliation. –n. 2. a severe, incisive, or witty reply.

**retrace, ** v., -traced, -tracing. to trace back; go back over.

**retract, ** v. 1. to draw back or in. 2. to withdraw or revoke (a decree, promise, etc.).

**retreat, ** n. 1. the act of withdrawing, as into safety or privacy. 2. a place of refuge or seclusion. –v. 3. to withdraw or retire, esp. for shelter or seclusion.

**retrench, ** v. 1. to dismiss, as part of an effort to economise. 2. to economise; reduce expenses.

**retribution, ** n. repayment according to merits or deserts, esp. for evil.

**retrieve, ** v., -trieved, -trieving 1. to recover or regain. 2. to bring back to a former and better state. – **retrieval, ** n.

**retro·active, ** adj. operative with respect to past occurrences, as a statute; retrospective.

**retro·grade, ** adj. returning to an earlier and inferior state.

**retro·spect, ** n. contemplation of the past. – **retrospection, ** n.

retrospective

retro·spec·tive, *adj.* 1. looking or directed backwards. 2. retroactive, as a statute. – **retrospectively**, *n.*

return, *v.* 1. to go or come back, as to a former place, position, state, etc. 2. to put, bring, take, give, or send back. 3. to make reply; retort. 4. to yield (a profit, revenue, etc.). 5. to elect, as to a legislative body. 6. to turn back or in the reverse direction. –*n.* 7. the act or fact of returning. 8. response or reply. 9. (*oft. pl.*). a yield or profit. 10. **by return**, by the next post. –*adj.* 11. sent, given, or done in return. 12. done or occurring again.

re·union, *n.* a gathering of relatives, friends, etc. after separation.

rev, *n.*, *v.*, **revved, revving.** –*n.* 1. a revolution (in an engine or the like). –*v.* 2. to change, esp. to increase the speed of.

re·value, *v.*, **-ued, -uing.** to value again, esp. to raise the legal value of (a currency).

revamp, *v.* to renovate.

reveal, *v.* 1. to make known; disclose; divulge. 2. to lay open to view; display. – **revelation**, *n.*

re·veille /rəˈvælɪ/, *n.* a signal to waken soldiers or sailors.

revel, *v.*, **-elled, -elling,** *n.* –*v.* 1. to take great pleasure or delight (*in*). –*n.* 2. (*oft. pl.*) an occasion of noisy festivity with dancing, etc. – **revelry**, *n.*

re·venge, *n.*, *v.*, **-venged, -venging.** –*n.* 1. retaliation for injuries or wrongs; vengeance. –*v.* 2. to take vengeance on behalf of (a person, etc.) or for (a wrong, etc.).

revenue, *n.* 1. the income of a government from taxation, excise duties, customs, etc. 2. a regular income, as the return or yield from any kind of property.

rever·berate, *v.*, **-rated, -rating.** to re-echo or resound.

revere, *v.*, **-vered, -vering.** to regard with respect and awe; venerate. – **reverence**, *n.* – **reverent**, *adj.*

rever·end, *adj.* 1. (*oft. cap.*) a title of respect for a clergyman. –*n.* 2. *Colloq.* a clergyman.

rev·erie, *n.* a state of dreamy meditation.

re·verse, *adj.*, *n.*, *v.*, **-versed, -versing.** –*adj.* 1. opposite or contrary in position, direction, order, or character. 2. producing a backward motion. –*n.* 3. the opposite or contrary of something. 4. the back or rear of anything. 5. an adverse change of fortune. 6. *Motor Vehicles.* reverse gear. –*v.* 7. to turn (something) inside out or upside down. 8. to turn or move (something) in the opposite direction. 9. to revoke or annul (a decree, judgment, etc.). 10. to drive (a motor vehicle) backwards.

revert, *v.* 1. to return to a former habit, practice, etc. 2. *Law.* to go back to the former owner or his heirs. – **reversion**, *n.*

review, *n.* 1. a critical article or report on some literary work. 2. a periodical publication containing articles on current events, books, art, etc. 3. consideration of past events, circumstances, or facts. 4. a general survey of something, esp. in words. –*v.* 5. to view or look over again. 6. to look back upon; view retrospectively. 7. to present a survey in speech or writing. 8. to discuss (a book, etc.) in a critical review.

revile, *v.*, **-viled, -viling.** to address, or

revile, speak of, abusively or contemptuously.

revise, v., -vised, -vising. 1. to amend or alter. 2. to go over or study (a subject, book, etc.) again. – **revision**, n.

revive, v., -vived, -viving. 1. to bring back into notice, use, or currency. 2. to restore to life or consciousness. – **revival**, n.

revoke, v., -voked, -voking. to take back or withdraw; annul. – **revocation**, n.

revolt, v. 1. to break away from or rise against constituted authority. 2. to turn away in mental rebellion or abhorrence. 3. to affect with disgust or abhorrence. –n. 4. an insurrection or rebellion. 5. aversion, disgust, or loathing. 6. the state of those revolting.

revolution, n. 1. a complete overthrow of an established government. 2. a complete or radical change. 3. procedure or course as if in a circuit. 4. a single turn of this kind.

revolutionary, adj., n., pl. -ries. –adj. 1. pertaining to a revolution. –n. 2. one who advocates or takes part in a revolution.

revolutionise, v., -volved, -nising. to bring about a revolution in.

revolve, v., -volved, -volving. 1. to rotate, as on an axis. 2. to move in a circular or curving course, or orbit.

revolver, n. a pistol which can be fired repeatedly without reloading.

revue, n. any group of skits, dances, and songs.

revulsion, n. a violent dislike or aversion for something or someone.

reward, n. 1. something given or received in return for service, merit, hardship, etc. –v. 2. to give something (to someone) in return for service, etc.

rewarding, adj. giving satisfaction that the effort made was worth while.

rhapsody, n., pl. -dies. 1. an exaggerated expression of enthusiasm. 2. Music. an instrumental composition suggestive of improvisation.

rhetoric, n. 1. the art of literary uses of language. 2. (in prose or verse) the use of exaggeration in an unfavourable sense.

rheumatism, n. a disease commonly affecting the joints. – **rheumatic**, adj.

rhinestone, n. an artificial gem made of glass.

rhinoceros, n., pl. -roses, (esp. collectively) -ros. any of various large mammals with one or 2 upright horns on the snout. Also, **rhino**.

rhizome, n. a rootlike horizontal underground stem.

rhodium, n. a silvery white metallic element of the platinum family. Symbol: Rh

rhododendron, n. any of several ornametal, flowering shrubs and trees.

rhombus, n., pl. -buses, -bi. an oblique-angled equilateral parallelogram.

rhubarb, n. a garden plant with edible leafstalks.

rhyme, n., v., rhymed, rhyming. –n. 1. agreement in the terminal sounds of lines of verse, or of words. 2. **rhyme or reason**, logic; explanation; meaning. –v. 3. to form a

rhyme

rhyme, as one word or line with another.

rhythm, *n.* any movement or procedure marked by the regular recurrence of particular elements or phases, as the recurring beat, accent, etc. in music. – **rhythmic, rhythmical,** *adj.*

rib[1], *n., v.,* **ribbed, ribbing.** –*n.* 1. one of a series of long, slender, curved bones, more or less enclosing the chest. 2. something resembling a rib in form, position, or use, as a supporting or strengthening part. –*v.* 3. to furnish or strengthen with ribs.

rib[2], *v.,* **ribbed, ribbing.** *Colloq.* to tease; ridicule; make fun of.

ribald /'rɪbəld, 'raɪ-/, *adj.* coarsely mocking or abusive. – **ribaldry**, *n.*

ribbon, *n.* 1. a band of fine material, used for ornament, tying, etc. 2. anything resembling a ribbon or woven band. 3. a band of material supplying ink, as in a typewriter.

ribo·flavin /raɪbou'fleɪvən/, *n.* one of the vitamins included in the vitamin B complex.

rice, *n.* the starchy grain of a species of grass, used for food.

rich, *adj.* 1. abundantly supplied with resources, means, or funds. 2. abounding (*in* or *with*). 3. of great value or worth; valuable. 4. (of wine, gravy, etc.) strong and full flavoured. 5. (of colour) deep, strong, or vivid. 6. (of sound, the voice, etc.) full and mellow in tone. 7. *Colloq.* ridiculous or absurd. –*n.* 8. rich people collectively (usu. prec. by *the*).

riches, *n.pl.* wealth.

rick·ets, *n.* a childhood disease,

ridicule

caused by malnutrition and often resulting in bone deformities.

rick·ety, *adj.* liable to fall or collapse; shaky.

rick·shaw, *n.* a small two-wheeled vehicle drawn by one or two men.

ri·co·chet /'rɪkəʃeɪ/, *n.* the motion of an object which rebounds once or more times from a flat surface.

ri·cot·ta, *n.* a soft unripened cheese with a fresh bland flavour.

rid, *v.,* **rid** or **ridded, ridding.** –*v.* 1. to clear or free (*of*) something objectionable. –*adj.* 2. **get rid of**, to get free, or relieved of.

rid·dle[1], *n.* 1. a question or statement so framed as to exercise one's ingenuity in answering it. 2. a puzzling question, problem, or matter.

rid·dle[2], *v.,* **-dled, -dling.** to pierce with many holes.

ride, *v.,* **rode, ridden, riding**, *n.* –*v.* 1. to sit on and control (a horse, bicycle, etc.) in motion. 2. to be carried on something as if on horseback or in a vehicle. 3. to ride over, along or through (a road, boundary, region, etc.). 4. to be based or rely on something. 5. to work or move (*up*) from the proper position, as a skirt, or the like. **ride out**, to sustain or endure successfully. –*n.* 7. a journey or excursion on a horse, etc., or on or in a vehicle.

rid·er, *n.* 1. one who rides. 2. an addition or amendment to a document, etc.

ridge, *n., v.,* **ridged, ridging.** –*n.* 1. a long, narrow elevation of land. 2. any raised narrow strip. –*v.* 3. to provide with or form into a ridge or ridges.

ri·di·cule, *n., v.,* **-culed, -culing.** –*n.* 1.

ridicule

words or actions intended to excite contemptuous laughter at a person or thing. -v. 2. to deride; make fun of.

ridicu·lous, adj. absurd, preposterous, or laughable.

rife, adj. of common occurrence; prevalent.

riffle, v., **-fled, -fling**. to flutter and shift, as pages.

riff-raff, n. worthless or low persons.

rifle[1], n. a shoulder firearm.

rifle[2], v., **-fled, -fling**. to ransack and rob (a place, receptacle, etc.).

rift, n. 1. an opening made by splitting. 2. a break in friendly relations as between people or countries etc.

rig, v., **rigged, rigging**, n. -v. 1. to provide with equipment, etc.; fit (*out* or *up*). 2. to prepare or put together, esp. as a makeshift (*up*). 3. to manipulate fraudulently. -n. 4. apparatus for some purpose; equipment. 5. Also, **rig-out**. *Colloq*. costume or dress, esp. when odd or conspicuous.

rigging, n. the ropes, chains, etc., which operate the masts, yards, sails, etc., on a ship.

right, adj. 1. in accordance with what is just or good. 2. in conformity with fact, reason, or some standard or principle; correct. 3. in good health or spirits, as persons. 4. in good order. 5. most convenient, desirable, or favourable. 6. belonging or pertaining to the side which is turned towards the east when a person or thing is facing north (opposed to *left*). 7. socially and politically conservative. 8. *Geom*. having the axis perpendicular to the base. 9. *Colloq*. unquestionable; unmistakeable; true. -n. 10. a just claim or title to anything. 11. that which is due to anyone by just claim. 12. that which is ethically good and proper and in conformity with the moral law. 13. that which accords with fact, reason, or propriety. 14. the right side or what is on the right side. 15. a body of persons, political party, etc., holding conservative views. -adv. 16. quite or completely. 17. immediately. 18. exactly, precisely, or just. 19. correctly or accurately. 20. properly or fittingly. 21. advantageously, favourably, or well. 22. towards the right hand; to the right. 23. very (used in certain titles). -v. 24. to bring or restore to, or resume an upright or the proper position. 25. to set in order or put right. 26. to redress (wrong, etc.).

right angle, n. an angle of 90°.

right·eous, adj. characterised by uprightness or morality; virtuous.

rigid, adj. stiff or unyielding; not pliant or flexible; hard.

rigma·role, n. a long and complicated process.

rigour /ˈrɪgə/, n. 1. strictness or harshness, as in dealing with persons. 2. severity of life; hardship. – **rigorous**, adj.

rile, v., **riled, riling**. *Colloq*. to irritate or vex.

rim, n., v., **rimmed, rimming**. -n. 1. the outer edge, border, or margin, esp. of a circular object. -v. 2. to furnish with a rim, border, or margin.

rind, n. a thick and firm coat or covering, as of fruits, cheeses, etc.

ring[1], n., v., **ringed, ringing**. -n. 1. a circular band of metal etc., any one for wearing on the finger. 2. anything having the form of a circular band. 3. a circular course. 4. an enclosed circular or other area, as one in which some sport or exhibition takes place. **5.** a group of persons cooperating for selfish or illegal purposes. –v. **6.** to surround with a ring; encircle. **7.** to form (into) a ring. **8.** to move in a ring or a constantly curving course.

ring², v., **rang**, **rung**, **ringing**, n. –v. **1.** to (cause to) give forth a clear, resonant sound when set in sudden vibration by a blow or otherwise, as a bell. **2.** to be filled with sound; re-echo with sound, as a place. **3.** to proclaim, summon, signal, etc., by or as by the sound of a bell. **4.** to telephone. **5.** to seem (true, false, etc.) in the effect produced on the mind. **6.** to arouse a memory; sound familiar. **7. ring off**, to end a telephone conversation. **8. ring the changes**, to vary the manner of performing an action. **9. ring up**, **a.** to telephone. **b.** to record (the cost of an item) on a cash register. –n. **10.** a resonant sound or note. **11.** a telephone call. **12.** a characteristic or inherent quality.

ring·bark, v. to cut away the bark in a ring around a tree trunk or branch, in order to kill the tree or the affected part.

ringer, n. Colloq. **1.** an athlete, horse, etc., entered in a competition under false representations as to identity or ability. **2.** a person or thing that closely resembles another.

ring-in, n. Colloq. a person or thing substituted for another at the last moment.

ring·let, n. a curled lock of hair.

ringmaster, n. a person in charge of performances in a ring or circular stage (e.g. a circus ring).

ring road, n. a road which bypasses a town or city, designed to reduce urban traffic congestion.

ring·worm, n. any of certain contagious skin diseases.

rink, n. **1.** an area of ice for skating. **2.** a smooth floor for roller-skating.

rinse, –v., **rinsed**, **rinsing**. n. –v. **1.** to put through clean water, as a final stage in cleansing. –n. **2.** an act or instance of rinsing. **3.** any liquid preparation used for impermanently tinting the hair.

riot, n. **1.** any disturbance of the peace by an assembly of persons. **2.** a violent outbreak, as of emotions, passions, etc. **3.** a brilliant display. **4.** Colloq. one who or that which causes great amusement, enthusiasm, etc. **5. run riot**, to act without control or restraint. –v. **6.** to take part in a riot or disorderly public outbreak. – **riotous**, adj.

RIP, abbrev. may he, or she, rest in peace. Inscription often used in epitaphs.

rip, v., **ripped**, **ripping**. –v. **1.** to cut or tear apart roughly or vigorously. **2.** Colloq. to move along with violence or great speed. –n. **3.** a rent made by ripping; a tear.

riparian, adj. of or on the riverbank.

rip·cord, n. a cord or ring which opens a parachute during a descent.

ripe, adj., **riper**, **ripest**. complete in natural growth or development.

ripen, v. to make or become ripe.

rip-off, n. an excessive charge or exorbitant price; swindle. – **rip off**, v.

rip·oste /ri'pəʊst/, n. a quick, sharp return in speech or action. Also, **ripost**.

ripple, v., **-pled**, **-pling**. to form small waves on the surface, as water.

rise, v., rose, risen, rising, n. –v. 1. to get up from a reclining, sitting, kneeling position. 2. to get up from bed. 3. to become active in opposition or resistance; rebel. 4. to spring up or grow. 5. to move upwards or ascend. 6. to come above the horizon, as a heavenly body. 7. to extend directly upwards. 8. to attain higher rank, importance, etc. 9. to prove oneself equal (to) a demand, emergency, etc. 10. to become animated or cheerful, as the spirits. 11. to swell or puff up, as dough from the action of yeast. 12. to increase in amount, as prices, etc. 13. to increase in degree, intensity, or force; as colour, fever, etc. 14. to become louder or of higher pitch, as the voice. 15. to adjourn, or close a session, as a parliament or court. –n. 16. the act of rising; upward movement or ascent. 17. elevation or advance in rank, fortune, etc. 18. an increase in amount, as of wages, etc. 19. an increase in degree or intensity, as of temperature. 20. origin, source, or beginning. 21. extension upwards. 22. upward slope, as of ground or a road. 23. a piece of rising or high ground. 24. **get or take a rise out of**, to provoke to anger, annoyance, etc., by banter, mockery, deception, etc.

risk, n. 1. a hazard or dangerous chance. –v. 2. to expose to the chance of injury or loss, or hazard. 3. to venture upon; take or run the risk of. – **risky**, adj.

risqué /'rɪskeɪ, rɪs'keɪ/, adj. daringly close to indelicacy or impropriety.

ris·sole, n. a small fried ball of minced meat or fish.

rite, n. a ceremonial act or procedure customary in religious or other solemn use.

ritual, n. 1. (the act of following) an established procedure, form, etc., for a religious or other rite. 2. any solemn or customary action, code of behaviour, etc., regulating social conduct.

rival, n., adj., v., -valled, -valling. –n. 1. one who strives to equal or outdo another; a competitor. –adj. 2. being a rival. –v. 3. to strive to equal or outdo.

river, n. 1. a considerable natural stream of water flowing in a definite course. 2. any abundant stream or copious flow.

rivet, n. 1. a metal pin or bolt. –v. 2. to fasten or fix firmly.

rivu·let, n. a small stream.

road, n. 1. a way, usu. open to the public for the passage of vehicles, persons, and animals. 2. a way or course.

roam, v. to walk, go, or travel about without fixed purpose or direction.

roan, adj. (chiefly of horses) brown in colour with splashes of grey or white.

roar, v. 1. to utter or express (in) a loud, deep sound, esp. of excitement, distress, or anger. 2. to laugh loudly or boisterously. 3. to make a loud noise or din, as thunder, cannon, waves, wind, etc. –n. 4. the sound of roaring.

roast, v. 1. to bake and brown (meat, coffee etc.) by dry heat, as in an oven. 2. *Colloq.* to criticise, rebuke or ridicule severely. –n. 3. a piece of roasted meat.

rob, v., robbed, robbing. to steal something from by unlawful force or threat of violence.

robe

robe, *n.* any long, loose garment.

robot, *n.* a manufactured device capable of performing some human-like functions.

robust, *adj.* **1.** strong and healthy, hardy, or vigorous. **2.** suited to or requiring bodily strength or endurance.

rock[1], *n.* **1.** *Geol.* mineral matter assembled in masses or considerable quantities in nature. **2.** stone in the mass. **3.** something resembling or suggesting a rock. **4.** a firm foundation for support. **5.** a stone of any size. **6. on the rocks, a.** *Colloq.* into or in a state of disaster or ruin. **b.** (of drinks) with ice-cubes.

rock[2], *v.* **1.** to (cause to) move or sway to and fro or from side to side. **2.** →**rock music**. **3.** →**rock'n'roll**.

rocker, *n.* **1.** one of the curved pieces on which a cradle or a rocking chair rocks. **2.** any of various devices that operate with a rocking motion. **3. off one's rocker,** *Colloq.* crazy; demented.

rock·ery, *n., pl.* **-ries.** a mound of rocks and earth for growing ferns or other plants.

rocket, *n.* **1.** *Aeron.* a structure propelled by an emission of heated gas from the rear. –*v.* **2.** to move like a rocket.

rock music, *n.* contemporary music which is derived basically from the blues.

rock'n'roll, *n.* a form of pop music of the 1950s. Also, **rock-and-roll, rock-'n'-roll.**

rococo, *n.* **1.** an ornate style of art, architecture and decoration of the 18th century. –*adj.* **2.** decorated in exaggeratedly elaborate style.

roll

rod, *n.* **1.** a stick, shaft, etc., of wood, metal, or other material. **2.** a pole used in fishing. **3.** a stick used as an instrument of punishment. **4.** a wand or staff carried as a symbol of office, authority, power, etc.

rode, *v.* past tense of *ride*.

rodent, *n.* one of the order of gnawing or nibbling mammals, that include the mice, squirrels, beavers, etc.

rodeo /ˈrouˈdeɪou, ˈoudiou/, *n., pl.* **-deos.** an exhibition of the skills of cowboys.

roe, *n.* the mass of eggs of the female fish.

Rogation Day, *n.* any of the days of prayer observed on the three days before Ascension Day, and by Roman Catholics also on 25 April.

roger, *interj.* message received and understood (used in telecommunications).

rogue, *n.* **1.** a dishonest person. **2.** a playfully mischievous person; rascal; scamp.

role, *n.* **1.** the character which an actor presents in a play. **2.** proper or customary function.

roll, *v.* **1.** to (cause to) move along a surface by turning over and over, as a ball or a wheel. **2.** to move or be moved on wheels, as a vehicle or its occupants (*along*). **3.** to extend in undulations, as land. **4.** to continue in or have a deep, prolonged sound, as thunder, etc. **5.** to turn over, or over and over, as a person or animal lying down. **6.** to sway or rock from side to side, as a ship. **7.** to form into a roll, or curl up from itself. **8.** to spread (*out*, etc.) from being rolled up; unroll. **9.** to spread out as under a roller. **10.** to cause to turn round in different directions, as the eyes. **11.**

446

roll — to make by forming a roll. **12.** to wrap, enfold, or envelop, as in some covering. **13.** to operate upon with a roller or rollers, as to spread out, level, compact, etc. —*n.* **14.** a list, register, or catalogue. **15.** anything rolled up in cylindrical form. **16.** a small cake of bread. **17.** a deep, prolonged sound, as of thunder, etc. **18.** the continuous sound of a drum rapidly beaten. **19.** a single throw of dice. **20.** *Colloq.* a wad of paper currency.

rolled gold, *n.* metal covered with a thin coating of gold.

roller, *n.* **1.** a cylinder wheel, or the like, upon which something is rolled along. **2.** a cylinder of plastic, wire, etc., around which hair is rolled to set it. **3.** a cylindrical body, as one for rolling over something to be spread out, levelled, crushed, etc.

roller-coaster, *n.* an amusement park ride, on a steep twisting track.

roller-skate, *n.*, *v.*, **-skated**, **-skating**. —*n.* **1.** a form of skate running on small wheels or rollers. —*v.* **2.** to move on roller-skates.

rol·lick·ing, *adj.* swaggering and jolly.

ROM, *abbrev.* read-only memory.

romance, *n.*, *v.*, **-manced**, **-mancing**. —*n.* **1.** a tale depicting heroic or marvellous achievements. **2.** a made-up story; fanciful or extravagant invention. **3.** romantic character or quality. **4.** a romantic affair or experience. —*v.* **5.** to think or talk romantically.

Roman numerals, *n.pl.* the numerals used by the ancient Romans still used for certain purposes. The common basic symbols are I(=1), V(=5), X(=10), L(=50), C(=100), D(=500), and M(=1000).

roman·tic, *adj.* **1.** of, pertaining to, or of the nature of romance. **2.** proper to romance rather than to real life. **3.** displaying or expressing love, emotion, etc. **4.** imaginary or fictitious. —*n.* **5.** a romantic person. – **romanticise**, *v.*

romp, *v.* **1.** to play or frolic in a lively or boisterous manner. **2. romp home** or **in**, to win easily.

roof, *n.*, *pl.* **roofs**. **1.** the external upper covering of any building. **2.** something which resembles this in form or position.

rook[1], *n.* **1.** a black European crow. —*v.* **2.** to cheat; fleece; swindle.

rook[2], *n.* a chess piece.

rook·ery, *n.*, *pl.* **-ries**. **1.** a breeding place or colony. **2.** any instance of cheating, sharp practice, exorbitant prices, etc.

rookie, *n. Colloq.* a raw recruit.

room, *n.* **1.** a portion of space within a building, separated by walls from other parts. **2.** space, or extent of space, occupied by or available for something. **3.** opportunity or scope for or to do something. —*v.* **4.** to occupy a room or rooms; to share a room; lodge.

roomy, *adj.*, **-mier**, **-miest**. affording ample room; spacious; large.

roost, *n.* **1.** a perch upon which domestic fowls rest at night. —*v.* **2.** to settle or stay, esp. for the night.

roos·ter, *n.* a domestic cock.

root[1], *n.* **1.** a part of the plant which grows downward into the soil, fixing the plant and absorbing nutriment and moisture. **2.** the embedded part of a hair, tooth, nail, etc. **3.** the fundamental or essential part. **4.** the base or point of origin

447

root

of something. **5.** (*pl.*) a person's real home and environment. **6.** *Maths.* a quantity which, when multiplied by itself a certain number of times, produces a given quantity. –*v.* **7.** to send out roots and begin to grow. **8.** to become fixed or established. **9.** to fix by, or as if by, roots. **10.** to pull, tear, or dig (*up*, *out*, etc.) by the roots. **11.** *Colloq.* to have sexual intercourse with.

root², *v.* **1.** to poke or search (*around*) as if to find something. **2.** to unearth; bring to light (*up*, etc.).

rope, *n.*, *v.*, **roped**, **roping.** –*n.* **1.** a strong, thick line or cord. **2.** death by hanging as a punishment. **3.** (*pl.*) methods of operation of a business, etc. –*v.* **4.** to tie, bind, or fasten with a rope. **5.** *Colloq.* to draw or entice (*into*) something.

ropy, *adj.*, **-ier**, **-iest.** poor in quality.

Roquefort, *n.* strong-flavoured crumbly French cheese with bluish-green veins.

rosary, *n.*, *pl.* **-ries.** a string of beads used for counting prayers in reciting them.

rose¹, *n.* **1.** (the flower of) any of various showy-flowered shrubs. **2.** an ornament shaped like or suggesting a rose. **3.** the traditional reddish colour of the rose. **4.** a perforated cap, as at the end of the spout of a watering-can, etc., to break a flow of water into a spray.

rose², *v.* past tense of **rise**.

rosé, *n.* a light, pale red wine.

roseate, *adj.* **1.** resembling a rose, esp. in colour. –*adj.* **2.** marked by unrealistic optimism.

rosemary, *n.* an aromatic herb used in cooking.

rosette, *n.* any arrangement, part, object, or formation more or less resembling a rose.

rosewood, *n.* dark purplish red wood from various tropical trees. Often used in furniture.

rosin, *n.* a hard, brittle resin used for rubbing on violin bows, etc.

roster, *n.* a list of persons or groups showing their periods of duty.

rostrum, *n.*, *pl.* **-trums**, **-tra.** any platform, stage, etc., for public speaking.

rosy, *adj.*, **rosier**, **rosiest.** **1.** pink or pinkish red. **2.** (of persons, the cheeks, lips, etc.) having a fresh, healthy redness. **3.** bright or promising. **4.** cheerful or optimistic.

rot, *v.*, **rotted**, **rotting**, *n.* –*v.* **1.** (to cause to) undergo decomposition; decay. –*n.* **2.** rotting or rotten matter. **3.** any of various diseases characterised by decomposition. **4.** *Colloq.* nonsense.

rotary, *adj.* **1.** turning round as on an axis, as an object. **2.** having a part or parts that rotate, as a machine.

rotate, *v.*, **-tated**, **-tating.** **1.** (to cause to) turn round like a wheel on its axis. **2.** to proceed in a fixed routine of succession: *The seasons rotate.* – **rotation**, *n.*

rote, *n.* in the phrase **by rote**, in a mechanical way without thought of the meaning.

rotisserie, *n.* a mechanical rotating spit on which food can be cooked.

rotten, *adj.* **1.** in a state of decay; putrid. **2.** *Colloq.* wretchedly bad, unsatisfactory or unpleasant. **3.** contemptible.

rotund, *adj.* rounded; plump.

rotunda, *n.* a round building, esp. one with a dome.

rouge /ruʒ/, *n.*, *v.*, **rouged**, **rouging.** –*n.* **1.** a red cosmetic for colouring

rouge the cheeks or lips. —*v.* **2.** to colour with rouge.

rough, *adj.* **1.** uneven of surface; not smooth. **2.** shaggy. **3.** acting with or characterised by violence. **4.** unmannerly or rude. **5.** *Colloq.* severe, hard, or unpleasant. **6.** without ordinary comforts or conveniences. **7.** requiring exertion or strength rather than intelligence or skill, as work. **8.** unpolished, as language, verse, style, etc. **9.** made or done without any attempt at exactness, completeness, or thoroughness. —*n.* **10.** that which is rough. **11.** the rough, hard, or unpleasant side or part of anything. —*adv.* **12.** in a rough manner; roughly. —*v.* **13.** to treat roughly or harshly (*up*). **14.** to cut, shape, or sketch roughly (*in* or *out*).

rough·age, *n.* the coarser parts of food, of little nutritive value, but aiding digestion.

rough·ly, *adv.* **1.** in a crude, harsh or violent manner. **2.** approximately; about.

rou·lette, *n.* **1.** a gambling game. **2.** a small toothed wheel, mounted in a handle, for making lines of marks, dots, or perforations.

round, *adj.* **1.** circular, as a disc. **2.** ring-shaped, as a hoop. **3.** curved like part of a circle, as an outline. **4.** spherical or globular, as a ball. **5.** free from angularity; curved, as parts of the body. **6.** full, complete, or entire. **7.** roughly correct. **8.** (of a literary character) described in depth. **9.** something round. **10.** any complete course, series, or succession. **11.** (sometimes *pl.*) a circuit of any place, series of places, etc., covered in a customary way. **12.** a single outburst, as of applause, cheers, etc. **13.** a distribution of drink, etc., to all the members of a company. **14. a.** (of bread) a sandwich. **b.** a slice. —*adv.* **15.** in a circle, ring, etc., or so as to surround something. **16.** on all sides or about. **17.** in a circular or rounded course. **18.** throughout a period of time: *all year round*. **19.** by a roundabout course. **20.** with change to another direction, course, opinion, etc.: *to look round.* —*prep.* **21.** so as to encircle, surround, or envelop. **22.** around; about. **23.** in the vicinity of. **24.** so as to make a turn or partial circuit about or to the other side of. **25. round the bend** or **twist**, *Colloq.* insane. —*v.* **26.** to free or become free from angularity or flatness; become plump. **27.** to encircle or surround. **28.** to develop to completeness or perfection. **29. round on** or **upon**, to attack, usu. verbally, with sudden and often unexpected vigour. **30. round up**, to collect (cattle, people, etc.) in a particular place.

round·about, *n.* **1.** →**merry-go-round**. **2.** a road junction at which the traffic moves in one direction only round a circular arrangement. —*adj.* **3.** circuitous or indirect.

roundel, *n.* circular panel, window, mark, disc, or medallion.

roundelay, *n.* a simple song or poem with a repeated refrain.

roun·ders, *n.pl.* (construed as *sing.*) a game played with bat and ball.

round·ly, *adv.* vigorously or briskly.

rouse /rauz/, *v.*, **roused**, **rousing**. to bring or come out of a state of sleep, inactivity, depression, etc.

roustabout *n.* labourer on an oil rig; unskilled or casual labourer, e.g. on fairground.

rout¹, *n.* **1.** a defeat attended with disorderly flight. **2.** a clamour or fuss. –*v.* **3.** to defeat utterly.

rout², *v.* to poke, search, or rummage.

route, *n.* a way or road taken or planned for passage or travel.

rou·tine, *n.* **1.** a customary or regular course of procedure. –*adj.* **2.** of the nature of, proceeding by, or adhering to routine.

rove, *v.*, **roved, roving.** to wander about without definite destination.

row¹ /rou/, *n.* a number of persons or things arranged in a straight line.

row² /rou/, *v.* **1.** to propel (a boat, etc.) by or as by the use of oars. –*n.* **2.** an act of rowing.

row³ /rau/, *n.* **1.** a noisy dispute or quarrel; commotion. **2.** *Colloq.* noise or clamour.

rowdy, *adj.*, **-dier, -diest.** rough and disorderly.

row·lock /'rolək/, *n.* a device on which an oar rests and swings.

royal, *adj.* of, pertaining to, established by, or existing under the patronage of, a sovereign.

royal·ist, *n.* a supporter or adherent of a monarch or monarchy.

royalty, *n., pl.* **-ties. 1.** royal persons collectively. **2.** royal status, dignity, or power; sovereignty. **3.** an agreed portion of the proceeds from his work, paid to an author, composer, etc.

rub, *v.*, **rubbed, rubbing,** *n.* –*v.* **1.** to subject (an object) to pressure and friction, esp. in order to clean, smooth, polish, etc. **2.** to move, spread, or apply (something) with pressure and friction over something else. **3.** to move (things) with pressure and friction over each other (*together*, etc.). **4.** to remove or erase by rubbing (*off, out*, etc.). **5.** to chafe or abrade. **6.** to admit of being rubbed (*off*, etc.). **7. rub it in**, to remind someone repeatedly of his mistakes, failures or shortcomings. **8. rub off on**, to be transferred to, esp. as a result of repeated close contact. –*n.* **9.** the act of rubbing. **10.** a source of doubt or difficulty.

rubber¹, *n.* **1.** an elastic substance, derived from the latex of certain plants. **2.** a synthetic material resembling rubber. **3.** a piece of such material as used for erasing pencil marks, etc.

rubber², *n.* Bridge, Whist, *etc.*, a set of games.

rub·bish, *n.* **1.** waste or refuse material; debris; litter. **2.** nonsense. –*v.* **3.** to speak of scornfully; criticise; denigrate.

rub·ble, *n.* rough fragments of broken stone.

rubella, *n.* →**German measles.**

rubric, *n.* a title, heading, direction, etc., in a manuscript, book, etc.

ruby, *n., pl.* **-bies. 1.** a red gemstone. **2.** deep red; carmine. –*adj.* **3.** ruby-coloured. **4.** made from or containing a ruby.

ruck¹, *n.* **1.** *Aus. Rules.* a group of 3 players who do not have fixed positions. **2.** *Rugby Football.* a group of players struggling for the ball in no set pattern of play.

ruck², *n.* a fold, crease, or wrinkle.

ruck·sack, *n.* a kind of knapsack carried by hikers, etc.

ruc·tion, *n.* *Colloq.* a disturbance, quarrel or row.

rudder, *n.* a board of wood or metal

rudder

at the stern of a boat used as a means of steering.

ruddy, *adj.,* **-dier, -diest,** *adv. -adj.* **1.** reddish in colour, as from good health. –*adv.* **2.** *Colloq.* extremely.

rude, *adj.,* **ruder, rudest. 1.** discourteous or impolite. **2.** without culture, learning, or refinement.

rudi·ments, *n.pl.* the elements or first principles of a subject.

rue, *v.,* **rued, ruing.** to feel sorrow over; repent of.

ruf·fian, *n.* a violent, lawless man; a rough brute.

ruffle, *v.,* **-fled, -fling,** *n. –v.* **1.** to destroy the smoothness or evenness of. **2.** to annoy or disturb. **3.** to draw up (cloth, lace, etc.) into a ruffle. **4.** to be or become ruffled. –*n.* **5.** a break in the smoothness or evenness of some surface. **6.** a strip of cloth, lace, etc., drawn up by gathering along one edge.

rug, *n.* **1.** a small, often thick, carpet. **2.** a thick, warm blanket. –*v.* **3.** to dress (oneself) (*up*) in thick clothing, etc.

Rugby football, *n.* either of 2 forms of football, **Rugby League,** and **Rugby Union.**

rugged, *adj.* **1.** roughly broken, rocky, hilly, or otherwise difficult of passage. **2.** severe, hard, or trying.

ruin, *n.* **1.** (*pl.*) the remains of a fallen building, town, etc. **2.** a ruined building, town, etc. **3.** fallen and wrecked or decayed state. **4.** the complete loss of means, position, or the like. –*v.* **5.** to reduce to ruin. –**ruinous,** *adj.*

rule, *n., v.,* **ruled, ruling.** –*n.* **1.** a principle or regulation governing

rumple

conduct, action, procedure, etc. **2.** that which customarily occurs or holds good. **3.** control, government, or dominion. –*v.* **4.** to control or direct. **5.** to declare judicially; decree. **6.** to mark with lines, esp. parallel straight lines, with the aid of a ruler or the like. **7.** to prevail or be current. **8.** **rule out,** to exclude; refuse to admit.

ruler, *n.* **1.** one who or that which rules or governs. **2.** a strip of wood, metal, or other material with a graduated straight edge, used in drawing lines, measuring, etc.

rum, *n.* an alcoholic spirit.

rumble, *v.,* **-bled, -bling.** –*v.* **1.** to make a deep, continuous, resonant sound, as thunder, etc. –*n.* **2.** *Colloq.* a fight, esp. between teenage gangs.

ruminant, *n.* any of a group of four-footed cud-chewing animals, such as cattle, sheep, deer, etc.

rumi·nate, *v.,* **-nated, -nating. 1.** to chew the cud, as a ruminant does. **2.** to meditate or muse; ponder.

rum·mage, *v.,* **-maged, -maging,** *n. –v.* **1.** to search thoroughly or actively through (a place, receptacle, etc.). **2.** to find (*out* or *up*) by searching. –*n.* **3.** miscellaneous articles; odds and ends. **4.** a rummaging search.

rummy, *n.* a card game.

rumour, *n.* **1.** a story or statement in general circulation without confirmation or certainty as to facts. –*v.* **2.** to circulate, report, or assert by a rumour.

rump, *n.* the hind part of the body of an animal.

rumple, *v.,* **-pled, -pling. 1.** to draw or

451

rumple

crush into wrinkles. 2. to become wrinkled or crumpled.

rumpus, *n. Colloq.* disturbing noise; uproar.

run, *v.*, **ran**, **run**, **running**, *n.* –*v.* 1. to move quickly on foot, so as to go more rapidly than in walking. 2. to (cause to) move easily or swiftly. 3. to make a short journey, as for a visit, etc. 4. to stand as a candidate for election. 5. to traverse a route, as a public conveyance. 6. to melt, flow, or stream, as a liquid. 7. to recur or be inherent. 8. to come undone, as knitted fabric; ladder. 9. to be or keep in operation, as a machine. 10. to exist or occur within a specified range of variation. 11. to pass into a certain state or condition; become: *to run wild*. 12. to cause (an animal, etc.) to move quickly on foot. 13. to cause (a vehicle, etc.) to move. 14. to traverse (a distance or course) in running. 15. to perform by or as by running. 16. to run or get past or through: *to run a blockade.* 17. to keep (livestock), as on pasture. 18. to convey or transport, as in a vessel or vehicle. 19. to expose oneself to or be exposed to (a risk, etc.) 20. to bring, lead, or force into some state, action, etc.: *to run oneself into debt.* 21. to conduct, as a business, experiment, etc. 22. **run down, a.** to slow up before stopping, as a clock or other mechanism. **b.** to knock down and injure, as a vehicle or driver; run over. **c.** to denigrate. **d.** to find, esp. after extensive searching. 23. **run in, a.** to operate (new machinery), esp. a motor vehicle) carefully for an initial period. **b.** *Colloq.* →**arrest.** 24. **run off, a.** to depart quickly. **b.** to produce by a printing process. **c.** to write or otherwise create quickly. 25. **run over, a.** to knock down and injure, as a vehicle or the like. **b.** to exceed (a time-limit or the like). **c.** to review, rehearse, or recapitulate. 26. **run up, a.** to amass or incur, as a bill. **b.** to make, esp. quickly, as something sewn. –*n.* 27. an act, instance, or spell of running. 28. a running pace. 29. an act or instance of escaping, running away, etc. 30. a quick, short trip. 31. the amount of something produced in any uninterrupted period of operation. 32. a place in knitted or sewn work where a series of stitches have slipped or come undone; a ladder. 33. freedom to range over, go through, or use. 34. any rapid or easy course or progress. 35. a continuous course of some condition of affairs, etc. 36. a continuous series of something. 37. any continued or extensive demand, call, or the like. 38. the ordinary or average kind. 39. an enclosure within which domestic animals may range about. 40. the area and habitual route covered by a vendor who delivers goods to houses, etc. 41. a large area of grazing land. 42. **in the long run,** ultimately. 43. **the runs,** *Colloq.* →**diarrhoea.**

rung[1], *v.* past tense and past participle of **ring**[2].

rung[2], *n.* 1. one of the rounded crosspieces forming the steps of a ladder. 2. a horizontal supporting rod, as between the legs of a chair.

runner, *n.* 1. one whose business it is to solicit patronage or trade. 2. something in or on which something else runs or moves. 3. a long, narrow strip, as of material.

runner-up, *n.* the competitor, or team finishing in 2nd place.

running

run·ning, *n.* 1. the managing or directing, as of a business, etc. 2. **in the running**, having a chance of success. –*adj.* 3. moving or passing rapidly or smoothly. 4. creeping or climbing, as plants. 5. sliding easily, as a knot or a noose. 6. operating, as a machine. 7. cursive, as handwriting. 8. going or carried on continuously. 9. following in succession: *2 days running*.

runny, *adj.* 1. (of matter) fluid or tending to flow. 2. tending to flow with or discharge liquid.

run-of-the-mill, *adj.* ordinary; mediocre; commonplace.

runt, *n.* the smallest in a litter.

runway, *n.* a paved or cleared strip on which aeroplanes land and take off.

rup·ture, *n., v.*, **-tured, -turing.** –*n.* 1. the state of being broken or burst. –*v.* 2. to break or burst (a blood vessel, etc.). 3. to cause a breach of (relations, etc.).

rural, *adj.* 1. of, pertaining to, or characteristic of the country (as distinguished from towns or cities). 2. pertaining to agriculture.

ruse, *n.* a trick, stratagem, or artifice.

rush[1], *v.* 1. to (cause to) move or go with speed or violence. 2. to perform, complete, or organise (some process or activity) with special haste. 3. to attack with a rush. –*n.* 4. the act of rushing; a rapid, impetuous, or headlong onward movement. 5. a sudden coming or access. 6. a hurried state, as from pressure of affairs. 7. a period of intense activity. 8. a great demand for a commodity, etc. (*on*). –*adj.* 9.

rye

requiring or performed with haste. 10. characterised by rush or press of work, traffic, etc.

rush[2], *n.* 1. a hollow-stemmed grasslike herb found in marshy places. 2. a stem of such a plant, used for making chair seats, baskets, etc.

rusk, *n.* a crisp biscuit, given esp. to babies when teething, and invalids.

russet, *n., adj.* light reddish or yellowish brown.

rust, *n.* 1. the red or orange coating which forms on the surface of iron when exposed to air and moisture. 2. rust colour; reddish brown or orange. –*v.* 3. to become covered with rust. 4. to deteriorate as through inaction or disuse. – **rusty**, *adj.*

rustic, *adj.* 1. rural. 2. made of rough timber, as garden seats, etc. –*n.* 3. an unsophisticated country person.

rustle, *v.*, **-tled, -tling**, *n.* –*v.* 1. to (cause to) make a succession of slight, soft sounds, as of parts rubbing gently one on another, as leaves, silks, papers, etc. 2. to steal (cattle, etc.). 3. *Colloq.* to move, bring, get, etc., by energetic action (*up*). –*n.* 4. the sound made by anything that rustles.

rut[1], *n.* 1. any furrow, groove, etc. 2. a fixed or established way of life.

rut[2], *n.* the periodically recurring sexual excitement of the deer, goat, sheep, etc.

ruth·less, *adj.* without pity or compassion; pitiless; merciless.

rye, *n.* 1. (the seed of) a widely cultivated cereal grass. 2. an American whisky distilled from rye.

Ss

S, s, *n.*, *pl.* **S's** or **Ss, s's** or **ss.** the 19th letter of the English alphabet.

Sab·bath, *n.* the day of the week reserved for rest and religious observance.

sab·bat·i·cal, *n.* (in certain universities, etc.) study and research leave for teaching staff.

sable, *n.* **1.** a weasel-like mammal. *–adj.* **2.** made of the dark brown fur of the sable.

sabo·tage, *n.*, *v.*, **-taged, -taging.** *–n.* **1.** malicious injury to work, tools, machinery, etc. **2.** any malicious attack on or undermining of a cause. *–v.* **3.** to attack by sabotage. **– saboteur,** *n.*

sabre, *n.* **1.** a heavy one-edged sword. **2.** a light sword for fencing.

sac, *n.* a baglike structure in an animal or plant.

sac·cha·rin, *n.* a very sweet crystalline compound. Also, **saccharine.**

sachet, *n.* a small sealed bag used for packaging.

sack[1], *n.* **1.** a large bag of stout woven material. **2.** *Colloq.* dismissal from employment. *–v.* **3.** *Colloq.* to dismiss from employment.

sack[2], *v.* **1.** to pillage or loot after capture. *–n.* **2.** the plundering of a captured place.

sacra·ment, *n.* an outward sign signifying something spiritual or religious.

safety

sacred, *adj.* **1.** pertaining to or connected with religion. **2.** immune from violence, interference, etc.

sacri·fice, *n.*, *v.*, **-ficed, -ficing.** *–n.* **1.** the offering of life or some material possession to a deity, as in propitiation or homage. **2.** the surrender or destruction of something prized for the sake of a benefit expected. **3.** the thing so surrendered or offered. *–v.* **4.** to make a sacrifice or offering of. **– sacrificial,** *adj.*

sacri·lege, *n.* the violation or profanation of anything held sacred. **– sacrilegious,** *adj.*

sacro·sanct, *adj.* especially sacred or inviolable.

sad, *adj.*, **sadder, saddest. 1.** sorrowful or mournful. **2.** causing sorrow.

saddle, *n.*, *v.*, **-dled, -dling.** *–n.* **1.** a seat for a rider on the back of a horse, bicycle, etc. **2.** something resembling a saddle. *–v.* **3.** to put a saddle upon (a horse, etc.). **4.** to load or charge, as with a burden.

sadism, *n.* **1.** sexual gratification gained through causing physical pain and humiliation. **2.** any morbid enjoyment in inflicting mental or physical pain. **– sadist,** *n.* **– sadistic,** *adj.*

safari, *n.*, *pl.* **-ris.** a journey; an expedition, esp. for hunting.

safe, *adj.*, **safer, safest.** *n.* *–adj.* **1.** secure from harm, injury, danger, or risk. **2.** involving no risk. *–n.* **3.** a receptacle for the storage or preservation of articles.

safe·guard, *n.* **1.** something ensuring safety. *–v.* **2.** to guard; protect.

safety, *n.*, *pl.* **-ties.** the state of being safe; freedom from danger.

saf·flower, *n.* a herb cultivated for its oil which is used in cookery, etc.

saf·fron, *n.* an orange-coloured plant product used in cooking.

sag, *v.*, **sagged**, **sagging**. –*v.* 1. to bend downwards by weight or pressure, esp. in the middle. –*n.* 2. the degree of sagging. 3. a place where anything sags.

saga, *n.* any narrative or legend of heroic exploits.

saga·cious, *adj.* having acute mental discernment and keen practical sense; shrewd. – **sagacity**, *n.*

sage[1], *n.*, *adj.*, **sager**, **sagest**. –*n.* 1. a profoundly wise man. –*adj.* 2. wise, judicious, or prudent.

sage[2], *n.* a herb used in cookery.

sago, *n.* a starchy foodstuff used in making puddings, etc.

said, *v.* 1. past tense and past participle of **say**. –*adj.* 2. named or mentioned before.

sail, *n.* 1. an expanse of canvas or similar material spread to the wind to make a vessel move through the water. 2. some similar piece or apparatus. 3. a voyage or excursion, esp. in a sailing vessel. –*v.* 4. to travel in a ship. 5. to move along like a sailing vessel. 6. to sail upon, over, or through. 7. to navigate (a ship, etc.). – **sailor**, *n.*

saint, *n.* a person of great holiness.

sake[1] /seik/, *n.* 1. cause, account, or interest. 2. purpose or end.

sake[2] /'saki/, *n.* a Japanese alcoholic drink made from rice.

sala·cious, *adj.* lustful or lecherous.

salad, *n.* a dish of uncooked vegetables or fruits.

sala·man·der, *n.* 1. any of various tailed amphibians, most of which have an aquatic larval stage but are terrestrial as adults. 2. a mythical being supposed to be able to live in fire.

salami, *n.* a kind of sausage, often flavoured with garlic.

salary, *n.*, *pl.* **-ries**. a fixed periodical payment for work. – **salaried**, *adj.*

sale, *n.* 1. the act of selling. 2. the quantity sold. 3. a special disposal of goods at reduced prices.

sali·ent, *adj.* prominent or conspicuous.

saline, *adj.* 1. containing or tasting like common table salt. –*n.* 2. a health drink or medicine.

saliva, *n.* the fluid secretions produced by glands in the mouth.

sallow, *adj.* of a yellowish, sickly hue or complexion.

sally, *v.*, **-lied**, **-lying**. to set out briskly or energetically.

salmon, *n.*, *pl.* **-mons**, *(esp. collectively)* **-mon**. 1. a marine and freshwater food fish with pink flesh. 2. a light yellowish-pink.

salon, *n.* 1. a drawing room or reception room in a large house. 2. a fashionable business establishment or shop.

saloon, *n.* a room or place for public use for a specific purpose.

salt, *n.* 1. a crystalline compound, sodium chloride, NaCl, used for seasoning food, as a preservative, etc. 2. *Chem.* a compound formed when an inorganic acid and a base react with each other. 3. wit; pungency. –*v.* 4. to season with salt. 5. to cure, preserve, or treat with salt. –*adj.* 6. containing salt.

salt·bush, *n.* any of various drought-resistant plants used as grazing plants in arid areas.

salt·cellar

salt·cellar, *n.* a shaker or vessel for salt.

salt·petre, *n.* a white salt used in making gunpowder, etc.

salu·bri·ous, *adj.* (esp. of air, climate, etc.) favourable to health.

saluki, *n.* tall slender keen-eyed hunting dog.

salu·tary, *n.* promoting some beneficial purpose.

salu·tation, *n.* something uttered, written, or done as a greeting.

salute, *v.,* **-luted, -luting.** *–n.* **1.** to address with expressions of goodwill, respect, etc; greet. **2.** *Mil., Navy.* to pay respect to or honour by some formal act, etc. *–n.* **3.** an act of saluting.

sal·vage, *n., v.,* **-vaged, -vaging.** *–n.* **1.** the saving of anything from fire, danger, etc., or the property so saved. *–v.* **2.** to save from shipwreck, fire, etc.

sal·vation, *n.* **1.** the state of being saved or delivered. **2.** a source or means of deliverance.

salve, *n., v.,* **salved, salving.** *–n.* **1.** a healing ointment. *–v.* **2.** to soothe as if with salve.

salver, *n.* a tray for drinks, letters, etc. Often made of silver.

salvo, *n., pl.* **-vos, -voes.** a discharge of artillery or other firearms.

same, *adj.* **1.** identical. **2.** being one or identical, though having different names, aspects, etc. **3.** agreeing in kind, amount, etc. **4.** unchanged in character, condition, etc. *–pron.* **5.** the same person or thing. **6. the same,** with the same manner (used adverbially).

sample, *n., adj., v.,* **-pled, -pling.** *–n.* **1.** a small part of anything or one of a number, intended to show the quality, style, etc., of the whole. *–adj.* **2.** serving as a specimen. *–v.* **3.** to take or test a sample or samples of.

sane

sana·torium, *n., pl.* **-toriums, -toria.** an establishment for the treatment of invalids, convalescents, etc.

sancti·moni·ous, *adj.* making a show of holiness.

sanc·tion, *n.* **1.** support given to an action, etc. *–v.* **2.** to authorise or allow. **3.** to ratify or confirm.

sanc·tity, *n., pl.* **-ties. 1.** holiness. **2.** sacred or hallowed character.

sanc·tuary, *n., pl.* **-ries. 1.** a sacred or holy place. **2.** (a place of) protection from something.

sand, *n.* **1.** the fine debris of rocks, consisting of small, loose grains. **2.** a dull reddish yellow colour. *–v.* **3.** to smooth or polish with sand or sandpaper.

sandal, *n.* any of various kinds of low open shoes.

sandal·wood, *n.* the fragrant inner wood of certain Asian and Aust. trees.

sand·bar, *n.* a bar of sand formed in a river or sea.

sand·paper, *v.,* *n.* (to smooth or polish with) a strong paper coated with a layer of sand.

sand·shoe, *n.* a rubber-soled canvas shoe, worn esp. for sports, etc.

sand·soap, *n.* a soap with mildly abrasive power.

sand·stone, *n.* a rock formed by the consolidation of sand.

sand·wich, *n.* **1.** 2 slices of bread with a layer of meat, cheese, etc., between. *–v.* **2.** to insert or hem in between 2 other things.

sane, *adj.,* **saner, sanest. 1.** free from mental derangement. **2.** having or

456

sane

showing reason, sound judgment, or good sense. – **sanity**, n.

sang, v. past tense of **sing**.

san·guine, adj. hopeful or confident.

sani·tary, adj. 1. of or pertaining to health. 2. free from dirt, germs, etc.

sani·tation, n. (the protection of public health, esp. by) drainage systems.

sank, v. past tense of **sink**.

sap[1], n. 1. the vital circulating fluid of a woody plant. 2. *Colloq.* a fool or weak person.

sap[2], v., **sapped**, **sapping**. to undermine; weaken or destroy insidiously.

sap·ling, n. a young tree.

sapph·ire, n. 1. a transparent blue gemstone. 2. a deep blue. –adj. 3. deep blue.

sar·casm, n. harsh or bitter derision or irony. – **sarcastic**, adj.

sar·coma, n., pl. -**mata**. a malignant tumour attacking esp. the bones.

sar·cophagus, n., pl. -**gi**, -**guses**. a stone coffin.

sar·dine, n., pl. -**dines**, (esp. collectively) -**dine**. the young of the common pilchard, often preserved in oil and canned for food.

sar·donic, adj. bitterly ironical; sneering.

sari, n., pl. -**ris**. a long piece of cotton or silk, the principal outer garment of Hindu women.

sarong, n. the piece of cloth worn like a skirt as the main garment by both sexes in the Malay Archipelago.

sarsa·pa·rilla, n. 1. a climbing plant having a root used medicinally. 2. an extract made of it.

satyr

sar·torial, adj. of or pertaining to clothes or dress, generally men's.

sash[1], n. a long band or scarf of silk, etc.

sash[2], n. a movable framework in which panes of glass are set, as in a window.

sassa·fras, n. any of several Aust. trees with fragrant bark.

sat, v. past tense of **sit**.

satanic, adj. characterised by evil; extremely wicked. Also, **satanical**.

satchel, n. a bag with a shoulder-strap, used for carrying schoolbooks.

sate, v., **sated**, **sating**. to satisfy (any appetite or desire) to the full.

satel·lite, n. 1. a small body which revolves round a planet. 2. a man-made device for launching into orbit round the earth, etc.

sati·ate /ˈseɪʃieɪt/, v., -**ated**, -**ating**. to supply with anything to excess. – **satiety**, n.

satin, n. 1. a very smooth, glossy fabric. –adj. 2. smooth; glossy.

satire, n. the use of irony, sarcasm, ridicule, etc., in exposing vice, folly, etc. – **satirical**, **satiric**, adj.

sati·rise, v., -**rised**, -**rising**. to make the object of satire.

satis·fac·tion, n. 1. the state of being satisfied. 2. something that satisfies. 3. payment, as for debt. – **satisfactory**, adj.

sat·isfy, v., -**fied**, -**fying**. 1. to fulfil (the desires, expectations, etc.) of. 2. to discharge fully (a debt, etc.).

satu·rate, v., -**rated**, -**rating**. to soak, or imbue thoroughly.

satur·nine, adj. gloomy; taciturn.

satyr /ˈsætə, ˈseɪtə/, n. 1. in classical

457

satyr

mythology, a god, part human and part goat. 2. a lascivious man.

sauce, *n.* any preparation, usu. liquid or soft, eaten as an accompaniment to food.

sauce·pan, *n.* a container for boiling, stewing, etc.

saucer, *n.* a small, round, shallow dish to hold a cup.

saucy, *adj.*, **-cier**, **-ciest**. *Colloq.* 1. impertinent. 2. pert.

sauer·kraut, *n.* cabbage cut fine, salted, and allowed to ferment.

sauna, *n.* (a room or device for taking) a type of steam bath.

saun·ter, *v.* 1. to walk with a leisurely gait. –*n.* 2. a leisurely walk or ramble.

saus·age, *n.* minced meats packed into a special skin.

sauté /'souteɪ/, *v.*, **-téed**, **-téeing**. to cook in a small amount of fat.

sau·terne /sou'tɜːn, sə-/, *n.* a rich, sweet, white, table wine.

savage, *adj.*, *n.*, *v.*, **savaged, savaging**. –*adj.* 1. uncivilised; barbarous. 2. fierce or cruel. –*n.* 3. an uncivilised human being. –*v.* 4. to assail violently; maul. – **savagery**, *n.*

save[1], *v.*, **saved, saving**, *n.* –*v.* 1. to rescue from danger. 2. to avoid the spending, consumption, or waste of. 3. to set apart or reserve. 4. to prevent the occurrence, use, or necessity of. 5. to accumulate or put aside (money, etc.) as the result of economy. –*n.* 6. the act or instance of saving, esp. preventing a goal being scored in soccer, etc.

save[2], *prep.*, *conj.* except; but.

sav·eloy, *n.* frankfurt.

saving, *adj.* 1. that saves; rescuing; preserving. 2. redeeming. –*n.* 3. a reduction or lessening of expenditure. 4. (*pl.*) sums of money saved by economy. –*prep.* 5. except.

saviour, *n.* one who saves, rescues, or delivers.

savour, *n.* 1. a particular taste or smell. 2. distinctive quality or property. –*v.* 3. to perceive by taste or smell, esp. with relish. 4. to give oneself to the enjoyment of.

sav·oury, *adj.*, *n.*, *pl.* **-vouries**. –*adj.* 1. piquant, pungent, or salty to the taste. –*n.* 2. a usu. salty, bite-sized morsel on a small biscuit.

savvy, *v.*, **-vied, -vying**. *Colloq.* to know; understand.

saw[1], *n.*, *v.*, **sawed, sawn** or **sawed, sawing**. –*n.* 1. a tool or device for cutting, typically a thin serrated metal blade. –*v.* 2. to cut with a saw.

saw[2], *v.* past tense of **see**[1].

saxo·phone, *n.* a musical brass wind instrument.

say, *v.*, **said, saying**. –*v.* 1. to utter or pronounce. 2. to express in words. 3. to assume as a hypothesis or an estimate. 4. to declare; express an opinion. –*v.* 5. *Colloq.* the right or opportunity to say, speak or decide.

saying, *n.* something said, esp. a proverb.

scab, *n.*, *v.*, **scabbed, scabbing**. –*n.* 1. the crust which forms over a sore during healing. 2. one who continues to work during a strike. –*v.* 3. to act or work as a scab.

scab·bard, *n.* a sheath or cover for the blade of a sword, dagger, etc.

sca·bies, *n.* an infectious skin disease occurring in animals or man, caused by parasitic mites.

scaf·fold, *n.* a raised framework or platform.

scald, v. 1. to burn or affect painfully with hot liquid or steam. –n. 2. a burn caused by hot liquid or steam.

scale[1], n., v., **scaled, scaling**. –n. 1. one of the thin, flat, horny or hard plates that form the covering of certain animals, as fishes. 2. any thin piece such as peels off from a surface. –v. 3. to remove the scale(s) from.

scale[2], n. (usu. pl.) a device for weighing; balance.

scale[3], n., v., **scaled, scaling**. –n. 1. a succession of steps or degrees. 2. a graduated line, as on a map, representing proportionate size. 3. an instrument with graduated spaces, for measuring, etc. 4. the proportion which the representation of an object bears to the object. 5. *Music*. a succession of notes ascending or descending according to fixed intervals. –v. 6. to climb (as) by a ladder; climb up or over. 7. to reduce in amount according to a fixed scale or proportion (*down*).

scal·lop, n. 1. a bivalve mollusc with fluted shells. 2. one of a series of rounded projections along the edge of pastry, a garment, etc. 3. potato dipped in batter and fried. –v. 4. to finish (an edge) with scallops.

scally·wag, n. (*oft. used indulgently of children*) a scamp; rascal.

scalp, n. 1. the skin of the upper part of the head. –v. 2. to cut or tear the scalp from.

scal·pel, n. a light knife used in surgery.

scamp, n. a mischievous child.

scam·per, v. to run or go quickly and playfully.

scan, v., **scanned, scanning**, n. –v. 1. to glance at or run through hastily. 2. *Radar*. to sweep a region with a beam from a radar transmitter. 3. (of verse) to conform to the rules of metre. –n. 4. close examination or scrutiny.

scan·dal, n. 1. a disgraceful or discreditable action, circumstance, etc. 2. damage to reputation. 3. malicious gossip.

scan·da·lise, v., **-lised, -lising**. to shock or horrify by something considered immoral or improper.

scant, *adj*. 1. barely sufficient. 2. barely amounting to as much as indicated.

scape·goat, n. one who is made to bear the blame for others.

scap·ula, n., pl. **-lae**. the flat bone in each shoulder.

scar, n., v., **scarred, scarring**. –n. 1. the mark left by a healed wound. –v. 2. to mark with a scar.

scar·ab, n. a type of beetle.

scarce, *adj*., **scarcer, scarcest**. seldom met with; not plentiful.

scarce·ly, *adv*. barely; hardly.

scare, v., **scared, scaring**. –v. 1. to strike with sudden fear. 2. to become frightened. –n. 3. a sudden fright or alarm.

scare·crow, n. a figure of a man set up to frighten birds away from crops.

scarf, n., pl. **scarfs, scarves**. a long, broad strip of fabric worn about the neck, shoulders, or head for ornament or protection.

scar·ify, v., **-fied, -fying**. to make scratches or superficial incisions in.

scar·let, *adj*., n. (of a) bright red colour inclining towards orange.

scarlet fever, *n.* a contagious disease, now chiefly of children.

scat, *v.*, **scatted**, **scatting**. *Colloq.* to go off hastily (usu. in the imperative).

scath·ing, *adj.* intended to hurt the feelings.

scat·ter, *v.* 1. to throw loosely about. 2. to separate and drive off in various directions. 3. to go in different directions. –*n.* 4. the act of scattering. 5. something scattered.

scav·enge, *v.*, **-enged**, **-enging**. to search for, and take (anything useable) from discarded material.

scen·ario, *n., pl.* **-narios**. an outline of the plot of a dramatic work.

scene, *n.* 1. the place where any action, real or fictional, occurs. 2. any view or picture. 3. an exhibition or outbreak of excited or violent feeling before others. 4. a unit of dramatic action within a play. 5. an episode or situation as described in writing.

scen·ery, *n., pl.* **-neries**. 1. the general appearance of a place. 2. the setting on a stage to represent some place.

scenic, *adj.* of or pertaining to natural scenery; having fine scenery.

scent, *n.* 1. distinctive smell, esp. when agreeable. 2. a track or trail as indicated by such a smell. 3. →**perfume**. –*v.* 4. to perceive or recognise by the sense of smell. 5. to sprinkle with perfume.

scep·tic, *n.* one who has a doubting, pessimistic attitude towards people, plans, ideas, etc. – **sceptical**, *adj.*

scep·tre, *n.* a rod or wand carried as an emblem of royal power.

sched·ule, *n., v.*, **-uled**, **-uling**. –*n.* 1. a plan of procedure. 2. a list of items to be dealt with during a specified time. 3. a timetable. –*v.* 4. to enter in a schedule. 5. to plan for a certain date.

scheme, *n., v.*, **schemed**, **scheming**. –*n.* 1. a plan or design. 2. a policy or plan officially adopted by a company, business, etc. 3. an underhand plot; intrigue. 4. any system of correlated things, parts, etc., or the manner of its arrangement. –*v.* 5. to plan. 6. to plot; intrigue.

schism, *n.* division into mutually opposed parties.

schizo·phrenia, *n.* a severe mental illness.

schnap·per, *n.* →**snapper**.

schnapps, *n.* a type of gin.

scholar, *n.* 1. a learned or erudite person. 2. a student; pupil.

scholar·ship, *n.* 1. knowledge acquired by study. 2. the sum of money or other aid granted to a scholar.

schol·as·tic, *adj.* of or pertaining to schools, scholars, or education.

school[1], *n.* 1. a place or establishment where instruction is given, esp. one for children. 2. a department or faculty in a university, etc. 3. a body of scholars, artists, writers, etc., united by a similarity of method, style, principles, etc. –*v.* 4. to educate in or as in a school.

school[2], *n.* a large number of fish, porpoises, whales, etc., swimming together.

schoon·er, *n.* 1. a sailing vessel. 2. a beer glass.

sci·atica, *n.* any painful disorder extending from the hip down the back of the thigh and surrounding area.

science

science, *n.* 1. systematised knowledge in general. 2. the systematic study of man and the physical world.

science fiction, *n.* a form of fiction which draws imaginatively on scientific speculation.

scien·tific, *adj.* 1. of or pertaining to science or the sciences. 2. systematic or accurate.

scien·tist, *n.* one versed in or devoted to science.

scin·til·late, *v.*, -lated, -lating. 1. to twinkle, as the stars. 2. to be witty, brilliant in conversation.

scion /ˈsaɪən/, *n.* a descendant.

scis·sors, *n.pl. or sing.* a cutting instrument with 2 blades whose edges work against each other.

scoff[1], *v.* to jeer (*at*).

scoff[2], *v. Colloq.* to eat greedily and quickly.

scold, *v.* 1. to find fault (with). *—n.* 2. a person, esp. a woman, addicted to abusive speech.

scone, *n.* 1. a small light plain cake. 2. *Colloq.* the head.

scoop, *n.* 1. a ladle or similar utensil. 2. an item of news, etc., published or broadcast in advance of, or to the exclusion of, rivals. *—v.* 3. to take up or out with, or as with a scoop.

scoot, *v. Colloq.* to go swiftly or hastily.

scooter, *n.* a child's vehicle with 2 wheels.

scope, *n.* 1. extent or range of view, operation, etc. 2. space for movement or activity.

scorch, *v.* 1. to affect in colour, taste, etc., by burning slightly. 2. to parch or shrivel with heat. 3. to be or become scorched.

scraggy

score, *n., v.*, scored, scoring. *—n.* 1. the record of points made by the competitors in a game or match. 2. a notch or scratch. 3. a group or set of 20. 4. account, reason, or ground. 5. *Music.* a written or printed piece of music. *—v.* 6. to make a score of. 7. to make notches, cuts, or lines in or on. 8. to make a point or points in a game or contest. 9. to keep score, as of a game.

scorn, *n.* 1. open or unqualified contempt. *—v.* 2. to treat or regard with scorn.

scor·pion, *n.* any of numerous arachnids having a long narrow tail with a venomous sting.

scotch, *v.* to injure so as to make harmless.

scot-free, *adj.* free from penalty.

scoun·drel, *n.* an unprincipled, dishonourable man.

scour[1], *v., n.* to (cleanse or polish by) a hard rubbing.

scour[2], *v.* to range over, as in search.

scourge, *n., v.*, scourged, scourging. *—n.* 1. a cause of affliction or calamity. *—v.* 2. to punish or chastise severely; afflict.

scout, *n.* 1. a person sent out to obtain information. *—v.* 2. *Colloq.* to seek; search (for) (*out* or *round*).

scowl, *v.* 1. to have a gloomy or threatening look. *—n.* 2. a scowling expression.

scrab·ble, *v.*, -bled, -bling, *n.* *—v.* 1. to scratch or scrape, as with the claws or hands. *—n.* 2. a scrabbling or scramble.

scrag·gly, *adj.*, -glier, -gliest. irregular; ragged; straggling.

scraggy, *adj.*, -gier, -giest. 1. lean or thin. 2. meagre.

461

scram

scram, *v.*, **scrammed, scramming.** *Colloq.* to get away quickly.

scram·ble, *v.*, **-bled, -bling.** *–v.* 1. to make one's way hurriedly by use of the hands and feet (*over*). 2. to struggle with others for possession. 3. to mix together confusedly. *–n.* 4. a climb or progression over rough, irregular ground, etc. 5. any disorderly struggle or proceeding.

scrap[1], *n., adj., v.*, **scrapped, scrapping.** *–n.* 1. a small piece. *–adj.* 2. consisting of scraps. 3. discarded or left over. *–v.* 4. to discard as useless.

scrap[2], *n. Colloq.* a fight or quarrel.

scrape, *v.*, **scraped, scraping**, *n. –v.* 1. to free from an outer layer by rubbing with a sharp instrument. 2. to remove (an outer layer, adhering matter, etc.) in this way. 3. to rub harshly on or across (something). 4. to collect by or as by scraping, or laboriously (*up* or *together*). 5. to practise laborious economy. *–n.* 6. a scraped place. 7. an embarrassing situation.

scratch, *v.* 1. to dig, scrape, or to tear (*out, off*, etc.) with the claws, the nails, etc. 2. to rub or scrape lightly with the fingernails, etc. 3. to erase or strike (*out*). 4. to use the nails, claws, etc., for tearing, digging, etc. 5. to relieve itching by scratching. 6. to make a slight grating noise. *–n.* 7. a mark produced by scratching. 8. an act of scratching. 9. **from scratch**, from the beginning. 10. **up to scratch**, satisfactory.

scrawl, *v.* 1. to write or draw in a sprawling awkward manner. *–n.* 2. awkward or careless handwriting.

scrawny, *adj.*, **-nier, -niest.** lean; thin; scraggy.

scream, *v.* 1. to utter a loud, sharp,

scripture

piercing cry. *–n.* 2. a loud, sharp, piercing cry or sound. 3. *Colloq.* someone or something very funny.

screech, *v., n.* (to utter) a harsh, shrill cry.

screed, *n.* long speech or piece of writing.

screen, *n.* 1. a covered frame serving as a shelter, partition, etc. 2. a surface for displaying films, slides, etc. 3. films collectively. 4. anything that shelters, protects, or conceals. *–v.* 5. to shelter, protect, or conceal with a screen. 6. to project (pictures, etc.) on a screen.

screw, *n.* 1. a metal nail-like device with a slotted head and a spiral ridge. 2. to force, press, etc., by or as by means of a screw. 3. to twist; contort. 4. to force. 5. to turn as or like a screw. 6. to be adapted for being connected or taken apart by means of a screw or screws (*on, together, off*, etc.).

screw·driv·er, *n.* a tool for driving in or withdrawing screws.

scrib·ble, *v.*, **-bled, -bling.** *–v.* 1. to write hastily or carelessly. 2. to make meaningless marks. *–n.* 3. a hasty or careless piece of writing or drawing.

scribe, *n.* a penman or copyist who, formerly, made copies of manuscripts, etc.

scrimp, *v.* to be sparing of or in; stint.

scrip, *n.* 1. a writing, esp. a receipt or certificate. 2. *Finance.* shares or stock issued to shareholders.

script, *n.* the working text of a play, film, etc.

scrip·ture, *n.* any writing or book, of a sacred nature, esp. (*cap.*) the Bible.

scroll

scroll, *n.* **1.** a roll of parchment or paper. **2.** an ornament with a spiral or coiled form.

scrooge, *n.* a miserly, ill-tempered person.

scrotum, *n., pl.* **-ta.** the pouch of skin that contains the testicles.

scrounge, *v.*, **scrounged, scrounging.** to obtain by borrowing, foraging, or pilfering.

scrub[1], *v.*, **scrubbed, scrubbing**, *n.* –*v.* **1.** to wash by rubbing hard with a brush, cloth, etc. **2.** *Colloq.* to cancel; get rid of. –*n.* **3.** the act of scrubbing.

scrub[2], *n.* **1.** low trees or shrubs, collectively. **2.** tall, thick rainforest in eastn Aust.

scruff, *n.* the nape or back of the neck.

scruffy, *adj. Colloq.* unkempt or dirty.

scrum, *n. Rugby Football* a formation for restarting play after a rule has been broken.

scrumptious, *adj. Colloq.* deliciously tasty.

scrupulous, *adj.* minutely careful, precise, or exact.

scrutineer, *n.* one who is authorised to inspect the counting of votes.

scrutinise, *v.*, **-nised, -nising.** to examine closely or critically. – **scrutiny**, *n.*

scuba, *n.* a portable breathing device for divers.

scud, *v.*, **scudded, scudding.** to run or move quickly or hurriedly.

scuff, *v.* **1.** to mar by scraping or hard use. –*n.* **2.** a type of slipper or sandal without a back.

scuffle, *v.*, **-fled, -fling,** *n.* –*v.* **1.** to struggle or fight in a confused manner. –*n.* **2.** a confused struggle or fight.

scullery, *n., pl.* **-leries.** a small room where the rough, dirty work of a kitchen is done.

sculpture, *n.*, *v.*, **-tured, -turing.** –*n.* **1.** the fine art of making three-dimensional figures or designs. **2.** a piece of such work. –*v.* **3.** to carve or make by sculpture. – **sculptor**, *n.*

scum, *n.* a film of foul or extraneous matter on a liquid.

scurrilous, *adj.* grossly or indecently abusive.

scurry, *v.*, **-ried, -rying,** *n., pl.* **-ries.** –*v.* **1.** to go or move quickly. –*n.* **2.** a quick movement.

scurvy, *n., adj.*, **-vier, -viest.** –*n.* **1.** a disease caused by lack of vitamin C. –*adj.* **2.** low, mean, or contemptible.

scuttle, *n.*, *v.*, **-tled, -tling,** *n.* –*v.* **1.** to run with quick, hasty steps (*off, away,* etc.). –*n.* **2.** a short, hurried run.

scythe, *n.* an agricultural implement for mowing grass, etc., by hand.

sea, *n.* **1.** the salt waters that cover the greater part of the earth's surface. **2.** a division of these waters. **3.** a large lake. **4.** a huge quantity or expanse. **5. at sea,** in a state of perplexity.

seafood, *n.* any saltwater fish or shellfish used for food.

seagull, *n.* a web-footed marine bird.

seahorse, *n.* a type of small fish with a prehensile tail and a head at right angles to the body.

seal[1], *n.* **1.** a device affixed to a document as evidence of authenticity or attestation. **2.** anything that

seal

effectively closes a thing. 3. a road surface of hard material. –v. 4. to approve, authorise, or confirm. 5. to close by any form of fastening that must be broken to open it. 6. to surface a road with tar, bitumen, etc.

seal², n., pl. **seals**, (esp. collectively) **seal**. any of several furred, amphibious mammals with flippers for limbs.

seam, n. 1. the line formed by sewing together pieces of cloth. 2. any line between abutting edges; a crack or fissure. –v. 3. to join with a seam. 4. to furrow; mark with wrinkles. 5. to become cracked, fissured, or furrowed.

seam·stress, n. a woman whose occupation is sewing. Also, **sempstress**.

seamy, adj., -mier, -miest. bad; sordid.

seance, n. a meeting of people seeking to make contact with spirits.

sear, v. to burn or char the surface of.

search, v. 1. to go or look carefully to find something. 2. to examine (a person) for concealed objects. 3. to bring or find (out) by a search. 4. to seek. –n. 5. the act of searching.

sea·sick·ness, n. nausea caused by the motion of a vessel at sea.

season, n. 1. a period of the year characterised by particular conditions of weather, etc. 2. the period of the year when something is past or available. 3. any period or time. 4. Agric. the time for mating in female stock. –v. 5. to heighten or improve the flavour of (food) with condiments, etc. 6. to dry and harden (timber). 7. to become seasoned, matured, hardened.

season·able, adj. 1. suitable to the season. 2. timely; opportune.

seas·onal, adj. periodical.

season·ing, n. 1. something that seasons, esp. salt, spices, herbs, or other condiments. 2. a savoury filling for poultry, etc.; stuffing.

seat, n. 1. something for sitting on, as a chair or bench. 2. the buttocks. 3. manner of sitting, as on horseback. 4. an established place or centre, as of government. 5. a parliamentary constituency. –v. 6. to place on a seat or seats. 7. to find seats for.

seat belt, n. a belt attached to the frame of a motor vehicle to hold the driver, passenger securely in the seat. Also, **safety belt**.

sea·weed, n. any plant or plants growing in the ocean.

seb·aceous, adj. 1. fatty; greasy. 2. secreting a fatty substance.

secant, Maths. n. a straight line which cuts a circle or other curve.

seca·teurs, n.pl. a scissor-like cutting instrument for pruning shrubs, etc.

secede, v., -ceded, -ceding. to withdraw formally from an alliance or association. – **secession**, n.

seclude, v., -cluded, -cluding. to shut off or keep apart; withdraw into solitude. – **seclusion**, n.

second

second¹ /'sɛkənd/, adj. 1. next after the first in order, quality, etc.; the ordinal of 2. alternate: *every second day*. 3. additional; a second chance. –n. 4. that which comes after the first, in order, etc. 5. (sometimes pl.) Comm. a product that is below the normal or

464

second

required standard. –v. **6.** to support, back up, or assist. –adv. **7.** in the second place, group, etc.

second² /'sɛkənd/, n. **1.** a 60th part of a minute of time. **2.** *Geom.*, *etc.* the 60th part of a minute of a degree. **3.** a moment or instant.

second³ /sə'kɒnd/, v. to transfer (someone) temporarily to another post or organisation.

secon·dary, adj. **1.** next after the first in order, place, time, importance, etc. **2.** derived; not primary or original. **3.** of or pertaining to the processing of primary products. **4.** of minor importance; subordinate.

second cousin, n. See cousin.

second-hand, adv., adj. (after having been) previously used or owned.

secret, adj. **1.** done or made without the knowledge of others. –n. **2.** something secret or hidden. – **secretive**, adj.

secre·tariat, n. the officials or office entrusted with maintaining records, etc., esp. for an international organisation.

secre·tary, n., pl. **-taries**. a person who conducts correspondence, keeps records, etc., for an individual or an organisation.

secrete, v., **-creted, -creting. 1.** *Biol.* to separate off or convert from the blood, as in the physiological process of secretion. **2.** to hide or conceal. – **secretion**, n.

secret service, n. **1.** a government department concerned with security. **2.** espionage.

sect, n. a body of persons adhering to a particular religious faith.

sec·tion, n. **1.** one of a number of parts that fit together to make a whole. **2.** the act of cutting; separation by cutting. **3.** a representation of an object as it would appear if cut across.

sector, n. any field or division of a field of activity.

secu·lar, adj. of or pertaining to the world, or to things not religious; temporal.

secure, adj., v., **-cured, -curing.** –adj. **1.** free from or not exposed to danger. **2.** not liable to fall, yield, become displaced, etc. **3.** free from care or anxiety. **4.** sure. –v. **5.** to get hold or possession of. **6.** to make secure or certain. **7.** to assure a creditor of (payment) by a pledge or mortgage.

sedan, n. a four-door passenger car. Also, **saloon car**.

sedate, adj., v., **-dated, -dating.** –adj. **1.** calm, quiet, or composed. –v. **2.** to calm or put to sleep by means of sedatives.

seda·tive, adj. **1.** tending to calm or soothe. –n. **2.** a sedative agent or remedy.

seden·tary /'sɛdəntri/, adj. characterised by or requiring a sitting posture.

sedi·ment, n. matter which settles to the bottom of a liquid.

sedi·tion, n. incitement of rebellion against the government.

seduce, v., **-duced, -ducing. 1.** to induce to have sexual intercourse. **2.** to win over; entice. – **seduction**, n. – **seductive**, adj.

see¹, v., **saw, seen, seeing. 1.** to observe or be aware of. **2.** to perceive or be aware of with any or all of the senses. **3.** to view, or visit or attend as a spectator. **4.** to discern with the intelligence. **5.** to find out, or learn, as by enquiry. **6.** to visit. **7.** to accompany or escort. **8.** to ensure. **9.** to have or use the power of sight. **10.** to enquire or find out. **11.** to give attention or care.

see[2], *n.* the centre of jurisdiction of a bishop.

seed, *n., pl.* **seeds, seed,** *v.* –*n.* **1.** the part of a plant that propagates, including ovules, tubers, bulbs, etc. **2.** (*usu. pl.*) the germ or beginning of anything. **3.** *Sport.* a player who has been seeded. –*v.* **4.** to sow (land) with seed. **5.** *Sport.* to distribute certain outstanding players so that they will not meet in the early rounds of play: *Jones is seeded number 3 this year.* **6.** to produce or shed seed.

seed·ling, *n.* a young plant developed after germination of a seed.

seedy, *adj.,* **-dier, -diest.** rather disreputable or shabby.

seek, *v.,* **sought, seeking. 1.** to go in search of. **2.** to try or attempt (fol. by an infinitive): *He seeks to please.* **3.** to ask for.

seem, *v.* to appear or look to be; appear (to be, feel, do, etc.).

seemly, *adj.,* **-lier, -liest** fitting or becoming with respect to propriety or good taste.

seep, *v.* to pass gradually, as liquid, through a porous substance.

seer, *n.* one who foretells future events; prophet.

seesaw, *n.* **1.** a plank or beam balanced at the middle so that its ends may rise and fall alternately. –*v.* **2.** to move up and down or back and forth.

seethe, *v.,* **seethed, seething.** to surge or foam, as a boiling liquid.

seg·ment, *n.* **1.** one of the parts into which anything naturally separates or is naturally divided. –*v.* **2.** to separate or divide into segments.

segre·gate, *v.* to separate, or set or go apart from the others or from the main body.

seis·mic /ˈsaɪzmɪk/, *adj.* pertaining to an earthquake. Also, **seismal, seismical.**

seize, *v.,* **seized, seizing. 1.** to lay hold of suddenly or forcibly. **2.** to take possession of by legal authority. **3.** to take advantage of promptly. **4.** to become jammed, as an engine through excessive heat (*up*).

sei·zure, *n.* **1.** the act of seizing. **2.** a sudden attack, as of disease.

seldom, *adv.* not often; rarely.

select, *v.* **1.** to choose in preference to another or others. –*adj.* **2.** specially chosen; excellent.

selec·tion, *n.* **1.** the act of selecting or the fact of being selected. **2.** a thing or a number of things selected. **3.** a range of things from which selection may be made.

self, *n., pron., pl.* **selves.** –*n.* **1.** a person or thing referred to with respect to individuality; one's own person. –*pron.* **2.** myself, himself, etc.

self-conscious, *adj.* excessively conscious of oneself as observed by others.

self-evident, *adj.* evident in itself without proof.

self-government, *n.* political independence of a country, people, region, etc.

self-interest

self-interest, *n.* excessive regard for one's own interest or advantage.

selfish, *adj.* devoted to or caring only for oneself.

self-opinionated, *adj.* obstinate in one's own opinion.

self-possessed, *adj.* having or showing control of one's feelings, behaviour, etc.

self-raising flour, *n.* wheat flour with baking powder already added.

self·same, *adj.* (the) very same; identical.

self-seeking, *adj.* selfish.

self-service, *adj.* of or pertaining to a restaurant, lift, etc., in which the customers, etc., serve themselves. Also, **self-serve**.

sell, *v.*, **sold, selling**, *n.* –*v.* **1.** to dispose of to a purchaser for a price. **2.** to deal in. **3.** to be on sale; find purchasers. **4. sell out**, **a.** to sell all of. *Colloq.* to betray. **5. sell up**, to liquidate by selling the assets (of). –*n.* **6.** *Colloq.* an act of selling or salesmanship.

sel·vedge, *n.* the edge of woven fabric finished to prevent fraying. Also, **selvage**.

seman·tic, *adj.* pertaining to meaning. – **semantics**, *n.*

sema·phore, *n.* a system of signalling by hand-held flags.

sem·blance, *n.* an outward aspect or appearance.

semen, *n.* the impregnating fluid produced by male reproductive organs.

sem·ester, *n.* (in educational institutions) one of 2 divisions of the academic year. See **term**.

semi·colon, *n.* a mark of punctuation (;) used to indicate a more distinct separation between parts of a sentence than that indicated by a comma.

sensation

semi-detached, *adj.* of or pertaining to a pair of houses joined by a common wall but detached from other buildings.

sem·inal, *adj.* **1.** pertaining to semen. **2.** highly original and influential.

sem·inar, *n.* a meeting organised to discuss a specific topic.

semi·nary, *n.*, *pl.* **-naries**. *Rom. Cath. Ch.* a college for the training of priests.

semi·tone, *n. Music.* the smallest interval in the chromatic scale of Western music.

semi-trailer, *n.* an articulated goods vehicle.

semo·lina, *n.* the large, hard parts of wheat grains used for making puddings, etc.

sen·ate, *n.* **1.** a legislative assembly. **2.** a governing or disciplinary body, as in certain universities. – **senator**, *n.*

send, *v.*, **sent, sending. 1.** to cause to go. **2.** to cause (a message, messenger) to be conveyed or transmitted to a destination. **3.** to give (*forth, out,* etc.), as light, smell, or sound. **4. send up**, *Colloq.* to mock or ridicule.

senile, *adj.* mentally or physically infirm due to old age.

senior, *adj.* **1.** older or elder. **2.** of higher rank or standing. –*n.* **3.** a person who is older than another. – **seniority**, *n.*

sen·sation, *n.* **1.** the operation or function of the senses; perception through the senses. **2.** a (cause of) state of excited feeling or interest.

467

sense

sense, *n., v.,* **sensed, sensing.** –*n.* **1.** each of the special faculties connected with bodily organs, commonly reckoned as sight, hearing, smell, taste, and touch. **2.** a feeling or perception produced through these organs. **3.** any more or less vague perception or impression. **4.** sound practical intelligence. **5.** what is sensible or reasonable. **6.** the meaning of a word, statement, etc. **7. in a sense,** according to one interpretation. –*v.* **8.** to perceive by or as by the senses.

sen·si·bil·i·ty, *n., pl.* **-ties. 1.** mental susceptibility or responsiveness. **2.** (*pl.*) emotional capacities.

sen·si·ble, *adj.* **1.** having, using, or showing good sense. **2.** keenly aware (*of*).

sen·si·tive, *adj.* **1.** readily affected by external agencies or influences. **2.** easily affected, pained, annoyed, etc. **3.** (of an issue, topic, etc.) arousing strong feelings.

sensor, *n.* a device which detects a variable quantity and converts it into a signal.

sen·sory, *adj.* pertaining to sensation.

sen·sual, *adj.* pertaining to or given to the gratification of the senses or the indulgence of appetite.

sen·su·ous, *adj.* readily affected through the senses.

sent, *v.* past tense and past participle of **send.**

sen·tence, *n., v.,* **-tenced, -tencing.** –*n.* **1.** a word or a sequence of words expressing an independent statement, inquiry, command, as, *Fire!* or *Summer is here* or *Who's there?* **2.** *Law.* **a.** the judicial determination of the punishment to be inflicted on a convicted criminal. **b.** the punishment itself. –*v.* **3.** to pronounce sentence upon.

septum

sen·ten·tious, *adj.* moralising or given to using maxims.

senti·ent, *adj.* having the power of sense perception.

senti·ment, *n.* **1.** mental attitude with regard to something; opinion. **2.** refined or tender emotion. **3.** the thought or feeling intended to be conveyed by words.

senti·men·tal, *adj.* **1.** pertaining to or dependent on sentiment. **2.** weakly emotional.

senti·nel, *n.* a person on watch.

sentry, *n., pl.* **-tries.** a soldier stationed at a place to keep guard.

sepa·rate, *v.,* **-rated, -rating,** *adj.* –*v.* **1.** to keep apart or divide. **2.** to part or divide (an assemblage, mass, compound, etc.) into individuals, components, or elements. **3.** to take (*from* or *out*) by such parting or dividing. **4.** to part company (*from*). **5.** to become disconnected or disengaged. **6.** to become parted from a mass or compound. –*adj.* **7.** separated, disconnected, or disjoined. **8.** unconnected or distinct.

sepia, *n.* **1.** a brown pigment. **2.** *Photog.* a brown-coloured image. –*adj.* **3.** brown.

sepsis, *n.* bacterial invasion of the body.

septic, *adj.* infected.

septi·cae·mia, *n.* a bacterial invasion of the bloodstream.

septic tank, *n.* a tank in which solid organic sewage is decomposed and purified by anaerobic bacteria.

septum, *n., pl.* **septa.** *Biol.* a dividing wall, membrane, or the like in a plant or animal structure.

sepul·chre, *n.* a tomb, grave, or burial place.

sequel, *n.* 1. a literary work, film, etc., continuing a preceding work. 2. an event or circumstance following something.

se·quence, *n.* 1. the following of one thing after another. 2. order of succession. 3. a continuous or connected series. – **sequential**, *adj.*

seques·ter, *v.* to remove or withdraw into solitude or retirement.

sequin, *n.* a small shining disc or spangle used to ornament a dress, etc.

seren·ade, *n., v.,* -naded, -nading. –*n.* 1. a song sung in the open air at night, usu. by a lover to his lady. –*v.* 2. to entertain with a serenade.

serene, *adj.* calm; peaceful; tranquil. – **serenity**, *n.*

serf, *n. Hist.* a person required to render services to his lord.

serge, *n.* cotton, rayon, wool, or silk in a twill weave.

serial, *n.* 1. anything published, broadcast, etc., in regular instalments. –*adj.* 2. published in instalments. 3. of, pertaining to, or arranged in a series.

serial number, *n.* an individual number given for identification.

series, *n., pl.* -ries. a number of things, events, etc., ranged or occurring in succession; sequence.

seri·ous, *adj.* 1. of thoughtful or solemn disposition or character. 2. being in earnest. 3. weighty or important.

sermon, *n.* 1. a talk for the purpose of religious instruction, usu. delivered from a pulpit. 2. a long, tedious speech.

ser·pent, *n.* a snake. – **serpentine**, *adj.*

ser·rated, *adj.* having a notched or grooved edge.

serum, *n., pl.* **sera, serums.** the clear, pale yellow liquid forming the basis of blood.

ser·vant, *n.* a person in the paid service of another.

serve, *v.,* **served, serving,** *n.* –*v.* 1. to act as a servant. 2. to hand food to (guests). 3. to render assistance (to). 4. *Tennis, etc.* to put the ball in play. 5. to work for. 6. to go through (a term of service, imprisonment, etc.). 7. to answer the requirements of; suffice. 8. to wait upon. 9. (of a male animal) to mate with. 10. *Law.* to make legal delivery of (a process or writ). –*n.* 11. the act, manner, or right of serving, as in tennis.

ser·very, *n.* an area in which food is set out on plates.

ser·vice, *n., adj., v.,* -viced, -vicing. –*n.* 1. an act of helpful activity. 2. the supplying or supplier of any articles, commodities, activities, etc. 3. occupation or employment as a servant. 4. *Mil.* (*pl.*) the armed forces. 5. the act of keeping a piece of machinery, esp. a motor vehicle, in operation. 6. public religious worship. 7. *Tennis, etc.* the act or manner of putting the ball in play. –*adj.* 8. of, pertaining to, or used by, servants, tradesmen, etc. 9. of pertaining to the armed forces. –*v.* 10. to make fit for use. 11. (of a male animal) to inseminate (a female animal). 12. to meet interest and other payments on, as a debt.

service·able, *adj.* capable of doing good service.

service station, *n.* commercial pre-

service station

mises selling petrol, oil, etc., and for repairing cars. Also, **petrol station.**

servi·ette, *n.* a piece of cloth or paper used at table to protect the clothes, etc. Also, **table napkin, napkin.**

ser·vile, *adj.* obsequious.

serv·ing, *n.* a portion of food or drink.

servi·tude, *n.* slavery; bondage.

sesame, *n.* the small edible seeds of a tropical plant.

session, *n.* a period of time during which an activity is performed.

set, *v.,* **set, setting,** *n., adj.* –*v.* 1. to put in a particular place, position, condition or relation. 2. to apply. 3. to incite to attack. 4. to fix or appoint. 5. to prescribe or assign, as a task. 6. to adjust or arrange. 7. to cause to sit. 8. to put into a fixed, rigid, or settled state: *to set the jaw.* 9. to cause (something, as mortar) to become firm or hard. 10. to cause (hair, etc.) to assume a desired shape. 11. *Surg.* to put (a broken or dislocated bone) back in position. 12. *Music.* to fit, as words to music. 13. (of the sun or moon) to pass below the horizon. 14. to become set. 15. **set about,** to begin. 16. **set off, a.** to explode. **b.** to begin, as on a journey. **c.** to intensify or improve by contrast. 17. **set out, a.** to arrange. **b.** to state or explain methodically. **c.** to start, as on a journey. 18. **set to, a.** to apply oneself. **b.** to start to fight. –*n.* 19. the act or state of setting. 20. a number of things customarily used together or forming a complete collection or series. 21. a group of persons associating or classed together. 22. fixed direction, as of the mind, etc. 23. a radio or television receiving apparatus. 24. a construction representing a place in which action takes place in a play, etc. –*adj.* 25. fixed beforehand. 26. fixed; rigid. 27. resolved or determined; habitually or stubbornly fixed. 28. ready. 29. **dead set,** *Colloq.* true; certain.

set square, *n.* a flat piece of plastic, etc., in the shape of a right-angled triangle.

settee, *n.* a seat for 2 or more persons.

setter, *n.* a long-haired hunting dog.

set·ting, *n.* 1. the surroundings or environment of anything. 2. the articles required for setting a single place at a table.

settle, *v.,* **-tled, -tling.** 1. to agree upon (a time, price, conditions, etc.). 2. to pay (a bill, account due, etc.). 3. to (cause to) take up residence in a country, etc. 4. to establish in a way of life, a business, etc. 5. to bring to rest. 6. to (cause to) sink down gradually. 7. to decide; arrange (*on* or *upon*). 8. to come to rest in a particular place.

settle·ment, *n.* 1. the act of settling. 2. a colony, esp. in its early stages.

seven, *n.* a cardinal number, 6 plus 1.

seven·teen, *n.* a cardinal number, 10 plus 7.

sev·enty, *n., pl.* **-ties.** a cardinal number, 10 times 7.

sever, *v.* 1. to divide into parts, esp. forcibly; cut. 2. to break off or dissolve (ties, relations, etc.). – **sever·ance,** *n.*

sev·eral, *adj.* 1. being more than 2 or 3, but not many. 2. respective; individual. 3. separate; different.

severance

sever·ance, *n.* a breaking off, as relations.

severe, *adj.,* **-verer, -verest. 1.** harsh; harshly extreme. **2.** serious; stern. **3.** rigidly restrained in style or taste. **4.** rigidly exact. **– severity,** *n.*

sew, *v.,* **sewed, sewn** or **sewed, sewing. 1.** to join or attach by stitching. **2.** to make (a garment) by such means. **3.** to work with a needle and thread, or with a sewing machine.

sewage, *n.* the waste matter which passes through sewers.

sewer, *n.* an artificial conduit, usu. underground, for carrying off waste water and refuse, as from a town or city.

sewer·age, *n.* **1.** the removal of waste water and refuse by means of sewers. **2.** the pipes and fittings conveying sewage.

sex, *n.* **1.** the sum of the physical differences which distinguish the male and the female. **2.** men collectively or women collectively. **3.** *Colloq.* sexual intercourse. *–v.* **4.** to ascertain the sex of.

sexist, *adj.* **1.** of an attitude which stereotypes a person according to gender. *–n.* **2.** a person who displays sexist attitudes.

sextet, *n.* any group or set of 6.

sexual, *adj.* **1.** of or pertaining to sex. **2.** occurring between or involving the 2 sexes.

sexual intercourse, *n.* the insertion of the penis into the vagina followed by ejaculation; coitus.

sex·ual·ity, *n.* sexual character.

sexy, *adj.,* **-ier, -iest.** sexually interesting or exciting.

shabby, *adj.,* **-bier, -biest. 1.** having the appearance impaired by wear, use, etc. **2.** meanly ungenerous or unfair.

shack, *n.* **1.** a rough cabin. *–v.* **2. shack up,** to live (*with*).

shackle, *n., v.,* **-led, -ling.** *–n.* **1.** a metal ring or fastening for securing the wrist, ankle, etc.; fetter. **2.** something that prevents freedom of procedure, thought, etc. *–v.* **3.** to confine or restrain.

shade, *n., v.,* **shaded, shading.** *–n.* **1.** the comparative darkness caused by the blocking of light. **2.** anything used for protection against excessive light, heat, etc. **3.** degree of darkening of a colour. **4.** a slight variation, amount, or degree. *–v.* **5.** to produce shade in or on. **6.** to screen. **7.** to pass or change by slight graduations.

shadow, *n.* **1.** a dark shape cast by a body intercepting light. **2.** an area of comparative darkness. **3.** a slight suggestion; trace. *–v.* **4.** to follow (a person) about secretly. *–adj.* **5.** *Govt.* of or pertaining to members of the chief opposition party, as **shadow cabinet.**

shaft, *n.* **1.** a long pole or rod forming the body of a spear, lance, etc. **2.** something directed in attack. **3.** a ray or beam. **4.** the handle of a long implement. **5.** either of the parallel bars of wood between which the animal drawing a vehicle is placed. **6.** any vertical enclosed space.

shag[1], *n.* rough, matted hair, wool, or the like.

shag[2], *n.* →**cormorant.**

shake, *v.,* **shook, shaken, shaking,** *n.* *–v.* **1.** to move or sway with short, quick, irregular vibratory movements. **2.** to tremble. **3.** to become unsteady. **4.** to shake, brandish, or

shake

471

shake

flourish (something). **5.** to bring, throw, force, rouse, etc., by shaking. **6.** to agitate or disturb profoundly. —*n.* **7.** the act of shaking. **8.** tremulous motion. **9.** a drink made by shaking ingredients together. **10.** (*pl.*) *Colloq.* a state of trembling.

shale, *n.* a layered, easily split rock formed by the consolidation of clay.

shall, *aux. v., pres. sing.* **shall**; *pt.* **should. 1.** (used, generally, in the first person to indicate simple future time): *I shall go tomorrow.* **2.** (used generally in the 2nd and 3rd persons), to indicate promise or determination).

shal·lot, *n.* a plant of the lily family whose small bulbs are used in cookery.

shal·low, *adj.* **1.** of little depth. —*n.* **2.** (*usu. pl.*) a shallow part of a body of water.

sham, *n., adj., v.,* **shammed, shamming.** —*n.* **1.** something that is not what it purports to be. —*adj.* **2.** pretended. —*v.* **3.** to assume the appearance of.

sham·ble, *v.,* **-bled, -bling.** to walk or go awkwardly; shuffle.

sham·bles, *n.* any place or thing in confusion or disorder.

shame, *n., v.,* **shamed, shaming.** —*n.* **1.** the painful feeling arising from the consciousness of something dishonourable, improper, ridiculous, etc., done by oneself or another. **2.** disgrace. —*v.* **3.** to cause to feel shame.

sham·poo, *v.,* **-pooed, -pooing,** *n.* —*v.* **1.** to wash (the hair, carpets, etc.) with a cleaning preparation. —*n.* **2.** a preparation used for shampooing.

472

sharp

sham·rock, *n.* a plant with trifoliate leaflets.

shandy, *n.* a mixed drink of beer with ginger beer or lemonade.

shang·hai, *v.,* **-haied, -haiing.** *Naut.* to obtain (a man) for the crew of a ship by kidnapping.

shank, *n.* **1.** that part of the leg in man between the knee and the ankle. **2.** the corresponding part in an animal.

shantung, *n.* a kind of silk.

shanty, *n., pl.* **-ties.** a roughly built hut.

shape, *n., v.,* **shaped, shaping.** —*n.* **1.** the quality of a thing depending on its outline or external surface. **2.** a particular or definite form. **3.** something used to give form, as a mould. —*v.* **4.** to give definite form, shape, or character to. **5.** to develop; assume a definite form or character (*up*).

shard, *n.* a fragment, esp. of broken earthenware.

share, *n., v.,* **shared, sharing.** —*n.* **1.** the portion belonging to, or contributed or owed by, someone. **2.** one of the equal parts into which the capital stock of a limited company is divided. —*v.* **3.** to use, participate in, enjoy, etc., jointly.

share·broker, *n.* →**stockbroker**.

shark, *n.* a type of fish, certain species of which are large and ferocious.

sharp, *adj.* **1.** having a thin cutting edge or a fine point. **2.** not blunt or rounded. **3.** clearly outlined; distinct. **4.** keen or acute: *sharp eyesight.* **5.** shrewd to the point of dishonesty. —*adv.* **6.** keenly or acutely. **7.** abruptly or suddenly. **8.** punctually. —*n. Music.* **9.** (the sign

sharp

#, indicating) a note raised one semitone above another.

shat·ter, v. to break suddenly into fragments.

shave, v., **shaved, shaved** or **shaven, shaving**, n. —v. 1. to remove hair from (the face, legs, etc.). 2. to cut or scrape away the surface of with a sharp-edged tool. —n. 3. the act or process of shaving. 4. a narrow miss or escape.

shaving, n. (oft. pl.) a very thin piece or slice, esp. of wood.

shawl, n. a piece of material, worn as a covering for the shoulders, head, etc.

she, pron., poss. **her**, obj. **her**, pl. **they**; n., pl. **shes**; adj. —pron. 1. the female in question or last mentioned. —n. 2. any woman or any female person or animal (correlative to **he**). —adj. 3. female or feminine, esp. of animals.

sheaf, n., pl. **sheaves**. a bundle into which wheat, etc., is tied after being cut.

shear, v., **sheared** or **shorn, shearing**; n. —v. 1. to remove by or as by cutting with a sharp instrument. 2. to cut the hair, fleece, wool, etc., from. —n. 3. (pl.) scissors of large size.

sheath, n. 1. a case for the blade of a sword, dagger, etc. 2. any similar covering.

shed[1], n. a structure, sometimes open at the sides or end, built for shelter, storage, etc.

shed[2], v., **shed, shedding**. 1. to emit and let fall (tears). 2. to cast off or let fall by natural process.

sheen, n. lustre; brightness; radiance.

sheep, n., pl. **sheep**. 1. a ruminant mammal, valuable for its flesh, fleece, etc. 2. a meek, timid, or stupid person.

sheep·ish, adj. awkwardly bashful or embarrassed.

sheep·shank, n. a kind of knot made on a rope to shorten it temporarily.

sheer[1], adj. 1. transparently thin. 2. unmixed with anything else. 3. very steep.

sheer[2], v. to deviate from a course, as a ship.

sheet, n. 1. a large rectangular piece of linen, cotton, etc., used as an article of bedding. 2. a broad, thin mass, layer, or covering. 3. a rectangular or square piece of paper.

sheikh, n. a chief or head of an Arab or Muslim religious group, tribe, etc.

shelf, n., pl. **shelves**. 1. a thin slab of wood or other material fixed horizontally to a wall, or in a frame, for supporting objects. 2. a shelf-like surface or projection; ledge.

shell, n., pl. **shells** or (for def 6) **shell**, v. —n. 1. a hard outer covering of an animal, as a mollusc, turtle, etc. 2. an object resembling a shell. 3. the hard exterior of an egg. 4. an enclosing case or cover. 5. a cartridge (def. 1) for a gun. 6. to take out of the shell, pod, etc. 7. to remove the shell of.

shell·fish, n., pl. **-fishes**, (esp. collectively) **-fish**. an aquatic animal having a shell, as the oyster, lobster, etc.

shel·ter, n. 1. a place of refuge or safety. —v. 2. to be a shelter for. 3. to take shelter.

shelve, v., **shelved, shelving**. to put aside from consideration.

shepherd

shep·herd, *n.* **1.** a man who minds sheep. **2.** one who watches over or protects a group of people. –*v.* **3.** to tend or guard as a shepherd.

sher·bet, *n.* **1.** a powdered confection. **2.** Also, **sorbet**, a frozen fruit-flavoured mixture.

she·riff, *n. Law.* an executive officer of the Supreme Court.

sher·ry, *n., pl.* **-ries.** a fortified and blended wine.

shield, *n.* **1.** anything used or serving to protect, esp. a piece of armour carried on the left arm. **2.** a shield-shaped device on which a coat of arms is displayed. –*v.* **3.** to protect (as) with a shield.

shift, *v.* **1.** to move or transfer from one place, position, etc., to another. –*n.* **2.** a transfer. **3.** the portion of the day scheduled as a day's work when a factory, etc., operates day and night. **4.** an expedient. **5.** a woman's loose-fitting dress.

shift·less, *adj.* lacking in resource or ambition; lazy.

shift·y, *adj.,* **-ti·er, -ti·est.** furtive.

shil·ling, *n.* (formerly) a coin equal to $\frac{1}{10}$ of a pound.

shim·mer, *n.* **1.** a subdued, tremulous light or gleam. –*v.* **2.** to shine with a shimmer.

shin, *n., v.,* **shinned, shin·ning.** –*n.* **1.** the front part of the leg between the knee to the ankle. –*v.* **2.** to climb by holding fast with the hands or arms and legs and drawing oneself up.

shine, *v.,* **shone** or **shined, shin·ing,** *v.* **1.** to give forth, or glow with, light. **2.** to be bright with reflected light. **3.** to excel. **4.** to cause to shine. –*n.* **5.** radiance. **6.** lustre; polish. **7.** sunshine. **8.** *Colloq.* a liking; fancy.

shock

shin·er, *n. Colloq.* a black eye.

shin·gle¹, *n.* a thin piece of wood, slate, etc., used to cover the roofs and sides of houses.

shin·gle², *n.* small, water-worn stones or pebbles such as on the seashore.

shin·gles, *n. sing.* or *pl.* a painful disease of the skin.

ship, *n., v.,* **shipped, ship·ping.** –*n.* **1.** a large vessel for navigating deep water, propelled by sail, steam, etc. **2.** an aircraft. –*v.* **3.** to send or transport by ship, rail, etc. **4.** to bring (an object) into a ship or boat.

ship·ment, *n.* **1.** the act of shipping goods, etc. **2.** that which is shipped.

ship·shape, *adj.* in good order.

shi·ra·lee, *n.,* →**swag.**

shire, *n.* an area of land administered by local government.

shirk, *v.* to evade (work, duty, etc.).

shirt, *n.* a garment for the upper part of the body.

shish kebab, *n.* cubes of meat grilled on a skewer, often with vegetables, etc.

shit, *v.,* **shit·ted, shat** or **shit; shit·ting;** *n., interj. Colloq.* –*v.* **1.** to defecate. –*n.* **2.** faeces; dung. **3.** the act of defecating. –*interj.* **4.** (an exclamation expressing anger, disgust, surprise, etc.).

shiv·er, *v.* **1.** to shake or tremble with cold, fear, excitement, etc. –*n.* **2.** a trembling movement.

shoal¹, *n.* a sandbank or sandbar in the bed of a body of water.

shoal², *n.* a massed group of fish.

shock¹, *n.* **1.** a sudden and violent blow or impact. **2.** something that shocks mentally, emotionally, etc. **3.** *Pathol.* a sudden collapse of the nervous mechanism caused by trauma. 4. the physiological effect produced by the passage of an electric current through the body. –v. 5. to strike with intense surprise, horror, disgust, etc. 6. to cause a shock in. –adj. 7. causing intense surprise, horror, etc.

shock[2], n. a thick, bushy mass, as of hair.

shoddy, adj., -dier, -diest. of poor quality or badly made.

shoe, n., pl. **shoes**, v., **shod, shoeing**. –n. 1. a covering, usu. of leather, for the foot. 2. some thing or part resembling a shoe in form, position, or use. –v. 3. to provide or fit with a shoe or shoes.

shoe·horn, n. a shaped device held at the heel of a shoe to make it slip on more easily.

shook, v. past tense of **shake**.

shoot, v., **shot, shooting**. –v. 1. to hit, wound, or kill with a missile discharged from a weapon. 2. to send forth (arrows, bullets, etc.). 3. to discharge (a weapon). 4. to send forth like an arrow or bullet. 5. to pass rapidly along with. 6. *Photog.* to photograph or film. 7. to move suddenly or swiftly; dart; be propelled (*ahead, away, into, off,* etc.). 8. to grow, esp. rapidly (*up*). –n. 9. an expedition for shooting animals. 10. a young branch, stem, twig, or the like.

shop, n., v., **shopped, shopping**. –n. 1. a building where goods are sold retail. 2. a place for doing certain work. 3. **talk shop**, to discuss one's trade, profession, or business. –v. 4. to visit shops to buy goods.

shop·front, n. that part of an organisation which deals directly with the public.

shop·lift, v. to steal (goods) from a shop while appearing to be a legitimate shopper.

shop steward, n. a trade-union official representing workers in a factory, workshop, etc.

shore[1], n. land along the edge of a sea, lake, large river, etc.

shore[2], v., **shored, shoring**. to support or prop (*up*).

shorn, v. past participle of **shear**.

short, adj. 1. having little length. 2. having little height. 3. brief. 4. rudely brief; curt. 5. below the standard in extent, quantity, duration, etc. 6. deficient in (*on*). –adv. 7. on the nearer side of an intended or particular point. 8. something that is short. 9. **for short**, by way of abbreviation. 10. **in short**, briefly.

short·age, n. deficiency in quantity.

short·bread, n. a thick, crisp biscuit, rich in butter.

short-change, v., -**changed, -changing**. *Colloq.* to give less than proper change to.

short circuit, n. an accidental connection between 2 points of different potential in an electrical circuit, thus enabling excess current to bypass the normal path. –**short-circuit**, v.

short·coming, n. a failure or defect in conduct, condition, etc.

short cut, n. a shorter or quicker way.

short·en·ing, n. any fat used to make pastry, etc.

short·hand, n. 1. a method of rapid handwriting using simple strokes in place of letters. –adj. 2. using shorthand. 3. written in shorthand.

short·ly, adv. in a short time.

shorts, *n.pl.* short trousers, not extending beyond the knee.

short-sighted, *adj.* unable to see far.

short-tempered, *adj.* having a hasty temper.

short-winded, *adj.* short of breath; liable to difficulty in breathing.

shot[1], *n., pl.* **shots**. 1. the act of shooting. 2. small pellets of lead as used in a sportsman's gun. 3. a person who shoots. 4. a heavy metal ball which competitors cast as far as possible in shot-putting contests. 5. an aimed stroke, throw, or the like, as in games, etc. 6. an attempt or try. 7. *Colloq.* an injection of a drug, vaccine, etc. 8. *Photog.* a photograph.

shot[2], *v.* past tense and past participle of **shoot**. –*adj.* 2. woven so as to present a play of colours, as silk.

shot·gun, *n.* a gun for firing small shot.

shot-put, *n.* the athletic exercise of putting the shot. See **shot**[1] (def. 4).

should, *v.* past tense of **shall**. 2. (specially used) **a.** to denote duty, propriety, or expediency: *You should work.* **b.** to make a statement less direct or blunt: *I should like you to do it.* **c.** to emphasise the uncertainty in conditional and hypothetical clauses: *if she should come.*

shoul·der, *n.* 1. either of 2 corresponding parts of the human body extending on either side of the neck to the upper joint of the arm. 2. a corresponding part in animals. 3. a shoulder-like part or projection. 4. either of 2 strips of land bordering a road. –*v.* 5. to push, as with the shoulder, esp. roughly. 6. to take upon or support with the shoulder. 7. to assume as a burden, or responsibility.

shoulder-blade, *n.* →scapula.

shout, *v.* 1. to call or cry out loudly and vigorously. 2. to pay for something for another person. –*n.* 3. a loud call or cry. 4. one's turn to pay.

shove, *v.*, **shoved**, **shoving**, *n.* –*v.* 1. to move along by force from behind. 2. to push roughly or rudely. –*n.* 3. an act of shoving.

shovel, *n., v.*, **-elled**, **-elling**. 1. an implement similar to a spade but with a scooped blade. –*v.* 2. to take up and remove with a shovel.

show, *v.*, **showed**, **shown** or **showed**, **showing**, *n.* –*v.* 1. to cause or allow to be seen. 2. to point out. 3. to guide. 4. to indicate. 5. to make evident by appearance, behaviour, etc. 6. to be or become visible. 7. **show off**, to exhibit for approval or admiration, or ostentatiously. –*n.* 8. a display. 9. ostentatious display. 10. an indication. 11. any undertaking, organisation, etc.

show·down, *n.* a final confrontation.

shower, *n.* 1. a brief fall, as of rain, etc. 2. **a.** an apparatus for spraying water for bathing. **b.** a washing of the body under such an apparatus. –*v.* 3. to pour (something) down in a shower. 4. to rain in a shower. 5. (of a person) to take a shower (def. 2).

shower tea, *n.* a party for a bride-to-be at which she receives household gifts.

show-off, *n. Colloq.* one given to pretentious display.

show·room, *n.* a room used for the display of goods or merchandise.

shrapnel

shrap·nel, *n.* shell (def. 5) fragments.

shred, *n., v.*, **shredded** or **shred, shredding**. –*n.* **1.** a narrow strip cut or torn off. –*v.* **2.** to cut or tear into small strips. **3.** to be reduced to shreds.

shrew, *n.* **1.** a small, insectivorous mouse-like mammal. **2.** a woman of violent temper and speech.

shrewd, *adj.* astute or sharp.

shriek, *n.* **1.** a loud, sharp, shrill cry. –*v.* **2.** to cry out sharply in a high voice.

shrift, *n. in the phrase,* **short shrift**, little consideration in dealing with someone or something.

shrill, *adj.* **1.** high-pitched and piercing. –*v.* **2.** to cry shrilly.

shrimp, *n.* **1.** any of various small, long-tailed, edible shellfish. **2.** *Colloq.* a diminutive or insignificant person.

shrine, *n.* any structure or place consecrated or devoted to some deity or revered person(s).

shrink, *v.*, **shrank** or **shrunk** or **shrunken**, **shrinking**. **1.** to draw back, as in retreat or avoidance. **2.** to become reduced in extent. **3.** to cause to shrink or contract. – **shrinkage**, *n.*

shri·vel, *v.*, **-elled**, **-elling**. to contract and wrinkle, as from great heat or cold.

shroud, *n.* **1.** a cloth in which a corpse is wrapped for burial. **2.** something which covers or conceals. –*v.* **3.** to cover; hide from view.

shrub, *n.* a woody perennial plant smaller than a tree, usu. branching from or near the ground.

shrug, *v.*, **shrugged, shrugging**, *n.* –*v.* **1.** to raise and lower (the shoulders), expressing indifference, disdain, etc. –*n.* **2.** this movement.

shud·der, *v., n.* (to tremble with) a sudden convulsive movement.

shuf·fle, *v.*, **-fled, -fling**, *n.* –*v.* **1.** to walk without lifting the feet. **2.** to mix (cards in a pack). –*n.* **3.** the act of shuffling.

shuf·ti, *n. Colloq.* an investigative look or inspection.

shun, *v.*, **shunned, shunning**. to keep away from.

shunt, *v.* **1.** to move or turn aside or out of the way.

shush, *interj.* hush (a command to be quiet or silent).

shut, *v.*, **shut, shutting**. **1.** to put (a door, cover, etc.) in position to close or obstruct. **2.** to close the doors of (*up*). **3.** to close by bringing together or folding. **4.** to confine; enclose (*in*). **5.** to bar; exclude (*out*). **6.** to become shut or closed. **7.** *shut up, Colloq.* to stop talking.

shut·ter, *n.* a hinged or otherwise movable cover for a window or other opening.

shut·tle, *n., v.*, **-tled, -tling**. *n.* **1.** the sliding container that carries the lower thread in a sewing machine. –*v.* **2.** to move quickly to and fro like a shuttle.

shut·tle·cock, *n.* a piece of cork with feathers stuck in one end, used in badminton.

shy, *adj.*, **shyer, shyest** or **shier, shiest**, *v.*, **shied, shying**. –*adj.* **1.** bashful, retiring. **2.** easily frightened away. –*v.* **3** to draw back.

SI, *n.* the International System of Units.

sib·i·lant, *adj.* hissing.

sib·ling, *n.* a brother or sister.

sic

sic, *adv.* so; thus (often used parenthetically to show that something has been copied exactly from the original).

sick, *adj.* **1.** affected with nausea. **2.** affected with any disorder of health. **3.** of or appropriate to sick persons. **4.** morbid; macabre. *–v.* **5.** vomit.

sickie, *n. Colloq.* a day taken off work with pay, because of genuine or feigned illness.

sickle, *n.* a short-handled implement with a curved blade for cutting grain, etc.

sickly, *adj.*, **-ier**, **-iest**. liable to frailty or illness; mawkish or sentimental.

side, *n., adj., v.*, **sided**, **siding**. *–n.* **1.** one of the surfaces or lines bounding a thing. **2.** one of the 2 surfaces of an object other than the front, back, top, and bottom. **3.** either of the 2 lateral (right and left) parts of a thing. **4.** the space immediately beside someone or something. **5.** one of 2 or more parties concerned in a case, contest, etc. *–adj.* **6.** being at or on one side. **7.** coming from or directed towards one side. **8.** subordinate. *v.* **9. side with** or **against**, to place oneself with or against (a side or party).

side·board, *n.* a piece of furniture for holding articles of table service.

side·car, *n.* a small car attached to one side to a motorcycle and supported on the other by a wheel of its own.

side effect, *n.* any effect produced other than those originally intended.

side·long, *adj.* **1.** directed to one side. *–adv.* **2.** towards the side; obliquely.

side·ways, *adv.* **1.** with the side foremost. **2.** towards or from one side. *–adj.* **3.** towards or from one side. Also **sidewise**.

siding, *n.* a short sidetrack off a railway line used for moving, loading, etc. goods trucks.

sidle, *v.*, **-dled**, **-dling**. to edge along furtively.

siege, *n.* the attacking, surrounding of, and cutting off of supplies to a fortified place in order to capture it.

sie·mens, *n., pl.* **siemens**. the SI unit of electrical conductance. Symbol: S

siesta, *n.* a midday or afternoon rest or nap.

sieve, *n.* an instrument, with a meshed or perforated bottom which holds back coarse or solid matter while allowing fine matter or liquid to pass through.

sift, *v.* **1.** to separate the coarse parts of (flour, ashes, etc.) with a sieve. **2.** to scatter by means of a sieve. **3.** to examine closely.

sigh, *v.* **1.** to let out one's breath audibly, as from sorrow, etc. **2.** to yearn or long. **3.** to express with a sigh. *–n.* **4.** the act or sound of sighing.

sight, *n.* **1.** the power or faculty of seeing. **2.** the act or fact of seeing. **3.** range of vision. **4.** a view; glimpse. **5.** something seen or to be seen. *–v.* **6.** to get sight of.

sign

sign, *n.* **1.** a token; indication. **2.** a symbol used instead of words in science, trade, etc. **3.** an inscribed board, space, etc., serving for information, advertisement, warn-

signing, etc. –*v.* 4. to affix a signature to. 5. to communicate by a sign or signal. 6. to write one's signature.

signal, *n., adj., v.,* **-nalled, -nalling**. –*n.* 1. a gesture, act, light, etc., serving to warn, direct, command, or the like. 2. an act, event, or the like, which precipitates an action. 3. a token; indication. 4. *Radio, etc.* the impulses, waves, sounds, etc., transmitted or received. –*adj.* 5. serving as a sign. –*v.* 6. to make a signal to. 7. to make known by a signal. 8. to make communication by a signal or signals.

sig·na·tory, *adj., n., pl.* **-ries**. –*adj.* 1. that has signed a document. –*n.* 2. one who has signed a document.

sig·na·ture, *n.* 1. a person's name written by himself. 2. the act of signing a document.

signet, *n.* a small official seal.

sig·nif·i·cance, *n.* 1. importance. 2. meaning. – **significant**, *adj.*

sig·ni·fy, *v.,* **-fied, -fying**. 1. to make known by signs, speech, or action. 2. to be a sign of; mean. 3. to be of importance.

silence, *n., v.,* **-lenced, -lencing**, *interj.* –*n.* 1. absence of any sound or noise. –*v.* 2. to cause to be silent. –*interj.* 3. be silent! – **silent**, *adj.*

sil·hou·ette, *n.* a dark image outlined against a lighter background.

silica, *n.* a silicon dioxide, appearing as quartz, sand, flint, and agate.

sil·i·con, *n.* a non-metallic element used in steel-making, etc. Symbol: Si

silk, *n.* 1. (the thread or cloth made from) the fine, soft, lustrous fibre obtained from the cocoon of a caterpillar. 2. any fibre resembling silk. 3. **to take silk**, to become a Queen's or King's Counsel. –*adj.* 4. made of silk. 5. of or pertaining to silk. – **silken**, *adj.*

silk-screen, *n.* 1. a process of printing from stencils through a fine mesh of silk, metal or other material. –*v.* 2. to print using this process.

sill, *n.* the horizontal piece beneath a window or door.

silly, *adj.,* **-lier, -liest**, *n., pl.* **-lies**. –*adj.* 1. lacking good sense; foolish. 2. absurd or ridiculous. –*n.* 3. *Colloq.* a silly person.

silo, *n., pl.* **-los**. a tower-like structure for storing grain.

silt, *n.* earthy matter deposited as a sediment by moving water.

silver, *n.* 1. *Chem.* a white ductile metallic element. Symbol: Ag 2. coin made of silver or of a metal resembling silver; money. 3. table articles made of silver or plated with silver. 4. a lustrous greyish-white or whitish-grey. –*adj.* 5. made of or plated with silver. 6. of or pertaining to silver. 7. (of coins) made of a metal or alloy resembling silver. 8. having the colour silver. 9. indicating the 25th event of a series, as a wedding anniversary.

silver·fish, *n., pl.* **-fish, -fishes**, (*esp. collectively*) **-fish**. any of certain small, wingless insects damaging to books, wallpaper, etc.

silver·side, *n.* a cut of beef from the outside portion of a full butt.

simi·lar, *adj.* having a general likeness or resemblance.

simile, *n.* a figure of speech directly expressing a resemblance, as *a man like an ox.*

sim·il·i·tude, *n.* 1. likeness; resemblance. 2. a likening or comparison.

479

simmer, v. 1. to cook in a liquid just below the boiling point. 2. **simmer down**, *Colloq.* to become calm or calmer. – n. 3. state or process of simmering.

simper, v. to smile in a silly, self-conscious way.

simple, adj., -pler, -plest. 1. easy to understand, deal with, use, etc. 2. not complex. 3. sincere. 4. unlearned. – **simplicity**, n. – **simplify**, v.

simple·ton, n. a fool.

sim·plis·tic, adj. oversimplified.

simu·lation, n. 1. assumption of a particular appearance or form. 2. the practice of constructing a model of a machine in order to test behaviour. – **simulate**, v.

simul·cast, n. simultaneous broadcast by a radio and a television station.

simul·tan·eous, adj. existing, occurring, or operating at the same time.

sin, n., v., sinned, sinning. – n. 1. (an act of) transgression of divine law. – v. 2. to do a sinful act.

since, adv. 1. from then till now (oft. prec. by *ever*). 2. between a particular past time and the present; subsequently. 3. ago. – prep. 4. continuously from or counting from: *since noon*. 5. between (a past time or event) and the present: *since the war*. – conj. 6. in the period following the time when: *tired since the party*. 7. because.

sin·cere, adj., -cerer, -cerest. free from any element of deceit or hypocrisy. – **sincerity**, n.

sine, n. *Maths.* a trigonometric function defined for an acute angle in a right-angled triangle as the ratio of the side opposite the angle to the hypotenuse.

sinec·ure, n. a well-paid office requiring little or no work.

sinew, n. 1. a tendon. 2. strength; vigour.

sing, v., sang or sung, sung, singing. 1. to utter (words or sounds) in succession with musical modulations of the voice. 2. to produce melodious sounds, as certain birds, insects, etc. 3. to make a short ringing, whistling, or whizzing sound. 4. to bring, send, put, etc., with or by singing.

singe, v., singed, singeing. – v. 1. to burn superficially. – n. 2. a superficial burn.

single, adj., v., -gled, -gling. n. – adj. 1. one only; separate. 2. of or pertaining to one person, family, etc. 3. alone; solitary. 4. unmarried. 5. consisting of one part, element, or member. – v. 6. to pick or choose from others (*out*). – n. 7. something single or separate.

single-handed, adj. acting or working alone or unaided.

single-minded, adj. having or showing undivided purpose.

sing·let, n. a short garment, with or without sleeves, usu. worn next to the skin.

sing·song, n. 1. an informal gathering at which the company sing. – adj. 2. characterised by a regular rising and falling intonation.

singu·lar, adj. 1. being the only one of the kind. 2. out of the ordinary. 3. *Gram.* designating the number category that normally implies one person, thing, or collection.

sin·is·ter, *adj.* threatening or portending evil.

sink, *v.,* **sank** or **sunk, sunk** or **sunken, sinking,** *n.* —*v.* 1. to descend gradually to a lower level. 2. to become submerged. 3. to pass or fall into some lower state. 4. to enter or permeate (*in, into,* etc.) the mind. 5. to fall in, as the cheeks. 6. to degenerate (*in* or *into*). 7. to cause to sink. 8. to make (a hole, shaft, well, etc.) by excavating or boring downwards. —*n.* 9. a basin with a water supply and outlet. 10. a low-lying area where waters collect.

sinker, *n.* a weight of lead, etc., on a fishing line, net, etc.

sinu·ous, *adj.* having many curves, bends, or turns; winding.

sinus, *n., pl.* **-nuses.** one of the hollow cavities in the skull connecting with the nasal cavities.

sip, *v.,* **sipped, sipping,** *n.* —*v.* 1. to drink a little at a time. 2. an act of sipping. 3. a small quantity taken by sipping.

siphon, *n.* 1. a tube through which liquid flows over the side of a container to a lower level by atmospheric pressure. —*v.* 2. to convey or pass through a siphon. Also, **syphon.**

sir, *n.* a respectful or formal term of address used to a man.

sire, *n., v.,* **sired, siring.** —*n.* 1. the male parent of an animal. —*v.* 2. to beget.

siren, *n.* 1. *Class Myth.* a sea nymph, part woman and part bird, supposed to lure mariners to destruction by their seductive singing. 2. a device used as a warning sound.

sir·loin, *n.* the portion of the loin of beef in front of the rump.

sissy, *n.* a timid or cowardly person.

sister, *n.* 1. a daughter of the same parents. 2. a female associate. 3. a female member of a religious community. 4. a senior nurse. —*adj.* 5. being a sister; related by, or as by, sisterhood.

sister-in-law, *n., pl.* **sisters-in-law.** 1. the sister of one's spouse. 2. the wife of one's brother. 3. the wife of one's spouse's brother.

sit, *v.,* **sat, sitting.** 1. to rest on the lower part of the body. 2. to be situated. 3. to fit or be adjusted, as a garment. 4. to occupy a seat in an official capacity, as a judge or bishop. 5. to be convened or in session, as an assembly. 6. to cause to sit; seat (*down*). 7. to sit upon (a horse, etc.). 8. to provide seating room for.

site, *n., v.,* **sited, siting.** —*n.* 1. the area on which anything, as a building, is, has been or is to be situated. —*v.* 2. to locate; place.

situ·ate, *v.,* **-ated, -ating.** to give a site to; locate.

situ·ation, *n.* 1. a location or position with reference to environment. 2. a place or locality. 3. the state of affairs. 4. a position or post of employment.

six, *n.* a cardinal number, 5 plus one.

six·teen, *n.* a cardinal number, 10 plus 6.

sixth sense, *n.* a power of perception beyond the 5 senses; intuition.

sixty, *n.* a cardinal number, 10 times 6.

size¹, *n., v.,* **sized, sizing.** —*n.* 1. the dimensions or magnitude of anything. —*v.* 2. to separate or sort

size

according to size. **3.** to make of a certain size. **4. to size up,** to form an estimate of.

size¹, *n., v.,* **sized, sizing.** –*n.* **1.** any of various gelatinous or glutinous preparations used for glazing or coating paper, cloth, etc. *v.* **2.** to treat with size.

siz·zle, *v.,* **-zled, -zling.** –*v.* **1.** to make a hissing sound, as in frying or burning. –*n.* **2.** a sizzling sound.

skate, *n., v.,* **skated, skating.** –*n.* **1.** a steel blade attached to the bottom of a shoe, enabling a person to glide on ice. **2.** →**roller-skate.** *v.* **3.** to glide over ice, the ground, etc., on skates.

skate·board, *n.* a short plank on roller-skate wheels, ridden standing up.

skedaddle, *v. Colloq.* **-ling.** run away, retreat in haste.

skein, *n.* a length of thread or yarn wound in a coil.

skele·ton, *n.* **1.** the bones of a human or other animal body considered together. **2.** *Colloq.* a very lean person or animal. **3.** a supporting framework. –*adv.* **4.** of or pertaining to a skeleton. – **skeletal,** *adj.*

skeleton key, *n.* a key which may open various locks. Also, **pass key.**

sketch, *n.* **1.** a simply or hastily executed drawing. **2.** a rough plan or draft, as of a literary work. **3.** a brief or hasty outline of facts, occurrences, etc. –*v.* **4.** to make a sketch (of).

skew, *v.* **1.** to turn aside or swerve. **2.** to give an oblique direction to; shape or form obliquely.

skewer, *n.* **1.** a long pin of wood or metal for holding meat together while being cooked. –*v.* **2.** to fasten (as) with skewers.

skin

ski, *n., pl.* **skis, ski,** *v.,* **ski'd** or **skied, skiing.** –*n.* **1.** one of a pair of long, slender pieces of hard wood, metal, or plastic, one fastened to each shoe, used for travelling or gliding over snow. –*v.* **2.** to travel on or use skis.

skid, *n., v.,* **skidded, skidding.** –*n.* **1.** a plank or log on which something heavy may be slid or rolled along. **2.** an act of skidding. **3.** to slide along without rotating, as a vehicle to which a brake has been applied. **4.** to slide forward under its own momentum, usu. out of control, as a car.

skiff, *n.* a small sailing or rowing boat.

skill, *n.* the ability to do something well that comes from knowledge, practice, etc. – **skilful,** *adj.*

skilled, *adj.* **1.** showing, involving, or requiring skill, as work. **2.** of or pertaining to workers specially trained in their trade.

skil·let, *n.* a frying pan.

skim, *v.,* **skimmed, skimming.** –*v.* **1.** to take up or remove (floating matter) from a liquid. **2.** to clear (liquid) thus. **3.** to move or glide lightly over or along the surface of. –*n.* **4.** the act of skimming.

skimp, *v.* **1.** to be sparing with; scrimp. **2.** to be extremely thrifty (on).

skin, *n., v.,* **skinned, skinning.** –*n.* **1.** the external covering of an animal body, esp. when soft and flexible. **2.** any outer coating, or surface layer, as the rind or peel of fruit, or a film on liquid. –*v.* **3.** to strip or deprive of skin.

skin-diving, *n.* underwater swimming with an aqualung or snorkel, and foot fins.

skin-flint, *n.* a mean person.

skin·ful, *n. Colloq.* the amount of alcohol needed to make a person drunk.

skink, *n.* any of various harmless, generally smooth-scaled lizards.

skinny, *adj.*, **-nier**, **-niest**. lean; emaciated.

skip, *v.*, **skipped**, **skipping**, *n.* –*v.* 1. to spring, jump, or leap lightly (over). 2. to pass from one point, thing, subject, etc. to another, disregarding or omitting what intervenes. 3. to miss out part of. 4. *Colloq.* to leave hastily, or flee from. –*n.* 5. a skipping movement.

skip·per, *n.* the leader of a team or crew.

skir·mish, *n.* 1. any brisk encounter, as for fighting or argument. –*v.* 2. to engage in a skirmish.

skirt, *n.* 1. (the lower part of) a garment, hanging from the waist. 2. some part resembling or suggesting the skirt of a garment. –*v.* 3. to pass along or around the border or edge of. 4. to be, lie, live, etc., on or along the edge of something.

skir·ting board, *n.* a line of boarding on an interior wall next to the floor.

skit, *n.* a slight parody or satire, esp. dramatic or literary.

skit·tish, *adj.* restlessly or excessively lively.

skit·tle, *n., v.*, **skittled**, **skittling**. –*n.* 1. (*pl.*) a game of bowling using nine pins. –*v.* 2. to knock over.

skiv·vy, *n. Colloq.* (*derog.*) domestic servant, usu. a female cleaner.

skul·dug·ger·y, *n.* dishonourable proceedings. Also, **skullduggery**.

skulk, *v.* to lie or keep in hiding, as for some evil or cowardly reason.

skull, *n.* the bony framework of the head, enclosing the brain, etc.

skunk, *n.* 1. a small Nth American mammal which ejects a stinking fluid when attacked. 2. *Colloq.* a thoroughly contemptible person.

sky, *n.* (*oft. pl.*) the region of the clouds or the upper air.

sky-div·ing, *n.* the sport of free-falling from an aeroplane for a great distance before releasing one's parachute.

sky-lark, *v.* to frolic or play about, esp. boisterously.

sky-light, *n.* an opening in a roof or ceiling, fitted with glass.

sky-scrap·er, *n.* a tall building of many storeys.

slab, *n.* a broad, flat, somewhat thick piece of some solid material.

slack, *adj.* 1. not tense or taut. 2. indolent, negligent or inactive. –*n.* 3. a slack condition, interval, or part. –*v.* 4. to neglect or shirk (some matter, duty, etc.).

slacks, *n.pl.* long trousers, worn by either men or women as informal wear.

slag, *n.* waste matter separated during the reduction of a metal from its ore.

slain, *v.* past participle of **slay**.

slake, *v.*, **slaked**, **slaking**. to satisfy (thirst, desire, wrath, etc.).

sla·lom, *n.* a skiing or canoe race over a winding obstacle course.

slam, *v.*, **slammed**, **slamming**, *n.* –*v.* 1. to shut with force and noise. 2. to dash, strike, etc., with noisy impact. –*n.* 3. a violent and noisy closing, dashing, or impact.

slander

slander, *n.* 1. a malicious, false, and defamatory statement. –*v.* 2. to utter slander concerning.

slang, *n.* language differing from and more informal than standard or written language, and sometimes regarded as being inferior.

slant, *v.* 1. to slope; be oblique. 2. to direct or turn so as to make (something) oblique. 3. to distort or give partisan emphasis to (a newspaper story, article, etc.). –*n.* 4. slanting or oblique direction. 5. a mental leaning or tendency, esp. unusual or unfair; bias.

slap, *v.,* **slapped, slapping,** *n.* (to strike with) a smart blow, esp. with the open hand.

slap·dash, *adv., adj.* carelessly hasty or offhand.

slap·stick, *n.* comedy featuring rough play and clowning.

slap-up, *adj. Colloq.* first-rate; excellent.

slash, *v.* 1. to cut with a violent or random sweep. 2. to cut, reduce, or alter, esp. drastically. –*n.* 3. (a cut or wound made with) a sweeping stroke.

slat, *n., v.,* **slatted, slatting.** –*n.* 1. a long, thin, narrow strip of wood, metal, etc. –*v.* 2. to furnish or make with slats.

slate[1], *n., v.,* **slated, slating.** –*n.* 1. a fine-grained rock that tends to split along parallel cleavage planes. 2. a thin piece or plate of this rock or a similar material, used esp. for roofing, or for writing on. 3. a dull, dark bluish grey. –*v.* 4. to cover with slate.

slate[2], *v.,* **slated, slating.** to censure or reprimand severely.

slather, *v.* 1. to use in large quantities. –*n.* 2. **open slather,** complete freedom.

sleeper

slaugh·ter, *n.* 1. the killing or butchering of cattle, sheep, etc., for food. 2. the killing by violence of great numbers of people. –*v.* 3. to kill (people or animals).

slave, *n., v.,* **slaved, slaving.** –*n.* 1. one who is the property of, and wholly subject to, another. –*v.* 2. to work like a slave; drudge. – **slavery**, *n.* – **slavish,** *adj.*

slaver, *v.* to let saliva run from the mouth.

slay, *v.,* **slew, slain, slaying.** to kill by violence.

sleazy, *adj.,* **-zier, -ziest.** shabby, shoddy, untidy, or dirty.

sled, *n.* a small sledge or toboggan.

sledge, *n.* a vehicle drawn by horses or dogs and mounted on runners, for travelling or conveying loads over snow, ice, rough ground, etc.

sledge-hammer, *n.* a very large heavy hammer.

sleek, *adj.* 1. smooth; glossy, as hair, an animal, etc. 2. well-fed or well-groomed. 3. suave.

sleep, *v.,* **slept, sleeping,** *n.* –*v.* 1. to take the repose or rest afforded by the natural suspension of consciousness. 2. to be dormant or inactive. 3. to have beds or sleeping accommodation for. 4. to spend or pass (time, etc.) in sleep (*away* or *out*). –*n.* 5. the state of one that sleeps. 6. a period of sleeping.

sleeper, *n.* 1. a cross beam (usu. timber) serving as a foundation for the rails of a railway track. 2. a bed or compartment in a carriage on a passenger train. 3. a small ring, bar, etc., worn in the ear lobe after piercing.

sleet, *n.* snow or hail and rain falling together.

sleeve, *n.* 1. the part of a garment that covers the arm. 2. something resembling this.

sleigh, *n.* a sledge.

sleight /slaɪt/, *n.* skill; dexterity.

slen·der, *adj.* 1. small in circumference in proportion to height or length. 2. small in size, amount, extent, etc.

sleuth, *n. Colloq.* a detective.

slew[1], *v.* past tense of **slay**.

slew[2], *v.* 1. to turn or twist (something), esp. upon its own axis or without moving it from its place. 2. to (cause to) swing round. 3. to swerve awkwardly. –*n.* 4. such a movement.

slice, *n., v.,* **sliced, slicing.** –*n.* 1. a thin, broad, flat piece cut from something. 2. any of various implements with a thin, broad blade. –*v.* 3. to cut into slices. 4. to cut (*off, away, from,* etc.) as or like a slice.

slick, *adj.* 1. smooth of manners, speech, etc. 2. ingenious or adroit. –*n.* 3. a patch or film of oil, as on the sea.

slide, *v.,* **slid, slid** or **slidden, sliding.** –*v.* 1. to (cause to) move along in continuous contact with a smooth or slippery surface. 2. to slip, as one losing foothold or as a vehicle skidding. 3. to go quietly, or unobtrusively (*in, out, away,* etc.). –*n.* 4. the act of sliding. 5. a single image for projection in a projector. 6. any sliding part.

slide rule, *n.* a device for rapid arithmetic calculation, marked with logarithmic scales.

slight, *adj.* 1. small in amount, degree, etc. 2. frail; flimsy. –*v.* 3. to treat with indifference; ignore or snub. –*n.* 4. an affront.

slim, *adj.,* **slimmer, slimmest,** *v.,* **slimmed, slimming.** –*adj.* 1. slender, as in girth or form. –*v.* 2. to make oneself slim, as by dieting, exercise, etc.

slime, *n.* 1. thin, glutinous mud. 2. a viscous secretion of animal or vegetable origin. – **slimy, slimey,** *adj.*

sling, *n., v.,* **slung, slinging.** –*n.* 1. an instrument for hurling stones, etc., by hand. 2. a strap, band, or the like forming a loop by which something is suspended or carried. –*v.* 3. to throw, cast or hurl. 4. to suspend. 5. to give money as a bribe.

slink, *v.,* **slunk; slinking.** to move stealthily, as to evade notice.

slip[1], *v.,* **slipped; slipping.** –*v.* 1. to pass or go smoothly or easily; glide; slide. 2. to lose one's footing. 3. to move or slide from place, a fastening, etc. 4. to go, come, get, etc., easily or quickly. 5. to go quietly. 6. to cause to slip. 7. to untie or undo (a knot). 8. to escape (one's memory, notice, knowledge, etc.). 9. **slip up**, to make a mistake. –*n.* 10. the act of slipping. 11. a mistake, as in speaking or writing. 12. the eluding of a pursuer, etc. 13. a woman's sleeveless undergarment. 14. a pillowcase.

slip[2], *n.* 1. any long, narrow piece or strip, as of wood, paper, land, etc. 2. a young person, esp. one of slender form.

slip·per, *n.* a light shoe for indoor wear.

slip·per·y, *adj.,* **-perier, -periest.** 1. tending to cause slipping or slid-

485

slippery

ing, as ground, surfaces, etc. **2.** likely to slip away or escape.

slippy, *adj.*, *Colloq.* slippery.

slip-shod, *adj.* untidy, or slovenly; careless.

slip-stitch, *n.* one of a series of stitches used for dress hems, etc.

slip-stream, *n.* an air current behind any moving object.

slip-way, *n.* a ramp used for the landing and repairing of nets.

slit, *v.*, **slit, slitting.** *-v.* **1.** to cut apart or open along a line. *-n.* **2.** a straight, narrow cut or opening.

slither, *v.* to slide down or along a surface, esp. unsteadily or noisily.

sliver, *n.* a slender piece, as of wood, split, broken, or cut off.

slob, *n.* *Colloq.* a stupid, clumsy, uncouth, or slovenly person.

slob-ber, *v.* **1.** to let saliva, etc., run from the mouth. **2.** to indulge in mawkish sentimentality. *-n.* **3.** saliva or liquid dribbling from the mouth.

sloe, *n.* small blue fruit of blackthorn.

slog, *v.*, **slogged, slogging.** *n.* *Colloq.* *-v.* **1.** to hit hard, as in boxing, cricket, etc. **2.** to toil. *-n.* **3.** a strong crude blow. **4.** a spell of hard work or walking.

slogan, *n.* a distinctive cry or phrase of any party, class, body, or person.

slop, *v.*, **slopped, slopping.** *n.* *-v.* **1.** to spill or splash. *-n.* **2.** (*oft. pl.*) the dirty water, liquid refuse, etc., of a household, etc.

slope, *v.*, **sloped, sloping.** *-v.* **1.** to take or have an inclined direction from the horizontal. **2.** to direct at a slope or inclination. *-n.* **3.** inclination or slant. **4.** an inclined surface.

486

slug

sloppy *adj.*, **-pier, -piest.** **1.** muddy, slushy, or very wet. **2.** *Colloq.* weak, silly, or maudlin. **3.** *Colloq.* loose, careless, or slovenly.

sloppy joe, *n.* a loose, thick sweater.

slosh, *n.* →**slush.** *-v.* **2.** to splash in slush, mud, or water. **3.** to pour, stir, spread, etc., a liquid (*in, on, round,* etc.).

slot, *n., v.*, **slotted, slotting.** *-n.* **1.** a narrow, elongated depression or aperture, esp. one to receive or admit something. **2.** a position within a system. *-v.* **3.** to provide with a slot or slots. **4.** to insert into a slot (*in*).

sloth-ful, *adj.* indolent; lazy.

slouch, *v.* **1.** to sit, stand, or walk in an awkward, drooping posture. **2.** to cause to droop or bend down. *-n.* **3.** a drooping of the head and shoulders.

slouch hat, *n.* an army hat of soft felt.

slough /slʌf/, *v.* to cast (*off*).

sloven, *n.* one who is habitually untidy or dirty. — **slovenly,** *adj.*

slow, *adj.* **1.** taking or requiring a comparatively long time. **2.** sluggish. **3.** dull of perception or understanding. **4.** slack, as trade. **5.** showing a time earlier than the correct time. *-adv.* **6.** in a slow manner. *-v.* **7.** to make or become slow or slower.

sludge, *n.* mud, mire.

slug[1], *n.* **1.** any of various small, slimy, gastropods related to the snails, but having no shell. **2.** a piece of lead or other metal for firing from a gun.

slug[2], *v.*, **slugged, slugging.** *n.* *-v.* **1.** to strike heavily. *-n.* **2.** a heavy blow, esp. with the fist.

slug·gard, *n.* one who is habitually lazy.

slug·gish, *adj.* inactive, slow, or of little energy or vigour.

sluice, *n., v.*, **sluiced, sluicing.** –*n.* 1. any contrivance for regulating a flow of water. 2. a channel or a drain. –*v.* 3. to flush or cleanse with a rush of water.

slum, *n.* (*oft. pl.*) an overpopulated, squalid part of a city.

slum·ber, *v.* 1. to sleep, esp. deeply. –*n.* 2. (*oft. pl.*) sleep, esp. deep sleep.

slump, *v.* 1. to drop heavily and limply. 2. to fall suddenly and markedly, as prices. –*n.* 3. a decline in prices or sales.

slur, *v.*, **slurred, slurring.** *n.* –*v.* 1. to pass over lightly, or without due mention or consideration (*over*). 2. to pronounce (a syllable, word, etc.) indistinctly. –*n.* 3. a disparaging remark. 4. a blot or stain, as upon reputation.

slurp, *v.* 1. to eat or drink noisily. –*n.* 2. the noise produced in this way.

slush, *n.* 1. snow in a partly melted state. 2. *Colloq.* silly, sentimental, or weakly emotional writing, talk, etc.

slut, *n.* a dirty, slovenly woman.

sly, *adj.*, **slyer, slyest** or **slier, sliest.** cunning or wily.

smack[1], *n.* 1. a slight taste or flavour, suggestive of something. –*v.* 2. to have a taste, flavour, trace, or suggestion (*of*).

smack[2], *v.* 1. to strike smartly, esp. with the open hand. 2. to bring, put or throw with a sharp, resounding blow. 3. to come or strike smartly or forcibly, as against something. –*n.* 4. a smart, resounding blow. 5. a resounding or loud kiss. 6. *Colloq.* heroin. –*adv.* 7. *Colloq.* directly; straight.

small, *adj.* 1. of limited size; not big. 2. not great in amount, degree, extent, duration, value, etc. 3. of minor importance. –*adv.* 4. in a small manner. 5. into small pieces. –*n.* 6. the lower central part of the back.

small fry, *n.* young or unimportant persons or objects.

small·goods, *n. pl.* 1. processed meats, as salami, frankfurts. 2. (imported) foods found in a delicatessen.

small·pox, *n.* an acute, highly contagious disease characterised by pustular sores.

smarmy, *adj.* flattering; unctuous.

smart, *v.* 1. to be a source of sharp, local, and usu. superficial pain, as a wound. 2. to suffer keenly from wounded feelings. –*adj.* 3. sharp or keen, as pain. 4. sharply severe, as blows. 5. sharply brisk, vigorous, or active. 6. clever. 7. dashingly or effectively neat or trim in appearance. 8. socially elegant, or fashionable. –*n.* 9. sharp local pain, usu. superficial.

smash, *v.* 1. to break to pieces, often with a crashing sound. 2. to break to pieces from a violent blow or collision. –*n.* 3. a smashing or shattering, or the sound of it. 4. a destructive collision.

smash·ing, *adj. Colloq.* extremely fine; first-rate.

smat·ter·ing, *n.* a slight or superficial knowledge of something.

smear, *v.* 1. to rub or spread with oil, dirt, etc. –*n.* 2. a mark or stain made by, or as by, smearing.

smell

smell, *v.*, **smelled** or **smelt, smelling**, *n.* –*v.* **1.** to perceive through the nose. **2.** to test by the sense of smell. **3.** to search or find as if by smell (*out*). **4.** to search or investigate (*around*). **5.** to give out an odour, esp. as specified (*of*). **6.** to seem to be unpleasant or bad. –*n.* **7.** the faculty or sense of smelling. **8.** that quality of a thing which is or may be smelled. **9.** the act of smelling.

smid·gin, *n.* a very small quantity. Also **smidgen, smidgeon**.

smile, *v.*, **smiled, smiling**, *n.* –*v.* **1.** to widen the mouth, turn up the lips, etc., in pleasure, amusement, scorn, etc. **2.** to assume or give (a smile). **3.** to express by a smile. **4.** to look with favour or support (*on* or *upon*). –*n.* **5.** the act of smiling; a smiling expression of the face.

smirk, *v.* **1.** to smile in a condescending or know-all way. –*n.* **2.** such a smile.

smite, *v.*, **smote, smitten** or **smit, smiting**. **1.** to strike or hit hard. **2.** to affect suddenly and strongly with a specified feeling.

smith, *n.* a worker in metal.

smith·er·eens, *n.pl. Colloq.* small fragments.

smock, *n.* any loose overgarment.

smog, *n.* a mixture of smoke and fog.

smoke, *n.*, *v.*, **smoked, smoking**. –*n.* **1** the visible exhalation given off by a burning or smouldering substance. **2.** something resembling this, as vapour or mist. **3.** an act or spell of smoking tobacco, or the like. **4.** that which is smoked, as a cigar or cigarette. –*v.* **5.** to give off or emit smoke. **6.** to draw into the mouth and puff out the smoke of (tobacco or the like). **7.** to expose to smoke.

smooch, *v. Colloq.* kiss; dance slowly.

smooth, *adj.* **1.** free from irregularities of surface. **2.** of uniform consistency. **3.** pleasant, agreeable, or ingratiatingly polite. –*v.* **4.** to make smooth of surface, as by scraping, pressing, etc. (*down*). **5.** to remove (projections, etc.) (*away* or *out*). –*n.* **6.** a smooth part or place.

smor·gas·bord, *n.* a buffet meal of various dishes.

smother, *v.* **1.** to stifle or suffocate, esp. by smoke or by depriving of air. **2.** to extinguish or deaden (fire, etc.) by excluding air. **3.** to oppress by giving too much, as of love, kindness. –*n.* **4.** an overspreading profusion of anything.

smoul·der, *v.* **1.** to burn or smoke without flame. **2.** to exist or continue in a suppressed state or without outward demonstration.

smudge, *v.*, **smudged, smudging**, *n.* (to mark with) a dirty mark or smear.

smug, *adj.*, **smugger, smuggest**. complacently proper, righteous, clever, etc.

smug·gle, *v.*, **-gled, -gling**. to import or export (goods) secretly, and illegally.

smut, *n.* **1.** a black or dirty mark. **2.** indecent talk or writing.

snack, *n.* **1.** a small portion of food or drink; a light meal. **2.** *Colloq.* anything easily done.

snag, *n.*, *v.*, **snagged, snagging**. –*n.* **1.** any sharp or rough projection. **2.** any obstacle or impediment. **3.** a small hole caused by a snag. **4.**

snag

—v. 4. to catch upon, or damage by, a snag.

snail, n. 1. a land gastropod having a single, usu. spirally coiled shell. 2. a slow or lazy person.

snake, in., v., **snaked, snaking.** —n. 1. a scaly, limbless, usu. slender reptile, sometimes venomous. 2. a treacherous person. 3. something resembling a snake in form or manner. —v. 4. to move, twist, or wind in the manner of a snake.

snap, v., **snapped, snapping**, n., adj. —v. 1. to move, strike, shut, catch, etc. with a sharp sound. 2. to break suddenly. 3. to make a quick or sudden bite or snatch. 4. to utter a quick, sharp screech, reproof, retort, etc. 5. to seize with, or as with, a quick bite or snatch (up or off). 6. Photog. to take a snapshot of. —n. 7. (an action causing) a sharp, crackling or clicking sound. 8. a quick or sudden bite or snatch. 9. a short spell, as of cold weather. 10. →**snapshot.** —adj. 11. denoting devices closing by pressure on a spring catch. 12. made, done, taken, etc., suddenly.

snap·per, n. a marine food fish. Also **schnapper.**

snappish, adj. curt, ill-tempered, impatient.

snap·shot, n. an informal photograph.

snare, n. anything serving to entrap, entangle, or catch unawares.

snarl[1], v. 1. to growl angrily or viciously. —n. 2. the act of snarling.

snarl[2], n. 1. a tangle, as of thread or hair. —v. 2. to bring into a tangled condition, as thread, hair, etc.

snatch, v. 1. to make a sudden effort to seize something (at). 2. to seize by a sudden or hasty grasp (up, from, out of, away, etc.). —n. 3. the act of snatching. 4. a bit, scrap, or fragment of something.

snazzy, adj., **-zier, -ziest.** Colloq. very smart, strikingly fashionable.

sneak, v., **sneaked** or Colloq. **snuck, sneaking.** n. —v. 1. to go in a stealthy or furtive manner (about, along, in, off, out, etc.). 2. to act in a furtive, underhand, or mean way. 3. to move, put, pass, etc., in a stealthy or furtive manner. —n. 4. one who gives furtive information about others.

sneaker, n. Colloq. a shoe with a rubber or other soft sole used esp. in gymnasiums; trainer.

sneer, v. 1. to smile or curl the lip in a manner that shows scorn, contempt, etc. —n. 2. an act of sneering.

sneeze, v., **sneezed, sneezing**, n. —v. 1. to emit air or breath suddenly, forcibly, and audibly through the nose and mouth by involuntary spasmodic action. —n. 2. an act or sound of sneezing.

snick, v. to cut, snip, or nick.

snide, adj. derogatory in a nasty, insinuating manner.

sniff, v. 1. to draw air through the nose in short, audible inhalation. 2. to draw in or through the nose by sniffing, as air, smells, liquid, powder, etc. —n. 3. an act of sniffing.

snif·fle, v., **-fled, -fling.** to sniff repeatedly, as from a cold, etc.

snig·ger, v. to laugh in a half-suppressed, disrespectful manner.

snip, v., **snipped, snipping**, n. —v. 1. to cut with a small, quick stroke. —n. 2. the act of snipping. 3. a small

489

snip

cut, notch, slit, etc., made by snipping.

snipe, *v.,* **sniped, sniping.** to shoot at individual soldiers, etc., as opportunity offers from a concealed or long-range position.

snip·pet, *n.* a small piece snipped off.

snivel, *v.,* **-elled, -elling. 1.** to weep or cry with sniffing. **2.** to draw up mucus audibly through the nose.

snob, *n.* one who affects social importance and exclusiveness.

snoo·ker, *n.* a game played on a billiard table.

snoop, *Colloq. v.* **1.** to prowl or pry; go about in a sneaking, prying way. *–n.* **2.** an act or instance of snooping. **3.** one who snoops.

snooze, *v.,* **snoozed, snoozing,** *n., Colloq. –v.* **1.** to sleep; doze. *–n.* **2.** a rest; short sleep.

snore, *v.,* **snored, snoring,** *n. –v.* **1.** to breathe during sleep with hoarse or harsh sounds. *–n.* **2.** the sound made.

snor·kel, *n.* a tube enabling an underwater swimmer to breathe.

snort, *v.* **1.** to force the breath violently and noisily through the nostrils, as a horse, etc. **2.** to express contempt, indignation, etc., by such a sound. *–n.* **3.** the act or sound of snorting.

snot, *n. Colloq.* mucus from the nose.

snout, *n.* the part of an animal's head projecting forward and containing the nose and jaws.

snow, *n.* **1.** the aqueous vapour of the atmosphere, partially frozen, and falling to the earth in white flakes. **2.** something resembling snow. *–v.* **3.** to send down snow;

soak

fall as snow. **4.** to descend like snow. **5.** to cover, obstruct, isolate, etc., with snow (*in, over, under, up,* etc.).

snub, *v.,* **snubbed, snubbing,** *n., adj. –v.* **1.** to treat with disdain or contempt. **2.** to check or rebuke sharply. *–n.* **3.** an act of snubbing. *–adj.* **4.** (of the nose) short, and turned up at the tip.

snuff[1], *n.* a preparation of powdered tobacco inhaled into the nostrils.

snuff[2], *v.* to extinguish (*out*).

snuf·fle, *v.,* **-fled, -fling,** *n. –v.* **1.** to speak through the nose or with a nasal twang. **2.** to sniff; snivel. *–n.* **3.** an act of snuffling.

snug, *adj.,* **snugger, snuggest. 1.** comfortable or cosy, as a place. **2.** fitting closely, but comfortably, as a garment.

snug·gle, *v.,* **-gled, -gling,** *n. –v.* **1.** to lie or press closely, as for comfort or from affection (*up, in,* etc). *–n.* **2.** a cuddle.

so, *adv.* **1.** in the way or manner indicated, described, or implied. **2.** as stated or reported. **3.** to that extent; in that degree. **4.** for a given reason; hence; therefore. **5.** in the way that follows; in this way. **6. and so on,** et cetera. **7. or so,** about thus: *a day or so ago. –conj.* **8.** *Colloq.* consequently; with the result that. **9.** under the condition that (*that*). *–pron.* **10.** such as has been stated: *to be good and stay so.*

soak, *v.* **1.** to lie in and become saturated or permeated with a liquid. **2.** to pass, as a liquid, through pores or openings (*in, through, out,* etc.). **3.** to place and keep in liquid in order to saturate thoroughly. **4.** to permeate thoroughly, as liquid or moisture. **5.** to

soak

absorb (*up*). –*n.* **6.** the act of soaking.

soap, *n.* **1.** a substance used for washing and cleansing. –*v.* **2.** to rub, cover or treat with soap.

soap·box, *n.* (formerly) a wooden box used as a temporary platform by street speakers.

soar, *v.* to fly at a great height, without visible movements of the pinions, as a bird.

sob, *v.*, **sobbed, sobbing,** *n.* –*v.* **1.** to weep with a sound caused by a convulsive catching of the breath. –*n.* **2.** a convulsive catching of the breath in weeping.

sober, *adj.* **1.** not intoxicated or drunk. **2.** quiet or sedate in demeanour, as persons. **3.** free from excess, extravagance, or exaggeration. –*v.* **4.** to make or become sober. – **sobriety,** *n.*

soccer, *n.* a form of football in which the use of the hands and arms is prohibited except to the goalkeeper.

socia·ble, *adj.* enjoying the company of others.

social, *adj.* **1.** pertaining to friendly companionship or relations. **2.** of or pertaining to the life and relation of human beings in a community. –*n.* **3.** a social gathering or party.

socia·lise, *v.*, **-lised, -lising. 1.** to educate to conform to society. **2.** to go into society.

socia·lism, *n.* a theory or system of social organisation which advocates public ownership and control of the means of production, capital, land, etc. – **socialist,** *adj., n.*

socia·lite, *n.* a member of the social elite.

social work, *n.* organised work directed towards the betterment of social conditions, esp. among the disadvantaged in the community.

soci·ety, *n., pl.* **-ties,** *adj.* –*n.* **1.** a body of individuals living as members of a community. **2.** people regarded as a body divided into classes according to worldly status. **3.** an association for religious, benevolent, literary, scientific, etc., purposes. –*adj.* **4.** of or pertaining to polite society.

soci·ology, *n.* the science or study of the development, organisation, and functioning of human society.

sock[1]**,** *n.* a short stocking reaching about halfway to the knee, or only above the ankle.

sock[2]**,** *v. Colloq.* to strike or hit hard.

socket, *n.* a hollow part or piece for receiving and holding some part or thing.

sod, *n.* a cut piece of turf with its soil and roots.

soda, *n.* **1.** sodium (in phrases). **2.** soda-water. **3.** a drink made with soda-water, served with fruit or other syrups, ice-cream, etc.

soda-water, *n.* an effervescent drink consisting of water charged with carbon dioxide.

sodden, *adj.* soaked with liquid or moisture.

sodium, *n.* a soft, silver-white metallic element which oxidises rapidly in moist air. *Symbol:* Na

sodium chloride, *n. Chem.* common salt, NaCl.

sodomy, *n.* any sexual practice regarded as unnatural or perverted.

sofa, *n.* a long upholstered seat, or couch.

soft, *adj.* **1.** yielding readily to touch, cutting or pressure; not hard or stiff. **2.** smooth and agreeable to the touch. **3.** producing agreeable sensations. **4.** gentle, mild. **5.** not strong or robust. **6.** *Colloq.* involving little effort. **7.** (of water) relatively free from mineral salts that interfere with the action of soap. **8.** (of drugs) non-addictive, as marijuana and LSD. – **softness**, *n.*

soft·ball, *n.* a form of baseball played with a larger and softer ball.

soft drink, *n.* a drink which is not alcoholic or intoxicating.

soft·ware, *n.* a collection of programs used to instruct a computer (opposed to *hardware*).

soggy, *adj.*, **-gier, -giest. 1.** soaked; thoroughly wet. **2.** damp and heavy, as ill-baked bread.

soil[1], *n.* **1.** the ground or earth in which plants grow. **2.** a particular kind of earth.

soil[2], *v.* to make or become dirty or foul, esp. on the surface.

so·journ, *v.* **1.** to dwell for a time in a place. –*n.* **2.** a temporary remaining in a place.

solace, *n., v.,* **-aced, -acing.** –*n.* **1.** comfort in sorrow or trouble. **2.** something that gives comfort. –*v.* **3.** to comfort, console, or cheer (someone).

solar, *adj.* **1.** of, pertaining to, or determined by the sun. **2.** proceeding from the sun, as light or heat. **3.** operating by the light or heat of the sun.

solar plexus, *n.* a network of nerves situated at the upper part of the abdomen.

sold, *v.* past tense and past participle of **sell**.

solder, *n.* **1.** melted alloys applied to metal surfaces, joints, etc., to unite them. –*v.* **2.** to unite with solder.

sol·dier, *n.* **1.** one who serves in an army for pay. –*v.* **2.** to act or serve as a soldier.

sole[1], *adj.* **1.** being the only one or ones. **2.** belonging or pertaining to one individual or group to the exclusion of all others.

sole[2], *n.* **1.** the bottom or under surface of the foot. **2.** the corresponding under part of a shoe, boot, or the like.

sole[3], *n., pl.* **soles,** (*esp. collectively*) **sole.** a flatfish with a hooklike snout.

sol·ecism, *n.* any error, impropriety, or inconsistency.

solemn, *adj.* **1.** grave, sober, or mirthless. **2.** serious or earnest. **3.** formal or ceremonious. – **solemnity,** *n.*

sol·enoid, *n.* a coiled electrical conductor which, when a current passes through, establishes a magnetic field.

solfa, *n. Music.* a system of syllables used to represent the notes of the scale.

sol·icit, *v.* **1.** to seek for by entreaty, earnest or respectful request, etc. **2.** to accost another with immoral intention. **3.** to endeavour to obtain orders or trade. – **solicitation,** *n.*

sol·ici·tor, *n.* a lawyer who advises clients, represents them in lower courts and prepares cases for barristers to conduct in the higher courts.

sol·ici·tous, *adj.* anxious or concerned.

solid, *adj.* **1.** having 3 dimensions (length, breadth, and thickness). **2.** having the interior completely

solid

filled up. 3. without openings or breaks. 4. firm, hard, or compact in substance. 5. dense, thick, or heavy in nature or appearance. 6. whole or entire. 7. financially sound. —*n.* 8. a body or magnitude having length, breadth, and thickness. 9. a solid substance or body.

soli·darity, *n.* union or fellowship arising from common responsibilities and interests.

solid-state, *adj.* of or pertaining to electronic devices which are composed of components in the solid state, as transistors, integrated circuits, etc.

sol·il·oquy, *n., pl.* **-quies.** the act of talking when alone or as if alone.

soli·taire, *n.* 1. a game played by one person alone. 2. a precious stone set by itself.

soli·tary, *adj.* 1. without companions. 2. done without assistance or accompaniment. 3. secluded, or lonely.

soli·tude, *n.* the state of being or living alone.

solo, *n., pl.* **-los, -li,** *adj., adv.* —*n.* 1. any performance by one person. —*adj.* 2. performed alone. —*adv.* 3. alone.

sol·stice, *n. Astron.* the shortest (winter) or longest (summer) day of the year.

solu·ble, *adj.* 1. capable of being dissolved. 2. capable of being solved or explained.

solu·tion, *n.* 1. an explanation or answer. 2. the fact of being dissolved. 3. a homogeneous molecular mixture of 2 or more substances.

solve, *v.*, **solved, solving.** 1. to clear up or explain. 2. to work out the answer or solution to.

sol·vent, *adj.* 1. able to pay all just debts. 2. having the power of dissolving. —*n.* 3. the component of a solution which dissolves the other component. — **solvency,** *n.*

sombre, *adj.* gloomily dark, shadowy, or dimly lit

som·brero, *n., pl.* **-ros.** a broad-brimmed hat, as worn in Mexico.

some, *adj.* 1. being an undetermined or unspecified one. 2. certain (with plural nouns). 3. of a certain unspecified number, amount, degree, etc. —*pron.* 4. certain persons, instances, etc., not specified.

some·body, *pron., n., pl.* **-bodies.** —*pron.* 1. some person. —*n.* 2. a person of some note or importance.

some·how, *adv.* in some way not specified, apparent, or known.

some·one, *pron., n.* somebody.

somer·sault, *n.* an acrobatic movement of the body in which it describes a complete revolution, heels over head.

some·what, *adv.* in some measure or degree; to some extent.

some·where, *adv.* in, at or to some place not specified, determined, or known.

som·nam·bu·lism, *n.* sleepwalking.

som·nolent, *adj.* (tending to make one) drowsy or sleepy.

son, *n.* 1. a male child or person in relation to his parents. 2. any male descendant. 3. one related as if by ties of sonship.

sonar, *n.* an echo sounder. Also, **SONAR.**

sonata, *n.* an extended instrumental composition.

song, *n.* 1. a short metrical com-

song

position combining words and music. **2.** poetical compositions. **3.** the musical or tuneful sounds produced by certain birds, insects, etc.

song·ster, *n.* singer; songbird.

son·ic, *adj.* **1.** of or pertaining to sound. **2.** denoting a speed approximating that at which sound travels.

son-in-law, *n., pl.* **sons-in-law.** the husband of one's daughter.

son·net, *n.* a poem of 14 lines.

so·no·rous, *adj.* loud, deep, or resonant, as a sound.

soon, *adv.* **1.** within a short period after this (or that) time, event, etc. **2.** promptly or quickly.

soot, *n.* a black carbonaceous substance produced during the imperfect combustion of coal, wood, oil, etc.

soothe, *v.,* **soothed, soothing. 1.** to tranquillise or calm. **2.** to mitigate or allay, as pain, sorrow, doubt, etc.

sop, *n., v.,* **sopped, sopping.** –*n.* **1.** something given to pacify or quiet, or as a bribe. –*v.* **2.** to drench or become drenched. **3.** to take (water, etc.) by absorption (*up*).

soph·is·ti·cat·ed, *adj.* **1.** (of a person, ideas, manners, etc.) altered by education, experience, etc., to be worldly-wise. **2.** of intellectual complexity; reflecting a high degree of skill, intelligence, etc.; subtle. – **sophisticate,** *n.*

soph·is·ti·ca·tion, *n.* **1.** sophisticated character, ideas, tastes or ways. **2.** advanced refinement or complexity.

soph·is·try, *n.* specious reasoning.

so·po·rif·ic, *adj.* causing or tending to cause sleep.

sought

sop·py, *adj.,* **-pier, -piest.** *Colloq.* excessively sentimental.

so·pra·no, *n., pl.* **-pranos, -prani.** the highest singing voice in women and boys.

sor·bet /ˈsɔːbeɪ/, *n.* an iced dessert made with fruit.

sor·cer·y, *n., pl.* **-ceries.** magic, esp. black magic. – **sorcerer,** *n.*

sor·did, *adj.* **1.** filthy; squalid. **2.** morally mean or ignoble.

sore, *adj.,* **sorer, sorest.** –*adj.* **1.** physically painful or sensitive, as a wound. **2.** suffering bodily pain. **3.** causing very great suffering, misery, hardship, etc. –*n.* **4.** a sore spot or place on the body.

sor·row, *n.* **1.** distress caused by loss, affliction, disappointment, etc. **2.** a cause or occasion of grief or regret. –*v.* **3.** to feel sorrow.

sor·ry, *adv.,* **-rier, -riest.** feeling regret, compunction, sympathy, pity, etc. **2.** of a deplorable, pitiable, or miserable kind.

sort, *n.* **1.** a particular kind, species, variety, class, or group. **2.** of sorts, of a mediocre or poor kind. **3.** out of sorts, not in a normal condition of good health, spirits, or temper. **4.** sort of, to a certain extent; in some way. –*v.* **5.** to arrange according to sort, kind, or class. **6.** to separate or take (*out*) from other sorts, or from others.

sot·to vo·ce /sɒtoʊ ˈvoʊtʃeɪ/, *adv.* in a low tone intended not to be overheard.

souf·flé /ˈsuːfleɪ/, *n.* a light savoury or sweet (baked or unbaked) dish made fluffy with beaten egg-whites.

sought, *v.* past tense and past participle of **seek**.

soul, *n.* 1. the spiritual part of man. 2. the seat of the feelings or sentiments. 3. the embodiment of some quality. 4. a human being.

sound[1], *n.* 1. the sensation produced in the organs of hearing by certain vibrations in the surrounding air. 2. a noise, vocal utterance, musical note, or the like. 3. mere noise, without meaning. –*v.* 4. to (cause to) make or emit a sound. 5. to be heard, as a sound. 6. to convey a certain impression when heard or read. 7. to give forth (a sound).

sound[2], *adj.* 1. free from injury, defect, etc. 2. financially strong, secure, or reliable.

sound[3], *v.* 1. to measure or try the depth of (water, a deep hole, etc.) by letting down a lead or plummet at the end of a line. 2. to seek to elicit the views or sentiments of (a person) by indirect inquiries, etc. (*out*).

sound[4], *n.* an inlet (usu. narrow) of the sea.

soup, *n.* a liquid food made of various ingredients boiled together.

sour, *adj.* 1. having an acid taste, such as that of vinegar, lemon juice, etc. 2. rendered acid or affected by fermentation. 3. distasteful or disagreeable.

source, *n.* any thing or place from which something comes, arises, or is obtained.

souse, *v.*, **soused, sousing.** to plunge into water or other liquid.

south, *n.* 1. a cardinal point of the compass directly opposite to the north. –*adj.* 2. directed or proceeding towards the south. 3. coming from the south, as a wind. –*adv.* 4. towards or in the south. Also, **esp.** *Naut.*, **sou'.** –*southerly, adj., – southern, adj.*

sou·venir, *n.* something given or kept for remembrance.

sove·reign, *n.* 1. a monarch. 2. a former British gold coin. –*adj.* 3. belonging to or characteristic of a sovereign. – **sovereignty,** *n.*

sow[1] /sou/, *v.*, **sowed, sown** or **sowed, sowing.** 1. to scatter (seed) for growth. 2. to scatter seed over (land, earth, etc.).

sow[2] /sau/, *n.* an adult female pig.

soya bean, *n.* a leguminous plant with an oil-yielding seed used as food. Also, **soy, soybean.**

soya sauce, *n.* a salty dark brown sauce, made by fermenting soya beans in brine. Also, **soy sauce.**

spa, *n.* 1. a mineral spring, or a locality in which such springs exist. 2. an enclosed section of a swimming pool through which heated, aerated water is pumped.

space, *n., v.*, **spaced, spacing.** –*n.* 1. the unlimited expanse extending in all directions in which the universe is placed. 2. that part of the universe which lies outside the earth's atmosphere. 3. (a particular) extent or area. 4. extent, or for a particular extent, of time. –*v.* 5. to set some distance apart.

space·craft, *n.* a vehicle capable of travelling in space.

spa·cious, *adj.* containing much space, as a house, street, etc.

spade[1], *n.* 1. a tool for digging. 2. some implement, piece, or part resembling this.

spade[2], *n.* a black figure shaped like an inverted heart with a short stem used on playing cards.

spadework

spade·work, *n.* laborious or tedious preliminary work.

spa·ghet·ti, *n.* a kind of pasta.

span, *n., v.,* **spanned, spanning.** –*n.* **1.** the distance between the tip of the thumb and the tip of the little finger when the hand is fully extended. **2.** the distance or space between 2 supports of a bridge, beam, or similar structure. **3.** the full extent, stretch or reach of anything. –*v.* **4.** to encircle with the hand or hands. **5.** to extend over or across.

span·gle, *n., v.,* **-gled, -gling.** –*n.* **1.** a small, thin piece of sparkling material, usu. metal, for decorating clothes, etc. –*v.* **2.** to decorate with spangles.

span·iel, *n.* a small dog usu. with a long, silky coat and drooping ears.

spank, *v.* **1.** to strike (a person, usu. a child) with the open hand, a slipper, etc., esp. on the buttocks. –*n.* **2.** a blow given in spanking.

span·ner, *n.* a tool for gripping and turning the head of a bolt, a nut, a pipe, etc.

spar[1], *n. Naut.* a stout pole such as those used for masts, etc.; a mast, yard, boom, or the like.

spar[2], *v.,* **sparred, sparring.** to box with light blows, esp. while seeking an opening in an opponent's defense.

spare, *v.,* **spared, sparing,** *adj.* **sparer, sparest.** –*v.* **1.** to refrain from harming or destroying. **2.** to save from strain, discomfort, annoyance, or the like. **3.** to part with or let go, as from a supply, esp. without inconvenience. **4.** to use economically or frugally. **5.** to use economy; be frugal. –*adj.* **6.** kept in reserve. **7.** being in excess of present need. **8.** lean or thin, as a person. –*n.* **9.** an extra thing, part, etc.

spark, *n.* **1.** a fiery particle thrown off by burning wood, etc., or produced by one hard body striking against another. **2.** *Elect.* the light produced by a sudden discontinuous discharge of electricity. –*v.* **3.** to emit or produce sparks.

spar·kle, *v.,* **-kled, -kling.** –*v.* **1.** to emit little sparks, as burning matter. **2.** to shine with little gleams of light. **3.** to effervesce, as wine. –*n.* **4.** a little spark.

spark plug, *n.* a device inserted in the cylinder of an internal-combustion engine, containing 2 terminals between which passes the electric spark for igniting the explosive gases. Also, **sparking plug.**

spar·row, *n.* a small, hardy, pugnacious bird.

sparse, *adj.,* **sparser, sparsest.** thinly scattered or distributed.

Spar·tan, *adj.* rigorously simple, frugal or disciplined.

spasm, *n.* a sudden, involuntary muscular contraction.

spas·mod·ic, *adj.* like a spasm; intermittent.

spas·tic, *n.* one suffering from a condition, esp. cerebral palsy, involving paralysis and muscular spasm from birth.

spat[1], *n.* a petty quarrel.

spat[2], *v.* past tense and past participle of **spit.**

spate, *n.* a sudden, almost overwhelming outpouring.

spa·tial, *adj.* of or pertaining to space.

spatter

spat·ter, v. 1. to scatter or dash in small particles or drops. 2. to splash with small particles.

spat·ula, n. a broad, flexible blade, used for mixing and spreading.

spawn, v. 1. to shed the sex cells, esp. as applied to animals that shed eggs and sperm directly into water. 2. to give birth to; give rise to.

spay, v. to remove the ovaries of (a female animal).

speak, v., **spoke** or (*Archaic*) **spake**, **spoken** or (*Archaic*) **spoke**, **speaking**. 1. to utter words or articulate sounds. 2. to deliver an address. 3. to make communication by any means: *Her music speaks to me.* 4. to use, or be able to use, in oral utterance, as a language.

speaker, n. 1. (*usu. cap.*) the presiding officer of the lower house of a parliament. 2. a loudspeaker.

spear, n. 1. a weapon for thrusting or throwing, being a long staff with a sharp head, of iron or steel. –v. 2. to pierce with or as with a spear.

spear·mint, n. an aromatic herb.

special, adj. 1. of a distinct or particular character. 2. being a special one. 3. pertaining to or peculiar to a particular person, thing, instance, etc. 4. extraordinary. –n. 5. **on special**, *Colloq.* available at a bargain price.

specia·lise, v., **-lised**, **-lising**. 1. to pursue some special line of study, work, etc. 2. to invest with a special character, function, etc. 3. to adapt to special conditions. – **specialisation**, n.

specia·list, n. one who devotes himself to one subject, or to one particular branch of a subject or pursuit.

spectrum

specia·lity, n., pl. **-ties**. an article of unusual or superior design or quality.

special·ty, n., pl. **-ties**. 1. a special study, line of work, etc. 2. an article particularly dealt in, manufactured, etc.

spe·cies, n., pl. **-cies**. a group of individuals having some common characteristics or qualities; distinct sort or kind.

speci·fic, adj. 1. specified, precise, or particular. 2. peculiar or proper to something, as qualities, characteristics, effects, etc. 3. of a special or particular kind. –n. 4. something specific, as a statement, quality, etc. – **specificity**, n.

speci·fi·cation, n. the act of specifying. 2. a statement of particulars.

specify, v., **-fied**, **-fying**. 1. to mention or name specifically or definitely. 2. to name or state as a condition.

speci·men, n. something taken as an example or sample.

spe·cious, adj. apparently good or right but without real merit.

speck, n. 1. a small spot differing in colour or substance from its background. 2. a small particle. –v. 3. to mark with, or as with, a speck or specks.

speckle, n., v., **-led**, **-ling**. 1. a small speck, spot, or mark, as on skin. –v. 2. to mark with speckles.

spec·tacle, n. 1. something striking presented to the sight or view. 2. (*pl.*) →**glass** (def. 2). – **spectacular**, adj.

spec·tator, n. one who looks on; an onlooker.

spec·tre, n. a ghost; phantom.

spec·trum, n. *Physics.* 1. the band of

spectrum

colours (red, orange, yellow, green, blue, indigo, violet) revealed when white light passes through a prism. **2.** a range of interrelated values, objects, opinions, etc.

spec·u·late, *v.*, -lated, -lating. **1.** to engage in thought or reflection (*on*, or *upon*). **2.** to indulge in conjectural thought. **3.** *Comm.* to buy and sell commodities, shares, etc., in the expectation of profit. – **speculation**, *n.* – **speculative**, *adj.* – **speculator**, *n.*

sped, *v.* past tense and past participle of **speed**.

speech, *n.* **1.** the faculty or power of speaking. **2.** that which is spoken. **3.** a communication made by a speaker before an audience for a given purpose. **4.** a characteristic form of language or dialect. **5.** manner of speaking, as of a person.

speed, *n., v.,* **sped** or **speeded**, **speeding**. –*n.* **1.** rapidity in moving. **2.** the ratio of the distance covered to the time taken. **3.** *Colloq.* amphetamines. –*v.* **4.** to move or proceed with rapidity. **5.** to drive a vehicle faster than the maximum permitted. **6.** **speed up**, to increase the speed or progress (of).

speed·om·e·ter, *n.* a device attached to a motor vehicle or the like to record the rate of travel. Also, **speedo**.

spel·e·ol·o·gy, *n.* the exploration and study of caves. Also, **spelaeology**.

spell[1], *v.,* **spelt** or **spelled**, **spelling**. **1.** to name or write in order, the letters of (a word, syllable, etc.). **2.** (of letters) to form (a word, syllable, etc.). **3.** to name, write, or give the letters of words, etc.

spell[2], *n.* a combination of words supposed to possess magic power.

spell[3], *n.* **1.** a continuous course or period of work or other activity. **2.** *Colloq.* an interval or space of time, usu. indefinite or short. **3.** an interval or period of rest. –*v.* **4.** to give an interval of rest to.

spell·ing, *n.* the manner in which words are spelt.

spen·cer, *n.* a woman's undergarment, worn for extra warmth.

spend, *v.,* **spent**, **spending**. **1.** to pay out, disburse, or expend; dispose of (money, wealth, resources, etc.). **2.** to spend money, etc.

spend·thrift, *n.* one who spends his possessions or money extravagantly.

sperm, *n.* a male reproductive cell.

sper·ma·to·zo·on, *n., pl.* -**zoa**. a mature male reproductive cell.

spew, *v.* to vomit.

sphere, *n.* **1.** a round body whose surface is at all points equidistant from the centre. **2.** a field of activity. – **spherical**, *adj.*

sphinc·ter, *n.* a circular band of voluntary or involuntary muscle which encircles an orifice. of the body or one of its hollow organs.

spice, *n., v.,* **spiced**, **spicing**. –*n.* **1.** any of a class of pungent or aromatic substances of vegetable origin, used as seasoning or preservatives. **2.** piquancy, or interest. –*v.* **3.** to prepare or season with a spice or spices. – **spicy**, *adj.*

spick-and-span, *adj.* **1.** neat and clean. **2.** perfectly new; fresh.

spi·der, *n.* any of the eight-legged wingless, predatory, insectlike arachnids, most of which spin webs.

spiel /spiːl, ʃpiːl/, *n.* a salesman's, conjurer's, or swindler's patter.

spigot

spigot, *n.* a small peg or plug for stopping the vent of a cask, etc.

spike, *n., v.*, **spiked, spiking.** –*n.* 1. a stiff, sharp-pointed piece or part. –*v.* 2. to fasten or secure with a spike or spikes. 3. to pierce with a spike. 4. to set with something suggesting spikes. 5. to make ineffective, or frustrate the action or purpose of. 6. *Colloq.* to add alcoholic liquor to a drink.

spill, *v.*, **spilt** or **spilled, spilling**, *n.* –*v.* 1. to cause or allow (liquid, or any matter in grains or loose pieces) to run or fall from a container, esp. accidentally. 2. (of a liquid, loose particles, etc.) to run or escape from a container. –*n.* 3. a spilling. 4. a quantity spilt. 5. a throw or fall from a horse, vehicle, or the like.

spin, *v.*, **spun** or (*Archaic*) **span; spun; spinning**. –*v.* 1. to make (yarn) from fibres. 2. to form (any material) into thread. 3. to cause to turn round rapidly, as on an axis. 4. to make up or tell (a story): *He spins a good tale.* 5. to turn round rapidly, as on an axis, as the earth, a top, etc. 6. to produce a thread from the body, as spiders, silkworms, etc. –*n.* 7. a spinning motion given to a ball or the like when thrown or struck.

spin·ach, *n.* an annual herb cultivated for its succulent leaves.

spin·dle, *n.* 1. the rod on a spinning wheel by which the thread is twisted and on which it is wound. 2. any similar rod or pin.

spin·dly, *adj.*, **-dlier, -dliest.** long or tall and slender.

spine, *n.* 1. the vertebral or any backbone-like part. 2. a stiff, pointed process or appendage. 3. 4. the part of a book's cover that holds the front and back together. –**spi·nal**, *adj.*

spine·chilling, *adj.* terrifying.

spini·fex, *n.* spiny-leaved, tussock-forming grasses of coastal or inland Aust.

spin·naker, *n.* a large triangular sail with a light boom (**spinnaker boom**).

spin·ning wheel, *n.* a device for spinning wool, flax, etc., into yarn or thread.

spin-off, *n.* an object, product or enterprise derived as an incidental or secondary development of a larger enterprise.

spin·ster, *n.* a woman still unmarried beyond the usual age of marrying.

spiny anteater, *n.* →**echidna**.

spiral, *n., adj., v.*, **-ralled, -ralling.** –*n.* 1. a plane curve running continuously round a fixed point or centre while constantly receding from it. 2. a spiral object, formation, or form. 3. *Econ.* a reciprocal interaction of price and cost changes forming an overall economic change. –*adj.* 4. resembling or arranged in a spiral or spirals. –*v.* 5. to (cause to) take a spiral form or course.

spire, *n.* a tall, tapering structure erected on a tower, roof, etc.

spirit, *n.* 1. the vital principle in man, animating the body or mediating between body and soul. 2. a supernatural, incorporeal being. 3. (*pl.*) feelings with respect to exaltation or depression. 4. fine or brave vigour or liveliness. 5. the true intent of a statement, etc. 6. (*oft. pl.*) a strong distilled alcoholic

499

spirit

liquor. –*adj.* **7.** pertaining to something which works by burning alcoholic spirits. –*v.* **8.** to carry (*away, off,* etc.) mysteriously or secretly. – **spirited,** *adj.*

spir·i·tual, *adj.* **1.** of, pertaining to, or consisting of spirit or incorporeal being. –*n.* **2.** a traditional religious song, esp. of American Negroes.

spit[1], *v.,* **spat** or **spit, spitting,** *n.* –*v.* **1.** to eject saliva from the mouth. **2.** to sputter. **3.** to fall in scattered drops or flakes, as rain or snow. **4.** to eject (saliva, etc.) from the mouth. **5.** to throw out or emit, esp. violently. –*n.* **6.** saliva, esp. when ejected. **7.** the act of spitting. Also, **dead spit.** *Colloq.* the image, likeness, or counterpart of a person, etc.

spit[2], *n., v.,* **spitted, spitting.** –*n.* **1.** any of various rods, pins, or the like used for particular purposes. **2.** a narrow point of land projecting into the water. –*v.* **3.** to thrust a spit through, as roasting meat.

spite, *n., v.,* **spited, spiting.** –*n.* **1.** an ill-natured desire to humiliate or injure another. **2. in spite of,** in disregard or defiance of. –*v.* **3.** to annoy or thwart, out of spite.

spit·tle, *n.* saliva; spit.

spit·toon, *n.* a bowl, etc., for spitting into.

splash, *v.* **1.** to wet or soil by dashing masses or particles of water, mud, etc., against. **2.** to dash (water, etc.) about in scattered masses or particles. **3.** *Colloq.* to display or print very noticeably, as in a newspaper. **4.** to fall or move in scattered masses or particles. –*n.* **5.** the act or sound of splashing. **6.** a striking show, or an ostentatious display.

spoil

splat·ter, *v.* to splash.

splay, *v.* **1.** to spread out, expand, or extend. **2.** to spread or flare.

spleen, *n.* **1.** a glandlike organ, in the upper left of the abdomen, which modifies the blood. **2.** ill humour, peevish temper, or spite.

splen·did, *adj.* **1.** gorgeous; magnificent. **2.** strikingly admirable or fine.

splen·dour, *n.* brilliant or gorgeous appearance, colouring, etc.

splice, *v.,* **spliced, splicing.** to join together or unite, esp. by the interweaving of strands.

splint, *n.* **1.** a thin piece of wood or other rigid material used to immobilise a fractured or dislocated bone. –*v.* **2.** to support with splints.

splin·ter, *n.* **1.** a thin, sharp piece of wood, bone, etc., split or broken off from a main body. –*v.* **2.** to split or break into splinters.

split, *v.,* **split, splitting,** *n., adj.* –*v.* **1.** to divide into distinct parts or portions. **2.** to separate (a part) by such division. **3.** to break or part lengthways. **4.** to part, divide, or separate in any way. **5.** to become separated off as a piece or part from a whole. **6.** *Colloq.* to leave hurriedly. –*n.* **7.** the act of splitting. **8.** a crack, rent, or fissure caused by splitting. **9.** (*usu. pl.*) the feat of separating the legs at right angles to the body while sinking to the floor. –*adj.* **10.** that has undergone splitting.

splurge, *v.,* **splurged, splurging.** *Colloq.* to be extravagant.

splut·ter, *v.* **1.** to talk hastily and confusedly. **2.** to spatter, as a liquid.

spoil, *v.,* **spoiled** or **spoilt, spoiling,** *n.*

spoil

−*v.* **1.** to damage or impair (a thing) irreparably. **2.** to impair in character or disposition. **3.** to become spoiled, bad, or unfit for use. −*n.* **4.** (*oft. pl.*) booty, loot, or plunder taken in war or robbery. **5.** treasures won or accumulated.

spoil·sport, *n.* one who interferes with the pleasure of others.

spoke¹, *v.* past tense of **speak**.

spoke², *n.* one of the rungs radiating from the hub of a wheel.

spoken, *v.* **1.** past participle of **speak**. **2.** (in compounds) speaking, or using speech, as specified.

spokes·person, *n.* one who speaks for another or others.

sponge, *n.*, *v.*, **sponging**. −*n.* **1.** the light, porous, fibrous skeleton of certain marine animals which absorbs water readily, becoming soft but retaining toughness. **2.** one who or that which absorbs something freely, as a sponge does water. **3.** a light, sweet cake. −*v.* **4.** to wipe or rub with a wet sponge. **5.** to remove with a wet sponge (*off*, *away*, etc.). **6.** *Colloq.* to live at the expense of others.

spon·sor, *n.* **1.** one who vouches or is responsible for a person or thing. **2.** a person, firm, etc., that finances a radio or television program in return for advertisement. −*v.* **3.** to act as sponsor for.

spon·taneous, *adj.* **1.** natural and unconstrained. **2.** independent of external agencies.

spoof, *n.* *Colloq.* a parody.

spook, *n.* *Colloq.* a ghost; spectre.

spool, *n.* any cylindrical piece on which something is wound.

spoon, *n.* **1.** a utensil consisting of a bowl or concave part and a handle, for taking up or stirring liquid or other food. −*v.* **2.** to take up or transfer in or as in a spoon. **3.** *Colloq.* to show affection, esp. in an openly sentimental manner.

spooner·ism, *n.* the transposition of initial sounds of words, as in 'our queer old dean' for 'our dear old queen'.

spoor, *n.* a track or trail of a wild animal.

spo·radic, *adj.* appearing or happening at intervals.

spore, *n.* a germ, germ cell, seed, or the like.

spor·ran, *n.* (in Scottish Highland costume) a large pouch hanging from the belt over the front of the kilt.

sport, *n.* **1.** an energetic activity pursued for exercise or pleasure. **2.** a pleasant pastime. **3.** something sported with or tossed about like a plaything. **4.** *Colloq.* (a term of address, usu. between males). −*v.* **5.** to amuse oneself with some pleasant pastime. **6.** to have or wear, esp. ostentatiously.

sport·ing, *adj.* **1.** sportsmanlike. **2.** willing to take a chance. **3.** even or fair.

sports, *adj.* **1.** of, pertaining to, or devoted to a sport or sports. **2.** (of garments, etc.) suitable for outdoor or informal use.

sports car, *n.* a high-powered car with rakish lines, usu. a two-seater.

sports·man, *n.*, *pl.* **-men**. **1.** a man who engages in sport. **2.** one who exhibits qualities such as fairness, good humour when losing, willingness to take risks, etc.

spot, *n.*, *v.*, **spotted, spotting**. −*n.* **1.** a mark made by foreign matter.

spot

a blemish of the skin, as a pimple. 3. a relatively small, usu. roundish, part of a surface differing from the rest in appearance or character. 4. a moral blemish. 5. a place or locality. 6. *Colloq.* a small quantity of something. 7. *Colloq.* a predicament. –v. 8. to stain with spots. 9. to see or perceive, esp. suddenly, by chance, or when it is difficult to do so. 10. to make a spot.

spot·light, *n.* (in theatrical use) a strong light thrown upon a particular spot on the stage.

spot-on, *adj. Colloq.* absolutely right or accurate.

spouse, *n.* one's husband or wife.

spout, *v.* 1. to discharge or emit (a liquid, etc.) in a stream with some force. 2. to issue with force, as liquid through a narrow orifice. –*n.* 3. a tube by which a liquid is discharged or poured.

sprain, *v.* to overstrain or wrench (a joint), as an ankle, etc.

sprat, *n.* a small, herring-like marine fish.

sprawl, *v.* 1. to lie or sit with the limbs stretched out in a careless or ungraceful posture. 2. to spread out in a straggling or irregular manner, as vines, buildings, handwriting, etc. 3. to stretch out (the limbs) as in sprawling.

spray¹, *n.* 1. fine particles of water or other liquid blown or falling through the air. –*v.* 2. to scatter (as) in fine particles. 3. to direct a spray of particles, missiles, etc., upon. 4. to issue as spray.

spray², *n.* a single flower or small bouquet of flowers designed to be pinned to one's clothes.

spread, *v.*, **spread, spreading,** *n.* –*v.*

spring

1. to draw or stretch out to the full width. 2. to distribute in a sheet or layer. 3. to overlay or coat with something. 4. to diffuse or disseminate, as knowledge, news, disease, etc. 5. to become stretched out or extended. 6. to admit of being applied in a thin layer. 7. to become diffused abroad, or disseminated. –*n.* 8. expansion; extension; diffusion. 9. a stretch, expanse, or extent of something. 10. a cloth covering for a bed, table, etc. 11. any food preparation for spreading on bread, etc.

spread-eagle, *v.,* **-gled, -gling.** to stretch out with arms and legs wide apart. – **spread-eagled,** *adj.*

spree, *n.* a session or period of indulgence.

sprig, *n.* a shoot, twig, or small branch.

spright·ly, *adj.,* **-lier, -liest.** animated, vivacious, or gay.

spring, *v.,* **sprang** or **sprung, sprung, springing,** *n., adj.* –*v.* 1. to rise or move suddenly and lightly. 2. to go or come suddenly as if with a leap. 3. to come into being; rise or arise (*up*). 4. to cause to spring. 5. to bring out, disclose, produce, make, etc., suddenly. 6. to equip or fit with springs. 7. to make a surprise attack on (someone). –*n.* 8. a leap, jump, or bound. 9. elasticity or springiness. 10. an issue of water from the earth. 11. a beginning or cause of origin. 12. the season of the year between winter and summer. 13. the first and freshest period. 14. an elastic contrivance which recovers its shape after being compressed, bent, etc. –*adj.* 15. of or pertaining to the season of

spring

spring. **16.** resting on or containing springs. – **springy,** *adj.*

spring·board, *n.* a flexible board used as a take-off in vaulting, tumbling, etc.

sprin·kle, *v.,* -kled, -kling, *n.* –*v.* **1.** to scatter, as a liquid or a powder, in drops or particles. **2.** to disperse or distribute here and there. **3.** to overspread with drops or particles. –*n.* **4.** a sprinkling.

sprint, *v.* **1.** to race at full speed, esp. for a short distance, as in running, rowing, etc. –*n.* **2.** a short race at full speed.

sprite, *n.* an elf, fairy, or goblin.

sprock·et, *n. Mach.* one of a set of projections on the rim of a wheel which engage the links of a chain.

sprout, *v.* **1.** to begin to grow. **2.** (of a seed, plant, the earth, etc.) to put forth buds or shoots. –*n.* **3.** a shoot of a plant. **4.** →**brussels sprout.**

spruce[1], *n.* an evergreen tree with short angular needle-shaped leaves.

spruce[2], *adj.,* **sprucer, sprucest,** –*v.,* **spruced, sprucing.** –*adj.* **1.** smart in dress or appearance. –*v.* **2.** to make oneself smart (*up*).

spry, *adj.,* **spryer, spryest** or **sprier, spriest.** active; nimble.

spud, *n. Colloq.* a potato.

spume, *n.* foam; froth; scum.

spun, *v.* past tense and past participle of **spin.**

spunk, *n. Colloq.* pluck; spirit; mettle.

spur, *n., v.,* **spurred, spurring.** –*n.* **1.** a pointed device attached to a horseman's boot heel, for goading a horse onwards, etc. **2. on the spur of the moment,** suddenly; without premeditation. –*v.* **3.** to prick with, or as with, spurs or a spur.

square

spu·ri·ous, *adj.* not genuine or true.

spurn, *v.* to reject with disdain.

spurt, *v.* **1.** to gush or issue suddenly in a stream or jet. **2.** to show marked activity or energy for a short period. –*n.* **3.** a forcible gush of water, etc., as from a confined place. **4.** a sudden outburst, as of feeling.

sput·ter, *v.* **1.** to emit particles of anything in an explosive manner, as a candle does in burning. **2.** to emit (anything) in small particles, as if by spitting.

spy, *n., pl.* **spies,** *v.,* **spied, spying.** –*n.* **1.** one who keeps secret watch on the actions of others. **2.** one employed by a government to obtain secret information or intelligence. –*v.* **3.** to make secret observations. **4.** to find (*out*) by observation. **5.** to catch sight of; see.

squab·ble, *v.,* **-bled, -bling.** –*v.* **1.** to engage in a petty quarrel. *n.* **2.** a petty quarrel.

squad, *n.* any small group or party of persons engaged in a common enterprise, etc.

squad·ron, *n.* an airforce unit.

squal·id, *adj.* foul and repulsive.

squall[1], *n.* a sudden strong wind which dies away rapidly.

squall[2], *v.* to cry out loudly.

squal·or, *n.* filth and misery.

squan·der, *v.* to spend (money, time, etc) wastefully (*away*).

square, *n., v.,* **squared, squaring.** *adj.,* **squarer, squarest,** *adv.* –*n.* **1.** a right-angled, four-sided plane having all its sides equal. **2.** anything having this form or a form approximating to it. **3.** *Maths.* the 2nd power of a number or quantity. **4.**

503

square

Colloq. one who is ignorant of or uninterested in the latest fads. –*v.* **5.** to reduce to square, rectangular, or cubic form. **6.** *Maths.* to multiply (a number or quantity) by itself. **7.** to make straight, level, or even. **8.** to accord or agree (*with*). **9. square up**, to pay or settle a bill, debt, etc. –*adj.* **10.** of the form of a right angle. **11.** at right angles, or perpendicular. **12.** designating a unit representing an area in the form of a square. **13.** of a specified length on each side of a square. **14.** having all accounts settled. **15.** just, fair, or honest. **16.** conservative. –*adv.* **17.** in square or rectangular form.

square dance, *n.* a dance by couples arranged in a square or in some set form.

square root, *n. Maths.* the quantity of which a given quantity is the square (def. 3).

squash[1], *v.* **1.** to press into a flat mass or pulp. –*n.* **2.** the act or sound of squashing. **3.** the fact of being squashed. **4.** something squashed or crushed. **5.** Also, **squash racquets**, a game for 2 players, played in a small walled court with light racquets and a small rubber ball.

squash[2], *n.* a vegetable similar to the pumpkin.

squat, *v.*, **squatted** or **squat, squatting,** *adj.*, *n.* –*v.* **1.** to crouch close to the ground with the knees bent and the back more or less straight. **2.** to occupy a building without title or right. –*adj.* **3.** low and thick or broad. –*n.* **4.** a squatting position or posture.

squat·ter, *n.* **1.** one who occupies a building without right or title. **2.** (*Austral.*) (formerly) one who settled on Crown land to run stock.

squaw, *n.* a Nth American Indian woman or wife.

squawk, *v.* **1.** to utter a loud, harsh cry, as a duck. –*n.* **2.** a loud, harsh cry or sound.

squeak, *n.* **1.** a short, sharp, shrill cry. –*v.* **2.** to utter or emit a sound of this kind.

squeaky, *adj.*, **-ier, -iest.** making squeaking sound; clean, above criticism.

squeal, *n.* **1.** a more or less prolonged, sharp, shrill cry, as of pain, fear, etc. –*v.* **2.** to utter or emit a sound of this kind.

squeam·ish, *adj.* easily nauseated or sickened.

squeeze, *v.*, **squeezed, squeezing,** *n.* –*v.* **1.** to press forcibly together. **2.** to apply pressure to extract something. **3.** to thrust forcibly; force by pressure. **4.** to force out or extract by pressure (*out* or *from*). **5.** to exert a compressing force. **6.** to force a way through some narrow or crowded place (*through, in, out,* etc.). –*n.* **7.** the act of squeezing. **8.** a small quantity obtained by squeezing.

squelch, *v.* **1.** to strike or press with crushing sound. **2.** to make a splashing sound.

squid, *n.*, *pl.* **squids,** (*esp. collectively*) **squid.** any of various slender marine creatures with 10 tentacles.

squint, *v.* **1.** to look with the eyes partly closed. **2.** to look or glance obliquely or sideways. **3.** to close (the eyes) partly. –*n.* **4.** *Pathol.* a disorder of the eye. **5.** a looking obliquely. –*adj.* **6.** looking obliquely.

squire

squire, *n.*, *v.*, **squired, squiring.** –*n.* **1.**

squire a personal attendant of a person of rank. –*v.* 2. to attend as or in the manner of a squire.

squirm, *v.* 1. to wriggle or writhe.

squir·rel, *n.* 1. any of various arboreal, bushy-tailed rodents. 2. *Colloq.* a person who hoards objects of little value.

squirt, *v.* 1. to eject (liquid) in a jet from a narrow orifice. 2. to wet or spatter with a liquid so ejected. 3. to issue in a jetlike stream. –*n.* 4. a jet, as of water.

stab, *v.*, **stabbed, stabbing,** *n.* –*v.* 1. to pierce or wound with a pointed weapon. 2. to thrust or plunge (a knife, etc.) into something. 3. to thrust with a knife or other pointed weapon. –*n.* 4. the act of stabbing. 5. a sudden, usu. painful sensation.

stable[1], *n., v.,* **-bled, -bling.** –*n.* 1. a building for the lodging and feeding of horses. 2. a collection of horses belonging in such a building. 3. the people, or production centre(s), in the same large establishment. –*v.* 4. to put or lodge (as) in a stable.

stable[2], *adj.* not likely to give way, as a structure, support, etc. – **stability,** *n.* – **stabilise,** *v.*

stac·ca·to, *Music.* detached, disconnected, or abrupt.

stack, *n.* 1. an orderly pile or heap. 2. *Colloq.* a great quantity or number. 3. that part of a library in which the main holdings of a library are kept. 4. to pile in a stack. 5. to cover or load with something in stacks. 6. to bring a large number of one's own supporters to (a meeting) in order to outvote those of opposing views. 7. to accumulate (*up*).

stadium, *n., pl.* **-dia, -diums.** a sport-

stain ing facility, often enclosed, comprising an arena and tiers or seats for spectators.

staff, *n., pl.* **staffs, staves,** *v.* –*n.* 1. a pole or rod to aid in walking. 2. something which serves to support or sustain. 3. a body of persons charged with carrying out the work of an establishment. 4. *Music.* →**stave** (def. 1). –*v.* 5. to provide with a staff.

stag, *n.* 1. an adult male deer. –*adj.* 2. *Colloq.* for or of men only.

stage, *n., v.,* **staged, staging.** –*n.* 1. a single step or degree in a process; a particular period in a process of development. 2. a raised platform. 3. the theatre, the drama, or the dramatic profession. 4. the scene of any action. –*v.* 5. to put or represent on or as on a stage. 6. to arrange; set up, as for a particular event.

stage·coach, *n.* a coach that runs regularly over a fixed route.

stag·ger, *v.* 1. to walk, move, or stand unsteadily. 2. to cause to reel, as with shock. 3. to arrange in some order in which there is a continuous overlapping. –*n.* 4. the act of staggering.

stag·nant, *adj.* not running or flowing, as water, air, etc.

stag·nate, *v.,* **-nated, -nating.** 1. to become foul from standing, as a pool of water. 2. to become inactive, sluggish, or dull. 3. to make no progress; stop developing.

staid, *adj.* of settled or sedate character.

stain, *n.* 1. a discolouration produced by foreign matter. 2. a cause of reproach. 3. a solution or suspension of colouring matter in water, spirit, or oil. –*v.* 4. to discolour

505

stain

with spots or streaks of foreign matter. 5. to become stained.

stair, *n.* a series or flight of steps.

stair·case, *n.* a flight of stairs.

stair·well, *n.* the vertical opening containing a stairway.

stake[1], *n., v.,* staked, staking. —*n.* 1. a stick or post pointed at one end for driving into the ground. 2. a post to which a person is bound for execution. —*v.* 3. to mark with stakes (*off* or *out*). 4. to protect or separate by a barrier of stakes. 5. to support with a stake or stakes, as a plant. 6. to surround (a building, etc.) for the purposes of a raid or keeping watch (*out*).

stake[2], *n., v.,* staked, staking. —*n.* 1. that which is wagered. 2. an interest held in something. 3. **at stake**, involved; in a state of being at hazard. —*v.* 4. to put at risk upon the result of a game, venture, etc.

sta·lac·tite, *n.* a calcium deposit shaped like an icicle, hanging from the roof of a cave.

sta·lag·mite, *n.* a calcium deposit shaped like an inverted stalactite, formed on the floor of a cave.

stale, *adj.* having lost freshness or interest.

stale·mate, *n.* any position in which no action can be taken.

stalk[1], *n.* the stem or main axis of a plant.

stalk[2], *v.* 1. to pursue or approach game, etc., stealthily. 2. to walk with slow, stiff, or haughty strides. 3. to pursue (game, a person, etc.) stealthily.

stall, *n.* 1. a compartment in a stable or shed to accommodate one animal. 2. a booth or stand on which goods are displayed for sale. —*v.* 3.

stand

to come or bring to a standstill, esp. of a vehicle or an engine.

stal·lion, *n.* a male horse not castrated.

stal·wart /'stɔlwət/, *adj.* 1. strong and brave. 2. firm; steadfast.

sta·men, *n.* the pollen-bearing part of a flower.

stam·i·na, *n.* strength of physical constitution.

stam·mer, *v.* 1. to speak with spasmodic repetitions of syllables or sounds. —*n.* 2. a stammering mode of utterance.

stamp, *v.* 1. to strike or beat with a forcible downward thrust of the foot. 2. to bring (the foot) down forcibly or smartly on the ground, etc. 3. to impress with a particular mark or device. 4. to impress (a design, figure, words, etc.) on something; imprint deeply or permanently on anything. 5. to affix an adhesive paper stamp to (a letter, etc.). —*n.* 6. the act or an instance of stamping. 7. a die, engraved block, etc., for impressing a design, etc. 8. an official mark indicating genuineness, validity, etc., or payment of a duty or charge. 9. a small adhesive piece of paper for attaching to documents, goods subject to duty, letters, etc., to show that a charge has been paid.

stam·pede, *n., v.,* -peded, -peding. —*n.* 1. a sudden scattering or headlong flight. —*v.* 2. to (cause to) scatter or flee in a stampede.

stance, *n.* the position or bearing of the body while standing.

stan·chion, *n.* an upright bar or support.

stand, *v.,* stood, standing, *n.* —*v.* 1. (cause to) take or keep an upright

stand

position on the feet. **2.** (of things) to be in an upright position. **3.** to cease moving. **4.** to take a position or attitude. **5.** to have a specified height: *He stands 6 feet tall.* **6.** to be or remain in a specified position or condition. **7.** to resist change, decay, or destruction. **8.** to become or be a candidate, as for parliament. **9.** to tolerate. **10. stand by, a.** to wait in a state of readiness. **b.** to aid, uphold, or sustain. **11. stand down, a.** to withdraw, as from a contest. **b.** to dismiss (employees) who are not involved in direct strike action but who are not able to carry out their normal duties. **12. stand in,** to act as a substitute or representative. *-n.* **13.** the act of standing. **14.** a coming to a position of rest. **15.** a determined opposition to or support for some cause, etc. **16.** a raised platform. **17.** a framework on or in which articles are placed for support, exhibition, etc.

stan·dard, *n.* **1.** an approved model. **2.** a certain commodity in which the basic monetary unit is stated, historically usu. either gold or silver. **3.** a level of excellence, achievement, etc. **4.** a level of quality which is regarded as normal or acceptable. **5.** *Mil.* a flag. **6.** an upright support or supporting part. *-adj.* **7.** serving as a basis of weight, measure, value, comparison, or judgment. **8.** normal, adequate, acceptable, or average.

stan·dar·dise, *v.,* **-dised, -dising. 1.** to bring to or make of an established standard size, weight, quality, etc. **2.** to compare with or test by a standard.

stand-by, *n., pl.* **-bys. 1.** something or someone upon which one can rely. **2.** something kept in a state of readiness for use.

stand-in, *n.* a substitute.

stand·ing, *n.* **1.** position or status. **2.** good position, financial viability, or credit. **3.** length of existence, continuance, residence, membership, experience, etc. *-adj.* **4.** performed in or from a stationary or an erect position. **5.** continuing in operation, force, use, etc.

stand·point, *n.* the mental position from which one views something.

stanza, *n.* a group of lines of verse, forming a regularly repeated metrical division of a poem.

staphylo·coccus, *n., pl.* **-cocci.** any of certain species of bacteria.

staple[1], *n., v.,* **-pled, -pling.** *-n.* **1.** a bent piece of wire used to bind papers, sections of a book, etc., together. *-v.* **2.** to secure or fasten by a staple.

staple[2], *n.* **1.** a principal item, thing, feature, element, or part. *-adj.* **2.** principally used.

stapler, *n.* a stapling machine.

star, *n., adj., v.,* **starred, starring.** *-n.* **1.** any of the heavenly bodies appearing as apparently fixed luminous points in the sky at night. **2.** (*pl.*) a horoscope. **3.** a conventional five-pointed figure considered as representing a star of the sky. **4.** a prominent actor, singer, or the like. *-adj.* **5.** brilliant, prominent, or distinguished. *-v.* **6.** to set with, or as with, stars. **7.** to present or feature (an actor, etc.) as a star. **8.** to mark with a star or asterisk. **9.** (of an actor, etc.) to appear as a star.

star·board, *Naut. n.* the side of a ship to the right of a person look-

starboard

ing towards the bow (opposed to *larboard* and *port*).

starch, *n.* 1. a white, tasteless, solid, carbohydrate, occurring in plants. 2. a commercial preparation of this substance. 3. stiffness or formality, as of manner. –*v.* 4. to stiffen or treat with starch.

stare, *v.,* **stared, staring** *n.* –*v.* 1. to gaze fixedly, esp. with the eyes wide open. 2. to stand out boldly or obtrusively to view. –*n.* 3. a staring gaze.

star·fish, *n., pl.* **-fishes,** (*esp. collectively*) **-fish.** a marine animal in the form of a star.

stark, *adj.* 1. sheer, utter, downright, or arrant. 2. harsh, grim, or desolate to the view. –*adv.* 3. utterly or absolutely.

star·ling, *n.* a small, noisy bird with black, speckled feathers.

start, *v.* 1. to begin to move, go, or act. 2. to begin (any course of action). 3. (of a process or performance) to begin. 4. to move with a sudden, involuntary jerk or twitch, as from a shock. 5. to set in operation. –*n.* 6. the beginning or outset of anything. 7. the first part of anything. 8. a sudden, involuntary movement. 9. a lead or advance over competitors or pursuers. 10. a spurt of activity.

star·tle, *v.,* **-tled, -tling.** to cause to start involuntarily, as under a sudden shock.

starve, *v.,* **starved, starving.** 1. (cause to) die or perish from hunger. 2. to suffer for a lack of something specified (*for*). – **starvation,** *n.*

state, *n., adj., v.,* **stated, stating.** –*n.* 1. the condition of a person or thing, as to circumstances or attributes. 2. condition as to constitu-

station wagon

tion, structure, etc. 3. a particular condition of mind or feeling. 4. a particularly tense, nervous, or excited condition. 5. a body of people occupying a definite territory and organised under one government. –*adj.* 6. of or pertaining to the supreme civil government. 7. characterised by, attended with, or involving ceremony. –*v.* 8. to declare definitely. 9. to set forth formally in speech or writing.

stately, *adj.,* **-lier, -liest.** dignified or majestic.

state·ment, *n.* 1. something stated. 2. *Comm.* an account rendered to show the balance due.

states·man, *n., pl.* **-men.** a man who is versed in the management of affairs of state.

static, *adj.* Also, **statical.** 1. pertaining to or characterised by a fixed or stationary condition. –*n.* 2. (*pl.*) Also, **atmospherics.** *Radio.* extraneous noises, crackling, etc., caused by electrical currents picked up by the receiver.

station, *n.* 1. the place in which anything stands. 2. the place at which something stops. 3. a place equipped for some particular kind of work, service, or the like. 4. a property on which sheep or cattle are raised. 5. standing, as of persons in a social scale. 6. the wave-length on which a radio or television programme is broadcast. –*v.* 7. to place or post in a station or position.

station·ary, *adj.* standing still; not moving.

station·ery, *n.* writing materials, as pens, pencils, paper, etc. – **stationer,** *n.*

station wagon, *n.* a car with an

508

station wagon

extended interior behind the rear seat, and a door at the back.

statis·tics, *n.* 1. (construed as *sing.*) the science which deals with the collection, classification, and use of numerical facts or data, bearing on a subject or matter. 2. (construed as *pl.*) the numerical facts or data themselves. – **statistician**, *n.* – **statistical**, *adj.*

statue, *n.* a representation in the round of a person or an animal.

stat·ure, *n.* 1. the height of an animal body, esp. of man. 2. degree of development or achievement attained.

status, *n.* 1. condition, position, or standing socially, professionally, or otherwise. 2. the relative standing, position, or condition of anything.

status quo, *n.* the existing state or condition.

stat·ute, *n.* a permanent rule established by an institution, corporation, etc., for the conduct of its internal affairs. – **statutory**, *adj.*

staunch[1], *v.* to stop the flow of (a liquid, esp. blood).

staunch[2], *adj.* firm or steadfast.

stave, *n.*, *v.*, **staved** or **stove**, **staving**. –*n.* 1. Also, **staff**. *Music.* a set of horizontal lines on which music is written. –*v.* 2. to break a hole in; crush inwards (*in*). 3. **stave off**, to put, ward, or keep off.

stay[1], *v.*, **stayed** or **staid**, **staying**. –*v.* 1. to remain in a place, situation, company, etc. 2. to pause or wait. 3. to hold back, detain, or restrain. 4. to remain through or during (a period of time, etc.). 5. to remain to the end of. –*n.* 6. a sojourn or temporary residence.

steam

stay[2], *n.* 1. a prop; brace. 2. (*pl.*) a corset.

stead, *n.* the place of a person or thing as occupied by a successor or substitute.

stead·fast, *adj.* 1. firm in purpose, resolution, faith, attachment, etc. 2. unwavering, as resolution, faith, adherence, etc.

steady, *adj.*, **steadier**, **steadiest**, *n.*, *pl.* **steadies**, *v.*, **steadied**, **steadying**, *adv.* –*adj.* 1. firmly placed or fixed; stable. 2. uniform; continuous. 3. settled, staid, or sober. –*n.* 4. *Colloq.* a regular boyfriend or girlfriend. –*v.* 5. to make or become steady, as in position, etc. –*adv.* 6. in a firm or steady manner.

steak, *n.* a thick slice of meat or fish.

steal, *v.*, **stole**, **stolen**, **stealing**. –*v.* 1. to take or take away dishonestly or wrongfully, esp. secretly. 2. to move (something) secretly or quietly (*away*, *from*, *in*, *into*, etc.). 3. to commit or practise theft. 4. to move, go, or come secretly, quietly, or unobserved. –*n.* 5. *Colloq.* something acquired at a cost well below its true value.

stealth, *n.* secret, clandestine, or surreptitious procedure. – **stealthy**, *adj.*

steam, *n.* 1. water in the form of gas or vapour. 2. water changed to this form by boiling, and extensively used for the generation of mechanical power, for heating purposes, etc. –*v.* 3. to emit or give off steam or vapour. 4. to become covered with condensed steam, as a surface. 5. to expose to or treat with steam, as in order to heat, cook, soften, renovate, etc. –*adj.* 6. heated by or heating with steam. 7. operated by steam.

509

steamroller

steam·roller, *n.* a heavy locomotive, originally steam-powered, having a roller or rollers, for crushing or levelling materials in road-making.

steed, *n.* a horse, esp. one for riding.

steel, *n.* 1. iron in a modified form, artificially produced, and possessing hardness, elasticity and strength. –*adj.* 2. pertaining to or made of steel. 3. like steel in colour, hardness, or strength. –*v.* 4. to make (oneself) unfeeling, determined, etc.

steep¹, *adj.* 1. having a relatively high gradient, as a hill, stairs, etc. 2. *Colloq.* unduly high, or exorbitant, as a price or amount.

steep², *v.* to soak or lie soaking in water or other liquid.

steeple, *n.* a lofty tower, esp. one with a spire, attached to a church, etc.

steeple·chase, *n.* a horserace over a course furnished with artificial ditches, hedges, and other obstacles.

steer¹, *v.* to guide the course of (anything in motion) by a rudder, helm, wheel, etc.

steer², *n.* a castrated bull, esp. one raised for beef; ox; bullock.

stel·lar, *adj.* 1. of or pertaining to the stars; consisting of stars. 2. starlike.

stem¹, *n., v.,* **stemmed, stemming.** –*n.* 1. the ascending axis of a plant growing above the ground. 2. something resembling or suggesting this. –*v.* 3. to originate (*from*).

stem², *v.* to stop, hold back or plug.

stench, *n.* an offensive smell.

sten·cil, *n., v.,* **-cilled, -cilling.** –*n.* 1. a thin sheet of stiff material cut through so as to reproduce a design, letters, etc., when colour is rubbed through it. 2. the letters, designs, etc., produced. –*v.* 3. to produce (letters, etc.) by means of a stencil.

stereotype

steno·grapher, *n.* one who is skilled in taking dictation in shorthand.

sten·torian, *adj.* very loud or powerful in sound.

step, *n., v.,* **stepped, stepping.** –*n.* 1. a movement made by lifting the foot and setting it down again in a new position, as in walking, etc. 2. the space passed over or measured in making a step. 3. pace uniform with that of another or others, or in time with music. 4. a move or proceeding, as towards some end. 5. a degree on a scale. 6. a support for the foot in ascending or descending. –*v.* 7. to move by a step or steps. 8. to tread (*on* or *upon*). 9. to move or set (the foot) in taking a step. 10. to measure (a distance, ground, etc.) by steps (*off* or *out*). 11. to make or arrange in the manner of a series of steps. 12. **step down, a.** to decrease. **b.** to resign; relinquish a position.

step·ladder, *n.* a ladder having flat steps or treads in place of rungs and a hinged support to keep it upright.

steppe, *n.* an extensive plain, esp. one without trees.

stereo, *n., pl.* **stereos,** *adj.* –*n.* 1. stereophonic sound reproduction. 2. any system, equipment, etc., for reproducing stereophonic sound. –*adj.* 3. pertaining to stereophonic sound.

stereo·phonic, *adj.* of or pertaining to the multi-channel reproduction or broadcasting of sound.

stereo·type, *n., v.,* **-typed, -typing.**

stereotype

–*n.* **1.** a process for making metal plates for use in printing from moulds. **2.** a plate made by this process. **3.** a standardised idea or concept. –*v.* **4.** to make a stereotype of.

ster·ile, *adj.* **1.** free from living germs or micro-organisms. **2.** incapable of producing offspring. – **sterility,** *n.* – **sterilise,** *v.*

ster·ling, *adj.* **1.** consisting of or pertaining to British money. **2.** (of silver) being of standard quality, 92½ per cent pure silver.

stern[1], *adj.* firm, strict, or uncompromising.

stern[2], *n.* the hinder part of anything.

ster·num, *n., pl.* **-na, -nums.** the flat bone connecting the front of the true ribs.

stetho·scope, *n.* an instrument placed on the body, used to convey sounds within the body to the ear of the examiner.

steve·dore, *n.* a firm or individual engaged in the loading or unloading of a vessel.

stew, *v.* **1.** to cook (food) by simmering or slow boiling. **2.** to undergo cooking by simmering or slow boiling. –*n.* **3.** a preparation of food cooked by stewing.

steward, *n.* **1.** one who manages another's property or financial affairs. **2.** any attendant on a ship or aircraft who waits on passengers.

stick[1], *n.* **1.** a relatively long and slender piece of wood or similar material. **2. the sticks,** remote and little developed areas.

stick[2], *v.,* **stuck, sticking. 1.** to pierce or puncture with a pointed instrument. **2.** to thrust (something pointed) in, into, through, etc., as for fastening. **3.** to place in a specified position. **4.** to (cause to) cling together more or less permanently. **5.** to endure. **6.** to remain firm in resolution, etc. **7.** to keep steadily at a task, undertaking, or the like (*at* or *to*). **8.** to be at a standstill. **9.** to project or protrude (*through, from, out, up,* etc.). **10. stick up,** *Colloq.* to rob, esp. at gunpoint. **11. stick up for,** to speak or act in favour of.

sticker, *n.* an adhesive label, usu. with a message printed on it.

stickleback, *n.* a freshwater fish.

stick·ler, *n.* a person who insists on something unyieldingly (*for*).

stiff, *adj.* **1.** rigid or firm in substance. **2.** not moving or working easily. **3.** rigidly formal. **4.** severe, as a penalty. –*n. Colloq.* **5.** a dead body. –*adv.* **6.** in a rigid state.

stifle, *v.,* **-fled, -fling. 1.** to smother or suffocate. **2.** to suppress. **3.** to become stifled or suffocated.

stigma, *n., pl.* **stigmata, stigmas.** a mark of disgrace.

stile, *n.* a series of steps for getting over a fence, etc.

sti·letto, *n.* a dagger with a narrow blade.

still[1], *adj.* **1.** remaining at rest. **2.** tranquil or quiet. **3.** not effervescent, as wine. –*n.* **4.** a single photographic picture. –*adv.* **5.** up to this or that time: *It's still cold.* **6.** even or yet (with comparatives or the like): *The blue one is better still.* **7.** even then: *She was wealthy and still worried about money.* –*conj.* **8.** and yet: *He's old, still he goes out.* –*v.* **9.** to calm or allay.

still², *n.* a distilling apparatus.

still·birth, *n.* the birth of a dead child or organism.

still life, *n., pl.* **still lifes.** a picture representing inanimate objects, such as fruit, flowers, etc.

stilt, *n.* **1.** one of 2 poles, each with a support for the foot at some distance above the ground. **2.** one of several high posts underneath any structure built above land or over water.

stilted, *adj.* stiffly dignified or formal.

stimu·lant, *n.* any beverage, food, or drug that stimulates.

stimu·late, *v.*, **-lated, -lating. 1.** to rouse to action or effort. **2.** to invigorate as by an alcoholic or other stimulant.

stimu·lus, *n., pl.* **-li, -luses.** something that incites to action, etc.

sting, *v.*, **stung, stinging.** *n.* –*v.* **1.** to use or have a sting, as bees. **2.** to (cause to) feel a smarting pain. –*n.* **3.** any sharp pain (physical or mental). **4.** anything that wounds, pains, or irritates.

stingy /'stɪndʒɪ/, *adj.*, **-gier, -giest.** reluctant to give or spend.

stink, *v.*, **stank** or **stunk, stunk, stinking**, *n.* (to emit) a strong offensive smell.

stint, *v.* **1.** to limit, often unduly. **2.** to be frugal. –*n.* **3.** a period of time allotted to a particular activity.

sti·pend, *n.* fixed or regular pay.

stip·ple, *v.*, **-pled, -pling.** to paint, etc., by means of dots or small touches.

stipu·late, *v.*, **-lated, -lating. 1.** to make an express demand (*for*), as a condition of agreement. **2.** to require as an essential condition.

---

stock exchange

stir, *v.*, **stirred, stirring**, *n.* –*v.* **1.** to move or agitate (a liquid, etc.). **2.** to (cause to) move, esp. in some slight way. **3.** to rouse from inactivity (*up*). **4.** to excite. **5.** to incite a heated discussion deliberately. –*n.* **6.** the act of stirring or moving, or the sound made. **7.** a state or occasion of general excitement.

stir·rup, *n.* a loop suspended from the saddle of a horse to support the rider's foot.

stitch, *n.* **1.** a loop made by one movement in sewing, knitting, etc. **2.** a sudden, sharp pain, esp. in the muscles between the ribs. –*v.* **3.** to work upon or fasten with stitches.

stoat, *n.* the ermine in its brown summer phase.

stock, *n.* **1.** an aggregate of goods kept on hand by a merchant, etc. **2.** a quantity of something accumulated, as for future use. **3.** a race or other related group of animals or plants. **4.** the handle of a whip, etc. **5.** a pole used in skiing. **6.** (*pl.*) (formerly) a frame with holes for ankles and wrists, used to hold an offender exposed to public ridicule. **7.** *Finance.* **a.** the capital of a company converted from fully paid shares. **b.** the shares of a particular company. **8. take stock**, to make an appraisal of resources, prospects, etc. –*adj.* **9.** of common type or use. **10.** pertaining to livestock raising. –*v.* **11.** to furnish with stock.

stock·ade, *n.* a defensive barrier consisting of strong posts or timbers fixed upright in the ground.

stock·broker, *n.* a broker who buys and sells stocks and shares for customers for a commission.

stock exchange, *n.* **1.** (*oft. caps.*) a building or place where stocks and

stock exchange

shares are bought and sold. 2. an association of brokers in stocks and bonds.

stock·ing, *n*. a close-fitting covering for the foot and leg.

stock market, *n*. a stock exchange.

stock·pile, *n*., *v*. -piled, -piling. –*n*. 1. a large supply of essential materials, held in reserve. –*v*. 2. to accumulate for future use.

stocky, *adj*., -ier, -iest. of solid and sturdy form or build.

stodgy, *adj*. heavy, dull or uninteresting.

stoic, *n*. one who maintains or affects a mental attitude of austere fortitude. – **stoical**, *adj*.

stoke, *v*., **stoked**, **stoking**. to poke, stir up, and feed (a fire). – **stoker**, *n*.

stole[1], *v*. past tense of **steal**.

stole[2], *n*. a type of long scarf.

stolen, *v*. past participle of **steal**.

stolid, *adj*. not easily moved or stirred mentally; impassive; unemotional.

stomach, *n*. 1. (in man and other vertebrates) an organ of storage and digestion. 2. the part of the body containing the stomach. –*v*. 3. to endure or tolerate.

stomp, *v*. *Colloq*. to stamp.

stone, *n*., *pl*. **stones** (except **stone** for def. 3), *adj*., *v*., **stoned**, **stoning**. –*n*. 1. the hard substance of which rocks consist. 2. a piece of rock of small or moderate size. 3. a unit of mass in the imperial system, equal to 14 lb avoirdupois, or approx. 6.35 kg. 4. something resembling a small stone, as the central seed of certain fruits. –*adj*. 5. made of stone. –*v*. 6. to throw stones at. 7. to free from stones, as fruit.

stoned, *adj*. *Colloq*. completely

store

drunk or under the influence of drugs.

stood, *v*. past tense and past participle of **stand**.

stooge, *n*. one who acts on behalf of another.

stool, *n*. 1. a seat without arms or a back. 2. faeces.

stoop, *v*. 1. to bend (the head and shoulders, or the body generally) forwards and downwards. 2. to condescend; deign. –*n*. 3. a stooping position or carriage of body.

stop, *v*., **stopped**, **stopping**, *n*. –*v*. 1. to (cause to) cease. 2. to cut off, intercept, or withhold. 3. to prevent from continuing, etc. 4. to block (a passageway, duct, etc.) (*up*). 5. to stay. 6. **stop by**, to call somewhere briefly on the way to another destination. –*n*. 7. the act of stopping. 8. a stay or sojourn. 9. a place where buses or other vehicles halt. 10. any piece or device that serves to check or control movement or action in a mechanism. 11. →**full stop**. – **stoppage**, *n*.

stop·over, *n*. any brief stop in the course of a journey.

stop·per, *n*. a plug or piece for closing a bottle, tube, or the like.

stop press, *n*. news inserted in a newspaper after printing has begun.

stop·watch, *n*. a watch with a hand or hands that can be stopped or started at any instant.

stor·age, *n*. 1. the state or fact of being stored. 2. a place where something is stored.

store, *n*., *v*., **stored**, **storing**. –*n*. 1. a supply or stock (of something). 2. a shop, usu. large. 3. measure of

513

store

esteem or regard. –v. 4. to lay (up) or put (away), for future use.

storey, n., pl. -reys. one complete level or floor of a building.

stork, n. a long-legged, long-necked, long-billed wading bird.

storm, n. a heavy fall of rain, snow, or hail or a violent outbreak of thunder and lightning, often with strong winds. 2. a violent outburst or outbreak. –v. 3. to rage or complain with violence or fury. 4. to assault or attack.

story, n., pl. -ries. –n. 1. a narrative designed to interest or amuse the hearer or reader. 2. the plot of a novel, poem, drama, etc. 3. Colloq. a lie; fib.

stout, adj. 1. bulky or thickset. 2. bold or hardy. –n. 3. any of various beers darker and heavier than ales.

stove[1], n. an apparatus for supplying heat.

stove[2], v. a past tense and past participle of **stave**.

stow, v. to put in a place or receptacle; pack.

stow-away, n. one who conceals himself aboard a ship or other conveyance, as to get a free trip.

strad·dle, v., -dled, -dling. to walk, stand, or sit with one leg on each side of.

strafe, v., strafed, strafing. to bombard heavily.

strag·gle, v., -gled, -gling. to go, come, or spread in a scattered, irregular fashion.

straight, adj. 1. without a bend. 2. honest or upright. 3. right or correct. 4. undiluted, as an alcoholic beverage. –adv. 5. in a straight line. 6. honestly or virtuously. 7. in the proper order or condition, as a

strand

room. 8. directly or immediately. – **straighten**, v.

straight·away, adv. immediately.

straight·forward, adj. 1. free from deceit. 2. uncomplicated.

strain[1], v. 1. to exert to the utmost. 2. to impair by stretching or overexertion. 3. to make excessive demands upon. 4. to pass (liquid matter) through a filter, sieve, or the like, in order to hold back the denser or solid constituents. 5. to stretch one's muscles, nerves, etc., to the utmost. –n. 6. an injury due to excessive tension or use. 7. damaging or wearing pressure or effect. 8. (sing. or pl., oft. collective pl.) a passage of music or song as rendered or heard.

strain[2], n. 1. any of the different lines of ancestry united in a family or an individual. 2. a variety, esp. of micro-organisms.

strainer, n. a filter, sieve, or the like for straining liquids.

strait, n. 1. (oft. pl. with sing. sense) a narrow passage of water connecting two large bodies of water. 2. (oft. pl.) a position of difficulty, distress, or need.

strait·ened, adj. difficult, esp. financially.

strait·jacket, n. a kind of coat for confining the arms of violently insane persons, etc. Also, **straightjacket**.

strait·laced, adj. excessively strict in conduct or morality.

strand[1], v. 1. (usu. in the passive) to bring into a helpless position. 2. to be driven or run ashore.

strand[2], n. 1. each of a number of strings twisted together to form a

strand

rope, cord, etc. 2. a thread of the texture of anything.

strange, *adj.*, **stranger, strangest**. 1. unusual or extraordinary. 2. coming from outside one's own or a particular locality.

stran·ger, *n.* 1. a person with whom one has (hitherto) had no personal acquaintance. 2. a person or thing that is unaccustomed or new (*to*).

stran·gle, *v.*, **-gled, -gling**. to kill by stopping the breath.

strap, *n., v.*, **strapped, strapping**. *-n.* 1. a long, narrow piece or object. *-v.* 2. to secure with a strap.

strap·ping, *adj. Colloq.* tall, robust, and strongly built.

strat·a·gem, *n.* a plan or trick for deceiving the enemy.

strat·e·gy, *n., pl.* **-gies**. the method of conducting operations, esp. by the aid of manoeuvring or stratagem. – **strategic**, *adj.*

strat·i·fy, *v.*, **-fied, -fying**. to form in strata or layers.

stra·tum, *n., pl.* **strata, stratums**. a layer of material, often one of a number of parallel layers.

straw, *n.* 1. a single stalk or stem, esp. of certain species of grain. 2. a mass of such stalks used as fodder, etc. 3. a hollow tube used in drinking. *-adj.* 4. made of straw.

straw·ber·ry, *n., pl.* **-ries**. a small, red, fleshy fruit.

stray, *v.* 1. to wander (*away, off, from, into, to,* etc.). 2. to go astray. *-n.* 3. a domestic animal found wandering at large or without an owner. *-adj.* 4. wandering or lost. 5. found or occurring as an isolated or casual instance.

streak, *n.* 1. a long, narrow mark, smear, band of colour, or the like.

stretch

2. an admixture of anything. *-v.* 3. to make or become streaked. 4. to flash or go rapidly.

stream, *n.* 1. any flow of water or other liquid. 2. prevailing direction; drift. *-v.* 3. to (cause to) flow in a stream. 4. to run or flow (*with*).

streamer, *n.* a long, narrow strip of paper, usu. brightly coloured, thrown in festivities, or used for decorating.

stream·lined, *adj.* having a shape designed to offer the least possible resistance in passing through the air, etc.

street, *n.* a public way or road in a town or city.

strength, *n.* 1. the quality or state of being strong. 2. something that makes strong.

stren·u·ous, *adj.* characterised by vigorous exertion.

stress, *v.* 1. to emphasise. *-n.* 2. importance or significance attached to a thing. 3. emphasis in music, rhythm, etc. 4. the physical force exerted on one thing by another. 5. (a disturbing influence which produces) a state of severe tension in an individual.

stretch, *v.* 1. to draw out or extend. 2. to lengthen or enlarge by tension. 3. to force beyond the natural or proper limits. 4. to recline at full length (*out*). 5. to reach, as for something. 6. to extend over a distance, area, period of time, etc. 7. to stretch oneself by extending the limbs, straining the muscles, etc. 8. to become stretched, as any elastic material. *-n.* 9. capacity for being stretched. 10. a continuous length or expanse. 11. an extent in time or duration. *-adj.* 12. made to stretch, as clothing.

515

stretcher

stretch·er, n. a light, folding bed.

strew, v., **strewed**, **strewed** or **strewn**, **strewing**. to scatter or sprinkle.

striated /straɪˈeɪtəd/, adj. furrowed or striped.

stricken, adj. afflicted, as with disease or sorrow.

strict, adj. 1. in close conformity to requirements or principles. 2. rigorously enforced. 3. precise.

stric·ture, n. (a remark made in) adverse criticism.

stride, v., **strode**, **stridden**, **striding**, n. –v. 1. to take a long step. 2. to walk with long steps (along, on, through, over, etc.). –n. 3. a long step in walking. 4. (pl.) Colloq. trousers.

stri·dent, adj. making or having a harsh sound.

strife, n. conflict or discord.

strike, v., **struck**, **striking**, n. –v. 1. to deal a blow or stroke (to). 2. to deal or inflict (a blow, stroke, etc.). 3. to drive or thrust forcibly. 4. to produce (fire, sparks, light, etc.). 5. to come into forcible contact (with). 6. to fall upon (something), as light or sound. 7. to enter the mind of. 8. to impress strongly. 9. to come upon or find (ore, oil, etc.). 10. to efface (as) with the stroke of a pen (off, out, etc.). 11. to remove with a cut (off). 12. to indicate (the hour of day), as a clock. 13. to assume (an attitude or posture). 14. to reach by agreement, as a compromise. 15. to enter upon or form (an acquaintance, etc.). 16. (of an orchestra or band) to begin to play (up). 17. to take root. 18. to go, esp. in a new direction. 19. (of an employee or employees) to engage in a strike. –n. 20. the act of striking. 21. a concerted stopping of work to compel an employer to accede to demands.

string, n., **strung**, **stringing**. –n. 1. a cord used for tying parcels, etc. 2. a number of objects arranged on a cord. 3. any series of things following closely one after another. 4. (in musical instruments) a tightly stretched cord or wire which produces a note when caused to vibrate. –v. 5. to furnish with strings. 6. to extend or stretch (a cord, etc.) from one point to another. 7. to thread on to a string. 8. to arrange in a series. 9. **string along**, Colloq. to deceive (someone) repeatedly.

strin·gent, adj. narrowly binding.

strip[1], v., **stripped**, **stripping**. 1. to make bare or naked. 2. to take away or remove. 3. to take off one's clothes.

strip[2], n. a long, narrow piece.

stripe, n., **striped**, **striping**. 1. a relatively long, narrow, contrasting band. –v. 2. to mark with stripes.

strip·tease, n. an act in which someone strips before an audience.

strive, v., **strove**, **striven**, **striving**. 1. to make strenuous efforts towards any end. 2. to struggle vigorously, as in opposition.

stroke[1], n. 1. a blow. 2. something likened to a blow, as an attack of paralysis. 3. a repeated or characteristic movement, as in a machine, or in swimming, tennis, etc. 4. a movement of, or mark traced by a pen, etc.

stroke[2], v., **stroked**, **stroking**, n. –v. 1. to pass the hand or an instrument over (something) lightly or with little pressure. –n. 2. the act or an instance of stroking.

stroll

stroll, *v., n.* (to take) a leisurely walk.

stroller, *n.* a light collapsible chair on wheels, used for carrying small children. Also, **pushchair, pusher**.

strong, *adj.* 1. physically vigorous or robust. 2. mentally or morally powerful. 3. powerful in influence, authority, resources. 4. of great force, effectiveness, potency, or cogency. 5. containing alcohol, or much alcohol. 6. intense, as light or colour. 7. of an unpleasant or offensive flavour or smell. —*adv.* 8. in a strong manner. 9. in number: *The team was 15 strong.*

strong·hold, *n.* a strong or well-fortified place; a fortress.

stron·ti·um, *n.* a metallic element whose radioactive isotope is produced in some nuclear reactions.

strop, *n., v.,* **stropped, stropping**. —*n.* 1. material used for sharpening razors. —*v.* 2. to sharpen on a strop.

stroppy, *adj. Colloq.* rebellious or complaining.

strove, *v.* past tense of **strive**.

struck, *v.* past tense and a past participle of **strike**.

struc·ture, *n., v.,* **-tured, -turing**. —*n.* 1. arrangement of parts, elements or constituents. 2. something built or constructed. 3. anything composed of parts arranged together. —*v.* 4. to give form or organisation to. —**structural**, *adj.*

strug·gle, *v.,* **-gled, -gling**, *n.* —*v.* 1. to contend with an opposing force. —*n.* 2. the act or process of struggling.

strum, *v.,* **strummed, strumming**. 1. to play on (a stringed musical instrument) unskilfully or carelessly. 2. to play (chords, etc.), esp. on a guitar) by sweeping across the strings with the fingers or with a plectrum.

strung, *v.* past tense and past participle of **string**.

strut[1], *v.,* **strutted, strutting**. to walk with a vain, pompous bearing, as with head erect and chest thrown out.

strut[2], *n.* a structural part designed to take pressure.

strych·nine, *n.* a colourless crystalline poison.

stub, *n., v.,* **stubbed, stubbing**. —*n.* 1. a short remaining piece. —*v.* 2. to strike, as one's toe, against something. 3. to extinguish (a cigarette) by pressing the lighted end against a hard surface.

stub·ble, *n.* any short, rough growth, as of beard.

stub·born, *adj.* unreasonably obstinate.

stubby, *adj.,* **-bier, -biest**, *n., pl.* **-bies**. —*adj.* 1. short and thick. —*n.* 2. a small squat beer bottle.

stucco, *n.* cement, concrete, or plaster used to decorate exterior walls.

stuck, *v.* past tense and past participle of **stick**[2].

stud[1], *n., v.,* **studded, studding**. —*n.* 1. a small protuberance projecting from a surface or part, esp. as an ornament. 2. a kind of small button or fastener. —*v.* 3. to set with or as with studs. 4. to set or scatter (objects) at intervals over a surface.

stud[2], *n.* 1. an establishment in which horses cattle, etc., are kept for breeding. —*adj.* 2. retained for breeding purposes.

stu·dent, *n.* one who studies.

studio, *n., pl.* **-dios**. 1. a room or place in which some form of art is

studio

pursued. 2. a room or set of rooms for broadcasting radio or television programs or making recordings.

study, *n., pl.* **studies,** *v.,* **studied, studying.** —*n.* 1. application of the mind to the acquisition of knowledge; as by reading, investigation, or reflection. 2. a thorough examination and analysis of a particular subject. 3. a room set apart for private study, reading or writing. 4. something produced as an educational exercise. —*v.* 5. to apply oneself to acquiring knowledge (of). 6. to examine or investigate carefully and in detail. — **studious,** *adj.*

stuff, *n.* 1. the material of which anything is made. 2. matter or material indefinitely: *cushions filled with some soft stuff.* —*v.* 3. to fill (a receptacle), esp. by close packing. 4. to fill (poultry, meat, etc.) with seasoned breadcrumbs or other savoury matter. 5. to thrust or cram (something) tightly into a receptacle, etc. 6. to stop or plug (*up*). 7. *Colloq.* to cause to fail; render useless. 8. to cram (oneself) with food.

stuff·ing, *n.* that with which anything is or may be filled.

stuffy, *adj.,* **stuffier, stuffiest.** 1. close or ill-ventilated; as a room. 2. old-fashioned; immune to new ideas.

stum·ble, *v.,* **-bled, -bling,** *n.* —*v.* 1. to strike the foot against something so as to stagger or fall; trip. 2. to walk or go unsteadily. 3. to come accidentally or unexpectedly (*on, upon, across,* etc.). —*n.* 4. the act of stumbling.

stump, *n.* 1. something left after a part has been cut off or used up, as

style

of a tree, leg, pencil, etc. 2. *Cricket.* each of the 3 upright sticks which form a wicket. —*v.* 3. to embarrass or render completely at a loss. 4. to walk heavily or clumsily.

stun, *v.,* **stunned, stunning.** 1. to deprive of consciousness or strength by a blow, fall, etc. 2. to strike with astonishment.

stung, *v.* past tense and past participle of **sting.**

stunt[1], *v.* to check the growth or development of.

stunt[2], *n.* a performance serving as a display of skill, or the like; feat.

stu·pefy, *v.,* **-fied, -fying.** to put into a state of stupor.

stu·pen·dous, *adj.* such as to cause amazement.

stupid, *adj.* lacking ordinary activity and keenness of mind; dull.

stupor, *n.* a state of suspended or deadened sensibility.

sturdy, *adj.,* **-dier, -diest.** strongly built, stalwart, or robust.

stut·ter, *v.* 1. to utter (sounds) in which the rhythm is interrupted by blocks or spasms, repetitions, or prolongation. —*n.* 2. unrhythmical and distorted speech.

sty[1], *n., pl.* **sties.** a pen or enclosure for pigs.

sty[2], *n., pl.* **sties.** a small inflammation on the eyelid. Also, **stye.**

style, *n., v.,* **styled, styling.** —*n.* 1. a particular kind, sort, or type. 2. a particular, distinctive, or characteristic mode of action, speech, literary expression, etc. 3. a mode of fashion; elegance; smartness. 4. a descriptive or distinguishing title. —*v.* 5. to call by a particular title. 6. to design in accordance with a given or new style. — **stylistic,** *adj.*

styl·ise, v., -lised, -lising. to bring into conformity with a particular (esp. simplistic) style.

stylish, adj. smart; elegant.

stylus, n. 1. a needle tipped with diamond, sapphire, etc., for reproducing the sound of a gramophone record. 2. any instrument used in drawing, etc.

suave /swav/, adj. (of persons or their manner, speech, etc.) smoothly agreeable or polite.

sub, n. 1. subeditor. 2. submarine. 3. subscription.

sub·con·scious, adj. 1. existing or operating beneath or beyond consciousness. –n. 2. the totality of mental processes of which the individual is not aware.

sub·con·tract, Law. n. 1. a contract by which one agrees to render services necessary for the performance of another contract. –v. 2. to make a subcontract (for). – **subcontractor**, n.

sub·cu·ta·ne·ous, adj. situated or lying under the skin, as tissue.

sub·di·vide, v., -vided, -viding. to divide anew after a first division. – **subdivision**, n.

subdue, v., -dued, -duing. 1. to overpower by superior force. 2. to bring into mental subjection. 3. to reduce the intensity, force, or vividness of.

sub·ed·i·tor, n. 1. Journalism. one who edits and prepares copy for printing. 2. an assistant or subordinate editor.

sub·head·ing, n. a title or heading of a section in an essay, newspaper article, etc.

sub·ject, n. 1. something that forms a matter of thought, discourse, investigation, etc. 2. a branch of knowledge forming a course of study. 3. one who is under the dominion or rule of a sovereign, state, etc. 4. Gram. the word or words of a sentence which represent the person or object performing the action, as, he in *He raised his hat*. 5. one who or that which undergoes some action. –adj. 6. being under domination, control, or influence (to). 7. open or exposed (to). 8. being dependent or conditional upon something (to). –v. 9. to make subject (to). – **subjection**, n.

sub·jec·tive, adj. belonging to the thinking person rather than to the object of thought (opposed to *objective*).

sub·ju·gate, v., -gated, -gating. to bring under complete control; subdue; conquer.

sub·junc·tive, adj. Gram. the mood expressing hypothetical action.

sub·li·mate, v., -mated, -mating. Psychol. to deflect (sexual or other biological energies) into socially constructive or creative channels.

sub·lime, adj. supreme or perfect.

sub·lim·i·nal, adj. (of stimuli, etc.) being or operating below the threshold of consciousness or perception.

sub·ma·rine, n. 1. a type of vessel that can operate under water. –adj. 2. operating, or living under the surface of the sea.

sub·merge, v., -merged, -merging. to sink or plunge under water.

submit, v., -mitted, -mitting. 1. to yield in surrender, compliance, or obedience. 2. to state or urge with deference (usu. fol. by a clause). 3. to refer to the decision or judgment

submit

of another or others. – **submission**, n. – **submissive**, adj.

sub·or·di·nate, adj., n., v., -nated, -nating. –adj. 1. of lesser importance; secondary. 2. subject to the authority of a superior. –n. 3. a subordinate person or thing. –v. 4. to place in a lower order or rank. 5. to make subordinate.

sub·poe·na /səˈpinə/, v., -naed, -naing, n. Law. (to serve with) a writ for the summoning of witnesses.

sub·scribe, v., -scribed, -scribing. 1. to sign (one's name) to a document, etc., esp. as a sign of assent. 2. to obtain a subscription to a magazine, newspaper, etc. 3. to give or pay money as a contribution, payment, etc.

sub·scrip·tion, n. 1. a monetary contribution towards some object or a payment for shares, a book, a periodical, etc. 2. the dues paid by a member of a club, society, etc.

sub·se·quent, adj. occurring or coming later or after.

sub·ser·vi·ent, adj. excessively submissive; obsequious.

sub·side, v., -sided, -siding. to sink to a low or lower level.

sub·sid·i·ar·y, adj. 1. serving to assist or supplement. 2. subordinate or secondary. –n. 3. a company whose controlling interest is held by another company.

sub·si·dy, n., pl. -dies. a direct pecuniary aid furnished by a government to a private organisation. – **subsidise**, v.

sub·sist, v. to live, as on food, resources, etc., esp. when these are limited. – **subsistence**, n.

sub·stance, n. 1. that of which a

suburb

thing consists; matter. 2. a matter of definite chemical composition. 3. substantial or solid character or quality. 4. the meaning or gist, as of speech or writing.

sub·stan·tial, adj. 1. real or actual. 2. of considerable amount, importance, size, etc. 3. of solid character or quality. 4. wealthy or influential.

sub·stan·ti·ate, v., -ated, -ating. to establish by evidence.

sub·stan·tive, n. 1. Gram. a word or phrase functioning as a noun. –adj. 2. Gram. of or pertaining to substantives. 3. real or actual. 4. of considerable amount or quantity.

sub·sti·tute, n., v., -tuted, -tuting. –n. 1. a person or thing acting or serving in place of another. –v. 2. to put or act in the place of another.

sub·sume, v., -sumed, -suming. 1. to consider (an idea, etc.) as part of a more comprehensive one. 2. to bring (a case, instance, etc.) under a rule.

sub·ter·fuge, n. an artifice or expedient employed to evade or hide something etc.

sub·ter·ra·nean, adj. underground.

sub·ti·tle, n. 1. a secondary title of a literary work, usu. explanatory. 2. Films. a caption on the screen translating the dialogue of foreign language films.

sub·tle /ˈsʌtl/, adj. 1. fine or delicate, often when likely to elude perception. 2. requiring mental acuteness. 3. insidious in operation, as poison, etc. – **subtlety**, n.

sub·tract, v. to take away (something or a part) from a whole.

sub·urb, n. a more or less self-contained district of a town or city. – **suburban**, adj.

sub·vert, v. to cause the downfall, ruin, or destruction of.

subway, n. a pedestrian passage or tunnel beneath a street, railway line, etc.

suc·ceed, v. 1. to turn out or terminate according to desire. 2. to accomplish what is attempted or intended. 3. to follow or replace (another) by descent, election, appointment, etc. 4. to come next after (something else) in an order or series. – **succession**, n. – **successive**, adj.

suc·cess, n. 1. the favourable termination of attempts or endeavours. 2. the gaining of wealth, position, or the like. 3. a thing or a person that is successful. – **successful**, adj.

suc·ces·sor, n. one who or that which succeeds or follows.

suc·cinct, adj. concisely expressed.

suc·cour, n. help; relief; aid.

suc·cu·lent, adj. full of juice; juicy.

suc·cumb, v. to give way to superior force; yield.

such, adj. 1. of the kind, character, degree, extent, etc., indicated or implied: *You won't meet another such as her; oranges, apples and such fruit.* 2. of so extreme a kind: *He is such a liar.* 3. being as indicated: *The true facts are such.* 4. Also, **such and such**. particular, but not named or specified: *Ring me at such time as he arrives.* –adv. 5. so, or in such a manner or degree: *such dreadful events.* –pron. 6. the person or thing, or the persons or things, indicated. 7. **as such**, a. as being what is indicated; in that capacity. b. in itself or themselves.

suck, v. 1. to draw into the mouth by action of the lips and tongue. 2. to draw (water, moisture, air, etc.) by any process resembling this. 3. to apply the lips or mouth to, and draw upon for extracting fluid contents. 4. to hold in the mouth and absorb by action of the tongue, etc. –n. 5. the act or instance of sucking.

sucker, n. *Colloq.* a person easily deceived or imposed upon.

suckle, v., **-led**, **-ling**. 1. to nurse (a child) at the breast. 2. to suck milk at the breast.

suc·rose, n. the sugar obtained from the sugar cane, the sugar beet, etc.

suc·tion, n. 1. the act, process, or condition of sucking. 2. the process by which a substance is sucked into an interior space when the atmospheric pressure is reduced in the space.

sudden, adj. happening, coming, made, or done quickly or unexpectedly.

suds, n.pl. soapy water; lather.

sue, v., **sued**, **suing**. to take legal action against (someone), as to obtain reparation, divorce, etc.

suede /sweɪd/, n. kid or other leather finished on the flesh side with a soft, napped surface.

suet, n. hard animal fat used in cookery, etc.

suffer, v. 1. to undergo or feel (pain or distress). 2. to endure patiently or bravely. 3. to tolerate or allow.

suf·fer·ance, n. in the phrase **on sufferance**, reluctantly tolerated.

suf·fice, v., **-ficed**, **-ficing**. to be enough or adequate.

suf·fi·cient, adj. that suffices. – **sufficiency**, n.

suffix, n. *Gram.* a word part added

suffix

to the end of a word, as -ness in kindness.

suf·fo·cate, v., **-cated**, **-cating**. 1. to kill by preventing the access of oxygen to the blood through the lungs. 2. to become suffocated; stifle; smother.

suf·frage, n. the right of voting, esp. in political elections.

suf·fuse, v., **-fused**, **-fusing**. to overspread with or as with a liquid, colour, etc.

sugar, n. 1. a sweet crystalline substance used as food. 2. a member of the same class of carbohydrates. –v. 3. to cover or sweeten with sugar.

sugar beet, n. a variety of beet cultivated for the sugar it yields.

sugar-cane, n. a tall grass of tropical and warm regions, constituting the chief source of sugar.

sug·gest, v. 1. to put forward (an idea, etc.) for consideration or possible action. 2. to propose (a person or thing) as suitable or possible. – **suggestion**, n.

sug·gest·ible, adj. capable of being influenced by suggestion.

sug·gest·ive, adj. 1. tending to suggest thoughts, ideas, etc. 2. such as to suggest something improper or indecent.

sui·cide, n., v., **-cided**, **-ciding**. –n. 1. one who intentionally takes his own life. 2. the intentional taking of one's own life. –v. 3. to commit suicide. – **suicidal**, adj.

suit, n. 1. a set of garments intended to be worn together. 2. the act or process of suing in a court of law. 3. a number of things forming a series or set, as of cards. –v. 4. to make or be appropriate. 5. to be satisfactory, agreeable, or acceptable. – **suitable**, adj.

summer

suit·case, n. a travelling bag, usu. with stiffened frame, for carrying clothes, etc.

suite, n. 1. a company of followers or attendants. 2. a number of things forming a series or set.

sulk, v. to hold aloof in a sullen, morose, or offended mood. – **sulky**, adj.

sullen, adj. showing ill humour by a gloomy silence or reserve.

sully, v., **-lied**, **-lying**. to soil, stain, or tarnish.

sul·phur, n. Chem. a non-metallic element. Symbol: S

sultan, n. the sovereign of a Muslim country.

sul·tana, n. a small, green, seedless grape, often dried.

sultry, adj., **-trier**, **-triest**. oppressively hot and close or moist.

sum, n., v., **summed**, **summing**, adj. –n. 1. the aggregate of 2 or more numbers as determined by mathematical process. 2. a quantity or amount, esp. of money. 3. a series of numbers or quantities to be added up. 4. the total amount, or the whole. –v. 5. to combine into an aggregate or total (up). 6. to bring into or contain in a summary (up). –adj. 7. denoting or pertaining to a sum.

sum·mary, n., pl. **-ries**, adj. 1. a brief and comprehensive presentation of facts or statements. –adj. 2. brief and comprehensive. 3. direct and prompt; unceremoniously fast. – **summarise**, v.

summer, n. the warmest season of the year, between spring and autumn.

summit, *n.* 1. the highest point or part. –*adj.* 2. (in diplomacy) between heads of state.

summon, *v.* 1. to call, as with authority. 2. to call into action; rouse (*up*).

sum·mons, *n., pl.* **-monses**. an authoritative command, message, or signal by which one is summoned.

sump, *n.* a pit or receptacle in which water or other liquid is collected.

sump·tu·ous, *adj.* luxuriously fine.

sun, *n., v.*, **sunned**, **sunning**. *n.* 1. the star which is the central body of the solar system. 2. sunshine. –*v.* 3. to warm, dry, etc., in the sunshine.

sun·bake, *v.*, **-baked**, **-baking**. to expose one's body to the sun.

sun·burn, *n.* superficial inflammation of the skin, caused by excessive exposure to the sun's rays.

sundae, *n.* a portion of ice-cream with syrup poured over it.

sunder, *v.* to separate; part.

sun·dial, *n.* an instrument for indicating the time of day by the position of a shadow cast by the sun.

sun·dries, *n.pl.* sundry things or items.

sundry, *adj.* 1. various or divers. –*pron.* 2. **all and sundry**, everyone.

sun·flower, *n.* a tall plant grown for its showy flowers, and for its seeds, valuable as a source of oil.

sung, *v.* past participle of **sing**.

sun·glasses, *n.pl.* spectacles with tinted lenses to protect the eyes from glare.

sunk, *v.* a past tense and past participle of **sink**.

sun·rise, *n.* the rise of the sun above the horizon in the morning.

sunset, *n.* the setting of the sun below the horizon in the evening.

sun·shine, *n.* 1. the direct light of the sun. 2. cheerfulness, happiness, or prosperity.

sun·spot, *n.* 1. one of the relatively dark patches which appear periodically on the sun. 2. a discolouration and roughening of part of the skin, usu. as a result of exposure to the sun.

sun·stroke, *n.* a condition of physical weakness caused by excessive exposure to the sun.

super, *n.* *Colloq.* 1. →**superannuation**. 2. high-octane petrol. 3. →**superintendent**. –*adj.* 4. of a superior quality, grade, size, etc.

super·annuation, *n.* 1. a pension or allowance to a retired person. 2. a sum paid periodically as contribution to a pension fund.

superb, *adj.* admirably fine or excellent.

super·cilious, *adj.* haughtily disdainful or contemptuous.

super·ficial, *adj.* 1. being at, on, or near the surface. 2. concerned with or comprehending only what is on the surface or obvious; shallow. 3. apparent, rather than real.

super·fluous, *adj.* being over and above what is sufficient or required.

super·intend, *v.* to oversee and direct (work, etc.). – **superintendent**, *n.*

superior, *adj.* 1. higher in station, rank, degree, or grade. 2. of higher quality. 3. greater in quantity or amount. 4. showing a feeling of being better than others. –*n.* 5. one

superior

superior to another or others. – **superiority**, n.

superla·tive, adj. surpassing all others.

super·market, n. a large, usu. self-service, retail store or market.

super·natural, adj. 1. not explicable in terms of natural laws or phenomena. 2. of or pertaining to supernatural beings, as ghosts, spirits, etc. –n. 3. supernatural forces, effects, and beings collectively.

super·phos·phate, n. an artificial fertiliser.

super·sede, v., -seded, -seding. 1. to set aside, as void, useless, or obsolete. 2. to supplant.

super·sonic, adj. (of velocities) above the velocity of sound.

super·star, n. a showbusiness personality who is very famous.

super·stition, n. 1. a belief or notion entertained, regardless of reason or knowledge, of the ominous significance of a particular thing, circumstance, etc. 2. any blindly accepted belief or notion.

super·structure, n. all of an edifice above the basement or foundation.

super·vise, v., -vised, -vising. to oversee (a process, work, workers, etc.). – **supervision**, n.

supine, adj. lying on the back.

supper, n. 1. a light meal taken late at night. 2. *Chiefly Brit. and U.S.* the evening meal.

sup·plant, v. to take the place of (another).

supple, adj. bending readily or easily.

sup·ple·ment, n. 1. something added to complete or extend a thing. –v. 2. to complete or extend by a supplement; form a supplement to. – **supplementary**, adj.

sup·pli·cate, v., -cated, -cating. to make humble and earnest entreaty.

supply, v., -plied, -plying, n., pl. -plies. –v. 1. to furnish (a person, establishment, place, etc.) with what is lacking or required. 2. to furnish or provide (something wanting or requisite). –n. 3. the act of supplying. 4. a quantity of something provided or available, as for use or sale.

support, v. 1. to sustain or withstand (weight, etc.) without giving way. 2. to undergo or endure; tolerate. 3. to sustain (a person, the mind, etc.) under trial or affliction. 4. to maintain (a person, institution, etc.) by supplying with things necessary to existence; provide for. 5. to uphold (a person, cause, policy, etc.). –n. 6. the act of supporting. 7. the state of being supported. 8. a thing or a person that supports.

sup·pose, v., -posed, -posing. 1. to assume (something), without reference to its being true or false, for the sake of argument, etc. 2. to assume as true, or believe, in the absence of positive knowledge. 3. (of facts, circumstances, etc.) to require logically; presuppose. – **supposition**, n.

sup·posi·tory, n., pl. -ries. a medicinal substance inserted into the rectum or vagina to be dissolved therein.

sup·press, v. 1. to keep in or repress. 2. to vanquish or subdue.

sup·pu·rate, v., -rated, -rating. to produce or discharge pus.

supreme, adj. 1. highest in rank or authority. 2. greatest, utmost, or extreme. – **supremacy**, n.

524

surcharge

sur·charge, v., **-charged, -charging.** n. (to subject to) an additional sum added to the usual cost.

sure, adj., **surer, surest.** adv. –adj. 1. free from apprehension or doubt; confident. 2. worthy of confidence; reliable. 3. firm or stable. 4. never missing, slipping, etc. 5. inevitable. –adv. 6. *Colloq.* surely, undoubtedly, or certainly.

surely, adv. 1. in a sure manner. 2. (in emphatic utterances) it is unlikely to be otherwise (that). 3. inevitably or without fail.

surety, n., pl. **-ties.** security against loss or damage, non-payment of a debt, etc.

surf, n. 1. the swell of the sea which breaks upon a shore. –v. 2. to engage in surfing.

sur·face, n., adj., v., **-faced, -facing.** –n. 1. the outer face, or outside, of a thing. –adj. 2. of, on, or pertaining to the surface. 3. superficial; apparent, rather than real. 4. of, on, or pertaining to land and/or sea. –v. 5. to give a particular kind of surface to. 6. to rise to the surface.

surf·board, n. a long, narrow board used in riding waves towards the shore.

sur·feit, n. 1. an excessive amount. 2. general disgust caused by excess or satiety.

surf·ing, n. 1. the sport in which one attempts to ride on or with a wave towards the shore standing on a surfboard. 2. Also, **body-surfing.** the sport of riding waves without a surfboard.

surge, n., v., **surged, surging.** –n. 1. a strong forward or upward movement, as or like that of swelling or rolling waves. –v. 2. to rise or roll in waves, or like waves.

surrender

sur·geon, n. a doctor qualified to practise surgery.

sur·gery, n., pl. **-geries.** 1. the treating of diseases, injuries, or deformities by manual operation or instrumental appliances. 2. the consulting room of a medical practitioner, dentist, or the like. – **surgical,** adj.

surly, adj., **-lier, -liest.** churlishly rude or ill-humoured.

sur·mise, v., **-mised, -mising,** n. –v. 1. to think or infer without certain or strong evidence. –n. 2. a matter of conjecture.

sur·mount, v. 1. to get over or across (barriers, obstacles, etc.). 2. to be on top of or above.

sur·name, n. a family name, as distinguished from a Christian or first name.

sur·pass, v. to go beyond in amount, extent, or degree.

sur·plus, n. that which remains above what is used or needed.

sur·prise, v., **-prised, -prising,** n. adj. –v. 1. to catch (a person, etc.) in the act of doing something. 2. to assail without warning. 3. to strike with a sudden feeling of wonder. –n. 4. a sudden and unexpected event, action, or the like. 5. the state of feeling of wonder or alarm at something unexpected. –adj. 6. sudden and unexpected.

sur·real·ism, n. a movement in literature and art based on the expression of the uncontrolled subconscious mind. – **surreal,** adj.

sur·ren·der, v. 1. to give (something) up to the possession or power of another. 2. to give oneself

surrender

up to an emotion, course of action, etc. –n. 3. the act of surrendering.

sur·rep·ti·tious, adj. obtained, done, made, etc., by stealth.

sur·ro·gate, n. a substitute.

sur·round, v. 1. to enclose on all sides, or encompass. –n. 2. a border which surrounds.

sur·veil·lance, n. watch kept over a person, etc.

survey, v., n., pl. **-veys**. –v. 1. to take a general or comprehensive view of. 2. to inspect in detail, esp. officially. 3. to collect sample opinions, or the like in order to estimate the overall situation. 4. to determine the form, boundaries, etc., of (land). –n. 5. a comprehensive view. 6. a formal or official examination. 7. a gathering of sample opinions, etc., in order to estimate the overall situation. 8. the act of surveying land, or plans resulting from this.

sur·vive, v., **-vived, -viving**. to remain alive or in existence after the death of (someone) or after the cessation of (something). – **survivor**, n. – **survival**, n.

sus·cep·ti·ble, adj. 1. capable of receiving or being affected by, something (of or to). 2. impressionable. – **susceptibility**, n.

sus·pect, v. 1. to imagine to be guilty, defective, bad, etc., with insufficient or no proof. 2. to imagine something evil, wrong, or undesirable) to be the case. –n. 3. a person suspected of a crime, offence, or the like. –adj. 4. suspected; open to suspicion.

sus·pend, v. 1. to hang by attachment to something above. 2. to defer or postpone. 3. to (cause to) stop or stay, usu. for a time, as payment. 4. to debar, usu. for a time, from the exercise of an office or privilege.

swag

sus·pen·der, n. a strap with fastenings to support women's stockings.

sus·pense, n. a state of mental uncertainty, as in awaiting a decision or outcome, usu. with anxiety.

sus·pen·sion, n. 1. the act of suspending. 2. the state of being suspended. 3. something on or by which something else is hung. 4. the arrangement of springs, shock absorbers, hangers, etc., in a motor vehicle.

sus·pi·cion, n. 1. the act of suspecting. 2. a vague notion of something. 3. a slight trace. – **suspicious**, adj.

sus·tain, v. 1. to hold or bear up from below. 2. to bear (a burden, charge, etc.). 3. to suffer (injury, loss, etc.). 4. to keep going, as an action or process. 5. to supply with food and drink, or the necessities of life.

sus·te·nance, n. means of sustaining life; nourishment.

suture, n., v., **-tured, -turing**. –n. 1. a sewing together, or a joining as by sewing. –v. 2. to unite by or as by a suture.

swab, n., v., **swabbed, swabbing**. –n. 1. absorbent material used for cleaning wounds, etc. 2. matter collected with such material for medical testing, etc. –v. 3. to wipe or clean. 4. to take a swab (def. 2).

swag, n. a bundle or roll containing the personal belongings of a traveller through the bush, a miner, etc.

swag·ger, *v.* to walk or strut with a defiant or insolent air.

swal·low[1], *v.* 1. to take (food, etc.) into the stomach through the throat. 2. to take in so as to envelop. 3. *Colloq.* to accept without question or suspicion. —*n.* 4. the act of swallowing.

swal·low[2], *n.* a small, long-winged, migratory bird.

swamp, *n.* 1. a piece or tract of wet, spongy land. —*v.* 2. to flood or drench with water or the like.

swan, *n.* a large, stately swimming bird with a long, slender neck.

swank, *n. Colloq.* dashing smartness; ostentation or style.

swap, *v.*, **swapped**, **swapping**, *n.* —*v.* 1. to exchange, barter, or trade, as one thing for another. —*n.* 2. an exchange. Also, **swop**.

swarm, *n.* 1. a body of bees moving together. 2. a great number of things or persons, esp. in motion. —*v.* 3. to move in great numbers, as things or persons. 4. (of a place) to be thronged or overrun (*with*).

swar·thy, *adj.*, **-thier**, **-thiest**. dark in complexion.

swat, *v.*, **swatted**, **swatting**. *Colloq.* to hit with a smart or violent blow.

swathe, *v.*, **swathed**, **swathing**. to wrap or bind with bands of some material.

sway, *v.* 1. (cause to) move to and fro. 2. to fluctuate or vacillate, as in opinion. 3. to cause (the mind, etc., or the person) to incline or turn in a specified way. —*n.* 4. rule; dominion. 5. dominating power or influence.

swear, *v.*, **swore**, **sworn**, **swearing**. 1. to make a solemn declaration with an appeal to God or some sacred being. 2. to engage or promise on oath or in a solemn manner. 3. to use profane or taboo language. 4. to affirm or say with solemn earnestness or great emphasis. 5. **swear in**, to admit to office or service by administering an oath.

sweat, *v.*, **sweat** or **sweated**, **sweating**. —*v.* 1. to excrete (watery fluid through the pores of the skin), as from heat, exertion, etc. 2. *Colloq.* to exert oneself strenuously. 3. to send forth or get rid of like perspiration (*out* or *off*). 4. **sweat it out**, *Colloq.* to endure until the end. —*n.* 5. the process of sweating. 6. the secretions of sweat glands; perspiration.

sweat·ed, *adj.* underpaid and overworked.

sweat·er, *n.* a knitted jumper.

sweat-shirt, *n.* a loose pullover.

sweep, *v.*, **swept**, **sweeping**, *n.* —*v.* 1. to move, drive, or bring, by or as if by, passing a broom, brush, or the like over the surface occupied. 2. to pass or draw (something) over a surface, or about, along, etc., with a steady, continuous stroke. 3. to clear or clean (a floor, room, etc.) by means of a broom. 4. to move steadily and strongly or swiftly (*down*, *over*, etc.). 5. to walk in long, trailing garments. 6. to extend in a continuous or curving stretch, as a road, etc. —*n.* 7. the act of sweeping. 8. a swinging or curving movement or stroke. 9. a continuous or entire stretch.

sweep·stake, *n.* a method of gambling, as on the outcome of a horserace, in which each participant contributes a stake, the winnings being provided from the stake money. Also, **sweepstakes**.

sweet

sweet, *adj.* **1.** having the pleasant taste or flavour characteristic of sugar, honey, etc. **2.** pleasing or agreeable. **3.** pleasant in disposition or manners. **4.** dear; beloved. –*adv.* **5.** in a sweet manner; sweetly. –*n.* **6.** that which is sweet. **7.** Also, **sweetie**. any of various small confections made from sugar. **8.** (*oft. pl.*) any sweet dish served at the end of a meal. **9.** a beloved person; sweetheart.

sweet·bread, *n.* the pancreas or thymus gland of an animal, esp. a calf or a lamb, used for food.

sweet corn, *n.* the sweet and tender ears of maize, esp. when used as a table vegetable.

sweet·heart, *n.* a beloved person.

sweet·meat, *n.* a sweet delicacy.

sweet potato, *n.* a plant cultivated for its edible root.

swell, *v.*, **swelled**, **swollen** or **swelled**, **swelling**, *n.*, *adj.* –*v.* **1.** to grow in bulk, as by absorption of moisture, by distention, addition, or the like. **2.** to rise in waves, as the sea. **3.** to grow in amount, degree, force, or the like. **4.** to puff up with pride. –*n.* **5.** increase in bulk. **6.** a part that bulges out. **7.** a wave, esp. when long and unbroken, or such waves collectively. **8.** an elevation of the land. **9.** increase in amount, degree, force, etc. **10.** *Colloq.* a person of high social standing. –*adj. Colloq.* **11.** (of things) stylish; elegant. **12.** first-rate; excellent.

swell·ing, *n.* a swollen part.

swel·ter, *v.* to suffer or languish with oppressive heat.

swerve, *v.*, **swerved**, **swerving**. to turn aside abruptly in movement or direction.

swing

swift, *adj.* **1.** moving with great speed; rapid. –*n.* **2.** any of several rapidly flying birds.

swill, *n.* **1.** any liquid matter, esp. waste; slops. –*v.* **2.** to wash or cleanse by flooding with water.

swim, *v.*, **swam**, **swum**, **swimming**. –*v.* **1.** to move on or in water or other liquid in any way. **2.** to be immersed or flooded with a liquid. **3.** to be dizzy or giddy. –*n.* **4.** an act of swimming. **5. in the swim**, actively engaged in current affairs, social activities, etc.

swin·dle, *v.*, **-dled**, **-dling**, *n.* –*v.* **1.** to cheat (a person) out of money, etc. –*n.* **2.** a fraudulent transaction or scheme.

swine, *n.*, *pl.* **swine**. **1.** the domestic pig. **2.** a contemptible person.

swing[1], *v.*, **swung**, **swinging**. –*v.* **1.** to (cause to) move to and fro as something suspended from above. **2.** to (cause to) move in alternate directions about a fixed point, as a door on its hinges. **3.** to sway, influence, or manage as desired. **4.** to move to and fro on a swinging seat. **5.** to move in a curve, as around a corner. **6.** to change or shift one's attention, opinion, interest, etc. **7.** to aim at or hit something with a sweeping movement of the arm. –*n.* **8.** the act or the manner of swinging. **9.** the amount of such movement. **10.** active operation. **11.** a seat suspended from above by ropes, etc., in which one may sit and swing to and fro for amusement.

swing[2], *n.*, *v.*, **swung**, **swinging**. –*n.* **1.** Also, **swing music**. a smooth, orchestral type of jazz popular in the 1930s. –*v.* **2.** *Colloq.* to be lively or modern.

swipe, n., v., swiped, swiping. *Colloq.* —n. 1. a sweeping stroke. —v. 2. to strike with a sweeping blow. 3. to steal.

swirl, v. to move with a whirling motion.

swish, v. 1. to move with or make a hissing sound. —n. 2. a swishing movement or sound. —3. *Colloq.* Also, **swishy.** smart; stylish.

switch, n. 1. a slender, flexible rod used esp. in whipping, beating, etc. 2. *Elect.* a device for turning on or off or directing an electric current. 3. *Colloq.* →**switchboard.** —v. 4. to move, swing, or whisk (a cane, a fishing line, etc.) with a swift, lashing stroke. 5. to exchange; shift. 6. **switch on,** to cause (an electric current) to flow or (an electric appliance) to operate. 7. **switch off,** to cause (an electric current or appliance) to stop. 8. to change direction or course.

switch·board, n. an arrangement of switches, plugs, and jacks mounted on a board or frame enabling an operator to make temporary connections between telephone users.

swivel, n. a fastening device which allows the thing fastened to turn round freely upon it.

swoon, v. to faint; lose consciousness.

swoop, v. 1. to sweep through the air, as a bird upon prey. 2. to come down in a sudden swift attack (*down* or *on* or *upon*). 3. to take with, or as with, a sweeping motion (*up*). —n. 4. the act of swooping. 5. **at one fell swoop,** all at once.

sword, n. a weapon with a long, straight or slightly curved blade fixed in a hilt or handle.

swot, v., swotted, swotting. n. *Colloq.* —v. 1. to study hard. —n. 2. one who studies hard.

syco·phant, n. a self-seeking flatterer.

syl·lable, n. 1. *Phonet.* a segment of speech uttered with a single impulse of air-pressure from the lungs. 2. the least portion or amount of speech or writing. – **syllabic,** *adj.*

syl·la·bus, n., pl. **-buses, -bi.** an outline or summary of a course of studies, lectures, etc.

symbol, n. something used or regarded as representing something else. – **symbolic,** *adj.*

symbo·lise, v., **-lised, -lising.** 1. to be a symbol of. 2. to represent by a symbol or symbols.

sym·metry, n., pl. **-tries.** the correspondence, in size, form, and arrangement, of opposite parts. – **symmetrical,** *adj.*

sym·pa·thetic, *adj.* 1. characterised by, proceeding from, exhibiting, or feeling sympathy. 2. looking with favour or liking upon (*to* or *towards*).

sym·pa·thise, v., **-thised, -thising.** 1. to feel a compassionate sympathy (*with*). 2. to agree, correspond, or accord.

sym·pathy, n., pl. **-thies.** 1. agreement in feeling. 2. the fact or the power of entering into the feelings of another. 3. agreement, consonance, or accord.

sym·phony, n., pl. **-nies.** *Music.* an elaborate instrumental composition written for an orchestra.

sym·po·sium, n., pl. **-siums, -sia.** a meeting or conference for discussion of some subject.

symp·tom, *n.* a sign or indication of something.

symp·to·matic, *adj.* constituting a symptom; indicative (*of*).

syna·gogue, *n.* a Jewish house of worship.

syn·chro·nise, *v.*, **-nised, -nising.** to (cause to) occur at the same time, or coincide or agree in time. – **synchronisation,** *n.*

syn·di·cate, *n.*, *v.*, **-cated, -cating.** –*n.* 1. a combination of business associates, commercial firms, etc., formed for the purpose of carrying out some project. –*v.* 2. to combine into a syndicate. 3. to publish simultaneously in a number of newspapers or other periodicals in different places.

syn·drome, *n.* a number of characteristic symptoms occurring together, as in a disease.

syno·nym, *n.* a word having the same, or nearly the same, meaning as another, as *joyful, elated, glad.*

syn·op·sis, *n.*, *pl.* **-ses.** a brief or condensed statement giving a general view of some subject.

syntax, *n. Gram.* the patterns of formation of sentences and phrases from words in a particular language.

syn·thesis, *n.*, *pl.* **-ses.** 1. the combination of parts or elements into a complex whole (opposed to *analysis*). 2. a complex whole made up of parts or elements combined. – **synthetic,** *adj.*

syn·the·sise, *v.*, **-sised, -sising.** to make up by combining parts or elements.

syphi·lis, *n.* a chronic, infectious venereal disease.

syphon, *n.*, *v.* →**siphon.**

syr·inge, *n. Med.* a small tube used for injecting fluids into the body, etc.

syrup, *n.* any of various sweet, viscid liquids.

system, *n.* 1. an assemblage or combination of things or parts forming a complex or unitary whole. 2. a coordinated body of methods, or a complex scheme or plan of procedure. 3. the entire human or animal body. 4. a method or scheme of classification. – **systematise,** *v.*

sys·te·matic, *adj.* having, showing, or involving a system, method, or plan.

sys·temic, *adj.* relating to or affecting the whole bodily system.

Tt

T, t, *n., pl.* **T's** or **Ts, t's** or **ts.** the 20th letter of the English alphabet.

tab, *n.* **1.** a small strap, loop, etc. as on a garment, etc. **2.** a protruding label for ready identification.

tabby, *n., pl.* **-bies.** a cat with a striped or brindled coat.

taber·nacle, *n.* **1.** the tent used by the Jews as a portable sanctuary before their final settlement in Palestine. **2.** any (large) place of worship.

table, *n., v.,* **-bled, -bling.** –*n.* **1.** an article of furniture consisting of a flat top resting on legs or on a pillar. **2.** a flat surface. **3.** an arrangement of words, numbers, or signs to exhibit a set of facts in a compact form: *multiplication tables.* –*v.* **4.** to form into a table or list. **5.** to place on a table.

tab·leau, *n., pl.* **-leaux, -leaus.** a picturesque grouping of persons or objects.

table·land, *n.* an elevated, usu. level region.

table·spoon, *n.* a large spoon.

tablet, *n.* **1.** a pad of writing paper. **2.** a small, flat slab, esp. one bearing an inscription, carving, etc. **3.** a small, flat piece of some solid substance, as a drug, chemical, etc.

table tennis, *n.* an indoor small-scale tennis game, played on a table.

tab·loid, *n.* a newspaper, about ½ the ordinary page size, emphasising pictures and concise writing.

taboo, *adj., n., pl.* **-boos,** *v.,* **-booed, -booing.** –*adj.* **1.** forbidden to general use; prohibited or banned. –*n.* **2.** a prohibition or exclusion from use or practice. –*v.* **3.** to put under a taboo; prohibit or forbid.

tabu·lar, *adj.* pertaining to or arranged as a table (def. 3).

tabu·late, *v.,* **-lated, -lating.** to put or form into a table, scheme, or synopsis. **– tabulator,** *n.*

tacit, *adj.* **1.** silent. **2.** not openly expressed, but implied.

taci·turn, *adj.* inclined to silence, or reserved in speech.

tack, *n.* **1.** a short, sharp-pointed nail or pin. **2.** a long stitch used before permanent sewing. **3.** *Naut.* **a.** the direction or course of a ship in relation to the position of her sails. **b.** a course obliquely against the wind. **4.** a course of action, esp. one differing from some preceding course. **5.** all the equipment pertaining to the saddling and harnessing of horses. –*v.* **6.** to fasten by a tack. **7.** *Naut.* to change the course of a ship.

tackle, *n., v.,* **-led, -ling.** –*n.* **1.** equipment, esp. for fishing. **2.** apparatus, as a rope and block or a combination of these, for hoisting, lowering, etc. materials. **3.** an act of tackling, as in football. –*v.* **4.** to undertake to deal with, master, solve, etc. **5.** *Rugby Football, etc.* to seize and pull down (an opponent having the ball).

tacky, *adj.,* **-ier, -iest.** *Colloq.* **1.** shabby. **2.** superficially attractive but lacking quality or craftsmanship.

tact, *n.* a keen sense of what to say or do to avoid giving offence.

tactic

tac·tic, *n.* a plan for achieving a desired end.

tac·tile, *adj.* of or pertaining to the organs or sense of touch.

tad·pole, *n.* the aquatic larva of frogs, toads, etc.

tag[1], *n., v.,* **tagged, tagging.** –*n.* 1. a piece of strong paper, leather, etc., attached to something as a label. 2. any small loosely-attached part or piece. –*v.* 3. to attach as a tag to something else. 4. to follow closely (*along*).

tag[2], *n.* a type of wrestling.

tagliatelle, *n.* ribbon pasta.

tail, *n.* 1. the rear end of an animal, esp. when forming a distinct flexible appendage to the trunk. 2. something resembling this in shape or position. 3. the bottom or concluding part of anything. 4. *Colloq.* (*pl.*) the reverse of a coin. 5. *Colloq.* the buttocks. 6. *Colloq.* a person who follows another, esp. in order to observe or hinder escape. –*v.* 7. *Colloq.* to follow in order to hinder escape or to observe. 8. **tail off**, to decrease gradually.

tailor, *n.* one whose business it is to make or mend clothing, esp. men's suits.

taint, *n.* 1. a trace of infection, contamination, etc. –*v.* 2. to infect, contaminate, or corrupt. 3. to sully or tarnish.

taipan, *n.* a long-fanged, highly venomous snake.

take, *v.,* **took, taken, taking.** –*v.t.* 1. to get into one's hands, possession, control, etc. 2. to seize: *to take prisoners.* 3. to select: *Take which one you like.* 4. to obtain by making payment: *to take a holiday house.* 5. to carry off or remove

talc

(*away*, etc.). 6. to subtract or deduct: *take 2 from 4.* 7. to carry or convey. 8. to use (a vehicle, etc.) as a means of travel. 9. to conduct or lead: *This road will take you to the town.* 10. to absorb or be absorbed, as ink, etc. 11. to proceed to deal with: *to take a matter under consideration.* 12. to proceed to occupy: *to take a seat.* 13. to occupy or use up (space, material, time, etc.). 14. to attract and hold: *a display which takes one's eye.* 15. to write down (notes, a copy, etc.). 16. to make (a photograph, etc., of something). 17. to make (a measurement, observation, etc.). 18. to assume the obligation of (a vow, pledge, etc.). 19. to assume or adopt as one's own: *to take the credit for something.* 20. to comply with (advice, etc.). 21. *Gram.* to have by usage (a particular form, case, etc.). 22. to engage, as a mechanical device. 23. to begin to grow, as a plant. 24. to have the intended effect, as a medicine, inoculation, etc. 25. to become (sick or ill). 26. **take off, a.** to remove (clothing, etc.). **b.** to leave the ground, as an aeroplane. **c.** *Colloq.* to imitate or mimic. 27. **take place**, to happen; occur. –*n.* 28. an act or instance of taking. 29. that which is taken. 30. *Films, etc.* (a portion of) a scene photographed without any interruption. 31. *Colloq.* a cheat; swindle.

take·over, *n.* acquisition of control, esp. of a business company, by the purchase of the majority of its shares.

tak·ings, *n.pl.* receipts.

talc, *n.* Also, **talcum**. a soft greenish grey mineral used in making lubricants, powder, etc.

tale, *n.* a story about some real or imaginary event.

talent, *n.* a special natural ability.

tal·is·man, *n., pl.* **-mans.** any charm, esp. worn for magical effect.

talk, *v.* 1. to perform the act of speaking. 2. to make known by means of spoken words. 3. to express in words: *to talk politics.* 4. to discuss: *to talk politics.* —*n.* 5. speech; conversation, esp. of a familiar or informal kind. 6. a lecture or informal speech. 7. report or rumour; gossip.

tall, *adj.* of more than average height.

tallow, *n.* the fatty tissue of animals, used in making candles, soap etc.

tally, *n., pl.* **-lies,** *v.,* **-lied, lying.** —*n.* 1. an account or record of a score. —*v.* 2. to count or reckon up.

talon, *n.* a claw, esp. of a bird of prey.

tam·bour·ine, *n.* a small hand-held drum with pairs of metal discs inserted into the frame.

tame, *adj.,* **tamer, tamest,** *v.,* **tamed, taming.** —*adj.* 1. changed from the wild state; domesticated. 2. tractable, docile, or submissive. 3. spiritless. —*v.* 4. to make tame; subdue. 5. to soften; tone down.

tamp, *v.* to force in or down by repeated, somewhat light strokes.

tamper, *v.* to meddle, esp. for the purpose of altering, damaging, etc. (*with*).

tampon, *n.* 1. a plug of cotton put into an opening, wound, etc., as to stop haemorrhage. 2. a similar device used internally to absorb menstrual flow.

tan, *v.,* **tanned, tanning,** *n.* —*v.* 1. to convert (a hide) into a leather. 2. to make brown by exposure to the sun. 3. *Colloq.* to beat or thrash. —*n.* 4. the brown colour of skin exposed to the sun.

tandem, *adv.* 1. one behind another. —*n.* 2. a bicycle for 2 riders.

tang, *n.* 1. a strong taste or flavour. 2. a pungent or distinctive smell.

tan·gent, *adj.* 1. touching. —*n.* 2. a sudden divergence from one course, thought, etc., to another.

tan·ger·ine, *n.* a type of mandarin.

tan·gi·ble, *adj.* 1. discernible by the touch; material or substantial. 2. real rather than imaginary.

tangle, *v.,* **-gled, -gling,** *n.* —*v.* 1. to bring or be brought together into a mass of twisted threads, etc. —*n.* 2. a tangled condition.

tango, *n., pl.* **-gos,** *v.,* **-goed, -going.** —*n.* 1. a dance of Spanish-American origin. —*v.* 2. to dance the tango.

tank, *n.* 1. a large container for holding liquid or a gas. 2. *Mil.* an armoured combat vehicle, armed with cannon and machine-guns and moving on continuous tracks.

tank·ard, *n.* a large drinking cup, now usu. with a handle and (sometimes) a hinged cover.

tanker, *n.* a ship or vehicle designed to carry liquid in bulk.

tannin, *n.* a substance used in tanning.

tan·ta·lise, *v.,* **-lised, -lising.** to torment or tease (as) with the sight of something desired but out of reach.

tan·ta·mount, *adj.* equivalent, as in value, effect, etc. (*to*).

tan·trum, *n.* a fit of ill temper or passion.

tap[1], *v.,* **tapped, tapping,** *n.* —*v.* 1. to strike with slight, audible blows. —*n.* 2. a light blow.

tap

tap[2], *n., v.*, **tapped, tapping.** –*n.* 1. any device for controlling the flow of liquid from a pipe, etc., by opening or closing an orifice; cock. –*v.* 2. to draw off (liquid) by opening a tap, or by piercing the container. 3. to gain secret access to. 4. to open outlets from (power lines, roads, pipes, etc.).

tape, *n., v.*, **taped, taping.** –*n.* 1. a long narrow strip of fabric used for tying garments, etc. 2. a long narrow strip of paper, metal, etc. –*v.* 3. to furnish with a tape. 4. to record on a tape-recorder.

taper, *v.* 1. to make or become gradually thinner towards one end. 2. to reduce gradually. –*n.* 3. gradual decrease of width, thickness, force, capacity, etc. 4. a long, narrow candle.

tape-recorder, *n.* a device for recording sound on magnetic tape.

tapestry, *n., pl.* **-tries.** an open weave fabric upon which coloured threads are woven by hand to produce a decorative design.

tapeworm, *n.* a parasitic flat or tapelike worm.

tapioca, *n.* a granular, starchy food used for making puddings, etc.

tap root, *n.* a main root descending downwards and branching into small lateral roots.

tar, *n., v.*, **tarred, tarring.** –*n.* 1. any of various dark, sticky products obtained by processing substances, such as coal, wood, etc. –*v.* 2. to smear (as) with tar.

tar·an·tula, *n., pl.* **-las, -lae.** a large spider.

tardy, *adj.*, **-dier, -diest.** 1. slow; sluggish. 2. late.

tare, *n.* 1. the weight of the container holding goods. 2. the weight of a vehicle without cargo, passengers, etc.

target, *n.* 1. a device, usu. marked with concentric circles, to be aimed at in shooting practice or contests. 2. a goal to be reached.

tariff, *n.* (an official list showing) the duties or customs imposed by a government on exports or, esp., imports.

tarmac, *n.* 1. (a road or airport runway surfaced with) a mixture of gravel and tar.

tar·nish, *v.* 1. to (cause to) become dull or discoloured, as metals. 2. to destroy the purity of; stain; sully. –*n.* 3. tarnished or discoloured condition. 4. stain or blemish.

tarot /'tæroʊ/, *n.* a pack of cards, usu. used in fortune-telling.

tar·paulin, *n.* a protective waterproof covering of canvas or other material.

tar·ra·gon, *n.* a herb with aromatic leaves.

tarry, *v.*, **-ried, -rying.** 1. to remain or stay, as in a place. 2. to delay in acting, starting, coming, etc. 3. to wait.

tart[1], *adj.* sour or acid.

tart[2], *n.* 1. a shell of pastry, filled, as with cooked fruit, and having no top crust. 2. *Colloq.* a girl or woman, now esp. of low character.

tartan, *n.* a woollen or worsted cloth woven with stripes crossing at right angles, worn chiefly by the Scottish Highlanders.

tartar, *n.* 1. a hard substance deposited on the teeth. 2. the deposit from wines.

task

task, *n.* 1. a definite piece of work assigned to a person; duty. 2. a

task

demanding or difficult matter. –*v*. **3.** to subject to severe exertion; make great demands on.

tas·sel, *n*. **1.** a clasp consisting commonly of a bunch of threads, etc., hanging from a knob. **2.** something resembling this.

taste, *v*., **tasted**, **tasting**, *n*. –*v*. **1.** to try or perceive the flavour or quality of (something) by taking some into the mouth. **2.** to eat or drink a little of. **3.** to have or get a (slight) experience of. **4.** to smack or savour (*of*). –*n*. **5.** the act of tasting. **6.** the sense by which the flavour of things is perceived when they are brought into contact with special organs of the tongue. **7.** a small quantity tasted. **8.** a liking or predilection for something. **9.** the sense of what is appropriate, harmonious, or beautiful; the perception and enjoyment of excellence in the fine arts, literature, etc. **10.** a slight experience of something.

tasty, *adj*., **tastier**, **tastiest**. pleasing to the taste; savoury.

tat·ter, *n*. a torn piece hanging loose (or being separate) from the main part, as of a garment, etc.

tat·ting, *n*. (the making of) a kind of hand-made knotted lace.

tat·tle, *v*., **-tled**, **-tling**. to let out secrets.

tat·too[1], *n*., *pl*. **-toos**. an outdoor military pageant or display.

tat·too[2], *n*., *pl*. **-toos**. an indelible pattern made on the skin.

taught, *v*. past tense and past participle of **teach**.

taunt, *v*. to reproach or provoke in a sarcastic or insulting manner.

taut, *adj*. tightly drawn; tense.

teach

taut·ol·o·gy, *n*., *pl*. **-gies**. needless repetition of an idea.

tav·ern, *n*. premises where food and alcoholic drink are served.

taw, *n*. a choice or fancy marble (def. 3a.)

taw·dry, *adj*., **-drier**, **-driest**. (of finery, etc.) gaudy; showy and cheap.

taw·ny, *adj*., **-nier**, **-niest**. of a dark yellowish brown colour.

tax, *n*. **1.** a compulsory monetary contribution demanded by a government for its support, and levied on incomes, property, goods purchased, etc. –*v*. **2.** to impose tax on. **3.** to lay a burden on; make serious demands on. - **taxable**, *adj*.

tax·a·tion, *n*. **1.** the act of taxing. **2.** the revenue raised by taxes.

tax·i, *n*., *pl*. **taxis**, *v*., **taxied**, **taxiing** or **taxying**. –*n*. **1.** Also, **taxicab**. a motor car for public hire. –*v*. **2.** (of an aeroplane) to move over the surface of the ground or water under its own power.

tax·i·der·my, *n*. the art of preserving the skins of animals, and stuffing and mounting them in lifelike form. - **taxidermist**, *n*.

tax·on·o·my, *n*. scientific classification, esp. in relation to its laws.

tea, *n*. **1.** the dried and prepared leaves of an oriental shrub, from which a somewhat bitter, aromatic beverage is made by infusion in boiling water. **2.** a drink or medicine made from tea or other plants. **3.** a light meal taken in the late afternoon. **4.** the main evening meal.

teach, *v*., **taught**, **teaching**. **1.** to impart knowledge of or skill in; give instruction in (a subject). **2.** to

535

teach

give instruction to (someone). – **teacher,** n.

teak, n. a large tree with a hard, yellowish brown, resinous wood.

teal, n., pl. **teals,** (esp. collectively) **teal.** a small freshwater duck.

team, n. **1.** a number of persons associated in some joint action, esp. one of the sides in a match. **2.** 2 or more horses, oxen, etc., harnessed together to draw a vehicle, plough etc. –v. **3.** to join together in a team.

tear[1] /tɪə/, n. a drop of fluid flowing from the eye, chiefly as the result of sadness, pain, etc.

tear[2] /tɛə/, v., **tore, torn, tearing.** –v. **1.** to pull apart esp. so as to leave ragged edges. **2.** to pull violently or with force. **3.** to divide. **4.** to become torn. **5.** Colloq. to move with violence or great haste. –n. **6.** the act of tearing. **7.** a crack or split.

tease, v., **teased, teasing,** n. –v. **1.** to irritate by persistent petty requests, or other annoyances, often in jest. **2.** to pull apart the fibres of. **3.** to flirt. –n. **4.** the act of teasing. **5.** someone or something which teases.

teat, n. **1.** the protuberance on the breast or udder in female mammals where the milk ducts terminate; a nipple. **2.** something resembling a teat, esp. for feeding a baby from a bottle.

tech, n. Colloq. a technical college or school.

tech·ni·cal, adj. **1.** pertaining to an art, science, etc. **2.** having practical skills in a particular art, trade, etc., as a person. **3.** pertaining to the mechanical or industrial arts and the applied sciences.

telegraph

tech·ni·cal·i·ty, n., pl. **-ties.** a literal, often narrow-minded interpretation of a rule, etc.

tech·ni·cian, n. one skilled in the technique of an art or science.

tech·nique, n. method or performance.

tech·nol·o·gy, n. the branch of knowledge that deals with (the practice and application of) science and engineering.

tec·ton·ic, adj. of or pertaining to building or construction.

tedium, n. the state of being dull and tiresome. – **tedious,** adj.

tee, n., v., **teed, teeing.** Golf. –n. **1.** (the wooden, etc., holder at) the beginning of each fairway from which the ball is driven. –v. **2.** to strike the ball from a tee (off).

teem[1], v. to abound or swarm (with).

teem[2], v. to rain very hard.

teen·ager, n. a person aged between 12 and 20. – **teenage,** adj.

teeter, v. to move unsteadily.

teeth, n. plural of **tooth.**

teethe, v., **teethed, teething.** to have one's teeth grow and emerge through the gums.

tee·total, adj. pledged to total abstinence from alcohol. – **teetotaller,** n.

tele·cast, v., **-cast** or **-casted, -casting,** n. –v. **1.** to broadcast by television. –n. **2.** a television broadcast.

tele·communi·cations, n.pl. the science of sending information by line or radio transmission.

tele·gram, n. a message sent by telegraph.

tele·graph, n. **1.** an apparatus for transmitting messages or signals to a distance. –v. **2.** to send (a mes-

telegraph

sage, etc.) by telegraph. – **telegraphic**, *adj.* – **telegraphy**, *n.*

tel·epathy, *n.* communication of one mind with another by some means other than the normal use of the senses.

tele·phone, *n.* an (electrical) apparatus or system for sending sound or speech to a distant point. – **telephonist**, *n.* – **telephony**, *n.*

tele·photo, *adj.* relating to a photographic lens which produces magnified images.

tele·printer, *n.* an instrument having a typewriter keyboard which transmits and receives messages over distances or to and from a computer. Also, **teletype**.

tele·scope, *n., v.,* **-scoped, -scoping.** –*n.* 1. an optical instrument for making distant objects appear nearer and larger. –*v.* 2. to force or slide together, one into another, or into something else, in the manner of the sliding tubes of a jointed telescope. 3. to condense; shorten. – **telescopic**, *adj.*

tele·vision, *n.* 1. the broadcasting of images via radio waves to receivers which project them on a picture tube for viewing. 2. a television receiver. – **televise**, *v.*

telex, *n.* a service provided by postal authorities in which teleprinters are loaned to subscribers.

tell, *v.,* **told, telling.** 1. to give an account or report (of); relate (a story, etc.). 2. to make known by speech or writing (information, etc.); communicate. 3. to utter (the truth, a lie, etc.). 4. to recognise or distinguish: *You can't tell the difference between them.* 5. to give evidence (*of*): *Her handbag tells of her arrival.* 6. to play the informer (*on*). 7. to produce a marked effect: *The strain was telling on his face.*

tempest

teller, *n.* one employed in a bank to receive or pay out money over the counter.

tel·luric, *adj.* relating to the earth.

tem·erity, *n.* reckless boldness.

temper, *n.* 1. a particular state of mind or feelings. 2. passion, shown in outbursts of anger, resentment, etc. 3. the particular degree of hardness and elasticity imparted to steel, etc., by tempering. –*v.* 4. to moderate or mitigate. 5. to bring to a desirable state (as) by blending. 6. to heat and cool or quench (metal) to bring to the proper degree of hardness, elasticity, etc.

tem·pera, *n.* paint made from pigment ground in water and mixed with egg yolk or some similar substance.

tem·pera·ment, *n.* the individual character of a person, as shown by the manner of thinking, feeling, and acting.

tem·pera·men·tal, *adj.* 1. moody, irritable, or sensitive. 2. unstable; unreliable.

tem·per·ance, *n.* 1. habitual moderation. 2. total abstinence from alcohol.

tem·per·ate, *adj.* 1. moderate or self-restrained. 2. not excessive.

tem·pera·ture, *n.* 1. a measure of the degree of hotness or coldness of a body or substance. 2. *Physiol., Pathol.* **a.** the degree of heat of a living body, esp. the human body. **b.** the excess of this above the normal (37°C or about 98.4°F in adult humans).

tem·pest, *n.* a violent storm.

537

tem·pes·tu·ous, adj. of or like a storm.

tem·plate, n. a pattern, mould, or the like, usu. consisting of a thin plate of wood, etc., used as a guide in transferring designs, etc.

temple[1], n. a place of worship, esp. a large or imposing one.

temple[2], n. the flattened region on either side of the human forehead.

tempo, n., pl. **-pos**, **-pi**. Music. relative rate of movement.

tem·poral, adj. 1. of or pertaining to time. 2. pertaining to the present life or this world; worldly.

tem·po·rary, adj. lasting for a short time only; not permanent.

tem·po·rise, v., **-rised**, **-rising**. 1. to act indecisively to gain time or delay matters. 2. to (appear to) yield temporarily to the demands of the occasion.

tempt, v. 1. to persuade by enticement or allurement. 2. to cause to be strongly disposed (to do something). – **temptation**, n.

ten, n. a cardinal number, 9 plus one. – **tenth**, adj., n.

tena·ble, adj. capable of being held, maintained, or defended, as against attack or objection.

tena·cious, adj. 1. holding fast (of). 2. highly retentive, as memory. 3. persistent or obstinate. – **tenacity**, n.

tenant, n. one who leases a house, etc., from a landlord. – **tenancy**, n.

tend[1], v. to be inclined (to do something). – **tendency**, n.

tend[2], v. to attend to by work or services, etc. 2. to care for.

ten·den·tious, adj. presenting a particular bias or point of view.

tender[1], adj. 1. soft or delicate. 2. weak or fragile in constitution. 3. gentle. 4. painfully sensitive.

tender[2], v. 1. to offer formally for acceptance. –n. 2. an offer of something for acceptance. 3. Comm. an offer made in writing by one party to another to carry out work, supply certain commodities, etc., at a given cost.

tendon, n. a cord of dense, white fibrous tissue, connecting a muscle with a bone or part; a sinew. – **tendinous**, adj.

ten·dril, n. a leafless curly organ of climbing plants.

tene·ment house, n. a house divided into flats, esp. one in the poorer, crowded parts of a large city.

tenet, n. any opinion, doctrine, etc., held as true.

tennis, n. a game in which players with racquets hit a ball to each other over a net.

tenon, n. an end of a piece of wood, etc., shaped for insertion in a corresponding cavity (mortise) in another piece.

tenor, n. 1. the meaning which runs through something written or spoken; purport. 2. Music. the highest natural male voice.

tense[1], adj., **tenser**, **tensest**, v., **tensed**, **tensing**. –adj. 1. stretched tight; rigid. 2. in a state of nervous strain, as a person. –v. 3. to make or become tense.

tense[2], n. a form of a verb which specifies the time and length of the action or state expressed by the verb.

ten·sile, adj. 1. relating to tension. 2. capable of being stretched. – **tensility**, n.

ten·sion, n. 1. the act of stretching

or straining. 2. mental or emotional strain, as anxiety, suspense, or excitement. 3. *Elect.* electromotive force; potential.

tent, *n.* a portable shelter of skins or coarse cloth, esp. canvas.

ten·ta·cle, *n. Zool.* any of various slender, flexible appendages in animals, esp. invertebrates, used for grasping, touching, etc.

ten·ta·tive, *adj.* 1. experimental. 2. hesitant; diffident.

tenter·hooks, *n.pl. in the phrase* **on tenterhooks**, in a state of painful suspense or anxiety.

tenu·ous, *adj.* flimsy; lacking a sound basis; weak.

tenure, *n.* (the period or terms of) the possession of anything.

tepid, *adj.* moderately warm.

term, *n.* 1. any word or expression naming something, esp. as used in some particular field of knowledge. 2. the time through which something lasts or is fixed to last. 3. (in schools, universities, etc.) a period of the year during which instruction is regularly organised. 4. (*pl.*) conditions with regard to payment, price, etc. 5. (*pl.*) footing or standing: *to be on good terms with someone.* 6. **a contradiction in terms**, a statement which is self-contradictory. –*v.* 7. to name; call; designate.

ter·mi·nal, *adj.* 1. situated at or forming the end of something. 2. occurring at or causing the end of life. –*n.* 3. an end or extremity. 4. the end of a railway line, shipping route, air route, etc., at which loading and unloading of passengers, goods, etc., takes place. 5. *Elect.* the point of connection in an electrical circuit. 6. a keyboard or display unit used for entering data into a computer.

ter·mi·nate, *v.*, **-nated, -nating.** 1. to end, conclude, or cease (something). – **terminable**, *adj.*

ter·mi·nology, *n., pl.* **-gies.** the system of terms belonging to a subject; nomenclature.

ter·mi·nus, *n., pl.* **-ni, -nuses.** the station or town at the end of a railway line, bus route, etc.

ter·mite, *n.* a social insect, sometimes very destructive to buildings, etc.; white ant.

tern, *n.* a seabird.

ter·nary, *adj.* triple.

ter·race, *n.* 1. one of a series of raised level areas formed across a mountain side, etc., usu. for the purposes of cultivation. 2. an open (usu. paved) outdoor living area adjoining a house. 3. (a house in) a row of adjoining, identical houses.

terra cotta, *n.* a hard, usu. unglazed earthenware of fine quality.

ter·rain, *n.* an area of land, esp. as considered with reference to its natural features, military advantages, etc.

ter·res·trial, *adj.* 1. pertaining to, consisting of, or representing the earth. 2. of or pertaining to the land as distinct from the water.

ter·rible, *adj.* 1. exciting terror or great fear; dreadful; awful. 2. *Colloq.* very bad.

ter·rier, *n.* a small dog, originally bred for hunting.

ter·ri·fic, *adj.* 1. causing terror. 2. *Colloq.* very good.

ter·rify, *v.*, **-fied, -fying.** to fill with terror.

ter·ri·tory, *n., pl.* **-ries.** 1. any area of

territory

land; region or district. **2.** the land and waters belonging to or under the jurisdiction of a state, sovereign, etc. **3.** the field of action, thought, etc. – **territorial,** *adj.*

terror, *n.* **1.** intense, sharp, overpowering fear. **2.** *Colloq.* a person or thing that is a particular nuisance.

ter·ror·ise, *v.,* **-rised, -rising.** to fill with terror. – **terrorism,** *n.*

terry towelling, *n.* cotton fabric with loops on one or both sides.

terse, *adj.,* **terser, tersest. 1.** concise or brief, as language. **2.** abrupt or bad-tempered, esp. in one's speech.

ter·tiary, *adj.* of the 3rd order, rank, etc.

tes·sel·lated, *adj.* arranged in a chequered pattern.

test, *n.* **1.** a trial by which the presence, quality, or genuineness of anything is determined. **2.** *Educ.* a form of examination for evaluating the abilities of a student or class. –*v.* **3.** to subject to a test; try.

tes·ta·ment, *n.* **1.** *Law.* a formal declaration, usu. in writing, of a person's wishes as to the distribution of his property after his death. **2.** (*cap.*) either of the 2 main divisions of the Bible.

tes·ta·tor, *n.* one who makes a will.

tes·ti·cle, *n.* one of the paired male sex glands situated in the scrotum.

tes·ti·fy, *v.,* **-fied, -fying. 1.** to bear witness (to); give evidence (of). **2.** to make solemn declaration.

tes·ti·mo·ni·al, *n.* **1.** written evidence as to a person's character, conduct, or qualifications. **2.** something given or done as an expression of esteem, or gratitude.

tes·ti·mo·ny, *n., pl.* **-nies. 1.** *Law.* the statement of a witness under oath or affirmation, usu. in court. **2.** evidence.

testis, *n., pl.* **-tes.** →**testicle.**

test tube, *n.* a thin glass tube with one end closed, used in chemical tests.

testy, *adj.,* **-tier, -tiest.** touchy.

tet·a·nus, *n. Pathol.* an infectious, often fatal disease, marked by spasms and muscle rigidity.

tether, *n.* **1.** a rope, chain, etc., tied to an animal to limit its movement. **2. the end of one's tether,** the limit of one's patience or resources. –*v.* **3.** to fasten (as) with a tether.

text, *n.* **1.** the main body of matter in a book, etc. **2.** the actual wording of anything written or printed. **3.** a short passage of Scripture. – **textual,** *adj.*

text·book, *n.* a book used by students for a particular branch of study.

tex·tile, *n.* a woven material.

tex·ture, *n.* the characteristic appearance or structure of something, esp. as conveyed by the touch.

than, *conj.* **1.** a particle used after comparative adjectives and adverbs and certain other words, such as *other, otherwise, else,* etc., to introduce the second member of a comparison: *He is taller than I am.* –*prep.* **2.** in comparison with: *taller than me.*

thank, *v.* **1.** to give thanks to. –*n.* **2.** (*usu. pl.*) the expression of grateful feeling by words or otherwise.

that, *pron. and adj. pl.* **those;** *adv., conj.* –*pron.* **1.** (a demonstrative pronoun used to indicate: **a.** a person, thing, idea, etc., as pointed

that

out, mentioned, etc.: *That is my husband.* **b.** one of 2 or more persons, things, etc., already mentioned referring to the one more remote in place, time, or thought (often opposed to *this*): *That is the one I want.*) **2.** (a relative pronoun used as the subject or object of a relative clause: *How old was the car that was stolen?*) *–adj.* **3.** (a demonstrative adjective used to indicate: **a.** a person, place, thing, idea, etc., as pointed out, mentioned, etc.: *That man is my husband.* **b.** one of 2 or more persons, things, etc., already mentioned, referring to the one more remote in place, time, or thought (opposed to *this*): *It was that one, not this one.*) *–adv.* **4.** (an adverb used with adjectives and adverbs of quality or extent to indicate precise degree or extent: *that much; that far*). *–conj.* **5.** (a conjunction used to introduce a noun clause: *That he will come is certain.*).

thatch, *n.* **1.** a material, as straw, rushes, etc. used to cover roofs, haystacks, etc. *–v.* **2.** to cover (as) with thatch.

thaw, *v.* to pass from a frozen to a liquid or semi-liquid state; melt.

the, *def. art.* a word used esp. before nouns: **1.** with a specifying or limiting effect (opposed to *a* or *an*). **2.** denoting an individual, a class or an abstract notion: *to help the poor.*

the·a·tre, *n.* **1.** a building or room designed to stage dramatic presentations, screen films, etc. **2.** drama as a branch of art. **3.** a hall fitted with tiers of seats, as used for lectures, etc. **4.** a room in a hospital in which surgical operations are performed. **5.** a place of action; *theatre of war.*

the·at·ri·cal, *adj.* Also, **theatric. 1.** of or pertaining to the theatre. **2.** suggestive of the theatre or of acting.

theft, *n.* the act of stealing.

their, *adj.* the possessive form of *they* used before a noun.

theirs, *pron.* a form of the possessive *their* used after a verb or without a noun following.

the·ism, *n.* the belief in a god as the creator and ruler of the universe.

them, *pron.* the objective case of *they.*

theme, *n.* a subject of discussion, a composition, etc.

them·selves, *pron. pl.* **1.** a reflexive form of **them. 2.** an emphatic form of **them** or **they.**

then, *adv.* **1.** at that time. **2.** next in order of time. **3.** in that case.

thence, *adv.* **1.** from that place or time. **2.** for that reason; therefore.

the·od·o·lite, *n.* an instrument for measuring horizontal or vertical angles.

the·ol·o·gy, *n., pl.* **-gies.** the study of divine things or religious truth. **– theologian**, *n.*

the·o·rem, *n.* a rule or law, esp. one expressed by an equation or formula.

the·o·ret·i·cal, *adj.* **1.** of, pertaining to, or consisting in theory; not practical. **2.** hypothetical.

the·o·rise, *v.,* **-rised, -rising. 1.** to form a theory. **2.** to speculate or conjecture.

the·o·ry, *n., pl.* **-ries. 1.** a coherent group of propositions used to explain something. **2.** that department of a science or art which

theory

theory

deals with its principles or methods, as distinguished from practice. 3. conjecture or opinion.

thera·peu·tic, *adj.* pertaining to the treating or curing of disease.

therapy, *n., pl.* **-pies**. the treatment of disease, etc., as by some remedy. – **therapist**, *n.*

there, *adv.* in, at, to, or into that place.

there·by, *adv.* by means of that.

there·fore, *adv.* as a result; consequently.

there·upon, *adv.* immediately following that.

ther·mal, *adj.* of or pertaining to heat or temperature. Also, **thermic**.

thermo·dynamics, *n.* the science concerned with the relations between heat and mechanical energy and the conversion of one into the other.

ther·mom·eter, *n.* an instrument for measuring temperature.

thermo·nuclear, *adj.* capable of producing extremely high temperatures resulting from nuclear fusion.

ther·mo·stat, *n.* a device which establishes and maintains a desired temperature automatically.

thes·aurus, *n., pl.* **-sauri**. a dictionary of synonyms and antonyms.

these, *pron., adj.* plural of **this**.

thesis, *n., pl.* **-ses**. 1. a proposition laid down or stated, esp. one to be discussed and proved. 2. a subject for a composition or essay. 3. a dissertation, as one presented by a candidate for a postgraduate degree.

they, *pron. pl., poss.* **theirs**, *obj.* **them**. nominative plural of *he, she* and *it*.

thia·mine /ˈθaɪəmɪn/, *n.* a vitamin

think

(B_1) required by the nervous system.

thick, *adj.* 1. having relatively great extent from one surface or side to its opposite; not thin. 2. measuring as specified between opposite surfaces. 3. set close together; dense. 4. viscous. 5. (of an accent) very pronounced.

thicket, *n.* a thick or dense growth of small trees, etc.

thief, *n., pl.* **thieves**. one who steals.

thieve, *v.*, **thieved, thieving**. to take by theft; steal. – **thievery**, *n.*

thigh, *n.* that part of the leg between the hip and the knee in man.

thim·ble, *n.* a metal cap, worn on the finger to push the needle in sewing.

thin, *adj.*, **thinner, thinnest**, *v.*, **thinned, thinning**. –*adj.* 1. having relatively little extent from one surface or side to its opposite; not thick. 2. of small cross-section in comparison with the length; slender. 3. having little flesh; lean. 4. not dense; sparse. 5. without solidity; unsubstantial. 6. transparent, or flimsy: *a thin excuse*. –*v.* 7. to make or become thin or thinner (*down, out*, etc.).

thine, *pron., adj.* the possessive form corresponding to **thou** used with or without a noun following, or before a noun beginning with a vowel or *h*. Cf. **thy**.

thing, *n.* 1. a material object without life or consciousness. 2. that which is or may become an object of thought.

think, *v.*, **thought, thinking**. 1. to have in the mind as an idea, conception, or the like. 2. to form or have an idea or conception of (a thing, fact, circumstance, etc.). 3. to hold as an

think

opinion; believe; suppose. 4. to consider (something) to be (as specified). 5. to use the mind, esp. the intellect, actively; cogitate or meditate. 6. to reflect upon the matter in question.

third, adj. 1. next after the 2nd in order, quality, etc. -n. 2. someone or something which comes next after the 2nd. 3. one of 3 parts of a whole.

third party, n. any person other than those directly involved in some transaction, etc.

thirst, n. 1. a sensation of dryness in the mouth and throat caused by need of drink. 2. strong or eager desire; craving. - **thirsty**, adj.

thir·teen /θɜ'tin/, n. a cardinal number, 10 plus 3. - **thirteenth**, adj., n.

thirty, n., pl. -ties. a cardinal number, 10 times 3. - **thirtieth**, adj., n.

this, pron. and adj., pl. **these**; adv. -pron. 1. (a demonstrative pronoun used to indicate: **a.** a person, thing, idea, etc., as pointed out, present, or near, as before mentioned etc.: *This is my husband.* **b.** one of 2 or more persons, things, etc., already mentioned, referring to the one nearer in place, time, or thought: *This is the one.*) -adj. 2. (a demonstrative adjective used to indicate: **a.** a person, place, thing, idea, etc., as pointed out, present, or near, before mentioned, etc.: *This man is my husband.* **b.** one of 2 or more persons, things, etc., already mentioned, referring to one nearer in place, time, or thought: *not that one.*) -adv. 3. (an adverb used with adjectives and adverbs of quality or extent to indicate precise degree or extent: *this much; this far.*)

this·tle, n. a prickly plant.

thither, adv. to or towards that place.

thong, n. 1. a narrow strip of leather, used as a fastening, as the lash of a whip, etc. 2. a sandal held loosely on the foot by 2 strips of leather, rubber, etc.

thorax, n., pl. **thoraces**, **thoraxes**. (in man and the higher vertebrates) the part of the trunk between the neck and the abdomen; the chest. - **thoracic**, adj.

thorn, n. a sharp-pointed outgrowth on a plant; a prickle.

thor·ough, adj. 1. carried out through the whole of something; complete or perfect. 2. leaving nothing undone.

thorough·fare, n. a road, street, etc., open at both ends, esp. a main road.

those, pron., adj. plural of **that**.

thou, pron., sing., nom. **thou**, poss. **thy** or **thine**; obj. **thee**; pl., nom. **you** or **ye**; poss. **your** or **yours**; obj. **you** or **ye**. -pron. the personal pronoun of the 2nd person, in the singular number and nominative case, now replaced by **you**.

though, conj. 1. in spite of the fact that. 2. even if. 3. if (usu. in *as though*). -adv. 4. for all that; however. Also, **tho'**.

thought[1], n. 1. that which one thinks. 2. the capacity or faculty of thinking. 3. meditation.

thought[2], v. past tense and past participle of **think**.

thou·sand, n. a cardinal number, 10 times 100.

thrash, v. 1. to beat soundly by way of punishment. 2. to toss, or plunge violently about.

thread, *n.* 1. a fine cord, esp. that used for sewing. 2. the spiral ridge of a screw. 3. that which runs through the whole course of something, as the sequence of events in a narrative. –*v.* 4. to pass the end of a thread through (a needle, beads, etc.).

thread·bare, *adj.* 1. having the nap worn off so as to lay bare the threads, as a fabric. 2. meagre, scanty, or poor.

threat, *n.* 1. a declaration of an intention to inflict punishment, pain or loss on someone. 2. an indication of probable evil to come. – **threaten**, *v.*

three, *n.* a cardinal number, 2 plus one.

three-dimensional, *adj.* 1. having depth as well as height and breadth. 2. realistic; lifelike.

thresh, *v.* to separate the grain or seeds from (a cereal plant, etc.).

thres·hold, *n.* 1. the entrance to a house or building. 2. any place of entering or beginning. 3. *Psychol., Physiol.* the point at which a stimulus becomes perceptible or strong enough to produce an effect.

threw, *v.* past tense of **throw**.

thrice, *adv.* 3 times.

thrift, *n.* economical management; frugality. – **thrifty**, *adj.*

thrill, *v.* 1. to affect or be affected by a sudden wave of keen emotion, so as to produce a tingling sensation through the body. –*n.* 2. a tingling sensation passing through the body as the result of sudden keen emotion or excitement. 3. thrilling quality, as of a story.

thril·ler, *n.* a book, etc., dealing with crime, mystery, etc., in an exciting manner.

thrive, *v.*, **throve** or **thrived** or **thriven**, **thriving**. to grow strongly or flourish.

throat, *n.* 1. the passage from the mouth to the stomach or to the lungs. 2. the front of the neck below the chin and above the collarbones.

throb, *v.*, **throbbed**, **throbbing**, *n.* –*v.* 1. to beat with increased force or rapidity, as the heart. –*n.* 2. the act of throbbing. 3. any pulsation.

throe, *n.* 1. a violent spasm. 2. **in the throes of**, engaged in.

throm·bosis, *n.* coagulation of the blood in the heart or blood vessels.

throne, *n.* the seat occupied by a sovereign, or other important person on ceremonial occasions.

throng, *n.* many people crowded together.

throt·tle, *n., v.*, **-tled**, **-tling**. –*n.* 1. a device to control the amount of fuel being fed to an engine. –*v.* 2. to strangle.

through, *prep.* 1. in at one end, side, or surface, and out at the other, of. 2. by the means of. 3. because of: *He lost his job through no fault of his own.* –*adv.* 4. in at one end, side, or surface and out at the other. 5. from the beginning to the end. 6. to the end. –*adj.* 7. that goes through the whole of a long distance with little or no interruption. Also, **thro**, **thro'**, **thru**.

through·out, *prep.* 1. in or to every part of. –*adv.* 2. in every part.

throw, *v.*, **threw**, **thrown**, **throwing**, *n.* –*v.* 1. to propel forcibly through the air. 2. to put hastily. 3. to shape on a potter's wheel. 4. to deliver (a blow or punch). 5. to cast (dice). 6. (of a horse, etc.) to cause to fall off. 7. *Colloq.* to astonish; confuse. 8. to arrange: *to throw a party.* —*n.* 9. an act of throwing.

throw·back, *n.* reversion to an ancestral type.

thrush[1], *n.* a migratory songbird.

thrush[2], *n. Pathol.* a disease, esp. of the mouth and vagina, caused by a parasitic fungus.

thrust, *v.*, **thrust, thrusting.** —*v.* 1. to push forcibly (against something). 2. to make a lunge, or stab at something. —*n.* 3. the act of thrusting; a push, lunge or stab.

thud, *n.*, *v.*, **thudded, thudding.** —*n.* 1. a dull sound, as of a heavy blow. —*v.* 2. to strike with a dull sound.

thug, *n.* a brutal or murderous ruffian.

thumb, *n.* 1. the short, thick inner digit of the human hand, next to the forefinger. —*v.* 2. to turn quickly or wear (the pages of a book, etc.).

thump, *n.* 1. a heavy blow producing a dull sound. —*v.* 2. to strike or beat with something thick and heavy, so as to produce a dull sound. 3. *Colloq.* to punch; thrash severely.

thun·der, *n.* 1. the loud noise which accompanies a flash of lightning. —*v.* 2. to speak in a very loud tone.

thus, *adv.* 1. in this way. 2. accordingly; consequently.

thwack, *v.* to strike with something flat; whack.

thwart, *v.* to oppose successfully or frustrate (a purpose, etc.).

thy, *pron., adj.* the possessive form corresponding to **thou** and **thee**, used before a noun. Cf. **thine**.

thyme /taɪm/, *n.* a plant of the mint family, with aromatic leaves.

thymus, *n.* a ductless gland lying near the base of the neck.

thy·roid gland, *n.* a two-lobed gland lying on either side of the trachea which secretes a hormone stimulating bodily and mental activity.

tiara, *n.* a jewelled ornamental coronet worn by women.

tibia, *n., pl.* **tibiae, tibias.** *Anat.* the inner of the 2 bones which extend from the knee to the ankle.

tic, *n. Pathol.* a sudden, involuntary muscular contraction in the face or extremities.

tick[1], *n.* 1. a slight, sharp click or beat, as of a clock. 2. a small mark(✓), indicating that something has been done or is correct. —*v.* 3. to produce a tick, as a clock. 4. to mark (an item, etc.) with a tick. 5. **tick off**, to rebuke; scold.

tick[2], *n.* a blood-sucking animal like a mite.

ticket, *n.* 1. a small piece of paper serving as evidence of the holder's right to some service. 2. a label or tag. 3. a list of candidates nominated by a political party, etc. 4. a summons issued for a traffic or parking offence. 5. *Colloq.* the right, or proper thing: *That's the ticket.*

tickle, *v.*, **-led, -ling.** 1. to touch lightly so as to excite a tingling or itching sensation in. 2. to poke in some sensitive part of the body so as to excite spasmodic laughter.

tick·lish, *adj.* 1. sensitive to tickling. 2. requiring careful handling; risky.

tid·dler, *n.* a very small fish.

tiddly, *n. Colloq.* slightly drunk.

tide, *n., v.*, **tided, tiding.** —*n.* 1. the periodic rise and fall of the waters of the ocean due to the attraction

tide

of the moon and sun. **2.** a tendency or trend: *the tide of public opinion.* –*v.* **3. tide over**, to enable (a person, etc.) to cope with a period of distress, etc. – **tidal,** *adj.*

tid·ings, *n.pl.* *(sometimes construed as sing.)* news or information.

tidy, *adj.*, **-dier, -diest,** *v.*, **-died, -dying.** –*adj.* **1.** neat; trim; orderly. **2.** *Colloq.* considerable: *a tidy sum of money.* –*v.* **3.** to make tidy or neat.

tie, *v.*, **tied, tying.** –*v.* **1.** to bind or draw together (the parts of) with a knotted string or the like. **2.** to draw together into a knot, as a cord. **3.** to join, or connect in any way. **4.** to confine, restrict, or limit. **5.** to bind or oblige, as to do something. **6.** to make the same score in a contest. –*n.* **7.** a narrow strip of material worn round the neck and tied in front. **8.** anything that fastens, secures, or unites. **9.** something that restricts one's freedom of action. **10.** a state of equality in points, votes, etc., as among competitors.

tier, *n.* a row or rank.

tiff, *n.* a petty quarrel.

tiger, *n.* a large, carnivorous striped animal of the cat family.

tight, *adj.* **1.** firmly fixed in place; secure. **2.** stretched so as to be taut. **3.** fitting closely, esp. too closely. **4.** impervious to water, air, etc. **5.** strict. **6.** *Colloq.* stingy; parsimonious. **7.** *Colloq.* drunk. **8.** *Finance.* (of credit) not easily obtained.

tight·rope, *n.* a rope or wire stretched tight, on which acrobats perform feats of balancing.

tights, *n.pl.* a close-fitting garment covering the body from the waist to the feet.

timely

tile, *n.*, *v.*, **tiled, tiling.** –*n.* **1.** a thin slab of baked clay used for covering roofs, floors, etc. –*v.* **2.** to cover with tiles.

till[1], *prep.* **1.** up to the time of; until. **2.** (with a negative) before: *He cannot come till Thursday.* –*conj.* **3.** to the time that or when; until. **4.** (with a negative) before.

till[2], *v.* to cultivate (land).

till[3], *n.* (in a shop, etc.) a box, drawer, etc. in which cash is kept.

tilt, *v.* **1.** to (cause to) lean, incline, slope or slant. **2.** to strike or charge (*at*) with a lance etc. –*n.* **3.** an act or instance of tilting. **4.** the state of being tilted.

timber, *n.* wood, esp. for use in carpentry, joinery, etc.

timbre /'tɪmbə, 'tæmbə/, *n.* the characteristic quality of a sound.

time, *n.*, *adj.*, *v.*, **timed, timing.** –*n.* **1.** the system of those relations which any event has to any other as past, present, or future. **2.** a limited extent of time, as between 2 events: *a short time.* **3.** (*oft. pl.*) the era now (or then) present. **4.** an allotted period, as of one's life, for payment of a debt, etc.: *Your time is up.* **5.** a particular point: *in time.* **6.** a particular part of a year, day, etc. **7.** the period in which an action is completed: *The winner's time was 2 minutes.* **8.** each occasion of a recurring event: *He climbed the mountain 5 times.* **9.** (*pl.*) used in multiplication. **10.** *Music, etc.* tempo. –*adj.* **11.** relating to the passage of time. –*v.* **12.** to ascertain the duration, or rate of. **13.** to choose the moment or occasion for.

timely, *adj.*, **-lier, -liest.** occurring at a suitable time; opportune.

time·piece, *n.* a clock or a watch.

time·ta·ble, *n.* any plan listing the times at which certain things are due to take place, as the departure of buses, trains, etc.

timid, *adj.* subject to fear; shy.

timing, *n.* 1. the controlling of the speed of an action, event, etc. 2. the mechanism that ensures that the valves in an internal-combustion engine open and close at the correct time.

timo·rous, *adj.* fearful; timid.

tim·pani, *n.pl., sing.* **-no.** a set of kettledrums.

tin, *n., v.*, **tinned, tinning.** *-n.* 1. a low-melting, metallic element. *Symbol:* Sn 2. any shallow metal pan, esp. one used in baking. 3. a sealed container for food. *-v.* 4. to coat with a thin layer of tin. 5. to preserve in tins, as foodstuffs.

tinc·ture, *n. Pharm.* a solution of a medicinal substance in alcohol.

tinder, *n.* any dry substance that readily takes fire from a spark.

tine, *n.* a sharp prong, as of a fork.

tinea, *n.* a skin disease caused by fungi.

tinge, *v.*, **tinged, tingeing** or **tinging**, *n.* *-v.* 1. to impart a trace of colour to; tint. *-n.* 2. a trace of colour.

tingle, *v.*, **-gled, -gling**, *n.* *-v.* 1. to (have) a prickling or stinging sensation.

tinker, *n.* 1. a (travelling) mender of pots, kettles, pans, etc. *-v.* 2. to busy oneself with something, esp. an appliance, usu. without useful results.

tinkle, *v.*, **-kled, -kling**, *n.* *-v.* 1. to make a succession of short, light, ringing sounds. *-n.* 2. a tinkling sound.

tinny, *adj.*, **-nier, -niest.** 1. lacking resonance. 2. not strong or durable.

tinsel, *n.* (a strip of) cheap, glittering, metallic material.

tint, *n.* 1. (a variety of) a colour; hue. 2. a colour diluted with white. *-v.* 3. to colour slightly or delicately; tinge.

tiny, *adj.*, **-nier, -niest.** very small.

tip[1], *n.* 1. a slender, pointed end of anything long or tapered. 2. the top, summit, or apex.

tip[2], *v.*, **tipped, tipping**, *n.* *-v.* 1. to incline; tilt. 2. to tumble or topple (something) (*over*). *-n.* 3. a rubbish dump.

tip[3], *n., v.*, **tipped, tipping.** *-n.* 1. a small sum of money given to a waiter, porter, etc., for performing a service. 2. a useful hint or idea. *-v.* 3. to give a small sum of money to.

tipple, *v.*, **-pled, -pling.** to drink (wine, spirits, etc.), esp. to excess.

tipsy, *adj.*, **-sier, -siest.** slightly intoxicated.

tiptoe, *v.*, **-toed, -toeing.** to go on the tips of the toes, as with caution or stealth.

tirade, *n.* a prolonged outburst of denunciation.

tire, *v.*, **tired, tiring.** 1. to (cause to) become exhausted or wearied by exertion. 2. **tire of**, to have one's interest, patience, etc., exhausted.

tissue, *n.* 1. *Biol.* the substance of an organism. 2. a soft gauzelike paper. 3. a paper handkerchief.

tit[1], *n.* a small bird.

tit[2], *n. Colloq.* a female breast.

titanic, *adj.* of enormous size.

tita·nium, *n.* a metallic element. *Symbol:* Ti

titbit

titbit, *n.* a choice or delicate bit, esp. of food.

tithe, *n.* (*oft. pl.*) the 10th part of the annual produce of agriculture, etc., due or paid as a tax.

titian /ˈtɪʃən, ˈti-/, *n.* a reddish brown.

titil·late, *v.*, **-lated**, **-lating**. 1. to tickle. 2. to excite agreeably.

titi·vate, *v.*, **-vated**, **-vating**. *Colloq.* to make smart or spruce.

title, *n.* 1. the distinguishing name of a book, piece of music, etc. 2. a name given to a person by right of rank, office, attainment, etc. 3. *Sport.* the championship. 4. established or recognised right to something. 5. *Law.* (legal document giving the) right to the possession of property.

titter, *v.* to laugh in a low, half-restrained way, as from nervousness or in ill-suppressed amusement.

titu·lar, *adj.* 1. relating to a title. 2. existing in title only.

to, *prep.* 1. expressing motion or direction towards something. 2. indicating limit of movement or extent: *rotten to the core*. 3. expressing a point in time: *to this day*. 4. expressing aim, or intention: *going to the rescue*. 5. expressing limit in degree or amount: *goods to the value of $50*. 6. indicating addition or amount: *adding insult to injury*. 7. expressing comparison: *The score was 9 to 5*. 8. expressing reference or relation: *What will he say to this?* 9. expressing relative position: *next to the wall*. 10. indicating proportion or ratio: *one teacher to every 30 students*. 11. used as the ordinary sign or accompaniment of the infinitive. –*adv.* 12. towards a per-

toggle

son, thing, or point implied or understood. 13. to consciousness; to one's senses: *after he came to*.

toad, *n.* an amphibian similar to a frog.

toad·stool, *n.* a usu. poisonous fungus, similar to a mushroom.

toast[1], *n.* bread in slices browned on both surfaces by heat.

toast[2], *n.* 1. words of congratulation, loyalty, etc., spoken before drinking. –*v.* 2. to drink to the health of, or in honour of.

tob·acco, *n.*, *pl.* **-cos**, **-coes**. a plant whose leaves are prepared for smoking or chewing or as snuff.

tobog·gan, *n.* a light sledge with low runners.

today, *n.* 1. this present day. –*adv.* 2. on this present day.

toddle, *v.*, **-dled**, **-dling**. to go with short, unsteady steps, as a child.

toddy, *n.*, *pl.* **-dies**. a warm, sweet, alcoholic drink.

to-do, *n.*, *pl.* **-dos**. *Colloq.* bustle; fuss.

toe, *n.* 1. (in man) one of the digits of the foot. 2. an analogous part in other animals. 3. something like a toe in shape or position.

toff, *n.* *Colloq.* a rich, upper-class, usu. well-dressed person.

toffee, *n.* a sweet made of boiled sugar or treacle, often with butter, nuts, etc.

toga, *n.*, *pl.* **-gas**. the loose outer garment of the citizens of ancient Rome.

to·gether, *adv.* 1. in(to) one gathering, place, or body. 2. at the same time. 3. in cooperation. –*adj.* 4. capable and calm.

toggle, *n.* a transverse pin, etc.,

toggle

placed through an eye of a rope, etc., for various purposes.

togs, *n.pl. Colloq.* clothes.

toil, *n.* 1. hard and continuous work. *–v.* 2. to engage in exhausting and continuous work.

toilet, *n.* 1. a disposal apparatus of any type used for urination and defecation, esp. a water-closet. 2. the process of dressing, including bathing, arranging the hair, etc.

token, *n.* 1. something serving to represent or indicate some fact, event, feeling, etc.; sign. 2. a characteristic mark or indication; symbol. 3. a ticket, metal disc, etc. used instead of money for ferry fares, etc.

told, *v.* 1. past tense and past participle of **tell**. 2. **all told**, in all.

tol·erate, *v.*, **-rated, -rating.** 1. to allow; permit. 2. to bear; cope with. 3. *Med.* to endure or resist the action of (a drug, poison, etc.). **–tolerable**, *adj.* **–tolerance**, *n.* **–toleration**, *n.*

toll[1], *v.* (of a bell) to (cause to) sound with slow, regular, single strokes.

toll[2], *n.* Also, **tollage.** 1. a payment exacted by the government for the right to travel along a road. 2. cost etc., esp. in terms of death or loss.

toma·hawk, *n.* a small, short-handled axe.

tomato, *n., pl.* **-toes.** a widely cultivated plant bearing a slightly acid, pulpy, red, edible fruit.

tomb, *n.* an excavation in earth or rock to receive a dead body.

tomboy, *n.* a boisterous, romping girl.

tomb·stone, *n.* a stone, usu. bearing an inscription, set to mark a tomb or grave.

tonic

tome, *n.* a heavy, learned book.

tom·fool·ery, *n., pl.* **-eries.** foolish or silly behaviour.

to·morrow, *n.* 1. the day after this day. *–adv.* 2. on the day after this day.

tom-tom, *n.* a type of drum.

ton, *n.* 1. a unit of mass in the imperial system equal to 2240 lb. 2. →**tonne**.

tone, *n., v.,* **toned, toning.** *–n.* 1. any sound considered with reference to its quality, pitch, strength, source, etc. 2. quality or character of sound. 3. intonation of the voice. 4. *Music.* an interval equivalent to 2 semitones. 5. a tint or shade of colour. 6. *Physiol.* the state of firmness proper to the organs or tissues of the body. 7. style, distinction, or elegance. *–v.* 8. to sound with a particular tone. 9. to give the proper tone to. 10. to modify the tone or character of. 11. to harmonise in tone or colour (*with* or *in with*). **–tonal**, *adj.*

tongs, *n.pl.* an implement with 2 arms fastened together, for holding something.

tongue, *n.* 1. an organ situated in the mouth of man and most vertebrates, responsible for taste, and, in man, articulate speech. 2. the power of speech. 3. the language of a particular people, country, or locality. 4. something like an animal's tongue in shape, position, or function.

tonic, *n.* 1. a strengthening medicine. 2. anything invigorating physically, mentally, or morally. 3. *Music.* the first note of the scale; keynote. *–adj.* 4. restoring the tone or healthy condition of the body, as

tonic

a medicine. 5. invigorating physically, mentally, or morally.

to·night, n. 1. this present or coming night. –adv. 2. on this present night.

tonne, n. a unit of mass equal to 1000 kilograms. *Symbol:* t

tonsil, n. either of 2 masses of lymphoid tissue at the back of the throat.

ton·sure, n. the shaving of the head as a religious rite.

too, adv. 1. in addition; also. 2. to an excessive degree.

took, v. past tense of **take**.

tool, n. 1. a (hand-held) instrument for performing mechanical operations, as a hammer, saw, etc. 2. a person used by another for his own ends. –v. 3. to work with a tool.

toot, v. to (cause to) sound, as a horn.

tooth, n., pl. **teeth**. 1. (in most vertebrates) one of the hard bodies set in a row to each jaw, used for chewing, etc. 2. any projection like a tooth.

top[1], n., adj., v., **topped, topping.** –n. 1. the highest point or part of anything; summit. 2. the highest position, rank, etc.: *the top of the class.* 3. the highest pitch, or degree: *the top of one's voice.* 4. a covering or lid. 5. a garment to cover the torso. –adj. 6. highest; uppermost; upper. 7. greatest. 8. foremost or principal. 9. *Colloq.* the best; excellent. –v. 10. to put a top on. 11. to be at the top of. 12. to reach the top of. 13. to surpass. 14. to remove the top of; prune.

top[2], n. a child's toy, with a point on which it is made to spin.

topaz, n. a gem stone occurring in crystals of various colours.

topi·ary, adj. (of hedges, trees, etc.) clipped into (fantastic) shapes.

topic, n. a subject of conversation or discussion.

topi·cal, adj. 1. pertaining to current or local interest. 2. pertaining to the subject of a discourse, etc.

top·ography, n., pl. **-phies**. the geographical features of an area.

topple, v., **-pled, -pling**. to fall forwards from having too heavy a top.

top·soil, n. the upper layer of soil.

topsy-turvy, adj. upside down.

torch, n. 1. a small portable electric lamp powered by dry batteries. 2. a flame carried in the hand to give light. 3. a device which burns gas to produce a hot flame used for soldering, etc.

tore, v. past tense of **tear**[2].

tor·eador, n. a bullfighter.

tor·ment, v. 1. to afflict with great bodily or mental suffering. –n. 2. a state or source of great bodily or mental suffering; agony; misery.

torn, v. past participle of **tear**[2].

tor·nado, n., pl. **-does, -dos**. a violent whirlwind.

tor·pedo, n., pl. **-does**, v., **-doed, -doing.** –n. 1. a self-propelled cigar-shaped missile containing explosives. –v. 2. to damage, or destroy with a torpedo.

torpid, adj. slow or lethargic.

torpor, n. lethargy; apathy.

torque, n. *Mech.* that which produces torsion or rotation.

tor·rent, n. a stream of water flowing with great rapidity and violence. – **torrential**, adj.

torrid, adj. 1. (of regions) oppres-

torrid

sively hot or burning. **2.** ardent; passionate.

tor·sion, *n.* **1.** the act or result of twisting. **2.** *Mech.* **a.** the twisting of a body by 2 equal and opposite torques. **b.** the internal torque so produced.

torso, *n., pl.* **-sos.** the trunk of the human body.

tort, *n. Law.* **1.** any wrong other than a criminal wrong, as negligence, defamation, etc. **2.** (*pl.*) the field of study of torts.

tor·toise, *n.* a slow-moving reptile, with a hard shell covering its body and with toed feet rather than flippers. – **tortoiseshell,** *adj., n.*

tor·tu·ous, *adj.* **1.** full of twists, turns, or bends. **2.** not straightforward.

tor·ture, *n., v.,* **-tured, -turing.** *–n.* **1.** the act of inflicting excruciating pain. **2.** agony of body or mind. *–v.* **3.** to subject to torture. – **torturous,** *adj.*

toss, *v.* **1.** to throw, esp. lightly or carelessly. **2.** to pitch, rock, sway: *to toss on rough seas.* **3.** to move restlessly about. *–n.* **4.** the act of tossing.

tot[1]**,** *n.* a small child.

tot[2]**,** *v.,* **totted, totting.** *Colloq.* to add (*up*).

total, *adj., n., v.,* **-talled, -talling.** *–adj.* **1.** entire; whole. **2.** complete; absolute. *–n.* **3.** the total amount; sum. *–v.* **4.** to add up (*to*).

tota·li·sator, *n.* a form of betting, as on horseraces, in which those who bet on the winners divide the bets or stakes, less a percentage for the management, taxes, etc.

totali·tarian, *adj.* of or pertaining to a centralised government in which

toupee

those in control grant neither recognition nor tolerance to parties of differing opinion.

tota·lity, *n., pl.* **-ties. 1.** the entirety. **2.** total amount; whole.

tote, *v.,* **toted, toting.** *Colloq.* to carry.

totem, *n.* something in nature, often an animal, assumed as the emblem of a clan, family, etc. – **totemic,** *adj.*

totter, *v.* **1.** to walk falteringly or weakly. **2.** to sway or rock, as if about to fall.

toucan, *n.* a strikingly coloured bird with a huge beak.

touch, *v.* **1.** to put the hand, etc., on (something) to feel it. **2.** to come into or be in contact with (something). **3.** to reach; attain. **4.** to give rise to some emotion in (someone). **5.** to be a matter of importance to. **6.** *Colloq.* to apply for money. **7.** to speak or write (*on* or *upon*) briefly or casually. *–n.* **8.** the act of touching. **9.** that sense by which anything is perceived by means of the contact with the body. **10.** the sensation caused by touching something, regarded as a quality of the thing. **11.** a slight stroke or blow. **12.** a slight attack, as of illness or disease. **13.** manner of execution in artistic work. **14.** a slight amount. **15.** *Colloq.* a person from whom one can obtain money as a gift or loan.

touchy, *adj.,* **touchier, touchiest. 1.** irritable. **2.** risky.

tough, *adj.* **1.** not easily broken or cut. **2.** capable of great endurance. **3.** difficult to perform, accomplish, or deal with. **4.** vigorous; severe; violent.

toupee, *n.* a wig worn to cover a bald spot.

551

tour

tour, v. 1. to travel from place to place. –n. 2. a journey to a place or places. 3. *Chiefly Mil.* A period of duty at one place. – **tourist,** *adj., n.*

tour·na·ment, n. a meeting for contests in athletic or other sports.

tour·ni·quet /'tɔːnəkeɪ, 'tuə-/, n. any device for stopping bleeding by forcibly compressing a blood vessel.

tousle, v., **-sled, -sling.** to disorder or dishevel.

tout, v. 1. to solicit business, votes, etc., persistently. 2. *Racing.* to sell betting information, take bets, etc. –n. 3. one who touts.

tow, v. 1. to pull (a boat, car, etc.) with a rope or chain. –n. 2. the act of towing.

to·wards, prep. 1. in the direction of. 2. with respect to. 3. as a help or contribution to. Also, **toward.**

towel, n. a cloth for wiping and drying something wet.

towel·ling, n. any absorbent fabric used for towels, beachwear, etc.

tower, n. 1. a tall, narrow structure. 2. any tower-like objects. –v. 3. to extend far upwards. 4. to surpass, as in ability, etc. (*over, above,* etc.).

town, n. 1. a distinct densely-populated area, usu. smaller than a city. 2. urban life, opposed to rural. 3. the main shopping, business, or entertainment centre of a large town, contrasted with the suburbs. 4. the people of a town.

town house, n. a house in a small block of similar houses, each being sold under strata title, and each with ground floor access.

town·ship, n. a small town or settlement.

toxin, n. a poison produced by a

tract

disease-producing micro-organism. – **toxic,** *adj.* – **toxicity,** *n.*

toy, n. 1. a (children's) plaything. –*adj.* 2. of or like a toy, esp. in size. –v. 3. to act idly or absent-mindedly. 4. to trifle (*with*).

trace¹, n., v., **traced, tracing.** –n. 1. a mark or evidence of the former existence, or action of something; a vestige. 2. a very small amount. 3. a record traced by a self-registering instrument. –v. 4. to follow the footprints, track, or traces of. 5. to follow the course or development of. 6. to copy (a drawing, plan, etc.) by following the lines of the original on a superimposed transparent sheet. 7. to make a plan, diagram, or map of.

trace², n. each of the 2 straps by which a carriage, etc. is drawn by a horse, etc.

tra·cery, n., pl. **-ries.** any delicate interlacing work of lines, etc.

tra·chea, n., pl. **tracheae.** the main tube which conveys air to and from the lungs; the windpipe.

track, n. 1. a rough path, or trail. 2. the mark, or series of marks, left by anything that has passed along. 3. an endless jointed metal band around the wheels of some heavy vehicles. 4. a course of action or conduct. 5. a course laid out for racing. 6. one of the distinct sections of a gramophone record. –v. 7. to hunt by following the tracks of. 8. **track down,** to catch or find, after pursuit or searching. 9. to follow (a track, course, etc.).

track suit, n. a loose, two-piece overgarment worn by athletes.

tract¹, n. a stretch or extent, as of land, water, etc.

tract

tract², *n.* a brief treatise, esp. one dealing with religion.

trac·ta·ble, *adj.* easily managed, or docile.

trac·tion, *n.* 1. the act of drawing or pulling. 2. the adhesive friction which stops a body from slipping, as a tyre on the road.

trac·tor, *n.* a motor vehicle, usu. fitted with deeply treaded tyres, used to draw farm implements.

trade, *n., v.,* **traded, trading.** –*n.* 1. the buying and selling, or exchanging, of goods within a country or between countries. 2. market: *the tourist trade.* 3. commercial occupation (as against professional). –*v.* 4. to carry on trade. 5. to exchange; barter. 6. **trade in,** to give in part exchange: *to trade in an old car on a new one.*

trade·mark, *n.* the exclusive symbol, mark, etc. used by a manufacturer to distinguish his own goods from those manufactured by others.

trade name, *n.* 1. the name under which a firm does business. 2. a word or phrase used to designate a business or a particular class of goods but which is not technically a trademark. 3. the name by which an article is known to the trade.

trade-off, *n.* a concession made in a negotiation in return for one given.

trade union, *n.* an organisation of employees for mutual aid and protection, and for dealing collectively with employers. Also, **trades union.** – **trade unionism**, *n.* – **trade unionist**, *n.*

tra·di·tion, *n.* the handing down of beliefs, legends, customs, etc., from generation to generation, esp.

train

by word of mouth or by practice. – **traditional,** *adj.*

tra·duce, *v.* **-duced, -ducing.** to speak evil or maliciously of.

traf·fic, *n., v.,* **-ficked, -ficking.** –*n.* 1. the coming and going of persons, vehicles, ships, etc., along a way of passage or travel. 2. (commercial) dealings between parties, people, etc. –*v.* 3. to carry on dealings, esp. of an illicit or improper kind.

tra·ge·dy, *n., pl.* **-dies.** 1. a serious dramatic composition with an unhappy ending. 2. a disaster or calamity. – **tragic,** *adj.*

trail, *v.* 1. to draw or be drawn along the ground or behind. 2. to hang down loosely from something. 3. to follow, esp. slowly. –*n.* 4. a track made over rough country, by the passage of men or animals. 5. the track or scent left by an animal, person, or thing, esp. as followed in pursuit.

trail·er, *n.* 1. a vehicle designed to be towed by a motor vehicle, and used in transporting loads. 2. *Films.* an advertisement for a forthcoming film, usu. consisting of extracts from it.

train, *n.* 1. *Railways.* a set of carriages or wagons, whether self-propelled or connected to a locomotive. 2. a procession of persons, vehicles, etc. 3. a long, trailing part of a skirt or dress. 4. a succession of circumstances, etc. 5. a succession of connected ideas. –*v.* 6. to educate (a person) or become educated in some art, profession, or work. 7. to make or become fit by proper exercise, diet, etc., as for some athletic feat or contest. 8. to discipline and instruct (an animal) to perform specified actions.

trainee

train·ee, *n.* 1. one receiving training. –*adj.* 2. receiving training.

traipse, *v.*, **traipsed**, **traipsing**. to walk (about) aimlessly.

trait /treɪ, treɪt/, *n.* a distinguishing feature.

trai·tor, *n.* one who betrays his country by violating his allegiance.

tra·jec·to·ry, *n., pl.* **-ries.** the curved flight path of a projectile.

tram, *n.* a passenger vehicle moving on tracks laid in streets. Also, **tramcar.**

tram·mel, *n.* (*usu. pl.*) a restraint.

tramp, *v.* 1. to walk with a firm, heavy, resounding step. 2. to go about as a vagabond. –*n.* 3. the act of tramping. 4. a person who travels about on foot from place to place, esp. a vagabond living on occasional jobs or gifts of money or food.

tram·ple, *v.*, **-pled**, **-pling.** to tread heavily, roughly, or carelessly on or over.

tram·po·line, *n.* a canvas springboard attached to a horizontal frame used when performing acrobatics.

trance, *n.* 1. a dazed or bewildered condition. 2. a state of complete mental absorption. 3. an unconscious hypnotic condition.

tran·quil, *adj.*, **-quiller**, **-quillest.** 1. peaceful; quiet; calm. 2. unaffected by disturbing emotions. – **tranquillity**, *n.* – **tranquillise**, *v.*

trans·act, *v.* to carry through (affairs, business, negotiations, etc.) to settlement. – **transaction**, *n.*

tran·scend, *v.* to go over be above or beyond; surpass or exceed. – **transcendent**, *adj.*

tran·scen·den·tal, *adj.* transcend-

transient

ing ordinary experience, thought, or belief.

tran·scribe, *v.*, **-scribed**, **-scribing.** 1. to reproduce in writing or print (as from speech, etc.). 2. to write out in other characters. – **transcript**, *n.* – **transcription**, *n.*

trans·fer, *v.* 1. to convey or remove from one place, person, etc., to another. –*n.* 2. the means, system or act of transferring. 3. a drawing, pattern, etc., which may be transferred to a surface, esp. by direct contact. 4. *Law.* a conveyance, by sale, gift, or otherwise, of real or personal property, to another. – **transferable**, *adj.* – **transference**, *n.* – **transferral**, *n.*

trans·figure, *v.*, **-ured**, **-uring.** to change in outward form or appearance.

trans·fix, *v.* 1. to pierce through, (as) with a pointed weapon. 2. to make motionless with amazement, terror.

trans·form, *v.* to change in appearance, condition, nature, or character, esp. completely or extensively. – **transformation**, *n.*

trans·former, *n.* a device which transforms electric energy from circuit to circuit, usu. also changing voltage and current.

trans·fuse, *v.*, **-fused**, **-fusing.** 1. to pour from one container into another. 2. *Med.* to transfer (blood) from the veins or arteries of one person or animal into those of another. – **transfusion**, *n.*

trans·gress, *v.* to go beyond the limits imposed by (a law, command, etc.). – **transgression**, *n.*

tran·sient, *adj.* 1. not lasting or enduring. 2. temporary. –*n.* 3. one who or that which is transient. – **transience**, *n.*

554

tran·sis·tor, *n.* **1.** *Electronics.* a miniature solid-state device for amplifying or switching. **2.** a radio equipped with transistors.

tran·sit, *n.* passage or conveyance from one place to another.

tran·si·tion, *n.* passage from one position, state, stage, etc., to another.

tran·si·tive verb, *n.* a verb regularly having a direct object.

tran·si·to·ry, *adj.* passing away; not lasting or permanent.

trans·late, *v.*, **-lat·ed**, **-lat·ing**. **1.** to turn (something written or spoken) from one language into another. **2.** to interpret; explain. **– translation**, *n.*

trans·lu·cent, *adj.* transmitting light imperfectly, as frosted glass.

trans·mis·sion, *n.* **1.** the act of transmitting. **2.** that which is transmitted. **3.** *Mach.* a device for transmitting power from the engine to the wheels of a motor vehicle.

trans·mit, *v.*, **-mit·ted**, **-mit·ting**. **1.** to send over or along, as to a person or place. **2.** to communicate, as information, news, etc. **3.** to broadcast (a radio or television program). **4.** to allow (heat, light, etc.) to pass through.

tran·som, *n.* a lintel.

trans·par·en·cy, *n., pl.* **-cies**. Also, **transparence**. **1.** the property or quality of being transparent. **2.** a transparent positive photographic image used for projection onto a screen.

trans·par·ent, *adj.* **1.** transmitting light perfectly so that bodies situated beyond can be distinctly seen. **2.** open, frank, or candid. **3.** easily seen through or understood.

tran·spire, *v.*, **-spired**, **-spir·ing**. **1.** to occur or happen. **2.** to emit waste matter, etc., through the surface, as of the body, of leaves, etc.

trans·plant, *v.* **1.** to remove (a plant) from one place and plant it in another. **2.** *Surg.* to transfer (an organ or a portion of tissue) from one part of the body to another or from one person or animal to another. **–n. 3.** a transplanting. **4.** something transplanted.

trans·port, *v.* **1.** to carry from one place to another. **2.** to carry away by strong emotion. **–n.** **3.** the act, method, or system of transporting or conveying. **4.** a means of transporting, as a ship, large truck, aeroplane, etc. **5.** strong emotion, as ecstatic joy, bliss, etc. **– transportation**, *n.*

trans·pose, *v.*, **-posed**, **-pos·ing**. **1.** to alter the relative position or order of: *to transpose the letters in a word.* **2.** to cause (2 or more things) to change places. **3.** *Music.* to reproduce in a different key.

trans·verse, *adj.* lying or being in a crosswise direction.

trans·ves·tism, *n.* the abnormal desire to wear clothing appropriate to the opposite sex. **– transvestite**, *n., adj.*

trap, *n., v.*, **trapped**, **trap·ping**. **–n. 1.** a device used for catching game or other animals. **2.** any stratagem for catching someone unawares. **3.** a contrivance for preventing the passage of steam, water, etc. **4.** a light two-wheeled carriage. **–v. 5.** to catch in a trap.

trap·door, *n.* a door, etc., cut into the surface of a floor, ceiling, etc.

tra·peze, *n.* an apparatus for gymnastics, consisting of a short horizontal bar attached to the ends of 2 suspended ropes.

tra·pe·zium, n., pl. **-ziums, -zia.** a four-sided plane figure in which only one pair of opposite sides is parallel.

tra·pe·zoid, n. *Geom.* a four-sided plane figure of which no 2 sides are parallel.

trap·pings, n. pl. (ornamental) articles of equipment or dress.

trash, n. anything worthless or useless; rubbish.

trauma, n., pl. **-mata, -mas.** 1. *Pathol.* a bodily injury. 2. *Psychol.* a shock which has a lasting effect on mental life. – **traumatic**, *adj.*

tra·vail, n. (painful) physical or mental exertion.

travel, v., **-elled, -elling,** n. –v. 1. to move or go from one place to another. –n. 2. journeying, esp. in distant or foreign places. 3. (*pl.*) journeys. 4. *Mach.* the complete movement of a moving part in one direction, or the distance traversed.

tra·verse, v., **-ersed, -ersing,** n., adj. –v. 1. to pass across, over, or through. 2. to go to and fro over or along. 3. *Law.* to deny formally, in pleading at law. –n. 4. the act of traversing. 5. something that obstructs or thwarts. 6. a place where one may cross. –adj. 7. transverse.

trav·esty, n., pl. **-ties.** any grotesque or debased imitation.

trawl, n. 1. Also, **trawl net.** a strong net dragged along the sea bottom to catch fish. –v. 2. to fish with a trawl. 3. to troll.

tray, n. a flat piece of wood, metal, etc., with slightly raised edges used for carrying things.

treach·ery, n., pl. **-eries.** betrayal of trust; treason. – **treacherous**, *adj.*

trea·cle, n. the dark, sticky syrup obtained in refining sugar.

tread, v., **trod, trodden** or **trod; treading;** n. –v. 1. to step or walk on, about, in, or along. 2. to trample underfoot. 3. to domineer harshly; crush. –n. 4. (the sound of) treading, stepping, or walking. 5. manner of treading or walking. 6. a single step as in walking. 7. the horizontal upper surface of a step. 8. that part of a tyre, etc., which touches the road, etc.

trea·dle, n. a lever or the like worked by the foot to set a machine in motion.

tread·mill, n. a monotonous or wearisome round, as of work or life.

trea·son, n. violation by a subject of his allegiance to his sovereign or to the state; high treason.

treas·ure, n., v., **-ured, -uring.** –n. 1. accumulated riches, esp. precious metals or money. 2. any thing or person greatly valued. –v. 3. to regard as precious; cherish.

treas·urer, n. 1. one who has charge of the funds of a company, private society, or the like. 2. (*cap.*) government minister resposible for the Treasury.

treas·ury, n., pl. **-uries.** 1. a place where public money, or the funds of a company, etc., are kept. 2. (*cap.*) the department of government which has control over public revenue.

treat, v. 1. to act towards in some specified way: *to treat someone kindly.* 2. to deal with: *to treat a matter as unimportant.* 3. to subject to some, usu. chemical, agent in order to bring about a particular result. 4. to discuss terms of

treat

settlement or negotiate. –*n.* **5.** *Colloq.* anything that gives particular pleasure. **6.** one's turn to pay, as for a joint outing, etc. **– treatment**, *n.*

trea·tise, *n.* a book or writing on some particular subject.

treaty, *n., pl.* **-ties.** a formal agreement between 2 or more independent states in reference to peace, alliance, commerce, etc.

treble, *adj.* **1.** triple. **2.** *Music.* of the highest pitch or range.

tree, *n.* a perennial plant having a woody, self-supporting main stem or trunk, usu. growing to a considerable height, and usu. developing branches at some distance from the ground.

trek, *n.* a journey, esp. a difficult one on foot.

trel·lis, *n.* a lattice.

trem·ble, *v.*, **-bled, -bling. 1.** (of persons, the body, etc.) to shake with quick, short, involuntary movements, as from fear, excitement, weakness, cold, etc. **2.** to be tremulous, as light, sound, etc.

tre·men·dous, *adj. Colloq.* **1.** extraordinarily great in size, amount, degree, etc. **2.** extraordinary; unusual; remarkable.

tremor, *n.* **1.** involuntary shaking of the body or limbs, as from fear, weakness, etc. **2.** a vibration. **3.** a trembling or quivering effect, as of light, etc. **4.** a tremulous sound or note.

tremu·lous, *adj.* **1.** (of persons, the body, etc.) characterised by trembling. **2.** (of things) vibratory or quivering.

trench, *n.* a deep furrow, ditch, or cut.

tren·chant, *adj.* incisive or cutting, as language or a person.

trencher, *n.* →**mortarboard**.

trend, *n.* **1.** the general course, drift, or tendency. **2.** style; fashion. **– trendy**, *adj.*

trepi·dation, *n.* tremulous alarm or agitation.

tres·pass, *n.* **1.** *Law.* **a.** an unlawful act causing injury to the person, property, or rights of another, committed with force or violence. **b.** a wrongful entry upon the lands of another. **2.** an encroachment or intrusion. –*v.* **3.** to commit trespass.

tress, *n.* (usu. *pl.*) any long lock of hair.

tres·tle, *n.* a supporting frame, usu. consisting of a horizontal beam or bar fixed at each end to a pair of spreading legs.

trews, *n. Colloq.* tartan trousers.

triad, *n.* a group of 3.

trial, *n.* **1.** *Law.* **a.** the examination in a court of law of the facts of a case. **b.** the determination of a person's guilt or innocence by a court. **2.** the act of trying or testing. **3.** a contest. **4.** an attempt to do something. **5.** an experiment. **6.** an affliction or trouble.

tri·angle, *n.* **1.** a three-sided plane figure. **2.** *Music.* a triangular percussion instrument. **– triangular**, *adj.*

tribe, *n.* any group of people united by ties of descent from a common ancestor, community of customs and traditions, adherence to the same leaders, etc. **– tribal**, *adj.*

tribu·lation, *n.* grievous trouble.

tri·bunal, *n.* **1.** a court of justice. **2.** a place or seat of judgment.

tribu·tary, *n., pl.* **-taries**, *adj.* –*n.* **1.** a

tributary

stream flowing into a larger stream or other body of water. –*adj.* **2.** contributory; auxiliary. **3.** paying or required to pay tribute.

trib·ute, *n.* **1.** a personal offering given as if due, or in acknowledgment of gratitude or esteem of. **2.** an enforced payment made by one sovereign or state to another as the price of peace, security, etc.

trice, *n.* a very short time.

trick, *n.* **1.** a crafty or fraudulent expedient. **2.** the knack of doing something. **3.** a clever or dexterous feat, as for exhibition or entertainment. **4.** *Cards.* the cards which are played and won in one round. **5.** to deceive by trickery. – **trickery,** *n.*

trickle, *v.,* –**led, -ling.** *n.* –*v.* **1.** to flow or fall by drops, or in a small, gentle stream. **2.** to come, go, pass, or proceed bit by bit, slowly, irregularly, etc. –*n.* **3.** a trickling flow or stream.

tri·cycle, *n.* a cycle with 3 wheels.

tri·dent, *n.* a three-pronged instrument or weapon.

tried, *v.* past tense and past participle of **try.**

trifle, *n., v.,* –**fled, -fling.** –*n.* **1.** something of small value, amount or importance. **2.** a dessert of sponge, jelly, cream, etc. –*v.* **3.** to deal lightly or without due seriousness or respect (*with*).

trifling, *adj.* trivial.

trig·ger, *n.* **1.** (in firearms) a small projecting piece which, when pressed by the finger, discharges the weapon. –*v.* **2.** to start (*off*) (something), as a chain of events.

trigo·nometry, *n.* the branch of mathematics that deals with the relations between the sides and angles of triangles and the calculations, etc., based on these.

trill, *v.* **1.** to resound vibrantly, or with a rapid succession of sounds, as the voice, song, laughter, etc. **2.** to perform a trill with the voice or on a musical instrument. –*n.* **3.** the act or sound of trilling.

tril·ogy, *n., pl.* –**gies.** a group of 3 related dramas, operas, novels, etc.

trim, *v.,* **trimmed, trimming,** *n., adj.,* **trimmer, trimmest.** –*v.* **1.** to reduce to an orderly state by clipping, paring, pruning, etc. **2.** to modify (opinions, etc.) according to expediency. **3.** to decorate with ornaments, etc. –*n.* **4.** proper condition or order. **5.** dress, array, or equipment. **6.** material used for decoration. **7.** a trimming by cutting, clipping, or the like. **8. a.** the upholstery, knobs, handles, etc., inside a motor car. **b.** ornamentation on the exterior of a motor car. –*adj.* **9.** pleasingly neat or smart in appearance. **10.** in good condition or order.

tri·maran /'traɪməræn/, *n.* a boat with a main middle hull and 2 outer hulls.

trin·ity, *n., pl.* –**ties.** a group of 3.

trin·ket, *n.* any small fancy article, bit of jewellery, etc., usu. of little value. **2.** anything trifling.

trio, *n., pl.* **trios.** any group of 3 persons or things.

trip, *n., v.,* **tripped, tripping.** –*n.* **1.** a journey. **2.** *Colloq.* a period under the influence of a hallucinatory drug. **3.** a stumble. **4.** to (cause to) stumble. **5.** to step lightly or nimbly. **6.** trip up, to (cause to) make a slip or error.

tripartite

tri·par·tite, *adj.* consisting of 3 parts.

tripe, *n.* 1. part of the stomach of a ruminant, esp. the ox, prepared for use as food. 2. *Colloq.* anything poor or worthless, esp. written work.

triple, *adj.* 1. consisting of 3 parts. –*v.* 2. to multiply by 3.

trip·let, *n.* 1. one of 3 children born at one birth. 2. any group or combination of 3. 3. a thin bar of opal set between 2 layers of plastic, or one layer of potch and one of crystal.

tripli·cate, *v.*, **-cated, -cating**, *adj.* –*v.* 1. to triple. –*adj.* 2. triple.

tripod, *n.* a stool, stand, etc., with 3 legs, esp. as for a camera.

trip·tych /'triptɪk/, *n. Art.* a set of 3 panels side by side, bearing pictures, carvings, or the like.

trite, *adj.*, **triter, tritest.** made commonplace by constant use.

tri·umph, *n.* 1. victory; conquest. 2. a notable achievement; striking success. –*v.* 3. to achieve success. – **triumphal**, *adj.* **triumphant**, *adj.*

trivia, *n.pl.* unimportant, or inconsequential things; trifles. – **trivial**, *adj.*

tro·chee /'trouki/, *n.* (in poetry) a metrical foot of 2 syllables, a long followed by a short, or an accented followed by an unaccented. – **trochaic**, *adj.*

trod, *v.* past tense and past participle of **tread**.

trod·den, *v.* past participle of **tread**.

troll, *v.* to fish with a moving line, as one trailed behind a boat.

trol·ley, *n., pl.* **-leys**. *n.* a kind of low cart.

trouble

trol·lop, *n.* 1. an untidy or slovenly woman; a slattern. 2. a prostitute.

trom·bone, *n.* a brass wind instrument whose pitch is changed by use of a slide. – **trombonist**, *n.*

troop, *n.* 1. a company or band of persons or things. 2. (*pl.*) a body of soldiers, marines, etc. –*v.* 3. to walk as if on a march.

trophy, *n., pl.* **-phies.** anything taken in war, hunting, etc., esp. when preserved as a memento; a spoil or prize.

tropic, *n. Geog.* 1. either of 2 corresponding parallels of latitude on the terrestrial globe, one (**tropic of Cancer**) about 23½° nth, and the other (**tropic of Capricorn**) about 23½° sth of the equator, being the boundaries of the Torrid Zone. 2. **the tropics**, the regions lying between and near these parallels of latitude. – **tropical**, *adj.*

trot, *v.*, **trotted, trotting,** *n.* –*v.* 1. (of a horse, etc.) to go at a gait between a walk and a run. 2. to move briskly, bustle, or hurry. –*n.* 3. a jogging gait between a walk and a run. 4. (*pl.*) races for trotting or pacing horses. 5. (*pl.*) *Colloq.* diarrhoea.

troth, *n.* one's word or promise.

trot·ter, *n.* 1. a horse bred and trained for harness racing. 2. the foot of an animal, esp. of a sheep or pig, used as food.

trouba·dour, *n.* a minstrel.

trou·ble, *v.*, **-bled, -bling,** *n.* –*v.* 1. to distress; worry. 2. to put to inconvenience. –*n.* 3. molestation, harassment, annoyance, or difficulty. 4. misfortunes. 5. disturbance; disorder; unrest. 6. distur-

559

trouble

bance of mind, distress, or worry. – **troublesome**, adj.

trough, n. 1. an open, boxlike receptacle, usu. long and narrow, as for holding water or food for animals. 2. Meteorol. an elongated area of relatively low pressure.

trounce, v., trounced, trouncing. to beat or thrash severely.

troupe, n. a troop, esp. of actors or singers.

trou·sers, n. pl. an outer garment covering the lower part of the trunk and each leg separately, extending to the ankles.

trous·seau, n., pl. -seaux, -seaus. a bride's outfit of clothes, linen, etc.

trout, n., pl. trouts, (esp. collectively) trout. a game and food fish.

trowel, n. a tool with a metal plate fitted into a short handle, used for spreading, shaping, or smoothing plaster, etc.

truant, n. a pupil who stays away from school without permission. – **truancy**, n.

truce, n. (an agreement calling for) end to fighting between armies for a period; an armistice.

truck[1], n. 1. a vehicle for carrying goods, etc. –v. 2. to transport by truck.

truck[2], n. dealings.

truc·u·lent /ˈtrʌkjələnt/, adj. 1. fierce; cruel. 2. aggressive; belligerent.

trudge, v., trudged, trudging. to walk, esp. laboriously or wearily.

true, adj., truer, truest, adv. –adj. 1. being in accordance with the actual state of things; not false. 2. real or genuine. 3. loyal; faithful; trusty. 4. exact. 5. legitimate. 6. accurately shaped or placed, as a surface, instrument, or part of a mechan-

trust

ism. 7. Navig. (of a bearing) fixed in relation to the earth's axis rather than the magnetic poles. –adv. 8. in a true manner; truly or truthfully. 9. exactly or accurately. – **truly**, adv.

truf·fle, n. a subterranean edible fungus.

truism, n. a self-evident, obvious truth. – **truistic**, adj.

trump, n. Cards. 1. any playing card of a suit that for the time outranks the other suits. –v. 2. to take with a trump.

trum·pet, n. 1. a brass wind instrument with a cup-shaped mouthpiece. –v. 2. to sound on a trumpet.

trun·cate, v., -cated, -cating. to shorten by cutting off a part; mutilate.

trun·cheon, n. a short club carried by a policeman.

trun·dle, v., -dled, -dling. 1. to roll (a ball, hoop, etc.). 2. Colloq. to walk in a leisurely fashion.

trunk, n. 1. the main stem of a tree, as distinct from the branches and roots. 2. a chest for holding clothes etc. as for use on a journey. 3. the body of a human being or of an animal, excluding the head and limbs. 4. (pl.) shorts worn by swimmers, athletes, etc. 5. the long, flexible, boneless nose of the elephant.

trunk line, n. Telecom. a telephone line between 2 exchanges, which is used for long-distance calls.

truss, v. 1. to tie, bind, or fasten. –n. 2. Bldg Trades, etc. a combination of beams, bars, ties, etc., so arranged as to form a rigid framework. 3. Med. an apparatus for maintaining a hernia in a reduced state.

trust, n. 1. reliance on the integrity,

560

trust

justice, etc., of a person, or on some attribute of a thing; confidence. **2.** hope. **3.** the state of being relied on. **4.** the obligation imposed on one in whom confidence or authority is placed. **5.** *Law.* **a.** a relationship in which one person (the trustee) holds the title to property for the benefit of another (the beneficiary). **b.** a fund of securities, cash or other assets, held by trustees on behalf of a number of investors. –*v.t.* **6.** to have trust or confidence (in); rely on. **7.** to expect confidently, hope (usu. fol. by a clause or an infinitive).

trus·tee, *n.* **1.** a person appointed to administer the affairs of a company, institution, etc. **2.** a person who holds the title to property for the benefit of another.

trust·worthy, *adj.* reliable.

truth, *n.* **1.** the true or actual facts of a case. **2.** a verified or indisputable fact, proposition, etc.

try, *v.*, **tried**, **trying**, *n.*, *pl.* **tries**. –*v.t.* **1.** to attempt to do. **2.** to test the quality, accuracy, etc, of. **3.** *Law.* to examine and determine in a court of law, the guilt or innocence of (a person). **4.** to put to a severe test; strain the endurance, etc., of. –*n.* **5.** an attempt or effort. **6.** *Rugby Football.* a score of 3 points earned by putting the ball down behind the opposing team's goal line.

trying, *adj.* annoying; distressing.

tryst /trist/, *n.* an appointment, esp. between lovers.

tsar, *n.* **1.** an emperor or king. **2.** (*usu. cap.*) the emperor of Russia.

T-shirt, *n.* a lightweight, close-fitting, collarless shirt, with short sleeves. Also, **tee-shirt**.

tub, *n.* **1.** a large, open, flat-bottomed vessel used for bathing, washing clothes, etc. **2.** a vessel resembling a tub.

tuba, *n., pl.* **-bas**, **-bae**. a brass wind instrument of low pitch.

tubby, *adj.*, **-bier**, **-biest**. short and fat.

tube, *n.* **1.** a hollow, usu. cylindrical body of metal, glass, rubber, etc., used for conveying or containing fluids, etc. **2.** a small, soft metal cylinder closed at one end and capped at the other, for holding paint, toothpaste, etc., to be squeezed out by pressure. –*n.* **tubular**, *adj.*

tuber, *n. Bot.* a fleshy, long or rounded outgrowth (as the potato) of a subterranean stem.

tuber·cu·losis, *n.* an infectious disease, esp. of the lungs.

tuck, *v.* **1.** to thrust into some narrow or concealed space. **2.** to draw up in folds. –*n.* **3.** a tucked piece or part. **4.** *Sewing.* a fold made by doubling cloth upon itself, and stitching along the edge of the fold.

tucker[1], *n. Colloq.* food.

tucker[2], *v. Colloq.* to weary; tire (*out*).

tuft, *n.* a bunch of grass, feathers, hairs, etc., fixed at the base with the upper part loose.

tug, *v.*, **tugged**, **tugging**. to pull at forcefully.

tuition, *n.* teaching or instruction.

tulip, *n.* a plant with large, showy, cup-shaped or bell-shaped flowers.

tumble, *v.*, **-bled**, **-bling**. –*v.* **1.** to roll or fall down as by losing footing. **2.** to fall rapidly, as stock market prices. –*n.* **3.** a fall. **4.** disorder or confusion.

tummy, *n. Colloq.* stomach.

561

tumour

tumour, *n. Pathol.* an abnormal swelling in any part of the body.

tumult, *n.* 1. the noisy disturbance of a multitude; an uproar. 2. a mental or emotional disturbance. – **tumultuous**, *adj.*

tuna, *n.* a large, fast-swimming, marine food fish.

tundra, *n.* one of the vast, treeless plains of the arctic regions of Europe, Asia, and Nth America.

tune, *n., v.,* **tuned, tuning.** –*n.* 1. a succession of musical sounds forming a melody. 2. the state of being in the proper pitch. 3. accord; agreement. –*v.* 4. to adjust (a musical instrument) to a given standard of pitch (*up*). 5. to bring into harmony. 6. to adjust (an engine, etc.) for proper running (*up*). 7. *Radio.* to adjust a receiving apparatus so as to receive (the signals of a sending station).

tuner, *n.* the part of a radio receiver which produces an output suitable for feeding into an amplifier.

tungsten, *n.* a rare metallic element Symbol: W

tunic, *n.* 1. a coat worn as part of a military or other uniform. 2. a loose, sleeveless dress, esp. as worn by girls as part of a school uniform.

tunnel, *n., v.,* **-nelled, -nelling.** –*n.* 1. an underground passage. –*v.* 2. to make a tunnel through or under.

turban, *n.* a form of headdress consisting of a scarf wound around the head.

turbid, *adj.* 1. (of liquids) muddy with suspended particles. 2. disturbed; confused.

turbine, *n.* a hydraulic motor in which a vaned wheel is made to

turn

revolve by the pressure of liquid, gas, steam or air.

turbulent, *adj.* disturbed; agitated; troubled; stormy. – **turbulence**, *n.*

turd, *n. Colloq.* 1. a piece of excrement. 2. (*derog.*) an unpleasant person.

tureen, *n.* a large, deep, covered dish, for holding soup, etc.

turf, *n., pl.* **turfs, turves,** *v.* –*n.* 1. a surface of grass, etc., with its matted roots. 2. a piece cut from this; a sod. –*v.* 3. to cover with turf or sod. 4. **turf out**, *Colloq.* to throw out.

turgid /ˈtɜːdʒɪd/, *adj.* 1. pompous or bombastic, as language, style, etc. 2. swollen; distended.

turkey, *n.* a large, domesticated fowl.

turmeric /ˈtɜːmərɪk/, *n.* (a yellow powder prepared from) the aromatic rhizome of an East Indian plant, used as a seasoning, dye etc.

turmoil, *n.* a state of commotion, tumult or agitation.

turn, *v.* 1. to (cause to) move round on an axis or about a centre; rotate. 2. to reverse the position of: *to turn a page.* 3. to alter the course of; to divert. 4. to alter the nature, character, or appearance (of). 5. to change or be changed (*into* or *to*): *to turn water into ice.* 6. to put to some use. 7. to pass (a certain age, time, amount, etc.). 8. to bring into or assume a rounded or curved form. 9. to express gracefully: *to turn a phrase.* 10. to cause to go; send; drive: *to turn someone from one's door.* 11. to curve, bend, or twist. 12. to direct the gaze in a particular direction. 13. to direct one's course in a particular direction. 14. to devote oneself to something: *to turn to crime.* 15. to shift the body about as if on an

turn

axis. **16.** to be affected with nausea, as the stomach. **17. turn down, a.** to fold. **b.** to lessen the intensity of. **c.** to refuse or reject (a person, request, etc.). **18. turn off, a.** to stop the flow of (water, gas, etc.) as by closing a valve, etc. **b.** to switch off (a radio, light, etc.). **c.** to branch off; diverge. **d.** to arouse antipathy in. **19. turn on, a.** to cause (water, gas, etc.) to flow as by opening a valve, etc. **b.** to switch on (a radio, light, etc.). **c.** Also, **turn upon.** to attack without warning. *Colloq.* to excite or interest (a person). **20. turn out, a.** to extinguish or put out (a light, etc.). **b.** to become ultimately. **21. turn over, a.** to move or be moved from one side to another. **b.** to ponder. **c.** *Comm.* to purchase and then sell (goods or commodities). –*n.* **22.** a movement of rotation, whether total or partial. **23.** the time for action which comes in order to each of a number of persons, etc. **24.** a place where a road, river, etc., turns. **25.** a single revolution, as of a wheel. **26.** a change in nature, circumstances, etc. **27.** a twisting of one thing round another as of a rope around a mast. **28.** a distinctive form or style imparted: *a happy turn of expression.* **29.** a short walk, ride, etc. **30.** natural inclination or aptitude. **31.** a spell of action. **32.** an attack of illness or the like. **33.** an act of service or disservice (prec. by *good, bad, kind,* etc.). **34.** *Colloq.* a nervous shock, as from fright or astonishment. **35.** Also, **turnout.** a social entertainment; party.

turnip, *n.* a plant with a thick, fleshy, edible root.

turn·over, *n.* **1.** the total amount of business done in a given year. **2.** (the rate of) replacement of goods, personnel, etc.

turn·stile, *n.* a horizontally revolving gate which allows people to pass one at a time.

turn·table, *n.* the rotating disc on which the record in a gramophone rests.

tur·pen·tine, *n.* a resin derived from various trees, yielding a volatile oil.

tur·pi·tude, *n.* shameful wickedness.

tur·quoise, *n.* **1.** a sky blue or greenish blue mineral, used in jewellery. **2.** a greenish blue or bluish green.

turret, *n.* a small tower, esp. one at an angle of a building.

turtle, *n.* a reptile having the body enclosed in a shell from which the head, tail, and 4 flipper-like legs protrude.

tusk, *n.* a tooth developed to great length, usu. as one of a pair, as in the elephant, walrus, wild boar, etc.

tussle, *v.,* **-sled, -sling,** *n.* –*v.* **1.** to struggle or fight roughly; scuffle. –*n.* **2.** a rough struggle.

tus·sock, *n.* a tuft or clump of growing grass etc.

tutel·age, *n.* **1.** the office or function of a guardian. **2.** instruction. – **tutelary,** *adj.*

tutor, *n.* **1.** one employed to educate another, esp. a private instructor. **2.** a university teacher who supervises the studies of certain undergraduates assigned to him. –*v.* **3.** to act as a tutor to.

tut·orial, *n.* a period of instruction given by a university tutor to an individual student or a small group of students.

tutu, *n.* a short, full, ballet skirt.

563

tuxedo, *n., pl.* -dos. a dinner jacket.

twain, *adj., n. Archaic.* two.

twang, *v.* 1. to give out a sharp, ringing sound. *-n.* **2.** the sharp, ringing sound produced by plucking a tense string. **3.** a sharp, nasal tone, as of the human voice.

tweak, *v.* to seize and pull with a sharp jerk and twist.

twee, *adj. Colloq.* affected; excessively dainty.

tweed, *n.* a coarse wool cloth in a variety of weaves and colours.

tweez·ers, *n.pl.* small pincers for plucking out hairs, taking up small objects, etc.

twelve, *n.* a cardinal number, 10 plus 2. **– twelfth, *adj., n.***

twenty, *n., pl.* -ties. *n.* a cardinal number, 10 times 2. **– twentieth, *adj., n.***

twice, *adv.* 2 times.

twid·dle, *v.,* -dled, -dling. to turn round and round, esp. with the fingers.

twig¹, *n.* 1. a slender shoot of a plant. **2.** a small, dry, woody piece fallen from a branch.

twig², *v.,* twigged, twigging. to understand.

twi·light, *n.* the light when the sun is just below the horizon, esp. in the evening.

twill, *n.* a fabric woven so as to produce an effect of parallel diagonal lines.

twin, *n.* 1. one of 2 children or animals born at a single birth. *-adj.* **2.** being, or one of 2, such children or animals. **3.** forming a pair or couple.

twine, *n., v.,* twined, twining. *-n.* 1. a strong string composed of 2 or more strands twisted together. *-v.* **2.** to twist together. **3.** to wind in a sinuous course.

twinge, *n.* a sudden, sharp pain.

twin·kle, *v.,* -kled, -kling, *n. -v.* 1. to shine with quick, flickering, gleams of light, as stars, etc. **2.** to sparkle in the light. **3.** (of the eyes) to be bright with amusement, etc. *-n.* **4.** a twinkling with light. **5.** a twinkling brightness in the eyes.

twirl, *v.* (cause to) rotate rapidly; spin; whirl.

twist, *v.* 1. to combine or be combined by winding together, as threads. **2.** to wind or twine (something) about a thing. **3.** to (cause to) take a spiral form or course; wind, curve, or bend. **4.** to turn or rotate, as on an axis. **5.** to change the proper form or meaning; pervert. *-n.* **6.** a curve, bend, or turn. **7.** a peculiar bent, bias, etc., as in the mind or nature. **8.** an unexpected alteration to the course of events, as in a play. **9.** a vigorous dance of the 1960s.

twit¹, *v.,* twitted, twitting. 1. to taunt by references to anything embarrassing. **2.** to reproach or upbraid.

twit², *n. Colloq.* a fool.

twitch, *v.* 1. to give a short, sudden pull or tug at; jerk. *-n.* **2.** a quick, jerky movement of (some part of) the body.

twit·ter, *v.* to utter a succession of small, tremulous sounds, as a bird.

two, *n.* a cardinal number, one plus one.

two-dimensional, *adj.* having 2 dimensions, as height and width.

two-fold, *adj.* 1. having 2 parts. **2.** having twice the amount, etc.

two-up, *n.* a gambling game in

two-up

which 2 coins are spun in the air and bets are laid on whether they fall heads or tails.

ty·coon, *n.* a businessman having great wealth and power.

tyke, *n.* **1.** *Colloq.* a Roman Catholic. **2.** a mischievous child.

type, *n.*, *v.*, **typed, typing.** –*n.* **1.** a kind, class, or group as distinguished by a particular characteristic. **2.** the general style distinguishing a particular kind, class or group. **3.** the model from which something is made. **4.** *Print.* **a.** a rectangular metal piece, having on its upper surface a letter or character in relief. **b.** a printed character or printed characters. –*v.* **5.** to write (a letter, etc.) by means of a typewriter. **6.** to be a type or symbol of.

type·cast, *v.*, **-cast, -casting.** to cast (an actor, etc.) continually in the same kind of role.

type·face, *n.* →**face** (def. 6).

type·script, *n.* typewritten material, as distinct from handwriting or print.

type·set, *v.*, **-set, -setting.** *Print.* to set in type.

type·writer, *n.* a machine for writing mechanically in letters and characters.

ty·phoid fever, *n.* an infectious, often fatal, fever. Also, **typhoid.**

ty·phoon, *n.* a tropical cyclone or hurricane.

typhus, *n.* an acute infectious disease, transmitted by lice and fleas. Also, **typhus fever.** – **typhous**, *adj.*

typ·i·cal, *adj.* **1.** pertaining to type or emblem; symbolic. **2.** serving as a type or representative specimen. **3.** conforming to the type.

typ·i·fy, *v.*, **-fied, -fying.** to serve as the typical specimen of.

typist, *n.* one who operates a typewriter.

tyr·anny, *n.*, *pl.* **-nies. 1.** despotic abuse of authority. **2.** the government or rule of a tyrant. **3.** undue severity or harshness. – **tyrannical**, *adj.* – **tyrannise**, *v.*

tyrant, *n.* **1.** a king or ruler who uses his power oppressively or unjustly. **2.** any person who exercises power despotically.

tyre, *n.* a band of metal or (usu. inflated) rubber, fitted round the rim of a wheel as a running surface.

Uu

U, u, *n., pl.* **U's** or **Us, u's** or **us.** the 21st letter of the English alphabet.

ubi·quity, *n.* the state or capacity of being everywhere at the same time. – **ubiquitous,** *adj.*

udder, *n.* a mammary gland, esp. with more than one teat, as in cows.

UFO /ju εf 'oʊ, 'jufoʊ/, *n.* unidentified flying object.

ugly, *adj.,* **-lier, -liest. 1.** offensive to the sense of beauty. **2.** troublesome or dangerous.

uku·lele, *n.* a small guitar-like musical instrument. Also, **ukelele.**

ulcer, *n. Pathol.* a pus-filled sore open either to the surface of the body or to a natural cavity. – **ulcerous,** *adj.* – **ulcerate,** *v.*

ul·terior, *adj.* intentionally kept concealed: *ulterior motives.*

ulti·mate, *adj.* **1.** forming the final aim or object. **2.** coming at the end, as of a course of action, a process, etc. –*n.* **3.** the final point or result. **4.** a fundamental fact or principle.

ulti·matum, *n., pl.* **-tums, -ta.** a final proposal or statement of conditions.

ultra·marine, *n.* a deep blue colour.

ultra·sound, *n.* pressure waves like sound waves, but inaudible to the human ear. – **ultrasonic,** *adj.*

ultra·violet, *adj.* of the invisible rays of the spectrum lying outside the violet end of the visible spectrum.

ulu·late, *v.,* **-lated, -lating.** to howl, as a dog or wolf.

umber, *n.* a brown pigment.

umbi·li·cal cord /ʌm'bɪləkəl, ˌʌmbə'laɪkəl/, *n.* a cord connecting the embryo or foetus with the placenta of the mother, and transmitting nourishment from the mother.

umb·rage, *n.* offence given or taken; resentful displeasure.

um·brella, *n.* a portable shade or screen for protection from sunlight, rain, etc.

umpire, *n.* **1.** a person selected to see that a game is played in accordance with the rules. **2.** a person to whose decision a controversy between parties is referred; an arbiter or referee.

ump·teen, *adj.* a large, usu. indefinite, number.

unani·mous, *adj.* in complete accord; agreed.

un·assum·ing, *adj.* unpretending; modest.

uncalled-for, *adj.* unnecessary and improper.

un·canny, *adj.* **1.** such as to arouse superstitious uneasiness. **2.** abnormally good.

uncle, *n.* a brother of one's father or mother. **2.** an aunt's husband.

un·conscion·able, *adj.* **1.** not just or reasonable. **2.** not guided by conscience; unscrupulous.

un·con·scious, *adj.* **1.** not conscious; unaware. **2.** temporarily devoid of consciousness. **3.** occurring below the level of conscious thought. **4.** unintentional.

un·couth, *adj.* clumsy or rude.

unc·tion, *n.* the act of anointing, esp. for medical purposes or as a religious rite.

unc·tuous, *adj.* 1. oily; greasy. 2. insincerely smooth in manner; ingratiating.

under, *prep.* 1. beneath and covered by. 2. at a point or position lower than or farther down than. 3. subject to. 4. below in degree, amount, price, etc. 5. below in rank, dignity, or the like. 6. authorised, warranted, or attested by: *under licence.* 7. in accordance with: *under the rules.* –*adv.* 8. under or beneath something. 9. in a lower place. 10. in a lower degree, amount, etc. 11. in a subordinate position or condition. 12. **go under**, *Colloq.* a. to sink (as) in water. b. to fail, esp. of a business.

under·arm, *adj. Cricket, Tennis, etc.* executed with the hand below the shoulder as in bowling, service, etc.

under·carriage, *n.* the portions of an aeroplane beneath the body.

under·cut, *v.,* -cut, -cutting. to sell or work at a lower price than.

under·dog, *n.* 1. a victim of oppression. 2. the loser or expected loser in a competitive situation, fight, etc.

under·go, *v.,* -went, -gone, -going. 1. to be subjected to; experience. 2. to endure; sustain; suffer.

under·graduate, *n.* a student in a university or college who has not taken his first degree.

under·ground, *adj.* 1. existing, situated, operating, or taking place beneath the surface of the ground. 2. hidden or secret; not open. –*n.* 3. the place or region beneath the surface of the ground. 4. a secret organisation, etc.

under·growth, *n.* shrubs or small trees growing beneath or among large trees.

under·hand, *adj.* secret and crafty or dishonourable.

under·line, *v.,* -lined, -lining. to mark with a line or lines underneath, esp. for emphasis in writing, etc.

under·ling, *n.* (*usu. derog.*) a subordinate.

under·mine, *v.,* -mined, -mining. to weaken insidiously; destroy gradually.

under·neath, *prep.* 1. under; beneath. –*adv.* 2. beneath; below. –*adj.* 3. lower.

under·stand, *v.,* -stood, -standing. 1. to perceive the meaning of; grasp the idea of; comprehend. 2. to be thoroughly familiar with; apprehend clearly the character or nature of. 3. to regard or take as a fact, or as settled. 4. to perceive what is meant.

under·standing, *n.* 1. the act of one who understands; comprehension; personal interpretation. 2. superior intelligence; power of recognising the truth. 3. a mutual private agreement. –*adj.* 4. sympathetic and tolerant.

under·state, *v.,* -stated, -stating. to state or represent less strongly than is desirable or necessary. – **understatement**, *n.*

under·study, *n.* an actor or actress who stands by to replace a (sick) performer.

under·take, *v.,* -took, -taking. to take on oneself (some task, performance, etc.); attempt.

under·taker, *n.* one whose business

undertaker

it is to prepare the dead for burial or cremation and to take charge of funerals.

under·taking, *n.* a task, enterprise, etc., undertaken.

under·tone, *n.* 1. a low or subdued tone, as of utterance. 2. an underlying quality, element, or tendency.

under·tow, *n.* the backward flow or pull of the water, below the surface, from waves breaking on a beach.

under·wear, *n.* clothes worn under outer clothes, esp. those worn next to the skin.

under·world, *n.* 1. the lower or criminal part of human society. 2. *Myth.* the lower world of the dead.

under·write, *v.*, **-wrote, -written, -writing.** 1. to agree to meet the expense of. 2. to guarantee the sale of (shares or bonds to be offered to the public for subscription). 3. to accept liability in case of certain losses specified in (an insurance policy).

undo, *v.*, **-did, -done, -doing.** 1. to unfasten and open (something closed, tied, locked, barred, etc.). 2. to cause to be as if never done. 3. to bring to ruin or disaster.

undue, *adj.* excessive; unjustified. – **unduly**, *adv.*

undu·late, *v.*, **-lated, -lating.** to have a wavy motion or appearance.

un·earth, *v.* to uncover or bring to light by digging, searching, or discovery.

uneasy, *adj.*, **-easier, -easiest.** not at ease in body or mind; disturbed.

un·employed, *adj.* without work or employment.

un·erring, *adj.* 1. without error or mistake. 2. unfailingly right, exact, or sure.

un·feeling, *adj.* unsympathetic; callous.

un·fore·seen, *adj.* not predicted; unexpected.

un·gainly, *adj.* not graceful.

ungu·ent, *n.* any soft preparation or ointment.

uni, *n. Colloq.* a university.

uni·corn, *n.* a mythological animal with a single long horn.

uni·form, *adj.* 1. having always the same form or character; unvarying. 2. regular; even. 3. agreeing with one another in form, character, appearance, etc.; alike. –*n.* 4. a distinctive dress of uniform style, materials, and colour, worn by all the members of a group or organisation. – **uniformity**, *n.*

unify, *v.*, **-fied, -fying.** to form into one; reduce to unity. – **unification**, *n.*

uni·lateral, *adj.* 1. pertaining to, occurring on, or affecting one side only. 2. considering only one side of a matter or question.

union, *n.* 1. the act of uniting 2 or more things into one. 2. the state of being so united; conjunction. 3. something formed by uniting 2 or more things; combination. 4. a number of persons, societies, states, or the like, joined together or associated for some common purpose. 5. → **trade union**.

union·ise, *v.*, **-nised, -nising.** to organise into a trade union.

union·ist, *n.* a trade unionist.

unique, *adj.* 1. of which there is only one. 2. having no like or equal.

unisex, *adj.* without the traditional differentiations between the sexes.

unison

unison, *n.* **1.** coincidence in pitch of 2 or more notes, voices, etc. **2.** accord or agreement.

unit, *n.* **1.** a single thing or person; any group of things or persons regarded as an individual. **2.** any specified amount of a quantity by comparison with which any other quantity of the same kind is measured: *The metre is a unit of length.* **3.** a self-contained suite of rooms.

unite, *v.,* **united, uniting. 1.** to join, combine, or incorporate in one; cause to be one. **2.** to associate (persons, etc.) by some bond or tie; join in action, interest, opinion, feeling, etc.

unity, *n., pl.* **-ties. 1.** the state or fact of being one. **2.** the oneness of a complex or organic whole. **3.** freedom from diversity or variety. **4.** oneness of mind, feeling, etc.

uni·versal, *adj.* **1.** without exception. **2.** applicable to many individuals or single cases. **3.** affecting, concerning, or involving all. **4.** of or pertaining to the universe, all nature, or all existing things. **5.** adapted or adaptable for all or various uses, angles, sizes, etc. —*n.* **6.** that which may be applied throughout the universe to many things.

uni·verse, *n.* **1.** all of space, and all the matter and energy which it contains; the cosmos. **2.** a world or sphere in which something exists or prevails.

uni·ver·sity, *n., pl.* **-ties.** an institution of higher learning, conducting teaching and research at the undergraduate and postgraduate level.

until

un·kempt, *adj.* in a neglected, or untidy state.

unless, *conj.* except on condition that; except when.

un·likely, *adj.* not likely to happen; doubtful.

unload, *v.* to remove the burden, cargo, or freight from.

un·nerve, *v.,* **-nerved, -nerving.** to deprive of nerve, strength, or physical or mental firmness; upset.

unprin·cipled, *adj.* lacking sound moral principles.

un·ravel, *v.,* **-elled, -elling.** to disentangle; disengage the threads or fibres of.

unreal, *adj.* **1.** not real; imaginary; artificial; unpractical or visionary. **2.** *Colloq.* **a.** unbelievably awful. **b.** unbelievably wonderful.

unremit·ting, *adj.* not stopping or slackening.

un·requited, *adj.* (used esp. of affection) not returned or reciprocated.

unrest, *n.* strong, almost rebellious, dissatisfaction and agitation.

unruly, *adj.* not submissive or conforming to rule.

un·savoury, *adj.* unpleasant or offensive.

un·scathed, *adj.* not harmed in any way.

un·secured, *adj.* **1.** not fastened. **2.** not insured against loss, as by a mortgage, bond, etc.

un·settle, *v.,* **-tled, -tling.** to shake or weaken (beliefs, feelings, etc.); disturb.

un·sightly, *adj.* not pleasing to the sight.

until, *conj.* **1.** up to the time that or when; till. **2.** (with negatives)

until

before: *not until he is finished.* –*prep.* 3. onward to, or till (a specified time); up to the time of (some occurrence). 4. (with negatives) before: *not until evening.*

unto, *prep.* Archaic. to (in its various uses, especially as the accompaniment of the infinitive).

un·toward, *adj.* 1. unfavourable or unfortunate. 2. unseemly.

un·wieldy, *adj.* 1. not easily handled or used, due to size, shape, or weight. 2. ungainly; awkward.

un·witting, *adj.* unaware; unconscious.

up, *adv., prep., adj., v.*, upped, upping. –*adv.* 1. to, towards, or in a more elevated position. 2. into the air. 3. to or in an erect position. 4. out of bed: *Get up.* 5. to or at any point that is considered higher, as the north, a capital city, etc. 6. to or at a higher point or degree in a scale, as of rank, size, value, pitch, etc. 7. to or at a point of equal advance, extent, etc. 8. well advanced or versed, as in a subject. 9. to a state of maturity: *Grow up.* 10. to a state of completion. –*prep.* 11. to, towards, or at a higher place on or in. 12. to, towards, near, or at a higher condition or rank in. –*adj.* 13. going or directed upwards. 14. travelling towards a terminus or centre. 15. standing and speaking. 16. out of bed: *He is up.* 17. well informed or advanced, as in a subject. 18. appearing before a court on some charge. 19. in a leading position. –*v.* Colloq. 20. to put or take up. 21. to make larger; step up.

up·braid, *v.* to reproach for some fault or offence.

up·bringing, *n.* the bringing up or rearing of a person from childhood.

upset

update, *v.*, -dated, -dating. to bring up to date.

up-end, *v.* 1. to set on end. 2. to upset.

up·grade, *v.*, -graded, -grading. to improve.

up·heave, *v.*, -heaved or -hove, -heaving. 1. to heave or lift up. 2. to disturb or change violently or radically. – **upheaval**, *n.*

uphold, *v.*, -held, -holding. to support or maintain, as by advocacy or agreement.

uphol·stery, *n., pl.* -ries. the cushions, fabric and other material used to cover furniture.

upkeep, *n.* (the cost of) the maintenance of an establishment, machine, etc.

uplift, *v.* 1. to lift up. 2. to exalt emotionally or spiritually.

upon, *prep.* 1. upwards so as to get or be on. 2. on, in any of various senses.

upper, *adj.* 1. higher (than something implied) or highest, as in place, or position, or in a scale. 2. forming the higher of a pair. 3. (of a surface) facing upwards. –*n.* 4. anything which is higher or highest. 5. the part of a shoe or boot above the sole.

up·right, *adj.* 1. erect or vertical. 2. righteous, honest, or just.

up·rising, *n.* an insurrection or revolt.

uproar, *n.* violent and noisy disturbance.

up·roari·ous, *adj.* 1. characterised by or in a state of uproar. 2. extremely funny.

upset, *v.*, -set, -setting, *n., adj.* –*v.* 1. to overturn; knock or tip over. 2. to disturb (someone) mentally or

570

upset

upset emotionally; distress. **3.** to defeat (a competitor or opponent). –*n.* **4.** a physical upsetting. **5.** an emotional disturbance. **6.** a defeat, esp. unexpected. –*adj.* **7.** emotionally disturbed; distressed.

upshot, *n.* the final issue, the conclusion, or the result.

up·stage, *adv., adj.,* -**staged**, -**staging**. –*adv.* **1.** on or to the back of the stage. –*v.* **2.** to steal attention (from another).

up·stairs, *adv., adj.* –*adv.* **1.** to or on an upper floor. **2.** to or in a higher rank or office. –*adj.* **3.** on or pertaining to an upper floor.

up·stand·ing, *adj.* **1.** standing upright. **2.** straightforward, open, or honourable.

up·start, *n.* one who has risen suddenly in wealth or power.

uptake, *n.* the action of understanding.

up·tight, *adj. Colloq.* tense, nervous, or irritable.

up-to-date, *adj.* extending to the present time; modern.

upturn, *n.* an upward turn, as in prices, business, etc.

upward, *adj.* **1.** directed, tending, or moving upwards. –*adv.* **2.** upwards.

up·wards, *adv.* towards a higher position, degree, or standard.

ura·nium, *n.* a white, lustrous, radioactive, metallic element. Symbol: U

urban, *adj.* of, pertaining to, or comprising a city or town.

urbane, *adj.* civilised; sophisticated.

urchin, *n.* a mischievous or shabbily dressed youngster.

urethra, *n., pl.* -**thrae**, -**thras**. the membranous tube which extends from the bladder to the exterior. In the male it conveys semen as well as urine.

urge, *v.,* **urged, urging,** *n.* –*v.* **1.** to endeavour to induce or persuade. **2.** to press, push, or hasten (the course, activities, etc.). –*n.* **3.** the fact of urging or being urged. **4.** an involuntary, natural, or instinctive impulse.

urgent, *adj.* **1.** requiring immediate action or attention. **2.** insistent or earnest in solicitation. – **urgency,** *n.*

urinal /ˈjuːrənl, juˈraɪnəl/, *n.* a fixture, room, or building for discharging urine in.

uri·nate, *v.* to discharge urine.

urine, *n.* the secretion of the kidneys (in mammals, a fluid). – **urinary,** *adj.*

urn /ɜːn/, *n.* **1.** a kind of vase. **2.** a vessel with a tap, used for heating liquids in quantity.

ursine, *adj.* of or pertaining to bears.

us, *pron.* objective case of **we**.

usage, *n.* **1.** customary way of doing; a custom or practice. **2.** customary manner of using a language or any of its forms. **3.** usual conduct or behaviour. **4.** the act or fact of using or employing; use.

use, *v.,* **used, using,** *n.* –*v.* **1.** to employ for some purpose. **2.** to act or behave towards (a person). **3.** to exploit (a person) for one's own ends. –*n.* **4.** the act of employing or using, or putting into service. **5.** the state of being employed or used. **6.** a purpose for which something is used. **7.** the power, right, or privilege of using something. **8.** help; profit; resulting good. **9.** custom; practice. – **useful,** *adj.*

used[1] /juːzd/, *adj.* **1.** worn; showing signs of wear. **2.** second-hand.

571

used² /just/, *adj.* accustomed; inured (*to*).

usher, *n.* 1. one who escorts persons to seats in a church, theatre, etc. 2. an attendant who keeps order in a law court. –*v.* 3. to act as an usher to.

usher·ette, *n.* a female attendant, esp. one who shows people to their seats in a theatre.

usual, *adj.* 1. habitual or customary. 2. in common use; common. –*n.* 3. that which is usual or habitual. – **usually**, *adv.*

usurp, *v.* to seize and hold (an office or position, power, etc.) by force or without right.

usury, *n., pl.* -ries. (the practice of lending money at) an exorbitant rate of interest.

uten·sil, *n.* any instrument, vessel, or implement.

uterus, *n., pl.* uteri. that portion of the female reproductive system in which the fertilised ovum implants itself and develops until birth; womb. – **uterine**, *adj.*

uti·lise, *v.*, -lised, -lising. to put to use.

utili·tarian, *adj.* 1. concerning practical or material things. 2. having regard to usefulness rather than beauty.

util·ity, *n., pl.* -ties. 1. the state or character of being useful. 2. something useful; a useful thing. 3. a public service, as a railway, gas supply, etc.

utility truck, *n.* a small truck with an enclosed cabin and a rectangular tray with sides. Also, **ute**.

utmost, *adj.* 1. of the greatest degree, quantity, etc. 2. being at the farthest point or extremity; farthest. –*n.* 3. the greatest degree or amount. 4. the best of one's power. Also, **uttermost**.

utopia, *n.* (*sometimes cap.*) a place or state of ideal perfection. – **utopian**, *adj.*

utter¹, *v.* 1. to give audible expression to (words, etc.). 2. to express in any manner. 3. to make publicly known; publish. 4. to put into circulation, esp. counterfeit money, forged cheques, etc. – **utterance**, *n.*

utter², *adj.* complete; total; absolute. – **utterly**, *adv.*

uvula, *n., pl.* -las, -lae. the small, fleshy, conical body projecting downwards above the back of the tongue. – **uvular**, *adj.*

uxor·ious, *adj.* excessively fond of one's wife.

Vv

V, v, *n., pl.* **V's** or **Vs, v's** or **vs.** the 22nd letter of the English alphabet.

vacant, *adj.* **1.** having no contents; empty. **2.** having no occupant. **– vacancy,** *n.*

vacate, *v.,* **-cated, -cating. 1.** to make vacant; to empty. **2.** to give up the occupancy of.

vacation, *n.* **1.** a part of the year when schools, etc., are suspended or closed. **2.** a holiday.

vac·ci·nate, *v.,* **-nated, -nating.** to inoculate with a vaccine.

vaccine, *n.* the (modified) virus of any of various diseases, used for preventive inoculation.

vacil·late, *v.,* **-lated, -lating. 1.** to sway unsteadily. **2.** to fluctuate.

vacuous, *adj.* **1.** empty. **2.** empty of ideas or intelligence. **– vacuity,** *n.*

vacuum, *n., pl.* **vacuums, vacua.** a space entirely void of matter.

vagabond, *n.* a vagrant.

vagary, *n., pl.* **-ries. 1.** an extravagant idea or notion. **2.** a wild, capricious, or fantastic action.

vagina /vəˈdʒaɪnə/, *n., pl.* **-nas, -nae** /-niː/. the passage leading from the uterus to the vulva in a female mammal. **– vaginal,** *adj.*

vagrant /ˈveɪgrənt/, *n.* **1.** one who wanders with no settled home or means of support. *–adj.* **2.** wandering or roaming. **– vagrancy,** *n.*

vague, *adj.,* **vaguer, vaguest. 1.** not definite in statement or meaning. **2.** indistinct to the sight or other sense. **3.** (of persons, etc.) not clear in thought or understanding.

vain, *adj.* **1.** without real value or importance. **2.** futile; useless; ineffectual. **3.** having excessive pride in oneself; conceited.

valance, *n.* a short curtain.

valediction, *n.* a bidding farewell. **– valedictory,** *adj.*

valency, *n., pl.* **-cies.** the combining capacity of an atom.

valet /ˈvæleɪ, ˈvælət/, *n.* a personal attendant, caring for his employer's clothing, etc.

valiant, *adj.* brave; courageous.

valid, *adj.* **1.** sound, just, or well-founded. **2.** having force, weight, or cogency; authoritative. **3.** legally sound, effective, or binding. **– validity,** *n.* **– validate,** *v.*

valley, *n., pl.* **-leys.** an elongated depression between uplands, hills, or mountains, esp. one following the course of a stream.

valour, *n.* bravery or heroic courage, esp. in battle.

valu·able, *adj.* **1.** of monetary worth. **2.** of considerable use, service, or importance.

valu·ation, *n.* an estimating or fixing of the value of a thing.

value, *n., v.,* **-ued, -uing.** *–n.* **1.** (measure of) that quality which makes something esteemed, desirable, or useful; merit; worth. **2.** the worth of a thing as measured by the amount of other things, esp. money, for which it can be exchanged. *–v.* **3.** to estimate the value of; appraise. **4.** to regard or esteem highly.

valve, *n.* **1.** any device for controlling

valve

the flow of liquids, gases, etc. 2. *Anat.* a structure which permits blood to flow in one direction only.

vamp[1], *n.* 1. the front part of the upper of a shoe or boot. 2. anything patched up or pieced together. –*v.* 3. to patch (*up*); renovate.

vamp[2], *n. Colloq.* a woman who uses her charms to seduce and exploit men.

vam·pire, *n.* 1. a supernatural being, supposed to suck blood of sleeping persons at night. 2. Also, **vampire bat**. a bat which feeds on the blood of animals including man.

van, *n.* a covered vehicle for moving furniture, goods, etc.

vandal, *n.* one who wilfully destroys or damages anything. – **vandalism**, *n.* – **vandalise**, *v.*

vane, *n.* a flat piece of metal, etc., esp. one which moves with the wind and indicates its direction.

van·guard, *n.* the leading position in any field.

va·nil·la, *n.* a tropical orchid whose pod-like fruit is used in flavourings, perfumery, etc.

vanish, *v.* to become invisible, esp. by magic or quickly.

vanity, *n., pl.* **-ties.** the quality of being personally vain.

van·quish, *v.* to conquer or defeat.

van·tage point, *n.* a position affording a clear view.

vapid, *adj.* having lost life, sharpness, or flavour.

vapor·ise, *v.*, **-rised, -rising.** to make gaseous.

vapour, *n.* 1. a visible exhalation, as fog, mist, condensed steam. 2. a gas.

vari·able, *adj.* 1. apt or liable to vary or change. 2. inconsistent or fickle.

vassal

–*n.* 3. something variable. 4. *Maths.* a representation of a quantity or any one of a given set of numbers. – **variability**, *n.*

vari·ance, *n.* the state or fact of varying; divergence or discrepancy.

vari·ant, *adj., n.* (being) an altered or different form.

vari·ation, *n.* 1. change in condition, character, degree, etc. 2. amount or rate of change. 3. a different form; a variant.

vari·cose, *adj.* abnormally enlarged or swollen.

vari·egate, *v.*, **-gated, -gating.** to mark with different colours.

vari·ety, *n., pl.* **-ties.** 1. the state or character of being various or varied. 2. a number of things of different kinds. 3. a kind or sort. 4. a different form, condition, or phase of something.

vari·ous, *adj.* 1. differing one from another. 2. several or many.

var·nish, *n.* 1. a liquid which dries as a hard, glossy, usu. transparent, coating for wood, metal, etc. –*v.* 2. to apply varnish to.

vary, *v.*, **-ried, -rying.** 1. to change or alter, as in form, appearance, character, substance, degree, etc. 2. to (cause to) be different, one from another. 3. to relieve from uniformity or monotony. 4. to alternate. 5. to diverge; deviate (*from*).

vas·cu·lar, *adj.* pertaining to, composed of, or provided with vessels or ducts which convey fluids, as blood, lymph, or sap.

vase, *n.* a container for cut flowers.

vas·ec·tomy, *n., pl.* **-mies.** the cutting of the duct from testicle to penis, as a contraceptive measure.

vassal, *n.* (in the feudal system) a

person holding lands by the obligation to render (military) service to his lord.

vast, *adj.* of very great extent or area; immense.

vat, *n.* a large container for liquids.

vaude·ville, *n.* a light or amusing theatrical piece, interspersed with songs and dances.

vault[1], *n.* 1. an arched space, chamber, or passage. 2. a strongroom for storing and safeguarding valuables.

vault[2], *v.* to leap or spring, esp. over (something).

vaunt, *v.* 1. to speak boastfully of. –*n.* 2. boastful utterance.

veal, *n.* the flesh of the calf as used for food.

vector, *n.* 1. a quantity which possesses both magnitude and direction. 2. *Biol.* a transmitter of germs or disease.

veer, *v.* to change direction or course.

vegan /'vigən/, *n.* a strict vegetarian, whose diet excludes any animal product.

vege·table, *n.* 1. any herbaceous plant whose fruits, seeds, roots, bulbs, leaves, etc., are used as food. 2. *Colloq.* a person who is entirely dependent on others, usu. due to severe brain damage.

vege·tarian, *n.* one who eats only vegetable (and sometimes dairy) products.

vege·tate, *v.,* -tated, -tating. 1. to grow in the manner of plants. 2. to live in a passive or unthinking way.

vege·tation, *n.* the plant life of a particular region considered as a whole.

vehe·ment /'viəmənt/, *adj.* 1. eager, impetuous, or impassioned. 2. (of actions) marked by great energy or exertion.

vehi·cle, *n.* 1. any receptacle, or means of transport, in which something is carried or conveyed, or travels. 2. a medium by which ideas or effects are communicated. – **vehicular**, *adj.*

veil, *n.* 1. a piece of material worn over the head or face, as to conceal or protect the face. 2. something that covers, screens, or conceals. –*v.* 3. to cover or conceal (as) with a veil.

vein, *n.* 1. one of the branching vessels or tubes conveying blood to the heart. 2. one of the strands or bundles of vascular tissue forming the principal framework of a leaf. 3. any body or stratum of ore, coal, etc., clearly separated or defined. 4. a quality traceable in character or conduct, writing, etc.

velo·city, *n., pl.* -ties. 1. rapidity of motion or operation. 2. *Physics.* rate of motion, esp. when the direction of motion is also specified.

velo·drome, *n.* an arena with a suitably banked track for cycle races.

velour, *n.* any of various fabrics with a fine raised finish.

velvet, *n.* 1. a fabric with a thick, soft pile. 2. something likened to the fabric velvet in softness, etc.

venal, *adj.* accessible to bribery; corruptly mercenary.

vend, *v.* to sell. – **vendor**, *n.*

ven·detta, *n.* 1. a private feud. 2. any prolonged or persistent quarrel, rivalry, etc.

veneer, *n.* 1. a thin layer of wood or other material used for facing or

veneer

overlaying wood. 2. a superficially pleasing appearance or show.

vener·able, *adj.* worthy of veneration or reverence, as on account of high character or office.

vener·ate, *v.*, **-rated, -rating.** to regard with reverence. – **veneration,** *n.*

ven·ereal disease, *n.* any disease transmitted by sexual intercourse, esp. syphilis and gonorrhoea.

ven·geance, *n.* the avenging of wrong, injury, or the like. – **vengeful,** *adj.*

venial, *adj.* that may be forgiven or pardoned.

veni·son, *n.* the flesh of a deer or similar animal.

venom, *n.* the poisonous fluid which some animals, as certain snakes, spiders, etc., secrete and inject into their victims. – **venomous,** *adj.*

vent[1], *n.* an opening serving as an outlet for air, smoke, fumes, etc.

vent[2], *v.* to give free course or expression to (an emotion, passion, etc.).

venti·late, *v.*, **-lated, -lating.** 1. to provide (a room, mine, etc.) with fresh air. 2. to air or discuss (a problem, etc.).

ven·tral, *adj.* of or pertaining to the belly; abdominal.

ven·tri·cle, *n.* 1. any of various hollow organs or parts in an animal body. 2. one of the 2 main cavities of the heart.

ven·trilo·quism, *n.* the art or practice of speaking in such a manner that the voice appears to come from some other source, such as a dummy. Also, **ventriloquy.** – **ventriloquist,** *n.*

ven·ture, *n.*, *v.*, **-tured, -turing.** –*n.* 1.

verge

any undertaking or proceeding involving uncertainty as to the outcome. 2. a business enterprise or proceeding in which loss is risked in the hope of profit. –*v.* 3. to make a venture. 4. to take a risk; dare or presume (oft. fol. by *on* or *upon* an infinitive). – **venturesome,** *adj.*

venue, *n.* the scene of any action or event.

ver·acious, *adj.* truthful. – **veracity,** *n.*

ver·anda, *n.* an open or partly open portion of a building, roofed usu. by the main structure. Also, **verandah.**

verb, *n.* one of the major parts of speech, comprising words which express the occurrence of an action, existence of a state, and the like.

verbal, *adj.* 1. of or pertaining to words. 2. spoken, rather than written. 3. of, pertaining to, or derived from a verb.

verba·lise, *v.*, **-lised, -lising.** to express in words.

ver·batim /vɜ'beɪtəm/, *adv.* in exactly the same words.

ver·bi·age, *n.* abundance of useless words; wordiness.

ver·bose, *adj.* expressed in or using many or too many words; wordy.

ver·dant, *adj.* green with vegetation.

ver·dict, *n.* *Law.* the finding or answer of a jury. 2. a judgment or decision.

ver·dure, *n.* greenness, esp. of fresh, flourishing vegetation.

verge, *n.*, *v.*, **verged, verging.** –*n.* 1. the edge, rim, or margin of something. 2. the limit or point beyond which something begins or occurs. –*v.* 3. to be on the verge or border,

verge

or touch at the border. 4. to come close to, approach, or border (*on* or *upon*) some state or condition.

verger, *n.* an official who takes care of the interior of a church and acts as attendant.

verify, *v.,* **-fied, -fying.** 1. to prove (something) to be true; confirm or substantiate. 2. to ascertain the truth or correctness of, esp. by examination or comparison. – **verification,** *n.*

veri·table, *adj.* being truly such; genuine or real.

verity, *n., pl.* **-ties.** the quality of being true.

vermi·form, *adj.* like a worm in form; long and slender.

vermiform appendix, →**appendix** (def. 2).

ver·milion, *n.* brilliant scarlet red.

vermin, *n.pl. or sing.* noxious, troublesome, or objectionable animals collectively.

ver·mouth, *n.* a white wine in which herbs, roots, and other flavourings have been steeped.

ver·nacu·lar, *adj.* 1. native or originating in the place of its occurrence or use, as language or words (oft. as opposed to *literary* or *learned* language). –*n.* 2. the native speech or language of a place.

vernal, *adj.* of or appropriate to spring.

versa·tile, *adj.* capable of or adapted for a variety of tasks, subjects, etc. – **versatility,** *n.*

verse, *n.* 1. a stanza or other subdivision of a metrical composition. 2. one of the lines of a poem. 3. a short division of a chapter in the Bible.

vestal

versed, *adj.* experienced or skilled (*in*).

ver·sion, *n.* 1. a particular account of some matter, as contrasted with another. 2. a translation.

versus, *prep.* against; in opposition to. *Abbrev.:* v. or vs.

ver·te·bra, *n., pl.* **-brae, -bras.** any of the bones or segments composing the spinal column.

ver·te·brate, *n.* 1. a vertebrate animal. –*adj.* 2. having vertebrae; having a backbone or spinal column.

vertex, *n.* the highest point of something; apex.

ver·ti·cal, *adj.* 1. being in a position or direction perpendicular to the plane of the horizon; upright. –*n.* 2. a vertical line, plane, or the like.

ver·ti·go, *n., pl.* **vertigos, vertigines.** a feeling of dizziness.

verve, *n.* enthusiasm or energy, as in literary or artistic work.

very, *adv., adj.,* **-rier, -riest.** –*adv.* 1. in a high degree, extremely, or exceedingly. –*adj.* 2. precise or identical. 3. mere. 4. actual. 5. true, genuine or real.

ves·icle, *n.* a little sac or cyst.

vessel, *n.* 1. a craft for travelling on water. 2. a container for holding liquid or other contents. 3. a tube or duct, as an artery, vein, or the like, containing or conveying blood or some other body fluid.

vest, *n.* 1. a short, warm undergarment; singlet. 2. a waistcoat. –*v.* 3. to clothe, dress, or robe. 4. to place or settle (something, esp. property, rights, powers, etc.) (*in*) the possession or control of a person or persons.

vestal, *adj.* virginal; chaste.

vestibule

ves·ti·bule, *n.* an entrance passage, hall, or room.

ves·tige, *n.* a mark, trace, or visible evidence of something which is no longer present or in existence. – **vestigial**, *adj.*

vest·ment, *n.* an official or ceremonial robe.

vestry, *n., pl.* **-tries.** a room in or a building attached to a church.

vet, *n., v.,* vetted, vetting. *Colloq.* –*n.* 1. a veterinary surgeon. –*v.* 2. to examine with a view to acceptance, rejection, or correction.

vet·eran, *n.* 1. one who has seen long service in any occupation or office. –*adj.* 2. experienced through long service or practice.

vet·erin·ary science, *n.* that branch of medicine that concerns itself with animal diseases.

veterinary surgeon, *n.* one who practises veterinary science or surgery.

veto, *n., pl.* **-toes**, *v.,* **-toed, -toing.** –*n.* 1. the power or right of preventing action by a prohibition. –*v.* 2. to prevent (a proposal, legislative bill, etc.) being put into action by exercising the right of veto. 3. to refuse to consent to.

vex, *v.* to irritate; annoy; provoke. – **vexation**, *n.* – **vexatious**, *adj.*

via /'vaɪə/, *prep.* 1. by way of; by a route that passes through. 2. by means of.

viable, *adj.* 1. capable of living. 2. practicable; workable.

via·duct, *n.* a bridge for carrying a road, railway, etc., over a valley, etc.

vial, *n.* – **phial** (def. 1).

vibes, *n.pl. Colloq.* quality or atmosphere.

victory

vib·rant, *adj.* 1. moving to and fro rapidly; vibrating. 2. full of vigour; powerful.

vib·rate, *v.,* **-brated, -brating.** 1. to move to and fro, as a pendulum; oscillate. 2. to move to and fro or up and down quickly and repeatedly; quiver; tremble. – **vibratory**, *adj.* – **vibration**, *n.* – **vibrator**, *n.*

vib·rato, *n., pl.* **-tos.** *Music.* a pulsating effect produced by rapid small oscillations in pitch about the given note.

vicar, *n.* a clergyman acting as priest of a parish.

vic·arious, *adj.* performed, exercised, received, or suffered in place of another.

vice[1], *n.* 1. an immoral or evil habit or practice. 2. immoral conduct or life.

vice[2], *n.* a device used to hold an object firmly while work is being done upon it.

vice versa, *adv.* conversely; the order being changed (from that of a preceding statement).

vicin·ity, *n., pl.* **-ties.** the region near or about a place.

vicious, *adj.* 1. addicted to or characterised by vice or immorality; depraved; profligate. 2. spiteful or malignant. 3. unpleasantly severe.

vicis·si·tude, *n.* a change or variation occurring in the course of something.

victim, *n.* a sufferer from any destructive, injurious, or adverse action or agency.

vic·tim·ise, *v.,* **-mised, -mising.** 1. to make a victim of. 2. to discipline or punish selectively.

vic·tory, *n., pl.* **-ries.** 1. the ultimate

and decisive superiority in a battle or any contest. 2. any success or successful performance achieved over an adversary or opponent, opposition, difficulties, etc. – **victor**, n. – **victorious**, adj.

video, adj. Television. pertaining to or employed in the display, transmission, or reception of a televised image.

video·tape, n. magnetic tape upon which a video signal is recorded, used for storing a television program or film.

vie, v., **vied, vying.** to compete with another; to contend for superiority.

view, n. 1. a seeing or beholding; an examination by the eye. 2. range of sight or vision. 3. a sight or prospect of some landscape, scene, etc. 4. aim, intention, or purpose. 5. a conception, notion, or idea of a thing; an opinion or theory. –v. 6. to see or behold. 7. to look at, survey, or inspect. 8. to contemplate mentally; consider.

vigil, n. a keeping awake for any purpose during the normal hours of sleep.

vigi·lant, adj. keenly attentive to detect danger; wary. – **vigilance**, n.

vigi·lante /vɪdʒəˈlænti/, n. Chiefly U.S. a member of an unauthorised body organised for the maintenance of order.

vigour, n. 1. active strength, energy or force, as of body or mind. 2. active or effective force. – **vigorous**, adj.

vile, adj., **viler, vilest.** 1. wretchedly bad. 2. repulsive or disgusting. 3. of mean or low condition, as a person.

vilify, v., **-fied, -fying.** to speak evil of; defame; traduce.

village, n. a small community in a country district.

villain, n. a wicked person; scoundrel. – **villainous**, adj. – **villainy**, n.

vim, n. Colloq. force; energy; vigour in action.

vin·di·cate, v., **-cated, -cating.** 1. to clear, as from a charge, imputation, suspicion, or the like. 2. to uphold or justify by argument or evidence. – **vindicatory**, adj.

vin·dic·tive, adj. disposed or inclined to revenge; revengeful.

vine, n. a long, slender stem that trails or creeps on the ground or climbs by winding itself about a support. 2. a plant bearing such stems.

vin·egar, n. a sour acidic liquid used as a condiment, preservative, etc.

vine·yard, n. a plantation of grapevines for wine-making, etc.

vin·tage, n. 1. the wine from a particular harvest or crop. 2. an exceptionally fine wine from the crop of a good year. –adj. 3. of or pertaining to wine or wine-making. 4. (of wines) designated and sold as the produce of a specified year. 5. of high quality; exceptionally fine. 6. old-fashioned; out of date.

vint·ner, n. a wine merchant.

vinyl, n. a type of plastic.

viol, n. a musical instrument similar to the violin.

viola, n. a four-stringed musical instrument slightly larger than the violin.

vio·late, v., **-lated, -lating.** 1. to break, infringe, or transgress (a law, promise, instructions, etc.). 2. to deal with or treat in a violent or irreverent way.

vio·lent, adj. 1. acting with or char-

violent

acterised by uncontrolled, strong, rough force. **2.** intense in force, effect, etc.; severe. – **violence,** *n.*

violet, *n.* **1.** a small plant with purple, blue, yellow, white, or variegated flowers. **2.** a bluish purple colour.

violin, *n.* a bowed four-stringed instrument held nearly horizontal by the player's arm, with the lower part supported against the shoulder.

viper, *n.* a venomous snake.

virago /vəˈrɑːgoʊ/, *n., pl.* **-goes, -gos.** a violent or ill-tempered scolding woman.

viral, *adj.* pertaining to or caused by a virus.

virgin, *n.* **1.** a person, esp. a young woman, who has had no sexual intercourse. *–adj.* **2.** being a virgin. **3.** pure; unsullied. **4.** untouched or unused.

vir·ginal[1], *adj.* of, pertaining to, characteristic of, or befitting a virgin.

vir·ginal[2], *n.* a small harpsichord of rectangular shape.

virile, *adj.* **1.** of, pertaining to, or characteristic of a man. **2.** having masculine vigour, etc. **3.** sexually able. – **virility,** *n.*

virology, *n.* the study of viruses and the diseases caused by them.

virtual, *adj.* being such in power, force, or effect, although not actually or expressly such.

virtue, *n.* **1.** moral excellence or goodness. **2.** a particular moral excellence, as justice, prudence, etc. **3.** an excellence, merit, or good quality. **4.** **by** or **in virtue of,** by reason of; because of.

vir·tu·oso, *n., pl.* **-sos, -si.** one who

580

visionary

has special knowledge or skill in any field, as in music. – **virtuosity,** *n.*

vir·tu·ous, *adj.* morally excellent or good.

viru·lent, *adj.* **1.** actively poisonous, malignant, or deadly. **2.** *Med.* highly infective.

virus, *n.* **1.** an infective agent smaller than a common micro-organism, and requiring living cells for multiplication. **2.** any disease caused by a virus.

visa /ˈviːzə/, *n.* an endorsement made on a passport, permitting passage to the country making the endorsement.

visage, *n.* the face.

viscid, *adj.* sticky or adhesive.

vis·count /ˈvaɪkaʊnt/, *n.* a nobleman next below an earl or count and next above a baron.

viscous, *adj.* sticky, adhesive, thick, or glutinous. – **viscosity,** *n.*

visi·bil·ity, *n., pl.* **-ties. 1.** the state or fact of being visible. **2.** *Meteorol.* visual range.

vis·ible, *adj.* capable of being seen; perceptible by the eye.

vision, *n.* **1.** the power, faculty, or sense of sight. **2.** the act or power of perceiving what is not actually present to the eye. **3.** a mental view or image of what is not actually present or commonly accepted to exist in place or time. **4.** something perceived; an object of sight.

vision·ary, *adj., n., pl.* **-ries.** *–adj.* **1.** given to or characterised by radical, often unpractical ideas, views, or schemes. **2.** given to or concerned with seeing visions. *–n.* **3.** one who sees visions. **4.** one who is given to visionary ideas.

visit, v. 1. to go to see (a person, place, etc.) in the way of friendship, ceremony, duty, business, curiosity, or the like. 2. (in general) to come or go to. 3. to come upon or assail. –n. 4. an act of visiting. – **visitor**, n.

visi·tation, n. 1. a visit, esp. for an official inspection or examination. 2. an affliction or punishment from God.

visor, n. 1. the movable front parts of a helmet, esp. the uppermost part which protects the eyes. 2. a small shield in a car which may be swung down to protect a driver's eyes from glare.

vista, n. a view or prospect.

visual, adj. 1. of or pertaining to sight. 2. perceptible by the sight; visible.

visua·lise, v., -lised, -lising. to form a mental image of.

vital, adj. 1. of or pertaining to life. 2. having remarkable energy, enthusiasm, vivacity. 3. necessary to life, existence, continuance, or well-being; indispensable. 4. of critical importance.

vitality, n., pl. -ties. exuberant physical vigour; energy; enthusiastic vivacity.

vita·min, n. any of a group of food factors essential in small quantities to maintain life.

viti·ate /'vɪʃieɪt/, v., -ated, -ating. 1. to impair the quality of; mar. 2. to contaminate; spoil. 3. to make legally defective or invalid.

viti·culture, n. the culture or cultivation of the grapevine.

vit·reous, adj. of the nature of glass; resembling glass.

vit·rify, v., -fied, -fying. to make or become vitreous.

vit·riol, n. 1. sulphuric acid. 2. something highly caustic, or severe in its effects, as criticism. – **vitriolic**, adj.

vitu·perate, v., -rated, -rating. 1. to criticise abusively. 2. to address abusive language to.

viva·cious, adj. lively, animated, or sprightly. – **vivacity**, n.

vivid, adj. 1. strikingly bright, as colour, light, objects, etc. 2. lively or intense, as feelings, etc. 3. clearly perceptible to the eye or mind.

vivify, v., -fied, -fying. to enliven; render lively or animated; brighten.

vivi·parous, adj. Zool. bringing forth living young (rather than eggs), as most mammals and some reptiles and fishes.

vivi·sect, v. to dissect the living body of. – **vivisection**, n.

vixen, n. a female fox.

voca·bulary, n., pl. -ries. 1. the stock of words used by a people, or by a particular class or person. 2. a glossary, dictionary, or lexicon.

vocal, adj. 1. of or pertaining to the voice; uttered with the voice; oral. 2. rendered by or intended for singing, as music.

vocal cords, n.pl. folds of mucous membrane projecting into the cavity of the larynx, vibration of which produces vocal sound.

voca·lise, v., -lised, -lising. to make vocal; utter or articulate; sing.

voca·list, n. a singer.

vo·cation, n. a particular occupation, business, profession; calling. – **vocational**, adj.

voci·fer·ous, *adj.* crying out noisily; clamorous.

vodka, *n.* an alcoholic drink of Russian origin.

vogue, *n.* the fashion, as at a particular time.

voice, *n., v.,* **voiced, voicing.** –*n.* 1. the sound or sounds uttered through the mouth of living creatures, esp. of human beings. 2. such sounds considered with reference to their character or quality. 3. expressed opinion or choice. 4. the right to express an opinion or choice; vote. 5. *Phonet.* the sound produced by vibration of the vocal cords. 6. *Gram.* a verb form showing the relationship between the action expressed by the verb and the subject, as the passive and active voices. –*v.* 7. to give voice, utterance, or expression to; express; declare.

void, *adj.* 1. *Law.* without legal force or effect. 2. useless; ineffectual; vain. 3. completely empty; devoid; destitute (*of*). –*n.* 4. an empty space. 5. a place without the usual or desired occupant. 6. emptiness; vacancy. –*v.* 7. to make void or of no effect; invalidate; nullify. 8. to empty or discharge (contents).

vola·tile, *adj.* 1. evaporating rapidly. 2. light and changeable of mind; frivolous; flighty.

vol·cano, *n., pl.* **-noes, -nos.** an opening in the earth's crust through which molten rock (lava), steam, ashes, etc., are expelled. – **volcanic**, *adj.*

vole, *n.* a type of rodent.

vol·ition, *n.* the act of willing; exercise of choice to determine action.

volley, *n., pl.* **-leys,** *v.,* **-leyed, -leying.** *n.* 1. the discharge of a number of missiles or firearms simultaneously. 2. a burst or outpouring of many things at once or in quick succession. 3. *Tennis, etc.* a. a return of the ball before it touches the ground. b. a succession of such returns. –*v.* 4. to discharge in or as in a volley. 5. *Tennis, Soccer, etc.* to return, kick, etc., (the ball) before it strikes the ground.

volley·ball, *n.* a game in which a large ball is struck from side to side over a high net with the hands or arms.

volt, *n.* the derived SI unit of electric potential. *Symbol:* V

vol·tage, *n.* electromotive force or potential expressed in volts.

vol·uble, *adj.* characterised by a ready and continuous flow of words.

volume, *n.* 1. a collection of written or printed sheets bound together and constituting a book. 2. the size, measure, or amount of anything in 3 dimensions; the SI unit of volume is the cubic metre (m³). 3. a mass or quantity, esp. a large quantity, of anything. 4. loudness or softness.

volu·metric, *adj.* denoting, pertaining to, or depending upon measurement by volume. Also, **volumetrical**.

vol·umi·nous, *adj.* of ample size, extent, or fullness.

vol·un·tary, *adj., n., pl.* **-taries.** –*adj.* 1. done, made, brought about, undertaken, etc., of one's own accord or by free choice. 2. *Physiol.* subject to or controlled by the will. –*n.* 3. a piece of music, esp. organ

voluntary

music played before or after a church service.

vol·un·teer, n. 1. one who enters into any service of his own free will. –v. 2. to offer oneself for some service or undertaking.

vol·up·tuary, n., pl. -aries. one given up to luxurious or sensuous pleasures.

vol·up·tuous, adj. 1. full of, characterised by, directed towards, or ministering to pleasure or luxurious or sensuous enjoyment. 2. sensuously pleasing. 3. (of the female figure) attractively curved.

vomit, v. 1. to bring up (the contents of the stomach) by the mouth; spew. 2. to eject or be ejected with force or violence.

voodoo, n. a class of mysterious rites or practices, of the nature of sorcery or witchcraft.

voracious, adj. devouring or craving food in large quantities.

vortex, n., pl. -texes, -tices. a whirling movement or mass of water, as a whirlpool.

votary, n., pl. -ries. one who is bound by a vow, esp. to a religious life.

vote, n., v., voted, voting. –n. 1. a formal expression of will, wish, or choice in some matter, signified by voice, by ballot, etc. 2. the right to such expression; suffrage. 3. an expression of feeling, as approval, or the like. –v. 4. to express or signify choice in a matter undergoing decision, as by a voice, ballot, or otherwise. 5. to enact, establish, or determine by vote; bring or put (in, out, down, etc.) by vote.

votive, adj. offered, given, dedicated, etc., in accordance with a vow.

vouch, v. 1. to answer (for) as being true, certain, reliable, justly asserted, etc. 2. to give one's own assurance, as surety or sponsor (for).

vulva

voucher, n. 1. a document, receipt, stamp, or the like, which proves the truth of a claimed expenditure. 2. a ticket used as a substitute for cash.

vouchsafe, v., -safed, -safing. to grant or give, by favour or grace.

vow, n. 1. a solemn promise, pledge, or personal engagement. –v. 2. to promise by a vow, as to God or a saint. 3. to pledge oneself to do, make, give, observe, etc.

vowel, n. 1. Phonet. a voiced speech sound during the articulation of which air from the lungs is free to pass out through the middle of the mouth without causing undue friction. 2. a letter which usu. represents a vowel, as in English a, e, i, o and u, and sometimes y.

voyage, v., -aged, -aging, n. (to make or take) a passage, or course of travel, by sea or water.

voyeur, n. one who attains sexual gratification by looking at sexual objects or situations. – **voyeurism**, n. – **voyeuristic**, adj.

vulcanology, n. the study of volcanoes and volcanic phenomena.

vulgar, adj. 1. marked by ignorance of or lack of good breeding or taste. 2. crude; coarse; unrefined. 3. ostentatious; unsubtle. 4. common or ordinary. – **vulgarity**, n.

vulnerable, adj. susceptible to being hurt physically or emotionally. – **vulnerability**, n.

vulture, n. a large, carrion-eating bird related to the eagle.

vulva, n., pl. -vae, -vas. the external female genitalia.

583

Ww

W, w, *n., pl.* **W's** or **Ws**, **w's** or **ws**. the 23rd letter of the English alphabet.

wad, *n.* **1.** a small mass or lump of anything soft. **2.** a roll or bundle, esp. of banknotes.

wad·ding, *n.* any fibrous or soft material for padding, etc.

wad·dle, *v.,* **-dled, -dling.** to walk with short steps and swaying or rocking from side to side, as a duck.

wad·dy, *n., pl.* **-dies.** an Aboriginal heavy wooden war club.

wade, *v.,* **waded, wading.** to walk through any substance, as water, snow, sand, etc., that impedes free motion.

wa·fer, *n.* **1.** a thin, crisp cake or biscuit. **2.** any of various other thin, flat cakes, sheets, or the like.

waf·fle[1], *n.* a kind of batter cake.

waf·fle[2], *v.,* **-fled, -fling,** *n.* —*v. Colloq.* **1.** to speak or write vaguely, pointlessly, and at considerable length. —*n.* **2.** verbose nonsense.

waft, *v.* **1.** to bear or carry through the air or over water. **2.** to bear or convey lightly as if in flight. **3.** to float or be carried, esp. through the air.

wag[1], *v.,* **wagged, wagging,** *n.* —*v.* **1.** to move in different directions, rapidly and repeatedly. **2.** *Colloq.* to be absent from (school, etc.) without permission. —*n.* **3.** the act of wagging.

wag[2], *n.* a humorous person; joker.

wage, *n., v.,* **waged, waging.** —*n.* **1.** (*oft. pl.*) that which is paid for work or services; hire; pay. —*v.* **2.** to carry on (a battle, war, conflict, etc.).

wa·ger, *n.* **1.** something staked or hazarded on an uncertain event; bet. —*v.* **2.** to hazard (something) on the issue of a contest or any uncertain event or matter; stake; bet.

wag·gle, *v.,* **-gled, -gling,** *n.* —*v.* **1.** to wag with short, quick movements. —*n.* **2.** a waggling motion.

wag·on, *n.* any of various kinds of four-wheeled vehicles, esp. one designed for the transport of heavy loads, delivery, etc.

wag·tail, *n.* a small bird with a long, narrow tail.

waif, *n.* a person without home or friends, esp. a child.

wail, *v.* **1.** to utter a prolonged, inarticulate, mournful cry. —*n.* **2.** a wailing cry, as of grief, pain, etc.

wain·scot, *n.* wooden panels serving to line the walls of a room, etc. **– wainscoting,** *n.*

waist, *n.* the part of the human body between the ribs and the hips.

waist·coat, *n.* a close-fitting, sleeveless garment which reaches to the waist.

wait, *v.* **1.** to stay or rest in expectation (*for, till,* or *until*). **2. wait on** or **upon, a.** to perform the duties of an attendant or servant to. **b.** to supply the wants of (a person) at table. **3.** to continue stationary or inactive in expectation of; await. —*n.* **4.** an act, period or interval of waiting; delay.

wait·er, *n.* a man who serves cus-

waiter

tomers at table, as in a restaurant, etc. – **waitress**, *n. fem.*

waive, *v.*, **waived**, **waiving**. to forbear to insist on; relinquish; forgo.

waiver, *n.* (in law) an intentional relinquishment of some right, interest, or the like.

wake[1], *v.*, **woke**, **woken**, **waking**. –*v.* **1.** Also, **waken**. to rouse or become roused from sleep; awake (*up*). –*n.* **2.** a watching, or a watch kept, esp. for some solemn or ceremonial purpose. **3.** a watch, esp. at night, near the body of a dead person before burial, often accompanied by drinking and feasting.

wake[2], *n.* the track left by a ship or other object moving in the water.

walk, *v.* **1.** to go or travel by steps, or by advancing the feet in turn. **2.** to proceed through, over, or upon by walking. **3.** to lead, drive, or ride at a walk, as an animal. –*n.* **4.** the act or course of going on foot. **5.** a spell of walking for exercise or pleasure. **6.** a gait or pace. **7.** a department or branch of activity.

walk-about, *n.* a period of wandering as a nomad, esp. by Aborigines.

walkie-talkie, *n.* a lightweight combined radio transmitter and receiver.

walk-over, *n. Colloq.* an unopposed or easy victory.

wall, *n.* **1.** an upright structure of stone, brick, etc., serving for enclosure, division, support, protection, etc. **2.** anything which resembles or suggests a wall. –*v.* **3.** to enclose, shut off, divide, protect, etc., with or as with a wall (*in* or *off*).

wal·la·by, *n.*, *pl.* **-bies**, (*esp. collectively*) **-by**. any of various animals,

wane

many resembling small kangaroos, others more possum-like in size and appearance.

walla·roo, *n.* a stocky, coarse-haired kangaroo.

wallet, *n.* a small, booklike folding case for carrying papers, paper money, etc., in the pocket.

wall-eyed /ˈwɔlaɪd/, *adj.* having eyes with little or no colour or with an abnormal amount of white showing.

wallop, *v. Colloq.* to beat soundly; thrash.

wallow, *v.* **1.** to roll the body about, or lie, in water, snow, mud, dust, or the like. **2.** to indulge oneself (*in*).

wall·paper, *n.* coloured or patterned paper for covering the walls or ceilings of rooms, etc.

walnut, *n.* (a tree bearing) an edible nut.

walrus, *n.*, *pl.* **-ruses**, (*esp. collectively*) **-rus**. either of 2 large marine mammals having flippers, a pair of large tusks, and a thick, tough skin.

waltz, *n.* **1.** a ballroom dance. –*v.* **2.** to dance a waltz.

wan, *adj.*, **wanner**, **wannest**. of an unnatural or sickly pallor; pallid.

wand, *n.* a slender stick or rod, esp. one supposedly used for working magic.

wander, *v.* **1.** to ramble without any certain course or object in view; roam. **2.** to stray from a path, companions, etc.

wane, *v.*, **waned**, **waning**. –*v.* **1.** (of the moon) to decrease periodically in the extent of its illuminated portion after the full moon (opposed to *wax*). **2.** to decline in

wane

power, importance, prosperity, etc. –*n.* **3.** gradual decline.

wangle, *v.*, **-gled, -gling**. *Colloq.* to bring about or obtain by indirect or insidious methods.

want, *v.* **1.** to feel a need or a desire for; wish for. **2.** to be without or be deficient in. **3.** to wish; like; feel inclined (*to*). **4.** to be deficient by the absence of some part or thing: *to want for money.* **5.** to be lacking or absent, as a part or thing necessary to completeness. –*n.* **6.** something wanted or needed; a necessity. **7. in want**, poor or destitute.

wanton, *adj.* **1.** done maliciously or unjustifiably. **2.** reckless or disregardful of right, justice, humanity, etc. **3.** sexually unrestrained; lascivious.

war, *n., v.*, **warred, warring.** –*n.* **1.** a conflict carried on by force of arms, as between nations or between parties within a nation. **2.** active hostility or contention; conflict; contest. –*v.* **3.** to make or carry on war; fight.

warble, *v.*, **-bled, -bling.** to sing with trills, quavers, or melodic embellishments.

ward, *n.* **1.** an administrative division or district of a municipality, city or town. **2.** a division of a hospital or prison. **3.** *Law.* a person, esp. a minor, who has been legally placed under the care or control of a legal guardian. –*v.* **4.** to avert, repel, or turn aside, as danger, an attack, assailant, etc. (*off*).

warden, *n.* **1.** one charged with the care or custody of something; keeper. **2.** the head of certain colleges, hospitals, youth hostels, etc.

warp

warder, *n.* an official having charge of prisoners in a gaol; prison officer.

wardrobe, *n.* **1.** a stock of clothes or costumes. **2.** a piece of furniture for holding clothes.

wardship, *n.* tutelage.

ware, *n.* (*usu. pl.*) articles of merchandise or manufacture, or goods.

warehouse, *n.* a storehouse for wares or goods.

warfare, *n.* **1.** the act of waging war. **2.** armed conflict.

warlike, *adj.* soldierly, hostile, military.

warlock, *n.* one who practises magic arts by the aid of the devil; a sorcerer or wizard.

warm, *adj.* **1.** having or communicating a moderate degree of heat. **2.** (of colour) suggesting warmth; inclining towards red or orange, as yellow (rather than towards green or blue). **3.** having or showing lively feelings, passions, sympathies, etc. –*v.* **4.** to make or become warm; heat (*up*). **5.** to excite ardour, enthusiasm, or animation in. **6.** to inspire with kindly feeling. **7. warm up**, to prepare for a sporting event, musical or theatrical performance, etc. – **warmth**, *n.*

warn, *v.* **1.** to give notice to (a person, etc.) of danger, possible harm, etc. **2.** to admonish or exhort as to action or conduct – **warning**, *n.*

warp, *v.* **1.** to bend or become bent out of shape, esp. from a straight or flat form. **2.** to distort from the truth, fact, true meaning, etc.; bias or pervert. **3.** to turn or change from the natural or proper course, state, etc. –*n.* **4.** a bend or twist in something, as in wood that has dried unevenly. **5.** a mental twist or bias. **6.** yarns placed lengthwise in

warp

the loom, across the weft or woof, and interlaced.

war·rant, *n.* 1. authorisation, sanction, or justification. 2. that which serves to give reliable or formal assurance of something; guarantee. 3. a writing or document certifying or authorising something. –*v.* 4. to give authority to; authorise. 5. to afford warrant or sanction for, or justify. 6. to give a formal assurance, or a guarantee or promise, to or for; guarantee.

war·ran·ty, *n., pl.* **-ties.** 1. the act of warranting; warrant; assurance. 2. *Law.* an engagement, express or implied, in assurance of some particular in connection with a contract, as of sale.

warren, *n.* a place where rabbits breed or abound.

war·rior, *n.* a man engaged or experienced in warfare; soldier.

wart, *n.* 1. a small, usu. hard, abnormal elevation on the skin, caused by a virus. 2. a small protuberance.

wary, *adj.,* **warier, wariest.** watchful, or on the alert; cautious; careful.

was, *v.* first and 3rd person singular past tense indicative of **be**.

wash, *v.* 1. to apply water or some other liquid to for the purpose of cleansing. 2. to flow over or against. 3. to carry or bring, (as) with water or any liquid: *The tide washed up seaweed.* 4. to wear as water does (*out* or *away*). 5. *Colloq.* to stand being put to the proof; bear investigation. –*n.* 6. the act of washing with water or other liquid. 7. a quantity of clothes, etc., washed, or to be washed, at one time. 8. a liquid with which something is washed, wetted, coloured,

watch

etc. 9. the flow, sweep, dash, or breaking of water. 10. a broad, thin layer of colour, as in watercolour painting.

washer, *n.* 1. a flat ring used to give tightness to a joint, to prevent leakage, and to distribute pressure. 2. Also, **facecloth, flannel, washrag.** a small piece of towelling for washing the face or body.

wasp, *n.* a stinging insect.

wasp·ish, *adj.* quick to resent a trifling affront or injury; snappish.

wast·age, *n.* loss by use, wear, decay, wastefulness, etc.

waste, *v.,* **wasted, wasting,** *n., adj.* –*v.* 1. to consume, spend, or employ uselessly or without adequate return; squander. 2. to fail to use. 3. to wear down or reduce, esp. in health or strength. 4. to destroy or devastate. 5. to become physically deteriorated (*away*). 6. to diminish gradually, as wealth, power, etc. (*away*). –*n.* 7. useless consumption or expenditure, or use without adequate return. 8. neglect, instead of use. 9. gradual destruction or decay. 10. a desolate stretch of land. 11. anything left over, as excess materials, etc. –*adj.* 12. not used or in use. 13. (of land, etc.) uninhabited and wild; desolate. 14. left over or superfluous.

wast·rel, *n.* a wasteful person; spendthrift.

watch, *v.* 1. to be on the lookout, look attentively, or be closely observant. 2. to look or wait attentively and expectantly (*for*). 3. to view attentively or with interest. 4. to guard for protection or safekeeping. –*n.* 5. close, constant observation for the purpose of seeking or discovering something.

587

watch

6. a lookout, as for something expected. 7. vigilant guard, as for protection, restraint, etc. 8. a small, portable timepiece, usu. worn on the wrist.

watch·ful, *adj.* vigilant or alert; closely observant.

water, *n.* 1. the liquid which in a more or less impure state constitutes rain, oceans, lakes, rivers, etc., and which in a pure state is a transparent, odourless, tasteless compound of hydrogen and oxygen, H_2O. 2. (*pl.*) a body of water. 3. any liquid or watery organic secretion. –*v.* 4. to sprinkle, moisten, or drench with water. 5. to supply (animals) with water for drinking. 6. to dilute or adulterate (as) with water. 7. to produce a wavy lustrous pattern, marking, or finish on (fabrics, metals, etc.). 8. to fill with or secrete water or liquid, as the eyes, or as the mouth at the sight or thought of tempting food. – **watery**, *adj.*

water·bed, *n.* a heavy, durable, plastic bag filled with water, used as a mattress.

water·buffalo, *n.* a large buffalo widely used as a draught animal. Also, **water-ox**.

water·closet, *n.* a receptacle in which human excrement is flushed down a drain by water from a cistern.

water·colour, *n.* (a painting executed in) pigments dispersed in water-soluble gum.

water·course, *n.* (the bed of) a stream of water, as a river or brook.

water·cress, *n.* a plant, usu. growing in clear, running water, and bearing pungent leaves used in salads, etc.

wave

water·fall, *n.* a steep fall or flow of water from a height; cascade.

water·front, *n.* 1. land abutting on a body of water. 2. workers in industries using wharf facilities.

water·log, *v.*, **-logged**, **-logging**. to soak or saturate with water.

water·mark, *n.* 1. a mark indicating the height to which water rises or has risen, as in a river, etc. 2. a figure or design impressed in the fabric in the manufacture of paper and visible when the paper is held to the light.

water·melon, *n.* a large melon with pink, juicy flesh.

water·polo, *n.* a water game played by 2 teams of swimmers.

water·shed, *n.* the ridge or crest line dividing 2 drainage areas.

water·ski, *n.*, *v.*, **-ski'd** or **-skied**, **-skiing**. –*n.* 1. a type of ski used for gliding over water. –*v.* 2. to glide over water on water-skis by grasping a rope towed by a speedboat.

water·table, *n.* the upper limit of underground water-saturated layers of rock.

watt, *n.* the derived SI unit of power, defined as one joule per second. Symbol: W

wattle, *n.* 1. (*pl.* or *sing.*) rods or stakes interwoven with twigs or branches of trees, used for making fences, walls, roofs, etc. 2. any of the very numerous Aust. acacias, with spikes or globular heads of yellow or cream flowers. 3. a fleshy lobe hanging down from the throat or chin.

wattle and daub, *n.* wattles plastered with mud or clay and used as a building material.

wave, *n.*, *v.*, **waved**, **waving**. –*n.* 1.

wave

wave liquid rising as a ridge or swell, as water in the sea. **2.** a swell, surge, or rush, as of feeling, excitement, prosperity, etc. **3.** a widespread movement, feeling, opinion, tendency, etc. **4.** *Physics.* a progressive vibrational disturbance propagated through a medium, as air, without corresponding progress or advance of the parts or particles themselves, as in the transmission of sound or electromagnetic energy. –v. **5.** to (cause to) move loosely to and fro or up and down. **6.** to undulate. – **wavy,** *adj.*

wave·length, *n. Physics.* the length of each cycle or assail of a wave (def. 4).

waver, *v.* **1.** to sway to and fro; flutter. **2.** to feel or show doubt or indecision; vacillate.

wax¹, *n.* **1.** a solid, non-greasy, insoluble substance which has a low melting or softening point. **2.** a substance secreted by certain insects and plants. **3.** something suggesting wax as being readily moulded, worked upon, handled, managed, etc. –v. **4.** to rub, smear, stiffen, polish, etc., with wax.

wax², *v.,* **waxed;** *or (Poetic)* **waxen; waxing. 1.** to increase in extent, quantity, intensity, power, etc.. **2.** (of the moon) to increase in the extent of its illuminated portion before the full moon (opposed to *wane*). **3.** to grow or become (as stated): *to wax pale at the thought.*

wax·work, *n.* figures, ornaments, etc., made of wax.

way, *n.* **1.** manner, mode, or fashion. **2.** a course, plan, or means for attaining an end. **3.** respect or particular: *defective in several ways.* **4.** direction: *Look this way.* **5.** passage or progress on a course. **6.** a path or course leading from one place to another. **7.** (*oft. pl.*) a habit or custom: *his funny little ways.* **8.** course of life, action, or experience. **9. by the way,** incidentally; in the course of one's remarks. **10. give way to, a.** to yield to. **b.** to lose control of (one's emotions, etc.). **11. in the way,** forming an obstruction or hindrance. **12. make way for, a.** to allow to pass. **b.** to give up or retire in favour of. **13. under way,** in motion or moving along.

way·farer, *n.* a traveller.

waylay, *v.,* **-laid, -laying.** to fall upon or assail from ambush, as in order to rob, seize, or slay.

way·side, *n.* the border or edge of the road or highway.

way·ward, *adj.* turned or turning away from what is right or proper; perverse.

we, *pron., pl.; poss.* **our** *or* **ours;** *obj. us.* nominative plural of 'I'.

weak, *adj.* **1.** liable to yield, break, or collapse under pressure; fragile; frail. **2.** deficient in bodily strength; feeble; infirm. **3.** lacking in force, potency, or efficacy. **4.** deficient in amount, volume, loudness, intensity, etc.; faint; slight. – **weaken,** *v.*

weak·ling, *n.* a weak or feeble creature (physically or morally).

weal, *n.* **1.** a small burning or itching swelling on the skin. **2.** a welt (def. 1).

wealth, *n.* **1.** a great store of valuable possessions, property, or riches. **2.** a rich abundance or profusion of anything. – **wealthy,** *adj.*

wean, *v.* to accustom (a child or animal) to food other than its mother's milk.

589

weapon

weapon, *n.* any instrument for use in attack or defence in fighting.

wear, *v.,* wore, worn, wearing, *n.* –*v.* **1.** to carry or have on the body or about the person as a covering, equipment, ornament, or the like. **2.** to bear or have in the aspect or appearance. **3.** to cause or undergo gradual impairment, reduction, etc., by or from wear, use or attrition (*away, down, out,* or *off*). **4.** to make (a hole, channel, way, etc.) by such action. **5.** to hold out or last under wear, use, or any continued strain. –*n.* **6.** gradual impairment, wasting, diminution, etc., as from use.

weari·some, *adj.* tedious.

weary, *adj.,* -rier, -riest, *v.,* -ried, -rying. –*adj.* **1.** exhausted physically or mentally by labour, exertion, strain, etc.; fatigued; tired. **2.** impatient or dissatisfied at excess or overlong continuance (*of*). –*v.* **3.** to make or become weary; fatigue or tire. **4.** to make or grow impatient or dissatisfied at having too much (*of*) something. – **weariness,** *n.*

weasel, *n.* a small carnivore having a long, slender body, and feeding largely on small rodents.

weather, *n.* **1.** the state of the atmosphere with respect to wind, temperature, cloudiness, moisture, pressure, etc. –*v.* **2.** to bear up against and come safely through (a storm, danger, trouble, etc.). **3.** to undergo change, as discolouration or disintegration, as the result of exposure to atmospheric conditions.

weather·board, *n.* one of a series of thin boards nailed on an outside wall or a roof to form a protective covering.

weather·vane, *n.* a vane for indicating the direction of the wind.

weed

weave, *v.,* wove or (*esp.* for def. 2) weaved; woven or wove; weaving; *n.* –*v.* **1.** to interlace (threads, cloth) so as to form a fabric or texture. **2.** to follow in a winding course; to move from side to side. –*n.* **3.** a manner of interlacing yarns.

web, *n.* **1.** something formed as by weaving or interweaving. **2.** a thin silken fabric spun by spiders, and also by the larvae of some insects. **3.** a tangled intricate state of circumstances, events, etc. **4.** *Zool.* a membrane which connects the digits of some animals and birds.

wed, *v.,* wedded or wed, wedding. **1.** to bind oneself to (a person) in marriage; take for husband or wife. **2.** to unite (a couple) or (join (one person to another) in marriage or wedlock; marry.

wed·ding, *n.* the act or ceremony of marrying; marriage.

wedge, *n., v.,* wedged, wedging. –*n.* **1.** a device consisting of a piece of hard material with 2 principal faces meeting in a sharply acute angle. **2.** a piece of anything of like shape. **3.** something that serves to part, divide, etc. –*v.* **4.** to pack or fix tightly by driving in a wedge or wedges. **5.** to thrust, drive, or fix (in, between, etc.) like a wedge.

wed·lock, *n.* the state of marriage; matrimony.

wee, *adj.* little; very small.

weed, *n.* **1.** a plant growing wild, esp. where unwanted. **2.** a thin or weakly person, esp. one regarded as stupid or infantile. –*v.* **3.** to free

weed

from weeds. 4. to rid of what is undesirable or superfluous (*out*).

week, *n.* 1. a period of 7 successive days. 2. the working portion of this period. 3. 7 days after a specified day: *Tuesday week*.

week-end, *n.* the end of the working week, esp. the period from Friday night or Saturday to Monday, as a time for recreation.

weekly, *adj., adv., n.* -**lies**. –*adj.* 1. pertaining to a week, or to each week. 2. done, happening, appearing, etc., once a week, or every week. 3. once a week. 4. by the week. –*n.* 5. a periodical appearing once a week.

weep, *v.*, **wept**, **weeping**, *n.* –*v.* 1. to shed (tears) as from sorrow or any overpowering emotion; cry. 2. to exude water or liquid, as a plant stem, a sore, etc.

weevil, *n.* a type of beetle destructive to nuts, grain, fruit, etc.

weft, *n.* 1. yarns which run from selvage to selvage in a loom, interlacing with the warp; woof. 2. a woven piece.

weigh, *v.* 1. to find the weight of by means of a balance, etc. 2. to bear (*down*) by weight, heaviness, oppression, etc. 3. to consider carefully in order to reach an opinion, decision, or choice. 4. to raise or lift (now chiefly in the phrase *to weigh anchor*). 5. to have weight or heaviness.

weight, *n.* 1. amount of heaviness. 2. a piece of metal of a certain mass, for using on a balance or scale. 3. any heavy mass or object, esp. an object used because of its heaviness. 4. importance, moment, consequence, or effective influence. 5. something oppressive. –*v.* 6. to add weight to; load with additional weight.

weight-lifting, *n.* the sport of lifting steel bars with disc-shaped weights attached.

weighty, *adj.*, -**tier**, -**tiest**. having considerable weight; heavy.

weir, *n.* a dam in a river or stream.

weird, *adj.* 1. involving or suggesting the supernatural; unearthly or uncanny. 2. *Colloq.* startlingly or extraordinarily singular, odd, or queer.

wel·come, *n., v.*, -**comed**, -**coming**, *adj.* –*n.* 1. a kindly greeting or reception. –*v.* 2. to greet the coming of (a person, etc.) with pleasure or kindly courtesy. –*adj.* 3. gladly received.

weld, *v.* to unite or fuse (pieces of metal, etc.), esp. with the use of heat.

wel·fare, *n.* well-being.

well[1], *adv., adj., compar.* **better**, *super.* **best.** –*adv.* 1. in a satisfactory, favourable, or advantageous manner; fortunately or happily. 2. in a good or proper manner. 3. thoroughly or soundly. 4. easily; clearly. 5. to a considerable extent or degree. 6. **as well**, in addition. 7. **as well as**, in addition to; no less than. 8. **very well**, with certainty; undeniably. 9. a. (a phrase used to indicate consent, often with reluctance). b. (*ironic*) satisfactory; pleasing. –*adj.* 9. in good health. 10. satisfactory or good.

well[2], *n.* 1. a hole drilled into the earth for the production of water, petroleum, natural gas, etc. 2. a spring or natural source of water. –*v.* 3. to rise, spring, or gush, as water, from the earth (*up*, *out*, or *forth*).

well-being

well-being, *n.* good or satisfactory condition of existence; welfare.

well-heeled, *adj. Colloq.* wealthy; prosperous.

wel·ling·ton boot, *n.* a waterproof knee-high boot; gumboot.

well-off, *adj.* in good or easy circumstances as to money or means; moderately rich.

well-to-do, *adj.* having a sufficiency of means for comfortable living; well-off or prosperous.

welsh, *v. Colloq.* to cheat by evading payment, esp. of a gambling debt (*on*).

welt, *n.* 1. a ridge made on the surface of the body, as from the stroke of a stick or whip. 2. a strengthening or ornamental finish along a seam, the edge of a garment, etc.

welter, *n.* 1. a rolling or tumbling about. 2. commotion, turmoil, or chaos.

wench, *n.* 1. a girl, or young woman. 2. a rustic or working girl.

wend, *v.* to direct or pursue (one's way, etc.).

wept, *v.* past tense and past participle of **weep**.

were, *v.* past tense indicative plural and subjunctive of **be**.

were·wolf /'wɪəwʊlf, 'wɜ-, 'wɛə-/, *n., pl.* **-wolves.** (in old superstition) a human being turned into a wolf.

west, *n.* 1. a cardinal point of the compass corresponding to the point where the sun is seen to set. –*adj.* 2. directed or proceeding towards the west. 3. (of wind) coming from the west. –*adv.* 4. in the direction of the sunset; towards or in the west. – **westerly**, *adj., n.*

west·ern, *adj.* 1. lying towards or situated in the west. 2. directed or proceeding towards the west. 3. coming from the west, as a wind. –*n.* 4. (*usu. cap.*) a story or film about frontier life in the American west.

wet, *adj.,* **wetter, wettest,** *n., v.,* **wet** or **wetted, wetting.** –*adj.* 1. covered or soaked, wholly or in part, with water or some other liquid. 2. moist, damp, or not dry. 3. rainy; having a rainy climate. –*n.* 4. that which makes wet, as water or other liquid; moisture. 5. rain. –*v.* 6. to make wet.

wet blanket, *n.* a person or thing that has a discouraging or depressing effect.

wether, *n.* a ram castrated when young.

wet nurse, *n.* a woman hired to suckle another's infant.

wet·suit, *n.* a tight-fitting rubber suit worn by divers, surfers, etc.

whack, *v. Colloq.* to strike with a smart, resounding blow or blows.

whale, *n. Zool.* a large cetacean with fishlike body, modified foreflippers, and a horizontally flattened tail.

whale·bone, *n.* an elastic horny substance found in certain whales, used esp. in corsets.

wham, *v.* whammed, whamming. to hit forcefully.

wharf, *n., pl.* **wharves, wharfs.** a structure built on the shore of, or projecting out into, a harbour, stream, etc., so that vessels may be moored alongside to load or unload or to lie at rest; quay.

what, *interrog. pron.* 1. (asking for the specifying of some impersonal thing): *What is your name?* 2. (enquiring as to nature, character, class, origin, etc.): *What is that*

what

animal? **3.** (enquiring as to worth, usefulness, force, or importance): *What is wealth without health?* **4.** how much?: *What did it cost?* **5.** (an interjection expressing surprise, disbelief, indignation, etc.). –*rel. pron.* **6.** that which: *That is what he says.* **7.** the kind of thing or person that, or such: *The old man is not what he says.* **8.** anything that, or whatever: *Take what you like.* **9.** (in parenthetic clauses) something that: *He came, and what is more, he stayed.* **10.** (used adjectively) that or any ... which; such ... as: *Take what time you need.*

what·ev·er, *pron.* **1.** *indef. rel. pron.* **a.** anything that: *Do whatever you like.* **b.** any amount or measure (of something) that. **c.** no matter what: *Whatever happens, don't go.* –*adj.* **2.** any ... that: *whatever time I have.*

wheat, *n.* the grain of a cereal grass used for food.

whee·dle, *v.*, **-dled**, **-dling.** to endeavour to influence (a person) by smooth or flattering words.

wheel, *n.* **1.** a circular frame or solid disc arranged to turn on an axis, as in vehicles, machinery, etc. **2.** anything resembling or suggesting a wheel. **3.** (*pl.*) moving, propelling, or animating agencies. **4.** (*pl.*) *Colloq.* a motor vehicle. **5.** a wheeling or circular movement. **6.** *Colloq.* a person of considerable importance or influence. –*v.* **7.** to cause to rotate, as on an axis. **8.** to move, roll, or convey on wheels, castors, etc.. **9.** to revolve. **10.** to move in a circular or curving course. **11.** to turn or change in procedure or opinion (*about* or *round*).

wheel·bar·row, *n.* a barrow supported at one end by a wheel on which it is pushed along.

whereas

wheel·chair, *n.* a chair mounted on large wheels, and used by invalids or disabled people.

wheeze, *v.*, **wheezed**, **wheezing.** to breathe with difficulty and with a whistling sound.

whelk, *n.* a large spiral-shelled marine gastropod.

whelp, *n.* the young of the dog, or of the wolf, bear, lion, tiger, seal, etc.

when, *adv.* **1.** at what time: *When are you coming?* –*conj.* **2.** at what time: *to know when to be silent.* **3.** at the time that: *When we were young, life was fun.* **4.** whereas: *You rush ahead, when you should think first.* –*pron.* **5.** what time: *since when?* **6.** which time: *They left on Monday, since when we have heard nothing.*

when·ev·er, *conj.* at any time when: *Come whenever you like.*

where, *adv.* **1.** in or at what place?: *Where is he?* **2.** in what position or circumstances?: *Where are you without money?* **3.** to what place, point, or end?: *Where are you going?* **4.** from what source, or whence: *Where did you get that notion?* –*conj.* **5.** in or at what place, part, point, etc.: *Find where he is.* **6.** in or at the place, part, point, etc., in or at which: *It's where you left it.* –*pron.* **7.** what place: *from where?*

where·a·bouts, *adv.* **1.** about where? where? –*conj.* **2.** near or in what place. –*n.pl.* **3.** the place where a person or thing is; the locality of a person or thing.

where·as, *conj.* **1.** while on the contrary. **2.** it being the case that, or considering that.

593

whereby

where·by, *adv., conj.* by what or by which.

where·upon, *conj.* at or after which.

wher·ev·er, *conj.* in, at, or to whatever place.

where·with·al, *n.* means or supplies for the purpose or need, esp. money.

whet, *v.,* whetted, whetting. 1. to sharpen (a knife, tool, etc.) by grinding or friction. 2. to make keen or eager.

whether, *conj.* a word introducing the first of 2 or more alternatives (used in correlation with *or*).

whey, *n.* milk serum, separating as a watery liquid from the curd after coagulation, as in cheese-making.

which, *interrog. pron.* 1. what one (of a certain number mentioned or implied)?: *Which do you want?* –*rel. pron.* 2. (a simple relative with an antecedent which is a thing or body of persons): *I read the book, which was short.* 3. (in parenthetic clauses) a thing that: *and, which is worse, you've done it wrongly.* –*adj.* 4. what one of (a certain number mentioned or implied): *Which book do you want?*

which·ev·er, *pron.* 1. any one (of those in question) that: *Take whichever you like.* 2. no matter which: *Whichever you choose, someone will be offended.* –*adj.* 3. no matter which: *whichever book you like.*

whiff, *n.* 1. a slight blast or puff of wind or air. 2. a waft of scent or smell.

while, *n., conj., v.,* whiled, whiling. –*n.* 1. a space of time. –*conj.* Also, **whilst**. 2. during or in the time that. 3. throughout the time that, or as

whip

long as. 4. at the same time that (implying opposition or contrast). –*v.* 5. to cause (time) to pass, esp. in some easy or pleasant manner (*away*).

whim, *n.* an odd or fanciful notion.

whim·per, *v.* 1. to cry with low, plaintive, broken sounds, as a child, a dog, etc. –*n.* 2. a whimpering cry or sound.

whim·si·cal, *adj.* of an odd, quaint, or comical kind.

whim·sy, *n., pl.* -sies. an odd or fanciful notion.

whine, *v.,* whined, whining, *n.* –*v.* 1. to utter a nasal, complaining cry or sound, as from uneasiness, discontent, peevishness, etc. –*n.* 2. a whining utterance, sound, or tone.

whinge, *v.,* whinged, whingeing. to complain; whine.

whin·ny, *v.,* -nied, -nying. (of a horse) to utter its characteristic cry; neigh.

whip, *v.,* whipped or whipt, whipping, *n.* –*v.* 1. to strike with quick, repeated strokes of something slender and flexible; lash. 2. to beat with a whip or the like, esp. as punishment; flog; thrash. 3. to move quickly and suddenly; pull, jerk, snatch, seize, put, etc., with a sudden movement (*away, out, up, into,* etc.). 4. to beat (eggs, cream, etc.) to a froth with a whisk, fork, etc. 5. to beat or lash about, as a pennant in the wind. 6. **whip up, a.** to create quickly. **b.** to arouse to fury, intense excitement, etc. –*n.* 7. an instrument for striking or punishing, typically consisting of a flexible part with a more rigid handle. 8. *Parl.* a party manager who supplies information to members about the government busi-

594

whip

whip·lash, *n.* an injury to the spine caused by sudden movement forwards or backwards, as in a motor accident.

whip·pet, *n.* a dog similar to a small greyhound.

whirl, *v.* 1. to turn round, spin, or rotate rapidly. 2. to move rapidly along on wheels or otherwise. 3. to cause to turn or rotate rapidly. –*n.* 4. rapid rotation or gyration. 5. a short drive, run, walk, or the like; spin. 6. a rapid round of events, feelings, thoughts, etc.

whirl·pool, *n.* a whirling eddy or current, as in a river or the sea.

whirl·wind, *n.* a mass of rapidly rotating air.

whirr, *v.*, **whirred, whirring.** to go, fly, dart, revolve, or otherwise move quickly with a vibratory or buzzing sound.

whisk[1], *v.* 1. to sweep (dust, crumbs, etc. or a surface) with a brush, or the like. 2. to move with a rapid, sweeping stroke.

whisk[2], *v.* 1. to whip (eggs, cream, etc.) to a froth with a whisk or beating implement. –*n.* 2. a small bunch of grass, straw, hair, or the like, esp. for use in brushing. 3. an implement, in one form a bunch of loops of wire held together in a handle, for beating or whipping eggs, cream, etc.

whis·ker, *n.* 1. (*pl.*) the beard generally. 2. a single hair of the beard.

whisky, *n., pl.* **-kies.** a distilled spirit made from grain.

whis·per, *v.* 1. to speak or utter with soft, low sounds, using the breath, lips, etc., without vibration of the vocal cords. 2. (of trees, water, breezes, etc.) to make a soft, rustling sound. –*n.* 3. the mode of utterance, or the voice, of one who whispers. 4. a whispering sound. 5. confidential information; rumour.

whist, *n.* a card game.

whis·tle, *v.*, **-tled, -tling.** *v.* 1. to make a musical sound by forcing the breath through a small opening of the lips, helped by the tongue. 2. to make such a sound by blowing on a particular device. –*n.* 3. an instrument for producing such sounds. 4. a sound produced by or as by whistling.

white, *adj.*, **whiter, whitest**, *n.* –*adj.* 1. of the colour of pure snow, reflecting all or nearly all the rays of sunlight. 2. having a light-coloured skin. 3. pallid or pale, as from fear or other strong emotion, or pain or illness. 4. (of wines) light-coloured or yellowish (opposed to *red*). 5. (of coffee) with milk or cream. –*n.* 6. an achromatic visual sensation of relatively high luminosity. A white surface reflects light of all hues completely and diffusely. 7. lightness of skin pigment. 8. something white, or a white part of something. 9. a pellucid viscous fluid which surrounds the yolk of an egg; albumen. 10. the white part of the eyeball.

white ant, *n.* any of various species of wood-eating insects.

white-collar, *adj.* belonging or pertaining to non-manual workers, as those in professional and clerical work.

white flag, *n.* an all-white flag, used as a symbol of surrender, etc.

white gold, *n.* any of several gold

white gold

alloys possessing a white colour due to the presence of nickel or platinum.

white·goods, *n. pl.* electrical goods as refrigerators, washing machines, etc., which have a white enamel surface.

white heat, *n.* an intense heat at which a substance glows with white light.

white lie, *n.* a lie uttered from polite, amiable, or pardonable motives.

white·wash, *n.* 1. a composition, as of lime and water, used for painting walls, woodwork, etc., white. 2. anything used to cover up defects, gloss over faults or errors, or give a specious semblance of respectability, honesty, etc.

whither, *adv. Archaic;* now replaced by *where.* to what place?

whiting, *n.* a food and sport fish.

whit·tle, *v.,* **-tled, -tling.** 1. to cut, trim, or shape (a stick, piece of wood, etc.) by taking off bits with a knife. 2. to cut in order to reduce (*down*). – **whittler**, *n.*

whiz[1], *v.,* **whizzed, whizzing.** to make a humming or hissing sound, as an object passing rapidly through the air.

whiz[2], *n. Colloq.* a person who shows outstanding ability in a particular field or who is notable in some way; expert.

who, *pron.;* poss. **whose;** obj. **whom.** –*interrog. pron.* 1. what person? 2. (of a person) what as to character, origin, position, importance, etc.: *Who is that man?* –*rel. pron.* 3. the or any person that; any person: *I know who did it.* 4. (as a simple relative, with antecedent (a person, or sometimes an animal or a personified thing) expressed): *We saw men who were at work; the man who is wearing a blue tie.*

who·ever, *pron.;* possessive **whosever;** objective **whomever.** –*indef. rel. pron.* 1. whatever person, or anyone that. –*interrog. pron.* 2. *Colloq.* who ever? who? (used emphatically).

whole, *adj.* 1. comprising the full quantity, amount, extent, number, etc., without diminution or exception; entire, full, or total. 2. undivided, or in one piece. 3. uninjured, undamaged, or unbroken; sound; intact. –*n.* 4. the whole assemblage of parts or elements belonging to a thing; the entire quantity, account, extent, or number. 5. a thing complete in itself, or comprising all its parts or elements. – **wholly**, *adv.*

whole·hearted, *adj.* hearty; earnest; sincere.

whole·meal, *adj.* prepared with the complete wheat kernel, as flour or the bread baked with it.

whole number, *n.* an integer as 0, 1, 2, 3, 4, 5, etc.

whole·sale, *n., adj., adv., v.,* **-saled, -saling.** –*n.* 1. the sale of commodities in large quantities, as to retailers, rather than to consumers directly (distinguished from *retail*). –*adj.* 2. extensive and indiscriminate. –*adv.* 3. in a wholesale way. –*v.* 4. to sell by wholesale.

whole·some, *adj.* 1. conducive to or suggestive of moral or general well-being. 2. conducive to bodily health; salubrious.

whom, *pron.* objective case of **who.**

whoop, *n.* 1. a loud cry or shout, as one uttered by children or warriors. –*v.* 2. to utter a loud cry or shout,

whoop·ing cough, *n.* an infectious disease of the respiratory mucous membrane, esp. of children.

whoops, *interj.* (an exclamation of mild surprise, dismay, etc.). Also, **whoops-a-daisy.**

whoosh, *n.* a loud rushing noise, as of water or air.

whop·per, *n. Colloq.* 1. something uncommonly large of its kind. 2. a big lie.

whore, *n.* a prostitute.

whorl, *n.* 1. a circular arrangement of like parts, as leaves, flowers, etc., round a point on an axis. 2. anything shaped like a coil.

whose, *pron.* 1. possessive case of the relative and interrogative pronoun **who.** 2. possessive case of the relative pronoun **which** (historically, of **what**).

why, *adv.* 1. for what? for what cause, reason, or purpose? *–conj.* 2. for what cause or reason.

wick, *n.* a twist of soft threads, which draws up the melted tallow of a candle to the flame, or some similar device.

wicked, *adj.* evil or morally bad; iniquitous; sinful.

wicker·work, *n.* work consisting of plaited or woven hollow twigs.

wicket, *n.* 1. a small door or gate, esp. one beside, or forming part of, a larger one. 2. *Cricket.* **a.** either of the 2 frameworks, each consisting of 3 stumps with 2 bails in grooves across their tops, at which the bowler aims the ball. **b.** the area between the wickets, esp. with reference to the state of the ground. **c.** the achievement of a batsman's dismissal by the fielding side.

wide, *adj.,* **wider, widest,** *adv. –adj.* 1. having considerable or great extent from side to side; broad; not narrow. 2. of great range or scope. 3. open to the full or a great extent; expanded; distended. *–adv.* 4. to a great, or relatively great, extent from side to side. 5. to the full extent of opening. 6. away from or to one side of a point, mark, purpose, or the like; aside; astray. **– width,** *n.*

wide·spread, *adj.* 1. spread over or occupying a wide space. 2. distributed over a wide region, or occurring in many places or among many persons or individuals.

widow, *n.* a woman who has lost her husband by death and has not married again. **– widower,** *n.masc.*

wield, *v.* 1. to exercise (power, authority, influence, etc.), as in ruling or dominating. 2. to manage (a weapon, instrument, etc.) in use; handle or employ in action.

wife, *n., pl.* **wives.** a woman joined in marriage to a man as husband.

wig, *n.* an artificial covering of hair for the head.

wig·gle, *v.,* **-gled, -gling,** *n. –v.* 1. to (cause to) move or go with short, quick, irregular movements from side to side; wriggle. *–n.* 2. a wavy line.

wigwam, *n.* an American Indian hut or lodge.

wild, *adj.* 1. living in a state of nature, as animals that have not been tamed or domesticated. 2. growing or produced without cultivation or the care of man, as plants, flowers, fruit, honey, etc. 3. of unrestrained violence, fury, intensity, etc.; vio-

597

wild

lent; furious. **4.** extravagant or fantastic. **5.** disorderly or dishevelled. **6.** *Colloq.* intensely eager or enthusiastic. *–adv.* **7.** in a wild manner; wildly. *–n.* **8.** (*oft. pl.*) an uncultivated, uninhabited, or desolate region or tract; waste; wilderness; desert.

wilder·ness, *n.* a wild region, as of forest or desert.

wild·life, *n.* animals living in their natural habitat.

wile, *n.* a trick, artifice, or stratagem.

wilful, *adj.* **1.** willed, voluntary, or intentional. **2.** self-willed; perversely obstinate.

will¹, *v., pres.* will, *pt.* would. *–aux. v.* **1.** am (is, are, etc.) about or going to: *I will do that tomorrow; He will probably like that.* **2.** am (is, are, etc.) disposed or willing to. **3.** am (is, are, etc.) determined or sure to (used emphatically).

will², *n., v.*, willed, willing. *–n.* **1.** the faculty of conscious and esp. of deliberate action. **2.** the power of choosing one's own actions. **3.** wish or desire. **4.** purpose or determination. **5.** disposition (good or ill) towards another. **6.** *Law.* a legal declaration of a person's wishes as to the disposition of his (real) property, etc., after his death, usu. in writing. *–v.* **7.** to give by will or testament; bequeath or devise. **8.** to influence by exerting willpower. **9.** to purpose, determine on, or elect, by act of will.

will·ing, *adj.* **1.** disposed or consenting (without being particularly desirous). **2.** cheerfully consenting or ready.

willow, *n.* a tree or shrub with tough, pliable twigs or branches which are used for wickerwork, etc.

wind

will·power, *n.* control over one's impulses and actions.

wilt, *v.* to become limp and drooping, as a fading flower; wither.

wily, *adj.*, -lier, -liest. crafty.

wimple, *n.* a woman's headcloth drawn in folds about the chin.

win, *v.*, won, winning, *n.* **1.** to succeed by striving or effort. **2.** to gain the victory. **3.** to be placed first in a race or the like. **4.** to get by effort, as through labour, competition, or conquest. **5.** to be successful in (a game, battle, etc.). *–n.* **6.** an act of winning; success; victory.

wince, *v.*, winced, wincing. to shrink, as in pain or from a blow; start; flinch.

winch, *n.* the crank or handle of a revolving machine.

wind¹ /wind/, *n.* **1.** air in natural motion, as along the earth's surface. **2.** any stream of air, as that produced by a bellows, a fan, etc. **3.** a hint or intimation. **4.** gas generated in the stomach and bowels. *–v.* **5.** to expose to wind or air. **6.** to deprive momentarily of breath, as by a blow. *–adj.* **7.** (of a musical instrument) sounded by the breath of the player. – **windy**, *adj.*

wind² /waind/, *v.*, wound, winding. **1.** to change direction; bend; turn; meander. **2.** to have a circular or spiral course or direction. **3.** to proceed indirectly. **4.** to encircle, as with something twined, wrapped, or placed about. **5.** to roll or coil (thread, etc.) (*up*) into a ball or on a spool or the like. **6.** to adjust (a mechanism, etc.) for operation by some turning or coiling process (*up*).

wind·break, *n.* a growth of trees, a structure of boards, or the like, serving as a shelter from the wind.

wind·cheater, *n.* any close-fitting garment for the upper part of the body designed to give protection against the wind.

wind·fall, *n.* an unexpected piece of good fortune.

wind·lass, *n.* a device for raising weights, etc.

wind·mill, *n.* a mill or machine, as for grinding or pumping, operated by the wind.

window, *n.* 1. an opening in a wall or roof for the admission of air or light. 2. anything likened to a window in appearance or function.

wind·pipe, *n.* the trachea of an air-breathing vertebrate.

wind·screen, *n.* the sheet of glass which forms the front window of a motor vehicle.

wind·sock, *n.* a wind-direction indicator, installed at airports and elsewhere, consisting of an elongated truncated cone of textile material, flown from a mast. Also, **airsock**, **wind cone**, **wind sleeve**.

wine, *n.* the fermented juice of the grape.

wing, *n.* 1. either of the 2 appendages, of most birds and bats, which are adapted for flight. 2. any similar structure. 3. that portion of a main supporting surface confined to one side of an aeroplane. 4. a part of a building projecting on one side of, or subordinate to, a central or main part. 5. (*pl.*) the insignia or emblem worn by a qualified pilot. 6. *Sport.* a player to one side of a centre player or position. 7. *Theat.* the platform or space on the right or left of the stage proper. –*v.* 8. to equip with wings. 9. to wound or disable (a bird, etc.) in the wing. 10. to travel on or as on wings; fly.

wink, *v.* 1. to close and open (the eyes) quickly. 2. to close and open one eye quickly as a hint or signal or with some sly meaning (*at*). 3. to shine with little flashes of light, or twinkle. –*n.* 4. the act of winking. 5. the time required for winking once; an instant or twinkling.

winnow, *v.* 1. to free (grain, etc.) from chaff, refuse particles, etc., by means of wind or driven air; fan. 2. to subject to some process of separating or distinguishing; analyse critically; sift.

win·some, *adj.* winning, engaging, or charming.

winter, *n.* 1. the coldest season of the year. 2. a period like winter, as the last or final period of life; a period of decline, decay, inertia, dreariness, or adversity. –*adj.* 3. of, pertaining to, or characteristic of winter. 4. suitable for wear or use in winter.

wipe, *v.*, **wiped**, **wiping**, *n.* –*v.* 1. to rub lightly in order to clean or dry. 2. to remove by rubbing with or on something (*away*, *off*, *out*, etc.). 3. to destroy or eradicate, as from existence or memory. 4. **wipe out**, to destroy completely. –*n.* 5. the action of wiping.

wire, *n.*, *v.*, **wired**, **wiring**. *n.* 1. a long piece of slender, flexible metal. 2. a length of such material used as a conductor of electricity, usu. insulated in a flex. 3. *Orig. U.S. Colloq.* a telegram. –*v.* 4. to furnish with a wire or wires. 5. to install an electric system of wiring, as for

wire

lighting, etc. 6. *Colloq.* to send a telegraphic message to.

wire·less, *n.* radio.

wiry, *adj.*, **wirier**, **wiriest**. lean and sinewy.

wisdom, *n.* knowledge of what is true or right coupled with just judgment as to action; sagacity, prudence, or common sense.

wise, *adj.*, **wiser**, **wisest**. 1. having the power of discerning and judging properly as to what is true or right. 2. possessed of or characterised by scholarly knowledge or learning; learned; erudite. 3. having knowledge or information as to facts, circumstances, etc.

wish, *v.* 1. to want; desire. –*n.* 2. a distinct mental inclination towards something; a desire, felt or expressed. 3. that which is wished.

wish·bone, *n.* the forked bone in front of the breastbone in most birds.

wishy-washy, *adj.* lacking in substantial qualities; weak, feeble, or poor.

wisp, *n.* 1. a handful or small bundle of straw, hay, or the like. 2. anything small or thin, as a shred, bundle, or slip of something: *a wisp of cloud*.

wis·teria, *n.* a climbing shrub with handsome purple or white flowers.

wist·ful, *adj.* 1. pensive or melancholy. 2. showing longing tinged with melancholy; regretful; sad.

wit, *n.* 1. keen perception and cleverly apt expression of connections between ideas which may arouse pleasure and especially amusement. 2. a person endowed with or noted for such wit. 3. (*pl.*) mental faculties, or senses.

within

witch, *n.* a person, now esp. a woman, who professes or is supposed to practise magic, esp. black magic; sorceress. – **witchery**, *n.*

witch·etty, *n.* any of various large, white, edible, wood-boring grubs that are the larvae of certain Aust. moths and beetles.

with, *prep.* 1. accompanied by or accompanying: *to go with him*. 2. in some particular relation to: *to mix water with wine*. 3. (expressing similarity or agreement): *in agreement with him*. 4. characterised by or having: *a cat with green eyes*. 5. (of means or instrument) by the use of: *to write with a pen*. 6. (of manner) using or showing: *to sing with gusto*. 7. in correspondence or proportion to: *Their power increased with their number*. 8. against, as in opposition or competition: *to fight with someone*.

with·draw, *v.*, **-drew**, **-drawn**, **-drawing**. 1. to draw back or away; take back; remove. 2. to retire; retreat; go apart or away. 3. to retract (a statement). – **withdrawal**, *n.*

wither, *v.* 1. to shrivel; fade; decay. 2. to make flaccid, shrunken, or dry, as from loss of moisture; cause to lose freshness, bloom, vigour, etc.

with·ers, *n. pl.* the highest part of a horse's or other animal's back, behind the neck.

with·hold, *v.*, **-held**, **-holding**. 1. to hold back; restrain or check. 2. to refrain from giving or granting. – **withholder**, *n.*

with·in, *adv.* 1. in or into the interior or inner part, or inside. –*prep.* 2. in or into the interior of or the parts or space enclosed by 3. at or to some amount or degree not exceeding.

with·out, *prep.* **1.** not with; with no; with absence, omission, or avoidance of; lacking (as opposed to *with*). **2.** beyond the compass, limits, range or scope of (now used chiefly in opposition to *within*).

with·stand, *v.*, **-stood, -stand·ing.** to stand or hold out against; resist or oppose, esp. successfully.

wit·ness, *v.* **1.** to see or know by personal presence and perception. **2.** to be present at (an occurrence) as a formal witness or otherwise. –*n.* **3.** one who, being present, personally sees or perceives a thing; eyewitness. **4.** one who gives testimony, as in a court of law. **5.** one who signs a document in attestation of the genuineness of its execution.

wit·ti·cism, *n.* a witty remark.

wit·ty, *adj.*, **-ti·er, -ti·est.** possessing wit in speech or writing; amusingly clever in perception and expression.

wiz·ard, *n.* one who professes to practise magic; a magician or sorcerer.

wiz·ened, *adj.* dried-up; withered; shrivelled.

woad, *n.* a plant yielding blue dye; the dye.

wob·ble, *v.*, **-bled, -bling. 1.** to incline to one side and to the other alternately, as a wheel, top, or other rotating body, when not properly balanced. **2.** to move unsteadily from side to side.

woe, *n.* grievous distress, affliction, or trouble. – **woe·ful**, *adj.*

woe·be·gone, *adj.* beset with woe; mournful or miserable.

wog, *n.* Colloq. (*derog.*) a person of Mediterranean extraction, or of similar complexion and appearance.

wok, *n.* a bowl-shaped oriental cooking pan used esp. in Chinese cookery.

woke, *v.* a past tense of **wake**.

wok·en, *v.* past participle of **wake**.

wolf, *n., pl.* **wolves**, *v.* –*n.* **1.** a large, wild carnivore belonging to the dog family. **2.** Colloq. a man who is boldly flirtatious or amorous towards many women. –*v.* **3.** Colloq. to eat ravenously.

wol·ver·ine, *n.* N. American carnivorous mammal of the weasel family.

wom·an, *n., pl.* **women**, *adj.* –*n.* **1.** the female human being (distinguished from *man*). **2.** an adult female person (distinguished from *girl*).

womb, *n.* the uterus of the human female and some of the higher mammalian quadrupeds.

wom·bat, *n.* a large, heavily-built burrowing marsupial with short legs and a rudimentary tail.

wom·en, *n.* plural of **woman**.

won, *v.* past tense and past participle of **win**.

won·der, *v.* **1.** to think or speculate curiously. **2.** to be affected with wonder; marvel (*at*). **3.** to be curious about; be curious to know (fol. by a clause). **4.** to feel wonder at (now only fol. by a clause as object). –*n.* **5.** something strange and surprising; a cause of surprise, astonishment, or admiration. **6.** a feeling of surprised or puzzled interest, sometimes tinged with admiration.

won·der·ful, *adj.* excellent; delightful; extremely good or fine.

won·drous, *adj.* wonderful.

wonk·y, *adj.* Colloq. **1.** shaky; unsound. **2.** unwell; upset.

wont

wont, *adj.* **1.** accustomed; used (commonly followed by an infinitive). *n.* **2.** custom; habit; practice.

wonted, *adj.* habitual, usual, customary.

woo, *v.* **1.** to seek the favour, affection, or love of, esp. with a view to marriage. **2.** to seek to win.

wood, *n.* **1.** the hard, fibrous substance composing most of the stem and branches of a tree or shrub, and covered by the bark. **2.** the trunks of trees as suitable for architectural and other purposes; timber or lumber. **3.** (*oft. pl.*) a large and thick collection of growing trees, smaller than a forest. –*adj.* **4.** made of wood; wooden. **5.** used to cut, carve, or otherwise shape wood. –*v.* **6.** to cover or plant with trees. – **woody,** *adj.*

wooden, *adj.* **1.** consisting or made of wood. **2.** stiff, ungainly, or awkward. **3.** without spirit or animation.

wood·pecker, *n.* a bird with a hard, chisel-like bill for boring into wood after insects.

wood·wind, *n.* the group of wind instruments which comprises the flutes, clarinets, oboes, and bassoons.

wood·work, *n.* **1.** the interior wooden fittings of a house or the like. **2.** the art or craft of working in wood; carpentry.

woof[1], *n.* →**weft.**

woof[2], *n.* the sound of a dog barking, esp. deeply and loudly.

woofer, *n.* loudspeaker for low-frequency sound.

wool, *n.* **1.** a fibre produced from sheep's fleece. **2.** any finely fibrous or filamentary matter suggesting the wool of a sheep.

wool·len, *adj.* made or consisting of wool.

woolly, *adj.*, **-lier, -liest. 1.** consisting of wool. **2.** resembling wool. **3.** blurred, confused or indistinct, as thinking, expression, depiction.

wool·shed, *n.* a large shed for shearing and baling of wool.

woozy, *adj. Colloq.* **1.** muddled, or stupidly confused. **2.** dizzy, nauseous, etc.

Worcester sauce, *n.* a highly-seasoned savoury sauce.

word, *n.* **1.** a sound or a combination of sounds, or its written or printed representation, used in any language as the sign of a concept. **2.** (*pl.*) angry speech; a quarrel. **3.** warrant, assurance, or promise. **4.** news. –*v.* **5.** to express in words, or phrase.

word-break, *n.* the point of division in a word which runs over from one line to the next.

wording, *n.* phrasing or choice of words.

word processor, *n.* a computer usu. with keyboard and visual display unit, designed esp. for storing and editing text – **word processing,** *n.*

wordy, *adj.*, **wordier, wordiest.** characterised by or given to the use of many, or too many, words; verbose.

wore, *v.* past tense of **wear.**

work, *n., v.,* **worked** or **wrought, working.** –*n.* **1.** exertion directed to produce or accomplish something; labour; toil. **2.** something to be made or done; a task or undertaking. **3.** *Physics.* the product of the force acting upon a body and the distance through which the point of application of force moves. The derived SI unit of work is the joule. **4.** employment; a job, esp. that by which one earns a living. **5.** (*pl. oft. construed as sing.*) a place or establishment for carrying on some form of labour or industry. **6.** (*pl.*) *Theol.* acts performed in obedience to the law of God; righteous deeds. *-v.* **7.** to exert oneself (contrasted with *play*). **8.** to be employed. **9.** to be in operation, as a machine. **10.** to act or operate effectively. **11.** to have an effect or influence, as (*on*) a person or (*on*) the mind or feelings. **12.** to use or manage (an apparatus, contrivance, etc.) in operation. **13.** to bring, put, get, render, etc., by work, effort, or action (*in, off, out*, etc.): *to work a screw loose; to work a design into a rug.* **14.** to effect, accomplish, cause, or do. **15.** to expend work on; manipulate or treat by labour. **16.** to operate (a mine, farm, etc.). **17.** to move, stir, or excite in feeling, etc. (*up*). **18. work out, a.** to effect or achieve by labour. **b.** to solve (a problem) by a reasoning process. **c.** to (cause to) finish up, turn out, or culminate.

work·able, *adj.* practicable or feasible.

work·a·day, *n.* humdrum.

work·er, *n.* **1.** one employed in manual or industrial labour. **2.** an employee, esp. as contrasted with a capitalist or a manager.

work·load, *n.* the amount of work done or to be done in a specified time.

work·man·ship, *n.* the art or skill with which something is made.

world, *n.* **1.** the earth or globe. **2.** a particular section of the world's inhabitants. **3.** mankind; humanity. **4.** a particular class of mankind, with common interests, aims, etc. **5.** any sphere, realm, or domain: *the world of surfing.* **6.** the entire system of created things; the universe.

world·ling, *n.* one devoted to the interests and pleasures of this world; a worldly person.

world·ly, *adj.*, **-li·er, -li·est,** *adv.* **-ly. 1.** earthly or mundane (as opposed to *heavenly, spiritual,* etc.). **2.** devoted to, directed towards, or connected with the affairs, interests, or pleasures of this world. **3.** secular (as opposed to *ecclesiastical, religious,* etc.). *-adv.* **4.** in a worldly manner. **- worldliness,** *n.*

worm, *n.* **1.** *Zool.* a long, slender, soft-bodied invertebrate. **2.** (in popular language) any of numerous small creeping animals. **3.** something resembling or suggesting a worm in appearance, movement, etc. **4.** a grovelling, abject, or contemptible person. **5.** (*pl.*) *Pathol.* any disease or disorder arising from the presence of parasitic worms in the intestines or other tissues. *-v.* **6.** to creep, crawl, or advance slowly or stealthily. **7.** to make, cause, bring, etc., along by creeping or crawling, or by stealthy or devious advances.

worn, *v.* **1.** past participle of **wear**[1]. *-adj.* **2.** impaired by wear or use. **3.** wearied or exhausted.

worri·some, *adj.* worrying, annoying, or disturbing; causing worry.

worry, *v.*, **-ried, -ry·ing,** *n., pl.* **-ries.** *-v.* **1.** to feel uneasy or anxious; fret; torment oneself with or suffer from disturbing thoughts. **2.** to cause to feel uneasy or anxious; plague,

603

worry

pester, or bother. **3.** to harass by repeated biting, snapping, etc. –*n.* **4.** uneasiness or anxiety.

worse, *adj.*, used as compar. of **bad**. **1.** bad or ill in a greater or higher degree; inferior. –*n.* **2.** that which is worse. –*adv.* **3.** in a more disagreeable, evil, wicked, severe, or disadvantageous manner. **4.** with more severity, intensity, etc. **5.** in a less effective manner.

wor·ship, *n., v.*, **-shipped**, **-shipping**. –*n.* **1.** reverent honour and homage paid to God, or to any object regarded as sacred. **2.** adoring reverence or regard. **3.** (with *your, his, etc.*) a title of honour. –*v.* **4.** to render religious reverence and homage to.

worst, *adj.*, used as superl. of **bad**. **1.** bad or ill in the greatest or highest degree. **2.** most faulty, unsatisfactory, or objectionable. –*n.* **3.** that which is worst or the worst part. –*adv.* **4.** in the most evil, wicked, or disadvantageous manner. **5.** with the most severity, intensity, etc. **6.** in the least satisfactory, complete or effective manner.

wor·sted /'wustəd/, *n.* (cloth woven from) a type of woollen yarn.

worth, *adj.* **1.** good or important enough to justify (what is specified). **2.** having a value of, or equal in value to, as in money. –*n.* **3.** excellence of character or quality as commanding esteem. **4.** usefulness or importance, as to the world, to a person, or for a purpose. **5.** value, as in money.

worth·while, *adj.* such as to repay one's time, attention, interest, work, trouble, etc.

worthy, *adj.*, **-thier**, **-thiest**, *n.*, *pl.* **-thies**. –*adj.* **1.** of adequate merit or character. **2.** deserving: *worthy of merit.* –*n.* **3.** a person of eminent worth or merit or of social importance. **4.** (*oft. joc.*) a person.

would, *v.* past tense of **will**[1] used: **1.** specially in expressing a wish: *I would it were true.* **2.** often in place of *will*, to make a statement or question less direct or blunt: *That would be rather unkind.*

wound[1] /wund/, *n.* **1.** an injury to an organism due to external violence rather than disease. –*v.* **2.** to inflict a wound upon; injure; hurt.

wound[2] /waund/, *v.* past tense and past participle of **wind**[2] and **wind**[3].

wove, *v.* past tense and occasional past participle of **weave**.

woven, *v.* past participle of **weave**.

wow, –*interj. Colloq.* (an exclamation of surprise, wonder, pleasure, dismay, etc.)

wowser, *n. Colloq.* a prudish teetotaller; killjoy.

wraith, *n.* a visible spirit.

wran·gle, *v.*, **-gled**, **-gling**. to argue or dispute, esp. in a noisy or angry manner.

wrap, *v.*, wrapped or wrapt, wrapping, *n.* –*v.* **1.** to enclose, envelop, or muffle in something wound or folded about (*up*). **2.** to wind, fold, or bind (something) about as a covering. **3.** to surround, envelop, shroud, or enfold. **4.** **wrap up**, *Colloq.* to conclude or settle. –*n.* **5.** something to be wrapped about the person, as a shawl, scarf, or mantle.

wrap·ped, *adj.* enthused (about).

wrath, *n.* strong, stern, or fierce anger; deeply resentful indignation; ire.

wreak, *v.* to inflict or execute (vengeance, etc.).

wreath, *n.*, *pl.* **wreaths.** something twisted or bent into a circular form, esp. a circular band of flowers, foliage, etc.

wreathe, *v.*, **wreathed, wreathing.** 1. to encircle or adorn with or as with a wreath or wreaths. 2. to surround in curving or curling masses or form.

wreck, *n.* 1. a vessel in a state of ruin from disaster at sea, on rocks, etc. 2. the ruin or destruction of anything. –*v.* 3. to cause the wreck of (a vessel). 4. to cause the ruin or destruction of; spoil.

wren, *n.* a small bird with long legs and a long, almost upright tail.

wrench, *v.* 1. to pull, jerk, or force by a violent twist. –*n.* 2. a sudden, violent twist. 3. a sharp, distressing strain, as to the feelings. 4. a spanner.

wrest, *v.* 1. to twist or turn; pull, jerk, or force by a violent twist. 2. to take away by force.

wres·tle, *v.*, **-tled, -tling.** 1. to engage in wrestling. 2. to contend, as in a struggle for mastery; grapple.

wrest·ling, *n.* a sport in which 2 persons struggle hand to hand, each striving to throw or force the other to the ground.

wretch, *n.* a deplorably unfortunate or unhappy person.

wretched, *adj.* very unfortunate in condition or circumstances; miserable; pitiable.

wrick, *v.* to wrench or strain.

wrig·gle, *v.*, **-gled, -gling.** to twist to and fro, writhe, or squirm.

wring, *v.*, **wrung, wringing.** 1. to twist forcibly. 2. to twist and compress in order to force out moisture (*out*). 3. to clasp (one's hands) together, as in grief, etc.

wrin·kle, *n.*, *v.*, **-kled, -kling.** –*n.* 1. a ridge or furrow on a surface, due to contraction, folding, rumpling, or the like; crease. –*v.* 2. to form wrinkles in; crease.

wrist, *n.* the part of the arm between the forearm and the hand.

writ, *n. Law.* a formal order under seal, issued in the name of a sovereign, government, court, etc., directing the person to whom it is addressed to do or refrain from doing some specified act.

write, *v.*, **wrote** or **writ, written, writing.** 1. to express in writing; give a written account of. 2. to produce as author or composer. 3. to trace or form (characters, words, etc.) with a pen, etc. 4. to be a writer, journalist, or author for one's living. 5. to write a letter. 6. **write off** to cancel, as an entry in an account, as by an offsetting entry.

write-off, *n.* 1. *Accounting.* something written off from the books. 2. *Colloq.* something irreparably damaged, as an aircraft, car, etc.

write-up, *n.* a written description or account, as in a newspaper or magazine.

writhe, *v.*, **writhed, writhing.** to twist the body about, or squirm, as in pain, violent effort, etc.

wrong, *adj.* 1. not in accordance with what is morally right or good. 2. deviating from truth or fact; erroneous. 3. not correct; in error. 4. not suitable or appropriate. –*n.* 5. that which is not in accordance with morality, goodness, justice, truth, or the like; evil. 6. an unjust act; injury. –*adv.* 7. in a wrong manner; not rightly; awry or amiss.

wrong

—v. **8.** to do wrong to; treat unfairly or unjustly; injure or harm. **9.** impute evil to unjustly.

wrought, v. *Archaic.* a past tense and past participle of **work**. —adj. **2.** fashioned or formed by manufacture. **3.** produced or shaped by beating with a hammer, etc., as iron or silver articles. **4.** ornamented or elaborated.

wry, *adj.* **wryer, wryest** or **wrier, wriest**. **1.** distorted to show dislike, etc., as the features. **2.** ironically or bitterly amusing. **3.** twisted or crooked.

Xx

X, x, *n., pl.* **X's** or **Xs, x's** or **xs. 1.** the 24th letter of the English alphabet. **2.** a term often used to designate a person, thing, or the like, whose true name is unknown or withheld.

xeno·phobia, *n.* a fear or hatred of foreigners.

xero·graphy, *n.* a method of photographic copying. **– xerograph,** *n.* **– xerographic,** *adj.*

Xmas, *n.* Christmas.

X-ray, *n.* **1.** *Physics.* electromagnetic radiation of shorter wavelength than light, which is able to penetrate solids, expose photographic plates, etc. **2.** a picture produced by the action of X-rays. *v.* **3.** to examine by means of X-rays.

xylo·phone, *n. Music.* a percussion instrument consisting of a graduated series of wooden bars, usu. sounded by striking.

Yy

Y, y, *n., pl.* **Y's** or **Ys, y's** or **ys.** the 25th letter of the English alphabet.

yabber, *Colloq.* *–v.* **1.** to talk. *–n.* **2.** talk, conversation.

yacht /jɒt/, *n.* a sailing vessel mostly used for non-commercial purposes.

yachting, *n.* the action or pastime of sailing or racing a yacht.

yachtsman, *n.* a person who sails a yacht.

yahoo, *n.* an uncouth person.

yak, *n.* a long-haired wild ox.

yam, *n.* the starchy, tuberous root of certain climbing vines.

yank, *Colloq.* *v., n.* (to pull or move with) a sudden jerking motion.

yap, *v.,* **yapped, yapping. 1.** to yelp. **2.** *Colloq.* to talk snappishly, noisily, or foolishly.

yard^1**,** *n.* **1.** a common unit of linear measure in the imperial system defined as 0.9144 metres. **2.** *Naut.* a long cylindrical spar suspending a sail.

yard^2**,** *n.* **1.** a piece of enclosed ground next to a house, etc. **2.** an enclosure within which any work or business is carried on.

yard·arm, *n.* either end of a yard of a square sail.

yard·stick, *n.* any standard of measurement.

yarn, *n.* **1.** thread made by twisting fibres, as nylon, cotton or wool, and used for knitting and weaving. **2.** *Colloq.* a story, esp. a long one about incredible events. **3.** a talk, chat. *–v.* **4.** *Colloq.* to tell stories. **5.** to talk, chat.

yaw, *v.* to deviate temporarily from the straight course.

yawn, *v.* **1.** to open the mouth involuntarily with a prolonged deep intake of breath, as from drowsiness or weariness. **2.** to open

yawn

wide like a mouth. —n. 3. the act of yawning.

ye, pron. Archaic. you (esp. plural). See **thou**.

yea, adv. yes.

yeah, adv. Colloq. yes.

year, n. 1. a period of 365 or 366 days, now reckoned as beginning 1 January and ending 31 December (**calendar year**). 2. such a period reckoned from any point. 3. the true period of the earth's revolution round the sun. 4. a level or grade in an academic program. 5. (pl.) age, esp. of a person. 6. (pl.) time, esp. a long time.

year·ling, n. an animal one year old or in the 2nd year of its age.

yearly, adj., adv., n., pl. **-lies**. —adj. 1. done, made, happening, appearing, coming, etc., once a year or every year. —adv. 2. once a year; annually. —n. 3. a publication appearing once a year.

yearn, v. to have an earnest or strong desire.

yeast, n. a substance consisting of the cells of certain fungi, used to induce fermentation in the manufacture of beer, etc., to leaven bread, and in medicine.

yell, v., n. (to call out with) a strong, loud, clear cry.

yellow, adj. 1. of a bright colour like that of butter, lemons, etc.; between green and orange in the spectrum. 2. Colloq. cowardly. —n. 3. a hue between green and orange in the spectrum.

yellow·cake, n. uranium oxide in an unprocessed form.

yellow fever, n. a dangerous, infectious febrile disease.

yogi

yelp, v., n. (to give) a quick, sharp bark or cry.

yen, n. Colloq. desire; longing.

yes, adv., n., pl. **yeses**. —adv. 1. (used to express affirmation or assent or emphasis). —n. 2. an affirmative reply.

yester·day, adv., n. (on) the day preceding this day.

yet, adv. 1. at the present time: *Don't leave me yet.* 2. up to a particular time: *He had not gone yet.* 3. now or then as previously; still: *There is hope yet.* 4. in addition: *yet once more.* 5. even or still: *He could not run, nor yet walk.* 6. nevertheless: *strange yet true.* —conj. 7. nevertheless: *It was raining yet he came.*

yew, n. an evergreen coniferous tree.

yield, v. 1. to give forth or produce by a natural process or in return for cultivation. 2. to produce or furnish as payment, profit, or interest. 3. to give up, as to superior power or authority. 4. to give way to influence, entreaty, argument, or the like. —n. 5. the action of yielding or producing. 6. that which is yielded. 7. the quantity or amount yielded.

yob, n. Colloq. a loutish youth. Also, **yobbo**.

yodel, v., **-delled**, **-delling**. to sing with frequent changes from the natural voice to falsetto.

yoga, n. the use of meditation, often with unfamiliar postures, to attain the withdrawal of the senses from all external objects.

yog·hurt, n. a prepared food made from milk that has been curdled by the action of enzymes or other cultures. Also, **yoghourt**, **yogurt**.

yogi, n., pl. **-gis**. one who practises yoga.

yoke, *n.*, *v.*, **yoked, yoking.** –*n.* 1. a contrivance for joining a pair of draught animals. 2. something resembling a yoke in form or use. 3. a shaped piece in a garment from which the rest of the garment hangs. –*v.* 4. to put a yoke on.

yokel, *n.* a countryman.

yolk, *n.* the yellow and principal substance of an egg.

yonder, *adj.* 1. being the more distant. 2. being in that place or over there. –*adv.* 3. at, in, or to that place; over there.

yore, *n.* time long past, now only in the phrase of yore.

you, *pron.*, *poss.* **your** or **yours**, *obj.* **you.** 1. the ordinary pronoun of the 2nd person. 2. one; anyone; people in general.

young, *adj.* 1. being in the first or early stage of life, or growth. 2. of or pertaining to youth. 3. comparatively not far advanced in years. –*n.* 4. young offspring. 5. young people collectively.

young·ster, *n.* a young person.

your, *pron.* the possessive form of *you*, *ye*, used before a noun.

yours, *pron.* form of *your* used predicatively or without a noun following.

your·self, *pron.*, *pl.* **-selves.** 1. a reflexive form of *you*: You've cut yourself. 2. an emphatic form of *you* used **a.** as object. **b.** in apposition to a subject or object. 3. your proper or normal self.

youth, *n.*, *pl.* **youths**, (*collectively*) **youth.** 1. the condition of being young. 2. the time of being young. 3. the first or early period of anything. 4. a young person, esp. a young man. – **youthful**, *adj.*

yowl, *v.* to utter a long distressful cry.

yoyo, *n.*, *pl.* **-yos.** a round toy with a groove round the edge, in which a string is wound by which it can be spun up and down.

yuk, *interj.* (an expression of disgust).

yule, *n.* Christmas, or the Christmas season.

Zz

Z, z, *n.*, *pl.* **Z's** or **Zs, z's** or **zs.** the 26th letter of the English alphabet.

zany, *adj.* 1. extremely comical; clownish. 2. slightly crazy.

zeal, *n.* ardour for a person, cause, or object; enthusiastic diligence. – **zealous**, *adj.*

zealot, *n.* 1. one who displays zeal, esp. excessively. 2. *Colloq.* a religious fanatic.

zebra, *n.* a wild, horselike animal, with regular black and white stripes.

zenith, *n.* 1. the point in the heavens vertically above any place or observer. 2. any highest point or state.

zephyr, *n.* a soft, mild breeze.

zep·pelin, *n.* a large dirigible.

zero, *n.*, *pl.* **-ros** or **-roes**, *v.*, **-roed, -roing.** –*n.* 1. the figure or symbol 0, which stands for the absence of quantity. 2. the line or point from which anything is measured. 3. naught or nothing. 4. the lowest

zero

point or degree. –v. **5. zero in on, a.** to focus attention on. **b.** to adjust a rifle, etc., so as to aim directly at.

zest, n. **1.** (anything added to impart) agreeable or piquant flavour. **2.** piquancy, interest, or charm.

zigzag, n. a line, course, or progression characterised by sharp turns first to one side and then to the other.

zinc, n. Chem. a metallic element used in making alloys, and as a protective covering for roofs, etc. Symbol: Zn

zinnia, n. an annual plant with colourful flowers.

zip, n., v., **zipped, zipping.** –n. **1.** Also, **zipper.** a fastener consisting of an interlocking device set along 2 edges, which unites (or separates) them when an attached piece sliding between them is pulled. **2.** energy or vim. –v. **3.** to proceed with energy. **4.** to fasten (up) with a zip.

zircon, n. a common mineral used as a gem.

zither, n. a stringed musical instrument.

zodiac, n. an imaginary belt of the heavens, containing 12 constellations and hence 12 divisions (called signs). – **zodiacal,** adj.

zygote

zombie, n. **1.** a dead body brought to life by a supernatural force. **2.** (derog.) a person having no independent judgment, intelligence, etc. Also, **zombi.**

zone, n. **1.** any continuous distinguishable tract or area. **2.** an area or district where certain conditions or circumstances prevail. – **zonal,** adj.

zoning, n. the marking out of an area of land with respect to its use.

zoo, n. a park or other large enclosure in which live animals are kept for public exhibition.

zoo·logy, n., pl. **-gies.** the science that treats of animals or the animal kingdom. – **zoological,** adj.

zoom, v. **1.** to make, or move with, a continuous humming sound. **2.** (of prices) to rise rapidly. **3.** Films, Television, etc. to use a lens which makes an object appear to approach or recede from the viewer.

zounds, interj. Archaic. an exclamation of surprise, anger, etc.

zuc·chini, n., pl. **-ni, -nis.** a small vegetable marrow; courgette.

zygote, n. the cell produced by the union of 2 gametes. – **zygotic,** adj.

APPENDICES
Countries of the World

AFGHANISTAN
  Capital: Kabul
  Currency: afghani (pul)

ALBANIA
  Capital: Tirana
  Currency: lek (qindar)

ALGERIA
  Capital: Algiers
  Currency: dinar (centime)

ANGOLA
  Capital: Luanda
  Currency: kwanza (lwei)

ARGENTINA
  Capital: Buenos Aires
  Currency: peso (centavo)

ARMENIA
  Capital: Yerevan
  Currency: dram

AUSTRALIA
  Capital: Canberra
  Currency: dollar (cent)

AUSTRIA
  Capital: Vienna
  Currency: schilling (groschen)

AZERBAIDJAN
  Capital: Baku
  Currency: manat (gopik)

BANGLADESH
  Capital: Dhaka
  Currency: taka (paisa)

BELARUS
  Capital: Minsk
  Currency: rouble (copeck)

BELGIUM
  Capital: Brussels
  Currency: franc (centime)

BOLIVIA
  Capital: La Paz
  Currency: boliviano (centavo)

BOSNIA AND HERCEGOVINA
  Capital: Sarajevo
  Currency: dinar (para)

BOTSWANA
  Capital: Gaborone
  Currency: pula (thebe)

BRAZIL
  Capital: Brasilia
  Currency: cruzeiro (centavo)

BULGARIA
  Capital: Sofia
  Currency: lev (stotinka)

BURMA
  Capital: Rangoon
  Currency: kyat (pya)

CAMBODIA
  Capital: Phnom Penh
  Currency: riel (sen)

CAMEROON
  Capital: Yaounde
  Currency: franc (centime)

CANADA
  Capital: Ottawa
  Currency: dollar (cent)

CHILE
  Capital: Santiago
  Currency: peso (centavo)

CHINA
  Capital: Beijing
  Currency: yuan (fen)

COLOMBIA
  Capital: Bogotá
  Currency: peso (centavo)

COSTA RICA
  Capital: San José
  Currency: colón (céntimo)

COTE D'IVOIRE
  Capital: Yamoussoukro
  Currency: franc (centime)

CROATIA
  Capital: Zagreb
  Currency: dinar (para)

CUBA
  Capital: Havana
  Currency: peso (centavo)

CYPRUS
  Capital: Nicosia
  Currency: pound (cent)

CZECH REPUBLIC
  Capital: Prague
  Currency: koruna (haléřů)

DENMARK
  Capital: Copenhagen
  Currency: krone (öre)

DOMINICAN REPUBLIC
  Capital: Santo Domingo
  Currency: peso (centavo)

ECUADOR
  Capital: Quito
  Currency: sucre (centavo)

EGYPT
  Capital: Cairo
  Currency: pound (piastre)

EL SALVADOR
  Capital: San Salvador
  Currency: colón (centavo)

ERITREA
  Capital: Asmara

ESTONIA
  Capital: Tallinn
  Currency: kroon (cente)

ETHIOPIA
  Capital: Addis Ababa
  Currency: birr (cent)

FINLAND
  Capital: Helsinki
  Currency: markka (penni)

FRANCE
  Capital: Paris
  Currency: franc (centime)

GABON
  Capital: Libreville
  Currency: franc (centime)

THE GAMBIA
  Capital: Banjul
  Currency: dalasi (butut)

GEORGIA
Capital: Tbilisi

GERMANY
Capital: Berlin
Currency: Deutschmark (Pfennig)

GHANA
Capital: Accra
Currency: cedi (pesewa)

GREECE
Capital: Athens
Currency: drachma (lepton)

GUATEMALA
Capital: Guatemala City
Currency: quetzal (centavo)

GUINEA
Capital: Conakry
Currency: franc (centime)

HAITI
Capital: Port-au-Prince
Currency: gourde (centime)

HONDURAS
Capital: Tegucigalpa
Currency: lempira (centavo)

HONG KONG
Capital: Victoria
Currency: dollar (cent)

HUNGARY
Capital: Budapest
Currency: forint (filler)

ICELAND
Capital: Reykjavik
Currency: króna (eyrir)

INDIA
Capital: New Delhi
Currency: rupee (paisa)

INDONESIA
Capital: Jakarta
Currency: rupiah (sen)

IRAN
Capital: Tehran
Currency: rial (dinar)

IRAQ
Capital: Baghdad
Currency: dinar (fils)

IRELAND, REPUBLIC OF
Capital: Dublin
Currency: punt (pence)

ISRAEL
Capital: Jerusalem
Currency: shekel (agora)

ITALY
Capital: Rome
Currency: lira (centesimo)

JAMAICA
Capital: Kingston
Currency: dollar (cent)

JAPAN
Capital: Tokyo
Currency: yen (sen)

JORDAN
Capital: Amman
Currency: dinar (fils)

KAZAKHSTAN
Capital: Alma-Ata
Currency: tenge

KENYA
 Capital: Nairobi
 Currency: shilling (cent)

KOREA, DEMOCRATIC PEOPLE'S REPUBLIC OF
(North Korea)
 Capital: P'yŏngyang
 Currency: won (chon)

KOREA, REPUBLIC OF
(South Korea)
 Capital: Seoul
 Currency: won (jeon)

KUWAIT
 Capital: Kuwait
 Currency: dinar (fils)

KYRGYZSTAN
 Capital: Pishpek
 Currency: som

LAOS
 Capital: Vientiane
 Currency: kip (at)

LATVIA
 Capital: Riga
 Currency: lat

LEBANON
 Capital: Beirut
 Currency: pound (piastre)

LIBERIA
 Capital: Monrovia
 Currency: dollar (cent)

LIBYA
 Capital: Tripoli
 Currency: dinar (dirham)

LITHUANIA
 Capital: Vilnius
 Currency: litas

LUXEMBOURG
 Capital: Luxembourg
 Currency: franc (centime)

MACEDONIA
 Capital: Skopje
 Currency: denar

MADAGASCAR
 Capital: Antananarivo
 Currency: franc (centime)

MALAWI
 Capital: Lilongwe
 Currency: kwacha (tambala)

MALAYSIA
 Capital: Kuala Lumpur
 Currency: ringgit (sen)

MALI
 Capital: Bamako
 Currency: franc (centime)

MALTA
 Capital: Valletta
 Currency: lira (cent)

MAURITANIA
 Capital: Nouakchott
 Currency: ouguiya (khoum)

MAURITIUS
 Capital: Port Louis
 Currency: rupee (cent)

MEXICO
 Capital: Mexico City
 Currency: peso (centavo)

MOLDOVA
 Capital: Kishinev
 Currency: lei

MONGOLIA
 Capital: Ulan Bator
 Currency: tugrik (mongo)

MOROCCO
 Capital: Rabat
 Currency: dirham (centime)

MOZAMBIQUE
 Capital: Maputo
 Currency: metical (centavo)

NAMIBIA
 Capital: Windhoek
 Currency: dollar (cent)

NEPAL
 Capital: Kathmandu
 Currency: rupee (paisa)

NETHERLANDS
 Capital: Amsterdam
 Currency: guilder (cent)

NEW ZEALAND
 Capital: Wellington
 Currency: dollar (cent)

NICARAGUA
 Capital: Managua
 Currency: córdoba (centavo)

NIGER
 Capital: Niamey
 Currency: franc (centime)

NIGERIA
 Capital: Abuja
 Currency: naira (kobo)

NORWAY
 Capital: Oslo
 Currency: krone (öre)

OMAN
 Capital: Muscat
 Currency: rial

PAKISTAN
 Capital: Islamabad
 Currency: rupee (paisa)

PANAMA
 Capital: Panama City
 Currency: balboa (centesimo)

PAPUA NEW GUINEA
 Capital: Port Moresby
 Currency: kina (toea)

PARAGUAY
 Capital: Asunción
 Currency: guarani (céntimo)

PERU
 Capital: Lima
 Currency: sol (cent)

PHILIPPINES
 Capital: Manila
 Currency: peso (centavo)

POLAND
 Capital: Warsaw
 Currency: zloty (grosz)

PORTUGAL
 Capital: Lisbon
 Currency: escudo (centavo)

QATAR
 Capital: Doha
 Currency: riyal (dirham)

ROMANIA
  Capital: Bucharest
  Currency: leu (ban)

RUSSIA
  Capital: Moscow
  Currency: rouble (copeck)

RWANDA
  Capital: Kigali
  Currency: franc (centime)

SAUDI ARABIA
  Capital: Riyadh
  Currency: riyal (halalas)

SENEGAL
  Capital: Dakar
  Currency: franc (centime)

SEYCHELLES
  Capital: Victoria
  Currency: rupee (cent)

SIERRA LEONE
  Capital: Freetown
  Currency: leone (cent)

SINGAPORE
  Capital: Singapore City
  Currency: dollar (cent)

SLOVAKIA
  Capital: Bratislava
  Currency: koruna (haler)

SLOVENIA
  Capital: Ljublijana
  Currency: tolar

SOMALIA
  Capital: Mogadishu
  Currency: shilling (cent)

SOUTH AFRICA
  Capital: Pretoria
  Currency: rand (cent)

SPAIN
  Capital: Madrid
  Currency: peseta (cèntimo)

SRI LANKA
  Capital: Colombo
  Currency: rupee (cent)

SUDAN
  Capital: Khartoum
  Currency: pound (piastre)

SWAZILAND
  Capital: Mbabane
  Currency: lilangeni (cent)

SWEDEN
  Capital: Stockholm
  Currency: krona (öre)

SWITZERLAND
  Capital: Bern
  Currency: franc (centime)

SYRIA
  Capital: Damascus
  Currency: pound (piastre)

TAIWAN
  Capital: Taipei
  Currency: dollar (cent)

TAJIKSTAN
  Capital: Dushanbe
  Currency: rouble (copeck)

TANZANIA
  Capital: Dodoma
  Currency: shilling (cent)

THAILAND
Capital: Bangkok
Currency: baht (satange)

TOGO
Capital: Lome
Currency: franc (centime)

TUNISIA
Capital: Tunis
Currency: dinar (millieme)

TURKEY
Capital: Ankara
Currency: lira (kurus)

TURKMENISTAN
Capital: Ashkhabad
Currency: manat

UGANDA
Capital: Kampala
Currency: shilling (cent)

UKRAINE
Capital: Kiev

UNITED KINGDOM
Capital: London
Currency: pound (pence)

UNITED STATES OF AMERICA
Capital: Washington, DC
Currency: dollar (cent)

URUGUAY
Capital: Montevideo
Currency: peso (centésimo)

UZBEKISTAN
Capital: Tashkent
Currency: som

VENEZUELA
Capital: Caracas
Currency: bolivar (centimo)

VIETNAM
Capital: Hanoi
Currency: dong (xu)

YEMEN
Capital: Aden
Currency: riyal (fils)

YUGOSLAVIA
Capital: Belgrade
Currency: dinar (para)

ZAÏRE
Capital: Kinshasa
Currency: zaïre (maikuta)

ZAMBIA
Capital: Lusaka
Currency: kwacha (ngwee)

ZIMBABWE
Capital: Harare
Currency: dollar (cent)

Metric conversion

Quantity	Metric unit	Imperial unit
LENGTH	millimetre (mm) or centimetre (cm)	inch (in)
	centimetre (cm) or metric (m)	foot (ft)
	metre (m)	yard (yd)
	kilometre (km)	mile
MASS	gram (g)	ounce (oz)
	gram (g) or kilogram (kg)	pound (lb)
	tonne (t)	ton
AREA	square centimetre (cm^2)	square inch (in^2)
	square centimetre (cm^2) or square metre (m^2)	square foot (ft^2)
	square metre (m^2)	square yard (yd^2)
	hectare (ha)	acre (ac)
	square kilometre (km^2)	square mile (sq. mile)
VOLUME	cubic centimetre (cm^3)	cubic inch (in^3)
	cubic decimetre (dm^3) or cubic metre (m^3)	cubic foot (ft^3)
	cubic metre (m^3)	cubic yard (yd^3)
	cubic metre (m^3)	bushel (bus)
VOLUME (fluids)	millilitre (mL)	fluid ounce (fl oz)
	millilitre (mL) or litre (L)	pint (pt)
	litre (L) or cubic metre (m^3)	gallon (gal)
FORCE	newton (N)	pound-force (lbf)

Conversion factors (approximate)

Metric to Imperial units	Imperial to metric units
1 cm = 0.394 in	1 in = 25.4 mm
1 m = 3.28 ft	1 ft = 30.5 cm
1 m = 1.09 yd	1 yd = 0.914 m
1 km = 0.621 mile	1 mile = 1.61 km
1 g = 0.0353 oz	1 oz = 28.3 g
1 kg = 2.20 lb	1 lb = 454 g
1 tonne = 0.984 ton	1 ton = 1.02 tonne
1 cm^2 = 0.155 in^2	1 in^2 = 6.45 cm^2
1 m^2 = 10.8 ft^2	1 ft^2 = 929 cm^2
1 m^2 = 1.20 yd^2	1 yd^2 = 0.836 m^2
1 ha = 2.47 ac	1 ac = 0.405 ha
1 km^2 = 0.386 sq. mile	1 sq. mile = 2.59 km^2
1 cm^3 = 0.0610 in^3	1 in^3 = 16.4 cm^3
1 m^3 = 35.3 ft^3	1 ft^3 = 28.3 dm^3
1 m^3 = 1.31 yd^3	1 yd^3 = 0.765 m^3
1 m^3 = 27.5 bus	1 bus = 0.0364 m^3
1 mL = 0.0352 fl oz	1 fl oz = 28.4 mL
1 litre = 1.76 pint	1 pint = 568 mL
1 m^3 = 220 gallon	1 gal = 4.55 litre
1 N = 0.225 lbf	1 lbf = 4.45 N

Common Prefixes and Combining Forms

Prefix	Meaning or denoting	Example of base word (if applicable)	New word formed
a-[1]	on, in, into	shore, bed	ashore, abed
a-[2]	of	kin	akin
a-[3]	up	rise	arise
ab-, a-[4]	away, from	normal	abnormal
ad-, ac-, a-[5]	direction, tendency	(de)scend	ascend
an-, a-[6]	not, lacking	(mon)archy	anarchy
ante-	before in time or space	date	antedate
anti-	against	slavery	antislavery
auto-	self	biography	autobiography
be-	(to make or do) all over	calm	becalm
co-, com-, con-	together	habit	cohabit
contra-	against	(con)ception	contraception
de-	separation, negation, reversal down, reversal	horn, merit	dehorn, demerit
		(a)scend	descend
dis-	apart, negation, reversal	ability	disability
e-	variant of ex-	—	evict
en-, em-	in, into	gulf	engulf
equi-	equal	distant	equidistant
ex-	out of, from, thoroughly, former	(suc)ceed	exceed
		wife	ex-wife
extra-	outside, besides	curricular	extracurricular
hyper-	over	active	hyperactive
hypo-	under, less than	centre	hypocentre
il-	variant of in- — "not"	logical	illogical

620

Prefix	Meaning	Example base	Example word
in-¹, im-¹	in or into	land	inland
in-², im-²	not, negation	attention	inattention
infra-	below, beneath	structure	infrastructure
inter-	between, among	national	international
intra-	within	state	intrastate
intro-	inwardly, within	(in)vert	introvert
ir-	variant of in- "not"	regular	irregular
macro-	long, large	economy	macro-economy
magni-	large, great	—	magnify
mal-	bad, wrong	adjustment	maladjustment
micro-	very small	organism	micro-organism
mis-	fault, failure, negation	deed	misdeed
mono-	alone, single	chromatic	monochromatic
multi-	many	form	multiform
neo-	new, recent	classical	neoclassical
non-	exclusion, negation, failure	member	non-member
ob-	to, on, against	(con)struct	obstruct
omni-	all	benevolent	omnibenevolent
pan-	through, utterly	theism	pantheism
per-	through, utterly	(in)vade	pervade
poly-	much, many	clinic	polyclinic
post-	behind, after	graduate	postgraduate
pre-, prae-	(i) prior to	war	prewar
	(ii) early, beforehand	pay	prepay
pro-	(i) in favour of	Catholic	pro-Catholic
	(ii) projecting or advancing	—	proceed
quasi-	resembling	official	quasi-official
re-	again or back	(a)spect	redo
retro-	backwards	—	retrospect
self-	reflexive action	control	self-control

Prefix	Meaning or denoting	Example of base word (if applicable)	New word formed
semi-	half	circle	semicircle
sub-, sur-[1]	under, not quite	normal	subnormal
super-, sur-[2]	over	natural	supernatural
supra-	above	renal	suprarenal
trans-	across, beyond	(ex)port	transport
ultra-	(i) beyond in space or time	planetary	ultraplanetary
	(ii) excessively	conservative	ultraconservative
un-[1]	not	able	unable
un-[2]	reversal of an action, etc.	bend	unbend

Common Suffixes and Combining Forms

Suffix	Meaning or denoting	Example of base word (if applicable)	New word formed

A. NOUN-FORMING

Suffix	Meaning or denoting	Example of base word (if applicable)	New word formed
-age	(i) collectivity	leaf	leafage
	(ii) condition or state	bond	bondage
	(iii) process or result	wreck	wreckage
-al	an action	deny	denial
-an	person concerned with	republic	republican
-ance, -ancy	action, state or quality	assist	assistance
-ant	one who or to that which	serve	servant
-ary	(i) a place, person or relationship	grain	granary
		adverse	adversary
	(ii) (forming collective numeral nouns)		
-ate	(i) condition, office, etc.	consul	consulate
	(ii) result	—	mandate
-cy	(i) condition or character	accurate	accuracy
	(ii) rank	captain	captaincy
-dom	(i) domain	king	kingdom
	(ii) collection of persons	official	officialdom
	(iii) rank	earl	earldom
	(iv) condition	free	freedom
-ee	object of an action, etc.	donate	donee
-eer	one concerned with	engine	engineer
-en¹	plural	ox	oxen
-en²	diminutive	maid	maiden

623

Suffix	Meaning or denoting	Example of base word (if applicable)	New word formed
-ence	action, state, or quality	prudent	prudence
-ent	one who or that which	preside	president
-er¹	(i) one who or that which	harvest	harvester
	(ii) thing or person with a special characteristic	Island	Islander
-er²	person connected with something	office	officer
-er³	an action or process	remind	reminder
-ery	(i) type or place of work	bake	bakery
	(ii) character	prude	prudery
	(iii) activity	archer	archery
-ess	feminine form	count	countess
-et	diminutive form	isle	islet
-ette	(i) diminutive form	cigar	cigarette
	(ii) feminine form	usher	usherette
-ful	as much as will fill	spoon	spoonful
-hood	state, condition, character, etc.	child	childhood
-ian	one of, or connected with a place, person or thing	territory	territorian
-ics	a body of facts, principles	Christ	Christian
-ing	an action, result, product, etc.	ethos	ethics
-ion	a process, state, or result	build	building
-isc	quality or function	commune	communion
-ism	action, condition, principles, etc.	merchant	merchandise
-ist	one concerned with	baptise	baptism
-ite	one associated with a place, etc.	piano	pianist
-ity	condition, qualities, etc.	Israel	Israelite
-logy	science or knowledge, writing	active	activity
		(bio-)	biology

624

suffix	meaning	example	derived
-ment	an action, state or result, etc.	refresh	refreshment
-ness	quality or state, etc.	happy	happiness
-or	person who or thing that	act	actor
-ory	place or thing for	direct	directory
-ship	(i) condition	friend	friendship
	(ii) office, skill, etc.	leader	leadership
-sion	variant of -ion	compel	compulsion
-tion, also -ation, -ution, -ition	variant of -ion	seduce	seduction
		tempt	temptation
		revolve	revolution
		render	rendition

B. ADJECTIVE-FORMING

suffix	meaning	example	derived
-able	ability, likelihood, etc.	perish	perishable
-ac	pertaining to	elegy	elegiac
-al	connected with, like, etc.	nature	natural
-an	belonging or relating to	Australia	Australian
-ant	having quality or character of	ascend	ascendant
-ar, -ary	of or like	supplement	supplementary
-en	with appearance, made of	wood	wooden
-ent	having quality or character of	depend	dependent
-eous	variant of -ous	plenty	plenteous
-er	comparative degree	small	smaller
-ern	(added to words denoting direction)	south	southern
-est	superlative degree	small	smallest
-ful	full of, marked by	beauty	beautiful
-ible, -ile	variant of -able	reduce	reducible
-ic, -ical	characteristic of, belonging to	poet	poetic
-ish	(i) somewhat, rather	Britain	British
		red	reddish

625

Suffix	Meaning or denoting	Example of base word (if applicable)	New word formed
-ive	serving or able to	correct	corrective
-less	without	care	careless
-like	similar to, like	life	lifelike
-ly	(i) per	hour	hourly
	(ii) like	saint	saintly
-ory	having the effect of	contribute	contributory
-ous	full of, marked by	joy	joyous
-some	indicating a tendency	quarrel	quarrelsome

C. ADVERB-FORMING

Suffix	Meaning or denoting	Example of base word (if applicable)	New word formed
-er	comparative degree	fast	faster
-est	superlative degree	fast	fastest
-ly	manner	glad	gladly
-s	manner or direction	sideway	sideways
-ward(s)	direction	up(ward)	upwards
-ways	manner	length	lengthways
-wise	direction of, in respect of	length	lengthwise

D. VERB-FORMING

Suffix	Meaning or denoting	Example of base word (if applicable)	New word formed
-ate	cause or do	active	activate
-en	make or do	length	lengthen
-er	(forming verbs of repetition)	flick	flicker
-ise	make or do	legal	legalise